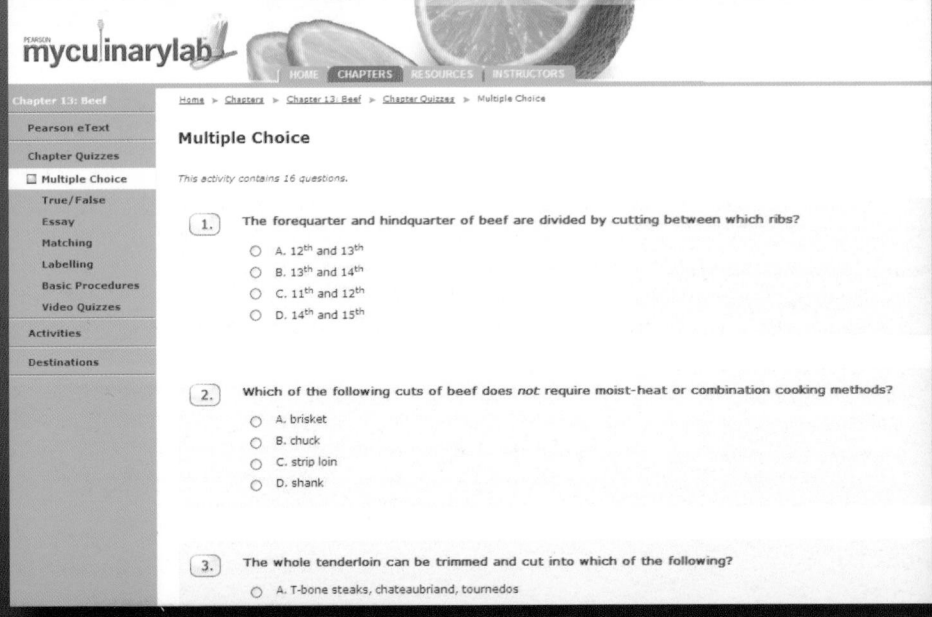

Test Yourself!

Test your knowledge with *MyCulinaryLab*'s Chapter Quizzes, Video Quizzes, and Preparation Exams, and get automatic grades to see your progress.

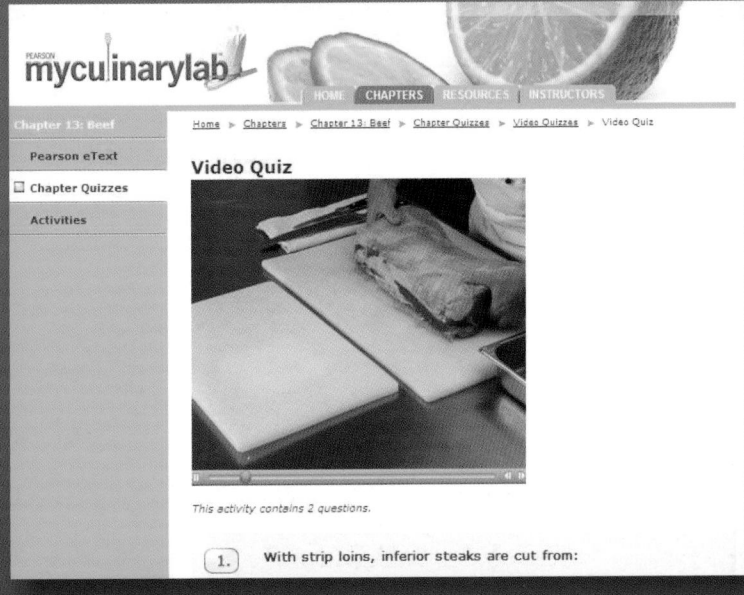

MyCulinaryLab provides

- An array of Chapter Quizzes that test your culinary knowledge and provide immediate grades
- A Video Library containing more than 100 videos that demonstrate in-depth procedures and techniques
- An Audio Glossary of selected terms from the text
- Fun, interactive Activities that help you learn key terms
- Two bonus chapters: Mise en Place and International Flavour Principles
- Information on culinary competitions, molecular gastronomy, and financial tools for the meat professional

Pearson eText

Pearson eText gives students access to the text whenever and wherever they have access to the internet. eText pages look exactly like the printed text, offering powerful new functionality for students and instructors.

Users can create notes, highlight text in different colours, create bookmarks, zoom, click hyperlinked words and phrases to view definitions, and choose single-page or two-page view.

Pearson eText allows for quick navigation using a table of contents and provides full-text search. The eText may also offer links to associated media files, enabling users to access videos, animations, or other activities as they read the text.

ONCOOKING

FIFTH CANADIAN EDITION

ONCOOKING

A Textbook of Culinary Fundamentals

Sarah R. LABENSKY, CCP

Alan M. HAUSE

Priscilla A. MARTEL

Fred L. MALLEY, SAIT Polytechnic

Anthony BEVAN, Georgian College – Owen Sound

Settimio SICOLI, Vancouver Community College

Photographs by Richard Embery
Drawings by William E. Ingram

Pearson Canada
Toronto

Library and Archives Canada Cataloguing in Publication

On cooking : a textbook of culinary fundamentals / Sarah R. Labensky ... [et al.] ; photographs by Richard Embery ; drawings by William E. Ingram. -- 5th Canadian ed.

Includes bibliographical references and index. ISBN 978-0-13-800918-2

1. Cookery. I. Labensky, Sarah R.

TX651.O53 2011 641.5 C2010-903699-9

ISBN 978-0-13-800918-2

Vice President, Editorial Director: Gary Bennett
Editor-in-Chief: Ky Pruesse
Acquisitions Editor: David Le Gallais
Sponsoring Editor: Carolin Sweig
Marketing Manager: Lisa Gillis
Supervising Developmental Editor: Suzanne Schaan
Project Managers: Lila Campbell, Cheryl Noseworthy
Production Editor: Susan Broadhurst
Copy Editor: Susan Broadhurst
Proofreaders: Susan Bindernagel, Kelli Howey
Compositor: Debbie Kumpf
Permissions Manager: Susan Wallace-Cox
Photo and Permissions Researcher: Karen Hunter
Art Director: Julia Hall
Cover and Interior Designer: Miriam Blier
Cover Image: Getty Images / Matthias Hoffmann

1 2 3 4 5   15 14 13 12 11

Printed and bound in the United States.

Foreword

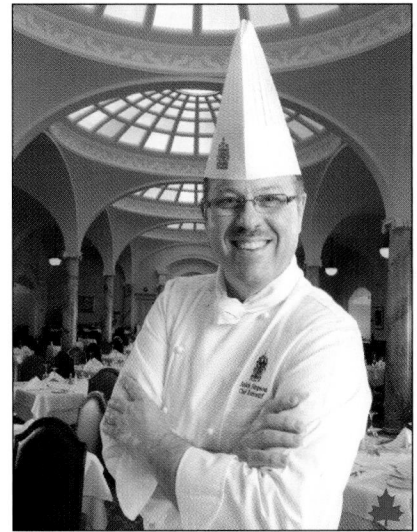

Judson Simpson, CCC

Born and raised in Toronto, Judson trained at George Brown College and worked at some of the city's landmarks, including the historic King Edward Hotel, before moving to Ottawa in 1991, as Executive Chef of Food Services at the House of Commons. Jud has managed regional and national teams at the World Culinary Olympics and is actively involved in many organizations, including Chefs Care Foundation, which he founded to help families learn about proper nutrition through community-based programs. As National President of the Canadian Culinary Federation since 2006, his main focus has been the promotion of Canadian chefs and cuisine, with specific interest in the development of Junior Chefs in Canada and abroad.

On Cooking is the resource I recommend first and foremost to aspiring young cooks or to anyone who loves cooking. Although there is no substitute for hands-on training through observation and practice, this textbook will help you understand the fundamental principles of the culinary arts and inspire you to embark on a lifelong journey of learning.

With their contributions to *On Cooking*, many of Canada's most successful chefs are showing their commitment to the next generation of cooks by their level of dedication to culinary instruction. Because of the different styles and philosophies of its contributors, this textbook is an excellent learning tool that you will use repeatedly now, as you prepare for a career in the food service industry, and always, as your quest for greater knowledge will never end. It will help you understand what it's like to work in a kitchen and be better equipped to face its many challenges, but also to benefit from its numerous rewards.

The career path you have chosen in hospitality and tourism may lead you down many different avenues. In many instances, you will have to work very hard under constant pressure for long hours. It is my hope that you will soldier on, despite the many obstacles and challenges you will face, because the rewards you will receive are well worth the effort. A culinary career can be a wonderful outlet for your artistic creativity while allowing you to indulge in your passion for cooking. Food, after all, is not only for sustenance—it is the universal language of love, friendship and sharing that knows no boundaries. Just think of how it will make you feel to know that the meal you have prepared has been the source of pleasure and enjoyment to all those who have partaken of it. I can't think of a better way to feel like you've *made a difference* in someone else's daily life.

As President of the Canadian Culinary Federation, I hope to welcome you someday as one of our members. As a former manager of Culinary Team Canada, I can assure you of Canada's most respected role on the international stage. That reputation is built on a solid foundation of dedicated culinary professionals in our workplaces across the country. With their help and guidance, and with *On Cooking* as the undisputed reference tool, you will be able to maximize your potential for success in the culinary career of your choice.

Judson W. Simpson, CCC
President, CCFCC

Brief Contents

Contents

Preface

Welcome to the fifth Canadian edition of *On Cooking: A Textbook of Culinary Fundamentals*. Learning to cook entails much more than simply learning to follow a recipe. Consequently, this is neither a cookbook nor a collection of recipes. It is a carefully designed text intended to teach you the fundamentals of the culinary arts and to prepare you for a rewarding career in the food service industry.

This book is extensively illustrated with photographs and line illustrations to help you identify foods and equipment. Throughout the book we emphasize culinary principles, not recipes (although we include close to 450 of them in the text, and more on the CD-ROM). Whenever possible, we focus on the general procedure, highlighting fundamental principles and skills, whether it be for preparing a yeast bread or grilling a piece of fish. We discuss both the *how* and the *why* of cooking. Only then are specific applications and sample recipes given. Many recipes include photographs of the finished dish, ready for service; many procedures are illustrated with step-by-step photographs as well.

Numerous hotel and restaurant chefs, as well as chef-instructors, from across Canada have contributed recipes to this book—usually accompanied by photographs and brief biographies of the chefs. These recipes allow you to explore the different techniques and styles used by a range of professionals and help to characterize Canadian cuisine.

In order to provide you with a sense of the rich tradition of cookery, informative sidebars on food history, chefs' profiles and other topics are scattered throughout the book. Also included are several short essays by prominent culinarians on topics ranging from tempering chocolate to tasting spicy foods.

We wish you much success in your culinary career and hope this text will continue to inform and inspire you long after graduation.

Approach and Philosophy of *On Cooking*

On Cooking, Fifth Canadian Edition, follows the model established in our previous editions, which have prepared thousands of students for successful careers in the culinary arts by building a strong foundation based in sound fundamental techniques. Students and instructors alike have praised *On Cooking* for its comprehensive yet accessible coverage of culinary skills and cooking procedures.

On Cooking focuses on teaching the hows and whys of cooking. *On Cooking* starts with general procedures, highlighting fundamental principles and skills, and then presents specific applications and sample recipes. Core cooking principles are explained as the background for learning proper cooking techniques. Once mastered, these techniques can be used to cook a wide array of foods. The culinary arts are shown in cultural and historical context as well so that students understand how different techniques form the basis for various cuisines.

Chapters focus on five areas essential to a well-rounded culinary professional:

- **Professionalism:** Background chapters introduce students to the field with material on food history, food safety, nutrition and menu planning. Food safety information has been updated to reflect the most recent regulations.
- **Preparation:** *On Cooking* covers those core subjects with which all culinary students should be familiar before stepping into the kitchen. Equipment and basic knife skills are presented. Staple ingredients such as eggs, dairy products, herbs and spices are covered.
- **Cooking:** Fundamental cooking techniques are explained and then demonstrated with a wide range of recipes. Individual chapters focus on different categories

of key ingredients: meats, poultry, fish, vegetables and so forth. A separate chapter on vegetarian cooking outlines the variations and presents specific ingredients and approaches to vegetarian cuisine.

- **Baking:** Several chapters cover the aspects of bread and pastry making that every student should know. The material is sufficient to support a stand-alone unit on bread baking and dessert preparation.
- **Meal Service and Presentation:** Brunch and appetizers are covered, and a separate chapter on beverages includes discussions of water, juice, coffee and tea, as well as wine and food pairings. A final chapter on plate presentation demonstrates traditional and contemporary techniques for enhancing the visual presentation of food.

New to the Fifth Canadian Edition

New to this edition is MyCulinaryLab, an interactive online site that offers demonstration videos, animations, assessment with personalized feedback and other resources. See page xiv for further information.

New information and topics in the text include the following:

- small plate presentation
- food substitutions for allergies
- equipment such as Japanese knives and sous vide machinery
- new safety equipment, such as mesh gloves
- organic certification
- molecular gastronomy
- additional step-by-step illustrated procedures, especially throughout Chapter 9, Principles of Cooking
- a variety of new "Safety Alerts" and informative sidebars
- "new" ingredients that are gaining in popularity, such as cured meats

The fifth Canadian edition also features improved four-colour illustrations, as well as more than 100 new photos, including new sequences illustrating specific processes, new ingredient photos and more photos of completed dishes. A number of new recipes are included in the text, and the selection in the MasterCook *On Cooking* Canadian archive has been expanded.

A Note on the Recipes

Recipes are important and useful as a means of standardizing food preparation and recording information. We include recipes that are primarily designed to reinforce and explain techniques and procedures presented in the text. Many recipe yields have been standardized to 10 servings, although some variety has been maintained to accommodate different needs.

All ingredients are listed in both metric and U.S. measurements. The metric recipes have been written to reinforce the simplicity of the system. Weights for ingredients are used to make food costing easier and to professionalize the recipes. Electronic scales are readily available and inexpensive. U.S. equivalents have been left in volume measures in most cases. Please do not directly compare the metric conversions against U.S. measurements; they are not intended to be identical and adjustments have been made. We strongly recommend that you work only in one system, as switching back and forth leads to disappointment in the end product. Each product is unique and there are no magic conversions that work across the spectrum.

Temperature requirements may vary depending on equipment and altitudes. Different ovens will be more or less efficient in maintaining proper temperature, and oven temperature calibrations need to be verified on a regular basis. The temperatures given in recipes should be taken as guidelines and adjusted for these factors. Note that metric recipes tend to use finer calibrations, whereas U.S. measurements tend to work in increments of 25°F. Cooking times also may vary depending on the quality of the meat being prepared or other factors.

Throughout the text, standards from the Canadian Food Inspection Agency have been upheld, although real-world practices and customer preferences are also considered.

Throughout this book, unless otherwise noted, *mirepoix* refers to a preparation of 2 parts onion, 1 part celery and 1 part carrot by weight; *pepper* refers to ground black pepper, preferably freshly ground; *butter* refers to whole, unsalted butter; and *TT* means "to taste."

A nutritional analysis is provided with each recipe. This information is provided as a reference only. There is a 20% margin of error, due primarily to choices for specific ingredients and variations in the size of fruits and vegetables. When a recipe offers a choice of ingredients, the first-mentioned ingredient was the one used in the calculations. Ingredients listed as "to taste" (TT) and "as needed" are generally omitted from the analysis. In addition, canola oil and 2% milk are used throughout for "vegetable oil" and "milk," respectively. When the recipe gives a choice of serving or weight, the first mentioned is used.

Recipes marked with the rainbow symbol are considered healthful and may be low in calories, fat, saturated fat and/or sodium; some may also be a good source of vitamins, protein, fibre or calcium. These dishes are not necessarily dietetic; rather, they should be consumed as part of a well-balanced diet.

Vegetarian dishes are also indicated with an icon. These recipes do not contain meat, poultry, fish or shellfish, but may contain dairy products and/or eggs. Vegetarian dishes are not necessarily low in calories, fat or sodium, nor are they automatically good sources of vitamins, protein, fibre or calcium.

Detailed procedures for standard techniques (e.g., "deglaze the pan" or "monter au beurre") are presented in the text and generally are not repeated in each recipe. No matter how detailed the written recipe, we must assume that you have certain knowledge, skills and judgment.

Variations appear at the end of selected recipes. These give you the opportunity to see how one set of techniques or procedures can be used to prepare different dishes with only minor modifications. You should also rely upon the knowledge and skill of your instructor or chef for guidance. While some skills and an understanding of theory can be acquired through reading and study, no book can substitute for repeated, hands-on preparation and observation.

Student CD-ROM

This interactive CD-ROM comes with every new copy of the text and includes the following resources:

- MasterCook, a recipe software that allows scaling, generates shopping lists and offers other tools. It includes a complete archive of all recipes from this edition of *On Cooking*, recipes from the second, third and fourth Canadian editions that no longer appear in the text and new recipes provided by Canadian chefs.
- A separate printable archive of all recipes from the first Canadian edition of *On Cooking*.
- Two bonus chapters, "Mise en Place" and "International Flavour Principles." The latter includes coverage of the following cuisines: Chinese, Japanese, Indian, North African (including Ethiopian) and Middle Eastern, South American and Caribbean and Canadian Aboriginal.
- Additional information on food and wine pairings that supplements the material in Chapter 35, Beverages, including sample recipes with wine suggestions and detailed pairing charts. A chart on pairing beers with cheeses is also available in this section.

Additional Student Supplements

MyCulinaryLab (www.myculinarylab.ca). A dynamic online tool, MyCulinaryLab supports the many ways in which students learn, enabling them to study and master the content online on their own time and at their own pace. Media-rich personalized study plans are based on the student's performance using the site's interactive testing and games. The key features of MyCulinaryLab include the following:

- **Chapter quizzes** test students' knowledge of key points. Marks can be sent to the gradebook, or the quizzes can be used as self-assessment tools for students to check their own understanding of the material and concepts in the textbook.
- **Video clips**, with accompanying quizzes, demonstrate various kitchen techniques, such as knife skills.
- **Animations** are interactive activities that provide visual references, along with follow-up quizzing.
- **Interactive activities** use word and matching games to reinforce concepts and vocabulary.
- **Practice exams** help students prepare for the journeyperson's exam and Red Seal exam.
- Information on **culinary competitions** outlines the benefits of competition as an extension of learning and highlights opportunities for students and apprentices.

Study Guide (978-0-13-231756-6). The Study Guide provides an overview of the key concepts in *On Cooking* through self-tests, including multiple choice, fill-in-the-blank, short answer, matching and labelling questions.

CourseSmart for Students. CourseSmart goes beyond traditional expectations— providing instant, online access to the textbooks and course materials you need at an average savings of 60%. With instant access from any computer and the ability to search your text, you'll find the content you need quickly, no matter where you are. And with online tools such as highlighting and note-taking, you can save time and study efficiently. See all of the benefits at www.coursesmart.com/students.

Instructor Supplements

MyCulinaryLab (www.myculinarylab.ca). MyCulinaryLab is an easy-to-use online resource designed to supplement a traditional lecture course. It provides instructors with basic course management capabilities in the areas of course organization, grades, communication and personalization of content. Instructors benefit from course management tools such as a robust grade book, integrated course email and reporting tools.

Instructor's Resource CD-ROM (978-0-13-218328-4). This resource CD includes the following instructor supplements:
- Instructor's Manual: This manual includes chapter outlines, lists of key terms, additional discussion questions and learning activities.
- Test Item File: More than 1300 test questions, including multiple-choice, fill-in-the-blank, matching and true/false, are provided in Microsoft Word format. This test bank is also available in MyTest format (see below).
- PowerPoints: PowerPoint presentations offer outlines of the key concepts in each chapter as well as images from the text.
- Transparency Masters: Key information from the text, including selected figures and tables, are provided as transparency masters that can be reproduced for classroom use.

These instructor supplements may also be available for downloading from a password-protected section of Pearson Education Canada's online catalogue (vig.pearsoned.ca). See your local sales representative for details and access.

MyTest. MyTest from Pearson Education Canada is a powerful assessment generation program that helps instructors easily create and print quizzes, tests and exams, as well as homework or practice handouts. Questions and tests can be authored online, allowing instructors ultimate flexibility and the ability to efficiently manage assessments any time, from anywhere. MyTest for *On Cooking* includes more than 1300 test questions, including multiple-choice, fill-in-the-blank, matching and true/false. These questions are also available in Microsoft Word format on the Instructor's Resource CD-ROM.

Technology Specialists. Pearson's Technology Specialists work with faculty and campus course designers to ensure that Pearson technology products, assessment tools and online course materials are tailored to meet your specific needs. This highly qualified team is dedicated to helping schools take full advantage of a wide range of educational resources, by assisting in the integration of a variety of instructional materials and media formats. Your local Pearson Education sales representative can provide you with more details on this service program.

CourseSmart for Instructors. CourseSmart goes beyond traditional expectations— providing instant, online access to the textbooks and course materials you need at a lower cost for students. And even as students save money, you can save time and hassle with a digital eTextbook that allows you to search for the most relevant content at the very moment you need it. Whether it's evaluating textbooks or creating lecture notes to help students with difficult concepts, CourseSmart can make life a little easier. See how when you visit www.coursesmart.com/instructors.

Acknowledgments

The authors of the fifth Canadian edition would like to thank a number of people for their contributions to this edition. At Pearson Education Canada, the project was shaped by Carolin Sweig (Sponsoring Editor), Suzanne Schaan (Supervising Developmental Editor), Lila Campbell and Cheryl Noseworthy (Project Managers). Susan Broadhurst (Production Editor and Copy Editor) and Susan Bindernagel and Kelli Howey (Proofreaders) helped to correct and improve the manuscript. Miriam Blier's updated design was implemented by Debbie Kumpf (Composition). The Canadian version of MyCulinaryLab was overseen by Marisa D'Andrea (Media Content Developer).

We are grateful to the many Canadian chefs who have provided recipes for this and previous Canadian editions of the text. We are indebted to Howard Selig for his meticulous work on the nutritional analyses for the new and modified recipes. Special thanks to the following colleagues who have provided input on specific topics in previous editions: Ken Harper of Vancouver Island University, whose good suggestions helped make the baking and pastry chapters more student friendly; Master pâtissier Hermann Greineder of SAIT, who proved an invaluable resource for the baking chapters; and Gilbert Noussitou of Camosun College, who provided valuable comments on Chapters 10 (Stocks and Sauces), 12 (Principles of Meat Cookery), 13 (Beef) and 14 (Veal) as well as corrections throughout the text.

We would also like to thank all those instructors who provided feedback throughout the development of the new edition, including:

Allan Aikman, Vancouver Island University
Larry Bergeron, Nova Scotia Community College, Akerley Campus
Michael Bryanton, Holland College
Kim Coates, Cambrian College
David Hawey, Fleming College
Patrick Hersey, Fanshawe College
Michael Olson, Niagara Culinary Institute
Joerg Roth, Centennial College

Rossana Di Zio Magnotta of Magnotta Winery graciously allowed us to use the material on wine and food pairings found on the Student CD-ROM. Special thanks to Richard Embery, photographer, and to Stacey Winters Quattrone and William Ingram, illustrators, whose work for the American editions of this text has also enriched our Canadian editions. We are also grateful to the many chefs, restaurateurs, writers and culinary professionals who provided recipes and essays for this book. Generous donations of equipment and supplies by the following companies have helped to make the book possible: J.A. Henckels Zwillingswerk, Inc., All-Clad Metalcrafters, Inc. and Parrish's Cake Decorating Supplies, Inc. We also wish to thank Shamrock Foods Company, KitchenAid Home Appliances, Taylor Environmental Instruments, Hobart Corporation, Jeff and Sue Reising of Arizona Ostrich Fillet, Randy Dougherty of ISF International and TechneUSA.

Key Features

LEARNING OUTCOMES AND CHAPTER INTRODUCTION

Each chapter begins with clearly stated outcomes. Students can refer to these outcomes while reading to make sure they understand the material. The introduction provides a brief overview of the topics to be covered, and the MyCulinaryLab feature previews the chapter resources available online.

LEARNING OUTCOMES

After studying this chapter you will be able to:

- understand the basic principles of the physiology of the sense of taste and smell
- recognize a variety of herbs, spices, oils, vinegars, and other flavourings
- understand how to use flavouring ingredients to create, enhance or alter the natural flavours of a dish

These interactive online tools will help you master the skills in this chapter:

- Videos
- Quizzes
- Additional activities

It is the chef's role to consistently present well-flavoured foods—to excite the consumer's brain and palate. This can be accomplished by an act as simple as sprinkling a bit of salt over a ripe watermelon to enhance the melon's natural sweetness or as complicated as using a long-simmering stock made from wild mushrooms to enrich a sauce flavoured with herbs and wine. In either case, the chef must understand how to flavour foods and be able to recognize flavouring ingredients and know how to use them. This chapter looks at the sense of taste and smell and the flavouring ingredients used in the professional kitchen to enhance foods. Flavourings—the herbs, spices, salt, oils, vinegars and condiments typically used to create, enhance or alter the natural flavours of a dish—are featured. Flavourings used primarily for baked goods and desserts are discussed in Chapter 27, Principles of the Bakeshop.

MARGINAL DEFINITIONS

Important terms are defined in the margins to help students master new terminology. An end-of-text glossary provides an easy reference for all the key terms.

- **flavour** an identifiable or distinctive quality of a food, drink or other substance perceived with the combined senses of taste, touch and smell
- **taste** the sensations, as interpreted by the brain, of what we detect when food, drink or other substances come in contact with our taste buds
- **mouth-feel** the sensation created in the mouth by a combination of a food's taste, smell, texture and temperature

SAFETY ALERT

Tasting Food

To avoid cross-contamination, a two-spoon tasting method should be used when sampling in the professional kitchen. To safely taste food, use a clean spoon to remove some of the food from the pan in which it was made or stored. Pour that food into a second clean spoon before tasting it. This prevents the soiled spoon from going back into the food being prepared. Keep a supply of clean spoons for this purpose near all cooking and preparation stations.

SAFETY ALERTS

Brief notes remind students of safety concerns and encourage them to incorporate food safety and sanitation into their regular kitchen activities.

BOXES AND SIDEBARS

Boxes and sidebars present supplementary information, including notes on food history, food in culture and the background of professional foodservice. This material helps students understand the culinary arts in a wider social context. Extended profiles of Canadian chefs provide an inside look at the philosophy and daily life of successful chefs.

Cooking with Cheese

The Dairy Bureau of Canada promotes a concept of Evolutive Cuisine. It allows the chef creativity in blending techniques and nontraditional ingredients with original presentations and decorating practices. The objective is to preserve and enhance flavours while maintaining nutritional soundness. Effectively cooking with cheese is a part of this concept.

We need to remember that cheese is a living organism. Each type of cheese has characteristics that must be considered. These include fat content, moisture content, pH level, buffering capacity, thickening power and the reactions of proteins and minerals to other ingredients or heat. When creating or adapting a recipe, all of these factors must be consid-

ered. For example, if low-fat mascarpone is used to make a butterscotch sauce, you must add more fat (butter) for the sauce to have the right characteristics. To use a snow goat cheese to liaise a jus-based sauce, the alcohol in the wine must be evaporated and the reduction removed from the fire before the room temperature cheese is whisked in. Whipping cream may have to be added to a purée soup to buffer the liquid to achieve successful incorporation of the cheese.

For detailed information, *Fundamentals of Canadian Cheeses and Their Use in Fine Cuisine* by the Dairy Farmers of Canada (Montreal: les Éditions de la Chenelière Inc., 1992) is an excellent resource.

TABLES

Tables and charts offer visual support and organization of material to enhance students' understanding of the material.

TABLE 18.1	Using Furred Game		
Animal	**Commonly Purchased Cuts**	**Cooking Methods**	**Suggested Use**
Bison	Purchased and prepared in the same manner as lean beef		
Deer	Loin	Dry heat (roast; sauté; grill)	Sautéed medallions; whole roast loin; grilled steaks
	Leg	Combination (braise; stew)	Marinate and braise; pot roast with cranberries; chili; sausage; forcemeat
	Rack	Dry heat (roast; grill)	Grilled chops
Rabbit	Full carcass	Dry heat (sauté; pan-fry; roast; grill) Combination (braise; stew)	Pan-fried rabbit with cream gravy Braised rabbit with mushrooms
Wild Boar	Loin	Dry heat (roast)	Roast loin with mustard crust
	Chops	Combination (braise)	Marinate and braise; stew with red wine and sour cream; sausage; forcemeat

FIGURES

Detailed line drawings illustrate tools and equipment. Illustrations are also used to show students the skeletal structure of meat animals and fish.

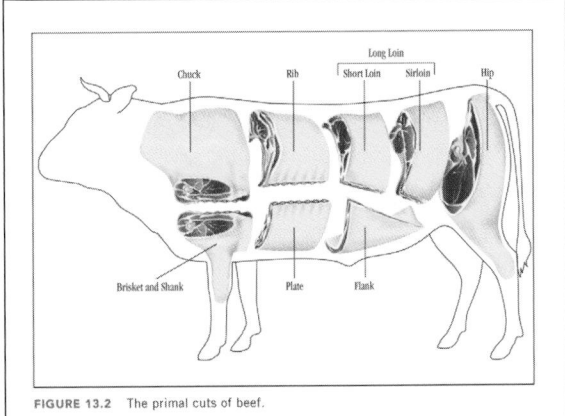

FIGURE 13.2   The primal cuts of beef.

PRODUCT IDENTIFICATION

Hundreds of original colour photographs help students recognize and identify ingredients. Students can explore a huge variety of items such as fresh herbs, fish, dried spices, game, meats and fine cheeses.

Herbs

Basil (Fr. *basilique*) is considered one of the great culinary herbs. It is available in a variety of "flavours"—cinnamon, garlic, lemon, even chocolate—but the most common is sweet basil. **Sweet basil** has light green, tender leaves and small white flowers. Its flavour is strong, warm and slightly peppery, with a hint of cloves. Basil is used in Asian and Mediterranean cuisines and has a special affinity for garlic and tomatoes. When purchasing fresh basil, look for bright green leaves; avoid flower buds and wilted or rust-coloured leaves. Dried sweet basil is readily available but has a decidedly weaker flavour.

Basil

Opal Basil

    Opal basil is named for its vivid purple colour. It has a tougher, crinkled leaf and a medium-strong flavour. Opal basil may be substituted for sweet basil in cooking and its appearance makes it a distinctive garnish.

BASIC PROCEDURES

Numbered steps outline the basic procedures that must be mastered. These procedures are often followed by "Applying the Basics" recipes that allow students to practise these skills.

BASIC PROCEDURE FOR SAUTÉING VEGETABLES

1. Wash and cut the vegetables into uniform shapes and sizes.

2. Heat a sauté pan and add enough fat to just cover the bottom. The pan should be large enough to hold the vegetables without overcrowding.

3. When preparing an assortment of vegetables, add the ingredients according to their cooking times (first add the vegetables that take the longest to cook). Plan carefully so that all vegetables will be done at the same time. Do not overcrowd the pan; maintain high enough heat so the vegetables do not cook in their own juices.

4. Toss the vegetables using the sloped sides of the sauté pan or wok to flip them back on top of themselves. Do not toss more than necessary. The pan should remain in contact with the heat source as much as possible to maintain proper temperatures.

5. Add any sauces or vegetables with high water content, such as tomatoes, last.

6. Season the vegetables as desired with herbs or spices, or add ingredients for a glaze.

ILLUSTRATED PROCEDURES

Step-by-step colour photographs of various stages in the preparation of dishes and ingredients help students visualize unfamiliar techniques and encourage them to review kitchen activities whenever necessary.

BASIC PROCEDURE FOR PAN-FRYING FOOD

1. Cut, pound or otherwise prepare the food to be pan-fried; then bread, batter or flour it as desired.

2. Heat a moderate amount of fat or oil in a heavy pan—usually enough to cover the item one-third to halfway up its sides.

3. Add the food to the pan, being careful not to splash the hot fat.

4. Fry the food on one side until brown. Using tongs, turn and brown the other side. Generally, pan-fried foods are fully cooked when they are well browned on both sides.

5. Remove the food from the pan and drain it on absorbent paper before serving.

1. Use tongs to carefully place the item being pan-fried into a moderate amount of hot oil.

2. Turn the item to brown the other side.

3. Drain the cooked item on absorbent paper.

QUESTIONS FOR DISCUSSION

Questions for Discussion appear at the end of each chapter to encourage students to integrate theory and technique into a broader understanding of the material.

Questions for Discussion

1. Explain the criteria used in grading eggs. Why might you prefer to use eggs with lower grades?

2. What are the differences between egg products and egg substitutes?

3. What is milkfat and how is it used in classifying milk-based products?

4. If a recipe calls for whole milk and you have only dried milk, what do you do? Explain your answer.

5. What is clarified butter and when is it used? Describe the procedure for clarifying butter.

6. The texture and shelf life of cheese depend on what two factors?

7. Cheeses are categorized as fresh or unripened, soft, semi-soft, firm, hard and light. Give two examples of each and explain how they are generally used.

RECITES

CHEF BIOGRAPHIES

Recipes by Canadian chefs are accompanied by brief biographies highlighting their training and achievements.

MEASUREMENTS

All recipes provide both metric and U.S. measurements.

STEP BY STEP INSTRUCTIONS

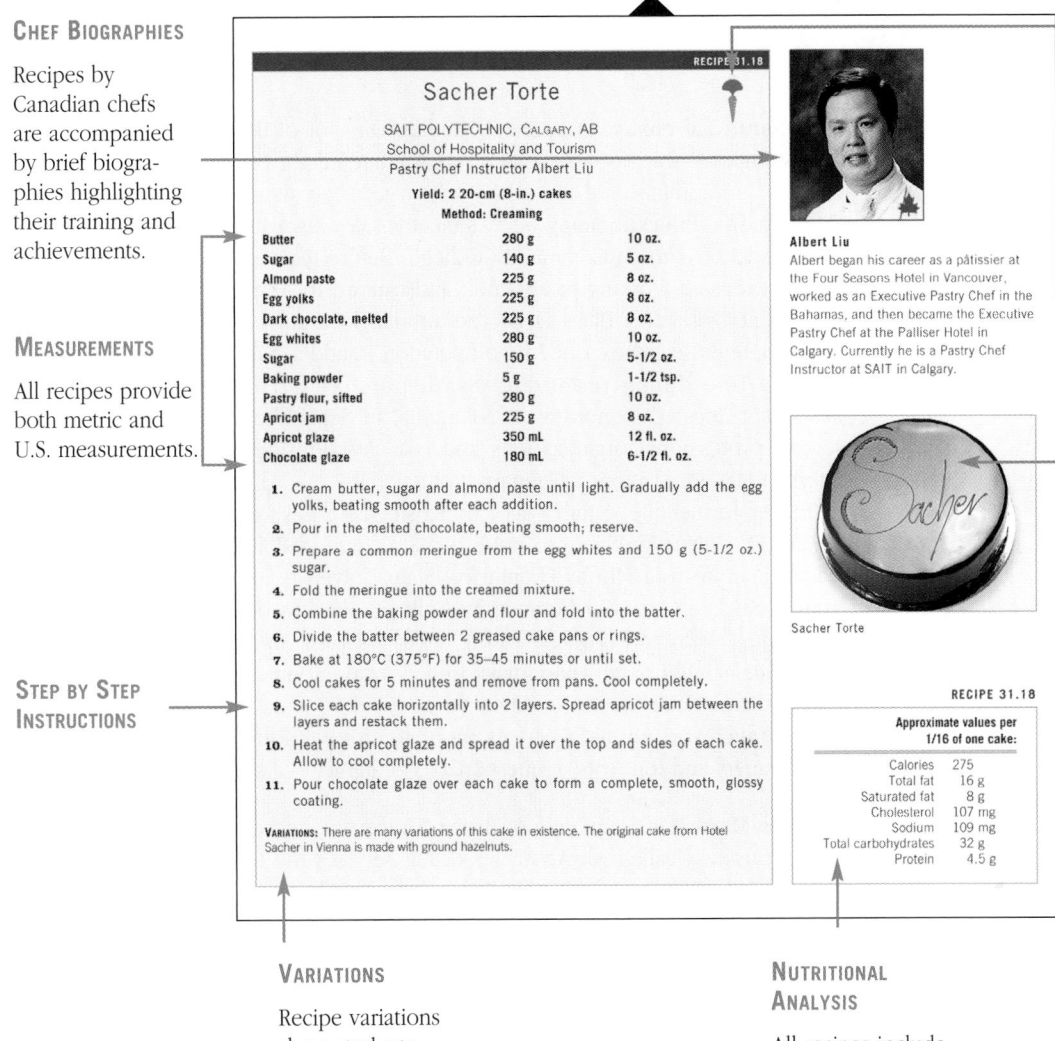

ICONS

Healthy recipes and vegetarian dishes are indicated with colourful icons.

FINISHED DISH

Some recipes are accompanied by a photograph of the finished dish, allowing students to see what the completed item should look like. These photographs can also help students understand different ways of presenting foods.

VARIATIONS

Recipe variations show students how to modify recipes to create new flavour profiles and new dishes.

NUTRITIONAL ANALYSIS

All recipes include a nutritional analysis prepared specifically for this text.

RECIPE 31.18

Sacher Torte

SAIT POLYTECHNIC, CALGARY, AB
School of Hospitality and Tourism
Pastry Chef Instructor Albert Liu

Yield: 2 20-cm (8-in.) cakes
Method: Creaming

Ingredient	Metric	U.S.
Butter	280 g	10 oz.
Sugar	140 g	5 oz.
Almond paste	225 g	8 oz.
Egg yolks	225 g	8 oz.
Dark chocolate, melted	225 g	8 oz.
Egg whites	280 g	10 oz.
Sugar	150 g	5-1/2 oz.
Baking powder	5 g	1-1/2 tsp.
Pastry flour, sifted	280 g	10 oz.
Apricot jam	225 g	8 oz.
Apricot glaze	350 mL	12 fl. oz.
Chocolate glaze	180 mL	6-1/2 fl. oz.

1. Cream butter, sugar and almond paste until light. Gradually add the egg yolks, beating smooth after each addition.
2. Pour in the melted chocolate, beating smooth; reserve.
3. Prepare a common meringue from the egg whites and 150 g (5-1/2 oz.) sugar.
4. Fold the meringue into the creamed mixture.
5. Combine the baking powder and flour and fold into the batter.
6. Divide the batter between 2 greased cake pans or rings.
7. Bake at 180°C (375°F) for 35–45 minutes or until set.
8. Cool cakes for 5 minutes and remove from pans. Cool completely.
9. Slice each cake horizontally into 2 layers. Spread apricot jam between the layers and restack them.
10. Heat the apricot glaze and spread it over the top and sides of each cake. Allow to cool completely.
11. Pour chocolate glaze over each cake to form a complete, smooth, glossy coating.

VARIATIONS: There are many variations of this cake in existence. The original cake from Hotel Sacher in Vienna is made with ground hazelnuts.

Albert Liu
Albert began his career as a pâtissier at the Four Seasons Hotel in Vancouver, worked as an Executive Pastry Chef in the Bahamas, and then became the Executive Pastry Chef at the Palliser Hotel in Calgary. Currently he is a Pastry Chef Instructor at SAIT in Calgary.

Sacher Torte

RECIPE 31.18

Approximate values per 1/16 of one cake:

Calories	275
Total fat	16 g
Saturated fat	8 g
Cholesterol	107 mg
Sodium	109 mg
Total carbohydrates	32 g
Protein	4.5 g

About the Authors

Chef Sarah Labensky, CCP, was Founding Director of the Culinary Arts Institute at Mississippi University for Women (MUW). She taught cooking and management courses and administered the school's four-year baccalaureate degree program in Culinary Arts. Prior to joining MUW's faculty, she was a Professor of Culinary Arts at Scottsdale (Arizona) Community College. Before teaching, Chef Labensky spent many years as a working pastry cook and caterer. In April 2006, Sarah purchased The Front Door and Back Door restaurants, located in downtown Columbus, Missouri. She quickly expanded the operation to add a gourmet retail shop and an evening fine dining restaurant. Sarah purchased The Green Olive Italian Restaurant, located in northwest Columbus, in September 2006. She is active in several professional organizations and is a Past President of the 4000-member International Association of Culinary Professionals.

In her former life, Sarah was a practising attorney, with a J.D. degree from Vanderbilt University. She also holds a B.S. degree in Political Science and Public Administration from Murray (Kentucky) State University and a Culinary Certificate from Scottsdale (Arizona) Community College. She has been repeatedly included in *Marquis' Who's Who in the World*, *Who's Who in America* and *Who's Who of American Women*. Sarah is originally from Murray, Kentucky, and has also lived in Phoenix and Nashville. In addition to good food, Chef Labensky is passionate about travel and animals. She is mom to three Rhodesian Ridgebacks, two Weimaraners and four cats of questionable pedigree.

Priscilla Martell is a graduate of Brown University, and currently operates a consulting business called All About Food that services the food, baking and restaurant industries. She's a prolific freelance writer and her articles have appeared in a number of newspapers and magazines, such as *Cooking Light*, *Food and Wine* and *Flavor & Menu*. Priscilla also works with the American Almond Products Company as Culinary Research Director and she has taught as an adjunct at Connecticut Culinary Academy and Boston University. She and her husband, Charlie van Over, opened and ran, for a number of years, an award-winning restaurant called Restaurant du Village in their hometown of Chester, Connecticut.

Allen "Skip" Hause is co-owner and directing executive of Fabulous Food, which he and his wife founded in 1995 to fulfil their vision of unique custom catering. A graduate of New York's renowned Culinary Institute of America, Skip has stellar credentials in all facets of the culinary world. His experience includes the noted Williamsburg Inn (Williamsburg, Virginia), corporate work for Omni International Hotels (Atlanta, Georgia) and 16 years as Executive Chef for a leading Phoenix catering company. As Fabulous Food's Executive Chef, Skip oversees all aspects of the business. He is ably assisted by an exceptional kitchen and planning staff, whose combined talents are the reason the company earns its name in both taste and presentation.

Fred Malley's career includes being an educator, chef, food and beverage manager, caterer and food stylist. His passion for food began early in life and has continually evolved. He instructs aspiring culinarians at SAIT Polytechnic in Calgary and mentors for professional designation. Curriculum development is a particular interest; as a Director of the Canadian Tourism Human Resource Council, he was actively involved in the development of National Occupational Standards for professional cook, line cook, kitchen helper, food and beverage manager and entry level cook training. One of his most recent projects has been working as a Curriculum Validation Expert for Alberta Apprenticeship and Industry Training. Fred co-authored *Food Safety and Sanitation* (SAIT), collaborated on *Fundamentals of Canadian Cheeses and Their Uses in Fine Cuisine* (Dairy Farmers of Canada) and provided input into Alberta's Apprentice Cook outline and exams. As a Director of the Canadian Federation of Chefs and Cooks, he chaired the Canadian Culinary Institute, the body responsible for professional certification of chefs throughout Canada, for five years.

Chef Malley is a certified chef de cuisine (CCC) and a DACUM facilitator; he is also certified for Evolutive Cuisine with Canadian Cheeses (ECCC) with Distinction. Fred is active in the Alberta Culinary Arts Foundation as a director and was a support member for Culinary Team Alberta in 1996. He is a member of Epsilon Pi Tau and holds a degree in Adult Education. His food styling appears internationally for major corporations and he has ventured into research and development for food companies.

Anthony Bevan, CCC, a native of Dublin, Ireland, graduated from the Dublin Institute of Technology's culinary program and continued his culinary training in Basel, Switzerland. Returning to Ireland, he worked his way through the ranks and became the youngest Executive Chef in a high-quality hotel. He led the culinary brigades of other fine hotels and restaurants until finally opening his own restaurant called Knocklofty House in Tipperary, Ireland.

Anthony moved to Canada and joined the culinary faculty team at Cambrian College, Sudbury, eventually becoming the Coordinator for Hospitality Studies. During his 10 years there, his achievements included winning the Teaching Excellence Award, being awarded an Aboriginal name (*Gaage Aan Kwod*, meaning "Clear Sky"), helping to establish Canada's accredited Aboriginal Culinary Program and Aboriginal Hotel Lodge Management DIP Program and writing a column for the *Sudbury Star*.

In 1997, Anthony joined the team at Humber College in Toronto. While there, he designed and implemented the Ontario Youth Apprenticeship Program (OYAP) for cooks; received the College Innovation of the Year Award; chaired the Curriculum Advisory Committee for the trade of cook for the Ministry of Training, Colleges and Universities; conceived, designed and led the development of Ontario's Chef Apprenticeship program; and hosted a television show called *School of Chef.*

In 2010, Anthony became head of the Culinary School at Georgian College in Owen Sound, Ontario, where he places an emphasis on local, sustainable, fresh, chemical-free foods. He also devotes time to creating national and international work placements for students and graduates of the culinary programs and continues his partnerships with First Nation community initiatives.

Settimio Sicoli graduated from the University of Victoria with majors in anthropology and psychology. His culinary journey began when he enrolled in the Professional Cook Training program at Vancouver Community College. He served his three-year apprenticeship at Hotel Vancouver, successfully attaining his Red Seal designation. He continued his culinary training in Europe, at the Hilton International Hotel in Mainz, Germany. Returning to Canada, he joined the kitchen brigade at the University Club of Vancouver, attaining the position of Executive Chef.

Settimio joined the faculty of Vancouver Community College's Culinary Arts Department in 1987. During his tenure there, Settimio has been instrumental in establishing the first Culinary Arts–ESL combined skills program and has obtained his provincial Instructor's Diploma with a post-secondary endorsement. He has held the positions of Assistant Department Head and Department Head of Culinary Arts, and is the former Associate Dean of the Tourism, Hospitality, and Business Division. He currently instructs various components of the Culinary Arts program.

Settimio has been active for years in many professional associations. He is Past President and Chair of the British Columbia Chefs' Association and Chef Director on the Vancouver branch's board. Settimio is also the Founding Director of British Columbia's Culinary Arts Foundation and former First Vice-President of Canadian Chef Educators. He has been director of both the B.C. Restaurant "FoodService Expo" and the Annual Food and Beverage Conference, chairman of the Provincial Cook Training Articulation Committee and board member of the Industry Training Advisory Commission (ITAC).

Professionalism 1

" Cookery is become an art, a noble science; cooks are gentlemen.

—Robert Burton, British author, 1621

LEARNING OUTCOMES

After studying this chapter you will be able to:

- name key historical figures responsible for developing food service professionalism

- discuss the development of the modern food service industry

- explain the organization of classical and modern kitchen brigades

- explain the role of the professional chef in modern food service operations

- identify the attributes an apprentice or student cook needs to become a professional chef

These interactive online tools will help you master the skills in this chapter:

- Chapter Quizzes
- Activities
- Molecular Gastronomy

Defining the Key Terms

Cooking—(1) The transfer of energy from a heat source to a food; this energy alters the food's molecular structure, changing its texture, flavour, aroma and appearance; (2) the preparation of food for consumption.

Cookery—The art, practice or work of cooking.

Professional cooking—A system of cooking based on a knowledge of and appreciation for ingredients and procedures.

Great cookery requires taste and creativity,

an appreciation of beauty and a mastery of technique. Like the sciences, successful cookery demands a certain level of knowledge and an understanding of basic principles. And, as with any vocation, today's professional chefs must exercise sound judgment and be committed to achieving excellence in their endeavours.

This book describes foods and cooking equipment, explains culinary principles and cooking techniques and provides recipes utilizing these principles and techniques. This book cannot, however, provide taste, creativity, commitment and judgment. For these you must strive for excellence and have the drive to succeed.

CHEFS AND RESTAURANTS

Cooks have produced food in quantity for as long as people have eaten together. For millennia, chefs have catered to the often elaborate dining needs of the wealthy and powerful, whether they be Asian, Native Canadian, European or African. And for centuries, vendors in China, Europe and elsewhere have sold to the public foods they prepared themselves or bought from others.

But the history of the professional chef is of relatively recent origin. Its cast is mostly French, and it is intertwined with the history of restaurants. For only with the development of restaurants during the late 18th and early 19th centuries were chefs expected to produce, efficiently and economically, different dishes at different or the same times for different diners.

The 18th Century—Boulanger's Restaurant

The word "restaurant" is derived from the French word *restaurer* (to restore). Since the 16th century, the word "restorative" had been used to describe rich and highly flavoured soups or stews capable of restoring lost strength. Restoratives, like all other cooked foods offered and purchased outside the home, were made by guild members. Each guild had a monopoly on preparing certain food items. For example, during the reign of Henri IV of France (1553–1610), there were separate guilds for *rôtisseurs* (who cooked *la grosse viande*, the main cuts of meat), *pâtissiers* (who cooked poultry, pies and tarts), *tamisiers* (who baked breads), *vinaigriers* (who made sauces and some stews, including some restoratives), *traiteurs* (who made ragouts) and *porte-chapes* (caterers who organized feasts and celebrations).

The French claim that the first modern restaurant opened one day in 1765 when a Parisian tavernkeeper, a Monsieur Boulanger, hung a sign advertising the sale of his special restorative, a dish of sheep feet in white sauce. His establishment closed shortly thereafter as the result of a lawsuit brought by a guild whose members claimed that Boulanger was infringing on their exclusive right to sell prepared dishes. Boulanger triumphed in court and later reopened.

Boulanger's establishment differed from the inns and taverns that had existed throughout Europe for centuries. These inns and taverns served foods prepared (usually off-premises) by the appropriate guild. The food—of which there was little choice—was offered by the keeper as incidental to the establishment's primary function: providing sleeping accommodations or drink. Customers were served family-style and ate at communal tables. Boulanger's contribution to the food service industry was to serve a variety of foods prepared on premises to customers whose primary interest was dining.

Several other restaurants opened in Paris during the succeeding decades, including the Grande Taverne de Londres in 1782. Its owner, Antoine Beauvilliers (1754–1817), advanced the development of the modern restaurant by offering his wealthy patrons a menu listing available dishes during fixed hours. Beauvilliers' impeccably trained wait staff served patrons at small, individual tables in an elegant setting.

The French Revolution (1789–1799) had a significant effect on the budding restaurant industry. Along with the aristocracy, guilds and their monopolies were generally abolished. The revolution also allowed the public access to the skills and creativity of the well-trained, sophisticated chefs who had worked in the aristocracy's private kitchens.

The Early 19th Century—Carême and *Grande Cuisine*

As the 19th century progressed, more restaurants opened, serving a greater selection of items and catering to a wider clientele. By mid-century, there were several large, grand restaurants in Paris serving elaborate meals, decidedly reminiscent of the *grande cuisine* (also known as *haute cuisine*) of the aristocracy. **Grande cuisine**, which arguably reached its peak of perfection in the hands of Antonin Carême, was characterized by meals consisting of dozens of courses of elaborately and intricately prepared, presented, garnished and sauced foods. Other restaurateurs blended the techniques and styles of *grande cuisine* with the simpler foods and tastes of the middle class (*cuisine bourgeoisie*) to create a new cuisine simpler than *grande cuisine* but more than mere home cooking.

● *grande cuisine* the rich, intricate and elaborate cuisine of the 18th- and 19th-century French aristocracy and upper classes. It is based on the rational identification, development and adoption of strict culinary principles. By emphasizing the how and why of cooking, *grande cuisine* was the first to distinguish itself from regional cuisines, which tend to emphasize the tradition of cooking.

The Late 19th Century—Escoffier and *Cuisine Classique*

Following the lead set by the French in both culinary style and the restaurant business, restaurants opened in the Americas and throughout Europe during the 19th century. Charles Ranhofer (1836–1899) was the first internationally renowned chef of an American restaurant, Delmonico's in New York City. In 1893 Ranhofer published his "franco-american" encyclopedia of cooking, *The Epicurean*, containing more than 3500 recipes.

One of the finest restaurants outside France was the dining room at London's Savoy Hotel, opened in 1898 under the directions of Cesar Ritz (1850–1918) and Auguste Escoffier. Escoffier is generally credited with refining the *grande cuisine* of Carême to create *cuisine classique* or **classic cuisine**. By doing so, he brought French cuisine into the 20th century.

● **classic cuisine** a late 19th- and early 20th-century refinement and simplification of French *grande cuisine*. Classic (or classical) cuisine relies on the thorough exploration of culinary principles and techniques, and emphasizes the refined preparation and presentation of superb ingredients.

The Mid-20th Century—Point and *Nouvelle Cuisine*

The mid-20th century witnessed a trend toward lighter, more naturally flavoured and more simply prepared foods. Fernand Point was a master practitioner of this movement. But this master's goal of simplicity and refinement was carried to even greater heights by a generation of chefs Point trained: principally, Paul Bocuse, Jean and Pierre Troisgros, Alain Chapel, François Bise and Louis Outhier. They, along with Michel Guérard and Roger Vergé, were the pioneers of **nouvelle cuisine** in the early 1970s.

● **nouvelle cuisine** French for "new cooking"; a mid-20th-century movement away from many classic cuisine principles and toward a lighter cuisine based on natural flavours, shortened cooking times and innovative combinations

Marie-Antoine (Antonin) Carême (1784–1833)

Carême, known as the "cook of kings and the king of cooks," was an acknowledged master of French *grande cuisine*. Abandoned on the streets of Paris as a child, he worked his way from cook's helper in a working-class restaurant to become one of the most prestigious chefs of his (or, arguably, any other) time. During his career he was chef to the famous French diplomat and gourmand Talleyrand, the Prince Regent of England (who became King George IV), Tsar Alexander I of Russia and Baron de Rothschild, among others.

His stated goal was to achieve "lightness," "grace," "order" and "perspicuity" in the preparation and presentation of food. As a *pâtissier*, he designed and prepared elaborate and elegant pastry and confectionery creations, many of which were based on architectural designs. (He wrote that "the fine arts are five in number, namely: painting, sculpture, poetry, music, architecture—the main branch of which is confectionery.") As a showman, he garnished his dishes with ornamental *hatelets* (skewers) threaded with colourful ingredients such as crayfish and intricately carved vegetables, and presented his creations on elaborate *socles* (bases). As a *saucier*, he standardized the use of roux as

Courtesy of Barbara Wheaton

a thickening agent, perfected recipes and devised a system for classifying sauces. As a *garde-manger*, Carême popularized cold cuisine, emphasizing moulds and aspic dishes. As a culinary professional, he designed kitchen tools, equipment and uniforms.

As an author, he wrote and illustrated important texts on the culinary arts,

including *Le Maître d'hôtel français* (1822), describing the hundreds of dishes he had personally created and cooked in the capitals of Europe; *Le Pâtissier royal parisien* (1825), containing fanciful designs for *les pièces montées*, the great decorative centrepieces that were the crowning glory of grand dinners; and his five-volume masterpiece on the state of his profession, *L'Art de la cuisine au XIXe siècle* (1833), the last two volumes of which were completed after his death by his associate, Plumerey. Carême's writings almost single-handedly refined and summarized 500 years of culinary evolution. But his treatises were not mere cookbooks. Rather, he analyzed cooking, old and new, emphasizing procedure and order and covering every aspect of the art known as *grande cuisine*.

Carême died before the age of 50, burnt out, according to Laurent Tailhade, "by the flame of his genius and the coal of the spits."

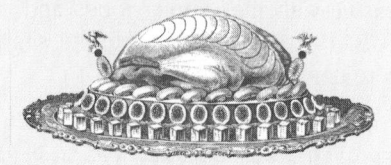

The nouvelle cuisine philosophy is premised on the rejection of overly rich, needlessly complicated dishes. These chefs emphasize healthful eating. The ingredients must be absolutely fresh and of the highest possible quality; the cooking methods should be simple and direct whenever possible. The accompaniments and garnishes must be light and must contribute to an overall harmony; the completed plates must be elegantly designed and decorated. Following these guidelines, some traditional cooking methods have been applied to untraditional ingredients, and ingredients have been combined in new and previously unorthodox fashions. For chefs with taste, skill, knowledge and judgment, this works.

The Late 20th Century—Regional, Slow Food and Fusion Cuisine

The late 20th century was characterized by a resurgence in regional cuisine with the emphasis on sourcing the best of local, seasonal products. Producers and chefs became partners. Marcel Kretz pioneered this concept in Canada while at La Sapinière in Quebec. Chez Panisse's Alice Waters led the American front, which included local producers raising many commodities previously imported (e.g., foie gras). Simple preparations highlighting foods' natural flavours were preferred.

Auguste Escoffier (1846–1935)

Escoffier's brilliant culinary career began at the age of 13 in his uncle's restaurant and continued until his death at the age of 89. Called the "Emperor of the world's kitchens," he is perhaps best known for defining French cuisine and dining during *La Belle Époque* (the "Gay Nineties").

Unlike Carême, Escoffier never worked in an aristocratic household. Rather, he exhibited his culinary skills in the dining rooms of the finest hotels in Europe, including the Place Vendôme in Paris and the Savoy and Carlton Hotels in London.

Escoffier did much to enhance the *grande cuisine* that arguably had reached its perfection under Carême. Crediting Carême with providing the foundation for great—that is, French—cooking, Escoffier simplified the profusion of flavours, dishes and garnishes typifying Carême's work. He also streamlined some of Carême's overly elaborate and fussy procedures and classifications. For example, he reduced Carême's elaborate system of classifying sauces into the five families of sauces still recognized today. Escoffier sought simplicity and aimed for the perfect balance of a few superb ingredients. Some consider his refinement of *grande cuisine* to have been so radical as to credit him with the development of a new cuisine referred to as *cuisine classique* (classic or classical cuisine).

His many writings include *Le Livre des menus* (1912), in which, discussing the principles of a well-planned meal, he analogizes a great dinner to a symphony with contrasting movements that should be appropriate to the occasion, the guests and the season, and *Ma cuisine* (1934), surveying *cuisine bourgeoisie*. But his most important contribution is a culinary treatise intended for the professional chef entitled *Le Guide culinaire* (1903). Still in use today, it is an astounding collection of more than 5000 classic cuisine recipes and garnishes. In it, Escoffier emphasizes the mastery of techniques, the thorough understanding of cooking principles and the appreciation of ingredients: attributes he considered the building blocks professional chefs should use to create great dishes.

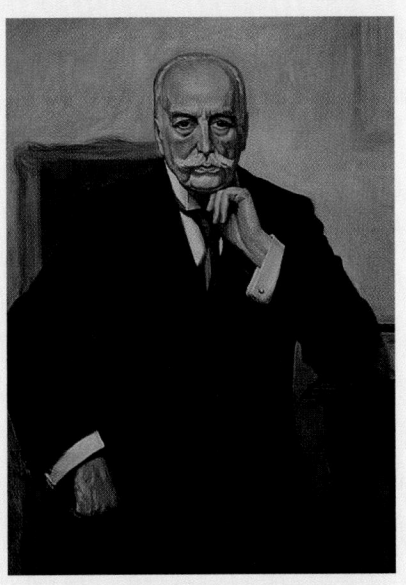

Escoffier was honoured as a Chevalier of the French Legion of Honour in 1920 for his work in enhancing the reputation of French cuisine.

Coupled with regionalism is the Slow Food movement. Started in 1986 by Carlo Petrini to counteract the proliferation of fast food, the Slow Food movement has spread globally from its origins in Rome. Its goals are to protect cultural regional food and drink and encourage the use of local ingredients. In 2004, Petrini and Massimo Montanari spearheaded the creation of the University of Gastronomic Sciences in Piedmont and Emilia-Romagna, Italy. The goal is to promote an awareness of good food and nutrition while sustaining ecological balances within an ecosystem.

A concept called **fusion cuisine** evolved during this time. Ingredients or methods from one region or ethnic base are combined with those of another; for example, a duck confit is flavoured with lemon grass, ginger and chiles. A thorough knowledge of ingredients and flavours is necessary to successfully create a great fusion dish.

● **fusion cuisine** the blending or use of ingredients and/or preparation methods from various ethnic, regional or national cuisines in the same dish; also known as transnational cuisine

Fernand Point (1897–1955)

A massive man with a monumental personality, Point refined and modernized the classic cuisine of Escoffier. By doing so, he laid the foundations for nouvelle cuisine.

Point received his early training in some of the finest hotel-restaurant kitchens in Paris. In 1922 he and his family moved to Vienne, a city in southeast France near Lyon, and opened a restaurant. Two years later his father left the restaurant to Fernand, who renamed it *La Pyramide*. During the succeeding years it became one of the culinary wonders of the world.

Point disdained dominating sauces and distracting accompaniments and garnishes. He believed that each dish should have a single dominant ingredient, flavour or theme; garnishes must be simple and match "like a tie to a suit." Procedure was of great importance. He devoted equal efforts to frying an egg and creating the marjolaine (a light almond and hazelnut spongecake filled with chocolate and praline buttercreams). His goal was to use the finest of raw ingredients to produce perfect food that looked elegant and simple. But simplicity was not easy to achieve. As he once said, "A béarnaise sauce is simply an egg yolk, a shallot, a little tarragon vinegar, and butter, but it takes years of practice for the result to be perfect."

At the same time that chefs are sourcing ingredients globally, they are also working in tandem with farmers to supply their diners with fresh flavours while preserving local agriculture and heirloom varieties. The concern for locally raised ingredients, referred to as the **farm-to-table movement**, has influenced chefs to serve fresh seasonal foods, such as wild greens or pastured pork, that is produced within 100 miles of their restaurants.

Beginning in the 1990s, chefs began to seriously explore the scientific aspect of cooking. The French scientist Hervé This coined the term **molecular gastronomy** to describe the re-engineering of cooking using industrial concepts and machines. Ferran Adrià of Spain's elBulli restaurant is the founding chef. Hallmarks include superb quality ingredients, intense flavours, dehydrators, espumas and freezer technologies.

Many chefs have been elevated to celebrity status; an entire cable television network is devoted to cooking. Bookstore and library shelves are jammed with cookbooks, and newspapers and magazines regularly review restaurants and report on culinary trends. With gourmet shops and cookware stores in most malls, cooking has become both a hobby and a spectator sport. All this has helped inspire a generation of Canadian teenagers to pursue careers behind the stove—and in front of the camera.

● **farm-to-table movement** an awareness of the source of ingredients with an emphasis on serving locally grown and minimally processed foods in season

● **molecular gastronomy** a contemporary scientific movement that investigates the chemistry and physics behind the preparation of foods and dishes

Ferran Adrià (1962–)

Cooking is a language through which all the following properties may be expressed: harmony, creativity, happiness, beauty, poetry, complexity, magic, humour, provocation and culture.
—Ferran Adrià

Ferran Adrià is an experimental Spanish chef called the Salvador Dalí of the kitchen. Adrià's restaurant, elBulli (slang for "the bulldog"), was voted World's Best Restaurant four times by Britain's *Restaurant* magazine. ElBulli also had three Michelin stars, the highest rating, an award it maintained since 1997.

Born near Barcelona, this food futurist planned a business career before a temporary dishwashing job redirected his path. Inspired by classic cuisine and an encouraging chef, Adrià began his self-education, reading from cover to cover *El Práctico*, a cooking manual edited by a Spanish chef heavily influenced by Escoffier. A month working at elBulli, a prestigious resort restaurant in the tiny town of Roses on the Costa Brava, was an experience so stimulating that he returned there upon completion of his military service in 1984.

At the time, the cuisine at elBulli was heavily influenced by nouvelle cuisine, then at its height. Working alongside the restaurant's

chef, Adrià created new versions of acclaimed French dishes, earning the restaurant its first star in the influential Michelin Guide. He enhanced his skills and knowledge of classic technique through brief apprenticeships in top kitchens in France. But in 1987, Adrià heard an expression that was to change his direction as a chef. "Creativity means not copying," said Jacques Maximin, then chef of Le Chanticleer in Nice, France. At that moment Adrià and his team committed themselves to reinventing cuisine as we know it.

The food served at elBulli engaged all of one's senses. Dinner was a tasting menu of up to 35 bite-sized dishes. What appeared to be cooked may actually have been flash

frozen. A herb clipped to a spoon allowed guests to smell the aroma before tasting the herb in the dish. Warm foam that tasted of carrots or mushrooms, hot gelatin, encapsulated mango purée that resembled egg yolks and ravioli filled with liquid were some of the show-stopping techniques for which Adrià became known. At the vanguard of experimental cooking, Adrià and staff spent six months each year working with food technologists, industrial designers and artists experimenting with new techniques. The chef and his staff documented their style of cooking in a 23-point synthesis. Using the freshest ingredients and mastery of technique are given, they write. But all foods are of equal gastronomic value, with a preference for vegetables and seafood to create a "light, harmonic cuisine" based on classic and modern technologies.

Among those who have worked at elBulli, Chef Grant Achatz of Alinea in Chicago and Chef Wylie Dufresne of wd50 in New York City have become leaders in this emerging modern style of cooking. Indicative of the appeal of this challenging cuisine, millions of prospective customers vied for one of only 8000 seats at the restaurant each year.

In 2010, Adrià announced that he would be temporarily closing elBulli and opening a professional academy.

INFLUENCES ON MODERN FOOD SERVICE OPERATIONS

From Monsieur Boulanger's humble establishment, a great industry has grown. Today there are more than 60 000 restaurants in Canada, as well as institutional and catering facilities. The dramatic growth and diversification of the food service industry are due in part to the Industrial Revolution and the social and economic changes it wrought, including the introduction of new technologies, foods, concerns and consumers.

New Technologies

Technology has always had a profound effect on cooking. For example, the development of clay and, later, metal vessels that could contain liquids and withstand as well as conduct heat offered prehistoric cooks the opportunity to stew, make soups and porridge, pickle and brine foods and control fermentation. But it was not until the rapid technological advances fostered by the Industrial Revolution that anything approaching the modern kitchen was possible.

One of the most important advancements was the introduction of the cast-iron stove. Prior to the 19th century, most cooking was done on spits or grills or in cauldrons or pots set on or in a wood- or coal-burning hearth. Hearthside cooking did not lend itself well to the simultaneous preparation of many items or to items requiring constant and delicate attention. With the introduction of cast-iron stoves during the 1800s (first wood- and coal-burning, then, by mid-century, gas and, by the early 20th century, electric), cooks could more comfortably and safely approach the heat source and control its temperatures. Cooks were also able to prepare efficiently and hold for later use or service a multitude of smaller amounts of items requiring different cooking methods or ingredients. This is a necessity at a restaurant simultaneously catering to different diners' demands.

Also of great importance were developments in food preservation and storage techniques. For thousands of years, food had been preserved by sun-drying, salting, smoking, pickling, sugar-curing or fermenting. Although useful, these procedures destroy or distort the appearance and flavour of most foods. By the early 19th century, preserving techniques that had minimal effect on appearance and flavour began to emerge. For example, by 1800 the Frenchman François Appert successfully "canned" foods by subjecting foods stored in sterilized glass jars to very high heat. An early mechanical refrigerator was developed by the mid-1800s; soon reliable iceboxes, refrigerators and, later, freezers were available. During the 20th century, freeze-drying, vacuum-packing and irradiation became common preservation techniques.

While advancements were being made in preservation and storage techniques, developments in transportation technology were also underway. During the 19th century, steam-powered ships and railroads were able to bring foods quickly to market from distant suppliers. Indeed, by the early 1900s, live Atlantic oysters were available on the western plains. During and since the 20th century, temperature-controlled cargo ships, trains, trucks and airplanes all have been used as part of an integrated worldwide food transportation network.

Combined with dependable food preservation and storage techniques, improved transportation networks have freed chefs from seasonal and geographic limitations in their choice of foods and have expanded consumers' culinary horizons.

Engineering advancements also have facilitated or even eliminated much routine kitchen work. Since the start of the Industrial Revolution, chefs have come to rely increasingly on mechanical and motorized food processors, mixers and cutters, as well as a wealth of sophisticated kitchen equipment such as high-carbon stainless steel knife blades, microwave ovens, convection-steamers, combitherm ovens and induction cooktops. More recently, new computer technologies have made managing restaurant kitchens more efficient. And with easy access to the Internet, chefs can now source ingredients from a world of suppliers.

New Foods

Modern food preservation, storage and transportation techniques have made both fresh and exotic foods regularly available to chefs and consumers. Many of these foods are themselves more wholesome as the result of progress in agriculture and animal husbandry.

Advancements in agriculture such as the switch from organic to chemical fertilizers and the introduction of pesticides and drought- or pest-resistant strains have resulted in increased yields of crops. Traditional hybridization techniques and, more recently, genetic engineering have produced new or improved grains and, for better or for worse, fruits and vegetables that have a longer shelf life and are more amenable to mass-production handling, storage and transportation methods.

Likewise, advancements in animal husbandry and aquaculture have led to a more reliable supply of leaner, healthier meat, poultry and fish. Moreover, foods found traditionally only in the wild (for example, game, wild rice and many mushrooms) are now being raised commercially and are routinely available.

Food preservation and processing techniques have led to the development of quality packaged, prepared convenience foods. Today's chef can rely on many of these products. They allow greater flexibility and more time to devote to other preparations.

New Concerns

Consumer concerns about nutrition and diet have fuelled changes in the food service industry. Obviously, what we eat affects our health. Adequate amounts of nutrients promote good health by preventing deficiencies and chronic diseases and increasing longevity.

The public has long been concerned about food safety. Federal, provincial and local governments have helped promote food safety by inspecting and grading meats and poultry, regulating label contents for packaged foods and setting sanitation standards. All these standards, especially sanitation standards, affect the way foods are prepared, stored and served.

Concerns about nutrition and food safety have resulted in renewed interest in organically grown fruits and vegetables and free-range-raised animals. Consumers are more aware of additives and preservatives used in commercial food production.

New Consumers

Demographic and social changes have contributed to the diversification of the food service industry by creating or identifying new consumer groups with their own desires or needs. By tailoring their menu, prices and decor accordingly, food service operations cater to consumers defined by age (baby boomers and seniors, in particular), type of household (singles, couples and families), income, education and geography.

Since the 20th century, especially in the decades following World War II, there has also been a rapid increase in the number and type of institutions providing food services. These include hospitals, schools, retirement centres, hotels and resorts (which may, in turn, have fine dining, coffee shop, banquet and room service facilities), factories, camps and office complexes. Each of these institutions presents the professional chef with unique challenges, whether they be culinary, dietary or budgetary.

Through travel or exposure to the many books and magazines about food, consumers are becoming better educated and more sophisticated. Educated consumers provide a market for new foods and cuisines (**global**, **national**, **regional** and **ethnic**) as well as an appreciation for a job well done.

Although some consumers may frequent a particular restaurant because its chef or owner is a celebrity or the restaurant is riding high on a crest of fad or fashion, most consumers choose a restaurant—whether it be a fast-food burger place or an elegant fine-dining restaurant—because it provides quality food at a cost they are willing to pay. To remain successful, then, the restaurant must carefully balance its commitment to quality with marketplace realities.

- **global cuisine** foods (often commercially produced items) or preparation methods that have become ubiquitous throughout the world; for example, curries and french-fried potatoes
- **national cusine** the characteristic cuisine of a nation
- **regional cuisine** a set of recipes based upon local ingredients, traditions and practices; within a larger geographical, political, cultural or social unit, regional cuisines are often variations of one another that blend together to create a national cuisine
- **ethnic cuisine** the cuisine of a group of people having a common cultural heritage, as opposed to the cuisine of a group of people bound together by geography or political factors

THE FOOD SERVICE OPERATION

To function efficiently, a food service operation must be well organized and staffed with appropriate personnel. This staff is traditionally called a **brigade**. Currently we refer to the "team," and sometimes the chef's title is kitchen leader. Although a chef will be most familiar with the back of the house or kitchen brigade, he or she should also understand how the dining room or front of the house operates. Staffing any food service facility ultimately depends on the type and complexity of the menu. (Types and styles of menus are discussed in Chapter 4, Menu Planning and Food Costing.)

- **brigade** a system of staffing a kitchen so that each worker is assigned a set of specific tasks; these tasks are often related by cooking method, equipment or the types of foods being produced

The Modern Kitchen Brigade

Today most food service operations utilize a simplified version of Escoffier's kitchen brigade.

The *executive chef*, working chef or kitchen leader is a team player who coordinates kitchen activities and directs the kitchen staff's training and work efforts. Taking into consideration factors such as food costs, food availability and popularity as well as labour costs, kitchen skills and equipment, the executive chef plans menus and creates recipes. He or she sets and enforces nutrition, safety and sanitation standards and participates in (or at least observes) the preparation and presentation of menu items to ensure that quality standards are rigorously and consistently maintained. The chef or kitchen leader may also be responsible for purchasing food items and, often, equipment. In some food service operations, the executive chef may assist in designing the menu, dining room and kitchen. He or she also educates the dining room staff so that they can correctly answer questions about the menu. The chef may also work with food purveyors to learn about new food items and products, as well as with equipment vendors, food stylists, restaurant consultants, public relations specialists, sanitation engineers, nutritionists and dietitians.

The executive chef is assisted by a *sous-chef* or *executive sous-chef*, who participates in, supervises and coordinates the preparation of menu items. His or her primary responsibility is to make sure that the food is prepared, portioned, garnished and presented according to the standards established by the executive chef. The sous-chef may be the cook principally responsible for producing menu items and supervising the kitchen.

The Dining Room

Like the back-of-the-house (i.e., kitchen) staff, the front-of-the-house (i.e., dining room) staff is also organized into a brigade. The dining room brigade is led by the *dining room manager* (French *maître d'hotel* or *maître d'*), who generally trains all service personnel, oversees wine selections and works with the chef to develop the menu. He or she organizes the seating chart and may also seat the guests. Working with this manager are the following:

The *wine steward* (French *chef de vin* or *sommelier*), who is responsible for the wine service, including purchasing wines, assisting guests in selecting wines and then serving the wines.

The *headwaiter* (French *chef de salle*), who is responsible for service throughout the dining room or a section of it. In smaller operations, his or her role may be assumed by the *maître d'* or a captain.

The *captains* (French *chefs d'étage*), who are responsible for explaining the menu to guests and taking their orders. They are also responsible for any table-side preparations.

The *front waiters* (French *chefs de rang*), who are responsible for ensuring that the tables are set correctly for each course, foods are delivered properly to the right tables and the needs of the guests are met.

The *backwaiters* (French *demi-chefs de rang* or *commis de rang*, also known as dining room attendants or buspersons), who are responsible for clearing plates, refilling water glasses and other general tasks appropriate for new dining room workers.

Whether a restaurant uses this entire array of staff depends upon the nature and size of the restaurant and the type of service

provided. With *American service* there is one waiter (also called a server) who takes the order and brings the food to the table. The table is then cleaned by a dining room attendant. With *French service* there are two waiters: a captain and a waiter. The captain takes the order, does the tableside cooking and brings the drinks, appetizers, entrees and desserts to the table. The waiter serves bread and water, clears each course, crumbs the table and serves the coffee. With *Russian service*, the entree, vegetables and potatoes are served from a platter onto a plate by the waiter. With *buffet service*, usually found in specialty restaurants and some institutional settings such as schools and correctional facilities, diners generally serve themselves or are served by workers assigned to specific areas of the buffet. Restaurants offering buffet service generally charge by the meal; if they charge by the dish they are known as cafeterias.

On Experience

Sight, feel, hearing, and smell taught me about food. By touching a piece of meat, I learned to determine its degree of doneness. Raw meat was spongy, well-done meat hard. I learned precisely how to determine all the stages in between by pushing a finger against the surface of the meat. Hearing was significant, too. The snap of an asparagus spear, the crunch of an apple, the pop of a grape are all indicators of freshness and quality. I learned to listen to the sizzling sound of a chicken roasting in the oven. When *le poulet chant* (the chicken sings), I knew that the layers of fat had clarified, signifying that the chicken was nearly done. Smell was of importance in recognizing quality. A fresh fish smells of the sea, seaweed, and salt. Fresh meat has a sweet smell, fresh poultry practically no smell at all. Melon, pears, tomatoes, raspberries, oranges and the like each have their own distinctive fragrance when perfectly ripe.

Large hotels and conference centres with multiple dining facilities may have several sous-chefs, each responsible for a specific facility or function. There could be, for instance, a restaurant chef and a banquet chef. Sous-chefs report to the executive chef, and each in turn has a brigade/team functioning with him or her.

Like Escoffier's station chefs, *line cooks* (or section cooks) are responsible for preparing menu items according to recipe specifications. Making the most of time, talent, space and equipment, the chef assigns responsibilities to each of the line cooks. Depending upon the size and type of operation, the sauté, broiler, fry, soup and vegetable stations may be combined into one position, as may the pantry, cold foods and salad stations.

The *pastry chef* is responsible for developing recipes for and preparing desserts, pastries, frozen desserts and breads. He or she is usually responsible for purchasing the food items used in the bake shop.

A restaurant may employ a certified chef or *master chef* (Fr. *maître cuisinier*), *master pastry chef* (Fr. *maître pâtissier*) or a *master baker* (Fr. *maître boulanger*, Gr. *bäckermeister*). These titles recognize the highest level of achievement; only highly skilled and experienced professionals who have demonstrated their expertise and knowledge in written and practical exams are entitled to use them. These titles are based on the European guild tradition still prevalent in some countries today. In Germany, for example, a chef, pastry chef or baker must pursue years of classroom and job training, work as an apprentice and pass numerous examinations before acquiring the right to call himself or herself a "master."

And, as in Escoffier's days, *apprentices* and *kitchen helpers* are assigned where needed in today's kitchens.

New styles of dining have created new positions since Escoffier's days. The most notable is the *line/short-order cook*, who is responsible for quickly preparing foods to order in smaller operations. He or she will work the

The Classic Kitchen Brigade

From the chaos and redundancy found in the private kitchens of the 19th century's aristocracy, Escoffier created a distinct hierarchy of responsibilities and functions for food service operations.

At the top is the *chef de cuisine* or chef, who is responsible for all operations, developing menu items and setting the kitchen's tone and tempo.

His or her principal assistant is the *sous-chef* (the under chef or second chef), who is responsible for scheduling personnel and replacing the chef and station chefs as necessary. The sous-chef also often functions as the *aboyeur* (expediter or announcer), who accepts the orders from the dining room, relays them to the various station chefs and then reviews the dishes before service.

The *chefs de partie* (station chefs) produce the menu items under the direct supervision of the chef or sous-chef. Previously, whenever a cook needed an item, he or his assistants produced it; thus several cooks could be making the same sauce or basic preparation. Under Escoffier's system, each station chef is assigned a specific task based on either the cooking method and equipment or the category of items to be produced. They include the following:

- The *saucier* (sauté station chef), who holds one of the most demanding jobs in the classical kitchen, is responsible for all sautéed items and most sauces.
- The *poissonier* (fish station chef) is responsible for fish and shellfish items and their sauces.
- The *grillardin* (grill station chef) is responsible for all grilled items.
- The *friturier* (fry station chef) is responsible for all fried items.
- The *rôtisseur* (roast station chef) is responsible for all roasted items and jus or other related sauces.
- The *potager* (soup station chef) is responsible for soups and stocks.
- The *légumier* (vegetable station chef) is responsible for all vegetable and starch items.
- The *potager* and *légumier* functions are often combined into a single vegetable station whose chef is known as the *entremetier*. *Entremets* were the courses served after the roast; they usually comprised vegetables, fruits, fritters or sweet items (the sorbet served before the main course in some contemporary restaurants is a vestigial entremet).

- The *garde-manger* (pantry chef) is responsible for cold food preparations, including salads and salad dressings, cold appetizers, charcuterie items, pâtés, terrines and similar dishes. The garde-manger supervises the boucher (butcher), who is responsible for butchering meats and poultry, as well as the chefs responsible for hors d'oeuvre and breakfast items.
- The tournant, also known as the roundsman or swing cook, works where needed.
- The *pâtissier* (pastry chef) is responsible for all baked items, including breads, pastries and desserts. Unlike the several station chefs, the pâtissier is not necessarily under the sous-chef's supervision. The pâtissier supervises the boulanger (bread baker), who makes the breads, rolls and baked dough containers used for other menu items (for example, *bouchées* and *feuilletés*); the confiseur, who makes candies and petit fours; the glacier, who makes all chilled and frozen desserts; and the décorateur, who makes showpieces and special cakes.
- Depending on the size and needs of any station or area, there may be one or more demi-chefs (assistants) and commis (apprentices) who work with the station chef or pastry chef to learn the area.

broiler, deep-fat fryer and griddle as well as make sandwiches and even some sautéed items.

Another new position is the *institutional cook*, who generally works with large quantities of prepackaged or prepared foods for a captive market such as a school, hospital, prison or camp.

Camp cooks often prepare food in remote locations with limited facilities. They usually work for an industrial catering firm contracting multiple sites. Many sites are very modern and have high standards for food preparation and service.

THE PROFESSIONAL CHEF

Although there is no one career ladder for producing a good professional chef, we believe that with training, skill, taste, judgment, dedication and pride, a student cook or apprentice will develop into a professional chef.

Training

Chefs must be able to identify, purchase, utilize and prepare a wide variety of foods. They should be able to train and supervise a safe, skilled and efficient staff. To do all this successfully, chefs must possess a body of knowledge and

The Vocabulary of Eating Well

Gastronomy—The art and science of eating well.

Gourmet—A connoisseur of fine food and drink.

Gourmand—A connoisseur of fine food and drink, often to excess.

Gourmet foods—Foods of the highest quality, perfectly prepared and beautifully presented.

Cooking for Others

Each person has a set of preferred tastes and biases. When cooking for others, one must at times ignore one's own preference for some flavours. Salt and pepper are common ingredients in many dishes and each person tolerates different levels of seasoning. Remember to cook for your clients, not just yourself, and do not mask the taste of the principal ingredients by overseasoning. Superior taste is a balance of the elements—sweet, sour, salty, bitter and umami.

understand and apply certain scientific and business principles. Schooling helps. A professional culinary program—whether at the secondary or post-secondary level—should, at a minimum, provide the student cook with a basic knowledge of foods, food styles and the methods used to prepare foods. Student cooks must be able to apply sanitation, nutrition and business procedures such as food costing. They start their apprenticeship at this time. After approximately three years of work experience and technical training, they take the Journeyperson's exam and Interprovincial Red Seal. This can be followed by achieving Certified Chef de Cuisine (CCC) or Certified Master Chef (CMC) status.

This textbook is designed to help you learn these basics. Many chapters have extensive sections identifying foods and equipment. Throughout this book we emphasize culinary principles, not recipes. Whenever possible, whether it be preparing puff pastry or grilling a steak, we focus on the general procedure, highlighting fundamental principles and skills; we discuss both the how and the why of cooking. Only then are specific applications and sample recipes given. We also want you to have a sense of the rich tradition of cookery, so informative sidebars on food history, chef biographies and other topics are scattered throughout the book.

In this way, we follow the trail blazed by Escoffier, who wrote in the introduction to *Le Guide culinaire* that his book is not intended to be a compendium of recipes to be slavishly followed, but rather his treatise should be a tool that leaves his colleagues "free to develop their own methods and follow their own inspiration;... The art of cooking ... will evolve as a society evolves,... only basic rules remain unalterable."

As with any profession, an education does not stop at graduation. The acquisition of knowledge continues after the student cook joins the ranks of the employed. He or she should take additional classes on unique or ethnic cuisines, nutrition, business management or specialized skills. Apprentices and professionals should regularly review some of the many periodicals and books devoted to cooking and should travel and try new dishes to broaden their culinary horizons. The professional cook should also become involved in professional organizations in order to meet peers and exchange ideas.

Skill

Culinary schooling alone does not make a student a cook. Nothing but practical, hands-on experience will provide even the most academically gifted student with the skills needed to produce, consistently and efficiently, quality foods or to organize, train, motivate and supervise a staff.

Many food service operations recognize that new workers, even those who have graduated from culinary programs, need time and experience to develop and hone their skills. Therefore, many graduates start at entry-level positions. They should not be discouraged; advancement will come and the training pays off in the long run. Today culinary styles and fashions change frequently. What do not go out of fashion are well-trained, skilled and knowledgeable cooks. They can adapt.

Taste

No matter how knowledgeable or skilled the cook, he or she must be able to produce food that tastes great or the consumer will not return. A cook can only do so if confident about his or her own sense of taste.

Our total perception of taste is a complex combination of smell, taste, sight, sound and texture. All senses are involved in the enjoyment of eating; all must be considered in creating or preparing a dish. The cook should develop a taste memory by sampling foods, both familiar and unfamiliar. He or she should think about what is being tasted, make notes and experiment with flavour combinations and cooking methods. But a cook should not be inventive simply for the sake of invention. Rather, cooks must consider how the flavours, appearances, textures and aromas of various foods will interact to create a total taste experience. (See Chapter 7, Flavours and Flavourings, for further discussion of taste and flavours.)

Judgment

Selecting menu items, determining how much of what item to order, deciding whether and how to combine ingredients and approving finished items for service are all matters of judgment. Although knowledge and skill play a role in developing judgment, sound judgment comes only with experience. And real experience is often accompanied by failure. Do not be upset or surprised when a dish does not turn out as you expected. Learn from your mistakes as well as from your successes; only then will you develop sound judgment.

Dedication

Becoming a cook is hard work; so is being one. The work is often physically taxing, the hours are usually long and the pace is frequently hectic. Despite these pressures, the cook is expected to efficiently produce consistently fine foods that are properly prepared, seasoned, garnished and presented. To do so, the cook must be dedicated to the job.

The dedicated cook should never falter. The food service industry is competitive and dependent upon the continuing good will of an often fickle public. One bad dish or one off night can result in a disgruntled diner and lost business. The cook should always be mindful of the food prepared and the customer served.

The cook must also be dedicated to co-workers. Virtually all food service operations rely on teamwork to get the job done well. Good teamwork requires dedication to a shared goal as well as a positive attitude. The cook is the individual who provides leadership and mentoring to the team.

Pride

Not only is it important that the job be well done, but the professional cook should also have a sense of pride in doing it well. Pride should also extend to personal appearance and behaviour in and around the kitchen. The professional cook should be well groomed and in uniform when working.

The professional cook's uniform consists of comfortable shoes, trousers (either solid white, solid black, black-and-white checked or black-and-white striped), a white double-breasted jacket, an apron and a neckerchief usually knotted or tied cravat style. The uniform has certain utilitarian aspects: checked trousers disguise stains; the double-breasted white jacket can be rebuttoned to hide dirt, and the double layer of fabric protects from scalds and burns; the neckerchief absorbs facial perspiration; and the apron protects the uniform and insulates the body. Side towels are useful. This uniform should be worn with pride. Shoes should be polished; trousers and jacket should be pressed.

Chef Profile

Shawn Whalen

Current Position: Owner/Culinary Director of Liaison College Toronto West

Career: Executive Chef for 19 years, most recently with Marriott as Regional Executive Chef in charge of the daily operation of two hotels.

Some Highlights:
- Earning numerous culinary awards, including 50 gold medals, trophies and best-of-show awards
- Captaining seven international culinary teams
- Guiding apprentices and cooks to 200 gold medals and 26 best-of-show awards
- Winning Chef of the Year awards from the Escoffier Society

Culinary Philosophy: I am an avid supporter of the apprenticeship program for training young chefs and students. I take pride in teaching apprentices the culinary arts for competition, hoping to instill in them a passion for quality, self-esteem and attention to detail that will follow them throughout their careers.

La toque blanche

The crowning element of the uniform is the toque. The toque is the tall white hat worn by cooks and chefs almost everywhere. Although the toque traces its origin to the monasteries of the 6th century, the style worn today was introduced at the end of the 19th century. Most cooks now wear a standard 15- or 24-cm-high (6- or 9-in.) toque, but historically a cook's rank in the kitchen dictated the type of hat worn. Beginners wore flat-topped calottes; cooks with more advanced skills wore low toques and the master chefs wore high toques called *dodin-bouffants*. Culinary lore holds that the toque's pleats—101 in all—represented the 101 ways its wearer could successfully prepare eggs.

Some establishments are switching to other styles of hats. The change is usually part of a marketing plan. In addition, colours and designs have been introduced into uniforms. But functionality must always be kept in mind.

Conclusion

The art and science of cookery form a noble profession with a rich history and long traditions. With training, knowledge, skill, taste, judgment, dedication and pride, the student cook or apprentice can become part of this profession. In this book we provide you with the basic knowledge and describe the techniques at which you must become skilled. Dedicate yourself to learning this information and mastering your skills. Once you have done so, take pride in your accomplishments. Good luck.

Questions for Discussion

1. Describe the kitchen brigade system. How does the classic brigade compare with modern teams?
2. What are the roles of a chef, sous-chef and line cook in a modern kitchen?
3. Describe the differences in a meal prepared by Carême and one prepared by Point.
4. List and explain three technological advances affecting food preparation.
5. Discuss the societal changes that have contributed to diversification in the modern food service industry.
6. Discuss the pros and cons of using only locally grown food within the context of Canada.

2 Food Safety and Sanitation

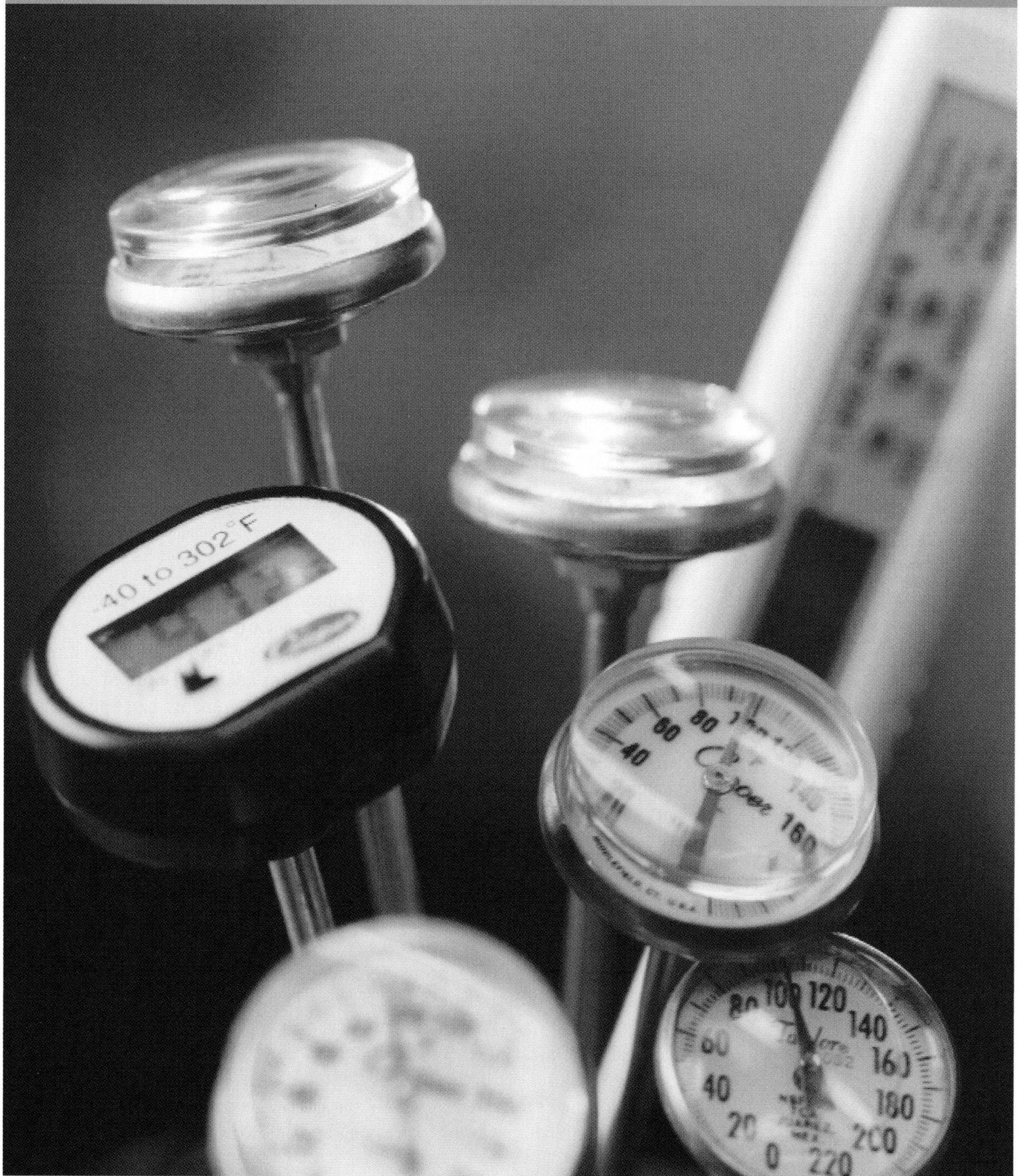

> "Our lives are not in the lap of the gods, but in the lap of our cooks.
>
> —Lin Yutang, Chinese-American writer, in *The Importance of Living*, 1937

● **sanitation** the creation and maintenance of conditions that control food contamination or food-borne illness

● **contamination** the presence, generally unintentional, of harmful organisms or substances

● **direct contamination** the contamination of raw foods in their natural settings or habitats

● **cross-contamination** the transfer of bacteria or other contaminants from one food, work surface or piece of equipment to another

● **microorganisms** single-celled organisms as well as tiny plants and animals that can be seen only through a microscope

The Canadian Food Inspection Agency has overall responsibility for setting and monitoring food safety standards. The industry is assuming more responsibility and accountability for food safety, and the role of health inspectors is evolving. Providing consumers with safe food is the food handler's most important responsibility. Food handlers include anyone coming into contact with food or food preparation equipment. Food handlers are also the primary cause of food-related illnesses.

By understanding how food-borne illnesses are caused and what can be done to prevent them, you will be better able to protect your customers. This chapter is not meant to be a complete discussion of sanitation in food service operations. It should, however, alert you to practices that can result in food-borne illnesses.

Federal, provincial and municipal health, building and other codes are designed in part to ensure that food is handled in a safe and proper manner. Always consult your local health department for information and guidance. Take an approved safe food handling course or upgrade your present certificate. And always be conscious of what you can do to create and maintain a safe product and safe environment for your customers, your fellow employees and yourself.

Sanitation refers to the creation and maintenance of conditions that will control food contamination or food-borne illness. **Contamination** refers to the presence, generally unintended, of harmful organisms or substances. Contaminants can be (1) **biological**, (2) **chemical** or (3) **physical**. When consumed in sufficient quantities, food-borne contaminants can cause illness or injury, long-lasting disease or even death.

Contamination occurs in two ways: direct contamination and cross-contamination. **Direct contamination** is the contamination of raw foods, or the plants or animals from which they come, in their natural settings or habitats. Chemical and biological contaminants such as bacteria and fungi are present in the air, soil and water. So foods can be easily contaminated by their general exposures to the environment: grains can become contaminated by soil fumigants in the field, and shellfish can become contaminated by ingesting toxic marine algae.

Chemicals and microorganisms generally cannot move on their own, however. They need to be transported, an event known as **cross-contamination**. The major cause of cross-contamination is people. Food handlers can transfer biological, chemical and physical contaminants to food while processing, preparing, cooking or serving it. It is therefore necessary to view sanitation as the correction of problems caused by direct contamination and the prevention of cross-contamination during processing and service.

DIRECT CONTAMINATION
Biological Contaminants

Biologically based food-borne illnesses can be caused by several **microorganisms**, primarily bacteria, parasites, viruses and fungi. By understanding how these organisms live and reproduce, you can better understand how to protect food from them.

Bacteria

Bacteria, which are single-celled microorganisms, are the leading cause of food-borne illnesses. (See Figure 2.1.) Most bacteria reproduce by binary fission: their genetic material is first duplicated and the nucleus then splits, each new nucleus taking some of the cellular material with it. (See Figure 2.2 on the next page.) Under favourable conditions each bacterium can divide every 15 to 30 minutes. Within 12 hours, 1 bacterium can become a colony of 72 billion bacteria, more than enough to cause serious illness.

Some rod-shaped bacteria are capable of forming spores. Spores are thick-walled structures used as protection against a hostile environment. The bacteria essentially hibernate within their spores, where they can survive extreme conditions that would otherwise destroy them. When conditions become favourable, the bacteria return to a viable state. This is important in food sanitation because bacterial spores may not be destroyed by heating or sanitizing techniques.

Some bacteria are beneficial, such as those that aid in digesting food or decomposing garbage. Other bacteria spoil food but without rendering it unfit for human consumption. These bacteria, called **putrefactives**, are not a sanitation concern. Indeed, in some cultures, they are not even a culinary concern. Cultures differ on what constitutes "bad" meat, for example, and red meat is sometimes hung for a time or "aged" to allow bacteria to tenderize the meat.

The bacteria that are dangerous when consumed by humans are called **pathogenic**. These are the bacteria that must be destroyed or controlled in a food service operation.

Intoxications and Infections

Depending upon the particular microorganism, pathogenic bacteria can cause illnesses in humans in one of three ways: by intoxication, infection or toxin-mediated infection.

Botulism is a well-known example of an **intoxication**. Certain bacteria produce **toxins**, byproducts of their life processes. You cannot smell, see or taste toxins. Ingesting these toxin-producing bacteria by themselves does not cause illness. But when their toxins are ingested, the toxins can poison the consumer. Proper food-handling techniques are critical in preventing an intoxication, because even if food is cooked to a sufficiently high temperature to kill all bacteria present, the toxins they leave behind are usually not destroyed.

The second type of bacterial illness is an **infection**. Salmonella is the most well-known example. An infection occurs when live pathogenic bacteria (infectants) are ingested. The bacteria then live in the consumer's intestinal tract. It is the living bacteria, not their waste products, that cause an illness. An infectant must be alive when eaten for it to do any harm. Fortunately, these bacteria can be destroyed by cooking foods to sufficiently high temperatures, usually 74°C (165°F) or higher, and maintaining the temperature for sufficient time.

The third type of bacterial illness has characteristics of both an intoxication and an infection, and is referred to as a **toxin-mediated infection**. Examples are *Clostridium perfringens* and *Escherichia coli 0157:H7*. When these living organisms are ingested, they establish colonies in human or animal intestinal tracts, where they then produce toxins. These bacteria are particularly dangerous for young children, the elderly, the infirm or immunosuppressed individuals.

Preventing Bacterial Intoxications and Infections

All bacteria, like other living things, need certain conditions in order to complete their life cycles. Like humans, they need food, a comfortable temperature, moisture, the proper pH, the proper atmosphere and time. The best way to prevent bacterial intoxications and infections is to control the factors bacteria need to survive and multiply.

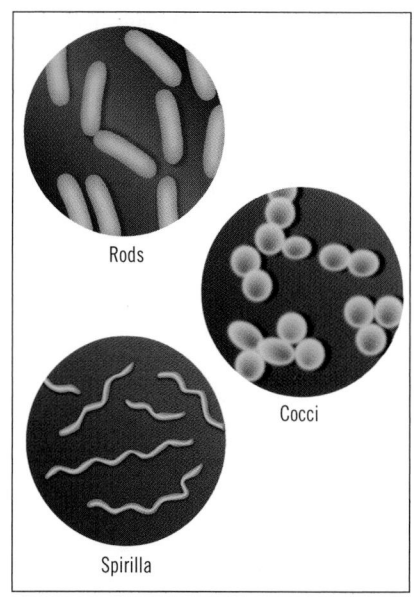

FIGURE 2.1 Bacteria can be classified by shape: rods are short, tubular structures; cocci are disks, some of which form clusters; and spirilla are corkscrews.

● **putrefactives** bacteria that spoil food without rendering it unfit for human consumption

● **pathogen** any organism that causes illness; usually refers to bacteria; undetectable by smell, sight or taste, pathogens are responsible for as much as 95% of all food-borne illnesses

● **intoxication** in the food safety context, an illness caused by the toxins that bacteria produce during their life processes

● **toxins** byproducts of living bacteria that can cause illness if consumed in sufficient quantities

● **infection** in the food safety context, an illness caused by the ingestion of live pathogenic bacteria that continue their life processes in the consumer's intestinal tract

● **toxin-mediated infection** illness from toxins produced in the intestine after ingesting living bacteria

potentially hazardous foods foods on which bacteria can thrive

temperature danger zone the broad range of temperatures between 4°C and 60°C (40°F and 140°F) at which bacteria multiply rapidly

Food Bacteria need food for energy and growth. The foods on which bacteria thrive are referred to as **potentially hazardous foods**. Potentially hazardous foods include those high in protein such as meat, poultry, fish and shellfish. Dairy products, eggs, grains and some vegetables (garlic and raw sprouts) are also sufficiently high in protein to support bacterial growth. These foods and items containing these foods (for example, custard, hollandaise sauce and quiche) must be handled with great care.

Temperature Temperature is the most important factor in the pathogenic bacteria's environment because it is the factor most easily controlled by food service workers. Most microorganisms are destroyed at high temperatures. Freezing slows, but does not stop, growth, nor does it destroy bacteria.

Most of the bacteria that cause food-borne illnesses multiply rapidly at temperatures between 16°C and 49°C (60°F and 120°F). Therefore, the broad range of temperatures between 4°C and 60°C (40°F and 140°F) is referred to as the **temperature danger zone**. (See Figure 2.3.) By keeping foods out of the temperature danger zone, you decrease the bacteria's ability to thrive and reproduce.

This is known as the *time-and-temperature principle*. Potentially hazardous foods should be heated or cooled quickly so that they are within the temperature danger zone as briefly as possible.

To control the growth of any bacteria that may be present, it is important to maintain the internal temperature of food at or above 60°C (140°F), or at 4°C (40°F) or below. Simply stated: ***Keep hot foods hot, cold foods cold***.

Keep hot foods hot. The high internal temperatures reached during cooking (74°C to 100°C/165°F to 212°F) kill most of the bacteria that can cause food-borne illnesses. When foods are reheated, the internal temperature should reach or exceed 77°C (170°F) for two minutes in order to kill any bacteria that may have grown during storage. Once properly heated, hot foods must be held at temperatures of 60°C (140°F) or above. Foods that are to be displayed or served hot must be heated rapidly to reduce the time within the temperature danger zone. When heating or reheating foods:

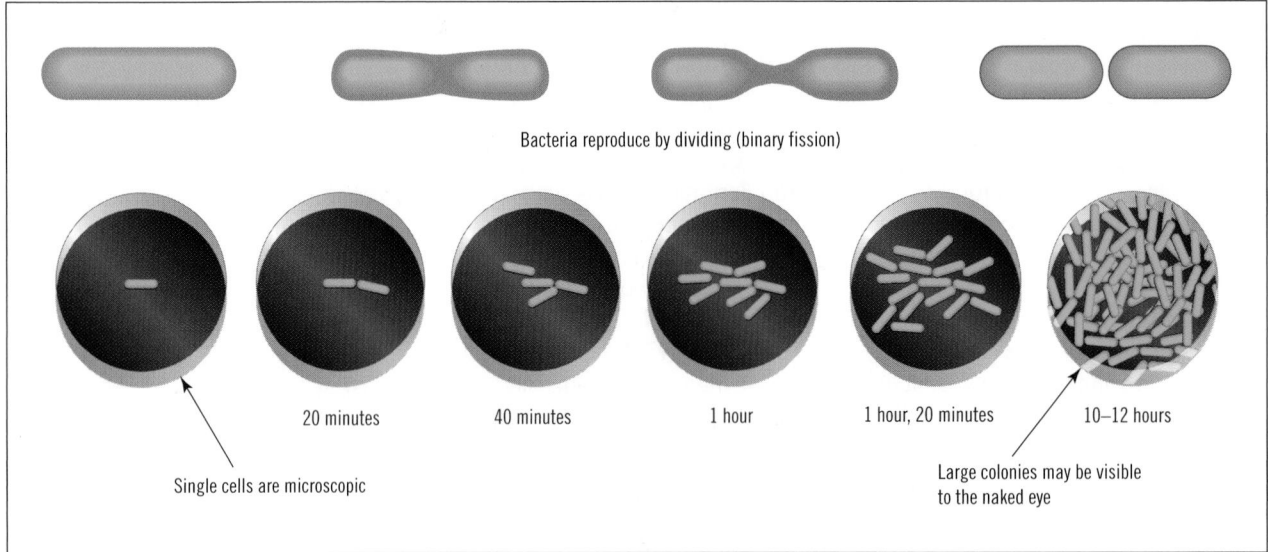

Bacteria reproduce by dividing (binary fission)

20 minutes   40 minutes   1 hour   1 hour, 20 minutes   10–12 hours

Single cells are microscopic

Large colonies may be visible to the naked eye

FIGURE 2.2 Binary fission: One bacterium divides into two; the two bacteria each divide, creating four; the four become 16 and so on. Under favourable conditons each bacterium can divide every 15 to 30 minutes. Within 12 hours, a colony of 72 billion bacteria is possible.

- Use shallow containers to promote rapid thermalization.
- Heat small quantities at a time.
- Stir frequently.
- Heat foods as close to service time as possible.
- Use preheated ingredients whenever possible to prepare hot foods.
- Never use a steam table for heating or reheating foods. Bring the food to an appropriate internal temperature (at least 77°C/170°F) for two minutes before placing it in the steam table for holding.

Keep cold foods cold. Foods that are to be displayed, stored or served cold must be cooled rapidly. When cooling foods:

- Refrigerate semisolid foods at 4°C (40°F) or below in containers that are less than 5 cm (2 in.) deep. (Increased surface area decreases cooling time.)
- Avoid crowding the refrigerator; allow air to circulate around foods.
- Vent hot foods in an ice water bath, as illustrated in Chapter 10, Stocks and Sauces. Stir frequently.
- Use prechilled ingredients, for example mayonnaise, to prepare cold foods.
- Store cooked foods above raw foods to prevent cross-contamination.

Keep frozen foods frozen. Freezing at –18°C (0°F) or below essentially stops bacterial growth but will not kill the bacteria. Do not place hot foods in a standard freezer. They will not cool more rapidly and the release of heat can raise the temperature of other foods in the freezer. Only a special blast or shock freezer can be used for chilling hot items. If one is not available, cool hot foods as described above before freezing them. When frozen foods are thawed, bacteria that are present will begin to grow. Therefore,

- Never thaw foods at room temperature.
- Thaw foods gradually under refrigeration. Place them in a container to prevent cross-contamination from dripping or leaking liquids.
- Thaw foods under cold running water if items are wrapped in plastic.
- Thaw foods in a microwave *only* if the food will be prepared and served immediately.

Time　When bacteria are moved from one place to another, they require time to adjust to new conditions. This resting period, during which very little growth occurs, is known as the **lag phase**. This phase averages two to four hours. It is followed by the **log phase**, a period of accelerated growth, which lasts until the bacteria begin to crowd others within their colony, creating competition for food, space and moisture. This begins the **decline** or **negative growth phase**, during which bacteria die at an accelerated rate. See Figure 2.4 on page 21.

Because of the lag phase, foods can be in the temperature danger zone for *very short periods* during preparation without an unacceptable increase in bacterial growth. Exposure to the temperature danger zone is cumulative, however, and should not exceed two hours total. The less time food is in the temperature danger zone, the less opportunity bacteria have to multiply.

Moisture　Bacteria need a certain amount of moisture, which is expressed as water activity or A_W. Water itself has an A_W of 1.0. Any food with an A_W of 0.85 or greater is considered potentially hazardous. Bacteria cannot flourish where the A_W is too low, usually below 0.85. This explains why dry foods such as flour, sugar or crackers are rarely subject to bacterial infestations. A low A_W only halts bacterial growth, however; it does not kill the microorganisms. When a dried food such as beans, eggs or rice is rehydrated, any bacteria present can flourish and the food may become potentially hazardous.

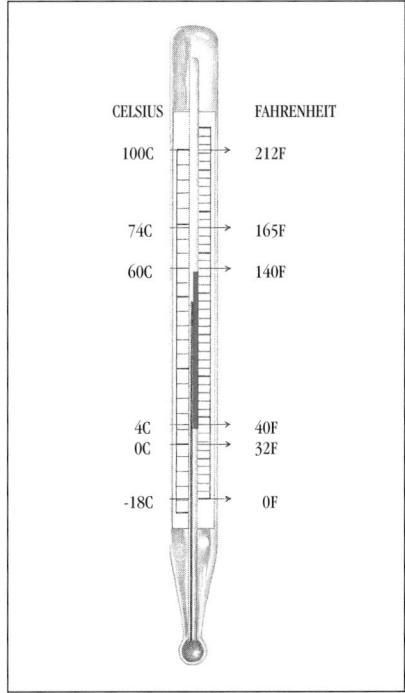

FIGURE 2.3　The temperature danger zone.

SAFETY ALERT

E. coli, Listeria, C. botulinum and *C. perfringens* can grow at refrigerator temperatures.

● **lag phase** a period, usually following transfer from one place to another, during which bacteria do not experience much growth

● **log phase** a period of accelerated growth for bacteria

● **decline phase** a period during which bacteria die at an accelerated rate, also known as the negative growth phase

TABLE 2.1	Characteristics of Bacterial Illnesses			
Common Name	**Organism Name**	**Form**	**Sources**	**Prevention**
Staph	*Staphylococcus aureus*	Toxin	Starchy foods, cold meats, bakery items, custards, milk products, humans with infected wounds or sores	Wash hands and utensils before use; exclude unhealthy food handlers; avoid having foods at room temperature
Perfringens or CP	*Clostridium perfringens*	Cells and toxin	Reheated meats, sauces, stews, casseroles	Keep cooked foods at an internal temperature of 60°C (140°F) or higher; reheat leftovers to internal temperature of 75°C (170°F) or higher
Botulism	*Clostridium botulinum*	Toxin, cells, spores	Cooked foods held for an extended time at warm temperatures with limited oxygen; rice, potatoes, smoked fish, canned vegetables	Keep internal temperature of cooked foods above 60°C (140°F) or below 4°C (40°F); reheat leftovers thoroughly; discard swollen cans
Salmonella	*Salmonella*	Cells	Poultry, eggs, milk, meats, fecal contamination	Thoroughly cook all meat, poultry, fish and eggs; avoid cross-contamination with raw foods; maintain good personal hygiene
Strep	*Streptococcus*	Cells	Infected food handlers	Do not allow employees to work if ill; protect foods from customers' coughs and sneezes
E. coli or 0157	*Escherichia coli 0157:H7* (enteropathogenic strains)	Cells and toxins	Any food, especially raw milk, raw vegetables, raw or rare beef (especially ground), humans (fecal contamination)	Thoroughly cook or reheat items
Listeria	*Listeria monocytogenes*	Cells	Milk products, deli meats, humans	Avoid raw milk and cheese made from unpasteurized milk; keep storage areas clean

● **pH** a measurement of the acid or alkali content of a solution, expressed on a scale of 0 to 14.0. A pH of 7.0 is considered neutral or balanced. The lower the pH value, the more acidic the substance. The higher the pH value, the more alkaline the substance.

● **aerobic bacteria** those that thrive on oxygen

● **anaerobic bacteria** those that are able to live and grow without the presence of oxygen

● **facultative bacteria** those that can adapt and will survive with or without oxygen

Acid/Alkaline Balance   Bacteria are affected by the **pH** of their environment. Although they can survive in a wider range, they prefer a neutral environment with a pH of 6.6 to 7.5. Growth is usually halted if the pH is 4.6 or less. Acidic foods such as lemon juice, tomatoes and vinegar create an unfavourable environment for bacteria. Simply adding an acidic ingredient to foods should not, however, be relied upon to destroy bacteria or preserve foods. The amount of acidity appropriate for flavouring is not sufficient to ensure the destruction of bacteria.

Atmosphere   Bacteria need an appropriate atmosphere. Some bacteria, known as **aerobes**, thrive on oxygen, while others, known as **anaerobes**, do not require the presence of oxygen. Others, known as **facultative**, can adapt and will survive with or without oxygen. Unfortunately, most pathogenic bacteria are facultative. (See Table 2.1.)

Canning, which creates an anaerobic atmosphere, destroys bacteria that need oxygen. But it also creates a favourable atmosphere for anaerobic and facultative bacteria. A complete vacuum need not be formed for anaerobic bacteria to thrive, however. A tight foil covering, a complete layer of fat, even a well-fitting lid can create an atmosphere sufficiently devoid of oxygen to permit growth of anaerobic bacteria. *Clostridium botulinum* is anaerobic and is one of the most deadly forms of food poisoning.

Parasites

Parasites are tiny organisms that depend on nutrients from a living host to complete their life cycle. Meat animals, fish, shellfish and humans can all play host to parasites. Several types of very small parasitic worms can enter an animal through contaminated feed, then settle in the host's intestinal tract or muscles, where they grow and reproduce. The ones most commonly found in foods are *trichinella spiralis* and *anisakis*.

Trichinosis is an illness caused by eating undercooked game or pork infected with trichina larvae. Trichinosis has been virtually eradicated by grain-feeding hogs and testing them before slaughter. Traditionally, it was thought that pork must be cooked to internal temperatures of 77°C (170°F) or higher to eradicate the larvae. This generally resulted in a dry, tough product. Scientists have now determined that trichina larvae are killed if held at 58°C (137°F) for 10 seconds. The Canadian Food Inspection Agency currently recommends cooking pork products to an internal temperature of 66°C (150°F). All commercially packaged cured or smoked pork products must be heated to an internal temperature of 68°C (155°F) during processing.

Anisakiasis is an illness caused by parasitic roundworms. Anisakis worms reside in the organs of fish, especially bottom feeders or those taken from contaminated waters. Raw or undercooked fish is most often implicated in anisakiasis. Fish should be thoroughly cleaned immediately after being caught so that the parasites do not have an opportunity to spread. Cooking to a minimum internal temperature of 63°C (145°F) for at least 15 seconds or freezing at –20°C (–4°F) for 7 days is recommended, as the parasites can survive even highly acidic marinades.

Cyclospora infections are caused by a single-celled parasite found in water or food contaminated by infected feces. Produce from undeveloped countries is a common source of cyclospora parasites, as is untreated water. Avoiding such products is the best prevention method.

Viruses

Other biologically based food-borne illnesses such as hepatitis A and Norwalk virus are caused by viruses. Viruses are the smallest known form of life. They invade the living cells of a host, take over those cells' genetic material and cause the cells to produce more viruses.

Viruses do not require a host to survive, however. They can survive—but not multiply—while lying on any food or food contact surface. Unlike bacteria, viruses can be present on any food, not just a potentially hazardous food. The food or food contact surface simply becomes a means of transportation between hosts.

Unlike bacteria, viruses are not affected by the water activity, pH or oxygen content of their environment. Some, however, can be destroyed by temperatures higher than 85°C (185°F) for one minute. Basically, the only way to prevent food-borne viral illnesses is to prevent contamination in the first place.

Hepatitis A often enters the food supply through shellfish harvested from sewage-polluted waters. The virus is carried by humans, some of whom may never know they are infected, and is transmitted by poor personal hygiene and cross-contamination. The actual source of contamination may be hard to establish, though, because it may take months for symptoms to appear.

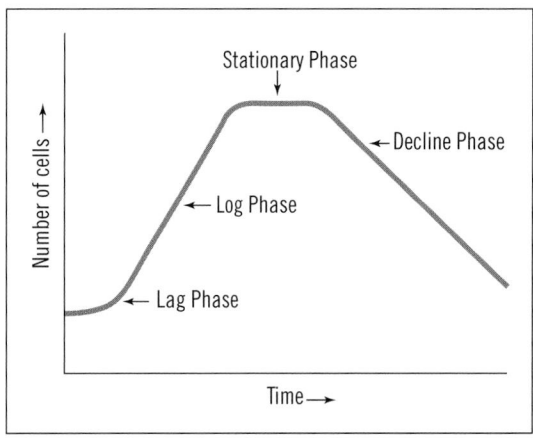

FIGURE 2.4   Bacterial growth curve.

Cryptosporidium parvum

Outbreaks in North America have been on the rise since 1993. The parasite contaminates drinking water and can affect entire communities. The protozoa are transmitted by the oral-fecal route. Personal hygiene is critical. Filtration and chemical disinfection are not always effective.

• **fermentation** the process by which yeast converts sugar into alcohol and carbon dioxide; it also refers to the time that yeast dough is left to rise

The *Norwalk virus* is spread almost entirely by poor personal hygiene among infected food handlers. The virus is found in human feces, contaminated water or vegetables fertilized by manure. The virus can be destroyed by high cooking temperatures but not by sanitizing solutions or freezing. In fact, Norwalk virus has even been found in ice cubes.

Foods most likely to transmit viral diseases are those that are not heated after handling. These include salads, sandwiches, milk, baked products, uncooked fish and shellfish and sliced meats. The best techniques for avoiding viral food-borne illnesses are to observe good personal hygiene habits, avoid cross-contamination and use only foods obtained from reputable sources.

Fungi

Fungi are a large group of plants ranging from single-celled organisms to giant mushrooms. Fungi are everywhere: in the soil, air and water. Poisonous mushrooms, a type of fungus, can cause illness or death if consumed. The most common fungi, however, are moulds and yeasts.

Moulds

Moulds are algae-like fungi that form long filaments or strands. These filaments often extend into the air, appearing as cottony or velvety masses on food. Large colonies of mould are easily visible to the naked eye. Although many food moulds are not dangerous, and some are even very beneficial, rare types known as mycotoxicoses do form toxins that have been linked to food-borne illnesses. For the most part, however, moulds only affect the appearance and flavour of foods. They cause discoloration, odours and off-flavours.

Unlike bacteria, moulds can grow on almost any food at almost any temperature, moist or dry, acidic or alkaline. Mould cells can be destroyed by heating to 60°C (140°F) for 10 minutes. Their toxins are heat resistant, however, and are not destroyed by normal cooking methods. Therefore, foods that develop mould should be discarded and any container or storage area cleaned and sanitized. The roots can grow 2.5 cm (1 in.) into the host product.

Yeasts

Yeasts require water and carbohydrates (sugar or starch) for survival. As the organisms consume carbohydrates, they expel alcohol and carbon dioxide gas through a process known as **fermentation**. Fermentation is of great benefit in making bread and alcoholic beverages.

Although naturally occurring yeasts have not been proven to be harmful to humans, they can cause foods to spoil, developing off-flavours, odours and discoloration. Yeasts are killed at temperatures of 58°C (136°F) or above.

Chemical Contaminants

The contamination of foods by a wide variety of chemicals is a very real and serious danger, one in which the public has shown a strong interest. Chemical contamination is usually inadvertent and invisible, making it extremely difficult to detect. The only way to avoid such hazards is for everyone working in a food service operation to follow proper procedures when handling foods or chemicals.

Chemical hazards include contamination with (1) the residual chemicals used in growing the food supply, (2) food service chemicals and cleaners and (3) toxic metals.

Residual Chemicals

Chemicals such as antibiotics, fertilizers, insecticides and herbicides have brought about great progress in controlling plant, animal and human diseases, permitting greater food yields and stimulating animal growth. The benefits derived from these chemicals, however, must be contrasted with the adverse effects on humans when chemicals are used indiscriminately or improperly.

The danger of these chemicals lies in the possible contamination of human foods, which occurs when chemical residues remain after the intended goal is achieved. Fruits and vegetables must be washed and peeled properly to reduce the risk of consuming residual chemicals.

Food Service Chemicals and Cleaners

A more common contamination problem involves the common chemicals found in most every food service operation. Cleaners, polishes, pesticides and abrasives are often poisonous to humans. Illness and even death can result from foods contaminated by such common items as bug spray, drain cleaner, oven cleaner or silver polish. These chemicals pose a hazard if used or stored near food supplies. Even improperly washing or rinsing dishes and utensils leaves a soap residue, which is then transmitted via food to anyone using the item.

To avoid food service chemical contamination, make sure all cleaning chemicals are clearly labelled and stored well away from food preparation and storage areas. Always use these products as directed by the manufacturer; never reuse a chemical container or package. Follow Workplace Hazardous Materials Information System (WHMIS) guidelines.

Cloth Towelling

The use of cloth towels or rags to cover, dry or wipe food products is not acceptable. They contain soap and other chemical residues and shed fibres or threads. There is a very real danger of causing choking. Use paper towels if food contact is involved and cover food products with plastic wrap.

Toxic Metals

Another type of chemical contamination occurs when metals such as lead, mercury, copper, zinc and antimony are dispersed in food or water. For example:

- Metals can accumulate in fish and shellfish living in polluted waters or in plants grown in soil contaminated by the metals.
- Using an acidic food such as tomatoes or wine in a zinc (galvanized) or unlined copper container causes metal ions to be released into the food.
- Antimony is used in bonding enamelware; it can be released into food when the enamel is chipped or cracked, so great care must be taken when using enamelware (terrines).
- Lead enters the water supply from lead pipes and solder and is found in the glaze on some imported ceramic items.

Consuming any of these metals can cause poisoning.

To prevent metal contamination, use only approved food service equipment and utensils and re-tin copper cookware as needed. Never serve fish or shellfish that was illegally harvested or obtained from uninspected sources.

Physical Contaminants

Physical contaminants include foreign objects that find their way into foods by mistake. Examples include metal shavings created by a worn can opener, pieces of glass from a broken container, hair, lubricants and dirt. Physical contaminants may be created by intentional tampering, but they are most likely the result of poor safety and sanitation practices or a lack of training.

CROSS-CONTAMINATION

Generally, microorganisms and other contaminants cannot move by themselves. Rather, they are carried to foods and food contact surfaces by humans, rodents or insects. This transfer is referred to as cross-contamination.

Cross-contamination is the process by which one item, such as your fingers or a cutting board, becomes contaminated and then contaminates a food or tool. For example, a chef's knife and cutting board are used in preparing a potentially hazardous food such as a chicken. In this case, the chicken has been directly contaminated with salmonella at the hatchery. If the knife and board are not cleaned *and sanitized* properly, anything that touches them can also become contaminated. So, even though cooking the chicken to an appropriate internal temperature may destroy the salmonella in the chicken, the uncooked salad greens cut on the same cutting board or with the same knife can contain live bacteria. Health regulations require separate cutting boards for raw and cooked products.

Cross-contamination can occur with bacteria or other microorganisms, chemicals, dirt and debris. Side towels are an especially common source of cross-contamination. If a cook uses a side towel to wipe a spill off the floor, then uses that same towel to dry his or her hands after visiting the restroom, the cook's hands are recontaminated with whatever bacteria or dirt was on the floor. Cross-contamination also occurs when raw foods come in contact with cooked foods. Never store cooked food below raw food in a refrigerator, and never return cooked food to the container that held the raw food. Cross-contamination can also occur easily from smoking, drinking or eating, unless hands are properly washed after each of these activities.

Reducing Cross-Contamination

Cross-contamination can be reduced or even prevented by (1) personal cleanliness, (2) dish and equipment cleanliness and (3) pest control.

Personal Cleanliness

To produce clean, sanitary food, all food handlers must maintain high standards of personal cleanliness and hygiene. This begins with good grooming.

Humans provide the ideal environment for the growth of microorganisms. Everyone harbours bacteria in the nose and mouth. These bacteria are easily spread by sneezing or coughing, by not disposing of tissues properly and by not washing hands frequently and properly. Touching your body, then touching food or utensils transfers bacteria. Human waste carries many dangerous microorganisms, so it is especially important to *wash your hands thoroughly* **for at least 30 seconds** *after visiting the toilet.* An employee who is ill should not be allowed in the operation.

Current research shows that the human immunodeficiency virus (HIV), the causative agent of AIDS, is not spread by food. According to the Canadian Food Inspection Agency (*Meat Manual of Procedures*, Ch. 1, section 1.5.2, AIDS in Food Processing Establishments, 1990), HIV will *not* survive in food. Even if contamination does occur in a food-processing establishment—which is unlikely—there is no risk to the general public. Government departments and agencies enforce strict standards for the sanitary production, preparation and handling of food. These standards of good personal hygiene and workplace sanitation were not developed in response to AIDS but have been in effect in one form or another for many years.

PROCEDURE FOR PROPER HANDWASHING

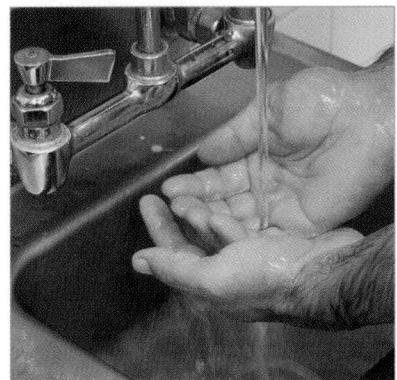

1. Using hot water (38°C/100°F), wet hands and forearms.

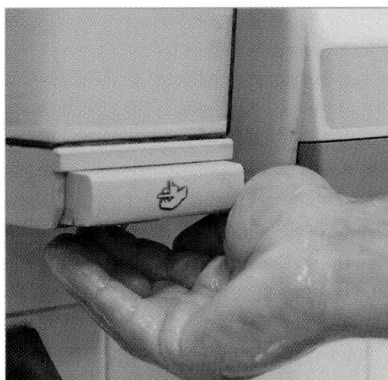

2. Apply an antibacterial soap.

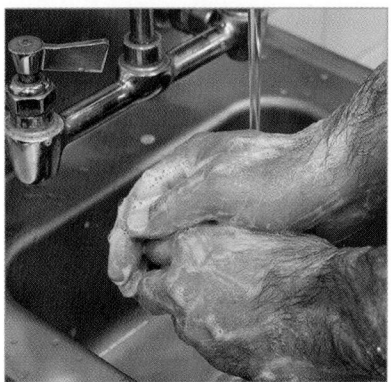

3. Rub hands and arms briskly with soapy lather for at least 30 seconds.

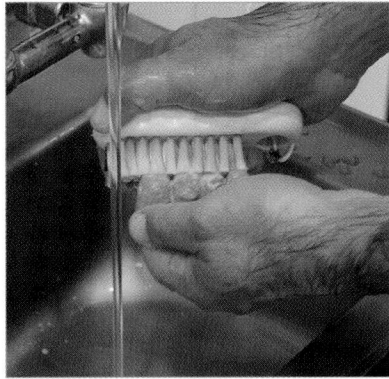

4. Scrub between fingers and clean nails with a clean nail brush.

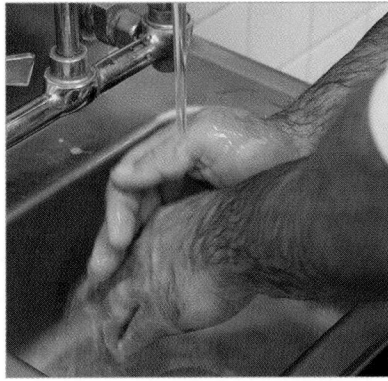

5. Rinse thoroughly under hot running water. Reapply soap and scrub hands and forearms for another 5 to 10 seconds. Rinse again.

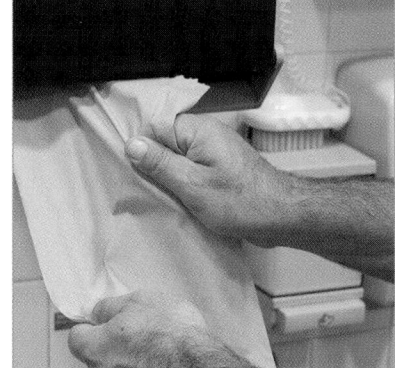

6. Dry hands and arms with a single-use towel, using the towel to turn off the water. Discard the towel in a trash receptacle after exiting the washroom.

There have been no documented or suspected cases of transmission of HIV through food. As a result, there is no medical or public health reason to restrict an HIV-infected person from working in food production, preparation or handling establishments, unless the individual has another illness for which any worker would be restricted.

There are several things you can do to decrease the risk of an illness being spread by poor personal hygiene:

- Wash your hands frequently and thoroughly. Gloves are not a substitute for proper handwashing and may create a false sense of security.
- Keep your fingernails short, clean and neat. Do not bite your nails or wear nail polish.
- Keep any cut or wound antiseptically bandaged. An injured hand should also be covered with a disposable glove.
- Bathe daily, or more often if required.
- Keep your hair clean and restrained.

- Wear work clothes that are clean and neat. Avoid wearing jewellery or watches.
- Do not eat, drink, smoke or chew gum in food preparation areas.

Dish and Equipment Cleanliness

One of the primary requirements for any food service facility is cleanability. But there is an important difference between clean and sanitary. **Clean** means that the item has no visible soil on it. **Sanitary** means that harmful substances are reduced to safe levels. Thus, something may be clean without being sanitary; the visible dirt can be removed, but disease-causing microorganisms can remain. (**Sterilize** means that all living microorganisms are destroyed.)

The cleaning of dishes, pots, pans and utensils in a food service operation involves both removing soil and sanitizing. Soil can be removed manually or by machine. Sanitizing can be accomplished with heat or chemical disinfectants.

Procedures for manually washing, rinsing and sanitizing dishes and equipment generally follow the three-compartment sink setup shown in Figure 2.5. The dish/pot washer must do the following:

1. Scrape and pre-rinse the item to remove soil. Cutlery must be presoaked in a mild detergent solution.
2. Wash the item in the first sink compartment at a temperature not lower than 45°C (113°F) using an approved detergent. A brush or cloth may be used to remove any remaining soil.
3. Rinse the item in the second sink compartment using clear, hot water of at least 45°C (113°F).
4. Sanitize the item in the third sink compartment by either:
   a. immersing it in 77°C (170°F) water for at least two minutes, or
   b. immersing it in an approved chemical sanitizing solution according to the manufacturer's directions. Use test strips to verify adequate concentrations.
   Note: A basket or rack must be used for immersion and a test thermometer must be available.
5. Empty, clean and refill each sink compartment as necessary and check the water temperature regularly.

Food service items, dishes, silverware and utensils should always be allowed to air-dry, as towel-drying may recontaminate them.

Machine-washing dishes or utensils follows a similar procedure. The dishwasher should first scrape and rinse items as needed, then load the items into

---

- **clean** to remove visible dirt and soil
- **sanitize** to reduce pathogenic organisms to safe levels
- **sterilize** to destroy all living microorganisms

Chemical Sanitizers

At a temperature of 45°C (113°F) and for at least two minutes, utensils may be sanitized with solutions containing at least:

1. 100 mg of available chlorine per litre,
2. 25 mg of available iodine per litre, or
3. 200 mg of quaternary ammonium compound per litre.

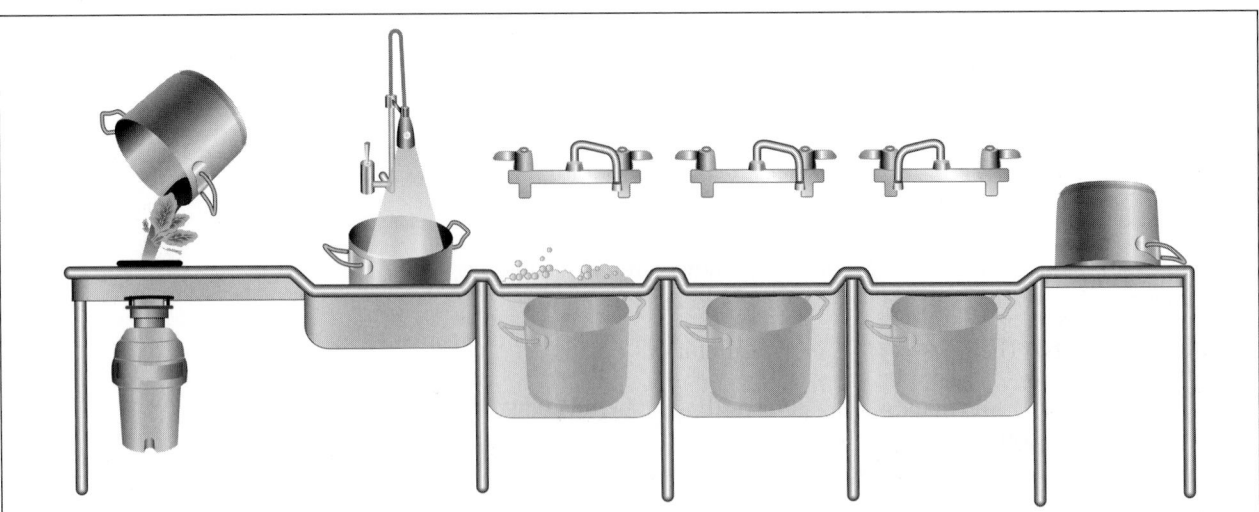

FIGURE 2.5 The three-compartment sink. Procedure—scrape, pre-rinse, wash, rinse, sanitize and air-dry each item.

dishwashing machine racks so that the spray of water will reach all surfaces. The machine cleans the items with a detergent in wash water of at least 60°C (140°F) for hot-temperature machines, then sanitizes them with either a hot-water rinse (at least 82°C/180°F) for 30 seconds or a suitable time-temperature combination or chemical disinfectant. When the machine cycle is complete, items should be inspected for residual soil, allowed to air-dry and stored in a clean area.

Work tables and stationary equipment must also be cleaned and sanitized properly. Equipment and surfaces, including floors, walls and work tables, should be easily exposed for inspection and cleaning and should be constructed so that soil can be removed effectively and efficiently with normal cleaning procedures. A thorough cleaning schedule should be implemented and closely monitored to prevent problems from developing.

The following points are important to the safety and cleanliness of any food service facility:

- Equipment should be disassembled for cleaning; any immersible pieces should be cleaned and sanitized like other items.

- All work tables or other food contact surfaces should be cleaned with detergent, then sanitized with a clean cloth dipped in a sanitizing solution. An acceptable sanitizing solution is made by combining 4.5 L (1 gal.) of lukewarm water with 15 mL (1 Tbsp.) of chlorine bleach. This solution must be replaced every two hours. Other chemical sanitizers should be prepared and used according to health department and manufacturer's directions.

- Surfaces, especially work surfaces with which food may come in contact, should be smooth and free of cracks, crevices or seams in which soil and microorganisms can hide.

- Floors should be nonabsorbent and should not become slippery when wet.

- Walls and ceilings should be smooth and light-coloured so that soil is easier to see.

- Light should be ample and well located throughout food preparation and storage areas. All light bulbs should be covered with a sleeve or globe to protect surroundings from shattered glass.

The design of a kitchen can also affect food safety and sanitation. Food preparation equipment should be arranged in such a way as to decrease the chances of cross-contamination. The work flow should eliminate crisscrossing and backtracking. Employees should be able to reach storage, refrigeration and cleanup areas easily. Dish- and pot-washing areas and garbage facilities should be kept as far from food preparation and storage areas as possible. Cleaning supplies and other chemicals should be stored away from foods.

In most communities, the design of a food service facility is controlled in part by public health regulations. The local health and building codes should be consulted when planning any construction or remodelling, or when purchasing and installing new equipment.

Pest Control

Food can be contaminated by insects (e.g., roaches and flies) and rodents (e.g., mice and rats). These pests carry many harmful bacteria on their bodies and defecate frequently, thus contaminating any surface with which they come in contact. An insect or rodent infestation is usually considered a serious health risk and should be dealt with immediately and thoroughly. Pests must be controlled by (1) building them out of the facility, (2) creating an environment in which they cannot find food, water or shelter and (3) relying on professional extermination.

Canadian Food Inspection Agency

Although the safety of agri-food products produced in Canada is the ultimate responsibility of the food industry, the role of the Canadian Food Inspection Agency's (CFIA's) food inspection programs is to ensure that in federally registered establishments, appropriate steps are taken by industry to produce a safe product for consumers.

The Food Safety Enhancement Program, established in 1996, is designed to encourage the adoption of Hazard Analysis Critical Control Points (HACCP) principles. HACCP has been recognized internationally as a logical tool toward a more modern, scientifically based inspection system. The key element of an HACCP-based system is its preventive nature and the exercising of control throughout the manufacturing process, at critical steps called critical control points. By doing so, defects that could affect the safety of the food being processed can be readily detected and corrected at these points before the product is completely processed and packaged.

Source: Adapted from Canadian Food Inspection Agency, FOOD SAFETY ENHANCEMENT PROGRAM (FSEP) IMPLEMENTATION MANUAL, Chapter 1, www.inspection.gc.ca/english/fssa/polstrat/haccp/manu/vol1/1-2e.shtml#ch1 (accessed August 31, 2004).

The best defence against pests is to prevent infestations in the first place by building them out. Any crack—no matter how small—in door frames, walls or windowsills should be repaired immediately and all drains, pipes and vents should be well sealed. Inspect all deliveries thoroughly and reject any packages or containers found to contain evidence of pests.

Flies are a perfect method of transportation for bacteria because they feed and breed on human waste and garbage. Use screens or "fly fans" (also known as air curtains) to keep them out in the first place. Control of garbage is also essential because moist, warm, decaying organic material attracts flies and provides favourable conditions for eggs to hatch and larvae to grow.

Pest control also requires creating an inhospitable environment for pests. Store all food and supplies at least 15 cm (6 in.) off the floor and 5 cm (2 in.) away from walls. **Rotate stock** often to disrupt nesting places and breeding habits. Provide good ventilation in storerooms to remove humidity, airborne contaminants, grease and fumes. Do not allow water to stand in drains, sinks or buckets, as cockroaches are attracted to moisture. Clean up spills and crumbs immediately and completely to reduce the pests' food supply.

Despite your best efforts to build pests out and maintain proper housekeeping standards, it is still important to watch for the presence of pests. For example, cockroaches leave a strong, oily odour and feces that look like large grains of pepper. Cockroaches prefer to search for food and water in the dark, so seeing any cockroach on the move in the daylight is an indication of a large infestation.

Rodents (mice and rats) tend to hide during the day, so an infestation may be rather serious before any creature is actually seen. Rodent droppings, which are shiny black to brownish grey, may be evident, however. Rodent nests made from scraps of paper, hair or other soft materials may be spotted.

Should an infestation occur, consult a licensed pest control operator immediately. With early detection and proper treatment, infestations can be eliminated. Be very careful in attempting to use pesticides or insecticides yourself. These chemicals are toxic to humans as well as to pests. Great care must be used to prevent contaminating food or exposing workers or customers to the chemicals.

HACCP SYSTEMS

Now that you understand what contaminants are and how they can be destroyed or controlled, it is necessary to put this information into practice during day-to-day operations. Although local health departments inspect all food service facilities on a regular basis, continual self-inspection and control are essential for maintaining sanitary conditions.

Hazard Analysis Critical Control Points (HACCP) continues to be an effective and efficient method for managing and maintaining sanitary conditions in all types of food service operations. Developed by Pillsbury in 1971 for NASA to ensure food safety for astronauts, HACCP—and a similar system adopted by the National Restaurant Association known as Sanitary Assessment of the Food Environment/S.A.F.E.—is a rigorous system of self-inspection. It focuses on the *flow of food* through the food service facility, from the decision to include an item on the menu through service to the consumer.

An HACCP **critical control point** is any step during the processing of a food at which a mistake can result in the transmission, growth or survival of pathogenic bacteria. At each of these steps there is some hazard of contamination. The HACCP process begins by identifying the steps and evaluating the type and severity of hazard that can occur. It then identifies what actions can be taken to reduce or prevent each risk of hazard. (See Table 2.2.) The activities that present the highest risk of hazard should be monitored most closely. For example, a cook's failure

● rotate stock to use products in the order in which they were received; all perishable and semi-perishable goods, whether fresh, frozen, canned or dry, should be used according to the first in, first out (FIFO) principle

● critical control point any step in the food-handling process at which a prescribed action will reduce the likelihood of a food-borne illness or hazard

TABLE 2.2	HACCP Analysis—The Flow of Food		
Control Point	**Hazards**	**Standards**	**Critical Actions**
Selecting the menu and recipes	PHF; human hands involved in food preparation	Analyze menus and recipes for control points; wash hands frequently; use single-use gloves as appropriate	Plan physical work flow; train employees
Receiving	Contaminated or spoiled goods; PHF in the temperature danger zone	Do not accept torn bags, dented cans, broken glass containers or leaking or damaged packages; frozen food should be received at −18°C (0°F) or below and refrigerated food at 4°C (40°F) or below	Inspect all deliveries and reject as necessary
Storing	Cross-contamination to and from other foods; bacterial growth; spoilage; improper holding temperatures	Avoid crowding and allow air to circulate in freezers and refrigerators; rotate stock and keep storage areas clean, dry and well lit; store frozen food at −18°C (0°F) or below and refrigerated food at 4°C (40°F) or below	Maintain proper temperatures and other storage conditions; discard if necessary
Preparing	Cross-contamination; bacterial growth	Keep PHF at 4°C (40°F) or below or 60°C (140°F) or above; thaw frozen foods under refrigeration or under cold running water (21°C/70°F) for no more than 2 hours	Avoid the temperature danger zone; maintain good personal hygiene and use sanitary utensils
Cooking	Bacterial survival; physical or chemical contamination	Heat foods to the appropriate internal temperature; reheat leftover foods to at least 77°C (170°F)	Cook foods to their proper temperatures
Holding and service	Bacterial growth; contamination	Maintain hot holding temperatures at 60°C (140°F) or above and cold holding temperatures at 4°C (40°F) or below; do not mix new product with old and discard food after 2 hours of being held at room temperature	Maintain proper temperatures and use sanitary equipment
Cooling leftovers	Bacterial growth	Spread food into clean, shallow, metal containers; use an ice bath; stir periodically during cooling; cool to 21°C (70°F) within 2 hours, then cool to 4°C (40°F) or below within 4 hours; cover and refrigerate; store cooked food above raw	Cool foods quickly; label and store them properly
Reheating	Bacterial survival and growth	Use leftovers within 4 days; heat leftovers to 77°C (170°F) within 2 hours; do not mix old product with new and discard secondary leftovers	Reheat food quickly (do not use a steam table) and as close to serving time as possible; reheat smaller quantities as needed; discard if necessary

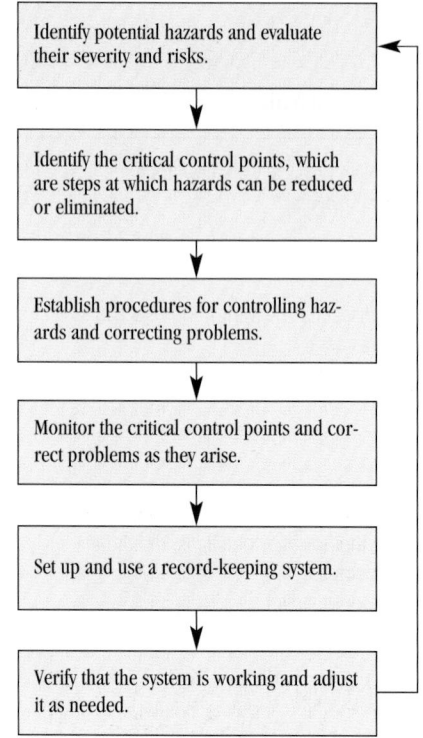

Identify potential hazards and evaluate their severity and risks.

↓

Identify the critical control points, which are steps at which hazards can be reduced or eliminated.

↓

Establish procedures for controlling hazards and correcting problems.

↓

Monitor the critical control points and correct problems as they arise.

↓

Set up and use a record-keeping system.

↓

Verify that the system is working and adjust it as needed.

FIGURE 2.6 An HACCP system flowchart.

to wash his or her hands before handling cooked food presents a greater risk of hazard than does a dirty floor. In other words, hazards must be prioritized and correction of critical concerns should take priority. (See Figure 2.6.)

Whatever system is followed, however, all personnel must be constantly aware of and responsive to problems and potential problems associated with the safety of the food they are serving. Accurate record keeping is a requirement of an effective HACCP program.

THE SAFE WORKER

Kitchens are filled with objects that can cut, burn, break, crush or sprain the human body. The best way to prevent work-related injuries is through proper training, adherence to good work habits and careful supervision.

The federal government enacted legislation designed to reduce hazards in the work area, thereby reducing accidents. The Occupational Health and Safety Act (OHSA) covers a broad range of safety matters. Employers who fail to follow its rules can incur financial penalties. Unfortunately, human error is the leading cause of accidents, and no amount of legislation can protect someone who doesn't work in a safe manner.

Personal Safety

Safe behaviour on the job reflects pride, professionalism and consideration for fellow workers. The following list should alert you to conditions and activities aimed at preventing accidents and injuries:

- Clean up spills as soon as they occur.
- Learn to operate equipment properly; always use guards and safety devices.
- Wear clothing that fits properly; avoid wearing jewellery, which may get caught in equipment.
- Use knives and other equipment for their intended purpose only.
- Walk, do not run.
- Keep exits, aisles and stairs clear and unobstructed.
- Always assume a pot or pan is hot; handle with dry towels.
- Position pot and pan handles out of the aisles so they do not get bumped.
- Get help or use a cart when lifting or moving heavy objects.
- Avoid back injury by lifting with your leg muscles; stoop, do not bend, when lifting.
- Use a well-placed ladder or stool for climbing; do not use a chair, box, drawer or shelf.
- Keep breakable items away from food storage or production areas.
- Warn people when you must walk behind them, especially when carrying a hot pan.

Fire Safety

From grease flare-ups on cooktops to major fires caused by dirty ventilation hoods, fires can develop into serious threats in busy professional kitchens. Understanding the danger posed by fires and having a proper fire safety program in place is of utmost importance in a professional kitchen. Fire extinguishers contain different types of chemicals effective on various types of fires. (See Chapter 5, page 91.) Learn which types of fire extinguishers to use for specific combustible materials. Regulations require that commercial kitchens be outfitted with ventilation hoods and fire suppressant systems. Grease fires in ventilation hoods are the primary cause of restaurant fires; thorough and regular cleaning prevents hazardous grease buildup. All fire suppression systems should be inspected regularly. When faced with a serious fire, immediately call for help. Shut off all exhaust fans and turn off kitchen equipment if time permits. Close the kitchen doors and evacuate the premises.

Deep-fat fryers pose a serious fire threat and employee training should include instruction on the proper operation and cleaning of such equipment. In addition, large quantities of hot fat can cause severe burns if not properly handled. When liquids come into contact with the heated fat, hot steam is released. Take care when adding foods to deep-fat fryers to prevent getting burned. The threat is more extreme when a large quantity of liquid hits the hot grease. Keep containers of liquids and aerosol canisters away from deep-fat fryers to avoid accidentally spilling liquid into the hot fat and causing a hazardous explosion.

Chef uniforms were designed with comfort and safety in mind; the double front panels and long sleeves help prevent burns. Clothing and towels can catch on fire, however. If an employee's garments catch on fire, use a safety blanket to wrap the person and smother the flames. Although it is generally best to use an appropriate fire extinguisher to douse kitchen fires, some simple measures can be useful for extinguishing a small flame in a pan. Immediately cover a pan in which a small oil flare-up occurs; lack of oxygen will extinguish the flame. To extinguish a small grease flare-up in a pan or on a cooktop, douse it quickly with a generous amount of baking soda or salt.

First Aid

Some accidents will inevitably occur, and it is important to act appropriately in the event of an injury or emergency. This may mean calling for help or providing first aid. Every food service operation should be equipped with a complete first-aid kit. Municipal regulations may specify the exact contents of the kit. Be sure that the kit is conveniently located and well stocked at all times.

The Canadian Red Cross, St. John Ambulance and other agencies offer approved training in first aid, approved procedures for treating choking victims and cardiopulmonary resuscitation (CPR). All employees should be trained in basic emergency procedures. A list of emergency telephone numbers should be posted by each telephone.

Conclusion

All food service workers are responsible for supplying food that is safe to eat. Microorganisms that cause food-borne illnesses are found in all types of food; they can be destroyed or their growth can be severely limited by proper food handling procedures. By learning about food contaminants, how they are spread and how they can be prevented or controlled, you can help ensure customer safety. You are also responsible for your own physical safety as well as that of your customers and fellow workers. Maintaining sanitary and safe facilities and high standards of personal hygiene is a necessary part of this responsibility.

Storage and Food Labelling

Proper food labelling and good record keeping are as important as safe food handling practices to prevent cross-contamination and food spoilage. Food labels should be used to date all foods that are made for kitchen use as well as leftovers. Systems for labelling foods vary in every operation. Once placed in clean sanitized storage containers, food prepared for later use should be labelled with the product name and the date and time it was made. Some health department regulations require that food be labelled with the day or date by which the food must be consumed on premises, sold or discarded. Once labelled and then refrigerated or frozen, products will be easily identifiable by the entire kitchen staff.

Sample of a label used to identify and date foods after preparation

Questions for Discussion

1. Foods can be contaminated in several ways. Explain the differences between biological, chemical and physical contamination. Give an example of each.
2. Under what conditions will bacteria thrive? Explain what you can do to alter these conditions.
3. What is the temperature danger zone? What is its significance in food preparation?
4. Explain how improper or inadequate pest control can lead to food-borne illnesses.
5. What does the initialism HACCP stand for? How is this system used in a typical food service facility?
6. Discuss the use of latex or plastic gloves in food preparation. Are they a guarantee of food safety?

" If we could give every individual the right amount of nourishment and exercise, not too little and not too much, we would have found the safest way to health.

—Hippocrates, Greek physician and father of medicine (c. 460–377 B.C.E.)

After studying this chapter you will be able to:

- identify categories of nutrients and explain their importance in a balanced diet

- explain the evolution of Canada's Food Guide and its significance in planning nutritious menus

- describe the effects storage and preparation techniques have on various foods' nutritional values

- identify the use of ingredient substitutes and alternatives

- understand product nutrition labels

- provide diners with nutritious foods

PEARSON
myculinarylab

These interactive online tools will help you master the skills in this chapter:

- Chapter Quizzes

● **essential nutrients** nutrients that must be provided by food because the body cannot or does not produce them in sufficient quantities

Since the days of prehistoric hunters and gatherers, people have understood that some animals and plants are good to eat and others are not. For thousands of years, cultures worldwide have attributed medicinal and beneficial effects to certain foods, particularly plants, and have recognized that foods that might otherwise be fine to eat may be unhealthy if improperly prepared or stored. But not until the past few decades have people become increasingly concerned about how foods affect their health and which foods promote good health and longevity. Because of national health concerns about overconsumption leading to obesity, cardiovascular disease and diabetes, Canadians are looking to dine out in a healthier way. At the same time, people with certain health conditions that limit the intake of sugar, fat or wheat are looking for foods that will taste good and meet their diet regimens.

This chapter sets forth basic information about nutrients and guidelines for planning a diet for healthy people. The chapter also introduces the framework for understanding ingredient substitution for those following a particular diet because of personal preference or allergies. Guidelines for chefs seeking to incorporate healthy dishes into their menus are provided. As well, vegetarian eating patterns and ingredients are discussed.

Nutrition is the science that studies nutrients, (chemical) substances found in food that nourish the body by promoting growth, maintenance and repair and by facilitating body functions. Some nutrients also provide energy (calories).

The six categories of nutrients are carbohydrates, fats, proteins, water, vitamins, and minerals. **Essential nutrients** are those that must be provided by food because the body does not produce them in sufficient quantities or cannot make them at all. (See Table 3.1.) Some nutritional components are considered nonessential because healthy, well-nourished bodies can make them in sufficient quantities to satisfy their needs. Scientists, however, are beginning to understand that even some nonessential nutrients might be needed in amounts greater than formerly thought, in order to provide protection against chronic diseases such as cancer, diabetes and heart disease.

Our bodies depend upon the various nutrients for different purposes and require different amounts of each depending on age, sex and health. In addition, some nutrients depend on one another for proper functioning. For example, calcium and vitamin D work together in the body: vitamin D promotes the absorption of the calcium that the body utilizes for proper bone growth. Because foods differ with regard to their nutritional content, it is important to eat a variety of foods in order to achieve a proper nutritional balance.

TABLE 3.1	Essential Nutrients

Essential nutrients are those that must be provided because the human body does not produce them in sufficient quantities:

Energy Nutrients	Carbohydrates (starches and sugars)
	Fats (linoleic and linolenic acids)
	Proteins (the amino acids: histidine, isoleucine, leucine, lysine, methionine, phenylalanine, threonine, tryptophan and valine)
Water	
Vitamins	Thiamin, riboflavin, niacin, pantothenic acid, biotin, vitamin B_6, vitamin B_{12}, folate, vitamin C, vitamin A, vitamin D, vitamin E and vitamin K
Minerals	Calcium, chloride, magnesium, phosphorus, potassium, sodium, sulphur, selenium, zinc, chromium, copper, fluoride, iodine, iron, manganese and molybdenum

ESSENTIAL NUTRIENTS

Three of the essential nutrients provide calories or energy. Sometimes referred to as macronutrients, they are carbohydrates, fats and proteins.

A **calorie** (abbreviated *kcal*) is the way we describe the amount of energy in food. The number of calories in a food is measured by a device called a calorimeter, which burns the food and measures the heat the food gives off. From that measurement, an estimate for how the food would be burned in the body is calculated. The results of the calculation are the calorie designations assigned to the energy nutrients.

One gram of pure fat supplies 9 kcal; one gram of pure carbohydrate supplies 4 kcal, as does one gram of pure protein. Most foods are a combination of carbohydrates, proteins and fats; their kcal content may not be easily determined unless we know how much of each nutrient the food contains.

Vitamins and minerals are essential nutrients and must be provided through the diet because the body cannot manufacture them in quantities adequate to ensure good health. They have no calories. Because they are needed in smaller amounts than the other nutrients, they are sometimes referred to as micronutrients.

● **calorie** for nutritional purposes, the amount of heat necessary to raise 1 kg of water 1°C; calories may be expressed as joules; one calorie (kilocalorie) equals 4185.5 joules

Energy from Essential Nutrients
1 gram pure fat = 9 calories
1 gram pure carbohydrate = 4 calories
1 gram pure protein = 4 calories

Carbohydrates

Carbohydrates comprise carbon, hydrogen and oxygen and are found exclusively in plant foods and milk sugars. **Simple carbohydrates** include monosaccharides (single sugars) and disaccharides (double sugars). (See Table 3.2.) Simple carbohydrates are found in the naturally occurring sugars in fruit, vegetables and milk, as well as in sweeteners such as honey, corn syrup and table sugar. **Complex carbohydrates** comprise long chains of the monosaccharide glucose. Starch is a complex carbohydrate. Complex carbohydrates are found in vegetables, fruits and cereal grains such as wheat, barley and oats. The body digests (or breaks down) these sugars and starches into glucose. Glucose, also known as blood sugar, is a very important source of energy for the body.

Another complex carbohydrate is fibre. **Dietary fibre**, which generally comes from the seeds and cell walls of fruits, vegetables and cereal grains, plays an important role in health because it is not digested. There are two types of fibre: *soluble* and *insoluble*. Fibre-containing foods are usually composed of both kinds with one kind predominating. Because the body cannot digest dietary fibre, it passes through the digestive system almost completely unchanged. This helps keep the digestive tract running smoothly. Insoluble fibre, such as that found in whole wheat, increases fecal bulk, which encourages proper elimination of waste products from the large intestines and helps avoid some forms of gastrointestinal distress. In addition, because of its action in speeding up the passage of waste materials, insoluble fibre may prevent colon cancer by reducing the time that potentially dangerous carcinogens stay in contact with the walls of the intestines. Soluble fibre, which forms a gel-type substance in the digestive tract, helps reduce serum cholesterol by helping to remove the cholesterol from the body, thereby lessening the risk for heart disease.

TABLE 3.2	Sugars	
Monosaccharides	**Disaccharides**	
Glucose (blood sugar)	Lactose (milk sugar)	
Fructose (fruit sugar)	Maltose (malt sugar)	
Galactose (part of milk sugar)	Sucrose (table sugar)	

● **carbohydrates** a group of compounds comprising oxygen, hydrogen and carbon that supply the body with energy (4 calories per gram); carbohydrates are classified as **simple** (including certain sugars) and **complex** (including starches and fibre)

● **dietary fibre** indigestible carbohydrates found in grains, fruits and vegetables; fibre aids digestion

Lipids

Lipids, like carbohydrates, comprise carbon, hydrogen and oxygen. The differences between carbohydrates and lipids are the number and arrangement of the carbon, hydrogen and oxygen atoms. Fats and cholesterol are considered

Trans Fatty Acids

Hydrogenated fat is created when hydrogen is pumped through super-heated liquid fats. Unsaturated fats become saturated with significant levels of trans fat. Margarine and most short-enings are made this way. Manu-facturers like them because they give cookies their crunch and the shelf life of many "cream-filled" confections is extended. These fatty acids increase LDL (low-density lipoproteins) and lower beneficial HDL (high-density lipopro-teins). Canadian food labels must quan-tify the amount of trans fatty acids (trans fats) to allow consumers to make informed choices. In 2007 municipal jurisdictions began to ban foods with trans fats. Restaurants and food manu-facturers are affected by these new laws and many food items need to be reformulated.

● **trans fat** a type of fat created when vegetable oils are solidified through hydrogenation

lipids. Fats are found in both animal and plant foods, although fruits contain very little fat. Fats provide calories, help carry fat-soluble vitamins and give food a creamy, pleasant mouth-feel. A healthy diet contains a moderate amount of fat; in fact, some forms of fat are considered essential.

Cholesterol, also a lipid, is found only in foods of animal origin. Cholesterol is not considered an essential nutrient and it does not contribute calories. Cholesterol is, however, an important component of the body, although it is not necessary to eat foods containing cholesterol as the body can manufacture all it needs from the fat in the diet.

Depending upon their structure, the fats in foods can be classified as satu-rated, monounsaturated or polyunsaturated. Most foods contain a combination of the three kinds of fats, although one kind may predominate. If saturated fat is the most abundant kind (as in the fat surrounding muscle meats), the food is classified as being high in saturated fat even though it contains a mixture of all three kinds of fats.

Saturated fats are found mainly in animal products such as milk, eggs and meats, as well as in tropical oils such as coconut and palm. Monounsaturated fats come primarily from plants and plant foods such as avocados and olives and the oils made from them. Polyunsaturated fats come from plants (soy and corn, for example) and fish.

Vegetable oils such as rapeseed (canola) and olive are high in monounsatu-rated fat. Cottonseed, sunflower, corn and safflower oils are high in polyunsat-urated fat. All oils, however, are a combination of the three kinds of fat. All vegetable oils are cholesterol-free, however, as cholesterol is not found in plants.

Saturated fats such as butter, lard and other animal fats are usually solid at room temperature. Monounsaturated and polyunsaturated fats are usually soft or liquid at room temperature. Hydrogenation is a process by which a liquid fat is made more solid (or saturated) by the addition of hydrogen atoms. Hydrogenation increases the percentage of saturated fatty acids, resulting in a more solid product (e.g., margarine made from a liquid polyunsaturated oil such as corn oil). Hydrogenation has positive effects as well; it reduces the tendency to rancidity, thus increasing shelf life. For this reason, it is a process used frequently in the food manufacturing industry.

Research suggests that high-fat diets, especially diets high in saturated fat and **trans fat**, may be linked to heart disease, obesity and certain forms of cancer. Saturated fats are also linked to high levels of blood cholesterol, which are associated with arteriosclerosis (hardening of the arteries). Although the liver can produce all the cholesterol the body needs, additional cholesterol is often provided in the diet from meats, poultry, fish, eggs and dairy products. The combination of a diet high in saturated fat and a diet high in cholesterol can increase the risk of heart disease.

Proteins

Proteins are found in both animal and plant foods. They differ from carbohy-drates and fats in that they contain nitrogen as well as carbon, hydrogen and oxygen. Protein chains comprise amino acids, the building blocks of protein. There are 20 amino acids, 9 of which are essential. People who eat a varied diet with adequate calories and protein can easily get all of the essential amino acids. The specific combination of amino acids gives each protein its unique characteristics and properties.

Proteins are necessary for manufacturing, maintaining and repairing body tissues. They are essential for the periodic replacement of the outer layer of skin as well as for blood clotting and scar tissue formation. Hair and nails, which provide a protective cover for the body, are composed of proteins.

Another important function of protein is the regulation of body processes. Proteins regulate the balance of water, **acids** and **bases** and move nutrients in and out of cells. Proteins contribute to the immune system by producing antibodies, which are necessary for combatting diseases. Proteins also form the enzymes that act as catalysts for body functions and the hormones that help direct body processes.

- **acid** a substance that neutralizes a base (alkaline) in a liquid solution; foods such as citrus juice, vinegar and wine that have a sour or sharp flavour (most foods are slightly acidic); acids have a pH of less than 7

- **base** a substance that neutralizes an acid in a liquid solution; ingredients such as sodium bicarbonate (baking soda) that have an alkaline or bitter flavour; bases have a pH of more than 7

Water

The human body is approximately 60% water. Water is necessary for transporting nutrients and wastes throughout the body. It cushions the cells, lubricates the joints, maintains stable body temperatures and assists waste elimination. It also promotes functioning of the nervous system and muscles.

Although the principal sources of water are beverages, water is also the predominant nutrient by weight in most foods. Some foods such as tomatoes, oranges, watermelon and iceberg lettuce are particularly high in water. Others such as dried fruits, nuts and seeds are lower. Water is also formed by the body when other nutrients are metabolized.

The average adult should consume at least 8 to 10 glasses (2 L or 64 fl. oz.) of water a day to ensure adequate intake. People who perspire a lot should drink more water to replace body water lost through sweat.

Vitamins

Vitamins are vital dietary substances needed to regulate **metabolism** and for normal growth and body functions. They are essential and noncaloric, needed in the body in small amounts.

- **metabolism** all the chemical reactions and physical processes that occur continuously in living cells and organisms

There are 13 vitamins. Table 3.3 on the next page lists them, their principal functions in the human body, the foods that contain high concentrations of these nutrients and some of the preparation and storage techniques that help retain the maximum amount of the various vitamins in their food sources.

Vitamins are divided into two categories: fat soluble and water soluble. The fat-soluble vitamins are A, D, E and K and are found in foods containing fat. Excess supplies of these vitamins may be stored in fatty tissues and the liver. Water-soluble vitamins are vitamin C and the B-complex vitamins, including thiamin (B_1), riboflavin (B_2), niacin (B_3), cyano-cobalamin (B_{12}), pyridoxine (B_6), pantothenic acid, biotin and folate. Vitamins B_1 and B_2 are commonly referred to by their names, thiamin and riboflavin, respectively, whereas cobalamin and pyridoxine are commonly referred to by their letter designations, B_{12} and B_6, respectively. **Coenzyme** formulations are often recommended as dietary supplements, particularly for migraine sufferers. Water-soluble vitamins are not stored to the extent that fat-soluble vitamins are, and excesses may be excreted in the urine. Because of these differences, deficiencies in water-soluble vitamins usually develop more rapidly.

- **coenzyme** any of various small substances, many of which contain a B vitamin, that promote or assist an enzyme's activities

Virtually all foods contain some vitamins. Many factors contribute to a particular food's vitamin concentration. An animal's feed; the manner by which the produce is harvested, stored or processed; even the type of soil, sunlight, rainfall and temperature have significant effects on a food's vitamin content. For example, tomatoes have a higher concentration of vitamin C when picked ripe from the vine rather than when picked green. Also, different varieties of fruits and vegetables have different vitamin contents. A Wegener apple, for example, has 19 mg of vitamin C, while a Red Delicious has only 6 mg.

TABLE 3.3	Vitamins: Their Functions and Sources and Techniques for Retaining Maximum Nutrient Content		
Vitamin	**Functions in the Human Body**	**Sources**	**Techniques for Nutrient Retention**
Vitamin A	Keeps the skin healthy; protects eyes; protects mouth and nose linings; supports immune functioning	Deep yellow and orange vegetables, leafy green vegetables, deep orange fruits, egg yolks, liver, fortified milk	Serve fruits and vegetables raw or lightly cooked; store vegetables covered and refrigerated; steam vegetables; roast or broil meats
Vitamin D	Helps body absorb calcium; regulates calcium and phosphorus in the bones; assists bone mineralization	Fortified milk, butter, some fish oils, egg yolks (exposure to sunlight produces vitamin D in the body)	It is stable under heat and insoluble in water; therefore it is unaffected by cooking
Vitamin E	Antioxidant; protects membranes and cell walls	Vegetable oils, whole grains, dark leafy vegetables, wheat germ, nuts, seeds, whole grains	Use whole grain flours; store foods in airtight containers; avoid exposing the food to light and air
Vitamin K	Assists blood-clotting proteins	Liver, dark green leafy vegetables (bacteria in the intestinal tract also produce some vitamin K)	Steam or microwave vegetables; do not overcook meats
Vitamin C (Ascorbic acid)	Supports immune system functioning; repairs connective tissues; promotes healing; assists amino acid metabolism	Citrus fruits, green vegetables, strawberries, cantaloupes, tomatoes, broccoli, potatoes	Serve fruits and vegetables raw; steam or microwave vegetables
Thiamin (Vitamin B_1)	Assists energy metabolism; supports nervous system functioning	Meats (especially pork), legumes, whole grains	Use enriched or whole grain pasta or rice; do not wash whole grains before cooking or rinse afterwards; steam or microwave vegetables; roast meats at moderate temperatures; cook meats only until done
Riboflavin (Vitamin B_2)	Assists energy metabolism	Milk, cheese, yogurt, fish, enriched grain breads and cereals, dark green leafy vegetables	Store foods in opaque containers; roast or broil meats or poultry
Niacin (Vitamin B_3)	Promotes normal digestion; supports nervous system functioning; assists energy metabolism	Meats, poultry, fish, dark green leafy vegetables, whole grain or enriched breads and cereals, nuts	Steam or microwave vegetables; roast or broil beef, veal, lamb and poultry (pork retains about the same amount of niacin regardless of cooking method)
Vitamin B_6	Necessary for protein metabolism and red blood cell formation	Meats, fish, poultry, shellfish, whole grains, dark green vegetables, potatoes, liver	Serve vegetables raw; cook foods in a minimum amount of water and for the shortest possible time; roast or broil meats and fish
Vitamin B_{12}	Helps produce red blood cells; assists metabolism	Animal foods only, particularly milk, eggs, poultry and fish	Roast or broil meats, poultry and fish
Folate	Necessary for protein metabolism and red blood cell formation	Orange juice, dark green leafy vegetables, organ meats, legumes, seeds	Serve vegetables raw; steam or microwave vegetables; store vegetables covered and refrigerated
Biotin	Coenzyme in energy metabolism, glycogen synthesis and fat metabolism	Widespread in foods	
Pantothenic acid	Coenzyme in energy metabolism	Widespread in foods	

You can control vitamin concentration and retention through careful food preparation:

1. Prepare vegetables as close to service time as possible; vegetables cut long before service lose more vitamins than those cut immediately before cooking.

2. Whether a vegetable is boiled, steamed or microwaved also determines the amount of vitamins it retains. Because the B-complex vitamins and vitamin C are water soluble, they are easily leached (washed out) or destroyed by food processing and preparation techniques involving high temperatures and water. Steaming and microwaving help retain nutrients (when steaming, keep the water level below the vegetables). But microwave cooking is best because it cooks vegetables with minimal water in less time.

3. In general, roasting and grilling meats, poultry, fish and shellfish preserve more vitamins than stewing and braising. The temperatures to which foods are cooked and length of time they are cooked may affect vitamin retention as well.

4. Storage affects vitamin concentrations. For example, long exposure to air may destroy vitamin C. Using airtight containers prevents some of this loss. Riboflavin is sensitive to light, so milk products (which are good sources of riboflavin) should be stored in opaque containers.

Minerals

Minerals cannot be manufactured by the body. They are obtained by eating plants that have drawn minerals from the ground or the flesh of animals that have eaten such plants.

Minerals are a critical component in hard and soft tissues (e.g., the calcium, magnesium and phosphorus present in bones and teeth). Minerals also regulate certain necessary body functions. For example, nerve impulses are transmitted through an exchange of sodium and potassium ions in the nerve cells.

Minerals are divided into two categories: trace minerals and major minerals. Trace minerals such as iron are needed in only very small amounts. Major minerals such as calcium are needed in relatively larger quantities. Table 3.4 on the next page lists some minerals, their principal functions in the human body and the foods that contain high concentrations of these nutrients.

As with vitamins, food processing and preparation can reduce a food's mineral content. Soaking or cooking in large amounts of water can leach out small quantities of water-soluble minerals. Processing or refining grains, such as the wheat used to make white flour, also removes minerals.

Phytochemicals

Recent scientific research has identified non-nutritive components of plant foods called phytochemicals, which may be important in preventing some forms of cancer, diabetes, Alzheimer's, heart disease and other degenerative diseases. More than 900 of these chemicals have been identified, including plant estrogens, carotenoids and flavonoids. The health benefits of these substances appear to depend on consumption of a varied diet that includes plenty of grains, fruits and vegetables. The importance of phytochemicals to human health and well-being should not be minimized even though they do not constitute a nutrient category. Phytochemicals such as **flavonoids** and other compounds found in blueberries, pomegranates, green tea and cooked tomato products may act as antioxidants in the body to help eliminate free

Dieting

There are many diets promoted in the marketplace today. Some, like the Mediterranean diet, are a reflection of the eating habits of a region in general. The proliferation of fad diets is a concern, and many are not based on sound eating practices for health. So before you embark on low-carbohydrate, high-protein, grapefruit, cabbage or any of the mass-marketed concepts, check with your doctor. There are no quick fixes that produce permanent results. Healthful eating practices coupled with a regular exercise program are the best approach to achieving and maintaining a safe and healthy body weight. One needs to consume a nutritionally balanced diet that matches one's lifestyle and activity level while enhancing the benefits accrued by making healthful food choices such as increased consumption of omega-3 lipids.

● **flavonoids** plant pigments that dissolve readily in water, found in red, purple and white vegetables such as blueberries, red cabbage, onions and tea

TABLE 3.4	Minerals: Their Functions and Sources	
Mineral	Functions in the Human Body	Sources
Major Minerals		
Calcium	Helps build bones and teeth; helps blood clot; promotes muscle and nerve functions	Dairy products, canned salmon and sardines, broccoli, kale, tofu, turnips
Magnesium	Muscle contraction; assists energy metabolism; bone formation	Green leafy vegetables, whole grains, legumes, fish, shellfish, cocoa
Phosphorus	Helps build bones and teeth; assists energy metabolism; formation of DNA	All animal tissues, milk, legumes, nuts
Potassium	Maintains electrolyte and fluid balance; promotes normal body functions; assists protein metabolism	Meats, poultry, fish, fruits (especially bananas, oranges and cantaloupes), legumes, vegetables
Sodium	Maintains normal fluid balance; necessary for nerve impulse transmission	Salt, soy sauce, processed foods, MSG
Chloride	With sodium, involved in fluid balance; component of stomach acid	Salt, soy sauce, meats, milk, processed foods
Sulphur	A component of some proteins, insulin and the vitamins biotin and thiamin	All protein-containing foods
Trace Minerals		
Iron	Part of hemoglobin (the red substance in blood that carries oxygen); prevents anemia	Liver, meats, shellfish, enriched breads and cereals, legumes
Zinc	A component of insulin; enhances healing; a component of many enzymes; involved in taste perception; bone formation	Protein foods, whole grain breads and cereals, fish, shellfish, poultry, vegetables
Selenium	Antioxidant	Fish, shellfish, meats, eggs, grains (depends on soil conditions)
Iodine	Component of thyroid hormone	Iodized salt, fish, shellfish, bread, plants grown in soil
Copper	Facilitates iron absorption; part of enzymes	Meats, fish, shellfish, nuts, seeds
Fluoride	Necessary for bone and teeth formation; helps teeth resist tooth decay	Fluoridated drinking water, fish, shellfish
Chromium	Insulin cofactor	Liver, whole grains, brewer's yeast, nuts, oils
Molybdenum	Cofactor in metabolism	Legumes, cereals
Manganese	Cofactor in metabolism	Whole grains, nuts, organ meats
Cobalt	Component of vitamin B_{12} (cobalamin)	

radicals (unstable potentially harmful substances produced naturally in the body during metabolism). It is believed that antioxidants can reduce the potential for developing certain forms of cancer and heart disease as well as slowing down the aging process. Eating more plant foods such as fruits and vegetables and whole grains that provide a variety of phytochemicals will go a long way to preventing the incidence of many of the debilitating diseases of modern man.

EATING FOR HEALTH

It is generally recognized that a balanced diet is an important component of a healthy lifestyle. Eating well and exercising can contribute to a longer, healthier life.

Planning a diet to enhance health is made simpler by diet and exercise recommendations from organizations such as the Heart and Stroke Foundation of Canada and the Canadian Cancer Society. Both stress the importance of controlling the amount of fat in the diet and consuming in greater quantities plant foods such as vegetables, fruits and whole grains.

Another useful planning tool is *Eating Well with Canada's Food Guide* (2007), published by Health Canada, which can be seen on pages 42 to 43. The Food Guide recommends moderating the consumption of fats, cholesterol, sugar, salt and alcohol while increasing the consumption of grains, fruits and vegetables. Variety, energy, balance and moderation are the four central principles. Although some details of this guide are unique to Canada, the basic healthy eating principles that it promotes are much the same as the Food Pyramid used in the U.S. and the food guides of other international societies. By illustrating what foods are important and recommending a range of servings, these guides eliminate the guesswork of eating nutritiously. The latest version of the guide is intended to reflect the most up-to-date science on the power of nutrition—and how the foods we put on our plates can promote healthy bodies and minds, and assist in preventing diseases. The new guide also introduces more ethnic foods and is age- and sex-specific, advising how many servings in each of the four food groups should be eaten daily by pre-schoolers to seniors. Remember that each person is unique and specific dietary plans require a professional nutritionist to ensure that the diet is healthful and appropriate for the individual.

The goal of healthy eating is to promote the shift from the traditional Canadian diet that is based heavily on protein-rich, higher-fat foods to one that includes more complex carbohydrates, fibre, key vitamins and minerals. This shift is presented visually in the Food Guide by the rainbow design illustrated in Figure 3.1 on page 42. The larger outside arcs encourage eating proportionally more grain products, vegetables and fruits; the smaller inside arcs represent the smaller amounts required of milk and meat products. (See page 42.)

INGREDIENT SUBSTITUTES AND ALTERNATIVES

More and more people are becoming health-conscious consumers. Many are trying to cut down on foods high in salt, fat, added sugar and cholesterol. To a degree, people can accomplish their goals—and cooks can assist them—by turning to ingredient substitutes and alternatives where possible.

Here we use the term "ingredient substitute" to mean the replacement of one ingredient with another of presumably similar—although not necessarily identical—flavour, texture, appearance and other characteristics. The substitute may be more nutritious, however. So, someone who is avoiding fats can use reduced fat or nonfat sour cream in place of regular sour cream when baking quick breads. The differences in flavour, texture, appearance and baking quality should be minimal.

We use the term "ingredient alternative" to mean the replacement of one ingredient with another of different flavour, texture, appearance or other characteristic, but one that will not compromise—although it may change—the flavour of the dish. As with the ingredient substitute, the ingredient alternative may be more nutritious. Lemon juice and herbs, for instance, can be used as flavouring alternatives to salt; a salsa of fresh vegetables can replace a cream-based sauce. The dishes will not taste the same, but they will still taste good.

In attempting to modify a recipe, the cook should first identify the ingredient(s) and/or cooking method(s) that may need to be changed. He or she can then use the following principles—reduce, replace or eliminate—to make a dish healthier:

Recommended Number of Food Guide Servings per Day

Age in Years	2-3	4-8	9-13	Teens 14-18		Adults 19-50		51+	
Sex	Girls and Boys			Females	Males	Females	Males	Females	Males
Vegetables and Fruit	4	5	6	7	8	7-8	8-10	7	7
Grain Products	3	4	6	6	7	6-7	8	6	7
Milk and Alternatives	2	2	3-4	3-4	3-4	2	2	3	3
Meat and Alternatives	1	1	1-2	2	3	2	3	2	3

The chart above shows how many Food Guide Servings you need from each of the four food groups every day.

Having the amount and type of food recommended and following the tips in *Canada's Food Guide* will help:

- Meet your needs for vitamins, minerals and other nutrients.
- Reduce your risk of obesity, type 2 diabetes, heart disease, certain types of cancer and osteoporosis.
- Contribute to your overall health and vitality.

Health Canada Santé Canada

Your health and safety... our priority.

Votre santé et votre sécurité... notre priorité.

Eating Well with Canada's Food Guide

Canada

FIGURE 3.1 *Eating Well with Canada's Food Guide. Visit Health Canada's Web site for further information.*

Source: Health Canada. *Eating Well with Canada's Food Guide*, www.hc-sc.gc.ca/fn-an/alt_formats/hpfb-dgpsa/pdf/food-guide-aliment/print_eatwell_bienmang_e.pdf (revised 2007).

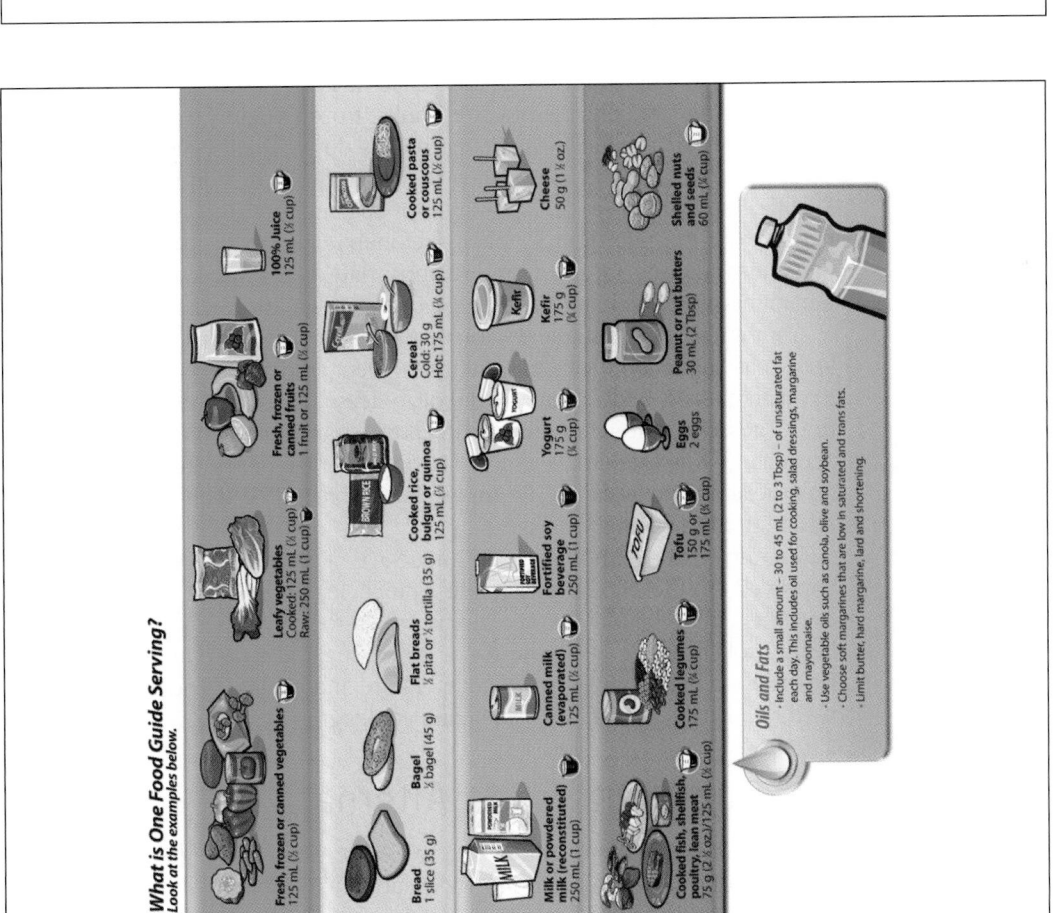

FIGURE 3.1 Eating Well with Canada's Food Guide (continued).

Back to Organic

Great strides in agriculture have been made during the past two centuries. Pesticides, fungicides and herbicides now eliminate or control pests that once would have devoured, ruined or choked crops. Chemical fertilizers increase yields of many of the world's staples. But not everyone has greeted these developments with open arms.

During the past few decades, scientific and medical investigators have documented, or at least suggested, health risks associated with certain synthetic pesticides, fertilizers and other products. These findings have led to a renewed interest in a back-to-the-basics approach to farming: organic farming. Specialty farms, orchards and even wineries now offer organically grown products (or, in the case of wineries, wines made from organically grown grapes). These products come with few, if any, intentional additives and should be free of any incidental additives. Proponents argue that these products are better for consumers and better for the health of the farm workers.

The National Standard of Canada for Organic Agriculture was introduced in 1999. There are still some provincial variances but in order to market a product as organic, the following requirements must be met: no use of antibiotic drugs in livestock feed; no use of chemical fertilizers or fertilizers that contain industrial or human waste; no use of synthetic pesticides; no use of genetically modified materials in seed for crops or in livestock feed; livestock must be grown in humane conditions (free range); and manure must be composted before use. Farms must be inspected annually for compliance and labelling claims are monitored by the Canadian Food Inspection Agency. There are numerous certifying bodies, and the chef needs to be aware of the standards adhered to when sourcing organic products.

1. Reduce the amounts of the ingredient(s); or
2. Replace the ingredient(s) with a substitute that will do the least to change the flavour and appearance of the dish; or
3. Eliminate the ingredient(s).

Salt Substitutes and Alternatives

A concern in the Canadian diet is excessive sodium (salt). Research has linked excessive amounts of sodium to hypertension (high blood pressure), heart and kidney diseases and strokes.

Cooks can contribute to a more healthful diet by decreasing the amount of salt and other high-sodium products such as soy sauce. Salt substitutes, which contain potassium chloride instead of sodium chloride, are available. "Lite" salt has a portion of the sodium content replaced by potassium but still contains some real salt for a truer flavour.

In addition, pepper, lemon, herbs, spices, fruits and flavoured vinegars can be used as salt alternatives to heighten flavour.

Sugar Substitutes

Saccharin, the oldest artificial sugar substitute, has been used for nearly a century. A petroleum derivative, it has no calories and tastes 300 times sweeter than table sugar. Saccharin has a bitter aftertaste, however, and many people find it unpalatable. Along with its sweetness come health concerns: some studies have linked saccharin with tumours in rats.

Aspartame (also known as Nutrasweet®), approved in Canada in 1982, is composed of the amino acids aspartic acid and phenylalanine. Unlike saccharin, aspartame does not have an aftertaste. It is 180 times sweeter than table sugar. It is now widely used in soft drinks, frozen yogurts, fruit spreads, candies and similar products. Aspartame breaks down when heated, so it cannot be used in cooked foods. According to the Health Protection Branch of Health Canada, aspartame is a safe substitute for sugar, although it is a risk for those people with the rare disorder phenylketonuria (PKU) who cannot metabolize the phenylalanine in aspartame. Appropriate warnings are printed on all aspartame-sweetened foods. It is not recommended for pregnant women.

Another sugar substitute is acesulfame K or acesulfame potassium (also known as Sunnette®), which is the most recent artificial sweetener to come on the market. The body cannot metabolize acesulfame K, so it passes through the digestive system unchanged. Like aspartame, it has no aftertaste. Acesulfame K is used in chewing gum, dry beverage mixes, instant coffees and teas, gelatins and nondairy creamers. It is more stable than aspartame, so it can be used in baking.

Sucralose (also known as Splenda®) is a noncaloric sugar substitute approved by the Health Protection Branch in 1991. Made from processed sugar, its tightly bound chlorine atoms pass through the body quickly without being broken down. Sucralose has a clean, sugar-like taste and no aftertaste. Because it remains stable in any temperature and storage conditions, it can be used in beverages, canning, baking and cooking.

Fat Substitutes and Alternatives

Several types of fat substitutes are available; they are either synthetic or derived from naturally occurring food substances. Some of the more recent products are Olestra®, Simplesse®, Oatrim and salatrim.

Olestra is made of sucrose and vegetable oil. The two are bonded together and the final product consists of molecules too large to be digested. Because it cannot be digested, Olestra does not add any calories. It may become a useful substitute for fats in baking or cooking, but health concerns have kept it from being widely available. Olestra is not approved for use or import in Canada.

Simplesse is a fat substitute used in frozen desserts such as ice creams and yogurt. Simplesse, made from egg whites or milk proteins, has a rich, creamy texture similar to fat but is fat free. Products made with Simplesse are not usually fat free, however, because other fat-containing ingredients are added.

Caprenin and salatrim are fat substitutes used in the candy industry and are not available for home or restaurant use.

Other Ingredient Substitutes and Alternatives

There are many other ingredient substitutes, some of which are identified in Table 3.5. Often ingredient substitutes and alternatives have a dramatic impact on the nutritional values of a completed dish. For example, in Figures 3.2A and 3.2B we list the ingredients for a sheet pan of traditional fudge brownies and one made with ingredient substitutes. Note the differences.

Lactose intolerance may be accommodated by using lactose-free dairy products. Soy or nut milk can be used if one is not allergic to either, but they are heat sensitive. Two egg whites (60 g) can be substituted for some whole eggs in many recipes. Use caution with egg substitutes. Gluten intolerance is common

TABLE 3.5	Ingredient Substitutes
For	**Use**
Bacon	Well-cooked, drained bacon or soy-based bacon
Butter	Powdered butter granules plus liquid (either skim milk or water) or butter-flavoured oil sprays
Chocolate	Cocoa (vegetable oil may be added as needed)
Cream cheese	Reduced-fat cream cheese or fat-free cream cheese
Emulsified salad dressing	Start with a base of reduced-fat or nonfat yogurt, sour cream or mayonnaise, then thin with skim milk; or use a slurry-thickened broth or juice as the oil and add vinegar and other seasonings; or blend silken tofu with other ingredients for a creamy dressing
Light cream	Equal portions of 1% milk and skim evaporated milk
Mayonnaise	Reduced-fat mayonnaise (it can be mixed with reduced-fat or nonfat sour cream)
Sour cream	Reduced-fat or nonfat sour cream; drained reduced-fat or nonfat plain yogurt without gelatin
Whipped cream	Whipped chilled evaporated skim milk; the milk and beaters need to be very cold (needs to be stabilized)
Whole eggs	Liquid egg substitutes; use 1 egg white for every third whole egg called for in a batter; fruit purées alone or combined with starches in quick bread batters

Traditional Fudge Brownies

Yield: 88 5-cm (2-in.) squares

Unsweetened chocolate	1 kg	2 lb.
Butter	1 kg	2 lb.
Eggs	22	22
Sugar	2.9 kg	5 lb. 12 oz.
Vanilla extract	60 mL	2 fl. oz.
All-purpose flour	750 g	1 lb. 10 oz.
Pecan pieces	500 g	1 lb.

Nutritional values per 5-cm (2-in.) square:

Calories	343
Total carbohydrates	41 g
Total fat	17 g
Protein	4 g
Saturated fat	9 g
Sodium	16 mg
Cholesterol	70 mg
Vitamin C	0

FIGURE 3.2A Traditional recipe.

Calorie-Reduced Brownies

Yield: 88 5-cm (2-in.) squares

Unsweetened chocolate	125 g	4 oz.
Cake flour	500 g	1 lb.
Cocoa powder	275 g	9 oz.
Salt substitute	10 g	2 tsp.
Egg whites	12	12
Whole eggs	10	10
Granulated sugar	1 kg	2 lb. 2 oz.
Corn syrup	1 kg	2 lb.
Unsweetened applesauce	725 mL	1-1/2 pt.
Canola oil	200 mL	7 fl. oz.
Vanilla extract	30 mL	2 Tbsp.

Nutritional values per 5-cm (2-in.) square:

Calories	150
Total carbohydrates	26 g
Total fat	5 g
Protein	2 g
Saturated fat	0.8 g
Sodium	82 mg
Cholesterol	19 mg
Vitamin C	4 mg

FIGURE 3.2B Calorie-reduced recipe.

and a gluten-free diet is often recommended for autistic or hyperactive disorders. Rice or corn pasta and starches to replace roux are easy solutions. Baked goods are a challenge to achieve acceptable texture and crumb. Developing recipes requires the use of alternate flours, vegetable gums and more eggs.

Ingredient substitutes and, especially, ingredient alternatives change the nutritional values of a dish; they may also change its flavour, texture or appearance. Sometimes these changes will be acceptable; sometimes they will not. Because some ingredient substitutes and alternatives result in unsatisfactory flavours, textures or appearance, many recipes may not be suitable for substitution or alteration. Prepare a test batch first if you are unsure.

PACKAGE LABELLING

To ensure that consumers have accurate information about packaged foods, the Consumer Packaging and Labelling Act and the Food and Drug Regulations require that most food products be clearly labelled. The language that may be used on these labels is closely regulated; even the minimum type size of the information is specified. The *Guide to Food Labelling and Advertising*, published by the Canadian Food Inspection Agency (1996), spells out requirements and is the source of most of the information that follows.

Mandatory Information

With few exceptions (such as one-bite confections sold individually), prepackaged products must be labelled. The label must include the common name of the product (e.g., "orange juice from concentrate," "mixed vegetables"), the net quantity, the name and address of the manufacturer or dealer and a list of ingredients, in descending order of proportion by weight in the food. Certain ingredients used in small amounts, such as seasonings, vitamins, minerals and additives, may be given in any order at the end of the list. Most products with a durable life of less than 90 days must have a "best before" date. The net quantity must be given in metric measures—grams or millilitres—and may also be given in imperial or U.S. measures such as ounces or fluid ounces. If the package suggests a natural flavour (e.g., a picture of an apple) but an artificial flavour is used, this information must be given next to the image. In most cases, mandatory information must be shown in both French and English.

Nutritional Information

A breakdown of nutritional content is not required. However, if it is given, it must follow specific formats set out in the *Guidelines on Nutrition Labelling* (Health Canada, 1996) and the Food and Drug Regulations and must not be misleading or deceptive. Nutritional labelling must be given in both official languages. A serving size must be given in grams or millilitres, and a household measure (e.g., 1 cup) should be used.

Nutrient information must include a "core list": energy (in both calories and kilojoules), and protein, fat and carbohydrates (in grams). Other information is optional. If one fat component (e.g., monounsaturates) is given, the other three components (polyunsaturates, saturates, cholesterol) must be given as well. If vitamins and minerals are listed, they must be given as a percentage of recommended daily intake. The United States' "Nutrition Facts" information is not permitted on foods sold in Canada, since the two countries use different methods of calculating nutrient values. New Canadian regulations came into effect on January 1, 2003.

Nutritional Claims

Many products carry nutritional claims, such as "a good source of...," "low in...," "sugar-free" or "low calorie." Such terms have specific definitions that must be used accurately. A food may not be listed as a source of a nutrient, for example, unless it contains at least 5% of the recommended daily intake for that nutrient. Standards for foods described as "a good source of" or "high in" a nutrient are specific to each nutrient. Figure 3.3 on the next page shows a label giving nutrient information and making appropriate nutritional claims.

As consumers express increasing concern about fat consumption, the term "fat free" has become particularly important. In 1997, Health Canada relaxed the definition of "fat free" to include foods that contain nutritionally insignificant amounts of fat: less than 0.5 grams of fat in a serving, and in a "reference amount" defined by regulation as the amount a person would typically consume at one time. The new definition matches U.S. and international standards.

Health Claims

Beyond simply making a claim about content, manufacturers sometimes want to claim certain benefits for a food. The language of health claims, too, is tightly regulated. For example, a food may be described as "wholesome" but should not be described as "healthy" or "healthful" where the word may suggest that simply eating the food will bring health. Manufacturers must not claim that a specific food may prevent a disease. Claims must be based on *Nutrition Recommendations for*

Recipe Nutritional Analyses

A registered dietitian has analyzed all of the recipes in this book using nutritional analysis software that incorporates data from the USDA, research laboratories and food manufacturers. The nutrient information provided here should be used only as a reference, however. A margin of error of approximately 20 percent can be expected because of natural variations in ingredients; the federal government permits food manufacturers and other suppliers to use this same margin of error in their food labelling efforts. Preparation techniques and serving sizes may also significantly alter the values of many nutrients. For the nutritional analysis, if a recipe offers a choice of ingredients, the first-mentioned ingredient was the one used. Ingredients listed as "to taste" (TT) and "as needed" were omitted from the analysis. Canola oil and 2% milk were used throughout for "vegetable oil" and "milk," respectively. When given a range of ingredient quantities or numbers of servings, the average was used.

Similar food products now list similar portion sizes, making nutritional comparison easier. The serving-size declaration must be given in grams or millilitres and should also include a common or household measure.

If this food contained a smaller amount of fat then it could be labelled "fat free," because the amount would be nutritionally insignificant: for example, only 0.5 grams of fat per serving and per reference amount.

No individual food may be called "essential" but nutrients assigned recommended daily intakes (RDI or RNI, recommended nutrient intake) may be. A food may not be called a "source" of a nutrient unless it contains at least 5% of the RDI.

Macronutrients are listed in grams; micronutrients are given as a percentage of RNI. RNI are usually for adult males and may be misleading for children or pregnant or lactating women.

Most mandatory information must be shown in both English and French.

Nutrition Facts / Valeur nutritive

Per 1/4 package (22 g) / pour 1/4 d'emballage (22 g)
About 1/2 cup prepared / environ 1/2 tasse préparé

Amount / Teneur	Dry Mix / Poudre	Prepared† / Préparé†
Calories / Calories	100	140
% Daily Value / % valeur quotidienne		
Fat / Lipides 2 g*	3 %	3 %
Saturated / saturés 1 g + Trans / trans 1 g	10 %	10 %
Cholesterol / Cholestérol 0 mg		
Sodium / Sodium 80 mg	3 %	6 %
Carbohydrate / Glucides 20 g	7 %	9 %
Fibre / Fibres 1 g	4 %	4 %
Sugars / Sucres 14 g		
Protein / Protéines 4 g		
Vitamin A / Vitamine A	0 %	6 %
Vitamin C / Vitamine C	0 %	2 %
Calcium / Calcium	0 %	15 %
Iron / Fer	2 %	2 %

* Amount in dry mix / Teneur de la poudre
† 1/2 cup skim milk adds 40 Calories, 65 mg sodium, 6 g carbohydrate (6 g sugars) and 4 g protein. / 1/2 tasse de lait écrémé ajoute 40 Calories, 65 mg sodium, 6 g glucides (6 g sucres) et 4 g protéines.

7.2 cm x 9.4 cm = 67.7 cm²

FIGURE 3.3   A product label showing nutritional information in approved format.

Canadians or *Eating Well with Canada's Food Guide*, and must be substantiated by nutrient information. For example, it would be acceptable to claim: "Consuming a variety of fibre-containing foods is part of a healthful diet; this product is high in fibre." The package would then have to give the fibre content, which would have to meet criteria for "high." Table 3.6 shows the health claims that may be made for specific nutrients.

Nutritional Labelling for Restaurant Menus

Restaurants are not required to give nutritional information on menu items. If they do, the information must be accurate and meet the same standards as packaging material. Some restaurateurs like to use a heart symbol or claim that particular menu items are "heart smart choices." Such claims may be prohibited because they suggest that the food will prevent disease. However, a check mark may be used to identify menu items as healthy choices if it is part of a clearly identified nutrition information program.

CONSUMER CONCERNS ABOUT FOOD AND NUTRITION

Many food ingredients have been linked to medical conditions. Some of the links are tenuous at best; others may be well supported by research. Nutrition is a science, and new information about the relationship of food to health and disease is always emerging.

Canadians have voiced concerns about the possible links of certain fats and dietary cholesterol to heart disease; they want to know if sugar intake is related

TABLE 3.6	Acceptable Biological Role Claims for Nutrients		
Protein	Helps build and repair body tissues Helps build antibodies	**Thiamin (Vitamin B$_1$)**	Releases energy from carbohydrate Aids normal growth
Fat	Supplies energy Aids in the absorption of fat-soluble vitamins	**Riboflavin (Vitamin B$_2$)**	Factor in energy metabolism and tissue formation
DHA	DHA, an omega-3 fatty acid, supports the normal development of the brain, eyes and nerves	**Niacin**	Aids in normal growth and development Factor in energy metabolism and tissue formation
Carbohydrate	Supplies energy Assists in the utilization of fats	**Vitamin B$_6$**	Factor in energy metabolism and tissue formation
Vitamin A	Aids normal bone and tooth development Aids in the development and maintenance of night vision Aids in maintaining the health of the skin and membranes	**Folate**	Aids in red blood cell formation
		Vitamin B$_{12}$	Aids in red blood cell formation
		Pantothenic acid	Factor in energy metabolism and tissue formation
		Calcium	Aids in the formation and maintenance of bones and teeth
Vitamin D	Factor in the formation and maintenance of bones and teeth Enhances calcium and phosphorus absorption and utilization	**Phosphorus**	Factor in the formation and maintenance of bones and teeth
		Magnesium	Factor in energy metabolism, tissue formation and bone development
Vitamin E	Protects the fat in body tissues from oxidation	**Iron**	Factor in red blood cell formation
Vitamin C	Factor in the development and maintenance of bones, cartilage, teeth and gums	**Zinc**	Factor in energy metabolism and tissue formation
		Iodine	Factor in the normal function of the thyroid gland

Source: Canadian Food Inspection Agency, *2003 Guide to Food Labelling and Advertising*, Chapter 8, Table 8.2, www.inspection.gc.ca/english/fssa/labeti/guide/ch8e.shtml#tab8-2.

to obesity, diabetes and heart disease. Some people are concerned that pesticide residues in produce may be dangerous, and they will seek out restaurants that serve organically grown produce.

There is a heightened awareness of genetically modified foods. While the jury is still out, many people refuse to consume them. Ethics and animal husbandry are also causing concerns.

The tremendous public interest in nutrition presents a special challenge to chefs. They should be able to prepare and serve food that meets the high standards for health demanded by some patrons, while maintaining the flavour and appearance important to everyone.

Food Allergies

The incidence of adverse reactions to food ingredients is prevalent in today's society. Whether a true food allergy or a food intolerance, the consequences to a restaurant patron can be deadly. Chefs, cooks and servers must be aware of the ingredients used in dishes and present in the establishment. Patrons who ask questions about ingredients must be given complete and accurate information. You are liable if you provide inaccurate information.

Foods Causing Allergies

Some Definitions

Food allergy—Adverse reaction to foods that involves an immune response; also called food hypersensitivity reaction.

Food intolerance—Adverse reaction to a food that does not involve the immune system.

Labelling of Foods Causing Allergies and Sensitivities

A variety of foods contain ingredients that can cause adverse reactions in hypersensitive individuals. Most adverse food reactions are caused by the following foods and products made from them:

- Peanuts
- Tree nuts (almonds, Brazil nuts, cashews, hazelnuts [filberts], macadamia nuts, pecans, pine nuts, pistachios, walnuts)
- Sesame seeds
- Milk
- Eggs
- Fish, crustaceans (e.g., crab, crayfish, lobster, shrimp) and shellfish (e.g., clams, mussels, oysters, scallops)
- Soy
- Wheat
- Sulphites

The Canadian Food Inspection Agency (CFIA) is working with the food industry to ensure that the foods listed above are always declared in the list of ingredients on the food label and to develop allergen-prevention strategies to manage the allergy risk. Menu descriptions must include the listed items to inform customers.

Source: Adapted from "Foods Causing Allergies and Sensitivities" on the Canadian Food Inspection Agency Web site www.inspection.gc.ca/english/corpaffr/ foodfacts/allergense.shtml

Gluten Allergy

Celiac disease, the inability to digest gluten, is one of the few diseases that is treated exclusively with diet. By removing all wheat, rye, and barley from the diet, people with celiac disease return to living a normal, healthy life. However, the most minute amount of gluten can cause symptoms to return. The problem is the gluten protein that is present in wheat, rye and barley.

Staying gluten-free is quite a challenge and requires a quick education about foods and ingredients. Gluten is hidden in many places including soy sauce (fermented with wheat), sauces, soups and even some spice blends. Wheat is also used in the glue on most envelopes. Many different flours are safe: rice flour, corn flour, cornstarch, potato flour and potato starch, tapioca starch, quinoa, soy, sorghum, bean flours, buckwheat, millet and amaranth. Teff and oats can be safe as long as the source is free of cross-contamination from wheat.

Baking without gluten defies most of the principles of food chemistry. It's best to use a blend of two to three different gluten-free flours and starches, usually rice flour, sorghum, buckwheat or millet with the addition of at least 30% starch—corn, potato or tapioca. Some of the protein and elasticity of gluten can be replaced with gums—xanthan, guar or locust bean gum. Usually one teaspoon per cup [5 mL per 225 mL] is used for pastries and 3 teaspoons per cup [15 mL per 225 mL] is recommended for creating a blend that is used for bread flour. The addition of eggs helps build up the protein in the mixture. Also, adding a small amount of a flour that is high in protein (amaranth, soy or other bean flour) helps to produce moisture in the final product.

Although gluten-free baking takes a bit of extra effort, the rewards outweigh the challenges as gluten-free consumers are very appreciative and will remain customers for life!

—BETH HILLSON, Founder,
The Gluten-Free Pantry

Because of metabolic, digestive, religious or allergic conditions, patrons will request that their meals be prepared in specific ways or that certain ingredients be deleted or substituted. The Canadian Food Inspection Agency identifies nine ingredients (see sidebar) that must be disclosed to the consumer as priority food allergens. They account for 95 percent of reactions. One must be aware of and disclose the ingredients even if they are part of another product (e.g., a condiment or a mix). Some ingredients are not in their common form. For example, miso and lecithin are soy derivatives. Some people are so dangerously allergic that even a trace amount of a particular ingredient can cause a deadly reaction or anaphylactic shock.

The CFIA is currently examining labelling and disclosure requirements. The regulations will be enhanced and enforcement will be implemented. Monosodium glutamate (MSG) is not on the list, but it is a common trigger and should be disclosed.

NUTRITION AND THE CHEF

Eating Well with Canada's Food Guide was designed to guide food consumption for a more healthful life. It presents a plan for a balanced diet. Chefs can use it to plan balanced menus as well. As the Food Guide suggests, chefs do not need to use only meat as the centre of the plate presentation. It demands that a variety of breads, pasta and grains be included on the menu along with an interesting selection of vegetable dishes. And it cautions against the use of too much fat and sugar. The rainbow symbol is used in this text to identify healthful food offerings (see Figure 3.4).

FIGURE 3.4 The symbol for a healthful recipe.

Many consumers are modifying eating patterns to reduce body weight and/or prevent states associated with obesity. Chefs are called upon to adjust offerings to reduce calories, fat and allergens. Half or split orders, broiling or baking instead of frying and sauces served on the side are common requests. Ingredient substitution is requested and often necessary.

Although not every food service operation can (or should) be devoted to "health food," to the extent appropriate you should offer healthful dining alternatives. Your ability to do so depends, of course, upon your facility. Chefs at hospitals, prisons and schools have much greater control over the foods they offer. Chefs at most restaurants, however, do not have such captive audiences. But that does not mean that you can shirk your responsibilities.

You assist customers when you do the following:

1. Use proper purchasing and storage techniques in order to preserve nutrients.
2. Offer a variety of foods from each arc of the Food Guide rainbow so that customers have a choice.
3. Offer entrees that emphasize plant instead of animal foods.
4. Offer dishes that are considerate of special dietary needs.
5. Use cooking procedures that preserve rather than destroy nutrients.
6. Use cooking procedures that minimize the use of added fat (e.g., stocks, sauces and soups can be cooled and the congealed fats removed; foods can be browned in the oven instead of being sautéed in hot fat).
7. Use equipment that minimizes the use of added fat (e.g., nonstick pans).
8. Train the wait staff to respond properly to nutritional questions diners may have about menu items.
9. Post notices on menus or label products that may contain allergens.
10. Use ingredient alternatives or substitutes where appropriate. If a dish does not lend itself to ingredient alternatives or substitutes, consider creating a new dish that replaces less nutritious traditional foods or preparations with more nutritious ones. For example, instead of serving a sauce made with butter, flour and cream, you can reduce an appropriately seasoned wine, stock or juice and then thicken it with fruit or vegetable purées or starches.

Sample Healthy Restaurant Meal

Chefs are increasingly challenged to create healthy menus for their establishments, menus that conform to current nutritional guidelines. Because health intakes vary by individual based on age, gender, level of physical activity and other variables, this cannot easily be determined. As a general guideline, an overall healthy meal comprising a first course, entree and dessert should offer the following components:

- The meal should consist of a total of 1000 calories.
- Fifteen to 25% of the calories should be from protein, which can be from an animal or plant-based source.
- Forty-five to 65% of the calories should come from carbohydrates, including whole grains and sugars from natural sources such as fruits.
- Twenty to 35% of the calories should be from fat. Of the total fat, less than 10% of the total calories should be from saturated fats such as that found in butter and animal fats. More of the fat should be from monounsaturated sources such as olive oil, fatty fish or nuts.

Keeping Halal

Many Muslims follow dietary laws based on the Koran (the revealed book), the Hadith (the sayings or traditions of the Prophet Muhammad) and the collective wisdom of Muslim scholars. *Halal*, which means "allowed" or "lawful," refers to foods and beverages that can be consumed by observant Muslims. Foods and beverages that are *haram* are not allowed, and those that are of a questionable or suspect nature are referred to as *mushbooh*.

As all fruits and vegetables are halal, the majority of Muslim dietary laws address permitted and prohibited meats. Cooked (not raw) beef, lamb and chicken are halal, provided the animals are slaughtered and butchered according to certain rituals and methods. Fish and shellfish are also halal. Pork, game, carnivorous animals, birds of prey, carrion (the meat of animals that died of natural causes) and blood are haram, as are products derived from them. Eggs and dairy products from permitted animals are halal, as are baked goods made with ingredients from permitted animals. Any halal food contaminated with blood, pork or other haram product is deemed haram and cannot be eaten. Alcohol, whether consumed as a beverage, used as a flavouring or even present in a cleaning solution for dishes, is haram. Gelatin, emulsifiers, animal-based fats and certain dairy products are considered mushbooh unless certified as halal. Halal certification is often denoted as a capital H inside a triangle.

In food service operations, it is best if equipment dedicated solely to halal cooking is used. If this is impractical and the same equipment is used to cook halal and haram foods, the equipment must be thoroughly sanitized before it can be used for halal products. Normally, a careful visual inspection of the equipment suffices.

- The meal should offer 8 to 12 g of fibre.
- The total meal should contain no more than 1000 mg of sodium.
- As a reference, a healthy meal should include 225 to 350 mL (1 to 1-1/2 cups) fresh vegetables.

These are approximate recommendations to help you plan a menu and the appropriate portion sizes within established health guidelines. Throughout this book various recipes are marked with the rainbow symbol illustrated in Figure 3.4. This symbol identifies dishes that are particularly low in calories, fat, saturated fat or sodium; if appropriate, they may also be a good source of vitamins, protein, fibre or calcium. Menus that meet these guidelines can be created using many of these recipes and other recipes.

The tremendous public interest in nutrition presents a special challenge to chefs. Ultimately it is the consumer's responsibility to choose wisely and eat properly. But chefs should be able to prepare and serve food that meets the high standards for health demanded by some patrons, while maintaining the flavour and appearance important to everyone.

Keeping Kosher

To one degree or another, many observant Jews keep kosher; that is, they adhere to dietary laws rooted in the Torah (the first five books of the Old Testament) and developed over the centuries by Jewish scholars. These laws (1) categorize foods and (2) define basic dietary principles.

Kosher foods—Only meat from animals that chew their cud and have split hooves can be eaten. These include cattle, goats, deer and other game; swine are not a kosher species. Poultry can be kosher, provided it is not from a bird of prey; thus, chicken, duck, goose and turkey are allowed, but hawk and eagle are not. Even if the species is kosher, the animal must still be slaughtered and butchered according to religious rules. For fish to be kosher, it must have both scales and gills; this eliminates catfish and eel, and no shellfish can be kosher. Dairy products are kosher if the species from which they come is kosher; for cheese to be kosher, it must be made without rennet. Fresh fruits and vegetables are always kosher, as are baked goods, provided they are not made with animal fats. Commercially prepared foods marked with U, K or a similar symbol (often in a circle) indicate that the food product is kosher, the producer having used appropriate ingredients and met certain standards and its facilities having been inspected and approved by a rabbi.

Kosher dietary principles—All foods are either (1) meat, (2) dairy or (3) pareve (parve). The principal dietary rule for keeping kosher is that meat and dairy foods cannot be cooked or eaten together. Over the centuries, this rule has been refined to the point that people keeping kosher will have two sets of cooking utensils, dishes and even dishcloths, one devoted to meat, the other to dairy, so that there is no accidental mixing. Particularly observant Jews will even wait for one to six hours after eating a meat dish before consuming a dairy dish. Pareve refers to neutral (neuter) foods such as fruits, vegetables, breads, fish, eggs and certain commercially prepared foods that can be eaten with either meat or dairy items.

Not all Jews keep strictly kosher. Those who do will dine out only in a restaurant that regularly observes the same religious laws that they do at home, or in one that has been specially inspected and approved by a rabbi for the particular occasion (an option often used by catering facilities to accommodate kosher weddings, bar mitzvahs, bat mitzvahs and other Jewish celebrations). Other Jews will keep kosher by not eating any shellfish, meat, poultry or fish from nonkosher species or mixing dairy and meat, but they will not insist that separate meat and dairy cooking and eating utensils be used. They will generally dine in nonkosher restaurants, provided that the menu (sometimes referred to as "kosher-style") offers appropriate selections from kosher species.

Conclusion

A basic understanding and appreciation of nutrition are important for both the consumer and those who prepare the foods consumed.

What you serve is important. Carbohydrates, proteins, fats, water, vitamins and minerals, in varying amounts, are all necessary for good health. *Eating Well with Canada's Food Guide* can guide selections to create and maintain a healthful diet.

How foods are prepared is also important. Remember that some cooking and storage techniques preserve nutrients; others do not. In addition, by substituting or modifying ingredients and preparation methods, many dishes can be made more nutritious.

Questions for Discussion

1. Identify the six categories of nutrients and list two sources for each.

2. What are the differences between saturated fats and unsaturated fats? Identify two sources for each.

3. List four things you can do to reduce the loss of minerals and vitamins when storing or preparing foods.

4. Describe *Eating Well with Canada's Food Guide*. Explain how a chef can use the guide to plan well-balanced meals and how a consumer can use the guide to establish a healthful diet. What other diet planning tools can be used along with the Food Guide?

5. Create two menus for a Thanksgiving dinner, both nutritionally balanced, but one high in calories, fat and so on, and the other including the traditional foods but reduced in fat, calories, cholesterol and sodium.

6. Identify four common food allergens and provide suggestions for ingredient substitutes.

4 Menu Planning and Food Costing

"My mother's [recipes] don't do me as much good as they might because she never included directions. Her reasoning, often expressed, was that any cook worth her salt would know, given a list of ingredients, what to do with them, and if she did come to a momentary loss while stirring up a dish—taste it! Cooking was a matter of born sense, ordinary good judgment, enough experience, materials worth the bothering about, and tasting.

—Eudora Welty, American author (1909–2001) in her introduction to *The Jackson Cookbook*, 1971

Today's professional cook must master more than the basics of béchamel, butchering and bread baking. You must be equally skilled in the business of food services. This means knowing what products cost and how much an operation should charge for its menu items.

Although computers are almost as common in kitchens as whisks, no machine can ever replace a cook's hands-on ability to apply food cost controls. Accurate measurements, portion control and proper food handling directly affect the food service operation's bottom line. In addition, cooks must, at the very least, be able to conduct yield tests, calculate recipe costs and use food cost percentages appropriately.

This chapter first introduces you to various types and styles of menus. It then explains a standardized recipe format and presents the basics of food cost controls as well as information on measurements and techniques for changing or converting recipe yields. It then describes methods for determining unit and recipe costs, including calculations for raw yield tests. It concludes with a discussion of the methods for pricing menus and controlling food costs. This chapter does not attempt to cover menu design, accounting principles or computer applications. It will, however, provide a foundation of practical techniques to be used by anyone with common sense and a calculator.

THE MENU

Whether it lists ethnic dishes, hamburgers, just desserts or classic cuisine, and whether the prices range from inexpensive to exorbitant, the menu is the soul of every food service operation. Its purposes are to identify for the consumer the foods and beverages the operation offers, to create consumer enthusiasm and to increase sales. When combined with excellent food and great service, a well-planned menu helps ensure success.

Most menus offer consumers sufficient selections to build an entire meal. A typical Canadian or American main meal consists of three courses. The first course may be a hot or cold appetizer, soup or salad. The second course is the **entree** or main dish, usually meat, poultry, fish or shellfish accompanied by a vegetable and starch. The third course is dessert, either a sweet preparation or fruit and cheese. For a more formal meal, there may be a progression of first courses, including a hot or cold appetizer and soup, as well as a fish course served before the main dish (which, in this case, would not be fish). For some meals sorbet or granité may follow the fish course as a palate cleanser. Occasionally, a light salad will be presented as a palate cleanser after the main dish and before dessert, cheese and friandises.

Types of Menus

Menus are classified according to the regularity with which the foods are offered:

1. **Static menu**—All patrons are offered the same foods every day. Once a static menu is developed and established, it rarely changes. Static menus are

● **entree** the main dish of a North American meal, usually meat, poultry, fish or shellfish accompanied by a vegetable and starch; in France, the first course, served before the fish and meat courses

● **static menu** a menu offering patrons the same foods every day

The Tasting Menu

In addition to their à la carte menus, restaurants are increasingly offering tasting menus (Fr. *menu dégustation*, It. *degustazione*), small portions served in four, five or more courses for a fixed price. A tasting menu allows consumers the opportunity to sample a wider range of dishes than would normally be eaten in one meal. The best examples of such menus are carefully crafted by the chef so that each dish complements the next and courses are not merely a hodgepodge of everything in the kitchen. Chefs frequently design tasting menus with a theme such as "spring asparagus" in which each course highlights the ingredient in a new guise. A selection of wines can accompany a tasting menu. For ease of service restaurants usually require that the tasting menu be ordered by the entire table.

● **cycle menu** a menu that changes every day for a certain period and then repeats the same daily items in the same order (e.g., on a seven-day cycle, the same menu is used every Monday)

● **market menu** a menu based on product availability during a specific period; it is written to use foods when they are in peak season or readily available

● **hybrid menu** a menu combining features of a static menu with a cycle menu or a market menu of specials

● **à la carte** a menu on which each food and beverage is listed and priced separately

● **semi à la carte** a menu on which some foods (usually appetizers and desserts) and beverages are priced and ordered separately, while the entree is accompanied by and priced to include other dishes such as a salad, starch or vegetable

● **prix fixe** French for "fixed price"; a menu offering a complete meal for a set price; also known as **table d'hôte**

typically found in fast-food operations, ethnic restaurants, steakhouses and the like.

Static menus can also be used in institutional settings. For example, a static menu at an elementary school could offer students, along with a vegetable and dessert, the same luncheon choices every school day: a cheeseburger, fish sticks, chicken tacos, pizza wedges or a sandwich.

2. **Cycle menu**—A cycle menu is developed for a set period; at the end of that period it repeats itself (i.e., on a seven-day cycle, the same menu is used every Monday). Some cycle menus are written on a seasonal basis, with a new menu for each season to take advantage of product availability. Cycle menus are used commonly in schools, hospitals and other institutions. Although cycle menus may be repetitive, the repetition is not necessarily noticeable to diners because of the length of the cycles.

3. **Market menu**—A market menu is based upon product availability during a specific period; it is written to use foods when they are in peak season or readily available. Market menus are becoming increasingly popular with chefs (and consumers) as they challenge the chef's ingenuity in using fresh, seasonal products. Market menus are short-lived, however, because of limited product availability and perishability. In fact, they often change daily.

4. **Hybrid menu**—A hybrid menu combines a static menu with a cycle menu or a market menu of specials.

Food service operations may have separate menus for breakfast, lunch or dinner. If all three meals are available all day and are listed on the same menu, the menu is often called a California menu; California menus are typically found in 24-hour restaurants. Depending on the food service operation's objectives, separate specialty menus for drinks, hors d'oeuvre, desserts, brunch or afternoon tea, for example, are used.

Regardless of whether the menu is static, cycle, market or hybrid, it can offer consumers the opportunity to purchase their selections à la carte, semi à la carte, table d'hôte or some combination of the three.

1. **À la carte**—Every food and beverage item is priced and ordered separately.

2. **Semi à la carte**—With this popular menu style, some food items (particularly appetizers and desserts) are priced and ordered separately, while the entree is accompanied by and priced to include other items, such as a salad, starch or vegetable.

3. **Table d'hôte** or **prix fixe**—This menu offers a complete meal at a set price. (The term *table d'hôte* is French for "host's table" and is derived from the innkeeper's practice of seating all guests at a large communal table and serving them all the same meal.) A table d'hôte meal can range from very elegant to a diner's blue-plate special.

Many menus combine à la carte, semi à la carte and table d'hôte choices. For example, appetizers, salads and desserts may be available à la carte; entrees may be offered semi à la carte (they come with a salad, starch and vegetable), while the daily special is a complete (table d'hôte or prix fixe) meal.

Menu Language

The menu is the principal way in which the food service operation, including the chef, communicates with the consumer. A well-designed menu often reflects the input of design, marketing, art and other consultants as well as the chef and management. The type of folds, cover, artwork, layout, typefaces, colours and paper are all important considerations. But the most important consideration is the language.

The menu should list the foods offered. It may include descriptions such as the preparation method, essential ingredients and service method as well as the quality, cut and quantity of product. For example, the menu can list "Striploin Steak" or "Mesquite Grilled 250 g Certified Canadian Angus Beef Striploin Steak."

Truth in Menu Advertising

Federal laws require that certain menu language be accurate. Areas of particular concern include statements about quantity, quality, grade and freshness as well as dietary and nutritional claims. Accurate references to an item's source are also important. If brand names are used, those brands must be served. If the restaurant claims to be serving "Fresh Dover Sole," it must be just that, not frozen sole from New England. (On the other hand, like French or Russian dressing, "English mint sauce" is a generic name for a style of food, so using that geographical adjective is appropriate even if the mint sauce is not made in England.) A reference to "our own fresh-baked" desserts means that the restaurant regularly bakes the desserts on premises, serves them soon after baking and does not substitute commercially prepared or frozen goods. Purchasing invoices must substantiate any claims.

STANDARDIZED RECIPES

Menu writing and **recipe** development are mutually dependent activities. Once the menu is created, standardized recipes should be prepared for each item. A **standardized recipe** is one that will produce a known quality and quantity of food for a specific operation. It specifies (1) the type and amount of each ingredient, (2) the preparation and cooking procedures and (3) the yield and portion size.

Standardized recipes may be found in books or provided by manufacturers, but usually they are recipes customized to your operation—cooking time, temperature and utensils should be based on the equipment actually available. Yield should be adjusted to an amount appropriate for your operation. A recipe must be tested repeatedly and adjusted to fit your facility and your needs before it can be considered standardized. Some recipes cannot be increased or decreased in yield very successfully. Exercise caution.

Standardized recipes are a tool for the chef and management. The written forms assist with training cooks, educating service staff and controlling financial matters. They also help ensure that the customer will receive a consistent quality and quantity of product. Accurate recipe costing and menu pricing depend on having and using standardized recipes.

Although formats differ, a standardized recipe form will usually include:

- Name of product
- Yield
- Portion size
- Presentation and garnish
- Ingredient quality and quantity
- Preparation procedures
- Cooking time and temperature
- Holding procedures

● **recipe** a set of written instructions for producing a specific food or beverage; also known as a formula

● **standardized recipe** a recipe producing a known quality and quantity of food for a specific operation

The form may also include information on costing and a photograph of the finished dish. Each form should be complete, consistent and simple to read and follow. The forms should be stored in a readily accessible place. Index cards, notebook binders or a computerized database may be used, depending on the size and complexity of the operation.

MEASUREMENTS AND CONVERSIONS
Measurement Formats

Accurate measurements are among the most important aspects of food production. Ingredients and portions must be measured correctly to ensure consistent product quality. In other words, the cook must be able to prepare a recipe the same way each time, and portion sizes must be the same from one order to the next.

In a kitchen, measurements may be made in three ways: weight, volume and count.

weight the mass or heaviness of a substance; weight measurements are commonly expressed as kilograms, grams, ounces and pounds

Weight refers to the mass or heaviness of a substance. It is expressed in terms such as kilograms, grams, ounces and pounds. Weight may be used to measure liquid or dry ingredients (for example, 800 g of eggs for a bread recipe) and portions (for example, 85 g of sliced turkey for a sandwich). As weight is generally the most accurate form of measurement, portion scales or balance scales are commonly used in kitchens.

volume the space occupied by a substance; volume measurements are commonly expressed as millilitres, litres, cups, quarts, gallons, teaspoons, fluid ounces and bushels

Volume refers to the space occupied by a substance. This is mathematically expressed as *height × width × length*. It is expressed in terms such as millilitres, litres, cups, quarts, gallons, teaspoons, fluid ounces and bushels. Volume is most commonly used to measure liquids. It may also be used for dry ingredients when the amount is too small to be weighed accurately (for example, 1 mL or 1/4 tsp. of salt). Although measuring by volume is somewhat less accurate than measuring by weight, volume measurements are generally quicker to do.

Frequently, mistakes are made in food preparation by cooks who assume wrongly that weight and volume are equal. Do not be fooled—250 mL of solid food does not equal 250 g. For example, the weight of 250 mL of diced apples will vary depending on the size of the apple pieces. Errors are commonly made in the bakeshop by cooks who assume that 250 g of flour is the same as 250 mL of flour. In fact, 225 mL (1 cup) of flour may weigh from 100 to 140 g (3-1/2 to 5 oz.) depending on type and conditions.

It is not unusual to see both weight and volume measurements used in a single recipe. When a recipe ingredient is expressed in weight, weigh it. When it is expressed as a volume, measure it. Like most rules, however, this one has exceptions. The weight and volume of water is essentially the same. For this ingredient you may use whichever measurement is most convenient.

count the number of individual items in a given measure of weight or volume

Count refers to the number of individual items. Count is used in recipes (for example, 4 eggs) and in portion control (for example, 2 fish fillets or 1 ear of corn). Count is also commonly used in purchasing to indicate the size of the individual items. For example, a "96 count" case of lemons means that an 18 kg (40 lb.) case contains 96 individual lemons; a "115 count" case means that the same 18 kg (40 lb.) case contains 115 individual lemons. So, each lemon in the 96-count case is larger than those in the 115-count case. Shrimp is another item commonly sold by count. Depending on the size of the individual pieces, 450 g (1 lb.) of shrimp may contain from 8 to several hundred shrimp. When placing an order, the chef must specify the desired count. For example, when ordering 450 g (1 lb.) of 21–25-count shrimp, the chef expects to receive not fewer than 21 nor more than 25 shrimps.

Measurement Systems

The measurement formats of weight, volume and count are used in the imperial, U.S. and metric measurement systems. Because each of these systems is used in modern food service operations, you should be able to prepare recipes written in any of the three.

The *imperial system* originated in Great Britain but is no longer used. It used pounds and ounces for weight, and pints and fluid ounces for volume.

The *U.S. system* is the most difficult system to understand. It uses pounds for weight and cups for volume.

The *metric system*, used in Canada, is the most commonly used system in the world. Developed in France during the late 18th century, it is a mathematically rational and uniform system of measurement. The metric system is a decimal system in which the gram, litre and metre are the basic units of weight, volume and length, respectively. Larger or smaller units of weight, volume and length are formed by adding a prefix to the words "gram," "litre" or "metre." Some of the more commonly used prefixes in food service operations are deca- (10), hecto- (100), kilo- (1000), deci- (1/10), centi- (1/100) and milli- (1/1000). Thus, a kilogram is 1000 grams; a decametre is 10 metres; a millilitre is 1/1000 of a litre. Because the metric system is based on multiples of 10, it is extremely easy to increase or decrease recipe amounts.

The most important thing for a cook to know about the metric system is that *you do not need to convert between the metric system and the U.S. or imperial system in recipe preparation.* If a recipe is written in metric units, use metric measuring equipment; if it is written in U.S. units, use U.S. measuring equipment. Most Canadian measuring equipment is calibrated in both U.S. and metric increments. The need to convert amounts will arise only if the proper equipment is unavailable.

Converting Grams and Ounces

As you can see from Table 4.1 on the next page, 1 ounce equals 28.35 grams. So, *to convert ounces to grams, multiply the number of ounces by 28* (rounded for convenience).

$$8 \text{ ounces} \times 28 = 224 \text{ grams (225 g for practical use)}$$

And *to convert grams to ounces, divide the number of grams by 28.*

$$224 \text{ grams} \div 28 = 8 \text{ ounces}$$

To help you develop a framework for judging conversions, remember:

- A kilogram is about 2.2 pounds
- A gram is about 1/30 ounce
- A pound is about 450 grams
- A litre is slightly more than a quart
- A centimetre is slightly less than 1/2 inch
- 0° Celsius is the freezing point of water (32°F)
- 100° Celsius is the boiling point of water (212°F) at sea level

These approximations are not a substitute for accurate conversions, however. The back endpapers of this textbook contain additional information on equivalents and metric conversions. Try to avoid converting weights and measures, especially for baking and pastry. The results may be substandard. Remember that most recipes are based on proportions of ingredients.

TABLE 4.1	Common Abbreviations and Conversions

teaspoon	= tsp.
tablespoon	= Tbsp.
cup	= c.
pint	= pt.
quart	= qt.
gram	= g
millilitre	= mL
litre	= L
ounce	= oz.
fluid ounce	= fl. oz.
pound	= lb.
kilogram	= kg
3 teaspoons	= 1 tablespoon
2 tablespoons	= 1 fl. oz.
2 cups	= 1 pint (16 fl. oz.)
2 pints	= 1 quart (32 fl. oz.)
4 quarts	= 1 gallon (128 fl. oz.)*
1 ounce	= 28.35 grams
454 grams	= 1 pound
2.2 pounds	= 1 kilogram (1000 grams)
1 teaspoon	= 5 millilitres
1 tablespoon	= 15 millilitres

*Note that the fluid ounce measures in this book are based on the U.S. system.

$$\frac{\text{New Yield}}{\text{Old Yield}} = \text{Conversion Factor}$$

$$\text{Old Quantity} \times \text{Conversion Factor} = \text{New Quantity}$$

● **yield** the total amount of a product made from a specific recipe; also, the amount of food item remaining after cleaning or processing

● **conversion factor (C.F.)** the number used to increase or decrease ingredient quantities and recipe yields

RECIPE CONVERSIONS

Whether 6 servings or 60, every recipe is designed to produce or **yield** a specific amount of product. A recipe's yield may be expressed in *volume*, *weight* or *servings* (for example, 1 litre of sauce; 4 kg of bread dough; eight 100-mL servings). If the expected yield does not meet your needs, you must convert (i.e., increase or decrease) the ingredient amounts. Recipe conversion is sometimes complicated by *portion size conversions*. For example, it may be necessary to convert a recipe that initially produces twenty-four 250-mL servings of soup into a recipe that produces sixty-two 180-mL servings.

It is just as easy to change yields by uneven amounts as it is to double or halve recipes. The mathematical principle is the same: *Each ingredient is multiplied by a* **conversion factor**. Do not take shortcuts by estimating recipe amounts or conversion factors. Inaccurate conversions lead to inedible foods, embarrassing shortages or wasteful excesses. Take the time to learn and apply proper conversion techniques. Most recipes can be doubled or halved without too much quality being lost. Seasonings may need further adjustments when doing larger conversion factors.

Converting Total Yield

When portion size is unimportant or remains the same, recipe yield is converted by a simple two-step process:

STEP 1: Divide the desired (new) yield by the recipe (old) yield to obtain the conversion factor (C.F.).

new yield ÷ old yield = conversion factor

STEP 2: Multiply each ingredient quantity by the conversion factor to obtain the new quantity.

old quantity × conversion factor = new quantity

EXAMPLE 4.1

You need to convert a recipe for cauliflower soup. The present recipe yields 6 L; you need to make only 3 L.

STEP 1: Determine the conversion factor:

$$3\text{ L} \div 6\text{ L} = 0.5$$

STEP 2: The conversion factor is applied to each ingredient in the soup recipe:

Cauliflower Soup

	old quantity	×	C.F.	=	new quantity
Cauliflower, chopped	2.5 kg	×	0.5	=	1.25 kg (or 1250 g)
Celery stalks	300 g	×	0.5	=	150 g
Onion	250 g	×	0.5	=	125 g
Chicken stock	2 L	×	0.5	=	1 L
Heavy cream	1300 mL	×	0.5	=	650 mL

Converting Portion Size

A few additional steps are necessary to convert recipes when portion sizes must also be changed.

STEP 1: Determine the total yield of the existing recipe by multiplying the number of portions by the portion size.

original portions × original portion size = total (old) yield

$$\text{Number of Portions} \times \text{Portion Size} = \text{Yield}$$

STEP 2: Determine the total yield desired by multiplying the new number of portions by the new portion size.

desired portions × desired portion size = total (new) yield

STEP 3: Obtain the conversion factor as described above.

total (new) yield ÷ total (old) yield = conversion factor

$$\frac{\text{New Yield}}{\text{Old Yield}} = \text{Conversion Factor}$$

STEP 4: Multiply each ingredient quantity by the conversion factor.

old quantity × conversion factor = new quantity

EXAMPLE 4.2

Returning to the cauliflower soup: The original recipe produced 6 L or 48 servings of 125 mL. Now you need 72 servings of 180 mL.

STEP 1: Total original yield is 48 × 125 = 6000 mL

STEP 2: Total desired yield is 72 × 180 = 12 960 mL

STEP 3: Conversion factor is calculated by dividing total new yield by total old yield:

$$12\ 960 \div 6000 = 2.25 \text{ (rounded)}$$

STEP 4: Old ingredient quantities are multiplied by conversion factor to determine new quantities:

Cauliflower Soup

	old quantity	×	C.F.	=	new quantity
Cauliflower, chopped	2.5 kg	×	2.25	=	5.625 kg
Celery stalks	300 g	×	2.25	=	675 g
Onion	250 g	×	2.25	=	550 g (rounded)
Chicken stock	2 L	×	2.25	=	4.5 L
Heavy cream	1300 mL	×	2.25	=	2.925 L

Additional Conversion Problems

When making very large recipe changes—for example, from 5 to 50 portions or 600 to 36 portions—you may encounter additional problems. The mathematical conversions described above do not take into account changes in equipment, evaporation rates, unforeseen recipe errors or cooking times. Chefs learn to use their judgment, knowledge of cooking principles and skills to compensate for these factors.

Equipment

When you change the size of a recipe, you must often change the equipment used as well. Problems arise, however, when the production techniques previously used no longer work with the new quantity of ingredients. For example, if you normally make a muffin recipe in small quantities by hand and you increase the recipe size, it may be necessary to prepare the batter in a mixer. But if mixing time remains the same, the batter may become overmixed, resulting in poor-quality muffins. Trying to prepare a small amount of product in equipment that is too large for the task can also affect its quality.

Evaporation

Equipment changes can also affect product quality because of changes in evaporation rates. Increasing a soup recipe may require substituting a tilt skillet for a saucepan. But because a tilt skillet provides more surface area for evaporation than does a saucepan, reduction time must be decreased to prevent overthickening the soup. The increased evaporation caused by an increased surface area may also alter the strength of the seasonings.

Recipe Errors

A recipe may contain errors in ingredients or techniques that are not obvious when it is prepared in small quantities. When increased, however, small mistakes often become big (and obvious) ones, and the final product suffers. The only solution is to test recipes carefully and rely on your knowledge of cooking principles to compensate for unexpected problems.

Time

Do not multiply time specifications given in a recipe by the conversion factor used with the recipe's ingredients. *All things being equal, cooking time will not change* when recipe size changes. For example, a muffin requires the same amount of baking time whether you prepare 1 dozen or 14 dozen. Cooking time will be affected, however, by changes in evaporation rate or heat conduction caused by equipment changes. *Mixing time* may change when recipe size is changed. Different equipment may perform mixing tasks more or less efficiently than previously used equipment. Again, rely on experience and good judgment or ask your supervisor.

CALCULATING UNIT COSTS AND RECIPE COSTS

Unit Costs

Food service operations purchase most foods from suppliers in bulk or wholesale packages. For example, canned goods are purchased by the case; produce by the flat, case or lug; and flour and sugar by 10- or 20-kg bags. Even fish and meats are often purchased in large cuts, not individual serving-sized portions. The purchased amount is rarely used for a single recipe, however. It must be broken down into smaller units such as kilograms, litres, grams or millilitres.

In order to allocate the proper ingredient costs to the recipe being prepared, it is necessary to convert **as-purchased costs or prices** to **unit costs or prices**. To find the unit cost (i.e., the cost of a particular unit, say a single egg) in a package containing multiple units (e.g., a 30-dozen case), divide the as-purchased (A.P.) cost of the package by the number of units in the package.

A.P. cost ÷ number of units = cost per unit

Calculating Unit Costs

When calculating unit costs, it is vital that the unit size and the unit required be expressed in the same measurement unit. For example, if the can is measured in fluid ounces, then the unit required must also be in fluid ounces. In the example opposite, if the volume remains the same but the can size is 795 mL, and you want to know how much 225 mL costs, you need to recalculate cost based on the new as-purchased (A.P.) cost. Costing problems arise when products are purchased by weight and recipes are expressed by volume. Water is the only substance with a one to one relationship of volume and weight (1 mL = 1 g).

● **as purchased (A.P.)** the condition or cost of an item as it is purchased or received from the supplier

● **unit cost** the price paid to acquire one of the specified units

$$\frac{\text{A.P. \$}}{\text{\# of Units}} = \text{\$ per Unit}$$

EXAMPLE 4.3

A case of #10 (2.84 L) tomato paste cans contains 6 individual cans. If a case of tomato paste costs $23.50, then each can costs $3.92.

$$\$23.50 \div 6 = \$3.92$$

If your recipe uses less than the total can, you must continue dividing the cost of the can until you arrive at the appropriate unit amount. Continuing with the tomato paste example, if you need only 0.225 L, or 225 mL, find out how much 1 litre costs by dividing the cost per item by the volume.

$$\$3.92 \div 2.84 \text{ L} = \$1.38 \text{ per L}$$

To calculate how much 225 mL costs, multiply this figure by the desired unit amount (0.225 L):

$$1.38 \times 0.225 = 0.3105 \text{ (to 4 decimal places)}$$

The whole operation can be expressed by the formula

$$\frac{\text{cost per item (\$3.92)} \times \text{unit required (0.225 L)}}{\text{unit size (2.84 L)}} = \$0.31$$

Recipe Costs

With a typical recipe, you calculate the **total recipe cost** with the following two-step procedure:

STEP 1: Determine the cost for the given quantity of each recipe ingredient with the unit costing procedures described above.

STEP 2: Add all of the ingredient costs together to obtain the total recipe cost.

The total recipe cost can then be broken down into the **cost per portion**, which is the most useful figure for food cost controls. To arrive at cost per portion, divide the total recipe cost by the total number of servings or portions produced by that recipe.

total recipe cost ÷ number of portions = cost per portion

The recipe costing form shown in Figure 4.1 on the next page is useful for organizing recipe costing information. It provides space for listing each ingredient, the quantity of each ingredient needed, the cost of each unit (known as **edible portion** or **E.P.**) and the total cost for the ingredient. Total yield, portion size and cost per portion are listed at the bottom of the form. Note that there is no space for recipe procedures, as these are irrelevant in recipe costing.

YIELD TESTS

Computing the cost of recipe ingredients is a simple matter if the foods are used the way they are received and there is no waste or trim. This is rarely the case, however. The amount of a food item as purchased (A.P.) and the amount of the edible portion (E.P.) of that same item may vary considerably, particularly with meats and fresh produce. In this context, yield is the usable or edible quantity remaining after processing the as-purchased quantity of the food item. That is, yield refers to the amount of usable lettuce after the case of iceberg is cleaned, or the amount of meat that is served after trimming. The yield factor or percentage is the ratio of the usable quantity to the purchased quantity. It is always less than 100% and may be calculated in dollars or weight/volume amounts.

total recipe cost the total cost of ingredients for a particular recipe; it does not reflect overhead, labour, fixed expenses or profit

cost per portion the amount of the total recipe cost divided by the number of portions produced from that recipe; the cost of one serving

$$\frac{\text{Recipe \$}}{\text{\# of Portions}} = \$ \text{ per Portion}$$

edible portion (E.P.) the amount of a food item available for consumption or use after trimming or fabrication; a smaller, more convenient portion of a larger or bulk unit

RECIPE COSTING FORM

Menu Item _Maple Glazed Carrots_   Date _May 2011_

Ingredient	Quantity	As Purchased	Yield %	Edible Portion	TOTAL COST
Carrots	2.2 kg	16.35/22.68 kg	85	.848/kg	1.866
Butter	125 g	3.51/454 g	100	7.73/kg	.966
Salt	10 g	6.25/20 kg	100	.3125/kg	.003
Pepper	1.5 g	8.73/540 g	100	.0162/kg	.025
Maple Syrup	125 mL	13.90/1 L	100	13.90/L	1.73
Parsley, chop.	20 g	0.31/150 g bunch	50	.0042/g	.083

TOTAL COST OF RECIPE $ _4.64_

Total Yield _2 kg_

Portion _100 g_

Cost per Portion _.234_

F.C.% _28%_

Sell Price _.84_

FIGURE 4.1   Recipe costing form.

Because purchase specifications and fabrication techniques vary from operation to operation, there are no precise, standard yield amounts. Each kitchen must determine its own yield factors. Yield tests must be conducted on A.P. items as they are received from purveyors. To be effective, several tests must be conducted and the results averaged to arrive at a specific operation's yield factor for that item.

The method of calculating yield varies depending on whether the item's trim is all waste (for example, vegetable peelings) or whether the trim creates usable or saleable byproducts (for example, meat and poultry).

Raw Yield Tests without Byproducts

The simplest yield test procedure is for items that have no usable or saleable byproducts. These items include most produce as well as some fish and shellfish. Unless these items are ready to serve *as received* from the purveyor, trimming is required and some trim is waste. For example, 450 g of apples may yield only 360 g of flesh after peeling and coring. If the recipe requires 450 g of peeled, cored apples, the chef must start with more than 450 g of A.P. apples. In order to determine accurate costs for such items, the trim loss must be taken into account. Even seedless grapes do not have a 100% yield factor. The weight of stems and bad grapes must be calculated and deducted from the A.P. weight to determine the correct price per 450 g of servable fruit.

There are three steps for calculating yield when all trim is waste:

STEP 1:   Calculate the total weight of the trim produced from the specified A.P. quantity. This is known as trim loss.

STEP 2:   Subtract the trim loss from the A.P. weight to arrive at the total yield weight.

STEP 3:   Divide the yield weight by the A.P. weight to determine the yield factor.

EXAMPLE 4.4

Nine hundred grams of fresh garlic generate 126 g of trim loss. Therefore, the yield weight is 774 g and the yield factor is 86% or 0.86:

$$900 \text{ g} - 126 \text{ g} = 774 \text{ g}$$

$$774 \div 900 = 0.86 = 86\%$$

Remember, subtract trim loss from A.P. weight, then divide yield weight by A.P. weight to arrive at the yield percentage. Note that the yield factor will always be some number less than 1, and the yield percentage will always be less than 100%.

Because each operation has its own standards for cleaning and trimming raw products, yield factors should be customized. Lists of common yield factors are available, however, as an indication of industry norms. Some of these are included in Table 4.2.

Applying Yield Factors

Now that you understand what yield factors are and how to calculate them, we look at how they are used in costing recipes. First, yield factors are used for accurate recipe costing.

EXAMPLE 4.5

Carrots cost $6.50 per 10-kg bag and have a yield factor of 78%. In other words, 22% of that 10-kg bag is waste. The price should be recalculated to account for that waste; that is, the A.P. (as purchased) unit cost must be converted to an E.P. (edible portion) unit cost. This is done by dividing A.P. cost by the yield percentage.

A.P. cost ($) ÷ yield percentage = E.P. cost ($)

0.65/kg (6.50 ÷ 10) ÷ 0.78 = 0.84/kg

Thus, the carrots have an E.P. unit cost of $0.84 per kilogram (as compared with an A.P. price of $0.65 per kilogram). Note that E.P. cost is always greater than A.P. cost. When costing a recipe, you should use the $0.84-per-kilogram price as the accurate ingredient cost.

Second, yield factors are necessary for accurate purchasing. Most recipes list ingredients in E.P. quantities. Therefore, the chef must consider waste or trim amounts when ordering these items. If only the amounts listed in the recipe are ordered and then the item requires trimming, the number of portions (or recipe yield) will be less than the desired amount.

EXAMPLE 4.6

A recipe requires 12 kg of shredded cabbage. The yield factor for cabbage is 79%. Therefore, 12 kg is 79% of the A.P. quantity. Divide the amount needed by the yield factor to determine the minimum A.P. quantity.

E.P. quantity ÷ yield percentage = A.P. quantity

12 kg ÷ 0.79 = 15.19 kg

It will take 15.2 kg of cabbage to provide the 12 kg of shredded cabbage. (This figure will be increased to an even amount for purchasing because yield factors are, at best, only an estimate.) Note that the A.P. figure must always be greater than the E.P. figure in this formula.

TABLE 4.2	Common Produce Yield Factors
Produce	**Yield Factor (%)**
Apples	75
Apricots	94
Artichokes	48
Avocados	75
Bananas	70
Berries	95
Broccoli	70
Cabbage	79
Carrots	78
Cauliflower	55
Celery	75
Cherries	82
Corn, cob	28
Cucumbers	95
Eggplant	85
Garlic	88
Grapefruit	45
Grapes	90
Kiwi	80
Leeks	50
Lemons	45
Lettuce	75
Limes	45
Melons	55
Mushrooms	90
Nectarines	86
Okra	82
Onions	90
Oranges	60
Papayas	65
Parsley	85
Pea pods	90
Peaches	75
Pears	75
Peppers	82
Pineapple	50
Plums	75
Potatoes	80
Radishes	90
Rhubarb	85
Scallions	65
Spinach	60
Squash, summer	90
Squash, winter	70
Tomatoes	90
Turnips	75
Watercress	90
Watermelon	45

FOOD COST

● **food cost** the cost of the materials that go directly into the production of menu items

● **cost of goods sold** the total cost of food items sold during a given period; calculated as beginning inventory plus purchases minus ending inventory; also known as raw food cost

Perhaps no other cost is emphasized as much by food service managers as **food cost**. Food cost refers to the cost of all foods used in the fabrication of menu items. This figure is also known as the **cost of goods sold** or **raw food cost** ("raw" is a bit misleading, as food cost includes precooked and packaged foods as well as uncooked foods).

Food costs are calculated in two ways: (1) as a total cost of all foods used during a given period, and (2) as a cost of one particular portion or menu item. Total cost is used as a general guideline for budgeting and menu planning. The portion or item cost is used to calculate menu prices; it helps the chef stay within cost limitations.

Cost of Goods Sold

● **inventory** the listing and accounting of all foods in the kitchen, storerooms and refrigerators

The "goods" sold by a food service operation are, of course, the foods used in producing menu items. Before you can calculate cost of goods sold, you must take a physical inventory of all foodstuffs on hand. **Inventory** should be taken periodically: at the end of each week, month, quarter or other accounting period. Taking inventory requires listing and counting all foods in the kitchen, storerooms and refrigerators. The quantities are then *extended*; that is, multiplied by the unit cost. The extended prices are then added to calculate the total inventory value.

Whether prepared foods or open containers are included in the inventory depends on the operation. Often small quantities of prepared foods or open containers are not inventoried on the theory that a certain amount of such items is always on hand, the value of which is minimal but fairly consistent from one accounting period to the next.

To properly calculate the cost of goods sold, you must conduct an inventory at the beginning and end of the desired period and maintain records of all purchases during the period. The time period covered by this calculation could be any duration: week, month, quarter or year. After the total value of the inventory for both the beginning and the end of the period has been established, cost of goods sold is calculated as follows:

	Value of food inventory at beginning of period
PLUS	**Food purchased during period**
MINUS	**Inventory at end of period**
MINUS	**Staff meals, promotions, writeoffs and returns**
	Cost of food sold

Example 4.7 (Simplified)

The total value of food in inventory on December 1 is $7600. The restaurant purchases $23 000 worth of food during December and the inventory on January 1 is worth $5600. The cost of goods sold during the month of December is $25 000 (in other words, the food produced during the month of December cost $25 000):

$$(7600 + 23\ 000) - 5600 = 25\ 000$$

Once management knows the cost of goods sold, it can compare this figure with the dollar value of sales for the same period. This comparison gives management an indicator of performance for that period compared with budget.

Food Cost Percentages

● **food cost percentage** the ratio of the cost of foods served to the food sales dollars during a given period

The **food cost percentage** is the ratio of costs to sales. It shows what each dollar of sales costs. For example, a 35% food cost means that $0.35 of each dollar received went to pay for the foods the operation used. Food cost percentage is determined by dividing food cost by sales.

food cost ÷ sales = food cost percentage

EXAMPLE 4.8

Refer back to Example 4.7 and assume that sales for December totalled $62 500. The food cost percentage for the month would be 40%:

$$25\ 000 \div 62\ 500 = 0.40 = 40\%$$

By itself a single food cost percentage is meaningless. To be useful, it should be compared with the food cost percentages for other months of the same year or the same month in previous years. It is also helpful to know the food cost percentages for other similarly situated food service operations.

Food cost percentages can also be calculated on individual menu items. If the food items in a sliced turkey sandwich cost $2.80 and the sandwich sells for $5.25, the food cost percentage is 53% (2.80 divided by 5.25). Many operations would find this unacceptably high. To reduce the percentage and increase gross profits, the operation must either increase the selling price or decrease the ingredient costs. Changing menu price, raw food cost or portion size will affect the food cost percentage. **Contribution margin** is the critical concept in profitability. This is the money that pays for everything except food cost. More importantly, it includes profit. A higher food cost item such as lobster may have a generous contribution margin, making it a desirable item to have on the menu despite its 50% food cost. Remember, you cannot bank a percentage. In addition, not all menu categories are marked up by the same amount. Food cost percentage is the average of all the menu items combined. Appetizers, desserts and beverages tend to have a lower food cost percentage than the budgeted figure. The result is a higher contribution margin—meaning servers should be promoting these items. Periodic evaluations are necessary to ensure that the desired objective is actually maintained. Operations may rationalize a higher food cost for partially or fully prepared items due to labour savings.

● **contribution margin** the money, including profit, that pays for all costs except food

ESTABLISHING MENU PRICES

After determining the cost of food items, you can calculate menu prices. A few of the many methods for setting menu prices are explained below. Some techniques are highly structured and closely related to food costs; others are unstructured and unrelated to actual food costs. As a practical matter, no one method is right for every operation, and a combination of methods may provide the best pricing information.

Cost-Based Pricing

Food Cost Percentage Pricing

For this technique, you must first determine the food cost percentage desired for the particular facility. After calculating each item's raw food cost (remember to include side dishes and condiments) you determine the selling price with the following formula:

cost per portion ÷ food cost percentage = selling price

EXAMPLE 4.9

If the raw food cost for 1 sandwich is $1.70 and the desired food cost percentage is 23%, the selling price must be at least $7.39:

$$1.70 \div 0.23 = 7.391$$

In this situation, 23% of the sales price for each item will go to cover the raw food cost for that item. The higher the food cost percentage, the lower the portion of the sales price available for labour, fixed expenses, overhead or profit. Determining the appropriate food cost percentage for the operation and menu category is critical to the successful use of this method.

Factor Pricing

A variation on food cost percentage pricing is factor pricing. First, you take the desired food cost percentage and divide it into 100 to arrive at a cost factor. The cost of each item is then multiplied by the cost factor to arrive at the menu price. Using the previous example, the factor is 4.35 (100 ÷ 23 = 4.35), and the menu price for a $1.70 item is $7.39 (1.70 × 4.35 = 7.39).

Both food cost percentage and factor pricings are fast and easy to use. But these methods are sometimes unreliable because they assume that other costs associated with preparing food stay the same for each menu item. These systems wrongly assume that the costs for labour, energy and overhead are the same for a rack of lamb entree and a seafood salad. These methods may be fine-tuned somewhat by adjusting the desired food cost percentage according to the type of food or menu category. Appetizers may be assigned a lower food cost percentage than, say, desserts or side dishes.

Prime Cost Pricing

The food service industry uses a figure known as prime cost to refer to the total of raw food cost plus direct labour. Direct labour is the labour actually required for an item's preparation. If, for example, food cost is $2.10 and direct labour is $1.50, then prime cost is $3.60. As with the food cost percentage example above, the prime cost percentage can be divided into the prime cost amount to determine menu price.

EXAMPLE 4.10

The raw food cost for a rack of lamb portion is $11.00; it takes a cook a total of 9 minutes to clean and trim it for service. If that cook is paid $12.60 per hour (0.21 per minute), the direct labour cost is $1.89 (12.60 per hour = 0.21 per minute; 0.21 × 9 = 1.89).

The prime cost of the rack of lamb is $12.89 (11.00 + 1.89). The selling price is then determined by dividing prime cost by the desired prime cost percentage. If management decided that the desired prime cost percentage is 48%, then the rack of lamb should be priced at $26.85 (12.89 ÷ 0.48 = 26.85). Note that we have not included starch, vegetables, sauces and condiments, which would result in a selling price in the $35.00-plus range depending on the establishment.

Perceived Value Pricing

This is a rather backwards way of setting prices based on what a customer will perceive as an appropriate price. First determine what the market price is for the same or a similar item. Then calculate what you can serve for that price. Assume, for example,

1. the market price for a complete fried chicken dinner is $9.95,
2. the desired profit is 7% of sales,
3. overhead expenses are 27% of sales, and
4. labour is approximately 23% of sales.

Subtract the total of these items (57%) from the $9.95 selling price, and you find that your total food cost for the fried chicken dinner must not be more than $4.28. This technique requires a thorough knowledge of the market and good historical information on labour and overhead costs. With the necessary information, you can determine how much to spend on raw product for each menu item and still make the desired profit.

Noncost-Based Pricing

Noncost-based pricing techniques rely on nonmonetary factors to set menu prices. Traditional prices in the area for the same or similar items may affect an operation's ability to set prices. This is particularly true for special or loss-leader items such as 99-cent jumbo sodas or $3.99 breakfast specials.

Although the competition's prices are an important consideration, you should not simply copy them. Your competition's costs are not your costs no matter how similar the final food items appear. If you must charge higher prices than your competition, seek out some way to differentiate your product or service.

Virtually all food service operations are seeking to charge the highest price possible without a loss of sales. The customer's perception of value is therefore critical. The menu can be used as a tool for educating customers. Descriptive language or an explanation of unique or special dishes can be included. Customers who understand the value of service, atmosphere, out-of-season foods and specialty products will tolerate higher prices for those items. Premium resort properties often use this approach.

Psychological Impact of Pricing

Regardless of how you arrive at a menu price, you may wish to round the figure up or down for psychological impact. It is human nature to perceive some prices as higher or lower than they actually are. For example, using a 9 or 5 as the last digit in a price creates the impression of a discount; prices ending in a 9 or 5 appeal to price-conscious customers. Prices ending in a 0 are perceived as more expensive and higher quality and so are often used on fine-dining menus.

The number of digits in a price is also important: $9.95 seems much less expensive than $10.25. Likewise, the first numeral in a price affects perception. When changing menu prices, an increase from $5.95 to $6.45 is seen as greater than an increase from $6.25 to $6.75, although both are 50-cent increases.

Patrons do not like to see a large spread in menu prices. It may make them think something is wrong with one of the items or may cause confusion. For example, a lobster dinner for $34.50 may be a reasonable price, but it may be inappropriate on a menu where all other items are less than $15.00. In general, the highest price should not be more than double the lowest price within the same food category. If the least expensive appetizer is $6.00, then the most expensive appetizer should not exceed $12.00.

Establishing menu prices is one of the most difficult yet important things a chef or manager can do to affect the facility's success. No one method is best for all operations, so careful study of several approaches is recommended.

CONTROLLING FOOD COSTS

Many things affect food costs in any given operation; most can be controlled by the chef or manager. These controls do not require mathematical calculations or formulas, just basic management skills and a good dose of common sense. The following factors all have an impact on the operation's bottom line:

- Menu
- Purchasing/ordering
- Receiving
- Storing
- Issuing

- Kitchen procedures
  – establishing standard portions
  – waste
- Sales and service

Chefs tend to focus their control efforts in the area of kitchen preparation. Although this may seem logical, it is not adequate. A good chef will be involved in all aspects of the operation to help prevent problems from arising or to correct those that may occur.

Menu

A profitable menu is based upon many variables including customer desires, physical space and equipment, ingredient availability, cost of goods sold, employee skills and competition. All management personnel, including the chef, should be consulted when planning the menu. Menu changes, although possibly desirable, must be executed with as much care as the original design.

Purchasing/Ordering

● **parstock (par)** the amount of stock necessary to cover operating needs between deliveries

Purchasing techniques have a direct impact on cost controls. On the one hand, **parstock** must be adequate for efficient operations; on the other hand, too much inventory wastes space and resources and may spoil. Generally, inventory should turn over on a regular basis. Approximately two and a half times per month ensures good cash flow and should minimize spoilage. Each operation must establish appropriate inventory and purchasing levels. Before any items are ordered, purchasing specifications should be established and communicated to potential purveyors. Specifications should precisely describe the item, including grade, quality, packaging and unit size. Each operation should design its own form to best meet its specific needs. A sample specification form is shown in Figure 4.2. This information can be used to obtain price quotes from several purveyors. Update these quotes periodically to ensure that you are getting the best value for your money.

Menu Item: *Beef Striploin (220–300 g)*

Product: *Angus Beef Striploin, fresh*   Date: *May 2011*

Grade/Quality: *AAA, Certified Canadian Angus, 21 days age*

Weight/Size: *10/12; 0 × 1 Trim*   Product Code: *CMC #180*

Packaging: *Vacuum*

Delivery Conditions: *Refrigerated truck; 0–4°C*
Product to be 4°C or less

Comments:
Open boxes to verify product, weight and condition (i.e., no broken bags/leakers)

FIGURE 4.2   Specification form.

Receiving

Whether goods are received by a full-time clerk, as they are in a large hotel, or by the chef or kitchen manager, certain standards should be observed. First, the person signing for merchandise should confirm that the items were actually ordered. Second, determine whether the items listed on the invoice are the ones being delivered and whether the price and quantity listed are accurate. Third, check the items, especially meats and produce, for quality, freshness, temperature and weight. Established purchase specifications should be readily available.

Storing

Proper storage of foodstuffs is crucial in order to prevent spoilage, pilferage and waste. Stock must be rotated so that the older items are used first. Such a system for rotating stock is referred to as **FIFO: First In, First Out** (mark dates on packaging). Storage areas should be well ventilated and lit to prevent infestation and mould. High-cost items and liquor are often locked up separately from standard groceries.

● **FIFO** first in, first out; a system of rotating inventory, particularly perishable and semiperishable goods, in which items are used in the order in which they are received

Issuing

It may be necessary, particularly in larger operations, to limit storeroom access to specific personnel. Maintaining ongoing inventory records or parstock sheets helps the ordering process. Controlling issuances eliminates waste caused by multiple opened containers and ensures proper stock rotation.

Kitchen Procedures: Establishing Standard Portions

Standardizing portions is essential to controlling food costs. Unless portion quantity is uniform, it will be impossible to compute portion costs accurately. Portion discrepancies can also confuse or mislead customers.

Actual portion sizes depend on the food service operation itself, the menu, the prices and the customers' desires. Some items are generally purchased preportioned for convenience (for example, steaks are sold in uniform cuts, baking potatoes are available in uniform sizes, butter comes in preportioned pats and bread comes sliced for service). Other items must be portioned by the establishment prior to service. Special equipment makes consistent portioning easy. There are machines to slice meats, cutting guides for cakes and pies and portion scales for weighing quantities. Standardized portion scoops and ladles are indispensable for serving vegetables, soups, stews, salads and similar foods. Many of these items are discussed and illustrated in Chapter 5, Tools and Equipment.

Once acceptable portion sizes are established, employees must be properly trained to present them. If each employee of a sandwich shop prepared sandwiches the way he or she would like to eat them, customers would probably never receive the same sandwich twice. Customers may become confused and decide not to risk a repeat visit. Obviously, carelessness in portioning can also drastically affect food cost.

Kitchen Procedures: Waste

The chef must also control waste from overproduction, poor trimming practices or failure to use leftovers. With an adequate sales history, the chef can accurately estimate the quantity of food to prepare for each week, day or meal. If the menu is designed properly, the chef can also use leftovers and trim from product fabrication. The less waste generated in food preparation, the lower the overall food cost will be. A periodic inspection of waste receptacles allows for monitoring of waste or carelessness. Checking refrigerators regularly helps to ensure efficient product use and handling.

Sales and Service

An improperly trained sales staff can undo even the most rigorous of food cost controls. Front-of-the-house personnel are, after all, ultimately responsible for the sales portion of the food cost equation. Proper training is once again critical. Prices charged must be accurate and complete. Poor service can lead to the need to serve for free ("comp") an excessive amount of food. Dropped or spilled foods do not generate revenues. It is important to record these items for tracking purposes. A good server will also promote high-contribution items.

Conclusion

No food service operation can become successful based on the chef's cooking ability alone. A well-designed, enticing and accurately priced menu is also necessary. By following a standardized recipe you should be able to repeatedly produce a known quality and quantity of food for your specific food service operation. Based upon the regularity with which you offer these foods, your menu can be classified as static, cycle, market or hybrid. You can offer your menu items either à la carte, semi à la carte or table d'hôte.

You must be able to understand and apply proper techniques for converting recipes, costing food, pricing the menu and controlling loss. Although computers are useful and are becoming more common in kitchens, no machine can substitute for a chef's watchful eye and hands-on controls.

Questions for Discussion

1. Describe the four types of menus. Can each type of menu offer foods à la carte, semi à la carte and/or table d'hôte? Explain your answer.
2. Discuss three factors in food preparation that affect successful recipe size changes.
3. Why is it important to calculate the portion cost of a recipe in professional food service operations? Why is the full recipe cost inadequate?
4. List several factors that might cause one operation's yield factor for lettuce to be higher than another operation's. Explain why standardized yield factor lists are unreliable.
5. How is food cost percentage calculated? How can this figure be used (or misused) to evaluate the success of an operation?
6. Discuss three psychological factors used in setting menu prices.
7. Explain how a high food cost item can be more profitable than a lower food cost item.

Tools and Equipment 5

"And, indeed, is there not something holy about a great kitchen?... The scoured gleam of row upon row of metal vessels dangling from hooks or reposing on their shelves till needed with the air of so many chalices waiting for the celebration of the sacrament of food.

—Angela Carter, British novelist (1940–1992)

Having the proper tools and equipment for a particular task may mean the difference

between a job well done and one done carelessly, incorrectly or even dangerously. This chapter introduces some of the tools and equipment typically used in a professional kitchen. Items are divided into categories according to their function: hand tools, knives, measuring and portioning devices, cookware, strainers and sieves, processing equipment, storage containers, heavy equipment, buffet equipment and safety equipment.

A wide variety of specialized tools and equipment is available to today's chef. Breading machines, mandolines and food processors are designed to speed production by reducing handwork. Other devices—for instance, a duck press or a couscousière—are used only for unique tasks in preparing a few menu items. Much of this specialized equipment is quite expensive and found only in food manufacturing operations or specialized kitchens; a discussion of it is beyond the scope of this chapter. Brief descriptions of some of these specialized devices are, however, found in the Glossary. Knife care is addressed in Chapter 6, Knife Skills. Baking pans and tools are discussed in Chapter 27, Principles of the Bakeshop.

Before using any equipment, study the operator's manual or have someone experienced with the particular item instruct you on proper procedures for its use and cleaning. And remember, always practise safety.

STANDARDS FOR TOOLS AND EQUIPMENT

Well-designed tools and equipment have characteristics that are beneficial to the overall efficiency and safety of the operation.

1. Equipment must be easily cleaned.
2. All food contact surfaces must be nontoxic (under intended end-use conditions), nonabsorbent, corrosion resistant and nonreactive.
3. All food contact surfaces must be smooth, that is, free of pits, cracks, crevices, ledges, rivet heads and bolts.
4. Internal corners and edges must be rounded and smooth; external corners and angles must be smooth and sealed.
5. Coating materials must be nontoxic and easily cleaned; coatings must resist chipping and cracking.
6. Waste and waste liquids must be easily removed.
7. Look for the CSA International symbol.

SELECTING TOOLS AND EQUIPMENT

In general, only commercial food service tools and equipment should be used in a professional kitchen. Household tools and appliances may not withstand the rigours of a professional kitchen. Look for tools that are well constructed. For example, joints should be welded, not bonded with solder; handles should be comfortable, with rounded borders; plastic and rubber parts should be seamless.

Before purchasing or leasing any particular piece of equipment, you should evaluate several factors:

1. Is this equipment necessary for producing menu items?
2. Will this equipment perform the job required in the space available?
3. Is this equipment the most economical for the operation's specific needs?
4. Is this equipment easy to clean, maintain and repair?

HAND TOOLS

Hand tools are designed to aid in cutting, shaping, moving or combining foods. They have few, if any, moving parts. Knives, discussed separately, are the most important hand tools. Others are metal or rubber spatulas, spoons, whisks, tongs and specialized cutters. In addition to the items shown in Figure 5.1, many hand tools designed for specific tasks, such as pressing tortillas or pitting cherries, are available. Sturdiness, durability and safety are the watchwords when selecting hand tools. Choose tools that can withstand the heavy use of a professional kitchen and those that are easily cleaned.

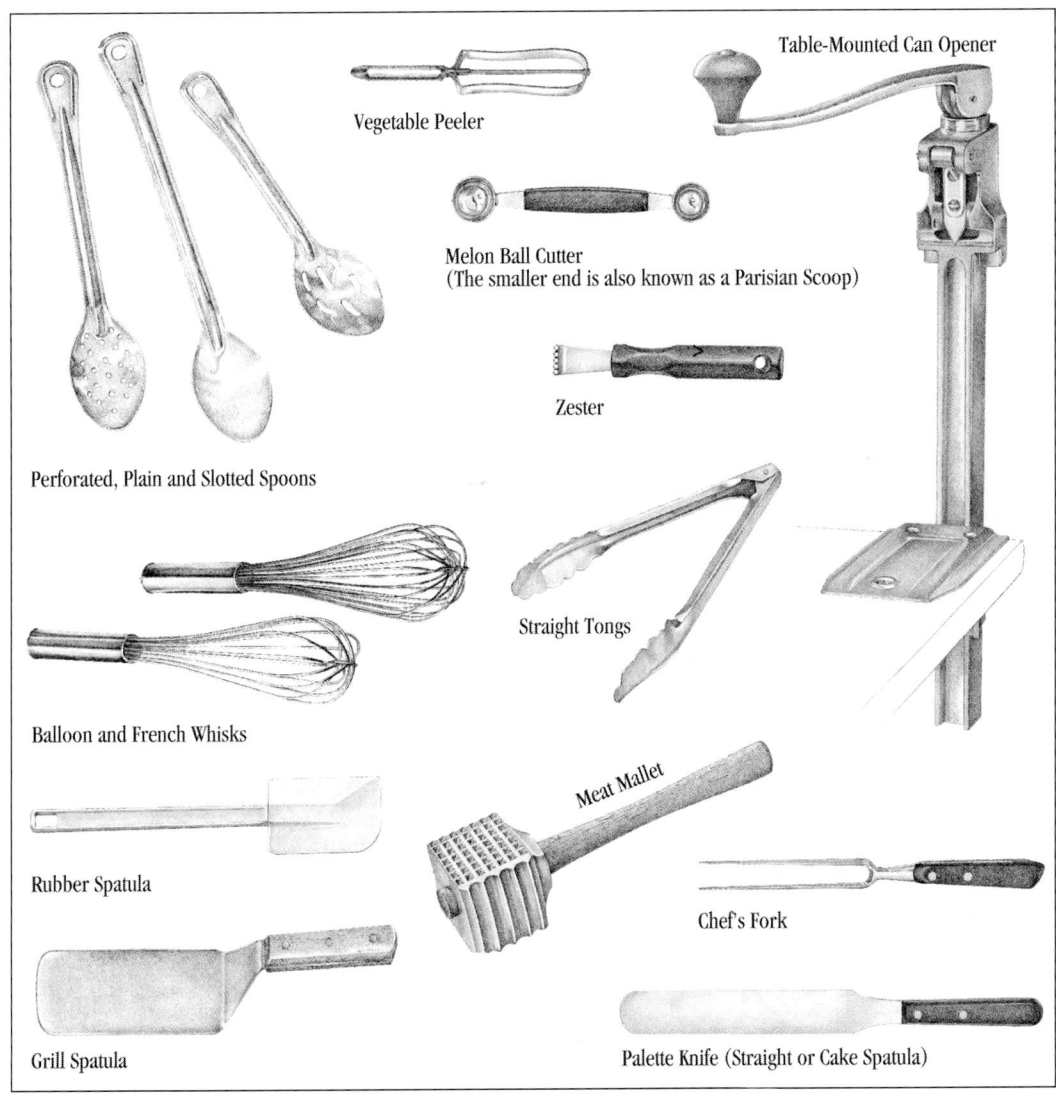

FIGURE 5.1   Hand tools.

KNIVES

Knives are the most important items in your tool kit. With a sharp knife, the skilled cook can accomplish a number of tasks more quickly and efficiently than any machine. Good-quality knives are expensive but will last for many years with proper care. Select easily sharpened, well-constructed knives that are comfortable and balanced in your hand. Knife construction and commonly used knives are discussed here; knife safety and care as well as cutting techniques are discussed in Chapter 6, Knife Skills.

Knife Construction

A good knife begins with a single piece of metal, stamped, cut or—best of all—forged and tempered into a blade of the desired shape. The metals generally used for knife blades are as follows:

1. **Carbon steel**—An alloy of carbon and iron, it was traditionally used for blades because it is soft enough to be sharpened easily. It corrodes and discolours easily, however, especially when used with acidic foods. It is not recommended for food service applications.

2. **Stainless steel**—It will not rust, corrode or discolour and is extremely durable. But a stainless steel blade is much more difficult to sharpen than a carbon steel one, although once an edge is established it lasts longer than the edge on a carbon steel blade.

3. **High carbon stainless steel**—An alloy combining the best features of carbon steel and stainless steel, it neither corrodes nor discolours and can be sharpened almost as easily as carbon steel. It is now the most frequently used metal for blades.

4. **Ceramic**—A ceramic called zirconium oxide is now used to make knife blades that are extremely sharp, very easy to clean, rustproof and nonreactive. With proper care, ceramic blades will remain sharp for years, but when sharpening is needed, it must be done professionally on special diamond wheels. Material costs and tariffs make ceramic-bladed knives very expensive. Although this ceramic is highly durable, it does not have the flexibility of metal, so never use a ceramic knife to pry anything, to strike a hard surface (for example, when crushing garlic or chopping through bones) or to cut against a china or ceramic surface.

A portion of the blade, known as the tang, fits inside the handle. (See Figure 5.2.) The best knives are constructed with a full tang running the length of the handle; they also have a bolster where the blade meets the handle (the bolster is part of the blade, not a separate collar). Less expensive knives may have a 3/4-length tang or a thin "rattail" tang. Neither provide as much support, durability or balance as a full tang.

Knife handles are often made of composite plastic materials. Moulded polypropylene handles are permanently bonded to a tang without seams or rivets. Any handle should be shaped for comfort and ground smooth to eliminate crevices where bacteria can grow.

FIGURE 5.2 Parts of a knife.

Knife Shapes and Sharpening Equipment

You will collect many knives during your career, many with specialized functions not described here. This list includes only the most basic knives and sharpening equipment.

French or Chef's Knife

An all-purpose knife used for chopping, slicing and mincing. Its rigid 20- to 35-cm-long (8- to 14-in.) blade is wide at the heel and tapers to a point at the tip.

French or Chef's Knife

Utility Knife

An all-purpose knife used for cutting fruits and vegetables and carving poultry. Its rigid 15- to 20-cm-long (6- to 8-in.) blade is shaped like a chef's knife but narrower.

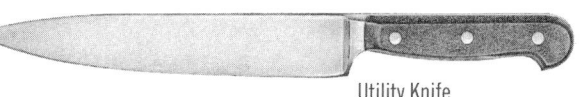

Utility Knife

Boning Knife

A smaller knife with a thin blade used to separate meat from bone. The blade is usually 12.5 to 17.5 cm (5 to 7 in.) long and may be flexible or rigid.

Rigid Boning Knife

Paring Knife

A short knife used for detail work or cutting fruits and vegetables. The rigid blade is from 5 to 10 cm (2 to 4 in.) long. A turning or bird's beak knife is similar to a paring knife but with a curved blade; it is used for shaping curved surfaces or turning vegetables.

Paring Knife

Cleaver

The large, heavy rectangular blade of this knife is used for chopping or cutting through bones.

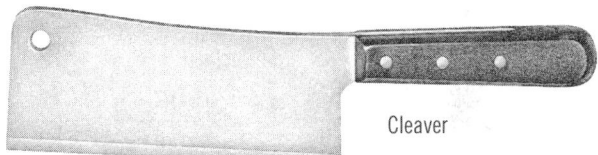

Cleaver

Slicer

A knife with a long, thin blade used primarily for slicing cooked meat. The tip may be round or pointed and the blade may be flexible or rigid. A similar knife with a serrated edge is used for slicing bread or pastry items.

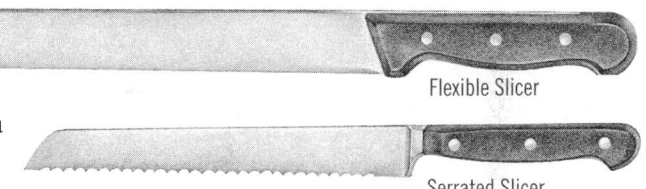

Flexible Slicer

Serrated Slicer

Butcher Knife

Sometimes known as a scimitar because the rigid blade curves up in a 25-degree angle at the tip, this knife is used for fabricating raw meat and is available with 15- to 35-cm (6- to 14-in.) blades.

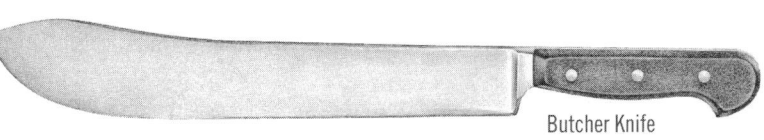

Butcher Knife

Oyster and Clam Knives

The short, rigid blades of these knives are used to open oyster and clam shells. The tips are blunt; only the clam knife has a sharp edge.

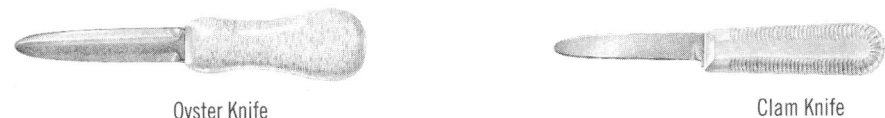

Oyster Knife

Clam Knife

Japanese Knives

Numerous specialized knives used in Japanese cooking are popular additions to a chef's tool kit. Traditional Japanese knives have an asymmetrical blade, basically flat on one side and bevelled to a sharp edge on the other side, which facili-tates precise cutting. The *usuba* has a rectangular blade and is used to cut thin vegetable garnishes. The *yanagiba* has a thin 20- to 35-cm-long (8- to 14-in.) straight blade traditionally used to cut translucent slices of raw fish fillets called sashimi and sushi rolls. The *deba* has a wide, sturdy 12.5- to 17.5-cm-long (5- to 7-in.) wedge-shaped blade used for butchering and boning fish.

Usuba Knife

Yanagiba Sashimi Knife

Deba Knife

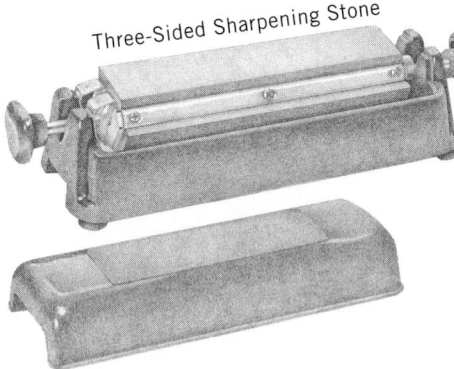

Three-Sided Sharpening Stone

Sharpening Stone

Also known as a whetstone, a sharpening stone is used to put an edge on a dull blade.

Steel

A steel is used to hone or straighten a blade immediately after and between sharpenings.

Steel

Measuring Precisely

Although many measuring devices are routinely used in kitchens, the most precise way to measure is by weight. Volume measures appear in this text for the convenience of the user.

MEASURING AND PORTIONING DEVICES

Recipe ingredients must be measured precisely, especially in the bakeshop, and foods should be measured when served to control portion size and cost. The devices used to measure and portion foods are, for the most part, hand tools designed to make food preparation and service easier and more precise. The accuracy they afford prevents the cost of mistakes made when accurate measurements are ignored.

Measurements may be based upon weight (e.g., grams, ounces, pounds) or volume (e.g., millilitres, litres, quarts). Therefore it is necessary to have available several measuring devices, including liquid and dry measuring cups and a variety of scales. Thermometers and timers are also measuring devices and are discussed here. When purchasing measuring devices, look for quality construction and accurate markings.

Commonly Used Devices

Scales

Scales are necessary to determine the weight of an ingredient or a portion of food (for example, the sliced meat for a sandwich). Portion scales use a spring mechanism, round dial and single flat tray. They are available calibrated in grams, ounces or pounds. Electronic scales also use a spring

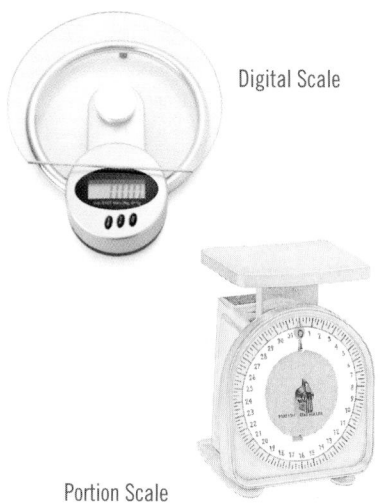

Digital Scale

Portion Scale

of care and is often quite heavy. Moreover, because copper may react with some foods, copper cookware usually has a tin lining, which is soft and easily scratched. Because of these problems, copper is now often sandwiched between layers of stainless steel or aluminum in the bottom of pots and pans.

Aluminum

Aluminum is the metal used most commonly in commercial utensils. It is light-weight and, after copper, conducts heat best. Aluminum is a soft metal, though, so it should be treated with care to avoid dents. Do not use aluminum containers for storage or for cooking acidic foods because the metal reacts chemically with many foods. Light-coloured foods, such as soups or sauces, may be discoloured when cooked in aluminum, especially if stirred with a metal whisk or spoon.

Anodized aluminum has a hard, dark, corrosion-resistant surface that helps prevent sticking and discoloration.

Stainless Steel

Although stainless steel conducts and retains heat poorly, it is a hard, durable metal particularly useful for holding foods and for low-temperature cooking where hot spots and scorching are not problems. Stainless steel pots and pans are available with aluminum or copper bonded to the bottom or with an aluminum-layered core. Although expensive, such cookware combines the rapid, uniform heat conductivity of copper and aluminum with the strength, durability and nonreactivity of stainless steel. Stainless steel is also ideal for storage containers because it does not react with foods.

Cast Iron

Cast-iron cookware distributes heat evenly and holds high temperatures well. It is often used in griddles and large skillets. Although relatively inexpensive, cast iron is extremely heavy and brittle. It must be kept properly conditioned and dry to prevent rust and pitting.

Glass

Glass retains heat well but conducts it poorly. It does not react with foods. Tempered glass is suitable for microwave cooking, provided it does not have any metal band or decoration. Commercial operations rarely use glass cookware because of the danger of breakage.

Ceramics

Ceramics, including earthenware, porcelain and stoneware, are used primarily for baking dishes, casseroles and baking stones because they conduct heat uniformly and retain temperatures well. Ceramics are nonreactive, inexpensive and generally suitable for use in a microwave oven (provided there is no metal in the glaze). Ceramics are easily chipped or cracked, however, and should not be used over a direct flame. Also, quick temperature changes may cause the cookware to crack or shatter.

Plastic

Plastic containers are frequently used in commercial kitchens for food storage or service, but they cannot be used for heating or cooking except in a microwave oven. Plastic microwave cookware is made of phenolic resin. It is easy to clean, relatively inexpensive and rigidly shaped, but its glasslike structure is brittle and it can crack or shatter.

continued

contributed to the Empire's decline. There is also ample evidence that from ancient times until just a few hundred years ago, wine was heated in lead vessels to sweeten it. This had a disastrous effect on the drinker and, for several centuries in countries throughout Europe, on the wine purveyor as well. The former could be poisoned and the latter could be punished by death for selling adulterated wine. More recently it was found that much of the moonshine whisky produced in the American South contained lead in potentially toxic ranges. The source was determined to be the lead solder used in homemade stills, some of which even included old lead-containing car radiators as condensers.

Although commercially available cookware will not contain lead, be careful of imported pottery and those lovely hand-thrown pots found at craft fairs—there could be lead in the glaze.

Silicone Bakeware

In the 1980s, flexible silicone baking materials became available for use in the professional kitchen. Made from pure silicone or fibreglass impregnated with food-grade silicone, this light material resists sticking and can withstand temperatures from freezing to 250°C (485°F). Baking pan liners made from silicone materials rarely require greasing and are useful for baking as well as candy and chocolate work. Heat-resistant spatulas and pot holders made from silicone are effective and popular. Sheets of baking moulds made from these materials are used to form individual cakes, petit fours and desserts, as well as ice cream and frozen desserts. Often these pans are called by the brand names used by their manufacturers, among them Silpats, Flexipan, Gastroflex, Silform and Elastomolds.

Enamelware

Pans lined with enamel should not be used for cooking; in many areas, their use in commercial kitchens is prohibited by law. The enamel can chip or crack easily, providing good places for bacteria to grow. Also, the chemicals used to bond the enamel to the cookware can cause food poisoning if ingested.

Nonstick Coatings

Without affecting a metal's ability to conduct heat, a polymer (plastic) known as polytetrafluoroethylene (PTFE) and marketed under the trade names Teflon® and Silverstone® may be applied to many types of cookware. It provides a slippery, nonreactive finish that prevents food from sticking and allows the use of less fat in cooking. Cookware with nonstick coatings requires a great deal of care, however, as the coatings can scratch, chip and blister. Do not use metal spoons or spatulas in cookware with nonstick coatings, and do not use intense heat.

Common Cookware

Pots

Pots are large round vessels with straight sides and two loop handles. Available in a range of sizes based on volume, they are used on the stove top for making stocks or soups, or for boiling or simmering foods, particularly where rapid evaporation is not desired. Flat or fitted lids are available.

Stockpot with Spigot

Pans

Pans are round vessels with one long handle and straight or sloped sides. They are usually smaller and shallower than pots. Pans are available in a range of diameters and are used for general stove-top cooking, especially sautéing, frying or reducing liquids rapidly.

Sauce Pot

Sautoir (Straight Sides)

Rondeau/Brazier

Cast-Iron Skillet (Griswold)

Sauteuse (Sloped Sides)

Saucepan

Woks

Originally used to prepare Asian foods, woks are now found in many professional kitchens. Their round bottoms and curved sides diffuse heat and make it easy to toss or stir contents. Their large domed lids retain heat for steaming vegetables. Woks are useful for quickly sautéing strips of meat, simmering a whole fish or deep-frying appetizers. Stove-top woks range in diameter from 30 to 75 cm (12 to 30 in.); larger built-in gas or electric models are also available.

Wok

Hotel Pans

Hotel pans (also known as steam-table pans) are rectangular stainless steel pans designed to hold food for service in steam tables. Hotel pans may also be used for baking, roasting or poaching inside an oven. Perforated pans useful for draining, steaming or icing down foods are also available. The standard full-size pan is 30 by 50 cm (12 by 20 in.), with pans one-half, one-third, one-sixth and other fractions of this size available. Hotel-pan depth is standardized at 5 cm (2 in.) (referred to as a "200 pan"), 10, 15 and 20 cm (4, 6 and 8 in.).

Hotel Pans

Moulds

Pâté en Croûte Mould

Pâté moulds are available in several shapes and sizes and are usually made from tinned steel. Those with hinged sides, whether smooth or patterned, are more properly referred to as *pâté en croûte* moulds. The hinged sides make it easier to remove the baked pâté. Terrine moulds are traditionally lidded earthenware or enamelled cast-iron containers used for baking forcemeat mixtures. They may be round, oval or rectangular. Timbale moulds are small (about 75 to 120 mL [2-1/2 to 4 oz.]) metal or ceramic containers used for moulding aspic or baking individual portions of mousse, custard or vegetables. They may be round or oval and their slightly flared sides allow the contents to release cleanly when inverted.

Timbales

STRAINERS AND SIEVES

Strainers and sieves are used primarily to aerate and remove impurities from dry ingredients and drain or purée cooked foods. Strainers, colanders, drum sieves, conical strainers and étamine strainers are nonmechanical devices with a stainless steel mesh or screen through which food passes. The size of the mesh or screen varies from extremely fine to several millimetres wide; select the fineness best suited for the task at hand.

Étamine Strainer

Conical Strainer (Chinois) and Étamine Strainer

Both the étamine strainer and the conical strainer are cone-shaped metal strainers. The conical shape allows liquids to filter through small openings. An étamine strainer is made from a very fine mesh, while a conical strainer has a perforated metal body. Both are used for straining stocks and sauces, with the étamine strainer being particularly useful for consommé. A conical strainer can also be used with a pestle to purée soft foods.

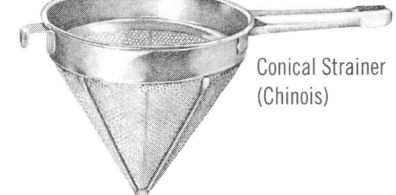

Conical Strainer (Chinois)

Skimmer and Spider

Both the skimmer and spider are long-handled tools used to remove foods or impurities from liquids. The flat, perforated disk of a skimmer is used for skimming stocks or removing foods from soups or stocks. The spider has a finer mesh disk, which makes it better for retrieving items from hot fat. Wooden-handled spiders are available but are less sturdy and harder to clean than all-metal designs.

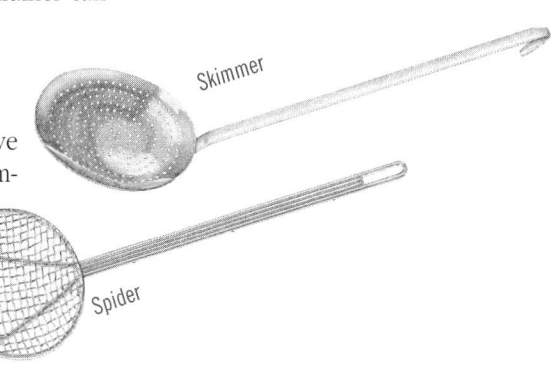

Skimmer

Spider

Round Mesh Strainer (Sieve)

Colander

Drum Sieve (Tamis)

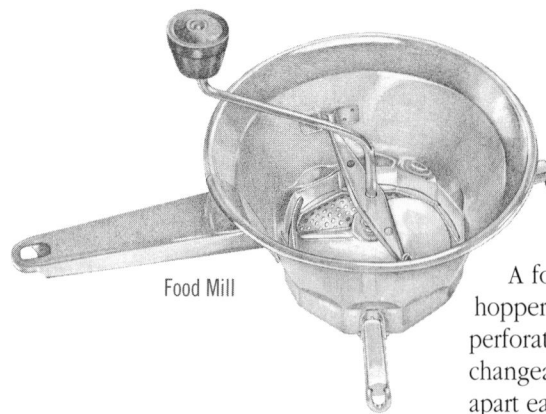
Food Mill

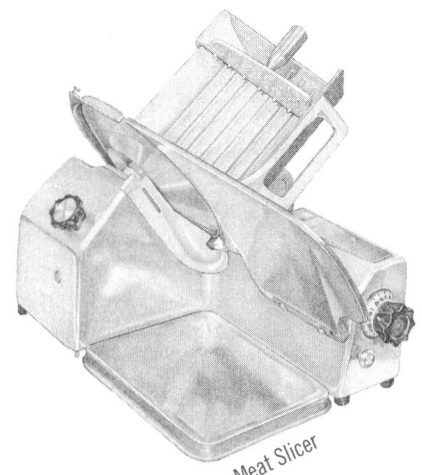
Flour Sifter

Meat Slicer

Cheesecloth

Cheesecloth is a loosely woven cotton gauze used for straining stocks and sauces and wrapping poultry or fish for poaching. Cheesecloth is also indispensable for making sachets. Always rinse cheesecloth thoroughly before use; this removes lint and prevents the cheesecloth from absorbing other liquids.

Food Mill

A food mill purées and strains food at the same time. Food is placed in the hopper and a hand-crank mechanism turns a blade in the hopper against a perforated disk, forcing the food through the disk. Most models have interchangeable disks with various-sized holes. Choose a mill that can be taken apart easily for cleaning.

Flour Sifter

A sifter is used for aerating, blending and removing impurities from dry ingredients such as flour, cocoa and leavening agents. The 2 L (8-cup) hand-crank sifter uses 4 curved rods to brush the contents through a curved mesh screen. The sifter should have a medium-fine screen and a comfortable handle.

PROCESSING EQUIPMENT

Processing equipment includes both electrical and nonelectrical devices used to chop, purée, slice, grind or mix foods. Before using any such equipment, be sure to review its operating procedures and ask for assistance if necessary. Always turn the equipment off and disconnect the power before disassembling, cleaning or moving the appliance. Any problems or malfunctions should be reported to your supervisor immediately. *Never place your hand into any machinery when the power is on. Processing equipment is powerful and can cause serious injury.*

Commonly Used Processing Equipment

Slicer

An electric slicer is used to cut meat, bread, cheese or raw vegetables into uniform slices. It has a circular blade that rotates at high speed. Food is placed in a carrier, then passed (manually or by an electric motor) against the blade. Slice thickness is determined by the distance between the blade and the carrier. Because of the speed with which the blade rotates, foods can be cut into extremely thin slices very quickly. An electric slicer is convenient for preparing moderate to large quantities of food, but the time required to disassemble and clean the equipment makes it impractical when slicing only a few items.

Mandoline

A mandoline is a manually operated slicer made of stainless steel with adjustable slicing blades. It is also used to make julienne and waffle-cut slices. Its narrow, rectangular body sits on the work counter at a 45-degree angle. Foods are passed against a blade to obtain uniform slices. It is useful for slicing small quantities of fruits or vegetables when using a large electric slicer would be unwarranted. To avoid injury, always use a hand guard or steel glove when using a mandoline.

Food Chopper or Buffalo Chopper

This chopper is used to process moderate to large quantities of food to a uniform size, such as chopping onions or grinding bread for crumbs. The food is placed in a large bowl rotating beneath a hood where curved blades chop it. The size of the cut depends on how long the food is left in the machine. Buffalo choppers are available in floor or tabletop models. The motor can usually be fitted with a variety of other tools such as a meat grinder or a slicer/shredder, making it even more useful.

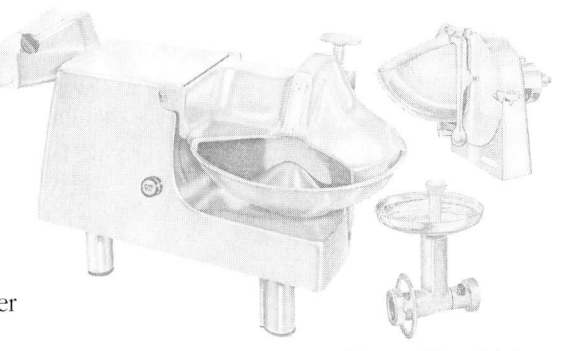

Buffalo Chopper with Slicer and Meat Grinder Attachments

Food Processor

A food processor has a motor housing with a removable bowl and S-shaped blade. It is used, for example, to purée cooked foods, chop nuts, prepare compound butters and emulsify sauces. Special disks can be added that slice, shred or julienne foods. Bowl capacity and motor power vary; select a model large enough for your most common tasks.

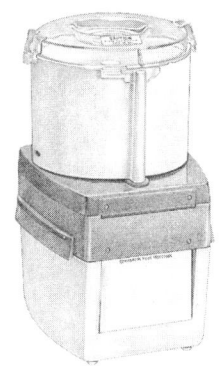

Food Processor

Blender

Though similar in principle to a food processor, a blender has a tall, narrow food container and a four-pronged blade. Its design is better for processing liquids or liquefying foods quickly. A blender is used to prepare smooth drinks, purée soups and sauces, blend batters and chop ice. A vertical cutter/mixer (VCM) operates like a very large, powerful blender. A VCM is usually floor-mounted and has a capacity of 55 to 300 L (15 to 80 gal.). Motorized blender blades at the end of a shaft are available for blending products in large containers.

Immersion Blender

An immersion blender—as well as its household counterpart, called a hand blender or wand—is a long shaft fitted with a rotating four-pronged blade at the bottom. Operated by pressing a button in the handle, an immersion blender is used to purée a soft food, soup or sauce directly in the container in which it was prepared, eliminating the need to transfer the food from one container to another. This is especially useful when working with hot foods. Small cordless, rechargeable models are convenient for puréeing or mixing small quantities or beverages, but larger heavy-duty electric models are more practical in commercial kitchens.

Immersion Blender

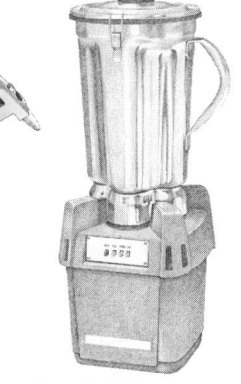
Heavy-Duty Blender

Flat Paddle

Dough Hook

Whip

20-L Mixer and Attachments

Mixer

A vertical mixer is indispensable in the bakeshop and most kitchens. The U-shaped arms hold a metal mixing bowl in place; the selected mixing attachment fits onto the rotating head. The three common mixing attachments are the whip (used for whipping eggs or cream), the paddle (used for general mixing) and the dough hook (used for kneading bread). Most mixers have several operating speeds. Bench models range in capacity from 4.5 to 20 L (4-1/2 to 20 qt.), while floor mixers can hold as much as 140 L (140 qt.). Some mixers can be fitted with shredder/slicers, meat grinders, juicers or power strainers, making the equipment more versatile.

Juicer

Two types of juicers are available: reamers and extractors. Reamers, also known as citrus juicers, remove juice from citrus fruits. They can be manual or electric. Manual models use a lever arm to squeeze the fruit with increased pressure. They are most often used to prepare small to moderate amounts of juice for cooking or beverages. Juice extractors are electrical devices that create juice by liquefying raw fruits, vegetables and herbs. They use centrifugal force to filter out fibre and pulp.

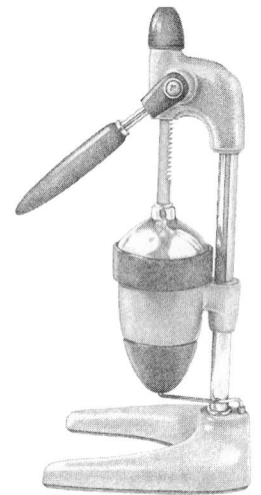

Citrus Juicer

STORAGE CONTAINERS

Proper storage containers are necessary for keeping leftovers, overproduction and opened packages of food safe for consumption. Proper storage can also reduce the costs incurred by waste or spoilage.

Although stainless steel pans such as hotel pans are suitable and useful for some items, the expense of stainless steel and the lack of airtight lids makes these pans impractical for general storage purposes. Aluminum containers are not recommended because the metal can react with even mildly acidic items. Glass containers are generally not allowed in commercial kitchens because of the hazards of broken glass. The most useful storage containers are those made of high-density plastic (such as polyethylene and polypropylene).

Storage containers must have well-fitting lids and should be available in a variety of sizes, including some that are small enough to hold even minimal quantities of food without allowing too much exposure to oxygen. Round and square plastic containers are widely available. Flat, snap-on lids allow containers to be stacked for more efficient storage. Containers may be clear or opaque white, which helps protect light-sensitive foods. Larger containers may be fitted with handles and spigots, making them especially suited for storing stock. Some storage containers are marked with graduated measurements, so content quantity can be determined at a glance.

Large quantities of dry ingredients, such as flour, sugar and rice, can be stored in rolling bins. The bins should be seamless with rounded corners for easy cleaning. They should have well-fitting but easy-to-open lids and should move easily on well-balanced casters.

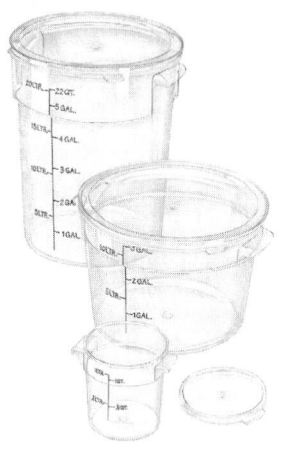

Storage Containers

HEAVY EQUIPMENT

Heavy equipment includes the gas-, electric- or steam-operated appliances used for cooking, reheating or holding foods. Heavy equipment also includes dishwashers and refrigeration units. Heavy equipment should be installed in a fixed location determined by the kitchen's traffic flow and space limitations.

Heavy equipment may be purchased or leased new or used. Used equipment is most often purchased in an effort to save money. Although the initial cost is generally less for used equipment, the buyer should also consider the lack of a manufacturer's warranty or dealership guarantee and how the equipment was maintained by the prior owner. Functional used equipment is satisfactory for back-of-the-house areas, but it is usually better to purchase new equipment if it will be visible to the customer. Leasing equipment may be appropriate for some operations. The cost of leasing is less than purchasing and, if something goes wrong with the equipment, the operator is generally not responsible for repairs or service charges.

Commonly Used Heavy Equipment

Stove Tops

Stove tops or ranges are often the most important cooking equipment in the kitchen. They have one or more burners powered by gas or electricity. The burners may be open or covered with a cast-iron or steel plate. Open burners supply quick, direct heat that is easy to regulate. A steel plate, known as a flat top, supplies even but less intense heat. Although it takes longer to heat than a burner, the flat top supports heavier weights and makes a larger area available for cooking. Many stoves include both flat tops and open burner arrangements. (See Figure 5.3 on the next page.)

Griddles are similar to flat tops except they are made of a thinner metal plate. Foods are usually cooked directly on the griddle's surface, not in pots or pans, which can nick or scratch the surface. The surface should be properly cleaned and conditioned after each use. Griddles are popular for short-order and fast-food-type operations.

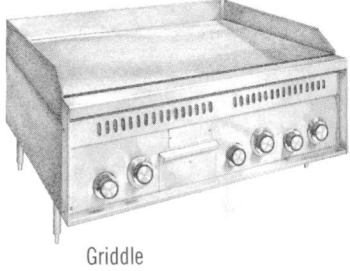
Griddle

Induction

Induction cooking uses a special induction coil placed below the stove top's surface in combination with specially designed cookware made of cast iron or magnetic stainless steel. The coil generates a magnetic current so that the cookware is heated rapidly with magnetic friction. Heat energy is then transferred from the cookware to the food by conduction. The cooking surface, which is made of a solid ceramic material, remains cool. Only the cookware and its contents get hot.

Induction cooking is a relatively new process, more popular in Europe than in Canada. But it is gaining acceptance in professional kitchens because of the speed with which foods can be heated and the ease of cleanup.

Portable induction burners are useful on buffets and cafeteria lines and for table service because they maintain a safer, cooler environment for both chefs and customers.

Induction Cooktop

Ovens

An oven is an enclosed space where food is cooked by being surrounded with hot, dry air. Conventional ovens are often located beneath the stove top. They have a heating element located at the unit's bottom or floor, and pans are placed on wire racks inside the oven's cavity. (See Figure 5.3.) Conventional ovens may

Stack Oven

Combitherm Oven

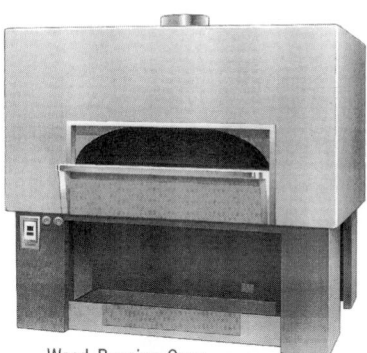

Wood-Burning Oven

Rotisserie

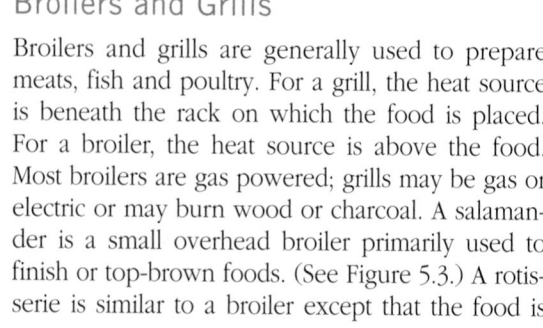

Overhead Broiler

also be separate, free-standing units or decks stacked one on top of the other. In stack ovens, pans are placed directly on the deck or floor and not on wire racks.

Convection ovens use internal fans to circulate the hot air. This tends to cook foods more quickly and evenly. Convection ovens are almost always free-standing units, powered either by gas or electricity. Because convection ovens cook foods more quickly, temperatures may need to be reduced by 12°C to 15°C (25°F to 30°F) from those recommended for conventional ovens. Fan speed will also affect the temperature.

Combitherm ovens are very versatile. They can function as a low-pressure steamer, convection oven or a combination of the two. The programmable features allow for performing complex cooking procedures to achieve superior end products.

Humidity levels in conjunction with temperature can be adjusted to simulate poaching and range to dry roasting. Some ovens have smoker attachments, and larger models may feature roll-in racks.

Wood-Burning Ovens

The ancient practice of baking in a retained-heat masonry oven has been revived in recent years, with many upscale restaurants and artisan bakeries installing brick or adobe ovens for baking pizzas and breads as well as for roasting fish, poultry and vegetables. These ovens have a curved interior chamber that is usually recessed into a wall. Although gas-fired models are available, wood-firing is more traditional and provides the aromas and flavours associated with brick ovens. A wood fire is built inside the oven to heat the brick chamber. The ashes are then swept out and the food is placed on the flat oven floor. The combination of high heat and wood smoke adds distinctive flavours to foods.

Microwave Ovens

Microwave ovens are electrically powered ovens used to cook or reheat foods. They are available in a range of sizes and power settings. Microwave ovens will not brown foods unless fitted with special browning elements. Microwave cooking is discussed in more detail in Chapter 9, Principles of Cooking.

Broilers and Grills

Broilers and grills are generally used to prepare meats, fish and poultry. For a grill, the heat source is beneath the rack on which the food is placed. For a broiler, the heat source is above the food. Most broilers are gas powered; grills may be gas or electric or may burn wood or charcoal. A salamander is a small overhead broiler primarily used to finish or top-brown foods. (See Figure 5.3.) A rotisserie is similar to a broiler except that the food is

Gas Grill

placed on a revolving spit in front of the heat source. The unit may be open or enclosed like an oven; it is most often used for cooking poultry or meats.

Tilting Skillets

Tilting skillets are large, free-standing, flat-bottomed pans about 15 cm (6 in.) deep with an internal heating element below the pan's bottom. They are usually made of stainless steel with a cover, and have a hand-crank mechanism that turns or tilts the pan to pour out the contents. Tilting skillets can be used as stockpots, braziers, fry pans, griddles or steam tables, making them one of the most versatile of modern commercial appliances.

Steam Kettles

Steam kettles (also known as steam-jacketed kettles) are similar to stockpots except they are heated from the bottom and sides by steam circulating between layers of stainless steel. The steam may be generated internally or from an outside source. Because steam heats the kettle's sides, foods cook more quickly and evenly than they would in a pot sitting on the stove top. Steam kettles are most often used for making sauces, soups, custards or stock. Steam kettles are available in a range of sizes, from a 9-L (2-gal.) tabletop model to a 450-L (100-gal.) floor model. Some models have a tilting mechanism that allows the contents to be poured out; others have a spigot near the bottom through which liquids can be drained.

Steamers

Pressure and convection steamers are used to cook foods rapidly and evenly, using direct contact with steam. Pressure steamers heat water above the boiling point in sealed compartments; the high temperature and sealed compartment increase the internal pressure in a range of 1.8 to 6.8 kg (4 to 15 lb.) per square inch. The increased pressure and temperature cook the foods rapidly. Convection steamers generate steam in an internal boiler, then release it over the foods in a cooking chamber. Both types of steamer are ideal for cooking vegetables with a minimal loss of flavour or nutrients.

Deep Fryers

Deep fryers are used only to fry foods in hot fat. The fryers may be either gas or electric and should have thermostatic controls to maintain the fat at a preset temperature. Frying procedures are discussed in Chapter 9, Principles of Cooking.

Refrigerators

Proper refrigeration space is an essential component of any kitchen. Many foods must be stored at low temperatures to maintain quality and safety. Most commercial refrigeration is of two types: walk-in units and reach-in or upright units.

A walk-in is a large, room-sized box capable of holding hundreds of kilograms of food on adjustable shelves. A separate freezer walk-in may be positioned nearby or even inside a refrigerated walk-in.

Reach-ins may be individual units or parts of a bank of units, each with shelves approximately the size of a full sheet pan. Reach-in refrigerators and

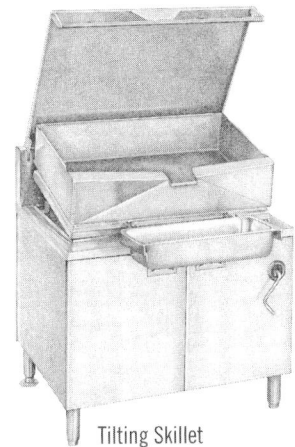

Tilting Skillet

Steam Kettle

Convection Steamer

Deep Fryer

freezers are usually located throughout the kitchen to provide quick access to foods. Small units may also be placed beneath the work counters. Freezers and refrigerators are available in a wide range of sizes and door designs to suit any operation.

Other forms of commercial refrigeration include chilled drawers located beneath a work area that are just large enough to accommodate a hotel pan, and display cases used to show foods to the customer.

Dishwashers

Mechanical dishwashers are available to wash, rinse and sanitize dishware, glassware, cookware and utensils. Small models clean one rack of items at a time, while larger models can handle several racks simultaneously on a conveyor belt system. Sanitizing may be accomplished with either extremely hot water (82°C/180°F) or chemicals automatically dispensed during the final rinse cycle. Any dishwashing area should be carefully organized for efficient use of equipment and employees and to prevent recontamination of clean items.

Insulated
Carrier

BUFFET EQUIPMENT

Food service operations that prepare buffets or cater off-premises events need a variety of specialized equipment to ensure that food is handled safely and efficiently and displayed appropriately. Proper temperatures must be maintained during transportation, display and service.

Insulated carriers hold food at its current temperature for a time. They are designed to hold hotel pans or sheet pans and are available with wheels for easy movement. Some are available with a spigot for serving hot or cold beverages. Any carrier should be easy to clean and of a convenient size for the space available and the type of operation.

Chafing Dish

Temperature remains a concern when arranging food on a buffet table. Chafing dishes are commonly used for keeping hot foods hot during service. Chafing dishes are designed so that cans of solid fuel can be placed under a deep hotel pan of hot water. Like a double boiler or bain marie, the hot water then helps maintain the temperature of food placed in a second hotel pan suspended over the first. Chafing dishes, however, should never be used to heat food. Chafing dishes are available in several sizes and shapes, but the most convenient are those based on the size of a standard hotel pan. Round, deep chafing dishes are useful for serving soups or sauces. Exteriors can be plain or ornate and made of silver, copper or stainless steel.

Roast beef, turkey, ham or other large cuts of meat are sometimes carved on a buffet in front of guests. Heat lamps can be used to keep these foods warm. Heat lamps are also useful for maintaining the temperature of pizza or fried foods, which might become soggy if held in a chafing dish.

Heat Lamp

Pastries, breads and cold foods can be arranged on a variety of platters, trays, baskets and serving pieces, depending on the size and style of the buffet. Some of the most elegant and traditional serving pieces are flat display mirrors. These may be plastic or glass and are available in a wide variety of shapes and sizes. The edges should be sealed in an easy-to-clean plastic to prevent chipping.

Although many of these items can be rented, operations that regularly serve buffets may prefer to invest in their own transportation and serving equipment.

Specialized Equipment for New and Emerging Culinary Techniques

Chefs are adopting new tools and cooking equipment to facilitate many modern and experimental cooking techniques. One of the more widely discussed new techniques is sous vide (French for "under vacuum"), a type of low-temperature cooking in which foods are vacuum-sealed in pouches, then cooked for an extended period in a water bath. Chefs such as Thomas Keller have discovered that this method, also known as cook-chill, which has been used since the 1960s for preparing cured and frozen meats, also produces tender, flavourful fresh meat, fish and seafood. The reduced oxygen environment of foods packaged under vacuum concentrates flavours and extends the shelf life of dishes prepared using this method. In addition, the temperatures for sous vide cooking, ranging from 51°C (125°F) to 90°C (195°F), rarely exceed the desired temperature of the finished dish, resulting in foods that are precisely cooked but not overcooked. (Food safety is ensured by cooking the foods the proper length of time at a constant temperature.)

Two essential pieces of equipment are required for sous vide cooking: a chamber vacuum machine and a thermal circulator or immersion circulator. The chamber vacuum machine allows solids and liquids to be packaged in food-grade polyethylene bags in order to seal in flavour and prevent water from touching the food to be cooked. A thermal circulator is attached to a vessel of water, where the pouched foods are then cooked in the warm flowing bath. The heating element and temperature controls on the circulator maintain the precise and constant temperatures required for sous vide cooking. Because foods cooked sous vide resemble poached or braised foods, they are often finished for service by browning conventionally in a pan or using a handheld propane torch.

Accurate temperature control and proper cooking time is essential when cooking foods sous vide at the low temperatures in which bacteria can thrive. The Food Code requires that a detailed HAACP program including time and temperature monitoring be in place in any food service operation using sous vide cooking methods. Before employing sous vide techniques in any food service operation, consult local health authorities to learn what technical training, licensing and record keeping is required.

Among the tools migrating from the chemistry laboratory to the kitchen are microscopically fine heat-resistant filters. With perforations a mere 100 microns (0.1 mm/0.004 in.) thick, these filters can be used for clarifying stock and making clear colourless consommé. The vacuum rotary evaporator, a costly lab instrument

Immersion Heat Circulator and Thermal Bath

used to distill mixtures, has been adapted for kitchen use to reduce liquids without applying heat and to impregnate foods with flavours. One device inspired by the science lab is the anti-griddle, which resembles a flat top on which food is frozen, not cooked. The surface of the anti-griddle, chilled to –34°C (–30°F), "sears" food with cold. Hot purées and liquids can be sealed on the outside with cold and still be warm or liquid inside.

SAFETY EQUIPMENT

There are certain items that are critical to the well-being of a food service operation, although they are not used in food preparation. These are safety devices, many of which are required by provincial or local law. Failing to include safety equipment in a kitchen or failing to maintain it properly endangers workers and customers.

Types of Equipment

Fire Extinguishers

Fire extinguishers are canisters of foam, dry chemicals (such as sodium bicarbonate or potassium bicarbonate) or pressurized water used to extinguish small fires. They must be placed within sight of and be easily reached from the work areas in which fires are most likely to occur. Different classes of extinguishers use different chemicals to fight different types of fire. The appropriate

P.A.S.S. Technique for Fire Extinguishers

Remember the acronym **P.A.S.S.** for the four steps to follow when using any fire extinguisher:

- **Pull**—Pull the safety pin on the extinguisher.
- **Aim**—Aim the extinguisher hose at the base of the fire.
- **Squeeze**—Squeeze the handle to discharge the material.
- **Sweep**—Sweep the hose from side to side across the base of the fire.

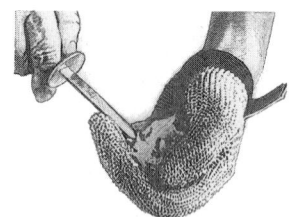

Mesh Safety Gloves

class must be used for the specific fire. (See Table 5.2.) Class K extinguishers are being phased in as the required standard for restaurants. Fire extinguishers must be recharged and checked from time to time. Be sure they have not been discharged, tampered with or otherwise damaged.

Ventilation Systems

Ventilation systems (also called ventilation hoods) are commonly installed over cooking equipment to remove vapours, heat and smoke. Most systems include fire extinguishing agents or sprinklers. A properly operating hood makes the kitchen more comfortable for the staff and reduces the danger of fire. The system must be designed, installed and inspected by professionals, then cleaned and maintained regularly. A return or makeup air system is installed to ensure air quality and good circulation.

First-Aid Kits

First-aid supplies should be stored in a clearly marked box conspicuously located near food preparation areas. Occupational health and safety guidelines may specify the kit's exact contents. Generally, it should include a first-aid manual, bandages, gauze dressings, adhesive tape, antiseptics, scissors, cold packs and other supplies. The kit should be checked regularly and items replaced as needed. In addition, cards with emergency telephone numbers should be placed inside the first-aid kit and near a telephone. Emergency response procedures must be communicated to staff and a copy of the procedures must be available for quick reference.

Protective Gear

All kitchens should be equipped with high quality heat-resistant gloves or pot holders to be used when handling hot pans and other equipment. In kitchens where a large quantity of shellfish is opened or a meat slicer is used, steel-mesh safety gloves may be required. Made from stainless steel woven into a fine fibre, these gloves recall medieval armour and are effective at preventing puncture or slicing wounds.

TABLE 5.2	Fire Extinguishers	
Class	**Symbol**	**Use**
Class A	▲	Fires involving wood, paper, cloth or plastic
Class B	■	Fires involving oil, grease or flammable chemicals
Class C	●	Fires involving electrical equipment or wiring
Class K	⬡	Fires involving cooking oils or fat and fats in commercial cooking equipment
Combination extinguishers—AB, BC and ABC—are also available.		

THE PROFESSIONAL KITCHEN

The kitchen is the heart of the food service operation. There, food and other items are received, stored, prepared and plated for service; dining room staff members place orders, retrieve foods ready for service and return dirty service items; dishes and other wares are cleaned and stored; and the chef conducts business. But commercial space is expensive, and most food service operators recognize that the greater the number of customers served, the greater the revenues. Often this translates into a large dining area and small kitchen and storage facilities. Therefore, when designing a kitchen, it is important to use the space wisely so that each of its functions can be accomplished efficiently.

Regardless of the kitchen's size, its design begins with a consideration of the tasks to be performed. Analyzing the menu identifies these tasks. A restaurant featuring steaks and chops, for example, will need areas to fabricate and grill meats. If it relies on commercially prepared desserts and breads, it will not need a bakeshop but will still need space to hold and plate baked goods.

Once all food preparation tasks are identified, a work area for each particular task is designated. These work areas are called **work stations**. At a steak restaurant, an important work station is the broiler. If the restaurant serves fried foods, it will also need a fry station. The size and design of each work station is determined by the volume of food the operation intends to produce.

Usually work stations using the same or similar equipment for related tasks are grouped together into **work sections**. (See Table 5.3. Note that work stations correspond to the kitchen brigade system discussed in Chapter 1, Professionalism.) For example, in a typical full-service restaurant, there will be a single hot-foods section. It can consist of broiler, fry, griddle, sauté and sauce stations. Both advance preparation and last-minute cooking may be performed in the hot-foods section. The principal cooking equipment (a range, broiler, deep-fat fryer, oven, griddle, etc.) will be arranged in a line under a ventilation hood. Although each work station within the hot-foods section may be staffed by a different line cook, the proximity of the stations allows one line cook to cover more than one station if the kitchen is short-handed or when business is slow.

Merely considering the plan of the work station or section is not enough, however. When designing the work area, you must also consider the elevation. That is, a kitchen designer not only examines what equipment should be placed next to the other (for example, the range next to the deep-fat fryer), but also what equipment and storage facilities can be placed beneath or on top of the other. For example, in a bakeshop, rolling storage carts for flour and sugar or an under-the-counter refrigerator for eggs and dairy products may be located beneath the work surface, while mixing bowls and dry ingredients are stored on shelves above. Ideally, each station should be designed so that the cook takes no more than three steps in any direction to perform all assigned station tasks.

TABLE 5.3	Work Sections and Their Stations
Sections	**Stations**
Hot-foods section	Broiler station Fry station Griddle station Sauté/sauce station Holding
Garde-manger section	Salad greens cleaning Salad preparation Cold foods preparation Sandwich station Showpiece preparation
Bakery section	Mixing station Dough holding and proofing Dough rolling and forming Baking and cooling Dessert preparation* Frozen dessert preparation* Plating desserts*
Banquet section	Steam cooking Dry heat cooking (roasting, broiling) Holding and plating
Short-order section	Griddle station Fry station Broiler station
Beverage section	Hot-beverage station Cold-beverage station Alcoholic-beverage station

*These stations are sometimes found in the garde-manger section.

● **work station** a work area in the kitchen dedicated to a particular task, such as broiling or salad making; work stations using the same or similar equipment for related tasks are grouped into **work sections**

In addition to the work sections at which the menu items are produced, a typical restaurant kitchen includes areas dedicated to the following:

1. *Receiving and storing foods and other items.* There should be separate freezer, refrigerator and dry-goods storage facilities. Each should have proper temperature, humidity and light controls in order to maintain the stored items properly and safely. Depending upon the operation's size and the work stations' specific needs, there can be either a central storage area, or each station or section can maintain its own storage facilities. Typically, however, there is a combination of central and section storage. For example, up to 45 kg (100 lb.) of flour and sugar can be stored in rolling bins under a work table in the bakeshop, while several hundred kilograms or pounds remain in a central dry goods area. Similarly, one box of salt can be stored near the hot line for immediate use, while the remainder of the case is stored in a central dry goods area. Additional storage space will be needed for cleaning and paper supplies, dishes and other service ware. *Never store cleaning supplies and other chemicals with foods.*

2. *Washing dishes and other equipment.* These dish- and equipment-washing facilities should have their own sinks. Food-preparation and handwashing sinks should be separate.

3. *Employee use.* Restrooms, locker facilities and an office are also found in most food service facilities.

The guiding principle behind a good kitchen design is to maximize the flow of goods and staff from one area to the next and within each area itself. Maximizing flow creates an efficient work environment and helps reduce preparation and service time.

Figure 5.4 shows the several sections of a professional kitchen. It includes an area for front-of-the-house staff to circulate, drop off orders, retrieve finished dishes and return dirty dishes. The design allows for the flow of foods from receiving to storage, to food preparation areas, to holding and service areas and then to the dining room as well as the flow of dirty dishes from the dining room back into the kitchen. The work sections are arranged to take advantage of shared equipment. For instance, by placing the bakeshop next to the hot-foods section, these sections can share ovens. The garde-manger and dessert sections, both of which rely on refrigerated foods, are conveniently located near the walk-in refrigerator and freezer area. The beverage station is located near the dining room entrance so that food servers do not have to walk through food preparation areas to fill beverage orders. The office is next to receiving so that the chef can easily check and receive orders. The central storage areas are easily accessible to the receiving area as well as to the food production areas, while the cleaning-supply storage is near the dishwashing area. In general, the design eliminates the need for staff from one work station or section to cross through another station or section.

Governmental building, health, fire and safety codes will dictate, to a degree, certain aspects of a professional kitchen's design. But to make the most of these spaces, the well-designed kitchen should reflect a sound understanding of the tasks to be performed and the equipment necessary to perform them. Hiring a professional kitchen designer is a good investment when building or retrofitting a food service facility.

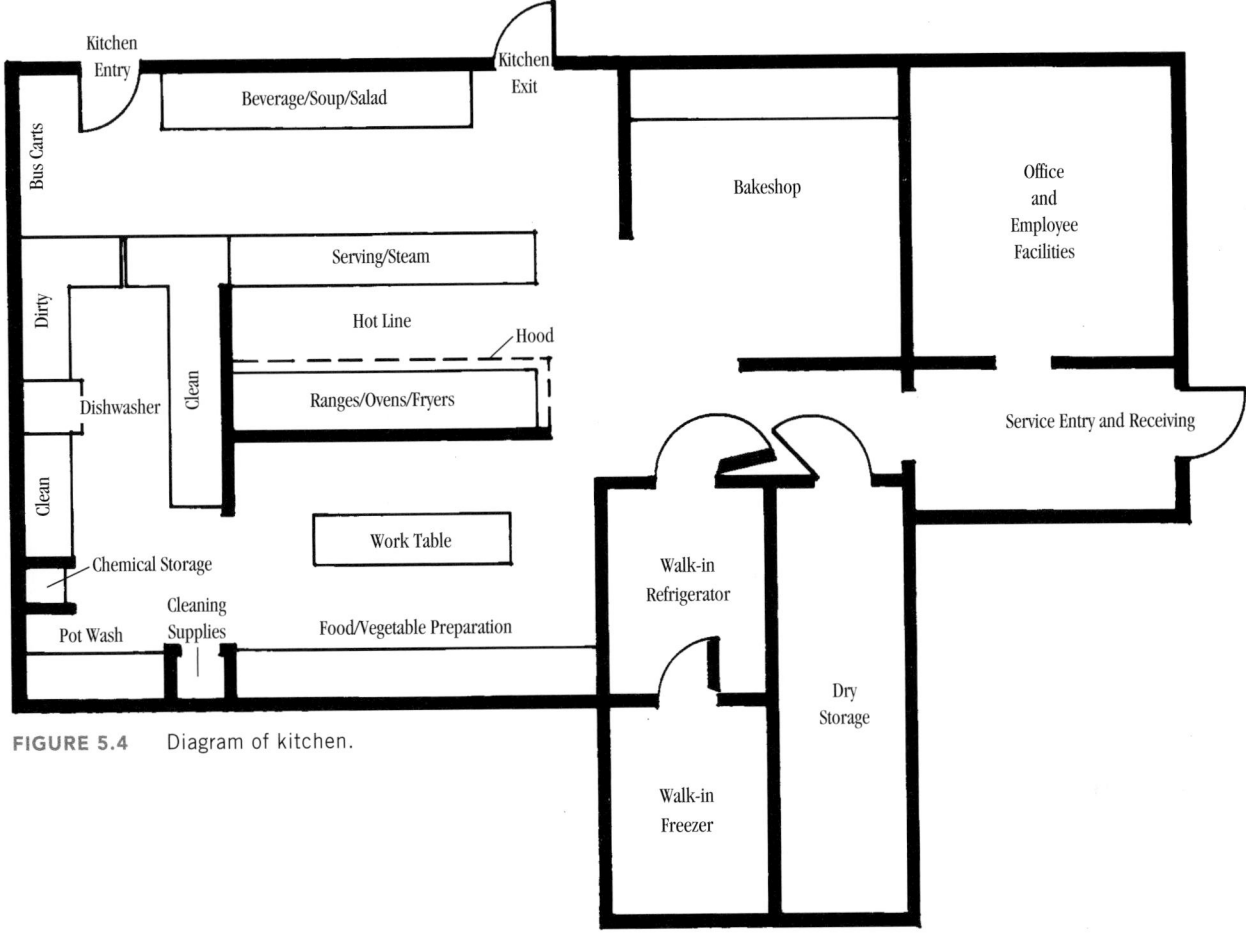

FIGURE 5.4 Diagram of kitchen.

Conclusion

There are hundreds of tools and pieces of equipment that can help you prepare, cook, store and present food. Every year, manufacturers offer new or improved items. Throughout your career you will use many of them. Select those that are well constructed, durable and best suited for the task at hand. Then use them in a safe and efficient manner.

The way in which equipment is arranged and stored in a kitchen is also important. Good kitchen design emphasizes the efficient flow of goods and staff from one work section to another as well as within each work section or station.

Questions for Discussion

1. What six characteristics should be considered in the selection of tools and equipment?
2. List the parts of a chef's knife and describe the knife's construction.
3. List six materials used to make commercial cookware and describe the advantages and disadvantages of each.
4. Describe six pieces of equipment that can be used to slice or chop foods.
5. List four classes of fire extinguishers. For each one, describe its designating symbol and identify the type or types of fire it should be used to extinguish.
6. Explain the relationship between work sections and work stations and the kitchen brigade system discussed in Chapter 1, Professionalism.

Knife Skills 6

 Every morning one must start from scratch, with nothing on the stoves. That is cuisine.

—Fernand Point, French restaurateur (1897–1955)

LEARNING OUTCOMES

After studying this chapter you will be able to:

- care for knives properly
- use knives safely and properly
- cut foods into a variety of classic shapes

These interactive online tools will help you master the skills in this chapter:

- Videos
- Chapter Quizzes
- Activities

Every professional must become skilled in the use of certain tools. The professional cook is no exception. One of the most important tools the apprentice cook must master is the knife. Good knife skills are critical to a cook's success because the knife is the most commonly used tool in the kitchen. Every cook spends countless hours slicing, dicing, mincing and chopping. Learning to perform these tasks safely and efficiently is an essential part of your training.

At first, professional knives may feel large and awkward and the techniques discussed below may not seem all that efficient. But as you become familiar with knives and practise your knife skills, using knives correctly will become second nature. Knives are identified in Chapter 5, Tools and Equipment. Here we show how they are used to cut vegetables. The techniques presented, however, can be used for most any food that holds its shape when cut. Knife skills for butchering and fabricating meat, poultry, fish and shellfish are discussed in Chapters 12, Principles of Meat Cookery, through 19, Fish and Shellfish.

A note about language: Many of the classic cuts are known by their French names: julienne, for example. Although these words are nouns and entered the English language as nouns (e.g., a julienne of carrot), they are also used as verbs (to julienne a carrot) and adjectives (julienned carrots).

USING YOUR KNIFE SAFELY

The first rule of knife safety is to *think about what you are doing*. Other basic rules of knife safety are as follows:

1. Use the correct knife for the task at hand.
2. Always cut away from yourself.
3. Always cut on a cutting board. Do not cut on glass, marble or metal.
4. Keep knives sharp; a dull knife is more dangerous than a sharp one.
5. When carrying a knife, hold it point down, parallel to and close to your leg as you walk.
6. A falling knife has no handle. Do not attempt to catch a falling knife; step back and allow it to fall.
7. Never leave a knife in a sink of water; anyone reaching into the sink could be injured, or the knife could be dented by pots or other utensils.
8. Never place items on top of your knives—that is, towels, boxes, food, cutting boards, etc.
9. Wash knives by hand; dishwashers may cause damage to the blade or handle.
10. To wipe a blade safely, place the knife in a folded towel with the cutting edge pointing away from you. Pull the knife through the towel with your palm on top of the towel.

CARING FOR YOUR KNIFE
Knife Sharpening and Care

A sharpening stone called a whetstone is used to put an edge on a dull knife blade. To use a whetstone, place the heel of the blade against the whetstone at a 20-degree angle. Keeping that angle, press down on the blade while pushing it away from you in one long arc, as if to slice off a thin piece of the stone. The entire length of the blade should come in contact with the stone during each sweep. Repeat the procedure on both sides of the blade until sufficiently sharp. With a triple-faced stone, such as that shown to the right, you progress from the coarsest to the finest surface. Any whetstone can be moistened with either water or mineral oil, but not both. Do not use vegetable oil on a whetstone as it will soon become rancid and gummy.

A steel generally does not sharpen a knife. Instead, it is used to hone or straighten the blade immediately after and between sharpenings. To use a steel, place the blade against the steel at a 20-degree angle. Then draw the blade along the entire length of the steel. Repeat the technique several times on each side of the blade. Diamond sharpening steels are available.

Do not wash knives in commercial dishwashers. The heat and harsh chemicals can damage the edge and the handle. The blade can also be damaged if it knocks against cookware or utensils. The knife could injure an unsuspecting worker if left in a sink of water. Always wash, sanitize, and dry your knives by hand immediately after each use to reduce cross-contamination issues. Store knives in sleeves or slotted trays. A magnetic wall rack is useful at work stations.

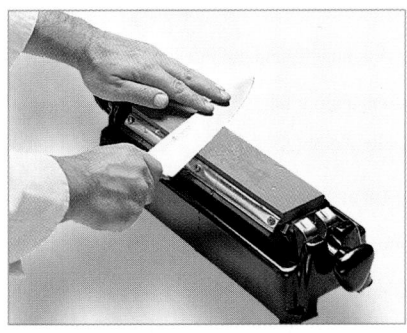

When sharpening a knife against a three-sided whetstone, go from the coarsest to the finest surface.

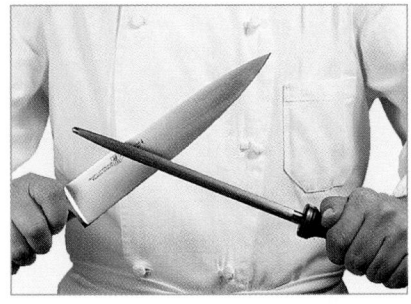

Honing a knife against a steel straightens the blade between sharpenings.

GRIPPING YOUR KNIFE

There are several ways to grip a knife. Use the grip that is most comfortable for you or the one dictated by the job at hand. Whichever grip you use should be firm but not so tight that your hand becomes tired. Gripping styles are shown below.

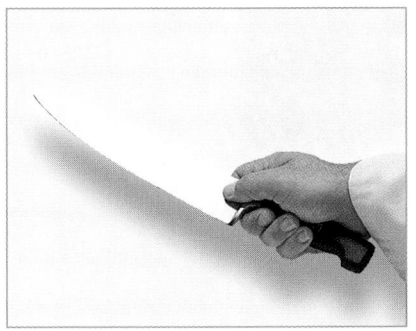

The most common grip: Hold the handle with three fingers while gripping the blade between the thumb and index finger.

A variation on the most common grip: Grip the handle with four fingers and place the thumb on the front of the handle.

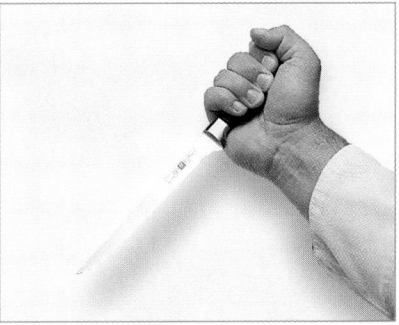

The underhand grip for a rigid boning knife: Grip the handle in a fist with four fingers and thumb. This grip allows you to use the knife tip to cut around joints and separate flesh from bone when boning meat and poultry.

CONTROLLING YOUR KNIFE

To safely produce even cuts, you must control (or guide) your knife with one hand and hold the item being cut with the other. Always allow the blade's sharp edge to do the cutting. Never force the blade through the item being cut. Smooth, even strokes should be used. Using a dull knife or excessive force with any knife produces, at best, poor results and, at worst, a significant safety risk. Cutting without using your hand as a guide may also be dangerous. Two safe cutting methods that produce good results are shown here.

METHOD A

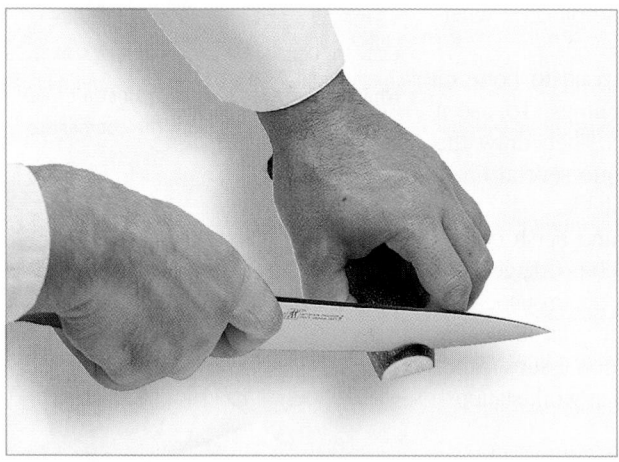 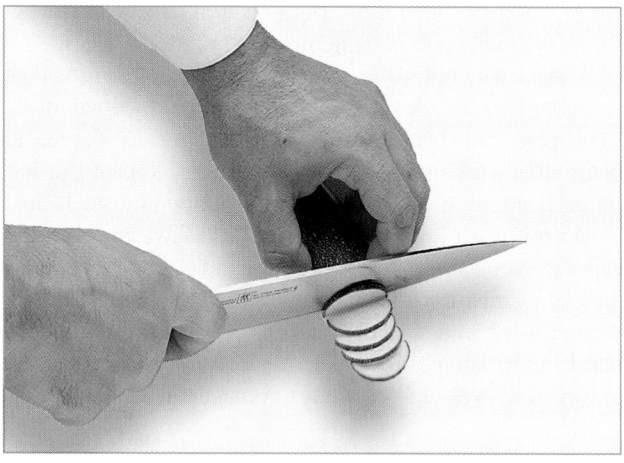

1. Keep your fingertips curled back, then grip the item being cut with three fingertips and your thumb. Hold the knife in the other hand. While keeping the knife's tip on the cutting board, lift the heel of the knife.

2. Use the second joint of your index finger as a guide and cut a slice using a smooth, even, downward stroke. Adjust the position of the guiding finger after each slice to produce slices of equal size. After a few cuts, slide your fingertips and thumb down the length of the item and continue slicing. For this slicing technique, the knife's tip acts as the fulcrum.

METHOD B

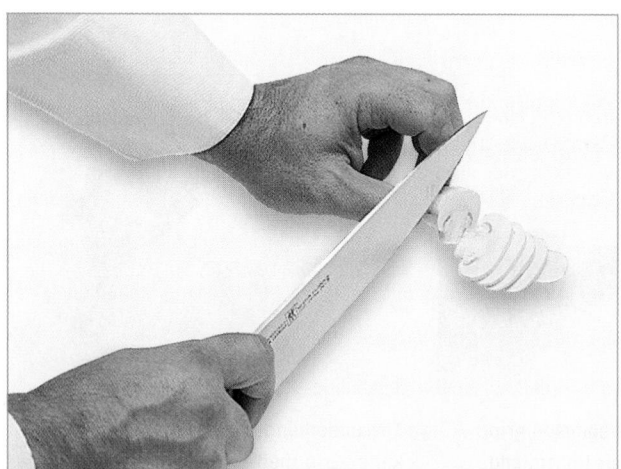 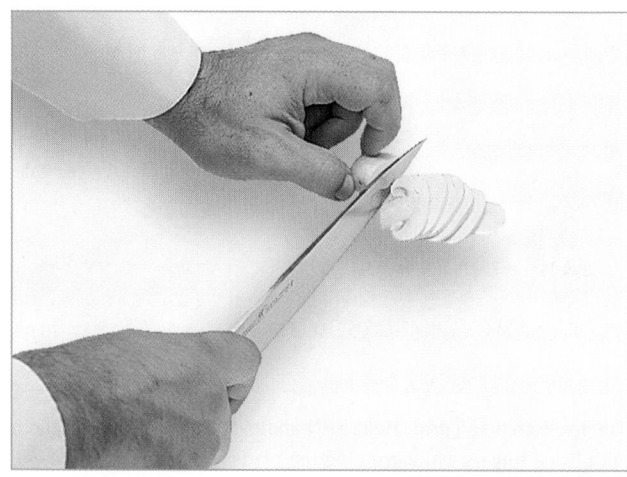

1. Grip the item as described above. Using the second joint of your index finger as a guide, lift the knife's tip and slice by drawing the knife slightly back toward you and down through the item, cutting the item to the desired thickness.

2. The motion of the knife should come almost entirely from the wrist, not the elbow. Allow the weight of the knife to do most of the work; very little downward pressure needs to be applied to the knife. For this slicing technique, your wrist should act as the fulcrum.

CUTTING WITH YOUR KNIFE

A knife is used to shape and reduce an item's size. Uniformity of size and shape ensures even cooking and enhances the appearance of the finished product. Items are shaped by slicing, chopping, dicing, mincing or by other special cutting techniques.

Slicing

To slice is to cut an item into relatively broad, thin pieces. Slices may be either the finished cut or the first step in producing other cuts. Slicing is typically used to create three specialty cuts: the chiffonade, rondelle and diagonal. Slicing skills are also used to produce oblique or roll cuts and lozenges.

A **chiffonade** is a preparation of finely sliced or shredded leafy vegetables used as a garnish or a base under cold presentations. As shown here, slicing spinach *en chiffonade* is a relatively simple process.

● **chiffonade** a preparation of finely sliced or shredded leafy vegetables or herbs

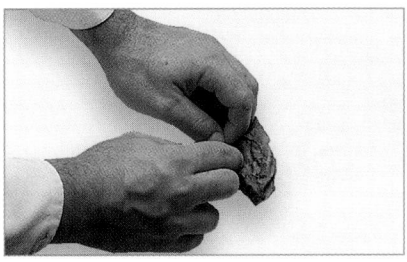 

1. Wash and destem the leaves as necessary. Stack several leaves on top of each other and roll them tightly like a cigar.

2. Make fine slices across the leaves while holding the leaf roll tightly.

As we see here, **rondelles** or **rounds** are easily made disk-shaped slices of cylindrical vegetables or fruits.

● **rondelles** disk-shaped slices

Peel the item (if desired) and place it on a cutting board. Make even slices perpendicular to the item being cut.

Diagonals are elongated or oval-shaped slices of cylindrical vegetables or fruits. They are produced with a cut similar to that used to cut rondelles except that the knife is held at an angle to the item being cut.

● **diagonals** oval-shaped slices

Peel the item (if desired) and place it on a cutting board. Position the knife at the desired angle to the item being cut and slice it evenly.

● **oblique cuts** small pieces with two angle-cut sides

Oblique or roll-cut items are small pieces with two angle-cut sides. This relatively simple cut is most often used on carrots and parsnips.

Place the peeled item on a cutting board. Holding the knife at a 45-degree angle, make the first cut. Roll the item a half turn, keeping the knife at the same angle, and make another cut. The result is a wedge-shaped piece with two angled sides.

● **lozenges** diamond-shaped pieces, usually of firm vegetables

Lozenges are diamond-shaped cuts prepared from firm vegetables such as carrots, turnips, rutabagas and potatoes.

1. Slice the item into long slices of the desired thickness. Then cut the slices into strips of the desired width.

2. Cut the strips at an angle to produce diamond shapes.

Horizontal Slicing

● **butterfly** to slice boneless meat, poultry or fish nearly in half lengthwise so that it spreads open like a book; used to increase surface area and speed cooking

To horizontal slice is to **butterfly** or cut a **pocket** into meats, poultry or fish. It is also a method of cutting used to thinly slice soft vegetables.

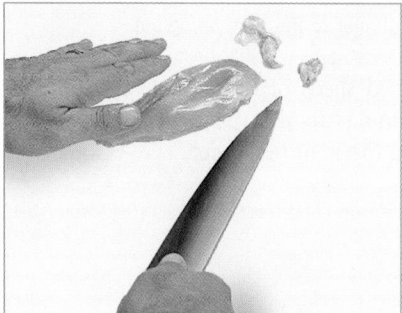

1. With your hand opened and your fingers arched upward, hold the item to be cut firmly in the centre of your palm.

2. Holding the knife parallel to the table, slice a pocket to the desired depth or cut through the item completely.

Chopping

To **chop** is to cut an item into small pieces where uniformity of size and shape is neither necessary (for example, coarsely chopped onions for a mire-poix that will be removed from the stock before service) nor feasible (for example, parsley).

● **chop** to cut into pieces where uniformity of size and shape is not important

Coarse Chopping

Coarse chopping does not mean carelessly hacking up food. Rather, the procedure is identical to that used for slicing but without the emphasis on uniformity. Coarsely chopped pieces should measure approximately 2 cm × 2 cm × 2 cm (3/4 in. × 3/4 in. × 3/4 in.).

Grip the knife as for slicing. Hold the item being chopped with your other hand. It may not be necessary to use your finger as a guide because uniformity is not crucial.

Chopping Parsley and Similar Foods

Parsley can be cut very coarsely or very finely. As shown below, it is easy to chop parsley and similar foods properly regardless of the desired fineness.

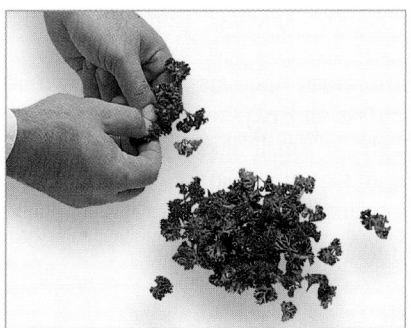

1. Wash the parsley in cold water; drain well. Remove the parsley sprigs from the stems.

2. Grip the knife in one hand. With the other hand spread flat, hold the knife's tip on the cutting board. Keeping the knife's tip on the board, chop the parsley sprigs by rocking the curved blade of the knife up and down while moving the knife back and forth over the parsley.

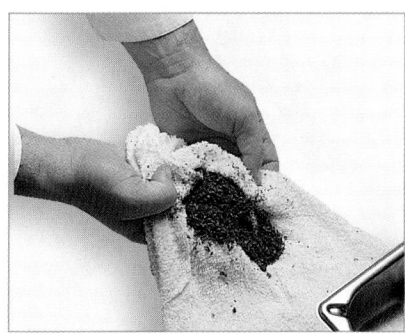

3. Place the chopped parsley in a double layer of cheesecloth. Rinse it under cold water and squeeze out as much water as possible. The chopped parsley should be dry and fluffy.

Chopping Garlic

A daily chore in many food service facilities, peeling and chopping garlic is a simple job made easy with the procedure shown here. Garlic paste can also be made.

 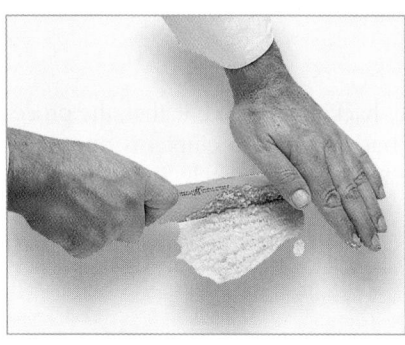 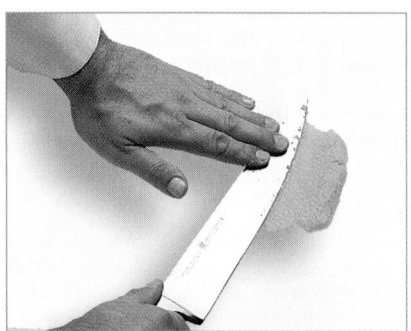

1. Break the head of garlic into individual cloves with your hands. Lightly crush the cloves using the flat edge of a chef's knife or a mallet. They will break open, and the peel can be separated easily from the garlic flesh.

2. With a flat hand, hold the knife's tip on the cutting board. Using a rocking motion, chop the garlic cloves to the desired size. Garlic is usually chopped very finely.

3. Garlic paste can be made by first finely chopping the garlic and then turning the knife on an angle and repeatedly dragging the edge of the knife along the cutting board, mashing the garlic.

Cutting Sticks and Dicing

To dice is to cut an item into cubes. Before an item can be diced, it must first be cut into certain-sized sticks. These techniques are most often used when uniformity of size and shape are important (for example, julienned carrots for a salad or brunoised vegetables for a garnish).

The dicing technique is typically used to create the classic cuts known as brunoise, small dice, medium dice, large dice and paysanne. Although most cooks have some notion of what size and shape "small diced" potatoes or julienne carrots may be, there are size ranges and specific shapes for these cuts.

Exact size will depend on the use or appearance desired.

Julienne—a stick-shaped item with dimensions of 1 to 2 mm × 1 to 2 mm × 2.5 to 4 cm (1/16 in. × 1/16 in. × 1 to 2 in.).

Brunoise—a cube-shaped item with dimensions of 1 to 2 mm × 1 to 2 mm × 1 to 2 mm (1/16 in. × 1/16 in. × 1/16 in.).

Allumette—a stick-shaped item, originally pertaining to potatoes only, with dimensions of 3 mm × 3 mm × 5 to 6 cm (1/8 in. × 1/8 in. × 2 to 2-1/2 in.).

Small dice—a cube-shaped item with dimensions of 3 mm × 3 mm × 3 mm (1/8 in. × 1/8 in. × 1/8 in.).

Batonnet—a stick-shaped item with dimensions of 6 mm × 6 mm × 5 to 6 cm (1/4 in. × 1/4 in. × 2 to 2-1/2 in.).

Medium dice—a cube-shaped item with dimensions of 6 mm × 6 mm × 6 mm (1/4 in. × 1/4 in. × 1/4 in.).

Baton—a stick-shaped item with dimensions of 12 mm × 12 mm × 6 cm (1/2 in. × 1/2 in. × 2-1/2 in.).

Large dice—a cube-shaped item with dimensions of 12 mm × 12 mm × 12 mm (1/2 in. × 1/2 in. × 1/2 in.).

Paysanne—a flat, rectangular or triangular-shaped item with dimensions of 12 mm × 12 mm × 3 mm thick (1/2 in. × 1/2 in. × 1/8 in.).

Cutting Julienne, Allumette and Batonnet

Julienne, allumette and batonnet are matchstick-shaped cuts prepared using the same procedure as cutting sticks for dicing.

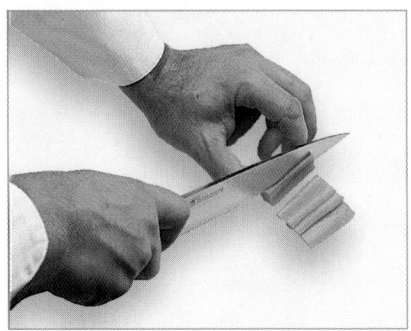 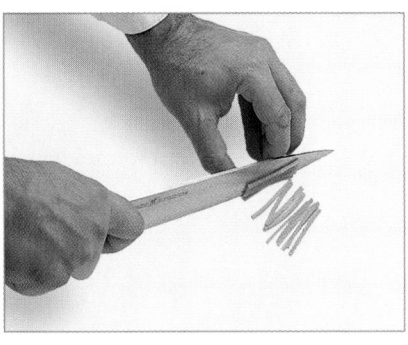

1. Peel the item (if desired) and square off the sides. Trim the item so that the slices cut from it will be the proper length. Cut even slices of the desired thickness, 1 to 2 mm (1/16 in.) for julienne, 3 mm (1/8 in.) for allumette or 6 mm (1/4 in.) for batonnet.

2. Stack the slices and cut them evenly into sticks (also referred to as "planks") that are the same thickness as the slices.

Cut Sizes

Most cuts have a range to their size depending on the use for the item or the desired look. Generally, Canadian standards are more closely aligned with European dimensions. The cook should verify dimensions with the chef. Some terms you may encounter include:

Macedoine—A small to medium dice, depending on use.

Jardinière—Garden vegetables in various shapes.

Matignon—A small to medium diced mirepoix with bacon used for flavouring and garnishing braises.

All cuts must be consistent in size to ensure a *uniform appearance* and, more importantly, *uniform cooking*.

Cutting Brunoise and Small, Medium and Large Dice

Brunoise as well as small, medium and large dice are made by first cutting the item into sticks following the procedure for cutting julienne, allumette or batonnet, then making cuts perpendicular to the length of the sticks to produce small cubes. Making a 1- to 2-mm (1/6-in.) cut perpendicular to the length of a julienne produces a brunoise. Making a 3-mm (1/8-in.) cut perpendicular to the length of a batonnet produces a small dice. A 6-mm (1/4-in.) cut from a 6-mm (1/4-in.) baton produces a medium dice and a 12-mm (1/2-in.) cut from a 12-mm (1/2-in.) baton produces a large dice.

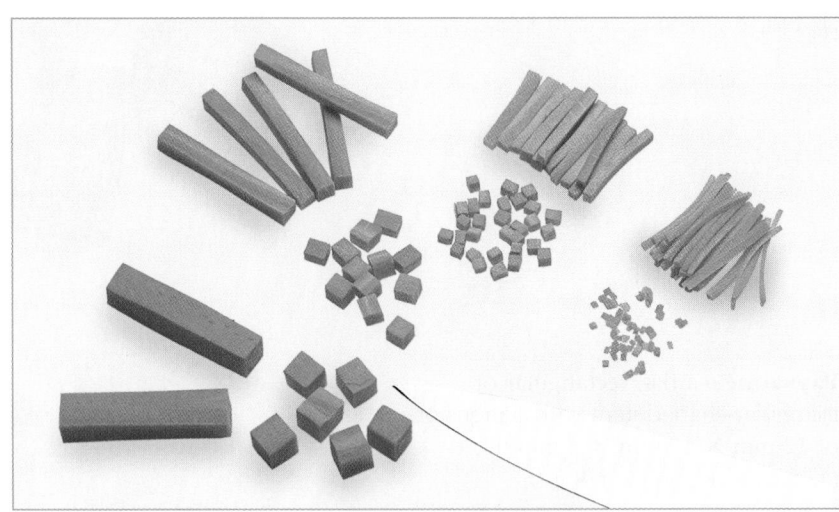

Baton, batonnet, allumette and julienne and the large, medium, small and brunoise dice cut from them.

Cutting Paysanne

Paysanne is a classic vegetable cut for garnishing soups and other dishes. It resembles a 12-mm (1/2-in.) dice that has been cut in thin slices. It is produced by following the procedures for dicing, but in the final step the 12-mm × 12-mm (1/2-in. × 1/2-in.) sticks are cut into slices 3-mm (1/8-in.) thick. It may also be rectangular or triangular shaped, like tiles.

Dicing an Onion

Onions are easily peeled and diced to any size desired using the procedure shown here.

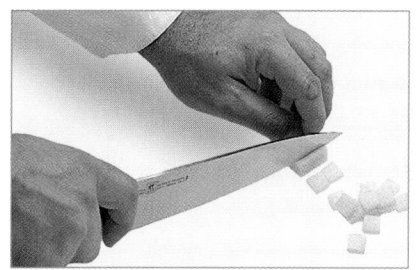

Cutting paysanne from a 12-mm × 12-mm (1/2-in. × 1/2-in.) stick.

1. Use a paring knife to remove the stem end. Trim the root end but leave it nearly intact (this helps prevent the onion from falling apart while being diced). Peel away the outer skin; be careful not to remove and waste too much onion.

2. Cut the onion in half through the stem and root. Place the cut side down on the cutting board.

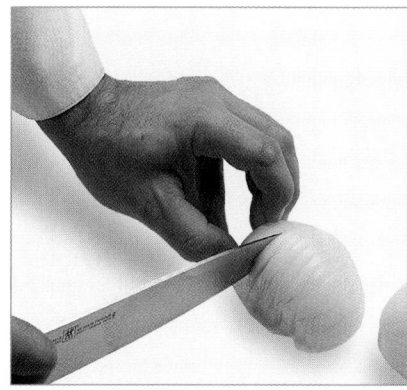

3. Cut parallel slices of the desired thickness vertically through the onion from the root toward the stem end without cutting completely through the root end.

4. Make a single horizontal cut on a small onion or two horizontal cuts on a large onion through the width of the onion, again without cutting through the root end.

5. Turn the onion and cut slices perpendicular to the previous slices to produce diced onion.

Mincing

To **mince** is to cut an item into very small pieces. The terms "finely chopped" and "minced" are often used interchangeably and are most often used when referring to garlic, shallots, herbs and other foods that do not have to be uniform in shape.

Mincing Shallots

The procedure for mincing shallots is shown here.

1. Peel and dice the shallots, following the procedure for peeling and dicing an onion.

2. With a flat hand, hold the knife's tip on the cutting board. Using a rocking motion, mince the shallots with the heel of the knife.

Turning (Shaping)

Turning (**tourner**, "to turn" in French) is a cutting technique that results in a football-shaped finished product. The carrots illustrated here have seven equal sides and blunt ends. The size of the finished product may vary, the most common being 5-cm (2-in.) long. Some products are partially turned or shaped

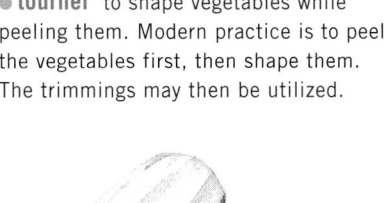

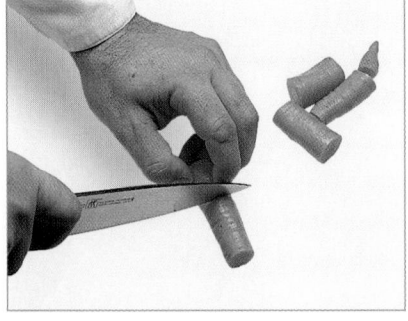

1. Cut the item being "turned" into pieces 5 cm × 2 to 2.5 cm (2 in. × 3/4 to 1 in.). Each piece should have flat ends. (Potatoes, turnips and beets may be cut into as many as 6 or 8 pieces; carrots can simply be cut into 5-cm/2-in. lengths.) Peeling is optional because in most cases the item's entire surface area is trimmed away.

2. Holding the item between the thumb and forefinger, use a turning knife or a paring knife to cut 7 curved sides on the item, creating a flat-ended, football-shaped product.

to achieve a better yield or for variety (crescents, mushrooms). Turned vegetables are generally associated with finer dining establishments. Due to higher labour and food cost, the practice is not prevalent. This is a more complicated procedure than other cuts and takes considerable practice to produce good results.

Parisiennes

A melon ball cutter or Parisienne scoop can be used to cut fruits and vegetables into uniform spheres, or **Parisiennes**. Small balls or spheres of fresh melon can be used in fruit salad, while tiny spheres of carrot, turnip, squash and so on can be used as a side dish or to garnish soup or an entree. Melon ball cutters are available in a range of sizes, the smallest of which has an approximately 9-mm (3/8-in.) diameter and is known as a Parisienne (or Parisian) scoop. Oval-shaped or olivette cutters are also available.

● **Parisienne** a sphere of fruit or vegetable cut with a small melon ball cutter

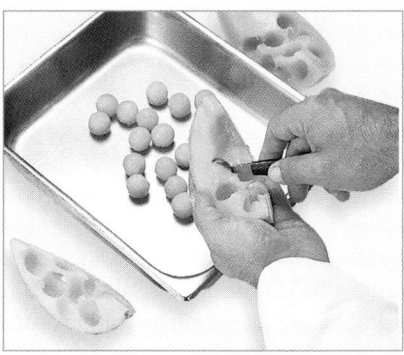

1. Cut each scoop with a pressing and twisting motion.

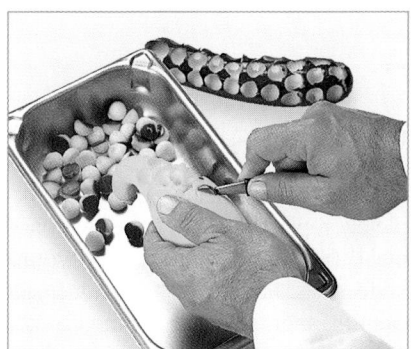

2. Make the cuts as close together as possible in order to minimize trim loss.

Using a Mandoline

The mandoline is a nonmechanical cutting tool. It does the jobs that can be done with a chef's knife, such as producing very thinly sliced apples or large quantities of julienned vegetables, quickly, easily and very accurately. It can also make cuts such as a ridged slice or **gaufrette** that cannot be done with a conventional chef's knife.

When using the mandoline, always use the guard or a steel-mesh glove to protect your hand.

● **gaufrette** ridged slices of potato, usually cut in a waffle pattern

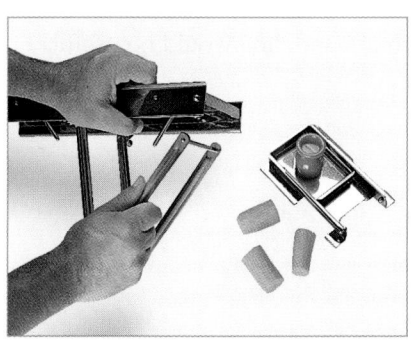

1. To use the mandoline, position the legs and set the blade to the desired shape and thickness.

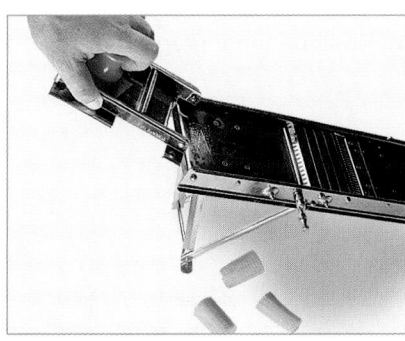

2. Slide the guard into place.

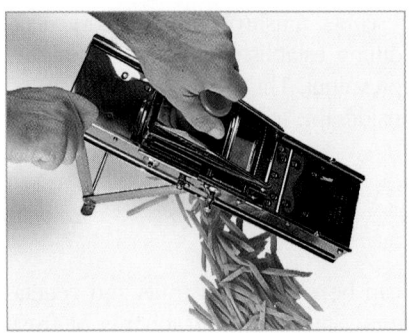

3. To slice, slide the item against the blade with a single, smooth stroke.

4. To cut gaufrette, select the ridged blade and set it to the desired thickness. Make the first slice, turn the item 60 degrees to 90 degrees and make the second slice. Turn the item back to the original position and make another slice, and so on.

Conclusion

Although many slicing and dicing machines are available, none can ever completely replace a skilled chef with a sharp knife. As an apprentice, you should make becoming efficient with your knives a high priority. Possessing good knife skills allows you to produce more attractive products in a safe and efficient manner. You will use the classic cuts and techniques outlined in this chapter throughout your career. You should memorize the procedures and practise them often. And remember, a dull or carelessly handled knife is dangerous.

Questions for Discussion

1. Explain the step-by-step procedures for sharpening a knife using a three-sided whetstone.
2. What is the purpose of a steel?
3. Why is it necessary to cut vegetables into uniform shapes and sizes?
4. Describe the following cutting procedures: slicing, chopping and dicing.
5. Identify the dimensions of the following cuts: julienne, batonnet, brunoise, small dice, medium dice, large dice and paysanne.
6. Describe the procedure for making turned or shaped vegetables.
7. Describe three preparations for which a mandoline would be useful.

After studying this chapter you will be able to:

- understand the basic principles of the physiology of the sense of taste and smell
- recognize a variety of herbs, spices, oils, vinegars, and other flavourings
- understand how to use flavouring ingredients to create, enhance or alter the natural flavours of a dish

These interactive online tools will help you master the skills in this chapter:

- Videos
- Chapter Quizzes
- Activities

● **flavour** an identifiable or distinctive quality of a food, drink or other substance perceived with the combined senses of taste, touch and smell

● **taste** the sensations, as interpreted by the brain, of what we detect when food, drink or other substances come in contact with our taste buds

● **mouth-feel** the sensation created in the mouth by a combination of a food's taste, smell, texture and temperature

● **aroma** the sensations, as interpreted by the brain, of what we detect when a substance comes in contact with sense receptors in the nose

● **palate** (1) the complex of smell, taste and touch receptors that contribute to a person's ability to recognize and appreciate flavours; (2) the range of an individual's recognition and appreciation of flavours

It is the chef's role to consistently present well-flavoured foods—to excite the consumer's brain and palate. This can be accomplished by an act as simple as sprinkling a bit of salt over a ripe watermelon to enhance the melon's natural sweetness or as complicated as using a long-simmering stock made from wild mushrooms to enrich a sauce flavoured with herbs and wine. In either case, the chef must understand how to flavour foods and be able to recognize flavouring ingredients and know how to use them. This chapter looks at the sense of taste and smell and the flavouring ingredients used in the professional kitchen to enhance foods. Flavourings—the herbs, spices, salt, oils, vinegars and condiments typically used to create, enhance or alter the natural flavours of a dish—are featured. Flavourings used primarily for baked goods and desserts are discussed in Chapter 27, Principles of the Bakeshop.

FLAVOURS

From the simplest grunt of pleasure upon biting into a chunk of meat fresh from the fire to the most sophisticated discourse on the fruity top notes of a full-bodied Cabernet Sauvignon, people have long attempted to describe the flavours of food. This is done by describing physical perceptions ("it tastes tart or sugary" or "it feels greasy") or the recognition of the flavour ("I can sense the rosemary" or "there is a hint of strawberries"). In either case, the terms "flavour" and "taste" are often confused. Although often used interchangeably, they are not synonymous.

A **flavour** is a combination of the tastes, aromas and other sensations caused by the presence of a foreign substance in the mouth. **Tastes** are the sensations we detect when a substance comes in contact with the taste buds on the tongue (sweet, sour, salt, bitter and umami). Some substances irritate other nerves on the tongue or embedded in the fleshy areas of the mouth. These nerves respond to sensations of pain, heat or cold, or sensations our brain interprets as spiciness, pungency or astringency. **Mouth-feel** refers to the sensation created in the mouth by a combination of a food's taste, smell, texture and temperature. **Aromas** are the odours that enter the nose or float up through the back of the mouth to activate smell receptors in the nose. Whenever a particular taste, sensation and/or aroma is detected, a set of neurons in the brain is excited and, with experience, we learn to recognize these patterns as the flavour of bananas, chocolate, grilled lamb or sour milk. Each person has a unique ability to recognize and appreciate thousands of these patterns. This compendium of flavours and the ability to recognize them is sometimes referred to as the **palate**.

Tastes: Sweet, Sour, Salty, Bitter and Now Umami

Over the centuries, various cultures have developed complex philosophies based, in part, on the basic tastes they found in the foods they ate. For example, as early as 1000 B.C.E., the Chinese were describing the five-taste scheme that they still adhere to today. For them, each of the basic tastes—sweet, sour, salty, bitter and pungent/hot/spicy—is associated with a vital organ of the body, a certain season, a specific element of nature or an astrological sign. Maintaining the proper balance of tastes in a dish or during a meal assists in the maintenance of good health and good fortune.

About the same time, in what is now India, the practice of ayurvedic medicine was developing. Indians recognized six tastes (and still do): sweet, sour, salty, spicy/pungent, bitter and astringent. Based on the tastes of various herbs and spices, practitioners of ayurvedic medicine associate them with specific vital organs or bodily systems. Indian cooks attempt to create dishes with a balance of all six tastes, in part to encourage good health.

A continent away and several hundred years later, the Greek philosopher Aristotle identified seven tastes in his epic work, *De Anima* (*On the Soul*, ca. 350 B.C.E.). He arranged the various tastes on a sort of continuum with the two primary and contrasting tastes, sweet and bitter, at either end. He placed a secondary taste next to each primary taste: succulent to the right of sweet and salty to the left of bitter. Between these secondary tastes he placed—from left to right—pungent, harsh and astringent. Each taste gave way to the next, creating, along with the other senses, the perception of flavours.

As the understanding of the human body evolved, the definition of taste came to be based more on science than on a balancing of elements. Today, taste is defined as the sensations detected when substances come in contact with the taste buds on the tongue, a process described more fully in the box on page 114. For many years, Western cultures have identified four tastes:

- *Sweet*—For most people, sweetness is the most pleasurable and most often sought-after taste, although, ironically, the fewer sweet-tasting foods we consume, the more enhanced our ability to recognize sweetness becomes. A food's sweetness comes from the naturally occurring sugars it contains (for example, sucrose and fructose) or sweeteners added to it. This sweetness can sometimes be enhanced by adding a small amount of a sour, bitter or salty taste. Adding too much sourness, bitterness or saltiness, however, will lessen our perception of the food's sweetness.

- *Sour*—Considered the opposite of sweet, a sour taste is found in acidic foods and, like sweetness, can vary greatly in intensity. Many foods with a dominant sour taste, such as red currants or sour cream, will also contain a secondary or slight sweetness. Often a sour taste can be improved by adding a little sweetness or negated by adding a large amount of a sweet ingredient.

- *Salty*—With the notable exception of oysters and other shellfish and seaweed, the presence of a salty taste in a food is the result of the cook's decision to add the mineral sodium chloride, known as salt, or to use a previously salted ingredient such as salt-cured fish or soy sauce. Salt helps finish a dish, heightening or enhancing its other flavours. Dishes that lack salt often taste flat. Like the taste of sweetness, the less salt consumed on a regular basis, the more saltiness we can detect in foods.

- *Bitter*—Although the bitterness associated with tasting alkaloids and other organic substances may occasionally be appreciated, such as when tasting chocolate or coffee, a bitter-flavoured ingredient unbalanced by something sour or salty is generally disliked and, as a survival mechanism, is believed to serve as a warning of inedibility or unhealthfulness.

In the past several years, many Western researchers have begun to recognize a fifth taste, akin to the **savoury** taste long recognized as the fifth taste in Japanese cuisine. Called *umami* (from the Japanese word *umai*, meaning "delicious"), this fifth taste does not have a simple English translation. Rather, for some people it refers to a food's savoury characteristic; for others to the richness or fullness of a dish's overall taste, and still others, the meatiness or meaty taste of a dish.

Taste buds sense umami in the presence of several substances, including the naturally occurring amino acid glutamate and its commercially produced counterpart known as monosodium glutamate (MSG). Cheeses, meats, rich stocks,

● **savoury** a food that is not sweet

How We Experience Taste and Smell

The smallest functional unit of taste is the taste bud. These specialized sensory organs can be found on the tongue within three different kinds of *papillae* (see Figure 7.1), as well as the back of the throat and the roof of the mouth. Each taste bud contains several *taste receptor cells,* and *taste compounds* interact with the tops of these specialized cells, which then transmit taste information through a nerve to the brain. The process of tasting begins when a substance is placed in the mouth and taste compounds begin to dissolve in saliva. Mastication, or chewing, further breaks down the substance and increases the concentration of taste compounds dissolved in the saliva. Once dissolved in saliva, the taste compounds have the potential to stimulate taste receptors and ultimately elicit taste sensations. Because compounds must dissolve in the saliva in order to reach the taste receptors, taste compounds must be water-soluble.

The process of smelling begins when odour compounds reach the olfactory neurons, the specialized sensing organs

of smell. Olfactory neurons are located at the top of the nasal cavity and are clustered together in the *olfactory bulb* (see Figure 7.2). A separate olfactory bulb rests at the bottom of each hemisphere of the brain and at the top of each nasal cavity. Odour compounds can reach these receptors through two different pathways: orthonasally via the external nares (or *nostrils*) or retronasally via the internal nares. When we sniff or experience odours that are external to our bodies, we are smelling orthonasally. Once we place a substance in our mouths, the aromas we are experiencing are being delivered through the *retronasal path*. Regardless of route, in order for odour compounds to reach the olfactory receptors they must be able to volatilize, or dissolve in air. Since air is hydrophobic, this means most odour compounds do not dissolve well in water, dissolving better in oils.

A pervasive myth (based upon misinterpretation of an article written in German in the 1800s) is that you experience certain taste qualities on only certain

areas of the tongue (sweet on the tip, bitter in the back, salt on the front sides and sour on the back sides). In fact, you can taste all taste compounds everywhere on your tongue, and it is easy to prove this to yourself by placing various items representative of sweet, sour, salty, bitter and even umami on the tip of your tongue. You will be able to immediately perceive any taste at the tongue tip (or anywhere else you have taste buds) and will not need to wait for bitter compounds to diffuse to the back, sour to the back sides or salt to the front sides.

Jeannine Delwiche, Ph.D., is the head of the Ohio State University Sensory Science Group. She teaches courses on sensory science (which covers the proper way to conduct taste tests) and on wine and beer. Her research focuses on taste, smell and flavour perception, as well as on some of the underlying principles that influence sensory evaluation methodologies. She has also conducted a variety of studies that examine factors that affect product differences and consumer assessments.

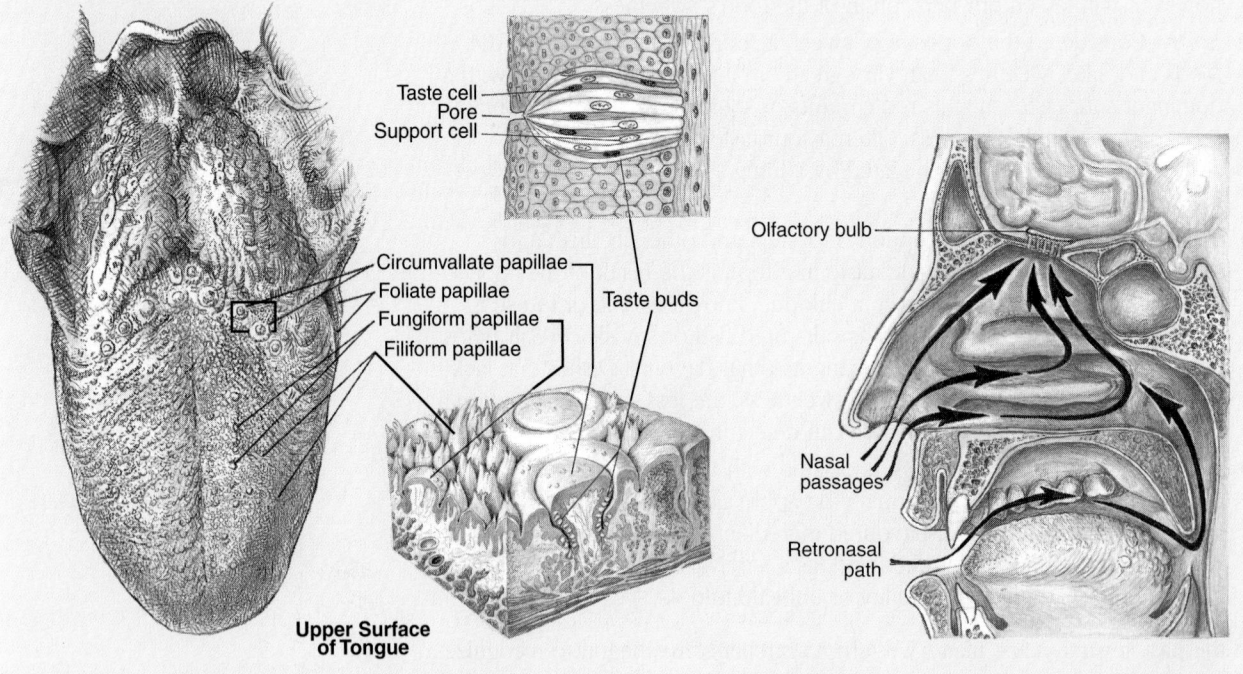

Taste cell
Pore
Support cell

Circumvallate papillae
Foliate papillae
Fungiform papillae
Filiform papillae

Taste buds

Upper Surface of Tongue

Olfactory bulb

Nasal passages

Retronasal path

FIGURE 7.1   The human tongue and taste buds.

FIGURE 7.2   The human olfactory system.

soy sauce, shellfish, fatty fish, mushrooms, tomatoes and wine are all high in glutamate and produce the taste sensation of umami. Aged or fermented foods also provide umami.

Often food professionals and others refer to tastes in addition to sweet, sour, salty, bitter and umami. Typically, they describe something as pungent, hot, spicy or piquant or something that is astringent, sharp or dry. None of these terms, however, fit the definition of a taste, as none are detected solely by taste buds. Rather, these sensations are detected by nerve endings embedded in the fleshy part of the mouth. These nerves, when "irritated" by the presence of compounds such as piperine (the active ingredient in black peppercorns) or capsaicin (the active ingredient in chiles), register a burning sensation that the brain translates as the hot and spicy "taste" of Szechuan or Mexican cuisines, for example.

Factors Affecting Perception of Flavours

Obviously, the most important factors affecting the flavour of a dish are the quantity, quality and concentration of the flavouring ingredients. (With practice, a chef gains a feel for the proper proportions.) Other factors that affect one's perception of flavours include the following:

- *Temperature*—Foods at warm temperatures offer the strongest tastes. Heating foods releases volatile flavour compounds, which intensifies one's perceptions of odours. This is why fine cheese is served at room temperature to improve its eating quality and flavour. Foods tend to lose their sour or sweet tastes both the colder and the hotter they become. Saltiness, however, is perceived differently at extreme cold temperatures; the same quantity of salt in a solution is perceived more strongly when very cold than when merely cool or warm. Therefore, it is best to adjust a dish's final flavours at its serving temperature. That is, *season hot foods when they are hot and cold foods when they are cold.*

- *Consistency*—A food's consistency affects its flavour. Two items with the same amount of taste and smell compounds that differ in texture will differ in their perceived intensity and onset time; the thicker item will take longer to reach its peak intensity and will have a less intense flavour. For example, two batches of sweetened heavy cream made from the same ingredients in the same proportions can taste different if one is whipped and the other is unwhipped; the whipped cream has more volume and therefore a milder flavour.

- *Presence of contrasting tastes*—Sweet and sour are considered opposites, and often the addition of one to a food dominated by the other will enhance the food's overall flavour. For example, adding a little sugar to vinaigrette reduces the dressing's sourness, or adding a squeeze of lemon to a broiled lobster reduces the shellfish's sweetness. But add too much, and the dominant taste will be negated. Likewise, adding something sweet, sour or salty to a dish with a predominantly bitter flavour will cut the bitterness.

- *Presence of fats*—Many of the chemical compounds that create tastes and aromas are dissolved in the fats naturally occurring in foods or added to foods during cooking. As these compounds are slowly released by evaporation or saliva, they provide a sustained taste sensation. If, however, there is too little fat, the flavour compounds may not be released efficiently, resulting in a dish with little sustained flavour. Too much fat poses another problem; it can coat the tongue and interfere with the ability of taste receptors to perceive flavour compounds.

- *Colour*—A food's colour affects how the consumer will perceive the food's flavour before it is even tasted. When foods or beverages lack their customary colour, they are less readily identified correctly than when appropriately coloured. As colour level changes to match normal expectations, our

Flavour Principles for Ethnic Cuisines

In *Ethnic Cuisine: The Flavour Principle Cookbook*, Elisabeth Rozin writes: "Every culture tends to combine a small number of flavouring ingredients so frequently and so consistently that they become definitive of that particular cuisine" (p. xiv). She calls these defining flavours "flavour principles" and notes that they are "designed to abstract what is absolutely fundamental about a cuisine and thus, to serve as a guide in cooking and developing new recipes" (p. xvii). She identifies the following "flavour principles":

Central Asia: cinnamon, fruit and nuts

China: generally—soy sauce, rice wine and ginger root

> Northern China (Mandarin/Peking)—miso and/or garlic and/or sesame

> Western China (Szechuan)—sweet, sour and hot

> Southern China (Canton)—black beans, garlic

Eastern Europe (Jewish): onion and chicken fat

Eastern and Northern Europe: sour cream and dill or paprika or allspice or caraway

France: generally—olive oil, garlic and basil *or* wine and herb *or* butter and/or sour cream and/or cheese plus wine and/or stock

> Southern France—olive oil, garlic, parsley and/or anchovy plus tomato as a variation

> Provence—olive oil, thyme, rosemary, marjoram, sage plus tomato as a variation

> Normandy—apple, cider, Calvados

Greece: tomato, cinnamon or olive oil, lemon, oregano

India: Northern—cumin, ginger, garlic

> Southern—mustard seed, coconut, tamarind, chile

Italy: generally—olive oil, garlic, basil

> Northern Italy—wine vinegar, garlic

> Southern Italy—olive oil, garlic, parsley and/or anchovy plus tomato as a variation

Japan: soy sauce, sake, sugar

Mexico: generally—tomato and chile *or* lime and chile

> Yucatan—sour orange, garlic, achiote

North Africa: cumin, coriander, cinnamon, ginger, onion and/or tomato and/or fruit

Spain: olive oil, garlic, nut oil, onion, pepper, tomato

Thailand: fish sauce, curry, chile

West Africa: tomato, peanut, chile

Supertasters, Medium Tasters and Nontasters

Recent research into the physiology of taste has shown that some people detect a greater degree of a taste in foods than others. Called *supertasters* by Professor Linda Bartoshuk at Yale University, these people may have more taste buds than average, possibly twice as many as *nontasters* or *medium tasters*. In addition to detecting strongly bitter flavours where many people do not (for example, in coffee, broccoli, Brussels sprouts, grapefruit juice and green tea), supertasters also tend to perceive artificial sweeteners as sweeter than do the rest of the population and with a bitter aftertaste that most people miss. Similarly, supertasters find the spicy heat generated by capsaicin to be more pronounced, sometimes unbearably so, than does the average person.

A person's responsiveness to tastes appears to influence food choices. Supertasters tend to avoid strong-tasting foods such as coffee, rich or very sweet desserts, greasy or spicy meats, green leafy vegetables and so on. They also tend not to crave fats or sugars. Cooks who are nontasters may not realize when a food would be too sweet or too bitter to medium- or super-tasters. And supertaster cooks may unconsciously avoid using foods that would be perfectly delicious to everyone else. It is easy to determine one's taste level with special chemically treated test papers.

perception of taste and flavour intensity increases. A miscue created by the perceived flavour (the flavour associated with the colour) can have an adverse impact on the consumer's appreciation of the actual flavour. For example, if the predominant flavour of a dessert is lemon, the dessert or some component of the dessert should be yellow; a green colour will trigger an expectation of lime and the possible disappointment of the consumer. Similarly, the dark ruby-red flesh of a blood orange looks different from the bright orange flesh of a Valencia orange. This tonal difference can create the expectation of a different, non-orangey flavour, even though the blood orange's flavour is similar to that of other sweet orange varieties. Likewise, a sliced apple that has turned brown may suggest an off-flavour, although there is none.

Compromises to the Perception of Taste

The sense of taste can be challenged by factors both within and beyond one's control. Age and general health can diminish one's perception of flavour, as can fatigue and stress. Chefs need to be aware of the age and health of their clientele, adjusting the seasoning of foods served according to their needs. Here are some factors, described by Jeannine Delwiche, Ph.D., that can affect one's taste perceptions.

- *Age.* "The bad news is that taste and smell sensitivity does decline as we age. The good news is that it declines at a slower rate than our vision and hearing. The sense of smell tends to decline earlier than the sense of taste. There is a great deal of variance across individuals, with some showing declines earlier than others."

- *Health.* "An acute condition, such as a cold, can result in a temporary loss of smell. The presence of mucus can prevent airflow, preventing the odour compounds from reaching the olfactory receptors. In contrast, the sense of taste would remain largely unaffected. Medications can also alter the perception of taste and smell. Some medications suppress the perceptions of saltiness, while others result in chronic perception of bitterness. Still other medications alter salivary flow, making it difficult to swallow dry foods. A further complication is the underlying conditions for taking medication. If an individual is taking high blood pressure medications, not only may the medication have a direct impact on perceived taste, but the same individual is likely to be on a sodium-restricted diet."

- *Smoking.* "Anecdotal reports from those who quit smoking strongly indicate that smoking diminishes odour sensitivity. This is further supported by evidence indicating that people who smoke generally are less sensitive to odours than those who do not. In contrast, evidence indicates that if one waits two hours after smoking, the sense of taste is unaltered. Immediately after smoking, however, taste sensitivity is lowered."

Describing Aromas and Flavours in Food

Food scientists and professional tasters make their living describing the smell and taste of foods. Many have attempted to standardize the language used to describe positive and negative aromas and flavours in foods such as beer, cheese, chocolate, coffee and fish. Frequently they employ flavour wheels or other charts to identify types of flavours and tastes found in foods.

One useful list employed by chemists to describe 16 broad categories of tastes and smells that correspond to the major chemicals found in aromas and tastes is shown in Table 7.1. Such a list is helpful when trying to analyze and describe the flavours in a dish.

TABLE 7.1	Common Flavour Descriptions
Type of Aroma or Flavour	**Foods with Such Characteristics**
Green, grassy	Green bell peppers, raw apple skins
Fruity, esterlike	Bananas, apples
Citrus, terpenic	Lemons, limes
Minty, camphoraceous	Fresh mint, rosemary
Floral, sweet	Roses, violets, honey
Spicy, herbaceous	Allspice, cinnamon, nutmeg
Woody, smoky	Smoked foods
Roasty, burnt	Coffee, toasted bread
Caramel, nutty	Burnt sugar, molasses
Bouillon, high vegetable protein	Meat stock
Meaty, animalic	Roasted meat
Fatty, rancid	Fishy smell
Sulphurous, alliaceous	Onions, garlic, rotten egg
Mushroom, earthy	Cooked mushrooms, damp soil, yeasty bread
Celery, soupy	Celery, parsnip
Dairy, buttery	Cheese

Describing Food Using Flavour Profiles

A food's flavour profile describes its flavour from the moment the consumer gets the first whiff of its aroma until he or she swallows that last morsel. It is a convenient way to articulate and evaluate a dish's sensory characteristics as well as identify contrasting or complementing items that could be served with it.

A food's flavour profile consists of one or more of the following elements:

- *Top notes or high notes*—the sharp, first flavours or aromas that come from citrus, herbs, spices and many condiments. These top notes provide instant impact and dissipate quickly.
- *Middle notes*—the second wave of flavours and aromas. More subtle and more lingering than top notes, middle notes come from dairy products, poultry, some vegetables, fish and some meats.
- *Low notes or bass notes*—the most dominant, lingering flavours. These flavours consist of the basic tastes (especially sweetness, sourness, saltiness and umami) and come from foods such as anchovies, beans, chocolate, dried mushrooms, fish sauce, tomatoes, most meats (especially beef and game) and garlic. Or they can be created by smoking or caramelizing the food's sugars during grilling, broiling and other dry heat cooking processes.
- *Aftertaste or finish*—the final flavour that remains in the mouth after swallowing; for example, the lingering bitterness of coffee or chocolate or the pungency of black pepper or a strong mustard.
- *Roundness*—the unity of the dish's various flavours achieved through the judicious use of butter, cream, coconut milk, reduced stocks, salt, sugar and the like; these ingredients cause the other flavourings to linger without necessarily adding their own dominant taste or flavour.
- *Depth of flavour*—whether the dish has a broad range of flavour notes.

About Flavours

Flavour is to *food* what hue is to colour. It is what timbre is to music. (*Flavour* is adjective; *food* is noun.) Each ingredient has its own particular character, which is altered by every other ingredient it encounters. A secret ingredient is one that mysteriously improves the flavour of a dish without calling attention to itself. It is either undetectable or extremely subtle, but its presence is crucial because the dish would not be nearly as good without it.

Primary flavours are those that are obvious, such as the flavours of chicken and tarragon in a chicken tarragon, shrimp and garlic in a shrimp scampi, or beef and red wine in a beef à la Bourguignonne. Secret ingredients belong to the realm of secondary flavours. However obvious it is that you need tarragon to prepare a chicken tarragon, you would not achieve the most interesting result using only tarragon. Tarragon, in this case, needs secondary ingredients—a hint of celery seed and anise—to make it taste more like quintessential tarragon and at the same time more than tarragon. In this way, primary flavours often depend on secret ingredients to make them more interesting and complex. Using only one herb or spice to achieve a certain taste usually results in a lackluster dish—each mouthful tastes the same. Whether they function in a primary or secondary way, flavours combine in only three different ways: They marry, oppose, or juxtapose.

When flavours marry, they combine to form one taste. Some secondary flavours marry with primary ones to create a new flavour greater than the sum of its parts, and often two flavours can do the job better than one. It may sound like an eccentric combination, but vanilla marries with the flavour of lobster, making it taste more like the essence of lobster than lobster does on its own. And when ginger and molasses marry, they create a flavour superior to either alone.

Opposite flavours can highlight or cancel each other; they can cut or balance each other. Sweet/sour, sweet/salty, sweet/hot, salty/sour, and salty/tart are all opposites. Salt and sugar are so opposed, in fact, that when used in equal amounts they cancel each other entirely. Sweet relish helps cancel the salty flavour of hot dogs. Chinese sauces usually contain some sugar to help balance the saltiness of soy sauce.

Knowing how to combine many flavours and aromas to achieve a simple and pure result (and knowing when not to combine flavours) will make you a better, more confident cook. Good cooks over the centuries have known these things intuitively—but they've had neither the huge variety of ingredients nor the knowledge of world cuisines that we have today.

—CHEF MICHAEL ROBERTS
is the author of *Secret Ingredients*

● **flavouring** an item that adds a new taste to a food and alters its natural flavours; flavourings include herbs, spices, vinegars and condiments. The terms "seasoning" and "flavouring" are often used interchangeably

● **herb** any of a large group of aromatic plants whose leaves, stems or flowers are used as a flavouring; used either dried or fresh

● **aromatic** a food added to enhance the natural aromas of another food; aromatics include most flavourings, such as herbs and spices, as well as some vegetables

● **spice** any of a large group of aromatic plants whose bark, roots, seeds, buds or berries are used as a flavouring; usually used in dried form, either whole or ground

● **condiment** traditionally, any item added to a dish for flavour, including herbs, spices and vinegars; now also refers to cooked or prepared flavourings such as prepared mustards, relishes, bottled sauces and pickles

These expressions can be applied to any dish to describe its sensory characteristics. For example, Chicken Sauté with Tomato, Garlic and Basil (page 366) has a flavour profile with a top note of basil. Its middle notes are contributed by the chicken, and the low notes from the tomato, shallots and garlic. There is an aftertaste of garlic and lemon. The sauce adds roundness to the chicken, thus creating a dish with a fine depth of flavour. An experienced chef is able to taste and evaluate a version of this dish, adjusting flavourings, ingredients and cooking technique as needed to maintain the balance of flavours in the original recipe.

FLAVOURINGS: HERBS AND SPICES

Herbs and spices are the kitchen staples used as **flavourings**. **Herbs** refer to the large group of **aromatic** plants whose leaves, stems or flowers are used to add flavours to other foods. Most herbs are available fresh or dried. Because drying alters their flavours and aromas, fresh herbs are generally preferred and should be used if possible. **Spices** are strongly flavoured or aromatic portions of plants used as flavourings, **condiments** or aromatics. Spices are the bark, roots, seeds, buds or berries of plants, most of which grow naturally only in tropical climates. Spices are almost always used in their dried form, rarely fresh, and can usually be purchased whole or ground. Some plants—dill, for example—can be used as both a herb (its leaves) and a spice (its seeds).

Herbs

Basil (Fr. *basilique*) is considered one of the great culinary herbs. It is available in a variety of "flavours"—cinnamon, garlic, lemon, even chocolate—but the most common is sweet basil. **Sweet basil** has light green, tender leaves and small white flowers. Its

Basil

flavour is strong, warm and slightly peppery, with a hint of cloves. Basil is used in Asian and Mediterranean cuisines and has a special affinity for garlic and tomatoes. When purchasing fresh basil, look for bright green leaves; avoid flower buds and wilted or rust-coloured leaves. Dried sweet basil is readily available but has a decidedly weaker flavour.

Opal basil is named for its vivid purple colour. It has a tougher, crinkled leaf and a medium-strong flavour. Opal basil may be substituted for sweet basil in cooking and its appearance makes it a distinctive garnish.

Opal Basil

Bay (Fr. *laurier*), also known as sweet laurel, is a small tree from Asia that produces tough, glossy leaves with a sweet balsamic aroma and peppery flavour. Bay symbolized wisdom and glory in ancient Rome; the leaves were used to form crowns or "laurels" worn by emperors and victorious athletes. In cooking, dried bay leaves are often preferred over the more bitter fresh leaves. Essential in French cuisine, bay leaves are part of the traditional bouquet garni and court bouillon. Whole dried leaves are usually added to a dish at the start of cooking, then removed when sufficient flavour has been extracted.

Bay Leaves

Chervil (Fr. *cerfeuil*), also known as sweet cicely, is native to Russia and the Middle East. Its lacy, fernlike leaves are similar to parsley and can be used as a garnish. Chervil's flavour is delicate, similar to parsley but with the distinctive aroma of anise. It should not be heated for long periods. Chervil is commonly used in French cuisine and is one of the traditional *fines herbes*.

Chervil

Chives (Fr. *ciboulette*) are perhaps the most delicate and sophisticated members of the onion family. Their hollow, thin grass-green stems grow in clumps and produce round, pale purple flowers, which are used as a garnish. Chives may be purchased dried, quick-frozen or fresh. They have a mild onion flavour and bright green colour. Chives complement eggs, poultry, potatoes, fish and shellfish. They should not be cooked for long periods or at high temperatures. Chives make an excellent garnish when snipped with scissors or carefully chopped and sprinkled over finished soups or sauces.

Chives

Garlic chives, also known as Chinese chives, actually belong to another plant species. They have flat, solid (not hollow) stems and a mild garlic flavour. They may be used in place of regular chives if their garlic flavour is desired.

Garlic Chives

Cilantro (Fr. *coriandre*) is the green leafy portion of the plant that yields seeds known as coriander. The flavours of the two portions of this plant are very different and cannot be substituted for each other.

Curry leaves (Hindi *karipatta*; *kitha neem*; Fr. *feuille de cari*) are the distinctively flavoured leaves of a small tree that grows wild in the Himalayan foothills, southern India and Sri Lanka. They look like small shiny bay leaves and have a strong currylike fragrance and a citrus-curry flavour. Often added to a preparation whole, then removed

Cilantro

Curry Leaves

before serving, they can also be minced or finely chopped for marinades and sauces. Choose fresh bright green leaves, if possible, or frozen leaves; dried leaves have virtually no flavour. Although used in making southern Indian and Thai dishes, curry leaves (also known as neem leaves) must not be confused with curry powder, which is discussed later.

Dill

Dill (Fr. *aneth*), a member of the parsley family, has tiny, aromatic, yellow flowers and feathery, delicate blue-green leaves. The leaves taste like parsley, but sharper, with a touch of anise. Dill seeds are flat, oval and brown, with a bitter flavour similar to caraway. Both the seeds and the leaves of the dill plant are used in cooking. Dill is commonly used in Scandinavian and Central European cuisines, particularly with fish and potatoes. Both leaves and seeds are used in pickling and sour dishes. Dill leaves are available fresh or dried but lose their aroma and flavour during cooking, so add them only after the dish is removed from the heat. Dill seeds are available whole or ground and are used in fish dishes, pickles and breads.

Epazote, also known as wormseed or stinkweed, grows wild throughout the Americas. It has a strong aroma similar to kerosene and a wild flavour. Fresh epazote is used in salads and as a flavouring in Mexican and Southwestern cuisines. It is often cooked with beans to reduce their gaseousness. Dried epazote is brewed to make a beverage.

Lavender is an evergreen with thin leaves and tall stems bearing spikes of tiny purple flowers. Although lavender is known primarily for its aroma, which is widely used in perfumes, soaps and cosmetics, the flowers are also used as a flavouring, particularly in Middle Eastern and Provençale cuisines. These flowers have a sweet, lemony flavour and can be crystallized and used as a garnish. Lavender is also used in jams and preserves and to flavour teas and tisanes.

Epazote

Lavender

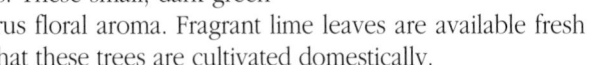

Lemon Grass

Lemon grass, also known as citronella grass, is a tropical grass with the strong aroma and taste of lemon. It is similar to scallions in appearance but with a woody texture. Only the lower base and white leaf stalks are used. Available fresh or quick-frozen, lemon grass is widely used in Indonesian and Southeast Asian cuisines.

Marjoram

Lime leaves from a species of thorny lime trees (*citrus hystrix*) are used much like bay leaves to flavour soups and stews in Thai and other Asian cuisines. These small, dark green leaves have a bright citrus floral aroma. Fragrant lime leaves are available fresh in North America now that these trees are cultivated domestically.

Fragrant Lime Leaves

Lovage (Fr. *celeri bâtard*, "false celery") has tall stalks and large, dark green celery-like leaves. The leaves, stalks and seeds have a strong celery flavour.

Marjoram (Fr. *marjolaine*), also known as sweet marjoram, is a flowering herb native to the Mediterranean and used since ancient times. Its flavour is similar to thyme but sweeter; it also has a stronger aroma. Marjoram is now used in many European cuisines. Although it is available fresh, marjoram is one of the few herbs whose flavour increases when dried. Wild marjoram is more commonly known as oregano.

Mint (Fr. *menthe*), a large family of herbs, includes many species and flavours (even chocolate). **Spearmint** is the most common garden and commercial variety. It has soft, bright green leaves and a tart aroma and flavour.

Spearmint

Mint does not blend well with other herbs, so its use is confined to specific dishes, usually fruits or fatty meats such as lamb. Mint has an affinity for chocolate. It can also be brewed into a beverage or used as a garnish. **Peppermint** has thin, stiff, pointed leaves and a sharper menthol flavour and aroma. Fresh peppermint is used less often in cooking or as a garnish than spearmint, but peppermint oil is a common flavouring in sweets and candies.

Peppermint

Oregano (Fr. *origan*), also known as wild marjoram, is a pungent, peppery herb used in Mediterranean cuisines, particularly Greek and Italian, as well as in Mexican cuisine. It is a classic complement to tomatoes. Oregano's thin, woody stalks bear clumps of tiny, dark green leaves, which are available dried and crushed.

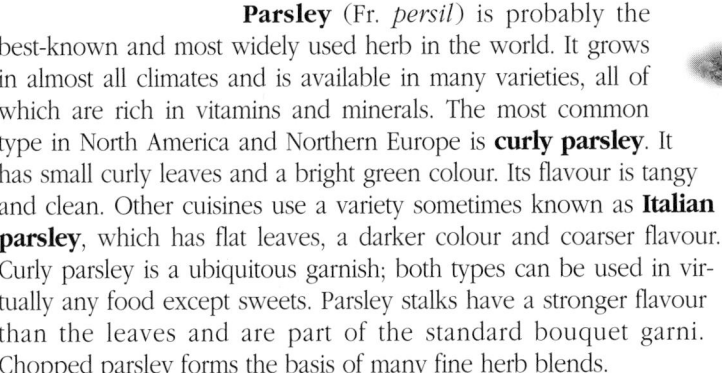
Oregano

Parsley (Fr. *persil*) is probably the best-known and most widely used herb in the world. It grows in almost all climates and is available in many varieties, all of which are rich in vitamins and minerals. The most common type in North America and Northern Europe is **curly parsley**. It has small curly leaves and a bright green colour. Its flavour is tangy and clean. Other cuisines use a variety sometimes known as **Italian parsley**, which has flat leaves, a darker colour and coarser flavour. Curly parsley is a ubiquitous garnish; both types can be used in virtually any food except sweets. Parsley stalks have a stronger flavour than the leaves and are part of the standard bouquet garni. Chopped parsley forms the basis of many fine herb blends.

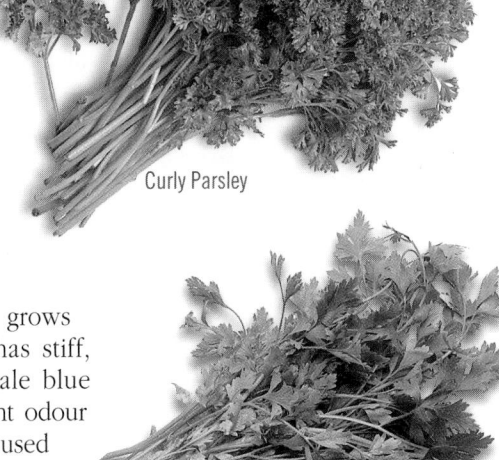
Curly Parsley

Rosemary (Fr. *romarin*) is an evergreen bush that grows wild in warm, dry climates worldwide. It has stiff, needlelike leaves; some varieties bear pale blue flowers. It is highly aromatic, with a slight odour of camphor or pine. Rosemary is best used fresh. When dried, it loses flavour and its leaves become very hard and unpleasant to chew. Whole rosemary stems may be added to a dish such as a stew and then removed when enough flavour has been imparted. They may also be added to a bouquet garni. Rosemary has a great affinity for roasted and grilled meats, especially lamb.

Rosemary

Italian Parsley

Sage (Fr. *sauge*) was used as a medicine for centuries before it entered the kitchen as a culinary herb. Culinary sage has narrow, fuzzy, grey-green leaves and blue flowers. Its flavour is strong and balsamic, with notes of camphor. Sage is used in poultry dishes, with fatty meats or brewed as a beverage. Sage's strong flavour does not blend well with other herbs. It dries well and is available in whole or chopped leaves or rubbed (coarsely ground).

Sage

Savory

Savory (Fr. *sariette*), also known as summer savory, has been used since ancient times. Its leaves are small and narrow and it has a sharp, bitter flavour, vaguely like thyme. It dries well and is used in bean dishes, sausages and herb mixtures.

Tarragon (Fr. *estragon*), another of the great culinary herbs, is native to Siberia. It is a bushy plant with long, narrow, dark green leaves and tiny grey flowers. Tarragon goes well with fish and tomatoes and is essential in many French dishes such as béarnaise sauce and fine herb blends. Its flavour is

Tarragon

Thyme

Aleppo Pepper

Allspice

Anise
Seeds

Star Anise

Annatto
Seeds

Capers

strong and diffuses quickly through foods. It is available dried, but drying may cause haylike flavours to develop.

Thyme (Fr. *thym*) has been popular since 3500 B.C.E., when Egyptians used it as a medicine and for embalming. Thyme is a small, bushy plant with woody stems, tiny green-grey leaves and purple flowers. Its flavour is strong but refined, with notes of sage. Thyme dries well and complements virtually all types of meat, poultry, fish, shellfish and vegetables. It is often included in a bouquet garni or added to stocks.

Spices

Aleppo pepper (ah-LEHP-oh) is made from bright red chiles grown in Turkey and northern Syria. The sun-dried Aleppo chiles are seeded and crushed, then used as a condiment. It has a sharp, but sweet, fruity flavour, with only mild heat (15 000 Scoville units, discussed in Chapter 22, Vegetables). Although a member of the *capsicum* family, Aleppo pepper is used more like ground peppercorns (*piper nigrum*) than a chile. Also known as Halaby pepper, it adds an authentic Mediterranean flavour and fragrance to foods.

Allspice (Fr. *toute-épice*), also known as Jamaican pepper, is the dried berry of a tree that flourishes in Jamaica and one of the few spices still grown exclusively in the New World. Allspice is available whole; in berries that look like large, rough, brown peppercorns; or ground. Ground allspice is not a mixture of spices, although it does taste like a blend of cinnamon, cloves and nutmeg. Allspice is now used throughout the world, in everything from cakes to curries, and is often included in peppercorn blends.

Anise (Fr. *anis*) is native to the eastern Mediterranean, where it was widely used by ancient civilizations. Today, it is grown commercially in warm climates throughout India, North Africa and southern Europe. The tiny, grey-green egg-shaped seeds have a distinctively strong, sweet flavour, similar to licorice and fennel. When anise seeds turn brown they are stale and should be discarded. Anise is used in pastries as well as fish, shellfish and vegetable dishes, and is commonly used in alcoholic beverages (e.g., Pernod and ouzo). The green leaves of the anise plant are occasionally used fresh as a herb or in salads.

Star anise, also known as Chinese anise, is the dried, star-shaped fruit of a Chinese magnolia tree. Although botanically unrelated, its flavour is similar to anise seeds but more bitter and pungent. It is an essential flavour in many Chinese dishes and one of the components of five-spice powder.

Annatto seeds (Fr. *roucou*) are the small, brick-red triangular seeds of a shrub from South America and the Caribbean. Annatto seeds add a mild, peppery flavour to rice, fish and shellfish dishes and are crushed to make Mexican achiote paste. Because they impart a bright yellow-orange colour to foods, annatto seeds are commonly used as a natural food colouring, especially in cheeses and margarine.

Asafetida (ah-sah-FEH-teh-dah; also spelled asafoetida) is a pale brown resin made from the sap of a giant fennel-like plant native to India and Iran. Also known as devil's dung, it has a garlicky flavour and a strong unpleasant fetid aroma (the aroma is not transferred to food being flavoured). Available powdered or in lump form, it is used—very sparingly—as a flavouring in Indian and Middle Eastern cuisines.

Capers (Fr. *capres*) come from a small bush that grows wild throughout the Mediterranean basin. Its unopened flower buds have been pickled and used as a condiment for thousands of years. Fresh capers are not used, as the sharp, salty-sour flavour develops only after curing in strongly salted white vinegar. The finest capers are the smallest, known as *nonpareils*, which are produced

A Pinch of History

Spices have been used for many purposes for thousands of years. Egyptian papyri dating back to 2800 B.C.E. identify several spices native to the Middle and Far East that were used by the ruling and priestly classes for therapeutic, cosmetic, medicinal, ritualistic and culinary purposes.

By 300 C.E. the Romans were regularly importing spices for use as perfumes, medicines, preservatives and ingredients from China and India via long, difficult caravan journeys over sea and land. Spices were extremely expensive and unavailable to all but the wealthiest citizens.

After Rome fell in the second half of the 5th century, much of the overland route through southern Europe became prey to bandits; and after Constantinople fell in 1453, the spice routes through the Middle East were controlled by the Ottoman Empire. Spice costs soared and economies based upon the spice trade, such as that of Venice, were at risk.

By then highly spiced food had become the norm, especially in wealthier households. So, in part to maintain their culinary norm, the Europeans set out to break the Ottoman Empire's monopoly. These efforts led to Columbus' discovery of the Americas and Vasco de Gama's discovery of a sea route to India. Although the New World contained none of the spices for which Columbus was searching, it provided many previously unknown foods and flavourings that changed European tables forever, including chiles, vanilla, tomatoes, potatoes and chocolate.

Formation of the Dutch East India Company in 1602 marked the start of the Dutch colonial empire and made spices widely available to the growing European middle classes. The transplantation and cultivation of spice plants eventually weakened the once-powerful trading empires until, by the 19th century, no European country could monopolize trade. Prices fell dramatically.

---

in France's Provence region. Capers are used in a variety of sauces (tartar, remoulade) and are excellent with fish and game. Capers will keep for long periods if moistened by their original liquid. Do not add or substitute vinegar, however, as this causes the capers to spoil.

Caraway (Fr. *carvi*) is perhaps the world's oldest spice. Its use has been traced to the Stone Age, and seeds have been found in ancient Egyptian tombs. The caraway plant grows wild in Europe and temperate regions of Asia. It produces a small, crescent-shaped brown seed with the peppery flavour of rye. Seeds may be purchased whole or ground. (The leaves have a mild, bland flavour and are rarely used in cooking.) Caraway is a very European flavour, used extensively in German and Austrian dishes, particularly breads, meats and cabbage. It is also used in cheeses and to flavour the liqueur kummel.

Caraway Seeds

Cardamom Seeds

Cardamom (Fr. *cardamone*) is one of the most expensive spices, second only to saffron in cost. Its seeds are encased in 6-mm-long (1/4-in.) light green or brown pods. Cardamom is highly aromatic. Its flavour, lemony with notes of camphor, is quite strong and is used in both sweet and savoury dishes. Cardamom is widely used in Indian and Middle Eastern cuisines, where it is also used to flavour coffee. Scandinavians use cardamom to flavour breads and pastries. Ground cardamom loses its flavour rapidly and is easily adulterated, so it is best to purchase whole seeds and grind your own as needed.

Chiles, including paprika, chile peppers, bell peppers and cayenne, are members of the *capsicum* plant family. Although cultivated for thousands of years in the West Indies and Americas, capsicum peppers were unknown in the Old World prior to Spanish explorations during the 15th century. Capsicum peppers come in all shapes and sizes, with a wide range of flavours, from sweet to extremely hot. Some capsicums are used as a vegetable, while others are dried, ground and used as a spice. Fresh chiles and bell peppers are discussed in Chapter 22, Vegetables. Capsicums are botanically unrelated to *piper nigrum*, the black peppercorns discussed later.

➤ For our purposes, *chile* refers to the plant, *chili* refers to the stewlike dish containing chiles and *chilli* refers to the commercial spice powder.

Cayenne, sometimes simply labelled "red pepper," is ground from a blend of several particularly hot types of dried red chile peppers. Its flavour is extremely hot and pungent; it has a bright orange-red colour and fine texture.

Paprika, also known as Hungarian pepper, is a bright red powder ground from particular varieties of red-ripened and dried chiles. The flavour ranges

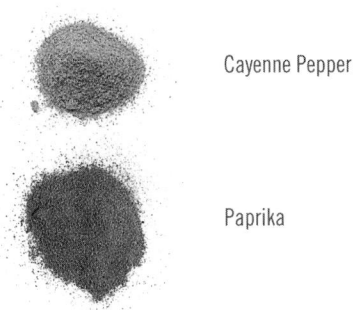

Cayenne Pepper

Paprika

Chilli Powder

Crushed Chiles

Ground Cinnamon
and Cinnamon Sticks

Cloves

Coriander
Seeds

Cumin

Fennel

Fenugreek

from sweet to pungent; the aroma is distinctive and strong. It is essential to many Spanish and eastern European dishes. Mild paprika is meant to be used in generous quantities and may be sprinkled on prepared foods as a garnish.

Chilli powders are made from a wide variety of dried chile peppers, ranging from sweet and mild to extremely hot and pungent. The finest pure chilli powders come from dried chiles that are simply roasted, ground and sieved. Commercial chilli powder, an American invention, is actually a combination of spices—oregano, cumin, garlic and other flavourings—intended for use in Mexican dishes. Each brand is different and should be sampled before using.

Crushed chiles, also known as chile flakes, are blended from dried, coarsely crushed chiles. They are quite hot and are used in sauces and meat dishes.

Cinnamon (Fr. *cannelle*) and its cousin **cassia** are among the oldest known spices: cinnamon's use is recorded in China as early as 2500 B.C.E., and Asia still produces most of these products. Both cinnamon and cassia come from the bark of small evergreen trees, peeled from branches in thin layers and dried in the sun. High-quality cinnamon should be pale brown and thin, rolled up like paper into sticks known as quills. Cassia is coarser and has a stronger, less subtle flavour than cinnamon. Consequently, it is cheaper than true cinnamon. Cinnamon is usually purchased ground because it is difficult to grind. Cinnamon sticks are used when long cooking times can be allowed in order to extract the flavour (for example, in stews or curries). Cinnamon's flavour is most often associated with pastries and sweets, but has a great affinity for lamb and spicy dishes. Labelling laws do not require that packages distinguish between cassia and cinnamon, so most of what is sold as cinnamon in North America is actually cassia, blended for consistent flavour and aroma.

Cloves (Fr. *clous de girofle*) are the unopened buds of evergreen trees that flourish in muggy tropical regions. When dried, whole cloves have hard, sharp prongs that can be used to push them into other foods, such as onions or fruit, in order to provide flavour. Cloves are extremely pungent, with a sweet, astringent aroma. A small amount provides a great deal of flavour. Cloves are used in desserts and meat dishes, preserves and liqueurs. They may be purchased whole or ground.

Coriander (Fr. *coriandre*) seeds come from the cilantro plant. They are round and beige, with a distinctive sweet, spicy flavour and strong aroma. Unlike other plants in which the seeds and the leaves carry the same flavour and aroma, coriander and cilantro are distinct. Coriander seeds are available whole or ground and are frequently used in Indian cuisine and pickling mixtures.

Cumin (Fr. *cumin*) is the seed of a small delicate plant of the parsley family that grows in North Africa and the Middle East. The small seeds are available whole or ground and look (but do not taste) like caraway seeds. Cumin has a powerful earthy flavour and tends to dominate any dish in which it is included. It is used in Indian, Middle Eastern and Mexican cuisines, in sausages and a few cheeses.

Fennel (Fr. *fenouil*) is a perennial plant with feathery leaves and tiny flowers long cultivated in India and China as a medicine and cure for witchcraft. Its seeds are greenish brown with prominent ridges and short, hairlike fibres. Their taste and aroma are similar to anise, though not as sweet. Whole seeds are widely used in Italian stews and sausages; Central European cuisines use fennel with fish, pork, pickles and vegetables. Ground seeds can also be used in breads, cakes and cookies. The same plant produces a bulbous stalk used as a vegetable.

Fenugreek (Fr. *fenugrec*), grown in Mediterranean countries since ancient times, is a small, beanlike plant with a tiny flower. The seeds, available whole or ground, are pebble-shaped and transfer their pale orange colour to the foods with which they are cooked. Their flavour is bittersweet, like burnt sugar with a bitter aftertaste. Fenugreek is a staple in Indian cuisine, especially curries and chutneys.

Filé powder (fee-LAY) is the dried, ground leaf of the sassafras plant. Long used by Choctaw Indians, it is now most commonly used as a thickener and flavouring in Cajun and Creole cuisines. Filé is also used as a table condiment to add a spicy note to stews, gumbo and the like. The powder forms strings if allowed to boil, so it should be added during the last minutes of cooking.

Galangal (guh-LANG-guhl) is the rhizome of a plant native to India and Southeast Asia. The rhizome has a reddish skin, an orange or whitish flesh and a peppery, gingerlike flavour and piney aroma. Also known as galanga root, Thai ginger and Laos ginger, it is peeled and crushed for use in Thai and Indonesian cuisines. Fresh ginger is an appropriate substitute.

Ginger (Fr. *gingembre*) is a well-known spice obtained from the root of a tall, flowering tropical plant. Fresh ginger root is known as a "hand" because it looks vaguely like a group of knobby fingers. It has greyish-tan skin and a pale yellow, fibrous interior. Fresh ginger should be plump and firm with smooth skin. It should keep for about a month under refrigeration. Its flavour is fiery but sweet, with notes of lemon and rosemary. Fresh ginger is widely available and is used in Indian and Asian cuisines. It has a special affinity for chicken, beef and curries. Ginger is also available peeled and pickled in vinegar, candied in sugar or preserved in alcohol or syrup. Dried, ground ginger is a fine yellow powder widely used in pastries. Its flavour is spicier and not as sweet as fresh ginger.

Grains of paradise are the seeds of a perennial reedlike plant indigenous to the West African coast. Related to cardamom, grains of paradise have a spicy, warm and slightly bitter flavour, similar to peppercorns. In fact, grains of paradise were traditionally used in place of black pepper and are also known as Guinea pepper or Melegueta pepper. Now enjoying a resurgence in popularity and increased availability, they are ground and used primarily in West African and Magreb dishes, and in the spice blend known as ras el hanout.

Horseradish (Fr. *cranson de Bretagne*) is the large off-white taproot of a hardy perennial (unrelated to radishes) that flourishes in cool climates. Fresh roots should be firm and plump; they will not have the distinctive horseradish aroma unless cut or bruised. The outer skin and inner core of a fresh horseradish root can have an unpleasant flavour and should be discarded. Typically used in Russian and Central European cuisines, especially as an accompaniment to roasted meats and fish and shellfish dishes, horseradish is usually served grated, creamed into a sauce or as part of a compound butter or mustard preparation. If horseradish is cooked, heat can destroy its flavour and pungency, so any horseradish should be added near the end of cooking.

Juniper (Fr. *genièvre*) is an evergreen bush grown throughout the northern hemisphere. It produces round purple berries with a sweet flavour similar to pine. Juniper berries are used for flavouring gin and other alcoholic beverages, and are crushed and incorporated in game dishes, particularly venison and wild boar.

Mustard seeds (Fr. *moutarde*), available in black, brown and yellow, come from three different plants in the cabbage family. Mustard seeds are small, hard spheres with a bitter flavour. The seeds have no aroma, but their flavour is sharp and fiery hot. Yellow seeds have the mildest and black seeds the strongest flavour. All are sold whole and can be crushed for cooking. Mustard seeds are a standard component of pickling spices and are processed and blended for prepared mustards, which are discussed later. Ground or dry mustard is a bright yellow powder made from a blend of ground seeds, wheat flour and turmeric.

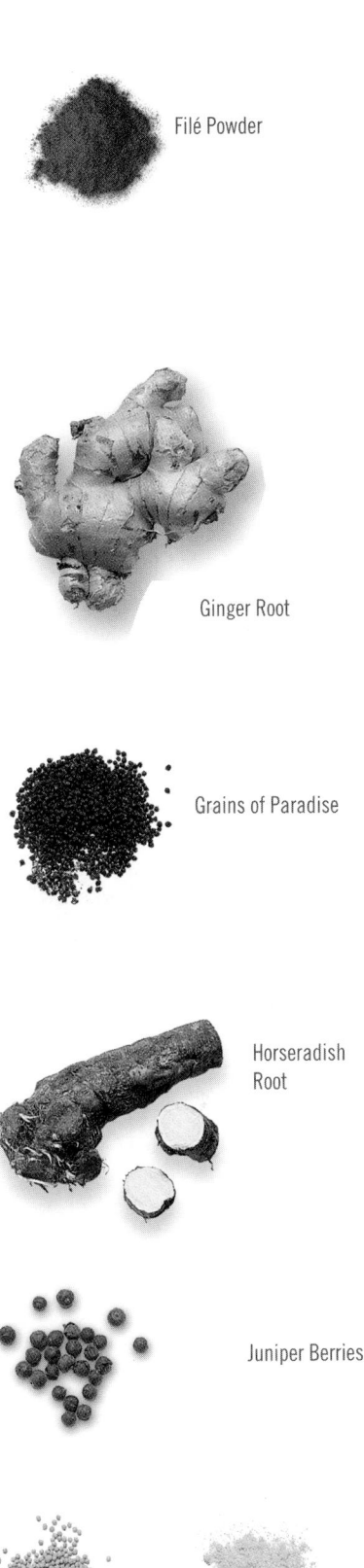

Filé Powder

Ginger Root

Grains of Paradise

Horseradish Root

Juniper Berries

Mustard Seeds

Ground Mustard

Mace (left),
Whole Nutmeg and Ground
Nutmeg (right)

Black Pepper (left) and
White Pepper (right)

Green Peppercorns

Pink Peppercorns

Szechuan Pepper

Poppy Seeds

Nutmeg (Fr. *muscade*) and mace come from the yellow plumlike fruit of a large tropical evergreen. These fruits are dried and opened to reveal the seed known as nutmeg. The seed is surrounded by a bright red lacy coating or aril; the aril is the spice mace. Whole nutmegs are oval and look rather like a piece of smooth wood. The flavour and aroma of nutmeg are strong and sweet, and a small quantity provides a great deal of flavour. Nutmeg should be grated directly into a dish as needed; once grated, flavour loss is rapid. Nutmeg is used in many European cuisines, mainly in pastries and sweets, but is also important in meat and savoury dishes.

Mace is an expensive spice, with a flavour similar to nutmeg but more refined. It is almost always purchased ground and retains its flavour longer than other ground spices. Mace is used primarily in pastry items.

Peppercorns (Fr. *poivre*) are the berries of a vine plant (*piper nigrum*) native to tropical Asia. Peppercorns should not be confused with the chile (capsicum) peppers discussed earlier. Peppercorns vary in size, colour, pungency and flavour. Many of these differences are the result of variations in climate and growing conditions. Good-quality pepper is expensive and should be purchased whole and ground fresh in a peppermill as needed. Whole peppercorns will last indefinitely if kept dry. They should be stored well covered in a cool, dark place.

Black and white **peppercorns** are produced from the same plant but are picked and processed differently. For black peppercorns, the berries are picked when green and simply dried whole in the sun. Black pepper has a warm, pungent flavour and aroma. Tellicherry peppercorns from the southwest coast of India are generally considered the finest black peppercorns in the world and are priced accordingly.

For **white peppercorns**, the berries are allowed to ripen until they turn red. The ripened berries are allowed to ferment, then the outer layer of skin is washed off. Nowadays, white pepper may be produced by mechanically removing the outer skin from black peppercorns. This is not true white pepper, and the resulting product should be labelled "decorticated." White pepper has less aroma than black pepper but is useful in white sauces or where the appearance of black speckles is undesirable.

Green peppercorns are unripened berries that are either freeze-dried or pickled in brine or vinegar. Pickled green peppercorns are soft, with a fresh, sour flavour similar to capers. They are excellent in spiced butters and sauces or with fish.

Pink peppercorns are actually the berries of a South American tree, not a vine pepper plant. Pink peppercorns are available dried or pickled in vinegar. Although attractive, their flavour is bitter and pinelike, with less spiciness than true pepper. Pink peppercorns are no longer available in some areas because of reported toxic side effects.

Szechuan pepper (also spelled Szechwan and Sichuan; Fr. *poivre anise*) is the dried red berries of the prickly ash tree native to China. Also known as anise pepper and Chinese pepper, the berries have an extremely hot, peppery, spicy flavour with citrus overtones and are used in Chinese cuisines and as part of Chinese five-spice powder.

Poppy seeds (Fr. *pavot*) are the ripened seeds of the opium poppy, which flourishes in the Middle East and India. (When ripe, the seeds do not contain any of the medicinal alkaloids found elsewhere in the plant.) The tiny blue-grey seeds are round and hard with a sweet, nutty flavour. Poppy seeds are used in pastries and breads.

Saffron (Fr. *safran*) comes from the dried stigmas of the saffron crocus. Each flower bears only three threadlike

Saffron

stigmas, and each must be picked by hand. It takes about 250 000 flowers to produce 450 g (1 lb.) of saffron, making it the most expensive spice in the world. Beware of bargains; there is no such thing as cheap saffron. Luckily, a tiny pinch is enough to colour and flavour a large quantity of food. Good saffron should be a brilliant orange colour, not yellow, with a strong aroma and a bitter, honeylike taste. Saffron produces a yellow dye that diffuses through any warm liquid. Valencia or Spanish saffron is considered the finest. It is commonly used with fish and shellfish (a necessity for bouillabaisse) and rice dishes such as paella and risotto. When using saffron threads, first crush them gently, then soak them in some hot liquid from the recipe. Powdered saffron is less expensive but more easily adulterated. It may be added directly to the other ingredients when cooking.

Sesame seeds, also known as benne seeds, are native to India. They are small, flat ovals, with a creamy white colour. Their taste is nutty and earthy, with a pronounced aroma when roasted or ground into a paste (known as tahini). Sesame seeds are the source of sesame oil, which has a mild, nutty flavour and does not go rancid easily. Sesame seeds are roasted and used in or as a garnish for breads and meat dishes. They are popular in Indian and Asian cuisines, with a black variety of seeds most popular as a Japanese condiment.

Tamarind (Fr. *tamarin*; Sp. and It. *tamarindo*), also known as an Indian date, is the brown, bean-shaped pod of the tamarind tree, which is native to Africa. Although naturally sweet, tamarind also contains 12% tartaric acid, which makes it extremely tart. It is commonly used in Indian curries and Mediterranean cooking as a souring agent and in the West Indies in fruit drinks. Tamarind is sold as a concentrate or in sticky blocks of crushed pods, pulp and seeds, which should be soaked in warm water for about five minutes, then squeezed through a sieve. Tamarind's high pectin content is useful in chutneys and jams, and it is often included in barbecue sauces and marinades. It is a key ingredient in Worcestershire sauce.

Turmeric, also known as Indian saffron, is produced from the roots of a flowering tropical plant related to ginger. Unlike ginger, fresh turmeric is not used in cooking. It is only available dried and usually ground. Turmeric is renowned for its vibrant yellow colour and is used as a food colouring and dye. Turmeric's flavour is distinctive and strong; it should not be substituted for saffron. Turmeric is a traditional ingredient in Indian curries, to which it imparts colour as well as flavour.

Wasabi is a pale green root similar, but unrelated, to horseradish. It has a strong aroma and a sharp, cleansing flavour with herbal overtones that is a bit hotter than that of horseradish. Fresh wasabi is rarely found outside Japan, but tins of powder and tubes of paste are readily available. It is commonly served with sushi and sashimi and can be used to add a spicy Asian note to other dishes, such as mashed potatoes or a compound butter.

Sesame Seeds

Tamarind Pods   Tamarind Paste

Turmeric

Wasabi

Herb and Spice Blends

Many countries and cuisines have created recognizable combinations of spice flavours that are found in a variety of dishes. Although many of these blends are available ready-prepared for convenience, most can be mixed by the chef as needed. A few of the more common spice blends are described here.

Chinese **five-spice powder** is a combination of equal parts finely ground Szechuan pepper, star anise, cloves, cinnamon and fennel seeds. This blend is widely used in Chinese and some Vietnamese foods and is excellent with pork and in pâtés.

Five-Spice Powder

Curry Powder

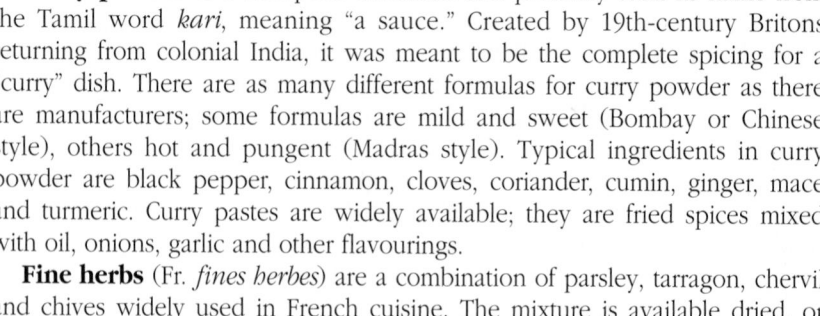

Curry powder is a European invention that probably took its name from the Tamil word *kari*, meaning "a sauce." Created by 19th-century Britons returning from colonial India, it was meant to be the complete spicing for a "curry" dish. There are as many different formulas for curry powder as there are manufacturers; some formulas are mild and sweet (Bombay or Chinese style), others hot and pungent (Madras style). Typical ingredients in curry powder are black pepper, cinnamon, cloves, coriander, cumin, ginger, mace and turmeric. Curry pastes are widely available; they are fried spices mixed with oil, onions, garlic and other flavourings.

Fine herbs (Fr. *fines herbes*) are a combination of parsley, tarragon, chervil and chives widely used in French cuisine. The mixture is available dried, or you can create your own from fresh ingredients.

Herbes de Provence is a blend of dried herbs commonly grown and used in southern France. Commercial blends usually include thyme, rosemary, bay leaf, basil, fennel seeds, savory and lavender. The herb blend is used with grilled or roasted meat, fish or chicken; in vegetable dishes; on pizza; and even in steamed rice and yeast breads.

Italian seasoning blend is a commercially prepared mixture of dried basil, oregano, sage, marjoram, rosemary, thyme, savory and other herbs associated with Italian cuisine.

Jamaican jerk seasoning is a powdered or wet mixture used on the Caribbean island of the same name made from a combination of spices that typically includes thyme, ground spices such as allspice, cinnamon, cloves, and ginger as well as onions and garlic. Chicken and pork are typically rubbed or marinated in the blend, then grilled.

Masala is a flavourful, aromatic blend of roasted and ground spices used in Indian cuisines. A **garam masala** is a masala made with hot spices (*garam* means "warm" or "hot"). A dry garam masala usually contains peppercorns, cardamom, cinnamon, cloves, coriander, nutmeg, turmeric, bay leaves and fennel seeds, and is added toward the end of cooking or sprinkled on the food just before service. A wet garam masala is made by adding coconut milk, oil or sometimes tamarind water to a dry garam masala. A wet garam masala is typically added at the start of cooking.

Pickling spice, as with other blends, varies by manufacturer. Most pickling spice blends are based on black peppercorns and red chiles, with some or all of the following added: allspice, cloves, ginger, mustard seeds, coriander seeds, bay leaves and dill. These blends are useful in making cucumber or vegetable pickles as well as in stews and soups.

Quatre-épices, literally "four spices" in French, is a peppery mixture of black peppercorns with lesser amounts of nutmeg, cloves and dried ginger. Sometimes cinnamon or allspice is included. Quatre-épices is used in charcuterie and long-simmered stews.

Ras el hanout (rass al ha-noot) is a common Moroccan spice blend varying greatly from supplier to supplier. It typically contains 20 or more spices, such as turmeric, cinnamon, cloves, grains of paradise, coriander, cumin, cardamom, peppercorns, dried chiles, dried flower petals and, allegedly, an aphrodisiac or two. It is sold whole and ground by the cook as necessary to flavour stews, rice, couscous and game dishes.

Seasoned salts are commercially blended products containing salt and one or more natural flavouring ingredients such as garlic, spices or celery seeds, and, often, monosodium glutamate (MSG).

Herbes de Provence

Pickling Spice

Storing Herbs and Spices

Fresh herbs should be kept refrigerated at 2°C–4°C (34°F–40°F). Large bouquets can be stored upright, their leaves loosely covered with plastic wrap and their stems submerged in water. Smaller bunches should be stored loosely covered with a damp towel. Excess fresh herbs can be dried for later use in an electric dehydrator or spread out on baking sheets in a 38°C (100°F) oven.

Dried herbs and spices should be stored in airtight, opaque containers in a cool, dry place. Avoid light and heat, both of which destroy delicate flavours. If stored properly, dried herbs should last for two to three months. Purchase only the amount of dried herbs that can be used within a short time.

Using Herbs and Spices

Herbs and spices are a simple, inexpensive way to bring individuality and variety to foods. Their proper use leads to better-flavoured and distinctively different dishes. They add neither fat nor sodium and virtually no calories to foods; most contain only 3 to 10 calories per 5 mL (1 tsp.). Table 7.2 lists just a few uses for some of the more common herbs and spices.

Although the flavours and aromas of fresh herbs are generally preferred, dried herbs are widely used because they are readily available and convenient. Use a smaller amount of dried herbs than you would of fresh herbs. The loss of moisture strengthens and concentrates the flavour in dried herbs. In general, you should use only one-half to one-third as much dried herb as fresh in any given recipe. For example, if a recipe calls for 15 mL/10 g (1 Tbsp.) of fresh basil, you should substitute only 5 mL/3 g (1 tsp.) of dried basil. You can usually add more later if necessary.

TABLE 7.2	Uses for Some Common Herbs and Spices	
Flavouring	**Form**	**Suggested Uses**
Allspice	Whole or ground	Fruits, relishes, braised meats
Anise	Whole or ground	Asian cuisines, pastries, breads, cheeses
Basil	Fresh or dried	Tomatoes, salads, eggs, fish, chicken, lamb, cheeses
Caraway	Whole or ground	Rye bread, cabbage, beans, pork, beef, veal
Chervil	Fresh or dried	Chicken, fish, eggs, salads, soups, vegetables
Chives	Fresh or dried	Eggs, fish, chicken, soups, potatoes, cheeses
Cilantro	Fresh leaves	Salsa, salads, Mexican cuisine, fish, shellfish, chicken
Cloves	Whole or ground	Marinades, baked goods, braised meats, pickles, fruits, beverages, stocks
Cumin	Whole or ground	Chili, sausages, stews, eggs
Dill	Fresh or dried leaves; Whole or ground seeds	Leaves or seeds in soups, salads; whole seeds in fish, shellfish, vegetables, breads; seeds in pickles, potatoes, vegetables
Fennel	Whole seeds	Sausages, stews, sauces, pickling, lamb, eggs
Ginger	Fresh or dried root	Asian, Caribbean and Indian cuisines, pastries, curries, stews, meats
Marjoram	Fresh or dried	Sausages, pâtés, meats, poultry, stews, green vegetables, tomatoes, game
Nutmeg	Ground	Curries, relishes, rice, eggs, beverages
Rosemary	Fresh or dried	Lamb, veal, beef, poultry, game, marinades, stews
Saffron	Threads or ground	Rice, breads, potatoes, soups, stews, chicken, fish, shellfish
Sage	Fresh or dried	Poultry, charcuterie, pork, stuffings, pasta, beans, tomatoes
Tarragon	Fresh or dried	Chicken, fish, eggs, salad dressings, sauces, tomatoes
Thyme	Fresh or dried	Fish, chicken, meats, stews, charcuterie, soups, tomatoes
Turmeric	Ground	Curries, relishes, rice, eggs, breads

Spices are often available whole or ground. Once ground, they lose their flavours rapidly, however. Whole spices should keep their flavours for many months if stored in airtight containers in a cool, dry place away from direct light. Stale spices lose their spicy aroma and develop a bitter or musty aftertaste. Discard them.

Because ground spices release their flavours quickly, they should be added to cooked dishes near the end of the cooking period. In uncooked dishes that call for ground spices (for example, salad dressings), the mixture should be allowed to stand for several hours to develop good flavour.

Although some combinations are timeless—rosemary with lamb, dill with salmon, nutmeg with spinach, caraway with rye bread—less common pairings can be equally delicious and far more exciting. A chef must be willing and able to experiment with new flavours. But first you must be familiar with the distinctive flavour and aroma of the herb or spice. Then you can experiment, always bearing in mind the following guidelines:

- Flavourings should not hide the taste or aroma of the primary ingredient;
- Flavourings should be combined in balance, so as not to overwhelm the palate; and
- Flavourings should not be used to disguise poor quality or poorly prepared products.

Even when following a well-tested recipe, the quantity of flavourings may need to be adjusted because of changes in brands or the condition of the ingredients. A cook should strive to develop his or her palate to recognize and correct subtle variances as necessary.

Bouquet Garni and Sachet

The bouquet garni and the sachet are used to introduce flavourings, seasonings and aromatics into stocks, sauces, soups and stews.

A **bouquet garni**, shown in Figure 7.3, is a selection of herbs (usually fresh) and vegetables tied into a bundle with twine. The twine makes it easy to remove the bouquet when sufficient flavour has been extracted. A standard bouquet garni consists of parsley stems, celery, thyme, leeks and carrots.

A **sachet** (also known as a **sachet d'épices**), shown in Figure 7.4, is made by tying seasonings together in cheesecloth. A standard sachet consists of peppercorns, bay leaves, parsley stems, thyme, cloves and, optionally, garlic. The exact quantity of these ingredients is determined by the amount of liquid the sachet is meant to flavour.

Bouquets garni and sachets are used to add flavours in such a way that the ingredients can be easily removed from a dish when the flavours have been extracted. A similar technique, although less commonly used, is an **oignon piqué** or **clouté** (studded onion). To prepare an oignon piqué, peel the onion and trim off the root end. Attach one or two dried bay leaves to the onion using whole cloves as pins. The oignon piqué is then simmered in milk or stock to extract flavours.

- **bouquet garni** fresh herbs and vegetables tied into a bundle with twine and used to flavour stocks, sauces, soups and stews

- **sachet d'épices** French for "bag of spices"; aromatic ingredients tied in a cheesecloth bag and used to flavour stocks and other foods; a standard sachet contains parsley stems, peppercorns, dried thyme, bay leaves, cloves and (optionally) garlic

- **oignon piqué** French for "pricked onion"; a bay leaf tacked with a clove to a peeled onion; used to flavour sauces and soups; also known as oignon clouté

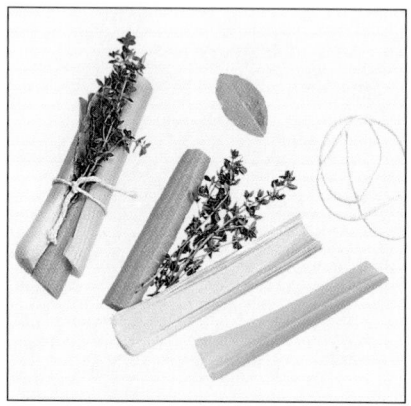

FIGURE 7.3 Bouquet garni.

FIGURE 7.4 Sachet.

SALT

Salt (Fr. *sel*) is the most basic seasoning, and its use is universal. It preserves foods, heightens their flavours and provides the distinctive taste of saltiness. The presence of salt can be tasted easily but not smelled. Salt suppresses bitter flavours, making the sweet and sour ones more prominent. The flavour of salt will not evaporate or dissipate during cooking so it should be added to foods carefully, according to taste. Remember, more salt can always be added to a dish but too much salt cannot be removed nor can its flavour be masked if too much salt has been added.

Culinary or **table salt** is sodium chloride (NaCl), one of the minerals essential to human life. Salt contains no calories, proteins, fats or carbohydrates. It is available from several sources, each with its own flavour and degree of saltiness.

Rock salt, mined from underground deposits, is available in both edible and nonedible forms. It is used in ice cream churns, for thawing frozen sidewalks and, in edible form, in salt mills.

Common **kitchen** or **table salt** is produced by pumping water through underground salt deposits, then bringing the brine to the surface to evaporate, leaving behind crystals. Chemicals are usually added to prevent table salt from absorbing moisture and thus keep it free-flowing. Iodized salt is commonly used in North America. The iodine has no effect on the salt's flavour or use; it is simply added to provide an easily available source of iodine, an important nutrient, to a large number of people.

Kosher salt has large, irregular crystals and is used in the "koshering" or curing of meats. It is purified rock salt that contains no iodine or additives. It can be substituted for common kitchen salt. Some chefs prefer it to table salt because they prefer its flavour and it dissolves more easily than other salts.

Sea salt is obtained, not surprisingly, by evaporating sea water. The evaporation can be done naturally by drying the salt in the sun (unrefined sea salt) or by boiling the salty liquid (refined sea salt). Unlike other table salts, unrefined sea salt contains additional mineral salts such as magnesium, calcium and potassium, which give it a stronger, more complex flavour and a greyish-brown colour. The region where it is produced can also affect its flavour and colour. For example, salt from the Mediterranean Sea will taste different from salt obtained from the Indian Ocean or the English Channel.

Sel gris is a sea salt harvested off the coast of Normandy, France. It is slightly wet and takes its grey colour from minerals in the clay from which it is collected. **Fleur de sel,** which means "flower of salt," is salt that collects on rocks in the sel gris marshes. It forms delicate crystals and has little colour because it has not come into contact with the clay.

Some **specialty salts** are actually mined from the earth, such as that from the foothills of the Himalayan Mountains. The presence of iron and copper along with other minerals gives Himalayan salt a pink hue and distinct flavour. Black salt, common in traditional Indian recipes, is mined rock salt; minerals and other components in the salt give it a dark colour and sulphurous taste. **Smoked salt** is a type of flavoured salt made by smoking the salt over a smouldering fire. It can also be made by adding liquid smoke to a salt solution before it is evaporated.

Sea salt is considerably more expensive than other table salts and is often reserved for finishing a dish or used as a condiment.

Because it is nonorganic, salt keeps indefinitely. It will, however, absorb moisture from the atmosphere, which prevents it from flowing properly. Salt is a powerful preservative; its presence stops or greatly slows down the growth of many undesirable organisms. Salt is used to preserve meats, vegetables and fish. It is also used to develop desirable flavours in bacon, ham, cheeses and fish products as well as pickled vegetables.

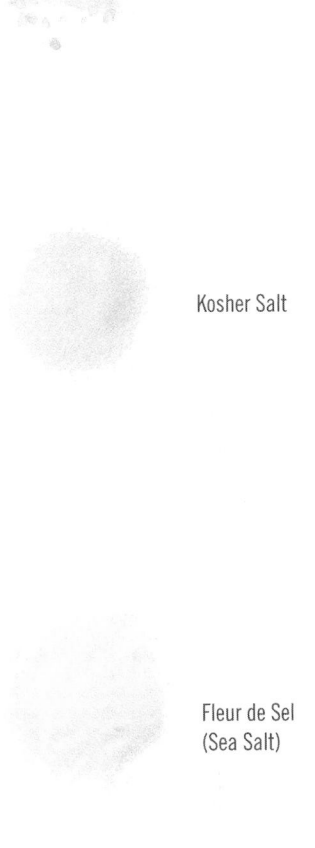

Rock Salt

Kosher Salt

Fleur de Sel
(Sea Salt)

OILS

Oils (Fr. *huile*) are a type of fat that remains liquid at room temperature. Cooking oils are refined from various seeds, plants and vegetables. (Other fats, such as

● **oil** a type of fat that remains liquid at room temperature

TABLE 7.3	The Smoke Points of Common Fats

Per 28 g (1 oz.) Serving	Smoke Point
Olive oil	225°C/437°F
Peanut oil	218°C/425°F
Lard	188°C/370°F
Canola oil	218°C/425°F
Walnut oil	163 to 204°C/ 325 to 400°F
Butter, clarified	204°C/400°F
Whole butter, unsalted	127°C/260°F

Source: *The Corinne T. Netzer Encyclopedia of Food Values 1992.*

● **shortening** (1) a white, flavourless, solid fat formulated for baking or deep-fat frying; (2) any fat used in baking to tenderize the product by shortening gluten strands

● **smoke point** the temperature at which a fat begins to break down and smoke

● **rancidity** a chemical change in fats caused by exposure to air, light or heat that results in objectionable flavours and odours

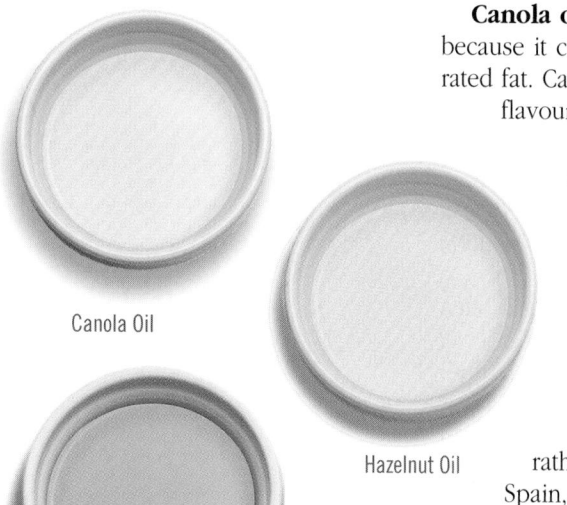

Canola Oil

Hazelnut Oil

Extra Virgin Olive Oil

butter and margarine, are discussed in Chapter 8, Eggs and Dairy Products; animal and solid fats are discussed in Chapter 27, Principles of the Bakeshop.)

When purchasing oils you should consider their use, smoke point, flavour and cost. Fats, including oils and **shortenings**, are manufactured for specific purposes such as deep-fat frying, cake-baking, salad dressings and sautéing. Most food service operations purchase different ones for each of these needs.

Fats break down at different temperatures. The temperature at which a given fat begins to break down and smoke is known as its **smoke point** (see Table 7.3). Choose fats with higher smoke points for high-temperature cooking such as deep-fat frying and sautéing. If a fat with a low smoke point is used for high-temperature cooking, it may break down, burn and impart undesirable flavours.

The flavour and cost of each oil must also be considered. For example, both corn oil and walnut oil may be used in a salad dressing. Their selection may depend on balancing cost (corn oil is less expensive) against flavour (walnut oil has a stronger, more distinctive flavour).

When fats spoil they are said to go rancid. **Rancidity** is a chemical change caused by exposure to air, light or heat. It results in objectionable flavours and odours. Different fats turn rancid at different rates, but all fats benefit from refrigerated storage away from moisture, light and air. (Some oils are packaged in coloured glass containers because certain tints of green and yellow block the damaging light rays that can cause an oil to go rancid.) Oils may become thick and cloudy under refrigeration. This is not a cause for concern. The oils will return to their clear, liquid states at room temperature. Stored fats should also be covered to prevent the absorption of odours.

Vegetable oils are extracted from a variety of plants, including corn, cottonseed, peanuts and soybeans, by pressure or chemical solvents. The oil is then refined and cleaned to remove unwanted colours, odours or flavours. Vegetable oils are virtually odourless and have a neutral flavour. Because they contain no animal products, they are cholesterol-free. If a commercial product contains only one type of oil, it is labelled "pure" (as in "pure corn oil"). Products labelled "vegetable oil" are blended from several sources. Products labelled "salad oil" are highly refined blends of vegetable oil.

Canola oil is processed from rapeseeds. Its popularity is growing rapidly because it contains no cholesterol and has a high percentage of monounsaturated fat. Canola oil is useful for frying and general cooking because it has no flavour and a high smoke point. Cold-pressed canola oil is flavourful.

Nut oils are extracted from a variety of nuts and are almost always packaged as a "pure" product, never blended. A nut oil should have the strong flavour and aroma of the nut from which it was processed. Popular examples are walnut and hazelnut oils. These oils are used to give flavour to salad dressings, marinades and other dishes. But heat diminishes their flavour, so nut oils are not recommended for frying or baking. Nut oils tend to go rancid quickly and therefore are usually packaged in small containers that must be refrigerated once opened.

Olive oil (Fr. *huile d'olive*) is an oil that is extracted from a fruit rather than a seed, nut or grain. Olive oil is produced primarily in Spain, Italy, France, Greece and North Africa. Like wine, olive oils vary in colour and flavour according to the variety of tree, the ripeness of the olives, the type of soil, the climate and the producer's preferences. Colours range from dark green to almost clear, depending on the ripeness of the olives at the time of pressing and the amount of subsequent refining. Colour is not a good indication of flavour, however. Flavour is ultimately a matter of personal preference. A stronger-flavoured oil may be desired for some foods, while a milder oil is better for others. Good olive oil should be thicker than refined vegetable oils, but not so thick that it has a fatty texture.

The label designations—extra virgin, virgin and pure—refer to the acidity of the oil (a low acid content is preferable) and the extent of processing used to extract the oil. The first cold-pressing of the olives results in virgin oil. (The designation "virgin" is used only when the oil is 100% unadulterated olive oil, unheated and without any chemical processing.) Virgin oil may still vary in quality depending on its acidity level. Extra virgin oil is virgin oil with an acidity level of not more than 1%; virgin oil may have an acidity level of up to 3%. Pure olive oil is processed from the pulp left after the first pressing using heat and chemicals. Pure oil is lighter in flavour and less expensive than virgin oil.

Flavoured oils, also known as **infused oils**, are an interesting and increasingly popular condiment. These oils may be used as a cooking medium or flavouring accent in marinades, dressings, sauces or other dishes. Flavours include basil and other herbs, garlic, citrus and spice. Flavoured oils are generally prepared with olive oil for additional flavour or canola oil, both considered more healthful than other fats.

Top-quality commercially flavoured oils are prepared by extracting aromatic oils from the flavouring ingredients and then emulsifying them with a high-grade oil; any impurities are then removed by placing the oil in a centrifuge. Using the aromatic oils of the flavouring ingredients yields a more intense flavour than merely steeping the same ingredients in the oil. Flavoured oils should be stored as you would any other high-quality oil.

VINEGARS

Vinegar (Fr. *vinaigre*) is a thin, sour liquid used for thousands of years as a preservative, cooking ingredient, condiment and cleaning solution. Vinegar is obtained through the fermentation of wine or other alcoholic liquid. Bacteria attack the alcohol in the solution, turning it into acetic acid. No alcohol will remain when the transformation is complete. The quality of vinegar depends upon the quality of the wine or other liquid on which it is based. Vinegar flavours are as varied as the liquids from which they are made.

Vinegars should be clear and clean looking, never cloudy or muddy. Commercial vinegars are pasteurized, so an unopened bottle should last indefinitely in a cool, dark place. Once opened, vinegars should last about three months if tightly capped. Any sediment that develops can be strained out; if mould develops, discard the vinegar.

Wine vinegars are as old as wine itself. They may be made from white or red wine, sherry or even champagne, and should bear the colour and flavour hallmarks of the wine used. Wine vinegars are preferred in French and Mediterranean cuisines.

Malt vinegar is produced from malted barley. Its slightly sweet, mild flavour is used as a condiment, especially with fried foods.

Distilled vinegar, made from grain alcohol, is completely clear, with a stronger vinegary flavour and higher acid content than other vinegars. It is preferred for pickling and preserving.

Cider vinegar is produced from unpasteurized apple juice or cider. It is pale brown in colour with a mild acidity and fruity aroma. Cider vinegar is particularly popular in North America.

Rice vinegar is a clear, slightly sweet product brewed from rice wine. Its flavour is clean and elegant, making it useful in a variety of dishes.

Flavoured vinegars are simply traditional vinegars in which herbs, spices, fruits or other foods are steeped to infuse their flavours. They are easily produced

Balsamic Vinegar

Raspberry Vinegar   Cider Vinegar

● **relish** a cooked or pickled sauce usually made with vegetables or fruits and often used as a condiment; can be smooth or chunky, sweet or savoury and hot or mild

● **pickle** (1) to preserve food in a brine or vinegar solution; (2) food that has been preserved in a seasoned brine or vinegar, especially cucumbers. Pickled cucumbers are available whole, sliced, in wedges, or chopped as a relish, and may be sweet, sour, dill-flavoured or hot and spicy.

from commercial wine or distilled vinegars, using any herb, spice or fruit desired. The use of flavoured vinegars is extremely popular but definitely not new. Clove, raspberry and fennel vinegars were sold on the streets of Paris during the 13th century. Making fruit-flavoured vinegars was also one of the responsibilities of North American housewives during the 18th and 19th centuries.

Balsamic vinegar (It. *aceto Balsamico)* is newly popular in North America, though it has been produced in Italy for more than 800 years. To produce balsamic vinegar, red wine vinegar is aged in a succession of wooden barrels made from a variety of woods—oak, cherry, locust, ash, mulberry and juniper—for at least 4, but sometimes up to 50, years. The resulting liquid is dark reddish-brown and sweet. Balsamic has a high acid level, but the sweetness covers the tart flavour, making it very mellow. True balsamic is extremely expensive because of the long aging process and the small quantities available. Most of the commercial products imported from Italy are now made by a quick caramelization and flavouring process. Balsamic is excellent as a condiment or seasoning and has a remarkable affinity for tomatoes and strawberries.

CONDIMENTS

Strictly speaking, a condiment is any food added to a dish for flavour, including herbs, spices and vinegars. Today, however, *condiments* more often refer to cooked or prepared flavourings, such as prepared mustards, **relishes**, bottled sauces and **pickles**. Several frequently used condiments are discussed here. These staples may be used to alter or enhance the flavour of a dish during cooking or added to a completed dish at the table by the consumer.

Chutney (from the Hindi word for *catnip)* is a pungent relish made from fruits, spices and herbs and is frequently used in Indian cooking.

Fermented black bean sauce is a Chinese condiment and flavouring ingredient made from black soybeans that have been heavily salted, then fermented and either slightly mashed (whole bean sauce) or puréed (paste). Both versions are usually mixed with hoisin, chile sauce or minced garlic to produce a sauce that has an intense, pungent, salty flavour. Yellow bean sauces are similar, but milder and sweeter.

Fish sauce (Viet. *nuoc mam;* Thai *nam pla)* is the liquid drained from fermenting salted anchovy-like fish. It is a thin, golden to light brown liquid with a very pungent, rotting odour and salty flavour. There is no substitute for the savoury richness that it adds to food and it is considered an essential flavouring and condiment throughout Southeast Asia, where it is used in and served with most every sort of dish.

Ketchup (also known as catsup) originated in Pakistan and referred to any salty extract from fish, fruits or vegetables. Prepared tomato ketchup, as we know it, is really a syrupy sauce, created in America and used worldwide as a flavouring ingredient or condiment. It is bright red and thick, with a tangy, sweet-sour flavour. Ketchup, with its high sugar content, can be stored either in the refrigerator or at room temperature; it should keep well for up to four months after opening. Ketchup does not turn rancid or develop mould, but it will darken and lose flavour as it ages.

Prepared mustard is a mixture of crushed mustard seeds, vinegar or wine and salt or spices. It can be flavoured in many ways—with herbs, onions, peppers and even citrus zest. It can be a smooth paste or coarse and chunky, depending on how finely the seeds are ground and whether the skins are strained out. Prepared mustard gets its tangy taste from an essential oil that forms only when the seeds are crushed and mixed with water. Prepared mustard can be used as a condiment, particularly with meat and charcuterie items, or as a flavouring ingredient in sauces, stews and marinades.

Fermented Black Bean Sauce

Fish Sauce

Yellow Mustard

Dijon Mustard

Whole-Grain Mustard

Brown Mustard

From Your Grocer's Shelf

Even the most sophisticated food service operation occasionally uses prepared condiments or flavourings. The products described here are widely used and available from grocery stores or wholesale purveyors. Some are brand-name items that have become almost synonymous with the product itself; others are available from several manufacturers.

Barbecue sauce—Like ketchup, commercial barbecue sauce is a mixture of tomatoes, vinegar and spices; it tends to be hotter and sweeter than ketchup, however. Commercial barbecue sauce is used primarily for marinating or basting meat, poultry or fish. A tremendous variety of barbecue sauces is available, with various flavours, textures and aromas. Sample several before selecting the most appropriate for your specific needs.

Fish sauce—Fish sauce is a thin, dark brown liquid made from anchovy extract and salt. It is the quintessential Thai seasoning, but is used throughout Southeast Asia. It is extremely salty with a powerful aroma. There is no substitute; only a small amount is necessary for most dishes.

Hoisin—Hoisin sauce is a dark, thick, salty-sweet sauce made from fermented soybeans, vinegar, garlic and caramel. It is used in Chinese dishes or served as a dipping sauce.

Old Bay® seasoning—Old Bay is a dry spice blend containing celery salt, dry mustard, paprika and other flavourings. It is widely used in shellfish preparations, especially boiled shrimp and crab.

Oyster sauce—Oyster sauce is a thick, dark sauce made from oyster extract. It has a salty-sweet flavour and rich aroma. Oyster sauce is often used with stir-fried meats and poultry.

Pickapeppa® sauce—Pickapeppa sauce is a dark, thick, sweet-hot blend of tomatoes, onions, sugar, vinegar, mango, raisins, tamarinds and spices. Produced in Jamaica, it is used as a condiment for meat, game or fish and as a seasoning in sauces, soups and dressings.

Tabasco® sauce—Tabasco sauce is a thin, bright red liquid blended from vinegar, chiles and salt. Its fiery flavour is widely used in sauces, soups and prepared dishes; it is a popular condiment for Mexican, southern and southwestern cuisines. Tabasco sauce has been produced in Louisiana since 1868. Other "Louisiana-style" hot sauces (those containing only peppers, vinegar and salt) may be substituted.

Worcestershire sauce—Worcestershire sauce is a thin, dark brown liquid made from malt vinegar, tamarind, molasses and spices. It is used as a condiment for beef and as a seasoning in sauces, soups, stews and prepared dishes. Its flavour should be rich and full, but not salty.

Dijon mustard takes its name from a town and the surrounding region in France that prepares about half of the world's mustard. French mustard labelled "Dijon" must, by law, be produced only in that region. Dijon and Dijon-style mustards are smooth with a rich, complex flavour. Western Canada grows the largest percentage of the world's mustard seed.

English and Chinese mustards are made from mustard flour and cool water. They are extremely hot and powerful. American or "ballpark" mustard is mild and vinegary with a bright yellow colour.

Mustard never really spoils, its flavour just fades away. Because of its high acid content, mustard does not turn rancid, but it will oxidize and develop a dark surface crust. Once opened, mustard should be kept well covered and refrigerated.

Soy sauce is a thin, dark brown liquid fermented from cooked soybeans, wheat and salt. Available in several flavours and strengths, it is ubiquitous in most Asian cuisines. Light soy sauce is thin, with a light brown colour and a very salty flavour. Dark soy sauce is thicker and dark brown, with a sweet, less salty flavour. Necessary for preparing many Asian dishes, soy sauce is also used in marinades and sauces and as an all-purpose condiment.

Tamari is a Japanese-style soy sauce made without wheat, although its name may be applied to a variety of Japanese-style soy sauces. Other common soy-based sauces and condiments include teriyaki sauce and fermented bean paste (miso), made by fermenting soybeans with a grain such as rice or barley.

Tahini is a thick, oily paste made of ground toasted sesame seeds. It is thick and slightly grainy, with an ivory to greyish-tan colour. Tahini can be bland or salty, depending on the manufacturer. Its toasted, nutty flavour is widely used in Middle Eastern and Mediterranean cuisine, especially in sauces and spreads such as hummus. Tahini is also useful in vegetarian dishes and is relatively high in protein and vitamins.

Conclusion

Much of the pleasure of eating comes from savouring the tastes and smells of well-flavoured, thoughtfully prepared foods. An understanding of how the human senses of taste and smell work helps a chef develop his or her own palate. With practice a chef will learn how to identify flavourings and learn to balance flavours when preparing recipes or creating new dishes.

Common flavourings include fresh and dried herbs, spices, salt, oils, condiments and vinegars. Chefs must be able to recognize, purchase, store and use many of these flavourings. The only way to determine which brands or types of flavourings are best for your particular needs is to taste, smell, sample and use a variety of those available. Cost, convenience and storage factors must also be considered. By maintaining a supply of flavourings, chefs will be able to create new dishes or enhance standard ones at a moment's notice.

Questions for Discussion

1. Identify the four western tastes and the Japanese addition. How does our olfactory system interpret these tastes?
2. What are some factors that can affect flavours? Discuss how this relates to cooking certain foods.
3. What is a flavouring? Does every kitchen keep the same flavourings on hand? Explain your answer.
4. What are the differences between a herb and a spice? Give an example of a plant that is used as both a herb and a spice.
5. If a recipe calls for a fresh herb and you have only the dried herb, what do you do? Explain your answer.
6. What is the difference between a sachet and a bouquet garni? Identify the ingredients in a standard sachet and a standard bouquet garni.

Eggs and Dairy Products

> Food history is as important as a Baroque church. Governments should recognize cultural heritage and protect traditional foods.
> A cheese is as worthy of preserving as a sixteenth-century building.
>
> —Carlo Petrini, Italian journalist (1950–)

After studying this chapter you will be able to:

- describe the composition of eggs

- purchase and store eggs properly

- prepare whipped egg whites

- identify, store and use a variety of milk-based products

- explain how to clarify butter

- identify, store and serve a variety of fine cheeses

Separating Eggs

The method preferred by health authorities for separating egg whites and yolks is to use the shell. Crack the egg so as to split the shell in two halves. Gently move the yolk from one shell half to the other to allow the albumen to separate and fall into a clean bowl.

The use of hands is not recommended due to the high potential for cross-contamination. The shell is deemed to be cleaner than a food worker's hands. Gloves are viewed as the same as hands.

Eggs and milk are unique in that they, along with seeds, are the only foods that are truly designed to support life: eggs support chick embryos; milk supports calves. Thus they are among the most nutritious of foods. Eggs as well as milk and milk-based products (known collectively as dairy products) are also extremely versatile. They are used throughout the kitchen, either served alone or as ingredients in everything from soups and sauces to breads and pastries. High quality and freshness are critical for their proper use. Learn to select the finest products, whether eggs, whole milk, butter or Brie, and handle them with care.

EGGS

Nature designed eggs to be the food source for developing chicks. Eggs, particularly chicken eggs, are also an excellent food for humans because of their high protein content, low cost and ready availability. Quail eggs are also used in food service operations. Duck and goose eggs are too fatty to be useful, however, except for preserved duck eggs.

Eggs can be cooked in a variety of ways, some of which are described in Chapter 33, Breakfast and Brunch. Eggs are also incorporated into other dishes to provide texture, structure, flavour, moisture and nutrition.

Composition

The primary parts of an egg are the shell, yolk and albumen. (See Figure 8.1.)

The shell, composed of calcium carbonate, is the outermost covering of the egg. It prevents microbes from entering and moisture from escaping, and protects the egg during handling and transport. Shell colour is determined by the breed of the hen; for chickens it can range from bright white to brown. Shell colour has no effect on quality, flavour or nutrition.

The yolk is the yellow portion of the egg. It constitutes just over one-third of the egg and contains three-fourths of the calories, most of the minerals and vitamins and all of the fat. The yolk also contains lecithin, the compound responsible for emulsification in products such as hollandaise sauce and mayonnaise. Egg yolk solidifies (coagulates) at temperatures between

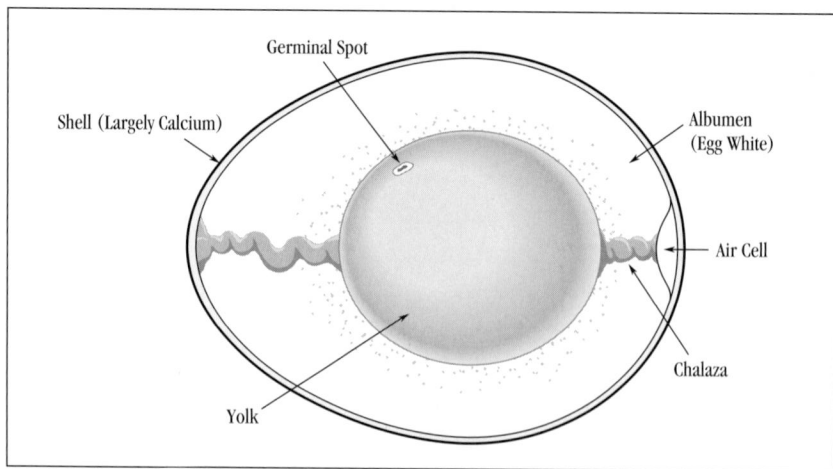

FIGURE 8.1 An egg.

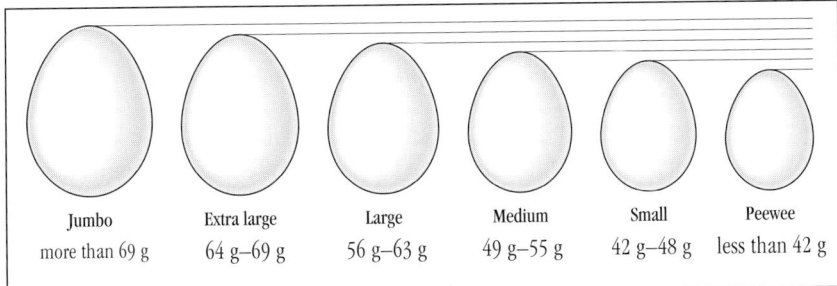

FIGURE 8.2 Egg sizes.

Jumbo	Extra large	Large	Medium	Small	Peewee
more than 69 g	64 g–69 g	56 g–63 g	49 g–55 g	42 g–48 g	less than 42 g

Omega-3 Eggs

More breakfast menus are offering omega-3 eggs. Chickens are fed flaxseed to enrich the omega-3 fatty acids in the yolk by up to 10 times that of regular eggs. EPA and DHA fatty acids are also increased, providing a triple benefit. Two omega-3 eggs contain more than half of Health Canada's recommended daily adult intake of omega-3 fatty acid.

65°C and 70°C (149°F and 158°F). Although the colour of a yolk may vary depending on the hen's feed, colour does not affect quality or nutritional content.

The **albumen** is the clear portion of the egg and is often referred to as the egg white. It constitutes about two-thirds of the egg and contains more than half of the protein and riboflavin. Egg white coagulates, becoming firm and opaque, at temperatures between 62°C and 65°C (144°F and 149°F).

An often misunderstood portion of the egg is the **chalazae cords**. These thick, twisted strands of egg white anchor the yolk in place. They are neither imperfections nor embryos. The more prominent the chalazae, the fresher the egg. Chalazae do not interfere with cooking or with whipping egg whites.

Eggs are sold in jumbo, extra large, large, medium, small and peewee sizes, as determined by weight per dozen. (See Figure 8.2.) Food service operations generally use large eggs and liquid whole egg for cost savings. Naturally enhanced omega-3 eggs are increasingly popular.

When separating eggs into whites and yolks, there is a range of weight for each component. Generally, medium eggs will have 32 g of albumen and 16 g of yolk. Large eggs will have approximately 35 g of albumen and 18 g of yolk.

● **albumen** the principal protein found in egg whites

● **chalazae cords** thick, twisted strands of egg white that anchor the yolk in place

Grading

Eggs are graded by the Canadian Food Inspection Agency (CFIA) (Egg and Egg Products Division). The grade A, B or C is given to an egg based upon interior and exterior quality, not size. The qualities for each grade are described in Table 8.1. Grade has no effect on nutritional values.

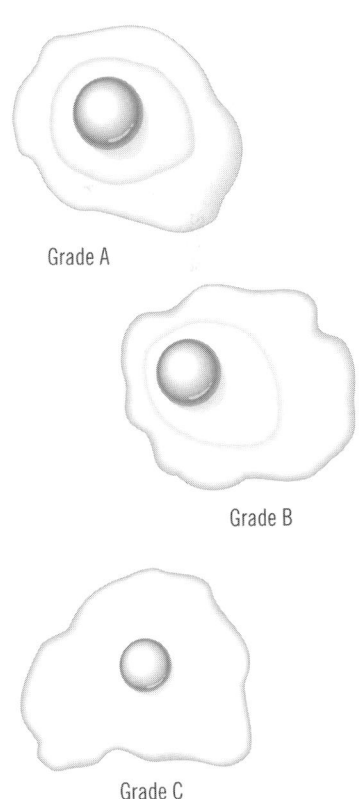

Grade A

Grade B

Grade C

TABLE 8.1	Egg Grades		
	Grade A	**Grade B**	**Grade C**
Albumen	Firm	Watery	Thin and watery
Yolk	Round, well centred	Slightly flattened	Loose
Shell	Clean, no cracks, normal shape	No cracks, but rough texture	May be cracked
Use	Sold at retail markets for household use	Used for commercial baking or further processing	Not sold to consumers; sold to commercial processors for further processing

Storage

Egg quality is quickly diminished by improper handling. Eggs should be stored at temperatures below 4°C (40°F) and at a relative humidity of 70% to 80%. Eggs will age more during one day at room temperature than they will during one week under proper refrigeration. As eggs age, the white becomes thinner and the yolk becomes flatter. Although this will change the appearance of poached or fried eggs, age has little effect on nutrition or behaviour during cooking procedures. Older eggs, however, should be used for hard-boiling, as the shells are easier to remove than those of fresh eggs.

Cartons of fresh, uncooked eggs will keep for at least four to five weeks beyond the pack date if properly refrigerated. Hard-boiled eggs left in their shells and refrigerated should be used within one week.

Store eggs away from strongly flavoured foods to reduce odour absorption. Rotate egg stock to maintain freshness. Do not use dirty, cracked or broken eggs as they may contain bacteria or other contaminants. Frozen eggs should be thawed in the refrigerator and used only in dishes that will be thoroughly cooked, such as baked products. Liquid egg must be refrigerated.

Sanitation

Eggs are a potentially hazardous food. Rich in protein, they are an excellent breeding ground for bacteria. Salmonella is of particular concern with eggs and egg products because this bacteria is commonly found in a chicken's intestinal tract. Although shells are cleaned at packing houses, some bacteria may remain. Therefore, to prevent contamination, it is best to avoid mixing a shell with the liquid egg.

Inadequately cooking or improperly storing eggs may lead to food-borne illnesses. **Pasteurization** is achieved when the whole egg stays at a temperature of 60°C (140°F) for 3.5 minutes. Hold egg dishes below 4°C (40°F) or above 63°C (145°F). Never leave an egg dish at room temperature for more than one hour, including preparation and service time. Never reuse a container after it has held raw eggs without thoroughly cleaning and sanitizing it. Do not use your fingers to separate eggs.

Egg Products

Food service operations often want the convenience of buying eggs out of the shell in the exact form needed: whole eggs, yolks only or whites only. These processed items are called *egg products* and are subject to strict pasteurization standards and CFIA inspections. Egg products can be frozen, refrigerated or dried. Precooked, preportioned and blended egg products are also available.

Egg Substitutes

Concerns about the cholesterol content of eggs have increased the popularity of egg substitutes. There are two general types of substitute. The first is a complete substitute made from soy or milk proteins. It should not be used in recipes in which eggs are required for thickening. The second substitute contains real albumen, but the egg yolk has been replaced with vegetable or milk products. Egg substitutes have a different flavour from real eggs but may be useful for persons on a restricted diet.

Nutrition

Eggs contain vitamins A, D, E and K and the B-complex vitamins. They are rich in minerals but also in cholesterol. The nutritional values of an egg are

Pasteurized Eggs

The potential risk of salmonella infection has resulted in many food service operations requiring the use of pasteurized egg products only. Whether liquid whole, albumen or yolks, fresh or frozen, they function in cooking the same as shell eggs. Pasteurized egg products contribute to HACCP compliance. Certified salmonella-free eggs and chickens are available in some parts of the world. Nutritionally enhanced omega-3 eggs are also available.

● **pasteurization** the process of heating a product to a specific temperature for a specific time to destroy pathogenic bacteria

TABLE 8.2	Nutritional Values of an Egg					
	Energy	Protein	Total Fat	Saturated Fat	Carbohydrates	Cholesterol
One large egg contains	75 calories	6 g	5 g	1.5 g	0.5 g	215 mg
Source: Canadian Egg Marketing Agency.						

listed in Table 8.2. Eggs are a good source of protein. Omega-3 eggs are widely available and have a significant level of omega-3 fatty acids, essential to a healthful diet.

Whipped Egg Whites

Egg whites are often whipped into a foam that is then incorporated into cakes, custards, soufflés, pancakes or other products. The air beaten into the egg foam gives products lightness and assists with leavening. Egg whites are usually whipped to a soft peak or stiff stage.

BASIC PROCEDURE FOR WHIPPING EGG WHITES

1. Use fresh egg whites that are completely free of egg yolk or other impurities. Warm the egg whites to room temperature before whipping; this causes a better foam to form.

2. Use a clean bowl and whisk. Even a tiny amount of fat can prevent the egg whites from foaming properly.

3. Whip the whites on medium speed until very foamy, then add salt or cream of tartar as directed.

4. Continue whipping until soft peaks form, then gradually add granulated sugar (or hot syrup, if preparing meringues) as directed.

5. Whip until stiff peaks form. Properly whipped egg whites should be moist and shiny; over-whipping will make the egg whites appear dry and spongy or curdled.

6. Use the whipped egg whites immediately. If liquid begins to separate from the whipped egg whites, discard them; they cannot be rewhipped successfully.

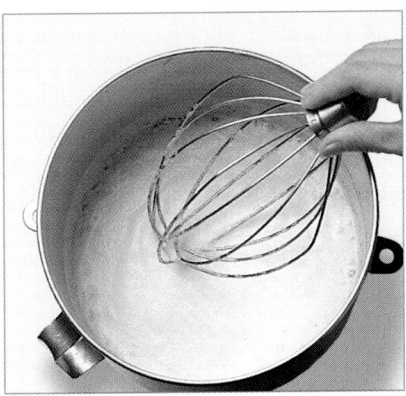

Egg whites whipped to soft peaks

Egg whites whipped to stiff peaks

Spongy, over-whipped egg whites

DAIRY PRODUCTS

Dairy products include cow's milk and foods produced from cow's milk such as butter, yogurt, sour cream and cheese. The milk of other mammals, namely goats, sheep and buffaloes, is also made into cheeses that are used in commercial food service operations. Regulations affecting dairy products are both federal and provincial, although they are being standardized under the Canadian Food Inspection Agency.

Milk

Milk is not only a popular beverage, but it is also used in the preparation of many dishes. It provides texture, flavour, colour and nutritional value for cooked or baked items. Indeed, milk is considered one of the most nutritious foods available, providing proteins, vitamins and minerals (particularly calcium). But milk is also highly perishable and is an excellent bacterial breeding ground. Care must be exercised in the handling and storage of milk and other dairy products.

Whole milk—that is, milk as it comes from the cow—is composed primarily of water (about 88%). It contains not less than 3.25% milkfat and at least 8% other milk solids (proteins, milk sugar [lactose] and minerals).

Fresh whole milk is not available raw but must be processed as described below, except for raw milk cheeses.

Processing Techniques

Pasteurization

By law, all milk must be pasteurized prior to retail sale. Pasteurization is the process of heating milk to a sufficiently high temperature for a sufficient length of time to destroy pathogenic bacteria. This typically requires holding milk at a temperature of 72°C (161°F) for 16 seconds. Pasteurization also destroys enzymes that cause spoilage, thus increasing shelf life. Milk's nutritional value is not significantly affected by pasteurization.

Ultra-Pasteurization

Ultra-pasteurization is a process in which milk is heated to a very high temperature (135°C/275°F) for a very short time (two to four seconds) in order to destroy virtually all bacteria. Ultra-pasteurization is most often used with whipping cream and individual creamers. Although the process may reduce cream's whipping properties, it extends its shelf life dramatically.

Ultra-High-Temperature Processing

Ultra-high-temperature processing (UHT) is a form of ultra-pasteurization in which milk is held at a temperature of 138°C to 150°C (280°F to 300°F) for two to six seconds. It is then packed in sterile containers under sterile conditions and aseptically sealed to prevent bacteria from entering the container. Unopened UHT milk can be stored without refrigeration for at least three months. Although UHT milk can be stored unrefrigerated, it should be chilled before serving and stored like fresh milk once opened. UHT processing may give milk a slightly cooked taste, but it has no significant effect on milk's nutritional value. It has long been available in Europe and Canada.

Homogenization

Homogenization is a process in which the fat globules in whole milk are reduced in size and permanently dispersed throughout the liquid. This prevents

---

● **dairy products** include cow's milk and foods produced from cow's milk such as butter, yogurt, sour cream and cheese; sometimes other milks and products made from them are included (e.g., goat's milk cheese)

Perfect Food?

Humans are the only mammal to regularly consume another mammal's milk. There is growing debate as to the prudence of this practice. The prevalence of lactose intolerance is now more widely documented, as well as intolerance to soy products, a widely accepted substitute. There may be an ethnocultural link to these conditions. It has also been suggested that although we regularly enjoy global access to almost any fruit or vegetable, our bodies may not be able to take full advantage of the nutrients due to inherited predispositions to certain foods. For example, those of northern European heritage may only derive sensory pleasure from a pineapple, as their bodies do not have the full capability to process the food completely. Likewise, Asians tend to have an intolerance for lactose and alcohol. Further research will help to clarify the situation and help us to understand how to best fuel our bodies.

the fat from clumping together and rising to the surface as a layer of cream. Although homogenization is not required, milk sold commercially is generally homogenized because it ensures a uniform consistency, a whiter colour and a richer taste.

Certification

Certification is a method of controlling the quality of milk by controlling the condition of the animals from which milk is obtained. Certification is not a true processing technique; rather, it requires frequent veterinary examinations of the cows and health department inspections of the dairy farm, the equipment and the employees who handle milk. Pasteurization has replaced the need for certification, but milk from certified herds is still available in a few areas.

Milkfat Removal

Whole milk can also be processed in a centrifuge to remove all or a portion of the milkfat, resulting in **lowfat milk** or partly **skim milk**.

Partly skim milk is whole milk from which sufficient milkfat has been removed to produce a liquid with 1% to 3.2% milkfat. (All lowfat milks must still contain at least 8% milk solids.) Vitamin A is added to lowfat milk to replace that removed along with the milkfat. It will be labelled with the fat content.

Skim milk, also referred to as lowfat milk, has had as much milkfat removed as possible. The fat content must be not more than 1%. Skim milk must also contain at least 8% milk solids and be fortified with vitamin A.

Storage

Fluid milk should be kept refrigerated at or below 4°C (40°F). Its shelf life is reduced by half for every 5-degree rise in temperature above 4°C (40°F). Keep milk containers closed to prevent absorption of odours and flavours. Freezing is not recommended.

Concentrated Milks

Concentrated or condensed milk products are produced by using a vacuum to remove all or part of the water from whole milk. The resulting products have a high concentration of milkfat and milk solids and an extended shelf life.

Evaporated milk is produced by removing approximately 60% of the water from whole, homogenized milk. Evaporated milk must contain at least 7.5% milkfat and 25% milk solids. Vitamins may be added as required. The concentrated liquid is canned and heat-sterilized. This results in a cooked flavour and darker colour. Evaporated skim milk has a milkfat content of not more than 0.3% and less than 17% milk solids other than fat. A can of evaporated milk requires no refrigeration until opened, although the can should be stored in a cool place. Evaporated milk can be reconstituted with an equal amount of water and used like whole milk for cooking or drinking.

Sweetened condensed milk is similar to evaporated milk in that 60% of the water has been removed. But unlike evaporated milk, sweetened condensed milk contains sweeteners and a minimum of 8% milkfat. Sweetened condensed milk is also canned; the canning process darkens the colour and adds a caramel flavour. Sweetened condensed milk cannot be substituted for whole milk or evaporated milk because of its sugar content. Its distinctive flavour is most often found in desserts and confections.

Dry milk powder is made by removing virtually all of the moisture from pasteurized milk. It is a graded product. The moisture content will vary depending on the process used. Milk powder graded as Canada #1 has less than 4%

Not Just from Cows

Cow's milk is by far the most widely used milk in North America, but other kinds of milk include:

Ewe's milk—Milk produced by a female sheep; it has approximately 7.9% milkfat, 11.4% milk solids and 80.7% water. It is naturally homogenized.

Goat's milk—Milk produced by a female goat; it has approximately 4.1% milkfat, 8.9% milk solids and 87% water.

Water buffalo milk—Milk produced by a female water buffalo; it has approximately 7.5% milkfat, 10.3% milk solids and 82.2% water.

SAFETY ALERT

Milk Storage

Canned milks, aseptically packaged milks and dry milk powders are shelf-stable products needing no refrigeration. After the can or box is opened or the powder is reconstituted with water, however, these become potentially hazardous foods and must be handled just as carefully as fresh milk. Do not store an open can of milk in its original container, and keep all milk products refrigerated at or below 4°C (40°F).

Imitation and Artificial Dairy Products

Coffee whiteners, imitation sour cream, whipped topping mixes and some whipped toppings in pressurized cans are made from nondairy products. These products usually consist of corn syrup, emulsifiers, vegetable fats, colouring agents and artificial flavours. These products are generally less expensive and have a longer shelf life than the real dairy products they replace, but their flavours are no match. Imitation and artificial products may be useful, however, for persons with allergies or on a restricted diet. If you choose to use these products, you cannot claim to be using real dairy products on menus or labels. Mislabelling or misrepresenting products is unethical and illegal.

moisture and 1.2% milkfat; Canada #2 has less than 1.29% milkfat and 5% moisture by weight. Dry whole milk contains a minimum of 2.6% milkfat. Nonfat milk powder is made from skim milk and must contain less than 1.2% milkfat by weight. Both types of dry milk are usually fortified with vitamins A and D.

The lack of moisture prevents the growth of microorganisms and allows dry whole and nonfat milk powders to be stored for extended periods without refrigeration. However, because of its high milkfat content, dried whole milk can turn rancid if not stored in a cool place. Either type of dry milk can be reconstituted with water and used like fresh milk. Milk powder may also be added to foods directly, with additional liquid included in the recipe. This procedure is typical in bread making and does not alter the function of the milk or the flavour in the finished product.

Cream

Cream is a rich, liquid milk product containing at least 18% milkfat. It must be pasteurized or ultra-pasteurized and may be homogenized. Cream has a slight yellow or ivory colour and is more viscous than milk. It is used throughout the kitchen to give flavour and body to sauces, soups and desserts. Whipping cream, containing not less than 30% milkfat, can be whipped into a stiff foam and used in pastries and desserts. Cream is marketed in several forms with different fat contents, as described here.

Table cream is a mixture of whole milk and cream containing not less than 18% milkfat. It is often served with cereal or coffee, but does not contain enough fat to whip into a foam.

Half-and-half, light cream or **coffee cream** are all products with more than 10% but less than 18% milkfat. These products are often used in baked goods or soups as well as with coffee, fruit and cereal. An 18% cream is now being marketed.

Whipping cream generally ranges from 30% to 36% milkfat, although higher percentages are available. It is generally used for thickening and enriching sauces and making ice cream. It can be whipped into a foam and used as a dessert topping or folded into custards or mousses to add flavour and lightness.

Storage

Ultra-pasteurized cream will keep for six to eight weeks if refrigerated. Unwhipped cream should not be frozen. Whipped, sweetened cream can be frozen, tightly covered, for up to three months, then slowly thawed in the refrigerator. Keep cream away from strong odours and bright lights, as they can adversely affect its flavour.

Cultured Dairy Products

Cultured dairy products such as yogurt, buttermilk and sour cream are produced by adding specific bacterial cultures to fluid dairy products. The bacteria convert the milk sugar **lactose** into lactic acid, giving these products their body and tangy, unique flavours. The acid content also retards the growth of undesirable microorganisms; thus, cultured products have been used for centuries to preserve milk.

Buttermilk originally referred to the liquid remaining after cream was churned into butter. Today buttermilk is produced by adding a culture (*Streptococcus lactis*) to fresh, pasteurized skim or lowfat milk. This results in a tart milk with a thick texture. Buttermilk is most often used as a beverage or in baked goods.

● **lactose** a disaccharide that occurs naturally in mammalian milk; milk sugar

Sour cream is produced by adding the same culture to pasteurized, homogenized light cream. The resulting product is a white, tangy gel used as a condiment or to give baked goods a distinctive flavour. Sour cream must have the milkfat content clearly labelled. Stabilizers may be added.

Crème fraîche is a cultured cream popular in French cuisine. Although thinner and richer than sour cream, it has a similar tart, tangy flavour. It is used extensively in soups and sauces, especially with poultry, rabbit and lamb dishes. It is easily prepared from the following recipe.

Crème Fraîche

APPLYING THE BASICS		RECIPE 8.1

Crème Fraîche

Yield: 500 mL (2 cups)

Whipping cream	500 mL	16 fl. oz.
Buttermilk, with active cultures	30 mL	1 fl. oz.

1. Heat the cream (preferably not ultra-pasteurized) to about 43°C (100°F).
2. Remove the cream from the heat and stir in the buttermilk.
3. Allow the mixture to stand in a warm place, loosely covered, until it thickens, approximately 12–36 hours.
4. Chill thoroughly before using. Crème fraîche will keep for up to 10 days in the refrigerator.

RECIPE 8.1

Approximate values per 30 g serving:	
Calories	90
Total fat	10 g
Saturated fat	6 g
Cholesterol	35 mg
Sodium	10 mg
Total carbohydrates	1 g
Protein	1 g

Yogurt is a thick, tart, custardlike product made from milk (either whole, lowfat or nonfat) cultured with *Lactobacillus bulgaricus* and *Streptococcus thermophilus*. Though touted as a health or diet food, yogurt contains the same amount of milkfat as the milk from which it is made. Yogurt may also contain a variety of sweeteners, flavourings and fruits. Yogurt is generally eaten as is, but may be used in baked products, salad dressings and frozen desserts. It is used in many Middle Eastern cuisines.

Storage

Cultured products should be kept refrigerated at 4°C (40°F) or below. Under proper conditions sour cream will last up to four weeks, yogurt up to three weeks and buttermilk up to two weeks. Freezing is not recommended for these products, but dishes prepared with cultured products generally can be frozen.

Butter

Butter is a fatty substance produced by agitating or churning cream. Its flavour is unequalled in sauces, breads and pastries. Butter contains at least 80% milkfat and not more than 20% moisture. It may or may not contain added salt. Butter is firm when chilled and soft at room temperature. It melts into a liquid at approximately 38°C (98°F) and reaches the smoke point at 127°C (260°F).

Government grading of dairy products, including butter, is mandatory as described in the Canada Agricultural Products Act—Dairy Products Regulations. The three grades of dairy products have grade names of Canada 1, Canada 2 and Canada 3. The Canada grade label on the butter package assures the consumer that the butter meets federal standards for the grade indicated.

Cultured Butter

Sometimes referred to as European butter, cultured butter contains 82% to 86% milk fat. Cultured butter is used to produce a rich, nutty flavour. It is not presently available in Canada.

Ghee

Ghee is an Indian version of clarified butter originally made from water buffalo milk. It has a long shelf life, a high smoke point and a nutty, caramel-like flavour. Ghee flavoured with ginger, peppercorns or cumin is also available.

- Canada 1: Butter of superior quality, with fresh, sweet flavour and aroma, a smooth creamy texture and good spreadability.
- Canada 2: Butter of very good quality, with pleasing flavour and fairly smooth texture.
- Canada 3: A processing grade used only for dairy products packed in bulk.

Salted butter is butter with up to 2.5% salt added. This not only changes the butter's flavour but also extends its keeping qualities. When using salted butter in cooking or baking, the salt content must be considered in the total recipe.

Whipped butter is made by incorporating air into the butter. This increases its volume and spreadability, but also increases the speed at which the butter will become rancid. Because of the change in density, whipped butter should not be substituted in recipes calling for regular butter.

Storage

With its high fat content, butter is extremely prone to **rancidity**. Rancid butter has a harsh, bitter taste and is deep yellow to brown in colour. To preserve its freshness, butter should be well wrapped and stored at temperatures between 0°C and 2°C (32°F and 35°F). Unsalted butter is best kept frozen until needed. If well wrapped, frozen butter will keep for up to nine months at a temperature of –18°C (0°F).

Clarified Butter

Clarified butter is butter that has had its water and milk solids removed by a process called clarification. Although **whole butter** can be used for cooking or sauce making, sometimes a more stable and consistent product will be achieved by using butter oil. It can be purchased commercially.

Clarified butter will keep for extended periods in either the freezer or the refrigerator.

Skimming milk solids from the surface of melted butter

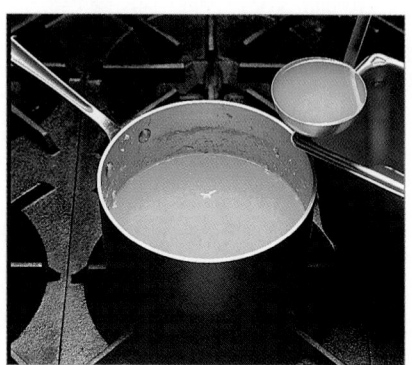

Ladling the butterfat into a clean pan

BASIC PROCEDURE FOR CLARIFYING BUTTER

1. Slowly warm the butter in a saucepan over low heat without boiling or agitating. As the butter melts, the milk solids rise to the top as a foam and the water sinks to the bottom.

2. When the butter is completely melted, skim just the milk solids from the top. Simmer until the oil clears.

3. When all the milk solids have been removed, ladle the butterfat into a clean saucepan, being careful to leave the water in the bottom of the pan.

4. The clarified butter is now ready to use. Four hundred and fifty-four grams (1 lb.) of whole salted butter will yield approximately 340 g (12 oz.) of clarified butter (a yield of 75%).

● **rancidity** the decomposition of fats by exposure to oxygen, resulting in off-flavours and destruction of nutritive components.

● **whole butter** butter that is not clarified, whipped or reduced fat

Margarine

Margarine is not a dairy product, but it is included in this section because it is so frequently substituted for butter in cooking, baking and table service. Margarine is manufactured from vegetable or animal fats or a combination of such fats. Flavourings, colourings, emulsifiers, preservatives and vitamins are added, and the mixture is firmed or solidified by exposure to hydrogen gas at very high temperatures, a process known as hydrogenation. Generally, the firmer the margarine, the greater the degree of hydrogenation and the longer its shelf life. Like butter, margarine is approximately 80% fat and 20% moisture. But even the finest margarine cannot match the flavour of butter.

Margarine packaged in tubs is softer and more spreadable than solid products and generally contains more water and air. Indeed, diet margarine is approximately 50% water. Because of their decreased density, these soft products should not be substituted for regular butter or margarine in cooking or baking.

Specially formulated and blended margarine or shortening is available for commercial use in making puff pastry, croissant doughs, frostings and the like.

Nutrition

Dairy products are naturally high in vitamins, minerals and protein. Often liquid products such as milk are fortified with additional vitamins and minerals. Their fat content varies depending upon the amount of milkfat left after processing.

Natural Cheeses

Cheese (Fr. *fromage*; It. *formaggio*) is one of the oldest and most widely used foods known. It is served alone or as a principal ingredient in or an accompaniment to countless dishes. Cheese is commonly used in commercial kitchens, appearing in everything from breakfast to snacks to desserts.

Literally hundreds of natural cheeses are produced worldwide. Although their shapes, ages and flavours vary according to local preferences and traditions, all natural cheeses are produced in the same basic fashion as has been used for centuries. Each starts with a mammal's milk; cows, goats and sheep are the most commonly used. The milk proteins (known as *casein*) are coagulated with the addition of an enzyme, usually rennet, which is found in calves' stomachs. As the milk coagulates, it separates into solid curds and liquid whey. After draining off the whey, either the curds are made into fresh cheese, such as ricotta or cottage cheese, or the curds are further processed by cutting, kneading and cooking. The resulting substance, known as "green cheese," is packed into moulds to drain. Salt or special bacteria may be added to the moulded cheeses, which are then allowed to age or ripen under controlled conditions to develop the desired texture, colour and flavour.

Cheeses are a product of their environment, which is why most fine cheeses cannot be reproduced outside their native locale. The breed and feed of the milk animal, the wild spores and moulds in the air and even the wind currents in a storage area can affect the manner in which a cheese develops. (Roquefort, for example, develops its distinctive flavour from aging in particular caves filled with crosscurrents of cool, moist air.) Canada has a thriving cheese industry and produces world-class products. They are unsurpassed in quality; Canada has among the strictest standards in the world.

Some cheeses develop a natural rind or surface because of the application of bacteria (bloomy rind) or by repeated washing with brine (washed rind). Most natural rinds may be eaten if desired. Other cheeses are coated with an inedible wax rind to prevent moisture loss. Fresh cheeses have no rind whatsoever.

Moisture and fat contents are good indicators of a cheese's texture and shelf life. The higher the moisture content, the softer the product and the more perishable

Margarine: From Laboratory Bench to Dinner Table

Margarine was invented by a French chemist in 1869 after Napoleon III offered a prize for the development of a synthetic edible fat. Originally produced from animal fat and milk, margarine is now made almost exclusively from vegetable fats.

In *On Food and Cooking, The Science and Lore of the Kitchen,* Harold McGee recounts the history of margarine. He explains that margarine caught on quickly in Europe and America, with large-scale production underway by 1880. But the American dairy industry and the U.S. government put up fierce resistance. First, margarine was defined as a harmful drug and its sale restricted. Then it was heavily taxed; stores had to be licensed to sell it and, like alcohol and tobacco, it was bootlegged. The U.S. government refused to purchase it for use by the armed forces. And, in an attempt to hold it to its true colours, some states did not allow margarine to be dyed yellow (animal fats and vegetable oils are much paler than butter); the dye was sold separately and mixed in by the consumer. World War II, which brought butter rationing, probably did the most to establish margarine's respectability. But it was not until 1967 that yellow margarine could be sold in Wisconsin or parts of Canada.

Today North Americans consume nearly three times as much margarine as butter. Both price and the concern about heart disease are responsible for this differential. Current research indicates that hydrogenated fats are potentially a greater health risk. Trans fats must now be identified on food product labels.

Making Mozzarella

In Italy, mozzarella is made every day; it is meant to be consumed just as often. Before there was refrigeration, the balls of mozzarella were stored in well water to keep them cool, which is where the tradition originated of storing fresh mozzarella in liquid.

Once the milk is coagulated and the curds are cut, the mass is slowly stirred to enhance the whey's expulsion. A few hours later, when the curds are mature, they are removed from the whey, chopped or shredded and then mixed with hot water.

To test the exact amount of maturity, a handful of curds is dipped into a bucket of hot water for 10 seconds. When the curds are removed, they should be kneaded briefly and then, holding the mass with two hands, it should be pulled and stretched out to determine its maturity. When it is exactly ready to be strung, it can be stretched as thin and opaque as tissue paper. At this point, small amounts of curd are dumped into a small vat and stirred with hot water using a paddle. This is known as "stringing" the cheese because as the curds are mixed with the water, they begin to melt somewhat and become stringy. The more the cheese is stirred the longer the strings are stretched. Eventually all the strings come together to make a large mass of satiny-smooth cheese. In Italian the word *filare* means "to string"; therefore, all cheeses that are strung are members of the *pasta filata* family.

When stringing is complete, the cheese is ready to be shaped and hand-formed into balls. The balls are tossed immediately into vats of cool water so they will maintain the desired shapes. When cool, the balls are immersed in brine solution and then wrapped in parchment paper.

Paula Lambert, owner
Mozzarella Company, Dallas, Texas

it will be. Low-moisture cheeses may be used for grating and will keep for several weeks if properly stored. (Reduced water activity levels prohibit bacterial growth.) Fat content ranges from low fat (less than 20% fat) to double cream (at least 60% fat) and triple cream (at least 72% fat). Cheeses with a high fat content will be creamier and have a richer taste and texture than lowfat products.

Most cheeses contain high percentages of fat and protein. Cheese is also rich in calcium, phosphorus and vitamin A. As animal products, natural cheeses contain cholesterol. Today, many lowfat, even nonfat, processed cheeses are available. Sodium has also been reduced or eliminated from some modern products.

Cheese Varieties

Cheeses can be classified by country of origin, ripening method, fat content or texture. Here we classify fine cheeses by texture. The Dairy Bureau of Canada recognizes six categories: fresh or unripened, soft, semi-soft, firm, hard and light. A separate section on goat's milk and other cheeses is also included.

Fresh or Unripened Cheeses

Fresh cheeses are uncooked and unripened. Referred to as *fromage blanc* or *fromage frais* in French, they are generally mild and creamy with a tart tanginess. They should not taste acidic or bitter. Fresh cheeses have a moisture content of 40% to 80% and are highly perishable.

Cream cheese is soft cow's milk cheese containing a minimum of 30% fat. It is available in various-sized solid white blocks or whipped and flavoured. It is used throughout the kitchen in baking, dips, dressings and confections and is popular as a spread for bagels or toast.

Mascarpone is a soft cow's milk cheese originally from Italy's Lombard region. It contains 70% to 75% fat and is extremely smooth and creamy. Mascarpone is highly perishable and is available in bulk or in 250- or 500-g (8- or 16-oz.) tubs. Its pale ivory colour and rich, sweet flavour are useful in both sweet and savoury sauces as well as desserts. It is also eaten plain, with fresh fruit, or spread on bread and sprinkled with cocoa or sugar.

Mascarpone

Ricotta is a soft cheese of Italian origin, similar to cottage cheese, made from the whey left when other cow's milk cheeses are produced. It contains from 0% to 10% fat. It is white or ivory in colour and creamy in texture, with a small grain and mellow, sometimes slightly tart, flavour. Ricotta is an important ingredient in many pasta dishes and desserts.

Ricotta

Soft Cheeses

Soft cheeses are characterized by their bloomy rinds and creamy centres. They are among the most delicious and popular of cheeses. They ripen quickly and are at their peak for only a few days, sometimes less. Canadian soft cheeses are not cooked or pressed. Moisture content ranges from 50% to 60%.

Bel paese is a 20th-century Italian creation made from cow's milk and containing approximately 50% fat. It is mild and creamy with a fruity flavour. The inside is yellowish and the outside is brown or grey. Bel paese is excellent for snacking and melts easily.

Brie is a surface-ripened cheese of French origin made with whole cow's milk and containing a minimum of 23% fat. Brie is made in round, flat disks weighing 1 or 2 kg (2 or 4 lb.); it is coated with a bloomy white rind. At the peak of ripeness it is creamy and rich, with a texture that oozes. Some Bries are called double or triple cream. Selecting a properly ripened Brie is a matter of judgment and experience. Select a cheese that is bulging a bit inside its rind; there should be just the beginning of brown colouring on the rind. If underripe, Brie will be bland with a hard, chalky core. Once the cheese is cut it will not ripen any further. If overripe, Brie will have a brownish rind that may be gummy or sagging and will smell strongly of ammonia. The rind (*penicillium camemberti*) is edible. The classic after-dinner cheese, Brie is also used in soups, sauces and hors d'oeuvre. Canada produces many fine Bries, particularly in Quebec.

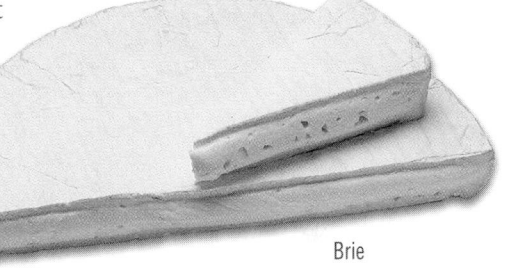
Brie

Boursin is a triple-cream cow's milk cheese from France containing approximately 75% fat. Boursin is usually flavoured with peppers, herbs or garlic. It is rindless, with a smooth, creamy texture, and is packed in small, foil-wrapped cylinders. Boursin is a good breakfast cheese and a welcome addition to any cheese board. It is also a popular filling for baked chicken.

Boursin

Camembert is a surface-ripened cheese originating in France and containing a minimum of 22% fat. Camembert is firmer than Brie, but milder. It is shaped in small round or oval disks and is coated with a white bloomy rind (*penicillium camemberti*). Selecting a properly ripened Camembert is similar to selecting a Brie, but Camembert will become overripe and ammoniated even more quickly than Brie. Camembert is an excellent dessert or after-dinner cheese and goes particularly well with fruit. Like Brie, double and triple cream varieties, as well as blue-veined varieties, are available.

Feta is a soft Greek or Italian product originally made from sheep's and/or goat's milk. Cow's milk fetas are common, too. Feta is a white, flaky cheese that is pickled (but not ripened) and stored in brine water, giving it a shelf life of four to six weeks. Its flavour becomes sharper and saltier with age. Feta is good for snacks and salads and melts easily for sauces and fillings. Limburger and Stella Alpine are other examples of this cheese type.

Feta

Semi-soft Cheeses

This large category is separated into groups based on the ripening method. Moisture content ranges between 40% and 60%, while fat content is between 10% and 30%.

Mozzarella

Havarti

Oka

Gorgonzola

Roquefort

Unripened Pasta filata or stretched curd cheeses make up most of this group. Many of these cheeses are of Italian origin but are produced in Canada. **Mozzarella** is the most prevalent type and is used extensively in pizza and pasta dishes. It has a smooth, elastic character and mild flavour. Fresh mozzarella is known as **bocconcini** and comes packed in brine. Mild and delicate, it goes well with ripe tomatoes, virgin olive oil and a little fresh basil. Scamorza, Trecce and Fior di Latte are other types; some of these unripened cheeses are smoked or aged for flavour.

Interior Ripened These cheeses have usually been pressed, cooked and ripened. The rind may be washed if it is firm enough as it forms. Most of these cheeses are mild and supple in texture. Monterey Jack is a widely used variety that originated in the United States. It comes in blocks and is mild on its own, but it is often flavoured with chiles and other seasonings. Havarti, Saint Paulin and Munster are three other interior-ripened cheeses.

Havarti is a cow's milk monastery-style cheese from Denmark containing 45% to 60% fat. Havarti is also known as **Danish Tilsit** or by the brand name **Dofino**. Pale yellow with many small, irregular holes, it is sold in small rounds, rectangular blocks or loaves. Havarti has a mild flavour and creamy texture. It is often flavoured with dill, caraway seeds or peppers. Havarti is very popular for snacking and on sandwiches.

Surface Ripened These cheeses ripen from the surface to the centre. They are turned, washed and kept in cold rooms. Some have a pungent smell and flavour. **Oka**, Canada's most famous and true cheese, is of this type. Oka has its origins with Trappist monks in France who produced Port Salut. The conditions in Quebec produced Oka instead. Only in recent years has the original production facility become commercial. The pale yellow to red rind containing a pale yellow interior has delighted connoisseurs the world over with its mellow, buttery, nutty flavour.

Port Salut is a monastery cow's milk product from France containing approximately 50% fat. Port Salut is smooth, rich and savoury. It is shaped in thick wheels with a dense, pale yellow interior and an edible, bright orange rind. The Danish version is known as **Esrom**.

Blue Cheese Blue cheese is a generic term for any cheese containing visible blue-green moulds that contribute a characteristic tart, sharp flavour and aroma, also known as a blue-veined cheese or bleu. It also refers to a group of Roquefort-style cheeses made in Canada and the United States from cow's or goat's milk rather than ewe's milk and injected with moulds (*penicillium roqueforti*) that form blue-green veins.

Gorgonzola is a blue-veined cow's milk cheese from Italy containing 48% fat. Gorgonzola has a white or ivory interior with bluish-green veins. It is creamier than Stilton or Roquefort, with a somewhat more pungent, spicy, earthy flavour. White Gorgonzola has no veins but a similar flavour, while aged Gorgonzola is drier and crumbly with a very strong, sharp flavour. The milder Gorgonzolas are excellent with fresh peaches or pears or crumbled in a salad. Gorgonzola is also used in sauces and in the *torta con basilico*, a cakelike cheese loaf comprising layers of cheese, fresh basil and pine nuts.

Roquefort is a blue-veined sheep's milk cheese from France containing approximately 45% fat. One of the oldest cheeses, Roquefort is intensely pungent with a rich, salty flavour and strong aroma. It is a white paste with veins of blue mould and a thin natural rind shaped into thick, foil-wrapped cylinders. Roquefort is always aged for at least three months in the limestone caves of Mount Combalou. Since 1926 no producer outside this region can legally use the name Roquefort or even "Roquefort-style." Roquefort is an excellent choice for serving before or after dinner and is, of course, essential for Roquefort dressing. Ermite is an excellent Canadian cheese produced in the Roquefort style.

Stilton is a blue-veined cow's milk cheese from Great Britain containing 45% fat. Stilton is one of the oldest and grandest cheeses in the world. It has a white or pale yellow interior with evenly spaced blue veins. Stilton's distinctive flavour is pungent, rich and tangy, combining the best of blues and cheddars. It is aged in cool ripening rooms for four to six months to develop the blue veining; it is then sold in tall cylinders with a crusty, edible rind. Stilton should be wrapped in a cloth dampened with salt water and stored at cool temperatures, but not refrigerated. It is best served alone, with plain crackers, dried fruit or vintage port.

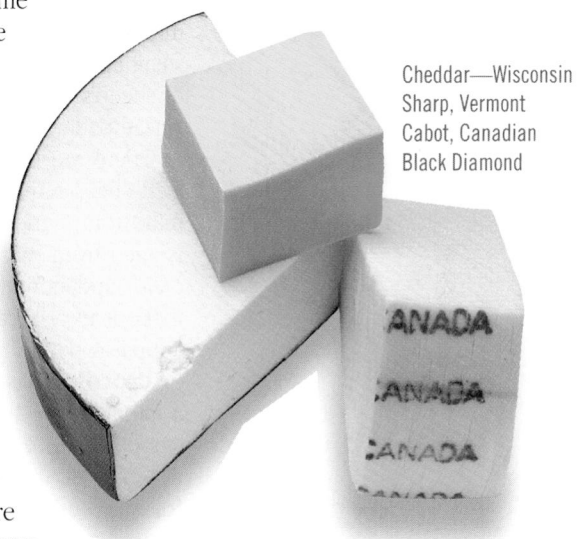

Stilton

Firm Cheeses

Firm cheeses are the largest Canadian cheese category. Some are close-textured and crumbly, like cheddar; others are dense, holey cheeses like Swiss Emmenthaler. All firm cheeses are interior ripened. Their moisture content ranges from 35% to 52%. Interior ripening is a common characteristic.

Cheddars are produced in both North America and Great Britain. Cheddar is a cow's milk cheese made primarily in the northern United States and most of Canada, containing a minimum of 31% fat. The best cheddars are non-coloured and aged two to five years. Hand-turned cheddars are now a rarity. Cheddars have a dense, crumbly texture and may be white or coloured orange with vegetable dyes, depending on local preference. "Marble" cheddar is popular in Western Canada. Flavours range from mild to very sharp, depending on the age of the cheese. **Colby** and **brick** are similar to cheddars. Cheddars are sold in a variety of shapes and sizes, often coated with wax. Good-quality cheddars are welcome additions to any cheese board, while those of lesser quality are better reserved for cooking and sandwiches. **English cheddar** is a variety of cow's milk cheese produced in Great Britain containing approximately 45% fat. Perhaps the most imitated cheese in the world, true English cheddar is available in Canada. Canadian cheese manufacturers have enhanced the original English recipe and Canadian cheddar has become famous the world over. It is a moist yet sliceable cheese, aged at least six months. It is a most versatile cheese, ideal for any time of day and with nearly any meal. It is used in numerous ways for desserts and in cooking.

Cheddar—Wisconsin Sharp, Vermont Cabot, Canadian Black Diamond

Emmenthaler (Swiss) is a cow's milk cheese of Swiss origin containing approximately 45% fat. Emmenthaler is the original Swiss cheese; it accounts for more than half of Switzerland's cheese production. It is mellow, rich and nutty with a natural rind and a light yellow interior full of large holes. It is ripened in three stages with the aid of fermenting bacteria. The holes or "eyes" are caused by CO_2 gases expanding inside the cheese during fermentation. Authentic Emmenthaler is sold in 90-kg (200-lb.) wheels with the word "Switzerland" stamped on the rind like the spokes of a wheel. Emmenthaler is popular for sandwiches, snacks and after dinner with fruit and nuts. **Gruyère** is used for **fondue** and quiche.

Gouda is a Dutch cheese containing approximately 48% fat. Gouda is sold in various-sized wheels covered with red or yellow wax. The cheese is yellow with a few small holes and a mild, buttery flavour. Gouda may be sold soon

Emmenthaler (Swiss)

● **fondue** a Swiss specialty made with melted cheese, wine and flavourings, eaten by dipping pieces of bread into the mixture with long forks

after production or it may be aged for several months, resulting in a firmer, more flavourful cheese. Gouda is widely popular for snacking.

Fontina is a cow's milk cheese from Italy's Piedmont region containing approximately 45% fat. The original, known as **fontina Val D'Aosta**, has a dark gold, crusty rind; the pale gold, dense interior has a few small holes. It is nutty and rich. The original must have a purple trademark stamped on the rind. Other fontinas (known as **fontal** or **fontinella**) are produced in Denmark, France, Sweden, North America and other regions of Italy. They tend to be softer, with less depth of flavour, and may have a rubbery texture. Fontina is a good after-dinner cheese; it also works well as a stuffing ingredient.

Jarlsberg is a Swiss-type cow's milk cheese from Norway containing approximately 45% fat. Jarlsberg closely resembles Swiss Emmenthaler in both taste and appearance. It is mild with a delicate, sweet taste and large holes. Jarlsberg has a pale yellow interior; it is coated with yellow wax and sold in huge wheels. It has a long shelf life and is popular for sandwiches and snacks and in cooking.

Manchego is the best-known and most widely available Spanish sheep's milk cheese. Its ivory to pale yellow interior is firm and compact with a few small air pockets. It has a buttery and slightly piquant flavour with an aftertaste of sheep's milk. The inedible rind is black, grey or beige, with a very distinctive zigzag pattern imprinted by the traditional esparto grass moulds.

There are two types of Manchego: farmhouse style, made with unpasteurized sheep's milk, and industrial, made with pasteurized milk. For both, only milk from Manchega sheep raised in the La Mancha region is used. Manchego is aged from two months (*fresco*) to one year (*curado*) to two years (*añejo* or *viejo*) and contains 45% to 57% fat. Its intense flavour and crumbly texture make it excellent for eating as is, with bread or fruit, or as the focal point of antipasto with a robust red wine or a dry sherry.

Provolone is a cow's milk cheese originating in southern Italy, containing a minimum of 24% fat. Provolone *dolce*, aged only two months, is mild, with a smooth texture. Provolone *piccante*, aged up to six months, is stronger, with a white-yellow fibrous interior. Smoked provolone is also popular, especially for snacking. Provolone is shaped in various ways, from huge salamis to plump spheres to tiny piglets shaped by hand. It is excellent in sandwiches and for cooking, and is often used for melting and in pizza and pasta dishes.

Other Canadian-produced cheeses in this category include Camosun, Edam, Friulano, New Bra and Saint André.

Manchego

Hard Cheeses

Hard cheeses are not simply cheeses that have been allowed to dry out. Rather, they are carefully aged for extended periods of time and have a moisture content from 5% to 30%. Hard cheeses are most often used for grating; the best flavour will come from cheeses grated as needed. Even the finest hard cheeses begin to lose their flavour within hours of grating. The most famous and popular of the hard cheeses are those from Italy, where they are known as *grana*. Hard cheeses can be served as a table cheese or garnish.

Asiago is a cow's milk cheese containing approximately 30% fat. After only one year of aging, Asiago is sharp and nutty with a cheddarlike texture. If aged for two years or more, Asiago becomes dry, brittle and suitable for grating. Either version should be an even white to pale yellow in colour with no dark spots, cracks or strong aromas. It is sold in small wheels and keeps for long periods if well wrapped. Asiago melts easily and is often used in cooking.

Parmigiano-Reggiano (Parmesan) is a cow's milk cheese made exclusively in the region near Parma, Italy, containing from 32% to 35% fat. Parmigiano-Reggiano is one of the world's oldest and most widely copied

Asiago

cheeses. Used primarily for grating and cooking, it is rich, spicy and sharp, with a golden interior and a hard oily rind. It should not be overly salty or bitter. Reggiano, as it is known, is produced only from mid-April to mid-November. It is shaped into huge wheels of about 36 kg (80 lb.) each, with the name stencilled repeatedly around the rind. Parmesan is produced in the United States, Argentina and elsewhere, but none can match the distinctive flavour of freshly grated Reggiano. Domestically produced Parmesan is widely available in Canada, grated, shredded or in block form. Premium products are now on the market.

Parmigiano-Reggiano (Parmesan)

Pecorino Romano is a sheep's milk cheese from central and southern Italy, containing approximately 35% fat. Romano is very brittle and sharper than other grating cheeses, with a "sheepy" tang. Its light, grainy interior is whiter than Parmesan or Asiago. It is packed in large cylinders with a yellow rind. Romano is often substituted for, or combined with, Parmesan in cooking but it is also good eaten with olives, sausages and red wine.

Light Cheese

Light cheese is defined as having a minimum 25% butterfat reduction compared with regular cheese. Light cheese tends to be less flavourful than regular cheese.

Other Types of Cheeses

Other types of cheeses include goat's milk cheeses and processed cheeses.

Because of their increasing popularity, cheeses made from **goat's milk** deserve a few words of their own. Although goats give less milk than cows, their milk is higher in fat and protein and richer and more concentrated in flavour. Cheeses made with goat's milk have a sharp, tangy flavour. They may range in texture from very soft and fresh to very hard, depending on age.

● **chèvre** French for "goat"; generally refers to a cheese made from goat's milk

Chèvre (French for "goat") refers to small, soft, creamy cheeses produced in a variety of shapes: cones, disks, pyramids or logs. Chèvres are often coated with ash, herbs or seasonings. They are excellent for cooking and complement a wide variety of flavours. Unfortunately, they have a short shelf life, perhaps only two weeks. Cheese labelled *pure chèvre* must be made with 100% goat's milk, while others may be a mixture of cow's and goat's milk. Canada's Natricia, Woolwich and Tournevent dairies produce excellent chèvre cheeses. French brands include Bucheron, Chevrotin and Montrachet.

Pasteurized processed cheese is made from a combination of aged and green cheeses that are mixed with emulsifiers and flavourings, pasteurized and poured into moulds to solidify. Manufacturers can thus produce cheeses with consistent textures and flavours. Processed cheeses are commonly used in food service operations because they are less expensive than natural cheeses. And, because they will not age or ripen, their shelf life is greatly extended. Nutritionally, processed cheeses generally contain less protein, calcium and vitamin A and more sodium than natural cheeses.

Processed cheese food contains less natural cheese (but at least 51% by weight) and more moisture than regular processed cheese. Often vegetable oils and milk solids are added, making cheese food soft and spreadable.

Assorted soft and goat's milk cheeses (clockwise starting from the top right): log of herb-coated French goat's cheese, French Banon wrapped in leaves, cinder-coated French Sainte Maure, French Chabichon goat's cheese, French Cabichou marinated in olive oil, herbs and peppercorns and, in the centre, French Camembert

Cold pack is a processed cheese product made primarily of old cheddar; it is not heated in processing. Sugars are usually added to mellow the flavour.

Imitation cheese is usually manufactured with dairy byproducts and soy products mixed with emulsifiers, colourings and flavouring agents and enzymes. Although considerably less expensive than natural cheese, imitation cheese tends to be dense and rubbery, with little flavour other than that of salt.

Serving Cheeses

Cheeses may be served at any time of day. In Northern Europe they are common for breakfast; in Great Britain they are a staple at lunch. Cheeses are widely used for sandwiches, snacks and cooking in Canada, and they are often served following the entree or instead of dessert at formal dinners.

The flavour and texture of natural cheeses are best at room temperature. So, except for fresh cheeses, all cheeses should be removed from the refrigerator 30 minutes to an hour before service to allow them to come to room temperature. Fresh cheeses, such as cottage and cream, should be eaten chilled.

Any selection of fine cheeses should include a variety of flavours and textures: from mild to sharp, from soft to creamy to firm. Use a variety of shapes and colours for visual appeal. Do not precut the cheeses, as this only causes them to become dry. Provide an adequate supply of serving knives so that stronger-flavoured cheeses will not combine with and overpower milder ones. Fine cheeses are best appreciated with plain bread and crackers, as salted or seasoned crackers can mask the cheese's flavour. Noncitrus fruits are also a nice accompaniment. Carefully pairing cheeses and wines can lead to a wonderful taste experience.

Canadian Cheese History

Some of the milk from cows arriving with Cartier in 1541 was likely made into cheese. The first North American dairy farm was the Champlain farm at Cap Tourmente in 1629. Nova Scotia's export of six tons of cheese in 1764 was the first documented production.

Originally produced from ewe's milk and coloured with marigolds, cheddar is a widely produced cheese in Canada, although it is made from cow's milk now. Black Diamond cheddar was the result of the wax coating protecting the cheese reacting with the mould it was transported in and turning black.

Some of Canada's finest cheeses are based on monastery production methods the monks brought with them from Europe. Oka is the most famous and is regarded as a true Canadian cheese.

Fine cheeses are now produced throughout Canada. They include Sir Laurier d'Artabaska, Miranda, Clos St. Ambroise, Migneron, Laracam, Cantonnier and Bénédictin, to name a few.

Cheeseboard ready for service (starting from the top right): Shropshire Blue from Great Britain, Layered Huntsman Cheese from Great Britain, Italian Pecorino Pepato and in the centre a wedge of ripe Brie cheese

Cooking with Cheese

The Dairy Bureau of Canada promotes a concept of Evolutive Cuisine. It allows the chef creativity in blending techniques and nontraditional ingredients with original presentations and decorating practices. The objective is to preserve and enhance flavours while maintaining nutritional soundness. Effectively cooking with cheese is a part of this concept.

We need to remember that cheese is a living organism. Each type of cheese has characteristics that must be considered. These include fat content, moisture content, pH level, buffering capacity, thickening power and the reactions of proteins and minerals to other ingredients or heat. When creating or adapting a recipe, all of these factors must be considered. For example, if low-fat mascarpone is used to make a butterscotch sauce, you must add more fat (butter) for the sauce to have the right characteristics. To use a snow goat cheese to liaise a jus-based sauce, the alcohol in the wine must be evaporated and the reduction removed from the fire before the room temperature cheese is whisked in. Whipping cream may have to be added to a purée soup to buffer the liquid to achieve successful incorporation of the cheese.

For detailed information, *Fundamentals of Canadian Cheeses and Their Use in Fine Cuisine* by the Dairy Farmers of Canada (Montreal: les Éditions de la Chenelière Inc., 1992) is an excellent resource.

Cheese Terminology

The following terms often appear on cheese labels and may help you identify or appreciate new or unfamiliar cheeses:

Affiné—French term for a washed-rind cheese.

Bleu—French for "blue."

Brique or briquette—A group of French brick-shaped cheeses.

Brosse—French term for cheeses that are brushed during ripening.

Capra—Italian term for goat's milk cheese.

Carré—French term for square, flat cheeses.

Cendré—French term for cheeses ripened in ashes.

Coulant—French for "flowing," used to describe Brie, Camembert and other cheeses when their interiors ooze or flow.

Ferme or fermier—French adjective used to indicate farm-produced cheeses.

Kaas—Dutch for "cheese."

Käse—German for "cheese."

Lait cru—French for "raw milk."

Laiterie or laitier—French for "dairy"; appears on factory-made cheeses.

Matières grasses—French for "fat content."

Mi chèvre—A French product so labelled must contain at least 25% goat's milk.

Ost—Term in several Scandinavian languages for "cheese."

Pecorino—Italian term for all sheep's milk cheeses.

Queso—Spanish for "cheese."

Râpé—French term applied to cheeses that are suitable for grating.

Tome or tomme—Term used by the French, Italians and Swiss to refer to mountain cheeses, particularly from the Pyrenees or Savoie regions.

Tyrophile—One who loves cheese.

Vaccino—Italian term for cow's milk cheese.

Vache—French term for cow's milk cheese.

Storage

Most cheeses are best kept refrigerated, well wrapped to keep odours out and moisture in. Firm and hard cheeses can be kept for several weeks; fresh cheeses will spoil in 7 to 10 days because of their high moisture content. Some cheeses that have become hard or dry may still be grated for cooking or baking. Freezing is possible but not recommended because it changes the cheese's texture, making it mealy or tough. Shock-freezing produces the best results due to the small size of the moisture crystals.

Conclusion

Eggs and dairy products are versatile foods used throughout the kitchen. They may be served as is or incorporated into many dishes, including soups, sauces, entrees, breads and desserts. Fine natural cheeses are useful in prepared dishes but are most important for buffets, as the cheese course during a meal or whenever cheese is the primary ingredient or dominant flavour. Eggs and dairy products spoil easily and must be handled and stored properly.

Questions for Discussion

1. Explain the criteria used in grading eggs. Why might you prefer to use eggs with lower grades?
2. What are the differences between egg products and egg substitutes?
3. What is milkfat and how is it used in classifying milk-based products?
4. If a recipe calls for whole milk and you have only dried milk, what do you do? Explain your answer.
5. What is clarified butter and when is it used? Describe the procedure for clarifying butter.
6. The texture and shelf life of cheese depend on what two factors?
7. Cheeses are categorized as fresh or unripened, soft, semi-soft, firm, hard and light. Give two examples of each and explain how they are generally used.

9 Principles of Cooking

"The qualities of an exceptional cook are akin to those of a successful tightrope walker: an abiding passion for the task, courage to go out on a limb and an impeccable sense of balance.

—Bryan Miller, American food writer

Cooking can be defined as the transfer of energy from a heat source to a food. This energy alters the food's molecular structure, changing its texture, flavour, aroma and appearance. But why is food cooked at all? The obvious answer is that cooking makes food taste better. Cooking also destroys undesirable microorganisms and makes foods easier to ingest and digest.

To cook foods successfully, you must first understand the ways in which heat is transferred: conduction, convection and radiation. You should also understand what the application of heat does to the proteins, sugars, starches, water and fats in foods.

Perhaps most importantly, you must understand the cooking methods used to transfer heat: broiling, grilling, roasting and baking, sautéing, pan-frying, deep-fat frying, poaching, simmering, boiling, steaming, braising and stewing. Each method is used for many types of food, so you will be applying one or more of them every time you cook. The cooking method you select gives the finished product a specific texture, appearance, aroma and flavour. A thorough understanding of the basic procedures involved in each cooking method helps you produce consistent, high-quality products.

This chapter discusses each of the cooking methods in general terms without applying them to any specific food. These methods will be discussed again in more detail as they are used in the following chapters.

HEAT TRANSFER

Heat is a type of energy. When a substance gets hot, its molecules have absorbed energy, which causes the molecules to vibrate rapidly, expand and bounce off one another. As the molecules move, they collide with nearby molecules, causing a transfer of heat energy. The faster the molecules within a substance move, the higher its temperature. This is true whether the substance is air, water, an aluminum pot or a sirloin steak.

Heat energy may be transferred *to* foods via conduction, convection or radiation. (See Figure 9.1 on the next page.) Heat then travels *through* foods by conduction. Only heat is transferred—cold is simply the absence of heat, so cold cannot be transferred from one substance to another.

Conduction

Conduction is the most straightforward means of heat transfer. It is simply the movement of heat from one item to another through direct contact. For example, when the flame of a gas burner touches the bottom of a sauté pan, heat is conducted to the pan. The metal of the pan then conducts heat to the surface of the food lying in that pan.

Some materials conduct heat better than others. Water is a better conductor of heat than air. This explains why a potato cooks much faster in boiling water than in an oven, and why you cannot place your hand in boiling water at a temperature of 100°C (212°F), but can place your hand, at least very briefly, into a 200°C (400°F) oven. Generally, metals are good conductors (as discussed in Chapter 5, Tools and Equipment, copper and aluminum are the best conductors), while liquids and gases are poor conductors.

● **conduction** the transfer of heat from one item to another through direct contact

FIGURE 9.1   Arrows indicate heat patterns during conduction, convection and radiation.

Conduction is a relatively slow method of heat transfer because there must be physical contact to transfer energy from one molecule to adjacent molecules. Consider what happens when a metal spoon is placed in a pot of simmering soup. At first the spoon handle remains cool. Gradually, however, heat travels up the handle, making it warmer and warmer, until it becomes too hot to touch.

Conduction is important in all cooking methods because it is responsible for the movement of heat from the surface of a food to its interior. As the molecules near the food's exterior gather energy, they move more and more rapidly. As they move, they conduct heat to the molecules nearby, thus transferring heat *through* the food (from the exterior of the item to the interior).

In conventional heating methods (nonmicrowave), the heat source causes food molecules to react largely from the surface inward, so that layers of molecules heat in succession. This produces a range of temperatures within the food, which means that the outside can brown and form a crust long before the interior is noticeably warmer. That is why a steak can be fully cooked on the outside but still rare on the inside.

Convection

convection the transfer of heat caused by the natural movement of molecules in a fluid (whether air, water or fat) from a warmer area to a cooler one

Convection refers to the transfer of heat through a fluid, which may be liquid or gas. Convection is actually a combination of conduction and a mixing in which molecules in a fluid (whether air, water or fat) move from a warmer area to a cooler one. There are two types of convection: natural and mechanical.

Natural convection occurs because of the tendency of warm liquids and gases to rise while cooler ones fall. This causes a constant natural circulation of heat. For example, when a pot of stock is placed over a gas burner, the molecules at the bottom of the pot are warmed. These molecules rise while cooler, heavier molecules sink. Upon reaching the pot's bottom, the cooler molecules are warmed and begin to rise. This ongoing cycle creates currents within the stock, and these currents distribute the heat throughout the stock.

Mechanical convection relies on fans or stirring to circulate heat more quickly and evenly. This explains why foods heat faster and more evenly when stirred. Convection ovens are equipped with fans to increase the circulation of air currents, thus speeding up the cooking process. But even conventional ovens (that is, not convection ovens) rely on the natural circulation patterns of heated air to transfer heat energy to items being baked or roasted.

● **natural convection** circulation caused by hot molecules rising and cool molecules falling

● **mechanical convection** the circulation of heat caused by fans or stirring

Radiation

Unlike conduction and convection, **radiation** does not require physical contact between the heat source and the food being cooked. Instead, energy is transferred by waves of heat or light striking the food. Two kinds of radiant heat are used in the kitchen: infrared and microwave.

Infrared cooking uses an electric or ceramic element heated to such a high temperature that it gives off waves of radiant heat that cook the food. Radiant heat waves travel at the speed of light in any direction (unlike convection heat, which only rises) until they are absorbed by a food. Infrared cooking is commonly used with toasters and broilers. The glowing coals of a fire are another example of radiant heat.

Microwave cooking relies on radiation generated by a special oven to penetrate the food, where it agitates water molecules, creating friction and heat. This energy then spreads throughout the food by conduction (and by convection in liquids). Microwave cooking is much faster than other methods because energy penetrates the food up to a depth of several centimetres, setting all water molecules in motion at the same time. Heat is generated quickly and uniformly throughout the food. Microwave cooking does not brown foods, however, and often gives meats a dry, mushy texture, making microwave ovens an unacceptable replacement for traditional ovens.

Because microwave radiation affects only water molecules, a completely waterless material (such as a plate) will not get hot. Any warmth felt in a plate used when microwaving food results from heat being conducted from the food to the plate.

Microwave cooking requires the use of certain types of utensils, usually heat-resistant glass or microwaveable plastic. Even heat-resistant glass can shatter, however, and it is not recommended for professional use. The aluminum utensils most common in professional kitchens cannot be used because metal deflects microwaves and this can damage the oven. Pure stainless steel is microwave safe.

● **radiation cooking** a heating process that does not require physical contact between the heat source and the food being cooked; instead, energy is transferred by waves of heat or light striking the food. Two kinds of radiant heat used in the kitchen are infrared and microwave.

● **infrared cooking** a heating method that uses an electric or ceramic element heated to such a high temperature that it gives off waves of radiant heat that cook the food

● **microwave cooking** a heating method that uses radiation generated by a special oven to penetrate the food: it agitates water molecules, creating friction and heat; this energy then spreads throughout the food by conduction (and by convection in liquids)

THE EFFECTS OF HEAT

Foods are composed of proteins, carbohydrates (starches and sugars), water and fats, plus small amounts of minerals and vitamins. Changes in shape, texture, colour and flavour of foods may occur when heat is applied to each of these nutrients. By understanding these changes and learning to control them, you will be able to prepare foods with the characteristics desired. Although volumes are written on these subjects, it is sufficient for you to know the following processes as you begin your study of cooking.

Proteins Coagulate

● **coagulation** the irreversible transformation of proteins from a liquid or semiliquid state to a drier, solid state; usually accomplished through the application of heat

The proper term for the cooking of proteins is **coagulation**. Proteins are large, complex molecules found in every living cell, plant as well as animal. Coagulation refers to the irreversible transformation of proteins from a liquid or semiliquid state to a solid state. As proteins cook, they lose moisture, shrink and become firm. Common examples of coagulation are the firming of meat fibres during cooking, the changing of egg whites from a clear liquid to a white solid when heated and the setting of the structure of wheat proteins (known as gluten) in bread during baking. Most proteins complete coagulation at 71°C to 85°C (160°F to 185°F).

Starches Gelatinize

● **gelatinization** the process by which starch granules are cooked; they absorb moisture. When placed in a liquid and heated, as the moisture is absorbed, the product swells, softens and clarifies slightly.

Gelatinization is the proper term for the cooking of starches. Starches are complex carbohydrates present in plants and grains such as potatoes, wheat, rice and corn. When a mixture of starch and liquid is heated, remarkable changes occur. The starch granules absorb water, causing them to swell, soften and clarify slightly. The liquid visibly thickens because of the water being absorbed into the starch granules and the granules themselves swelling to occupy more space.

Gelatinization occurs gradually over a range of temperatures—66°C to 100°C (150°F to 212°F)—depending on the type of starch used. Starch gelatinization affects not only sauces or liquids to which starches are added for the express purpose of thickening, but also any mixture of starch and liquid that is heated. For example, the flour (a starch) in cake batter gelatinizes by absorbing the water from eggs, milk or other ingredients as the batter bakes. This causes part of the firming and drying associated with baked goods.

Sugars Caramelize

● **caramelization** the process of cooking sugars; the browning of sugar enhances the flavour and appearance of foods

The process of cooking sugars is properly known as **caramelization**. Sugars are simple carbohydrates used by all plants and animals to store energy. As sugars cook, they gradually turn brown and change flavour. Caramelized sugar is used in many sauces, candies and desserts. Sucrose (common table sugar) begins to brown at about 160°C to 170°C (320°F to 338°F). The naturally occurring sugars in other foods such as maltose, lactose and fructose also caramelize, but at varying temperatures. Because high temperatures are required for browning (i.e., caramelizing), most foods will brown only on the outside and only through the application of dry heat. Because water cannot be heated above 100°C (212°F), foods cooked with moist-heat methods do not get hot enough to caramelize. Foods cooked with dry-heat methods, including those using fats, will reach the high temperatures at which browning occurs.

● **Maillard reactions** the process of browning of non-sugar foods

The **Maillard reactions** are the mechanism responsible for the browning of non-sugar foods such as meat, chocolate and bread crusts. It starts with a reaction between an amino acid and a starch molecule. When this unstable structure is subjected to heat, starting at 120°C (250°F), it results in meaty, savoury, earthy flavours. Depending on the product and as more heat is applied, caramelization flavours including sweet, sour, bitter, fruity, leafy and nutty develop. These complex flavour profiles add to our enjoyment of food.

Water Evaporates

All foods contain some water. Some foods, especially eggs, milk and leafy vegetables, are almost entirely water. Even as much as 75% of raw meat is water.

As the internal temperature of a food increases, water molecules move faster and faster until the water turns to a gas (steam) and vaporizes. This **evaporation** of water is responsible for the drying of foods during cooking.

Fats Melt

Fat is an energy source for the plant or animal in which it is stored. Fats are smooth, greasy substances that do not dissolve in water. Their texture varies from very firm to liquid. Oils are simply fats that remain liquid at room temperature. Fats **melt** when heated; that is, they gradually soften, then liquefy. Fats will not evaporate. Most fats can be heated to very high temperatures without burning, so they can be used as a cooking medium to brown foods.

COOKING METHODS

Foods can be cooked in air, fat, water or steam. These are collectively known as **cooking media**. There are two general types of cooking methods: dry heat and moist heat.

Dry-heat cooking methods are those using air or fat. They are broiling, grilling, roasting and baking, sautéing, pan-frying and deep-fat frying. Foods cooked using dry-heat cooking methods have a rich flavour caused by browning.

Moist-heat cooking methods are those using water or steam. They are poaching, simmering, boiling and steaming. Moist-heat cooking methods are used to emphasize the natural flavours of food.

Other cooking methods employ a combination of dry- and moist-heat cooking methods. The two most significant of these **combination cooking methods** are braising and stewing. (See Table 9.1.)

● **evaporation** the process by which heated water molecules move faster and faster until the water turns to a gas (steam) and vaporizes; evaporation is responsible for the drying of foods during cooking

● **melting** the process by which certain foods, especially those high in fat, gradually soften and then liquefy when heated

● **cooking medium** the air, fat, water or steam in which a food is cooked

● **dry-heat cooking methods** cooking methods, principally broiling, grilling, roasting and baking, sautéing, pan-frying and deep-fat frying, that use air or fat to transfer heat through convection; dry-heat cooking methods allow surface sugars to caramelize

● **moist-heat cooking methods** cooking methods, principally simmering, poaching, boiling and steaming, that use water or steam to transfer heat through convection; moist-heat cooking methods are used to emphasize the natural flavours of foods

● **combination cooking methods** cooking methods, principally braising and stewing, that employ both dry-heat and moist-heat procedures

TABLE 9.1	Cooking Methods	
Method	**Medium**	**Equipment**
Dry-Heat Cooking Methods		
Broiling	Air	Overhead broiler, salamander, rotisserie
Grilling	Air	Grill
Roasting	Air	Oven
Baking	Air	Oven
Sautéing	Fat	Stove
Pan-frying	Fat	Stove, tilt skillet
Deep-fat frying	Fat	Deep-fat fryer
Moist-Heat Cooking Methods		
Poaching	Water or other liquid	Stove, oven, steam-jacketed kettle, tilt skillet
Simmering	Water or other liquid	Stove, steam-jacketed kettle, tilt skillet
Boiling	Water or other liquid	Stove, steam-jacketed kettle, tilt skillet
Steaming	Steam	Stove, convection steamer
Combination Cooking Methods		
Braising	Fat then liquid	Stove (and oven), tilt skillet
Stewing	Fat then liquid	Stove (and oven), tilt skillet
Sous vide		Vacuum packer and others as needed
Cook–chill		Blast chiller and others as needed

Each of these cooking methods can be applied to a wide variety of foods—meats, fish, vegetables and even pastries. Here, we discuss only the general characteristics of these cooking methods. Detailed procedures for applying these methods to specific foods are found in subsequent chapters.

Dry-Heat Cooking Methods

Cooking by dry heat is the process of applying heat either directly, by subjecting the food to the heat of a flame, or indirectly, by surrounding the food with heated air or heated fat.

Broiling

Broiling uses radiant heat from an overhead source to cook foods. The temperature at the heat source can be as high as 1100°C (2000°F). The food to be broiled is placed on a preheated metal grate. Radiant heat from overhead cooks the food, while the hot grate below marks it with attractive crosshatch marks.

BASIC PROCEDURE FOR BROILING FOODS

1. Heat the broiler or salamander to its highest setting.

2. If necessary, use a wire brush to remove any charred or burnt particles that may be stuck to the broiler grate. The grate can be wiped with a lightly oiled towel to remove any remaining particles and to help season it.

3. Cut, trim or otherwise prepare the food to be broiled. (Thicker pieces of food will take longer to cook.) Marinate, rub or season it, as desired. Many foods can be brushed lightly with oil to keep them from sticking to the grate.

4. Place the food in the broiler, presentation side down. If necessary, use a fork or tongs to turn or flip the item without piercing its surface.

5. Cook the food to the desired degree of doneness while developing the proper surface colour. To do so, adjust the position of the item on the broiler, or adjust the distance between the grate and heat source. Doneness is often determined by touch, internal temperature or specific visual cues (for example, clear juices running from poultry).

1. Preheat the grate under the broiler, then pull it out and place the food on the hot grate, presentation side down. If the item is oblong, place it at a 45-degree angle to the bars on the cooking grate. Slide the grate back under the broiler and cook long enough for the food to develop lines where it touches the grate. Pull the sliding grate out again and turn the food over at a 90-degree angle, working from left to right.

2. Pull the sliding grate out of the broiler to turn the food as necessary in order to cook it evenly. Note the handle visible on the right, which can be used to adjust the distance between the grate and the heat source. Smaller pieces of food can often be cooked closer to the source of heat.

3. Remove the cooked item from the broiler grate.

Delicate foods that may be damaged by being placed directly on a metal grate, and foods on which crosshatch marks are not desirable, may be placed on a preheated heat-proof platter then placed under the broiler. Cooking will take place through indirect heat from the preheated platter as well as from the direct heat from the broiler's overhead heat source.

Grilling

Although similar to broiling, grilling uses a heat source located beneath the cooking surface. Grills may be electric or gas or they can burn wood or charcoal, which will add a smoky flavour to the food. Specific woods such as mesquite, hickory or vine clippings can be used to create special flavours. Grilled foods are often identified by crosshatch markings.

BASIC PROCEDURE FOR GRILLING FOODS

1. Heat the grill.

2. If necessary, use a wire brush to remove any charred or burnt particles that may be stuck to the grill grate. The grate can be wiped with a lightly oiled towel to remove any remaining particles and to help season it.

3. Cut, trim or otherwise prepare the food to be grilled. Marinate, rub or season it, as desired. Many foods can be brushed lightly with oil to keep them from sticking to the grate.

4. Place the food on the grill, presentation side down. If practical, rotate the food 90 degrees to produce the attractive crosshatch marks associated with grilling. Then use a fork or tongs to turn or flip the item without piercing its surface.

5. Cook the food to the desired degree of doneness while developing the proper surface colour. To do so, adjust the position of the item on the grill, or adjust the distance between the grate and heat source. Doneness is often determined by touch, internal temperature or specific visual cues (for example, clear juices running from poultry).

1. Decide which side of the grilled food will be presented face up to the customer. Place the food on the hot grill with this side facing down. If the item is oblong, place it at a 45-degree angle to the bars on the cooking grate. Cook long enough for the food to develop dark charred lines where it touches the grate.

2. Rotate the food 90 degrees and allow it to cook long enough for the grates to char it to the same extent as in Step 1.

3. Turn the food over and finish cooking it. It is usually unnecessary to create the crosshatch markings on the reverse side because the customer will not see this side.

Roasting and Baking

Roasting and baking are the processes of surrounding a food with dry, heated air in a closed environment. The term *roasting* is usually applied to meats and poultry, while *baking* is used when referring to fish, fruits, vegetables, starches, breads or pastry items. Heat is transferred by convection to the food's surface and then penetrates the food by conduction. The surface dehydrates and the food browns from caramelization, completing the cooking process.

● **baste** to moisten foods during cooking (usually grilling, broiling or roasting) with melted fat, pan drippings, a sauce or other liquids to prevent drying and to add flavour

● **carryover cooking** the cooking that occurs after a food is removed from a heat source; it is accomplished by the residual heat remaining in the food

BASIC PROCEDURE FOR ROASTING OR BAKING FOODS

1. Preheat the oven.

2. Cut, trim or otherwise prepare the food to be roasted or baked. Marinate or season as desired. Brush with oil or butter, as appropriate.

3. Place the food on a rack or directly in a roasting pan or baking dish.

4. Roast the food, generally uncovered, at the desired temperature. **Baste** as necessary.

5. Cook to the desired internal temperature or doneness, remembering that many foods will undergo **carryover cooking** after they are removed from the oven.

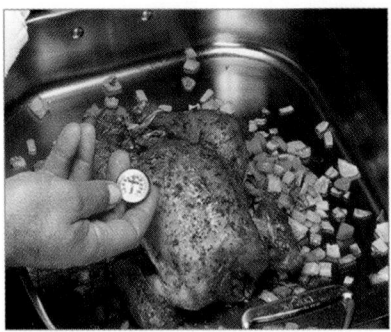

1. Season the item to be roasted, arrange it in an uncovered pan and place it in a preheated oven.

2. Use a thermometer to check the internal temperature of the item being roasted.

SAFETY ALERT

Cooking with Hot Oil

When hot oil comes into contact with liquid, it can spatter, causing severe burns. Use caution when placing foods into hot fat. When pan-frying, slide food into the heated pan, letting it fall away from you so that splatters do not cause burns. Pat moist foods dry with paper towels before adding them to a deep-fat fryer.

Oil heated to its flash point can ignite, causing burns or a serious kitchen fire. When oil is heated to its smoke point, it begins to break down, creating acreolin, a harsh-smelling chemical compound. This offensive smell is a good warning that hot oil may be close to its flash point. Turn off the heat and carefully remove the pan of oil from its heat source. Cover with a tight-fitting lid to smother any flames. Allow the oil to cool completely before discarding.

Sautéing

Sautéing is a dry-heat cooking method that uses conduction to transfer heat from a hot sauté pan to food with the aid of a small amount of fat. Heat then penetrates the food through conduction. High temperatures are used to sauté, and the foods are usually cut into small pieces to promote even cooking.

To sauté foods properly, begin by heating a sauté pan on the stove top, then add a small amount of fat. The fat should just cover the bottom of the pan. Heat the fat or oil to the point at which it just begins to smoke. The food to be cooked should be as dry as possible when it is added to the pan to promote browning and to prevent excessive spattering. Place the food in the pan in a single layer. The heat should be adjusted so the food cooks thoroughly; it should not be so hot that the outside of the food burns before the inside is cooked. The food should be turned or tossed periodically to develop the proper colour. Larger items should be turned using tongs without piercing the surface. Smaller items are often turned by using the sauteuse's sloped sides to flip them back on top of themselves. When tossing sautéed foods, keep the pan in contact with the heat source as much as possible to prevent it from cooling. Sautéing sometimes includes the preparation of a sauce directly in the pan after the main item has been removed.

Stir-frying is a variation of sautéing. A wok is used instead of a sauté pan; the curved sides and rounded bottom of the wok diffuse heat and facilitate

BASIC PROCEDURE FOR SAUTÉING FOODS

1. Cut, pound or otherwise prepare the food to be sautéed. Season it and dredge it in flour, if desired.

2. Heat a sauté pan and add enough fat (typically, oil or clarified butter) to just cover the pan's bottom.

3. Add the food to the sauté pan in a single layer, presentation side down. Do not crowd the pan.

4. Adjust the temperature so that the food's exterior browns properly without burning and the interior cooks. The heat should be high enough to complete the cooking process before the food begins to stew in its own juices.

5. Turn or toss the food as needed. Avoid burns by not splashing hot fat.

6. Cook until done. Doneness is usually determined by timing or touch.

1. Heat a small amount of oil in the sauté pan before adding the food.

2. The sloped edge of the pan can be used to toss the food.

3. The item being sautéed should be cooked quickly.

tossing and stirring. Otherwise, stir-frying procedures are the same as those outlined for sautéing and will not be discussed separately here.

Pan-Frying

Pan-frying shares similarities with both sautéing and deep-fat frying. It is a dry-heat cooking method in which heat is transferred by conduction from the pan to the food, using a moderate amount of fat. Heat is also transferred to the food from the hot fat by convection. Foods to be pan-fried are usually coated in breading. This forms a seal that keeps the food moist and prevents the hot fat from penetrating the food, causing it to become greasy.

To pan-fry foods properly, first heat the fat in a sauté pan. Use enough fat so that the food being cooked is immersed one-third to one-half in the fat. The fat should be at a temperature somewhat lower than that used in sautéing; it should not smoke but should be hot enough so that when the food is added it crackles and spatters from the rapid vaporization of moisture. If the temperature is too low, the food will absorb excessive amounts of fat; if it is too high, the food will burn on the outside before the interior is fully cooked. When the food is properly browned on one side, turn it without piercing it, using tongs. Always turn the food away from you to prevent being burned by any fat that may splash. When the food is fully cooked, remove it from the pan, drain it on absorbent paper and serve it immediately.

BASIC PROCEDURE FOR PAN-FRYING FOOD

1. Cut, pound or otherwise prepare the food to be pan-fried; then bread, batter or flour it as desired.

2. Heat a moderate amount of fat or oil in a heavy pan—usually enough to cover the item one-third to halfway up its sides.

3. Add the food to the pan, being careful not to splash the hot fat.

4. Fry the food on one side until brown. Using tongs, turn and brown the other side. Generally, pan-fried foods are fully cooked when they are well browned on both sides.

5. Remove the food from the pan and drain it on absorbent paper before serving.

1. Use tongs to carefully place the item being pan-fried into a moderate amount of hot oil.

2. Turn the item to brown the other side.

3. Drain the cooked item on absorbent paper.

Deep-Fat Frying

Deep-frying is a dry-heat cooking method that uses conduction and convection to transfer heat to food submerged in hot fat. Although conceptually similar to boiling, deep-frying is not a moist-heat cooking method because the liquid fat contains no water. A key difference between boiling and deep-frying is the temperature of the cooking medium. The boiling point, 100°C (212°F), is the hottest temperature at which food can be cooked in water. At this temperature, most foods require a long cooking period and surface sugars cannot caramelize. With deep-frying, temperatures up to 200°C (400°F) are used. These high temperatures cook food more quickly and allow the food's surface to brown.

Foods to be deep-fried are usually first coated in batter or breading. This preserves moisture and prevents the food from absorbing excessive quantities of fat. Foods to be deep-fried should be of a size and shape that allows them to float freely in the fat. Foods that are to be deep-fried together should be of uniform size and shape. Delicately flavoured foods should not be deep-fried in the same fat used for more strongly flavoured ones, as the former could develop an odd taste from residual flavours left in the fat. Deep-fried foods should cook thoroughly while developing an attractive deep golden-brown colour.

Today, most deep-frying is done in specially designed commercial fryers. These deep-fat fryers have built-in thermostats, making temperature control more precise. Deep-frying foods in a saucepan on the stove top is discouraged because it is both difficult and dangerous. **Recovery time** is usually very slow, and temperatures are difficult to control. Also, the fat can spill easily, leading to injuries or creating a fire hazard.

To deep-fry food, first heat the fat or oil to a temperature between 160°C and 190°C (325°F and 375°F). The cooking medium's temperature can be

● **recovery time** the length of time it takes a cooking medium such as fat or water to return to the desired cooking temperature after food is submerged in it

adjusted within this range to allow the interior of thicker foods or frozen foods to cook before their surfaces become too dark. The fat must be hot enough to quickly seal the surface of the food so that it does not become excessively greasy, yet it should not be so hot that the food's surface burns before the interior is cooked.

There are two methods of deep-frying: the basket method and the swimming method. The *basket method* uses a basket to hold foods that are breaded, are individually quick-frozen or otherwise will not tend to stick together during cooking. The basket is removed from the fryer and filled as much as two-thirds full of product. (Do not fill the basket while it is hanging over the fat, as this allows unnecessary salt and food particles to fall into the fat, decreasing its life.) The filled basket is then submerged in the hot fat. When cooking is completed, the basket is used to remove the foods from the fat and hold them while excess fat drains off.

A variation on this procedure is the *double-basket method*. It is used because many foods float as they deep-fry. This may produce undesirable results because the portion of the food not submerged may not cook. To prevent this and to promote even cooking, a second basket is placed over the food held in the first basket, keeping the food submerged in the fat.

Most battered foods initially sink to the bottom when placed in hot fat, then rise to the top as they cook. Because they would stick to a basket, the *swimming method* is used for these foods. With the swimming method, battered foods are carefully placed directly into the hot fat. (Baskets are not used.) They will rise to the top as they cook. When the surface that is in contact with the fat is properly browned, the food is turned over with a spider or a pair of tongs so that it can cook evenly on both sides. When done, the product is removed and drained, again using a spider or tongs.

Fats for Deep-Frying

Many types of fats can be used for deep-frying. By far the most common fats used for deep-frying are vegetable oils such as soybean, peanut and canola oil, all of which have high smoke points and are relatively inexpensive. Animal fats are not used commercially due to low smoke points, and dietary and religious concerns. Fryer fats are being reformulated to avoid hydrogenation, which increases trans fat. Trans fat is outlawed in some jurisdictions.

The basket method of deep-frying.

The double-basket method of deep-frying.

The swimming method of deep-frying.

BASIC PROCEDURE FOR DEEP-FRYING FOODS

1. Cut, trim or otherwise prepare the food to be deep-fried. Bread or batter it, as desired.
2. Heat the oil or fat to the desired temperature.
3. Using either the basket method or the swimming method, carefully place the food in the hot fat.
4. Deep-fry the food until done. Doneness is usually determined by timing, surface colour or sampling.
5. Remove the deep-fried food from the fryer and hold it over the cooking fat, allowing the excess fat to drain off.
6. Transfer the food to a hotel pan either lined with absorbent paper or fitted with a rack.
7. If the deep-fried items are to be held for later service, place them under a heat lamp; steam tables will not keep fried foods properly hot.

TABLE 9.2	Maintaining Fryer Fat

Fryer Fat Can Be Damaged By:
Salt
Water
Overheating
Food particles
Oxygen

Change Fryer Fat When It:

Becomes dark
Smokes
Foams
Develops off-flavours

Specially formulated deep-frying compounds are also available. These are usually composed of a vegetable oil or oils to which antifoaming agents, antioxidants and preservatives have been added. These additives increase the oil's usable life and raise its smoke point.

To choose the right fat, consider flavour, smoke point and resistance to chemical breakdown. High-quality frying fat should have a clean or natural flavour and a high smoke point and, when properly maintained, should be resistant to chemical breakdown.

Properly maintaining deep-fryer fat will greatly extend its useful life. (See Table 9.2.) To do so:

1. Store the fat in tightly sealed containers away from strong light; cover the deep-fat fryer when not in use. Prolonged exposure to air and light turns fat rancid.

2. Skim and remove food particles from the fat's surface during frying. Food particles cause fat to break down; if they are not removed, they will accumulate in the fryer and burn.

3. Do not salt food over the fat. Salt causes fat to break down chemically.

4. Prevent excessive water from coming into contact with the fat; pat-dry moist foods as much as possible before cooking and dry the fryer, baskets and utensils well after cleaning. Water, like salt, causes fat to break down.

5. Do not overheat the fat (turn the fryer down or off if not in use). High temperatures break down the fat.

6. Filter the fat each day or after each shift if the fryer is heavily used. Best results are obtained by using a filtering machine designed specifically for this purpose. Many large commercial fryers even have built-in filter systems. Less well-equipped operations can simply pour the hot fat through a paper filter. Exercise extreme caution when straining hot fat.

Moist-Heat Cooking Methods

Cooking with moist heat is the process of applying heat to food by submerging it directly into a hot liquid or by exposing it to steam. (See Table 9.3.)

Poaching

Poaching is a moist-heat cooking method that uses convection to transfer heat from a liquid to a food. For poaching, the food is submerged in a liquid held at temperatures between 71°C and 82°C (160°F and 180°F). The surface of the liquid should show only slight movement but no bubbles.

Poaching (71°C to 82°C/160°F to 180°F)

TABLE 9.3	Moist-Heat Cooking Methods		
Method	**Liquid's Temperature**	**Liquid's Condition**	**Uses**
Poaching	71°C–82°C/160°F–180°F	Liquid moves slightly but no bubbles	Eggs, fish, fruits
Simmering	85°C–96°C/185°F–205°F	Small bubbles break through the liquid's surface	Meats, stews, chicken
Boiling	100°C (sea level) 212°F	Large bubbles and rapid movement	Vegetables, pasta
Steaming	100°C or higher 212°F or higher	Food is in contact only with the steam generated by a boiling liquid	Vegetables, fish, shellfish

The flavour of the poaching liquid strongly affects the ultimate flavour of the finished product, so stock, court bouillon or broth is generally used. Poaching is most often associated with foods that do not require lengthy cooking to tenderize them, such as eggs or fish.

To poach food, first bring the poaching liquid to a boil in a suitably shaped cooking vessel. Add the food to be poached either by placing it directly into the liquid or by lowering it into the liquid using a specially designed rack. Adjust the heat as necessary to maintain the desired temperature throughout the cooking process. Do not allow the liquid to reach a boil, as the agitation will cause meats to become tough and stringy and will destroy tender foods such as fresh fruit or fish. For partially submerged foods, a cartouche is used to trap the steam. The liquid used to poach food is sometimes used to make an accompanying sauce.

BASIC PROCEDURE FOR POACHING FOODS

1. Cut, trim or otherwise prepare the food to be poached.

2. Bring an adequate amount of cooking liquid to the desired starting temperature. (For some items, the cooking liquid is first brought to a boil and then reduced to the poaching temperature.) Place the food in the liquid.

3. For submersion poaching, the liquid should completely cover the food.

4. For shallow poaching, the liquid should come approximately halfway up the side of the food. If shallow poaching, cover the pan with a piece of buttered parchment paper or a lid.

5. Maintaining the proper temperature, poach the food to the desired doneness in the oven or on the stove top. Doneness is generally determined by timing, internal temperature or tenderness.

6. Remove the food and hold it for service in a portion of the cooking liquid or, using an ice bath, cool it in the cooking liquid.

7. The cooking liquid can sometimes be used to prepare an accompanying sauce or reserved for use in other dishes.

1. Season the poaching liquid as desired and bring it to the correct temperature.

2. Carefully place the food item into the poaching liquid.

3. Remove the cooked food from the poaching liquid.

Simmering

Simmering is another moist-heat cooking method that uses convection to transfer heat from a liquid to a food. For simmering, the food is submerged in a liquid held at temperatures between 85°C and 96°C (185°F and 205°F). Because simmering temperatures are slightly higher than those used for poaching, there should be more action on the liquid's surface, with a few air bubbles breaking through.

Simmering (85°C to 96°C/185°F to 205°F)

As with poaching, the liquid used for simmering has a great effect on the food's flavour. Be sure to use a well-flavoured stock or broth and to add mirepoix, herbs and seasonings as needed. Simmered foods should be moist and very tender.

BASIC PROCEDURE FOR SIMMERING FOODS

1. Cut, trim or otherwise prepare the food to be simmered.

2. Bring an adequate amount of the cooking liquid to the appropriate temperature (some foods, especially smoked or cured items, are started in a cold liquid). There should be enough liquid to cover the food completely.

3. Add the food to the simmering liquid.

4. Maintaining the proper cooking temperature throughout the process, simmer the food to the desired doneness. Doneness is generally determined by timing or tenderness.

5. Remove the item and hold it for service in a portion of the cooking liquid or, using an ice bath, cool the food in its cooking liquid.

1. The item being simmered should be fully submerged in the seasoned liquid.

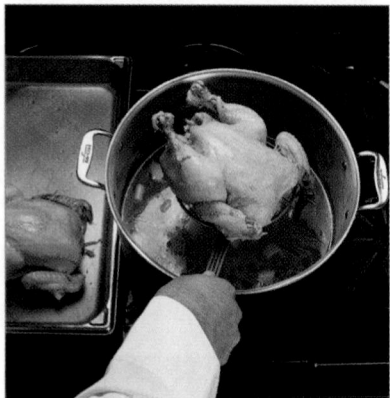

2. Remove the cooked item from the liquid.

Boiling

Boiling is another moist-heat cooking method that uses the process of convection to transfer heat from a liquid to a food. Boiling uses large amounts of rapidly bubbling liquid to cook foods. The turbulent waters and the relatively high temperatures cook foods more quickly than do poaching or simmering. Few foods, however, are cooked by true boiling. Most "boiled" meats are actually simmered. Even "hard-boiled" eggs are really only simmered. Starches such as pasta and potatoes are among the only types of food that are truly boiled.

Under normal atmospheric pressure at sea level, water boils at 100°C (212°F). The addition of other ingredients or a change in atmospheric pressure can change the boiling point, however. As altitude increases, the boiling point decreases because of the drop in atmospheric pressure. For every 305 m (1000 ft.) above sea level, the boiling point of water drops 1°C (2°F). In the city of Calgary at 1100 m, for example, water boils at 97°C (206°F). Because the boiling temperature is lower it will take longer to cook foods in Calgary than in, for example, Montreal.

The addition of alcohol also lowers the boiling point of water because alcohol boils at about 80°C (175°F). In contrast, the addition of salt, sugar or other substances raises the boiling point slightly. This means that foods cooked in salted water cook faster because the boiling point is one or two degrees higher than normal.

BASIC PROCEDURE FOR BOILING FOODS

1. Bring an appropriate amount of a liquid to a boil over high heat. Add oil or seasonings, if desired.

2. Add the food to be boiled to the rapidly boiling water. Bring the liquid back to a boil and adjust the temperature to maintain the boil.

3. Cook until done. Doneness is usually determined by timing or texture.

4. Remove the boiled food from the cooking liquid, draining any excess liquid.

5. Serve the boiled food immediately. Some boiled foods can be refreshed or shocked in ice water and held for later service.

1. Bring the cooking liquid to a full boil. When the item being cooked is added to the liquid, its temperature will fall.

2. After a boiled item such as pasta is cooked, it may be drained through a colander.

Steaming

Steaming is a moist-heat cooking method that uses the process of convection to transfer heat from the steam to the food being cooked. The food to be steamed is placed in a basket or rack above a boiling liquid. The food should not touch the liquid; it should be positioned so that the steam can circulate around it. A lid should be placed on the steaming pot to trap the steam and also create a slight pressure within the pot, which speeds the cooking process. The liquid used to steam the food is sometimes used to make a sauce served with the item.

Another type of steaming uses a low-pressure convection steamer. Convection steamers use steam to cook food very quickly in an enclosed chamber. Convection steamer cooking does not result in a flavoured liquid that can be used to make a sauce. High pressure steamers are also available.

BASIC PROCEDURE FOR STEAMING FOODS

1. Cut, trim or otherwise prepare the food to be steamed.

2. If a convection steamer is not being used, prepare a steaming liquid and bring it to a boil in a covered pan or doubleboiler.

3. Place the food to be steamed on a rack, in a basket or on a perforated pan in a single layer. Do not crowd the items. Place the rack, basket or pan over the boiling liquid.

4. Alternatively, place the food in a shallow pool of the cooking liquid.

5. Cover the cooking assemblage and cook to the desired doneness. Doneness is usually determined by timing, colour or tenderness.

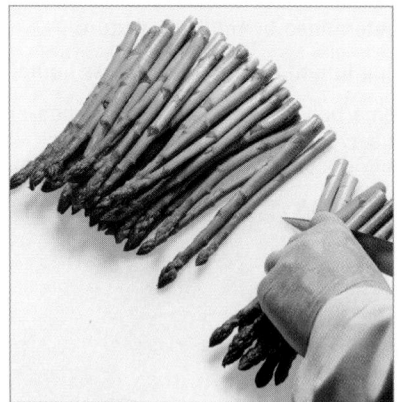

1. Trim items before steaming them so that they cook evenly.

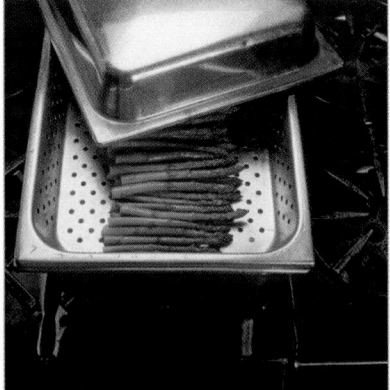

2. A perforated hotel pan can be set over a deeper pan of water, covered and used as a steamer.

Combination Cooking Methods

Some cooking methods employ both dry-heat and moist-heat cooking techniques. The two principal combination methods are braising and stewing. In both methods the first step is usually to brown the main item using dry heat. The second step is to complete cooking by simmering the food in a liquid. Combination methods are good for less tender but flavourful cuts of meat.

Braising and Poêléing

● **poêlé** a combination cooking method that involves browning the meat in butter and braising with a mirepoix

Braised foods, including **poêlé**, benefit from the best qualities of both dry- and moist-heat cooking methods. Foods to be braised are usually large pieces that are first browned in a small amount of fat at high temperatures. As with sautéing, heat is transferred from the pan to the food mainly by the process of conduction. Vegetables and seasonings are added and enough sauce or liquid is added to come one-third to one-half up the item being cooked. The pan is covered and the heat is reduced. The food is cooked at low heat, using a combination of simmering and steaming to transfer heat from the liquid (conduction) and the air (convection) to the food. This can be done on the stove top or in the oven. A long, slow cooking period helps tenderize the main item. Braised foods are usually served with a sauce made from the cooking liquid.

BASIC PROCEDURE FOR BRAISING FOODS

1. Cut, trim or otherwise prepare the food to be braised. Dredge it in flour, if desired.

2. Heat a small amount of fat in a heavy pan.

3. Sear the food on all sides. Some foods—notably, meats—should be removed from the pan after they are seared.

4. Add any other ingredients and sauté.

5. Add flour or roux, if used.

6. Add the cooking liquid; it should partially cover the food being braised.

7. Add aromatics and seasonings.

8. If the principal item was removed, return it to the pan.

9. Cover the pan and bring the cooking liquid to a simmer. Cook slowly, either on the stove top or in an oven at 120°C–150°C (250°F–300°F). Baste and turn the food as needed.

10. When the principal item is cooked, remove it from the pan and hold it in a warm place.

11. Prepare a sauce from the braising liquid if desired. This may be done by reducing the liquid on the stove top to intensify its flavours. If the food was braised in an unthickened stock, the stock may now be thickened using a roux, arrowroot or cornstarch. Strain the sauce or, if desired, purée the mirepoix and other ingredients and return them to the sauce. Adjust the sauce's consistency as desired.

  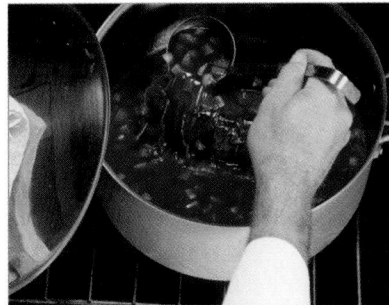

1. First brown the item being braised in fat.

2. Add liquid to the pan.

3. The item can be basted with the liquid during cooking.

Stewing

Stewing also uses a combination of dry- and moist-heat cooking methods. Stewing is most often associated with smaller pieces of food that are first cooked either by browning them in a small amount of fat or oil or by **blanching** them in a liquid. Cooking is then finished in a liquid or sauce. Stewed foods have enough liquid added to cover them completely and are simmered at a constant temperature until tender. Cooking time is generally shorter for stewing than for braising because the main items are smaller.

Sous Vide

Sous vide is a specialized cooking method that was developed by Georges Pralus, a French chef, in 1971. It means "under vacuum, cooked in a bag" and is characterized by fresh ingredients combined into various dishes, vacuum packed in individual portions, cooked under vacuum, then chilled. The item is later re-thermalized for service, still in the vacuum pack. Initially the process was primarily used by hotels, restaurants and caterers, but it has been widely adopted for the retail market.

BASIC PROCEDURE FOR STEWING FOODS

1. Trim and cut the food to be stewed into small, uniform-sized pieces. Dredge the pieces in flour, if desired.

2. Heat a small amount of fat in a heavy pan. Then sear the food on all sides, developing colour as desired.

3. Add any other ingredients and sauté.

4. Add flour or roux.

5. Gradually add the cooking liquid, stirring to prevent lumps. The liquid should completely cover the principal items.

6. Bring the stew to the appropriate temperature. Cover and place in the oven at 120°C–150°C (250°F–300°F) or continue to simmer on the stove top until the principal items are tender.

7. Remove the principal items and hold them in a warm place.

8. Thicken the sauce as desired.

9. Return the principal items to the stew. If not added during the cooking process, vegetables and other garnishes may be cooked separately and added to the finished stew.

1. First brown the item being stewed in a small amount of fat.

2. Add flour to make a roux.

3. Add liquid to the pan.

4. Degrease the finished stew as necessary.

Cost benefits of adopting the system include lower wastage due to extended shelf life, tighter portion controls and cutting food cost by reducing flavour-enhancing materials. Labour costs benefit from higher productivity in terms of food produced per labour hour. Staff recruitment can be easier and room service and banquet menus can require less preparation time. Overall product consistency and quality are maintained. There are fewer problems associated with oxygen and contamination due to vacuum packing.

Disadvantages begin with capital start-up costs associated with the equipment and systems needed to ensure strict quality controls. Staff training is more involved due to HACCP. There is a risk of food poisoning if the sous vide packages are temperature- or time-abused in preparation, storage and handling.

Typically, food vacuum packed for sous vide cooking is immersed in a hot water bath maintained at a temperature of 95°C (200°F). It is pasteurized at a temperature between 60°C and 95°C (140°F and 203°F), chilled rapidly in ice water and held at a temperature between 0°C and 3°C (32°F and 37°F). Each recipe varies, however, and lower temperatures for the water bath can be used if one pays strict attention to the integrity of the product being processed. For example, Daniel Boulud in New York has been known to cook braised beef short ribs for up to 30 hours at 66°C.

Maintaining food safety is critical in sous vide and other cook–chill systems. To ensure that a safe and wholesome product is served:

- Use only high-quality ingredients with low overall microbe counts.
- Ensure package integrity by using an appropriate sealing and packaging system.
- Process the product thermally with heat.
- Rapidly cool the heated product for storage between 2°C and 4°C (35°F and 40°F).
- Identify package leaks and discard the product.
- Date all products and consume within a specified time period.
- Implement a proper HACCP system to ensure correct preventative measures.

Cook–Chill Systems

Designed to increase productivity in food preparation and service, cook–chill and cook–freeze systems are increasingly employed in menu planning. Specialized equipment is used to ensure that food safety standards are met in cooking and reducing the core temperature of cooked foods. Home meal replacement items, also known as value-added products, employ this system. Airline production kitchens, convention centres, and hospitals use a precook and chill process in order to maximize the labour, operations and resources of large food service facilities. Cook–chill systems also preserve the nutritional integrity of the food better than other more conventional approaches.

There are a number of key concepts to be adhered to in employing a cook–chill system. One must start with a standardized recipe. HACCP principles should be integral to the recipes, identifying the critical control points (CCP) and necessary procedures to ensure compliance. Traditional cooking methods are used but may be enhanced with combitherm technology. The most critical element is the rapid chilling of the cooked food to between 0°C and 3°C (32°F and 37°F). A blast chiller is used to ensure that this happens. Factors to be considered include the size, shape, density and weight of the food item. Chilling may be achieved through clean, cold air circulation, non-oxidizing low temperature gases or appropriate refrigerated liquids in which prepackaged food is submerged (sous vide).

Essential benchmarks in the cook–chill system include:

- Food must be cooled from 60°C to 20°C (140°F to 68°F) in two hours or less.
- Food must be cooled from 20°C to 3°C (68°F to 37°F) in less than four hours.
- Food must spend less than six hours in the danger zone.

- Large or thick items should not exceed 2.5 kg (5-1/2 lb.) or maximum thickness of 100 mm (4 in.).
- After cooking, poultry should be cooled to 10°C (50°F) within 2.5 hours and then chilled to 0°C to 3°C (32°F to 37°F) for storage.
- Cooked menu items in trays should not exceed 50 mm (2 in.) in depth.
- Service of cook–chill items must occur within five days of initial production.

Storage of cook–chill products must be in adequate refrigeration to ensure that a temperature of 0°C to 3°C (32°F to 37°F) is maintained and not exceeded. The refrigerator must be used only for cook–chill items. If the internal temperature of the food reaches 5°C up to 9°C (41°F up to 48°F), it must be rethermalized and used within 12 hours. Once the internal temperature of the food reaches 10°C (50°F) or more, it must be destroyed. Particular care must be exercised in the transportation and distribution of cook–chill items to maintain the cold chain. Thorough product inspection upon receiving is important, as is rapid movement to a refrigerated storage area.

Reheating of cook–chill items requires attention as well. Regardless of whether the item is a single portion or a bulk pack, this CCP requires that the food be reheated to an internal temperature of 74°C (165°F) or hotter and held at this temperature for 15 minutes to maintain the integrity of the product.

Cook–freeze systems operate in much the same way as cook–chill. Shock freezers are the preferred technology, but blast freezers are also used. Core temperature of the food must reach at least –5°C (23°F) within 90 minutes. It is then lowered to at least –18°C (0°F) for storage. Shelf life of frozen products is eight weeks.

Conclusion

Cooking is the transfer of heat energy to foods by conduction, convection or radiation. Cooking changes the molecular structure of certain nutrients. When heat is applied, proteins coagulate, starches gelatinize, sugars caramelize, fats melt and water evaporates. Foods can be cooked using a variety of methods. Some use dry heat: broiling, grilling, roasting and baking, sautéing, pan-frying and deep-fat frying. Others use moist heat: poaching, simmering, boiling and steaming. Still others use a combination of the two: braising and stewing. Sous vide and cook–chill employ a variety of cooking methods, depending on the dish being prepared. The method used affects the texture, appearance and flavour of the cooked foods. You must understand these principles in order to ensure that foods are properly cooked.

Questions for Discussion

1. Describe the differences between conduction and convection. Identify four cooking methods that rely on both conduction and convection to heat foods. Explain your choices.
2. Identify two cooking methods that rely on infrared heat. What is the principal difference between these methods?
3. At the same temperature, will a food cook faster in a convection oven or a conventional oven? Explain your answer.
4. Describe the process of caramelization and its significance in food preparation. Will a braised food have a caramelized surface? Explain your answer.

5. Describe the process of coagulation and its significance in food preparation. Will a pure fat coagulate if heated? Explain your answer.

6. Describe the process of gelatinization and its significance in food preparation. Will a pure fat gelatinize? Explain your answer.

7. What qualities should be considered when choosing a fat for deep-fat frying?

8. List three signs that fryer fat has broken down and should be replaced. What causes fryer fat to break down? What can you do to extend the life of fryer fat?

9. Explain the differences between breading and battering foods for deep-fat frying.

10. Describe sous vide cooking.

11. Itemize the cooling process for a cook–chill system.

12. Do sous vide and cook–chill systems mean that less-skilled kitchen staff is needed?

10 Stocks and Sauces

"What I love about cooking is that after a hard day, there is something comforting about the fact that if you melt butter and add flour, then hot stock, it will get thick! It's a sure thing. It's a sure thing in a world where nothing is sure!

—Nora Ephron, American author and filmmaker (1941–)

A *stock* is a flavoured liquid; a good stock is the key to a great soup, sauce or braised dish. The French appropriately call a stock *fond* ("base"), as stocks are the basis for many classic and modern dishes.

A *sauce* is a thickened liquid used to flavour and enhance other foods. A good sauce adds flavour, moisture, richness and visual appeal. A sauce should complement food; it should never disguise it. A sauce can be hot or cold, sweet or savoury, smooth or chunky.

Although the thought of preparing stocks and sauces may be intimidating, the procedures are really quite simple. Carefully follow the basic procedures outlined in this chapter, use high-quality ingredients and, with practice and experience, you will soon be producing fine stocks and sauces.

This chapter addresses classical hot sauces as well as coulis, broths, oils, salsas and relishes. Cold sauces, generally based on mayonnaise, are discussed in Chapter 25, Salads and Salad Dressings; dessert sauces are discussed in Chapter 32, Custards, Creams, Frozen Desserts and Dessert Sauces.

STOCKS

All standard stocks are made from a combination of bones (protein-based stock only), flavouring vegetables (mirepoix), seasonings and liquids. Although they are all different, all stocks share four common quality characteristics regardless of the type:

- *Body:* Body is obtained from the dissolution of certain proteins (collagens) in protein-based stocks. *Note:* Vegetable stocks do not use bones and, as such, tend to have less body than regular stocks.

- *Flavour:* Flavour results from the use of flavouring vegetables (mirepoix), spices and herbs (sachet) or herbs and vegetables (bouquet garni). The caramelization and browning of bones and mirepoix for brown stocks also has a beneficial effect on flavour.

- *Clarity:* Clarity is achieved by removing impurities (scum) through blanching and refreshing the bones at the beginning of the cooking process and/or continually removing scum from the top of the stock. Adhere to these critical rules for clear stock production:

  1. Use only cold water.
  2. Never cover a stock with a lid during cooking.
  3. Always cook a stock at a simmer, not a boil.
  4. Never stir a stock.

- *Colour:* Many ingredients, such as carrots or leeks, may impart colour in a white stock. Overuse of such ingredients may have a negative impact on the colour of the finished product, making it too green or orange. With a brown stock, colour is achieved through browning bones and mirepoix, plus adding tomato purée.

There are several types of stocks:

A **white stock** is made by simmering chicken, veal, beef or game bird bones in water with vegetables and seasonings. The stock remains relatively colourless during the cooking process, as long as colourless vegetables are used.

● **white stock** a light-coloured stock made from chicken, veal, beef or game bird bones simmered in water with vegetables and seasoning

A **brown stock** is made from chicken, veal, beef or game bones and vegetables, all of which are browned before being simmered in water with seasonings. The stock has a rich, amber-brown colour.

A **fish stock** is made by sweating aromatic vegetables (white mirepoix), adding white, lean fish bones, water and seasonings, then simmering for 30 to 40 minutes. When making a **fumet**, dry white wine and sometimes a little lemon juice are used as part of the liquid. A fumet has a higher ratio of bones to liquid.

A **court bouillon** is made by simmering vegetables and seasonings in water and an acidic liquid such as vinegar or wine. It is used to poach fish, shellfish or vegetables.

A **vegetable stock**, made without meat products, is made with vegetables or parts of vegetables that do not contain excessive amounts of the following:

* starches—they make the stock cloudy

* chlorophyll—the green pigment of vegetables turns grey when cooked for a long time

* anthocyanins—the water-soluble pigment in vegetables such as red cabbage adds a strong, undesirable colour to the stock

* strong flavours (such as cabbage, cauliflower, etc.)

Ingredients

The basic ingredients of most stocks are bones, a flavouring vegetable mixture known as a *mirepoix*, seasonings and water.

Bones

Bones are the most important ingredient for producing a good, protein-based stock. Bones add flavour, body and colour. Traditionally, the kitchen or butcher shop saved the day's bones to make stock. However, because many meats and poultry items are now purchased previously cut or portioned, food service operations often purchase bones specifically for stock making.

Different bones release their flavour at different rates. Even though the bones are cut into 8- to 10-cm (3- to 4-in.) pieces, a stock made entirely of beef and/or veal bones requires 6 to 8 hours of cooking time, while a stock made entirely from chicken bones requires 3 to 4 hours.

Beef and Veal Bones

The best bones for beef and veal stock are from younger animals. They contain a higher percentage of **cartilage** and other **connective tissue** than do bones from more mature animals. Connective tissue has a high **collagen** content. Through the cooking process, the collagen is converted into **gelatin** and water. The gelatin adds richness and body to the finished stock.

The best beef and veal bones are knuckles, shank and long bones with marrow, as they have a high collagen content. Beef and veal bones should be cut with a meat saw into small pieces, approximately 8- to 10-cm (3- to 4-in.) long, so that they can release as much flavour and collagen as possible while the stock cooks.

Chicken Bones

The best bones for chicken stock are from the neck and back. If a whole chicken carcass is used, it can be cut up for easier handling. The bones may be washed well in cold water, rather than blanched and refreshed, to avoid losing too much of the flavour.

● **brown stock** a richly coloured stock made of chicken, veal, beef or game bones and vegetables, all of which are caramelized before they are simmered in water, flavourings and tomato purée

● **fumet** a stock made from fish bones and vegetables simmered in a liquid with flavourings

● **court bouillon** water simmered with vegetables, seasonings and an acidic product such as vinegar or wine; used for simmering or poaching fish, shellfish or vegetables

● **cartilage** also known as gristle, a tough, elastic, whitish connective tissue that helps give structure to an animal's body

● **connective tissue** tissue found throughout an animal's body that binds together and supports other tissues such as muscles

● **collagen** a protein found in nearly all connective tissue; it dissolves when cooked with moisture

● **gelatin** a tasteless and odourless mixture of proteins (especially collagen) extracted from boiling bones, connective tissue and other animal parts; when dissolved in a hot liquid and then cooled, it forms a jellylike substance used as a thickener and stabilizer

Fish Bones

The best bones for fish stock are from lean fish such as sole, halibut, cod or turbot. Bones from fatty fish (e.g., salmon and tuna) do not produce good stock because of their high fat content and distinctive flavours. However, if such bones are used, the resulting stock takes on the name of the fish bones that were used (i.e., salmon stock, tuna stock, etc.). The entire fish carcass can be used, but it should be cut up with a cleaver or heavy knife for easy handling and even extraction of flavours. After cutting, the pieces should be rinsed in cold water to remove blood, loose scales and other impurities.

Other Bones

Lamb, turkey, game and ham bones can also be used for white or brown stocks. Although mixing bones is generally acceptable, be careful of blending strongly flavoured bones, such as those from lamb or game, with beef, veal or chicken bones. The former's strong flavours may not be appropriate or desirable in the finished product. The use of pork bones is governed by customer profiles.

Mirepoix

A French classical flavouring agent made of "flavouring vegetables" is used to lay down a base flavour in stocks, soups, sauces, stews, braised dishes and pot roasts. The original mirepoix comprised carrots, onions, celery, lardons, sprig of thyme and bay leaves. For dietary reasons, many chefs often omit the lardons. A **matignon** is a standard mirepoix plus additional ingredients.

In many cases the mirepoix is removed before finishing or is puréed and mixed into the final product—for example, with puréed soups. For these reasons mirepoix does not have to be a precise cut. The length of cooking time dictates the size of the cut. Lengthy cooking requires large cuts while shorter times demand smaller cuts. The usual ratio is two parts onion to one part each of celery and carrot. To introduce colour and flavour, the mirepoix is browned either by sautéing or roasting it in the oven. The dry heat caramelizes the carbohydrates in the vegetables. For a white finished product, a white mirepoix is used, made up of onion, celery, white of leek and mushrooms.

Not all vegetables are suitable for laying a foundation of flavour, for some have overpowering flavours, such as turnip, fennel, peppers, and so on. Others will impart a bitter flavour, like cabbage, and some will affect colour—beets, for example. Certain root vegetables, such as potatoes, will release starch, which clouds the final product. The following vegetables are suitable to use as flavouring vegetables: carrots, celery, celeriac, mushrooms, garlic, leeks, onions, shallots and tomatoes.

Seasonings

Principal stock seasonings are peppercorns, bay leaves, thyme and parsley stems. These seasonings generally can be left whole. A stock is cooked long enough for all the seasoning flavours to be extracted so there is no reason to chop or grind them. Seasonings generally are added to the stock at the start of cooking. Some chefs do not add seasonings to beef or veal stock until midway through the cooking process, however, because of the extended cooking times. Seasonings can be added as a spice bag (sachet d'épices) or a bouquet garni.

Salt, an otherwise important seasoning, is not added to stock. Because a stock has a variety of uses, it is impossible for the chef to know how much salt to add when preparing it. If, for example, the stock was seasoned to taste with

Mirepoix Ingredients

Standard Ratio:
50% onions, 25% carrots,
25% celery by weight

● **matignon** a standard mirepoix plus diced smoked bacon or smoked ham and, depending on the dish, mushrooms and herbs; sometimes called an edible mirepoix, it is usually cut more uniformly than a standard mirepoix and left in the finished dish as a garnish

Start the stock in cold water.

Simmer the stock gently.

Skim the stock frequently.

Add mirepoix, herbs and spices.

Strain the stock carefully.

Cool the stock quickly.

Store the stock properly.

Degrease the stock.

FIGURE 10.1 Principles of stock making.

salt, the chef could not reduce it later; salt is not lost through reduction and the concentrated product would taste too salty. Similarly, seasoning the stock to taste with salt could prevent the chef from adding other ingredients that are high in salt when finishing a recipe. Unlike many seasonings whose flavours must be incorporated into a product through lengthy cooking periods, salt can be added at any time during the cooking process with the same effect.

Principles of Stock Making

The following principles apply to all stocks. You should follow them in order to achieve the highest quality stock possible. (See Figure 10.1.)

A. Start the Stock in Cold Water

The ingredients should always be covered with cold water. When bones are covered with cold water, impurities are drawn out and dissolve. As the water heats, the impurities coagulate and rise to the surface, where they can be removed easily by skimming. If the bones were covered with hot water, the impurities would coagulate more quickly and remain dispersed in the stock without rising to the top, making the stock cloudy and grey in colour.

If the water level falls below the bones during cooking, add water to cover them. Flavour and gelatin cannot be extracted from bones that are not under water, and bones exposed to the air will darken and discolour a white stock.

B. Simmer the Stock Gently

The stock should be brought to a boil and then reduced to a simmer, a temperature of approximately 85°C (185°F). While simmering, the ingredients release their flavours into the liquid. If kept at a simmer, the liquid will remain clear as it reduces and a stock develops (see sidebar for recommended cooking times).

Never boil a stock for any length of time. Rapid boiling of a stock, even for a few minutes, causes impurities and fats to blend with the liquid, making it cloudy. Never cover a stock with a lid.

C. Skim the Stock Frequently

A stock should be skimmed often to remove the impurities that rise to the surface during cooking. If they are not removed, they may make the stock cloudy.

D. Add Mirepoix, Herbs and Spices

Some chefs add the mirepoix, herbs and spices at the beginning of the cooking process, but, since the main reason for adding mirepoix, herbs and spices is to flavour the stock, many chefs prefer to add all flavourings two to three hours before the end of the cooking time, or long enough to release the flavours. This method also allows for skimming without removing the flavourings that are floating on the surface of the stock.

E. Strain the Stock Carefully

Once a stock finishes cooking, the liquid must be separated from the bones, vegetables and other solid ingredients. In order to keep the liquid clear, it is important not to disturb the solid ingredients when removing the liquid. This is easily accomplished if the stock is cooked in a steam kettle or stockpot with a spigot at the bottom.

If the stock is cooked in a standard stockpot, to strain it

1. Skim as much fat and as many impurities from the surface as possible before removing the stockpot from the heat. *Note:* Some chefs prefer to leave some fat in the stock as it rises to the top and solidifies to form a seal when the stock is cooled. It is then easily removed as a solid block before the stock is used. (See Figure 10.2.) Fat may be used to prepare roux.

2. After removing the pot from the heat, carefully ladle the stock from the pot without stirring it.

3. Strain the stock through a conical strainer lined with several layers of cheesecloth.

FIGURE 10.2   Lifting fat from the surface of a cold stock.

F. Cool the Stock Quickly

Most stocks are prepared in large quantities, cooled and held for later use. Great care must be taken when cooling a stock to prevent food-borne illnesses or souring. A stock can be cooled quickly and safely with the following procedure:

1. Keep the stock in a nonreactive metal container. A plastic container insulates the stock and delays cooling.

2. Vent the stockpot in an empty sink by placing it on blocks or a rack. This allows water to circulate on all sides and below the pot when the sink is filled with water. (See Figure 10.3.)

3. Install an overflow pipe in the drain and fill the sink with cold water or a combination of cold water and ice. Make sure that the weight of the stockpot is adequate to keep it from tipping over.

4. Let cold water run into the sink and drain out the overflow pipe. Stir the stock frequently to facilitate even, quick cooling.

SAFETY ALERT

Cooling and Handling Stocks

A two-stage cooling method is recommended for keeping stock out of the temperature danger zone. First cool the stock to 21°C (70°F) within 2 hours and from 21°C to below 4°C (70°F to below 40°F) in an additional 4 hours, for a total of 6 hours. To prevent bacterial growth if these temperatures have not been met, the stock must be reheated to 74°C (165°F) for 15 seconds within 2 hours or be discarded.

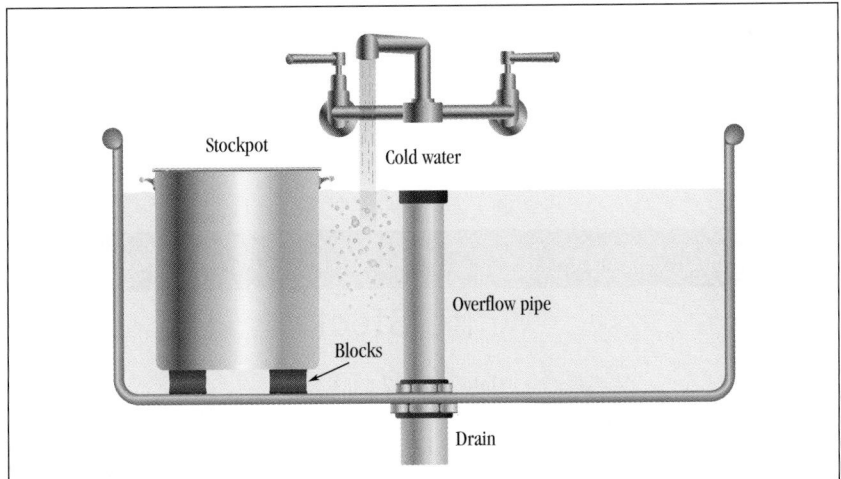

FIGURE 10.3   Venting a stockpot.

G. Store the Stock Properly

Once the stock is cooled, transfer it to a sanitized covered container (either food-grade plastic or nonreactive metal) and store it in the refrigerator. Stocks can be stored for up to one week under refrigeration or frozen for several months. Refrigerated stocks should be reheated after 3 or 4 days and simmered for 20 minutes. This will extend their shelf life by reducing bacterial counts. Chill quickly before storing again.

H. Degrease the Stock

● **degrease** to remove fat from the surface of a liquid such as a stock or sauce by skimming, scraping or lifting congealed fat

Degreasing a stock is simple: When a stock is refrigerated, fat rises to its surface, hardens and is easily lifted or scraped away before the stock is reheated. See Figure 10.2.

White Stock

A white stock may be made from beef, veal or chicken bones. The finished stock should have a good flavour, good clarity, high gelatin content and little or no colour. Veal bones are preferred usually, but any combination of beef, veal or chicken bones may be used.

Blanching and Refreshing Bones

Chefs disagree on whether the bones for a white stock should be blanched and refreshed to remove impurities. Some chefs argue that the process keeps the stock as clear and colourless as possible; others argue that blanching and refreshing removes flavour and advocate the continual removal of impurities from the stock by skimming.

1. Adding cold water to bones for white stock.

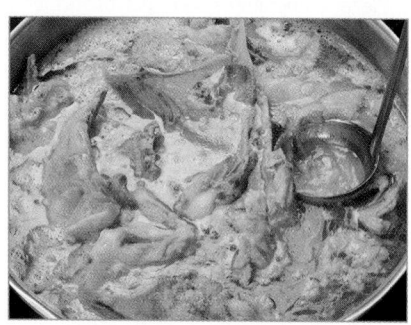

2. Skimming the white stock.

BASIC PROCEDURE FOR BLANCHING AND REFRESHING BONES

If you choose to blanch the bones:

1. Wash the cut-up bones; place them in a stockpot and cover them with cold water.

2. Bring the water to a boil over high heat.

3. As soon as the water boils, skim the rising impurities. Drain the water from the bones and discard it. Rinse the bones.

4. Refill the pot with cold water and proceed with the stock recipe.

3. Adding mirepoix to the white stock and seasonings.

APPLYING THE BASICS		RECIPE 10.1

White Stock

Yield: 10 L (2 gal.)

Bones: veal, chicken or beef	5 kg	10 lb.
Cold water	14 L	3 gal.
Mirepoix	1 kg	2 lb.

continued

RECIPE 10.1

Sachet:		
Bay leaves	2	2
Dried thyme	0.25 g	1/2 tsp.
Peppercorns, crushed	0.25 g	1/2 tsp.
Parsley stems	8	8

1. Cut the washed bones into pieces approximately 8- to 10-cm (3- to 4-in.) long.
2. Place the bones in a stockpot and cover them with cold water. If blanching, bring the water to a boil, skimming off the scum that rises to the surface. Drain off the water and the impurities. Rinse the bones, then add the 14 L (3 gal.) of cold water and bring to a boil. Reduce to a simmer.
3. If not blanching the bones, bring the cold water to a boil. Reduce to a simmer and skim the scum that forms.
4. Add the mirepoix and sachet to the simmering stock.
5. Continue simmering and skimming the stock for 6–8 hours. (If only chicken bones are used, simmer for 3–4 hours.)
6. Strain, cool and refrigerate.

Approximate values per 250 mL serving:	
Calories	32
Total fat	1.8 g
Saturated fat	0.6 g
Cholesterol	0.9 mg
Sodium	18 mg
Total carbohydrates	3.8 g
Protein	0.2 g

Brown Stock

A brown stock is made from chicken, veal, beef or game bones. The finished stock should have a good flavour, rich amber-brown colour and high gelatin content. Many chefs believe that a brown stock made from veal bones is superior.

The primary differences between a brown stock and a white stock are that for a brown stock, the bones and mirepoix are caramelized before being simmered and a tomato product is added. These extra steps provide the finished stock with a rich amber-brown colour and a more intense flavour. Burning the bones and mirepoix imparts a bitter flavour. The Maillard reactions also come into play.

Remouillage

French for "rewetting," remouillage is a stock produced by reusing the bones left from making another stock. After draining the original stock from the stockpot, add fresh mirepoix, a new sachet and enough water to cover the bones and mirepoix and a second stock can be made. A remouillage is treated like the original stock; allow it to simmer for 3–4 hours before straining. A remouillage will not be as clear or as flavourful, or have as much body as the original stock. It is often used to make braised or stewed products or in place of water when making stocks.

BASIC PROCEDURE FOR CARAMELIZING BONES

For browning, do not wash or blanch the bones, as this retards browning. To caramelize:

1. Place the cut-up bones in a roasting pan one layer deep. It is better to roast several pans of bones than to overfill one pan.
2. Roast the bones in a hot oven (190°C/375°F) until brown. Stirring occasionally, brown the bones thoroughly but do not allow them to burn.
3. Transfer the roasted bones from the pan to the stockpot.

Deglazing the Pan (Déglacer)

After the bones are caramelized, the excess fat should be removed and reserved for future use. The caramelized and coagulated proteins remaining in the roasting pan are very flavourful. To utilize them, **deglaze** the pan.

● **deglaze** to swirl or stir a liquid (usually wine or stock) in a sauté pan or other pan to dissolve cooked food particles remaining on the bottom; the resulting mixture often becomes the base for a sauce

1. Browning the bones.

2. Deglazing the pan with water.

3. Caramelizing the mirepoix.

4. Adding the proper amount of water.

BASIC PROCEDURE FOR DEGLAZING THE PAN

1. Place the pan on the stove top over medium heat and add enough water to cover the bottom of the pan approximately 1-cm (1/2-in.) deep.

2. Stir and scrape the pan bottom to dissolve and remove all of the caramelized materials while the water heats.

3. Pour the deglazing liquid (also known as the deglazing liquor) over the bones in the stockpot.

BASIC PROCEDURE FOR CARAMELIZING MIREPOIX

1. Add a little of the reserved fat from the roasted bones to the roasting pan after it has been deglazed. (Or use a sautoir large enough to contain all of the mirepoix comfortably.)

2. Sauté the mirepoix, browning all of the vegetables well and evenly without burning them. Alternatively, this may be done in an oven.

3. Add the caramelized mirepoix to the stockpot.

Almost any tomato product can be used in a brown stock: fresh tomatoes, canned whole tomatoes, crushed tomatoes, tomato purée or paste. If using a concentrated tomato product such as purée or paste, use approximately one-half or one-third the amount by weight of fresh or canned tomatoes. The tomato product should be added to the stockpot when the mirepoix is added.

APPLYING THE BASICS		RECIPE 10.2

Brown Stock

Yield: 10 L (2 gal.)

Bones: chicken, veal, beef or game		
cut in 8- to 10-cm (3- to 4-in.) pieces	5 kg	10 lb.
Cold water	14 L	3 gal.
Mirepoix, 5-cm (2-in.) pieces	1 kg	2 lb.
Tomato paste	250 mL	8 fl. oz.
Sachet:		
Bay leaves	2	2
Dried thyme	0.25 g	1/2 tsp.
Peppercorns, crushed	0.25 g	1/4 tsp.
Garlic cloves, crushed	10 g	3
Parsley stems	12	12

1. Place the bones in a roasting pan, one layer deep, and brown in a 190°C (375°F) oven. Turn the bones occasionally to brown them evenly.

2. Remove the bones and place them in a stockpot. Pour off the fat from the roasting pan and reserve it.

continued

3. Deglaze the roasting pan with part of the cold water.

4. Add the deglazing liquor and the rest of the cold water to the bones, covering them completely. Bring to a boil and reduce to a simmer.

5. Add a portion of the reserved fat to the roasting pan and sauté the mirepoix until evenly browned and caramelized. Then add it to the simmering stock.

6. Add the tomato paste and sachet to the stock and continue to simmer for 6–8 hours, skimming as necessary. (For brown chicken stock, simmer 3–4 hours.)

7. Strain, cool and refrigerate.

Approximate values per 250 mL serving:	
Calories	36
Total fat	1.8 g
Saturated fat	0.6 g
Cholesterol	0.9 mg
Sodium	52 mg
Total carbohydrates	4.6 g
Protein	0.3 g

Fish Stock and Fish Fumet

A fish stock and fish fumet are similar and can be used interchangeably in most recipes. Both are clear with a pronounced fish flavour and very light body. A fumet, however, is more strongly flavoured and aromatic. An essence results from reducing a fumet by half.

The fish bones used to make a fish stock or fumet should be washed but never blanched because blanching removes too much flavour. Because of the size and structure of fish bones, stocks and fumets made from them require much less cooking time than other stocks; 30 to 40 minutes is usually sufficient to extract full flavour. Mirepoix or other vegetables should be cut small so that all of their flavours can be extracted during the shorter cooking time. **Sweating** releases the flavour compounds quickly and mellows the onion/leek. *Note:* Use only bones from non-oily fish; flat fish bones are the best for stock production.

The procedure for making a fish stock is very similar to that for making a white stock.

French Terminology

White Stocks

Chicken: *Fond de volaille*
Veal: *Fond de veau*
Beef: *Fond de boeuf*
Vegetable: *Fond de légumes*
Fish: *Fond de poisson*

Brown Stocks

Chicken: *Fond de volaille brun*
Veal: *Fond de veau brun*
Beef: *Fond de boeuf brun*
Game: *Fond de gibier*

● **sweat** to cook a food in a pan (usually covered) without browning, over low heat until the item softens and releases moisture; sweating allows the food to release its flavour more quickly when cooked with other foods

APPLYING THE BASICS　　　　RECIPE 10.3

Fish Stock or Fumet

Yield: 8 L (2 gal.)

Clarified butter	50 g	2 oz.
White mirepoix, small dice	450 g	1 lb.
Parsley stems	12	12
Mushroom trimmings	75 g	3 oz.
Fresh thyme	2 sprigs	2 sprigs
Fish bones	8 kg	16 lb.
Dry white wine	750 mL	26 fl. oz.
Lemon juice (optional)	60 mL	2 fl. oz.
Cold water	8 L	8 qt.
Lemon slices (optional)	2–3	2–3

1. Melt the butter in a stockpot.

2. Add the mirepoix, parsley stems, mushroom trimmings and thyme and sweat 1 minute. Add fish bones. Cover the pot and sweat the bones on low heat. Do not stir.

3. Sprinkle the bones with the white wine and lemon juice (if using).

continued

RECIPE 10.3

Approximate values per 250 mL serving:	
Calories	300
Total fat	10 g
Saturated fat	1 g
Cholesterol	4 mg
Sodium	28 mg
Total carbohydrates	1.4 g
Protein	47 g

4. Add the cold water and lemon slices (if using). Bring to a simmer and cook approximately 30–40 minutes, skimming frequently.

5. Strain, cool and refrigerate.

NOTE: To make shellfish stock, replace fish bones with crustacean shells (i.e., shrimp, lobster, crab).

A lighter fish stock can be made by using half the bones and replacing the wine with water. A concentrated fumet becomes an essence.

1. Sweating the mirepoix, parsley stems, mushrooms, thyme and fish bones.

2. Adding cold water and simmering.

Vegetable Stock

A good vegetable stock should be clear and light-coloured. Because no animal products are used, it has no gelatin content. A vegetable stock can be used instead of a meat-based stock in most recipes. This substitution is useful when preparing vegetarian dishes or as a lighter, more healthful alternative when preparing sauces and soups. Although many combinations of vegetables can be used for stock making, more variety is not always better. Sometimes a vegetable stock made with one or two vegetables that complement the finished dish particularly well will produce better results than a stock made with too many vegetables. Peelings and onion skins are not acceptable.

See Table 10.1 for troubleshooting tips for stocks.

Adding cold water to the sweated vegetables.

APPLYING THE BASICS		RECIPE 10.4

Vegetable Stock

Yield: 4 L (1 gal.)

Vegetable oil	50 mL	2 fl. oz.
Mirepoix, small dice	600 g	1 lb. 4 oz.
Leek, whites and greens, chopped	125 g	4 oz.
Garlic cloves, chopped	4	4
Fennel, small dice	100 g	4 oz.
Tomato, diced	100 g	4 oz.

continued

Water	4.5 L	4-1/2 qt.
Sachet:		
Bay leaf	1	1
Dried thyme	0.25 g	1/2 tsp.
Peppercorns, crushed	0.25 g	1/4 tsp.
Parsley stems	8	8

1. Heat the oil. Add the vegetables and sweat for 10 minutes.
2. Add the water and sachet.
3. Bring the mixture to a boil, reduce to a simmer and cook for 30–40 minutes.
4. Strain, cool and refrigerate.

RECIPE 10.4

Approximate values per 250 mL serving:

Calories	37
Total fat	2.9 g
Saturated fat	0.2 g
Cholesterol	0 mg
Sodium	20 mg
Total carbohydrates	2.5 g
Protein	0.3 g

TABLE 10.1 Troubleshooting Tips for Stocks

Problem	Reason	Solution
Cloudy	Impurities	Start stock in cold water
	Stock boiled during cooking	Strain through layers of cheesecloth
Lack of flavour	Not cooked long enough	Increase cooking time
	Inadequate seasoning	Add more flavouring ingredients
	Improper ratio of bones to water	Add more bones or reduce liquid
Lack of colour	Improperly caramelized bones and mirepoix	Caramelize bones and mirepoix until darker
	Not cooked long enough	Cook longer
Lack of body	Wrong bones used	Use bones with a higher content of connective tissue
	Insufficient reduction	Cook longer
	Improper ratio of bones to water	Add more bones
Too salty	Commercial base used	Change base or make own stock
	Salt added during cooking	Do not salt stock

Court Bouillon

A court bouillon (acidic cooking liquid), although not actually a stock, is prepared in much the same manner as stocks so it is included here. A court bouillon (French for "short broth") is a flavoured liquid, usually water and wine or vinegar, in which flavouring vegetables and seasonings have been simmered to impart their flavours and aromas.

Court bouillon is most commonly used to poach foods such as fish and shellfish. Recipes vary depending upon the foods to be poached. Although a court bouillon can be made in advance and refrigerated for later use, its simplicity lends itself to fresh preparation whenever needed.

APPLYING THE BASICS **RECIPE 10.5**

Court Bouillon

Yield: 4 L (1 gal.)

| Water | 4.5 L | 5 qt. |
| White wine vinegar | 200 mL | 6 fl. oz. |

continued

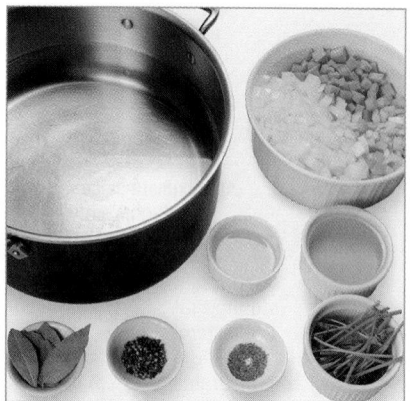

Mise en place for court bouillon

Lemon juice	50 mL	2 fl. oz.
Salt	10 g	1/4 oz.
Mirepoix	700 g	1 lb. 8 oz.
Peppercorns, crushed	15 g	1/2 oz.
Bay leaves	3	3
Dried thyme	0.25 g	1/2 tsp.
Parsley stems	8	8

1. Combine all ingredients and bring to a boil.

2. Reduce to a simmer and cook for 45 minutes.

3. Strain and use immediately or cool and refrigerate.

NOTE: This recipe can be used for poaching almost any fish, but it is particularly well suited to salmon, trout or shellfish. When poaching shellfish, replace the water and vinegar with equal parts white wine and water (nage).

Lime Leaves, Lemon Grass

Court bouillon lends itself to a variety of flavourings customized to the dish in which it is being used. Adding fragrant lime leaves, lemon grass or fresh ginger gives court bouillon an exotic flavour profile suitable for Asian fish dishes. Likewise, adding a mixture of mild dried chiles and cilantro to the preparation brings a Latin flair to the broth.

● **glaze** the dramatic reduction and concentration of stock

Nage

An aromatic court bouillon (nage) may be served as the accompanying sauce for poached items. Most often associated with fish and shellfish, the term may be used with other meats. It is preferable to make the court bouillon with citrus juice or verjus and wine rather than harsh vinegars. Clear stock may be used instead of water. Dishes described as *à la nage* (French for "swimming") are generally light but may be enriched by reducing the cooking liquid and finishing with cream or mounting with butter or extra virgin olive oil. Additional vegetables and herbs may be added to further complement the dish and provide garnish.

Glaze

A **glaze** is the reduction and concentration of a stock. Four litres (1 gallon) of stock produces only 250 to 500 mL (8 to 16 fl. oz.) of glaze. *Glace de viande* is made from brown stock, reduced until it becomes dark and syrupy. *Glace de volaille* is made from chicken stock and *glace de poisson* from fish stock or fumet.

Glazes are added to soups or sauces to increase and intensify flavours. They are also used as a source of intense flavouring for several of the derivative sauces discussed below. In many contemporary kitchens, glazes are used in place of traditional basic sauces such as demi-glace and veloutés.

1. A properly thickened glaze made from brown stock.

2. Chilled glace de viande.

BASIC PROCEDURE FOR REDUCING A STOCK TO A GLAZE

1. Simmer the stock over very low heat. Be careful not to let it burn. Skim it often.

2. As it reduces and the volume decreases, transfer the liquid into progressively smaller saucepans. Strain the liquid each time it is transferred into a smaller saucepan.

3. Strain it a final time, cool and refrigerate. A properly made glaze will keep for several months under refrigeration.

Commercial Bases

Commercially produced flavour (or convenience) bases are widely used in food service operations. They are powdered or paste flavourings added to water to create stocks or, when used in smaller amounts, to enhance the flavour of sauces and soups. Although inferior to well-made stocks, flavour bases do reduce the labour involved in the production of stocks, sauces and soups. Used properly, they also ensure a consistent product. Because bases do not contain gelatin, stocks and sauces made from them do not benefit from reduction.

Bases vary greatly in quality and price. Sodium (salt) is the main ingredient in most bases. Better bases are made primarily of meat, poultry or fish extracts. Combinations of sugars and specific amino acids can be heated to create flavour enhancers and substitutes. To judge the quality of a flavour base, prepare it according to package directions and compare the flavour with that of a well-made stock. A base can be improved by adding a mirepoix, standard sachet and a few appropriate bones to the mixture, then simmering for one or two hours. It can then be strained, stored and used like a regular stock.

Although convenience bases are widely used in the industry, it is important to remember that only high-quality bases/extracts are an acceptable substitute for well-made stocks.

SAUCES

With a few exceptions, a sauce is a liquid plus thickening agent plus seasonings. Any cook can produce fine sauces by learning to do the following:

1. Make good stocks;
2. Use thickening agents and/or techniques properly to achieve the desired texture, flavour and appearance; and
3. Use seasonings properly to achieve the desired flavours.

Classic hot sauces are divided into two groups: *basic* (or leading sauces) and *derivative* (small or compound sauces). The five classic basic sauces are béchamel, velouté, espagnole (brown), tomato and hollandaise. Except for hollandaise, basic sauces are rarely served as is; more often they are used to create the many derivative sauces.

Not all sauces fall into the traditional classifications, however. Some sauces use purées of fruits or vegetables as their base; they are known as **coulis**. Others, such as **beurre blanc** (French for "white butter") and **beurre rouge** ("red butter"), are based on an acidic reduction in which whole butter is incorporated. *Flavoured butters and oils, salsas, relishes,* and *pan gravy* are also used as sauces in modern food service operations.

Thickening Agents

Although there are exceptions, most sauces are thickened by the gelatinization of starches. As discussed in Chapter 9, Principles of Cooking, gelatinization is

Basic Sauces

- Béchamel
- Velouté: Fish
         Chicken
         Veal
- Espagnole—Demi-glace
- Tomato
- Hollandaise—Béarnaise

● **coulis** a sauce made from a purée of vegetables and/or fruit; may be served hot or cold

● **beurre blanc** French for "white butter"; an emulsified butter sauce made from shallots, white wine and butter

● **beurre rouge** French for "red butter"; an emulsified butter sauce made from shallots, red wine and butter

the process by which starch granules absorb moisture when placed in a liquid and heated. As the moisture is absorbed, the product thickens. Starches generally used to thicken sauces are flour, cornstarch, arrowroot and modified starches. Gelatinization may sound easy, but it takes practice to produce a good sauce that

- is clean, free of lumps and other impurities,
- has a good flavour that is not pasty or floury,
- has a consistency that will coat the back of a spoon (the French call this *nappé*) and a smooth texture, and
- will not separate or break when the sauce is held hot or reduced.

Roux

● **roux** a cooked mixture of equal parts flour and fat, by weight; used as a thickener for sauces and other dishes

Roux is the traditional means used to thicken sauces. It is a combination of equal parts, by weight, of flour and fat, cooked together to form a paste. Cooking the flour in fat coats the starch granules with the fat and prevents them from lumping together or forming lumps when introduced into a liquid. In some production kitchens, large amounts of roux are prepared and held for use as needed. Smaller operations may make roux as required for each recipe.

There are three types of roux, as shown in Figure 10.4:

1. *White roux* is cooked only briefly and should be removed from the heat as soon as it develops a frothy, bubbly appearance. It is used in white sauces, such as béchamel, or in dishes where little or no colour is desired.
2. *Blond roux* is cooked slightly longer than white roux and should begin to take on a little colour as the flour caramelizes. It is used in ivory-coloured sauces, such as velouté, or where a richer flavour is desired.
3. *Brown roux* is cooked until it develops a darker colour and a nutty aroma and flavour. Brown roux is used in brown sauces and dishes where a dark colour is desired. It is important to remember that cooking a starch before adding a liquid breaks down the starch granules and prevents gelatinization from occurring. Therefore, because brown roux is cooked longer than white roux, more brown roux is required to thicken a given quantity of liquid.

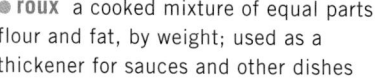

FIGURE 10.4 White, blond and brown roux.

Cook the roux.

BASIC PROCEDURE FOR MAKING ROUX

Whether it will be white, blond or brown, the procedure for making roux is the same:

1. Using a heavy saucepan to prevent scorching, heat the clarified butter or other fat.
2. Add all of the flour and stir to form a paste. Although all-purpose flour can be used, it is better to use cake or pastry flour because it contains a higher percentage of starch. (See Table 10.2.) Do not use high-gluten flour because of its lower starch content. (Flours are discussed in Chapter 27, Principles of the Bakeshop.)
3. Cook the paste over medium heat until the desired colour is achieved. It should have the consistency of wet cement. Stir the roux often to avoid burning. Burnt roux will not thicken a liquid; it will simply add dark specks and an undesirable flavour.

A Saucy History

The word *sauce* is derived from the Latin word *salus,* meaning "salted." This derivation is entirely logical. For millennia, salt has been the basic condiment for enhancing or disguising the flavour of many foods.

Cooks of ancient Rome flavoured dishes with *garum,* a golden-coloured sauce made from fermented fish entrails combined with brine, condiments, water and wine or vinegar. They also used a sauce referred to as a "single" made from oil, wine and brine. When boiled with herbs and saffron, it became a "double" sauce. To this the Byzantines later added pepper, cloves, cinnamon, cardamom and coriander or spikenard (a fragrant ointment made from grains).

Medieval chefs were fond of either very spicy or sweet-and-sour sauces. A typical sauce for roasted meat consisted of powdered cinnamon, mustard, red wine and a sweetener such as honey. Bits of stale or grilled bread were used as a thickener. Other sauces were based on verjuice, an acidic stock prepared from the juice of unripe grapes. To it were added other fruit juices, honey, flower petals and herbs or spices. Perhaps this was done to hide the taste of salt-cured or less-than-fresh meats, or, more likely, to showcase the host's wealth.

Guillaume Tirel (ca. 1312–1395), who called himself Taillevent, was the master chef for Charles V of France. Around 1375, Taillevent wrote *Le Viandier,* the oldest known French cookbook. It includes 17 sauces. Among them is a recipe for a sauce called *taillemaslée,* made of fried onions, verjuice, vinegar and mustard.

Sauces enjoyed in Renaissance Italy and France were prepared much like those of the Middle Ages, but in an important development for modern cuisine, many were based on broths thickened with cream, butter and egg yolks, and flavoured with herbs and spices. Recipes for some sauces of the Renaissance, such as poivrade and Robert, are recognizable today. Many consider François Pierre de La Varenne (1618–1678) to be one of the founding fathers of French cuisine. His treatises, especially *Le Cuisinier français* (1651), detail the early development, methods and manners of French cuisine. La Varenne is credited with introducing roux as a thickening agent for sauces, especially velouté sauces. He emphasized the importance of *fonds* and the reduction of cooking juices to concentrate flavours. He also popularized the use of bouquets garni to flavour stocks and sauces.

During the early 18th century, the chef to the French Duc de Lévis-Mirepoix pioneered the use of onions, celery and carrots to enhance the flavour and aroma of stocks. The mixture, named for the chef's employer, soon became the standard. An enriched stock greatly improves the quality of the sauces derived from it. Antonin Carême developed the modern system for classifying hundreds of sauces in the early 19th century. While it is unknown how many sauces Carême actually invented, he wrote treatises containing the theories and recipes for many of the sauces still used today. Carême's extravagant lists were simplified by chefs later in the 19th century, most notably by Auguste Escoffier.

TABLE 10.2	Proportions of Roux to Liquid						
Flour	+	Butter/Fat	=	Roux	+	Liquid	=	Sauce
175 g/6 oz.	+	175 g/6 oz.	=	350 g/12 oz.	+	4 L/1 gal.	=	light
250 g/8 oz.	+	250 g/8 oz.	=	500 g/1 lb.	+	4 L/1 gal.	=	medium
350 g/12 oz.	+	350 g/12 oz.	=	400 g/24 oz.	+	4 L/1 gal.	=	heavy

Variables: The starch content of a flour determines its thickening power. Cake flour, being lowest in protein and highest in starch, has more thickening power than bread flour, which is high in protein and low in starch. In addition, a dark roux has less thickening power than a lighter one, so more will be needed to thicken an equal amount of liquid.

The temperature and amount of roux being prepared determine the exact length of cooking time. Generally, however, a white roux needs to cook for only a few minutes, long enough to minimize the raw flour taste. Blond roux is cooked longer, until the paste begins to change to a slightly darker colour. Brown roux requires a much longer cooking time to develop its characteristic colour and aroma. A good roux will be stiff, not runny or pourable.

General Rule:

(a)

Warm Stock

Hot Roux

(b)

Hot Stock

Warm Roux

INCORPORATING ROUX INTO A LIQUID

There are two ways to incorporate roux into a liquid without causing lumps:

1. Warm or cold stock can be added to the hot roux while stirring vigorously with a whisk or wooden spoon.

2. Room-temperature roux can be added to a hot stock while stirring vigorously with a whisk.

When the roux and the liquid are completely incorporated and the sauce begins to boil, it is necessary to cook the sauce for a period of time to remove any raw flour taste that may remain. Most cooks feel a minimum of 20 minutes is necessary.

Note: Avoid using aluminum pots when using a whisk to incorporate a roux. Aluminum is a relatively soft metal and the whisk will scrape particles of aluminum into the sauce, causing discoloration and off-flavour.

GUIDELINES FOR USING ROUX

1. Avoid using aluminum pots. The scraping action of the whisk will turn light sauces grey and will impart a metallic flavour.

2. Use sufficiently heavy pots to prevent sauces from scorching or burning during extended cooking times.

3. Avoid extreme temperatures. Roux should be no colder than room temperature so that the fat is not fully solidified. Extremely hot roux is dangerous and can spatter when combined with a liquid. Stocks should not be ice cold when combined with roux; the roux will become very cold and the solidified pieces may be very difficult to work out with a whisk.

4. Avoid overthickening. Roux does not completely thicken a sauce until the sauce is at the simmering point; the thickening action continues for several minutes while the sauce simmers. If a sauce is to cook for a long time, it will also be thickened by reduction.

White Wash

When flour is used as a thickener, it can also be mixed with water instead of fat. The resulting solution is known as white wash and it is incorporated into a hot liquid in the same manner as cornstarch. Note that white wash is not a preferred thickening method because it weakens the flavour of the finished product.

Whisking cornstarch slurry into simmering liquid.

● **slurry** a mixture of raw starch and cold liquid used for thickening

Cornstarch

Cornstarch, a very fine white powder, is a pure starch derived from various species of corn. It is used widely as a thickening agent for hot and cold sauces and is especially popular in Asian cuisines for thickening sauces and soups. Liquids thickened with cornstarch have a glossy sheen and will gel when cooled.

One unit of cornstarch thickens about twice as much liquid as an equal unit of flour. Sauces thickened with cornstarch are less stable than those thickened with a flour-based agent because cornstarch breaks down (the starch molecules burst) and loses its thickening power after prolonged heating. Products thickened with regular cornstarch should not be reheated or frozen.

Incorporating Cornstarch

Cornstarch must be mixed with a cool liquid before it is introduced into a hot one. The cool liquid separates the granules of starch and allows them to begin absorbing liquid without lumping. A solution of starch and cool liquid is called a **slurry**.

The starch slurry is added to a hot liquid while stirring continuously to prevent lumping. Although the gelatinization point differs depending on the starch used, most starches begin to gelatinize at 60°C (140°F), while complete gelatinization occurs at, or just below, the simmering point. Simmer for two to three minutes.

Modified Starches and Pre-gelatinized Starches

Modified starches have been treated chemically to modify one or more of their physical or chemical properties. Because these starches are much more stable, especially at high temperatures and at freezing temperatures, they are typically used in commercially processed foods and in foods destined for the freezer. This category also includes natural starches, such as waxy maize (corn) or waxy rice starch, which contain amylopectin predominantly.

Cook–chill and sous vide food production for banquets and home meal replacement use modified starches for thickening sauces to yield better results on reheating.

Pre-gelatinized starches have been fully gelatinized and dried by the manufacturer before sale in a powdered form. They can be manufactured from either a native starch or a modified starch. Pre-gelatinized starches develop viscosity when dispersed in cold or warm liquid without the need for further heating, making them good candidates for thickening liquids that may lose colour or flavour during cooking (e.g., fruit juices).

Arrowroot

Arrowroot, derived from the roots of several tropical plants, is similar in texture, appearance and thickening power to cornstarch and is used in exactly the same manner. Although it is slightly more expensive, arrowroot does not break down as quickly as cornstarch and it produces a clearer finished product.

Beurre Manié

Beurre manié is a combination of equal amounts, by volume, of flour and soft whole butter. The flour and butter are kneaded together until smooth. The mixture is then formed into pea-sized balls and whisked into a simmering sauce. Beurre manié is used for quick thickening or adjusting at the end of the cooking process. The butter also adds shine and flavour to the sauce as it melts.

Liaison

Unlike the thickeners described above, a liaison does not thicken a sauce through gelatinization. A liaison is a mixture of egg yolks and heavy (whipping) cream, which adds richness and smoothness with minimal thickening.

Starches

Other starches used to thicken liquids include potato starch, tapioca, rice flour, instant wheat flour and sweet rice. Each imparts a unique flavour and texture to the sauce. Generally, you cannot substitute one starch for another without field-testing first.

Waxy maize is a type of cornstarch that can be frozen and reheated without breaking down. It is also more acid-tolerant than regular cornstarch. It is marketed as modified cornstarch. Some must be dissolved in a cold liquid first, while premium products can be incorporated into hot or cold liquids. They benefit from blending at high speeds.

Add the beurre manié in small pieces to finish a sauce.

1. Liaison: Add hot liquid to the egg yolks and cream mixture.

2. Add the tempered egg yolks and cream mixture to the hot liquid.

Special care must be taken to prevent the yolks from coagulating when they are added to a hot liquid because this could curdle the sauce. The ratio is generally 3 yolks to 200 mL (7 fl. oz.) cream.

BASIC PROCEDURE FOR USING A LIAISON

1. Whisk together one part egg yolk and three parts 35% whipping cream. Combining the yolk with cream raises the temperature at which the yolk's proteins coagulate, making it easier to incorporate them into a sauce without lumping or curdling.

2. **Temper** the egg yolk mixture by slowly adding a small amount of the hot liquid while stirring continuously.

3. When enough of the hot liquid has been added to the egg yolk mixture to warm it thoroughly, begin adding the warmed egg yolk mixture to the remaining hot liquid. Be sure to stir the mixture carefully to prevent the yolk from overcooking or lumping. Plain egg yolks fully coagulate at temperatures between 65°C and 70°C (149°F and 158°F). Mixing them with cream raises the temperatures at which they coagulate to approximately 82°C to 85°C (180°F to 185°F). Temperatures over 85°C (185°F) will cause the yolks to curdle. Liaison is preferably added to a sauce (or soup) just before service. However, it is sometimes necessary to hold the item for a while before service. In this case, great care must be taken to hold the sauce above 60°C (140°F) for food safety and sanitation reasons, yet below 85°C (185°F) to prevent curdling.

● **tempering** heating gently and gradually; refers to the process of slowly adding a hot liquid to eggs or other foods to raise their temperatures without causing them to curdle

Emulsification

Thickening sauces by emulsification is a process whereby two unmixable liquids such as oil and vinegar are stabilized into a uniform homogeneous state. Lecithin in egg yolks and trace amounts in butter acts as an emulsifying agent in mayonnaise, hollandaise and beurre blanc. Stirring or whisking, sometimes vigorously, the ingredients will result in an emulsion that is permanent, semi-permanent or temporary. The minute oil droplets are suspended in the liquid, resulting in a creamy smooth texture. Emulsified sauces are heat sensitive and the ratio of liquid to oil is critical to the stability of the mass. Pasteurized eggs are preferred from a health perspective but the shelf life of products without preservatives is limited. Mayonnaise is an example of a permanent emulsion. Hollandaise and beurre blanc are semi-permanent and vinaigrette is temporary, as it relies solely on the vigorous agitation of ingredients to suspend the oil.

Finishing Techniques

Reduction

● **reduction** cooking a liquid such as a sauce until its quantity decreases through evaporation. To reduce by one-half means that one-half of the original amount remains. To reduce by three-quarters means that only one-quarter of the original amount remains. To reduce au sec means that the liquid is cooked until nearly dry.

As sauces cook, moisture is released in the form of steam (evaporates). As steam escapes, the remaining ingredients concentrate, thickening the sauce and strengthening the flavours. This process, known as **reduction**, is commonly used to thicken sauces that require no starches or other flavour-altering ingredients. Sauces are often finished by allowing them to reduce until the desired consistency is reached.

Straining

Smoothness is important to the success of most sauces. They can be strained through either a conical strainer lined with several layers of cheesecloth or a fine mesh etâmine. As discussed below, often vegetables, herbs, spices and other seasonings are added to a sauce for flavour. Straining removes these ingredients as well as any undesirable lumps remaining in the sauce after the desired flavour and consistency have been reached.

Monter au Beurre

Monter au beurre is the process of swirling or whisking whole butter into a sauce to give it shine, flavour and richness. Compound or flavoured butters, discussed on page 209, can be used in place of whole butter to add specific flavours. Monter au beurre is widely used to enrich and finish derivative sauces.

Using a wire whisk to finish (mount) a sauce with whole butter.

Sauce Families

Basic (leading) *sauces* are the foundation for the entire classic repertoire of hot sauces. The five basic sauces—béchamel, velouté, espagnole (also known as brown), tomato and hollandaise—can be seasoned and garnished to create a wide variety of derivative or compound sauces. The five basic sauces are distinguished principally by the liquids and thickeners used to create them. See Table 10.3.

Derivative (small or compound) *sauces* are grouped together into families based on their basic sauce. Some derivative sauces have a variety of uses; others are traditional accompaniments for specific foods. A derivative sauce may be named for its ingredients, place of origin or creator. Although there are numerous classic derivative sauces, we have included only a few of the more popular ones following each of the basic sauce recipes.

TABLE 10.3	Sauce Families	
Basic Sauce	**Liquid**	**Thickener**
Béchamel	Milk	Roux—white
Velouté	White stock	Roux
Veal velouté	Veal stock	—blond
Chicken velouté	Chicken stock	—blond
Fish velouté	Fish stock	—white
Espagnole (brown sauce)	Brown stock	Roux—brown
Tomato sauce	Tomato	Roux optional
Hollandaise	Butter	Egg yolks

The Béchamel Family

Named for its creator, Louis de Béchamel (1630–1703), steward to Louis XIV of France, **béchamel** sauce is the easiest basic sauce to prepare. Traditionally it was made by adding heavy cream to a thick veal velouté. Although some chefs still believe a béchamel should contain veal stock, today the sauce is almost always made by thickening scalded milk (infused with a studded onion) with a white roux and adding seasonings. It is used for vegetable, egg, gratin and pasta dishes.

Quality Standard

A properly made béchamel is rich, creamy and absolutely smooth with no hint of graininess. The flavours of the onion and clove used to season it should be apparent but not overwhelm the sauce's clean, milky taste. The sauce should be the colour of heavy cream and have a deep lustre. It should be thick enough to coat foods lightly but should not taste like the roux used to thicken it.

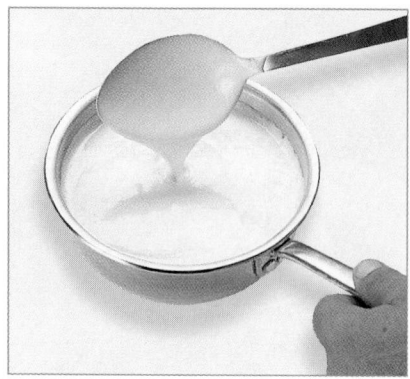

Béchamel

RECIPE 10.6

Approximate values per 100 mL serving:	
Calories	106
Total fat	6 g
Saturated fat	4 g
Cholesterol	19 mg
Sodium	168 mg
Total carbohydrates	9 g
Protein	4 g

APPLYING THE BASICS		RECIPE 10.6

Béchamel

Yield: 4 L (1 gal.)

Oignon piqué (studded onion)	150 g	5-1/2 oz.
Milk	4 L	1 gal.
Flour	200 g	7 oz.
Butter	200 g	7 oz.
Salt and white pepper	TT	TT
Nutmeg	TT	TT

1. Add the oignon piqué to the milk in a heavy saucepan and simmer/scald for 20 minutes over very low heat to infuse the flavours.
2. In a separate stainless steel pot, make a white roux with the flour and butter.
3. Remove the oignon piqué from the milk. Gradually add the hot milk to the roux while stirring constantly with a wooden spoon or whisk to prevent lumps. Bring to a simmer.
4. While simmerinig, add the seasonings and continue cooking for 20–30 minutes. Be cautious of burning or scorching.
5. Strain the sauce through a fine conical strainer. Melted butter can be carefully ladled over the surface of the sauce to prevent a skin from forming. Hold for service or cool in a water bath.

Béchamel Sauce Derivatives

With a good béchamel, producing the derivative sauces in its family is quite simple. The quantities indicated below are for 1 L (1 quart) of béchamel. The final step for each recipe is to season to taste with salt and pepper.

Anchovy/Anchois Add to béchamel 25 g (1 oz.) anchovy purée.

Cheddar Add to béchamel 250 g (8 oz.) grated old or medium cheddar cheese, a dash of Tabasco sauce and 7 g (1 Tbsp.) dry mustard.

Cream Sauce Add to béchamel 250 to 350 mL (8 to 12 fl. oz.) scalded cream and a few drops of lemon juice.

Egg/aux Oeufs (Écossaise) Add to béchamel 6 chopped hard-boiled eggs.

Mornay Add to béchamel 125 g (4 oz.) grated Gruyère cheese and 25 g (1 oz.) grated Parmesan cheese. Thin as desired with scalded cream. Remove the sauce from the heat and swirl in 60 g (2 oz.) whole butter.

Mustard/Moutard Add to béchamel 15 g (2 Tbsp.) dissolved dry mustard or 30 g (1 oz.) Dijon or English mustard.

Nantua Add to béchamel 125 mL (4 fl. oz.) heavy cream and 175 g (6 oz.) crayfish butter (see page 210). Add paprika to achieve the desired colour. Garnish the finished sauce with diced crayfish meat.

Parsley/Persil Add to béchamel 30 g (1 oz.) chopped parsley.

Soubise (modern) Sweat 250 g (8 oz.) diced, blanched onion in 25 g (1 oz.) butter. Add béchamel, 250 mL (8 fl. oz.) cream and 5 g (1 tsp.) sugar and simmer until the onions are fully cooked. Strain through a fine etâmine.

The Velouté Family

Velouté sauces are made by thickening a white stock or fish stock with roux. The white stock can be made from veal or chicken bones. A fish velouté

● **velouté** a basic sauce made by thickening a white stock (either fish, veal, or chicken) with roux

sauce, made from fish stock, is used to create a few derivative sauces. A velouté sauce made from veal or chicken stock is usually used to make one of two intermediary sauces—allemande and suprême—from which many sauces are derived. **Allemande** sauce is made by adding lemon juice, veal stock and mushrooms to a veal velouté and finishing it with a liaison. **Suprême** sauce is made by reducing cream and chicken stock in a chicken velouté. (See Table 10.4.)

Quality Standard

A properly made velouté should be rich, smooth and lump-free. If made from chicken or fish stock, it should taste of chicken or fish. A velouté made from veal stock should have a more neutral flavour. The sauce should be ivory-coloured, with a deep lustre. It should be thick enough to cling to foods without tasting like the roux used to thicken it.

● **allemande** a sauce made by adding lemon juice, mushrooms and a liaison to a velouté made from veal stock

● **suprême** a sauce made by adding cream to a velouté made from chicken stock

● **cuisson** the aromatic cooking liquid resulting from shallow poaching fish

● **vin blanc** an enriched sauce made by reducing the cooking liquid from shallow poaching fish and adding a velouté. Note that other methods exist.

TABLE 10.4	Velouté Sauces					
Fish stock	+ Roux	= Velouté	+	Cream and **cuisson**	=	**Vin blanc**
Chicken stock	+ Roux	= Velouté	+	Cream and mushroom	=	Suprême
Chicken stock	+ Roux	= Velouté	+	Wine and paprika	=	Hungarian
Veal stock	+ Roux	= Velouté	+	Liaison and lemon, mushroom and veal stock reduction	=	Allemande

APPLYING THE BASICS	RECIPE 10.7

Velouté

Yield: 4 L (1 gal.)

Clarified butter	250 g	8 oz.
Flour	250–300 g	8–10 oz.
Chicken, veal or fish stock, warm	5 L	5 qt.
Salt and white pepper (optional)*	TT	TT

1. Melt the butter in a heavy saucepan. Add the flour and cook to make a blond roux.
2. Gradually add the warm stock to the roux, stirring constantly with a whisk or wooden spoon to prevent lumps. Bring to a boil and reduce to a simmer.
3. Simmer and reduce to 4 L (1 gal.), approximately 30 minutes.
4. Strain through a fine conical strainer.
5. Melted butter may be carefully ladled over the surface of the sauce to prevent a skin from forming. Hold for service or cool in a water bath.

*Seasonings are optional; their use depends upon the seasonings in the stock and the sauce's intended use.

Velouté

RECIPE 10.7

Approximate values per 100 mL serving:	
Calories	109
Total fat	8 g
Saturated fat	4.4 g
Cholesterol	17 mg
Sodium	18 mg
Total carbohydrates	8.5 g
Protein	0.8 g

Fish Velouté Sauce Derivatives

A few derivative sauces can be made from fish velouté. The quantities given are for 1 L (1 qt.) fish velouté sauce. The final step for each recipe is to season to taste with salt and pepper.

Suprême Sauce

Allemande Sauce

RECIPE 10.8

Approximate values per 100 mL serving:	
Calories	53
Total fat	4.5 g
Saturated fat	2.5 g
Cholesterol	28 mg
Sodium	159 mg
Total carbohydrates	2.6 g
Protein	0.6 g

Bercy Sauté 60 g (2 oz.) finely diced shallots in butter. Then add 250 mL (8 fl. oz.) dry white wine and 250 mL (8 fl. oz.) fish stock. Reduce this mixture by one-third and add the fish velouté and 300 mL (10 fl. oz.) of heavy cream and reduce to 1 L (1 qt.). Finish with 100 g (3 oz.) butter and garnish with 30 g (3 Tbsp.) chopped parsley and 25 to 50 mL (1 to 2 fl. oz.) lemon juice.

Cardinal Add 250 mL (8 fl. oz.) fish fumet to 500 mL (1 pt.) fish velouté and 500 mL (1 pt.) béchamel. Reduce this mixture by half and add 500 mL (1 pt.) heavy cream and a dash of cayenne pepper. Bring to a boil and swirl in 45 g (1-1/2 oz.) lobster butter (see page 210) and 30 mL (1 fl. oz.) brandy. Garnish with chopped lobster coral at service time.

Normandy Add 125 g (4 oz.) mushroom trimmings, 125 mL (4 fl. oz.) shellfish liquor (oyster, clam, mussel) and 250 mL (8 fl. oz.) fish stock plus 10 mL (2 tsp.) lemon juice to 1 L (1 qt.) fish velouté. Reduce by one-third and finish with a 3–egg yolk and 250-mL (8 fl. oz.) cream liaison. Strain through a fine etâmine.

APPLYING THE BASICS		RECIPE 10.8

Allemande Sauce

Yield: 1 L (1 qt.)

Veal velouté	750 mL	24 fl. oz.
Veal stock	750 mL	24 fl. oz.
Mushrooms, chopped	60 g	2 oz.
Peppercorns, crushed	5 g	1 tsp.
Bay leaf	1	1
Salt and cayenne pepper	TT	TT
Lemon juice	30 mL	1 fl. oz.
Cream, 35%	250 mL	8 fl. oz.
Egg yolks	3	3

1. Combine velouté, stock, mushrooms, peppercorns and bay leaf.
2. Simmer to reduce liquid to 1 L (1 qt.).
3. Season with salt, cayenne and lemon juice.
4. Incorporate cream and egg yolk liaison.
5. Strain and do not allow to boil.

Allemande Sauce Derivatives

Several derivative sauces are easily produced from an allemande sauce made with a veal velouté. The quantities given are for 1 L (1 qt.) allemande sauce. The final step for each recipe is to season to taste with salt and pepper.

Horseradish Add to allemande 125 mL (4 fl. oz.) 35% cream and 5 g (1 tsp.) dry mustard. Just before service add 60 g (2 oz.) freshly grated horseradish. The horseradish should not be cooked with the sauce.

Mushroom Sauté 125 g (4 oz.) sliced mushrooms in 15 g (1/2 oz.) butter; add 25 mL (1 fl. oz.) white wine. Then add the allemande to the mushrooms. Do not strain. Garnish with 25 g (1 oz.) each chopped parsley and chives.

Poulette Sauté 250 g (8 oz.) sliced mushrooms and 15 g (1/2 oz.) diced shallots in 30 g (1 oz.) butter. Add to the allemande; then simmer and strain. Finish with 15 mL (1 Tbsp.) lemon juice and 15 g (1/2 oz.) chopped parsley.

APPLYING THE BASICS   **RECIPE 10.9**

Suprême Sauce

Yield: 2.5 L (2-1/2 qt.)

Chicken velouté sauce	2 L	2 qt.
Chicken stock	600 mL	24 fl. oz.
Cream, 35%	500 mL	16 fl. oz.
Salt and white pepper	TT	TT

1. Simmer the velouté sauce and stock until reduced to 2 L (2 qt.).
2. Stir in the cream and return to a simmer.
3. Adjust the seasonings.
4. Strain through a conical strainer lined with cheesecloth.

RECIPE 10.9

Approximate values per 100 mL serving:	
Calories	156
Total fat	14 g
Saturated fat	8 g
Cholesterol	40 mg
Sodium	209 mg
Total carbohydrates	8 g
Protein	1 g

Suprême Sauce Derivatives

The following derivative sauces are easily made from suprême sauce. The quantities given are for 1 L (1 qt.) suprême sauce. The final step for each recipe is to season to taste with salt and pepper.

Aurora Add 350 mL (12 fl. oz.) tomato sauce and 175 mL (6 fl. oz.) 35% cream. Simmer for 5 minutes, strain and mount with 250 g (8 oz.) butter.

Hungarian Sweat 90 g (3 oz.) diced onion in 60 g (2 oz.) butter. Add 15 g (1/2 oz.) paprika and sweat. Add 250 mL (8 fl. oz.) white wine and reduce. Stir in the suprême sauce. Cook for 2 to 3 minutes, strain and finish with 250 mL (8 fl. oz.) cream.

Ivory Add to suprême sauce 90 g (3 oz.) glace de volaille.

The Espagnole (Brown Sauce) Family

The basic sauce of the **espagnole** or **brown sauce** family is full bodied and rich. It is made from brown stock to which brown roux, mirepoix and tomato purée are added. Most often this sauce is used to produce demi-glace. Brown stock is also used to make jus lié. Demi-glace is used to create the derivative sauces of the espagnole family.

● **espagnole** also known as brown sauce; a basic sauce made of brown stock, mirepoix and tomatoes thickened with brown roux; often used to produce demi-glace

APPLYING THE BASICS   **RECIPE 10.10**

Espagnole (Brown Sauce)

Yield: 4 L (1 gal.)

Mirepoix, medium dice	500 g	1 lb.
Fat or clarified butter	200 g	7 oz.
Flour	250 g	8 oz.
Tomato purée	250 mL	8 fl. oz.
Brown stock	5 L	5 qt.

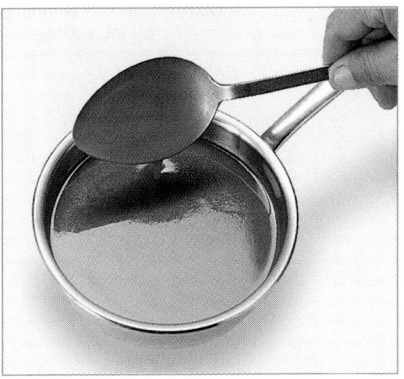

Espagnole (Brown Sauce)

continued

Sachet:		
Bay leaf	1	1
Dried thyme	2 g	1/2 tsp.
Peppercorns, crushed	2 g	1/2 tsp.
Parsley stems	8	8

1. Sauté the mirepoix in fat until well caramelized.
2. Add the flour and cook to make a brown roux.
3. Add the tomato purée. Stir to break up any lumps of roux. Add brown stock. Bring to a boil; reduce to a simmer.
4. Add the sachet.
5. Simmer for approximately 1–1.5 hours, allowing the sauce to reduce. Skim the surface as needed to remove impurities.
6. Strain the sauce through a fine conical strainer. Cool in a water bath or hold for service.

RECIPE 10.10

Approximate values per 100 mL serving:	
Calories	106
Total fat	6.8 g
Saturated fat	3.7 g
Cholesterol	14 mg
Sodium	79 mg
Total carbohydrates	10 g
Protein	1.1 g

Demi-Glace

Brown stock is used to make the espagnole or brown sauce described above. Espagnole sauce can then be made into **demi-glace**, which in turn is used to make the derivative sauces of the espagnole family. Demi-glace is half brown sauce and half brown stock, reduced by half. It is usually finished with a small amount of Madeira or sherry wine. Because demi-glace creates a richer, more flavourful base, it produces finer derivative sauces than those made directly from an espagnole (brown sauce).

● **demi-glace** French for "half glaze"; a mixture of half brown stock and half espagnole sauce, reduced by half

Quality Standard

A properly made demi-glace is rich, smooth and lump-free. Its prominent roasted flavour comes from the bones used for the brown stock. There should be no taste of roux. The caramelized bones and mirepoix as well as the tomato product contribute to its glossy dark brown, almost chocolate, colour. It should be barely thick enough to cling to food without being pasty or heavy.

Demi-Glace

RECIPE 10.11

Approximate values per 50 mL serving:	
Calories	69
Total fat	4.1 g
Saturated fat	2.1 g
Cholesterol	7.2 mg
Sodium	74 mg
Total carbohydrates	7.3 g
Protein	0.8 g

APPLYING THE BASICS   RECIPE 10.11

Demi-Glace

Yield: 1 L (1 qt.)

Brown stock	1 L	1 qt.
Espagnole (brown sauce)	1 L	1 qt.

1. Combine the stock and sauce in a saucepan over medium heat.
2. Simmer until the mixture is reduced by half (i.e., a yield of 1 L or 1 qt.).
3. Strain and cool in a water bath.

Espagnole (Brown Sauce) Derivatives

Demi-glace is used to produce many derivative sauces. The quantities given are for 1 L (1 qt.) demi-glace. The final step for each recipe is to season to taste with salt and pepper.

Bordelaise Sweat 100 g (3-1/2 oz.) chopped shallots, 1 bay leaf, 1 sprig of thyme and 5 g (1 tsp.) cracked peppercorns and add 500 mL (16 fl. oz.) dry red wine. Reduce by three-fourths, then add demi-glace and simmer for 15 minutes. Strain through a fine etâmine. Finish with 60 g (2 oz.) meat glaze, mount with 100 g (3-1/2 oz.) butter and garnish with sliced, poached beef marrow.

Chasseur (Hunter's Sauce) Sweat 30 g (1 oz.) diced shallots and 250 g (8 oz.) sliced mushrooms in butter. Add 250 mL (8 fl. oz.) white wine and 30 mL (1 fl. oz.) brandy and reduce by half. Add demi-glace and 250 g (8 oz.) tomato concassée and simmer 5 minutes. Finish with 30 g (1 oz.) meat glaze and 7 g (1/2 Tbsp.) each parsley and chives, chopped.

Chateaubriand Sweat 125 g (4 oz.) each sliced shallots and mushrooms in butter. Add 1 sprig of thyme, 2 bay leaves and 500 mL (16 fl. oz.) white wine. Reduce by two-thirds. Add demi-glace and reduce by half. Strain. Mount with 350 g (12 oz.) parsley butter and finish with 30 g (1 oz.) fresh chopped tarragon.

Madeira or Port Bring demi-glace to a boil, reduce slightly. Then add 125 mL (4 fl. oz.) Madeira wine or port. Mount with 60 g (2 oz.) butter.

Mushroom Sweat 50 g (2 oz.) shallots and 500 g (16 oz.) sliced mushrooms in 50 g (2 oz.) butter. Add 150 mL (5 fl. oz.) red, white or Madeira wine. Reduce liquid by two-thirds. Add demi-glace and reduce to desired consistency.

Périgueux Add finely diced truffles to Madeira sauce. *Périgourdine* sauce is the same, except that the truffles are cut into relatively thick slices.

Piquant Sweat 125 g (4 oz.) shallot and add 300 mL (10 fl. oz.) each white wine and white wine vinegar and 5 g (2 tsp.) cracked peppercorns. Reduce the mixture by three-quarters. Then add demi-glace and simmer for 10 minutes. Strain. Add 125 g (4 oz.) diced cornichons, 60 g (2 oz.) capers, 5 g (1/2 Tbsp.) fresh tarragon, 5 g (1/2 Tbsp.) fresh parsley and 5 g (1/2 Tbsp.) fresh chervil. Do not strain.

Poivrade Sweat 350 g (12 oz.) mirepoix in 30 g (1 oz.) butter. Add 2 bay leaves, a sprig of thyme, 4 parsley stems and 1 crushed garlic clove. Then add 500 mL (16 fl. oz.) white wine and 125 mL (4 fl. oz.) white wine vinegar. (Red wine vinegar and red wine are also often used.) Reduce by half, add demi-glace and reduce to 1 L (1 qt.). Then add 20 crushed peppercorns and 50 g (2 oz.) meat glaze and simmer for 5 more minutes. Strain through a fine etâmine and mount with up to 60 g (2 oz.) butter.

Robert Sauté 125 g (4 oz.) chopped onion in 30 g (1 oz.) butter. Add 250 mL (8 fl. oz.) dry white wine and reduce by two-thirds. Add demi-glace and simmer for 10 minutes. Strain and then add 5 g (2 tsp.) dry mustard dissolved in wine and 60 g (2 oz.) meat glaze. If the finished Robert sauce is garnished with sliced julienne of sour pickles, preferably cornichons, it is known as *charcuterie sauce*.

> ### Poivrade for Game
>
> Poivrade is also the name given a flavourful sauce traditionally made with game stock and seasoned with peppercorns. It is used for the wonderful *Sauce Grand Veneur*, one of the most complex derivative sauces in the classic repertoire. For *Grand Veneur*, game stock is flavoured with demi-glace and finished with cream and currant jelly. The sweetness balances the strong flavour of the game meats.

The Tomato Sauce Family

Classic **tomato sauce** is made from tomatoes, vegetables, seasonings and white stock and thickened with a blond or brown roux. In today's kitchens, however, most tomato sauces are not thickened with roux. Rather, they are tomatoes, herbs, spices, vegetables and other flavouring ingredients simmered together and puréed. A gastrique may be added to reduce the acidity of the tomatoes. **Gastrique** is made by caramelizing a small amount of sugar and deglazing with vinegar.

● **tomato sauce** a basic sauce made from tomatoes, vegetables, seasonings and white stock; it may or may not be thickened with a roux

● **gastrique** caramelized sugar deglazed with vinegar; used to flavour tomato or savoury fruit-based sauces

Quality Standard

A properly made tomato sauce is thick, rich and full-flavoured. Because it is a puréed sauce, its texture is somewhat coarser than other basic sauces, but it

1. Basic Tomato Sauce: Passing the sauce through a food mill.

2. The finished sauce.

RECIPE 10.12

Approximate values per 100 mL serving:	
Calories	92
Total fat	5.7 g
Saturated fat	1 g
Cholesterol	0.7 mg
Sodium	215 mg
Total carbohydrates	8.9 g
Protein	1.2 g

Use of Crushed vs. Puréed Tomatoes

Depending on whether you use crushed or puréed tomatoes, the simmering time and the amount of stock will vary. Monitor the quality of the tomato products carefully. There is a great difference in the concentration of the tomatoes. Low-quality brands are watery by comparison. Recipe outcomes will vary depending on the product used.

should still be smooth. The vegetables and other seasonings should add flavour, but none should be pronounced. Tomato sauce should not be bitter, acidic or overly sweet. It should be deep red and thick enough to cling to foods.

APPLYING THE BASICS		RECIPE 10.12

Basic Tomato Sauce

Yield: 2 L (2 qt.)

Carrot, cut in small dice	50 g	2 oz.
Celery, cut in small dice	50 g	2 oz.
Onion, cut in small dice	50 g	2 oz.
Garlic cloves, chopped or crushed	15 g	4
Olive oil	90–120 mL	3–4 fl. oz.
Tomato paste	500 g	1 lb.
White stock	2 L	2 qt.
Sugar	5 g	1 tsp.
Sachet:		
Bay leaf	1/2	1/2
Sage	0.25 g	1/4 tsp.
Thyme	0.5 g	1/2 tsp.
Rosemary	0.5 g	1/2 tsp.
Peppercorns	8	8
Fennel seeds, crushed		
(optional)	0.25 g	1/4 tsp.

1. Sweat the vegetables in the oil.

2. Add tomato paste and sweat for 2 minutes.

3. Add the remaining ingredients and simmer gently for about 1 hour.

4. Adjust the seasoning and press the sauce through a food mill, if desired, or blend in a food processor to purée.

Variations: Reduce the olive oil by half and sweat 100 g (4 oz.) of finely chopped bacon before adding vegetables. Be mindful that you may alienate some customers. Water or vegetable stock can be substituted for the white stock.

Tomato Sauce Derivatives or Variations

The following derivative sauces are made by adding the listed ingredients to 1 L (1 qt.) tomato sauce. The final step for each recipe is to season to taste with salt and pepper.

Creole Sauté 175 g (6 oz.) finely diced onion, 125 g (4 oz.) thinly sliced celery and 5 g (1 tsp.) garlic in 30 mL (1 fl. oz.) olive oil. Add tomato sauce, a bay leaf and a pinch of thyme; simmer for 15 minutes. Then add 125 g (4 oz.) finely diced green pepper, 100 g (3-1/2 oz.) diced okra, 100 g (3-1/2 oz.) sliced green olives and a dash of hot pepper sauce; simmer for 15 minutes longer. Remove bay leaf.

Spanish Sauté 150 g (5-1/2 oz.) sliced onions with 100 g (3-1/2 oz.) thinly sliced celery, 150 g (5-1/2 oz.) sliced sweet peppers and 5 g (1 clove) of garlic in 50 mL (2 fl. oz.) olive oil. Finish with 125 g (4 oz.) sliced mushrooms, sweated, and 125 g (4 oz.) **tomato concassée**. Season with chiles, salt and pepper to taste.

Milanaise Sauté 150 g (5 oz.) sliced mushrooms in 15 g (1 oz.) butter. Add tomato sauce then stir in 150 g (5 oz.) julienne ham and 150 g (5 oz.) julienne tongue. Bring to a simmer and adjust seasonings.

Provençale This sauce is not a derivative of tomato sauce. A simple version is 500 g (1 lb.) tomato concassée sautéed in 100 mL (4 fl. oz.) olive oil, flavoured with 5 g (1 clove) garlic, diced, and 50 g (2 oz.) chopped shallots. Season with salt and pepper and a pinch of sugar. Finish with 15 g (1/2 oz.) chopped fines herbes. It goes well with light-flavoured fish, meats or vegetables.

The Hollandaise Family

Hollandaise and the derivative sauces made from it are warm, **emulsified** sauces. Egg yolks, which contain large amounts of lecithin, a natural emulsifier, are used to emulsify warm butter and a small amount of water, lemon juice or vinegar. By vigorously whipping the egg yolks with the liquid over heat to form a soft foam, then folding in the warm butter, the lecithin coats the individual oil droplets and holds them in suspension in the liquid.

Béarnaise sauce is technically a separate sauce, not a derivative.

Quality Standard

A properly made hollandaise is smooth, buttery, pale lemon-yellow coloured and very rich, but light in texture. It is lump-free and should not exhibit any signs of separation. The buttery flavour should dominate but not mask the flavours of the egg, lemon and vinegar. The sauce should be frothy and light, not heavy like a mayonnaise. It should be able to be glazed under a salamander or broiler without breaking.

Temperatures and Food Safety Concerns

Temperatures play an important role in the proper production of a hollandaise sauce. As the egg yolks and liquid are whisked together, they are cooked over a bain marie until they thicken to the consistency of slightly whipped cream (ribbon stage). Do not overheat this mixture, because even slightly cooked yolks lose their ability to emulsify. The clarified butter used to make the sauce should be warm but not so hot as to cook the egg yolks further. Although hollandaise sauce can be made from whole butter, a more stable and consistent product will be achieved by using butter that has had the water and milk solids removed through clarification. (Clarification is described in Chapter 8, Eggs and Dairy Products.)

With practice, classic hollandaise can be produced quickly and efficiently. Many operations no longer make classic hollandaise due to health concerns or municipal regulations. These companies use a starch-based mixture that imitates hollandaise.

The right proportion of water and fat (butter) is critical to a light and stable emulsion. It is not the acid that creates the emulsion, just the liquid. The acid provides flavour.

● **tomato concassée** peeled, seeded and diced tomato

● **hollandaise** an emulsified sauce made of butter, egg yolks and flavourings (especially lemon juice)

● **emulsification** the process by which generally unmixable liquids, such as oil and water, are forced into a uniform distribution

SAFETY ALERT

Handling Emulsified Butter Sauces

Emulsified butter sauces must be held at the specific temperatures most conducive to bacterial growth: 4°C to 60°C (40°F to 140°F). If the sauce is heated above 65°C (150°F), the yolks will begin to cook and the sauce will break and become grainy. If the sauce temperature falls below 7°C (45°F), the butter will solidify, making the sauce unusable. In order to minimize the risk of food-borne illnesses:

- Always use clean, sanitized utensils.
- Schedule sauce production as close to the time of service as possible. Never hold hollandaise-based sauces more than 1-1/2 hours.
- Make small batches of sauce.
- Never mix an old batch of sauce with a new one.

Hollandaise

Yield: 750 mL (24 fl. oz.)

Black peppercorns, crushed	18	18
White wine vinegar	60 mL	2 fl. oz.
Lemon juice	30 mL	1 fl. oz.
Water	45 mL	1-1/2 fl. oz.
Egg yolks, pasteurized	6	6
Butter, clarified, warm	450 g	1 lb.
Lemon juice	TT	TT
Salt and white pepper	TT	TT
Cayenne pepper	TT	TT

1. Combine the peppercorns, vinegar and lemon juice in a small saucepan and reduce by one-half. Add the water.

2. Place the egg yolks in a stainless steel bowl. Strain the acidic reduction through a conical strainer and add to the egg yolks. There should be 15 mL (1/2 oz.) of moisture (reduction) per egg yolk.

3. Place the bowl over a doubleboiler, whipping the mixture continuously with a wire whip. As the yolks cook, the mixture will thicken. When the mixture is thick enough to leave a trail across the surface when the whip is drawn away (ribbon stage), remove the bowl from the doubleboiler. Continue whisking to stabilize the temperature. Do not overcook the egg yolks.

4. Begin to add the warm clarified butter to the egg yolk mixture a little at a time, while constantly whipping the mixture to form an emulsion. Once the emulsion is started, the butter may be added more quickly. Continue until all the butter is incorporated. Do not over-whisk.

5. Adjust the acidity of the sauce with a little lemon juice, if needed. Adjust the seasonings with salt, white pepper and cayenne pepper.

6. Strain the sauce through cheesecloth if necessary and hold for service in a warm (not simmering) bain marie. Too much heat will cause the hollandaise to break and separate.

RECIPE 10.13

Approximate values per 50 mL serving:	
Calories	282
Total fat	31 g
Saturated fat	19 g
Cholesterol	158 mg
Sodium	188 mg
Total carbohydrates	0.3 g
Protein	1.5 g

1. Hollandaise: Combine the egg yolks with the acidic reduction in a stainless steel bowl.

2. Whip the mixture over a doubleboiler until it is thick enough to leave a trail when the whip is removed.

3. Using a kitchen towel and sauce pot to firmly hold the bowl containing the yolks, add the butter slowly while whipping continuously.

4. Hollandaise at the proper consistency.

Procedure for Rescuing a Broken Hollandaise

Occasionally a hollandaise will break or separate and appear thin, grainy or even lumpy. A sauce breaks when the emulsion has not formed or the emulsified butter, eggs and liquid have separated. There are several reasons why this may happen: The temperature of the eggs or butter may have been too high or too low; the butter may have been added too quickly; the egg yolks may have been overcooked; too much butter may have been added; or the sauce may not have been whipped vigorously enough to start or may have been over-whipped.

Broken hollandaise can often be rescued and re-emulsified. To do so, you must first determine the cause of the problem.

Feel the bowl in which the sauce was prepared to determine if it is too hot or too cold. If the bowl is too hot, allow the sauce to cool. If it is too cold, reheat the sauce over a doubleboiler before attempting to rescue it.

For 1 L (1 qt.) of broken sauce, place 15 mL (1 Tbsp.) of water in a clean stainless steel bowl and slowly beat in the broken sauce. If the problem seems to be that the eggs were overcooked or too much butter was added, add a yolk to the water before incorporating the broken sauce.

Broken hollandaise separates, appearing thin and curdled.

Hollandaise Sauce Derivatives

The following derivative sauces are easily made by adding the listed ingredients to 750 mL (24 fl. oz.) of hollandaise. The final step for each recipe is to season to taste with salt and pepper.

Grimrod Infuse a hollandaise sauce reduction with a pinch of saffron.

Maltaise Add to hollandaise 50 mL (1-1/2 fl. oz.) blood orange juice and 5 g (2 tsp.) finely grated blood orange zest. Regular oranges may be used for this sauce.

Mousseline (Chantilly Sauce) Whip 125 mL (4 fl. oz.) 35% cream until stiff. Fold it into the hollandaise just before service. It is usually glazed under a broiler or salamander. Mousseline sauce is also used as a **glaçage** coating, and may be stabilized with velouté or béchamel sauce.

● **glaçage** browning or glazing a food, usually under a salamander or broiler

Béarnaise Sauce

Though some consider it a derivative of hollandaise sauce, béarnaise is presented here as a basic sauce since it has a unique tarragon flavour infused in the reduction.

BASIC PROCEDURE FOR MAKING BÉARNAISE SAUCE

1. Combine 25 g (1 oz.) chopped shallots, 10 g (1/3 oz.) chopped fresh tarragon, 5 g (1/4 oz.) chopped fresh chervil and 1 g (1 tsp.) crushed peppercorns with 100 mL (3 fl. oz.) white wine vinegar and 25 mL (1 fl. oz.) water. Reduce to 90 mL (3 fl. oz.) of liquid and strain.

2. Add this reduction to the egg yolks and proceed with the hollandaise recipe.

3. Season to taste with salt and cayenne pepper. Garnish with additional chopped fresh tarragon.

Béarnaise Sauce Derivatives

The following sauces are made by adding the listed ingredients to 750 mL (24 fl. oz.) of béarnaise. Season to taste with salt and pepper.

Choron Stir 60 g (2 oz.) tomato purée into a béarnaise.

Foyot Add to béarnaise 75 g (2-1/2 oz.) melted glace de viande.

More Butter Sauces

Additional butter sauces include:

Beurre noir—French for "black butter"; used to describe whole butter cooked until dark brown (not black). Beurre noir is sometimes flavoured with vinegar or lemon juice, capers and parsley, and served over fish, eggs and vegetables.

Beurre noisette—French for "brown butter"; used to describe butter cooked until it is a light brown colour. It is flavoured and used in much the same manner as beurre noir.

Beurre fondu—Melted butter, often served with asparagus.

Beurre Blanc and Beurre Rouge

Beurre blanc and beurre rouge are emulsified butter sauces made without egg yolks. The small amounts of lecithin and other emulsifiers naturally found in butter are used to form an oil-in-liquid emulsion. Although similar to hollandaise in concept, beurre blancs are a class in themselves. They are not classified as either basic or compound sauces. Beurre blancs are thinner and lighter than hollandaise and béarnaise. They should be smooth and slightly thicker than heavy cream.

Beurre blanc and beurre rouge are made from three main ingredients: shallots, white (Fr. *blanc*) wine or red (Fr. *rouge*) wine and whole butter (not clarified). The shallots and wine provide flavour, while the butter becomes the sauce. A good beurre blanc or beurre rouge is rich and buttery, with a light, acidic flavour that responds well to other seasonings and flavourings, thereby lending itself to the addition of herbs, spices and vegetable purées to complement the dish with which it is served. Its pale colour changes depending upon the flavourings added. It should be light and airy yet still liquid, while thick enough to cling to food.

● **au sec** reducing the liquid until it is nearly dry

BASIC PROCEDURE FOR MAKING BEURRE BLANC OR BEURRE ROUGE

1. Use a nonaluminum pan to prevent discolouring the sauce. Do not use a thin-walled or nonstick pan, as heat is not evenly distributed in a thin-walled pan and a nonstick pan makes it difficult for an emulsion to set.

2. Over medium heat, reduce the wine, shallots and herbs or other seasonings, if used, until **au sec**. Some cooks add a small amount of 35% cream at this point and reduce the mixture. Although not necessary, the added cream helps stabilize the finished sauce.

3. Whisk in cold butter a small amount at a time. The butter should be well chilled, as this allows the butterfat, water and milk solids to be gradually incorporated into the sauce as the butter melts and the mixture is whisked.

4. When all of the butter is incorporated, strain and hold the sauce in a bain marie.

Temperature

Do not let the sauce become too hot. At 58°C (136°F) some of the emulsifying proteins begin to break down and release the butterfat they hold in emulsion. Extended periods at temperatures over 58°C (136°F) will cause the sauce to separate. If the sauce separates, it can be corrected by cooling to approximately 43°C to 49°C (110°F to 120°F) and whisking to reincorporate the butterfat.

If the sauce is allowed to cool below 30°C (85°F), the butterfat will solidify. If the sauce is reheated, it will separate into butterfat and water; whisking will not re-emulsify it. Cold beurre blanc can be used as a soft, flavoured butter, however, simply by whisking it at room temperature until it smooths out to the consistency of mayonnaise.

APPLYING THE BASICS	RECIPE 10.14

Classic Beurre Blanc

Yield: 1 L (1 qt.)

White wine	30 mL	1 fl. oz.
White wine vinegar	125 mL	4 fl. oz.
Salt	7 g	1-1/2 tsp.
White pepper	0.5 g	1/2 tsp.
Shallots, minced	30 g	1 oz.
Whole butter, chilled	1 kg	2 lb.

1. Combine the white wine, white wine vinegar, salt, white pepper and shallots in a small saucepan. Reduce the mixture until approximately 30 mL (2 Tbsp.) of liquid remain. If more liquid than that is allowed to remain, the resulting sauce will be too thin. For a thicker sauce, reduce the mixture au sec.

2. Cut the butter into pieces approximately 30 g (1 oz.) in weight. Over low heat, whisk in the butter a few pieces at a time, using the chilled butter to keep the sauce between 43°C and 49°C (100°F and 120°F).

3. Once all of the butter has been incorporated, remove the saucepan from the heat. Strain through a conical strainer and hold the sauce between 38°C and 54°C (100°F and 130°F) for service.

VARIATIONS: LEMON-DILL—Heat 30 mL (2 Tbsp.) lemon juice and whisk it into the beurre blanc. Stir in 10 g (1/3 oz.) chopped fresh dill.

PINK PEPPERCORN—Add 10 g (1/3 oz.) coarsely crushed pink peppercorns to the shallot-wine reduction when making beurre rouge. Garnish the finished sauce with whole pink peppercorns.

RECIPE 10.14

Approximate values per 50 mL serving:	
Calories	372
Total fat	41 g
Saturated fat	25 g
Cholesterol	109 mg
Sodium	142 mg
Total carbohydrates	0.3 g
Protein	0.5 g

1. Classic Beurre Blanc: Reduce the shallots and wine au sec.

2. Whisk in the cold butter a little at a time.

3. Strain the sauce.

Compound Butters

A **compound butter** is made by incorporating various seasonings into softened whole butter. These butters, also known as *beurres composés*, give flavour and colour to derivative sauces or may be served as sauces or condiments in their own right. For example, a slice of maître d'hôtel butter (parsley butter) is often placed on a grilled steak or piece of fish at the time of service. The butter quickly melts, creating a sauce for the beef or fish.

Butter and flavouring ingredients can be combined in a blender, food processor or mixer. Using parchment paper or plastic wrap, the butter is then

● **compound butter** also known as *beurre composé*; a mixture of softened whole butter and flavourings used as a sauce or to flavour and colour other sauces

1. Place the compound butter on the plastic wrap.

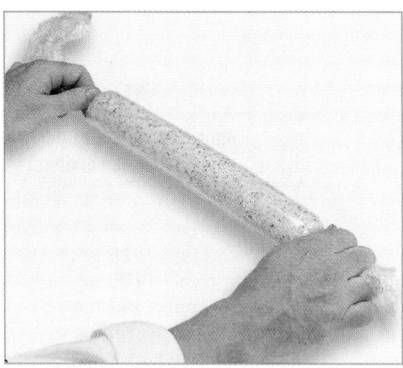

2. Roll the butter in the plastic wrap to form a cylinder.

rolled into a cylinder, chilled and sliced as needed. Or it can be piped into rosettes and refrigerated until firm. Most compound butters will keep for two to three days in the refrigerator, or they can be frozen for longer storage.

Recipes for Compound Butters

For each of the following butters, add the listed ingredients to 450 g (1 lb.) of softened, unsalted butter. The compound butter should then be seasoned with salt and pepper to taste.

Basil Butter   Mince 50 g (2 oz.) basil, 50 g (2 oz.) shallots and add to butter with 10 mL (2 tsp.) lemon juice.

Herb Butter   Add to the butter up to 150 g (5 oz.) of mixed chopped fresh herbs such as parsley, dill, chives, tarragon or chervil.

Lobster or Crayfish Butter   Grind 250 g (8 oz.) cooked lobster or crayfish meat, shells and/or coral with 450 g (1 lb.) butter. Place in a saucepan and clarify. Strain the butter through a fine conical strainer lined with cheesecloth. Refrigerate, then remove the butterfat when firm.

Maître d'Hôtel   Mix into the butter 8 g (1/4 oz.) finely chopped parsley, 45 mL (3 Tbsp.) lemon juice and a dash of white pepper.

Montpelier   Blanch 30 g (1 oz.) parsley, 30 g (1 oz.) chervil, 30 g (1 oz.) watercress and 30 g (1 oz.) tarragon in boiling water. Refresh thoroughly by immersing in ice water and removing as soon as the herbs are cold. Mince herbs, 2 hard-boiled egg yolks, 8 g (2) garlic cloves and 30 g (2) gherkin pickles. Blend everything into the butter.

Red Pepper Butter   Purée 250 g (8 oz.) roasted, peeled red bell peppers until liquid, cool, then add to the butter.

Shallot Butter   Blanch 250 g (8 oz.) of peeled shallots in boiling water. Dry and finely dice them and when cool, mix with the butter.

Jus and Pan Gravy

Drippings in roasting pans are used to make a number of sauces to be served with the roasted meat. They are lighter in texture and body than a demi-glace but have the distinctive flavour of the caramelized drippings. The term **jus lié** is used when the liquid is thickened with a starch. **Pan gravy** is roux thickened.

Jus de Rôti and Jus   A mirepoix is roasted with the drippings and the pan is deglazed with brown stock and a little wine if desired. The fat is removed after simmering and skimming. Always strain the jus. Traditionally, with larger roasts, additional small cut bones were added to the mirepoix to enhance flavour. Tomato purée may be added to boost flavour and colour.

● **jus lié** also known as fond lié; a sauce made by thickening brown stock with cornstarch or similar starch

● **pan gravy** a sauce made by deglazing pan drippings from roast meat or poultry and combining them with a roux or other starch and stock

Jus Lié   Jus thickened with arrowroot, cornstarch or modified starch. Fond lié refers to a reduced, thickened brown stock. It is traditionally served with roasted white meats.

Pan Gravy   Flour is added to the roasting fat and reduced drippings to make a roux. Stock is then added to make the gravy. The final product should have the characteristics of a good brown sauce with a meatier, richer flavour from the drippings.

BASIC PROCEDURE FOR MAKING PAN GRAVY

1. Remove the cooked meat or poultry from the roasting pan.

2. If mirepoix was not added during the roasting process, add it to the pan containing the drippings and fat.

3. Place the roasting pan on the stove top and clarify the fat by cooking off any remaining moisture.

4. Pour off the fat, reserving it to make the roux.

5. Deglaze the pan using an appropriate stock. The deglazing liquid may be transferred to a saucepan for easier handling or the gravy may be finished directly in the roasting pan.

6. Add enough stock or water to the deglazing liquid to yield the proper amount of finished gravy.

7. Determine the amount of roux needed to thicken the liquid and prepare it in a separate pan, using a portion of the reserved fat.

8. Add the roux to the liquid and bring the mixture to a simmer. Simmer until the mirepoix is well cooked, the flavour is extracted and the flour taste is cooked out.

9. Strain the gravy and adjust the seasonings.

1. Deglazing the roasting pan.

2. Thickening the gravy with a roux.

Quality Standard

A properly made jus lié or pan gravy is very rich and smooth. It shares many flavour characteristics with demi-glace. Its colour should be dark brown and glossy from the concentrated gelatin content. Its consistency is somewhat lighter than demi-glace, but it should still cling lightly to foods.

Coulis

The term *coulis* refers to a sauce made from a purée of vegetables or fruit thinned down to sauce consistency. A vegetable coulis can be served either as a hot or cold accompaniment to various food preparations. It is often made from a single vegetable base (popular examples include broccoli, tomatoes and sweet red peppers) cooked with flavouring ingredients such as onions, garlic, shallots, herbs and spices and then puréed. An appropriate liquid (stock, water or cream) may be added to thin the purée if necessary. Vegetable coulis are often prepared with very little fat and served as a healthful alternative to a heavier, classic sauce.

A fruit coulis, often made from fresh or frozen berries, is generally used as a dessert sauce. It is usually as simple as puréed fruit thinned to the desired consistency with sugar syrup and strained. (If heated and thickened with starches, it becomes a fruit sauce.)

Typically, both vegetable and fruit coulis have a texture similar to that of thin tomato sauce. Their textures can range from smooth to slightly grainy. The flavour and colour of a coulis should be that of the main ingredient. Herbs, spices and other flavouring ingredients should only complement and not dominate the coulis.

Coulis and Purées: Is There a Difference?

A coulis and a purée are two different things! A coulis should be as smooth as possible, thus the name coulis, which refers to what runs off the strainer. A puréed fruit or vegetable differs from a coulis in that a purée is generally thicker and coarser than a coulis.

BASIC PROCEDURE FOR MAKING COULIS

Here, we include a procedure for making a vegetable coulis. Procedures for making fruit coulis are included as recipes in Chapter 32, Custards, Creams, Frozen Desserts and Dessert Sauces.

1. Cook the main ingredient and any additional flavouring ingredients with an appropriate liquid.
2. Purée the main ingredient and flavouring ingredients in a food mill, blender or food processor.
3. Combine the purée with the appropriate liquid and simmer to blend the flavours.
4. Pass the purée through a sieve.
5. Thin and season the coulis as desired.

APPLYING THE BASICS　　　　　　　　　　**RECIPE 10.15**

 Red Pepper Coulis

Yield: 1 L (1 qt.)

Vegetable or olive oil	30 mL	1 fl. oz.
Garlic, chopped	15 g	1/2 oz.
Onion, small dice	90 g	3 oz.
Red bell pepper, medium dice	1.25 kg	3 lb.
White wine	250 mL	8 fl. oz.
Chicken stock	450 mL	1 pt.
Salt and pepper	TT	TT

1. Heat the oil and sauté the garlic and onion until translucent, without browning.
2. Add the red pepper and sauté until tender.
3. Deglaze the pan with the white wine.
4. Add the chicken stock, bring to a simmer and cook for 15 minutes. Season with salt and pepper.
5. Purée in a blender or food processor and strain through a sieve.
6. Adjust the consistency and seasonings and hold for service.

RECIPE 10.15

Approximate values per 50 mL serving:	
Calories	42
Total fat	1.9 g
Saturated fat	0.2 g
Cholesterol	0.2 mg
Sodium	296 mg
Total carbohydrates	5.5 g
Protein	0.7 g

1. Red Pepper Coulis: Sautéing the red peppers.

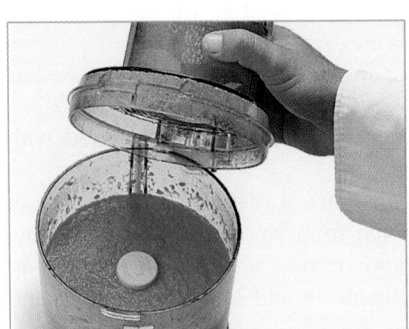

2. Puréeing the cooked peppers.

3. Straining the coulis.

CONTEMPORARY SAUCES

Modern chefs and menu writers are relying less on traditional sauces and more on salsas, relishes, juices, broths, essences and infused oils in their work. Unlike classic sauces, these modern accompaniments do not rely on meat-based stocks and starch thickeners, but rather on fresh vegetables, vegetable juices, aromatic broths and intensely flavoured oils. The names for these sauces are not codified, as are those in the classic sauce repertoire. Chefs apply various terms freely, using whatever name best fits the dish and the overall menu. Most of these contemporary sauces can be prepared more quickly than their classic counterparts, and the use of fresh fruits and vegetables enhances the healthfulness of the dish. These so-called modern sauces may have a lighter body and less fat than classic sauces, but they are still derived from classical culinary techniques and principles. Vinaigrettes are often used. The sauces should be appropriate in flavour, texture and appearance and should complement, not overwhelm, the food they accompany.

Vegetable Juice Sauces

Juice extractors make it possible to prepare juice from fresh, uncooked vegetables such as carrots, beets and spinach. Thinner and smoother than a purée, vegetable juice can be heated, reduced, flavoured and enriched with butter to create colourful, intensely flavoured sauces. (Note that chlorophyll discolours quickly.) Cream or stock can be added to finish the sauce. Sauces made from vegetable juices are sometimes referred to as an **essence** or **tea** on menus.

Juice from a single type of vegetable provides the purest, most pronounced flavour, but two or more vegetables sometimes can be combined successfully. Care must be taken, however, to avoid mixing too many flavours and colours. Also, flavours and colours may change or react during the cooling process. Juiced vegetable sauces are particularly appropriate with pasta, shellfish and poultry, and can be useful in vegetarian cuisine or as a healthier alternative to classic sauces.

BASIC PROCEDURE FOR MAKING A VEGETABLE JUICE SAUCE

1. Wash and peel vegetables as needed.
2. Process the vegetables through a juice extractor.
3. Place the juice in a saucepan and add stock, lemon juice, herbs or other flavourings as desired.
4. Bring the sauce to a simmer and reduce as necessary.
5. Strain the sauce through a fine etâmine.
6. Adjust the seasonings and whisk in whole butter to finish, if desired.

Broth

Broth, which also appears on menus as tea, essence or nage, is very similar to court bouillon (see page 189) but without the extra acidity. These thin, flavourful liquids are generally served in a pool beneath the main food. The broth should not be so abundant as to turn an entree into a soup, but it should provide moisture and flavour. The essence, broth or nage is often made by simply reducing and straining the liquid in which the main food was cooked. Alternatively, a

Jamie Kennedy's Tomato Consommé

2 kg ripe tomatoes
3 cloves garlic
1 leek, washed
2 celery stalks
12 basil leaves
5 mL nutmeg
4 egg whites
Salt and pepper

Coarsely chop the vegetables and herbs. Pulse 5 seconds in food processor. Transfer to heavy-bottomed pot and add remaining ingredients. Bring quickly to a boil. When raft forms, reduce heat and simmer 2 hours. Strain through cheesecloth. If not used immediately, freeze. Yield: 1.5 L.

—from *Jamie Kennedy's Seasons* (Vancouver: Whitecap Books Ltd., 2000).

● **essence** a sauce made from a concentrated vegetable juice

Jamie Kennedy

Jamie Kennedy has been one of Canada's pre-eminent chefs for two decades. He continues to amaze and delight diners who have followed his career from Scaramouche to Palmerston to JK at the Museum, in the Royal Ontario Museum. His current locations are Gilead Café and Bistro and the Gardiner Café, both in Toronto.

RECIPE 10.16

Approximate values per 125 mL serving:	
Calories	69
Total fat	0.9 g
Saturated fat	0.2 g
Cholesterol	0 mg
Sodium	292 mg
Total carbohydrates	13 g
Protein	2.2 g

Flavour Units for 250 mL (8 fl. oz.) Oil		
Nuts	75 g	2-1/2 oz.
Chile peppers (seedless)	15 g	1/2 oz.
Garlic	20 g	5 cloves
Citrus zest	40 g	1-1/4 oz.
Shallots	25 g	1 oz.
Herbs	30 g	1 oz.
Ginger root	25 g	1 oz.
Dried mushrooms	15 g	1/2 oz.
Peppercorns	10 each	10 each

Source: Adapted from Producers of Canadian Canola, "Canola Cooks."

specifically flavoured stock, tomato, for example, can be prepared, then clarified like consommé to create a broth or essence to accompany an appetizer or entree.

Oils with fresh puréed herbs are popular and colourful. Keep refrigerated and use within 2 days.

APPLYING THE BASICS　　　　　　　　　　**RECIPE 10.16**

Piquante Lemon Grass Bouillon

Chef Jamie Kennedy

Jamie Kennedy's Seasons (Vancouver: Whitecap Books Ltd., 2000)

Yield: 900 mL (30 fl. oz.)

Tomato consommé (see sidebar on page 213)	1 L	34 fl. oz.
Lemon grass, chopped	1 stalk	1 stalk
Green chiles, split lengthwise	2	2

1. Bring consommé to a simmer.
2. Add lemon grass and chiles and simmer 30 minutes to infuse. Strain through a fine sieve. Reserve.

NOTE: Jamie serves this with seared grouper marinated with lemon grass. Garnish is baked, diced sweet potato and leek combined with fresh, diced tomato.

Flavoured Oil

Small amounts of intensely flavoured oils can be used to dress or garnish a variety of dishes. Salads, soups, vegetable and starch dishes, as well as entrees, can be enhanced with a drizzle of colourful, appropriately flavoured oil. Because such small quantities are used, these oils provide flavour and moisture without adding too many calories or too much fat.

Unless the flavouring ingredient goes especially well with olive oil (for example, basil), select a high-quality but neutral oil such as sunflower, safflower or canola. The Producers of Canadian Canola have the Canadian Food Inspection Agency's approval for the following method of preparing a flavoured oil. No deviations from the procedure are acceptable due to the risk of botulism toxin developing. It is important that all moisture be evaporated. The more flavour units in the oil, the longer it will take to process.

Oils with fresh puréed herbs are popular and colourful. Keep refrigerated and use within two days.

BASIC PROCEDURE FOR MAKING A FLAVOURED OIL

Use a 500 to 750 mL (18 to 27 fl. oz) stainless steel insert.

1. Heat oil and flavouring ingredients in a 150°C (300°F) oven until the oil reaches a temperature of 120°C (250°F).
2. Remove from oven and cool on a rack for 30 minutes.
3. Strain the oil though a coffee filter presoaked with plain canola oil.
4. Store flavoured oil in a covered clean glass jar in a refrigerator. Use within 1 month.

Heating times: 1 unit—1 h 20 min; 2 units—1 h 40 min; 3 units—2 h; 4 units—2 h 20 min; 5 units—2 h 40 min; 6 units—3 h. Drier ingredients will reach temperature faster.

<table>
<tr><td>APPLYING THE BASICS</td><td>RECIPE 10.17</td></tr>
</table>

Rosemary Orange Oil

Yield: 225 mL (8 fl. oz.)

Canola oil	250 mL	8 fl. oz.
Orange zest	60 g	2 oz.
Rosemary	15 g	1/2 oz.

1. Preheat oven to 150°C (300°F).
2. Place all ingredients in a 500 mL (16 fl. oz.) stainless steel container.
3. Heat oil for 1 hour 40 minutes (2 units) to an internal temperature of 120°C (250°F).
4. Allow oil to cool for 30 minutes.
5. Strain into a glass jar, seal and store, refrigerated, for up to 1 month.

RECIPE 10.17

Approximate values per 15 mL serving:	
Calories	126
Total fat	14 g
Saturated fat	1 g
Cholesterol	0 mg
Sodium	0 mg
Total carbohydrates	0 g
Protein	0 g

Salsa, Relish and Chutneys

Salsa (Spanish for "sauce") is most commonly known as a chunky mixture of raw tomato, other vegetables, chiles and cilantro, eaten with chips or ladled over Mexican foods. It can also be puréed. **Relish** is commonly known as a sweet green condiment spooned on a hot dog, but the term refers to other preparations as well. **Chutneys** are known as a condiment served with curries. However, salsas, relishes and chutneys can be used as sauces with many meat, poultry, fish, shellfish or vegetable dishes. They can include many different fruits and vegetables such as oranges, pineapple, papaya, black beans, jicama and tomatillos.

Although not members of any classic sauce family, salsas and relishes are condiments currently enjoying great popularity because of their intense fresh flavours, ease of preparation, and low fat and calorie content. Salsas and relishes are often a riot of colours, textures and flavours, simultaneously cool and hot, spicy and sweet.

● **salsa** Spanish for "sauce"; generally a cold chunky mixture of fresh herbs, spices, fruits and/or vegetables used as a sauce for meat, poultry, fish or shellfish

● **relish** a cooked or pickled product usually made with vegetables or fruits and often used as a condiment

● **chutney** a sweet-and-sour condiment made of fruits and/or vegetables cooked in vinegar with sugar and spices; some chutneys are reduced to a purée; others retain recognizable pieces of their ingredients

BASIC PROCEDURE FOR MAKING A SALSA

1. Cut or chop the ingredients.
2. Precook and chill items as directed in the recipe.
3. Toss all ingredients together and refrigerate, allowing the flavours to combine for at least 30 minutes before service.

BASIC PROCEDURE FOR MAKING A RELISH

1. Clean, peel, trim and cut ingredients to desired size.
2. Precook, blanch or sauté items as directed in the recipe.
3. Combine all ingredients with the vinegar and sugar.
4. Cook gently until soft.

RECIPE 10.18

Approximate values per 50 mL serving:	
Calories	12
Total fat	0.1 g
Saturated fat	0 g
Cholesterol	0 mg
Sodium	101 mg
Total carbohydrates	2.4 g
Protein	0.4 g

Tomato Salsa

APPLYING THE BASICS   RECIPE 10.18

Tomato Salsa (Pico de Gallo)

Yield: 1 L (1 qt.)

Tomatoes, seeded, small dice	750 g	1-1/2 lb.
Green onions, sliced	1 bunch (6)	1 bunch (6)
Garlic cloves, minced	15 g	3
Cilantro, chopped	60 g	1/2 bunch
Jalapeño peppers, chopped fine	3	3
Lemon juice	60 mL	2 fl. oz.
Cumin, ground	1 g	1/2 tsp.
Salt and pepper	TT	TT

1. Combine all ingredients and gently toss.

2. Adjust seasonings and refrigerate.

VARIATION: To make a tomatillo salsa, substitute the tomatoes with tomatillo.

USING SAUCES

Although many classic sauces were designed for or intended to be used with specific dishes, modern chefs often mix and match sauces with foods in unique or nontraditional ways. Nonclassic sauces, such as salsa or relish, may be prepared in a range of flavours using a wide variety of ingredients.

The uses shown in Table 10.5 for classic and nonclassic sauces are just suggestions. Most sauces can be used in many different dishes. It depends on your taste, creativity and judgment.

TABLE 10.5	Using Sauces		
Sauce	**Qualities**	**Derivative Sauces or Flavourings**	**Use**
Béchamel	Smooth, rich and creamy; no graininess; cream-coloured with rich sheen	Cheddar	Vegetables, pasta
		Cream sauce	Vegetables, pasta, eggs, fish
		Mornay	Fish, shellfish, poultry, vegetables
		Nantua	Fish, shellfish
		Soubise	Veal, pork, eggs
Velouté	Smooth and rich; ivory-coloured; good flavour of the stock used; not pasty or heavy	Fish velouté	
		Bercy	Poached fish
		Cardinal	Lobster, white fish, crab, eggs
		Normandy	Delicate white fish, oysters
		Allemande (veal)	
		Horseradish	Roast beef, corned beef, baked ham
		Mushroom	Sautéed poultry, white meats
		Poulette	Vegetables, sweetbreads
		Suprême (chicken)	
		Aurora	Eggs, chicken, sweetbreads
		Hungarian	Eggs, chicken, chops, sweetbreads
		Ivory	Eggs, braised poultry
Espagnole/ Demi-glace	Smooth and rich; dark brown colour; good meat flavour	Bordelaise	Sautéed or grilled meats
		Chasseur	Sautéed or grilled meats and poultry
		Chateaubriand	Broiled meats

continued

TABLE 10.5	Using Sauces (*continued*)		
Sauce	**Qualities**	**Derivative Sauces or Flavourings**	**Use**
		Chevreuil	Roasted meats and game
		Madeira/Port	Grilled or roasted meats and game, ham
		Mushroom	Sautéed or grilled meats and poultry
		Périgueux/Périgourdine	Sautéed poultry, grilled meats and game, sweetbreads
		Piquant	Pork
		Poivrade	Grilled or roasted meats, game
		Robert	Pork
Tomato	Thick and rich; slightly grainy; full-flavoured	Tomato	Meats, poultry, vegetables, pasta and for making small sauces
		Milanaise	Pasta, grilled white meats
		Creole	Fish, eggs, chicken
		Provençale	Pasta, grilled or sautéed poultry and white meats
		Spanish	Eggs, fish
Hollandaise	Smooth and rich; buttery flavour; light and slightly frothy; pale yellow colour; no signs of separating	Grimrod	Grilled meats and fish
		Maltaise	Eggs, poached fish
		Mousseline	Poached fish, eggs, vegetables / Grilled or sautéed meats and fish / Grilled meats and fish
Béarnaise	Same as hollandaise	Choron	Grilled steak; grilled fish (e.g., salmon)
		Foyot	
Beurre blanc and beurre rouge	Rich and buttery; thinner than hollandaise; light and airy; pale-coloured	Wide variety of seasonings and flavourings may be used	Steamed, grilled or poached fish; chicken or vegetables
Compound butter	Flavour ingredients should be evenly distributed	Wide variety of seasonings and flavourings may be used	Grilled meats, poultry and fish; finishing sauces, condiment, spread
Jus de rôti, jus lié, pan gravy	Smooth; deep rich colour; meaty flavour	Made from pan drippings	Roasted meats and poultry
Coulis	Rich colour; moderately thin, grainy texture; strongly flavoured	Made with a wide variety of vegetables or fruits	Vegetables, grilled or poached meats, poultry and fish
Salsa, relish and chutney	Chunky; bright colours; not watery	Made with a wide variety of vegetables, fruits and seasonings	Meats, fish, vegetables and poultry; used as a sauce or condiment
Flavoured oil	Smooth, bright colour; intense flavours	Made with a variety of herbs, spices, and aromatics	Used as a garnish

Conclusion

In *Le Guide culinaire*, Auguste Escoffier wrote, "Indeed, stock is everything in cooking…. Without it, nothing can be done. If one's stock is good, what remains of the work is easy; if, on the other hand, it is bad or merely mediocre, it is quite hopeless to expect anything approaching a satisfactory result." Because stocks and the sauces made from them are still the basis for much of contemporary cuisine, Escoffier's words are as true today as when he wrote them.

Both the classic basic sauces and the derivative sauces made from them, as well as sauces such as beurre blanc and beurre rouge, coulis, salsas and relishes that are not based on classic recipes, all share two goals: to complement the foods with which they are served and to neither mask nor disguise poorly prepared foods. With practice and care (and the right ingredients), you will be able to make great sauces.

Questions for Discussion

1. Why are the bones of younger animals preferred for making stocks?
2. Why should a stock made from beef or veal bones cook longer than a stock made from fish bones? What is the result if a stock does not cook long enough?
3. What can cause a stock to become cloudy? How can you prevent this from happening?
4. List three differences in the production of a white stock and a brown stock.
5. List the five classic basic sauces and explain how they are used to prepare derivative sauces.
6. Why is demi-glace preferred when making brown sauces? Is jus lié different from classic demi-glace? Can they be used interchangeably?
7. Why are temperatures important when making hollandaise sauce? What precautions must be taken when holding hollandaise for service?
8. Compare a beurre blanc with a hollandaise sauce. How are they similar? How are they different?
9. How are compound butters used in making sauces? What are the ingredients for a traditional maître d'hôtel butter?
10. What are the differences among a salsa, chutney and relish? Can these items be used in place of classic sauces? Explain your answer.

Additional Sauce Recipes

Barbecue Sauce

RECIPE 10.19

Approximate values per 50 mL serving:	
Calories	170
Total fat	6.3 g
Saturated fat	0.5 g
Cholesterol	0 mg
Sodium	735 mg
Total carbohydrates	27 g
Protein	1.2 g

RECIPE 10.19

Barbecue Sauce

Yield: 1 L (1 qt.)

Onion, brunoise	50 g	2 oz.
Garlic, chopped	30 g	1 oz.
Vegetable oil	125 mL	4 fl. oz.
Cider vinegar	125 mL	4 fl. oz.
Molasses	125 mL	4 fl. oz.
Honey	125 g	4 oz.
Beer	125 mL	4 fl. oz.
Lemon juice	30 mL	1 oz.
Ketchup	1 L	32 fl. oz.
Dry mustard	15 g	1/2 oz.
Worcestershire sauce	30 mL	2 Tbsp.
Salt and pepper	TT	TT
Chilli powder	5 g	1 Tbsp.

1. Sweat the onion and garlic in the oil until tender.
2. Combine the remaining ingredients and simmer for 30 minutes.

VARIATION: Spices, herbs and other flavourings may be incorporated.

RECIPE 10.20

Four Cheese Cream Sauce

Yield: 5 L (5 qt.)

Cold milk	3.75 L	3-3/4 qt.
Ultra sperse M	95 g	1-1/4 cups
Cream, 35%	1 L	1 qt.
Salt	25 g	5 tsp.
Black pepper, ground	0.5 g	1 tsp.
Onion powder	8 g	2-1/2 tsp.
Nutmeg	2 g	1/2 tsp.
Cayenne	1 g	1/4 tsp.
Parmesan, finely grated	150 g	5-1/2 oz.
Asiago, finely grated	150 g	5-1/2 oz.
Fontina, finely grated	150 g	5-1/2 oz.
Romano, finely grated	150 g	5-1/2 oz.

1. Blend half the cold milk with ultra sperse M on high speed in a blender.
2. Combine the next six ingredients and remaining milk in a saucepan and whisk thoroughly.
3. Heat to a simmer, stirring constantly.
4. Whisk in grated cheeses and stir until completely blended.
5. Hold in a steam table for service or chill quickly for storage in refrigerator.

NOTE: Ultra sperse M is a pre-gelatinized modified starch with higher shear values and resistance to acids. The blending of the starch and liquid, initially, results in a smoother, finer-textured sauce.

RECIPE 10.20

Approximate values per 50 mL serving:	
Calories	80
Total fat	6 g
Saturated fat	4 g
Cholesterol	22 mg
Sodium	189 mg
Total carbohydrates	3 g
Protein	3 g

RECIPE 10.21

Oxtail Jus

HALIFAX, NS
Chef Michael Smith

Yield: 1.25 L (40 fl. oz.)

Butter	60 g	4 oz.
Onions, sliced	1.8 kg	4 lb.
Garlic, fine mince	10 g	4 cloves
Oxtail broth	1 L	32 fl. oz.
Red wine vinegar	5 mL	1 tsp.
Salt and pepper	TT	TT

1. Over medium heat, melt butter, add onions and begin cooking. Once the moisture has evaporated and the sugars begin to caramelize, lower the heat. Stir continuously and as the onions caramelize, gradually lower the heat. Stir continuously so the fonds do not burn.
2. When the onions are an even, deep golden-brown colour, stir in the garlic and cook for a few minutes until the garlic is fully aromatized.
3. Place onions in a blender with 250 mL (8 fl. oz.) of the broth and purée. Strain the purée into a clean pot and add remaining broth. Simmer to release the air and strain again through a fine mesh sieve.
4. Balance the flavours by adding the vinegar and adjust seasoning with salt and pepper.

NOTE: This recipe relies on a vegetable purée to lightly thicken the sauce instead of a traditional roux or cornstarch.

Michael Smith

Chef Michael Smith has dedicated his career to furthering the ideals of Canadian cuisine. He has hosted Food Network Canada's *Chef at Large, Chef at Home, Chef Abroad* and *The Inn Chef,* and frequently crisscrosses the country leading cooking classes. He has published a number of cookbooks, including *Open Kitchen: A Chef's Day at The Inn at Bay Fortune.*

RECIPE 10.21

Approximate values per 100 mL serving:	
Calories	93
Total fat	5.4 g
Saturated fat	2.9 g
Cholesterol	12 mg
Sodium	199 mg
Total carbohydrates	9.9 g
Protein	1.2 g

Nigel Webber

Nigel, a born and bred Edmontonian, graduated from NAIT in 1994, and was named top apprentice in Alberta the same year. He has won many awards, including two gold medals and top junior team awards with Team Alberta at the Culinary World Cup (1994), and two gold medals and second prize overall with Team Alberta at the World Culinary Olympics (1996). More recently, he led two teams of students to international culinary competitions in Singapore and Germany. Nigel is now a Chef Instructor at NAIT's Hokanson Centre for Culinary Arts.

RECIPE 10.22

Approximate values per 25 mL serving:	
Calories	95
Total fat	9.6 g
Saturated fat	1.3 g
Cholesterol	0 mg
Sodium	100 mg
Total carbohydrates	2.5 g
Protein	0.4 g

RECIPE 10.22

Charred Tomato Vinaigrette

NORTHERN ALBERTA INSTITUTE OF TECHNOLOGY
THE HOKANSON CENTRE FOR CULINARY ARTS
EDMONTON, AB
Chef Instructor Nigel Webber

Yield: 600 mL (20 fl. oz.)

Roma tomatoes, halved and seeded	900 g	6
Olive oil, extra virgin	250 mL	8 fl. oz.
Red wine vinegar	150 mL	5 fl. oz.
Shallots, brunoise	30 g	3 Tbsp.
Garlic, minced	10 g	2
Salt	TT	TT
Pepper, freshly ground	TT	TT

1. Brush tomatoes with some of the olive oil and grill until lightly charred and softening.
2. Cool, peel and dice fine.
3. Combine all ingredients and refrigerate overnight.

Mushroom Duxelles

Chopped mushrooms cooked with chopped shallots in butter with white wine until au sec. Used as a stuffing.

RECIPE 10.23

Approximate values per 50 mL serving:	
Calories	102
Total fat	7.9 g
Saturated fat	3.6 g
Cholesterol	15 mg
Sodium	174 mg
Total carbohydrates	6.6 g
Protein	1.2 g

RECIPE 10.23

Duxelles Sauce

Yield: 750 mL (1-1/2 pt.)

Mushrooms, chopped fine	250 g	8 oz.
Shallots, chopped fine	90 g	3 oz.
Clarified butter	30 mL	1 fl. oz.
Olive oil	30 mL	1 fl. oz.
Dry white wine	350 mL	12 fl. oz.
Demi-glace	500 mL	1 pt.
Cream, 35%	60 mL	2 fl. oz.
Salt and pepper	TT	TT
Parsley, chopped fine	15 mL	1 Tbsp.

1. Sauté the mushrooms and the shallots in the butter and oil. The mushrooms will release their liquid and darken. Cook until completely dry.
2. Deglaze with the white wine and reduce by two-thirds.
3. Add the demi-glace. Bring to a boil, then simmer for 5 minutes.
4. Stir in the cream. Adjust seasonings. Garnish with parsley.

RECIPE 10.24

Mole

*Mole sauce varies with each region of Mexico and was originally prepared with turkey.
Combinations of fresh and dried chiles may be used.*

Yield: 600 mL (20 fl. oz.)

Pasilla chiles, dry, seeded	250 g	8 oz.
Water, boiling	as needed	as needed
Anaheim chiles, fresh, seeded	250 g	8 oz.
Cinnamon, ground	3 g	1 tsp.
Cloves, ground	1 g	1/4 tsp.
Peppercorns, cracked	6	6
Fennel seed, ground	2 g	1/2 tsp.
Sesame seeds	50 g	1-1/2 oz.
Almonds, ground	50 g	1-1/2 oz.
Vegetable oil	50 mL	2 fl. oz.
Onion, brunoise	200 g	7 oz.
Garlic, minced	25 g	5
Epazote or oregano, dry	2 g	1 tsp.
Tomato concassée	450 g	1 lb.
Corn tortilla, broken, toasted	1	1
Chicken stock	500 mL	16 fl. oz.
Salt	TT	TT
Semi-sweet chocolate, grated	125 g	4 oz.

1. Cover pasilla chiles with boiling water and soak until soft. Drain and remove stem and seeds and scrape the flesh from the skins. Reserve flesh.
2. Combine spices, sesame seeds, almonds and dry-toast.
3. Sauté the onion and garlic in the oil until they start to colour. Add the toasted spices, nuts and epazote and fry for a moment.
4. Add the tomato concassée and sauté until nearly dry.
5. Add the tortilla and chicken stock. Simmer to thicken. Purée.
6. Adjust seasoning with salt and add the chocolate, stirring to incorporate.
7. Serve with turkey, chicken, rabbit or pork. This sauce freezes well.

1. Mise en place for mole.

2. The finished mole.

RECIPE 10.24

Approximate values per 50 mL serving:	
Calories	234
Total fat	11 g
Saturated fat	2.6 g
Cholesterol	0.5 mg
Sodium	226 mg
Total carbohydrates	31 g
Protein	6.6 g

11 Soups

"A first-rate soup is more creative than a second-rate painting.
—Abraham Maslow, American psychologist (1908–1970)

Soups are the universal comfort foods. The

variety of ingredients used in soup production is endless. Whether preparing a classic soup using specialized techniques or a simple purée, great soups can be made using the finest and most expensive ingredients or leftovers from the previous evening's dinner service and trimmings from the day's production. Seasonal and regional products can shine while contributing to a solid contribution margin.

This chapter extends to soups the skills and knowledge learned in Chapter 10, Stocks and Sauces. In Chapter 10 we discussed making stocks, thickening liquids, using a liaison and skimming impurities, techniques that apply to soup making as well. Here we discuss techniques such as clarifying consommés and thickening soups with vegetable purées. This chapter also covers cream soups, cold soups and guidelines for garnishing and serving a variety of soups.

Most soups can be classified by cooking technique and appearance as either clear or thick.

Clear soups include **broths** and **bouillons** made from meat, poultry, game, fish or vegetables, as well as **consommés**, which are stocks or broths clarified to remove impurities.

Thick soups include cream soups and purée soups. The most common **cream soups** are those made from vegetables cooked in a stock that is thickened with a roux; cream is then incorporated to add richness and flavour. Cream soups may also be made with a thin béchamel. **Purée soups** are generally made from starchy vegetables or legumes. After the main ingredient is simmered in a liquid, the mixture—or a portion of it—is puréed. Velouté soups are basically cream soups with the addition of a liaison.

Some soups (notably **bisques** and **chowders**, as well as cold soups such as gazpacho and fruit soup) are generally regarded as thick soups. They use special preparation methods or a combination of the methods mentioned above.

Quality Standard

A soup's quality is determined by its flavour, appearance and texture. A good soup should be full flavoured, with no off or sour tastes. Flavours from each of the soup's ingredients should blend and complement, with no one flavour overpowering another. Consommés should be crystal clear. The vegetables in vegetable soups should be brightly coloured, not grey. Garnishes should be attractive and uniform in size and shape. The soup's texture should be very precise. If it is supposed to be smooth, then it should be very smooth and lump-free. If the soft and crisp textures of certain ingredients are supposed to contrast, the soup should not be overcooked, as this causes all the ingredients to become mushy and soft.

Garnishing is an important consideration when preparing soups. When applied to soups, the word *garnish* has two meanings. The first is the one more typically associated with the word. It refers to foods added to the soup as decoration—for example, a broccoli floret floated on a bowl of cream of broccoli soup. The second refers to foods that may serve not only as decorations but also as critical components of the final product—for example, noodles in a bowl of chicken noodle soup. In this context, the noodles are not ingredients because they are not used to make the chicken soup. Rather they are added to chicken soup to create a different dish. These additional items are still referred to as garnishes, however.

● **clear soups** unthickened soups, including broths, consommés and broth-based soups

● **broth** a flavourful liquid obtained from the long simmering of meats and/or vegetables

● **consommé** a rich stock or broth that has been clarified with clearmeat to remove impurities

● **cream soup** a soup made from vegetables cooked in a stock that is thickened with a roux; cream is then incorporated to add richness and flavour

● **purée soup** a soup usually made from starchy vegetables or legumes; after the main ingredient is simmered in a liquid, the mixture, or a portion of it, is puréed

● **bisque** a purée soup made from crustacean shells; classic versions are thickened with rice

● **chowder** a hearty soup made from fish, shellfish and/or vegetables, usually containing milk and potatoes and often thickened with roux

● **garnish** (1) food used as an attractive decoration; (2) a subsidiary food used to add flavour or character to the main ingredient in a dish

Escoffier's Classification of Soups

In his 1903 culinary treatise *Le Guide culinaire*, Auguste Escoffier recognized many more categories of soups than we do today. They include:

Clear soups, which are always "clear consommés with a slight garnish in keeping with the nature of the consommé."

Purées, which are made from starchy vegetables and are thickened with rice, potato or soft bread crumbs.

Cullises, which use poultry, game or fish for a base and are thickened with rice, lentils, espagnole sauce or bread soaked in boiling salted water.

Bisques, which use shellfish cooked with a mirepoix as a base and are thickened with rice.

Veloutés, which use velouté sauce as a base and are finished with a liaison of egg yolks and cream.

Cream soups, which use béchamel sauce as a base and are finished with heavy cream.

Special soups, which do not follow the procedures for veloutés or creams.

Vegetable soups, which are usually paysanne or peasant-type and "do not demand very great precision in the apportionment of the vegetables of which they are composed, but they need great care and attention, notwithstanding."

Foreign soups, "which have a foreign origin whose use, although it may not be general, is yet sufficiently common."

Because of changes in consumer health consciousness and kitchen operations, many of the distinctions among Escoffier's classic soups have now become blurred and, in some cases, have been eliminated. As discussed in this chapter, for example, clear consommés and vegetable soups are now made with stocks or broths; most cream soups use velouté as a base and are finished with milk or cream rather than a liaison. But not everything has changed: the procedures for making purées and bisques are essentially the same today as they were when Escoffier haunted the great kitchens of Europe.

CLEAR SOUPS

All clear soups start as broth or as stock. Broths may be served as finished items, used as the base for other soups or refined (clarified) into consommés.

Broths and Bouillons

The techniques for making stocks, discussed in Chapter 10, are identical to those used for making broths and bouillons. Like stocks, broths are prepared by simmering flavouring ingredients in a liquid for long periods of time. Broths and stocks differ, however, in two ways. First, broths are made with meat instead of just bones. Second, broths (often with a garnish) can be served as finished dishes, while stocks are generally used to prepare other items.

Broths are made from meat, poultry, fish or vegetables cooked in a liquid. An especially full-flavoured broth results when a stock and not just water is used as the liquid. Cuts of meat from the shank, neck or shoulder result in more flavourful, full-bodied broths, as will the flesh of mature poultry. Proper temperature, skimming and straining help produce well-flavoured, clear broths.

1. Browning the meat.

BASIC PROCEDURE FOR PREPARING BROTHS

1. Truss or cut the main ingredient.
2. Brown the meat; brown or sweat the mirepoix or vegetables as necessary.
3. Place the main ingredient and mirepoix or vegetables in an appropriate stockpot and add enough cold water or stock to cover. Add a bouquet garni or sachet d'épices if desired.
4. Bring the liquid slowly to a boil; reduce to a simmer and cook, skimming occasionally, until the main ingredient is tender and the flavour is fully developed.

continued

5. Carefully strain the broth through a conical strainer lined with cheesecloth; avoid disturbing the flavouring ingredients in order to preserve the broth's clarity.

6. Cool and store following the procedures for cooling stocks. Or bring to a boil, garnish as desired and hold for service.

2. Adding mirepoix to the broth.

APPLYING THE BASICS   RECIPE 11.1

Beef Broth

Yield: 4 L (4 qt.)

Beef shank, neck or shoulder		
cut in 5-cm-thick (2-in.) pieces	2.25 kg	5 lb.
Vegetable oil	125 mL	4 fl. oz.
Beef stock	4 L	1 gal.
Mirepoix	500 g	1 lb.
Turnip, medium dice	125 g	4 oz.
Leeks, medium dice	125 g	4 oz.
Tomato, seeded and diced	125 g	4 oz.
Sachet:		
Bay leaf	1	1
Dried thyme	0.25 g	1/4 tsp.
Peppercorns, crushed	0.5 g	1/2 tsp.
Parsley stems	8	8
Garlic clove, crushed	1	1
Salt	TT	TT

1. Brown the meat in 60 mL (2 fl. oz.) of oil, then place it in a stockpot. Add the stock and bring to a simmer. Simmer gently for 2 hours, skimming the surface as necessary.

2. After the meat has simmered for 2 hours, caramelize the mirepoix in the remaining oil and add it to the liquid. Add the turnip, leeks, tomato and sachet.

3. Simmer until full flavour has developed, approximately 1 hour. Skim the surface as necessary.

4. Carefully strain the broth through cheesecloth and season to taste. Cool and refrigerate.

3. Straining the broth.

RECIPE 11.1

Approximate values per 175 mL serving:	
Calories	59
Total fat	5.2 g
Saturated fat	0.4 g
Cholesterol	0 mg
Sodium	97 mg
Total carbohydrates	2 g
Protein	1 g

Broth-Based Soups

Broths are often used as bases for such familiar soups as vegetable, chicken noodle or beef barley.

Transforming a broth into a broth-based vegetable soup, for example, is quite simple. Although a broth may be served with a vegetable (or meat) garnish, a broth-based vegetable soup is a soup in which the vegetables (and meats) are cooked directly in the broth, adding flavour, body and texture to the finished product. Any number of vegetables can be used to make a vegetable soup; it could be a single vegetable as in onion soup or a dozen different vegetables for a hearty minestrone. Making a mixed vegetable soup allows the cook to use his or her imagination and whatever produce may be on hand.

When making broth-based vegetable soups, each ingredient must be added at the proper time so that all ingredients are cooked when the soup is finished. The ingredients must cook long enough to add their flavours and soften sufficiently but not so long that they lose their identity and become too soft or mushy.

Because broth-based vegetable soups are made by simmering ingredients directly in the broth, they are generally not as clear as plain broths. But appearance is still important. So, when cutting ingredients for the soup, pay particular attention that the pieces are uniform and visually appealing. Small dice, julienne, batonnet or paysanne cuts are recommended.

BASIC PROCEDURE FOR PREPARING BROTH-BASED VEGETABLE SOUPS

1. Sweat long-cooking vegetables in butter or fat.
2. Add the appropriate stock or broth and bring to a simmer.
3. Add seasonings such as bay leaves, dried thyme, crushed peppercorns, parsley stems and garlic in a sachet, allowing enough time for the seasonings to fully flavour the soup.
4. Add additional ingredients according to their cooking times.
5. Simmer the soup to blend all the flavours.
6. If the soup is not going to be served immediately, cool and refrigerate it.
7. Just before service add any garnishes that were prepared separately or do not require cooking.

1. Sweating the vegetables.

2. The finished soup.

APPLYING THE BASICS		RECIPE 11.2

Hearty Vegetable Beef Soup

Yield: 5 L (5 qt.)

Butter or beef fat	170 g	6 oz.
Mirepoix, small dice	1.5 kg	3 lb.
Turnip, small dice	250 g	8 oz.
Garlic cloves, chopped	2	2
Beef broth or stock	4 L	4 qt.
Beef, small dice	450 g	1 lb.
Sachet:		
Bay leaf	1	1
Dried thyme	2 mL	1/2 tsp.
Peppercorns, crushed	1.5 g	1/2 tsp.
Parsley stems	8	8
Tomato concassée	350 g	12 oz.
Corn kernels, frozen or canned	350 g	12 oz.
Salt and pepper	TT	TT

1. In a soup pot, sweat the mirepoix and turnip in the butter or fat until tender.
2. Add the garlic and sauté lightly.
3. Add the broth or stock and the diced beef; bring to a simmer. Add the sachet. Skim or degrease as necessary.
4. Simmer until the beef and vegetables are tender, approximately 1 hour.
5. Add the tomato concassée and corn; simmer for 10 minutes. Season to taste with salt and pepper.
6. Cool and refrigerate or hold for service.

VARIATIONS: A wide variety of vegetables can be added or substituted in this recipe. If leeks, rutabagas, parsnips or cabbage are used, they should be sweated to bring out their flavours before the liquid is added. Potatoes, fresh beans, summer squash and other vegetables that cook more quickly should be added according to their cooking times. Rice, barley and pasta garnishes should be cooked separately and added just before service.

RECIPE 11.2

Approximate values per 180 mL serving	
Calories	183
Total fat	13 g
Saturated fat	5 g
Cholesterol	33 mg
Sodium	386 mg
Total carbohydrates	10 g
Protein	8 g

Consommés

A consommé is a stock or broth that has been clarified to remove impurities so that it is crystal clear. Traditionally, all clear broths were referred to as consommés; a clear broth further refined using the process described next was referred to as a double consommé. The term *double consommé* is still used occasionally to describe any strongly flavoured consommé.

Quality Standard

Well-prepared consommés should be rich in the flavour of the main ingredient. Beef and game consommés should be dark amber in colour; consommés made from poultry should have a golden to light amber colour. They should have substantial body as a result of their high gelatin content, and all consommés should be perfectly clear with no trace of fat.

Because a consommé is a clarified broth or stock, it is absolutely essential that the broth or stock used be of the highest quality. Although the clarification process adds some flavour to the consommé, the finished consommé will be only as good as the stock or broth from which it was made.

The Clarification Process

To make a consommé, you clarify a stock or broth. The stock or broth to be clarified must be cold and grease-free. To clarify, the cold degreased stock or broth is combined with a mixture known as a **clearmeat** or **clarification**. A clearmeat is a mixture of egg whites; ground meat, poultry or fish; mirepoix, herbs and spices; and an acidic product, usually tomatoes, lemon juice or wine. (An **oignon brûlé** may also be added to help flavour and add colour to the consommé as a remedial action.)

The stock or broth and clearmeat are then slowly brought to a simmer. As the albumen (protein) in the egg whites and meat begins to coagulate, it traps impurities suspended in the liquid. As coagulation continues, the albumen combines with the other clearmeat ingredients and rises to the liquid's surface, forming a **raft**. As the mixture simmers, the raft ingredients release their flavours, further enriching the consommé.

After simmering, the consommé is carefully strained through several layers of cheesecloth to remove any trace of impurities. It is then completely degreased, either by cooling and refrigerating, then removing the solidified fat, or by carefully brushing the top of the consommé with sheets of unbleached paper towel. The paper absorbs the fat and is discarded after one pass on top of the soup. The result is a rich, flavourful, crystal-clear consommé.

● **clarification** (1) the process of tranforming a broth into a clear consommé by trapping impurities with a clearmeat consisting of the egg white protein albumen, ground meat, an acidic product, mirepoix and other ingredients; (2) the clearmeat used to clarify a broth

● **oignon brûlé** French for "a burnt onion"; made by charring onion halves; used to flavour and colour stocks and sauces as a remedial action

● **raft** a crust formed during the process of clarifying consommé; it comprises the clearmeat and impurities from the stock, which rise to the top of the simmering stock and release additional flavours

BASIC PROCEDURE FOR MAKING CONSOMMÉS

1. In a suitable heavy-bottomed stockpot (one with a spigot makes it much easier to strain the consommé when it is finished), combine the ground meat, lightly beaten egg white and other clearmeat ingredients.
2. Add the cold stock or broth and stir to combine with the clearmeat ingredients.
3. Over medium heat, slowly bring the mixture to a simmer, stirring occasionally.
4. As the raft forms, make a hole in its centre so that the liquid can bubble through, cooking the raft completely and extracting as much flavour as possible from the raft ingredients.

continued

Classic Consommés

Beef Consommé

Brunoise—Brunoise of leeks, carrots, turnip, celery, peas and chervil.

Célestine—Julienne of savoury crepe, traditionally thickened with tapioca.

Julienne—Julienne of leeks, carrots, turnips, celery, cabbage, sorrel and chervil.

Chicken Consommé

Caroline—Royale, rice and chervil.

Mimosa—Sieved white and yolk of hard-boiled egg.

Royale—Royale and tapioca (royale is an egg and broth custard cut into cubes)

Fish Consommé

George Sand—White fish and crayfish quenelles, morels, carp soft roe on croutons made from French stick bread.

Game Consommé

Saint-Hubert—White wine, game and lentil royale, julienne of game.

5. Simmer the consommé until full flavour develops, approximately 1 to 1.5 hours.
6. Carefully strain the consommé through several layers of cheesecloth and degrease completely.
7. If the consommé will not be used immediately, it should be cooled and refrigerated, following the procedures for cooling stocks discussed in Chapter 10. When the consommé is completely cold, remove any remaining fat that solidified on its surface.
8. If, after reheating the consommé, small dots of fat appear on the surface, they can be removed by blotting with a small piece of paper towel.

APPLYING THE BASICS		RECIPE 11.3

Beef Consommé

Yield: 2.5 L (2-1/2 qt.) (10 servings)

Egg whites	175 g	5
Ground beef, lean, preferably shank, neck or shoulder	500 g	1 lb.
Mirepoix	250 g	1/2 lb.
Tomatoes, seeded and diced	200 g	6 oz.
Brown beef stock or broth, cold	2.5 L	2-1/2 qt.
Oignon brûlé (if required)	1 half	1 half
Sachet:		
Bay leaves	2	2
Dried thyme	1 g	1/2 tsp.
Peppercorns, crushed	1 g	1/2 tsp.
Parsley stems	8	8
Cloves, whole	2	2
Salt	TT	TT

1. Whip the egg whites until slightly frothy.
2. Combine the egg whites, beef, mirepoix and tomatoes in an appropriate stockpot.
3. Add the cold beef stock or broth; mix well and add the oignon brûlé and sachet.
4. Bring the mixture to a simmer over moderate heat, stirring occasionally. Stop stirring when the raft begins to form.
5. Break a hole in the centre of the raft to allow the consommé to bubble through.
6. Simmer until full flavour develops, approximately 1.5 hours.
7. Strain through several layers of cheesecloth, degrease and adjust the seasonings. Cool and refrigerate or hold for service.

RECIPE 11.3

Approximate values per 250 mL serving:	
Calories	71
Total fat	3.5 g
Saturated fat	1.1 g
Cholesterol	1.7 mg
Sodium	296 mg
Total carbohydrates	9.1 g
Protein	0.7 g

1. Beef Consommé: Combining the ingredients for the clearmeat.

2. Making a hole in the raft to allow the liquid to bubble through.

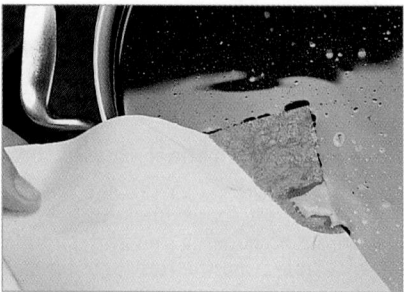

3. Degreasing the consommé with a paper towel.

Correcting a Poorly Clarified Consommé

A clarification may fail for a variety of reasons. For example, if the consommé is allowed to boil or if it is stirred after the raft has formed, a cloudy consommé can result. If the consommé is insufficiently clear, a second clarification can be performed using the following procedure. This second clarification should be performed only once, however, and only if absolutely necessary, because the eggs remove not only impurities but also some of the consommé's flavour and richness.

1. Thoroughly chill and degrease the consommé.
2. Lightly beat one egg white per litre (quart) of consommé and combine with the cold consommé.
3. Slowly bring the consommé to a simmer, stirring occasionally. Stop stirring when the egg whites begin to coagulate.
4. When the egg whites are completely coagulated, carefully strain the consommé.

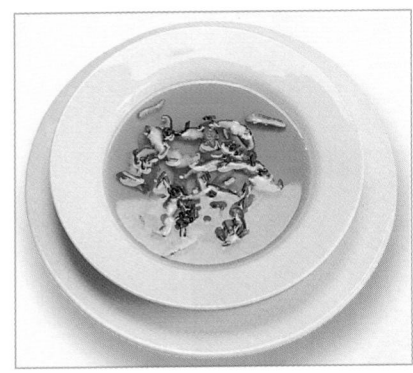

4. The finished consommé.

THICK SOUPS

There are two kinds of thick soups: cream velouté-based soups and purée soups. In general, cream velouté-based soups are thickened with a roux, while purée soups rely on a purée of the main ingredient for thickening. But in certain ways the two soups are very similar: some purée soups are finished with cream, and rice or potatoes may be used to help thicken the soup.

Cream Soups

Traditionally, cream soups were made with a thin béchamel. Velouté-based soups were finished with a liaison. Modern practice is to use a velouté base for cream soups and finish the soup with cream. The final strained product should have a smooth consistency similar to heavy cream, and may have a purée of the flavouring vegetables incorporated or recognizable pieces of the predominant vegetable flavour cooked separately and added as garnish (for example, cauliflower florets or slices of mushroom). Exercise caution when preparing cream soups from leafy greens; they will discolour badly if overcooked.

Two approaches are generally used in preparing a cream soup. The first is to sweat the aromatics and identifying vegetable and then add a hot velouté (or béchamel) and simmer to extract the flavours before straining. A second approach is to add flour to the sweated vegetables to make a white roux, then add hot stock and simmer to cook out the starch. The soup is strained and finished as desired. The cream or béchamel added to finish the soup must be heated before adding to maintain the temperature of the soup. If the soup is to be chilled for reconstitution later, do not add the cream or béchamel, as it shortens shelf life.

continued

Classic Velouté Soups

Velouté Agnès Sorel—Chicken velouté with mushrooms, julienne of mushrooms, white of chicken, ox tongue and liaison.

Bagration-Maigre—Fish velouté flavoured with mushrooms, julienne of sole, quenelles of white fish and crayfish, crayfish and liaison.

Classic Cream Soups

Crème Dubarry—Cauliflower
Crème de Céleri—Celery
Crème de Tomates—Tomato
Crème Solfèrino—Tomato and potato
Crème Portugaise—Tomato and rice
Crème Palestine—Artichoke
Crème Soubise—White onion
Crème de Poireaux—Leek

BASIC PROCEDURE FOR MAKING CREAM SOUPS

1. In a soup pot, sweat the mirepoix with firm chopped vegetables of choice (asparagus, broccoli, carrots, squash, etc.) in butter or oil without browning.
2. If using stock, add flour and cook out to a white roux stage before adding hot stock. Or, add hot velouté (or béchamel) and bring to a boil.

3. Simmer to cook out the roux and flavouring vegetables, approximately 30 to 40 minutes. Skim as needed. If making a soup with leafy greens, add them in the last 10 minutes of simmering.

4. Strain the soup into a clean pot and purée the mirepoix (use a blender, vertical chopper mixer [VCM], food processor or food mill) and flavouring vegetable, if returning to the soup.

5. Bring the soup back to a simmer and add either the purée and/or blanched pieces of garnishing vegetables. Adjust the consistency with hot stock or milk, if needed.

6. Finish the soup with hot cream or béchamel and adjust the seasoning for service.

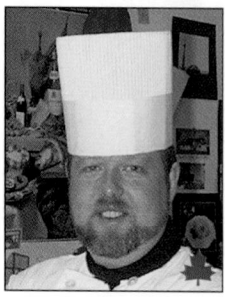

Anthony Bevan, CCC

Anthony is a native of Ireland, where he was Executive Chef at several five-star restaurants and chef-owner of Knocklofty House in Tipperary. He arrived in Canada in 1987 and played a major role in the development of Canada's first aboriginal culinary program. He currently teaches at Georgian College—Owen Sound.

Eric King

Born in Newfoundland, Eric started cooking at age 18 with the Canadian Air Force in Gander. After completing his cooking certification, he operated a bakery/restaurant and catering company before accepting a teaching position at the College of the North Atlantic. Eric has won medals in culinary competitions around the world and is an honorary member of the European Chefs Association.

RECIPE 11.4

Approximate values per 250 mL serving:	
Calories	228
Total fat	17 g
Saturated fat	10 g
Cholesterol	48 mg
Sodium	38 mg
Total carbohydrates	18 g
Protein	3.4 g

APPLYING THE BASICS   **RECIPE 11.4**

Cream of Mushroom Soup

SCHOOL OF HOSPITALITY, TOURISM AND RECREATION STUDIES,
GEORGIAN COLLEGE, OWEN SOUND, ON
Anthony Bevan, CCC

Yield: 2.5 L (2-1/2 qt.) (10 servings)

White mirepoix: onion, leek and celery	250 g	8 oz.
Butter	125 g	4 oz.
Mushrooms, stalks removed and retained	500 g	1 lb.
Flour, pastry	125 g	4 oz.
Chicken stock, warm	2.5 L	2.5 qt.
Sachet	1	1
Cream, 35%	150 mL	5 fl. oz.
Salt and pepper	TT	TT
Optional additions:		
White wine	90 mL	3 fl. oz.
or		
Dijon mustard	10 mL	2 tsp.
or		
Egg yolks (for liaison)	2	2

1. Sweat mirepoix in butter with mushroom stems. Do not brown.

2. Remove from heat, add flour and return to moderate heat and cook for 1 minute, stirring continuously. Remove from heat again.

3. Stir in warm chicken stock in 3 stages, bring to a boil and reduce to a simmer.

4. Add sachet and cook 30–40 minutes.

5. Strain the soup into a clean pot and bring back to a boil. Add wine or Dijon if using the optional additions.

6. Add sliced mushroom caps and return to a simmer for 10 minutes.

7. Add cream (or liaison) and adjust seasoning.

VARIATION: Varietal mushrooms may be used alone or in combination. Some chefs fine-chop or purée some of the mushrooms for more even distribution. If using a liaison to finish any cream soup, remember that it cannot be reboiled or the soup will curdle. Different primary vegetables may be substituted for the mushrooms to make other cream of vegetable soups—for example, broccoli, cauliflower, carrot or tomato.

Chef Eric King of the College of the North Atlantic in Newfoundland makes a similar Cream of Mushroom Soup with a slightly different spin: instead of white wine, add 60 mL (2 fl. oz.) of sherry.

Purée Soups

Purée soups are hearty soups made by cooking starchy vegetables or legumes in a stock or broth, then puréeing all or a portion of them to thicken the soup. The primary difference is that unlike cream soups, which are thickened with roux, purée soups generally do not use additional starch for thickening. Rather, purée soups depend on the starch content of the main ingredient for thickening. When finishing purée soups with cream, follow the guidelines discussed earlier for adding cream to cream soups.

Purée soups can be made with dried or fresh beans such as peas, lentils and navy beans, or with any number of vegetables including cauliflower, celery root, turnips, squashes and potatoes. Diced potatoes or rice are often used to help thicken vegetable purée soups.

BASIC PROCEDURE FOR MAKING PURÉE SOUPS

1. Sweat the mirepoix in butter or fat without browning.
2. Add the stock or cooking liquid.
3. Add the main ingredients and a sachet or bouquet garni.
4. Bring to a boil, reduce to a simmer and cook until all the ingredients are soft enough to purée easily. Skim as required. Remove and discard the sachet or bouquet garni.
5. Reserve a portion of the liquid to adjust the soup's consistency. Purée the rest of the soup by passing it through a food mill, food processor, blender or VCM.
6. Add enough of the reserved liquid to bring the soup to the correct consistency. If the soup is still too thick, add hot liquid as needed.
7. Return the soup to a simmer and adjust the seasonings and add any garnishes.
8. Add hot cream to the soup if desired.

Classic Purée Soups

Potage St. Germain—Green pea
Potage Crècy—Carrot
Potage Soissonnaise—Haricot bean
Potage Bonne Femme—Potato and leek
Potage Freneuse—Turnip
Potage Cressonière—Potato and watercress

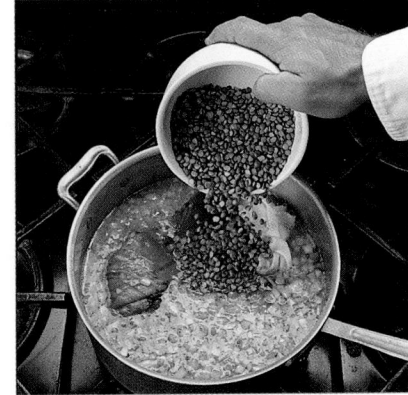

1. Purée of Split Pea Soup: Adding peas to the stockpot.

APPLYING THE BASICS   RECIPE 11.5

Purée of Split Pea Soup

Yield: 4 L (4 qt.)

Split peas, washed and soaked	800 g	1 lb. 12 oz.
Salt pork or bacon, diced	100 g	3 oz.
Mirepoix, medium dice	500 g	1 lb.
Garlic cloves, chopped	10 g	2
White stock	3 L	3 qt.
Ham hocks or meaty ham bones	700 g	1-1/2 lb.
Sachet:		
Bay leaves	2	2
Dried thyme	0.25 g	1/2 tsp.
Peppercorns, crushed	0.5 g	1/2 tsp.
Salt and pepper	TT	TT
Croutons, sautéed in butter	as needed for garnish	

1. Soak peas in water overnight.
2. In a stockpot, render the salt pork or bacon by cooking it slowly and allowing it to release its fat; sweat the mirepoix and garlic in the fat without browning them.

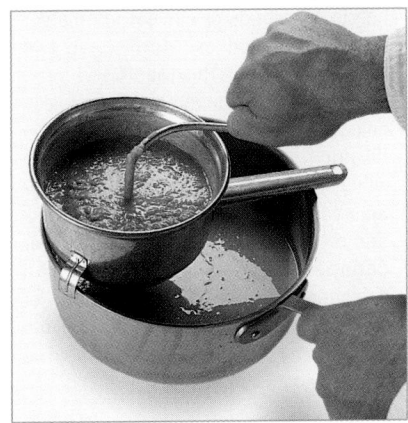

2. Puréeing the split pea soup.

continued

RECIPE 11.5

Approximate values per 175 mL serving:	
Calories	228
Total fat	6.9 g
Saturated fat	2.3 g
Cholesterol	23 mg
Sodium	109 mg
Total carbohydrates	26 g
Protein	16 g

3. Add the white stock, drained peas, ham hocks or bones and sachet. Bring to a boil, reduce to a simmer and cook until the peas are soft, approximately 1–1.5 hours.

4. Remove the sachet and ham hocks or bones. Pass the soup through a food mill and return it to the stockpot.

5. Remove the meat from the hocks or bones. Cut the meat into a medium dice and add it to the soup.

6. Bring the soup to a simmer and, if necessary, adjust the consistency by adding hot stock. Adjust the seasonings with salt and pepper and serve, garnished with croutons.

NOTE: White beans, yellow peas and other dried beans or lentils can be soaked overnight in water and used instead of split peas.

Adjusting the Consistency of Thick Soups

Cream and purée soups tend to thicken when made in advance and refrigerated. To dilute a portion being reheated, add a small amount of stock, broth or milk.

If the soup is too thin, additional roux, beurre manié or cornstarch mixed with cool stock can be used to thicken it. If additional starch is added to thicken the soup, it should be used sparingly and the soup should be simmered a few minutes to cook out the starchy flavour. A liaison of egg yolks and heavy cream can be used to finish cream soups when added richness is also desired. Remember, the soup must not boil after the liaison is added or it may curdle.

OTHER SOUPS

Several popular types of soup do not fit the descriptions of or follow the procedures for clear or thick soups. Soups such as bisques and chowders as well as many cold soups use special methods or a combination of the methods used for clear and thick soups.

Bisques

Traditionally, bisques were made from shellfish (crustaceans) or game, and thickened with cooked rice and the pulverized shells or bones (then strained through cheesecloth). Modern bisques are usually prepared using a combination of cream and purée soup methods without pulverizing the shells, but simmering for extended time periods. Roux is often the preferred thickener, as it produces a smoother-textured end product without the graininess imparted by rice. The term *bisque* is sometimes used to describe puréed vegetable soups (squash, for example).

Bisques are enriched with cream and may be mounted with butter (*monter au beurre*) for added richness. The garnish should be the diced flesh of the appropriate shellfish. Note that there are many traditional recipes for bisques and the base ingredients vary widely.

Croutons

A crouton is simply a piece of bread that is toasted, sautéed or dried. Two types are often used.

The more familiar ones are small seasoned cubes of bread that are baked or toasted and sprinkled over soups or salads.

A more classic variety is made by sautéing slices of bread in clarified butter or olive oil until brown and crisp. The bread may be rough slices from a baguette or cut into shapes (such as hearts, diamonds or circles) from larger slices. Sautéed croutons have two advantages over the toasted variety: They stay crisp longer after coming in contact with moist foods, and they gain flavour from the butter or olive oil in which they are cooked. Sautéed croutons can be used to decorate the border of a serving dish, as a base for canapés, a garnish for soups, an accompaniment to spreads or caviar or a base under some meat and game dishes. Dry toasted croutons may be referred to as sippets.

BASIC PROCEDURE FOR MAKING BISQUES

1. Sweat the mirepoix and crustacean shells in butter.

2. Flambé with brandy.

continued

3. Add tomato product, stock, wine, sachet and rice. Bring to a boil. Simmer and skim as needed until rice is soft.

4. Pass the mixture through a food mill, discarding larger pieces of shell.

5. Strain into a clean pot and return to a simmer. Adjust the consistency.

6. Finish with hot cream, mount with butter if desired and garnish with diced shellfish.

NOTE: A shrimp or lobster compound butter may be used for mounting. If desired, 100 mL (4 fl. oz.) of sherry may be added to 4 L (1 gallon) of soup just before service.

APPLYING THE BASICS   **RECIPE 11.6**

Lobster Bisque Scented with Vanilla and Basil

JW'S STEAKHOUSE, TORONTO, ON
Executive Chef Morgan Wilson

Yield: 2 L (2 qt.)

Ingredient	Metric	US
Lobster shells	2 kg	4-1/2 lb.
Olive oil, extra virgin	50 mL	2 fl. oz.
Brandy	200 mL	7 fl. oz.
Mirepoix (carrot, onion, celery, fennel)	500 g	1 lb.
Tomato paste	250 g	8 oz.
Vermouth	250 mL	8 fl. oz.
White wine, dry	750 mL	26 fl. oz.
White stock	4 L	4 qt.
Sachet	1	1
Rice, long grain	75 g	2-1/2 oz.
Basil	20 g	3/4 oz.
Vanilla bean, split	1	1
Cream, 35%	750 mL	26 fl. oz.
Sea salt	TT	TT
Black pepper, fresh	TT	TT
Lemon juice, fresh	TT	TT
Butter, unsalted, cold, cubed	150 g	5 oz.

1. Remove and discard any stomachs and bile sacs from lobster bodies. Rinse shells and chop roughly into 7–8-cm (3-in.) pieces.

2. Place shells on baking sheets and roast in a 180°C (375°F) oven until red and dry.

3. Preheat a large rondeau and add the olive oil and shells. Sauté for another minute and flame with brandy.

4. Add the mirepoix and sauté until tender.

5. Add the tomato paste and sweat.

6. Deglaze with vermouth, reduce au sec, add the white wine and reduce by one-third.

7. Add the stock and sachet and bring to a simmer for 1 hour. Skim often.

8. Add the rice and simmer 1 hour more.

9. Discard the large pieces of shell and pass the remaining mixture through a food mill.

10. Purée the bisque and strain through a fine etâmine.

11. Steep the basil and vanilla bean in the cream for 10 minutes, remove and add the cream to the bisque. Bring back to a simmer and adjust the seasoning with salt, pepper and lemon juice.

12. Mount with the butter. The bisque may be frothed with a wand mixer just before serving.

RECIPE 11.6

Approximate values per 200 mL serving:	
Calories	1130
Total fat	48 g
Saturated fat	26 g
Cholesterol	131 mg
Sodium	138 mg
Total carbohydrates	139 g
Protein	20 g

Chowders

Although chowders are usually associated with the eastern seaboard, where fish and clams are plentiful, they are of French origin. Undoubtedly the word *chowder* is derived from the Breton phrase *faire chaudière*, which means to make a fish stew in a cauldron. The procedure was probably brought to Nova Scotia by French settlers and later introduced into New England.

Chowders are hearty soups with chunks of the main ingredients (virtually always including diced potatoes) and garnishes. With some exceptions (notably Manhattan clam chowder), chowders contain milk or cream. Although there are thin chowders, most chowders are thickened with roux. The procedures for making chowders are similar to those for making cream soups except that chowders are not puréed and strained before the cream is added.

BASIC PROCEDURE FOR MAKING CHOWDERS

1. Render finely diced salt pork over medium heat.
2. Sweat mirepoix in the rendered pork.
3. Add flour to make a roux.
4. Add the liquid.
5. Add the seasoning and flavouring ingredients according to their cooking times.
6. Simmer, skimming as needed.
7. Add milk or cream.

New England–Style Clam Chowder

APPLYING THE BASICS   RECIPE 11.7

New England–Style Clam Chowder

Yield: 3.5 L (3-1/2 qt.)

Salt pork/bacon, diced	250 g	8 oz.
Butter	50 g	2 oz.
Onions, macedoine	100 g	3-1/2 oz.
Celery, macedoine	200 g	7 oz.
Flour, pastry	100 g	3-1/2 oz.
Fish stock, warm	1.5 L	60 fl. oz.
Clam nectar	600 mL	20 fl. oz.
Sachet	1	1
Potatoes, macedoine	125 g	4 oz.
Baby clams, tinned*	700 mL	28 fl. oz.
Cream, 35% or milk	250 mL	8 fl. oz.
Salt and pepper	TT	TT

1. Render salt pork/bacon with butter.
2. Sweat onions and celery until translucent.
3. Add flour and cook roux to white/blond stage.
4. Whisk in heated fish stock until smooth.
5. Stir in clam nectar, add sachet and simmer 15 minutes.

continued

RECIPE 11.7

6. Add potatoes and simmer until tender.

7. Stir in baby clams and juice.

8. Return to simmer, add cream and adjust seasoning.

*If using fresh clams for the chowder, wash and steam approximately 15 L (1/2 bushel) of chowder clams in a small amount of water to yield 1.25 L (1-1/4 qt.) of clam meat. Chop the clams. Strain the liquid through several layers of cheesecloth to remove any sand that may be present. Continue with the recipe, starting at Step 1.

VARIATION: Some chefs add red or green peppers or carrots. Corn is a popular addition in Western Canada. White wine or Pernod may also be added.

Approximate values per 225 mL serving:	
Calories	282
Total fat	24 g
Saturated fat	11 g
Cholesterol	78 mg
Sodium	782 mg
Total carbohydrates	9 g
Protein	7.4 g

Cold Soups

Cold soups can be as simple as a chilled version of a cream soup or as unique as a cold fruit soup blended with yogurt. Other than the fact that they are cold, cold soups are difficult to classify because many of them use unique or combination preparation methods. Regardless, they are divided here into two categories: those that require cooking and those that do not.

Cooked Cold Soups

Many cold soups are simply chilled versions of hot soups. For example, Consommé Madrilène and Consommé Portugaise are prepared hot and served cold. Vichyssoise, probably the most popular of all cold soups, is a cold version of purée of potato-leek soup. When serving a hot soup cold, there are several considerations:

1. If the soup is to be creamed, add the cream at the last minute. Although curdling is not as much of a problem as it is with hot soups, adding the cream at the last minute helps extend the soup's shelf life.

2. Cold soups should have a thinner consistency than hot soups. To achieve the proper consistency, use less starch if starch is used as the thickener, or use a higher ratio of liquid to main ingredient if the soup is thickened by puréeing. Consistency should be checked and adjusted at service time.

3. Cold dulls the sense of taste, so cold soups require more seasoning than hot ones. Taste the soup just before service and adjust the seasonings as needed.

4. Always serve cold soups as cold as possible.

SAFETY ALERT

Cooked Cold Soup

Cooked cold soups, especially those made with potatoes, beans, dairy products or other high-protein foods, are potentially hazardous foods and must be chilled quickly and held at or below 4°C (40°F). Because these soups will not be reheated for service, cross-contamination is also a concern. Keep the soup covered and store above any raw meat, poultry or seafood in the cooler.

APPLYING THE BASICS   **RECIPE 11.8**

Vichyssoise (Cold Potato-Leek Soup)

Yield: 2 L (2 qt.)

Leeks, white part only	500 g	1 lb.
Whole butter	125 g	4 oz.
Potatoes, large dice	500 g	1 lb.
Chicken stock	1.75 L	60 fl. oz.
Salt and white pepper	TT	TT
Cream, 35%	350 mL	12 fl. oz.
Chives, snipped	as needed	as needed

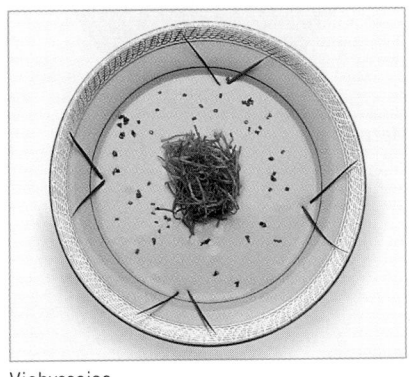
Vichyssoise

continued

RECIPE 11.8

Approximate values per 150 mL serving:	
Calories	256
Total fat	20 g
Saturated fat	12 g
Cholesterol	59 mg
Sodium	416 mg
Total carbohydrates	17 g
Protein	2 g

1. Split the leeks lengthwise and wash well to remove all sand and grit. Slice them thinly.

2. Sweat the leeks in the butter without browning them.

3. Add the potatoes and chicken stock, season with salt and pepper and bring to a simmer.

4. Simmer until the leeks and potatoes are very tender, approximately 45 minutes.

5. Purée the soup in a food processor, blender or food mill; strain through a fine sieve.

6. Chill the soup well.

7. At service time, incorporate the cream and adjust the seasonings. Serve in chilled bowls, garnished with snipped chives.

Many cooked cold soups use fruit juice (typically apple, grape or orange) as a base and are thickened with cornstarch or arrowroot as well as with puréed fruit. For additional flavour, wine is sometimes used in lieu of a portion of the fruit juice. Cinnamon, ginger and other spices that complement fruit are commonly added, as is lemon or lime juice, which adds acidity as well as flavour. Crème fraîche, yogurt or sour cream can be used as an ingredient or garnish to add richness.

Uncooked Cold Soups

Some cold soups are not cooked at all. Rather, they rely only on puréed fruits or vegetables for thickness, body and flavour. Cold stock is sometimes used to adjust the soup's consistency. Dairy products such as cream, sour cream or crème fraîche are sometimes added to enrich and flavour the soup.

Because uncooked cold soups are never heated, enzymes and bacteria are not destroyed and the soup can spoil quickly. When preparing uncooked cold soups, always prepare small batches as close to service time as possible.

Gazpacho

APPLYING THE BASICS   RECIPE 11.9

Gazpacho

Yield: 3 L (3 qt.)

Roma tomato, peeled and diced	500 g	1 lb.
Onion, medium dice	125 g	4 oz.
Green pepper, medium dice	50 g	2 oz.
Red pepper, medium dice	50 g	2 oz.
Cucumber, peeled, seeded, medium dice	250 g	8 oz.
Garlic, minced	15 g	1/2 oz.
Red wine vinegar	50 mL	1-1/2 fl. oz.
Lemon juice	30 mL	1 fl. oz.
Olive oil	50 mL	2 fl. oz.
Salt and pepper	TT	TT
Cayenne pepper	TT	TT
Fresh bread crumbs (optional)	50 g	2 oz.
Tomato or V-8 juice	1.5 L	1-1/2 qt.

continued

White stock	as needed	as needed
Garnish:		
Tomato, peeled, seeded,		
small dice	125 g	4 oz.
Red pepper, small dice	60 g	2 oz.
Green pepper, small dice	60 g	2 oz.
Yellow pepper, small dice	60 g	2 oz.
Cucumber, peeled, seeded,		
small dice	60 g	2 oz.
Green onion, sliced fine	30 g	1 oz.
Croutons	as needed	as needed

1. Combine and purée all ingredients except the tomato juice, stock and garnish in a VCM, food processor or blender.

2. Stir in the tomato juice.

3. Adjust the consistency with stock.

4. Stir in the vegetable garnishes and adjust the seasonings.

5. Serve in chilled cups or bowls garnished with croutons.

VARIATION: Gazpacho can be made without puréeing the ingredients. Use a small dice for everything.

RECIPE 11.9

Approximate values per 150 mL serving:	
Calories	56
Total fat	2.5 g
Saturated fat	0.3 g
Cholesterol	0 mg
Sodium	476 mg
Total carbohydrates	7.1 g
Protein	1.2 g

GARNISHING SOUPS

Garnishes can range from a simple sprinkle of chopped parsley on a bowl of cream soup to tiny profiteroles stuffed with foie gras adorning a crystal-clear bowl of consommé. Some soups are so full of attractive, flavourful and colourful foods that are integral parts of the soup (for example, vegetables and chicken in chicken vegetable soup) that no additional garnishes are necessary as either decoration or component. In others, the garnish determines the type of soup. For example, a beef broth garnished with cooked barley and diced beef becomes beef barley soup. See Table 11.1 on the next page.

Guidelines for Garnishing Soups

Although some soups (particularly consommés) have traditional garnishes, many soups depend on the chef's imagination and the kitchen's inventory for the finishing garnish. The only rules are as follows:

1. The garnish should be attractive and not hang over the spoon.

2. The meats and vegetables used should be neatly cut into an appropriate and uniform shape and size. This is particularly important when garnishing a clear soup such as a consommé, as the consommé's clarity highlights the precise (or imprecise) cuts.

3. The garnish's texture and flavour should complement the soup.

4. Starches and vegetables used as garnishes should be cooked separately, reheated and placed in the soup bowl before the hot soup is added. If they are cooked in the soup, they may cloud or thicken the soup or alter its flavour, texture and seasoning.

5. Garnishes should be cooked just until done; meat and poultry should be tender but not falling apart, vegetables should be firm but not mushy and

---

SAFETY ALERT

Uncooked Cold Soup

Because uncooked cold soups are never heated, enzymes and bacteria are not destroyed and the soup can spoil quickly. Many cold soups also contain dairy products, which makes them a potentially hazardous food. When preparing uncooked cold soups, always prepare small batches as close to service time as possible. Keep the soup at or below 4°C (40°F) at all times. Cover and store leftovers properly.

TABLE 11.1	Soups: Their Thickening Agents and Finishes		
Category	**Type**	**Thickening Agent or Method**	**Finish**
Clear soups	Broths	None	Assorted garnishes; any combination of julienne cuts of the same meat, poultry, fish or vegetable that provides the dominant flavour in the stock or broth, vegetables (cut uniformly into any shape), pasta (flat, small tortellini or tiny ravioli), gnocchi, quenelles, barley, spaetzle, white or wild rice, croutons, crepes, tortillas, or won tons
	Consommés	Usually none	Assorted garnishes
Thick soups	Cream soups	Roux	Assorted garnishes, cream or béchamel sauce; toasted slivered almonds, sour cream or crème fraîche, croutons, grated cheese or puff pastry fleurons; cream vegetable soups are usually garnished with slices or florets of the main ingredient
	Purée soups	Puréeing	Assorted garnishes; cream is optional; julienne cuts of poultry or ham, sliced sausage, croutons, grated cheese, bacon bits
Other soups	Bisques	Roux or rice and puréeing	Garnish of main ingredient, cream and/or butter
	Chowders	Roux	Cream
Cold soups	Cooked cold soups	Arrowroot, cornstarch, puréeing, sour cream, yogurt	Assorted garnishes, cream, crème fraîche or sour cream
	Uncooked cold soups	Puréeing	Assorted garnishes, cream, crème fraîche or sour cream
Any soup			Finely chopped fresh herbs, snipped chives, edible flower blossoms or petals, parsley or watercress

pasta and rice should maintain their identity. These types of garnishes are usually held on the side and added to the hot soup at the last minute to prevent overcooking.

SOUP SERVICE
Preparing Soups in Advance

Most soups can be made ahead of time and reheated as needed for service. To preserve freshness and quality, small batches of soup should be heated as needed throughout the meal service.

Clear soups are quite easy to reheat because there is little danger of scorching. If garnishes are already added to a clear soup, care should be taken not to overcook the garnishes when reheating the soup. All traces of fat should be removed from a consommé's surface before reheating.

Thick soups present more of a challenge. To increase shelf life and reduce the risk of spoilage, cool and refrigerate a thick soup when it is still a base (that is, before it is finished with milk or cream). When needed, carefully reheat the soup base just before service using a heavy-gauge pot over low heat. Stir often to prevent scorching and to rethermalize the soup more quickly. Then finish the soup (following the guidelines noted earlier) with boiling milk or cream, a light béchamel sauce or a liaison and adjust the seasonings. Always taste the soup after reheating and adjust the seasonings as needed.

A cream soup served in small glasses as a passed hors d'oeuvre.

Temperatures

The rule is simple: serve hot soup hot and cold soup cold. Hot clear soups should be served near boiling. Hot cream soups should be served at slightly lower temperatures: 90°C to 93°C (190°F to 200°F) is acceptable. Cold soups should be served at a temperature of 4°C (40°F) or below. Preheating or chilling service bowls is required.

Conclusion

Soup, often served as the first course, may determine the success or failure of an entire meal. Although a wide variety of ingredients can be used to make both clear and thick soups, including trimmings and leftovers, poor-quality ingredients make poor-quality soups. By using, adapting and combining the basic techniques described in this chapter with different ingredients, you can create an infinite number of new and appetizing hot or cold soups. But exercise good judgment when combining flavours and techniques; they should blend well and complement each other. Moreover, any garnishes that are added should contribute to the appearance and character of the finished soup. And remember, always serve hot soups hot and cold soups cold.

Questions for Discussion

1. What are the differences between a stock and a broth?
2. What are the differences between a beef consommé and a beef-based broth? How are they similar?
3. What are the differences between a cream soup and a purée soup? How are they similar?
4. Create a recipe for chicken consommé.
5. Discuss several techniques for serving soup. What can be done to ensure that soups are served at the correct temperature?
6. Explain how and why soups are garnished. Why is it sometimes said that the noodles in a chicken noodle soup are actually a garnish?

Additional Soup Recipes

RECIPE 11.10

French Onion Soup

Yield: 5 L (5 qt.)

Yellow onions, thinly sliced	3 kg	6-1/2 lb.
Garlic	10 g	2 cloves
Olive oil	25 mL	1 fl. oz.
Red wine	100 mL	3 fl. oz.
Brown stock	2.5 L	2-1/2 qt.
Chicken stock	2 L	2 qt.
Fresh thyme leaves	10 g	4 tsp.
Salt and pepper	TT	TT

RECIPE 11.10

Approximate values per 175 mL serving:	
Calories	84
Total fat	2.8 g
Saturated fat	0.9 g
Cholesterol	2.5 mg
Sodium	123 mg
Total carbohydrates	13 g
Protein	2.1 g

continued

| Toasted French bread slices | as needed for garnish |
| Gruyère cheese, grated | as needed for garnish |

1. Sauté the onions and garlic in the olive oil over low heat. Carefully caramelize them thoroughly without burning.

2. Deglaze the pan with the red wine. Cook au sec. The onions will be a very dark, even brown.

3. Add the stocks and thyme.

4. Bring to a simmer and cook 20 minutes to develop flavour. Adjust the seasonings.

5. Serve in warm bowls. Top each portion with a slice of toasted French bread and a thick layer of cheese. Place under the broiler or salamander until the cheese is melted and lightly browned.

VARIATION: Cook 50 g (2 oz.) flour with the cooked onions and moisten with stock. The soup will have a rustic quality with more body. This soup may be made with chicken or beef stock. White wine or sherry may be used. Some chefs use basil or marjoram. Other types of onions or combinations may be used.

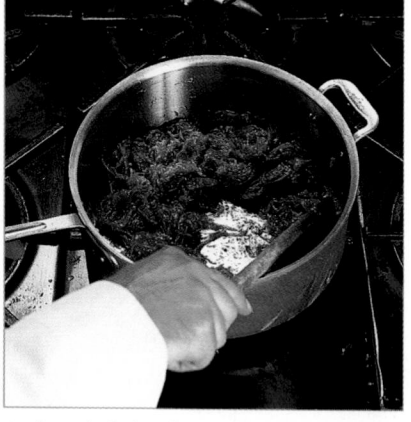

1. French Onion Soup: Caramelizing the onions thoroughly.

2. Sprinkling grated cheese on top of each serving of soup.

3. The finished soup after gratinéeing or baking.

RECIPE 11.11

🍂 Minestrone

Minestrone is a rich vegetable soup of Italian heritage. Northern Italian versions are made with beef stock, butter, rice and ribbon-shaped pasta. Southern Italian versions contain tomatoes, garlic, olive oil and tube-shaped pasta. The vegetables should be fresh and varied. Substitute or change those listed as necessary to reflect the season.

Yield: 4 L (4 qt.)

Dry white beans	150 g	5 oz.
Olive oil	25 mL	1 Tbsp.
Onions, paysanne	125 g	4 oz.
Garlic cloves, minced	5 g	1
Celery, paysanne	150 g	6 oz.
Carrot, paysanne	125 g	4 oz.
Zucchini, diced	250 g	8 oz.
Green beans, cut in 1.25-cm (1/2-in.) pieces	150 g	5 oz.
Cabbage, diced	250 g	8 oz.
White stock	2.5 L	2-1/2 qt.
Tomato concassée	250 g	8 oz.
Tomato paste, low-sodium	30 g	1 oz.
Orzo pasta, cooked	75 g	3 oz.
Fresh oregano, chopped	8 g	2 tsp.
Fresh basil, chopped	10 g	1 Tbsp.

Minestrone

continued

Fresh chervil, chopped	3 g	1 tsp.
Fresh parsley, chopped	20 g	2 Tbsp.
Salt and pepper	TT	TT
Parmesan cheese, grated (optional)	as needed for garnish	

1. Soak the beans in cold water overnight, then drain.

2. Cover the beans with water and simmer until tender, about 40 minutes.

3. Sauté the onions in the oil. Add garlic, celery and carrot and cook for 3 minutes.

4. Add the remaining vegetables, one type at a time, cooking each briefly.

5. Add the stock, tomatoes and tomato paste. Simmer for 45 minutes.

6. Add the drained beans and orzo pasta.

7. Stir in the chopped herbs and season to taste with salt and pepper.

8. Bring the soup to a simmer and simmer 15 minutes. Serve in warm bowls, garnished with Parmesan cheese.

NOTE: If substituting dry herbs, use one-third the amount.

RECIPE 11.11

Approximate values per 250 mL serving:

Calories	127
Total fat	4.0 g
Saturated fat	0.9 g
Cholesterol	1.1 mg
Sodium	406 mg
Total carbohydrates	19 g
Protein	3.7 g

RECIPE 11.12

Hungarian Gulyás Soup

Yield: 2.25 L (2-1/4 qt.)

Vegetable oil	100 mL	3-1/2 fl. oz.
Garlic, minced	20 g	4–5 cloves
Onion, macedoine	300 g	11 oz.
Caraway seeds, chopped	2.5 g	1 tsp.
Hungarian paprika	75 g	2/3 cup
Cayenne	1 g	1/4 tsp.
Beef shank, 6-mm cubes	400 g	14 oz.
Tomato purée	40 g	1-1/2 fl. oz.
Brown stock	2.75 L	2-3/4 qt.
Red wine vinegar	20 mL	4 tsp.
Red peppers, macedoine	110 g	4 oz.
Red potatoes, peeled, macedoine	250 g	8 oz.
Marjoram, ground	2.5 g	1 tsp.
Salt	15 g	1 Tbsp.
Black pepper, ground	5 g	2 tsp.
Spaetzle (3 eggs) (see Recipe 23.29)	250 g	8 oz.
Parsley, chopped	30 g	1 oz.

1. Heat oil in a heavy-bottomed brazier. Sweat garlic, onion and caraway.

2. Remove from heat and stir in paprika and cayenne thoroughly. Add drained beef and stir to coat meat. Return to heat and gently fry until mixture starts to dry. Exercise caution, as the mixture will burn easily.

3. Stir in tomato purée, brown stock and red wine vinegar. Bring to a boil and simmer for 1.5–2 hours until meat begins to tenderize.

4. Add peppers, potatoes, marjoram, salt and pepper. Simmer until potatoes are tender.

5. Add cooked spaetzle and chopped parsley. Adjust seasoning.

VARIATIONS: White stock may be used in this recipe. Mushrooms may be added, and it is common for smoked bacon or ham to be included as well.

RECIPE 11.12

Approximate values per 250 mL serving:

Calories	370
Total fat	20 g
Saturated fat	3.7 g
Cholesterol	100 mg
Sodium	761 mg
Total carbohydrates	29 g
Protein	21 g

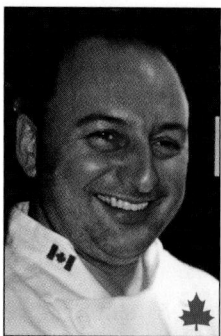

Larry Stewart, CCC

In 1996, Larry established Hardware Grill in Edmonton, an A-list dining spot with a reputation that travels beyond city and province. Providing excellent food, an award-winning wine list, outstanding service and serious respect for the history of Canadian cuisine, Chef/Owner Larry Stewart and his wife, Melinda, are pioneers in the development of a real Prairie food culture. His restaurant has a two-star rating in *Where to Eat in Canada* and has won *Wine Spectator's* Best Award of Excellence.

RECIPE 11.13

Approximate values per 175 mL serving:	
Calories	182
Total fat	9.3 g
Saturated fat	3.7 g
Cholesterol	12 mg
Sodium	249 mg
Total carbohydrates	19 g
Protein	5.5 g

RECIPE 11.13

Prairie Black Bean Soup with Cilantro Sour Cream

HARDWARE GRILL, EDMONTON, AB
Chef/Owner Larry Stewart, CCC

Yield: 5 L (5 qt.)

Dried black beans, washed	500 g	1 lb.
Chicken stock	4 L	4 qt.
Double-smoked bacon, diced	250 g	8 oz.
Onion, macedoine	175 g	6 oz.
Carrot, macedoine	175 g	6 oz.
Celery, macedoine	175 g	6 oz.
Garlic, minced	30 g	1-1/2 Tbsp.
Cumin, ground	2 g	1 tsp.
Chilli powder	25 g	3 Tbsp.
Cayenne pepper	0.25 g	1/3 tsp.
Salt	10 g	2 tsp.
Black pepper	2.5 g	1 tsp.

1. Combine the beans and stock and bring to a simmer, covered, for 2 hours.
2. Remove half of the beans from the pot with a slotted spoon. Purée in a food processor and return to the pot.
3. Add the remaining ingredients and simmer, covered, for 1 hour.
4. Serve in warmed bowls garnished with dollops of Cilantro Sour Cream (recipe follows).

Cilantro Sour Cream

Yield: 400 mL (14 fl. oz.)

Sour cream	250 mL	8 oz.
Cilantro, chopped	1 bunch	1 bunch
Lime juice	30 mL	1 fl. oz.
Roma tomato, diced	100 g	3 oz.

Combine all ingredients.

Photo by George Webber

Simon Dunn, CCC

Born and classically trained in Great Britain, Simon was most recently the Executive Chef at The Inn on Lake Bonavista, which was ranked as one of the top 100 restaurants in Canada for the duration of his tenure. Simon cooked for members of the British royal family during his career in the Royal Air Force and is currently a chef instructor at SAIT.

RECIPE 11.14

Celery and Quebec Blue Cheese (Bénédictin) Soup

SAIT POLYTECHNIC, CALGARY, AB
Chef Instructor Simon Dunn, CCC

Yield: 3 L (3 qt.)

Butter	100 g	3-1/2 oz.
Flour	125 g	4 oz.
Chicken stock, warm	3 L	3 qt.
Celery, macedoine	1 kg	2 lb.
Onion, macedoine	500 g	1 lb.
Butter	250 g	8 oz.

continued

Cream, 35%	150 mL	6 fl. oz.
Salt and white pepper	TT	TT
Bénédictin, crumbled	200 g	7 oz.

1. Prepare a blond roux.

2. Add warm chicken stock to make a velouté.

3. Sweat celery and onion in butter until tender. Add to velouté. Simmer for 10 minutes.

4. Blend in cream and adjust seasoning with salt and pepper.

5. Finish with crumbled Bénédictin (or substitute Stilton) or half the amount of Ermite.

RECIPE 11.14

Approximate values per 175 mL serving:

Calories	321
Total fat	26 g
Saturated fat	15 g
Cholesterol	67 mg
Sodium	531 mg
Total carbohydrates	17 g
Protein	4.8 g

RECIPE 11.15

Hot and Sour Soup

Yield: 3.25 L (3-1/2 qt.)

Shiitake mushrooms, stems removed, sliced thinly	8	8
Bamboo shoot, julienne	150 g	5-1/2 oz.
Green onion, bias cut	6	6
Peanut oil	75 mL	2-1/2 fl. oz.
Malt vinegar	150 mL	5-1/2 fl. oz.
White pepper, ground	8 g	1 Tbsp.
Soy sauce	40 mL	3 Tbsp.
Sambal olek (fresh, crushed chiles)	10 mL	2 tsp.
Sesame oil	10 mL	2 tsp.
Chicken stock, hot	3 L	3 qt.
Pork roast, diced or strips	150 g	5-1/2 oz.
Shrimp, raw, cleaned, diced	150 g	5-1/2 oz.
Salt	3 g	1/2 tsp.
Cornstarch, modified	50 g	2 oz.
Bean curd, cubed	150 g	5-1/2 oz.
Eggs, beaten	3	3

1. Sweat shiitake, bamboo shoot and green onion in peanut oil for 1 minute. Remove from heat.

2. Add vinegar, pepper, soy sauce, sambal and sesame oil. Reserve until ready to assemble soup.

3. Add hot chicken stock to reserved base mixture and bring to a boil. Add pork, shrimp and salt and simmer 1 minute.

4. Dissolve starch in a little water and stir into soup. Simmer for 2 minutes to thicken.

5. Add bean curd and swirl soup while pouring in beaten egg. Stop stirring and allow egg to set in streaks. Do not stir or reboil.

RECIPE 11.15

Approximate values per 250 mL serving:

Calories	170
Total fat	10 g
Saturated fat	2.2 g
Cholesterol	71 mg
Sodium	393 mg
Total carbohydrates	11 g
Protein	9 g

Rudi Fischbacher, CCC
Rudi trained in his native Austria and worked in Switzerland, Sweden, Spain and Germany before coming to Canada, where he started with the Fairmont Royal York Hotel. He currently is the Culinary Coordinator at Humber College and was part of the team that developed the Certified Master Chef program for the CCFCC.

RECIPE 11.16

Approximate values per 175 mL serving:	
Calories	308
Total fat	26 g
Saturated fat	23 g
Cholesterol	0 mg
Sodium	218 mg
Total carbohydrates	14 g
Protein	4.4 g

Robert Matthews
The year Bob began his professional chef training was also the year he represented Canada on the Men's Olympic Cycling Team. Twenty years later, he's an Olympic competitor in the culinary arena! After completing the Professional Cooking Program at the Southern Alberta Institute of Technology, Bob worked in Canada and abroad until finally becoming Personal Chef to the Canadian Ambassador for Japan, a position he held for five years. He returned to Canada in 1999 and became chef/co-owner of the highly regarded La Chaumière.

RECIPE 11.16

Thai Mushroom and Coconut Soup

HUMBER COLLEGE, TORONTO, ON
Culinary Arts Program Coordinator Rudi Fischbacher, CCC

Yield: 650 mL (24 fl. oz.)

Coconut milk	500 mL	16 fl. oz.
Ginger, minced	20 g	3/4 oz.
Garlic, puréed	5 g	2 cloves
Lemon grass, chopped	1 stalk	1 stalk
Kaffir leaves	4	4
Brown sugar	15 g	1 Tbsp.
Crushed chile/Sambal olek	2 g	1/2 tsp.
Cilantro root, chopped	10 g	2 tsp.
Mushroom caps, sliced	250 g	9 oz.
Salt and pepper	TT	TT
Lime juice, fresh	125 mL	4-1/2 fl. oz.
Cilantro leaves, chiffonade	1/2 bunch	1/2 bunch

1. Place first 8 ingredients in a sauce pot and bring to a boil. Simmer 5 minutes.
2. Strain and add mushrooms. Simmer 5–10 minutes. Adjust seasoning.
3. Add lime juice and cilantro leaves just before serving.

RECIPE 11.17

Melon Soup with Crisp Pancetta, Arugula and Borage

LA CHAUMIÈRE, CALGARY, AB
Chef/Co-Owner Robert Matthews

Yield: 1.25 L (44 fl. oz.)

Watermelon, skinless, seeded	1 kg	2-1/4 lb.
Salt and white pepper	TT	TT
Mint leaves, fine dice	10 g	1 Tbsp.
Lemon juice	50 mL	3 Tbsp.
Arugula leaves, stalk removed	10	10
Borage leaves, core spine removed	10	10
Cantaloupe, balls	10	10
Muskmelon, balls	10	10
Honeydew, balls	10	10
Port wine	20 mL	4 tsp.
Pancetta, crisp	50 g	1-1/2 oz.
Borage blossoms	30	30

1. Purée watermelon until smooth. Pass through sieve.
2. Season melon with salt, pepper, mint and lemon juice. Chill until very cold.
3. Cut arugula and borage leaves into fine chiffonade.
4. Marinate melon balls in port.

continued

RECIPE 11.17

Approximate values per 125 mL soup serving with 30 g melon balls:	
Calories	85
Total fat	3 g
Saturated fat	1 g
Cholesterol	4.3 mg
Sodium	670 mg
Total carbohydrates	12 g
Protein	2.6 g

5. To serve, ladle soup into rimmed soup plates. Set a complement of 3 melon balls in each plate. Set chiffonade in centre. Sprinkle with pancetta and borage blossoms.

NOTE: Borage is a Mediterranean herb with blue flowers and a cool, cucumber taste.

RECIPE 11.18

Strawberry Soup

Yield: 750 mL (25 fl. oz.)

Strawberries, washed, hulled	1 basket	1 basket
Sugar	50 g	2 oz.
Balsamic vinegar	25 mL	1 fl. oz.
Orange juice	100 mL	4 fl. oz.
Red wine	50 mL	2 fl. oz.
Orange liqueur	25 mL	1 fl. oz.
Cream, 18%	250 mL	8 fl. oz.
Crème fraîche	as needed	as needed
Strawberry pieces	as needed	as needed
Orange fillets	as needed	as needed
Mint sprigs	as needed	as needed

1. Place strawberries, sugar, balsamic vinegar, orange juice and red wine in food processor and blend until smooth.

2. Transfer to a bowl, stir in liqueur and cream and chill thoroughly.

3. For service, place a portion of the soup in a rimmed soup plate, drizzle with crème fraîche and arrange fruit and mint.

RECIPE 11.18

Approximate values per 175 mL serving:	
Calories	237
Total fat	12 g
Saturated fat	7.1 g
Cholesterol	39 mg
Sodium	28 mg
Total carbohydrates	27 g
Protein	2.5 g

RECIPE 11.19

Cream of Fennel and Gruyère Soup Scented with Sherry

FAIRMONT ROYAL YORK, TORONTO, ON
Executive Chef David Garcelon, CCC

Yield: 5 L (5 qt.)

Butter	375 g	12 oz.
Fennel, sliced	750 g	1 lb. 8 oz.
Onion, diced	375 g	12 oz.
Flour	375 g	12 oz.
Chicken stock, warm	4 L	4 qt.
Cream, 35%	1 L	1 qt.
Salt and pepper	TT	TT
Fennel, julienne	300 g	10 oz.
Gruyère, grated	450 g	1 lb.
Sherry	125 mL	4 fl. oz.

David Garcelon, CCC
A graduate of the Culinary Institute of Canada, David worked in Vancouver and Toronto before becoming Executive Chef at both Fairmont's Jasper Park Lodge and Delta's Lodge at Kananaskis. He then traded in his skis for sandals and snorkel gear to become an Executive Chef in Bermuda before moving back to Canada.

continued

RECIPE 11.19

Approximate values per 150 mL serving:	
Calories	338
Total fat	27 g
Saturated fat	16 g
Cholesterol	83 mg
Sodium	362 mg
Total carbohydrates	17 g
Protein	6.7 g

1. Melt butter in a pot. Sweat fennel and onions.
2. Add flour and cook out roux.
3. Add warm stock, stirring constantly. Bring to a boil and simmer until vegetables are tender.
4. Purée soup in a food processor.
5. Add cream, seasoning and julienne of fennel.
6. Whisk in the cheese and finish with sherry.
7. Serve immediately.

Christopher Ennew, CCC
Born and raised in Toronto, Chef Christopher Ennew attended Castle Frank High School before going on to George Brown College, where he earned his Red Seal Certificate. In 1990, Christopher became a Certified Chef de Cuisine. The past seven years Christopher has been the Executive Chef at Ste. Anne's Spa in Grafton. He is also a member of the Advisory Board of Liaison College of the Culinary Arts in Ontario.

RECIPE 11.20

Approximate values per 150 mL serving:	
Calories	365
Total fat	17 g
Saturated fat	1.6 g
Cholesterol	0 mg
Sodium	225 mg
Total carbohydrates	55 g
Protein	2.7 g

RECIPE 11.20

Pear and Parsnip Soup

STE. ANNE'S, A HALDIMAND HILLS SPA GRAFTON, GRAFTON, ON
Executive Chef Christopher Ennew, CCC

Yield: 6 portions

Parsnips, peeled	1 kg	2 lb.
Oil for deep frying	as needed	
Salt and pepper	T	TT
Olive oil	30 mL	2 Tbsp.
Shallot, minced	50 g	2 oz.
Pears, ripe, peeled, seeded, diced	3 each	3 each
Vegetable stock	1 L	1 qt.
Salt and pepper	TT	TT
Nutmeg, freshly ground	TT	TT
Maple syrup	60 mL	4 Tbsp.

1. Thinly slice six lengthwise strips of parsnip and fry in oil until crisp. Drain on paper towelling and season with salt and pepper.
2. Dice remaining parsnip.
3. Heat olive oil on medium heat and sweat shallots for 1 minute. Add the parsnips and sweat a further 5 minutes. Add 2/3 of the pears and the vegetable stock. Simmer for 20 minutes or until parsnips are tender.
4. Purée the soup and adjust the seasoning.
5. Sauté the remaining pears in a small amount of olive oil and portion in centre of service bowls.
6. Slowly pour in the soup and place a parsnip crisp on top of the pears.
7. Drizzle maple syrup around the perimeter of the soup.

NOTE: This soup can also be used as a sauce for a vegetarian meal, for example with grilled portobello mushrooms.

Principles of Meat Cookery

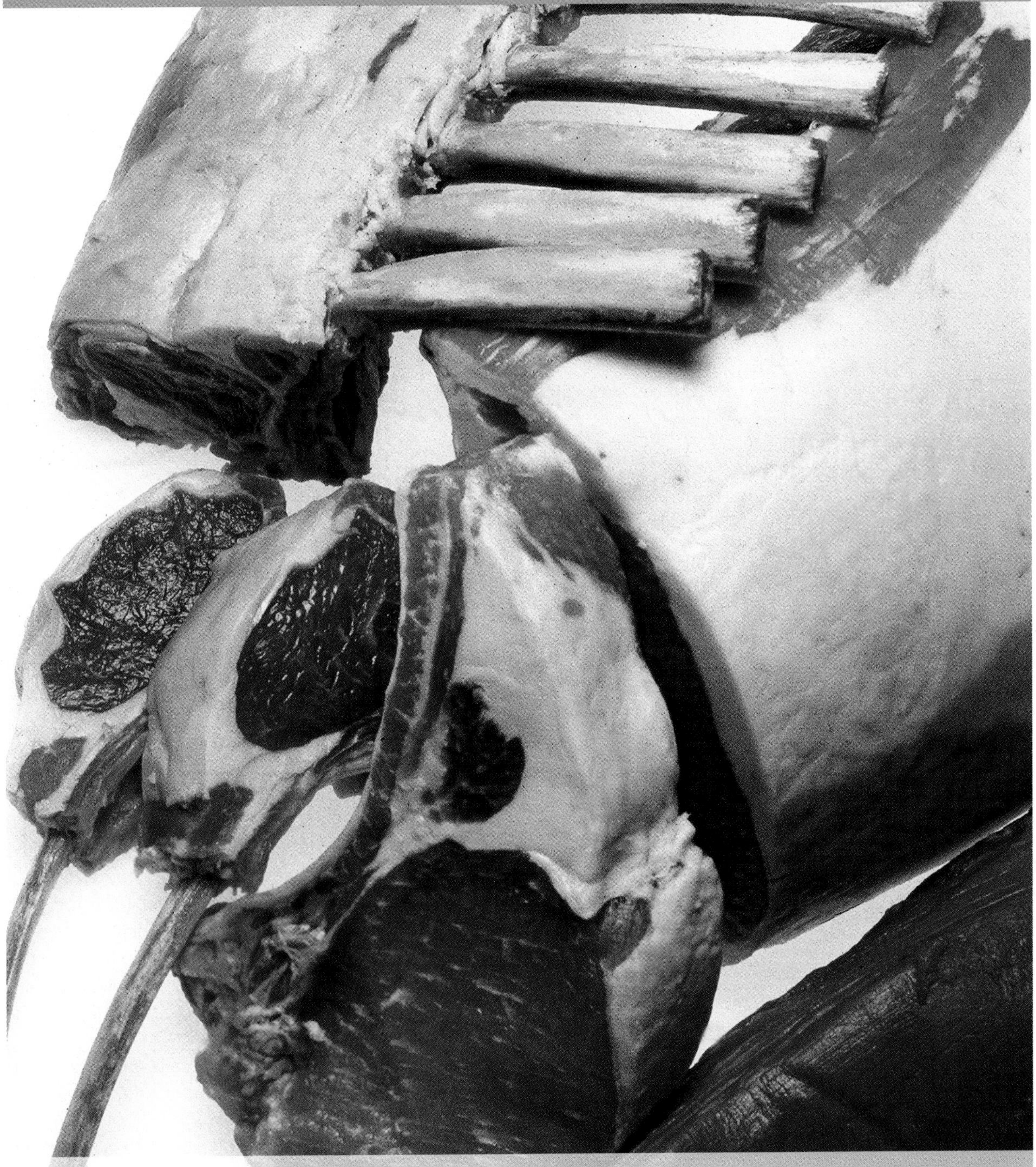

"
Cooking is at once one of the simplest
and most gratifying of the arts, but to
cook well one must love and respect food.

—Craig Claiborne, American food critic (1920–2000)

After studying this chapter you will be able to:

- identify the structure and composition of meats
- explain meat inspection and grading practices
- purchase meats appropriate for your needs
- store meats properly
- prepare meats for cooking
- apply various cooking methods to meats
- carve a beef hip or leg of lamb

These interactive online tools will help you master the skills in this chapter:

- Videos
- Chapter Quizzes
- Activities

● **primal cuts** primary divisions of muscle, bone and connective tissue produced by the initial breaking of the carcass

● **subprimal cuts** basic cuts produced from each primal

● **fabricated cuts** individual portions cut from a subprimal

● **marbling** whitish streaks of inter- and intramuscular fat

● **collagen** a protein found in connective tissue; it is converted into gelatin when cooked with moisture

● **elastin** a protein found in connective tissue, particularly ligaments and tendons. It also appears as a white or silver covering on meat known as silverskin.

Meats—beef, veal, lamb and pork—often consume the largest portion of your food-purchasing dollar. In this chapter we discuss how to protect your investment. You will learn how to determine the quality of meat, how to purchase meat in the form that best suits your needs and how to store it. We also discuss several of the dry-heat, moist-heat and combination cooking methods introduced in Chapter 9, Principles of Cooking, and how they can best be used so that a finished meat item is appealing to both the eye and the palate. Although each of the cooking methods is illustrated with a single beef, veal, lamb or pork recipe, the analysis is intended to apply to all meats.

In Chapters 13 through 16 you will learn about the specific cuts of beef, veal, lamb and pork typically used in food service operations, as well as some basic butchering procedures. Recipes using these cuts and applying the various cooking methods are included at the end of each of those chapters.

MUSCLE COMPOSITION

The carcasses of cattle, sheep, hogs and furred game animals consist mainly of edible lean muscular tissue, fat, connective tissue and bones. They are divided into large cuts called **primals**. Primal cuts are rarely cooked; rather, they are usually broken down to **subprimal cuts**, which, in turn, can be cooked as is or used to produce **fabricated cuts**. For example, the beef primal known as a short loin can be divided into subprimals including the strip loin. The strip loin can be fabricated into other cuts, including strip loin steaks. The primals, sub-primals and fabricated cuts of beef, veal, lamb and pork are discussed in Chapters 13 through 16, respectively; game is discussed in Chapter 18.

Muscle tissue gives meat its characteristic appearance; the amount of con-nective tissue determines the meat's tenderness. Beef muscle tissue is approxi-mately 72% water, 20% protein, 7% fat and 1% minerals. A single muscle comprises many bundles of muscle cells or fibres held together by connective tissue. (See Figures 12.1 and 12.2.) The thickness of the cells, the size of the cell bundles and the connective tissues holding them together form the grain of the meat and determine the meat's texture. When the fibre bundles are small, the meat has a fine grain and texture. Grain also refers to the direction in which the muscle fibres travel. When an animal fattens, some of the water and proteins in the lean muscle tissue are replaced with fat, which appears as **marbling**.

Connective tissue forms the walls of the long muscle cells and binds them into bundles. It surrounds the muscle as a membrane and also appears as the tendons and ligaments that attach the muscles to the bone. Most connective tissue is composed of either **collagen** or **elastin**. Collagen breaks down into water-soluble gelatin when cooked using moist heat. Elastin, on the other hand, will not break down under normal cooking conditions. Because elastin remains stringy and tough, tendons and ligaments should be trimmed away before meat is cooked.

Connective tissue develops primarily in the frequently used muscles. Therefore, cuts of meat from the shoulder (also known as the chuck), which the animal uses constantly, tend to be less tender than those from the back

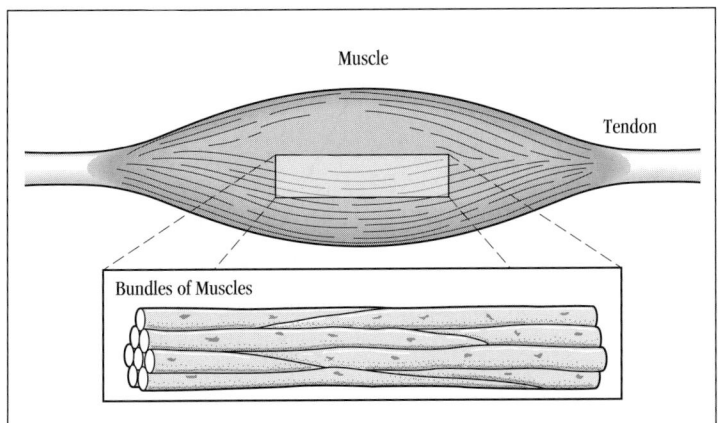

FIGURE 12.1 Muscle tissue.

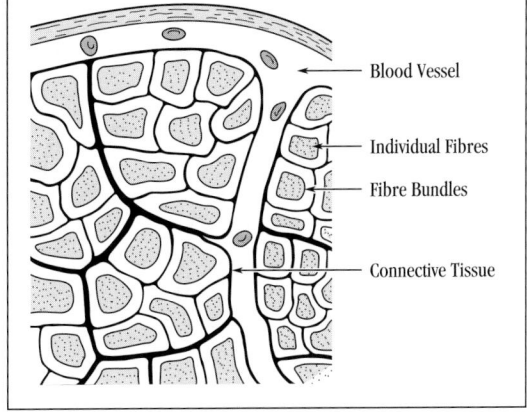

FIGURE 12.2 Crosscut of a bundle of muscle fibres.

(also known as the loin), which are used less frequently. As an animal ages, the collagen present within the muscles becomes more resistant to breaking down through moist-heat cooking. Therefore, the meat of an older animal tends to be less tender than that of a younger one.

NUTRITION

Although the nutritional content of beef, veal, pork and lamb differs, generally, all are high in protein, saturated fats and cholesterol. Consumed in moderate quantities, however, meat can be part of a healthful diet.

INSPECTION AND GRADING OF MEATS

Inspection

All meat produced for public consumption in Canada is subject to health inspection under the supervision of the Canadian Food Inspection Agency. Inspections ensure that products are processed under strict sanitary guidelines and are wholesome and fit for human consumption. Inspections do not indicate a meat's quality or tenderness. Whole carcasses of beef, pork, lamb and veal are labelled with a round stamp, which also identifies the processing facility. The stamp, which is shown in Figure 12.3, is also used for fabricated or processed meats and is found on either the product or its packaging. Imported products must also be inspected. The revised Canada Food Inspection System (CFIS) was implemented in 1998.

FIGURE 12.3 Canada meat inspection stamp.

Grading

Canadian grading provides a voluntary, uniform system by which producers, distributors and consumers can measure differences in the quality of meats and make price/quality comparisons. There are two parts to this grading system: quality grades and yield assessments. (See Figures 12.4 and 12.5 on the next page.)

Quality grades, provided and paid for by the industry, group meats of similar quality, yield and value.

● **quality grades** a guide to the eating qualities of meat—its tenderness, juiciness and flavour—based on an animal's age and the meat's colour, texture and degree of marbling

FIGURE 12.4 Grade stamp for Canada AAA beef.

FIGURE 12.5 Yield stamp Canada 1 means there is 59% or more lean meat; therefore, it has the best yield.

Grading takes into account five factors:

1. The animal's age, determined by the degree of bone ossification.
2. The colour of the meat.
3. The conformation of the muscling.
4. The fat colour.
5. The sex of the animal.

For beef, the intramuscular fat or marbling is taken into account also. It is assessed on the rib eye at the quarter break. For example, beef graded A or better must have at least "traces to slight" marbling and "good with some deficiency to excellent" muscling.

A Computer Vision System (CVS) uses cameras to assist in carcass sorting. The rib-eye camera takes a digitized picture of the rib eye. The computer software analyzes the marbling and can assist in grade assignment. The second camera takes a picture of the whole carcass and combines the information with the rib-eye scan. A yield score is calculated that provides an estimate of saleable yield. Testing has shown the computer-generated yield score to be twice as accurate as the yield ruler. A grader still assesses the final grade. Processors are using the CVS to differentiate the sub-levels within Prime and AAA. AAA has "small marbling" or better, while Prime exhibits "slightly abundant" marbling.

Carcass pasteurization is performed in large processing plants. The process involves three steps: removing water left on the carcass surface by the final

A History of Meat Regulations

1929: First beef grading policy inaugurated. Jointly proposed by producer, trade and governments, it was based on the belief that beef of good eating quality should be identified by branding and grading.

1941: All beef sold to the Department of National Defence had to be grade stamped. One year later, all beef to be branded had to be graded and stamped by official graders.

1947: National beef grading regulations were passed into law.

1958: Beef and veal grading regulations were revised under the Canada Agri-

cultural Products Standards Act. Grade descriptions reflected consumer demand for leaner beef.

1972: New beef grading system adopted. Based in part on partial ribbing and measurement of fat thickness only, with some visual appraisal of rib-eye muscle size and quality.

1984: Ribbing site relocated to between the twelfth and thirteenth ribs. Minimum carcass weight reintroduced. Metric measures introduced.

1988: Canada Agricultural Products Act proclaimed. Regulated marketing of agri-

cultural products in import, export, interprovincial trade and provincial national standards and grades.

1992: Grade names changed and marbling criteria used in harmony with USDA. Yield grades and stamps refined.

1995: Beef and poultry regulations amalgamated.

Late 1990s: Grading privatized. Canadian Food Inspection Agency created. Canada Prime grade added to beef system. HACCP legislated for federal plants. Computer Vision System developed.

wash, exposing the carcass to a hot-water or steam blanket and quickly chilling the carcass surface with a cold-water shower. A special chamber is used for the process.

Beef Canada has a well-defined beef grading system with A or higher being the best. The main grades are Canada Prime, AAA, AA, A, B1, B2, B3, B4, D and E grades. Approximately 82% (1999) of Canadian beef production is A grade or higher, and Canada Prime represents 1% of production. Systems are being developed to reward producers of higher grade meat.

Veal There are currently 10 grades of veal in Canada with A1, A2, A3 and A4 being the highest. Criteria include muscle conformation, flesh colour and fat deposits. Grading is carried out for the producer but consumers generally purchase based on colour (white to pink). Grading does not differentiate between milk- and grain-fed animals except in Quebec, where "milk-fed" is a regulated term. For menu terminology, the term "veal" is generally used, but if you specify "milk-fed" then you must have invoices to support your claim. "Baby beef" is not a recognized term, although "calf" is often used to describe veal liver. Graded carcasses are grade stamped. The minimum weight for a hide-off carcass is 80 kg (176 lb.) and the maximum is 160 kg (352 lb.). An ungraded veal carcass may weigh up to 180 kg (396 lb.) hide-off. The animal is generally a minimum of two weeks old.

Pork Pork grading is mainly done for the hog producer and for export. Domestic consumption does not show a grade stamp. The producer is paid according to the fat-to-lean ratio and most pork is trimmed at the plant. Of the 12 grades, Canada Yield Class is the most desirable. The carcass weighs 40 kg (88 lb.) or more and the yield percentage, by probe, of lean to fat on the loin meat must be between 54.7% and 64.3% or higher.

Sheep Most sheep are marketed as spring lamb or genuine spring lamb. Older sheep are generally processed into value-added products. Spring lamb is 5 to 12 months old and weighs 13.5 to 29.5 kg (30 to 65 lb.). The fat will be white and the flesh dark pink. The following characteristics are assessed and scored on a matrix grading: the appearance of the break joint, the yield, the fat level, the muscling, the colour of the pectoral muscle and the colour of the fat. For example, muscling is rated on a scale of 1 to 5, with M5 being the highest. Grading is done primarily for the producer as most lamb is sold ungraded.

AGING MEATS

When animals are slaughtered their muscles are soft and flabby. Within 6 to 24 hours rigor mortis sets in, causing the muscles to contract and stiffen. Rigor mortis dissipates within 48 to 72 hours under refrigerated conditions. All meats should be allowed to rest, or age, long enough for rigor mortis to dissipate completely. Meats that have not been aged long enough for rigor mortis to dissipate, or that have been frozen during this period, are known as "green meats." They will be very tough and flavourless when cooked. Current research verifies that aging contributes to the tenderness of beef. Little benefit is realized past 14 days. Marbling accounts for less than 5% of tenderness.

Typically, initial aging takes place while the meat is being transported from the slaughterhouse to the supplier or food service operation. Beef and lamb are sometimes aged for longer periods to increase their tenderness and flavour characteristics. Pork is not aged further because its high fat content turns rancid easily, and veal does not have enough fat to protect it during an extended aging period.

Yields and Grades

Yield assessments measure the amount of usable meat (as opposed to fat and bones) on a carcass and provide a uniform method of identifying differences among carcasses. Yield assessments are critical to producers and purveyors alike. Producers of hogs are paid more for higher yield carcasses. Purveyors and retailers want high-yield carcasses in order to reduce trim costs and increase profitability. Beef and pork are the carcasses with well-defined yield assessment criteria.

Grading of meats is a voluntary program paid for by the processing industry. Ungraded meat products can be purchased; however, consumers are willing to pay a premium for the assurance of graded, top-quality products. The development of private labelling systems by industry is growing, but these private systems do not necessarily conform to Agriculture Canada's regulations and can be a source of confusion to the consumer. Ask clear, direct and concise questions of your purveyor to ensure you are getting the product you require. Roller branding is only required for carcasses leaving the slaughter facility to be processed elsewhere.

Visit the Canadian Beef Grading Agency website at www.beefgrading agency.ca.

A Tender History

In *Food in History*, Reay Tannahill suggests that prehistoric hunters developed weapons and stealth tactics in order to kill their quarry without alerting it to danger and provoking fright, fight or flight. She notes that muscle tissues from animals that die placidly contain glycogen. At death, glycogen breaks down into various substances including lactic acid, a natural preservative. Animals experiencing fright, fight or flight just before death, however, use up their glycogen. Tannahill theorizes that prehistoric hunters recognized and responded to what science much later confirmed: meat from animals that die peacefully is sweeter and more tender.

● **vacuum packaging** a food preservation method in which fresh or cooked food is placed in an airtight container (usually plastic); virtually all air is removed from the container through a vacuum process, and the container is then sealed

Wet Aging

Today, most preportioned or precut meats are packaged and shipped in **vacuum-sealed** plastic packages, for example, Cryovac®. Wet aging is the process of storing vacuum-packaged meats under refrigeration for up to six weeks. This allows natural enzymes and microorganisms time to break down connective tissue, which tenderizes and flavours the meat. As this chemical process takes place, the meat develops a slight off-odour that is released when the package is opened and dissipates in a few minutes. Bag aging generally results in a yield loss of only 1% to 2%, significantly lower than dry (air) aging. A liquid called purge will be in the bag. Beef generally has the greatest capacity for aging. Exercise caution with the length of time. Most other meats must be used within a shorter time frame. Commercially vacuum-packaged and chilled pork, for example, has a shelf life of about 21 days.

Wet-Aged New York Strip

Dry Aging

Dry aging is the process of hanging fresh meats in an environment of controlled temperature, humidity and air flow for up to four weeks. This allows enzymes and microorganisms to break down connective tissues. Dry aging is actually the beginning of the natural decomposition process. Dry-aged meats can lose from 5% to 20% of their weight through moisture evaporation. Moisture loss combined with additional trimming can substantially increase the cost of dry-aged meats. Dry-aged meats are generally available only through smaller distributors and specialty butchers.

Dry-Aged Beef Short Loin

Irradiation

This process for meat is pending approval for use in Canada (2011; see Chapter 22, Vegetables). Other countries are irradiating meats and produce to increase shelf life by inhibiting the growth of some bacteria by altering the water activity (A_W) of the product. Changing the molecular structure of the water restricts microbial growth.

PURCHASING AND STORING MEATS

Several factors determine the cuts of meat your food service operation should use:

1. *Menu*—The menu identifies the types of cooking methods used. If meats are to be broiled, grilled, roasted, sautéed or fried, more tender cuts should be used. If they are to be stewed or braised, cuts with more connective tissue can be used to produce flavourful dishes.

2. *Menu price*—Cost constraints may prevent an operation from using the best quality meats available. Generally, the more tender the meat, the more expensive it is. But the most expensive cuts are not always the best choice for a particular cooking method. For example, a beef tenderloin is one of the most expensive cuts of beef. Although excellent grilled, it will not necessarily produce a better braised dish than the less tender chuck.

3. *Quality*—Often, several cuts of meat can be used for a specific dish, so each food service operation should develop its own quality specifications.

Purchasing Meats

Once you have identified the cuts of meat your operation needs, you must determine the forms in which they will be bought. Meats are purchased in a variety of forms: whole, sides, quarters, primal cuts or portion cuts (known as portion control or PC) ready to cook and serve. You should consider the following when deciding how to purchase meats:

1. *Employee skills*—Do your employees have the skills necessary to reduce large pieces of meat to the desired cuts?
2. *Menu*—Can you use the variety of bones, meat and trimmings that result from fabricating large cuts into individual portions?
3. *Storage*—Do you have ample refrigeration and freezer space so that you can be flexible in the way you purchase your meats?
4. *Cost*—Considering labour costs and trim usage, is it more economical to buy larger cuts of meat or PC units?

CMC/IMPS

The Canadian Meat Council (CMC) publishes full-colour manuals that name and number cuts of meat. The United States Department of Agriculture (USDA) publishes Institutional Meat Purchasing Specifications (IMPS). The CMC/IMPS system is a widely accepted and useful tool in preventing miscommunications between purchasers and purveyors. Meats are indexed by a numerical system: beef cuts are designated by the 100 series, lamb by the 200 series, veal by the 300 series, pork by the 400 series and portion cuts by the 1000 series. Commonly used cuts of beef, veal, lamb and pork and their CMC/IMPS numbers, as well as applicable cooking methods and serving suggestions, are discussed in Chapters 13 through 16. However, there are numbering differences in some cases and it is important to communicate clearly with your supplier to ensure the correct product is ordered and received.

Storing Meats

Meat products are highly perishable, so temperature control is the most important thing to remember when storing meats. Fresh meats should be stored at temperatures of –1°C to +2°C (30°F to 35°F). Vacuum-packed meats should be left in their packaging until they are needed. Under proper refrigeration, vacuum-packed meats with unbroken seals have a shelf life of three to four weeks. If the seal is broken, shelf life is reduced to only a few days. Meats that are not vacuum packed should be loosely wrapped or wrapped in air-permeable paper. Do not wrap meats tightly in plastic wrap, as this creates a good breeding ground for bacteria and will significantly shorten a meat's shelf life. Store meats on trays and away from other foods to prevent cross-contamination.

Meats freeze at about –2°C (28°F). When freezing meats, the faster the better. Slow freezing produces large ice crystals that tend to rupture the muscle tissues, allowing water and nutrients to drip out when the meat is thawed (see Figure 12.6). Most commercially packaged meats are frozen by blast freezing, which quickly cools by blasting –40°C (–40°F) air across the meat.

FIGURE 12.6 Meat damaged by freezer burn—freezer-burned bottom sirloin butt tri tip (top) and fresh bottom sirloin butt tri tip (bottom).

●**freezer burn** the surface dehydration and discoloration of food due to moisture loss at freezing temperatures. Poor or improper wrapping for storage is the main cause.

● **marinate** to soak a food in a seasoned liquid in order to tenderize the food or add flavour to it

● **barding** tying thin slices of fat, such as bacon or pork backfat, over meats or poultry that have little to no natural fat covering in order to protect and moisten them during roasting

● **larding** inserting thin slices of fat, such as pork backfat, into low-fat meats in order to add moisture

● **jacquarding** a process of piercing muscle tissue with needles to tenderize

● **tumbling** a process in which solid muscle meat is tumbled with crushed ice and/or a seasoned liquid until the meat absorbs a prescribed percentage of its weight in liquid. An emulsifier may be added or a vacuum used to promote faster, more complete absorption. The tumbling "releases" the protein and allows the liquid to emulsify with the fat in the muscle fibres. There are strict regulations governing the types of meats that may be tumbled (or pumped) and the allowable levels of moisture added. Sold as "seasoned" product or "water added."

● **needling** a process in which a solution is injected into the muscle to provide moisture and flavour. Products are referred to as marinated or enhanced. The moisture retention must be declared.

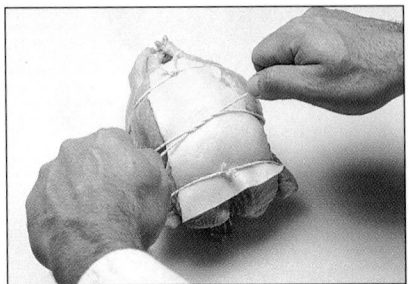
Barding a pheasant

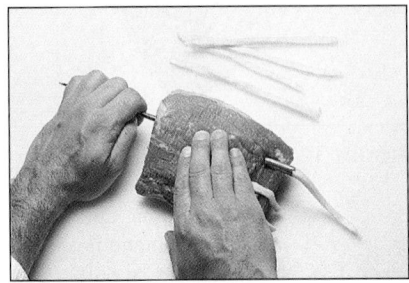
Larding meat

The ideal temperature for maintaining frozen meat is –45°C (–50°F). Frozen meat should not be maintained at any temperature warmer than –18°C (0°F). Moisture- and vapour-proof packaging will help prevent **freezer burn**. The length of frozen storage life varies with the species and type of meat. As a general rule, properly handled meats can be frozen for up to six months. Frozen meats should only be thawed at refrigerator temperatures, not at room temperature or in warm water.

PREPARING MEATS

Certain procedures are often applied to meats before cooking to add flavour and/or moisture, or to enhance tenderness. These include **marinating**, **barding**, **larding**, **jacquarding**, **tumbling** and **needling**.

Marinating—Wet and Dry

Wet marinating is the process of soaking meat in a seasoned liquid to flavour and tenderize it. Marinades can be simple blends (herbs, seasonings and oil) or a complicated cooked recipe (red wine, fruit and other ingredients). Mild marinades should be used on more delicate meats, such as veal. Game and beef require strongly flavoured marinades. In wine-based marinades, white wine is usually used for white meats and red wine for red meats. Not only does the wine add a distinctive flavour, the acids in it help break down connective tissues and tenderize the meat.

Veal and pork generally require less time to marinate than game, beef and lamb. Smaller pieces of meat take less time than larger pieces. When marinating meat, be sure to cover it completely and keep it refrigerated. Stir or turn the meat frequently to ensure that the marinade penetrates evenly.

Dry marinating generally involves rubbing herbs and spices into the surface of the meat, fish, poultry or game. Dry rubs may have sugar and salt in them as well, although both may draw moisture out of the product. Depending on the concentrations of salts and the use of nitrates and nitrites, dry marinating can become a form of curing. The product may be placed on a rack and sometimes is pressed as it undergoes the marinating process.

Barding

Barding is the process of covering the surface of meat or poultry with thin slices of pork backfat or bacon and tying them in place with butcher's twine. Barded meat or poultry is usually roasted. As the item cooks, the backfat continuously bastes it, protecting the meat from drying and enhancing moistness. A drawback to barding is that the backfat prevents the meat or poultry from developing the crusty exterior associated with roasting.

Larding

Larding is the process of inserting small strips of pork fat into meat with a larding needle to imitate marbling. Larded meat is usually cooked by braising. During cooking, the added fat melts and coats the meat fibres contributing to moistness. Although once popular, larding is rarely used today because advances in feeding practices and selective breeding produce better marbled meats.

APPLYING VARIOUS COOKING METHODS

Dry-Heat Cooking Methods

Dry-heat cooking methods subject food directly to the heat of a flame (broiling and grilling), hot air (roasting) or heated fat (sautéing and pan-frying, as well as deep-fat frying, which is covered in Chapter 9, Principles of Cooking). These cooking methods firm proteins without significant breakdown of connective tissue. They are not recommended for less tender cuts or those high in connective tissue.

Broiling and Grilling

To serve a good-quality broiled or grilled product, you must start with good-quality meat. The broiling or grilling process adds flavour; additional flavours are derived from seasonings. The broiler or grill should brown and sear the meat for flavour and appearance. The grill should leave distinctive crosshatch marks on the meat's surface.

Selecting Meats to Broil or Grill

Only the most tender cuts should be broiled or grilled because the high heat and short cooking times do not tenderize. Intramuscular fat adds flavour as the meat cooks, so the meat should be well marbled. Some external (**subcutaneous**) fat is also beneficial. Too much fat, however, will cause the broiler or grill to flare up, burning or discolouring the meat and adding objectionable flavours. Silverskin (elastin) toughens when meat is broiled or grilled. Trim away as much of it as possible.

Seasoning Meats to Be Broiled or Grilled

Meats that have not been marinated should be well seasoned with salt and pepper just before being placed on the broiler or grill. If they are seasoned and allowed to rest, the salt will dissolve and draw out moisture, making it difficult to brown the meat properly. Some chefs feel that broiled or grilled meats should be seasoned on the cooked surface only. Pork and veal, which have a tendency to dry out when cooked, should be basted with seasoned butter or oil during cooking to help keep them moist. Meats can be glazed or basted with sauces or marinade liquids as they cook, but observe food safety guidelines and excercise caution with high-sugar products that may burn.

Cooking Temperatures

Red meats should be cooked at sufficiently high temperatures to caramelize their surface, making them more attractive and flavourful. At the same time, the broiler or grill cannot be too hot or the meat's exterior will burn before the interior is cooked.

Because veal and pork are normally cooked to higher internal temperatures than are beef and lamb, they should be cooked at slightly lower temperatures so the exterior is a deep golden colour while the interior is cooked to the desired doneness but is still moist.

Degrees of Doneness

Consumers request and expect meats to be properly cooked to specific degrees of doneness. It is your responsibility to understand and comply with these requests. Meats can be cooked very rare (or bleu), rare, medium rare, medium, medium well or well done. Figure 12.7 on the next page shows the

● **subcutaneous fat** exterior fat; the fat between the hide and muscle

---

SAFETY ALERT

Serving Meat

The Canadian Food Inspection Agency recommends the following as safe internal temperatures for serving various meats. Note that these temperatures are approximately 5°C–8°C (10°F–15°F) higher than the temperatures generally preferred by chefs and diners. Most diners would find the CFIA's recommended 71°C (160°F) unacceptably overcooked for a "medium" steak. Each chef or meat cook must decide for themselves whether it is more important to their clientele to cook meat to the CFIA's safety standards or to diners' requests.

Fresh Beef, Veal and Lamb
Rare	not recommended
Medium rare	63°C (145°F)
Medium	71°C (160°F)
Well done	77°C (170°F)

Fresh Pork
Rare	not recommended
Medium rare	not recommended
Medium	71°C (160°F)
Well done	77°C (170°F)

Poultry	74°C (165°F)
Fresh Poultry	85°C (185°F)

Ground Meat and Meat Mixtures
Beef, veal, lamb and pork	71°C (160°F) or higher

FIGURE 12.7 Degrees of doneness: beef roasted very rare, rare, medium rare, medium, medium well and well done.

proper colour for these different degrees of doneness. This guide can be used for red meats cooked by any method.

Larger cuts of meat, such as a chateaubriand or thick chops, are often started on the broiler or grill to develop colour and flavour and then finished in a low-heat oven to ensure complete, even cooking.

Determining Doneness

Broiling or grilling meat to the proper degree of doneness is an art. Larger pieces of meat will take longer to cook than smaller ones, but how quickly a piece of meat cooks is determined by many other factors: the temperature of the broiler or grill, the temperature of the piece of meat when placed on the broiler or grill, the type of meat and the thickness of the cut. Because of these variables, timing alone is not a useful tool in determining doneness.

A thermometer is the most reliable method of determining doneness; however, its use is not very practical or accurate with cuts such as steaks. Cutting a steak to observe the colour is not acceptable to the customer. The most frequently used method of determining doneness is by pressing the piece of meat with tongs and gauging the amount of resistance it yields. Very rare (bleu) meat will offer almost no resistance and will feel almost the same as raw meat. Meat cooked rare will feel spongy and offer slight resistance to pressure. Meat cooked medium will feel slightly firm and springy to the touch. Meat cooked well done will feel quite firm and will spring back quickly when pressed. (See Table 12.1.) Many consumers prefer internal temperatures approximately 10°C cooler than those listed.

Accompaniments to Broiled and Grilled Meats

Because a broiler or grill cannot be deglazed to form the base for a sauce, compound butters or sauces such as béarnaise are often served with broiled or grilled meats. Brown sauces such as Bordelaise, chasseur, périgueux or brown mushroom sauce also complement many broiled or grilled items. Additional sauce suggestions are found in Table 10.5.

TABLE 12.1	Determining Doneness of Beef Steak and Roasts				
Degree of Doneness	**Colour**	**Degree of Resistance**	**Temperature (CFIA)**	**Temperature (Customer Preference)**
Very rare (bleu)	Very red and raw-looking centre (the centre is cool to the touch)	Almost no resistance		
Rare (saignant)	Large deep red centre	Spongy; very slight resistance	60°C (140°F)	52°C–54°C (125°F–130°F)
Medium rare	Bright red centre	Some resistance; slightly springy		
Medium (à point)	Rosy pink to red centre	Slightly firm; springy	68°C (155°F)	60°C–66°C (140°F–150°F)
Medium well	Very little pink at the centre, almost brown throughout	Firm; springy		
Well done (bien cuit)	No red	Quite firm; springs back quickly when pressed	77°C (170°F)	68°C–74°C (155°F–165°F)
Ground beef			71°C (160°F)	

Adapted from Beef Information Centre.

Note: • Roasts are generally cooked to higher temperatures than steaks.
     • Remember to allow for carryover cooking.

BASIC PROCEDURE FOR BROILING OR GRILLING MEATS

1. Heat the broiler or grill.

2. Use a wire brush to remove any charred or burnt particles that may be stuck to the broiler or grill grate. The grate can be wiped with a lightly oiled towel to remove any remaining particles and help season it.

3. Prepare the item to be broiled or grilled by trimming off excess fat and connective tissue and marinating or seasoning as desired. The meat may be brushed lightly with oil to help keep it from sticking to the grate, but excess fat will cause flare-ups.

4. Place the item in the broiler or on the grill. Following the example in Chapter 9, turn the meat to produce the attractive crosshatch marks associated with grilling. Use tongs to turn or flip the meat without piercing the surface in order to prevent valuable juices from escaping.

5. Cook the meat to the desired doneness while developing the proper surface colour. To do so, adjust the position of the meat on the broiler or grill or adjust the distance between the grate and heat source.

SAFETY ALERT

Grill Flare-Ups

Fat dripping onto a grill can cause flames to flare up and burn foods. Prevent flames by trimming excess fat from foods before cooking. Control the flame by moving the food to another section of the grill. The fat should burn off the coals within a few seconds. Should the flare-up become uncontrollable, suppress the flame with a lid or sheet tray.

APPLYING THE BASICS — RECIPE 12.1

Grilled Lamb Chops with Herb Butter

Yield: 2 servings

Lamb chops, loin or rib, approx. 2.5-cm (1-in.) thick	6	6
Salt and pepper	TT	TT
Oil	as needed	as needed
Herb butter	6 thin slices or 6 small rosettes	

1. Preheat the grill for 15 minutes or until the grate is sufficiently heated.

2. Season the lamb chops with salt and pepper; lightly brush with oil.

3. Place the lamb chops on the grill, turning as necessary to produce the proper crosshatching. Cook to the desired doneness.

4. Remove the lamb chops from the grill and place a slice or rosette of herb butter on each chop.

5. Serve immediately as the herb butter melts. The plate can be placed under the broiler for a few seconds to help melt the herb butter.

RECIPE 12.1

Approximate values per serving:	
Calories	524
Total fat	44 g
Saturated fat	20 g
Cholesterol	161 mg
Sodium	368 mg
Total carbohydrates	0.1 g
Protein	32 g

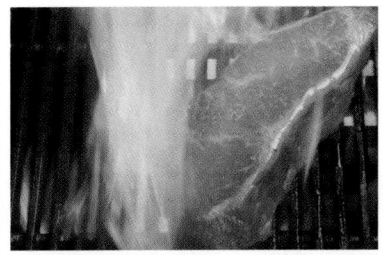

1. Grilled Lamb Chops: Brushing the lamb chops with oil.

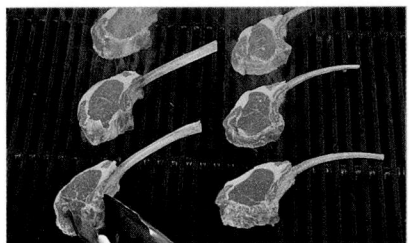

2. Placing the lamb chops on the grill.

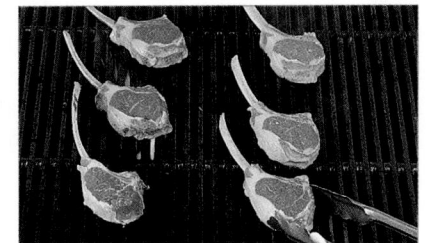

3. Rotating the lamb chops 90 degrees to create crosshatch marks.

4. Turning the chops over to finish them on the other side.

More about Roasting

Because roasting is a dry-heat cooking method, the best results come from using tender, well-marbled cuts from the rib, loin or leg. Larger or less tender cuts benefit from low-temperature roasting for longer times. This promotes moisture retention (better yield and flavour) and tenderness if the item is not cooked to medium well or well done.

The Challenge

Selecting the best oven temperature for a roast requires considering several factors. The size of the roast, degree of marbling, shape, equipment and time available all play a role. Too high a heat will result in a drier, lower yield, less tender product. Too low a temperature may not allow for browning or melting of the marbled fat or hydrolyzing of the collagen. Generally, large cuts are cooked with low heat for longer times and smaller cuts on higher heat for shorter times.

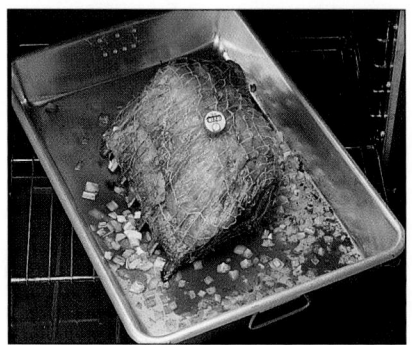

FIGURE 12.8 The proper placement of an instant-read thermometer.

Roasting

Properly roasted meats should be tender, juicy and evenly cooked to the appropriate degree of doneness. They should have a pleasant appearance when whole as well as when sliced and plated.

Seasoning Meats to Be Roasted

Seasonings are especially important with smaller roasts and roasts with little or no fat covering. With these roasts, some of the seasonings penetrate the meat, while the remainder help create the highly seasoned crust associated with a good roast. A large roast with a heavy fat covering (for example, a ponderosa hip or prime rib) does not benefit from being seasoned on the surface because the seasonings will not penetrate the fat layer, which is trimmed away before service.

When practical, a roast with excess fat should be trimmed, leaving just a thin fat layer so that the roast bastes itself while cooking. A lean roast can be barded or larded before cooking to add richness and moisture. Lamb legs are sometimes studded with garlic cloves by piercing the meat with a paring knife and then pressing slivers of raw garlic into the holes.

A roast is sometimes cooked on a bed of mirepoix, or mirepoix is added to the roasting pan as the roast cooks. The mirepoix raises the roast off the bottom of the roasting pan, preventing the bottom from overcooking. This mirepoix, however, does not add any flavour to the roast. Rather, it combines with the drippings to add flavour to the jus, sauce or gravy that is made with them.

Cooking Temperatures

Small roasts such as a rack of lamb or a beef tenderloin should be seared first to caramelize the surface and then roasted at 135°C to 165°C (275°F to 325°F) to ensure a tender, juicy product with a higher yield.

Traditionally, large roasts were started at high temperatures to sear the meat and seal in the juices; they were then finished at lower temperatures. Studies have proven, however, that roasts cooked at constant, low temperatures provide a juicier product with better yield and less shrinkage. Temperatures between 120°C and 135°C (250°F and 275°F) are ideal for large roasts. These temperatures will result in an evenly pink cooked centre portion.

Determining Doneness

The doneness of small roasts such as a rack of lamb is determined in much the same way as with broiled or grilled meats. With experience, the cook develops a sense of timing as well as a feel for gauging the amount of resistance by touching the meat. These techniques, however, are not infallible, especially with large roasts.

Although timing is useful as a general guide for planning purposes, there are too many variables for it to be relied upon exclusively. As a guideline, roasts will require 30 to 50 minutes per kilogram (15 to 20 minutes per pound), depending on the desired doneness, type and size of roast and internal temperature of the cut.

The best way to determine the doneness of a large roast is to use an instant-read thermometer, as shown in Figure 12.8. The thermometer is inserted into the centre or thickest part of the roast and away from any bones. The recommended finished temperatures for roasted meats are listed in Table 12.1. Customer and most chef preferences are usually 10°C cooler.

Carryover Cooking and Resting

Cooking does not stop the moment a roast is removed from the oven. Through conduction, the heat applied to the outside of the roast continues to penetrate, cooking the centre for several more minutes. Indeed, the internal temperature of a small roast can rise by as much as 3°C to 6°C (5°F to 10°F) after being removed from a hot oven. With a larger roast, such as a 20-kg (50-lb.) beef hip, it can rise by as much as 11°C (20°F). Therefore, remove roasted meats before they reach the desired degree of doneness and allow **carryover cooking** to complete the cooking process. The temperatures listed in Table 12.1 are internal temperatures after allowing for carryover cooking.

As meat cooks, its juices flow toward the centre. If the roast is carved immediately after it is removed from the oven, its juices would run from the meat, causing it to lose its colour and become dry. Letting the meat rest before slicing allows the juices to redistribute themselves evenly throughout the roast, so the roast will retain more juices when carved. Small roasts, like a rack of lamb, need to rest only 5 to 10 minutes; larger roasts such as a hip of beef require as much as an hour.

● **carryover cooking** the cooking that occurs after a food is removed from the heat source

Accompaniments to Roasted Meats

Roasts may be served with a sauce based on their natural juices (called *au jus*), as described in Recipe 12.2, Roast Prime Rib of Beef au Jus, or with a pan gravy made with drippings from the roast. Additional sauce suggestions are found in Table 10.5.

BASIC PROCEDURE FOR ROASTING MEATS

1. Trim excess fat, tendons and silverskin from the meat. Leave only a thin fat covering, if possible, so the roast bastes itself as it cooks.

2. Season the roast as appropriate and place it in a roasting pan. The roast may be placed on a bed of mirepoix, if small, or on a rack.

3. Roast the meat, uncovered, at the desired temperature (the larger the roast, the lower the temperature), usually 120°C to 165°C (250°F to 325°F).

4. If a jus or pan gravy is desired and a mirepoix was not added at the start of cooking, it may be added 45 to 60 minutes before the roast is done, thus allowing it to caramelize while the roast finishes cooking.

5. Cook to the desired temperature.

6. Remove the roast from the oven, allowing carryover cooking to raise the internal temperature to the desired degree of doneness. Allow the roast to rest before slicing or carving it. As the roast rests, prepare the jus, sauce or pan gravy.

APPLYING THE BASICS — RECIPE 12.2

Roast Prime Rib of Beef au Jus and Yorkshire Pudding Popovers

Yield: 18 250-g (8-oz.) boneless servings

Beef rib, cover off, CMC#109D, approx. 7.5 kg (16 lb.)	1	1
Salt and pepper	TT	TT
Garlic, chopped	120 g	4 oz.
Mirepoix	500 g	1 lb.
Brown stock	2 L	2 qt.

RECIPE 12.2

Approximate values per serving:	
Calories	883
Total fat	56 g
Saturated fat	24 g
Cholesterol	246 mg
Sodium	592 mg
Total carbohydrates	4 g
Protein	85 g

continued

1. Roast Prime Rib of Beef au Jus: Draining off the excess fat.

2. Caramelizing the mirepoix.

3. Deglazing the pan with brown stock.

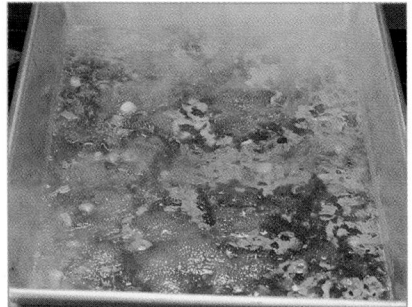

4. Simmering the jus, reducing it slightly and allowing the mirepoix to release its flavours.

5. Straining the jus through a conical strainer and cheesecloth.

1. Season the roast with the salt, pepper and chopped garlic. Place the roast in an appropriate-sized roasting pan. Roast at 120°C–135°C (250°F–275°F).

2. Add the mirepoix to the pan approximately 1 hour before the roast is finished cooking. Continue cooking until the internal temperature of the roast reaches 48°C (118°F), approximately 4–4.5 hours. Carryover cooking will raise the internal temperature of the roast to approximately 52°C (125°F), for medium rare as preferred by customers.

3. Remove the roast from the pan and allow it to rest in a warm place for 30 minutes.

4. Drain the excess fat from the roasting pan, reserving the mirepoix and any drippings in the roasting pan.

5. Caramelize the mirepoix on the stove top; allow the liquids to evaporate, leaving only brown drippings in the pan.

6. Deglaze the pan with brown stock. Stir to loosen all the drippings.

7. Simmer the jus, reducing it slightly and allowing the mirepoix to release its flavour; season with salt and pepper if necessary.

8. Strain the jus through a conical strainer lined with cheesecloth. Skim any remaining fat from the surface with a ladle.

9. Trim and slice the roast as described opposite and serve with approximately 30–60 mL (1–2 fl. oz.) jus per portion.

Yorkshire Pudding Popovers

Yield: 30 large

Method: Baking

Eggs, large	12	12
Water	675 mL	24 fl. oz.
Salt	30 g	1 oz.
All-purpose flour	300 g	3 cups
Nutmeg	1 g	1/2 tsp.
Vegetable oil	900 mL	30 fl. oz.

1. Beat eggs, water and salt thoroughly.

2. Add flour and nutmeg and beat until batter is smooth. Let batter rest for 1 hour.

3. Preheat oven to 200°C (400°F) and place conditioned muffin tins on baking sheets. Heat muffin tins with 30 mL (1 fl. oz.) of oil in each cup.

4. Pour 60 mL (2 fl. oz.) of batter into each heated cup. Return to oven and bake until puffed and beginning to crisp; approximately 15 minutes. Reduce heat to 175°C (350°F) and finish baking. Yorkshires should be hollow and crisp enough to hold their shape.

NOTE: Traditional Yorkshire pudding was baked in a baking pan placed under the roast to catch all the drippings. The end product is more pudding-like and is cut into squares.

Yorkshire Pudding Popovers— Approximate values per serving:	
Calories	310
Total fat	30 g
Saturated fat	3 g
Cholesterol	74 mg
Sodium	413 mg
Total carbohydrates	8 g
Protein	3 g

Carving Roasts

All the efforts that went into selecting and cooking a perfect roast will be wasted if the roast is not carved properly. Roasts are always carved against the grain; carving with the grain produces long stringy, tough slices. Cutting across the muscle fibres produces a more attractive and tender portion. Portions may be cut in a single thick slice, as with roast prime rib of beef, or in many thin slices. The photographs following illustrate several different carving procedures.

BASIC PROCEDURE FOR CARVING PRIME RIB (ROAST READY, CAP ON CMC#109)

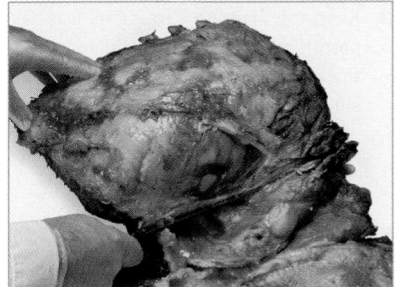

1. Remove the netting, cap fat and chine bones.

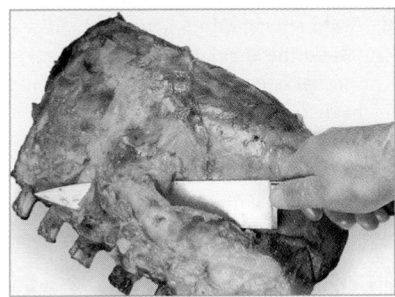

2. Trim the excess fat from the eye muscle.

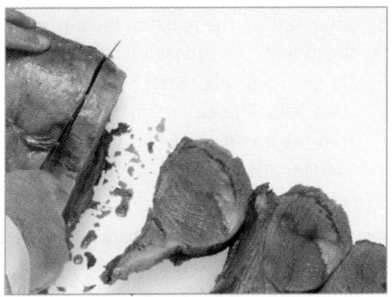

3. Slice the rib in long, smooth strokes, the first cut (end cut) without a rib bone, the second cut with a rib bone, and so on.

BASIC PROCEDURE FOR CARVING PRIME RIB ON THE SLICER

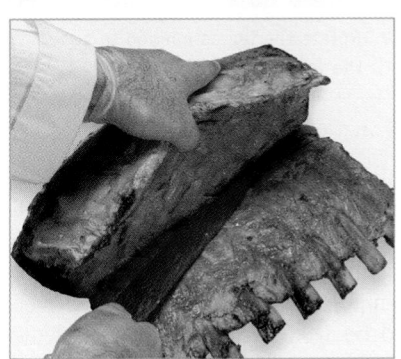

1. When producing large quantities of prime rib, it is often more practical to slice it on a slicing machine. Following the steps illustrated above, remove the netting, cap fat and chine bone; trim excess fat from the eye muscle. Then using a long slicer, completely remove the rib eye from the rib bones, being careful to stay as close as possible to the bones to avoid wasting any meat.

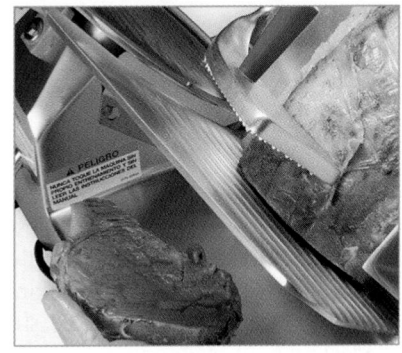

2. After placing the rib on the slicing machine, set the machine to the desired thickness. The blade will have to be adjusted often because a roast's shape fluctuates.

Carving pork tenderloin against the grain.

BASIC PROCEDURE FOR CARVING A BEEF HIP

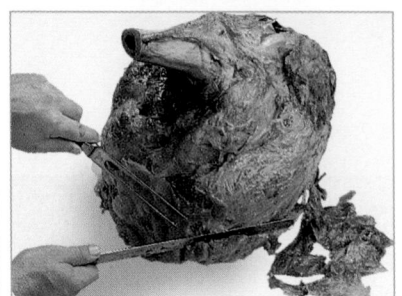

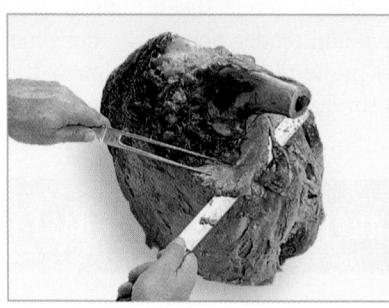

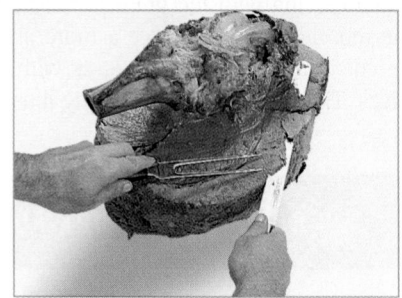

1. After setting the roast on the cutting board with the exposed femur bone (large end of the roast) down and the tibia (shank bone) or "handle" up, trim the excess exterior fat to expose the lean meat.

2. Begin slicing with a horizontal cut toward the shank bone, then make vertical cuts to release the slices of beef.

3. Keep the exposed surface as level as possible. Continue carving, turning the roast as necessary to access all sides.

BASIC PROCEDURE FOR CARVING A LEG OF LAMB

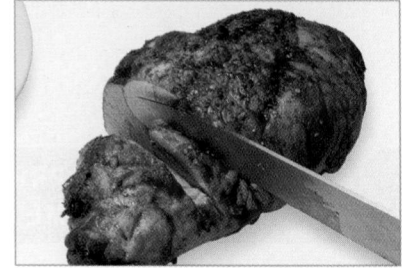

1. Holding the shank bone firmly, cut toward the bone.

2. Cut parallel to the shank bone to remove the slices.

3. Rotate the leg as needed to access the meat on all sides.

Sautéing

Sautéing is a dry-heat cooking method using high heat and selected for smaller cuts in which heat is conducted by a small amount of fat. Sautéed meats should be tender (a reflection of the quality of the raw product), of good colour (determined by proper cooking temperatures) and have a good overall flavour. Any accompanying sauce should be well seasoned and complement the meat without overpowering it.

Selecting Meats to Sauté

As with broiling, grilling and roasting, you should use tender meats of the highest quality in order to produce good results when sautéing. The cuts should be uniform in size and shape to promote even cooking.

Seasoning Meats to Be Sautéed

The meat can be marinated or simply seasoned with salt and pepper. If marinated, the meat must be patted dry before cooking to ensure proper browning. Some meats are dusted with flour before cooking to help dry the surface and promote even browning. Flour may provide some thickening of the sauce. The sauces that almost always accompany sautéed meats provide much of the flavour.

Determining Doneness

As with broiled and grilled meats, the doneness of sautéed meats is determined by touch and timing. Red meats should be well browned; veal and pork should be somewhat lighter.

Accompaniments to Sautéed Meats

Sauces served with sautéed meats are usually made directly in the sauté pan, utilizing the **fond**. They often incorporate a previously thickened sauce. Additional sauce suggestions for sautéed meats are found in Table 10.5.

● **fond** (1) French for "stock" or "base"; (2) the concentrated juices, drippings and bits of food left in a pan after foods are roasted or sautéed; it is used to flavour sauces made directly in the cooking pan

BASIC PROCEDURE FOR SAUTÉING MEATS

1. Heat a sauté pan and add enough oil or clarified butter just to cover the bottom. The pan should be large enough to hold the meat in a single layer. A pan that is too large may cause the fat or meat to burn.

2. Cut the meat into **cutlets, escallopes, émincés, medallions, mignonettes, noisettes, chops, paillardes** or small even-sized pieces. Season the meat and dredge in flour if desired.

3. Add the meat to the sauté pan in a single layer. Do not crowd the pan.

4. Adjust the temperature so that the meat's exterior browns properly without burning and the interior cooks. The heat should be high enough to complete the cooking process before the meat begins to stew in its own juices.

5. Small items may be tossed using the sauté pan's sloped sides to flip them back on top of themselves. Do not toss the meat more than necessary, however. The pan should remain in contact with the heat source as much as possible to maintain proper temperatures. Larger items should be turned using tongs or a kitchen fork. Avoid splashing hot fat.

6. Transfer the meat to another pan and proceed with preparing the sauce and/or garnish; combine the meat with the sauce and finish cooking.

● **cutlet** a relatively thick, boneless cut of meat

● **escallope** a thin, boneless slice of meat (paillarde, scallopini)

● **émincé** a small, thin, boneless piece of meat

● **medallion** a small, round, relatively thick slice of meat

● **mignonette** a small cut or medallion of meat

● **noisette** a small, usually round portion of meat cut from the rib

● **chop** a cut of meat including part of the rib

● **paillarde** a scallop of meat pounded until thin; usually grilled

BASIC PROCEDURE FOR MAKING A SAUCE IN THE SAUTÉ PAN

1. If a sauce is to be made in the sauté pan, hold the meat in a warm spot while preparing the sauce. When the meat is removed from the pan, leave a small amount of fat as well as the fond. If there is excessive fat, degrease the pan, leaving just enough to cover its bottom. Add ingredients such as garlic, shallots and mushrooms that will be used as garnishes and sauce flavourings; sauté them.

2. Deglaze the pan with wine or stock. Scrape the pan, loosening the fond and allowing it to dissolve in the liquid. Reduce the deglazing liquid by approximately three-quarters.

3. Add fond lié (or demi-glace) or stock to the pan. Cook and reduce the sauce to the desired consistency. Other sauces may be used.

4. Add any ingredients that do not require cooking such as herbs and spices. Adjust the seasonings with salt and pepper.

5. For service, the meat may be returned to the pan for a moment to reheat it and coat it with the finished sauce. The meat should remain in the sauce just long enough to reheat. Do not attempt to cook the meat in the sauce.

RECIPE 12.3

Approximate values per serving:	
Calories	432
Total fat	20 g
Saturated fat	11 g
Cholesterol	189 mg
Sodium	357 mg
Total carbohydrates	17 g
Protein	39 g

Sautéed Veal Scallopini with White Wine Lemon Sauce

Yield: 10 180-g (6-oz.) servings

Veal scallopini, 90 g (3 oz.) each	20	20
Clarified butter	100 g	3 fl. oz.
Flour	200 g	7 oz.
Salt and pepper	TT	TT
Shallots, chopped	35 g	3 Tbsp.
White wine	300 mL	10 fl. oz.
Lemon juice	80 mL	3 fl. oz.
Brown veal stock	200 mL	6-1/2 fl. oz.
Unsalted butter	80 g	3 oz.
Lemon wedges	20	20

1. Pound the scallopini to a uniform thickness, as described in Chapter 14, Veal.

2. Heat a sauté pan and add the clarified butter.

3. Dredge the scallopini in seasoned flour and add to the pan in a single layer. Sauté on each side for 1–2 minutes. As the first scallopini are done, remove them to a warm platter and sauté the remaining scallopini.

4. Add the chopped shallots to the pan and sauté.

5. Deglaze the pan with the white wine and lemon juice.

6. Add the brown veal stock and reduce by half.

7. Swirl in the unsalted butter (monter au beurre).

8. Adjust the seasonings with salt and pepper.

9. Serve 2 scallopini per person with approximately 30 mL (1 fl. oz.) of sauce. Garnish with lemon wedges.

VARIATIONS: The sauce may be modified to reduce the amount of butter. In Step 7, thicken the sauce with arrowroot or cornstarch and finish with 15 g (3 tsp.) butter. Pork, chicken or turkey cutlets may be used instead of veal. For other variations, omit the wine and lemon and try tomato sauce, zingara, Marsala or mushroom sauce. Add a vegetable or fruit garnish or fresh herbs or a bit of cream.

1. Veal Scallopini: Adding the veal cutlets to the pan. Note the relationship of scallopini to pan size.

2. Adding the chopped shallots to the pan and sautéing them.

3. Deglazing the pan with white wine and lemon juice.

4. Adding the brown veal stock and reducing by half.

5. Swirling in the butter and adjusting the seasonings.

Pan-Frying

Pan-frying is generally selected for larger cuts and uses more fat and lower heat than sautéing to conduct heat. Pan-fried meats should be tender (a reflection of the quality of the raw product), of good colour (determined by proper cooking temperatures) and with a good overall flavour. Meats to be pan-fried are usually breaded. In addition to providing flavour, breading seals the meat. The breading should be free from breaks, thus preventing the fat from coming into direct contact with the meat or collecting in a pocket formed between the meat and the breading. Pan-fried items should be golden in colour and the breading should not be soggy. Similar principles apply to deep-fat frying.

Selecting Meats to Pan-Fry

As with other dry-heat cooking methods, tender meats of high quality should be used because the meat will not be tenderized by the cooking process. Meats that are pan-fried are often cut into cutlets or escallopes and may be delicated, pounded or jacquarded to tenderize.

Seasoning Meats to Be Pan-Fried

Pan-fried meats are usually seasoned lightly with salt and pepper either by applying them directly to the meat or adding them to the flour used in the breading procedure.

Determining Doneness

The most accurate way to determine the doneness of a pan-fried item is by timing. The touch method is difficult to use because of the large amounts of hot fat. It also may not be as accurate as with broiled or grilled meats because pan-fried meats are often quite thin.

Accompaniments to Pan-Fried Meats

Any sauce served with pan-fried meats is usually made separately because there is often no fond (drippings) created during the pan-frying process. Sauce suggestions are listed in Table 10.5. Do not coat breaded items with sauce.

Standard Breading Procedure

A breaded item is any food that is coated with bread crumbs, cracker meal, cornmeal or other dry meal to protect it during cooking. Breaded foods are generally cooked by deep-fat frying or pan-frying. The breading makes a solid coating that seals during cooking to prevent the fat from coming in direct contact with the food and making it greasy.

Whether breading meats, poultry, fish, shellfish or vegetables, a three-step process is typically used. Called the **standard breading procedure**, it gives foods a relatively thick, crisp coating.

1. Pat the food dry and dredge it in seasoned flour. The flour adds seasoning to the food, helps seal it, and allows the egg wash to adhere.
2. Dip the floured food in an egg wash. The egg wash should contain whole eggs whisked together with up to 15 mL (1 Tbsp.) milk or water per egg. The egg wash will cause the crumbs or meal to completely coat the item and form a tight seal when the food is cooked.

3. Coat the food with bread crumbs, cracker crumbs or other dry meal. Shake off the excess crumbs and place the breaded item in a pan. As additional breaded items are added to the pan, align them in a single layer; do not stack them or the breadings will get soggy and the foods will stick together.

Figure 12.9 shows the proper setup for breading foods using the standard breading procedure.

The following procedure helps to bread foods more efficiently:

1. Assemble the mise en place as depicted in Figure 12.9.

2. With your left hand, place the food to be breaded in the flour and coat it evenly. With the same hand, remove the floured item, shake off the excess flour and place it in the egg wash.

3. With your right hand, remove the item from the egg wash and place it in the bread crumbs or meal.

4. With your left hand, cover the item with crumbs or meal and press lightly to make sure the item is completely and evenly coated. Shake off the excess crumbs or meal and place the breaded food in the empty pan for the finished product.

The key is to use one hand for the liquid ingredients and the other hand for the dry ingredients. This prevents your fingers from becoming coated with layer after layer of breading.

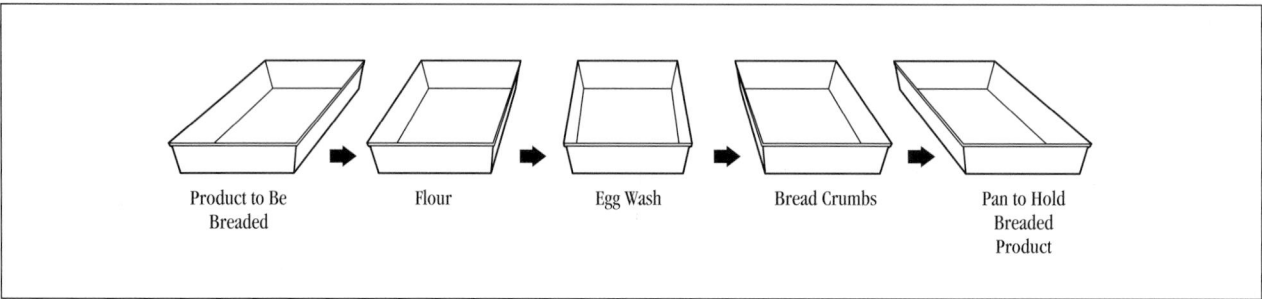

Product to Be Breaded → Flour → Egg Wash → Bread Crumbs → Pan to Hold Breaded Product

FIGURE 12.9 Setup for the standard breading procedure.

BASIC PROCEDURE FOR PAN-FRYING MEATS

1. Slice the meat into cutlets and pound, if required, as described in Chapter 14, Veal.

2. Bread the meat using the standard breading procedure detailed above.

3. Heat a moderate amount of fat or oil in a heavy pan. The temperature should be slightly lower than that used to sauté so that the breading will be nicely browned when the item is fully cooked.

4. Place the meat in the pan, being careful not to splash the hot oil. The meat should be immersed one-third. Fry until golden brown. Turn and brown the other side. Ideally, pan-fried meats should be fully cooked when they are well browned on both sides.

5. Remove the meat from the pan; drain it on absorbent paper before serving.

APPLYING THE BASICS	RECIPE 12.4

Breaded Pork Cutlets

Yield: 10 125-g (4-oz.) servings

Pork cutlet, 125 g (4 oz.) each	10	10
Salt and pepper	TT	TT
Standard breading:	as needed	as needed
Flour		
Egg wash		
Bread crumbs		
Vegetable oil	as needed	as needed
Butter (optional)	175 g	6 oz.
Lemon wedges	20	20

Approximate values per serving:

Calories	444
Total fat	24 g
Saturated fat	6.8 g
Cholesterol	155 mg
Sodium	590 mg
Total carbohydrates	19 g
Protein	38 g

1. Using a mallet, pound the cutlets to an even thickness, approximately 0.5 cm (1/4 in.). Season the cutlets with salt and pepper.

2. Bread the cutlets using the standard breading procedure described above.

3. Heat a heavy pan to moderate heat; add approximately 0.25 cm (1/8 in.) of oil.

4. Add the cutlets in a single layer. Do not crowd the pan. Brown on one side, then the other. Total cooking time should be approximately 4 minutes.

5. Remove the cutlets and drain on absorbent paper.

6. Melt the butter in a small pan until it foams.

7. Place 1 cutlet on each plate and pour approximately 15 mL (1/2 fl. oz.) butter over each portion. Garnish with lemon wedges.

NOTE: Chops, plain or stuffed, use this method, as does Cordon Bleu.

VARIATION: Veal, chicken or turkey may be substituted in this recipe.

1. Breaded Pork Cutlets: Adding the breaded cutlets to the hot pan. Note the amount of oil in the pan.

2. Turning the cutlets to brown on the second side.

3. Melting the butter in a separate pan until it foams.

4. Pouring the butter over the cutlet.

Moist-Heat Cooking Methods

Moist-heat cooking methods subject food to heat and moisture. Moist heat is often, but not always, used to tenderize tougher cuts of meat through long, slow cooking. Simmering is the only moist-heat cooking method discussed here as it is the one most frequently used with meat. Poaching is covered in fish (Chapter 19), poultry (Chapter 17) and breakfast (Chapter 33) cooking.

Simmering

Simmering is usually associated with specific tougher cuts of meat that need to be tenderized through long, slow, moist cooking. Quality simmered meats are moist and have good flavour and texture. The flavour is determined by the cooking liquid; the texture and moistness are a result of proper cooking temperatures and time.

Selecting Meats to Simmer

Meats such as fresh or corned beef brisket, fresh or cured hams and tongue are often simmered. Beef briskets and tongues, pork shoulder blades and hams are often simmered whole. The recipe name usually says "boiled."

Seasoning Meats to Be Simmered

If the meat to be simmered was cured and/or smoked (as with cured hams, ham hocks, smoked pork shoulder blades, corned beef or pickled tongue), the cooking liquid will not be used to make a sauce but should be seasoned with herbs and spices. Indeed, simmering cured meats helps leach out some of the excess salt, making the finished dish more palatable and healthful.

Cooking Temperatures

Moist-heat cooking methods generally use lower temperatures than dry-heat cooking methods. Meats are normally simmered at temperatures between 82°C and 93°C (180°F and 200°F). In larger food service operations, meats such as hams and corned beef are cooked at temperatures as low as 65°C (150°F) for up to 12 hours. Although lower cooking temperatures result in less shrinkage and a more moist and tender finished product, long cooking times may not always be practical, cost efficient or healthy.

Determining Doneness

Tougher cuts are almost always cooked well done, which is determined by tenderness. The size and quality of the raw product determines the cooking time. Undercooked meats will be tough and chewy. Overcooked meats will be stringy and may even fall apart.

To test large cuts of meat for doneness, insert a kitchen fork into the meat; the meat should slide easily off the fork. Smaller pieces of meat should be tender to the bite or easily cut with a table fork.

Accompaniments to Simmered Meats

Simmered meats are often served with boiled or steamed vegetables, for example, corned beef and cabbage. Pickled meats are often served with mustard or horseradish sauce on the side or perhaps a cider raisin sauce.

BASIC PROCEDURE FOR SIMMERING MEATS

1. Cut, trim or tie the meat according to the recipe.
2. Bring an adequate amount of liquid to a boil. There should be enough liquid to cover the meat completely. Too much liquid will leach off much of the meat's flavour; too little will leave a portion of the meat exposed, preventing it from cooking. Because the dish's final flavour is determined by the flavour of the liquid, use plenty of mirepoix, flavourings and seasonings.

continued

3. When simmering smoked or cured items, start them in cold water. This helps draw off some of the strong pickled or smoked flavours.

4. Add the meat to the liquid.

5. Reduce the heat to the desired temperature and cook until the meat is tender. Do not allow the cooking liquid to boil. Boiling results in a tough or overcooked and stringy product. If the simmered meat is to be served cold, a moister and juicier product can be achieved by removing the pot from the stove before the meat is fully cooked. The meat and the liquid can be cooled in a water bath like that for a stock, as described in Chapter 10, Stocks and Sauces. This allows the residual heat in the cooking liquid to finish cooking the meat.

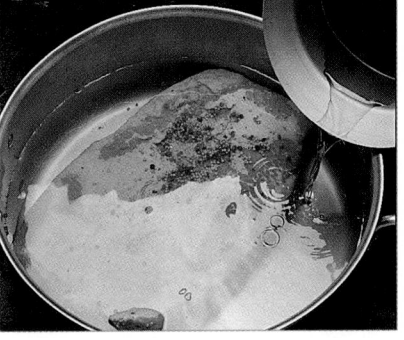

1. New England Boiled Dinner: Placing the corned beef and sachet in an appropriate pot and covering with stock.

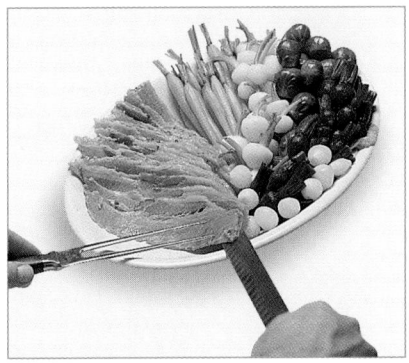

2. Presenting the carved beef with the vegetable garnish.

APPLYING THE BASICS		RECIPE 12.5

New England Boiled Dinner

Yield: 10 180-g (6-oz.) servings

Corned beef brisket, 3 kg (6-1/2 lb.)	1	1
White stock	as needed	as needed
Sachet:		
Bay leaves	2	2
Dried thyme	0.25 g	1/2 tsp.
Peppercorns, cracked	0.5 g	1/2 tsp.
Parsley stems	10	10
Mustard seeds	10 g	1 Tbsp.
Cinnamon sticks	10 g	2
Allspice berries (whole)	4	4
Baby red beets	20	20
Baby turnips	20	20
Baby carrots	20	20
Brussels sprouts	20	20
Pearl onions	20	20
Potatoes, Red Bliss	20	20
Salt and pepper	TT	TT

1. Place the beef in a pot and add enough stock to cover it. Add the sachet, bring to a boil and reduce to a simmer.

2. Simmer until the beef is tender, approximately 3 hours. Remove the beef and hold in a hotel pan in a small amount of the cooking liquid.

3. Peel or prepare the vegetables and potatoes as needed and cook separately in a portion of the cooking liquid.

4. Carve the beef and serve with 2 of each of the vegetables and horseradish sauce (see Chapter 10).

RECIPE 12.5

Approximate values per serving:	
Calories	727
Total fat	32 g
Saturated fat	10 g
Cholesterol	3 mg
Sodium	1155 mg
Total carbohydrates	60 g
Protein	50 g

Combination Cooking Methods

Braising and stewing are referred to as combination cooking methods because both dry heat and moist heat are used to achieve the desired results.

Braising

Braised meats are first browned and then cooked in a liquid that serves as a sauce for the meat. A well-prepared braised dish has the rich flavour of the

● **fork tender** describes braised meat
that is so tender it offers little resistance
when pierced with a fork

meat in the sauce and the moisture and flavour of the sauce in the meat. It
should be **fork tender** but not falling apart. The meat should have an attractive colour from the initial browning and final glazing.

Selecting Meats to Braise

Braising can be used for tender cuts but is better suited to tougher, lean cuts
such as shoulder, shank or some leg cuts. Traditionally, roasts were larded.

If tender cuts such as veal chops or pork chops are braised, the finished
dish has a uniquely different flavour and texture than if they were cooked by a
dry-heat method. Tender cuts require shorter cooking times than do tougher
cuts because lengthy cooking is not needed to break down connective tissue.

More often, braising is used with tougher cuts that are tenderized by the
long, moist cooking process. Cuts from the chuck, outside round and shank
are popular choices, as they are very flavourful and contain relatively large
amounts of collagen, which adds richness to the finished product.

Large pieces of meat can be braised, then carved like a roast (pot roast).
Portion-control cuts and diced meats can also be braised.

Seasoning Meats to Be Braised

The overall flavour of a braised dish is largely the result of using quality cooking liquids and the mirepoix, herbs, spices and other ingredients that flavour
the meat as it cooks. Braised meats can be marinated before they are cooked
to help tenderize them and add flavour. The marinade may be incorporated
into the braising liquid. Salt and pepper may be added to the flour if the meat
is dredged before it is browned, or the meat may be seasoned directly
(although the salt may draw out moisture and inhibit browning).

As a general rule, flavouring and seasoning ingredients, including tomato
products, are added at the start of simmering to ensure even flavour penetration during cooking. Care must be taken not to overseason too early, as the
sauce will reduce during cooking.

Cooking Temperatures

Braised meats are usually browned before simmering. As a general rule,
smaller cuts are floured before browning; larger cuts are not. Flouring dries the
surface of the meat, promotes even browning and provides some thickening to
the sauce that accompanies the meat. Whether floured or not, the meat is
browned in fat. After browning, white meats should be golden to amber in
colour; red meats should be dark brown. Do not brown the meat too quickly
at too high a temperature, as it is important to develop a well-caramelized surface. The caramelized surface adds colour and flavour to the final product.

The meat and the braising liquid are brought to a simmer over direct heat
and the pot is covered. Cooking can be finished in the oven or on the stove
top. The oven provides gentle, even heat without the risk of scorching. If the
braise is finished on the stove top, proper temperatures must be maintained
carefully throughout the cooking process and great care must be taken to prevent scorching or burning. Lower temperatures and longer cooking times
result in more even cooking and thorough penetration of the cooking liquid,
providing a more flavourful final product.

Finishing Braised Meats

Near the end of the cooking process, the lid may be removed from oven-braised
meats. Finishing braised meats without a cover serves two purposes. First, the
meat can be glazed by basting it often. (As the basting liquid evaporates, the
meat is browned and a strongly flavoured glaze is formed.) Second, removing

the lid allows the cooking liquid to reduce, thickening it and concentrating its flavours for use as a sauce.

Determining Doneness

Braised meats are done when they are tender. A fork inserted into the meat should meet little resistance. Properly braised meats should remain intact and not fall apart when handled gently.

Braised meats that fall apart or are stringy are overcooked. If the finished product is tough, it was probably undercooked or cooked at too high a temperature. If the entire dish lacks flavour, the meat may not have been properly browned or the cooking liquid may have been poorly seasoned.

Accompaniments to Braised Meats

Large braised items are often served like roasts. They are carved across the grain in thin slices and served with their sauce. Vegetables can be cooked with the braised meat, cooked separately and added when the main item has finished cooking or added at service. If the vegetables are cooked with the main item, they should be added at intervals based on their individual cooking times to prevent overcooking.

Paradox

Cooking any meat to achieve optimum palatability is a challenge. The product's characteristics and the customer's desires must be brought together. Longer cooking times, often associated with less tender cuts, usually mean the product will be well done. Well-done meat becomes dry and stringy. The hydrolyzed collagen (gelatin) ends up in the sauce as does any fat.

The cook must find a balance in controlling the cooking process to achieve the best results despite the chemistry. Careful thought must go into planning the menu, purchasing the appropriate product and applying the best cooking method to ensure customer satisfaction. Always analyze a recipe thoroughly and, if necessary, adapt the ingredients or method to have the chemistry working for you. Even very tender, well-marbled cuts can be ruined by applying inappropriate methodologies. Tenderloin can be tough!

BASIC PROCEDURE FOR BRAISING MEATS

The liquid used for braising is usually thickened in one of three ways:

1. With a roux added at the start of the cooking process; the roux thickens the sauce as the meat cooks.
2. Prethickened before the meat is added.
3. Thickened after the meat is cooked either by puréeing the mirepoix or by using roux, arrowroot or cornstarch.

The procedure for braising meats includes variations for whichever thickening method is selected.

1. Heat a small amount of oil in a heavy pan.
2. Dredge the meat to be braised in seasoned flour, if desired, and add it to the oil.
3. Brown the meat well on all sides and remove from the pan.
4. Add a mirepoix to the pan and caramelize it well. If using roux, it should be added at this time.
5. Add the appropriate stock or sauce so that when the meat is returned to the pan, it will be approximately one-third immersed.
6. Add aromatics and seasonings.
7. Return the meat to the sauce. Tightly cover the pot and bring it to a simmer. Cook slowly either on the stove top or by placing the covered pot directly in an oven at 120°C to 150°C (250°F to 300°F).
8. Cook the item, basting or turning it often so that all sides of the meat benefit from the moisture and flavour of the sauce.
9. When the meat is done, remove it from the pan and hold it in a warm place while the sauce is finished.
10. The sauce may be reduced on the stove top to intensify its flavours. If the meat was braised in a stock, the stock may be thickened using a roux, arrowroot or cornstarch. Strain the sauce or, if desired, purée the mirepoix and other ingredients and return them to the sauce. Adjust the sauce's consistency as desired.

Peter Schuster, CCC

Peter has had a long-standing relationship with apprentice training in Alberta. He was an Executive Chef for Four Seasons Hotels in Vancouver and Calgary in addition to working in Toronto for a number of years.

APPLYING THE BASICS		RECIPE 12.6

Braised Beef Roulade with Bread Dumplings

SAIT POLYTECHNIC, CALGARY, AB
Peter Schuster, CCC

Yield: 10 portions (225 g raw weight)

Beef, lean, ground	750 g	1 lb. 10 oz.
Eggs, beaten	2	2
Salt and pepper	TT	TT
Beef, inside round, cap removed, sliced thinly	10 × 120 g	10 × 4 oz.
Dijon mustard	50 mL	2 oz.
Bacon strips, par-cooked	10	10
Cornichons (sour gherkins)	20	20
Carrot, batons	10	10
Onion, julienne, sweated	200 g	6 oz.
Toothpicks	as needed	as needed
Canola oil	100 mL	3-1/2 fl. oz.
Flour	as needed	as needed
Onions, brunoise	200 g	7 oz.
Red wine or dark beer	300 mL	10 fl. oz.
Espagnole, thin	2 L	2 qt.
Bay leaves	2	2
Sachet:		
Peppercorns	10 g	1 Tbsp.
Thyme, dry	2 g	1 tsp.
Oregano, dry	2 g	1 tsp.
Marjoram	2 g	1 tsp.

1. Mix the ground beef with the eggs and season with salt and pepper.

2. Set the slices of beef out on a clean work surface. Season them lightly with salt and pepper.

3. Brush each slice with Dijon mustard and place a par-cooked bacon slice lengthwise.

4. Divide the ground beef into 10 portions and place a portion at one end of each beef slice.

5. Arrange 2 cornichons, a carrot baton and a portion of the onion next to the ground meat. Repeat on all slices.

6. Roll the meat snugly into a tightly closed package and secure with toothpicks.

7. Heat a braising pan (rondeau) and add the oil.

8. Dredge the roulades in flour and brown them in the hot oil.

9. Remove and reserve the browned roulades.

10. Add the onions to the pan and fry until golden.

11. Deglaze with the wine or beer and add the espagnole, bay leaves and sachet.

12. Bring to a boil and return the roulades to the pan. Cover.

13. Braise in a 200°C (400°F) oven for approximately 1 hour or until tender.

14. Place the cooked roulade in a hotel pan and remove the toothpicks. Reserve.

15. Adjust the seasoning and consistency of the sauce and strain over the meat.

16. For service, the roulade may be served whole or sliced. Arrange with dumplings and a portion of the sauce.

RECIPE 12.6

Approximate values per serving:	
Calories	813
Total fat	51 g
Saturated fat	20 g
Cholesterol	181 mg
Sodium	1125 mg
Total carbohydrates	33 g
Protein	49 g

Bread Dumplings (Bohemian)

Yield: 10 dumplings

Butter	150 g	5 oz.
Onion, brunoise	150 g	5 oz.
Slab bacon, rindless, small dice	150 g	5 oz.
White bread, day old	500 g	1 lb.
Milk	125 mL	4 fl. oz.
Parsley, chopped	50 g	2 oz.
Eggs, beaten	4	4
Salt	5 g	1 tsp.
Pepper, ground black	1 g	1/4 tsp.
Nutmeg	1 g	1/4 tsp.
Cornstarch	50 g	2 oz.

1. Melt the butter in a preheated pan and fry the onions and bacon until golden.
2. Cut the bread into 1-cm cubes and place in a mixing bowl.
3. Heat the milk to scalding.
4. Add the onion mixture and parsley to the bread and toss thoroughly.
5. Pour the hot milk over the bread mixture and add the beaten eggs and seasonings.
6. Mix well and let rest for 10 minutes. Taste and adjust seasoning.
7. Heat 6 litres (6 qt.) of water to a boil and add 10 g (2 tsp.) of salt.
8. Form 10 100-g (3-1/2-oz.) dumplings using an ice cream scoop. Roll each portion into a tight ball with no cracks.
9. Roll each dumpling in cornstarch and place in the simmering water.
10. Simmer for 25 minutes or until dry, not gummy, in the centre.

Bread Dumplings (Bohemian)— Approximate values per serving:	
Calories	337
Total fat	19 g
Saturated fat	9.4 g
Cholesterol	116 mg
Sodium	695 mg
Total carbohydrates	32 g
Protein	10 g

Stewing

Stewing is a combination cooking method. In many ways, the procedures for stewing and braising are identical, although stewing is usually associated with smaller or bite-sized pieces of meat.

There are two main types of stews: brown stews and white stews.

When making **brown stews**, the meat is first browned in fat; then a cooking liquid is added. The initial browning adds flavour and colour to the finished product. The same characteristics apply to a good brown stew that apply to a good braised dish: it should be fork tender and have an attractive colour and rich flavour.

There are two types of white stews: **fricassees**, in which the meat is first cooked in a small amount of fat without colouring, then combined with a cooking liquid; and **blanquettes**, in which the meat is first blanched, then rinsed and added to a cooking liquid. White stew should have the same flavour and texture characteristics as a brown stew but should be white or ivory in colour.

Vegetables to garnish stews are cut uniformly and attractively, as they are left in the dish for service. Flavourings such as a bouquet garni or sachet can easily be removed.

Selecting Meats to Stew

Stewing uses moist heat to tenderize meat just as braising does, therefore many of the same cuts can be used. Meats that are to be stewed should be

● **brown stew** a stew in which the meat is first browned in hot fat

● **fricassee** a white ragout usually made from white meat or small game, seared without browning and garnished with small onions and mushrooms

● **blanquette** a white stew in which the meat is first blanched, then added to a stock or sauce to complete the cooking and tenderizing process. Blanquettes are finished with a liaison of egg yolks and heavy cream.

Additional Stew Terminology

Ragout—A general term that refers to white or brown stews in which the meat is cooked by dry heat before liquid is added. In French, *ragoût* means "to bring back the taste."

Navarin—A brown ragout generally made with lamb, root vegetables, onions and peas.

Chili con carne—A ragout of ground or diced meat cooked with onions, chile peppers, cumin and other spices. Despite the objections of purists, chili sometimes contains beans.

Paprikash—A Hungarian stew thickened with onions, flavoured with paprika and garnished with potatoes. Pörkölt is braised and has more paprika and less liquid. Gulyás (goulash) is more like a soup.

Tagine—(tah-GEEN) A North African stew in which meat, poultry, fish or vegetables are flavoured with onions, cilantro, spices and aromatics and then braised over a fire in a covered earthenware vessel of the same name.

Adobo—A stew of Spanish origin in which meats are simmered with onions and spices in a savoury red chile sauce. In the Philippines, *adobo* refers to a stew in which ingredients including meats, poultry or fish are pickled in vinegar, oil and spices before cooking.

trimmed of excess fat and connective tissue and cut uniformly into 2.5- to 5-cm (1- to 2-in.) cubes.

Seasoning Meats to Be Stewed

Stews, like braised meats, get much of their flavour from their cooking liquid. A stew's seasoning and overall flavour are a direct result of the quality of the cooking liquid and the vegetables, herbs, spices and other ingredients added during cooking.

Cooking Temperatures

Meats for brown stews are first cooked at high temperatures over direct heat until well browned. Meats for fricassees are first sautéed at low temperatures so they do not develop colour.

Once the cooking liquid has been added and the moist-heat cooking process has begun, do not allow the stew to boil. Stews benefit from low-temperature cooking. If practical, stews can be covered and finished in the oven.

Determining Doneness

Stewed meats are done when they are fork tender. Test them by removing a piece of meat to a plate and cutting it with a fork. Any vegetables that are cooked with the meat should be added at the proper times so that they and the meat are completely cooked at the same time.

Accompaniments to Stewed Meats

Stews are often complete meals in themselves, containing meat, vegetables and starches in one dish. Stews that do not contain a starch are often served with pasta, rice, boiled potatoes or dumplings.

BASIC PROCEDURE FOR STEWING MEATS— BROWN STEWS

Red meats, lamb or game are most often used in brown stews. The procedure for making a brown stew is very similar to braising.

1. Trim the meat of excess fat and silverskin and cut into 2.5- to 5-cm (1- to 2-in.) pieces.

2. Dredge the meat in flour if desired. Heat an appropriate-sized pan and add enough oil to cover the bottom. Cook the meat in the oil, browning it well on all sides. Onions and garlic can be added at this time and browned.

3. Add flour to the meat and fat and cook to make a brown roux (optional—see step 6).

4. Gradually add the liquid to the roux, stirring to prevent lumps. Bring the stew to a boil and reduce to a simmer.

5. Add a tomato product and a sachet or a bouquet garni. Cover and place in the oven or continue to simmer on the stove top until the meat is tender. Add other ingredients such as vegetables or potatoes at the proper time so that they will be done when the meat is tender.

6. When the meat is tender, remove the sachet or bouquet garni. The meat may be strained out and the sauce thickened with roux, cornstarch or arrowroot or reduced to concentrate its flavours.

7. If not added during the cooking process, vegetables and other garnishes may be cooked separately and added to the finished stew.

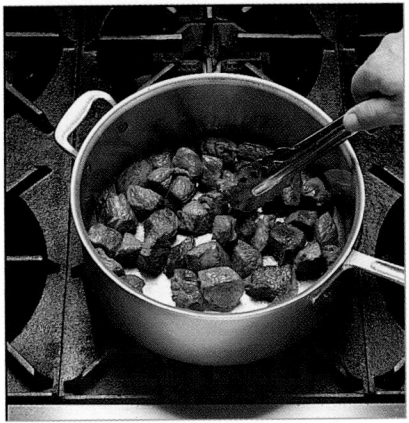

1. Brown Beef Stew: Browning the beef.

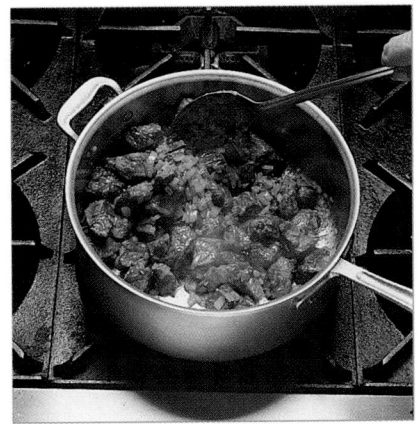

2. Sautéing the garlic and onions until slightly browned.

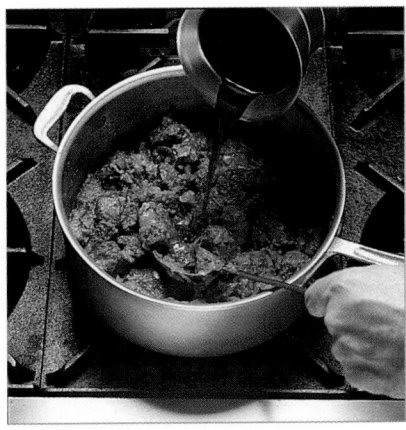

3. Adding the red wine and brown stock.

APPLYING THE BASICS   RECIPE 12.7

Brown Beef Stew

Yield: 10 250-mL (8-fl. oz.) servings

Oil	75 mL	2-1/2 fl. oz.
Beef chuck or shank, trimmed and cut into 3.5-cm (1-1/2-in.) cubes	2.5 kg	5 lb. 10 oz.
Salt	10 g	2 tsp.
Pepper	0.5 g	1/2 tsp.
Onion, small dice	375 g	12 oz.
Garlic clove, chopped	10 g	2
Red wine	300 mL	10 fl. oz.
Brown stock	1.25 L	1-1/4 qt.
Tomato purée	150 mL	5 fl. oz.
Sachet:		
Bay leaves	2	2
Dried thyme	0.25 g	1/2 tsp.
Peppercorns, crushed	0.5 g	1/2 tsp.
Parsley stems	10	10

1. Heat a heavy pot until very hot and add the oil.

2. Season the beef and add it to the pot, browning it well on all sides. Do not overcrowd the pot. If necessary, cook the beef in several batches.

3. Add the onion and garlic and sauté until the onion is slightly browned.

4. Add the red wine and brown stock.

5. Add the tomato purée and the sachet.

6. Bring to a simmer and cook until the beef is tender, approximately 1.5–2 hours.

7. Degrease the stew by skimming off the fat.

8. Optional: Remove the cooked beef from the sauce, strain the sauce and thicken slightly with a starch product. Return the beef to the sauce.

VARIATION: Vegetables such as mushrooms, turnips, carrots, celery and pearl onions can be cooked separately and added to the stew as garnish. Lardons (bacon) may be added.

4. Adding the tomato purée and sachet.

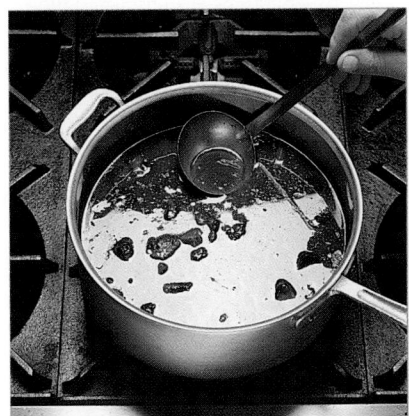

5. Degreasing the stew.

RECIPE 12.7

Approximate values per serving:	
Calories	618
Total fat	24 g
Saturated fat	6.5 g
Cholesterol	206 mg
Sodium	587 mg
Total carbohydrates	7.9 g
Protein	48 g

BASIC PROCEDURE FOR STEWING MEATS—BRAISED WHITE STEWS (FRICASSEES)

The procedure for making fricassees is similar to the procedure for brown stews. The primary difference is that the meat is sautéed but not allowed to brown. The braised white stew (fricassee) procedure outlined below is the basis for Recipe 17.7, Chicken Fricassee.

1. Trim meat of excess fat and silverskin and cut into 2.5- to 5-cm (1- to 2-in.) pieces.

2. Heat an appropriate-sized pan and add enough oil to cover the bottom. Add the meat (and often an onion) to the pan and cook without browning.

3. Sprinkle the meat (and onion) with flour and cook to make a blond roux.

4. Gradually add the liquid, stirring to prevent lumps. Bring the stew to a boil and reduce to a simmer.

5. Add a bouquet garni and seasonings. Cover the stew and place in the oven or continue to simmer on the stove top, being careful not to burn or scorch the stew.

6. Continue to cook until the meat is tender. If the sauce is too thin, remove the meat from the sauce and hold the meat in a warm place. Reduce the sauce to the proper consistency on the stove top or thicken it by adding a small amount of blond roux, cornstarch or arrowroot.

BASIC PROCEDURE FOR STEWING MEATS—SIMMERED WHITE STEWS (BLANQUETTES)

Unlike fricassees, blanquettes contain meat that is blanched, not sautéed. (Because the meat is cooked only by moist heat and never by dry heat, the blanquette cooking process is not a true combination cooking method; nevertheless, because of its striking similarities to stewing, it is included here.) The most common blanquette is made with veal and is known as blanquette de veau, but any white meat, poultry or lamb can be prepared in this manner using a variety of garnishes.

1. Trim meat of excess fat and silverskin and cut into 2.5- to 5-cm (1- to 2-in.) pieces.

2. Blanch the cubed meat by placing the meat in an appropriate pot, covering with cool water, adding salt and bringing it rapidly to a boil. Drain the water. Rinse the meat to remove any impurities.

3. Return the meat to the pot and add enough stock to cover. Add a bouquet garni, salt and pepper. Simmer until the meat is tender, approximately 1 to 1.5 hours.

4. Strain the meat from the stock. Discard the bouquet garni. Bring the stock to a boil, thicken it with a blond roux and simmer for 15 minutes.

5. Return the meat to the thickened stock and heat to just under 85°C (185°F). Remove from the heat and add the egg yolk and cream liaison just before service. Do not boil or the egg yolks will curdle.

6. If any vegetables are to be added, they should be cooked separately and added to the thickened stock with the meat.

7. Adjust the seasoning with a few drops of lemon juice, nutmeg or salt and pepper as needed.

RECIPE 12.8

Blanquette of Veal—Sous Vide

SAIT POLYTECHNIC, CALGARY, AB
Georg Windisch, CCC

Yield: 4 servings
Method: Sous vide

White wine, dry	50 mL	2 fl. oz.
Veal stock, white	150 mL	5 fl. oz.
Veal leg, trimmed and cut into 3-cm (1-1/4 in.) cubes	400 g	14 oz.
Blond roux	50 g	2 oz.
Cream, 35%	100 mL	3-1/2 fl. oz.
Pearl onions, fresh, butter glazed	60 g	2-1/2 oz.
Mushroom quarters, butter glazed	80 g	3 oz.
Salt	10 g	2 tsp.
White pepper, ground	2 g	1/4 tsp.

1. Combine white wine and veal stock and bring to a simmer. Blanch the veal cubes for 5 minutes.
2. Remove meat and reserve. Strain the stock and combine with the roux.
3. Add the cream and simmer for 5 minutes.
4. Add remaining ingredients, including reserved veal, and combine well. Adjust seasoning.
5. Portion the stew into cooking-grade vacuum bags and poach or steam at 85°C (185°F) for 2 hours. Remove and immediately chill in ice water.
6. Refrigerate at 1°C–3°C (34°F–37°F). Use within 5 days.
7. Rethermalize to 74°C (165°F) for 15 minutes for service.

Georg Windisch, CCC
Georg was born and professionally trained in Austria and has extensive work experience in the hotel industry in Europe, Australia, Asia and Canada. Before starting his own company and joining SAIT, he was the Executive Chef at the Pan Pacific Hotel in Singapore.

RECIPE 12.8

Approximate values per serving:	
Calories	308
Total fat	19 g
Saturated fat	11 g
Cholesterol	135 mg
Sodium	1128 mg
Total carbohydrates	9 g
Protein	23 g

Conclusion

Because meat may account for the largest portion of your food-cost dollar, it should be purchased carefully, stored properly and fabricated appropriately. The various cuts and flavours of meat (beef, veal, lamb and pork) can be successfully broiled, grilled, roasted, sautéed, pan-fried, simmered, braised or stewed, provided you follow a few simple procedures and learn which cuts respond best to the various cooking methods.

Questions for Discussion

1. Explain the difference between primals, subprimals and fabricated cuts of meat. Why is it important to be skilled in meat fabrication?
2. What is connective tissue composed of and where is it found? What happens to connective tissues at normal cooking temperatures?
3. Discuss the government's role in regulating the marketing and sale of meat.
4. Explain why meats are subject to a health inspection. What is the purpose of grading carcass meat?

5. At what temperature should fresh meat be stored? At what temperature should frozen meat be stored?

6. Would it be better to grill or braise a piece of meat that contains a great deal of connective tissue? Explain your answer.

7. List three ways to improve the cooking qualities of lean meats. What techniques can be used to compensate for the lack of fat?

8. Describe the similarities between sautéing meats and pan-frying them. Describe the differences.

9. Describe the similarities between braising meats and stewing them. Describe the differences.

10. Describe the similarities between the methods for preparing a traditional blanquette and one prepared sous vide. Describe the differences.

“ Beef is the soul of cooking.

—Marie-Antoine Carême, French chef (1784–1833)

PEARSON
myculinarylab

These interactive online tools will help you master the skills in this chapter:

- Videos
- Chapter Quizzes
- Activities

Not All Cattle Are Called "Daisy"

Cattle is the collective name for all domesticated oxen (genus *Bos*). Cattle are classified as follows:

Bulls—Male cattle, usually not raised to be eaten.

Veal—Young cows or bulls prized for their mild meat.

Cows—Female cattle after their first calving, raised in this country principally for milk and calf production. Cows are often processed for beef when they are no longer needed for milk.

Heifers—Young cows or cows before their first calving. Heifer meat is marketed with steer meat without identification.

Stags—Male cattle castrated after maturity, principally used for dog food.

Steers—Male cattle castrated prior to maturity and principally raised for beef.

Beef is the meat of domesticated cattle. Most of the beef Canadians eat comes from steers or heifers specifically raised for beef. Although Canadians are consuming less beef today than we once did, we still consume far more beef than any other meat. The beef we are eating is safe and healthy due to stringent regulations governing production, processing and importation.

PRIMAL AND SUBPRIMAL CUTS OF BEEF

After the steer or heifer is slaughtered, it is cut into four pieces (called quarters) for easy handling. This is done by first splitting the carcass down the backbone into two bilateral halves. Each half is divided into the forequarter (the front portion) and hindquarter (the rear portion) by cutting along the natural curvature between the twelfth and thirteenth ribs. The quartered carcass is then further reduced into the primal cuts and the subprimal and fabricated cuts.

The primal cuts of beef are the square chuck, point brisket and shank, rib, plate, short loin, sirloin, flank and hip. Figure 13.1 shows the relationship between a steer's bone structure and the primal cuts. Figure 13.2 shows the primal cuts of beef and their location on the carcass. Table 13.1 (page 286) identifies common beef cuts including their Canadian Meat Council (CMC) numbers (also shown in the captions of the illustrative photos) and suggests preparation methods. An entire beef carcass can range in weight from 225 kg to more than 360 kg (500 to 800 lb.).

Forequarter

Chuck (Square Cut Chuck)

The primal chuck is the animal's shoulder; it accounts for approximately 28% of carcass weight. It contains a portion of the backbone (which, in turn, consists of feather, finger and chine bones), five rib bones and portions of the blade and arm bones.

Because an animal constantly uses its shoulder muscles, chuck contains a high percentage of connective tissue and is quite tough. This tough cut of beef, however, is one of the most flavourful.

The primal chuck is used less frequently than other primal cuts in food service operations. If cooked whole, the chuck is difficult to cut or carve because of the large number of bones and relatively small muscle groups that travel in different directions.

The primal chuck produces several subprimal or fabricated cuts: shoulder clod, chuck roll, chuck tender, stew meat and ground chuck. Because the meat is tougher, the fabricated cuts usually benefit from moist-heat cooking or combination cooking methods such as stewing and braising. Flat iron is a popular exception.

Brisket (Full and Point) and Shank

The brisket and shank are located beneath the primal chuck on the front half of the carcass. Together, they form a single primal that accounts for approximately 8% of the carcass weight. This primal consists of the animal's breast (the brisket), which contains ribs and breast bone, and its arm (the foreshank), which contains only the shank bone.

The ribs and breast bone are always removed from the brisket before cooking. The boneless brisket is very tough and contains a substantial percentage of fat, both intermuscular and subcutaneous. It is well suited for moist-heat

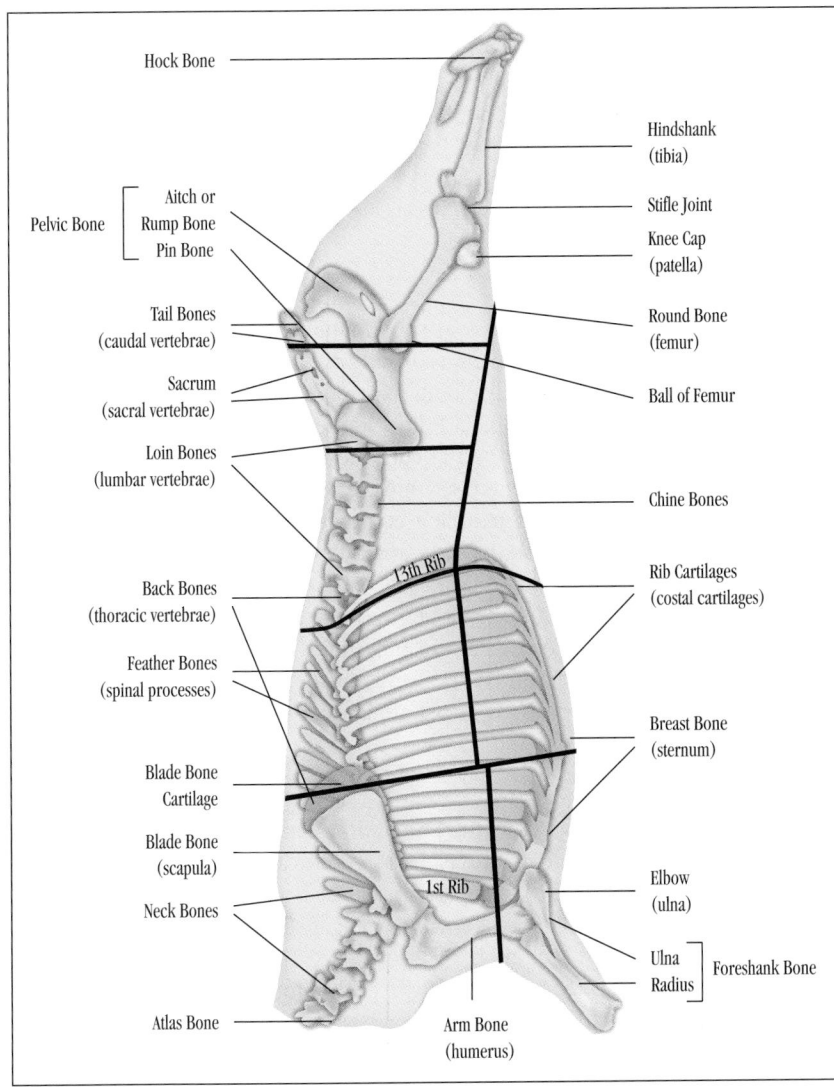

FIGURE 13.1 The skeletal structure of a steer.

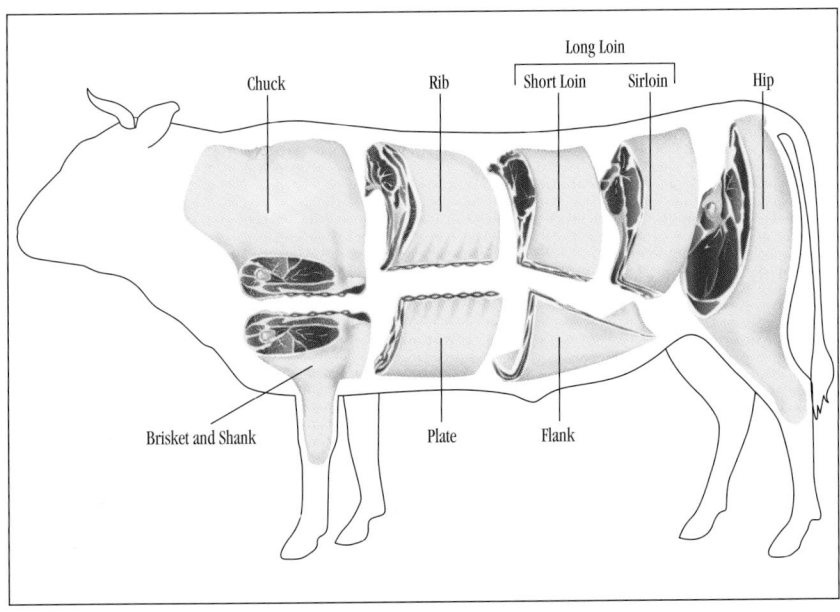

FIGURE 13.2 The primal cuts of beef.

Smaller Carcasses

Pressure and demand by restaurants is causing renewed interest in smaller carcasses. Thicker steaks can be cut from lighter animals and still meet portion standards. A premium price is being paid to acquire smaller muscles. However, the efficiencies and yields achieved from larger carcasses dictate that they will remain a strong market presence. New ways of fabricating and preparing the larger muscles are being developed.

"New" Beef Cuts

A number of secondary beef cuts are now being marketed, such as flat iron, medallions and chuck flat. Most of these cuts come from the front quarter. The Beef Information Centre provides technical sheets on these unfamiliar cuts that include recommendations on handling them and menu suggestions. Visit www.beefinfo.org for further information.

BSE (Mad Cow Disease)

Bovine spongiform encephalopathy (BSE) has caused global concerns over the safety of beef for human consumption. Canada has regulations in place to restrict the importation of live animals. The feeding of sheep- or cattle-based protein to cattle is banned. Canada has not imported meat or bone meal from the UK since 1982. In 1997, Canada banned the feeding of cattle with animal proteins. To further ensure a safe food supply, the Canadian Cattle Identification Program was introduced in January 2001. Canadian cattle are identified by a unique number on an ear tag.

As of 2008, several Canadian and American BSE cases were confirmed. Both countries have moved to improve the inspection processes for slaughter cattle and restore consumer confidence.

Blade Steak (Flat Iron), CMC#114D

Beef Rib Eye Roll Steak, CMC#1112

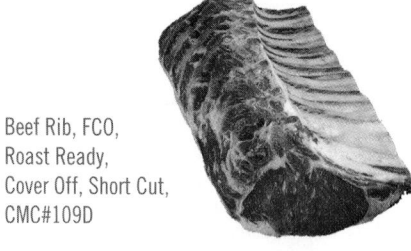

Beef Rib, FCO, Roast Ready, Cover Off, Short Cut, CMC#109D

Skirt Steak, Inner, CMC#121D

and combination cooking methods such as simmering or braising. It is often pickled or corned to produce corned beef brisket, or cured and peppered to make pastrami.

Beef foreshanks are very flavourful and high in collagen. Because collagen converts to gelatin when cooked using moist heat, foreshanks are excellent for making soups and stocks. Ground shank meat is often used to help clarify and flavour consommés because of its rich flavour and high collagen content.

Rib

The primal beef rib accounts for approximately 10% of carcass weight. It consists of ribs 6 through 12 as well as a portion of the backbone.

This primal is best known for yielding roast prime rib of beef. Prime rib is not named after the quality grade Canada Prime. Rather, its name reflects the fact that it constitutes the majority of the primal cut. The eye meat of the rib (the centre muscle portion) is not a well-exercised muscle and therefore is quite tender. It also contains large amounts of marbling compared with the rest of the carcass and produces rich, full-flavoured roasts and steaks. Although roasting the eye muscle on the rib bones produces a moister roast, the eye meat can be removed to produce a boneless rib eye roast or cut into rib eye steaks. The rib bones that are separated from the rib eye meat are quite meaty and flavourful and can be served as barbecued beef backribs. The ends of the rib bones that are trimmed off the primal rib to produce the rib roast are known as beef short ribs.

Plate

The plate is located directly below the primal rib on a side of beef; it accounts for only a small portion of the overall weight of the carcass, approximately 9%. The plate contains rib bones and cartilage and produces the meaty plate short ribs and inside and outside skirt steak (also known as hanger steak or hanging tenderloin).

Short ribs are meaty, yet high in connective tissue, and are best when braised. Skirt steak is often marinated and grilled for fajitas. Other, less meaty portions of the plate are trimmed and ground.

Hindquarter

Loin (Long Loin and Short Loin)

The long loin is the anterior (front) portion of the beef loin. It is located just behind the rib and becomes the first primal cut of the hindquarter when the side of beef is divided into a forequarter and hindquarter. It accounts for approximately 15% of carcass weight.

The short loin contains a single rib, the thirteenth, and a portion of the backbone. With careful butchering, this small primal can yield several subprimal and fabricated cuts, all of which are among the most tender, popular and expensive cuts of beef.

The loin eye muscle, a continuation of the rib eye muscle, runs along the top of the T-shaped bones that form the backbone. Beneath the loin eye muscle on the other side of the backbone is the tenderloin, the most tender cut of all.

When the short loin is cut in cross sections with the bone in, it produces—starting with the rib end of the short loin—club steaks (which do not contain any tenderloin), T-bone steaks (which

Beef Loin, T-bone Steak, CMC#173A

contain only a small portion of tenderloin) and porterhouse steaks (which are cut from the sirloin end of the short loin and contain a large portion of tenderloin).

The whole tenderloin also can be removed and cut into chateaubriand, filet mignon and tournedos. A portion of the tenderloin is located in the sirloin portion of the loin. When the entire beef loin is divided into the primal short loin and primal sirloin, the large end of the tenderloin (the butt tenderloin) is separated from the remainder of the tenderloin and remains in the sirloin; the smaller end of the tenderloin (the short tenderloin) remains in the short loin. If the tenderloin is to be kept whole, it must be removed before the short loin and sirloin are separated. The loin eye meat can be removed from the bones, producing a boneless strip loin, which is very tender and can be roasted or cut into boneless strip loin steaks. The sirloin is located in the hindquarter, between the short loin and the round. It accounts for approximately 7% of carcass weight and contains part of the backbone as well as a portion of the hip bone.

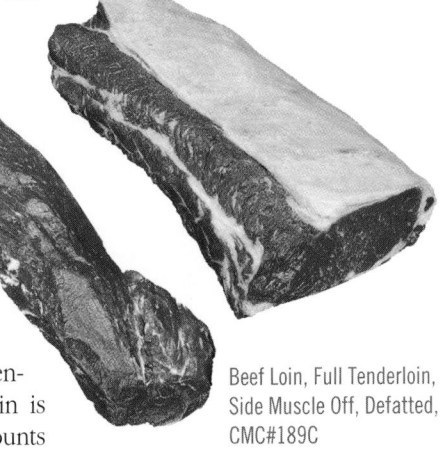

Beef Loin, Full Tenderloin, Side Muscle Off, Defatted, CMC#189C

The sirloin produces bone-in or boneless roasts and steaks that are flavourful and tender. With the exception of the tenderloin portion, however, these subprimals and fabricated cuts are not as tender as those from the strip loin. Innovative cuts from the sirloin include the flap, ball tip, tri tip, tenderloin roll and top cap muscle.

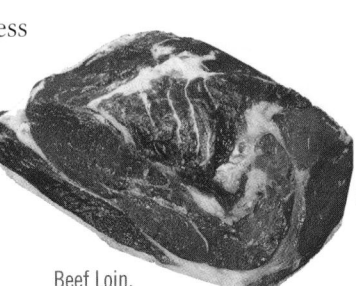

Beef Loin, Top Sirloin Butt, CMC#184

Beef Loin, Top Sirloin Butt Steak, Centre Cut, Boneless, CMC#184B

Flank

The flank is located directly beneath the loin, posterior to (behind) the plate. It accounts for approximately 6% of carcass weight. The flank contains minimal bones.

Although quite flavourful, it is tough meat with a good deal of fat and connective tissue. Flank meat is usually trimmed and ground, with the exception of the flank steak, which can be stuffed, rolled and braised or marinated and grilled to become a London broil. The flank also has a flap of meat called hanging tenderloin.

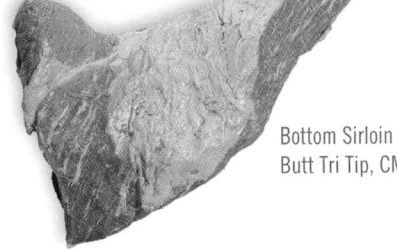

Bottom Sirloin Butt Tri Tip, CMC#184

Beef Flank Steak, CMC#193

Hip

The primal hip is very large, weighing as much as 90 kg (200 lb.) and accounting for approximately 24% of carcass weight. It is the hind leg of the animal and contains the round, aitch, shank and tail bones.

Meat from the hip is flavourful and fairly tender. The hip yields a wide variety of subprimal and fabricated cuts: the inside round, outside round flat, eye of round (the outside round flat and the eye of round together are called the bottom round), knuckle and shank. (See Figure 13.3 on the next page.) Steaks cut from the hip are tougher, but because they have large muscles and limited intermuscular fat, the top round and knuckle make good roasts. The outside round is best when braised. The hindshank is prepared in the same fashion as the foreshank.

Beef Round, Beef Top Round, Inside, CMC#168

Organ Meats

Several beef organ meats are used in food service operations. This group of products is known as **offal**. It includes the heart, kidney, tongue, tripe (stomach lining) and oxtail. They are thoroughly cleaned but have stronger flavours and are tough. Soaking in cold water with a little salt helps draw out impurities. Offal

● **offal** also called variety meats; the edible entrails and extremities of an animal

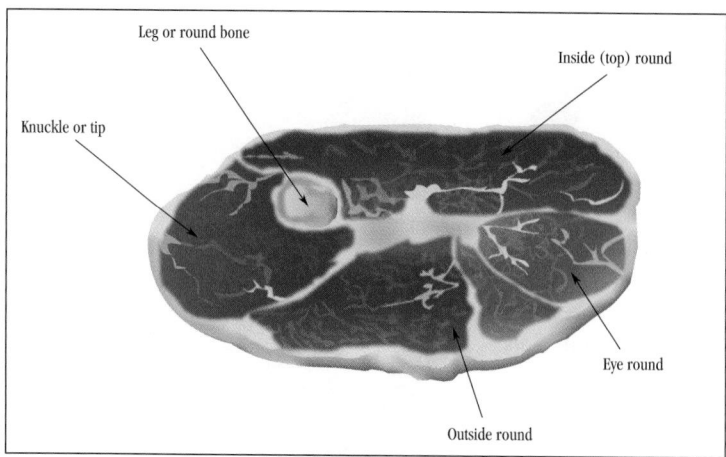

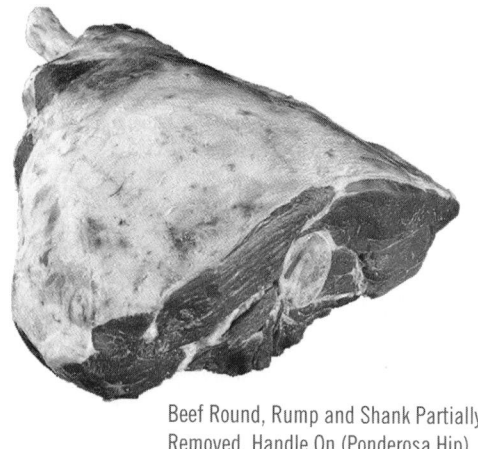

Beef Round, Rump and Shank Partially Removed, Handle On (Ponderosa Hip), CMC#164A

FIGURE 13.3 Crosscut of muscles in a whole hip.

benefit from moist-heat cooking and are often used in soup, stew or braised dishes. Tongue, technically a muscle, may be pickled and used for garnishing pâtés. Kidney, after blanching several times, is used for steak and kidney pies. Beef liver is used, but calves' liver is the most popular.

NUTRITION

Beef is a major source of protein and the primary food source of zinc as well as B vitamins, trace minerals and other nutrients. While well-marbled beef does contain a high percentage of saturated fat, lean cuts of beef such as eye round and top round roasts, top sirloin and shoulder pot roast have less fat than chicken thighs, a standard level of comparison. Excess fat should be trimmed as much as possible before cooking and serving.

BUTCHERING PROCEDURES

Although most food service operations buy their beef previously cut and portioned, cooks should be able to fabricate some cuts of beef and perform basic butchering tasks.

Kobe Beef

Kobe beef is an exclusive type of beef traditionally produced in Kobe, Japan. Wagyu cattle are fed a special diet, which includes beer to stimulate the animal's appetite during summer months. The animals are massaged with sake to relieve stress and muscle stiffness in the belief that calm, contented cattle produce better-quality meat. This special treatment produces meat that is extraordinarily tender and full-flavoured, and extraordinarily expensive. Kobe Beef America introduced Wagyu cattle to the United States in 1976. KBA's cattle are raised without hormones and the meat is dry-aged for 21 days prior to sale. Canada has some Wagyu ranchers as well.

BASIC PROCEDURE FOR CUTTING A STRIP LOIN STEAK FROM A BONELESS STRIP LOIN

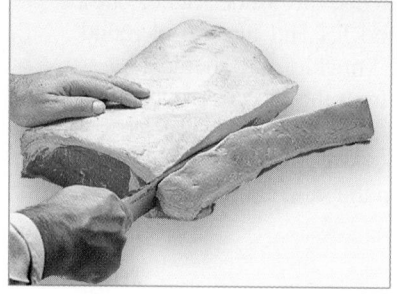

1. Square up the strip loin by trimming off the lip so it extends 2.5 to 5 cm (1 to 2 in.) from the eye muscle.

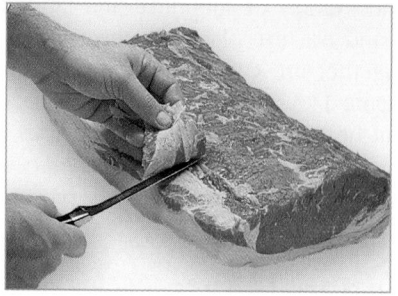

2. Turn the strip over and trim off any excess fat or connective tissue.

continued

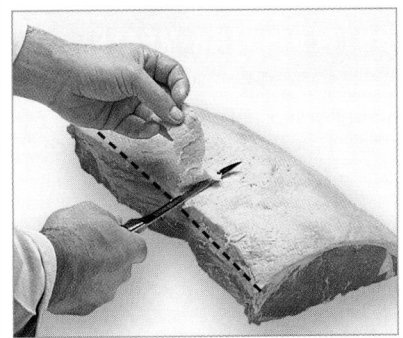

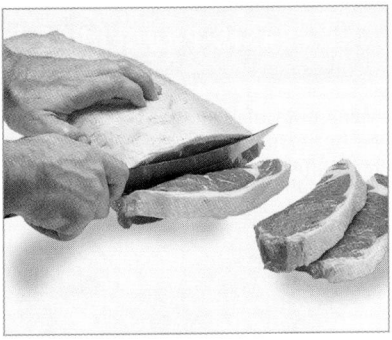

3. Turn the strip back over and trim the fat covering to a uniform thickness of 0.5 cm (1/4 in.). Many chefs also remove a 5-cm (2-in.) strip of backstrap and fat covering along the edge of the strip, as shown by the dotted line.

4. Cut the steaks to the thickness or weight desired.

5. The eye meat of steaks located on the sirloin end of the strip is divided by a strip of connective tissue. Steaks cut from this area are called vein steaks and are inferior to steaks cut from the rib end of the strip.

BASIC PROCEDURE FOR TRIMMING A FULL BEEF TENDERLOIN AND CUTTING IT INTO CHATEAUBRIAND, FILET MIGNON AND TENDER TIPS

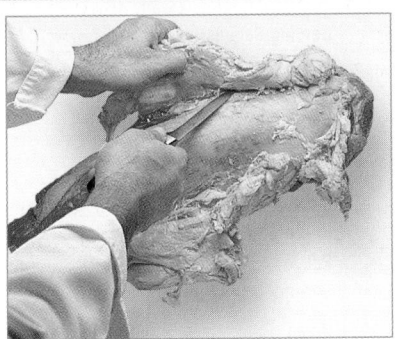

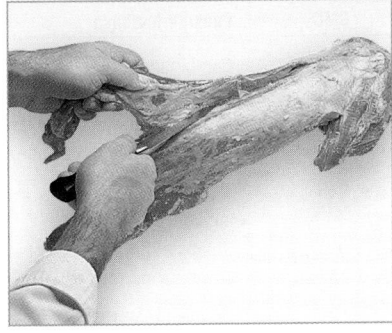

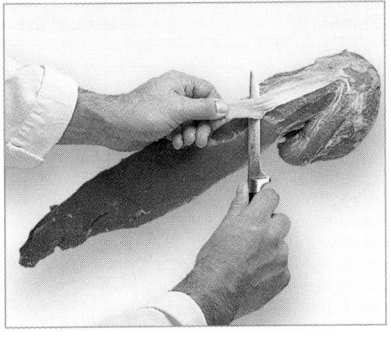

1. Cut and pull the excess fat from the entire tenderloin to expose the meat.

2. Remove the chain muscle from the side of the tenderloin. (Although it contains much connective tissue, the chain muscle may be trimmed and the meat used as tenderloin trimmings in various dishes.)

3. Trim away all the fat and silverskin. Do so by loosening a small piece of silverskin, then, holding the loosened silverskin tightly with one hand, cut it away in long strips, angling the knife up toward the silverskin slightly so that only the silverskin is removed and no meat is wasted.

4. Cut the tenderloin as desired into (left to right) tenderloin tips, tournedos, filet mignon, chateaubriand.

Boxed Beef

Boxed beef is the industry term for primal and subprimal cuts of beef that are vacuum sealed and packed into cardboard boxes for shipping from the packing plant to retail and food service operations.

BASIC PROCEDURE FOR BUTTERFLYING MEATS

Many cuts of boneless meats such as tenderloin and boneless loin steaks can be butterflied to create a thinner cut that has a greater surface area and cooks more quickly.

 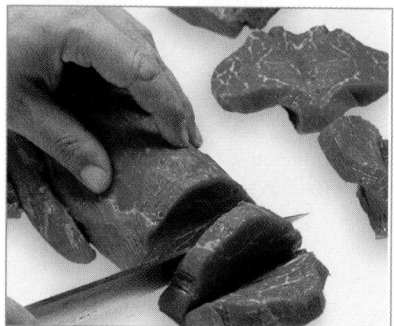

1. Make the first cut nearly all the way through the meat, keeping it attached by leaving approximately 0.5 cm (1/4 in.) uncut.

2. Make a second cut, this time cutting all the way through, completely removing the steak from the tenderloin. Flatten the meat to achieve uniform thickness.

TABLE 13.1   Using Common Cuts of Beef

Primal	Subprimal or Fabricated Cut	CMC	Cooking Methods	Serving Suggestions
Chuck	Chuck roll tied	116A	Combination (braise; stew)	Pot roast; beef stew
	Stew meat	135A	Combination (stew)	Beef stew
	Ground beef	136	Dry heat (broil or grill; roast)	Hamburgers; meatloaf
	Top blade (flat iron)	114D	Dry heat (broil, grill, sauté)	Steak sandwich, stir-fry
Brisket and Shank	Brisket	120	Moist heat (simmer) Combination (braise)	Corned beef; New England boiled dinner Pot roast
	Shank	117	Combination (braise)	Shredded beef for tamales or hash
Rib	Roast ready cap on	109	Dry heat (roast)	Roast prime rib
	Rib eye steak	1112	Dry heat (roast)	Rib eye steak
Plate	Skirt steak	121D	Dry heat (broil or grill)	Fajitas
	Short ribs	123A	Combination (braise)	Braised short ribs
Loin	Porterhouse or T-bone steaks	173 173A	Dry heat (broil or grill)	Steaks
	Strip loin	180	Dry heat (broil or grill; roast; sauté)	Strip loin steak; minute steak entrecôtes Bordelaise
	Tenderloin	189	Dry heat (broil or grill; roast)	Tournedos Rossini; Beef Wellington
	Top sirloin butt or tri tip	184	Dry heat Dry heat	Steak, roast Steak, stir-fry
Flank	Flank steak	193	Dry heat (broil or grill) Combination (braise)	London broil; stir-fry Braised stuffed flank steak
Hip	Ponderosa hip	164A	Dry heat (roast)	Roast beef
	Inside round	168	Dry heat (roast) Combination (braise)	Roast beef Braised beef roulade

Conclusion

Antonin Carême once said that "beef is the soul of cooking." It is also the most popular meat consumed in Canada and undoubtedly will play an important role on almost any menu. Beef's assertive flavour stands up well to a wide array of sauces and seasonings.

Prefabricated products are readily available. In fact, voluntary package-labelling conventions adopted by the beef industry in 1998 (such as "grilling steak" instead of just "steak") will make it easier for consumers to know how to cook the various cuts available at the meat counter. Performing basic fabrication procedures in restaurant kitchens is becoming a rarity. Each primal and subprimal cut has its own distinct characteristics. The primal rib, short loin and sirloin produce the most popular and most expensive cuts of beef. Once the beef is properly fabricated, choose the appropriate dry-heat, moist-heat or combination cooking method for that cut.

Maximum Fat Percentages for Ground Beef

Extra lean:	10%
Lean:	17%
Regular:	30%

One must choose the appropriate fat content for the dish being made. Fat adds moistness and flavour, which is important in a burger. However, extra fat may not be desirable in a taco preparation or for consommé.

Questions for Discussion

1. List each beef primal cut and describe its location on the carcass. For each primal cut, identify two subprimal or fabricated cuts taken from it.
2. Would it be better to use the chuck for grilling or stewing? Explain your answer.
3. Which fabricated cuts contain a portion of the tenderloin? What cooking methods are best suited for these cuts? Explain your answer.
4. Name four cuts that can be produced from a whole beef tenderloin. Describe a preparation procedure for each cut.
5. Most steaks are cut from the hindquarter. What popular steak is cut from the forequarter, and why is it tender when other cuts from the forequarter are relatively tough?

Beef Recipes

RECIPE 13.1

Grilled Western Steak

Yield: 10 150-g (5-oz.) servings
Method: Grilling

Mirepoix, minced	500 g	1 lb.
Canola oil	50 mL	2 fl. oz.
Thyme leaves, dry	2 g	1 tsp.
Marjoram leaves, dry	5 g	2 tsp.
Salt	8 g	1-1/2 tsp.
Pepper, ground black	5 g	1-1/2 tsp.
Bread crumbs	100 g	3-1/2 tsp.
Eggs, beaten	2	2
Worcestershire sauce	5 mL	1 tsp.
Tomato juice	100 mL	3-1/2 fl. oz.
Ground beef	1.5 kg	3 lb. 8 oz.
Bacon, sliced (optional)	10 pieces	10 pieces

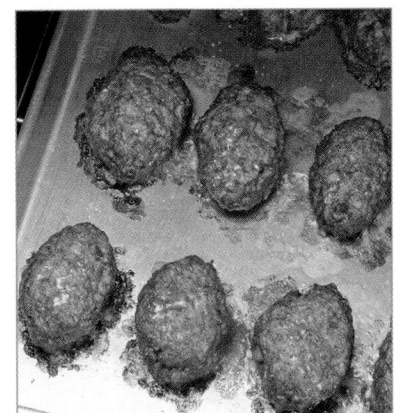

Grilled Western Steak

continued

1. Sauté the mirepoix in the oil until tender. Add the herbs, salt and pepper. Remove from the pan, cool and refrigerate thoroughly.

2. Place all the ingredients into a mixing bowl with a paddle attachment. Mix thoroughly on medium speed until the mixture binds well.

3. Form and cook a small test piece. Adjust seasonings if needed.

4. Scale 10 150-g (5-oz.) portions. Form each portion into a flattened puck shape.

5. Mark the "steaks" on a preheated, oiled grill. Place portions on a baking sheet.

6. Bake western steaks at 160°C (325°F) until done, approximately 10–15 minutes.

VARIATION: Wrap each "steak" wth a strip of bacon and secure with a toothpick. Serve with sautéed mushrooms or a mushroom sauce.

RECIPE 13.1

Approximate values per serving:	
Calories	427
Total fat	27 g
Saturated fat	9 g
Cholesterol	127 mg
Sodium	564 mg
Total carbohydrates	12 g
Protein	33 g

Michael Allemeier, CCC

Michael started cooking at the age of 15 at the St. Boniface Golf Club in Winnipeg. He later spent a number of years as Executive Chef at restaurants such as Bishop's in Vancouver and Teatro in Calgary, and Winery Chef at Mission Hill Family Estate in British Columbia. He has also been Host Chef on "Cook Like a Chef" (Food Network). Read more about his other culinary experiences in the profile on page 944.

RECIPE 13.2

Approximate values per serving:	
Calories	462
Total fat	31 g
Saturated fat	11 g
Cholesterol	108 mg
Sodium	186 mg
Total carbohydrates	7.7 g
Protein	38 g

RECIPE 13.2

Grilled Beef Flank Steak with Shallot Tomato Butter

SAIT POLYTECHNIC, CALGARY, AB
Chef Instructor Michael Allemeier, CCC

Yield: 6 servings
Method: Grilling

Beef flank steaks, each 175 g (6 oz.)	6	6
Paprika	35 g	6 Tbsp.
Fresh thyme, coarsely chopped	50 g	1/2 cup
Black pepper, fresh ground	7 g	1 Tbsp.
Canola oil	500 mL	16 fl. oz.

1. Mix paprika, thyme and pepper together and rub into the flank steaks.

2. Place steaks in a sealable container, add the canola oil and mix gently. Refrigerate, covered, for 3–6 days.

3. Preheat the grill or broiler on high heat. Remove steaks from fridge, drain and allow to come to room temperature (30 minutes).

4. Sear the steaks for 3–4 minutes per side, keeping them rare.

5. Rest steaks for 5–10 minutes and carve thinly across the grain.

Shallot Tomato Butter

Tomato concassée	1 kg	2 lb.
Olive oil	50 mL	1-1/2 fl. oz.
Butter	225 g	1/2 lb.
Shallots, fine dice	125 g	4 oz.

1. Stew the tomatoes in olive oil until au sec. Cool.

2. Place tomatoes and butter in food processor and purée. Fold in shallots.

3. Roll or pipe, then chill.

Beef Bourguignon

RECIPE 13.3

Beef Bourguignon

Yield: 10 250-g (8-oz.) servings
Method: Stewing

Marinade:

Garlic cloves, crushed	10 g	3
Onions, sliced	400 g	3
Carrots, sliced	150 g	2
Parsley stalks	10	10
Bouquet garni:		
Carrot stick, 10 cm (4 in.)	1	1
Leek, split, 10-cm (4-in.) piece	1	1
Fresh thyme	1 sprig	1 sprig
Bay leaf	1	1
Peppercorns, crushed	2 g	10
Salt	5 g	1 tsp.
Dry red wine, preferably Burgundy	750 mL	26 fl. oz.
Beef chuck, cubed for stew	2 kg	4 lb.
Vegetable oil	60 mL	2 fl. oz.
Flour	15 g	2 Tbsp.
Tomato paste	15 mL	1 Tbsp.
Tomatoes, quartered, seeded	4	4
Brown stock	500 mL	1 pt.
Mushrooms, quartered	500 g	1 lb.
Unsalted butter	50 g	1-1/2 oz.
Lardons of lean, double-smoked bacon	250 g	8 oz.
Pearl onions, boiled and peeled	30	30
Salt and pepper	TT	TT

1. Combine the garlic, onions, carrots, parsley, bouquet garni, peppercorns, salt and wine to make a marinade.
2. Marinate the meat for several hours under refrigeration.
3. Remove and drain the meat. Reserve the marinade.
4. Dry the beef and sauté it in the oil until well browned. Do this in several batches if necessary.
5. Return all the meat to the pot. Sprinkle with flour and cook to make a blond roux.
6. Stir in the tomato paste and cook for 5 minutes.
7. Add the reserved marinade, tomatoes and brown stock. Cook in a 180°C (350°F) oven until the meat is tender, approximately 2.5 hours.
8. Remove the meat from the sauce. Strain the sauce through a conical strainer, pressing to extract all of the liquid. Discard the solids. Return the liquid and beef to the pot.
9. Sauté the mushrooms in the butter and add them to the meat and sauce. Lightly sauté the lardons and add to stew. Add the onions and adjust the seasonings. Simmer for 10 minutes to blend the flavours.

RECIPE 13.3

Approximate values per serving:	
Calories	684
Total fat	52 g
Saturated fat	20 g
Cholesterol	158 mg
Sodium	650 mg
Total carbohydrates	13 g
Protein	41 g

RECIPE 13.4

Pepper Steak

Yield: 2 servings
Method: Sautéing

Boneless strip steaks, each approximately 250 g (8 oz.)	2	2
Salt, kosher	TT	TT
Peppercorns, cracked	25 g	2 Tbsp.
Clarified butter	25 mL	1 fl. oz.
Cognac	25 mL	1 fl. oz.
Cream, 35%	125 mL	4 fl. oz.
Meat glaze	25 mL	1 fl. oz.
Whole butter	50 g	2 oz.

1. Season the steaks with salt. Spread the peppercorns in a hotel pan and press the steaks into them, lightly coating each side.
2. Sauté the steaks in the clarified butter over high heat for 2–3 minutes on each side.
3. Remove the pan from the heat. Pour the cognac over the steaks, return the pan to the heat and flambé. When the flames subside, remove the steaks from the pan and keep them warm on a plate.
4. Add the cream and meat glaze to the pan. Bring to a boil and reduce for 2 minutes over high heat; monter au beurre. Pour this sauce over the steaks and serve immediately.

RECIPE 13.4

Approximate values per serving:	
Calories	939
Total fat	75 g
Saturated fat	41 g
Cholesterol	309 mg
Sodium	749 mg
Total carbohydrates	10 g
Protein	56 g

1. Flambé the cognac on the steaks.

2. Pour the finished sauce over each steak.

Beef Stroganoff

RECIPE 13.5

Beef Stroganoff

Yield: 8 250-g (8-oz.) servings
Method: Sautéing

Tenderloin tips, émincé	1 kg	2 lb.
Clarified butter	45 mL	1-1/2 fl. oz.
Onion, small dice or julienne	125 g	4 oz.
Paprika	30 g	5 Tbsp.
Mushrooms, sliced	450 g	1 lb.
Red wine	125 mL	4 fl. oz.

continued

Demi-glace	300 mL	10 fl. oz.
Sour cream	250 mL	8 fl. oz.
Cornichons, julienne	150 g	1 cup
Fresh parsley, chopped	10 g	1 Tbsp.
Salt and pepper	TT	TT
Egg noodles, cooked	700 g	24 oz.

1. Sauté the tenderloin tips in the butter, searing on all sides. Remove the meat and set aside.

2. Add the onion to the pan and sauté lightly, then add paprika and sweat. Add the mushrooms and sauté until soft.

3. Deglaze with red wine.

4. Add the demi-glace. Bring to a boil, reduce to a simmer and cook 5 minutes.

5. Add the sour cream, pickle and any meat juices that accumulated while holding the meat.

6. Return the meat to the sauce to reheat. Stir in the parsley. Adjust the seasonings and serve over egg noodles.

RECIPE 13.5

Approximate values per serving:

Calories	671
Total fat	27 g
Saturated fat	12 g
Cholesterol	182 mg
Sodium	630 mg
Total carbohydrates	67 g
Protein	40 g

RECIPE 13.6

Hungarian-Style Beef Goulash (Pörkölt)

Yield: 15 250-g (8-oz.) servings

Method: Stewing

Onion, fine dice	1.25 kg	2 lb. 12 oz.
Lard or vegetable oil	250 mL	8 fl. oz.
Hungarian paprika	120 g	1 cup
Beef stewing meat,		
cut in 2.5-cm (1-in.) cubes	2.25 kg	5 lb.
Salt	15 g	1 Tbsp.
White stock	2–3 L	2–3 qt.
Garlic, chopped	100 g	1/2 cup
Caraway seeds, crushed	3 g	1 tsp.
Red wine	250 mL	8 fl. oz.
Double-smoked bacon,		
1-cm (1/2-in.) cubes	500 g	1 lb.
Red pepper, diced	350 g	12 oz.
Tomato concassée	500 g	1 lb.
Pepper	TT	TT

1. Sauté the onion in the lard or oil until wilted.

2. Reduce the heat and add the paprika. Fry until fragrant.

3. Add the meat and salt, browning the meat while stirring it. Brown the meat well.

4. Moisten the meat with 1.5 L (1-1/2 qt.) of stock and then add the garlic, caraway seeds and wine. The meat should be just covered. Cover the pot and simmer. Stir occasionally. Add more liquid only if needed.

5. When the meat begins to soften (1 hour), add the bacon, red pepper, and tomato concassée. Simmer until the meat is tender (30–45 minutes).

6. Adjust seasoning with salt and pepper.

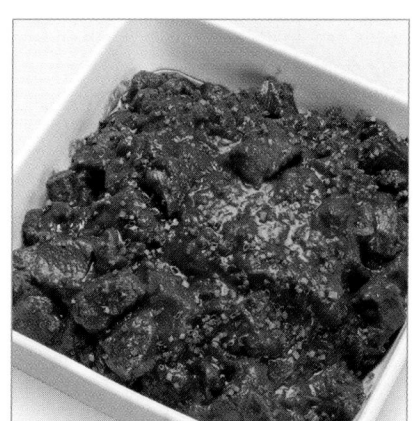

Hungarian-Style Beef Goulash (Pörkölt)

RECIPE 13.6

Approximate values per serving:

Calories	604
Total fat	44 g
Saturated fat	16 g
Cholesterol	124 mg
Sodium	853 mg
Total carbohydrates	17 g
Protein	35 g

Hungarian Style

The dish in Recipe 13.6 is more correctly called a pörkölt. Goulash or *gulyás* refers to soups that can be made from meats, fish, poultry or vegetables. *Paprikás* is a milder, more stew-like version of pörkölt.

Hungary produces many types of paprika, ranging from mild to spicy and with colours varying from yellow to crimson red. Experiment to achieve the balance of flavour and spiciness desired in a dish. Most recipes with paprika call for the spice to be lightly fried before the main ingredient is added. Much like preparing many curry dishes, gently frying the spice releases all the flavours and softens the harsh, grainy properties of the raw ground spice.

Felix Sano

Felix was born in the Dominican Republic and grew up on the nearby Caribbean island of Montserrat. His interest in cooking started at the age of 7 when he was allowed into the kitchen, accompanied by his dad, to cook for his visiting friends. Felix studied at Liaison College of the Culinary Arts in Toronto. After graduating, he apprenticed at the Toronto Board of Trade, where he honed various skills including fruit and vegetable carving and chocolate and ice sculptures. Felix is now Executive Chef at the Emerald Hills Golf Club.

RECIPE 13.7

Approximate values per serving:	
Calories	550
Total fat	63 g
Saturated fat	10 g
Cholesterol	152 mg
Sodium	332 mg
Total carbohydrates	2 g
Protein	63 g

Spicy Red Onion Marmalade Approximate values per 125 mL serving:	
Calories	188
Total fat	0 g
Saturated fat	0 g
Cholesterol	0 mg
Sodium	200 mg
Total carbohydrates	48 g
Protein	1 g

RECIPE 13.7

Grilled Beef Tenderloin with Spicy Red Onion Marmalade

EMERALD HILLS GOLF CLUB, STOUFFVILLE, ON
Executive Chef Felix Sano

Yield: 6 portions
Method: Grilling

Beef tenderloin, 225 g (8 oz.) fillets	6	6
Olive oil	50 mL	2 fl. oz.
Thyme, fresh, chopped	30 g	3 Tbsp.
Garlic, minced	15 g	3 cloves
Kosher salt	TT	TT
Fresh cracked black pepper	TT	TT

1. Place fillets in a bowl and add remaining ingredients. Coat thoroughly. They are best if marinated for 2 hours.
2. Grill steaks on a pre-heated grill to your desired doneness. Rest 2 minutes before plating.
3. Serve with Spicy Red Onion Marmalade.

Spicy Red Onion Marmalade

Red wine vinegar	225 mL	8 fl. oz.
Sugar	225 g	8 oz.
Tomato paste	15 g	1 Tbsp.
Red onions, julienne	525 g	3 medium
Salt	3 g	1/2 tsp.
Chile flakes	5 g	1 Tbsp.
Nutmeg	pinch	pinch

1. In a non-corrosive sauce pot, bring vinegar, sugar and tomato paste to a boil.
2. Add remaining ingredients, cook and reduce until thick and syrupy.
3. Cool and store until needed.

" Happy and successful cooking doesn't rely only on know-how; it comes from the heart, makes great demands on the palate and needs enthusiasm and deep love of food to bring it to life.

—Georges Blanc, French chef in *Ma Cuisine des Saisons*, 1984

These interactive online tools will help you master the skills in this chapter:

- Videos
- Chapter Quizzes
- Activities

Formula-Fed Veal vs. Free-Range Veal

Much of the veal produced today is known as formula-fed veal. Formula-fed calves are fed only nutrient-rich liquids; they are tethered in pens only slightly larger than their bodies to restrict their movements. Preventing the calves from eating grasses and other foods containing iron keeps their flesh white; restricting movement keeps their muscles from toughening. In recent years controversy and allegations of cruelty have arisen concerning these methods.

An alternative to formula-fed veal is free-range veal. Free-range veal is produced from calves that are allowed to roam freely and eat grasses and other natural foods. Because they consume feed containing iron, their flesh is a reddish pink and has a substantially different flavour from meat from formula-fed calves of the same age.

Opinions differ on which has the better flavour. Some chefs prefer the consistently mild, sweet taste of formula-fed veal. Others prefer the more substantial flavour of free-range veal. The two are interchangeable in recipes.

Cows must calve before they begin to give milk. Bull calves are the basis of today's veal industry. Veal is the meat of youthful bovine carcasses weighing less than 160 kg (350 lb.) hide-off. Quebec and Ontario produce 97% of the veal in Canada. Veal is lighter in colour than beef, has a more delicate flavour and is generally more tender. Veal has a firm texture, light pink colour and very little fat. As soon as a calf starts eating solid food, the iron in the food begins to turn the young animal's meat red. Grain-fed veal tends to be a deeper red, with some marbling and external fat.

Veal's low fat content makes it a popular meat, especially among those looking for an alternative to beef. Its delicate flavour is complemented by both classic and modern sauces.

PRIMAL AND SUBPRIMAL CUTS OF VEAL

The veal carcass is split down the backbone into two bilateral halves or sides. Each side may be separated into quarters or the shoulder, the foreshank, the flank, the breast, the rib, the loin and the leg. Occasionally, through special order, some other cuts such as saddles or whole loins are available.

Figure 14.1 shows the relationship between the animal's bone structure and the primal cuts. As with all meats, it is important to know the location of bones when cutting or working with veal. This makes meat fabrication and carving easier and aids in identifying cuts. Figure 14.2 shows the primal cuts of veal and their location. A graded veal carcass will also indicate the meat colour. Smaller muscles are available through imports. Table 14.1 (page 303) identifies common cuts of veal and suggests preparation methods.

Shoulder

The veal shoulder section of the front accounts for 21% of carcass weight. It contains six rib bones (as opposed to five in the beef chuck) and portions of the backbone, blade and arm bones, but not the neck, breast or shank.

The backbone, blade and arm bones are sometimes removed and the meat roasted or stuffed and braised. Although shoulder chops and steaks can be fabricated, they are inferior to the chops cut from more tender areas such as the loin or rib. Often the shoulder meat is ground or cubed for stew. Because of the relatively large amount of connective tissue it contains, meat from the shoulder is best braised or stewed.

Foreshank and Breast

The foreshank and breast are located beneath the shoulder and part of the rib section on the front half of the carcass. The shank is generally purchased separately, as is the breast. Combined, they account for approximately 16% of carcass weight. This section contains rib bones and rib cartilage, breast bones and shank bones. Because the calf is slaughtered young, many of the breast bones are cartilaginous rather than bony.

This cartilage, as well as the connective tissue present in the breast, breaks down during long moist cooking, thus making the breast a flavourful choice

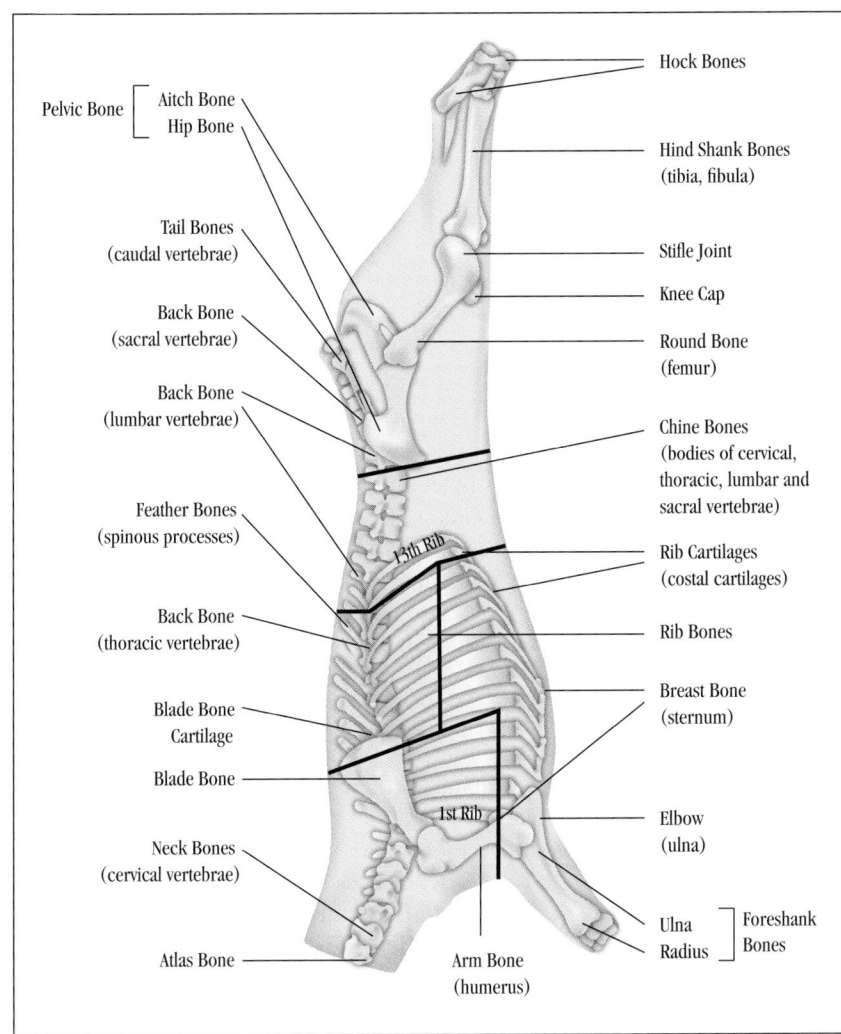

FIGURE 14.1   The skeletal structure of a calf.

Veal Grading

Veal carcasses are graded for quality on the basis of meat colour, overall muscling, and fat cover. There are A, B, and C grades. All carcasses are graded for meat colour. The veal grader uses a Minolta colour reflectance meter to do this. There are four colour classifications: 1—pale white colour, and 2, 3, and 4—assigned as the meat becomes more pink.

SOURCE: Adapted from Canada Beef Export Federation, February 19, 2002.

Classic Flavour Combinations for Veal

Veal is much more delicately flavoured than beef, with a finer texture and lighter colour. Its flavour blends well with a variety of sauces and other ingredients without overpowering them. Veal is often paired with light cream sauces flavoured with fresh mild-flavoured herbs such as chervil, chives, parsley and tarragon, with mustard or with paprika. Sautéed veal scallops or grilled veal chops are often finished with a simple squeeze of fresh lemon before serving. The acidity in fresh apples, sorrel or tomatoes also enhances the flavour of many classic veal dishes.

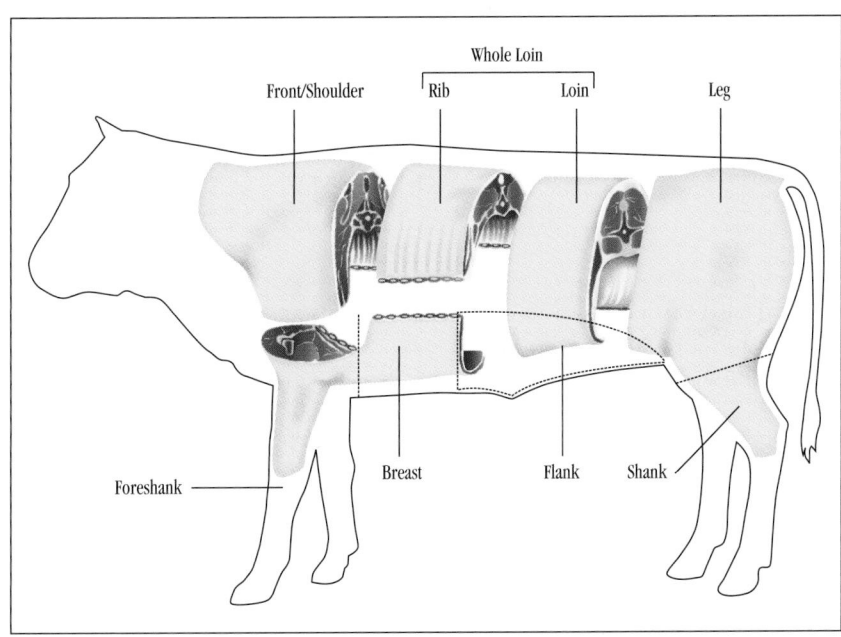

FIGURE 14.2   The primal cuts of veal.

for braising. Veal breast can also be cubed for stews such as veal fricassee and veal blanquette, rolled and stuffed, or trimmed and ground.

The foreshank is also very flavourful but tough. It can be braised whole or sliced perpendicular to the shank bone and braised to produce osso buco.

Whole Loin

The primal whole loin contains the ribs and loin sections of a side of veal. When purchased whole, it is often fabricated into chops, although it may be boned for roasting or preparing loin cutlets.

Rib

The rib, also known as a veal rack, is a very tender, relatively small cut, accounting for approximately 9% of carcass weight. It is relatively expensive. The double rack (or hotel rack) consists of both racks, each with seven rib bones and a portion of the backbone. It is a special order.

Veal hotel racks can be roasted either whole or split into two ribs. Veal ribs can be boned out to produce a veal rib eye. More often, veal ribs are trimmed and cut into chops, which can also be bone-in or boneless, to be grilled, sautéed or braised.

Veal Rib, Split, CMC#305

Loin

Veal Loin, CMC#331

The veal loin is posterior to the primal rib, contains no ribs and accounts for approximately 10% of carcass weight. The loin consists of the loin eye muscle on top of the chine bones and the tenderloin on the interior.

The veal loin is very tender and the tenderloin is, without a doubt, the most tender cut of veal. If the veal loin is separated from the primal leg before the tenderloin is removed, the tenderloin will be cut into two pieces. The small portion (short tenderloin) remains in the loin and the large portion (butt tenderloin) remains in the sirloin portion of the primal leg. The tenderloin is sometimes removed and cut into medallions. The veal loin is often cut into chops, bone-in or boneless. It is usually cooked using dry heat such as broiling, grilling, roasting or sautéing.

Boneless Strip Loin, CMC#344

Loin Chops, CMC#1332

Leg

The primal veal leg consists of both the sirloin and the leg. Together they account for approximately 42% of carcass weight. The primal leg is separated from the loin by a cut perpendicular to the backbone immediately anterior to the hip bone, and it contains portions of the backbone, tail bone, hip bone, aitch bone, round bone and hind shank.

Although it is tender enough to be roasted whole, the veal leg is typically fabricated into cutlets. To fabricate this cut, the leg is first broken down into its major muscles: the inside round, eye of round, knuckle, sirloin, bottom round (which includes the sirloin) and butt tenderloin. Each of these muscles can be reduced to cutlets by trimming all fat and visible connective tissue and slicing against the grain to the desired

Veal Leg, CMC#334

thickness. The cutlets may be pounded carefully to tenderize them further and to prevent them from curling when cooked.

The hindshank is somewhat meatier than the foreshank but both are prepared and cooked in the same manner.

Because the veal carcass is small enough to be handled easily, it is sometimes purchased in forms larger than the primal cuts described above. Depending on employee skill, available equipment and storage space and an ability to utilize fully all the cuts and trimmings that fabricating meat produces, you may want to special order veal in one of the following forms:

Inside Round, CMC#349

- *Foresaddle:* The anterior portion of the carcass after it is severed from the hindsaddle by a cut following the natural curvature between the eleventh and twelfth ribs. It contains the primal shoulder, foreshank and breast, and rib.
- *Hindsaddle:* The posterior portion of the carcass after it is severed from the foresaddle. It contains the primal loin and leg.
- *Back:* The trimmed rib and loin sections in one piece. The back is particularly useful for producing large quantities of veal chops.
- *Veal side:* One bilateral half of the carcass, produced by cutting lengthwise through the backbone.

Hindshank Cut for Osso Buco, CMC#337

Organ Meats

Several veal organ meats are used in food service operations.

Sweetbreads

Sweetbreads are the thymus glands of veal and lamb. As an animal ages, its thymus gland shrinks; therefore, sweetbreads are not available from older cattle or sheep. Veal sweetbreads (Fr. *ris de veau*) are much more popular than lamb sweetbreads in this country. Good-quality sweetbreads should be plump and firm, with the exterior membrane intact. Delicately flavoured and tender, they can be prepared by almost any cooking method. Clarify with your purveyor that you are purchasing veal and not beef sweetbreads.

Sweetbreads, CMC#3722

Veal (Calves') Liver

Veal liver is much more popular than beef liver because of its tenderness and mild flavour. Good-quality calves' liver should be firm and moist, with a shiny appearance and without any off-odour. It is most often sliced and sautéed or broiled and served with a sauce.

Calves' Liver, CMC#3724

Kidneys

Kidneys are more popular in other parts of the world than in Canada. Good-quality kidneys should be plump, firm and encased in a shiny membrane. Properly prepared kidneys have a rich, yet mild flavour and firm texture; they are best prepared by dry-heat cooking methods and are sometimes used in stew or steak and kidney pie.

Kidneys

NUTRITION

Like beef, veal is a major source of protein as well as niacin, zinc and B vitamins. Veal has less marbling than beef. When trimmed of any visible fat, veal is lower in fat and calories than comparable beef cuts. And it is leaner than many cuts of pork and poultry.

BUTCHERING PROCEDURES

Some food service operations purchase veal in primal or other large cuts and fabricate it in-house to their own specifications. There are several important veal fabrication and butchering techniques you should master.

BASIC PROCEDURE FOR BONING A LEG OF VEAL

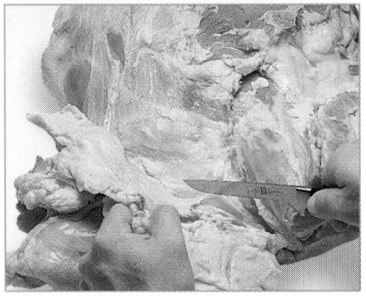

1. Remove the shank by cutting through the knee joint. Remove the excess fat and flank meat.

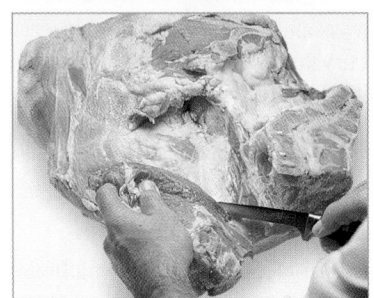

2. Remove the butt tenderloin from the inside of the pelvic bone.

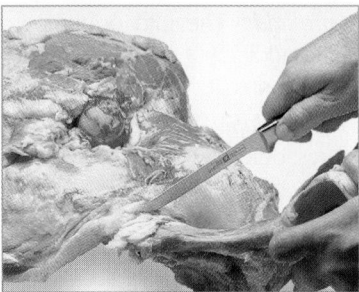

3. Remove the pelvic bone by carefully cutting around the bone, separating it from the meat. Continue until the bone is completely freed from the meat.

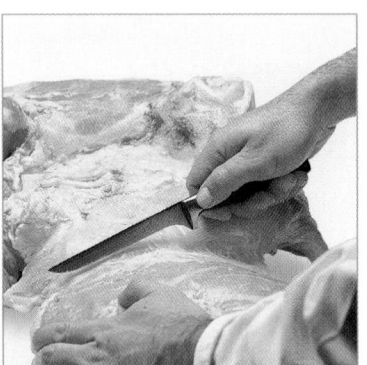

4. With the inside of the leg up, remove the inside (top) round by cutting along the natural seam.

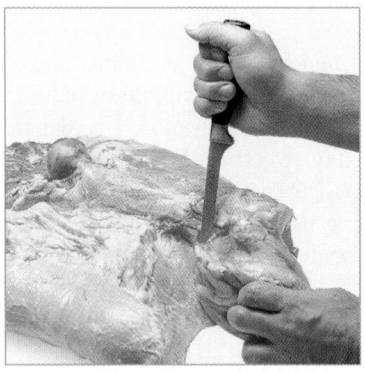

5. Remove the shank meat. (It is the round piece of meat lying between the eye of round and the bone, on the shank end of the leg.)

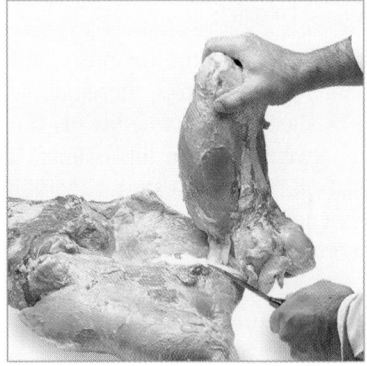

6. Remove the round bone and the knuckle together by cutting around the bone and through the natural seams separating the knuckle from the other muscles. Separate the knuckle meat from the bone.

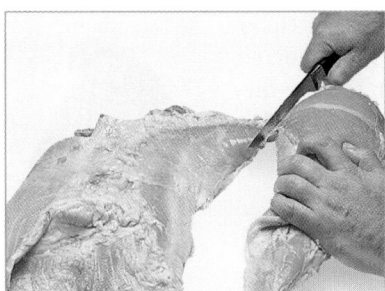

7. Remove the sirloin tip.

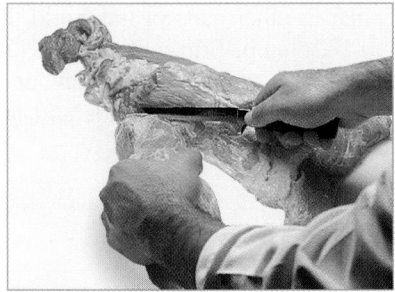

8. Remove the eye of round from the outside (bottom) round.

continued

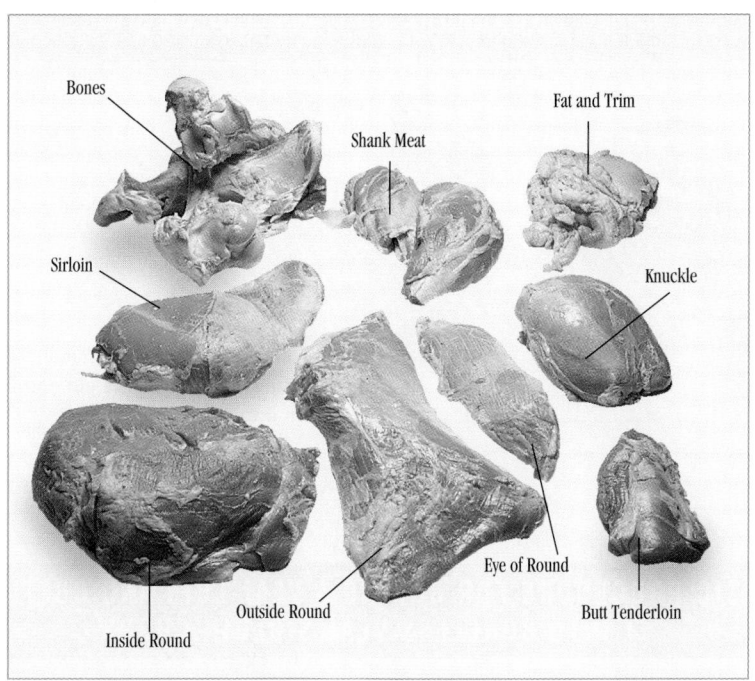

9. The completely boned-out veal leg, producing an inside round, eye of round, knuckle, shank meat, butt tenderloin, sirloin, outside round, bones and trimmings.

BASIC PROCEDURE FOR CUTTING AND POUNDING CUTLETS

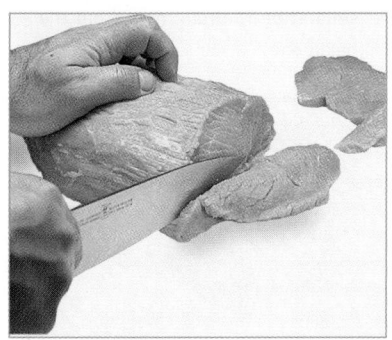

1. Veal cutlets are cut from relatively large pieces of veal (here, a portion of the inside round). All fat and silverskin must be trimmed. Going against the grain, cut slices approximately 0.5-cm (1/4-in.) thick; cut on the bias to produce larger pieces.

2. Place the cutlets between two pieces of plastic wrap and pound lightly to flatten and tenderize the meat. Be careful not to tear or pound holes in the meat.

Menu Terminology

Generally, if the word "veal" is used, there is not a problem with misrepresentation. However, a qualifier such as "milk-fed" must be supported by invoices to prove that is what is being served. A restaurant could face fraud charges. In Quebec, "grain-fed" is legally recognized, but this is not the case elsewhere in Canada. The CFIA does not recognize the term "baby beef." Technically, "calves'" liver should be called veal liver but the term currently enjoys general usage acceptance.

BASIC PROCEDURE FOR CUTTING ÉMINCÉ

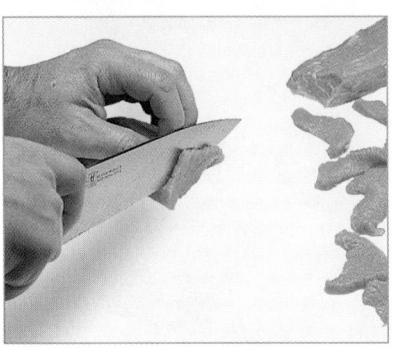

Émincé is cut from relatively small, lean pieces of meat. Here veal is cut across the grain into small, thin slices.

BASIC PROCEDURE FOR BONING A VEAL LOIN AND CUTTING IT INTO BONELESS VEAL SIRLOIN CHOPS

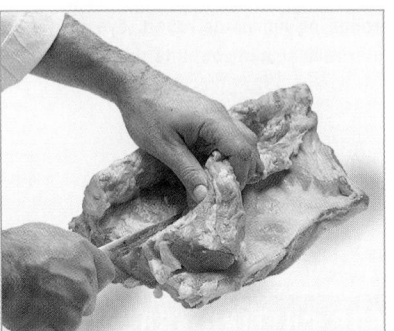

1. Remove the tenderloin in a single piece from the inside of the loin by following the vertebrae and cutting completely around the tenderloin.

2. From the backbone side, cut along the natural curve of the backbone, separating the loin meat from the backbone.

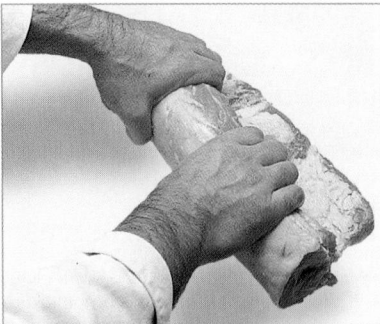

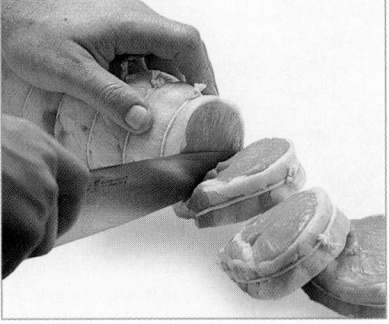

3. Trim any excess fat from the loin, and trim the flank to create a 7.5-cm (3-in.) lip. Tightly roll up the loin with the flank on the outside.

4. Tie the loin, using the procedure described next, at 2.5-cm (1-in.) intervals. Cut between the pieces of twine for individual boneless sirloin chops.

BASIC PROCEDURE FOR TYING (TRUSSING) MEATS

Here we apply the tying procedure to a boneless veal loin; the same procedure can be used on any type of meat.

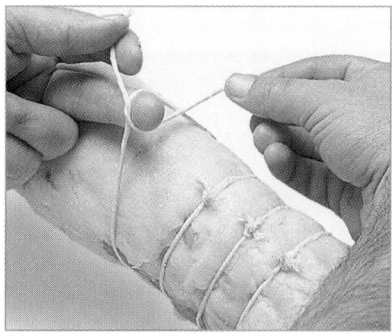

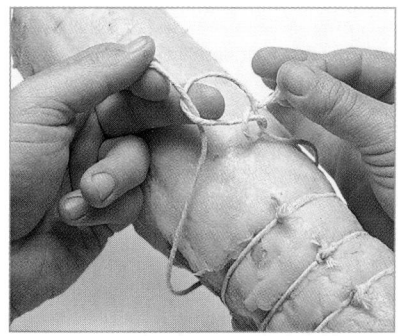

1. Cut a piece of string long enough to wrap completely around the loin. Holding one end between the thumb and forefinger, pass the other end around it and cross the strings. Loop the loose end of the string around your finger.

2. Wrap the string around itself and pass the loose end back through the hole (slip knot).

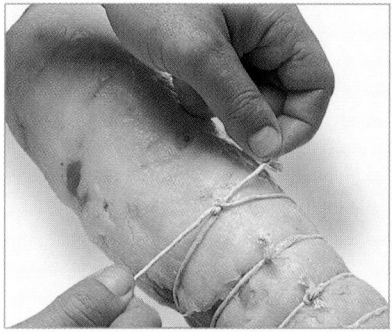

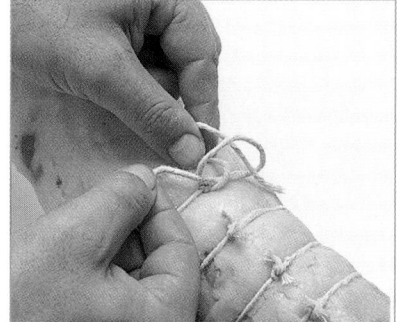

3. Pull to tighten the knot. Adjust the string so it is snug against the meat.

4. Loop one end of the string around your thumb and forefinger. Reach through with your thumb and fore-finger and pull the other string back through the loop. Pull both strings to tighten the knot, thus preventing the first knot from loosening (half hitch). Trim the ends of the strings.

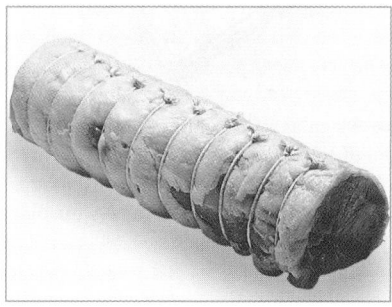

5. Continue in this fashion until the entire loin is tied. The strings should be tied at even intervals, just snug enough to hold the shape of the loin; they should not dig into or cut the meat.

All about Sweetbreads

Sweetbreads have a mild, neutral flavour. They combine well with various mushrooms, brown and white sauces and vinaigrettes. There are many classical and current styles that may be prepared. Sweetbreads are highly prized in Europe but tend to appear only in fine dining establishments in Canada. Two methods of preparing cleaned and pressed sweetbreads are as follows:

Grenoble style—Slices, sautéed in butter; finished with white wine, capers, lemon fillets and whole butter.

Jardinière style—Braised brown, with Madeira sauce and garden vegetables

BASIC PROCEDURE FOR CLEANING AND PRESSING SWEETBREADS

Before fabrication, you should submerge the sweetbreads in cold water with a little salt, cover them and place them in the refrigerator overnight to draw out any blood; then blanch them in a court bouillon for 5 minutes.

1. Remove the sweetbreads from the poaching liquid and allow them to cool.

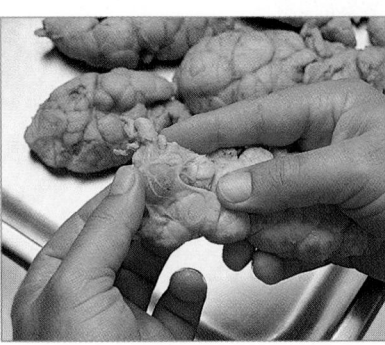

2. Using your hands, pull off any sinew or membranes that may be present on the surface of the sweetbreads.

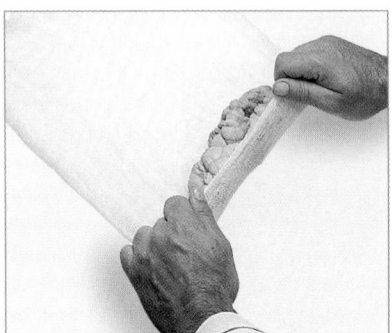

3. Wrap the sweetbreads in cheesecloth.

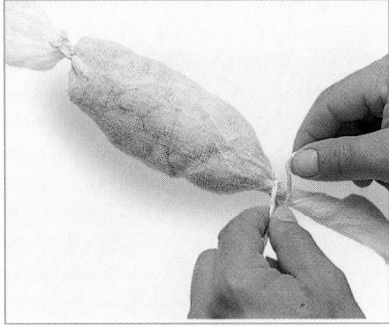

4. Tie the ends with butcher's twine.

5. Place the wrapped sweetbreads in a half hotel pan or similar container.

6. Place another half hotel pan on top of the sweetbreads; place a weight in the pan to press the sweetbreads. Pressing sweetbreads in this manner improves their texture.

BASIC PROCEDURE FOR CLEANING CALVES' LIVER

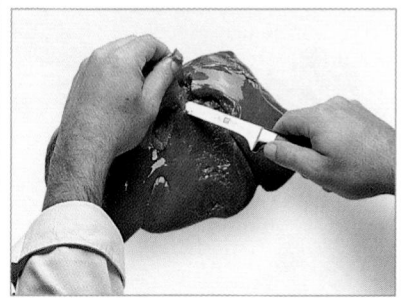

1. Trim the large sinew and outer membrane from the bottom of the liver.

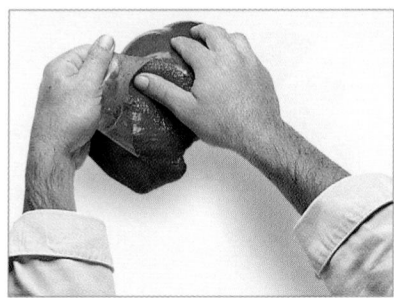

2. Turn the liver over and peel the membrane off with your hands.

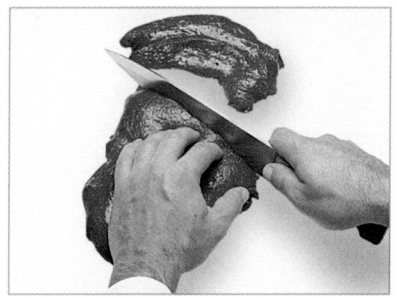

3. The liver can be cut into thick or thin slices as needed.

TABLE 14.1	Using Common Cuts of Veal			
Primal	**Subprimal or Fabricated Cut**	**CMC**	**Cooking Methods**	**Serving Suggestions**
Front/ Shoulder	Cubed veal		Combination (stew)	Blanquette or fricassee
	Ground veal	396	Dry heat (broil or grill)	Veal patties; pojarski
			Combination (braise)	Stuffing; meatballs
Foreshank and Breast	Foreshank	312	Combination (braise)	Osso buco
	Breast	313	Combination (braise)	Stuffed veal breast
Rib	Rack	305	Dry heat (broil or grill; roast)	Grilled veal chop; roast veal with porcini mushrooms
	Rib chops	1306	Dry heat (broil or grill)	Grilled veal chop
			Combination (braise)	Braised veal chop with risotto
	Rib eye	307	Dry heat (broil or grill; roast)	Broiled veal rib eye with chipotle sauce; roasted veal rib eye marchand de vin
			Combination (braise)	Braised rib eye
Loin	Veal loin	331	Dry heat (broil or grill; roast; sauté)	Roasted veal loin with wild mushrooms; sautéed veal medallions with green peppercorn sauce
	Loin chops	1332	Dry heat (broil or grill; sauté)	Broiled or sautéed veal chops with mushroom sauce
			Combination (braise)	Braised veal chops Lyonnaise
	Striploin, boneless	344	Dry heat (broil or grill; roast; sauté)	Roasted veal loin sauce poulette
	Veal tenderloin	345	Dry heat (broil or grill; roast; sauté)	Grilled tenderloin; roasted tenderloin; sautéed tenderloin with garlic and herbs
Leg	Leg	334	Dry heat (roast; sauté)	Veal scallopini
			Combination (stew)	Blanquette
	Inside round	349	Dry heat (roast; sauté)	Veal Marsala
	Outside round	350	Dry heat (sauté)	Sautéed cutlets with Calvados
			Combination (braise)	Stuffed veal cutlets
	Hindshank	337	Moist heat (simmer)	Veal broth
	Centre cut	1337	Combination (braise)	Osso buco
Offal	Sweetbreads	3722	Dry heat (pan-fry; sauté)	Sautéed sweetbreads beurre noisette
			Combination (braise)	Braised sweetbreads Madeira
	Calves' liver	3724	Dry heat (broil or grill; sauté)	Broiled or sautéed calves' liver with onion and bacon
	Kidneys		Combination (braise)	Kidney pie
	Tails			Soup and stock

BASIC PROCEDURE FOR CLEANING VEAL KIDNEYS

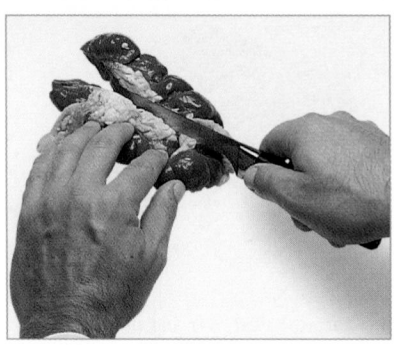

1. Split the kidneys lengthwise, exposing the fat and sinew.

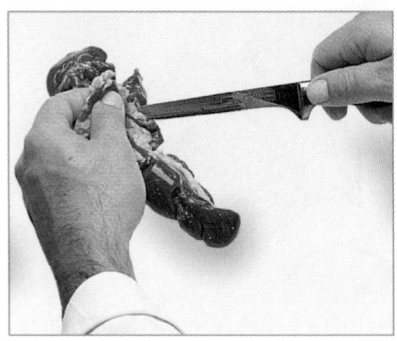

2. With a sharp knife, trim away the fat and sinew. The kidney is now ready for cooking.

Conclusion

Although veal may not be as popular as beef or pork, it is versatile and easy to cook and adds variety to menus. Veal is much more delicately flavoured than beef, with a finer texture and lighter colour. Its flavour blends well with a variety of sauces and other ingredients without overpowering them. Veal can be cooked by almost any dry-heat, moist-heat or combination cooking method.

Veal quality varies greatly among purveyors. Purchase only from reputable companies to be sure you are receiving a consistently high-quality product. Because veal carcasses are relatively small, they are sometimes purchased as primal cuts for your further fabrication.

Questions for Discussion

1. Compare and contrast the appearance and flavour of beef and veal.
2. What are the differences between formula-fed veal and free-range veal?
3. Describe two differences between a beef carcass and a veal carcass.
4. List each veal primal and describe its location on the carcass. For each primal, identify two subprimals or fabricated cuts taken from it.
5. Would it be better to use a veal loin for grilling or braising? Explain your answer.
6. What are veal sweetbreads? Describe how sweetbreads should be prepared for cooking.

Veal Recipes

Veal Blanquette

Yield: 10 250-mL (8-fl. oz.) servings
Method: Stewing

Veal stewing meat, trimmed, cut into 5-cm (2-in.) cubes	2.25 kg	5 lb.
Salt and white pepper	TT	TT
Veal stock, white, hot	2 L	2 qt.
Bouquet garni:		
Carrot baton, 10 cm (4 in.)	1	1
Leek (white), split, 10 cm (4 in.)	1	1
Thyme sprigs	2	2
Bay leaf	1	1
White roux	225 g	8 oz.
Button mushrooms	1 kg	2 lb.
Butter	100 g	3-1/2 oz.
Lemon juice	15 mL	1 Tbsp.
Pearl onions, cooked	500 g	1 lb.
Egg yolks	3	3
Cream, 35%	350 mL	12 fl. oz.

1. Place the veal into a pot and season lightly with salt and pepper.
2. Pour the hot stock over the meat and return to a simmer. Skim any impurities as they appear. Simmer for 1 hour and add the bouquet garni. Simmer approximately 30 minutes or until meat is tender.
3. Transfer the meat to a holding pan and keep warm.
4. Whisk the roux into the hot liquid and simmer until the raw starch taste is gone, 15–20 minutes, to make a velouté. Strain if necessary.
5. Meanwhile, stew the mushrooms in the butter and lemon juice until cooked but still white. Add the pearl onions and rethermalize.
6. Add the veal, any juices, mushrooms and pearl onions to the simmering velouté.
7. Simmer until the mixture is thoroughly heated and adjust seasoning.
8. The mixture may be chilled at this point for later service by placing it in a shallow hotel pan and rapidly cooling it. Cover and refrigerate. For service, rethermalize completely to an internal temperature of 75°C (170°F).
9. To serve, mix the egg yolks and cream to form a liaison. Temper the liaison with some of the hot velouté and incorporate the liaison into the stew. Heat to 73°C (165°F), stirring constantly. Do not boil or the sauce will curdle. Adjust seasoning with salt, pepper and lemon juice.

Approximate values per serving:	
Calories	661
Total fat	41 g
Saturated fat	16 g
Cholesterol	320 mg
Sodium	498 mg
Total carbohydrates	21 g
Protein	52 g

1. Veal Blanquette: Simmering the veal.

2. Whisking the roux into the reduced cooking liquid.

3. Adding the veal to the sauce.

4. Whisking a liaison into the sauce.

Cutlet Variations

Holstein style—Breaded, pan-fried, garnished with fried egg and anchovy fillets.

Viennese style—Breaded, pan-fried, garnished with lemon, grated egg white and yolk, capers and parsley.

Oscar—Floured, sautéed, garnished with crab meat, asparagus and hollandaise sauce.

Jäger schnitzel—Floured, sautéed, garnished with lardons, pearl onions and demi-glace.

Marsala—Floured, sautéed, pan deglazed with Marsala and brown veal stock, mounted with butter.

RECIPE 14.2

Approximate values per serving:

Calories	528
Total fat	32 g
Saturated fat	19 g
Cholesterol	269 mg
Sodium	286 mg
Total carbohydrates	16 g
Protein	41 g

RECIPE 14.2

Sautéed Veal Cutlets with Calvados

Yield: 10 170-g (6-oz.) servings
Method: Sautéing

Mushrooms, sliced	600 g	20 oz.
Clarified butter	200 mL	6-1/2 fl. oz.
Golden Delicious apples	5	5
Veal cutlets, pounded, each 170 g (6 oz.)	10	10
Salt and pepper	TT	TT
Shallots, brunoise	80 g	3
Calvados	80 mL	3 fl. oz.
Crème fraîche	400 mL	13 fl. oz.
Fresh parsley, chopped	15 g	2 Tbsp.

1. Sauté the mushrooms in a portion of the clarified butter until dry. Remove and reserve.
2. Peel and core the apples. Cut each into 12 wedges.
3. Sauté the apple wedges in a portion of the clarified butter until slightly browned and tender. Remove and reserve.
4. Season the veal cutlets with salt and pepper. Sauté in the remaining clarified butter. (This may be done in two or three batches.) Remove and reserve.
5. Add the shallots to the pan and sauté without browning.
6. Deglaze with the Calvados. Flambé the Calvados.
7. Add the sautéed mushrooms and crème fraîche. Bring to a boil and reduce until it thickens slightly.
8. Return the cutlets to the pan to reheat. Serve each cutlet with sauce, garnished with 6 apple slices and chopped parsley.

Sautéed Calves' Liver with Onions

RECIPE 14.3

Approximate values per serving:

Calories	292
Total fat	12 g
Saturated fat	2.7 g
Cholesterol	641 mg
Sodium	544 mg
Total carbohydrates	11 g
Protein	35 g

RECIPE 14.3

Sautéed Calves' Liver with Onions

Yield: 10 175-g (6-oz.) servings
Method: Sautéing

Onion, julienne	750 g	1 lb. 8 oz.
Clarified butter	100 mL	3 fl. oz.
Salt and pepper	TT	TT
White wine	250 mL	8 fl. oz.
Fresh parsley, chopped fine	10 g	1 Tbsp.
Calves' liver, 175-g (6-oz.) slices	10	10
Flour	as needed	as needed

1. Sauté the onion in 30 mL (1 fl. oz.) of butter until golden brown. Season with salt and pepper.
2. Add the white wine, cover and braise until the onions are tender, approximately 10 minutes. Stir in the chopped parsley.
3. Dredge the liver in flour seasoned with salt and pepper.
4. In a separate pan, sauté the liver in the remaining clarified butter until done. The liver should be slightly pink in the middle.
5. Serve the liver with a portion of the onion and its cooking liquid.

RECIPE 14.4

Veal Marengo

Yield: 10 300-g (10-oz.) servings
Method: Braising

Lean boneless veal, cut in 5-cm (2-in.) cubes	2 kg	4 lb.
Salt and pepper	TT	TT
Flour for dredging the veal	as needed	as needed
Vegetable oil	75 mL	2-1/2 fl. oz.
Clarified butter	150 mL	5 fl. oz.
Onion, julienne	600 g	20 oz.
Carrot, rondelles	500 g	16 oz.
Garlic cloves, crushed	15 g	3
Flour	30 g	3 Tbsp.
Tomato paste	50 mL	1-1/2 fl. oz.
Dry white wine	300 mL	10 fl. oz.
Brown veal stock	800 mL	26 fl. oz.
Bouquet garni:		
Carrot stick, 10 cm (4 in.)	1	1
Leek, split, 10-cm (4-in.) piece	1	1
Fresh thyme	2 sprigs	2 sprigs
Bay leaves	2	2
Mushrooms, washed and quartered	450 g	14 oz.
Tomato, diced	800 g	2 lb.
Pearl onions, boiled and peeled	450 g	40

1. Season the veal cubes with salt and pepper and dredge in flour.

2. Sauté the veal in 50 mL (2 fl. oz.) of oil and 50 g (2 oz.) of butter, browning well on all sides. Remove the meat and set aside.

3. Add 75 g (2 oz.) of butter and sauté the onion, carrot and garlic without colouring. Sprinkle with the 30 g (3 Tbsp.) flour and cook to make a blond roux. Stir in the tomato paste and return the veal to the pan.

4. Add the wine, stock and bouquet garni to the pan; bring to a boil. Cover and braise until the meat is tender, approximately 1.5 hours.

5. Sauté the mushrooms until dry in 20 mL (1 Tbsp.) of oil and 30 g (1 oz.) of butter without browning. Add the tomato to the pan and sauté over high heat for 3 minutes. Season with salt and pepper. Remove from the heat and reserve.

6. When the veal is tender, remove it from the pan with a slotted spoon and set aside. Strain the sauce.

7. Return the veal to the sauce along with the mushrooms, tomato and pearl onions. Bring to a boil and simmer for 5 minutes. Adjust the seasonings.

Veal Marengo

RECIPE 14.4

Approximate values per serving:	
Calories	557
Total fat	26 g
Saturated fat	9.8 g
Cholesterol	198 mg
Sodium	421 mg
Total carbohydrates	31 g
Protein	46 g

RECIPE 14.5

Veal Pojarski

Yield: 10 servings
Method: Pan-frying

Onion, brunoise	150 g	5 oz.
Garlic, minced	10 g	2 cloves
Butter	25 g	1 oz.
Marjoram, dry	2 g	1 tsp.

RECIPE 14.5

Approximate values per serving:	
Calories	674
Total fat	52 g
Saturated fat	24 g
Cholesterol	225 mg
Sodium	1012 mg
Total carbohydrates	17 g
Protein	33 g

continued

1. Pan-frying the patties.

2. The finished Veal Pojarski.

Thyme leaves, fresh	5 g	1-1/2 tsp.
Bread, fresh	3 slices	3 slices
Egg whites	2	2
Cream, 35%, cold	500 mL	16 fl. oz.
Veal, ground	1.5 kg	3 lb. 4 oz.
Salt	15 g	1 Tbsp.
Pepper, black	1 g	1/2 tsp.
Nutmeg	1 g	1/2 tsp.
Breading line, white crumbs	as needed	as needed
Butter, clarified	125 mL	4 fl. oz.
Canola oil	125 mL	4 fl. oz.

1. Sweat the onion and garlic in butter until soft and translucent. Add the marjoram and thyme. Chill thoroughly.

2. Combine the bread, egg whites and cream to form a panada (see Chapter 20).

3. Place the cold veal in a mixing bowl with a paddle attachment, add the seasonings and mix on medium speed to combine well. Add the panada in 3 stages, mixing well after each stage. The forcemeat should be smooth and firm and hold its shape.

4. Portion at 115 g (4 oz.) and form each piece into a chop shape about 1-cm (3/4-in.) thick. Chill well.

5. Pass each piece through a breading line, maintaining the chop shape.

6. Pan-fry the pojarski in a mixture of butter and oil until golden.

7. Finish in the oven if necessary.

8. Serve 2 pieces per portion with a chasseur sauce.

RECIPE 14.6

Veal Émincé Zurich Style

Yield: 8 servings
Method: Sautéing

Veal émincé	1 kg	2 lb. 4 oz.
Salt and pepper	TT	TT
Flour	as needed	as needed
Clarified butter	125 mL	4 fl. oz.
Shallots, brunoise	20 g	3/4 oz.
Field mushrooms, sliced	350 g	12 oz.
Porcini mushrooms, sliced	100 g	3 oz.
Brandy	25 mL	1 fl. oz.
White wine	125 mL	4 fl. oz.
Veal demi-glace	250 mL	8 fl. oz.
Cream, 35%	150 mL	5 fl. oz.

1. Dry veal with paper towelling. Season with salt and pepper. Lightly dust with flour.

2. In a hot sauteuse, heat clarified butter and sear veal quickly and reserve. Pour off excess fat.

3. Add shallots and mushrooms to pan. Sauté until almost dry. Flame with brandy and deglaze with wine.

4. Add demi-glace and cream to pan and reduce by one-third. Return veal and any juices to pan and heat thoroughly. Adjust seasonings.

5. Serve with spaetzle, noodles or rösti.

RECIPE 14.6

Approximate values per serving:	
Calories	357
Total fat	21 g
Saturated fat	12 g
Cholesterol	155 mg
Sodium	371 mg
Total carbohydrates	9.9 g
Protein	32 g

RECIPE 14.7

Osso Buco

VANCOUVER COMMUNITY COLLEGE, Vancouver, BC
Chef Instructor Settimio Sicoli
Yield: 8 servings
Method: Braising

Veal shank, cut in 2.5-cm (1-in.) pieces	16 pieces	16 pieces
Salt and pepper	TT	TT
Flour	150 g	5 oz.
Olive oil	75 mL	3 fl. oz.
Garlic clove, minced	10 g	2
Carrot, macedoine	200 g	6 oz.
Lemon zest	25 g	1-1/2 oz.
White wine	350 mL	12 fl. oz.
Brown veal stock	1.75 L	1-3/4 qt.
Tomato purée	50 mL	2 Tbsp.
Tomato concassée	300 g	10 oz.
Gremolada:		
Garlic clove, chopped fine	10 g	2
Lemon zest	25 g	1 oz.
Fresh Italian parsley, chopped	30 g	3 Tbsp.

1. Season the veal with salt and pepper and dredge the pieces in flour. Sauté them in olive oil until brown on both sides.

2. Add the garlic and carrot and sauté lightly.

3. Add the lemon zest, wine, stock and tomato purée and concassée. Bring to a boil and reduce to a simmer. Braise on the stove top or in a 160°C (325°F) oven until the meat is tender but not falling from the bone, approximately 40–60 minutes.

4. Remove the veal shanks, reserve, keeping warm, and reduce the sauce until thick. Adjust the seasonings.

5. At service time, transfer the meat to a serving platter and ladle the sauce over it. Combine the gremolada ingredients and sprinkle over the meat and sauce. Allow 2 pieces per person.

VARIATION: OSSO BUCO MILANESE—Add four minced anchovy fillets to gremolada and serve with saffron rice.

Settimio Sicoli
Settimio served his apprenticeship at Hotel Vancouver, then added to his culinary training overseas at the Hilton International Hotel in Mainz, Germany. Upon returning home in 1981, Settimio joined the kitchen brigade of the University Club of Vancouver, attaining the position of Executive Chef, until he was asked to join the Culinary Arts Department at Vancouver Community College in 1987.

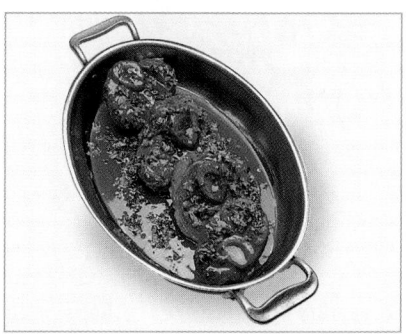

Osso Buco

RECIPE 14.7

Approximate values per serving:	
Calories	401
Total fat	17 g
Saturated fat	6 g
Cholesterol	103 mg
Sodium	363 mg
Total carbohydrates	26 g
Protein	27 g

RECIPE 14.8

Veal Sweetbread Picatta Milanese

Yield: 10 appetizers (5 mains)
Method: Pan-frying

Sweetbreads, blanched and pressed, membranes removed	750 kg	1 lb. 10 oz.
Eggs, beaten	5	5
Bread crumbs	30 g	1/4 cup
Parmesan, grated	50 g	2 oz.
Salt and pepper	TT	TT
Flour	as needed for dredging	
Clarified butter	200 mL	6 fl. oz.

continued

Linguine, cooked	625 g	20 oz.
Tomato sauce, light	625 mL	20 fl. oz.
Mushrooms, julienne, sweated	100 g	3-1/2 oz.
Ham, julienne	100 g	3-1/2 oz.

1. Slice the sweetbreads into medallions, 2 slices per order.
2. Combine eggs, bread crumbs and parmesan; reserve.
3. Season and lightly flour the sweetbreads.
4. Coat sweetbreads in the egg mixture and place immediately into a pre-heated frying pan with clarified butter.
5. Pan-fry the picatta until golden, turn over and cook second side.
6. To serve, mound a portion of the pasta on each plate, ladle a portion of the tomato sauce garnished with mushroom and ham julienne and top with 2 picatta.

RECIPE 14.8

Approximate values per serving:

Calories	435
Total fat	23 g
Saturated fat	12 g
Cholesterol	352 mg
Sodium	1100 mg
Total carbohydrates	32 g
Protein	26 g

Rosemary-Roasted Veal Chops with Porcini Mushrooms

RECIPE 14.9

Rosemary-Roasted Veal Chops with Porcini Mushrooms

THE FOUR SEASONS, NEW YORK, NY
Executive Chef Christian Albin

Yield: 4 350-g (12-oz.) servings
Method: Roasting

Veal chops, each 350 g (12 oz.)	4	4
Salt and pepper	TT	TT
Fresh rosemary	4 sprigs	4 sprigs
Flour	as needed	as needed
Paprika	TT	TT
Clarified butter	125 mL	4 fl. oz.
White wine	125 mL	4 fl. oz.
Brown veal stock	450 mL	16 fl. oz.
Unsalted butter	50 g	2 oz.

1. Season the veal chops with salt and pepper. Press a rosemary sprig onto one side of each chop. Mix the flour and paprika and dredge the chops (both sides) in this mixture.
2. Heat the clarified butter in a sauté pan. Place the chops in the pan, rosemary side down. Roast in a preheated 190°C (375°F) oven for 7 minutes. Turn the chops carefully to keep the rosemary sprigs intact. Roast for 5–6 minutes more. Remove the chops and keep warm.
3. To make the sauce, degrease the pan and deglaze with the white wine. Add the veal stock and any juices that have accumulated under the chops. Simmer to reduce to 250 mL (8 fl. oz.). Monter au beurre, strain and adjust the seasonings.
4. Serve the chops with grilled porcini mushrooms.

RECIPE 14.9

Approximate values per serving:

Calories	621
Total fat	45 g
Saturated fat	24 g
Cholesterol	238 mg
Sodium	728 mg
Total carbohydrates	9.9 g
Protein	44 g

“ I like a cook who smiles out loud when he tastes his own work. Let God worry about your modesty, I want to see your enthusiasm.

—Robert Farrar Capon

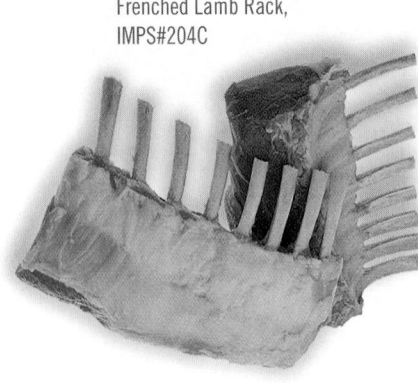

Frenched Lamb Rack, IMPS#204C

Lamb is the meat of sheep slaughtered under the age of

one year. Meat from sheep slaughtered after that age is called yearling or mutton. Spring lamb is young lamb that has not been fed grass. Because lamb is slaughtered at an early age, it is quite tender and can be prepared by almost any cooking method.

Lamb has a special and distinctive flavour. It goes well with boldly flavoured sauces and accompaniments.

PRIMAL AND SUBPRIMAL CUTS OF LAMB

After the young sheep is slaughtered, it is usually reduced to the primal cuts: front, breast, rack, loin and leg. Like veal, these primals are crosscut sections and contain both bilateral halves (for example, the primal leg contains both hind legs). Generally the pieces are sold separately. Lamb primals are not classified into a forequarter and hindquarter like beef, or a foresaddle and hindsaddle like veal.

Figure 15.1 shows the relationship between the lamb's bone structure and the primal cuts. As with all meats, it is important to know the location of bones when cutting or working with lamb. This makes meat fabrication and carving easier and aids in identifying cuts. Figure 15.2 shows the primal cuts of lamb and their location on the carcass. A lamb carcass generally weighs between 13 and 30 kg (30 and 65 lb.). Table 15.1 (see page 318) lists uses for common cuts of lamb.

Front

The primal lamb front is a relatively large cut, accounting for approximately 45% of carcass weight. The front contains the shoulder, which consists of six rib bones, the arm, blade and neck bones as well as many small, tough muscles whose grains travel in different directions. The breast and shank are also part of the front.

All the bone and muscle groups make it difficult to cook and carve a whole shoulder. It may be boned and rolled with or without stuffing. Cubing for stew is a common application. Although the shanks are excellent braised, they are often made into mince along with the breast.

Flank

Located below the whole loin, the primal flank is a small part of the carcass and is not generally marketed as is. It is ground for patties or shepherd's pie.

Whole Loin

The primal whole loin accounts for approximately 21% of carcass weight. It can be purchased as a saddle, but is usually broken down into ribs (racks) and loins.

Rib (Rack)

The lamb rib is located between the front and loin. Containing eight ribs and portions of the backbone, it accounts for approximately 8% of carcass weight.

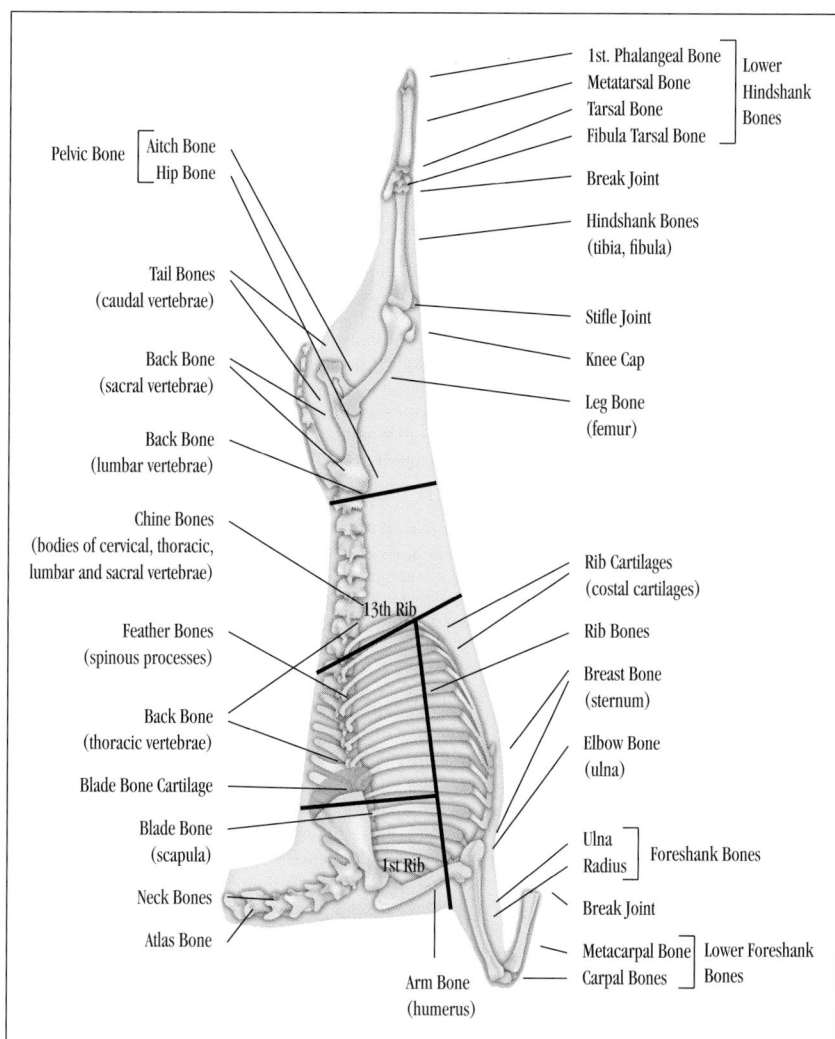

Pelvic Bone ⎡ Aitch Bone
⎣ Hip Bone

Tail Bones
(caudal vertebrae)

Back Bone
(sacral vertebrae)

Back Bone
(lumbar vertebrae)

Chine Bones
(bodies of cervical, thoracic,
lumbar and sacral vertebrae)

Feather Bones
(spinous processes)

Back Bone
(thoracic vertebrae)

Blade Bone Cartilage

Blade Bone
(scapula)

Neck Bones

Atlas Bone

1st. Phalangeal Bone ⎤ Lower
Metatarsal Bone   ⎥ Hindshank
Tarsal Bone   ⎥ Bones
Fibula Tarsal Bone ⎦

Break Joint

Hindshank Bones
(tibia, fibula)

Stifle Joint

Knee Cap

Leg Bone
(femur)

Rib Cartilages
(costal cartilages)

Rib Bones

Breast Bone
(sternum)

Elbow Bone
(ulna)

Ulna   ⎤ Foreshank Bones
Radius ⎦

Break Joint

Metacarpal Bone ⎤ Lower Foreshank
Carpal Bones   ⎦ Bones

Arm Bone
(humerus)

13th Rib

1st Rib

FIGURE 15.1   The skeletal structure of a lamb.

Classic Lamb Flavours

Lamb and its fat have a pronounced flavour, which lends itself to pairing with garlic and resinous herbs such as mint, oregano and rosemary. Many world cuisines incorporate some acid in their lamb preparations to balance fattiness; vinegar is the basic ingredient in mint sauce served with roasted lamb in Australia, Great Britain and New Zealand. Citrus juice, wine and yogurt are used to brighten the flavour in lamb stews and sauces served with lamb. The sweetness of dried fruits and root vegetables balances the fattiness of lamb and can be found in North African tagine, Indian curry and classic French lamb navarin.

Imported Lamb

Technologies that increase shelf life have made imported fresh lamb commonplace. Australian and New Zealand products account for most lamb consumed in Canada. New Zealand lamb is smaller than Canadian and Australian lamb in muscle size. Canada also produces a lamb similar to France's pré salé lambs in parts of Vancouver Island and the Gulf Islands. The salt marsh grasses impart a distinctive flavour.

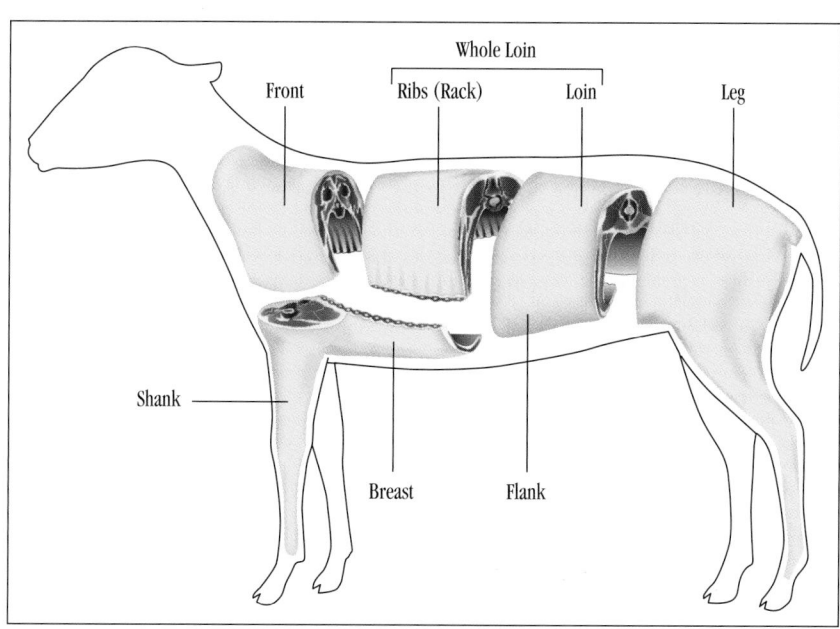

Whole Loin

Front   Ribs (Rack)   Loin   Leg

Shank

Breast   Flank

FIGURE 15.2   The primal cuts of lamb.

Lamb Rib,
IMPS#204

The rack is valued for its tender rib eye muscle. The hotel rack (rib double) is usually split in half and trimmed so that each set of ribs can be easily cut into chops. The split racks can then be grilled, broiled or roasted as racks or cut into single or double rib chops before cooking. Two racks are tied together to form a crown roast.

Loin

The loin is located between the rib and leg. It contains no rib but portions of the backbone as well as the loin eye muscle and tenderloin. It accounts for approximately 13% of carcass weight.

Lamb Loin Trimmed,
IMPS#232

The loin meat is very tender and is invariably cooked using a dry-heat method such as broiling, grilling or roasting. The loin may be boned to produce boneless roasts or chops or cut into chops with the bone in. The loin eye may be removed and cut into medallions or noisettes.

Leg

The primal legs are a large section accounting for approximately 34% of carcass weight. They are the posterior portion of the carcass, separated from the loin by a straight cut anterior to the hip bone cartilage. As with veal, the cut of meat that would be the sirloin on a beef carcass is separated from the lamb loin by this cut and becomes part of the primal leg. The lamb leg contains several bones: the backbone, tail, hip, aitch, round and shank bones.

Lamb Leg, IMPS#233A

The primal leg is rarely used as is. More often it is partially or fully boned. Lamb legs are quite tender—the sirloin end more so than the shank end—and are well suited to a variety of cooking methods. A bone-in leg is often roasted for buffet service or braised with vegetables or beans for a hearty dish. Steaks can also be cut from the bone-in leg, with the sirloin end producing the most tender cuts. A boneless leg can be tied and roasted, with or without stuffing, or trimmed and cut into kebabs. The shank end can be braised whole, diced for stew or ground for patties.

Special Cuts

Because lamb carcasses are so easily handled, purveyors often sell them whole or cut in a variety of ways to better meet their customers' needs. As well as whole carcass, primal and fabricated cuts, lamb can be purchased as a saddle. The saddle is the whole loin double in one piece. It is particularly useful for producing large quantities of lamb chops.

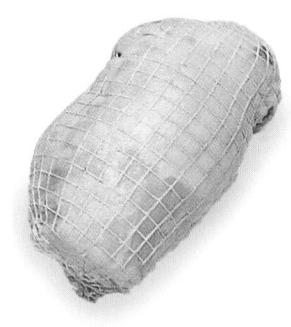

Boned, Rolled and Netted
Leg of Lamb, IMPS#233B

NUTRITION

Lamb, especially when purchased in subprimal cuts to be fabricated on-site, is an economical source of high-quality protein. Lean and lower in cholesterol than other red meat proteins, lamb is a good source of iron as compared with chicken, fish or poultry. Lamb has less marbling than other red meats. Its excess fat appears on the outside of many cuts and can easily be trimmed before cooking. Grass-fed lamb, like meat from other grass-fed ruminants, is high in the powerful antioxidant conjugated linoleic acid, identified as a cancer preventative.

BUTCHERING PROCEDURES

Lamb is unique among the common meat animals in that it is small enough to be handled easily in its carcass form. Thus, food service operations sometimes purchase lamb whole and fabricate the desired cuts themselves. This is practical if the operation has the necessary employee skills, equipment and storage space, as well as a need for all the various cuts and trimmings butchering a whole carcass produces. A few important lamb fabrication and butchering techniques follow.

BASIC PROCEDURE FOR FRENCHING A RACK OF LAMB

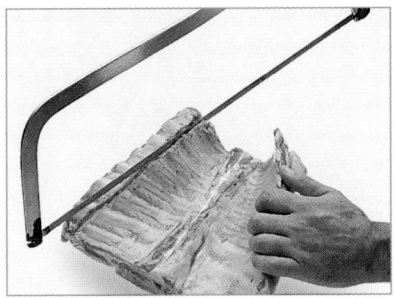

1. With a meat saw, trim the ribs to approximately 7.5 cm (3 in.), measuring from the rib eye on each side of the rack.

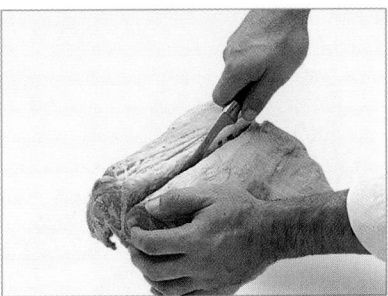

2. Turn the rack over and cut down both sides of the feather bones, completely separating the meat from the bone.

3. Turn the rack back over. Using a meat saw, cut between the ribs and the chine bone at a 45-degree angle, exposing the lean meat between the ribs and the vertebral junctures.

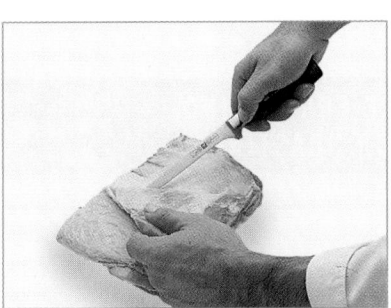

4. By pulling and cutting along the natural seam, remove the thick layers of fat and the meat between them from the rack's surface.

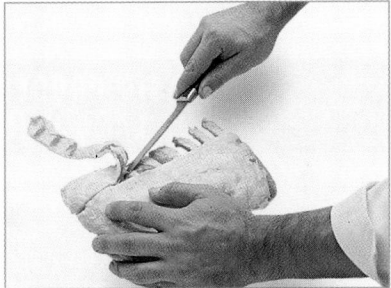

5. Make an even cut through the fat, perpendicular to the ribs, 2.5 cm (1 in.) from the rib eye. Trim away all meat and fat from the rib ends. The ribs should be completely clean.

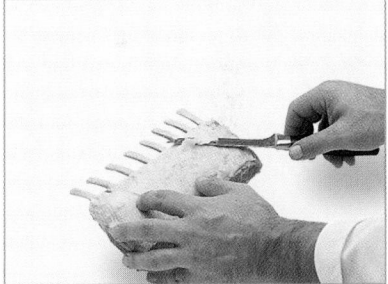

6. Trim away the fat covering. Leave either a thin layer to protect the meat during cooking or trim the fat away completely to produce a very lean rack. The rack can also be cut into chops.

BASIC PROCEDURE FOR TRIMMING AND BONING A LAMB LEG FOR ROASTING OR GRILLING

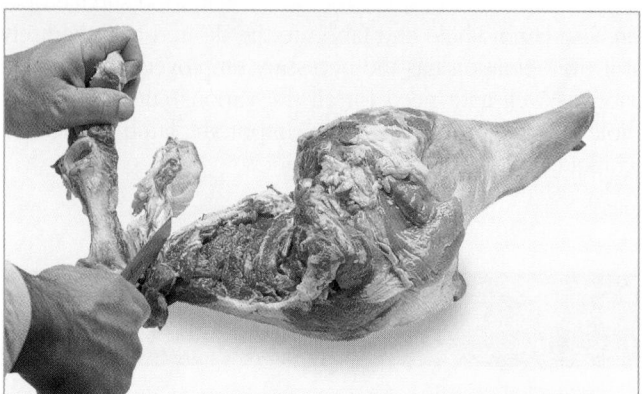

1. With the tip of the knife, trim around the pelvic bone; stay close to the bone to avoid wasting any meat. Cut the sinew inside the socket and remove the bone.

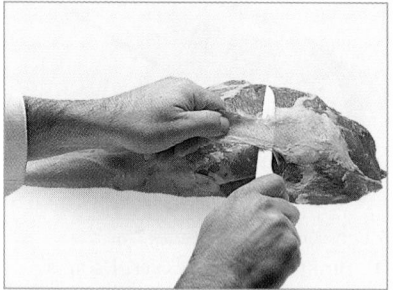

2. Trim away most of the exterior fat.

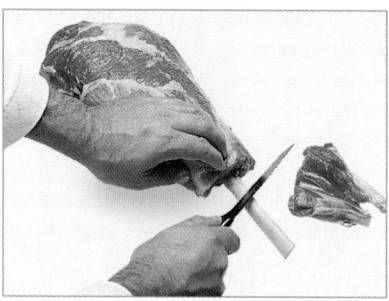

3. Cut off the shank portion completely and scrape the bone clean. This makes a handle to hold while carving the lamb.

4. Fold the flap of the sirloin over on top of the ball of the leg bone and tie with butcher's twine. This helps the leg cook evenly.

BASIC PROCEDURE FOR BONING A LAMB LOIN FOR ROASTING

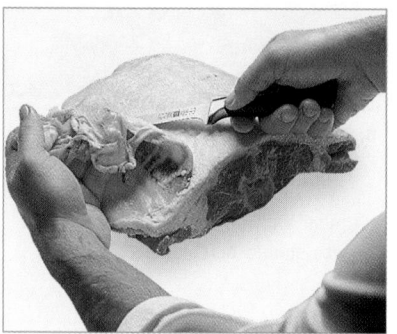

1. Start with a trimmed lamb loin (double). With the skin side up, trim the thin layer of connective tissue called the fell from the loin's surface.

2. Turn the loin over and trim the fat from around the tenderloins.

continued

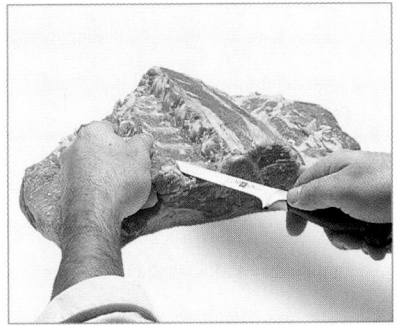

3. Starting in the middle of the back-bone, cut between the tenderloin and the vertebrae, separating them but leaving the tenderloin attached to the flank. Continue until you reach the end of the vertebrae. Repeat on the other side.

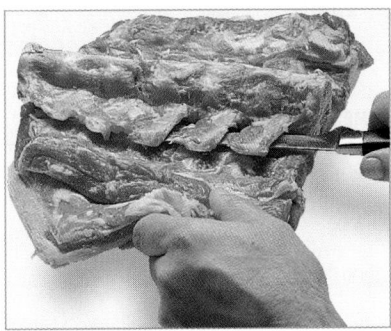

4. Slide the knife under the vertebrae and rib and cut back all the way to the backbone, separating the eye muscle from the vertebrae.

5. Pull the backbone out with your hands, keeping the loins intact.

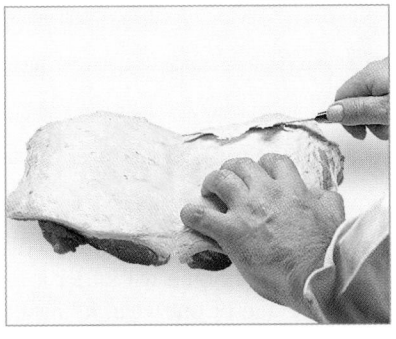

6. Turn the loins over and trim the sur-face fat to 0.6 cm (1/4 in.).

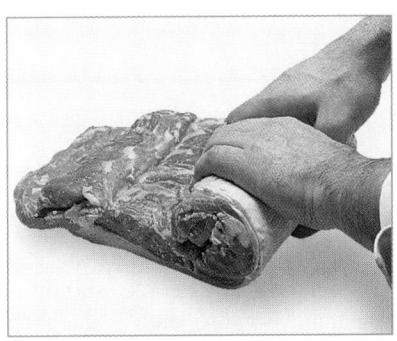

7. Roll the flank flaps under from each side.

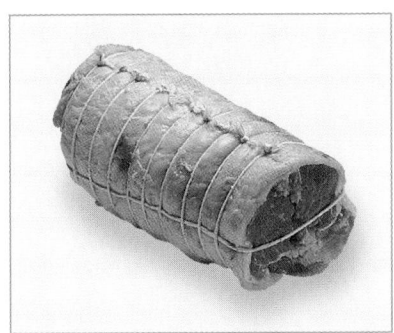

8. Tie the roast with butcher's twine at even intervals.

BASIC PROCEDURE FOR CUTTING LAMB NOISETTES FROM A LOIN

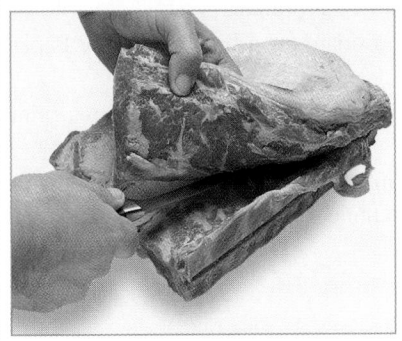

1. Remove the loin eye muscle by cut-ting down along the backbone and along the vertebrae. Trim the eye muscle, leaving a thin layer of fat if desired.

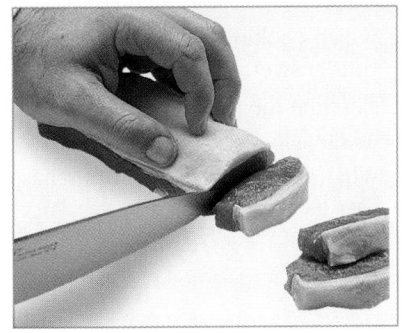

2. Cut the eye meat into noisettes of the desired thickness.

TABLE 15.1	Using Common Cuts of Lamb			
Primal	**Subprimal or Fabricated Cut**	**IMPS**	**Cooking Methods**	**Serving Suggestions**
Front	Shoulder lamb chop	1207	Dry heat (broil or grill)	Broiled or grilled lamb chops
	Diced lamb	1295	Combination (stew)	Lamb stew; lamb curry; navarin
	Ground lamb	1296	Dry heat (broil or grill; sauté)	Patties
Breast	Breast	209	Combination (braise)	Lamb breast stuffed with mushrooms
Rib	Lamb rack	204	Dry heat (broil or grill; roast; sauté)	Roast rack of lamb with garlic and rosemary
	Frenched lamb rack	204C	Dry heat (broil or grill; roast; sauté)	Broiled lamb with mustard and hazelnut crust
Loin	Lamb loin trimmed	232	Dry heat (broil or grill; roast; sauté)	Noisettes of lamb with roasted garlic sauce
	Loin chops	1232	Dry heat (broil or grill; sauté)	Broiled loin chops with herb butter
Leg	Lamb leg	233A	Dry heat (broil or grill; roast)	Kebabs; roast leg of lamb
	Boned, rolled, tied leg of lamb	233B	Dry heat (roast)	Roast leg of lamb

Conclusion

Even though lamb accounts for a small percentage of the meat consumed in this country, many people who do not prepare lamb at home will order it at a restaurant. Because lamb is slaughtered under the age of one year, its meat is tender and it can be prepared by almost any cooking method. Its distinctive flavour allows you to offer bold, robust sauces and accompaniments that might mask the flavours of other meats.

Questions for Discussion

1. Describe the basic differences between a lamb carcass and a beef carcass.
2. List each lamb primal and describe its location on the carcass. Identify two subprimals or fabricated cuts taken from each primal.
3. Which cooking methods are most appropriate for a breast of lamb? Explain your answer.
4. Describe the procedure for preparing a frenched rack of lamb from a primal hotel rack.
5. What is the best way to purchase lamb for a food service operation that cuts its own meat and uses large quantities of lamb chops? Explain your answer.

Lamb Recipes

Roast Rack of Lamb with Mint and Celeriac Sauce

GREENCHEF.CA, VANCOUVER, BC
Executive Chef Dennis Green

Yield: 4 125-g (4-oz.) servings
Method: Roasting

Lamb racks, cleaned and frenched, each 1 kg (2 lb.)	2	2
Salt and pepper	TT	TT
Fresh white bread cubes, crusts removed	150 g	2 cups
Fresh mint, chopped	20 g	2 Tbsp.
Fresh parsley, chopped	20 g	2 Tbsp.
Fresh chives, chopped	15 g	2 Tbsp.
Dijon mustard	30 mL	2 Tbsp.
Potato and Celeriac Purée (recipe follows)	as needed	as needed
Mint and Celeriac Sauce (recipe follows)	as needed	as needed
Fresh mint sprigs	2	2

1. Season the lamb racks with salt and pepper and sear on both sides.
2. Transfer the lamb to a roasting pan and roast in a 130°C (250°F) oven until medium rare, approximately 35–40 minutes.
3. Meanwhile, combine the bread cubes and the herbs in a food processor and process until well blended. Set aside.
4. Remove the lamb from the roasting pan and smear with the mustard. Coat the racks with the bread crumb mixture.
5. Allow the lamb to rest for 10 minutes before carving.
6. Serve with Potato and Celeriac Purée and Mint and Celeriac Sauce. Garnish with fresh mint.

Potato and Celeriac Purée

Yield: 8 120-g (4-oz.) servings

Potatoes, peeled and cut into pieces	750 g	1 lb. 8 oz.
Celeriac (celery root), peeled and cut into 2.5-cm (1-in.) pieces	250 g	8 oz.
Cream, 35%	250 mL	8 fl. oz.
Butter	30 mL	2 Tbsp.
Salt and pepper	TT	TT

1. Combine the potatoes and celeriac in a saucepan and cover with water. Bring to a boil, reduce the heat and simmer until tender, approximately 30 minutes.
2. Strain. Mash the potatoes and celeriac using a food mill or potato ricer.
3. Heat the cream and the butter just to a boil. Add to the hot potato mixture. Using an electric mixer fitted with the whip attachment, whip the purée until fluffy. Season to taste with salt and pepper.

Dennis Green
Dennis was raised in Vancouver and started cooking when he was 17. He served his apprenticeship at a small bistro named the Avenue Grill near his high school. He was Executive Chef at Bishop's Restaurant in Vancouver from 1997 to 2007. Since then, Dennis has run his own consulting business, greenchef.ca.

Roast Rack of Lamb

Approximate values per serving:	
Calories	764
Total fat	40 g
Saturated fat	20 g
Cholesterol	214 mg
Sodium	1202 mg
Total carbohydrates	53 g
Protein	48 g

Potato and Celeriac Purée— Approximate values per serving:	
Calories	231
Total fat	15 g
Saturated fat	9.1 g
Cholesterol	51 mg
Sodium	321 mg
Total carbohydrates	21 g
Protein	3.1 g

continued

Mint and Celeriac Sauce— Approximate values per 50 mL serving:	
Calories	110
Total fat	6.7 g
Saturated fat	3.6 g
Cholesterol	14 mg
Sodium	102 mg
Total carbohydrates	11 g
Protein	1.4 g

Mint and Celeriac Sauce

Yield: 500 mL (16 fl. oz.)

Butter	30 g	2 Tbsp.
Shallots, chopped fine	125 g	4 oz.
Garlic, minced	10 g	2 cloves
Celeriac (celery root), peeled and chopped	125 g	4 oz.
Red wine vinegar	30 mL	1 fl. oz.
Port	125 mL	4 fl. oz.
Fresh mint, chopped	100 mL	1/2 cup
Demi-glace	500 mL	16 fl. oz.

1. Melt the butter in a saucepan. Add the shallots, garlic and celeriac, and sauté until tender but not brown.
2. Add the vinegar and reduce au sec.
3. Add the port and mint and reduce by half.
4. Add the demi-glace and simmer for 30 minutes. Strain and keep warm for service. The sauce can be made up to 1 day in advance and refrigerated, then reheated as needed.

Shish Kebab

RECIPE 15.2

Approximate values per serving:	
Calories	554
Total fat	38 g
Saturated fat	8.7 g
Cholesterol	152 mg
Sodium	332 mg
Total carbohydrates	6 g
Protein	47 g

RECIPE 15.2

Shish Kebab

Yield: 10 225-g (7-1/2-oz.) servings
Method: Grilling or broiling

Marinade:		
Onion, small dice	350 g	12 oz.
Garlic, chopped	30 g	1 oz.
Lemon juice	125 mL	4 fl. oz.
Pepper	3 g	1 tsp.
Fresh oregano, chopped	5 g	2 tsp.
Olive oil	250 mL	8 fl. oz.
Cumin, ground	5 g	2 tsp.
Coriander, ground	6 g	1 Tbsp.
Fresh mint, chopped	8 g	2 tsp.
Lamb leg or shoulder, boneless, trimmed and cut in 5-cm (2-in.) cubes	2.2 kg	5 lb.
Salt	TT	TT

1. Combine the marinade ingredients and add the lamb. Marinate for 2 hours.
2. Place 3–4 cubes of lamb on each of 10 skewers. Season with salt. Grill or broil to the desired doneness. Serve with rice pilaf.

Irish Lamb Stew

RECIPE 15.3

Irish Lamb Stew

Yield: 10 250-g (8-oz.) servings
Method: Stewing

Lamb shoulder, in 4-cm		
(1-1/2-in.) cubes	1.5 kg	3 lb. 4 oz.
White stock	1.25 L	40 fl. oz.
Sachet:		
Bay leaf	1	1
Dried thyme	0.5 g	1/2 tsp.
Peppercorns, crushed	1 g	1/2 tsp.
Parsley stems	10	10
Garlic cloves, crushed	15 g	4
Onion, sliced	425 g	1 lb.
Leek, sliced	200 g	7 oz.
Potato, peeled, large dice	600 g	1 lb. 4 oz.
Salt and white pepper	TT	TT
Carrots, turned or baton	20	20
Turnips, turned or baton	20	20
Potatoes, turned or baton	20	20
Pearl onions, peeled	20	20
Parsley, chopped, fresh	15 g	1 Tbsp.

1. Combine the lamb, stock, sachet, onion, leek and potato. Season with salt and white pepper. Bring to a simmer and skim the surface. Simmer the stew on the stove or cover and cook in the oven at 180°C (350°F) until the lamb is tender, approximately 1 hour.

2. Degrease the stew; remove and discard the sachet.

3. Remove the pieces of potato and purée them in a food mill or ricer. Use the potato purée to thicken the stew to the desired consistency.

4. Simmer the stew for 10 minutes to blend the flavours.

5. Cook the turned or baton vegetables, potatoes and pearl onions separately. At service, heat the vegetable garnishes and add to each portion of stew.

6. Garnish with chopped parsley and serve.

RECIPE 15.3

Approximate values per serving:	
Calories	317
Total fat	9.3 g
Saturated fat	3.8 g
Cholesterol	107 mg
Sodium	300 mg
Total carbohydrates	24 g
Protein	33 g

RECIPE 15.4

Navarin of Lamb

Yield: 10 300-g (10-oz.) servings
Method: Stewing

Lean lamb shoulder, large dice	1.5 kg	3 lb.
Olive oil	50 mL	3 Tbsp.
Sugar	15 g	1 Tbsp.
Salt and pepper	TT	TT
Flour	25 g	3 Tbsp.
White stock	1 L	1 qt.
White wine	125 mL	4 fl. oz.
Tomato concassée	250 g	8 oz.

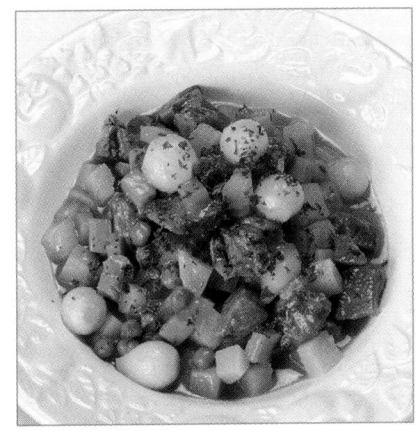

Navarin of Lamb

continued

RECIPE 15.4

Approximate values per serving:	
Calories	519
Total fat	23 g
Saturated fat	7.1 g
Cholesterol	144 mg
Sodium	197 mg
Total carbohydrates	32 g
Protein	46 g

Bouquet garni:		
Carrot stick, 10 cm (4 in.)	1	1
Leek, split, 10-cm (4-in.) piece	1	1
Fresh thyme	1 sprig	1 sprig
Bay leaf	1	1
Potato, peeled, medium dice	700 g	1 lb. 8 oz.
Carrot, medium dice	450 g	1 lb.
White turnip, peeled, medium dice	450 g	1 lb.
Pearl onions, peeled	12	12
Green peas, fresh	175 g	6 oz.

1. In a brazier, brown the meat in the olive oil.
2. Sprinkle the meat with the sugar and season with salt and pepper.
3. Add the flour and cook to make a blond roux.
4. Add the stock and wine. Add the tomatoes and bouquet garni; bring to a boil. Cover and cook in the oven at 190°C (375°F) until the meat is almost tender, approximately 1–1.5 hours.
5. Remove the meat and hold in a warm place. Strain the sauce and skim off any excess fat.
6. Combine the sauce, meat, potato, carrot, turnip and onions. Cover and cook until the vegetables are almost tender, approximately 25 minutes.
7. Add the peas and cook for 10 minutes more.
8. Serve in an individual casserole (cocotte) with accompaniments on the side.

NOTE: Some chefs prefer to turn (carve) the root vegetables for garnish.

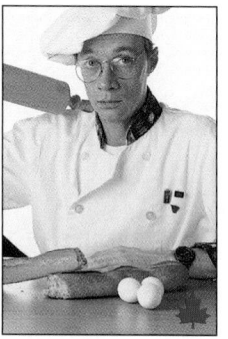

Carol Paradis

Born in Mont Joli, Quebec, Carol began his culinary career doing research on Canadian cooking for a Quebec culinary museum. Having taught at the Wolfgang Puck Cooking School and the French Culinary Institute in New York, Carol spent two years as Chef-Proprietor of Bistro du Lapin Agile, in Sutton, Quebec. As a chef-consultant, he was Executive Chef at the 2001 Tennis Masters Series and the 2001 International Meeting of Airports.

RECIPE 15.5

RECIPE 15.5

Braised Lamb Shanks with Rosemary Jus

LOEWS HOTEL VOGUE, MONTREAL, QC
Executive Chef Carol Paradis

Yield: 10 servings
Method: Braising

Lamb shanks	10	10
Lamb broth	1 L	1 qt.
Red wine	400 mL	15 fl. oz.
Bay leaves	7	7
Roasted garlic	20 g	6 cloves
Onion, brunoise	160 g	6 oz.
Fresh rosemary	75 g	2-1/2 oz.
Fresh marjoram	15 g	1/2 oz.
Black pepper, crushed	TT	TT
Salt	TT	TT

1. Sear lamb shanks on all sides until golden brown, about 2 minutes in a brazier.
2. Place all other ingredients into pan and bring to a simmer. Cover and place in oven.
3. Cook for approximately 2 hours at 160°C (350°F) until lamb is tender.
4. Strain jus and serve lamb in a rimmed plate with garlic mashed potatoes or polenta and the jus.

Approximate values per serving:	
Calories	312
Total fat	18 g
Saturated fat	7.7 g
Cholesterol	84 mg
Sodium	277 mg
Total carbohydrates	5.6 g
Protein	24 g

RECIPE 15.6

Roast Leg of Lamb

Yield: 12 150–180-g (5–6-oz.) servings
Method: Roasting

Leg of lamb, 2.7–3.6 kg (6–8 lb.)	1	1
Garlic, chopped	15 g	1 Tbsp.
Dijon mustard	30 mL	2 Tbsp.
Salt and pepper	TT	TT
Garlic heads	12	12
Fresh thyme	1 sprig	1 sprig
Fresh rosemary	1 sprig	1 sprig
Water	250 mL	8 fl. oz.
Chicken glaze	60 g	2 oz.

1. Bone and trim the leg of lamb, removing most of the fat; leave the shank bone intact.
2. Rub the leg with the chopped garlic and tie with twine.
3. Brush the lamb with Dijon mustard and season with salt and pepper.
4. Transfer the lamb to a roasting pan. Surround it with the garlic heads, thyme and rosemary. Roast at 135°C (275°F) for approximately 2–2.5 hours (internal temperature of 55°C/130°F), turning the leg 3–4 times. When the lamb is done, remove it and the garlic from the pan and set aside.
5. To make the sauce, add the water and chicken glaze to the pan and bring to a boil. Simmer 5 minutes and strain.
6. Cut the bottoms off the garlic heads. Serve 1 head with each lamb portion and top each serving with 15 mL (1 Tbsp.) of sauce.

RECIPE 15.6

Approximate values per serving:	
Calories	385
Total fat	27 g
Saturated fat	14 g
Cholesterol	132 mg
Sodium	312 mg
Total carbohydrates	3.4 g
Protein	32 g

RECIPE 15.7

Pan-Seared Lamb Loin with Rosemary Mousseline in Crispy Phyllo Crust

HUMBER COLLEGE, TORONTO, ON
Chef Konrad Weinbuch

Yield: 10 servings

Lamb loin, 120 g each	10	10
Olive oil	375 mL	12 fl. oz.
Garlic, chopped	50 g	10 cloves
Rosemary, chopped	7 g	2 tsp.
Thyme, chopped	7 g	2 tsp.
Black pepper, cracked	5 g	2 tsp.
Veal, lean, ground	625 g	1 lb. 5 oz.
Salt	10 g	2 tsp.
Pepper, ground	0.25 g	1/4 tsp.
Nutmeg	0.25 g	1/4 tsp.
Egg white	50 g	3
Cream, 35%	375 mL	12 fl. oz.
Shallots, brunoise	125 g	4 oz.

Konrad Weinbuch
Born in Germany into a family of restaurateurs, Konrad developed a passion for cooking at an early age. He trained and worked in several hotels in Europe before coming to Canada. Highlights of his career include joining the culinary team of the Fairmont Château Frontenac in Quebec City. Konrad currently teaches at Humber College in Toronto.

continued

Rosemary, chopped	10 g	1 Tbsp.
Chives, chopped	5 g	1 Tbsp.
Phyllo dough	20 sheets	20 sheets
Butter, clarified	375 g	12 oz.
Shallots, sliced	200 g	6-1/2 oz.
Butter	150 g	5 mL
Red wine	500 mL	16 fl. oz.
Black pepper, cracked	5 g	1-1/2 tsp.
Thyme	5 g	3 sprigs
Lamb glace de viande	500 mL	16 fl. oz.
Salt	TT	TT

1. Rub the lamb with olive oil, garlic, rosemary, thyme and pepper. Marinate for 6–8 hours.

2. Prepare a mousseline with the veal, salt, pepper, nutmeg, egg white, cream and shallots. Garnish with rosemary and chives.

3. Sear the lamb loins in olive oil and set aside to cool.

4. Brush 2 sheets of phyllo with butter and fold in half to obtain 4 layers. Repeat.

5. Spread one-tenth of the mousseline forcemeat on each set of sheets in a square approximately 10 cm × 10 cm × 8 mm (4 in. × 4 in. × 1/3 in.) thick.

6. Place the cooled lamb loin in the centre of the mousseline and wrap the phyllo to form a roll, ensuring that the mousseline encloses the loin completely. Fold the ends under and brush with clarified butter.

7. Bake in a 200°C (425°F) oven for 7 minutes for rare, 8 minutes for medium rare and 9 minutes for medium.

8. Allow to rest for at least 5 minutes in a warmer.

9. Caramelize the shallots in 25 g of the butter, add the red wine, pepper and thyme and reduce by three-quarters. Add the lamb glace de viande, bring back to a simmer and monter au beurre with the remaining butter. Adjust seasoning.

10. To serve, dress the plate with a portion of the sauce. Cut the lamb loin in half on a bias and arrange on sauce. Garnish appropriately.

RECIPE 15.7

Approximate values per serving:	
Calories	1062
Total fat	81 g
Saturated fat	41 g
Cholesterol	317 mg
Sodium	877 mg
Total carbohydrates	35 g
Protein	44 g

Takashi Ito, CCC

Takashi has been a Certified Chef de Cuisine since 1992, and has won several medals in competition, including the gold at the 1993 Grand Salon Culinaire in Vancouver. He is particularly notable for his skill and creativity in carving ice sculptures, for which he has also won numerous awards.

RECIPE 15.8

Cumin Coriander Crusted Lamb Loin, Basil Mascarpone and Chèvre, Truffled Lamb Jus

THE FAIRMONT EMPRESS, VICTORIA, BC
Executive Chef Takashi Ito, CCC

Yield: 2 150-g (5-1/2-oz.) servings
Method: Pan-frying

Lamb spice:

Cumin, ground	7 g	1 Tbsp.
Fennel, ground	3 g	1-1/2 tsp.
Coriander, ground	3 g	1-1/2 tsp.
Chilli powder	3 g	1-1/2 tsp.
Garlic, minced	10 g	2 cloves
Orange zest	5 g	1 strip
Rosemary, finely chopped	5 g	1-1/2 tsp.

continued

Lamb loin, cleaned	300 g	10 oz.
Salt and pepper	TT	TT
Mascarpone cheese	40 g	1-1/2 oz.
Chèvre cheese	40 g	1-1/2 oz.
Fresh basil, chopped	2 g	1/2 tsp.
Black pepper, coarsely ground	pinch	pinch
Sauce:		
Lamb glaze	60 mL	2 fl. oz.
Truffle oil	5 mL	1 tsp.

1. Combine spice mix.
2. Season lamb with salt and pepper and rub spice mix on lamb.
3. Pan-fry loins to desired doneness.
4. Combine mascarpone, chèvre, basil and pepper. Pipe onto 2 plates.
5. Slice lamb and arrange on cheese.
6. Combine sauce ingredients and drizzle sauce on plate.

RECIPE 15.8

Approximate values per serving:	
Calories	678
Total fat	50 g
Saturated fat	21 g
Cholesterol	156 mg
Sodium	723 mg
Total carbohydrates	19 g
Protein	38 g

RECIPE 15.9

Noisettes of Lamb with Garlic Sauce

Yield: 10 servings
Method: Sautéing

Lamb noisettes, each 60–90 g		
(2–3 oz.)	20	20
Salt and pepper	TT	TT
Fresh thyme	10 g	3 tsp.
Garlic heads	5	5
Rosemary, fresh	3 sprigs	3 sprigs
Olive oil	100 mL	3 fl. oz.
Red wine	300 mL	10 fl. oz.
Jus lié	1.5 L	40 fl. oz.

1. Season the noisettes with salt, pepper and thyme.
2. Break the garlic into cloves. Cook the cloves with the rosemary in 50 mL (1-1/2 fl. oz.) of oil over low heat until they are very soft, approximately 10 minutes.
3. Deglaze with the wine. Add the jus lié; simmer and reduce by half.
4. Strain the sauce through an etâmine, pushing to extract some of the garlic. Return the sauce to the saucepan and adjust the consistency and seasonings.
5. Sauté the noisettes to the desired degree of doneness in the remaining oil; serve with the sauce.

Noisettes of Lamb with Garlic Sauce

RECIPE 15.9

Approximate values per serving:	
Calories	307
Total fat	15 g
Saturated fat	3.8 g
Cholesterol	96 mg
Sodium	282 mg
Total carbohydrates	9.6 g
Protein	26 g

Simon Dunn, CCC

Born and classically trained in Great Britain, Simon was most recently the Executive Chef at The Inn on Lake Bonavista, which was ranked as one of the top 100 restaurants in Canada for the duration of his tenure. Simon cooked for members of the British royal family during his career in the Royal Air Force and is currently a chef instructor at SAIT.

RECIPE 15.10

Approximate values per serving:	
Calories	625
Total fat	40 g
Saturated fat	6.9 g
Cholesterol	116 mg
Sodium	335 mg
Total carbohydrates	31 g
Protein	38 g

RECIPE 15.10

Lamb Rogan Josh

SAIT POLYTECHNIC, CALGARY, AB
Chef Instructor Simon Dunn, CCC

Yield: 10 280-g (10-oz.) servings
Method: Stewing

Onions, brunoise	1.4 kg	3 lb.
Vegetable oil	300 mL	10 fl. oz.
Lamb shoulder, diced	1.6 kg	3 lb. 8 oz.
Garlic, crushed	30 g	7 cloves
Ginger, grated	75 g	2-1/2 oz.
Red chile, minced	4	4
Tomato paste	40 mL	2-1/2 Tbsp.
Black pepper	20 g	6 tsp.
Stock or water	3.5 L	3-1/2 qt.
Whole cloves	10	10
Cinnamon stick	3	3
Tomato, diced	1.2 kg	2-1/2 lb.
Salt	TT	TT
Yogurt	250 mL	8 fl. oz.

1. Brown onions in hot oil and remove from pan. Add lamb and brown on high heat.
2. Add garlic, ginger, chile, tomato paste and pepper. Return onions and stir well.
3. Add stock, cloves and cinnamon stick and stew until very tender.
4. Add fresh tomato and adjust seasoning. Finish with yogurt.

Pork 16

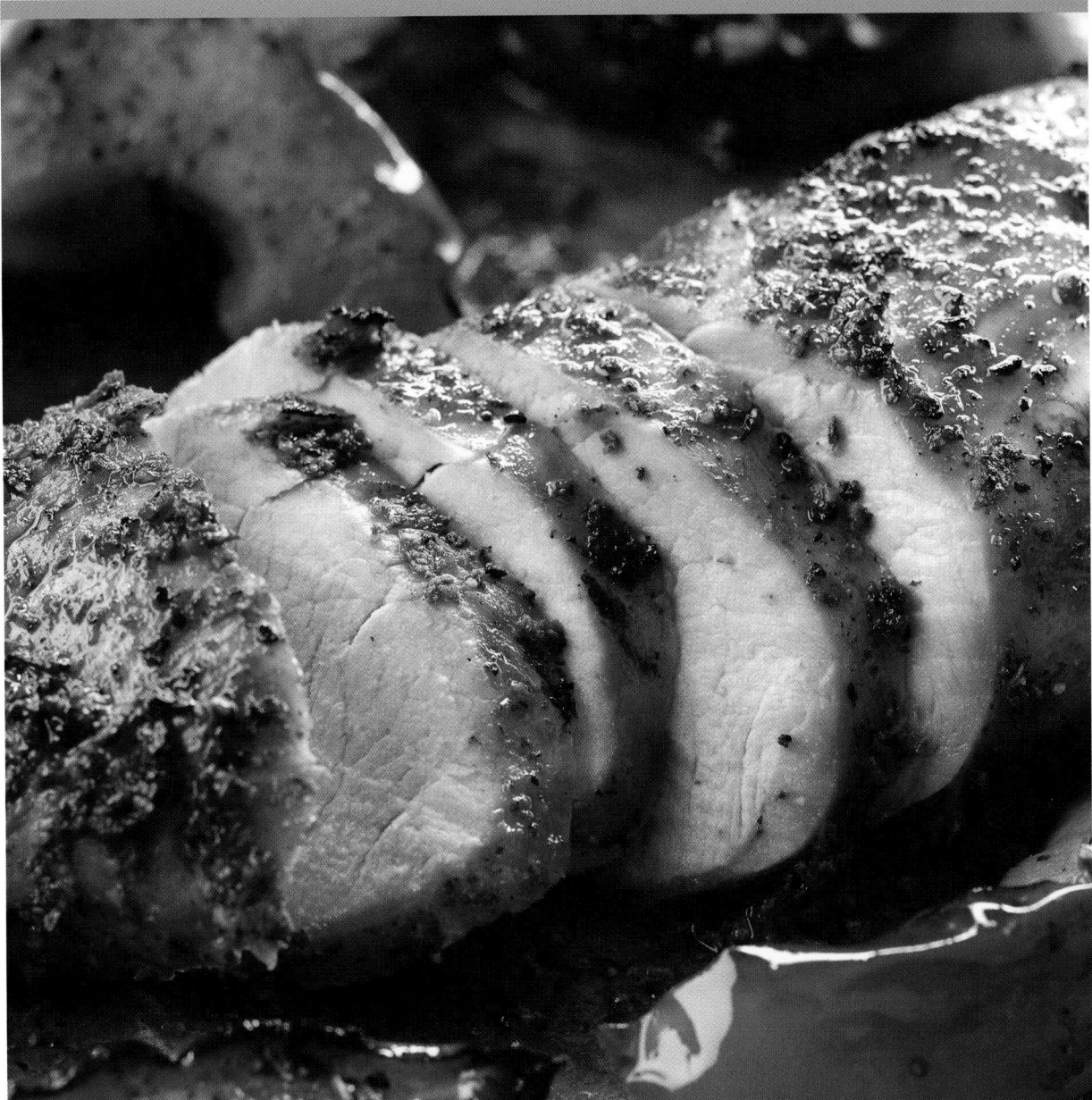

> But I will place this carefully
> fed pig
> Within the crackling oven;
> and, I pray,
> What nicer dish can e'er be given
> to man.

—Aeschylus, ancient Greek poet (c. 525–456 B.C.E.)

After studying this chapter you will be able to:

- identify the primal, subprimal and fabricated cuts of pork

- perform basic meat-cutting procedures: boning a pork loin, tying a pork roast, cutting a chop from a loin, cutting a pocket in a pork chop, trimming a pork tenderloin

- apply appropriate cooking methods to several common cuts of pork

These interactive online tools will help you master the skills in this chapter:

- Chapter Quizzes
- Activities

Shoulder Blade, CMC/Export#C320

Pork is the meat of hogs usually butchered before they are

one year old. With the exception of beef, Canadians consume more pork than any other meat. World pork consumption constitutes more than 70% of all meats eaten. The pork we eat is leaner and healthier than it once was because of advances in animal husbandry.

Because hogs are butchered at a young age, their meat is generally very tender and has a delicate flavour. It is well suited to a variety of cooking methods. A great deal of the pork marketed in North America is cured to produce products such as smoked hams and smoked bacon. Cured pork products are discussed in Chapter 20, Charcuterie.

PRIMAL AND SUBPRIMAL CUTS OF PORK

After a hog is slaughtered, it is generally split down the backbone, dividing the carcass into bilateral halves. Like the beef carcass, each side of the hog carcass is then further broken down into the primal cuts: shoulder, belly, loin and fresh leg.

Hogs are bred specifically to produce long loins. The loin contains the highest-quality meat and is the most expensive cut of pork. Pork is unique in that the ribs and loin are considered a single primal cut. They are not separated into two different primals as are the ribs and loin of beef, veal and lamb.

Figure 16.1 shows the relationship between the hog's bone structure and the primal cuts. As with all meats, it is important to know the location of bones when cutting or working with pork. This makes meat fabrication and carving easier and aids in identifying cuts. Figure 16.2 shows the primal cuts of pork and their location on the carcass. Table 16.1 (page 334) identifies common cuts of pork and suggests preparation methods. A hog carcass generally weighs in a range of 55 to 95 kg (120 to 210 lb.).

Shoulder

Pork Shoulder Picnic

The picnic is the lower portion of the hog's foreleg; it accounts for approximately 20% of carcass weight. The shoulder contains the arm and shank bones and has a relatively high ratio of bone to lean meat.

Because all pork comes from hogs slaughtered at a young age, the shoulder is tender enough to be cooked by any method. It is, however, one of the toughest cuts of pork. It is available smoked or fresh. The shoulder is fairly inexpensive and, when purchased fresh, it can be cut into shoulder blade steaks or boned and cut for stir-fry or stew.

The foreshank is called the pork hock and is almost always smoked. Cured and smoked pork hocks are often simmered for long periods in soups, stews and braised dishes to add flavour and richness.

Pork Shoulder Blade

The shoulder blade is a square cut located just above the shoulder picnic. It accounts for approximately 7% of carcass weight.

The shoulder blade is very meaty and tender, with a good percentage of lean meat to fat. Containing only a small portion of the blade bone, the blade

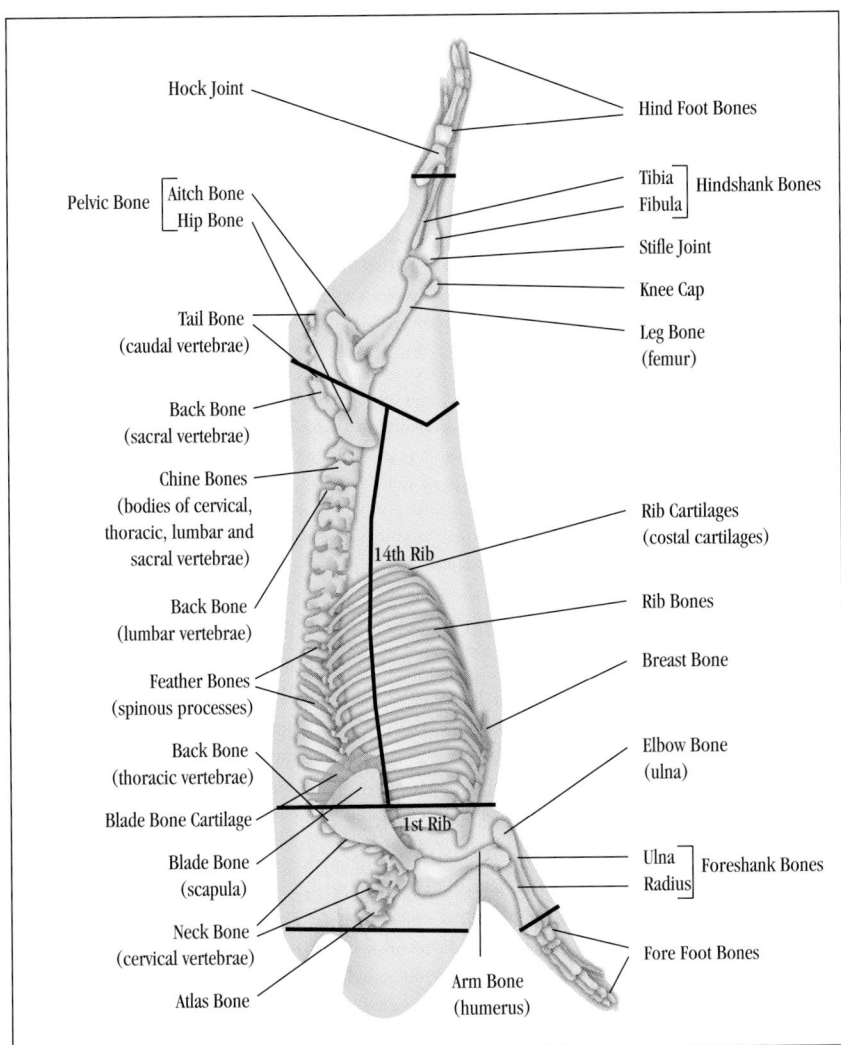

FIGURE 16.1 The skeletal structure of a hog.

Cooking Canadian Pork

Cooking pork to well done is not necessary or recommended in Canada. Trichinosis has virtually been eradicated in domestic pork and there has not been a reported case in more than three decades. Wild game is still a concern, however.

Today's leaner pork benefits greatly in palatability and yield through low-temperature cooking and cooking to medium doneness. Tougher cuts will require more cooking to achieve tenderness, although they are usually braised or stewed anyway.

Berkshire Pork

Berkshire pork is a breed of black pig named for the region of Great Britain where it was discovered. It is also known as Kurobuta in Japan. Considered a rare and endangered breed, Berkshire hogs produce pork that is well-marbled, moist and tender. Some producers feed the hogs sweet potatoes or beer to enhance their fat content, although this is not standard practice. Like Kobe beef, with which it is often compared, Berkshire pork is expensive and scarce.

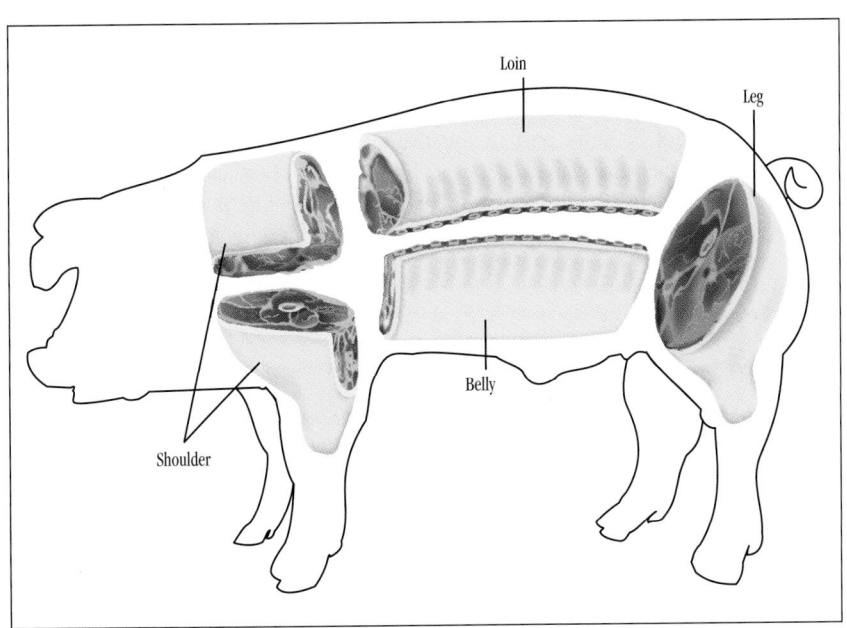

FIGURE 16.2 The primal cuts of pork.

Classic Pork Flavours

With a heavy layer of fat and many well-marbled cuts, pork benefits from robust seasonings. Shoulder and fresh leg roasts can be studded with garlic and strong herbs such as marjoram, oregano, rosemary or thyme before slow roasting. These cuts lend themselves to the flavours of American barbecue (smoke, whisky, sugar and salt curing), as well as spices used in Asian grilling (lemon grass, star anise, ginger, sesame oil and soy sauce). Lean cuts such as pork loin pair well with mild cream sauces flavoured with mustard or herbs such as tarragon, as well as richer brown sauces and caramelized apples, stone fruits or mushrooms.

Pork Side Ribs,
CMC/Export
#C500/502

Pork Loin,
CMC/Export
#C200

Pork Tenderloin,
CMC/Export#C227

Pork Backribs,
CMC/Export
#C505

Pork Rib Chops

is a good choice when a recipe calls for a solid piece of lean pork. The fresh shoulder blade is sometimes cut into steaks or chops to be broiled or sautéed. When the blade is smoked, it is usually boneless and called a cottage ham. The jowl may be cured for salt pork or smoked.

Belly

The primal pork belly is located below the loin. Accounting for approximately 16% of carcass weight, it is very fatty, with only streaks of lean meat. It contains the spareribs, which are always separated from the rest of the belly before cooking.

Spareribs usually are sold fresh but can also be smoked. Long, slow cooking and a dry-rub spice mixture yield tender, flavourful ribs. Radiant-heat slow-cooker-type ovens are very effective for cooking these cuts. The remainder of the pork belly is nearly always cured and smoked to produce side bacon.

Loin

The loin is cut from directly behind the shoulder blade and includes the entire rib section as well as the loin and a portion of the sirloin area. The primal loin accounts for approximately 20% of carcass weight. It contains a portion of the blade bone on the shoulder end, a portion of the hip bone on the leg end, all of the ribs and most of the backbone.

The primal pork loin is the only primal cut of pork not typically smoked or cured. Most of the loin is a single, very tender eye muscle. It is quite lean but contains enough intramuscular and subcutaneous fat to make it an excellent choice for a moist-heat cooking method such as braising. Or it can be prepared with dry-heat cooking methods such as roasting or sautéing. The loin also contains the pork tenderloin, located on the inside of the rib bones on the sirloin end of the loin. The tenderloin is the most tender cut of pork; it is very versatile and can be trimmed, cut into medallions and sautéed, or the whole tenderloin can be roasted or braised. The most popular cut from the loin is the pork chop. Chops can be cut from the entire loin, the choicest being centre-cut chops (or steaks) from the primal loin after the rib and sirloin portions at the front and rear of the loin are removed. The pork loin can be purchased boneless or boned and tied as a roast. A boneless pork loin is cured and smoked to produce Canadian back bacon. The rib bones, when trimmed from the loin, can be served as barbecued pork backribs.

Although not actually part of the primal loin, backfat is the thick layer of fat—sometimes more than 2.5 cm (1 in.) thick—between the skin and the lean eye muscle. It has a variety of uses in the kitchen, especially in the preparation of charcuterie items.

Fresh Leg

The primal fresh leg is the hog's hind leg. It is a rather large cut, accounting for approximately 24% of carcass weight. The leg contains the aitch, leg and hindshank bones. Like the legs of other meat animals, it contains large muscles with relatively small amounts of connective tissue.

Like many other cuts of pork, legs are often cured and smoked. But fresh legs also produce great roasts. When boned and seamed like veal, cutlets and kebabs can be fabricated. When cured and often smoked, hams are available in a variety of styles; they can be purchased bone-in, shankless or boneless, and partially or fully cooked. Fully cooked hams are also available canned. Each style of ham has specific applications, flavours and textures. See "Pork Products" on page 485 for further information.

The shank portion of the leg is called the leg shank. It is used in the same manner as the shoulder hock.

Pork Leg, Whole, CMC/Export #C100/101

NUTRITION

Like other meats, pork is a good source of protein, B vitamins and other essential nutrients, but it is also high in fat, especially saturated fats. Through new breeding and feeding techniques, the fat content of pork has been lowered in recent years. Cuts from the loin, such as the tenderloin and boneless loin chops, are among the leaner cuts of meat available with reduced levels of saturated fat. Sodium content of smoked and preserved pork products such as bacon, ham and sausage, which are discussed in Chapter 20, Charcuterie, is high but reduced-sodium preserved and smoked products are increasingly available.

FABRICATING PROCEDURES

Other than **suckling pigs** (which are very young, small whole pigs used for roasting or barbecuing), pork products generally are not purchased in forms larger than the primal cuts described previously. There are a few important pork fabrication techniques that you should master, however.

● **suckling pig** (Fr. *cochon de lait*) very young, small whole pig used for roasting or barbecuing whole

---

BASIC PROCEDURE FOR BONING A PORK LOIN

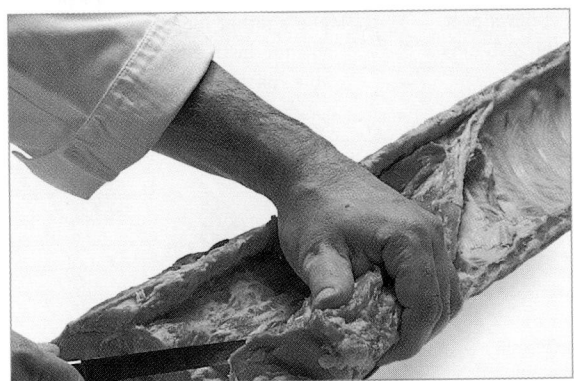

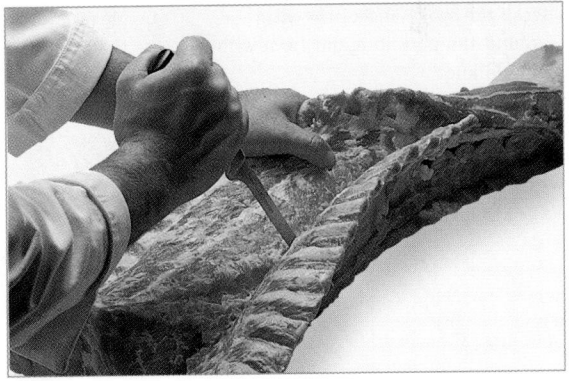

1. Starting on the sirloin end of a full pork loin, remove the tenderloin in one piece by making smooth cuts against the inside of the rib bones. Pull gently on the tenderloin as you cut.

2. Turn the loin over and cut between the ribs and the eye meat. Continue separating the meat from the bones, following the contours of the bones, until the loin is completely separated from the bones.

continued

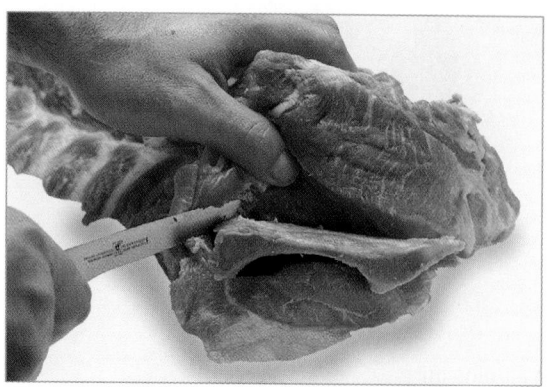

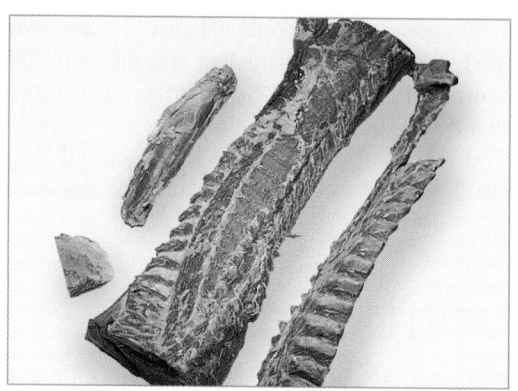

3. Trim around the blade bone on the shoulder end of the loin and remove it.

4. The fully boned loin will consist of (from left to right) the tenderloin, boneless loin and loin bones (backribs).

BASIC PROCEDURE FOR TYING A BONELESS PORK ROAST WITH THE HALF-HITCH METHOD

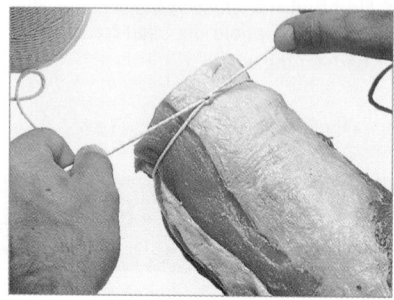

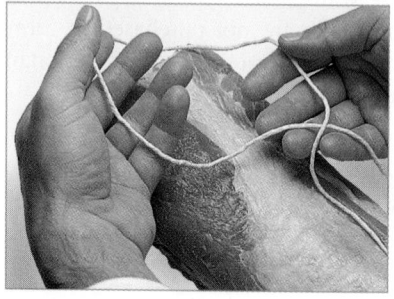

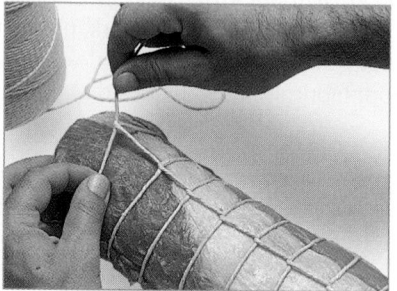

1. Wrap the loose end of the string around the pork loin and tie it with a double knot.

2. Make a loop and slide it down over the roast to approximately 2.5 cm (1 in.) from the first knot.

3. Make another loop and slide it down. Continue in this fashion until the whole roast has been tied.

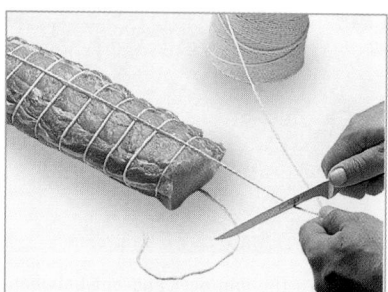

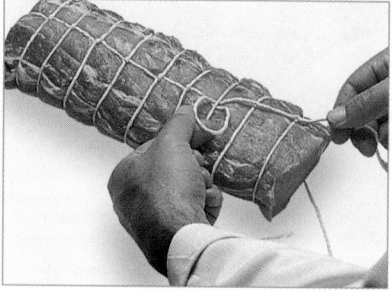

4. Turn the roast over and cut the string, leaving enough to wrap lengthwise around the roast to the original knot.

5. Wrap the string around the end of the roast, then around the string that formed the last loop. Continue in this fashion for the length of the roast, pulling the string tight after wrapping it around each loop.

continued

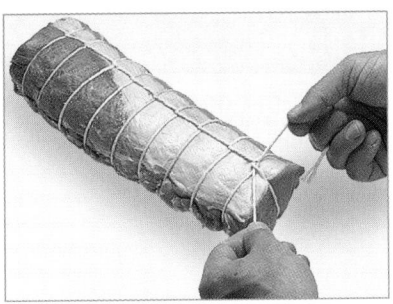 

6. Turn the roast back over. Wrap the string around the front end of the roast and secure it to the first loop at the point where you tied the first knot.

7. The finished roast. Note the even intervals at which the strings are tied. They should be just snug enough to hold the shape of the roast; they should not dig into or cut the meat.

Using Power Equipment

Pork loins are often cut into chops or steaks using a power band saw. The loin may be fresh or frozen. With fresh meat it is necessary to scrape the meat surface to remove bone and fat particles. Always follow proper safety and sanitation procedures when using power equipment.

BASIC PROCEDURE FOR CUTTING A CHOP FROM A PORK LOIN

Centre-cut pork chops can be cut from the centre portion of a bone-in pork loin without the aid of a saw by using a boning knife and a heavy cleaver. Trim the excess fat from the loin, leaving a 0.5-cm (1/4-in.) layer to protect the meat during cooking.

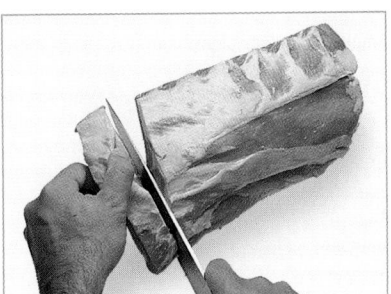 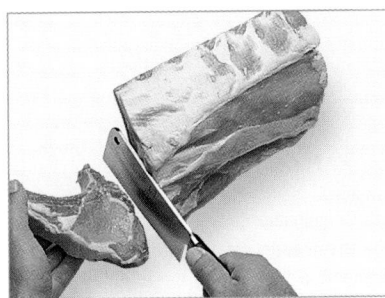 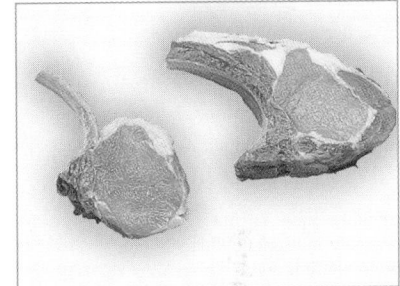

1. Cut through the meat with the knife.

2. Use the cleaver to chop through the chine bone.

3. To produce a cleaner chop, trim (french) the meat from the end of the rib bone. Then, with the boning knife, separate the loin meat from the chine bones and separate the chine bone from the rib with the cleaver.

BASIC PROCEDURE FOR CUTTING A POCKET IN A PORK CHOP

To make a pocket in a pork chop for stuffing, start with a thick chop or a double rib chop. Cut the pocket deep enough to hold ample stuffing, but be careful not to puncture either side of the chop.

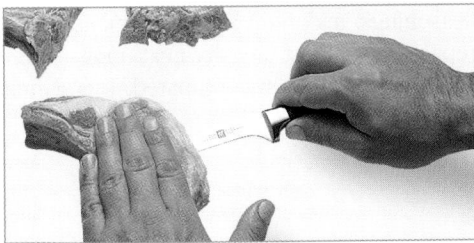

Use the tip of a boning knife to cut a pocket.

BASIC PROCEDURE FOR TRIMMING A PORK TENDERLOIN

As with a beef tenderloin, the pork tenderloin must be trimmed of all fat and silverskin. Follow the procedures outlined in Chapter 13, Beef, for trimming a beef tenderloin.

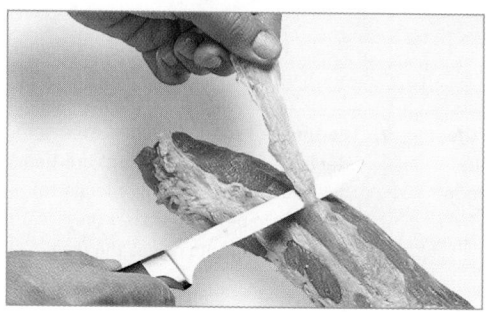

Use a boning knife to remove the silverskin from a pork tenderloin. Keep the silverskin tight and maintain a slight upward pressure on the knife to trim only the silverskin.

TABLE 16.1	Using Common Cuts of Pork			
Primal	**Subprimal or Fabricated Cut**	**CMC/ Export**	**Cooking Methods**	**Serving Suggestions**
Shoulder	Shoulder picnic	C311	Dry (baked)	Smoked shoulder picnic
	Shoulder blade	C320	Dry heat (broil or grill; sauté) Moist heat (simmer)	Broiled shoulder blade steaks Choucroûte
Belly	Bacon —fresh	C400	Dry heat (sauté) Moist heat (simmer) Combination (braise)	Breakfast meat Seasoning Seasoning
	Side spareribs	C500/502	Dry heat (low temperature)	Barbecued spareribs
Loin	Pork loin	C200	Dry heat (roast)	Roast pork
	—boneless	C201	Combination (braise)	Braised pork chops
	Pork tenderloin	C227	Dry heat (broil or grill; sauté; roast)	Roast pork tenderloin
	Pork backribs	C505	Combination (steam then grill)	Barbecued backribs
	Pork loin chops		Dry heat (broil or grill) Combination (braise)	Broiled loin chop with mushroom sauce Braised loin chop with leeks and fennel
Fresh Leg	Fresh leg	C100/101	Dry heat (roast)	Roast pork with apricots and almonds

Conclusion

Pork can be enjoyed cured, processed or fresh. The mild flavour of fresh pork blends well with many different seasonings, making it a popular menu item. It is naturally tender and can be prepared by almost any dry-heat, moist-heat or combination cooking method. Properly fabricated and prepared, it is a nutritious, healthy meat.

Questions for Discussion

1. List each pork primal cut and describe its location on the carcass. Identify two subprimals or fabricated cuts taken from each primal.
2. What is unique about the primal pork loin as compared with the beef or veal loin?
3. Are backfat and bacon taken from the same primal? How are they different?
4. What is the only primal cut of pork that is not typically smoked or cured? How is it best cooked? Explain your answer.

Pork Recipes

Brining Pork

Brining in a salty marinade is often associated with cured and smoked products. The heavy brine helps preserve the product. Light brining is popular today for lean cuts of meat, poultry or fish. Soaking the cuts in a 3% to 5% solution for a few hours or overnight increases moisture retention and promotes tenderness. Season items carefully to avoid oversalting. Some brines contain sweeteners to offset the salt. Avoid making pan gravy from brined meats.

Approximate ratios of salt to water for a light brine are:

- 3% solution: 15 g salt to 500 mL water
- 5% solution: 25 g salt to 500 mL water

RECIPE 16.1

Barbecued Ribs

Yield: 8 servings (approx. 4 ribs each)
Method: Baking

Salt	30 g	2 Tbsp.
Black pepper, ground	8 g	1 Tbsp.
Crushed red pepper flakes	6 g	1 Tbsp.
Pork backribs, 1.3–1.8 kg (3–4 lb.) slab	2	2
Cider vinegar	175 mL	6 fl. oz.
Water	300 mL	10-1/2 fl. oz.
Sauce:		
Onion, chopped coarse	150 g	5 oz.
Garlic cloves	10 g	3
Green bell pepper, chopped coarse	125 g	4 oz.
Plum tomatoes, canned	500 mL	16 fl. oz.
Vegetable oil	30 mL	2 Tbsp.
Frank's RedHot or other hot sauce	250 mL	8 fl. oz.
Brown sugar	250 g	10 oz.
Lemon juice	50 mL	2 fl. oz.

1. Combine the salt, pepper and red pepper flakes. Rub this mixture over both sides of the ribs, coating them well.
2. Place the ribs in a nonreactive pan and add the vinegar and water. Cover and refrigerate several hours or overnight.
3. Drain the ribs, turn the presentation side up and bake in a 120°C (250°F) oven for 2–2.5 hours or until tender.
4. Prepare the sauce by puréeing the onion, garlic, green pepper and tomatoes in a food processor or blender. Sweat this mixture in a nonreactive saucepan in the vegetable oil and add the remaining sauce ingredients.
5. Simmer the sauce over low heat until it thickens, approximately 15–20 minutes.
6. Brush the ribs with the sauce and return to a hot oven for 15 minutes to glaze the ribs. Serve additional sauce on the side. Serve with Creamy Coleslaw, Recipe 25.25, and Baked Beans, Recipe 22.6.

Barbecued Ribs

RECIPE 16.1

Approximate values per serving:	
Calories	736
Total fat	48 g
Saturated fat	17 g
Cholesterol	175 mg
Sodium	787 mg
Total carbohydrates	38 g
Protein	38 g

RECIPE 16.2

Approximate values per serving:

Calories	370
Total fat	14 g
Saturated fat	5 g
Cholesterol	94 mg
Sodium	2411 mg
Total carbohydrates	25 g
Protein	36 g

RECIPE 16.2

Maple Baked Ham

Yield: 25 175-g (6-oz.) servings
Method: Roasting

Ham, fully cooked, bone in, 5.4–6.3 kg (12–14 lb.)	1	1
Brown or maple sugar	175 g	6 oz.
Cloves, ground	1 g	1/2 tsp.
Crushed pineapple, with juice	500 g	16 oz.
Maple syrup	250 mL	8 fl. oz.
Orange marmalade	250 g	8 oz.

1. Peel the rind from the ham and trim the exterior fat to an even thickness of 0.5 cm (1/4 in.). Score the fat surface decoratively.

2. Combine the sugar and cloves and pat this mixture evenly over the top of the ham. Roast the coated ham at 135°C (275°F) for 1 hour.

3. Combine the pineapple, maple syrup and marmalade in a saucepan over medium heat.

4. Brush some of the sauce over the ham and cook until heated through, basting frequently, approximately 2 hours.

5. Remove the ham from the roasting pan. Keep it warm and allow it to rest 30 minutes before carving.

1. Stuffed Pork Chops: Stuffing the pork chops.

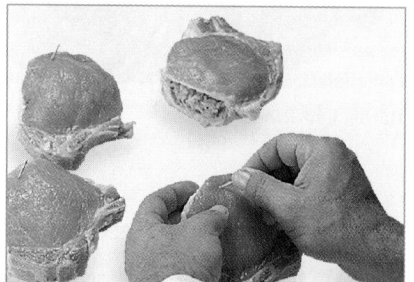

2. Closing the stuffed chops with tooth-picks.

RECIPE 16.3

Approximate values per serving:

Calories	661
Total fat	53 g
Saturated fat	22 g
Cholesterol	147 mg
Sodium	440 mg
Total carbohydrates	16 g
Protein	30 g

RECIPE 16.3

Stuffed Pork Chops

Yield: 10 servings
Method: Braising

Thick-cut pork chops, each approx. 225 g (8 oz.)	10	10
Celery, small dice	100 g	3 oz.
Onion, small dice	150 g	5 oz.
Apple, small dice	50 g	2 oz.
Whole butter, melted	175 g	6 oz.
Fresh bread cubes, 1.25 cm (1/2 in.)	225 g	8 oz.
Parsley, chopped	10 g	1 Tbsp.
Sage, fresh, chopped	5 g	2 tsp.
Salt and pepper	TT	TT
Lemon juice and zest	1/2 lemon	1/2 lemon
White stock	approx. 150 mL	approx. 5 fl. oz.
Canola oil	50 mL	2 fl. oz.
Demi-glace	1 L	1 qt.

1. Cut pockets in the chops.

2. Sauté the celery, onion and apple in 60 g (2 oz.) of butter until tender.

3. Combine the celery, onion, apple and remaining butter with the bread cubes, parsley, sage, salt and pepper, lemon juice and zest. Add enough stock to moisten the dressing.

4. Stuff the mixture into each of the pork chops. Seal the pockets with tooth-picks and tie with butcher's twine.

continued

5. In a brazier, brown the stuffed chops well on each side in the canola oil.

6. Add the demi-glace. Bring to a simmer, cover and place in a 165°C (325°F) oven. Cook until tender, approximately 45 minutes.

7. Remove the chops from the pan. Degrease the sauce and reduce to the desired consistency. Strain the sauce and adjust the seasonings.

3. The finished chops.

RECIPE 16.4

Pork Loin with Apricots/Prunes

Yield: 6 200-g (7-oz.) servings
Method: Roasting

Boneless pork loin roast, 1.5 kg (3 lb.)	1	1
Salt and pepper	TT	TT
Apricots, dry, or prunes, pitted	350 g	12 oz.
Carrot, chopped coarse	100 g	3 oz.
Onion, chopped coarse	175 g	6 oz.
Vegetable oil	15 mL	1 Tbsp.
Clarified butter	15 mL	1 Tbsp.
Fresh rosemary	3 g	1 tsp.
Fresh thyme	2 g	1 tsp.
Bay leaf, crushed	1	1
Garlic cloves	10 g	2
Apple juice	250 mL	8 fl. oz.
White stock	250 mL	8 fl. oz.
Sugar	60 g	2 oz.
Vinegar	60 mL	2 fl. oz.

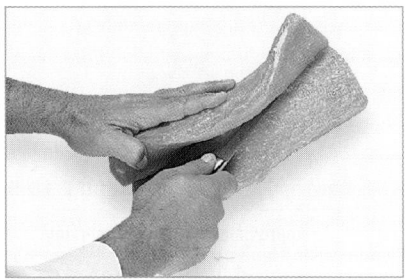

1. Pork Loin with Apricots/Prunes: Butterflying the pork loin.

1. Trim and butterfly the pork loin; reserve the trimmings. (To butterfly the loin, slice it partway through the centre and open it like a book, then flatten it into a rectangular shape.) Season with salt and pepper.

2. Reserve 12 apricots/prunes and arrange the remaining fruit pieces along the length of the loin. Roll up the loin and tie with butcher's twine.

3. Brown the pork roll and pork trimmings, carrot and onion in the oil and butter.

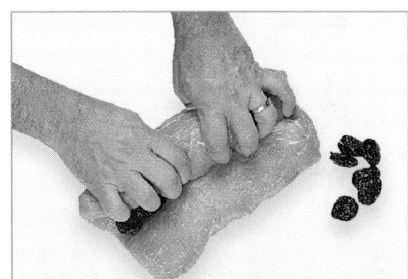

2. Rolling the pork loin around the filling.

4. Add the herbs and garlic and roast the pork on the bed of trimmings and vegetables at 135°C (275°F), basting frequently with the fat that accumulates in the pan, to an internal temperature of 60°C (110°F) (approximately 60 minutes).

5. Poach the reserved apricots in the apple juice until plump; set aside.

6. Remove the roast from the pan and keep it warm. Degrease the pan and deglaze with white stock. Simmer for 15 minutes, then strain.

7. Combine the sugar and vinegar in a saucepan. Bring to a boil and cook without stirring until the mixture turns a caramel colour. Immediately remove it from the heat and add the juices from the roasting pan. When the sputtering stops, return the pan to the heat and skim any fat from the surface; keep the sauce warm over low heat.

8. Drain the apricots. Remove the twine from the roast. Slice and serve the meat with the sauce and apricots.

VARIATION: Use apples or cranberries instead of apricots.

3. The cooked loin sliced for service.

RECIPE 16.4

Approximate values per serving:	
Calories	711
Total fat	27 g
Saturated fat	10 g
Cholesterol	132 mg
Sodium	313 mg
Total carbohydrates	70 g
Protein	47 g

RECIPE 16.5

Chinese Barbecued Pork

Yield: 6 servings
Method: Roasting

Pork loin	1 kg	2 lb.
Salt	5 g	1 tsp.
Garlic, chopped	15 g	3 cloves
Ginger, grated	10 g	1 Tbsp.
Spring onion, chopped	1	1
Light soy sauce	50 mL	2 fl. oz.
Sugar	50 g	2 oz.
Five-spice powder	4 g	1 tsp.
Chinese wine or sherry	50 mL	2 fl. oz.
Red colour	3 drops	3 drops
Honey	75 g	2-1/2 oz.

1. Cut loin lengthwise into 2.5-cm (1-in.) strips.
2. Combine all remaining ingredients and coat pork strips. Marinate 30 minutes.
3. Place a wire rack over a roasting pan half filled with water.
4. Place pork strips on rack and roast for 20 minutes in a 200°C (400°F) oven.
5. Turn strips over and brush with a bit of honey and any remaining marinade.
6. Cook a further 10–15 minutes.

RECIPE 16.5

Approximate values per serving:	
Calories	378
Total fat	19 g
Saturated fat	6.7 g
Cholesterol	103 mg
Sodium	906 mg
Total carbohydrates	20 g
Protein	34 g

Pork Chimichurri Kebabs

RECIPE 16.6

Pork Chimichurri Kebabs

Yield: 10 servings
Method: Grilling

Chimichurri Sauce:		
Garlic, peeled	8 cloves	8 cloves
Onion, chopped	125 g	4 oz.
Lemon juice, fresh	50 mL	3 Tbsp.
Oregano, dry, crushed	4 g	2 Tbsp.
Parsley, Italian	1 bunch	1 bunch
Olive oil	200 mL	7 fl. oz.
Sherry wine vinegar	60 mL	2 fl. oz.
Salt	5 g	1 tsp.
Red pepper flakes	1 g	1/2 tsp.
or		
Sambal olek (crushed fresh chiles)	5 g	1 tsp.
Black pepper, ground	2 g	1 tsp.
Pork loin, trimmed	1 kg	2 lb. 4 oz.

1. Place the sauce ingredients in a food processor and pulse until the ingredients are blended but still have some texture (not puréed).
2. Cut the pork into 2-cm (3/4-in.) cubes and place them in a nonreactive pan. Coat the meat thoroughly with two-thirds of the chimichurri sauce. Cover and refrigerate for 4–6 hours.
3. Reserve the remaining sauce for the kebabs in the refrigerator.

RECIPE 16.6

Approximate values per serving:	
Calories	357
Total fat	29 g
Saturated fat	6.1 g
Cholesterol	67 mg
Sodium	294 mg
Total carbohydrates	3.3 g
Protein	21 g

continued

4. Remove the pork from the marinade, discarding any remaining marinade in the pan.

5. Divide the pork among 10 presoaked bamboo skewers. Cook on a hot grill, turning as necessary to cook the pork and brown evenly. Serve with rice and black beans and the reserved chimichurri sauce.

VARIATION: Boneless chicken or lamb shoulder cubes may be used in place of the pork.

RECIPE 16.7

Pork Tenderloin Medallions Wrapped in Prosciutto and Sage with Brie Sauce, Apple Chutney and Pork Jus

NORTHERN LIGHTS COLLEGE, DAWSON CREEK, BC
Michael French, CCC, Program Head

Yield: 4 180-g (6-oz.) servings
Method: Pan-searing and roasting

Pork tenderloin medallions, 50 g each	12	12
Salt and pepper	TT	TT
Prosciutto ham, thinly sliced	200 g	6-1/2 oz.
Sage leaves, fresh	30 g	1 oz.
Pork jus	200 mL	7 fl. oz.
Brie Sauce (recipe follows)	200 mL	7 fl. oz.
Apple Chutney (recipe follows)	225 mL	8 fl. oz.

1. Sear the pork medallions on all sides, season with salt and pepper and let cool.
2. Deglaze the pan and reserve the liquid for jus.
3. Set prosciutto out and cut into strips matching the width of the medallions.
4. Place sage leaves lengthwise in the middle of the prosciutto and place a medallion at one end.
5. Roll the medallion in the prosciutto/sage to form a tight bundle.
6. Roast the medallions in a 180°C (375°F) oven for 12–15 minutes.

Brie Sauce

Cream, 35%	200 mL	7 fl. oz.
White wine, dry	50 mL	1-1/2 fl. oz.
Brie, grated	80 g	3 oz.
Salt and pepper	TT	TT

1. Reduce cream and wine by half.
2. Whisk in the Brie slowly to incorporate the cheese.
3. Strain and season with salt and pepper.

Apple Chutney

Spanish onion, macedoine	60 g	2 oz.
Butter	20 g	1 Tbsp.
Granny Smith apples, peeled and diced macedoine	450 g	1 lb.
Apple juice	100 mL	3-1/2 fl. oz.
White wine, sweet	40 mL	1-1/2 fl. oz.

Michael French, CCC
Michael began his career at the Banff Springs Hotel as an Apprentice in the early 1980s. He then moved to Europe where he was Chef de Partie in leading hotels in Switzerland and Austria. Some highlights of his 20-year career have been working as Executive Chef at the Oak Bay Beach Hotel and the Bedford Hotel in Victoria, BC, instructing at Northern Lights College, and being part of the Sheraton Salzburg Team international competition. Michael takes pride in mentoring the next generation of Canadian chefs.

RECIPE 16.7

Approximate values per serving, with sauce and chutney:	
Calories	582
Total fat	33 g
Saturated fat	18 g
Cholesterol	204 mg
Sodium	1155 mg
Total carbohydrates	19 g
Protein	50 g

Brie Sauce—Approximate values per 50 mL serving:	
Calories	241
Total fat	23 g
Saturated fat	14 g
Cholesterol	85 mg
Sodium	338 mg
Total carbohydrates	1.8 g
Protein	5.2 g

continued

Apple Chutney—Approximate values per 55 g serving:	
Calories	43
Total fat	1.5 g
Saturated fat	0.9 g
Cholesterol	4.3 mg
Sodium	14 mg
Total carbohydrates	7.2 g
Protein	0.2 g

Cumin, ground	1 g	1/4 oz.
Salt and pepper	TT	TT

1. Sweat onions in butter until translucent and then add apples and sweat briefly.
2. Add apple juice, white wine and cumin. Simmer on low heat until a relish consistency is achieved.
3. Let cool overnight to infuse the flavours and adjust seasoning with salt and pepper. Warm for service.

ASSEMBLY: Arrange 3 medallions in the centre of the plate and glaze with each of the sauces.

Otto R. Daniels, Jr.
Currently a teacher of professional cooking and coach/coordinator of culinary competitions, Otto is also studying for his Bachelor of Education degree. He has personally won medals and trophies in numerous competitions, and under his tutelage the St. Pius X team won four consecutive provincial championships from 1994 to 1997.

RECIPE 16.8

Approximate values per serving:	
Calories	620
Total fat	35 g
Saturated fat	11 g
Cholesterol	135 mg
Sodium	635 mg
Total carbohydrates	28 g
Protein	48 g

RECIPE 16.8

Smoked Loin of Pork, Hazelnut and Maple Syrup Crust, Apple Cider Sauce

ST. PIUS X CULINARY INSTITUTE, MONTREAL, QC
Chef Otto R. Daniels, Jr.

Yield: 10 servings
Method: Hot-smoking

Pork loin, boneless centre cut	2 kg	5 lb.
Sesame oil	100 mL	3-1/2 fl. oz.
Salt and pepper	TT	TT
Maple syrup	150 mL	5 fl. oz.
Dijon mustard	90 mL	3 fl. oz.
Hazelnuts, finely chopped	125 g	1 cup
Maple or apple wood chips	as needed	as needed
Sparkling apple cider	125 mL	4 fl. oz.
Demi-glace	500 mL	16 fl. oz.
Gorgonzola cheese, grated	100 g	3 oz.
Cream, 15%	50 mL	2 fl. oz.
Chives, finely chopped	15 g	1/2 oz.

1. Sear the pork loin in the sesame oil to a light golden-brown colour. Season with salt and pepper.
2. Combine the maple syrup and mustard and coat the loin with this mixture. Coat the loin with the hazelnuts, fat side up.
3. Place the pork in a roasting pan. Hot smoke in a smoker oven at 150°C (300°F) to an internal temperature of 65°C (150°F).
4. Remove from oven and place loin in a separate pan. Keep warm.
5. Deglaze the roasting pan with the cider and add the demi-glace, cheese and cream. Reduce the sauce to a coating consistency.
6. Strain sauce through a fine strainer and garnish with chives.
7. Adjust seasoning, and add cider if consistency is too thick.

Mie Goreng (Indonesian Fried Noodles with Pork and Shrimp)

Yield: 10 servings, each approximately 250 g (8 oz.)

Method: Stir-frying

Ingredient	Metric	U.S.
Egg noodles, fine	500 g	1 lb.
Vegetable oil	125 mL	4 fl. oz.
Onions, brunoise	350 g	12 oz.
Garlic, minced	30 g	6–8 cloves
Sambal olek (crushed fresh chiles)	10 g	2 tsp.
Blacan (trasi) (dry shrimp paste)	5 g	1 tsp.
Pork émincé	1 kg	2 lb.
Shrimp, peeled and deveined	500 g	1 lb.
Celery, sliced thin on bias	150 g	4 ribs
Napa cabbage, julienne	500 g	1 lb.
Salt	10 g	2 tsp.
Pepper	3 g	1 tsp.
Soy sauce	50 mL	3 Tbsp.
Onion flakes, deep fried, crisp	20 g	3 Tbsp.
Green onion, diagonal cut	6	6

1. Break noodles into halves or thirds and cook in rapidly boiling water until al dente. Drain, rinse with cold water and reserve.

2. Heat wok or heavy brazier and add oil.

3. Add onions, garlic and sambal olek. Fry until golden, add blacan, pork and shrimp. Stir-fry until meat is cooked and then add celery and cabbage. Fry just until vegetables are heated through but still crisp. Season with salt and pepper.

4. Add noodles, mixing well and heating through. Finish with soy sauce.

5. Place on plates and garnish with fried onion flakes and green onion.

VARIATION: For nasi goreng, use 1.3 kg (8 cups) cooked rice; omit cabbage and celery; add 15 g (2 Tbsp.) turmeric to onions, mix onion flakes and green onions into rice and garnish with thin strips of egg omelette (5 eggs).

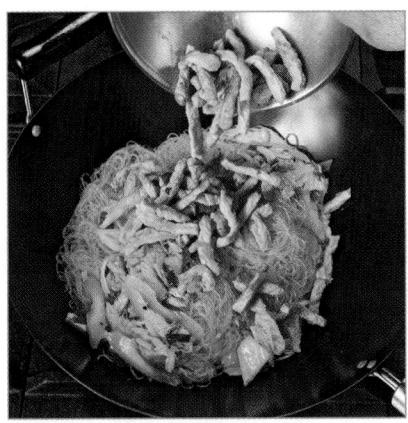

Mie Goreng

Approximate values per serving:	
Calories	657
Total fat	36 g
Saturated fat	9 g
Cholesterol	196 mg
Sodium	870 mg
Total carbohydrates	47 g
Protein	36 g

About Cassoulet

Cassoulet originates in the south of France. The contents vary widely: beans are a common ingredient, along with a meat stew and duck confit. Lamb is often used. The recipe presented here is a more straightforward method with a twist. One could add some fresh tomato concassée as a garnish. The traditional baked crust is not here, but a crusty bread on the side and a simple salad will round out the meal.

Cassoulet

dee Hobsbawn-Smith

dee—a Calgary-based professional chef, caterer, culinary educator and author—has been delighting Calgary diners and readers since 1983. She studied cooking at Vancouver Vocational Institute, completed her Red Seal in Calgary and studied with eminent chef and educator Madeleine Kamman in Annecy, France. Since selling her restaurant, Foodsmith, in 1994, dee has turned to food writing and now has four cookbooks and many magazine articles and columns under her belt.

RECIPE 16.10

Approximate values per serving:

Calories	749
Total fat	25 g
Saturated fat	8.1 g
Cholesterol	85 mg
Sodium	853 mg
Total carbohydrates	88 g
Protein	43 g

RECIPE 16.10

Cassoulet

CALGARY, AB

Chef dee Hobsbawn-Smith

Yield: 8 servings
Method: Stewing

Great Northern beans	750 g	3 cups
Onion, large dice	350 g	12 oz.
Leeks, large dice	350 g	12 oz.
Carrots, large dice	200 g	7 oz.
Celery rib, large dice	175 g	6 oz.
Garlic, sliced	30 g	8 cloves
Olive oil	15 mL	1 fl. oz.
Leek and cabbage sausage (or other)	2 links	2 links
Bay leaves	2	2
Fresh rosemary	2–3 sprigs	2–3 sprigs
Fresh thyme	4–5 sprigs	4–5 sprigs
Sage, fresh	2–3 sprigs	2–3 sprigs
Oregano, dry	0.5 g	1 tsp.
Basil, dry	0.5 g	1 tsp.
Star anise	1–2	1–2
Cinnamon stick	5 g	1/2 stick
Lemon zest	10 g	1 Tbsp.
Black peppercorns, cracked	8 g	1 Tbsp.
Allspice berries	2 g	1/2 tsp.
Cloves, whole	5	5
Red wine	250 mL	8 fl. oz.
Pomegranate molasses	125 mL	4 fl. oz.
Duck legs	1 kg	4–6
Pork hocks	1 kg	2
Brown chicken or beef stock	2 L	2 qt.
Herb-infused wine vinegar	25 mL	1 fl. oz.
Kosher salt and pepper	TT	TT

1. Soak beans in 3 times as much water overnight.

2. In heavy-bottomed brazier, cook the onion, leeks, carrots, celery and garlic in the olive oil. Add small amounts of water to prevent burning. When tender, allow liquid to evaporate and brown the vegetables.

3. Add the sausage, herbs and spices, wine, molasses, beans, duck legs, pork hocks and stock. Stir well, bring to a boil, cover tightly and continue to cook in a 190°C (375°F) oven for approximately 3 hours. The flavour will be mellowed and the beans tender.

4. Skim any fat from the surface, add the vinegar and adjust seasoning.

5. Skin the pork hocks and shred the meat.

6. Serve generous portions with the duck leg, sausage and shredded pork arranged attractively.

> The fact is that it takes more than ingredients and technique to cook a good meal. A good cook puts something of himself into the preparation—he cooks with enjoyment, anticipation, spontaneity, and he is willing to experiment.

—Pearl Bailey, American entertainer (1918–1990) in *Pearl's Kitchen*, 1973

LEARNING OUTCOMES

After studying this chapter you will be able to:

- recognize the structure and composition of poultry

- identify various kinds and classes of poultry

- explain poultry inspection and grading practices

- purchase poultry appropriate for your needs

- store poultry properly

- prepare poultry for cooking

- apply various cooking methods to poultry

- carve a turkey, capon or other large bird, or a chicken or other small bird

These interactive online tools will help you master the skills in this chapter:

- Videos
- Chapter Quizzes
- Activities

Poultry is the collective term for domesti-cated birds bred for eating.

They include chickens, ducks, geese, guineas, pigeons and turkeys. (Game birds such as pheasant, quail and partridge are described in Chapter 18, Game.) Poultry is generally the least expensive and most versatile of all main dish foods. It can be cooked by almost any method and its mild flavour goes well with a wide variety of sauces and accompaniments.

In this chapter we discuss the different kinds and classes of poultry and how to choose those that best suit your needs. You will learn how to store poultry properly to prevent food-borne illnesses and spoilage, how to process birds to produce the specific cuts you need and how to apply a variety of cooking methods properly.

Many of the cooking methods discussed here have been applied previously to meats. Although there are similarities with these methods, there are also many distinct differences. As you study this chapter, review the corresponding cooking methods for meats and note the similarities and differences.

MUSCLE COMPOSITION

The muscle tissue of poultry is similar to that of mammals in that it contains approximately 72% water, 20% protein, 7% fat and 1% minerals; it consists of bundles of muscle cells or fibres held together by connective tissue. Unlike red meat, poultry does not contain the intramuscular fat known as marbling. Instead, a bird stores fat in its skin, abdominal cavity and the fat pad near its tail. Poultry fat is softer and has a lower melting point than other animal fats. It is easily rendered during cooking.

As with red meats, poultry muscles that are used more often tend to be tougher than those used less frequently. Also, the muscles of an older bird tend to be tougher than those of a younger one. Because the majority of poultry is marketed at a young age, however, it is generally very tender.

Free-Range Chickens

Chicken has become increasingly popular in recent years, in part because it is inexpensive, versatile and considered more healthful than red meat. Indeed, more than 10 million chickens are processed weekly in this country. To meet an ever-increasing demand, chickens are raised indoors in huge chicken houses that may contain as many as 20 000 birds. They are fed a specially formulated mixture comprising primarily corn and soybean meal. Animal protein, vitamins, minerals and small amounts of antibiotics are added to produce quick-growing, healthy birds.

Many consumers feel that chickens raised this way do not have the flavour of chickens that are allowed to move freely and forage for food. Some consumers are concerned about the residual effects of the vitamins, minerals and antibiotics added to the chicken feed. To meet the demand for chickens raised the "old-fashioned way," some farmers raise (and many fine establishments offer) free-range chickens.

Although the CFIA has not standardized regulations for free-range chicken, generally the term *free-range* applies to birds that are allowed unlimited access to the area outside the chicken house. Often they are raised without antibiotics, fed a vegetarian diet (no animal fat or byproducts), processed without the use of preservatives and raised under more humane growing methods than conventionally grown birds. Most free-range chickens are marketed at 9 to 10 weeks old and weigh 2 to 2.5 kg (4-1/2 to 5 lb.)—considerably more mature and heavier than conventional broilers. They are generally sold with heads and feet intact and are more expensive than conventionally raised chickens.

Many consumers (in both the dining room and the kitchen) feel that free-range chicken is superior in flavour and quality. Others find no perceptible differences. As a consumer, you will have to decide whether any difference is worth the added expense.

The breast and wing flesh of chickens and turkeys is lighter in colour than the flesh of their thighs and legs. This colour difference is due to a higher concentration of the protein myoglobin in the thigh and leg muscles. Myoglobin is the protein that stores oxygen for the muscle tissues to use. More active muscles require more myoglobin and tend to be darker than less active ones. Because chickens and turkeys generally do not fly, their breast and wing muscles contain little myoglobin and are therefore a light colour. Birds that do fly have only dark meat. Dark meat also contains more fat and connective tissue than light meat, and its cooking time is longer.

Skin colour may vary from white to golden yellow, depending on what the bird was fed. Such colour differences are not an indication of overall quality.

IDENTIFYING POULTRY

Agriculture Canada recognizes nine categories or kinds of poultry: chicken, duck, goose, pheasant, quail, ostrich, guinea, pigeon and turkey. Each poultry kind is divided into classes based predominantly on the bird's age and tenderness. The sex of young birds is not significant for culinary purposes. It does matter, however, with older birds: older male birds are tough and stringy and have less flavour than older female birds. Table 17.1 lists identifying characteristics and suggested cooking methods for each of the various kinds and classes of poultry.

Chicken

Chicken (Fr. *poulet*) is the most popular and widely eaten poultry in the world. It contains both light and dark meat and has relatively little fat. A young, tender chicken can be cooked by almost any method; an older bird is best stewed or braised. Chicken is extremely versatile and may be flavoured, stuffed, basted or garnished with almost anything. Chicken is inexpensive and readily available, fresh or frozen, in a variety of forms.

Duck

The duck (Fr. *canard*) used most often in commercial food service operations is a young **duckling**. It contains only dark meat and large amounts of fat. In order to make the fatty skin palatable, it is important to render as much fat as possible. Duck has a high percentage of bone and fat to meat; for example, a 2-kg (4-lb.) duck will serve only two people, while a 2-kg (4-lb.) roasting chicken will serve four people.

Goose

A goose (Fr. *oie*) contains only dark meat and has very fatty skin. It is usually roasted at high temperatures to render the fat. Roasted goose is popular at holidays and is often served with an acidic fruit-based sauce to offset the fattiness.

Cornish Game Hen

Chicken Broiler/
Fryer

Capon

Young Duckling

Young Goose

Duck Terminology

Magret—A moulard duck breast.
Moulard—A breed of duck used for foie gras.
Muscovy—A domesticated musk duck with a rich flavour and tender texture.

● **duckling** a duck slaughtered before it is eight weeks old

TABLE 17.1	Poultry Classes (CFIA)			
Class	**Description**	**Age**	**Weight**	**Cooking Method**
Chicken Classes				
Game Hen	Young or immature progeny of Cornish chickens or of a Cornish chicken and a White Rock chicken; very flavourful	4–5 weeks	300–450 g (8 oz.–1 lb.)	Split and broil or grill; roast
Broiler/Fryer	Young with soft, smooth-textured skin; relatively lean; flexible breastbone	Under 10 weeks	up to 2 kg (4 lb.)	Any cooking method; very versatile
Roaster	Young with tender meat and smooth-textured skin; breastbone is less flexible than broiler's	10–12 weeks	2 kg (4 lb.) and over	Any cooking method
Capon	Surgically castrated male (Caponette—chemically castrated); tender meat with soft, smooth-textured skin; bred for well-flavoured meat; contains a high proportion of light to dark meat and a relatively high fat content	4 months	2–4 kg (6–10 lb.)	Roast
Fowl	Mature female; flavourful but less tender meat; nonflexible breastbone	Over 10 months	1 kg (2 lb.) and over	Stew or braise
Duck Classes				
Duckling	Young bird with tender meat; rich flavour; easily dented windpipe	8 weeks or less	2–2.5 kg (4–6 lb.)	Roast
Mature	Old bird with tough flesh; hard bill and windpipe	6 months or older	2–2.5 kg (4–6 lb.)	Braise
Goose Classes				
Young start,	Rich, tender dark meat with large amounts of fat; easily dented windpipe	6 months or less	2.5–5.5 kg (6–12 lb.)	Roast at high temperature to accompany with acidic sauces
Mature	Tough flesh and hard windpipe	Over 6 months	4.5–7 kg (10–16 lb.)	Braise or stew
Guinea Classes				
Young	Tender meat; flexible breastbone	3 months	0.3–0.7 kg (12 oz.–1 lb. 8 oz.)	Bard and roast; sauté
Mature	Tough flesh; hard breastbone	Over 3 months	0.5–1 kg (1–2 lb.)	Braise or stew
Pigeon Classes				
Squab	Immature pigeon; very tender, dark flesh and a small amount of fat	4 weeks	0.3–0.7 kg (12 oz.–1 lb. 8 oz.)	Broil, roast or sauté
Pigeon	Mature bird; coarse skin and tough flesh	Over 4 weeks	0.5–1 kg (1–2 lb.)	Braise or stew
Turkey Classes				
Young		24 weeks	7–12 kg (16–30 lb.) and under	Roast or cut into cutlets and sauté or pan-fry
Mature		15+ months	12+ kg (30+ lb.)	Roast or stew

Guinea

A guinea or guinea fowl (Fr. *pintade*) is the domesticated descendant of a game bird. It has both light and dark meat and a flavour similar to pheasant. Guinea is tender enough to sauté. Because it contains little fat, a guinea is usually barded prior to roasting. Guinea, which is relatively expensive, is not as popular here as it is in Europe.

Pigeon

The young pigeon (Fr. *pigeon*) used in commercial food service operations is referred to as squab. Its meat is dark, tender and well suited for broiling, sautéing or roasting. Squab has very little fat and benefits from barding.

Turkey

Turkey (Fr. *dinde*) is the second most popular poultry kind in Canada. It has both light and dark meat and a relatively small amount of fat. Younger turkey is economical and can be prepared in almost any manner. Males may be referred to as toms and females as hens.

Livers, Gizzards, Hearts and Necks

Livers, gizzards, hearts and necks are commonly referred to as **giblets**. Although most poultry kinds are sold with giblets, chickens can be purchased with or without them, depending on your needs.

Giblets can be used in a variety of ways. Gizzards (a bird's second stomach), hearts and necks are most often used to make giblet gravy or to fortify a stock. Necks are very flavourful and can be added to stocks for flavour and richness. Livers are not added to stocks, however, because of their strong flavour.

Chicken livers are often used in pâtés, sautéed or broiled with bacon and served as an appetizer.

Foie Gras

Foie gras is the enlarged liver of a duck or goose. Considered a delicacy since Roman times, it is now produced in many parts of the world. Foie gras is produced by methodically fattening the birds by force-feeding them specially

Young Guinea

Squab

Turkey

Chicken
Giblets

● **giblets** the collective term for edible poultry viscera, including gizzards, hearts, livers and necks

● **foie gras** liver of specially fattened geese or ducks

A Turkey by Any Other Name ...

In *Food in History*, Reay Tannahill explains why we call a turkey a turkey and not a peru. Turkeys were known as *uexolotl* to 16th-century native Central Americans. They were first brought to Europe by returning Spanish explorers early in the 1500s. Turkish merchants visiting Seville, Spain, on their journeys to and from the eastern Mediterranean brought these exotic birds to England, where the English dubbed them "turkie-cocks." This was eventually shortened to "turkeys." The Turks called these birds "hindi," suggesting that they believed the birds originated in India (as opposed to the Indies). This was a belief shared by the French, who called the bird *coq d'Inde*, which was later corrupted to *dinde* or *dindon*. The Germans followed suit, calling the bird *indianische Henn*, as did the Italians, who called it *galle d'India*. Meanwhile, in India, the bird was called a peru—which was a little closer to the geographical mark.

Duck Foie Gras

Frogs

Frogs are amphibians that can be prepared like poultry or fish. Their texture and flavour are similar to those of chicken. Most of the frogs used in food service operations are farm-raised, so their meat is quite tender. Typically, only the legs are eaten. They are sold frozen, in pairs, attached by a small portion of backbone.

Ostrich Fan

The Ostrich News in 1995 reported the following nutritional values per 28 g (1 oz.):		
	Ostrich	**Emu**
Protein	6.3 g	6.6 g
Calories	28.0 g	30.0 g
Cholesterol	18.1 mg	16.3 mg
Fat	0.28 g	0.48 g
Saturated fat	0.07 g	0.17 g
Sodium	18.0 mg	17.0 mg
Calcium	0.5 mg	0.3 mg
Iron	2.3 mg	1.4 mg

prepared corn while limiting their activity. Fresh foie gras consists of two lobes that must be separated, split and deveined. Good foie gras will be smooth, round and putty-coloured. It should not be yellow or grainy. Goose foie gras is lighter in colour and more delicate in flavour than that of duck. Duck foie gras has a deeper, winey flavour and is far more common than goose foie gras.

Fresh foie gras can be grilled, roasted, sautéed or made into pâtés or terrines. No matter which cooking method is used, care must be taken not to overcook the liver. Foie gras is so high in fat that overcooking will result in the liver actually melting away. Fresh foie gras is available from Quebec, but most foie gras used in this country is frozen, pasteurized or canned. Canned foie gras may consist of solid liver or small pieces of liver compacted to form a block. Canned foie gras mousse is also available. Truffles are a natural accompaniment to foie gras and are used in many tinned preparations.

In 2007, foie gras was banned in some jurisdictions and a movement started to ban it completely due to allegations of animal cruelty.

Ratites

Ratites are a family of flightless birds with small wings and flat breastbones. They include the ostrich, emu and rhea. These exotic animals are farm raised and the meat is commercially available, but much of their value is in their hides, which are tanned for leather. Butchering them is specialized due to their unique bone and muscle structure.

Ratite meat, which is classified as red meat, is a dark cherry-red colour with a flavour similar to beef but a little sweeter. Low in fat and calories, it is considered one of the healthiest red meats to eat. Most ratite meat is from animals slaughtered at 10 to 13 months of age. It is generally cut from the back, which contains a cut called tenderloin, the thigh (also known as the fan) and the leg. Market forms include steaks, filets, medallions, roasts, émincé, cubes or ground. A product called Activa™ TG is a vegetable-based binder that can be used to prepare consistently sized steaks and rolls of meat products and improve texture in protein products.

Ratite meat is often prepared like veal or wild game. The more tender cuts can be marinated and then cooked by dry-heat cooking methods, especially broiling, grilling, pan-frying and sautéing. Because this meat has little fat, care must be taken to avoid overcooking; these products are usually served rare to medium. Tougher cuts, such as those from the leg, are best ground or prepared with combination cooking methods. The meat lends itself well to charcuterie preparations and makes a fine dry cured and smoked product.

NUTRITION

Poultry is an economical source of high-quality protein. Poultry's nutritional value is similar to other meats, except that skinless chicken and turkey breast meat is lower in fat and higher in niacin than other lean meats. Generally, dark meat contains more niacin and riboflavin than white meat.

INSPECTION AND GRADING OF POULTRY
Inspection

All poultry produced for public consumption in Canada is subject to health inspection. Inspections ensure that products are processed under strict sanitary guidelines and are wholesome and fit for human consumption. Inspections do not indicate a product's quality or tenderness.

Grading

Grading poultry is voluntary. Birds are graded according to their overall quality with the grade (Canada A, utility, B or C) shown on the packaging. (See Figures 17.1 and 17.2.)

According to Agriculture Canada, Grade A poultry is free from deformities, with thick flesh and a well-developed fat layer. It is free of pinfeathers, cuts or tears and broken bones. The carcass is free from discoloration and, if it is frozen, free from defects that occur during handling or storage. Nearly all poultry used in wholesale and retail outlets is Grade A or utility. Grade B and C birds are used primarily for processed poultry products. In addition, poultry may be sold as "ungraded."

Quality grades have no bearing on the product's tenderness or flavour. A bird's tenderness is usually indicated by its class (for example, a "young turkey" is younger and more tender than a yearling). Its grade (Canada A, utility, B or C) within each class is determined by its overall quality.

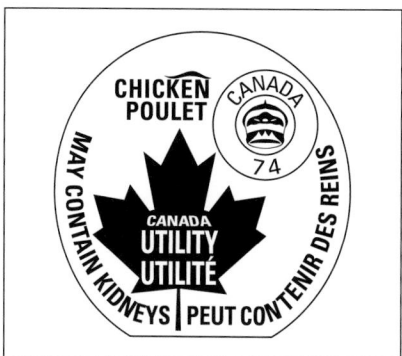

FIGURE 17.1 Grade stamp for utility grade.

PURCHASING AND STORING POULTRY
Purchasing Poultry

Poultry can be purchased in many forms: fresh or frozen, whole or cut up, bone-in or boneless, portion controlled (PC), individually quick frozen (IQF), tumbled or ground. Chicken and turkey are also widely used in prepared and convenience items and are available fully cooked and vacuum-wrapped or boned and canned. Although purchasing poultry in a ready-to-use form is convenient, it is not always necessary; poultry products are easy to fabricate and portion. Whole fresh poultry is also less expensive than precut or frozen products.

As with meats, you should consider your menu, labour costs, storage facilities and employee skills when deciding whether to purchase whole fresh poultry or some other form.

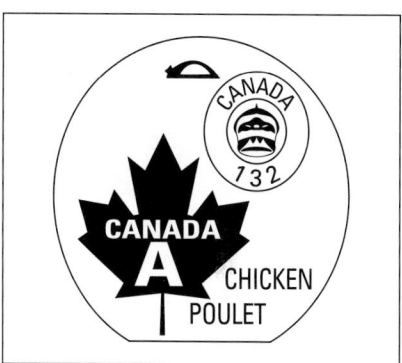

FIGURE 17.2 Grade stamp for Canada Grade A poultry.

Storing Poultry

Poultry is highly perishable and particularly susceptible to contamination by salmonella bacteria. It is critical that poultry be stored at the correct temperatures.

Fresh chickens and other small birds can be stored on ice or at 0°C to 2°C (32°F to 34°F) for up to two days; larger birds can be stored up to four days at these temperatures. Frozen poultry should be kept at –18°C (0°F) or below (the colder the better) and can be held for up to six months. Poultry should be thawed gradually under refrigeration, allowing two days for chickens and up to four days for larger birds. Never attempt to cook poultry that is still partially frozen: It will be impossible to cook the product evenly and the areas that were still frozen may not reach the temperatures necessary to destroy harmful bacteria. Never partially cook poultry one day and finish cooking it later. Bacteria are more likely to grow under such conditions and result in food poisoning. Poultry should be rinsed in clear, running water before processing.

Sanitation and Cross-Contamination

Review the information in Chapter 2, Food Safety and Sanitation, before butchering any poultry. Be sure that all work surfaces, cutting boards, knives, hands and other equipment used to prepare poultry products are clean and sanitary. Be careful that juices and trimmings from poultry do not come in contact with other foods. Anything coming in contact with raw poultry should

Poultry Safety Measures

Although generally following U.S. guidelines up to 1970, Canada streamlined its inspection system for poultry in the late 1970s and early 1980s. Based on a process-controlled environment, industry assumed some of the responsibility. The Canada Poultry Inspection Program was introduced in April 1996 and was revised in 1999.

be cleaned and sanitized with a chlorine solution of 200 parts per million or 200 mg of quaternary ammonium compound per litre before it comes in contact with any other food. Cooked foods should never be placed in containers that were used to hold the raw product. Kitchen towels that are used to handle poultry or clean up after butchering should be sanitized before being reused to prevent cross-contamination. Separate colour-coded cutting boards are recommended for raw and cooked product. Some operations use colour-coded knives as well.

FABRICATING PROCEDURES

Poultry is easier to fabricate than meats are and is often processed on-site. You should be able to perform the following commonly encountered procedures. Because the different kinds of poultry are similar in structure, these procedures apply to a variety of birds.

BASIC PROCEDURE FOR CUTTING A BIRD IN HALF

Often the first step in preparing poultry is to cut the bird in half. Broiler and fryer chickens are often split to make two portions. This procedure removes the backbone and breastbone (also known as the keel bone) for a neat finished product.

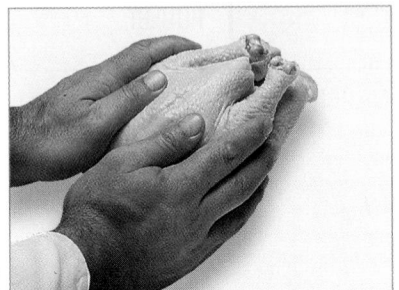

1. Square up the bird by placing it on its back and pressing on the legs and breast to create a more uniform appearance.

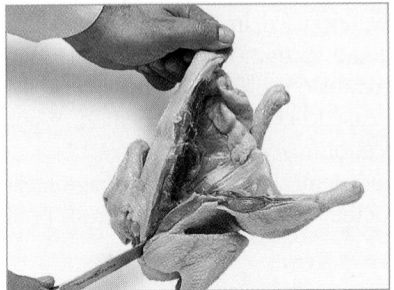

2. Place the bird on its breast and hold the tail tightly with the thumb and forefinger of one hand. Using a rigid boning knife, in a single swift movement cut alongside the backbone from the bird's tail to neck.

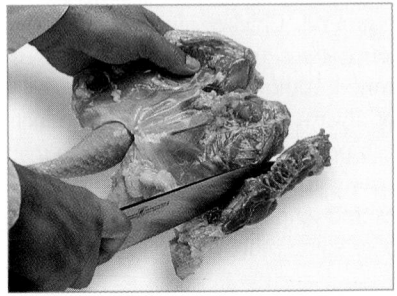

3. Lie the bird flat on the cutting board and remove the backbone by cutting through the ribs connecting it to the breast.

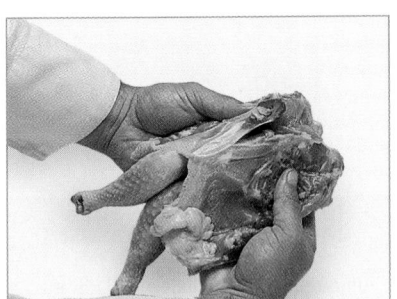

4. Bend the bird back, breaking the breast bone free.

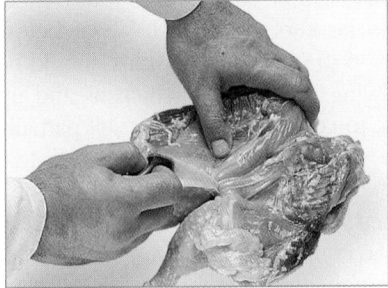

5. Run your fingers along the bone to separate the breast meat from it; pull the bone completely free. Be sure to remove the flexible cartilage completely.

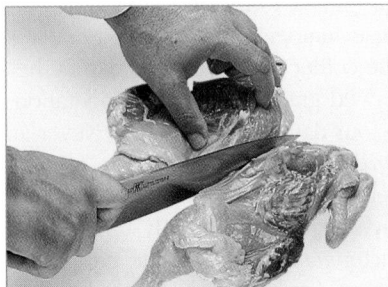

6. Cut through the skin to separate the bird into two halves. The halves are ready to be cooked; for a more attractive presentation, follow Steps 7 and 8.

continued

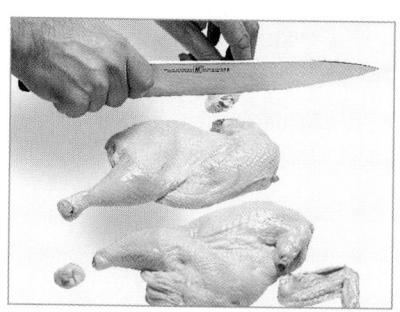

7. Trim off the wing tips and the ends of the leg bone.

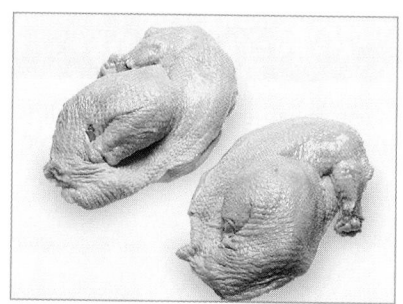

8. Make a slit in the skin below the leg and tuck the leg bone into the slit.

BASIC PROCEDURE FOR CUTTING A BIRD INTO PIECES

This is one of the most common butchering procedures. It is also very simple once you understand the bird's structure and are able to find each of its joints.

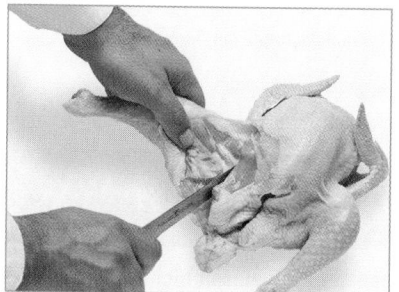

1. Remove the leg by pulling the leg and thigh away from the breast and cutting through the skin and flesh toward the thigh joint.

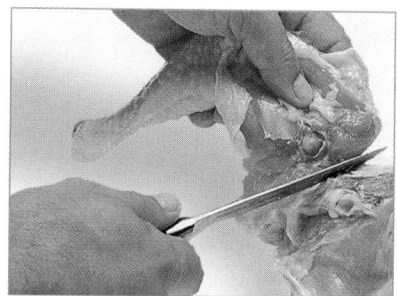

2. Cut down to the thigh joint, twist the leg to break the joint and cut the thigh and leg from the carcass. Be careful to trim around the oyster meat (the tender morsel of meat located next to the backbone); leave it attached to the thigh. Repeat with the other leg.

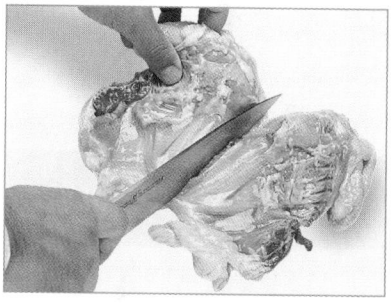

3. To split the breast, follow Steps 2 through 6 for cutting a bird in half. Cut the breast into two halves.

4. The bird is now cut into four pieces.

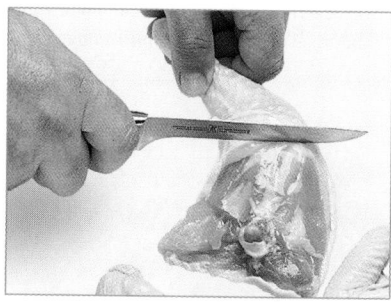

5. To cut the bird into six pieces, separate the thigh from the leg by making a cut guided by the line of fat on the inside of the thigh and leg.

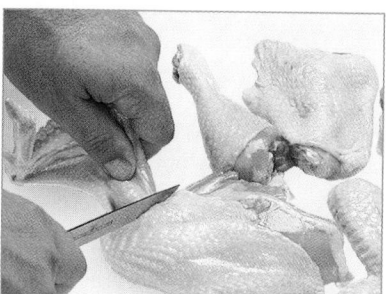

6. To cut the bird into eight pieces, separate the wing from the breast by cutting through the joint, or split the breast, leaving a portion of the breast meat attached to the wing.

BASIC PROCEDURE FOR PREPARING A BONELESS BREAST

A boneless chicken breast is one of the most versatile and popular poultry cuts. It can be broiled, grilled, baked, sautéed, pan-fried or poached. Boneless turkey breast can be roasted or sliced and sautéed in a manner similar to veal. The skin can be removed or left intact.

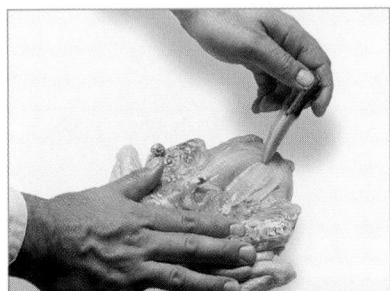

1. Remove the keel bone from the bone-in breast, following Steps 4, 5 and 6 for cutting a bird in half.

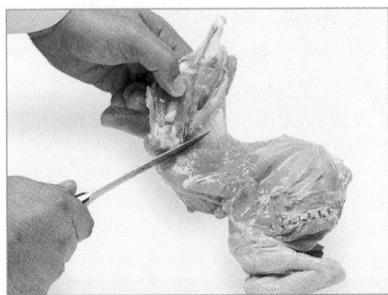

2. With the chicken breast lying skin side down, separate the rib bones, wing and wishbone from the breast. Leave the two tender pieces of meat known as the tenderloins attached to the breast. Repeat the procedure on the other side, being sure to remove the small wishbone pieces from the front of the breast.

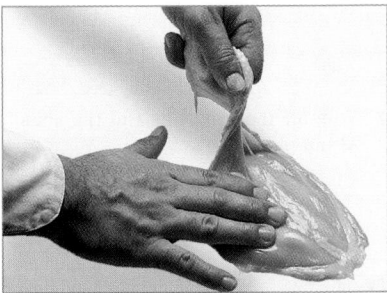

3. The skin may be left intact or removed to produce a skinless boneless breast, which can then be split into single breasts.

BASIC PROCEDURE FOR PREPARING A SUPRÊME OR FRENCHED BREAST

A chicken suprême or frenched breast is half of a boneless chicken breast with the first wing bone attached. The tip of the wing bone is removed, yielding a neat and attractive portion that can be prepared by a variety of cooking methods. The skin can be left on or removed.

1. Remove the legs from a chicken following Steps 1 and 2 for cutting a bird into pieces. Place the bird on its back. Locate the wishbone, trim around it and remove it.

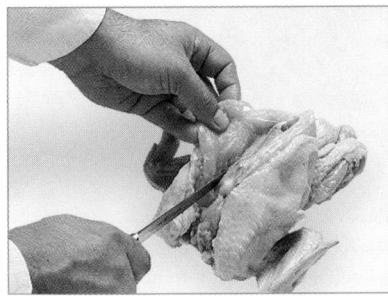

2. Cut along one side of the breast bone, separating the meat from the bone.

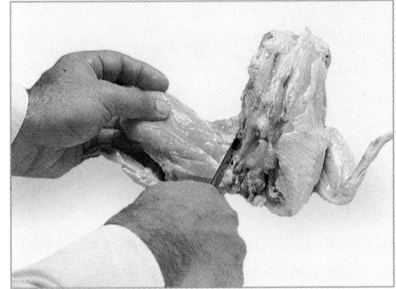

3. Following the natural curvature of the ribs, continue cutting to remove the meat from the bones.

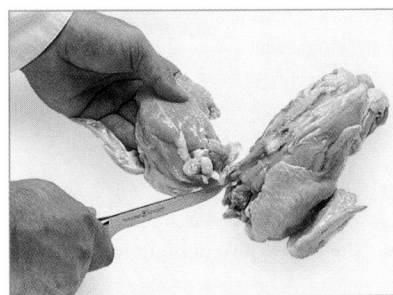

4. When you reach the wing joint, cut through the joint, keeping the wing attached to the breast portion. Cut the breast free from the carcass.

continued

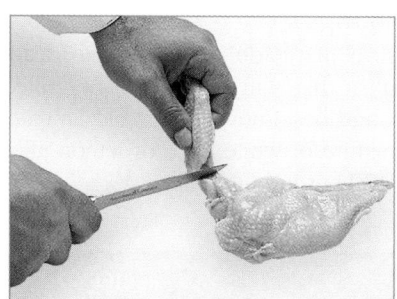

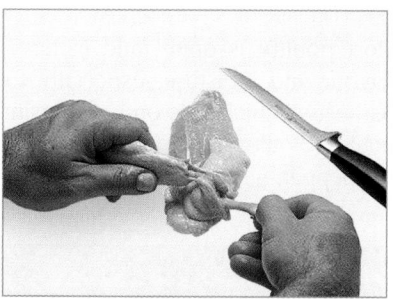

5. Make a cut on the back of the joint between the first and second wing bones.

6. Break the joint and pull the meat and skin back to expose a clean bone. Trim the wing bone.

7. The suprême can be prepared skin-on or skinless.

BASIC PROCEDURE FOR BONING A CHICKEN LEG

Chicken breasts are usually more popular than legs and thighs. There are, however, uses for boneless, skinless leg and thigh meat: they can be stuffed for ballotines or cut for stir-fry or cutlets, for example.

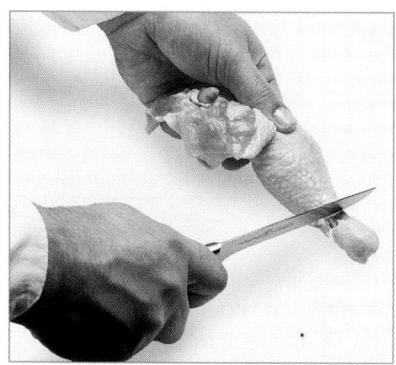

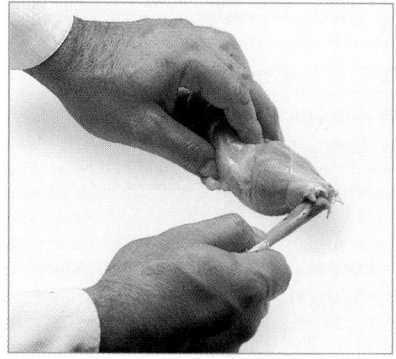

1. Carefully cut through the skin, meat and tendons at the base of the leg. Be sure to cut through completely to the bone.

2. Pull the skin off the leg with your hands, then break the joint between the leg and thigh. Twist and pull out the leg bone.

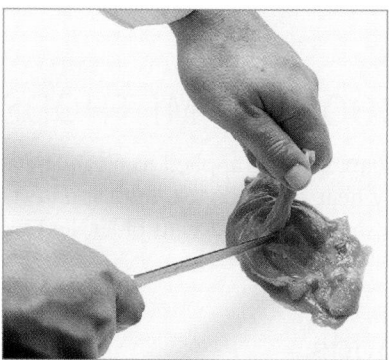

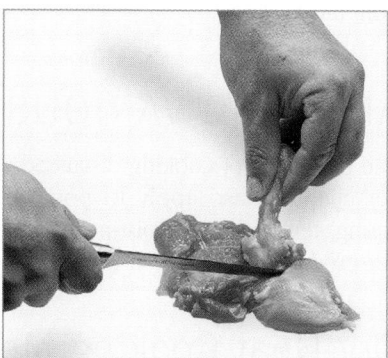

3. Working from the inside of the thigh, cut along both sides of the thigh bone, separating it from the meat.

4. Cut around the cartilage at the joint between the leg and thigh and remove the thigh bone and cartilage.

MARINATING POULTRY

Most poultry is quite mild in flavour, so a marinade is often used to add flavour and moisture, especially to poultry that will be broiled or grilled. Barbecued chicken is one of the simplest and best-known forms of marinated poultry. Poultry is often marinated in a mixture of white wine or lemon juice, oil, pepper, herbs and spices (see Recipe 17.1) or in buttermilk.

Marinating chicken breasts

APPLYING THE BASICS		RECIPE 17.1
Apple Citrus Marinade		
Yield: 750 mL (26 fl. oz.)		
Brown sugar	75 g	2-1/2 oz.
Kosher salt	100 g	3-1/2 oz.
Apple juice	300 mL	12 fl. oz.
Oranges, sliced	4	4
Lemon, sliced	1/2	1/2
Ginger, fresh, sliced	15 g	1/2 oz.
Whole cloves	2	2
Bay leaves	2	2
Garlic, chopped	5 g	1 clove
Water, cold	400 mL	14 fl. oz.

1. Dissolve sugar and salt in apple juice by boiling. Skim any foam.
2. Cool mixture.
3. Add remaining ingredients.

Poultry absorbs flavours quickly, so if pieces are left too long in an acidic marinade they may take on undesirable flavours. Two hours is often sufficient, with smaller pieces requiring less time in the marinade than larger ones.

If the marinade contains oil, drain it well to avoid flare-up when the item is placed on the broiler or grill. Use a clean paper towel to wipe excess moisture from the poultry's surface so that it browns more easily. The marinade can be used to baste the item during cooking, but leftover marinade should not be served uncooked or reused because of the danger of bacterial contamination from the raw poultry.

APPLYING VARIOUS COOKING METHODS

The principles of cooking discussed in Chapter 9 and applied to meats in earlier chapters also apply to poultry. Dry-heat methods are appropriate for young, tender birds. Moist-heat methods should be used with older, less tender products.

Dry-Heat Cooking Methods

Cooking poultry with dry-heat methods—broiling and grilling, roasting, sautéing, pan-frying and deep-fat frying—presents some unique challenges. Large birds such as turkeys benefit from low-heat cooking but are better when served with the crispy skin gained through higher temperatures. Duck and goose skin contains a great deal of fat that must be rendered during the cooking process. Small birds such as squab must be cooked at sufficiently high temperatures to crisp their skins but can be easily overcooked. Boneless chicken breasts, particularly flavourful and popular when broiled or grilled, are easily overcooked and become dry because they do not contain bones to help retain moisture during cooking. Proper application of the following dry-heat cooking methods will help meet these challenges and ensure a good-quality finished product.

Broiling and Grilling

Broiled and grilled poultry should have a well-browned surface and can show crosshatched grill marks. It should be moist, tender and juicy throughout. It may be seasoned to enhance its natural flavours or marinated or basted with any number of flavoured butters or sauces.

Selecting Poultry to Broil or Grill

Smaller birds such as Cornish hens, chickens and squab are especially well suited for broiling or grilling. Whole birds should be split or cut into smaller pieces before cooking; their joints may be broken so that they lie flat. Quail and other small birds can be skewered before being broiled to help them cook evenly and retain their shape. Be especially careful when cooking breast portions or boneless pieces: the direct heat of the broiler or grill can overcook the item very quickly.

Seasoning Poultry to Be Broiled or Grilled

Poultry is fairly neutral in flavour and responds well to marinating. Poultry may also be basted periodically during the cooking process with flavoured butter, oil or barbecue sauce. At the very least, broiled or grilled poultry should be well seasoned with salt and pepper just before cooking.

Determining Doneness

With the exception of duck breasts and squab, which are sometimes left pink, broiled or grilled poultry is always cooked well done. This makes the poultry particularly susceptible to becoming dry and tough because it contains little fat and is cooked at very high temperatures. Particular care must be taken to ensure that the item does not become overcooked.

Four methods are used to determine the doneness of broiled or grilled poultry:

1. *Touch*—When the item is done, it will have a firm texture, resist pressure and spring back quickly when pressed with tongs.

2. *Temperature*—Use an instant-read thermometer to determine the item's internal temperature. This may be difficult, however, because of the item's size and the heat from the broiler or grill. Insert the thermometer in the thickest part of the item away from any bones. It should read 74°C to 77°C (165°F to 170°F) at the coolest point. The higher temperature (77°C/170°F) is recommended for safety.

3. *Looseness of the joints*—When bone-in poultry is done, the leg will begin to move freely in its socket.

4. *Colour of the juices*—Poultry is done when its juices run clear. Quail and pheasant may be cooked **à point** (with traces of pink).

● *à point* (ah PWEN) (1) French term for cooking to the ideal degree of doneness; (2) when applied to meat, refers to cooking it medium rare

Accompaniments to Broiled and Grilled Poultry

If the item was basted with a herb butter, it can be served with additional butter; if the item was basted with barbecue sauce, it should be served with the

RECIPE 17.2

Approximate values per serving:	
Calories	314
Total fat	19 g
Saturated fat	8 g
Cholesterol	125 mg
Sodium	415 mg
Total carbohydrates	0 g
Protein	35 g

same sauce. Be careful, however, that any marinade or sauce that came in contact with the raw poultry is not served unless it is cooked thoroughly to destroy harmful bacteria. Additional sauce suggestions are found in Table 10.5.

Broiled or grilled poultry is very versatile and goes well with almost any side dish. Seasoned and grilled vegetables are a natural accompaniment, and deep-fat-fried potatoes are commonly served.

BASIC PROCEDURE FOR BROILING OR GRILLING POULTRY

As with meats, broiled or grilled poultry can be prepared by placing it directly on the grate. Poultry is also often broiled using a rotisserie.

1. Heat the broiler or grill.

2. Use a wire brush to remove any charred or burnt particles that may be stuck to the broiler or grill grate. The grate can be wiped with a lightly oiled towel to remove any remaining particles and help season the grate.

3. Prepare the item to be broiled or grilled by marinating or seasoning as desired; it may be brushed lightly with oil to keep it from sticking to the grate.

4. Place the item on the grate, presentation side (skin side) down. Following the example in Chapter 9, turn the item to produce the attractive cross-hatch marks associated with broiling or grilling. Baste the item often. Use tongs to turn or flip the item without piercing the surface so that valuable juices do not escape.

5. Develop the proper surface colour while cooking the item until it is done *à point*. To do so, adjust the position of the item on the broiler or grill or adjust the distance between the grate and heat source. Large pieces and bone-in pieces that are difficult to cook completely on the broiler or grill can be finished in the oven.

A commonly used procedure to cook a large volume of poultry is to place the seasoned items in a broiler pan or other shallow pan and then place the pan directly under the broiler. Baste the items periodically, turning them once when they are halfway done. Items begun this way can be easily finished by transferring the entire pan to the oven.

APPLYING THE BASICS   RECIPE 17.2

Grilled Chicken Breast with Basil Butter

Yield: 10 servings
Method: Grilling

Apple Citrus Marinade (see Recipe 17.1)	750 mL	26 fl. oz.
Chicken breasts, 150 g (5-1/2 oz.), boneless, skinless	10	10
Salt and pepper	TT	TT
Vegetable oil	50 mL	2 fl. oz.
Basil butter (see Chapter 10)	150 g	5 oz.

continued

1. Place marinade in a noncorrosive hotel pan.

2. Trim any excess fat from breasts and place in marinade. Marinate in refrigerator for 2 hours. Drain and pat breasts dry with paper towelling.

3. Heat and prepare grill.

4. Coat the breasts with oil, season with salt and pepper and place on the preheated grill.

5. Grill breasts until done and turn to produce crosshatch markings.

6. Remove the breasts from the grill and place on service plate. Set a 15-g (1/2-oz.) slice or rosette of basil butter on top of each breast (to make basil butter, see the instructions on p. 210). If necessary, heat the plate under a salamander to start melting the butter.

1. Grilled Chicken Breast: Seasoning the chicken breasts.

2. Placing the chicken on the grill at a 45° angle to the grates.

3. Using tongs, turn the chicken to cook the other side.

4. The cooked chicken is topped with basil butter.

Roasting

Properly roasted (or baked) poultry is attractively browned on the surface and tender and juicy throughout. Proper cooking temperatures ensure a crisp exterior and juicy interior. Most roasted poultry is cooked until the juices run clear. Squab and duck breasts are an exception: they are often served medium rare or pink.

Selecting Poultry to Roast

Almost every kind of poultry is suitable for roasting, but younger birds produce a more tender finished product. Because of variations in fat content, different kinds of poultry require different roasting temperatures and procedures.

BASIC PROCEDURE FOR TRUSSING POULTRY

Trussing is tying a bird into a more compact shape using string or butcher's twine. This allows the bird to cook more evenly, helps the bird retain moisture and improves the appearance of the finished product. There are many methods for trussing poultry, some of which require a special tool called a trussing needle. Here we show a simple method using butcher's twine.

● **truss** to tie poultry with butcher's twine into a compact shape for cooking

continued

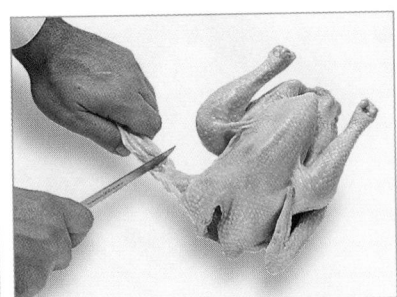

1. Square up the bird by pressing it firmly with both hands. Tuck the first joint of the wing behind the back or trim off the first and second joints as shown.

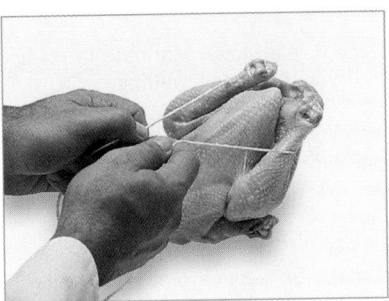

2. Cut a piece of butcher's twine approximately three times the bird's length. With the breast up and the neck toward you, pass the twine under the bird approximately 2.5 cm (1 in.) in front of the tail.

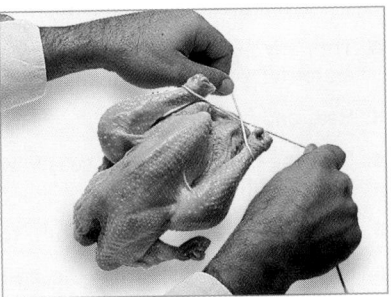

3. Bring the twine up around the legs and cross the ends, creating an × between the legs. Pass the ends of the twine below the legs.

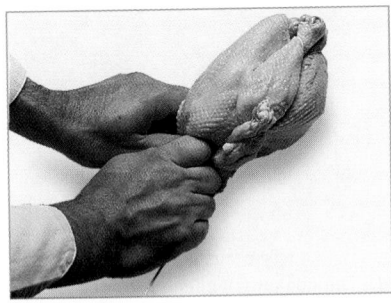

4. Pull the ends of the twine tightly across the leg and thigh joint and across the wing if the first and second joint were trimmed off or just above the wings if they are intact.

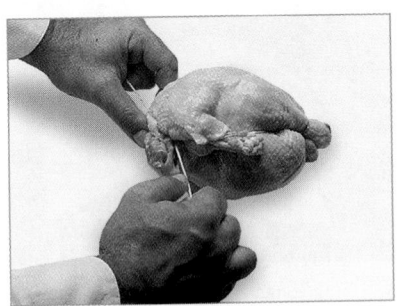

5. Pull the string tight and tie it securely just above the neck.

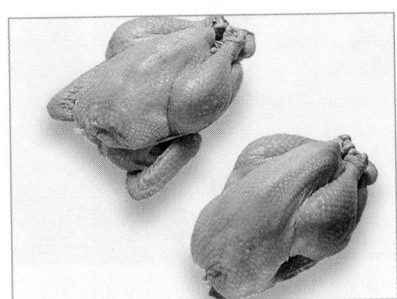

6. Two examples of properly trussed birds: one with the wings intact and one with the first and second wing joints removed.

Seasoning Poultry to Be Roasted

Although the mild flavour of most poultry is enhanced by a wide variety of herbs and spices, roasted poultry is often only lightly seasoned with salt and pepper. Poultry that is roasted at high temperatures should never be seasoned with herbs on its surface because the high cooking temperatures will burn them. If herbs or additional spices are used, they should be stuffed into the cavity. A mirepoix or a bouquet garni may also be added to the cavity for additional flavour. The cavities of dark-meated birds such as ducks and geese are often stuffed with fresh or dried fruits.

Cooking Temperatures

Small birds such as squab and Cornish game hens should be roasted at the relatively high temperatures of 190°C to 200°C (375°F to 400°F). These temperatures help produce crisp, well-coloured skins without overcooking the flesh. Chickens are best roasted at temperatures between 180°C and 190°C (350°F and 375°F). This temperature range allows the skin to crisp and the flesh to cook without causing the bird to stew in its own juices. Large birds such as capons and turkeys are started at high temperatures of 200°C to 220°C (400°F to 425°F) to brown the skin, then finished at lower temperatures of 135°C to 160°C (275°F to 325°F) to promote even cooking and produce a moister product. Ducks and geese, which are very high in fat, must be roasted at the high temperatures of 190°C to 220°C (375°F to 425°F) to render as much fat from the skin as possible. Duck and goose skin is often pricked before roasting so the rendered fat can escape; this helps to create crispy skin.

Barding Poultry to Be Roasted

Guineas, squabs or any skinless birds without an adequate fat covering to protect them from drying out during roasting can be barded. Bard the bird by covering its entire surface with thin slices of pork backfat, securing them with butcher's twine. See page 254.

Basting Roasted Poultry

With the exception of fatty birds such as ducks and geese, all poultry items should be basted while they roast to help retain moisture. To baste a bird, spoon or ladle the fat that collects in the bottom of the roasting pan over the bird at 15- to 20-minute intervals. Lean birds that are not barded will not produce enough fat for basting and may be brushed with butter in the same manner.

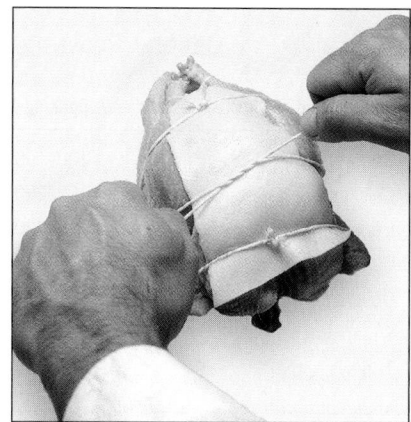

Barding a pheasant

Determining Doneness

Four methods are used to determine the doneness of roasted poultry. It is best to use a combination of these methods.

1. *Temperature*—Test the internal temperature of the bird with an instant-read thermometer. The thermometer should be inserted in the bird's thigh, which is the last part to become fully cooked. It should not touch the bone and should read a minimum of 74°C (165°F). To ensure a safer product, it is recommended that poultry be cooked to 77°C (170°F) and as high as 85°C (185°F) for stuffed birds. This method works best with large birds such as capons and turkeys. Large birds are subject to some degree of carryover cooking. This is not as much of a concern with poultry as it is with meat, because large birds are always cooked well done.

2. *Looseness of the joints*—The thigh and leg will begin to move freely in their sockets when the bird is done.

3. *Colour of the juices*—This method is used with birds that are not stuffed. Use a kitchen fork to tilt the bird, allowing some of the juices that have collected in the cavity to run out. Clear juices may indicate that the bird is done. If the juices are cloudy or pink, the bird is undercooked.

4. *Time*—Because there are so many variables, timing alone is less reliable than other methods. It is useful, however, for planning production when large quantities are roasted and as a general guideline when used with other methods. Table 17.2 gives some general timing guidelines for roasting several kinds of poultry.

Accompaniments to Roasted Poultry

The most common accompaniments to roasted poultry are bread stuffing (**dressing**) and gravy. Large birds, such as capons and turkeys, produce adequate drippings for making sauce or pan gravy. Small birds, such as squab and Cornish game hens, are often stuffed with wild rice or other ingredients and served with a sauce that is made separately.

● **dressing** another name for a bread stuffing used with poultry

Ducks and geese are complemented by stuffings containing rice, fruits, berries and nuts. They are very fatty and if stuffed they should be roasted on a rack or mirepoix bed to ensure that the fat that collects in the pan during roasting does not penetrate the cavity, making the stuffing greasy. Ducks and geese are often served with a citrus- or fruit-based sauce. Its high acid content complements these rich, fatty birds.

TABLE 17.2	General Roasting Temperatures and Times			
Poultry Kind or Class	**Cooking Temperatures**		**Minutes**	
Capons	180–190°C	350–375°F	35–40 min. per kg	18–20 min. per lb.
Chickens	190–200°C	375–400°F	30–35 min. per kg	15–18 min. per lb.
Ducks and geese	190–220°C	375–425°F	25–30 min. per kg	12–15 min. per lb.
Game hens	190–200°C	375–400°F	45–60 min. total	45–60 min. total
Guineas	190–200°C	375–400°F	35–40 min. per kg	18–20 min. per lb.
Squab	200°C	400°F	30–40 min. total	30–40 min. total
Turkeys (large)	160°C	325°F	25–30 min. per kg	12–15 min. per lb.

SAFETY ALERT

Handling Stuffed Poultry

Stuffing is a potentially hazardous food. All ingredients used to make stuffing must be cold and stay below 4°C (40°F) when mixing and stuffing into poultry. Stuff a bird as close to cooking time as possible to keep it out of the temperature danger zone. Observe proper cooking temperatures and roast until the bird reaches an internal temperature of 74°C (165°F) as indicated by an instant-read thermometer placed deep into the stuffing. Remove all stuffing from the bird's cavity promptly. If left in the cavity, stuffing will not cool and will become a potential breeding ground for bacteria.

BASIC PROCEDURE FOR STUFFING POULTRY

Small birds such as Cornish game hens, small chickens and squab can be stuffed successfully. Stuffing larger birds, especially for volume production, is impractical and can be dangerous for the following reasons:

1. *Safety*—Stuffing is a good bacterial breeding ground and, because it is difficult to control temperatures inside a stuffed bird, there is a risk of foodborne illness.

2. *Practicality*—Stuffing poultry is labour intensive.

3. *Quality*—Stuffed poultry must be cooked longer to cook the stuffing properly; this may cause the meat to be overcooked, becoming dry and tough.

When stuffing any bird, use the following guidelines.

1. Always be aware of temperatures when mixing the raw ingredients. All ingredients should be cold when they are mixed together, and the mixture's temperature should never be allowed to rise above 4°C (40°F).

2. Stuff the bird as close to roasting time as possible.

3. The neck and main body cavities should be loosely stuffed. The stuffing will expand during cooking.

4. After the cavities are filled, their openings should be secured with skewers and butcher's twine or by trussing.

5. After cooking, remove the stuffing from the bird and store separately.

BASIC PROCEDURE FOR ROASTING POULTRY

1. Season, bard, stuff and/or truss the bird as desired.

2. Place the bird in a roasting pan. It may be placed on a rack or mirepoix bed to prevent scorching and promote even cooking.

3. Roast uncovered, basting every 15 minutes.

4. Allow the bird to rest before carving to allow even distribution of juices. As the bird rests, prepare the pan gravy or sauce.

APPLYING THE BASICS   RECIPE 17.3

Roast Turkey with Chestnut Dressing and Giblet Gravy

Yield: 16 servings: each 120 g (4 oz.) turkey,
90 g (3 oz.) dressing, 120 mL (4 fl. oz.) gravy

Approximate values per serving:	
Calories	651
Total fat	31 g
Saturated fat	10 g
Cholesterol	171 mg
Sodium	691 mg
Total carbohydrates	48 g
Protein	45 g

Young turkey, 5.5–6.5 kg (12–15 lb.) with giblets	1	1
Salt and pepper	TT	TT
Mirepoix	600 g	21 oz.
Onion, small dice	250 g	8 oz.
Celery, small dice	175 g	6 oz.
Whole butter	125 g	4 oz.
Fresh bread cubes	1 kg	2 lb.
Eggs, beaten	2	2
Fresh parsley, chopped	10 g	1 Tbsp.
Chicken stock	2 L	2-1/4 qt.
Chestnuts, cooked and peeled, chopped coarse	250 g	8 oz.
Pastry flour	90 g	3 oz.

1. Remove the giblets from the turkey's cavity and set aside. Season the turkey inside and out with salt and pepper. Truss the turkey.

2. Place the turkey in a roasting pan. Roast at 200°C (400°F) for 30 minutes. Reduce the temperature to 160°C (325°F) and continue cooking the turkey to an internal temperature of 77°C (170°F), approximately 2.5–3 hours. Baste the turkey often during cooking. Approximately 45 minutes before the turkey is done, add the mirepoix to the roasting pan. If the turkey begins to overbrown, cover it loosely with aluminum foil.

3. To make the dressing, sauté the diced onion and celery in the butter until tender.

4. In a large bowl, toss together the bread cubes, salt, pepper, eggs, parsley, sautéed onions and celery, 125 mL (4 fl. oz.) of chicken stock and the chestnuts.

5. Place the dressing in a buttered hotel pan and cover with aluminum foil or buttered parchment paper. Bake at 175°C (350°F) to an internal temperature of 65°C (150°F), approximately 45 minutes.

6. As the turkey roasts, simmer the giblets (neck, heart and gizzard) in 1 L (1 qt.) of the chicken stock until tender, approximately 1.5 hours.

7. When the turkey is done, remove it from the roasting pan and set aside to rest. Degrease the roasting pan, reserving 90 g (3 oz.) of the fat to make a roux.

continued

1. Roast Turkey: Placing the turkey in the roasting pan.

2. Adding the mirepoix to the roasting pan.

3. Tossing the dressing ingredients together.

4. Browning the mirepoix.

5. Deglazing the roasting pan.

8. Place the roasting pan on the stove top and brown the mirepoix.

9. Deglaze the pan with a small amount of chicken stock. Transfer the mirepoix and stock to a saucepot and add the remaining stock and the broth from the giblets. Bring to a simmer and degrease.

10. Make a blond roux with the reserved fat and the flour. Add the roux to the liquid, whisking well to prevent lumps. Simmer 15 minutes. Strain the gravy through a conical strainer lined with cheesecloth.

11. Remove the meat from the turkey neck. Trim the gizzard. Finely chop the neck meat, heart and gizzard and add to the gravy. Adjust the seasonings.

12. Carve the turkey and serve with a portion of chestnut dressing and giblet gravy.

6. Transferring the mirepoix and stock to a saucepot.

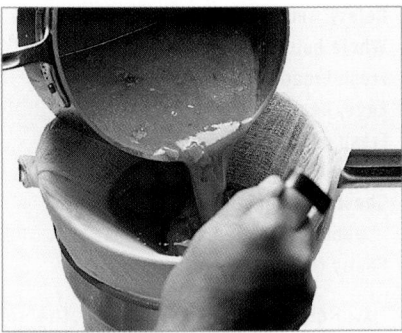

7. Straining the gravy through a conical strainer and cheesecloth.

Carving Roasted Poultry

Poultry can be carved in the kitchen, at tableside or on a buffet in a variety of manners. The carving methods described below produce slices of both light and dark meat.

BASIC PROCEDURE FOR CARVING A TURKEY, CAPON OR OTHER LARGE BIRD

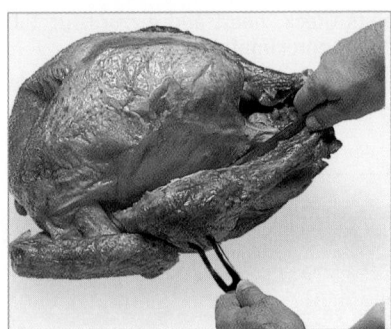

1. After roasting, allow the turkey to stand for 20 minutes so the juices can redistribute themselves. Holding the turkey firmly with a carving fork, pry a leg outward and locate the joint. Remove the leg and thigh in one piece by cutting through the joint with the tip of a knife.

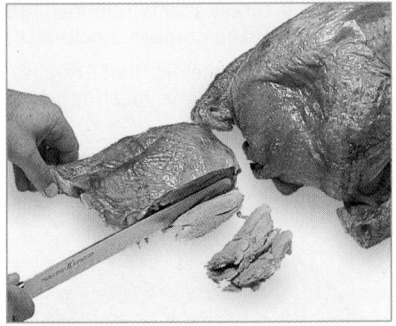

2. Repeat the procedure on the other side. Once both legs and thighs have been removed, slice the meat from the thigh by holding the leg firmly with one hand and slicing parallel to the bone.

continued

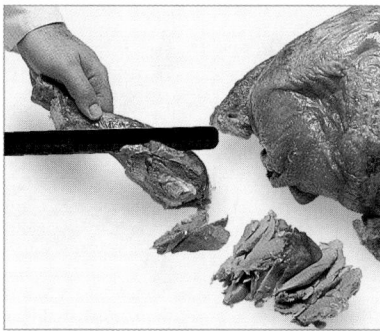

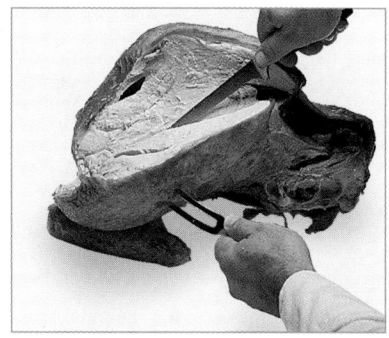

3. Separate the thigh from the leg bone by cutting through the joint. Slice the meat from the leg by cutting parallel to the bone.

4. Cut along the breastbone, following the natural curvature of the bones to separate the breast meat from the ribs.

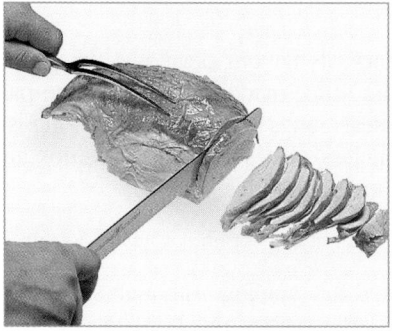

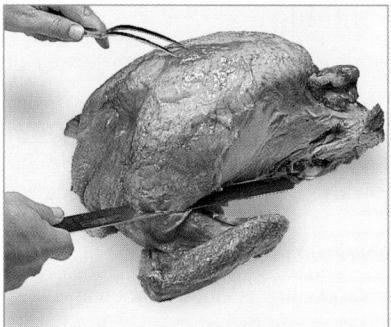

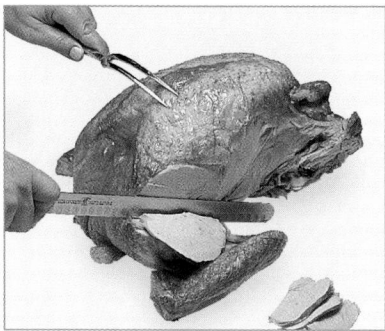

5. Remove an entire half breast and slice it on the cutting board as shown. Cut on an angle to produce larger slices.

6. Alternatively, the breast can be carved on the bird. Make a horizontal cut just above the wing in toward the rib bones.

7. Slice the breast meat as shown.

BASIC PROCEDURE FOR CARVING A CHICKEN OR OTHER SMALL BIRD

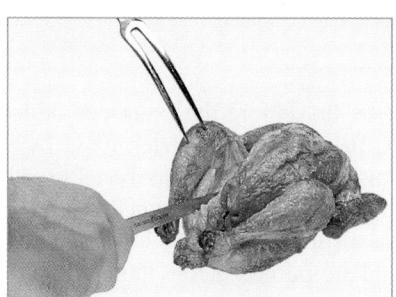

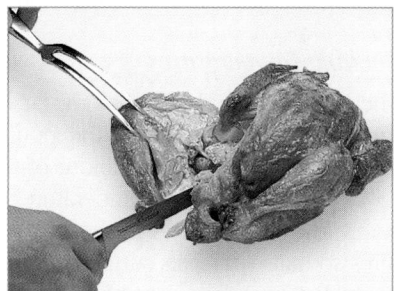

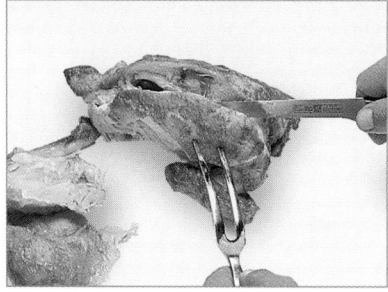

1. After allowing the chicken to rest for 15 minutes so the juices can redistribute themselves, cut through the skin between the leg and breast.

2. Use a kitchen fork to pry the leg and thigh away from the breast. Locate the thigh's ball joint and cut through it with the knife tip, separating it completely from the rest of the chicken. Be sure to cut around the delicate oyster meat, leaving it attached to the thigh.

3. With the knife tip, cut through the skin and meat on one side of the breastbone. Cut and pull the meat away from the bones with the knife.

continued

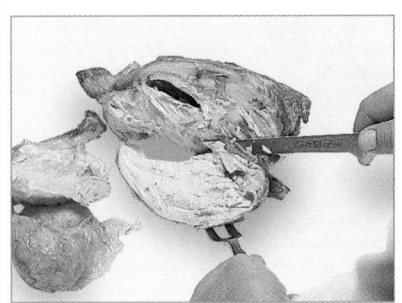

4. Cut through the wing joint, separating the breast and wing from the carcass. Repeat this procedure on the other side of the bird.

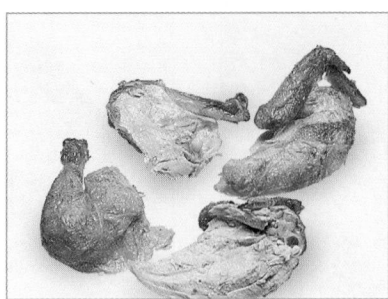

5. The chicken is now quartered.

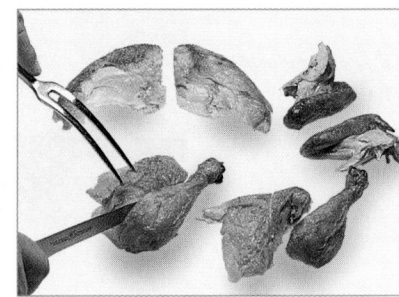

6. To cut it into eight pieces, separate the wings from the breasts and the thighs from the legs.

Sautéing

Sautéed poultry should be tender and juicy, its flavour developed by proper browning. Additional flavours come from a sauce made by deglazing the pan, usually with wine, and adding garnishes, seasonings and liquids. Stir-frying is a popular method of sautéing poultry; boneless pieces are cut into strips and quickly cooked with assorted vegetables and flavourings.

Selecting Poultry to Sauté

Most poultry is quite tender and well suited for sautéing. Although small birds such as squab can be sautéed bone-in, large pieces and bone-in cuts from larger birds should not be sautéed. Boneless breasts, suprêmes and cutlets are the most common and practical cuts for sautéing. An exception is boneless duck breast, which is cooked on the fat side on moderate heat to render the fat and crisp the skin, then turned and cooked on low heat.

Seasoning Poultry to Be Sautéed

Poultry has a delicate flavour that is enhanced by a wide variety of herbs, spices, condiments and marinades. Flavour combinations are limited only by your imagination. When poultry items are dusted with flour before sautéing, the seasonings may first be added to the flour.

Cooking Temperatures

The sauté pan and the cooking fat must be hot before the poultry is added. The temperature at which the poultry is then sautéed is determined by its thickness and the desired colour of the finished product. A thin, boneless slice requires relatively high temperatures so that its surface is browned before the centre is overcooked. A thicker cut such as a suprême requires lower temperatures so that neither its surface nor the fond are burned before the item is fully cooked. Adjust the temperature throughout the cooking process to achieve the desired results, never letting the pan become too cool.

If the pan is overcrowded or otherwise allowed to cool, the poultry will cook in its own juices and absorb oil from the pan, resulting in a poor-quality product.

Determining Doneness

Thin cuts of poultry cook very quickly, so timing is a useful practice; it is less useful with thicker cuts. Experienced cooks can tell the doneness of an item by judging the temperature of the sauté pan and the colour of the item being cooked.

A more practical method is to press the item with tongs and judge the resistance. Very undercooked poultry will offer little resistance and feel mushy. Slightly underdone poultry will feel spongy and will not spring back when the tongs are removed. Properly cooked poultry will feel firm to the touch and will spring back when the tongs are removed. Overcooked poultry will feel very firm, almost hard, and will spring back quickly.

Accompaniments to Sautéed Poultry

Sautéed poultry is usually served with a sauce made directly in the pan in which the item was cooked. The sauce uses the fond for added flavour. A wide variety of ingredients, including garlic, onions, shallots, mushrooms and tomatoes, are commonly added to the pan, as well as wine and stock. Table 10.5 suggests several sauces for sautéed poultry.

Sautéed items are often served with a starch such as pasta, rice or potatoes.

BASIC PROCEDURE FOR SAUTÉING POULTRY

1. Heat a sauté pan and add enough fat or oil just to cover the bottom.

2. Add the poultry item, presentation side down, and cook until browned.

3. Turn the item using tongs or by tossing the item back upon itself using the pan's sloped sides.

4. Larger items can be finished in an oven. Either place the sauté pan in the oven or transfer the poultry to another pan. The latter procedure allows a sauce to be made in the original pan as the poultry cooks in the oven. Reserve smaller pieces that are thoroughly cooked in a holding cabinet so that the pan can be used for making the sauce.

BASIC PROCEDURE FOR MAKING A SAUCE IN THE SAUTÉ PAN

1. Pour off any excess fat or oil from the sauté pan, leaving enough to sauté the sauce ingredients.

2. Add ingredients such as garlic, shallots and mushrooms that will be used as garnishes and sauce flavourings; sauté them.

3. Deglaze the pan with wine, stock or other liquids. Scrape the pan, loosening the fond and allowing it to dissolve in the liquid. Reduce the liquid.

4. Add any ingredients that do not require long cooking times such as herbs and spices. Adjust the sauce's consistency and seasonings.

5. For service, the poultry can be returned to the pan for a moment to reheat it and coat it with the sauce. The poultry should remain in the sauce just long enough to reheat. Do not attempt to cook the poultry in the sauce.

6. Serve the poultry with the accompanying sauce.

APPLYING THE BASICS

RECIPE 17.4

Chicken Sauté with Tomato, Garlic and Basil

Yield: 10 175-g (6-oz.) servings

Chicken breasts, boneless, skinless, each approximately 175 g (6 oz.)	10	10
Salt and pepper	TT	TT
Flour	as needed	as needed
Clarified butter	50 mL	2 fl. oz.
Shallots, small dice	100 g	3-1/2 oz.
Garlic cloves, chopped	40 g	8
Dry white wine	200 mL	7 fl. oz.
Lemon juice	25 mL	2 Tbsp.
Tomato concassée	300 g	10 oz.
Chicken stock	200 mL	7 fl. oz.
Fresh basil leaves, chiffonade	10	10

1. Season the chicken with salt and pepper; dredge in flour.

2. Sauté the breasts in the butter, browning them and cooking *à point*. Reserve in a holding cabinet.

3. Add the shallots and garlic to the fond and butter in the pan; sauté until the shallots are translucent.

4. Deglaze the pan with the white wine and lemon juice.

5. Add the tomato and the chicken stock. Sauté to combine the flavours; reduce the sauce to the desired consistency.

6. Add the basil to the sauce and return the chicken breasts for reheating. Adjust the seasonings and serve 1 breast per serving with a portion of the sauce.

RECIPE 17.4

Approximate values per serving:	
Calories	285
Total fat	7.2 g
Saturated fat	3.3 g
Cholesterol	112 mg
Sodium	207 mg
Total carbohydrates	9.3 g
Protein	41 g

1. Chicken Sauté: Sautéing the breasts in butter.

2. The fond left in the pan after sautéing the chicken.

3. Sautéing the shallots and garlic.

4. Deglazing the pan with white wine and lemon juice.

5. Adding the tomatoes and chicken stock and simmering to combine the flavours.

6. Returning the chicken to the pan to reheat.

Pan-Frying

Pan-fried poultry should be juicy. Its coating or batter should be crispy, golden-brown, not excessively oily and free from any breaks that allow fat to penetrate. Both the poultry and the coating should be well seasoned.

Selecting Poultry to Pan-Fry

The most common pan-fried poultry is fried chicken. Young tender birds cut into small pieces produce the best results. Other cuts commonly pan-fried are boneless portions such as chicken breasts and turkey cutlets.

Seasoning Poultry to Be Pan-Fried

Pan-fried poultry is usually floured, breaded or battered before cooking. Typically, the seasonings are added to the flour, breading or batter before the poultry item is coated. Seasonings can be a blend of any number of dried herbs and spices, but often only salt and pepper are required because the poultry will be served with a sauce or other accompaniments for additional flavours.

Cooking Temperatures

The fat should always be hot before the poultry is added. The temperature at which it is cooked is determined by the length of time required to cook it thoroughly. Pan-frying generally requires slightly lower temperatures than those used for sautéing. Within this range, thinner items require higher temperatures to produce good colour in a relatively short time. Thicker items and those containing bones require lower cooking temperatures and longer cooking times.

Determining Doneness

Even the largest pan-fried items may be too small to be accurately tested with an instant-read thermometer, so timing and experience are the best tools to determine doneness. Thin cutlets cook very quickly, so it is relatively easy to judge their doneness. On the other hand, fried chicken can take as long as 30 to 45 minutes to cook, requiring skill and experience to determine doneness.

Accompaniments to Pan-Fried Poultry

Because pan-frying does not produce fond or drippings that can be used to make a sauce, pan-fried poultry is usually served with lemon wedges, a vegetable garnish or a separately made sauce. Fried chicken is an exception: it is sometimes served with a country gravy made by degreasing the pan, making a roux with a portion of the fat and adding milk and seasonings.

BASIC PROCEDURE FOR PAN-FRYING POULTRY

1. Heat enough fat in a heavy sauté pan to immerse the item to be cooked one-quarter to halfway. The fat should be at approximately 160°C (325°F).

2. Add the floured, breaded or battered item to the hot fat, being careful not to splash. The fat must be hot enough to sizzle and bubble when the item is added.

3. Turn the item when the first side is the proper colour; it should be half cooked at this point. Larger items may need to be turned more than once to brown them properly on all sides.

4. Remove the browned poultry from the pan and drain it on absorbent paper.

APPLYING THE BASICS   RECIPE 17.5

Pan-Fried Chicken with Pan Gravy

Yield: 8 2-piece servings

Frying chickens, each 1.1–1.4 kg (2 lb. 8 oz.–3 lb.), cut in 8 pieces	2	2
Salt and pepper	TT	TT
Garlic powder	10 g	2 tsp.
Onion powder	6 g	2 tsp.
Dried oregano	0.5 g	1 tsp.
Dried basil	1 g	1 tsp.
Flour	300 g	9-1/2 oz.
Buttermilk	250 mL	8 fl. oz.
Oil	as needed	as needed
Onion, small dice	125 g	4 oz.
Chicken stock	750 mL	1-1/2 pt.

1. Season the chicken with salt and pepper.

2. Add the herbs and spices to 250 g (8 oz.) of the flour.

3. Dip the chicken pieces in the buttermilk.

4. Dredge the chicken in the seasoned flour.

5. Pan-fry the chicken in 1 cm (1/2 in.) of oil until done, approximately 40 minutes, turning so it cooks evenly. Reduce the heat as necessary to prevent the chicken from becoming too dark. Or remove the chicken when well browned, drain it and finish cooking it in the oven.

6. To make the pan gravy, pour off all but 50 mL (1-1/2 fl. oz.) of oil from the pan, carefully reserving the fond.

7. Add the diced onions and sauté until translucent.

8. Add 50 g (1-1/2 oz.) of flour and cook to make a blond roux.

9. Whisk in the stock and simmer approximately 15 minutes.

10. Strain through cheesecloth and adjust the seasonings.

11. Serve one-quarter chicken (2 pieces) per person with 125 mL (4 fl. oz.) gravy.

RECIPE 17.5

Approximate values per serving:

Calories	536
Total fat	32 g
Saturated fat	6.7 g
Cholesterol	92 mg
Sodium	642 mg
Total carbohydrates	34 g
Protein	28 g

1. Pan-Fried Chicken: Dipping the chicken pieces in the buttermilk.

2. Dredging the chicken in the flour mixture.

3. Adding the chicken to the oil. The bubbling fat indicates the proper cooking temperature.

4. Turning the chicken so it cooks evenly.

5. Sautéing the diced onions until translucent.

6. Adding the liquid to the roux.

Moist-Heat Cooking Methods

The moist-heat cooking methods most often used with poultry are poaching and simmering. Poaching is used to cook tender birds for short periods of time. Simmering is used to cook older, tougher birds for longer periods to tenderize them. Poaching and simmering are similar procedures, the principal differences being the temperature of the cooking liquid and the length of cooking time.

Poaching and Simmering

Poached or simmered poultry should be moist, tender and delicately flavoured. Although cooked in stock, poultry will be dry and tough if over-cooked. During cooking, some of the poultry's flavour is transferred to the cooking liquid, which can be used to make a sauce for the finished product.

Selecting Poultry to Poach or Simmer

Young birds are best suited for poaching; boneless chicken pieces are the most commonly used parts. Older, tougher birds are usually simmered. Duck and geese are rarely poached or simmered because of their high fat content.

Seasoning Poultry to Be Poached or Simmered

When poaching poultry, it is especially important to use a well-seasoned and highly flavoured liquid in order to infuse as much flavour as possible into the item being cooked. Either strong stock with a sachet or a mixture of stock or water and white wine with a bouquet garni or oignon piqué produces good results. The poultry should be completely covered with liquid so that it cooks evenly. However, if too much liquid is used and it is not strongly flavoured, flavours may be leached out of the poultry, resulting in a bland finished product.

Poultry is often simmered in water instead of stock. A sachet and a generous mirepoix should be added to help flavour it. Typically, simmering birds results in a strong broth that may be used to complete the recipe or reserved for other uses.

Cooking Temperatures

For best results, poultry should be poached at low temperatures, between 75°C and 80°C (165°F and 175°F). Cooking poultry to the proper doneness at these temperatures produces a product that is moist and tender.

Simmering is done at slightly higher temperatures, between 85°C (185°F) and just below the boiling point. When simmering, do not allow the liquid to boil, as this may result in a dry, tough and stringy finished product.

Determining Doneness

Poached poultry, whether whole or boneless, is cooked just until done. An instant-read thermometer inserted in the thigh or thicker part of the bird should read 77°C (170°F). Any juices that run from the bird should be clear.

Simmered poultry is usually cooked for longer periods to allow the moist heat to tenderize the meat. A chicken that weighs 1.5 kg (3 lb. 8 oz.), for example, may take 2.5 hours to cook, depending on its age.

Accompaniments to Poached or Simmered Poultry

Poached or simmered poultry can be served hot or cold. The meat from these birds can be served cold in salads, or hot in casseroles or used in any dish that calls for cooked poultry.

Poached items are typically served with a flavoured mayonnaise or a sauce made from the reduced poaching liquid, such as sauce suprême. Poultry is also often poached as a means of producing a low-calorie dish. If so, a vegetable coulis makes a good sauce or the poultry can be served with a portion of its cooking liquid and a vegetable garnish.

Simmered poultry to be served cold will be more moist and flavourful if it is cooled in its cooking liquid. To do so, remove the pot containing the bird and the cooking liquid from the heat when the bird is still slightly under-cooked. Cool the meat and broth in a water bath following the procedures in Chapter 10, Stocks and Sauces. Once cooled, remove the meat and wipe off any congealed broth before proceeding with the recipe.

BASIC PROCEDURE FOR POACHING OR SIMMERING POULTRY

1. Cut or truss the item to be cooked as directed in the recipe.

2. Prepare the cooking liquid and bring it to a simmer. Submerge the poultry in the cooking liquid, or arrange the items to be poached in an appropriate pan and add the poaching liquid to the pan.

3. Poach or simmer the item to the desired doneness in the oven or on the stove top. Maintain the proper cooking temperature throughout the process.

4. Remove the item and hold it for service in a portion of the cooking liquid or, using an ice bath, cool the item in its cooking liquid.

5. The cooking liquid may be used to prepare an accompanying sauce or reserved for use in other dishes.

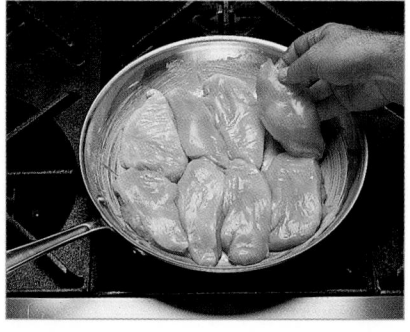

1. Poached Breast of Chicken: Arranging the breasts in an appropriate pan.

2. Adding the white wine, chicken stock and seasonings to the pan.

APPLYING THE BASICS   **RECIPE 17.6**

Poached Breast of Chicken with Tarragon Sauce

Yield: 10 175-g (6-oz.) servings

Chicken breasts, boneless, skinless, each approximately 175 g (6 oz.)	10	10
Whole butter	60 g	2 oz.
Salt and white pepper	TT	TT
White wine, warm	150 mL	5 fl. oz.
Chicken stock	625 mL	20 fl. oz.
Bay leaf	1	1
Dried thyme	0.3 g	1/2 tsp.
Dried tarragon	0.5 g	1 tsp.
Flour, pastry	40 g	1-1/2 oz.
Cream, 35%	175 mL	6 fl. oz.
Fresh tarragon sprigs	as needed	as needed

1. Trim any rib meat and fat from the breasts.

2. Select a pan that will just hold the breasts when they are placed close together. Rub the pan with approximately 20 g (1/2 oz.) of butter.

continued

3. Covering the breasts with a piece of buttered parchment paper (cartouche).

4. Adding the cream to the thickened sauce.

5. Plating the poached chicken breast.

3. Season the chicken breasts with salt and pepper and arrange them in the buttered pan, presentation side up.

4. Add the preheated white wine, stock, bay leaf, thyme and dried tarragon.

5. Cut and butter a piece of parchment paper and cover the chicken breasts.

6. Bring the liquid to a simmer and reduce the temperature to poach the chicken.

7. Make a blond roux with 40 g (1-1/2 oz.) of butter and the flour; set aside to cool.

8. When the breasts are done, remove them from the liquid. Thicken the liquid with the roux. Add the cream. Simmer and reduce to the desired consistency.

9. Strain the sauce through cheesecloth and adjust the seasonings.

10. Serve each breast nappéd with approximately 60 mL (2 fl. oz.) of sauce; garnish each portion with a sprig of fresh tarragon.

RECIPE 17.6

Approximate values per serving:	
Calories	326
Total fat	14 g
Saturated fat	7.6 g
Cholesterol	140 mg
Sodium	369 mg
Total carbohydrates	4.8 g
Protein	41 g

Combination Cooking Methods

Braising, stewing and poêlé use both dry and moist heat to produce a moist, flavourful product. One difference between braising and stewing when applied to meats is the size of the cut being cooked: large cuts of meat are braised, smaller ones are stewed. Because most poultry is relatively small, this distinction does not readily apply in poultry cookery.

Braising, Stewing and Poêlé

Braised, stewed and poêléd poultry should be moist and fork tender. The poultry is always served with the liquid in which it was cooked. Ducks and geese are braised or stewed in much the same way as red meats. Chicken cacciatore, coq au vin and chicken fricassee are examples of braised or stewed chicken dishes. Recipe 17.8 is a chicken poêlé.

Selecting Poultry to Braise, Stew or Poêlé

Braising and stewing, being slow, moist cooking processes, are often thought of as means to tenderize tough meats. Although they can be used to tenderize older, tougher birds, these cooking methods are more often selected as a way to add moisture and flavour to poultry that is inherently tender, such as young ducks and chickens. Typically, the birds are disjointed and cooked bone-in, just until done, so that they retain their juiciness. For poêlé, the bird is typically whole.

Seasoning Poultry to Be Braised, Stewed or Poêléd

Braised or stewed items obtain much of their flavour from the cooking liquid and other ingredients added during the cooking process. The main item and the cooking liquid should be well seasoned. If other seasonings such as an oignon piqué, sachet, bouquet garni or dried herbs and spices are required, they should be added at the beginning of the cooking process rather than at the end. This allows the flavours to blend and penetrate the larger pieces of poultry. If the poultry is dredged in flour prior to browning, seasonings may be added directly to the flour. As with all dishes using combination cooking methods, the finished dish should have the flavour of the poultry in the sauce and the moisture and flavour of the sauce in the poultry.

Cooking Temperatures

Some recipes, such as chicken cacciatore and coq au vin, require the main item to be thoroughly browned during the initial stages; others, such as chicken fricassee, do not. In either case, after the addition of the liquid it is important to maintain a slow simmer rather than a rapid boil. This can be done on the stove top or in the oven. Low temperatures control the cooking and produce a tender, juicy finished product.

Determining Doneness

Tenderness is the key to determining doneness. It can be determined by inserting a kitchen fork into the poultry. There should be little resistance and the poultry should freely fall off the fork. The pieces should retain their shape, however; if they fall apart, they are overdone. Small boneless pieces can be tested by cutting into them with a fork.

Accompaniments to Braised, Stewed or Poêléd Poultry

All braises, stews and poêlés are cooked in a liquid that results in a sauce or broth served as part of the finished dish. Rice, pasta or boiled potatoes are natural accompaniments to such dishes, as are steamed vegetables.

BASIC PROCEDURE FOR BRAISING, STEWING OR POÊLÉING POULTRY

1. Sear the main item in butter or oil, developing colour as desired.

2. Add vegetables and other ingredients as called for in the recipe and sauté.

3. Add the appropriate liquid.

4. Cover and simmer on the stove top or in the oven until done. Baste if poêlé.

5. Add seasonings and garnishes at the appropriate times during the cooking process.

6. If the dish requires a thickened sauce, pour off two-thirds of the liquid into another pot. Thicken this liquid with an appropriate starch product, simmer to cook starch, strain and recombine with other ingredients.

7. Finish the dish by adding cream or a liaison, if needed, or by adjusting its consistency. Adjust the seasonings.

8. Serve a portion of the main item with the sauce and appropriate garnish.

APPLYING THE BASICS   RECIPE 17.7

Chicken Fricassee

Yield: 8 2-piece servings

Frying chickens, each 1.1–1.4 kg (2 lb. 8 oz.–3 lb.), cut into 8 pieces	2	2
Salt and white pepper	TT	TT
Clarified butter	90 mL	3 fl. oz.
Onion, macedoine	300 g	10 oz.
Flour (see Variation)	90 g	3 oz.
Dry white wine	250 mL	8 fl. oz.
Chicken stock	1 L	1 qt.
Sachet:		
Bay leaf	1	1
Dry thyme	0.5 g	1/2 tsp.
Peppercorns, cracked	1 g	1/2 tsp.
Parsley stems	8	8
Garlic clove, crushed	5 g	1
Cream, 35%	250 mL	8 fl. oz.
Nutmeg	TT	TT

1. Season the chicken with salt and white pepper.

2. Sauté the chicken in the butter without browning. Add the onions and continue to sauté until they are translucent.

3. Alternative step: Sprinkle the flour over the chicken and onions and stir to make a roux. Cook the roux for 2 minutes without browning.

4. Deglaze the pan with white wine. Add the chicken stock and sachet; season with salt. Cover the pot and simmer until done, approximately 30–45 minutes.

5. Remove the chicken from the pot and reserve in a holding cabinet. Strain the sauce through cheesecloth and return it to a clean pan.

6. Add the cream and bring the sauce to a simmer. Add the nutmeg and adjust the seasonings. Return the chicken to the sauce to reheat it for service.

VARIATION: Some chefs prefer to thicken the braising/stewing liquid after the product is cooked. You have more control of the consistency of the sauce and more choices of thickening agents. You may also add flour after Step 2 to prepare a roux.

Approximate values per serving:

Calories	541
Total fat	41 g
Saturated fat	19 g
Cholesterol	159 mg
Sodium	635 mg
Total carbohydrates	18 g
Protein	25 g

1. Chicken Fricassee: Sautéing the chicken and onions in butter.

2. Sprinkling the flour over the chicken.

3. Deglazing the pan with white wine.

4. Removing the chicken from the pot.

5. Straining the sauce through cheesecloth.

6. Returning the chicken to the sauce to reheat it for service.

1. Poêlé of Chicken: Placing the chicken on the matignon.

2. Basting the chicken with fat from the pan during cooking.

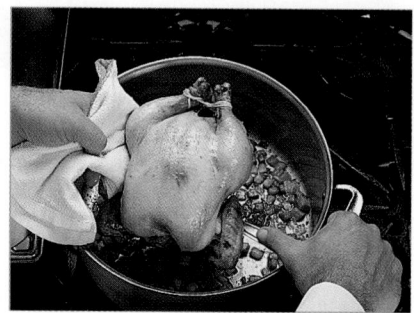

3. Carefully removing the cooked chicken from the pan.

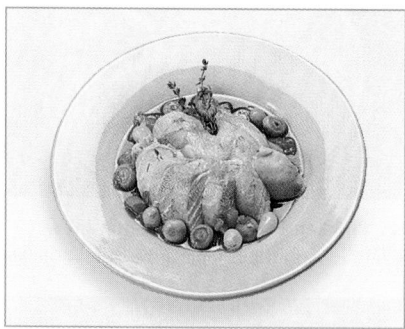

4. The plated poêlé of chicken.

APPLYING THE BASICS		RECIPE 17.8

Poêlé of Chicken with Pearl Onions and Mushrooms

Yield: 10 servings of 1/2 chicken each

Chickens, fryers, small (1 kg)	5	5
Salt and pepper	TT	TT
Herbs, fresh, assorted	5 bouquets	5 bouquets
Butter, clarified	125 g	4 fl. oz.
Matignon:		
Smoked ham or slab bacon	250 g	8 oz.
Onion, macedoine	350 g	12 oz.
Celery, macedoine	175 g	6 oz.
Carrot, macedoine	175 g	6 oz.
Garlic cloves	8	8
Pearl onions, blanched and peeled	250 g	8 oz.
Button mushrooms, stemmed	500 g	1 lb.
White wine	250 mL	8 fl. oz.
Demi-glace	1 L	1 qt.
Tomato concassée	250 g	8 oz.
Herbs, fresh, assorted, chopped	30 g	3 Tbsp.

1. Season the chicken cavities with salt and pepper and place a herb bouquet in each.

2. Heat the butter in a pan just large enough to hold the birds without crowding. Add the matignon and sauté briefly to begin caramelizing.

3. Place the trussed chickens on top of the matignon and baste. Cover the pan with a lid or foil and place in a 160°C (325°F) oven for approximately 1.5 hours or until done, basting the chickens every 20 minutes. Remove the lid for the last 30 minutes to allow the chickens to brown slightly.

4. Remove the chickens from the pan and reserve in a warmer. Place the roasting pan on the stove top. Remove a small amount of fat from the pan and place in a sauté pan. Sauté the onions and mushrooms to cook and colour them.

5. Bring the liquid in the pot to a simmer and skim to remove any excess fat or scum. Add the wine and reduce by half. Add the demi-glace and bring to a simmer. Adjust the thickness of the sauce. Strain out the matignon, if desired, and add the onions, mushrooms, tomato concassée and herbs. Bring to a simmer and adjust seasonings.

6. Carve the chickens and serve with a portion of the sauce.

RECIPE 17.8

Approximate values per serving:

Calories	977
Total fat	65 g
Saturated fat	24 g
Cholesterol	283 mg
Sodium	1041 mg
Total carbohydrates	27 g
Protein	65 g

Conclusion

The renowned French gastronome and author Jean-Anthelme Brillat-Savarin (1755–1826) once observed that "poultry is for the cook what canvas is for the painter." He meant, of course, that poultry, including chicken, duck, goose, guinea, pigeon and turkey, are wonderfully versatile foods that can be cooked by almost any method and with almost any seasonings, and can be served with many accompaniments and garnishes.

Questions for Discussion

1. List the nine categories or kinds of poultry recognized by Agriculture Canada. How are these categories then divided into classes?

2. How should fresh poultry be stored? Discuss several procedures that should be followed carefully when working with poultry to prevent cross-contamination.

3. What is a suprême? Describe the step-by-step procedure for preparing a chicken suprême.

4. What is trussing? Why is this technique used with poultry?

5. Which poultry items are best suited for broiling or grilling? Explain your answer.

6. Describe the characteristics of properly roasted poultry. Which classes of poultry are recommended for roasting?

7. What is foie gras? Why must you be extremely careful when cooking foie gras?

Additional Poultry Recipes

Turkey Scallopini with Capers and Lemon

RECIPE 17.9

Turkey Scallopini with Capers and Lemon

Yield: 10 servings
Method: Sautéing

Turkey breast, cut into 3-mm (1/8-in.) scallopini, each 90 g (3 oz.)	20	20
Salt and white pepper	TT	TT
Flour	as needed	as needed
Clarified butter	125 mL	4 fl. oz.
Dry white wine	250 mL	8 fl. oz.
Fresh lemon juice	125 mL	4 fl. oz.
Capers	50 g	5 Tbsp.

1. Gently pound each turkey slice with a meat mallet. Season with salt and pepper and dredge in flour.

2. Sauté the turkey in the clarified butter until golden brown. Remove and hold in a warm place.

3. Deglaze the pan with the wine, then add the lemon juice and capers. Return the turkey to the pan to coat with the sauce and reheat.

4. Serve 2 slices with a portion of the sauce for each serving.

RECIPE 17.9

Approximate values per serving:	
Calories	327
Total fat	13 g
Saturated fat	7.1 g
Cholesterol	118 mg
Sodium	465 mg
Total carbohydrates	5.7 g
Protein	41 g

Chicken and Snow Peas in Black Bean Sauce

RECIPE 17.10

Approximate values per serving:

Calories	426
Total fat	22 g
Saturated fat	3.8 g
Cholesterol	97 mg
Sodium	688 mg
Total carbohydrates	13 g
Protein	44 g

RECIPE 17.10

Chicken and Snow Peas in Black Bean Sauce

Yield: 8 servings
Method: Stir-frying

Chicken breasts, boneless, skinless	1 kg	2 lb.
Egg white	1	1
Chinese rice wine	175 mL	6 fl. oz.
Cornstarch	15 g	2 Tbsp.
Soy sauce	50 mL	2 fl. oz.
Onions, small	175 g	2
Peanut or canola oil	125 mL	4 fl. oz.
Garlic, minced	15 g	1 Tbsp.
Fresh ginger, minced	10 g	2 tsp.
Fermented black beans, mashed	50 g	3 Tbsp.
Snow peas, fresh	125 g	4 oz.

1. Slice the chicken into thin strips, approximately 4 cm × 0.6 cm (1-1/2 in. × 1/4 in.).
2. Combine the egg white, 60 mL (2 fl. oz.) of the wine and 8 g (1 Tbsp.) of the cornstarch. Add the chicken, coat evenly and refrigerate for 2 hours.
3. For the sauce, mix the soy sauce and the remaining wine and cornstarch.
4. Quarter the onions and separate the layers.
5. In a wok, stir-fry the chicken in 90 mL (3 fl. oz.) of oil. Remove and set aside.
6. If necessary, add all of the remaining oil and stir-fry the garlic and ginger for 10 seconds. Add the onions and mashed beans and stir-fry for 30 seconds. Add the snow peas and cook for 1 minute.
7. Return the chicken to the wok, add the sauce mixture and stir-fry until hot and the sauce has thickened.
8. Serve immediately with short-grain white rice.

VARIATION: Add 60 g (2 oz.) sliced mushrooms and reduce the amount of snow peas by half or substitute broccoli.

Chicken Yakitori

RECIPE 17.11

Chicken Yakitori

Yield: 8 servings
Method: Grilling

Soy sauce	250 mL	8 fl. oz.
Mirin	250 mL	8 fl. oz.
Granulated sugar	25 g	1 oz.
Ginger, grated	10 g	2 tsp.
Garlic, chopped	15 g	3 cloves
Chicken breasts, boneless	1 kg	2 lb.
Cornstarch	10 g	1 Tbsp.
Green onions, sliced	50 g	2
Sesame seeds	15 g	1 Tbsp.

continued

1. Combine the soy sauce, mirin, sugar, ginger and garlic. Reserve 250 mL (8 fl. oz.) of the mixture. Marinate chicken for 30 minutes.

2. Grill chicken over hot charcoal until done. Brush the chicken with soy sauce mixture, basting regularly.

3. To make the sauce, combine 60 mL (2 fl. oz.) of the soy sauce mixture with the cornstarch. Bring the remainder of the mixture to a boil in a small saucepan and stir in the cornstarch slurry. Stirring constantly, continue boiling until the sauce thickens. Simmer 1 minute. Add green onions.

4. Serve with short-grain white rice and garnish with sesame seeds.

RECIPE 17.11

Approximate values per serving:

Calories	293
Total fat	13 g
Saturated fat	3.5 g
Cholesterol	80 mg
Sodium	1678 mg
Total carbohydrates	14 g
Protein	30 g

RECIPE 17.12

Chicken Cacciatore

Yield: 8 2-piece servings
Method: Braising

Frying chickens, each 1.1–1.4 kg (2 lb. 8 oz.–3 lb.)	2	2
Flour	60 g	2 oz.
Salt and pepper	TT	TT
Olive oil	60 mL	2 fl. oz.
Onion, macedoine	125 g	4 oz.
Garlic cloves, minced	15 g	3
Mushrooms, sliced	250 g	8 oz.
Dried thyme	0.25 g	1/4 tsp.
White wine	50 mL	2 fl. oz.
Brandy	30 mL	1 fl. oz.
Demi-glace, veal or chicken	450 mL	16 fl. oz.
Tomato concassée	350 g	12 oz.

1. Cut each chicken into 8 pieces and dredge in flour seasoned with salt and pepper.

2. Heat the oil in a heavy brazier and brown the chicken well. Remove the chicken from the pan. Degrease the pan, leaving 15 mL (1 Tbsp.) of fat.

3. Add the onion and garlic and sauté lightly. Add the mushrooms and thyme and continue sautéing until the mushrooms are tender.

4. Deglaze the pan with the white wine and brandy. Add the demi-glace and tomato.

5. Return the chicken to the pan and season with salt and pepper. Cover and cook until the chicken is done, approximately 30 minutes.

6. Serve 2 pieces of chicken with a portion of sauce.

RECIPE 17.12

Approximate values per serving:

Calories	446
Total fat	30 g
Saturated fat	8.4 g
Cholesterol	98 mg
Sodium	642 mg
Total carbohydrates	19 g
Protein	25 g

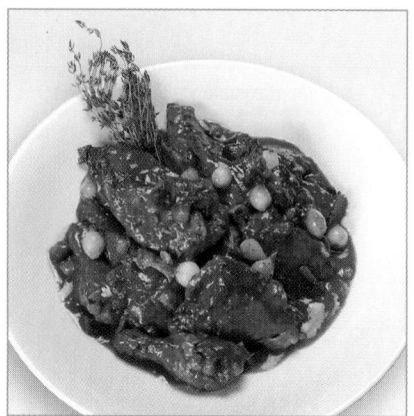

Coq au Vin

Coq au Vin

Yield: 8 2-piece servings
Method: Braising

Chickens, each 1–1.4 kg (2–3 lb.)	2	2
Flour for dredging	as needed	as needed
Salt and pepper	TT	TT
Clarified butter	60 mL	2 fl. oz.
Brandy	125 mL	4 fl. oz.
Bouquet garni:		
Carrot stick, 10 cm (4 in.)	1	1
Leek, split, 10-cm (4-in.) piece	1	1
Fresh thyme	1 sprig	1 sprig
Bay leaf	1	1
Garlic cloves, peeled and crushed	25 g	6
Red wine	750 mL	26 fl. oz.
Chicken stock	250 mL	8 fl. oz.
Bacon lardons, double smoked	125 g	4 oz.
Pearl onions, peeled	16	16
Mushroom caps, medium, quartered	10	10
Beurre manié	as needed	as needed
Large triangular croutons	8	8

1. Cut each chicken into 8 pieces and dredge in flour seasoned with salt and pepper.
2. Heat the clarified butter in a braising pan; brown the chicken.
3. Add the brandy and ignite. When the flame dies, add the bouquet garni, garlic, red wine and chicken stock. Bring to a boil, then reduce to a simmer.
4. Cover the pan and simmer until the chicken is tender, approximately 40 minutes.
5. In a separate pan, sauté the bacon until the fat begins to render. Add the onions and sauté until they begin to brown. Cook the bacon and onions covered, over low heat, until the onions are tender. Add the mushroom caps and cook them until tender.
6. Remove the chicken from the pan and adjust the sauce's consistency with the beurre manié. Strain the sauce through a conical strainer and adjust the seasonings.
7. Spoon the bacon, onions and mushrooms onto a serving platter, place the chicken over them and ladle the sauce over the finished dish. Serve with triangular croutons.

RECIPE 17.13

Approximate values per serving:	
Calories	568
Total fat	40 g
Saturated fat	17 g
Cholesterol	128 mg
Sodium	830 mg
Total carbohydrates	26 g
Protein	26 g

Chicken Curry

Yield: 4 servings
Method: Stir-frying

Masala:		
Onion, brunoise	250 g	8 oz.
Garlic, finely chopped	10 g	2 tsp.
Ghee (or clarified butter)	30 mL	2 Tbsp.
Fresh ginger, grated	60 g	2 oz.
Turmeric	5 g	1-1/2 tsp.

continued

Coriander seeds, ground	3 g	1-1/2 tsp.
Cumin seeds, ground	2 g	1 tsp.
Cayenne pepper	2 g	1 tsp.
Fenugreek, ground	2 g	1/2 tsp.
Coconut milk	575 mL	20 fl. oz.
Roasting chicken, 1.3 kg (3 lb.), cut into 8 pieces	1	1
Salt	5 g	1 tsp.
Jalapeño, split and seeded	1	1
Lemon juice	30 mL	1 fl. oz.

1. Fry the onion and garlic in the ghee until the onions are pale golden and the oil "returns" to the pan.

2. To make the wet masala, mix the ginger, turmeric, coriander, cumin, cayenne pepper and fenugreek; add just enough of the coconut milk to form a paste.

3. Add the wet masala to the onion and garlic and fry for 8 minutes, or until the mixture is fragrant.

4. Add the chicken pieces and cook, turning them frequently, for 6–8 minutes.

5. Add the remaining coconut milk, salt and jalapeño. Bring to a boil, cover and reduce to a simmer. Cook until the chicken is done, approximately 45 minutes.

6. Just before service, stir in the lemon juice and adjust the seasonings. Serve with rice and a chutney or sambals.

Chicken Curry

RECIPE 17.14

Approximate values per serving:	
Calories	706
Total fat	58 g
Saturated fat	36 g
Cholesterol	123 mg
Sodium	608 mg
Total carbohydrates	15 g
Protein	31 g

RECIPE 17.15

Roast Cornish Chickens with Wild Rice Stuffing

Yield: 10 servings
Method: Roasting

Onion, fine dice	100 g	3 oz.
Mushrooms, sliced	175 g	6 oz.
Whole butter, melted	175 g	6 oz.
Cooked wild rice	350 g	1-1/2 cups
Dried thyme, crushed	0.5 g	1/2 tsp.
Dried marjoram, crushed	0.5 g	1/2 tsp.
Salt and pepper	TT	TT
Cornish chickens, boned	5	5

1. Sauté the onion and mushrooms in 60 g (2 oz.) of melted butter until tender. Cool.

2. Stir in the rice and herbs and season to taste with salt and pepper.

3. Stuff the cavity of each hen loosely with the rice mixture. Shape the hen, secure with a strip of buttered parchment and place in a roasting pan.

4. Brush the hens with the remaining butter and season with salt and pepper. Roast at 200°C (400°F) for 15 minutes.

5. Reduce the oven temperature to 150°C (300°F) and roast until the juices run clear, approximately 30 minutes. Baste 2–3 times with melted butter.

6. Serve the hens with a pan gravy or a sauce made separately, such as mushroom sauce.

VARIATION: A mixture of white and wild rice also works well. If Cornish game hens are available, use a bird per serving.

RECIPE 17.15

Approximate values per serving:	
Calories	504
Total fat	38 g
Saturated fat	15 g
Cholesterol	214 mg
Sodium	443 mg
Total carbohydrates	9.2 g
Protein	31 g

Shawn Whalen, CCC, CEC
At age 25, Shawn became the youngest chef in Canada to achieve the Certified Chef de Cuisine designation. He has captained seven international culinary teams and has won numerous awards, including the Grand Gold Best of Show Award at the 126th Annual Salon of Culinary Arts of New York City. Shawn was an Executive Chef for 19 years, including 12 years with Marriott. Along with two partners, he is currently Owner and Culinary Director of Liaison College, Toronto West.

RECIPE 17.16

Duck Breast—
Approximate values per serving:

Calories	133
Total fat	2.5 g
Saturated fat	0.6 g
Cholesterol	136 mg
Sodium	197 mg
Total carbohydrates	0 g
Protein	26 g

Duck Leg Confit—
Approximate values per serving:

Calories	200
Total fat	11 g
Saturated fat	3 g
Cholesterol	105 mg
Sodium	101 mg
Total carbohydrates	0 g
Protein	25 g

RECIPE 17.16

Muscovy Duck Breast and Confit Leg à l'Orange

LIAISON COLLEGE, TORONTO WEST, TORONTO, ON
Director and Executive Chef Shawn Whalen, CCC, CEC

Yield: 2 servings
Method: Roasting and Pan-frying

Muscovy duck single breast, boned, trimmed	2	2
Shallot, peeled and minced	25 g	1 oz.
Garlic, peeled and minced	5 g	1 clove
Black peppercorn, whole, toasted	10 g	1 Tbsp.
Coriander seeds, whole, toasted	5 g	1 Tbsp.
Juniper berries, whole, toasted	5 g	1 Tbsp.
Lemon zest, pith removed, julienne	10 g	2 Tbsp.
Orange zest, pith removed, julienne	10 g	2 Tbsp.
Kosher salt	TT	TT
Black pepper, ground	TT	TT
Fleur de sel	pinch	pinch
Grand Marnier	30 mL	1 fl. oz.
à l'Orange Sauce (recipe follows)		
Orange fillets	6–8	6–8
Duck Leg Confit (recipe follows)		

1. Coat the duck breast with shallots, garlic, peppercorn, coriander, juniper berries and lemon and orange zest. Marinate for 24 hours.
2. To cook the duck breast, clean the marinade off the breast, rinse lightly and pat dry with a paper towel.
3. With a knife, lightly score the skin on the breast in a cross/diamond pattern. This will allow heat to penetrate and render down the fat.
4. Season the duck breast with kosher salt and pepper, then place into a cold pan over low heat. This will allow the fat between the skin and the flesh to render down.
5. As the fat renders down, slowly increase the heat to brown and crisp the skin.
6. Once the skin is crisp, turn the duck breast over and quickly sear the bottom.
7. Place the duck breast on a wire rack in the oven and roast slowly at 122°C (250°F) until the breast reaches an internal temperature of 61°C (142°F), or medium doneness.
8. Remove the breast and let rest for 10 minutes, then slice thinly against the natural grain of the meat.
9. Garnish with fleur de sel.
10. At service time, deglaze the pan used to roast the duck breast with the Grand Marnier, add à l'Orange Sauce and garnish with orange fillets. Serve sauce over the Duck Leg Confit topped with sliced duck breast.

Duck Leg Confit

Kosher salt	15 g	4 tsp.
Fresh bay leaf	1/2	1/2
Thyme, chopped	2 g	1 tsp.
Italian parsley	10 g	1 Tbsp.
Black peppercorns	1 g	1/2 tsp.
Duck legs, bone-in	2	2
Duck fat	750 mL	26 fl. oz.

1. Blend salt, bay leaf, thyme, parsley and peppercorns in a coffee grinder or food processor until coarsely ground.

continued

2. Coat the duck legs with the cure and refrigerate for 24 hours.

3. Rinse the legs under cold running water and dry thoroughly.

4. Heat the duck fat until it just liquefies.

5. In a sauce pot or small pan, cover the duck legs with the duck fat so that they are completely immersed.

6. Cook in an oven at 85°C–90°C (180°F–190°F) for approximately 6–8 hours or until legs are very fork tender.

7. Let the duck legs cool in the fat to preserve.

8. To cook the confit duck legs, remove from duck fat, season with salt and pepper and pan-sear until the skin is crisp and well browned. Finish in a 165°C (350°F) oven until hot.

à l'Orange Sauce

Sugar	90 g	3-1/2 oz.
Sherry vinegar	30 mL	1 fl. oz.
Orange juice	90 mL	3-1/2 fl. oz.
Veal stock reduction or duck glace	250 mL	9 fl. oz.
Salt	TT	TT
Pepper	TT	TT

1. Heat the sugar, sherry vinegar and orange juice in a nonreactive pot. Reduce until thick.

2. Add the duck glace and reduce to desired consistency.

3. Season the sauce.

à l'Orange Sauce—Approximate values per serving:	
Calories	236
Total fat	0 g
Saturated fat	0 g
Cholesterol	0 mg
Sodium	253 mg
Total carbohydrates	57 g
Protein	3 g

Sauce Bigarade

Roast duckling can be served with a bigarade sauce made from veal jus lié reduced with orange and lemon juice. Drain excess fat from the roasting pan, deglaze with fruit juices, add jus and simmer. Strain and garnish with blanched citrus zest.

RECIPE 17.17

Baked Chicken in a Sea-Salt Crust

CULINARY INSTITUTE OF CANADA, CHARLOTTETOWN, PEI
Chef Instructor Joerg Soltermann

Yield: 4 to 6 servings
Method: Baking

Roasting chicken, whole	1.5–2 kg	3-1/2 to 4-1/2 lb.
Rosemary sprig	1	1
Black peppercorn, crushed	3 g	1 tsp.
Butter	50 g	2 oz.
Garlic, crushed	10 g	2 cloves
Rosemary sprigs, chopped	2	2
Coarse sea salt, brown variety	3 kg	7 lb.

1. Place the rosemary, pepper and butter in the chicken's washed cavity. Truss the chicken with butcher's twine.

2. Rub the skin with crushed garlic.

3. Mix the chopped rosemary with the sea salt.

4. Line an ovenproof dish (just slightly larger than the chicken) with foil. The foil must overhang the dish generously.

5. Place a 1-cm (1/4-in.) layer of salt on the bottom of the foil-lined dish.

6. Place the chicken, breast side up, on the salt. Encase the whole chicken in the remaining salt and wrap with the foil.

7. Bake in a 200°C (425°F) oven for 1 hour and 45 minutes.

8. To serve, remove the foil and place the salt-encrusted chicken on a platter garnished with fresh herbs and roasted garlic. Crack open the salt crust in front of the guests and portion the chicken.

Joerg Soltermann
Joerg received his culinary training in his native Switzerland. His first taste of Canada came during a summer season at the Jasper Park Lodge. He has since cooked at restaurants such as Canadian Pacific's Hotel Newfoundland, St. John's, and its Prince Edward Hotel, Charlottetown. Joerg's skills have earned him numerous awards, including Chef of the Year 1990 (Newfoundland and Labrador) and Chef of the Year 2000 (PEI). Joerg is now Chef Instructor at the Culinary Institute of Canada.

RECIPE 17.17

Approximate values per serving:	
Calories	363
Total fat	17 g
Saturated fat	8 g
Cholesterol	189 mg
Sodium	855 mg
Total carbohydrates	1 g
Protein	48 g

Colin Maxwell, CCC

Currently an Instructor at SAIT, Colin had much of his training in England. He came to Canada in 1979 and quickly became the Executive Sous Chef at the Chateau Airport Hotel, where he helped run the Flight Kitchen. He was a member of Team Calgary in the 1987 World Culinary Arts Show in Vancouver and sat on the Red Seal Exam Revision Committee in 1998.

RECIPE 17.18

Approximate values per serving, not including fennel sauce:	
Calories	341
Total fat	20 g
Saturated fat	6.1 g
Cholesterol	108 mg
Sodium	565 mg
Total carbohydrates	5.3 g
Protein	35 g

Fennel Tomato Basil Cream Sauce—Approximate values per 85 mL serving:	
Calories	213
Total fat	19 g
Saturated fat	12 g
Cholesterol	67 mg
Sodium	232 mg
Total carbohydrates	8.7 g
Protein	1.8 g

RECIPE 17.18

Chicken Breast Stuffed with Smoked Scallops, Fennel Tomato Basil Cream Sauce

SAIT POLYTECHNIC, CALGARY, AB
Chef Instructor Colin Maxwell, CCC

Yield: 4 servings
Method: Smoking and Pan-roasting

Wood chips		
Scallops	250 g	8
Salt and black pepper	TT	TT
Lemon juice	30 mL	1 fl. oz.
Chicken breasts, frenched, skin on, each 175 g (6 oz.)	4	4
Flour	as needed	as needed
Vegetable oil	30 mL	1 fl. oz.
Butter	30 g	1 oz.
Fennel Tomato Basil Cream Sauce (recipe follows)		

1. Place wood chips in a pan, cover with foil poked with holes and place on a heat source.
2. Season scallops with salt, pepper and lemon juice on a perforated tray and place above the smoke from the wood chips. Lightly smoke each side for about 5 minutes.
3. Trim the chicken breasts neatly and cut a deep pocket in the thick end by the bone.
4. Once the scallops are cooled, insert 2 scallops into the pocket in each chicken breast.
5. Season the chicken with salt and pepper and lightly dust with flour. Sear the chicken in a pan with oil and butter. Finish cooking the breasts in a 150°C (300°F) oven to an internal temperature of 77°C (140°F).
6. When the chicken is finished, squeeze some lemon juice on it, cut on the bias to reveal the scallops inside and serve with Fennel Tomato Basil Cream Sauce.

Fennel Tomato Basil Cream Sauce

Fennel, thin slices, roughly chopped	350 g	2 bulbs
Shallots, diced	15 g	4 tsp.
Garlic, diced	10 g	2 tsp.
Butter	50 g	2 oz.
Vermouth	200 mL	7 fl. oz.
Roma tomatoes, peeled, seeded, chopped	250 g	8 oz.
Pernod	60 mL	2 fl. oz.
Cream, 35%	500 mL	16 fl. oz.
Salt and white pepper	TT	TT
Worcestershire sauce	TT	TT
Tabasco sauce	TT	TT
Lemon juice	1 lemon	1 lemon
Basil, shredded	100 g	1 cup

continued

1. In a braising pot, sweat the fennel, shallots and garlic in butter.

2. Add the vermouth and reduce a small amount.

3. Add the tomatoes and blend the sauce until desired smoothness.

4. Add the Pernod and cream and reduce to desired consistency.

5. Season with salt, white pepper, Worcestershire sauce, Tabasco sauce and lemon juice.

6. Add the basil.

RECIPE 17.19

Fried Frog Legs in Fines Herbes Butter

HERBSAINT BAR AND RESTAURANT, NEW ORLEANS, LA
Chef Donald Link

Yield: 24 legs (4 servings)
Method: Deep-frying

Fried Frog Legs in Fines Herbes Butter

Fines herbes butter:		
Butter, soft	250 g	8 oz.
Italian parsley, chopped	10 g	1 Tbsp.
Tarragon, fresh, chopped	3 g	1 tsp.
Chervil, fresh, chopped	3 g	1 tsp.
Chives, sliced finely	3 g	1-1/2 tsp.
Garlic, minced	3 g	1/2 tsp.
Cayenne pepper	2 g	1/2 tsp.
Frog leg pairs, split	12	12
Salt and pepper	TT	TT
Flour	450 g	1 lb.
Buttermilk	250 mL	8 fl. oz.

1. Combine all ingredients for the fines herbes butter and mix well. Refrigerate.

2. Dry the frog legs with paper towelling and season them with salt and pepper. Dredge the frog legs in flour, dip into buttermilk and dredge in flour again.

3. Deep-fry the frog legs until golden brown and cooked through, approximately 5–7 minutes. Drain, place in a stainless steel bowl and coat generously with the fines herbes butter.

4. Arrange the frog legs on plates, garnish and serve hot.

RECIPE 17.19

Approximate values per serving:	
Calories	963
Total fat	53 g
Saturated fat	32 g
Cholesterol	210 mg
Sodium	839 mg
Total carbohydrates	91 g
Protein	31 g

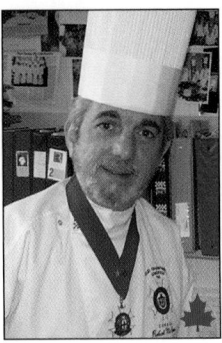

Robert McCann, CCC

Robert is a fellow of the Epicurean World Master Chefs Society and vice-chair of the Canadian chapter. In addition to instructing at Humber College, he judges international competitions.

RECIPE 17.20

Approximate values per serving:	
Calories	318
Total fat	14 g
Saturated fat	4 g
Cholesterol	100 mg
Sodium	570 mg
Total carbohydrates	18 g
Protein	30 g

RECIPE 17.20

Ostrich Steak Mandela

HRT ALLIANCE, HUMBER COLLEGE, Toronto, ON
Chef Instructor Robert McCann, CCC

Yield: 4 servings
Method: Pan-frying

Sunflower oil	30 mL	1 fl. oz.
Ostrich, sliced into thin steaks	500 g	1 lb.
Onion, fine chopped	125 g	4 oz.
Fennel, fine chopped	125 g	4 oz.
Full-bodied red wine	300 mL	10 fl. oz.
Brown game stock	300 mL	10 fl. oz.
Tomato purée	5 mL	1 tsp.
Lovage (to flavour stock and for garnish)	8 leaves	8 leaves
Brown roux (to thicken sauce)	30 g	1 oz.
Ground mace	pinch	pinch
Ground cinnamon	pinch	pinch
Mushrooms, turned	4	4
Mushroom stalks, diced	10 g	1 Tbsp.
Salt and pepper	TT	TT
Cherries, pitted	8	8
Chives, with buds on	4 strands	4 strands
Button onions, cooked	8	8

1. In a fry pan, heat oil and fry meat for 4 minutes until brown. Remove.
2. Add onion and fennel and fry for 4 minutes.
3. Discard surplus oil and add wine, stock, tomato purée and 4 lovage leaves.
4. Simmer for 8 minutes and thicken with roux, then boil for 4 minutes and strain.
5. Return strained liquid to a boil and add spices, turned mushrooms and diced mushrooms and season.
6. Return meat to sauce and serve.
7. Use the cherries, lovage, chives and button onions to garnish the plate.

"One can never know too much; the more one learns, the more one sees the need to learn more and that study as well as broadening the mind of the craftsman provides an easy way of perfecting yourself in the practice of your art.

—Auguste Escoffier, French chef (1846–1935)

**After studying this chapter
you will be able to:**

- identify a variety of game
- explain how to disjoint a rabbit
- explain game inspection practices
- purchase game appropriate for your needs
- store game properly
- prepare game for cooking
- apply various cooking methods to game

These interactive online tools will help you master the skills in this chapter:

- Chapter Quizzes
- Activities

The Daring Diner

Although venison, boar and pheasant may seem unusual to many people, even rarer meats are available to the daring diner. Zebra, bear, wildebeest and other "big game" animals are sometimes available through exotic game purveyors based in major metropolitan areas. Most often the meat is grilled, roasted or stewed.

Reptiles, particularly rattlesnake, crocodile and alligator, are now also being raised on farms to meet increased demand. Reptiles may be braised, or sliced and deep-fat fried. They have a mild flavour with a texture similar to lobster.

Bison Steak

Game (Fr. *gibier*) are animals hunted for sport or food.

Traditionally, game supplies depended upon the season and the hunter's success. But game's increasing popularity in food service operations has led to farm-raising techniques. As a result, pheasant, quail, deer, rabbit and other animals, although still considered game, are now ranch-raised and commercially available throughout the year.

The life of game creatures is reflected in their flesh's appearance, aroma, flavour and texture. Generally, game flesh has a dark colour and a strong but not unpleasant aroma. It has a robust flavour, less fat than other meats or poultry and is more compact, becoming quite tough in older animals.

Selecting the best cooking methods for game depends on the animal's age and the particular cut of flesh. Younger animals will, of course, be more tender than older ones. Flesh from the loin or less-used muscles will also be tender and therefore can be prepared with dry-heat cooking methods. Flesh from much-used muscles, such as the leg and shoulder, will be tougher and should be prepared with combination cooking methods. Less-tender cuts can also be used in sausages, pâtés and forcemeats, as discussed in Chapter 20, Charcuterie.

IDENTIFYING GAME

Canada has an abundance of wild game both large and small, as well as feathered. Truly wild game is not permitted for sale to the public; however, hunters may share their kill with friends. Private clubs are allowed to prepare and serve game to hunters and their parties. Strict sanitation practices are necessary to avoid cross-contamination. Game served by restaurants is farm-raised, therefore subject to health inspection and processing in approved facilities.

Big game and ground game hunted in Canada include deer, elk, bison, moose, reindeer, caribou, musk ox, bear, big horn sheep, goat and rabbit. Herd management in the Arctic and Newfoundland provides the only true wild game available. Farming provides deer, elk, bison, wild boar and rabbit. Reptile meat such as alligator and snake is farm-raised and imported, and there is a domestic market in ostrich and emu. Table 18.1 suggests some uses for game meat.

Bison

Once found in huge herds roaming the plains, bison were hunted into near extinction during the 19th century. Bison now live on reservations or ranches, where they are raised like beef cattle. Wood Buffalo National Park on the Alberta–Nunavut border is home to the largest herd of free-roaming bison.

TABLE 18.1	Using Furred Game		
Animal	**Commonly Purchased Cuts**	**Cooking Methods**	**Suggested Use**
Bison	Purchased and prepared in the same manner as lean beef		
Deer	Loin	Dry heat (roast; sauté; grill)	Sautéed medallions; whole roast loin; grilled steaks
	Leg	Combination (braise; stew)	Marinate and braise; pot roast with cranberries; chili; sausage; forcemeat
	Rack	Dry heat (roast; grill)	Grilled chops
Rabbit	Full carcass	Dry heat (sauté; pan-fry; roast; grill) Combination (braise; stew)	Pan-fried rabbit with cream gravy Braised rabbit with mushrooms
Wild Boar	Loin Chops	Dry heat (roast) Combination (braise)	Roast loin with mustard crust Marinate and braise; stew with red wine and sour cream; sausage; forcemeat

Bison meat is juicy and flavourful and may be prepared in the same manner as lean beef.

Deer

The deer family includes elk, moose, reindeer, red-tailed deer, white-tailed deer (Fr. *chevreuil*) and mule deer. Meat from any of these animals is known as **venison** (Fr. *venaisan*). Farm-raised venison, particularly from the Scottish red deer bred in New Zealand, Canada and the United States, is commercially available all year. Venison is typically dark red with a mild aroma. It is leaner than other meats, having almost no intramuscular fat or marbling.

The most popular commercial venison cuts are the loin, leg and rack. The loin is tender enough to roast, sauté or grill to medium rare. It can be left attached along the backbone to form a cut known as the saddle. The leg is often marinated in red wine and prepared with combination cooking methods. Other cuts can also be stewed or braised or used in sausages and pâtés. Butchering procedures for venison are similar to those for lamb discussed in Chapter 15.

Venison Saddle

Rabbit

Rabbits (Fr. *lapin*) are small burrowing animals that have long been raised for food. Rabbit has mild, lean and relatively tender flesh. Its taste and texture are similar to chicken. Ranch-raised rabbit is available all year, either whole or cut, fresh or frozen. The average weight of a whole dressed rabbit is 1.2 to 1.4 kg (2 lb. 8 oz. to 3 lb.). Young rabbit can be roasted, pan-fried, stewed or braised and is popular in rustic "country-style" dishes, especially casseroles and pâtés.

● **venison** flesh from any member of the deer family, including antelope, elk, moose, reindeer, red-tailed deer, white-tailed deer, mule deer and axis deer

BASIC PROCEDURE FOR DISJOINTING A RABBIT

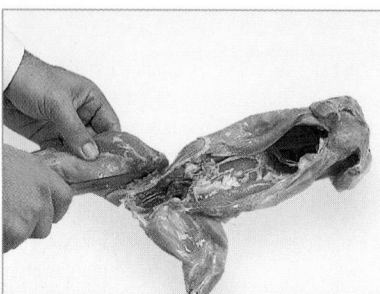

1. Place the rabbit on its back. Remove the hind legs by cutting close to the backbone and through the joint on each side. Each thigh and leg can be separated by cutting through the joint.

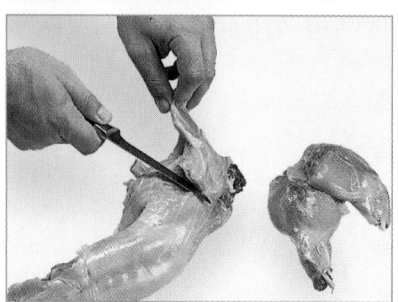

2. Remove the forelegs by cutting beneath the shoulder blades.

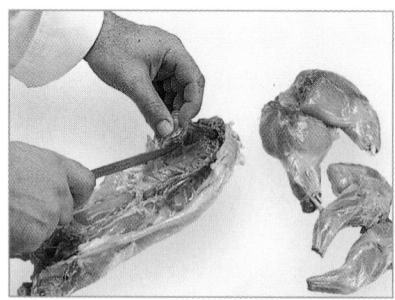

3. Cut through the breast bone and spread open the rib cage. Using a boning knife, separate the flesh from the rib bones and remove the bones.

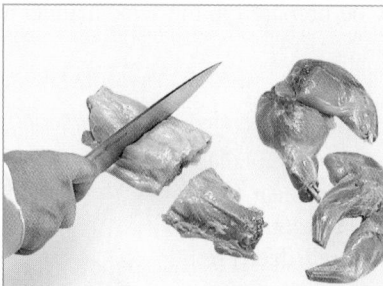

4. Cut through the backbone to divide the loin into the desired number of pieces.

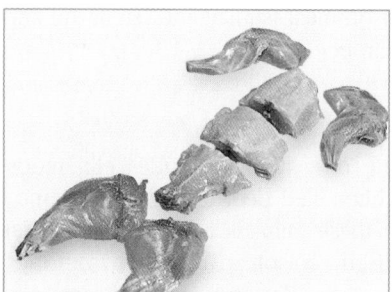

5. The cut-up rabbit: hind legs, thighs, loin in three pieces, forelegs.

Boar Saddle

Wild Boar

A close relative of the domesticated hog, wild boar (Fr. *sanglier*) is leaner, with a stronger flavour. Though plentiful in Europe and parts of America, wild boar is available only during autumn. A limited supply of farm-raised boar is available all year, however.

Baby boar (under six months old) is considered a delicacy, but mature animals (one to two years old) have the best flavour. The meat is most often roasted and may be used in sausages or terrines. Boar can often be substituted in recipes for venison or pork.

Upland Game Birds/Waterfowl

Feathered game includes upland birds such as wild turkeys, pheasants, quails, doves and woodcocks; songbirds such as larks; and waterfowl such as wild geese and ducks. Wild birds cannot be sold in Canada but may be prepared in some private clubs. An ever-increasing number of these birds, such as Muscovy duck, are being farm-raised to meet increased consumer demand, however.

Game birds are available whole or precut into pieces, fresh or frozen. Butchering techniques will not be shown in this chapter, as they are the same as those for domesticated poultry discussed in Chapter 17.

Because game birds tend to have less fat than other poultry, they are often barded with fat and cooked to medium rare. If cooked well done, they become dry and stringy.

Partridge

The Hungarian and chukar partridges (Fr. *perdrix*) of Europe were introduced into the United States and Canada during the 19th century. Now found principally in the prairie and western mountain regions, partridges are widely raised on game preserves and farms, producing a good commercial supply.

Their flavour is less delicate than pheasant and the meat tends to be tougher. Partridge may be roasted or cut into pieces and sautéed or braised. Each bird weighs about 450 g (1 lb.) dressed.

Chukar Partridge

Pheasant

The most popular of game birds, the pheasant (Fr. *faisan*) was introduced into Europe from Asia during the Middle Ages. Its mild flavour is excellent for roasting, stewing or braising. The hen is smaller and more tender than the cock. Stock made from the carcass is often used for consommé or sauce.

Farm-raised birds are available fresh or frozen. A dressed bird weighs about 680 g to 1 kg (1 lb. 8 oz. to 2 lb.) and serves two to four people.

Pheasant

Quail

The quail (Fr. *caille*) is a migratory game bird related to the pheasant. The more popular European and Californian species are farm-raised and available all year.

Quail are rather small, with only about 30 to 60 g (1 to 2 oz.) of breast meat each. Quail may be grilled (especially on skewers), roasted, broiled or sautéed and are often boned and served whole with a stuffing of forcemeat or rice. Because they are so lean, roasted quail benefit from barding.

Quail

NUTRITION

Even ranch-raised game animals live in the wild and are generally more active and less well fed than domesticated animals. This lifestyle produces animals whose meat has less fat than that of domesticated animals. Most game is also lower in cholesterol and has approximately one-third fewer calories than beef. Game is also generally high in protein and minerals.

INSPECTION OF GAME

The Canada Food Inspection Agency and most provinces restrict the sale of wild game. Truly wild game may be served only by those who hunt and share their kill or where a special import permit is obtained, again for private consumption. Special care must be taken to avoid cross-contamination.

Domestic Game

For resale of caribou, reindeer and farm- or ranch-raised game, mandatory federal and provincial inspections are conducted for wholesomeness. Generally, however, game is processed under the same federal inspection requirements as domesticated meats and poultry. Unlike meat and poultry from domesticated animals, game is not graded for quality except for bison.

Imported Game

The Canada Food Inspection Agency accepts game only from countries that have an approved inspection system. The plant processing the meat must also be an approved source. Exotic species may be subject to controls related to handling and cooking after they arrive in Canada.

How to Hang Game

The following information may be useful if you find yourself with a need to hang freshly killed game. Most game should be eviscerated (drawn or gutted) as soon as possible, then suspended by either the hind legs or the head in a dry, well-ventilated place. Because the fur or feathers help prevent bacterial contamination, they should be left intact during hanging; game should be skinned or plucked just before butchering.

The length of time necessary for hanging depends on the species and age of the animal. Two days may be sufficient for a rabbit, while up to three weeks may be necessary for a deer or boar. Hanging is generally complete when the first whiff of odour is detected (although traditionalists prefer pheasant to be hung until extremely ripe).

● **hanging** the practice of allowing eviscerated (drawn or gutted) game to age in a dry, well-ventilated place; hanging helps tenderize the flesh and strengthen its flavour

PURCHASING AND STORING GAME
Purchasing Game

Game is most often sold pre-portioned or as subprimals. Furred game meats are available fresh, usually in vacuum-sealed packaging, or frozen. Game birds are available cleaned and boned, fresh or frozen. Use the same criteria to determine the freshness of game as you would for any other meat or poultry: the flesh should be firm, without slime or an off-odour.

Fresh game is sometimes hung before cutting to allow the meat to mature or age. During **hanging**, carbohydrates (glycogen) stored in muscle tissues are converted to lactic acid. This process tenderizes the flesh and strengthens its flavour. But hanging is not necessary, especially if you object to "gamy" flavours. Commercially sold game is generally fully aged and ready to use when delivered. It does not need nor will it benefit from hanging.

Storing Game

As with any fresh or frozen meat, game should be well wrapped and stored under refrigeration at temperatures below 4°C (40°F). Because the flesh is generally dry and lean, frozen game should be used within four months. Thaw frozen game slowly under refrigeration to prevent moisture loss.

MARINATING FURRED GAME

Tradition calls for marinating game, particularly furred game, in strong mixtures of red wine, herbs and spices. Commercially raised game does not necessarily have to be marinated. Modern animal husbandry techniques used at game ranches assure the cook of receiving meat from young, tender animals. Farm-raised game animals also have a naturally milder flavour than their truly wild cousins.

For those preferring the flavours imparted by traditional marinades, the following red-wine marinade is included. After the meat is removed, the marinade may be added to the cooking liquid or reduced and used in a sauce. Do not serve uncooked marinade.

Wild Game—Delicious, Nutritious and Available

Wild game is now widely available for use in restaurants and at home. The best of wild game provides a safe, delicious and nutritious dining experience....

Game meat is available from farmed (domesticated) deer and from free-ranging (ranched) deer and antelope. Most farmed deer are taken to a fixed conventional slaughterhouse where they are slaughtered and processed in the same way as cattle, sheep, and goats. Ranched deer can be properly harvested only by an elaborate procedure which involves taking a mobile slaughter facility and meat inspector to the field where the animals are killed by shooting them with a high powered rifle under the supervision of the meat inspector. The carcass is then processed inside the mobile facility to avoid any contamination of the meat. This field harvesting eliminates any stress which might occur in transport of farmed deer to the slaughterhouse.

Farmed deer tend to be relatively more uniform in size and flavor. Free-ranging deer and antelope produce meat of more complex flavor due to the variety of their diet. The difference is somewhat like the difference in cultivated mushrooms and wild mushrooms, or pen-raised chickens compared with free-range chickens. Meat from free-range animals is more expensive due to higher labor and inspection costs.

Meat from both deer and antelope can be legally labeled "venison." All venison is relatively lean when compared with conventional red meats and requires special attention when cooking to avoid drying out the meat and toughening it. Tender cuts should be cooked as little as possible (rare to medium rare) to retain the maximum amount of moisture. Quick sautéing, grilling or roasting to retain a medium rare center is most satisfactory for tender cuts such as the loin, tenderloin, and leg.

Braising is the most effective method for cooking the less tender cuts such as the shoulder, ribs and shanks. Beef broth or red wine are good liquids for braising. The toughest cut of meat will be very satisfactorily tenderized if braised for a sufficient period of time (which may be as long as two or three hours). When properly cooked, these cuts can surpass the more tender cuts in flavor.

Mike Hughes, Broken Arrow Ranch,
Ingram, Texas (abridged)

APPLYING THE BASICS   **RECIPE 18.1**

Red-Wine Game Marinade

Yield: 1.5 L (1-1/2 qt.)

Carrot, chopped fine	75 g	2 oz.
Onion, chopped fine	75 g	2 oz.
Garlic, minced	15 g	1 Tbsp.
Dried thyme	0.25 g	1 tsp.
Bay leaves	2	2
Juniper berries, whole	5 g	2 tsp.
Peppercorns, whole	10 g	1 Tbsp.
Sage, ground	0.25 g	1/2 tsp.
Red wine	1 L	1 qt.
Red wine vinegar	125 mL	4 fl. oz.

1. Combine all ingredients in a noncorrosive container.

2. Place the meat in the marinade and marinate for the desired time. Tender, farm-raised game may need only 30 minutes; older, wild animals may need 1–2 days.

Conclusion

Game is becoming increasingly popular because of consumer desires for leaner, more healthful meats. Only inspected, farm-raised game can be used in food service operations. Luckily, many popular game items are now farm-raised, government-inspected and readily available. Generally, game flesh has a dark colour, a strong but not unpleasant aroma and a robust flavour. You should butcher, prepare and cook game according to the comparable guidelines for other meats and poultry.

Questions for Discussion

1. Explain the differences between truly wild game and ranch-raised game.
2. What is hanging? Is it necessary for modern food service operations to hang game?
3. Which cuts of furred game are best suited to dry-heat cooking methods? Which are best for combination cooking methods?
4. Can game birds be purchased whole? How are they fabricated?
5. What degree of doneness is best suited for game birds? Explain your answer.

Additional Game Recipes

Photo by George Webber

Fred Malley, CCC, B.Ed.

Fred's career includes being an educator, chef, food and beverage manager, caterer and food stylist. He currently instructs aspiring culinarians at SAIT, mentors for professional designation, and is actively involved in curriculum development. His food styling appears internationally for major corporations, and he has ventured into research and development for food companies.

RECIPE 18.2

Bison Chili

CARMEN CREEK™ GOURMET MEATS
Wild Rose Bison, CALGARY, AB

Chef Fred Malley, CCC, B.Ed.

Yield: 10 servings
Method: Stewing

Pasilla chiles	6	6
Jalepeño peppers, seeded	2	2
Bison or beef broth	450 mL	16 fl. oz.
Taco shells, broken	2 large	2 large
Canola oil	75 mL	2-1/2 fl. oz.
Bison, small cubes	1.125 kg	2-1/2 lbs.
Canola oil	30 mL	1 fl. oz.
Onions, brunoise	500 g	1 lb. 3 oz.
Garlic, minced	30 g	6 cloves
Cumin, ground	20 g	8 tsp.
Coriander, ground	2 g	1-1/4 tsp.
Cinnamon, ground	0.5 g	pinch
Tomato concassée	450 g	1 lb.
Bison broth	1 L	1 qt.
Guinness™ beer	1 tin	1 tin
Salt	5 g	1 tsp.
Black pepper, ground	1 g	1/4 tsp.
Lime juice, fresh	50 mL	2 fl. oz.
Cilantro, chopped (optional)	15 g	1-1/2 Tbsp.

Garnish: diced red onion, sliced
  black olives, avocado,
  grated Monterey Jack cheese

1. Toast the pasilla chiles over an open flame and remove stem and seeds.
2. Place the peppers and 450 mL (16 fl. oz.) bison broth in a saucepan and simmer for 10 minutes. Cool and place in food processor.
3. Add broken taco shells and purée mixture. Reserve.
4. Heat 75 mL (2-1/2 fl. oz.) of oil in a large sauté pan until smoking and add bison. Sear until the meat browns and reserve the meat.
5. In the same pan, add the remaining 30 mL (1 fl. oz.) of canola oil and the onions. Fry until golden, add the garlic and fry 1 minute more.

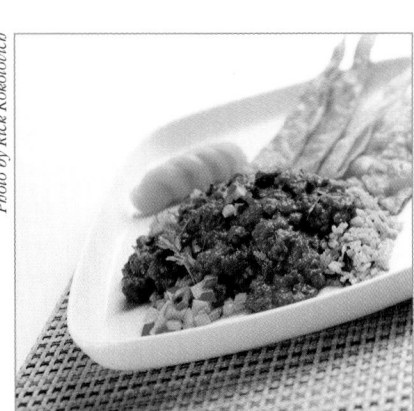

Photo by Rick Kokotovich

Bison Chili

continued

6. Add the cumin, coriander and cinnamon and fry 1 minute more.

7. Add the tomato concassée and puréed pepper mixture and continue frying and stirring until the mixture starts to brown. Do not scorch.

8. Return the bison to the pan with the remaining 1 L (1 qt.) bison broth and Guinness. Add salt and pepper and simmer for 45 minutes to 1 hour until chili thickens.

9. Finish with lime juice and cilantro at service time. This dish is excellent reheated. Garnish with diced red onion, sliced black olives, avocado and grated Monterey Jack cheese.

RECIPE 18.2

Approximate values per serving:

Calories	342
Total fat	17 g
Saturated fat	2 g
Cholesterol	70 mg
Sodium	358 mg
Total carbohydrates	17 g
Protein	28 g

RECIPE 18.3

Roasted Pheasant with Prairie Baby Lettuce Leaves, Walnut Oil and Balsamic Vinaigrette

ST. CHARLES COUNTRY CLUB, WINNIPEG, MB
Executive Chef Tony Murakami, CMC, CM

Yield: 10 servings
Method: Roasting

Whole pheasant, each 1.2–1.5 kg (2-1/2 to 3-1/2 lb.)	3	3
Butter, unsalted, room temperature	375 g	14 oz.
Salt and pepper	TT	TT
White wine, dry	350 mL	12 fl. oz.
Mirepoix	400 g	3-1/2 cups
Juniper berries	10 g	1 Tbsp.
Mignonette (coarsely ground black pepper)	3 g	1 tsp.
Pheasant or chicken stock	350 mL	12 fl. oz.
Gin	5 mL	1 tsp.
Walnut Oil and Balsamic Vinaigrette:		
Dijon mustard	15 mL	1 Tbsp.
Walnut oil	350 mL	12 fl. oz.
Balsamic vinegar	100 mL	3-1/2 fl. oz.
Shallots, finely chopped	20 g	2 Tbsp.
Dry red chile pepper, crushed	0.5 g	1 tsp.
Salt and pepper	TT	TT
Salad:		
Assortment of baby lettuce leaves, spinach leaves or other leaves	10 portions, each 75 g	10 portions, each 1 cup
Potato chips (small-sized baker-chipped as garnish)	30 pieces	30 pieces
Tomato petals, skinless	30 pieces	30 pieces

Tony Murakami, CMC, CM
Tony started out in Tokyo and then came to Canada, where he worked his way up to Executive Chef and joined the St. Charles Country Club. Tony is a Certified Master Chef. Highlights of his career include nine gold medals and four grand golds in international competition. He has been recognized by the federal and Manitoba governments for his work. Tony was awarded the Order of Canada in 2006.

1. Brush pheasant all over with butter and salt and pepper to season. Roast at 200°C (400°F) for 10 minutes. Reduce heat to 150°C (300°F) for 15–20 minutes. Next, pour the white wine over the bird. Take the pheasant out of the oven and let rest for 15 minutes.

2. Sauté the mirepoix until brown. Bone the pheasant and reserve the bones and skin. Set it aside and keep it warm.

continued

RECIPE 18.3

Approximate values per serving:	
Calories	550
Total fat	50 g
Saturated fat	12 g
Cholesterol	77 mg
Sodium	373 mg
Total carbohydrates	8.9 g
Protein	16 g

3. In a heavy stainless steel pan over medium heat, add pheasant skin, bone, mirepoix, juniper berries, mignonette and anything from the roasting pan. Add stock. Simmer for 20 minutes and skim the fat.

4. Strain the stock and reduce by half or to a syrupy consistency. Add the gin.

5. Make the vinaigrette dressing. Whip the ingredients except salt and pepper with the reduction of the stock. Add salt and pepper to taste.

6. Wash the salad leaves and spin dry. Toss the salad leaves with the vinaigrette. Arrange the greens on a chilled plate, then arrange thinly sliced pheasant on the plate with small potato chips and tomato petals. To make the tomato petals, peel the tomatoes then cut them into quarters or sixths. Seed them and cut away interior flesh to produce a petal- or leaf-like shape.

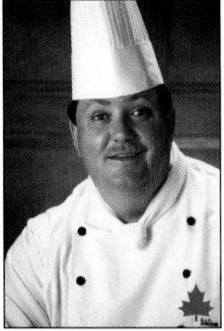

William McIlroy

William has a colourful culinary background that has taken him across the globe. After studying at Niagara College and cooking with Ramada hotels in Belleville and Toronto, he moved to Switzerland to become Banquet Sous Chef at the Mövenpick Hotel in Regensdorf. Next stop was Ecuador, where one of his greatest memories was planning a banquet for the presidents of Ecuador and Peru, an event intended to begin a peace process between the two countries. William eventually returned to Canada and became Executive Chef at The Fairmont Newfoundland. From there, he moved on to The Fairmont New Orleans.

RECIPE 18.4

Approximate values per serving:	
Calories	269
Total fat	17 g
Saturated fat	8.4 g
Cholesterol	72 mg
Sodium	382 mg
Total carbohydrates	16 g
Protein	13 g

RECIPE 18.4

Wild Rabbit and Chanterelle Potage

THE FAIRMONT NEW ORLEANS, NEW ORLEANS, LA
Executive Chef William McIlroy

Yield: 12–15 servings
Method: Stewing

Wild rabbit meat, boneless, no fat, 6-mm (1/4-in.) dice	500 g	1 lb.
Oil	as needed	as needed
Chanterelles, cleaned, 6-mm (1/4-in.) dice	500 g	1 lb.
Butter, unsalted	80 g	3 oz.
Shallots, fine dice	100 g	3-1/2 oz.
Celery, fine dice	100 g	3-1/2 oz.
Leek, white, fine dice	100 g	3-1/2 oz.
Flour	80 g	3 oz.
Brown rabbit stock, warm	2 L	2 qt.
Fresh sage, fine chop	1.5 g	1/2 tsp.
Fresh thyme, fine chop	1.5 g	1/2 tsp.
Dry sherry	50 mL	1-1/2 fl. oz.
Cream, 35%, lightly whipped	200 mL	7 fl. oz.
Salt and pepper	TT	TT

1. Season the rabbit meat and sear in a very hot pot in a little oil. Reserve the meat.

2. Add a little more oil and sauté the chanterelles. Reserve.

3. Reduce the heat to medium, add the butter and sweat the shallots, celery and leek.

4. Add the flour and cook out the roux for 4–6 minutes. Let cool slightly.

5. Incorporate the warm rabbit stock into the roux in batches, stirring constantly to a smooth consistency. Bring to a boil.

6. Add the rabbit meat and chanterelles and simmer for 45 minutes.

7. Five minutes before service, add the herbs, sherry and cream. Bring back to a boil and adjust seasoning.

Christophe Luzeux, CCC

Christophe comes from Marcq-en-Baroeul in the north of France and is a graduate of Lycée Michel Servet in Lille, France. He honed his skills in several of France's top establishments. His culinary achievements include winning silver in the Individual Competition in the 2000 Culinary Team Canada Competition and functioning as the captain of Team Nova Scotia when it won silver in both 1998 and 1999. Most recently, Christophe was a Gold Medal member of Culinary Team Canada 2004.

RECIPE 18.5

Guinea Fowl Basquaise

WORLD TRADE AND CONVENTION CENTRE, HALIFAX, NS

Executive Chef Christophe Luzeux, CCC

Yield: 4 servings

Method: Braising

Guinea fowl breasts, each 160 g (6 oz.)	4	4
Butter	50 g	1-1/2 oz.
Premium cured ham, diced (0.5 cm/1/4 in.)	300 g	10 oz.
Onions, julienne	350 g	12 oz.
Peppers, red, green and yellow, julienne (0.5 cm/1/4 in.)	500 g	3
Hot pepper, small	1	1
Tomato concassée	750 g	1-1/2 lb.
White wine	250 mL	8 fl. oz.
Cognac	125 mL	4 fl. oz.
Salt and pepper	TT	TT
Parsley, freshly chopped	TT	TT

1. Sear the breasts in butter for 3 minutes on each side. Remove and reserve.
2. Sauté the ham for 1 minute in the same pot. Remove and reserve.
3. Sauté the onions and peppers in the same pot for 8 minutes. Add the tomato, wine and cognac. Simmer for 15 minutes.
4. Add the guinea fowl and ham and simmer another 10 minutes. Season with salt and pepper.
5. Garnish with freshly chopped parsley for service.

RECIPE 18.5

Approximate values per serving:	
Calories	627
Total fat	31 g
Saturated fat	12 g
Cholesterol	203 mg
Sodium	1529 mg
Total carbohydrates	28 g
Protein	59 g

Georg Windisch, CCC

Georg was born and professionally trained in Austria and has extensive work experience in the hotel industry in Europe, Australia, Asia and Canada. Before starting his own company and joining SAIT, he was the Executive Chef at the Pan Pacific Hotel in Singapore.

RECIPE 18.6

Bison Medallions on Roasted Parsnip and Onion Bread and Butter Pudding, Espresso Jus

SAIT POLYTECHNIC, CALGARY, AB

Chef Instructors Georg Windisch, CCC, and Simon Dunn, CCC

Yield: 1 serving

Method: Pan-frying

Pudding (4–6 portions):		
Parsnips, roasted	125 g	2
Red onion, roasted	125 g	1/2
Eggs, medium	5	5
Cream, 35%	200 mL	7 fl. oz.
Milk	200 mL	7 fl. oz.
Brioche, buttered	6 slices	6 slices
Sauce:		
Shallots, brunoise	50 g	2 oz.
Clarified butter	5 mL	1 tsp.
Espresso	5 mL	1 tsp.

continued

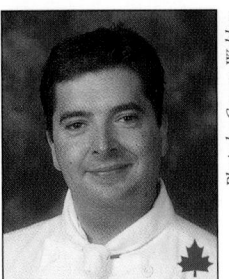

Photo by George Webber

Simon Dunn, CCC
Simon was born and classically trained in Great Britain. Most recently, he was the Executive Chef at the renowned Inn on Lake Bonavista.

RECIPE 18.6

Approximate values per serving, including 1/6th of pudding:	
Calories	922
Total fat	66 g
Saturated fat	30 g
Cholesterol	384 mg
Sodium	825 mg
Total carbohydrates	44 g
Protein	38 g

Fred Zimmermann, CCC
A patriarch among Canadian chefs, Fred has more than 35 years of experience in the food service industry. Having completed his culinary apprenticeship in his native Switzerland, he went on to cook in many of Canada's finest hotels before his 23-year career as Executive Chef at the Westin Calgary. Fred is now retired but still involved in competition, both as a coach and as an international judge. The latter represents a high commendation from Fred's international peers of his professional credentials, knowledge, expertise and accomplishments.

Merlot	50 mL	2 fl. oz.
Game stock	100 mL	3 fl. oz.
Bison tenderloin medallions, each 60 g (2 oz.)	2	2
Kosher salt	TT	TT
Crushed black pepper	TT	TT
Clarified butter	10 mL	2 tsp.
Butter, unsalted	10 g	2 tsp.
Garnish: parsnip chips, deep-fried sage leaves, onion straw		

1. To make the pudding, season and roast the parsnips and onion until caramelized; purée and cool.
2. Whisk eggs, cream and milk together, strain and incorporate the parsnip-onion purée.
3. Layer the buttered brioche in a well-buttered pan and add the custard.
4. Bake at 175°C (350°F) until top is golden and crisp and custard is set, approximately 25 minutes.
5. To make the sauce, caramelize the shallots in 5 mL (1 tsp.) clarified butter, add the espresso and reduce on low heat.
6. Deglaze with Merlot and reduce by one-third. Add the stock and reduce to 75 mL (2-1/2 fl. oz.).
7. Season the bison with salt and pepper. Sear in 10 mL (2 tsp.) clarified butter on high heat to develop colour and flavour. Do not cook past medium rare. Reserve meat.
8. Deglaze the meat pan with the sauce, whisk in the unsalted butter (mount) and adjust seasoning.
9. Place a wedge of pudding in centre of plate, arrange medallions and drizzle sauce.
10. Garnish with parsnip chips, deep-fried sage leaves and onion straw.

RECIPE 18.7

Venison Loin in Wild Rice Mantle

CULINARY TEAM ALBERTA, Calgary, AB
Chef Fred Zimmermann, CCC, retired
Yield: 4–6 servings
Method: Roasting

Venison loin, trimmed, silverskin removed	600–800 g	1-1/4 to 1-3/4 lb.
Salt and pepper	TT	TT
Vegetable oil or butter	30 mL	1 fl. oz.
Pork shoulder, fine grind	150 g	5 oz.
Shallots, diced	50 g	2 oz.
Garlic	5 g	1 clove
Nutmeg or mace	pinch	pinch
Cloves, ground	pinch	pinch
Allspice	pinch	pinch
Egg	1	1
Raw wild rice, cooked	100 g	3 oz.

continued

1. Season and sear the venison loin in a hot skillet and cool.

2. In a food processor, place pork, shallots, garlic, nutmeg, cloves, allspice, egg, salt and pepper and process for 1 minute.

3. Place forcemeat in a bowl and mix in wild rice.

4. Coat the venison loin evenly with the wild rice forcemeat. Roll in plastic wrap and then in foil.

5. Bake in a 140°C (285°F) oven for 45–55 minutes to an internal temperature of 55°C (130°F) for medium rare to medium.

6. Remove from oven and let rest 30 minutes.

7. Unwrap and pan-fry evenly in oil to brown the mantle. Let rest again for a few minutes before carving.

RECIPE 18.7

Approximate values per serving:	
Calories	432
Total fat	16 g
Saturated fat	3.4 g
Cholesterol	206 mg
Sodium	416 mg
Total carbohydrates	24 g
Protein	48 g

RECIPE 18.8

Star Anise- and Cardamom-Braised Bison Short Ribs

BELGO BRASSERIE, CALGARY, AB
General Manager and Executive Chef Shaun Desaulniers

Yield: 4 servings
Method: Braising

Bison short ribs	4	4
Vegetable oil	50 mL	2 fl. oz.
Braising Liquid (recipe follows)	750 mL	24 fl. oz.
Beef stock, brown	as needed	as needed
Thickening agent		
(roux or cornstarch)	as needed	as needed

1. Sear short ribs in a hot brazier with the oil. Drain off any excess oil.

2. Add the braising liquid and beef stock to cover the ribs. Place in a 175°C (350°F) oven and braise until the meat pulls away from the bone and is tender, approximately 2 hours.

3. Remove ribs from liquid and reserve in a warm place.

4. Taste the remaining liquid. If it has reduced too much and tastes salty, add some beef stock.

5. Thicken the liquid with roux or starch and simmer to cook out the starch taste.

6. Add the ribs back to the liquid and heat thoroughly.

Braising Liquid

Soy sauce	175 mL	6 fl. oz.
Garlic, minced	25 g	2 Tbsp.
Black peppercorns, crushed	5	5
Lemon juice, fresh	125 mL	2 lemons
Onion, diced	300 g	11 oz.
Ginger root, minced	25 g	2 Tbsp.
Sugar	125 g	4 oz.
Lemon grass, bruised	2 stalks	2 stalks
Water	250 mL	8 fl. oz.

Shaun Desaulniers
Shaun completed his apprenticeship at SAIT in Calgary. He has brought his commitment to fresh, local ingredients and innovative cuisine to hotels such as the Delta Lodge at Kananaskis and the Fairmont Waterfront in Vancouver. He was appointed Executive Chef at the Fairmont Palliser in Calgary in 2003. Shaun has won a number of awards for his cooking, including two gold medals at the Alberta Salon Culinaire (1999 and 2001). He opened Belgo Brasserie in 2005 and is currently Executive Chef at Wild Ginger in Calgary.

RECIPE 18.8

Approximate values per serving:	
Calories	559
Total fat	9 g
Saturated fat	2.1 g
Cholesterol	149 mg
Sodium	1578 mg
Total carbohydrates	65 g
Protein	57 g

continued

Braising Liquid— Approximate values per serving:	
Calories	272
Total fat	1.7 g
Saturated fat	0.2 g
Cholesterol	0.1 mg
Sodium	1448 mg
Total carbohydrates	64 g
Protein	5.6 g

Beef stock, brown	125 mL	4 fl. oz.
Coriander, ground	17 g	3 Tbsp.
Star anise, roasted	6 pieces	6 pieces
Cardamom seed	30 mL	2 Tbsp.
Chiles, dry, seeded	5 g	1 Tbsp.

Combine all ingredients and let macerate for 30 minutes. Strain.

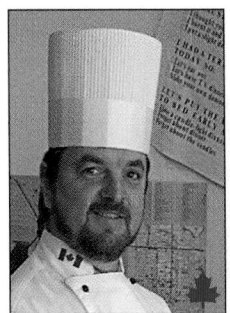

David Jones, CCC

David was born in Wales and trained in Canada. His career has been varied, from running hotel kitchens to developing a property in a Cree community on the shores of James Bay, to providing training to the U.S. Navy in Hong Kong, Hawaii and California. David has instructed in the culinary programs at Humber College and with the Toronto District School Board. He is currently the coordinator of culinary programs at Georgian College.

RECIPE 18.9

Brine for Smoking Wild Game

GEORGIAN COLLEGE, BARRIE, ON
Chef David Jones, CCC

Yield: 1.5 L (48 fl. oz.)

Cider vinegar	500 mL	16 fl. oz.
Water	1 L	1 qt.
Salt, non-iodized	250 g	8 oz.
Black peppercorns, cracked	10 g	1 Tbsp.
Brown sugar	100 g	3 oz.
Mace	0.75 g	1/2 tsp.
Parsley, chopped	3 g	1 tsp.
Onions, chopped	700 g	2 medium
Carrot, sliced	75 g	1 medium
Red wine, dry	250 mL	8 fl. oz.

1. Bring all ingredients except wine to a boil. Simmer for 30 minutes.
2. Strain and add wine. Chill.

Fish and Shellfish 19

> In the hands of an able cook, fish can become an inexhaustible source of perpetual delight.
>
> —Jean-Anthelme Brillat-Savarin (1755–1826)

After studying this chapter you will be able to:

- describe the structure and composition of fish and shellfish
- identify a variety of fish and shellfish
- purchase fish and shellfish appropriate to your needs
- store fish and shellfish properly
- prepare fish and shellfish for cooking
- apply various cooking methods to fish and shellfish

PEARSON
myculinarylab

These interactive online tools will help you master the skills in this chapter:

- Videos
- Chapter Quizzes
- Activities
- Simulations

● **round fish** fish with round, oval or compressed bodies that swim in a vertical position and have eyes on both sides of their heads, including salmon, swordfish and cod

● **flatfish** fish with asymmetrical, compressed bodies that swim in a horizontal position and have both eyes on the top of their heads, including sole, flounder and halibut

● **mollusks** shellfish characterized by a soft, unsegmented body, no internal skeleton and a hard external shell

● **univalves** single-shelled mollusks with a single muscular foot, such as abalone

● **bivalves** mollusks such as clams, oysters and mussels that have two bilateral shells attached at a central hinge

● **cephalopods** mollusks with a single, thin internal shell called a pen or cuttlebone, well-developed eyes, a number of arms that attach to the head and a sac-like fin-bearing mantle, including squid and octopus

● **crustaceans** shellfish characterized by a hard outer skeleton or shell and jointed appendages, including lobsters, crabs and shrimp

Fish are aquatic vertebrates with fins for swimming and gills for breathing. Of the more than 30 000 species known, most live in the seas and oceans; freshwater species are far less numerous. Shellfish are aquatic invertebrates with shells or carapaces. They are found in both fresh and salt water.

Always an important food source, fish and shellfish have become increasingly popular in recent years, due in part to demands from health-conscious consumers. Because of increased demand and improved preservation and transportation techniques, good-quality fish and shellfish, once found only along seacoasts and lakes, are now readily available to almost every food service operation.

Many fish and shellfish species are very expensive; all are highly perishable. Because their cooking times are generally shorter and their flavours more delicate than those of meat or poultry, special attention must be given to fish and shellfish to prevent spoilage and to produce high-quality finished products.

In this chapter, you will learn how to identify a large assortment of fish and shellfish as well as how to properly purchase and store them, fabricate or prepare them for cooking and cook them by a variety of dry-heat and moist-heat cooking methods. This chapter presents many of the cooking methods applied to meats and poultry in the previous chapters. Review the corresponding procedures for meats and poultry and note the similarities and differences.

STRUCTURE AND MUSCLE COMPOSITION

The fish and shellfish used in food service operations can be divided into three categories: fish, mollusks and crustaceans.

Fish (Fr. *poisson*) include both fresh- and saltwater varieties. They have fins and an internal skeleton of bone and cartilage. Based on shape and skeletal structure, fish can be divided into two groups: round fish and flatfish. **Round fish** swim in a vertical position and have eyes on both sides of their heads. Their bodies may be truly round, oval or compressed. (See Figure 19.1.) **Flatfish** have asymmetrical, compressed bodies, swim in a horizontal position and have both eyes on top of their heads. Flatfish are bottom dwellers; most are found in deep ocean waters around the world. The skin on top of their bodies is dark, to camouflage them from predators, and can change colour according to their surroundings. Their scales are small and their dorsal and anal fins run the length of their bodies. (See Figure 19.2.)

Mollusks (Fr. *mollusque*) are shellfish characterized by soft, unsegmented bodies with no internal skeleton. Most mollusks have hard outer shells. Single-shelled mollusks such as abalone are known as **univalves**. Those with two shells, such as clams, oysters and mussels, are known as **bivalves**. Squid and octopus, which are known as **cephalopods**, do not have a hard outer shell. Rather, they have a single thin internal shell called a *pen* or *cuttlebone*.

Crustaceans (Fr. *crustacé*) are also shellfish. They have a hard outer skeleton or shell and jointed appendages. Crustaceans include lobsters, crabs and shrimp.

The flesh of fish and shellfish consists primarily of water, protein, fat and minerals. Fish flesh comprises short muscle fibres separated by delicate sheets of connective tissue. Fish, as well as most shellfish, are naturally tender, so the purpose of cooking is to firm proteins and enhance flavour. The absence of the oxygen-carrying protein myoglobin makes fish flesh very light or white in colour. (The

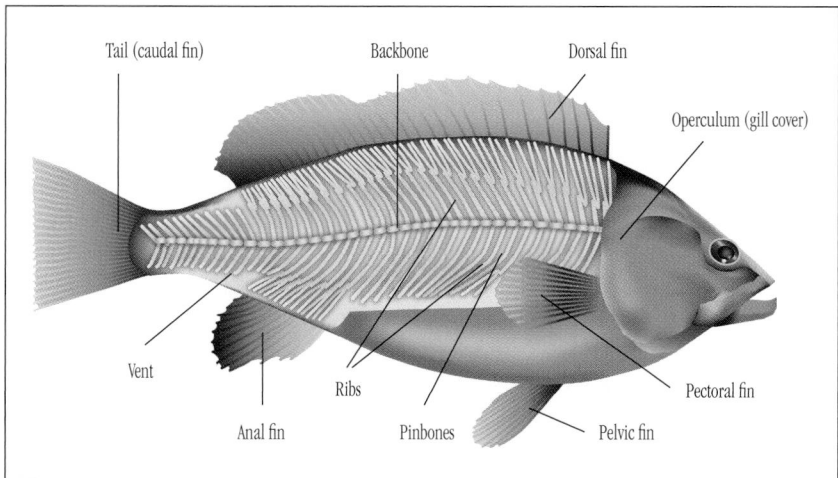

FIGURE 19.1 Bone structure of a round fish.

orange colour of salmon and some trout comes from pigments found in their food.) Compared with meats, fish do not contain large amounts of intermuscular fat. But the amount of fat a fish does contain affects the way it responds to cooking. Fish containing a relatively large amount of fat, such as salmon and mackerel, are known as fatty or oily fish. Fish such as cod and haddock contain very little fat and are referred to as lean fish. Shellfish are also very lean.

IDENTIFYING FISH AND SHELLFISH

Identifying fish and shellfish properly can be difficult because of the vast number of similar-appearing fish and shellfish that are separate species within each family. Adding confusion are the various colloquial names given to the same fish or the use of the same name for different fish in different localities. Fish with an unappealing name may also be given a catchier name or the name of a similar but more popular item for marketing purposes. Moreover, some species are referred to by a foreign name, especially on menus.

The Canadian Food Inspection Agency publishes regulations concerning acceptable nomenclature for fish and fish products.

Seafood

"Seafood" means different things to different people. For some, the term applies just to shellfish or to shellfish and other small edible marine creatures. For others, it is limited to saltwater shellfish or to saltwater shellfish and fish. For yet others, it refers to all fish and shellfish, both freshwater and saltwater. Because of the term's vagueness, it is not used here.

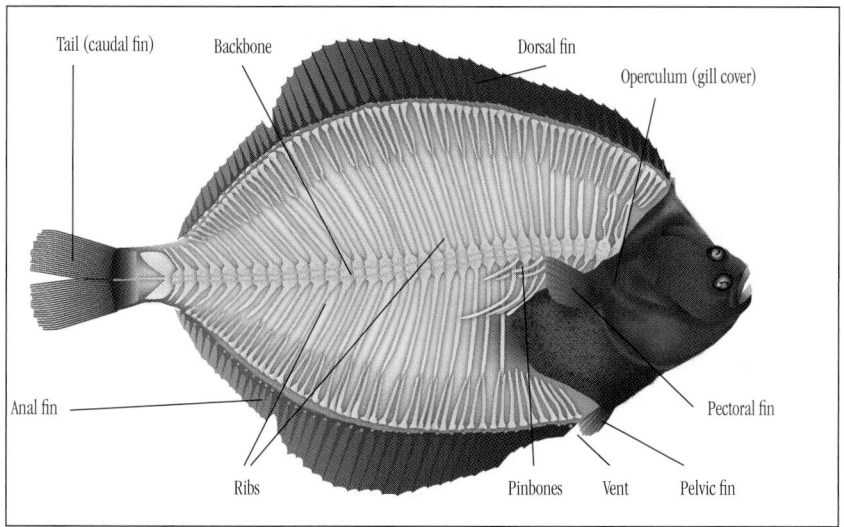

FIGURE 19.2 Bone structure of a flatfish.

Fish

Round Fish

Bass (Fr. *bar*) commonly refers to a number of unrelated fish. The better-known freshwater bass varieties (largemouth, smallmouth, redeye and black) are actually members of the sunfish family. They are lean and delicate but, as game, not commercially available in Canada. The saltwater bass varieties (black sea bass and striped bass) are popular commercial items.

Black Sea Bass

Black sea bass are sometimes referred to as rock sea bass. They have a lean, firm white flesh with a mild flavour and flaky texture. They usually weigh 675 g to 1.3 kg (1-1/2 to 3 lb.) and are most prevalent in the Atlantic Ocean between New York and North Carolina. Black sea bass can be prepared by almost any cooking method and are often served whole in Chinese and Italian cuisines.

Striped Bass

Striped bass, often erroneously referred to as rockfish, are **anadromous**: ocean fish that depend on freshwater rivers to reproduce. True striped bass cannot be marketed because pollution and overfishing have damaged the supply. A hybrid of striped bass and either white bass or white perch is being **aquafarmed** for commercial use, however. It is this hybrid that food service operations receive as striped bass. Whole fish weigh 450 g to 2.2 kg (1 to 5 lb.). Striped bass have a rich, sweet flavour and firm texture. They can be steamed, baked, poached or broiled.

Catfish

Catfish are scaleless freshwater fish common in southern lakes and rivers and now aquafarmed extensively. Aquafarm raising eliminates the "muddy" taste once associated with catfish and ensures a year-round supply. The flesh is pure white with a moderate fat content, a mild, sweet flavour and firm texture. Channel catfish are the most important commercially. They usually weigh 675 g to 2.2 kg (1-1/2 to 5 lb.). The smaller of these fish are known as **fiddlers**; they are often deep-fat fried and served whole. Catfish may be prepared by almost any cooking method, but are especially well suited to frying.

Arctic char are a type of salmon found in the far northern rivers. Brook trout and lake trout are also chars. They are lean and pink fleshed. Wild char is available fresh only in August, September, March and April. They are being farm raised.

The **cod** (Fr. *cabillaud*) family includes Atlantic and Pacific cod as well as pollock, haddock, whiting and hake. Cod have a mild, delicate flavour and lean, firm white flesh that flakes apart easily. Cod can be prepared by most cooking methods, although grilling is not recommended because the flesh is too flaky.

Atlantic Cod

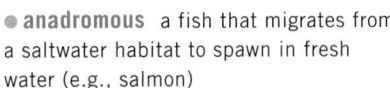

Atlantic cod are the best-selling fish in the Americas. They are available fresh, whole or drawn, or cut into fillets or steaks. They are also available frozen and are often used for precooked or prebreaded sticks or portions. Smoked cod and salt cod are also available. Although cod may reach 90 kg (200 lb.), most market cod weigh 4.5 kg (10 lb.) or less. **Scrod** is a marketing term for cod weighing less than 1.1 kg (2-1/2 lb.).

Haddock, the second most commercially important fish, look like thin, small Atlantic cod and weigh about 900 g to 2.3 kg (2 to 5 lb.). They have a stronger flavour and more delicate texture than Atlantic cod. They are available smoked.

Pacific cod, also known as grey cod, are found in the northern Pacific Ocean and are not as abundant as their Atlantic cousins. Pacific cod are most often available frozen; they should be labelled "true cod" to distinguish them from rock cod and black cod (sable fish), which are unrelated.

● **anadromous** a fish that migrates from a saltwater habitat to spawn in fresh water (e.g., salmon)

● **aquafarming** also known as aquaculture, the business, science and practice of raising large quantities of fish and shellfish in tanks, ponds or ocean pens. Health and food safety issues are critical.

Surimi

Surimi is made from a highly processed fish paste coloured, flavoured and shaped to resemble shrimp, lobster, crab or other shellfish. Most surimi is based on Alaskan pollock, but some blends include varying amounts of real crab, shrimp or other items. Available chilled or frozen, surimi is already fully cooked and ready to add to salads, pasta, sauces or other dishes. Surimi is very low in fat and relatively high in protein. Because of processing techniques, however, it has more sodium and fewer vitamins and minerals than the real fish or shellfish it replaces. North Americans now consume more than 45 million kilograms (100 million pounds) of surimi each year, and its popularity continues to grow. The Canadian Food Inspection Agency requires that all surimi products be labelled "imitation."

Pollock, also known as Boston bluefish or blue cod, are plentiful in the northern Atlantic and Pacific oceans. Their flesh is grey-pink when raw, turning white when cooked. Pollock are often frozen at sea, then reprocessed into surimi. They can also be salted or smoked. They are used extensively for battered fish and chips.

Pollock

Eels (Fr. *anguille*) are long, snakelike freshwater fish with dorsal and anal fins running the length of their bodies. (The conger eel is from a different family and has little culinary significance.) North American and European eels are available live, whole, gutted or as fillets. Eels have a high fat content and firm flesh; they are sweet and mildly flavoured. Their tough skin should be removed before cooking. Eels may be steamed, baked, fried or used in stews. Baby eels are a springtime delicacy, especially in Spain, where they are pan-fried in olive oil and garlic with hot red peppers. Smoked eels are also available.

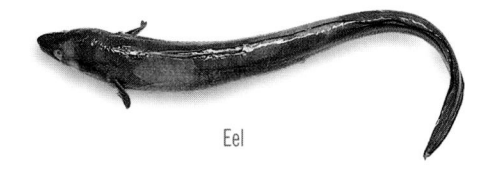
Eel

The **grouper** family includes almost 400 varieties found in temperate waters worldwide. The more common Atlantic Ocean varieties are the yellowfin grouper, black grouper, red grouper and gag; the Pacific Ocean varieties are the sea bass (also known as jewfish and different from the black sea bass) and spotted cabrilla. Although some species can reach 360 kg (800 lb.) or more, most commercial varieties are sold in the 2.2- to 9-kg (5- to 20- lb.) range. They have lean white flesh with a mild to sweet flavour and very firm texture. Their skin, which is tough and strongly flavoured, is generally removed before cooking. Grouper fillets may be baked, deep-fat fried, broiled or grilled.

Grouper

Herring (Fr. *hareng*) are long, silvery-blue fish found in both the northern Atlantic and Pacific oceans. Their strongly flavoured flesh has a moderate to high fat content. Whole herring weigh up to 225 g (8 oz.). Fresh herring may be butterflied or filleted and roasted, broiled or grilled. But because herring are very soft and tend to spoil quickly, they are rarely available fresh. More often, they are smoked (known as kippers) or pickled in brine.

Sardines (Fr. *sardine*) are young, small herring with fatty, oily flesh that has a flaky texture. Sardines are usually sold canned, whole or as skinned and boned fillets, or fried or smoked and packed in oil or sauce. Sardines are used primarily for sandwiches and salads.

Sardines

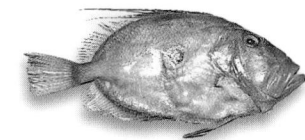

John Dory

Mackerel

Mahi-mahi

Monkfish Tail

Orange Roughy

Red Snapper

Atlantic Salmon

John Dory, also known as St. Peter's fish, have a distinctive round, black spot with a yellow halo on each side of the body. Their flesh is white, firm and finely flaked. They may be filleted and prepared like flounder and are a classic bouillabaisse ingredient.

Mackerel (Fr. *maquereau*) of culinary importance include king and Spanish mackerel as well as tuna and wahoo, which are discussed separately later. The species known as Atlantic and Pacific mackerel are not generally used for food because of their small size and high fat content. Mackerel flesh has a high fat content, grey to pink colouring, a mild flavour and flaky texture. The flesh becomes firm and off-white when cooked. Mackerel are best broiled, grilled, smoked or baked.

Mahi-mahi is the more commonly used name for dolphin or dolphinfish; this Hawaiian name is used to distinguish them from the marine mammal of the same name. (Dolphins and porpoises are marine mammals.) Also known by their Spanish name, *dorado*, mahi-mahi are brilliantly coloured fish found in tropical seas. Mahi-mahi weigh about 6.6 kg (15 lb.) and are sold whole or as fillets. Their flesh is off-white to pink, lean and firm with a sweet flavour. Mahi-mahi can be broiled, grilled or baked. The meat may become dry when cooked, however, so sauce or marinade is recommended.

Monkfish are also known as angler fish, goosefish, rape and lotte. These extraordinarily ugly fish are rarely seen whole, for the large head is usually discarded before reaching market. Only the tail is edible; monkfish are available in fillets, fresh or frozen. The scaleless skin must be removed. The flesh is lean, pearly white and very firm. Their texture and flavour have earned monkfish the nickname of "poor man's lobster." Monkfish absorb flavours easily and are baked, steamed, fried, grilled or broiled. They are also used for stews and soups.

Orange roughy are caught in the South Pacific off the coasts of New Zealand and Australia. They have bright orange skin and firm, pearly-white flesh with a low fat content and extremely bland flavour. Fresh-frozen fillets are widely available year round. Orange roughy are almost always marketed as skinless, boneless frozen fillets, averaging 170- to 225-g (6- to 8-oz.) each. They can be broiled, steamed, grilled or prepared in the same manner as cod.

Red snapper is also known as the American or northern red snapper. Although there are many members of the snapper family, only one is the true red snapper. Red-skinned rockfish are often mislabelled as the more popular red snapper or Pacific snapper, a practice that is currently legal only in California. True red snapper has lean, pink flesh that becomes white when cooked; it is sweet-flavoured and flaky. They are sold whole or as fillets with the skin left on for identification. Red snapper may reach 15 kg (35 lb.), but most are marketed at only 1.8 to 2.7 kg (4 to 6 lb.) or as 450-g to 1.3-kg (1- to 3-lb.) fillets. Red snapper can be prepared using almost any cooking method. The head and bones are excellent for stock.

Salmon (Fr. *saumon*) flourish in both the northern Atlantic and the Pacific oceans, returning to the freshwater rivers and streams of their birth to spawn. Salmon flesh gets its distinctive pink-red colour from fat-soluble carotenoids found in the crustaceans on which the fish feed. Salmon is the most popular fish in Canada. It is high in omega-3 fatty acids.

Atlantic salmon are the most important commercially, accounting for one-quarter of all salmon produced worldwide. Extensive aquafarms in Canada, Norway and Scotland produce a steady supply of Atlantic salmon. For marketing purposes, the fish's point of origin is often added to the name (for example, Norwegian, Scottish or Shetland Atlantic salmon). Atlantic salmon have a rich pink colour and moist flesh. Their average weight is from 1.8 to 5.4 kg (4 to 12 lb.). Wild Atlantic salmon are almost never available.

Chinook or King Salmon

Chinook or **king salmon** from the Pacific are also highly desirable. They average 2.2 to 13 kg (5 to 30 lb.) and have red-orange flesh with a high fat content and rich flavour. Like other salmon, their flesh separates into large flakes when cooked. Chinooks are often marketed by the name of the river from which they are harvested (for example, Columbia, Yukon or Copper Chinook salmon). They are distinguished by the black interior of their mouth.

Coho or **silver** salmon have pinkish flesh and are available fresh or frozen, wild or from aquafarms. Wild coho average 1.3 to 5.4 kg (3 to 12 lb.), while aquafarmed coho are much smaller, usually less than 450 g (1 lb.).

Other varieties, such as chum, sockeye, red, blueback and pink salmon, are usually canned but may be available fresh or frozen.

Mini Coho Salmon

Salmon can be prepared by many cooking methods: broiling, grilling, poaching, steaming or baking. Frying is not recommended, however, because of their high fat content. Salmon fillets are often cured or smoked. **Gravlax** is salmon that has been cured for one to three days with salt, sugar and dill. **Lox** is salmon that is cured in a salted brine and then typically cold-smoked. **Nova** is used in the eastern United States to refer to a less-salty, cold-smoked salmon.

Sharks provide delicious eating, despite their less-than-appealing appearance and vicious reputation. Mako and blue sharks are the most desirable, with mako often being sold as swordfish. Sand shark, sharpnose, blacktip, angel and thresher are also available commercially. Most sharks have lean flesh with a mild flavour and firm texture. The flesh is white with tinges of pink or red when raw, turning off-white when cooked. Makos weigh 13 to 110 kg (30 to 250 lb.); other species may reach as much as 450 kg (1000 lb.). All sharks have cartilaginous skeletons and no bones; therefore, they are not actually fish, but rather marine invertebrates. Sharks are usually cut into loins or wheels, then into steaks or cubes. They can be broiled, grilled, baked or fried. An ammonia smell indicates that the shark was not properly treated when caught. Do not buy or eat it.

Blacktip Shark

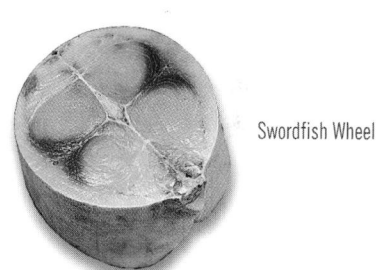

Swordfish Wheel

Swordfish take their name from the long, swordlike bill extending from their upper jaw. These game fish average about 110 kg (250 lb.). Their flesh is lean and sweet, with a very firm, meatlike texture; it may be grey, pink or off-white when raw, becoming white when cooked. Swordfish are available cut into wheels or portioned into steaks for grilling or broiling. Swordfish are becoming endangered.

Tilapia is the name given to several species of freshwater, aquafarm-raised fish bred worldwide. They grow quickly in warm water, reaching about 1.3 kg (3 lb.); they are available whole or filleted, fresh or frozen. The flesh is similar to catfish—lean, white and sweet, with a firm texture.

Tilapia

Trout (Fr. *truite*) are members of the *Salmonidae* family. Most of the freshwater trout commercially available are aquafarm-raised rainbow trout, although brown trout and brook trout are also being aquafarmed. Some trout species spend part of their lives at sea, returning to fresh water

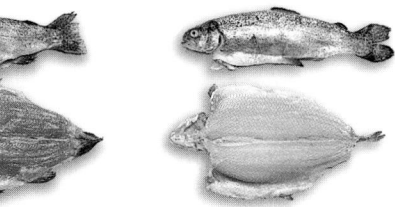

Red Mountain Trout   Rainbow Trout

Yellowfin Tuna

to spawn. On the west coast, these are called salmon trout or steelhead. Trout have a low to moderate fat content, a flaky texture and a delicate flavour that can be easily overwhelmed by strong sauces. The flesh may be white, orange or pink. Trout are usually marketed at 225- to 280-g (8- to 10-oz.) each, just right for an individual portion. Lake trout are not aquafarmed but are appearing on specialty menus, when available, as a cured and smoked product. Trout can be baked, pan-fried, smoked or steamed.

Tuna (Fr. *thon*) varieties include the bluefin, yellowfin, bonito, bigeye and blackfin. Ahi is the popular market name for either yellowfin or bigeye tuna. All are members of the mackerel family and are found in tropical and subtropical waters around the world. Tuna are large fish, weighing up to several hundred pounds each. Bluefin, the finest and most desirable for sashimi, are becoming very scarce because of overfishing. Regular canned tuna is usually prepared from yellowfin or skipjack; canned white tuna is prepared from albacore, also known as longfin tuna. Pacific tuna that is frozen at sea to preserve its freshness is referred to as clipper fish. Any of these species may be found fresh or frozen, however. Tuna is usually cut into four boneless loins for market. The loins are then cut into steaks, cubes or chunks. The flesh has a low to moderate fat content (a higher fat content is preferred for sashimi) and a deep red colour. The dark, reddish-brown muscle that runs along the lateral line is very fatty and can be removed. Tuna flesh turns light grey when cooked and is very firm, with a mild flavour. Tuna work well for grilling or broiling and may be marinated or brushed with seasoned oil during cooking. Tuna are often prepared medium rare to prevent dryness.

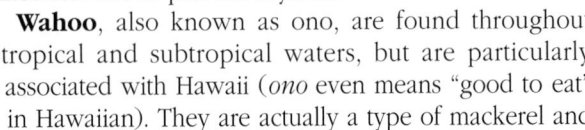

Wahoo

Wahoo, also known as ono, are found throughout tropical and subtropical waters, but are particularly associated with Hawaii (*ono* even means "good to eat" in Hawaiian). They are actually a type of mackerel and are cooked like any other mackerel.

Whitefish species inhabit the freshwater lakes and streams of North America. Lake whitefish, the most important commercially, are related to salmon. They are marketed at up to 3.2 kg (7 lb.) and are available whole or filleted. The flesh is firm and white, with a moderate amount of fat and a sweet flavour. Whitefish may be baked, broiled, grilled or smoked and are often used in processed fish products. They are the source for golden caviar.

Whitefish

Trash Fish

Ocean pout are considered a "trash fish," or fish that fishermen throw away because there is little or no consumer demand and therefore no market value.

Long ago, lobster were considered trash and good for nothing but chicken feed. More recently, monkfish was a trash fish in the U.S., and now we can't get enough. Obscure species are often trash fish until someone somewhere tastes them and realizes that they offer some incredible flavors and textures.

Searobins, dogfish, skate, and whiting are still considered trash fish in America, though they are gradually becoming more popular and will someday be readily available at fish markets.

From The Great American Seafood Cookbook by Susan Herrmann Loomis

Flatfish

Flounder (Fr. *flet*) have lean, firm flesh that is pearly or pinkish-white with a sweet, mild flavour. Although they are easily boned, most are deheaded and gutted at sea and sold as fresh or frozen fillets. These fillets are very thin and can dry out or spoil easily, so extra care should be taken in handling, preparing and storing them. Recipes that preserve moisture work best with flounder; poaching, steaming or frying are recommended. Many types of flounder are marketed as sole, perhaps in an attempt to cash in on the popularity of true sole. The Canadian Federal Fisheries permits this practice. (See Table 19.1 on the next page.)

English Sole

English sole are actually flounder caught off the west coast of Canada and the United States. They are usually marketed simply as "fillet of sole." They are a plentiful species of fair to average quality.

Petrale sole, another west coast flounder, are generally considered the finest of the domestic "soles." They are most often available as fillets, which tend to be thicker and firmer than other sole fillets.

Petrale Sole

Domestic Dover sole are also Pacific flounder. They are not as delicate or flavourful as other species of sole or flounder. Moreover, they are often afflicted with a parasite that causes the meat to have a slimy, gelatinous texture. Domestic Dover sole are not recommended if other sole or flounder are available.

Lemon sole are the most abundant and popular east coast flounder. They are also known as blackback or winter flounder (during the winter they migrate close to shore from the deeper, colder waters). They average 900 g (2 lb.) in weight.

Lemon Sole

Halibut are among the largest flatfish; they often weigh up to 135 kg (300 lb.). The Canadian Federal Fisheries recognizes only two halibut species: Atlantic (eastern) and Pacific (northern, Alaskan, western) halibut. Both have lean, firm flesh that is snow-white with a sweet, mild flavour. California halibut, which are actually flounder, are similar in taste and texture but

Alaskan Halibut

average only 5.4 kg (12 lb.) each. Halibut may be cut into boneless steaks or skewered on brochettes. The flesh, which dries out easily, can be poached, baked, grilled or broiled and is good with a variety of sauces.

Sole (Fr. *sole*) are probably the most flavourful and finely textured flatfish. Indeed, because of the connotations of quality associated with the name, "sole" is widely used for many species that are not members of the sole (*Soleidae*) family. Even though the Canadian Federal Fisheries allows many species of flatfish to be called "sole" for marketing purposes, no true sole is commercially harvested in North American waters. Any flatfish harvested in North American waters and marketed as sole is actually flounder.

True Dover Sole

True **Dover sole**, a staple of classic cuisine, are a lean fish with pearly-white flesh and a delicate flavour that can stand up to a variety of sauces and seasonings. They are a member of the *Soleidae* family and come only from the waters off the coasts of England, Africa and Europe. They are imported into this country as fresh or frozen fillets and whole fish.

Turbot are a Pacific flatfish of no great culinary distinction. In Europe, however, the species known as turbot (Fr. *turbot*) are large diamond-shaped fish highly prized for their delicate flavour and firm, white flesh. Although turbot and brill are separate species, turbot are also marketed as brill. Japanese markets sell brill for fine dining.

Turbot

Snails

Although snails (more politely known by their French name, *escargots*) are univalve land animals, they share many characteristics with their marine cousins. They can be poached in court bouillon or removed from their shells and boiled or baked briefly with a seasoned butter or sauce. They should be firm but tender; overcooking makes snails tough and chewy. The most popular varieties are the large white Burgundy snail and the small garden variety called *petit gris*.

Fresh snails are available from snail ranches through specialty suppliers. The great majority of snails, however, are purchased canned; most canned snails are produced in France or Taiwan.

Snail (left) and Snail Shell (right)

TABLE 19.1	Flounder (Also Known as Sole)

Atlantic Ocean	Pacific Ocean
Blackback/winter flounder/lemon sole	Arrowtooth
Fluke/summer flounder	Petrale sole
Starry flounder	Rex sole
Yellowtail	English sole
Windowpane flounder	Rock sole
Grey sole/witch flounder	Sand sole
	Yellowfin sole
	Domestic Dover sole/Pacific flounder
	Butter sole

Mollusks

Univalves

Univalves are mollusks with a single shell in which the soft-bodied animal resides. They are actually marine snails with a single foot, used to attach the creature to fixed objects such as rocks.

Abalone have brownish-grey, ear-shaped shells. They are harvested in California, but California law does not permit canning abalone or shipping it out of state. Some frozen abalone is available from Mexico; canned abalone is imported from Japan. Abalone are lean with a sweet, delicate flavour similar to that of clams. They are too tough to eat unless tenderized with a mallet or rolling pin. They may then be eaten raw or prepared seviche-style. Great care must be taken when grilling or sautéing abalone, as the meat becomes very tough when overcooked.

Conch are found in warm waters off the Florida Keys and in the Caribbean. The beautiful peachy-pink shell of the queen conch is prized by beachcombers. Conch meat is lean, smooth and very firm, with a sweet-smoky flavour and chewy texture. The meat can be sliced and pounded to tenderize it, eaten raw with lime juice, or slow-cooked whole.

Bivalves

Bivalves are mollusks with two bilateral shells attached by a central hinge.

Clams (Fr. *clovisses*) are harvested along both the east and the west coasts, with Atlantic clams being more significant commercially. Atlantic Coast clams include hard-shell, soft-shell and surf clams. Clams are available all year, either live in the shell or fresh-shucked (meat removed from the shell). Canned clams, whether minced, chopped or whole, are also available.

Atlantic hard-shell clams or **quahogs** have hard, blue-grey shells. Their chewy meat is not as sweet as other clam meat. Quahogs have different names, depending upon their size. **Littlenecks** are generally under 5 cm (2 in.) across the shell and usually are served on the half shell or steamed. They are the most expensive clams. **Cherrystones** are generally under 7.5 cm (3 in.) across the shell and are sometimes eaten raw but are more often cooked. **Topnecks** are usually cooked and are often served as stuffed clams. **Chowders**, the largest quahogs, are always eaten cooked, especially minced for chowder or soup.

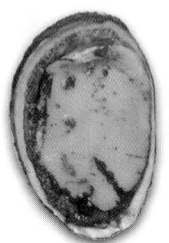

Abalone

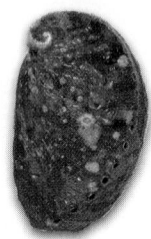

Littlenecks

Cherrystones

Topnecks

Soft-shell Clams

Soft-shell clams, also known as Ipswich, steamer and long-necked clams, have thin, brittle shells that do not completely close because of the clam's protruding black-tipped siphon. Their meat is tender and sweet. They are sometimes fried but are more often served steamed.

Surf clams are deep-water clams that reach sizes of 20-cm (8-in.) across. They are most often cut into strips for frying or are minced, chopped, processed and canned.

Pacific clams are generally too tough to eat raw. The most common is the **Manila clam**, which was introduced along the Pacific Coast during the 1930s. Resembling a quahog with a ridged shell, it can be served steamed or on the half shell. **Geoducks** are the largest Pacific clam, sometimes weighing up to 4.5 kg (10 lb.) each. They look like huge soft-shell clams with a large, protruding siphon. Their tender, rich bodies and briny flavour are popular in Asian cuisines.

Manila Clams

A freshwater **Red River clam** is commercially available in Canada.

Cockles are small bivalves, about 2.5-cm (1-in.) long, with ridged shells. They are more popular in Europe than in North America and are sometimes used in dishes such as paella and fish soups or stews.

Cockles

Mussels (Fr. *moule*) are found in waters worldwide. They are excellent steamed in wine or seasoned broth and can be fried or used in soups or pasta dishes.

Blue Mussels

Blue mussels are the most common edible mussel. They are found in the wild along the Atlantic Coast and are aquafarmed on both coasts. Their meat is plump and sweet with a firm, muscular texture. The orangish-yellow meat of cultivated mussels tends to be much larger than that of wild mussels and therefore worth the added cost. Blue mussels are sold live in the shell and average from 10 to 20 per pound. Although available all year, the best-quality blue mussels are harvested during the winter months.

Greenshell (or greenlip) **mussels** from New Zealand and Thailand are much larger than blue mussels, averaging 8 to 12 mussels per 450 g (1 lb.). Their shells are paler grey, with a distinctive bright-green edge.

Greenshell Mussels

Oysters (Fr. *huître*) have a rough grey shell; their soft, grey, briny flesh can be eaten raw or cooked. Most oysters available in this country are commercially grown and sold either live in the shell or shucked. Oysters are excellent live, eaten directly from the shell. They can also be steamed or baked in the shell or shucked and fried, sautéed or added to stews or chowders. There are four main domestic species.

European Flat Oysters

Atlantic oysters, also called American or Eastern oysters, have darker, flatter shells than other oysters. Malpeque oysters from Prince Edward Island are considered the finest.

Bluepoint Oysters

European flat oysters are often incorrectly called Belon (true Belon oysters live only in the Belon river of France); they are very round and flat and look like giant brownish-green Olympias.

Olympias are the only oysters native to the Pacific Coast; they are tiny (about the size of a loonie).

Olympias

Pacific oysters, also called Japanese oysters, are aquafarmed along the Pacific Coast; they have curly, thick striated shells and silvery-grey to gold to almost-white meat.

Florida Gulf Oysters

Sea Scallops

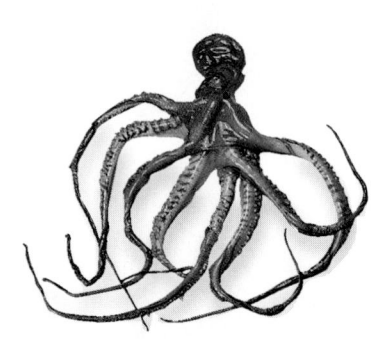

Octopus

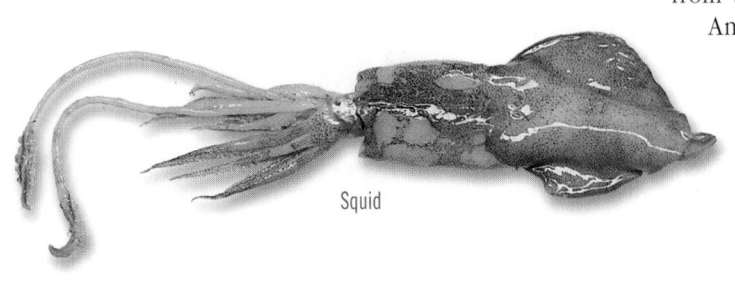

Squid

Although it may seem as if there are hundreds of oyster species on the market, there are only two that are commercially significant: the Atlantic oyster and the Pacific oyster. These two species yield dozens of different varieties, however, depending on their origin. For example, Atlantic oysters may be referred to as bluepoints, Malpeque, Florida Gulf, Long Island and so on, while Pacific oysters include Penn Cove Select, Westcott Bay, **Hamma-hamma** and Kumamoto, among others. An oyster's flavour reflects the minerals, nutrients and salts in its water and mud bed, so a Bristol from Maine and an Apalachicola from Florida will taste very different, even though they are the same Atlantic species. Oysters are at their prime in the winter months, particularly from Christmas to Easter.

Hamma-Hamma Oysters

Scallops contain an edible white adductor muscle that holds together the fan-shaped shells. Because they die quickly, they are almost always shucked and cleaned onboard ship. The sea scallop and the bay scallop, both cold-water varieties, and the calico scallop, a warm-water variety, are the most important commercially. Sea scallops are the largest, with an average count of 20 to 30 per pound. Larger sea scallops are also available. Bay scallops average 70 to 90 per pound; calico scallops average 70 to 110 per pound. Fresh or frozen shucked, cleaned scallops are the most common market form, but live scallops in the shell and shucked scallops with roe attached (very popular in Europe) are also available. Scallops are sweet, with a tender texture. Raw scallops should be a translucent ivory colour and nonsymmetrically round and should feel springy. They can be steamed, broiled, grilled, fried, sautéed or baked. When overcooked, however, scallops quickly become chewy and dry. Only absolutely fresh scallops should be eaten raw. Remember to remove the catch muscle if still attached. It becomes very tough when cooked.

Cephalopods

Cephalopods are marine mollusks with distinct heads, well-developed eyes, a number of arms that attach to the head near the mouth and a saclike fin-bearing mantle. They do not have an outer shell; instead, there is a thin internal shell called a *pen* or *cuttlebone*.

Octopus is generally quite tough and requires mechanical tenderization or long, moist-heat cooking to make it palatable. Most octopus is imported from Portugal, though fresh ones are available on the east coast during the winter. Octopus is sold by the kilogram or pound, fresh or frozen, usually whole. Octopus skin is grey when raw, turning purple when cooked. The interior flesh is white, lean, firm and flavourful.

Squid, known by their Italian name, *calamari*, are becoming increasingly popular in this country. Similar to octopus but much smaller, they are harvested along both North and South American coasts and elsewhere around the world (the finest are the east coast loligo or winter squid). They range in size from an average of 8 to 10 per pound to the giant South American squid that is sold as tenderized steaks. The squid's tentacles, mantle (body tube) and fins are edible. Squid meat is white to ivory in colour, turning darker with age. It is moderately lean, slightly sweet, firm and tender, but it toughens quickly if overcooked. Squid are available either fresh, or frozen and packed in blocks. Their ink is used for making black noodles.

Crustaceans

Crustaceans are found in both fresh and salt water. They have a hard outer shell and jointed appendages, and they breathe through gills.

Crayfish (Fr. *écrevisse*), generally called *crayfish* in the North and *crawfish* or *crawdad* in the South, are freshwater creatures that look like miniature lobsters. They are harvested from the wild or aquafarmed in Louisiana and the Pacific Northwest. They are from 8 to 17.5 cm (3-1/2 to 7 in.) in length when marketed and may be purchased live or precooked and frozen. The lean meat, found mostly in the tail, is sweet and tender. Crayfish can be boiled whole and served hot or cold. The tail meat can be deep-fat fried or used in soups, bisques or sauces. Crayfish are a staple of Cajun cuisine, often used in gumbo, étouffée and jambalaya. Whole crayfish become brilliant red when cooked and may be used as a garnish. Caribbean crayfish tails are often erroneously sold on menus as lobster tails. They are also found in Europe and especially Australia. Sizes range from 100 g (3-1/2 oz.) to 4.5 kg (10 lb.) for the Tasmanian crayfish.

Crabs (Fr. *crabe*) are found along the North American coasts in great numbers and are shipped throughout the world in fresh, frozen and canned forms. Crab meat varies in flavour and texture and can be used in a range of prepared dishes,

King Crab Legs

from chowders to curries to casseroles. Crabs purchased live should last up to five days; dead crabs should not be used.

King crabs are very large crabs (usually around 4.5 kg or 10 lb.) caught in the very cold waters of the North Pacific. Their meat is very sweet and snow-white. King crabs are always sold frozen, usually in the shell. In-shell forms include sections or clusters, legs and claws or split legs. The meat is also available in "fancy" packs of whole leg and body meat, or shredded and minced pieces. It is becoming rarer.

Dungeness crabs are found along the west coast. They weigh 675 g to 1.8 kg (1-1/2 to 4 lb.) and have delicate, sweet meat. They are sold live, precooked and frozen, or as picked meat, usually in 2.2-kg (5-lb.) vacuum-packed cans.

Blue crabs are found along the entire eastern seaboard and account for approximately 50% of the total weight of all crab species harvested in the United States. Their meat is rich and sweet. Blue crabs are available as hard-shell or soft-shell. Hard-shell crabs are sold live, precooked and frozen, or as picked meat. Soft-shell crabs are those harvested within six hours after moulting and are available live (generally only from May 15 to September 15) or frozen.

Snow Crab Legs

They are often steamed and served whole. Soft-shells can be sautéed, fried, broiled or added to soups or stews. Blue crabs are sold by size, with an average diameter of 10 to 18 cm (4 to 7 in.).

Snow or **spider crabs** are an abundant species, most often used as a substitute for the scarcer and more expensive king crab. They are harvested from Alaskan and British Columbian waters and along the eastern coast of Canada. Snow crab is sold precooked, usually frozen. The meat can be used in soups, salads, omelettes or other prepared dishes. Legs are often served cold as an appetizer.

Stone crabs are generally available only as cooked claws, either fresh or frozen (the claws cannot be frozen raw because the meat sticks to the shell).

Crayfish

Dungeness Crab

Blue Crab

Soft-Shell Crabs

Stone Crab Claws

Atlantic Lobster

In stone-crab fishery only the claw is harvested. After the claw is removed, the crab is returned to the water, where in about 18 months it regenerates a new claw. Claws average 75 to 165 g (2-1/2 to 5-1/2 oz.) each. The meat is firm, with a sweet taste similar to lobster. Cracked claws are served hot or cold, usually with cocktail sauce, lemon butter or other accompaniments.

Lobsters have brown to blue-black outer shells and firm, white meat with a rich, sweet flavour. Lobster shells turn red when cooked. They are usually poached, steamed, simmered, baked or grilled, and can be served hot or cold. Picked meat can be used in prepared dishes, soups or sautés. Lobsters must be kept alive until just before cooking. Dead lobsters should not be used. The Atlantic, also known as clawed lobster, and the spiny lobster are the most commonly marketed species. The coral (eggs) are a prized delicacy.

Atlantic lobsters have edible meat in both their tails and claws; they are considered superior in flavour to all other lobsters. They come from the cold waters along the northeast coast and are most often sold live. Atlantic lobsters may be purchased by weight (i.e., 525 g [1-1/4 lb.], 650 g [1-1/2 lb.] or 900 g [2 lb.] each), or as chix (i.e., less than 450 g [1 lb.]). (See sidebar on page 411.) Lobsters may also be purchased as culls (lobsters with only one claw) or bullets (lobsters with no claws). They are available frozen or as cooked, picked meat.

Figure 19.3 shows a cross-section of an Atlantic lobster and identifies the stomach, tomalley (the olive-green liver) and coral (the roe). The stomach is not eaten; the tomalley and coral are very flavourful and are often used in the preparation of sauces and other items.

Spiny lobsters have very small claws and are valuable only for their meaty tails, which are notched with short spines. Nearly all spiny lobsters marketed in this country are sold as frozen tails, often identified as rock lobster. Harvested in many parts of the world, those found off Florida, Brazil and in the Caribbean are marketed as warm-water tails; those found off South Africa, Australia and New Zealand are called cold-water tails. Cold-water spiny tails are considered superior to their warm-water cousins.

Slipper lobster, lobsterette and **squat lobster** are all clawless species found in tropical, subtropical and temperate waters worldwide. Although popular in some countries, their flavour is inferior to both Atlantic and spiny lobsters.

Shrimp (Fr. *crevette*) are found worldwide and are widely popular. Gulf whites, pinks, browns and black tigers are just a few of the dozens of shrimp varieties used in food service operations. Although fresh, head-on shrimp are available, the most common form is raw, head-off (also called green headless) shrimp with the shell on. Most shrimp are deheaded and frozen at sea to preserve freshness. Shrimp are available in many forms: raw, peeled and deveined; cooked, peeled and deveined; individually quick frozen; and in a variety of processed, breaded or canned products. Shrimp are graded by size, which can range from 400 per pound (450 g) (titi) to 8 per pound (450 g) (extra-colossal), and are sold in counts per pound. For example, shrimp marketed as "21–26 count"

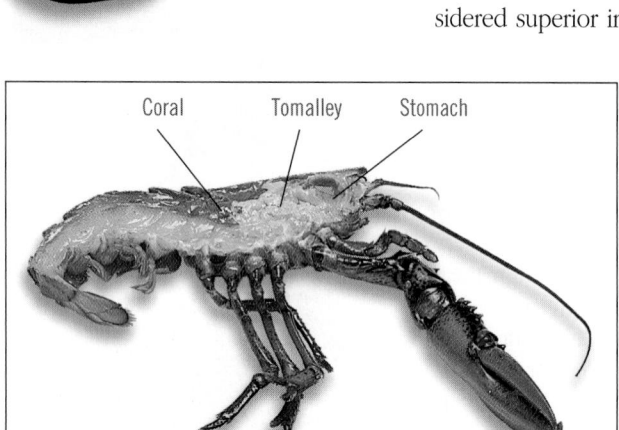
Coral   Tomalley   Stomach

FIGURE 19.3   Cross-section of an Atlantic lobster.

Green Headless Shrimp

Tiger Shrimp

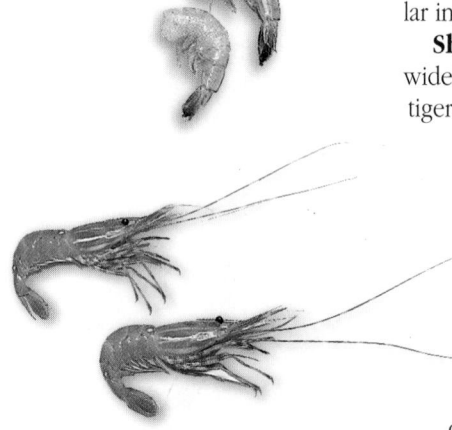
Shrimp

means that there is an average of 21 to 26 shrimp per pound; shrimp marketed as "U-10" means that there are under 10 shrimp per pound.

Prawn is often used interchangeably with the word "shrimp" in English-speaking countries. Although it is perhaps more accurate to refer to freshwater species as prawns and marine species as shrimp, in commercial practice prawn refers to any large shrimp. Equally confusing, *scampi* is the Italian name for the Dublin Bay prawn (which is actually a species of miniature lobster), but in this country *scampi* often refers to shrimp sautéed in garlic butter. The CFIA recognizes "shrimp" as the proper nomenclature for menu writing. **Langoustine** are small North Atlantic (Norway) lobsters.

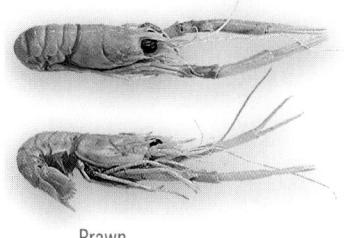
Prawn

NUTRITION

Fish and shellfish are low in calories, fat and sodium, and are high in vitamins A, B and D and protein. Fish and shellfish are also high in minerals, especially calcium (particularly in canned fish with edible bones), phosphorus, potassium and iron (especially mollusks). Some fish are high in a group of polyunsaturated fatty acids called omega-3, which may help combat high blood cholesterol levels and aid in preventing some heart disease. It also promotes fetal brain and eye development. Shellfish are not as high in cholesterol as was once thought. Crustaceans are higher in cholesterol than mollusks, but both have considerably lower levels than red meat or eggs.

The cooking methods used for fish and shellfish also contribute to their healthfulness. The most commonly used cooking methods—broiling, grilling, poaching and steaming—add little or no fat.

INSPECTION AND GRADING OF FISH AND SHELLFISH

Inspection

It is necessary to purchase fish and shellfish from approved sources only. The approval-granting agency is the Canadian Food Inspection Agency. For an operation to be an approved facility under federal regulations, it must demonstrate a Quality Management Program, which consists of a prerequisite program for the physical plant and an adherence to Hazard Analysis Critical Control Point (HACCP) principles. Verify the presence of a tag or stamp as illustrated in Figure 19.4. The new fish tag specifies the actual source of the fish (see Figure 19.5). In addition, there are guidelines for product quality, record keeping and a recall process.

Grading

No grading protocol for fish exists in Canada, so a buyer must rely on the integrity of the supplier. Ask the supplier if the fish are inspected and if it is an approved facility. The assurance of quality for yourself and the customer is well worth the extra you may pay for a superior, safe and wholesome product.

PURCHASING AND STORING FISH AND SHELLFISH

Determining Freshness

Because fish and shellfish are highly perishable, an inspection stamp does not necessarily ensure top quality. A few hours at the wrong temperature or a

Red Tide

Paralytic seafood poisoning is caused by a protozoan called *Gonyaulax*. Red-coloured tide waters are an indication of its presence. Exercise caution when harvesting your own shellfish in coastal waters; heed posted signs and local fisheries warnings.

FIGURE 19.4 CFIA mark and statements.

FIGURE 19.5 Fish Tag

couple of days in the refrigerator can turn high-quality fish or shellfish into garbage. It is important that you be able to determine for yourself the freshness and quality of the fish and shellfish you purchase or use. Freshness should be checked before purchasing and again just before cooking.

Freshness can be determined by the following:

1. *Smell*—Smell is by far the easiest way to determine freshness. Fresh fish should have a slight sea smell or no odour at all. Any off-odours or ammonia odours are a sure sign of aged or improperly handled fish.

2. *Eyes*—The eyes should be clear and full. Sunken eyes mean that the fish is drying out and is probably not fresh.

3. *Gills*—The gills should be intact and bright red. Brown gills are a sign of age.

4. *Texture*—Generally, the flesh of fresh fish should be firm. Mushy flesh or flesh that does not spring back when pressed with a finger is a sign of poor quality or age.

5. *Fins and scales*—Fins and scales should be moist and full without excessive drying on the outer edges. Dry fins or scales are a sign of age; damaged fins or scales may be a sign of mishandling.

6. *Appearance*—Fish cuts should be moist and glistening, without bruises or dark spots. Edges should not be brown or dry.

7. *Movement*—Shellfish should be purchased alive and should show movement. Lobsters and other crustaceans should be active. Clams, mussels and oysters that are partially opened should snap shut when tapped with a finger. (Exceptions are geoduck, razor and steamer clams whose siphons protrude, preventing the shell from closing completely.) Ones that do not close are dead and should not be used. Avoid mollusks with broken shells or heavy shells that might be filled with mud or sand.

Purchasing Fish and Shellfish

Fish are available from wholesalers in a variety of market forms:

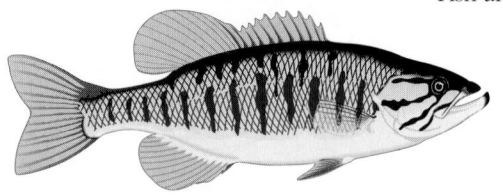

Whole or Round

- **Whole** or **round**—as caught, intact.

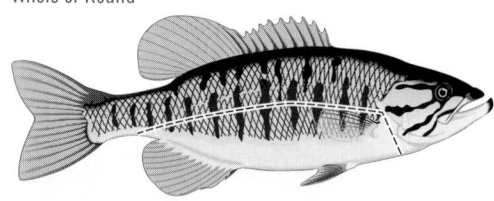

Drawn

- **Drawn**—viscera (internal organs) are removed; most whole fish are purchased this way.

Dressed or Pan-Dressed

- **Dressed**—viscera, gills, fins and scales are removed.
- **Pan-dressed**—viscera and gills are removed; fish is scaled and fins and tail are trimmed. The head is usually removed, although small fish, such as trout, may be pan-dressed with the head still attached. Pan-dressed fish are then pan-fried.

- **Butterflied**—a pan-dressed fish, boned and opened flat like a book. The two sides remain attached by the back or belly skin.

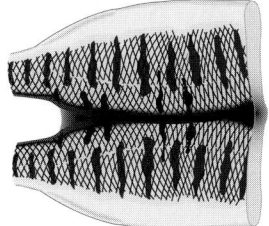

Butterflied Fillets

- **Fillet**—the side of a fish removed intact, boneless or semi-boneless, with or without skin.

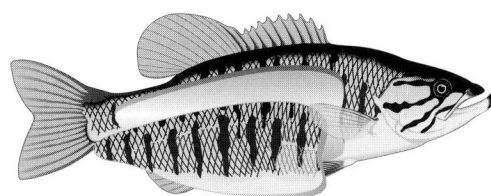

Fillets

- **Steak** or **darne**—cross-section slice, with a small section of backbone attached; usually prepared from large round fish.

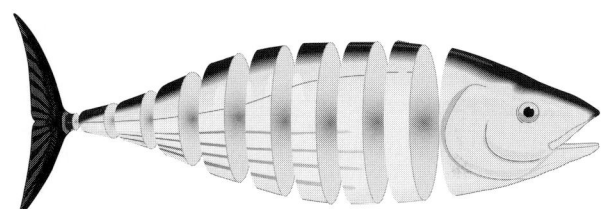

Steaks

- **Wheel** or **centre-cut**—used for swordfish and sharks, which are cut into large boneless pieces from which steaks are then cut.

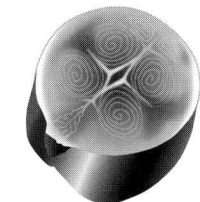

Wheel or Centre-Cut

You should purchase fish in the market forms most practical for your operation. Although fish fabrication is a relatively simple chore requiring little specialized equipment, before you decide to cut your own fish you should consider the following:

1. the food service operation's ability to utilize the bones and trim that cutting whole fish produces,
2. the employees' ability to fabricate fillets, steaks or portions as needed,
3. the storage facilities, and
4. the product's intended use.

Most shellfish can be purchased live in the shell, shucked (the meat removed from the shell) or processed. Both live and shucked shellfish are usually purchased by counts (i.e., the number per volume). For example, standard live Eastern oysters are packed 200 to 250 (the count) per bushel (the unit of volume: approximately 35 L); standard Eastern oyster meats are packed 350 per gallon. Crustaceans are sometimes packed by size based on the number of pieces per pound; for example, crab legs or shrimp are often sold in counts per pound. Or they are sold either by grades based on size (whole crabs) or by weight (lobsters).

Storing Fish and Shellfish

The most important concern when storing fish and shellfish is temperature. All fresh fish should be stored at temperatures between –1°C and 1°C (30°F and 34°F). Fish stored in a refrigerator at 4°C (40°F) will have approximately half the shelf life of fish stored at 0°C (32°F).

Most fish are shipped on ice and should be stored on ice in the refrigerator immediately upon receipt. Whole fish should be layered directly in crushed or shaved ice in a perforated pan so that the melted ice water drains away. If crushed or shaved ice is not available, cubed ice may be used provided it is put in plastic bags and gently placed on top of the fish to prevent bruising and denting. Fabricated and portioned fish may be wrapped in moisture-proof packaging before icing to prevent the ice and water from damaging the exposed flesh. Fish stored on ice should be drained and re-iced daily.

Fresh scallops, fish fillets that are purchased in plastic trays and oyster and clam meats should be set on or packed in ice. Do not let the scallops, fillets or meats come in direct contact with the ice.

Clams, mussels and oysters should be stored at 4°C (40°F), at high humidity and left in the boxes or net bags in which they were shipped. Under ideal conditions, shellfish can be kept alive for up to one week. Never store live shellfish in plastic bags and do not ice them.

If a saltwater tank is not available, live lobsters, crabs and other crustaceans should be kept in boxes with seaweed or damp newspaper to keep them moist. Most crustaceans circulate salt water over their gills; icing them or placing them in fresh water will kill them. Lobsters and crabs will live for several days under ideal conditions, but flesh volume diminishes.

Like most frozen foods, frozen fish should be kept at temperatures of –18°C (0°F) or colder. Colder temperatures greatly increase shelf life. Frozen fish should be thawed in the refrigerator; once thawed, they should be treated like fresh fish.

Whole fish properly stored in a perforated pan and covered with crushed ice.

FABRICATING PROCEDURES

As discussed, fish and shellfish can be purchased in many forms. Here we demonstrate several procedures for cutting, cleaning and otherwise fabricating or preparing fish and shellfish for cooking and service.

BASIC PROCEDURE FOR SCALING FISH

This procedure is used to remove the scales from fish that will be cooked with the skin on.

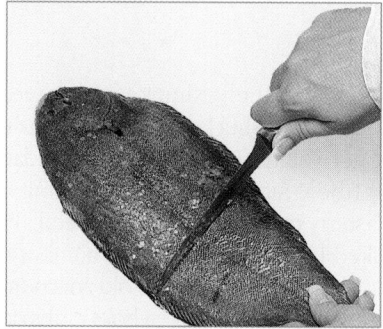

Place the fish on a work surface or in a large sink. Grip the fish by the tail and, working from the tail toward the head, scrape the scales off with a fish scaler or the back of a knife. Be careful not to damage the flesh by pushing too hard. Turn the fish over and remove the scales from the other side. Rinse the fish under cold water.

BASIC PROCEDURE FOR PAN-DRESSING FLATFISH

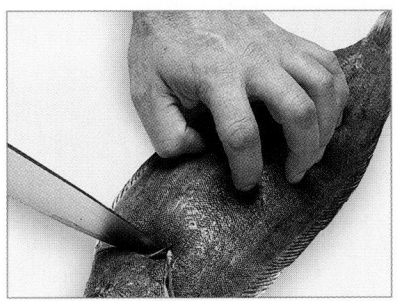

1. Scale the flatfish. Place the fish on a cutting board and remove the head by making a V-shaped cut around it with a chef's knife. Pull the head away and remove the viscera.

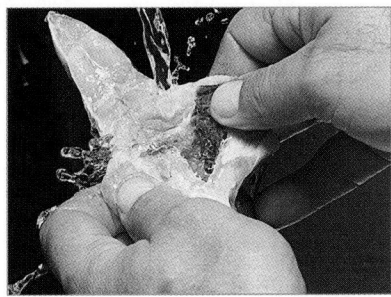

2. Rinse the fish under cold water, removing all traces of blood and viscera from the cavity.

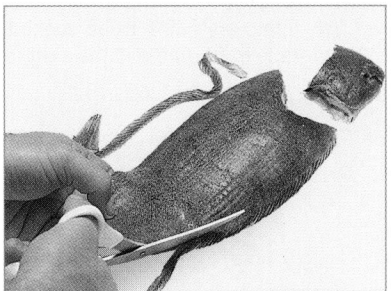

3. Using a pair of kitchen shears, trim off the tail and all of the fins.

BASIC PROCEDURE FOR FILLETING ROUND FISH

Round fish produce two fillets, one from either side.

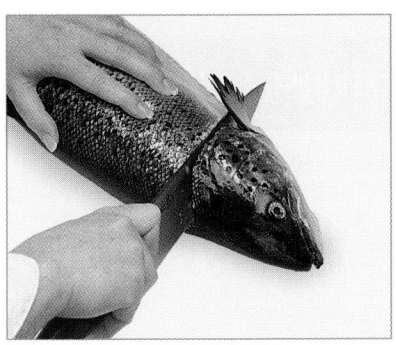

1. Using a chef's knife, cut down to the backbone just behind the gills. Do not remove the head.

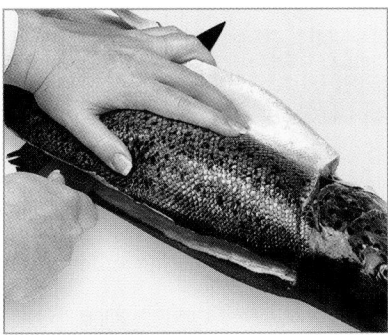

2. Turn the knife toward the tail; using smooth strokes, cut from head to tail parallel to the backbone. The knife should bump against the backbone so that no flesh is wasted; you will feel the knife cutting through the small pin bones. Cut the fillet completely free from the bones. Repeat on the other side.

3. Trim the rib bones from the fillet with a flexible filleting knife.

4. The finished fillet. (Pin bones still must be removed.)

BASIC PROCEDURE FOR FILLETING FLATFISH

Flatfish produce four fillets: two large bilateral fillets from the top and two smaller bilateral fillets from the bottom. If the fish fillets are going to be cooked with the skin on, the fish should be scaled before cooking (it is easier to scale the fish before it is filleted). If the skin is going to be removed before cooking, it is not necessary to scale the fish.

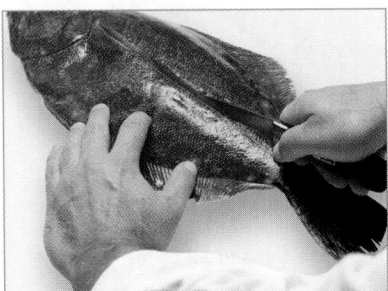

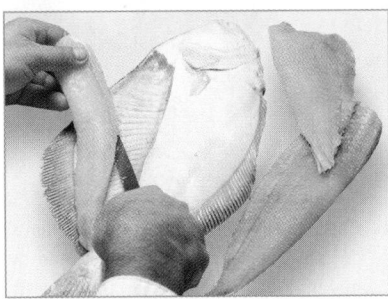

1. With the dark side of the fish facing up, cut along the backbone from head to tail with the tip of a flexible filleting knife.

2. Turn the knife and, using smooth strokes, cut between the flesh and the rib bones, keeping the flexible blade against the bone. Cut the fillet completely free from the fish. Remove the second fillet, following the same procedure.

3. Turn the fish over and remove the fillets from the bottom half of the fish, following the same procedure.

BASIC PROCEDURE FOR SKINNING DOVER SOLE

Dover sole is unique in that its skin can be pulled from the whole fish by following this procedure. The flesh of other small flatfish such as flounder, petrale sole and other types of domestic sole is more delicate; pulling the skin away from the whole fish could damage the flesh. These fish should be skinned using a filleting knife after they are filleted.

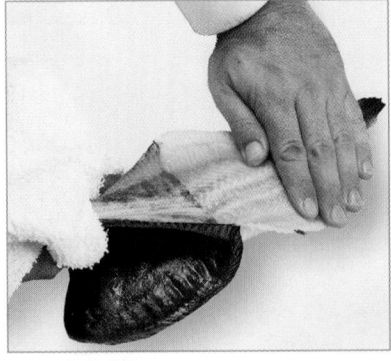

Make a shallow cut in the flesh perpendicular to the length of the fish, just in front of the tail and with the knife angled toward the head of the fish. Using a clean towel, grip the skin and pull it toward the head of the fish. The skin should come off cleanly, in one piece, leaving the flesh intact.

BASIC PROCEDURE FOR SKINNING FISH FILLETS

Here we use a salmon fillet to demonstrate the procedure for skinning fish fillets. Use the same procedure to skin all types of fish fillets.

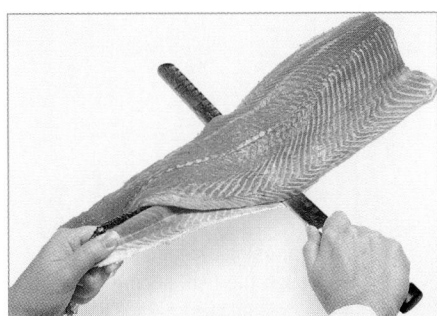

Place the fillet on a cutting board with the skin side down. Starting at the tail, use a meat slicer or a chef's knife to cut between the flesh and skin. Angle the knife down toward the skin, grip the skin tightly with one hand and use a sawing motion to cut the skin cleanly away from the flesh. Keep the skin taut.

BASIC PROCEDURE FOR PULLING PIN BONES FROM A SALMON FILLET

Round fish fillets contain a row of intramuscular bones running the length of the fillet. Known as pin bones, they are usually cut out with a knife to produce boneless fillets. In the case of salmon, they can be removed with salmon tweezers or small needle-nose pliers.

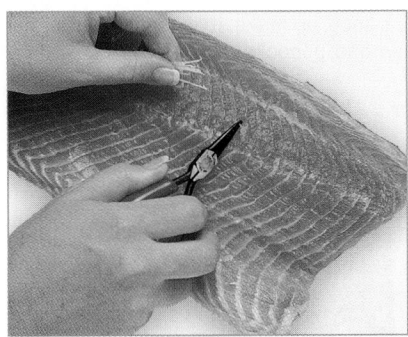

Place the fillet (either skinless or not) on the cutting board, skin side down. Starting at the front or head end of the fillet, use your fingertips to locate the bones and pull them out one by one with the pliers. Pull at an angle so as not to tear the flesh.

BASIC PROCEDURE FOR CUTTING A FILLET

A fillet is a boneless cut from a large flat or round fish. Usually cut on an angle, fillets or escallopes look larger and increase plate coverage.

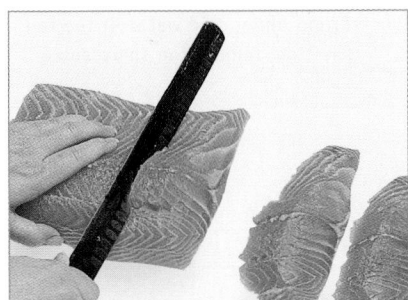

Place the fillet on the cutting board, skin side down. Using a slicer or chef's knife, cut slices of the desired weight. The fillet can be cut to the desired size by adjusting the angle of the knife. The more shallow the angle, the greater the surface area of the fillet.

BASIC PROCEDURE FOR CUTTING STEAKS FROM SALMON AND SIMILARLY SIZED ROUND FISH

Steaks, or darnes, are produced from salmon and similarly sized round fish by simply making crosscuts of the whole fish. First scale, gut and remove the fins from the fish.

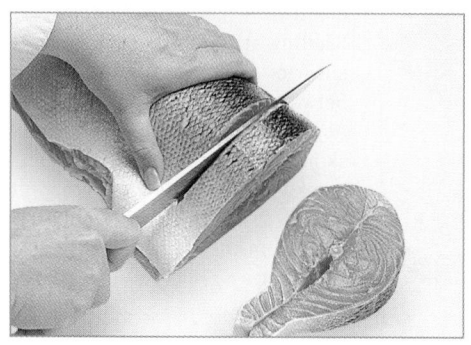

Then, using a chef's knife, cut through the fish, slicing steaks of the desired thickness. The steaks will contain some bones that are not necessarily removed.

BASIC PROCEDURE FOR PEELING AND DEVEINING SHRIMP

Peeling and deveining shrimp is a simple procedure done in most commercial kitchens. The tail portion of the shell is often left on the peeled shrimp to give it an attractive appearance or make it easier to eat. This procedure can be used on both cooked and uncooked shrimp.

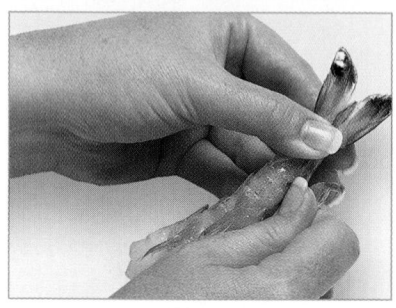

1. Grip the shrimp's tail between your thumb and forefinger. Use your other thumb and forefinger to grip the legs and the edge of the shell.

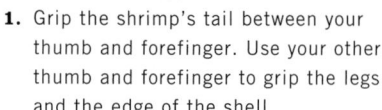

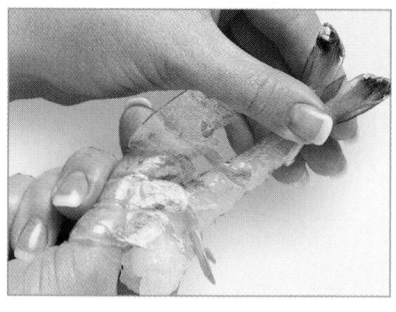

2. Pull the legs and shell away from the flesh, leaving the tail and first joint of the shell in place if desired.

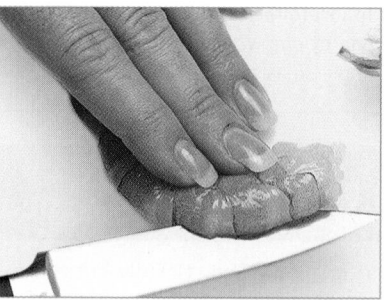

3. Place the shrimp on a cutting board and use a paring knife to make a shallow cut down the back of the shrimp, exposing the digestive tract or "vein."

4. Pull out the vein while rinsing the shrimp under cold water. If the tail is left on, remove the sharp spike.

BASIC PROCEDURE FOR BUTTERFLYING SHRIMP

Butterflying raw shrimp improves their appearance and increases their surface area for even cooking. To butterfly shrimp, first peel them using the procedure outlined on page 420.

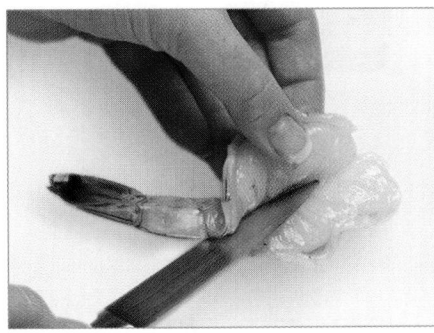

Then, instead of making a shallow cut to expose the vein, make a deeper cut that nearly slices the shrimp into two bilateral halves. Pull out the vein while rinsing the shrimp under cold water.

Shrimp for Sushi and Barbecue

To keep the shrimp straight during cooking, insert a skewer or heavy tooth-pick just under the shell, along the belly of the shrimp. This will prevent the shrimp from curling up. Remove the sand vein by opening the top of the shell at the first joint by the tail. Insert a bamboo skewer just under the flesh and lift to extract the vein.

BASIC PROCEDURE FOR PREPARING LIVE LOBSTER FOR BROILING

A whole lobster can be cooked by plunging it into boiling water or court bouillon. If the lobster is to be broiled, it must be split lengthwise before cooking.

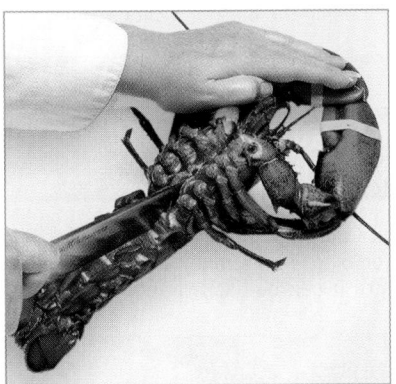

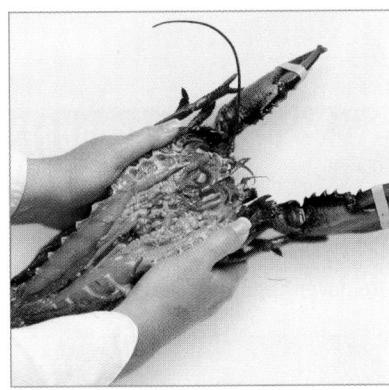

1. Place the live lobster on its back on a cutting board and pierce its head with the point of a chef's knife. Then, in one smooth stroke, bring the knife down and cut through the body and tail without splitting it completely in half.

2. Use your hands to crack the lobster's back so that it lies flat. Crack the claws with the back of a chef's knife.

3. Cut through the tail and curl each half of the tail to the side. Remove and discard the stomach and brain. The tomalley (the olive-green liver) and, if present, the coral (the roe) may be removed and saved for a sauce or other preparation.

BASIC PROCEDURE FOR PREPARING LIVE LOBSTER FOR SAUTÉING

A whole lobster may also be cut into smaller pieces for sautéing or other preparations.

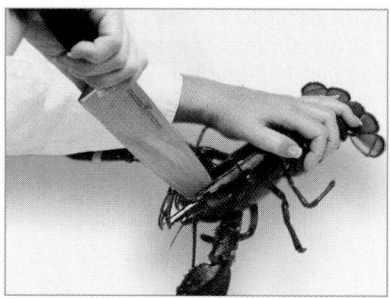

1. Use the point of a chef's knife to pierce the lobster's head.

2. Cut off the claws and arms.

3. Cut the tail into cross-sections.

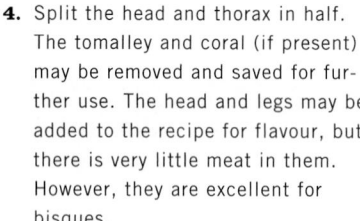

4. Split the head and thorax in half. The tomalley and coral (if present) may be removed and saved for further use. The head and legs may be added to the recipe for flavour, but there is very little meat in them. However, they are excellent for bisques.

5. Crack the claws with a firm blow, using the back of a chef's knife.

BASIC PROCEDURE FOR REMOVING COOKED LOBSTER MEAT FROM THE SHELL

Many recipes call for cooked lobster meat. Cook the lobster by plunging it into a boiling court bouillon and simmering for 6 to 8 minutes per 450 g (1 lb.). Remove the lobster and allow it to cool until it can be easily handled.

1. Pull the claws and large legs away from the body. Break the claw away from the leg. Split the legs with a chef's knife and remove the meat, using your fingers or a pick.

2. Carefully crack the claw with a mallet or the back of a chef's knife without damaging the meat. Pull out the claw meat in one piece.

continued

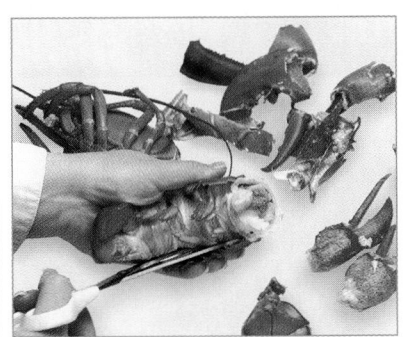

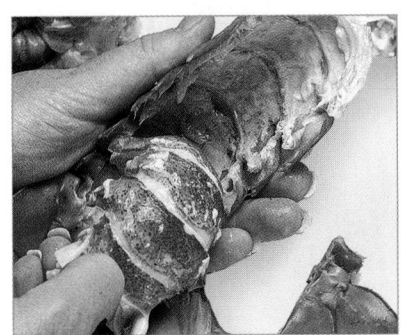

3. Pull the lobster's tail away from its body and use kitchen shears to trim away the soft membrane on the underside of the tail.

4. Pull the meat out of the shell in one piece.

BASIC PROCEDURE FOR OPENING CLAMS

Opening raw clams efficiently requires practice. Like all mollusks, clams should be cleaned under cold running water with a brush to remove all mud, silt and sand that may be stuck to their shells. A knife may be more easily inserted into a clam if the clam is washed and allowed to relax in the refrigerator for at least one hour before it is opened.

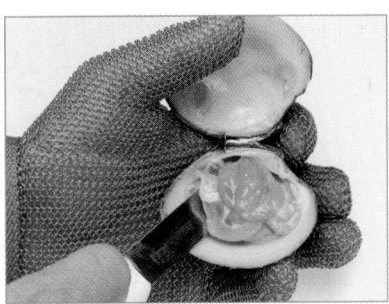

1. Wearing a mesh safety glove, hold the clam firmly in the palm of your hand; the notch in the edge of the shell should be toward your thumb. With the fingers of the same hand, squeeze and pull the blade of the clam knife between the clamshells. Do not push on the knife handle with your other hand; you will not be able to control the knife if it slips and you can cut yourself.

2. Pull the knife between the shells until it cuts the muscle. Twist the knife to pry the shells apart. Slide the knife tip along the top shell and cut through the muscle. Twist the top shell, breaking it free at the hinge; discard it.

3. Use the knife tip to release the clam from the bottom shell.

BASIC PROCEDURE FOR OPENING OYSTERS

1. Clean the oyster by brushing it under running water.

2. Wearing a mesh safety glove, hold the cleaned oyster firmly in the palm of your hand. Insert the tip of an oyster knife in the hinge and use a twisting motion to pop the hinge apart. Do not use too much forward pressure on the knife; it can slip and you could stab yourself.

3. Slide the knife along the top of the shell to release the oyster from the shell (sever the adductor muscle). Discard the top shell. Do not lose any of the juices. Reserve, strain and serve with the oysters on the half shell.

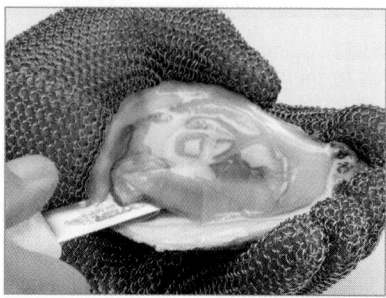

4. Use the knife tip to release the oyster from the bottom shell.

5. Fresh raw oysters on the half shell with seaweed garnish.

BASIC PROCEDURE FOR CLEANING AND DEBEARDING MUSSELS

Mussels are not normally eaten raw. Before cooking, a clump of dark threads called the beard must be removed. Because this could kill the mussel, cleaning and debearding must be done as close to cooking time as possible.

1. Clean the mussel with a brush under cold running water to remove sand and grit.

2. Pull the beard away from the mussel with your fingers or a small pair of pliers.

APPLYING VARIOUS COOKING METHODS

Fish and shellfish can be prepared by the dry-heat cooking methods of broiling and grilling, roasting (baking), sautéing, pan-frying and deep-fat frying, as well as the moist-heat cooking methods of steaming, poaching and simmering. These cooking methods are discussed below.

Determining Doneness

Unlike most meats and poultry, nearly all fish and shellfish are inherently tender and should be cooked just until done. Indeed, overcooking is the most common mistake made when preparing fish and shellfish. The Canadian Department of Fisheries recommends that all fish be cooked 10 minutes for every 2.5 cm (1 in.) of thickness, regardless of cooking method. Although this may be a good general policy, variables such as the type and the form of fish and the exact cooking method used suggest that one or more of the following methods of determining doneness are more appropriate for professional food service operations.

1. *Translucent flesh becomes opaque*—The raw flesh of most fish and shellfish appears somewhat translucent. As the proteins coagulate during cooking, the flesh becomes opaque.
2. *Flesh becomes firm*—The flesh of most fish and shellfish firms as it cooks. Doneness can be tested by judging the resistance of the flesh when pressed with tongs. Raw or undercooked fish or shellfish will be mushy and soft. As the fish cooks, the flesh offers more resistance and springs back quickly.
3. *Flesh separates from the bones easily*—The flesh of raw fish remains firmly attached to the bones. As the fish cooks, the flesh and bones separate easily.
4. *Flesh begins to flake*—Fish flesh consists of short muscle fibres separated by thin connective tissue. As the fish cooks, the connective tissue breaks down and the groups of muscle fibres begin to flake; that is, they separate from one another. Fish is done when the flesh *begins* to flake. If the flesh flakes easily the fish will be overdone and dry.

Remember, fish and shellfish are subject to carryover cooking. Because they cook quickly and at low temperatures, it is better to undercook the item and allow carryover cooking or residual heat to finish the cooking process. Cook to an internal temperature of 57°C (135°F).

Dry-Heat Cooking Methods

Dry-heat cooking methods are those that do not require additional moisture at any time during the cooking process. The dry-heat cooking methods used with fish and shellfish are broiling and grilling, roasting (usually referred to as baking when used with fish and shellfish), sautéing, pan-frying and deep-fat frying.

Broiling and Grilling

After brushing with flavoured (infused) oil or butter, fish can be grilled directly on the grate or placed on a heated platter under the broiler. Broiled or grilled fish should have a lightly browned surface and a slightly smoky flavour as a result of the intense radiant heat of the broiler or grill. The interior should be moist and juicy. Broiled or grilled shellfish meat should be moist and tender, with only slight coloration from the grill or broiler.

Selecting Fish and Shellfish to Broil or Grill

Nearly all types of fish and shellfish can be successfully broiled or grilled. Salmon, trout, swordfish and other oily fish are especially well suited to grilling, as are lean fish such as bass and snapper. Fillets of lean flatfish with delicate textures, such as flounder and sole, are better broiled. They should be placed on a preheated broiling (sizzler) platter before being placed under the broiler.

Oysters and clams are often broiled on the half shell with flavoured butters, bread crumbs or other garnishes and served sizzling hot. Squid can be stuffed, secured with a toothpick and broiled or grilled. Brushed with butter, split lobsters, king crabs and snow crabs are often broiled or grilled. Whole lobsters can be split and broiled or grilled, or their tails can be removed, split and cooked separately. Large crab legs can also be split and broiled or grilled. Shrimp and scallops are often marinated and broiled in flavoured butters or grilled on skewers for easy handling.

Seasoning Fish and Shellfish to Be Broiled or Grilled

All fish should be brushed lightly with butter or oil before being placed on the grill or under the broiler. The butter or oil prevents sticking and helps leaner fish retain moisture. For most fish, a simple seasoning of salt and pepper suffices. But most fish do respond well to marinades, especially those made with white wine and lemon juice. Because most fish are delicately flavoured, they should be marinated for only a brief period of time. (Even marinated fish should be brushed with butter or oil before cooking.) Herbs should be avoided because they will burn from the intense heat of the broiler or grill.

Clams, oysters and other shellfish that are stuffed or cooked with butters, vegetables, bacon or other accompaniments or garnishes gain flavour from these ingredients. Be careful, however, not to overpower the delicate flavours of the shellfish with the addition of too many strong flavourings.

Accompaniments to Broiled and Grilled Fish and Shellfish

Broiled fish and shellfish are served with sauces made separately. Butter sauces such as a beurre blanc are popular, as the richness of the sauce complements the lean fish. Vegetable coulis are a good choice for a healthful, lower-fat accompaniment. Additional sauce suggestions are found in Table 10.5.

If the item is cooked on a broiler platter with a seasoned butter, it is often served with that butter. Lemon or lime wedges are the traditional accompaniment to any broiled or grilled fish.

Almost any side dish goes well with broiled or grilled fish or shellfish. Fried or boiled potatoes, pasta and rice are all good choices. Grilled vegetables are a natural choice.

BASIC PROCEDURE FOR BROILING OR GRILLING FISH AND SHELLFISH

All fish is delicate and must be carefully handled to achieve an attractive finished product. When broiling whole fish or fillets with their skin still on, score the skin by making several diagonal slashes approximately 5-mm (1/4-in.) deep at even intervals. This prevents the fish from curling during cooking, promotes even cooking and creates a more attractive finished product. Be especially careful not to overcook the item. It should be served as hot as possible as soon as it is removed from the broiler or grill.

continued

1. Heat the broiler or grill.

2. Use a wire brush to remove any charred or burnt particles that may be stuck to the broiler or grill grate. The grate can be wiped with a lightly oiled towel to remove any remaining particles and help season the grate.

3. Prepare the item to be broiled or grilled. For example, cut the fish into steaks or fillets of even thickness; split the lobster; peel and/or skewer the shrimp. Season or marinate the item as desired. Brush the item with oil or butter.

4. Place the item (presentation side down) on a grill. If using a broiler, place the item directly on the grate or on a preheated broiler platter. Tender fish are usually broiled presentation side up on a broiler platter.

5. If practical, turn the item to produce the attractive crosshatch marks associated with grilling that are discussed in Chapter 9, Principles of Cooking. Items less than 12-mm (1/2-in.) thick cooked on a preheated broiler platter do not have to be turned over.

6. Cook the item to the desired doneness and serve immediately.

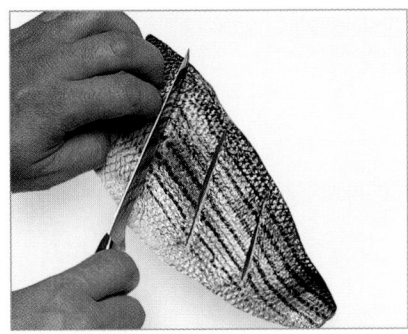

1. Broiled Black Sea Bass: Scoring the skin of the fish.

2. Placing the fish on a broiler platter, under the broiler.

APPLYING THE BASICS   **RECIPE 19.1**

Broiled Black Sea Bass with Herb Butter and Sautéed Leeks

Yield: 1 serving

Black sea bass fillet, skin on, approximately 200 g (7 oz.)	1	1
Salt and pepper	TT	TT
Whole butter, melted	as needed	as needed
Leeks, julienne	100 g	3-1/2 oz.
Lemon juice	10 mL	2 tsp.
Herb butter (p. 210)	30 g	1 oz.

1. Score the skin of the bass with three diagonal cuts approximately 5-mm (1/4-in.) deep.

2. Season the bass fillet with salt and pepper and brush with melted butter.

3. Place the fillet on a preheated broiler platter, skin side up, and place under the broiler.

4. Blanch the julienned leeks in boiling water until nearly tender.

5. Drain the leeks and sauté them in 15 mL (2 Tbsp.) of whole butter until tender. Add the lemon juice; season with salt and pepper.

6. Remove the fish from the broiler when done. Top with the herb butter and serve on a bed of sautéed leeks.

3. Serving the fish on a bed of sautéed leeks.

RECIPE 19.1

Approximate values per serving:	
Calories	512
Total fat	33 g
Saturated fat	17 g
Cholesterol	171 mg
Sodium	638 mg
Total carbohydrates	16 g
Protein	39 g

Baking

The terms *baking* and *roasting* are used interchangeably when applied to fish and shellfish. One disadvantage of baking fish is that the short baking time does not allow the surface of the fish to caramelize. To help correct this problem, fish can be browned in a sauté pan with a small amount of butter to achieve the added flavour and appearance of a browned surface, and then finished in an oven.

Selecting Fish and Shellfish to Bake

Fatty fish produce the best baked fish. Fish fillets and steaks are the best market forms to bake, as they cook quickly and evenly and are easily portioned. Although lean fish can be baked, it tends to become dry and must be basted often.

Seasoning Fish and Shellfish to Be Baked

The most popular seasonings for baked fish are lemon, butter, salt and pepper. Fish can also be marinated before baking for added flavour. But baked fish usually depend on the accompanying sauce for much of their flavour.

Shellfish are often stuffed or mixed with other ingredients before baking. For example, raw oysters on the half shell can be topped with spinach, watercress and Pernod (Oysters Rockefeller, Recipe 19.15) and baked. Shrimp are often butterflied, stuffed and baked; lobsters are split, stuffed and baked. Many food service operations remove clams from their shells, mix them with bread crumbs, seasonings or other ingredients, refill the shells and bake the mixture.

Accompaniments to Baked Fish and Shellfish

Baked fish is often served with a flavourful sauce such as a Creole sauce (p. 204) or a beurre blanc (Recipe 10.14). Additional sauce suggestions are found in Table 10.5. Almost any type of rice, pasta or potato is a good accompaniment, as is any variety of sautéed vegetable.

BASIC PROCEDURE FOR BAKING FISH AND SHELLFISH

1. Portion the fish and arrange on a well-oiled or buttered pan, presentation side up.

2. Season as desired and brush the surface of the fish or shellfish generously with melted butter; add garnishes or flavourings as desired or directed in the recipe. Sear, if desired, to develop colour.

3. Place the pan in a preheated oven at approximately 65°C (150°F).

4. Baste periodically during the cooking process (more often if the fish is lean). Remove from the oven when the fish is slightly underdone.

APPLYING THE BASICS		RECIPE 19.2

Baked Red Snapper

Yield: 10 servings

Red snapper fillets, 175 g (6 oz.) each	10	10
Salt and white pepper	TT	TT
Whole butter, melted	125 g	4 oz.
Mint leaves, chopped	25 g	2-1/2 Tbsp.
Garlic, minced	10 g	2 tsp.
Tomato concassée	300 g	10 oz.
White wine	100 mL	3 fl. oz.
Lemon juice	100 mL	3 fl. oz.

RECIPE 19.2

Approximate values per serving:	
Calories	411
Total fat	13 g
Saturated fat	6.8 g
Cholesterol	97 mg
Sodium	592 mg
Total carbohydrates	36 g
Protein	38 g

continued

1. Place the snapper on a buttered baking pan. Season the fillets with salt and white pepper; brush with butter.

2. Combine the mint, garlic and tomatoes and spoon on top of each portion of the fish.

3. Add the white wine and lemon juice to the pan.

4. Bake at 65°C (150°F), basting once halfway through the cooking process, until done, approximately 25 minutes.

1. Baked Red Snapper: Brushing the fillets with butter.

2. Topping each portion with mint, garlic and tomato concassée.

3. The finished fish.

Sautéing

Sautéing is a very popular cooking method for fish and shellfish. It lightly caramelizes the food's surface, giving it additional flavour. Typically, other ingredients such as garlic, onions, vegetables, wine and lemon juice are added to the fond to make a sauce.

Selecting Fish and Shellfish to Sauté

Both fatty and lean fish may be sautéed. Flatfish are sometimes dressed and sautéed whole, as are small round fish such as trout. Larger fish such as salmon can be cut into steaks or filleted and cut into fillets. The portions should be relatively uniform in size and thickness and fairly thin to promote even cooking. Although clams, mussels and oysters are not often sautéed, scallops and crustaceans are popular sauté items.

Seasoning Fish and Shellfish to Be Sautéed

Many types of fish—especially sole, flounder and other delicate, lean fish fillets—are often dredged in flour before sautéing. Seasoned butter is used to sauté some items, such as scampi-style shrimp. These items derive their flavour from the butter; additional seasonings should not be necessary.

Cooking Temperatures

The sauté pan and cooking fat must be hot before the fish or shellfish are added. Do not add too much fish or shellfish to the pan at one time or the pan and fat will cool, letting the foods simmer in their own juices. Thin slices and small pieces of fish and shellfish require a short cooking time, so use high temperatures in order to caramelize their surfaces without overcooking. Large, thick pieces of fish or shellfish being cooked in the shell may require slightly lower cooking temperatures to ensure that they are cooked without overbrowning their surfaces. (See Figure 19.6.)

FIGURE 19.6 A properly sautéed fish fillet (top) is lightly brown and holds its shape without sticking to the pan. An improperly sautéed fish fillet (bottom) is pale, falls apart and sticks to the pan.

Accompaniments to Sautéed Fish and Shellfish

Sautéed fish and shellfish are nearly always served with a sauce made directly in the sauté pan. This sauce may be as simple as browned butter (beurre noisette) or a complicated sauce flavoured with the fond. In some cases, seasoned butter is used to sauté the fish or shellfish and the butter is then served with the main item. See Table 10.5 for additional sauce suggestions.

Mildly flavoured rice and pasta are good choices to serve with sautéed fish or shellfish.

BASIC PROCEDURE FOR SAUTÉING FISH AND SHELLFISH

1. Cut or portion the fish or shellfish.

2. Season the item and dredge in seasoned flour if desired.

3. Heat a suitable sauté pan over moderate heat; add enough oil or clarified butter to cover the bottom to a depth of about 3 mm (1/8 in.).

4. Add the fish or shellfish to the pan (fish should be placed presentation side down); cook until done, turning once halfway through the cooking process. Add other foods as called for in the recipe.

5. Remove the fish or shellfish. If a sauce is to be made in the sauté pan, follow the procedures discussed in Chapter 17, Poultry.

APPLYING THE BASICS   RECIPE 19.3

Sautéed Halibut with Three-Colour Peppers and Spanish Olives

Yield: 4 servings

Halibut fillets, 175 g (6 oz.) each	4	4
Salt and pepper	TT	TT
Olive oil	60 mL	2 fl. oz.
Onion, sliced	100 g	3 oz.
Garlic, minced	10 g	2 tsp.
Green bell pepper, julienne	100 g	3 oz.
Red bell pepper, julienne	100 g	3 oz.
Yellow bell pepper, julienne	100 g	3 oz.
Tomato, peeled and diced	250 g	8 oz.
Spanish olives, pitted and quartered	60 g	2 oz.
Fresh thyme, chopped	8 g	2 tsp.
Lemon juice	60 mL	2 fl. oz.
Fish stock	60 mL	2 fl. oz.

1. Season the fillets with salt and pepper.

2. Heat a sauté pan and add the olive oil.

3. Sauté the halibut, turning once. Remove and reserve in a warm place.

4. Add the onion and garlic to the same pan and sauté for approximately 1 minute. Add the peppers and sauté for 1–2 minutes more.

RECIPE 19.3

Approximate values per serving:	
Calories	442
Total fat	21 g
Saturated fat	3 g
Cholesterol	72 mg
Sodium	775 mg
Total carbohydrates	13.5 g
Protein	49 g

continued

5. Add the tomato, olives and thyme; sauté briefly.

6. Add the lemon juice and deglaze the pan. Add the fish stock, simmer for 2 minutes to blend the flavours and adjust the seasonings.

7. Return the fish to the pan to reheat. Serve each fish fillet on a bed of vegetables with sauce and an appropriate garnish.

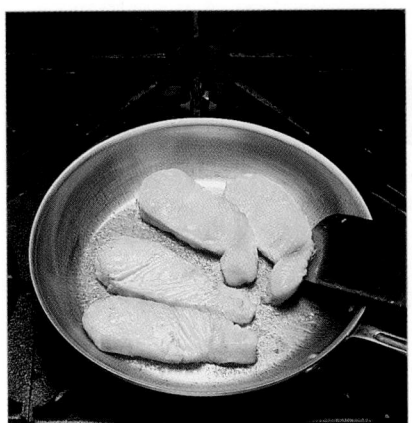

1. Sautéed Halibut: Sautéing the halibut fillets.

2. Sautéing the onion, garlic and peppers.

3. Adding the fish stock.

Pan-Frying

Pan-frying is very similar to sautéing, but it uses more fat to cook the main item. Pan-fried fish is always coated with flour, batter or breading to help seal the surface and prevent the flesh from coming in direct contact with the cooking fat. Properly prepared pan-fried fish and shellfish should be moist and tender with a crisp surface. If battered or breaded, the coating should be intact with no breaks.

Selecting Fish and Shellfish to Pan-Fry

Both fatty and lean fish may be pan-fried. Trout and other small fish are ideal for pan-frying, as are portioned fillets of lean fish such as halibut. Pan-fried fish and shellfish should be uniform in size and relatively thin so they cook quickly and evenly.

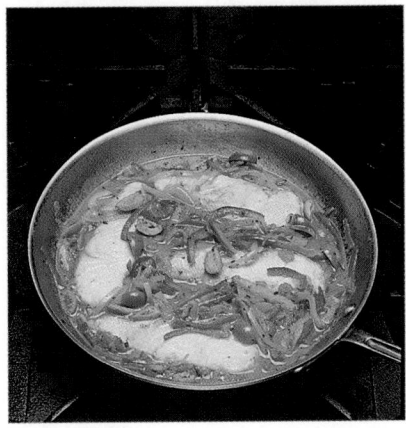

4. Returning the fish to the pan to reheat.

Seasoning Fish and Shellfish to Be Pan-Fried

Although fish and shellfish can be marinated or seasoned directly, it is more common to season the flour, batter or breading that will coat them. Batters, for example, can contain cheese, and breadings can contain nuts and other ingredients to add different flavours to the fish or shellfish. Additional seasonings come from sauces and other accompaniments served with the pan-fried fish or shellfish.

Cooking Temperatures

The fat should always be hot before the fish or shellfish are added. Breaded or battered fish fillets cook very quickly, and the fat should be hot enough to brown the coating without overcooking the interior. Whole pan-fried fish take longer to cook and therefore require a slightly lower cooking temperature so the surface does not become too dark before the interior is cooked. Oven finishing may be necessary.

Accompaniments to Pan-Fried Fish and Shellfish

Lemon or lime wedges are the classic accompaniment to pan-fried fish and shellfish. Sauces that accompany pan-fried items are made separately. Mayonnaise-based sauces such as Tartar Sauce (Recipe 25.14) and rémoulade sauce are especially popular; rich wine-based sauces should be avoided. Vegetable coulis, such as tomato, also complement many pan-fried items. Additional sauce suggestions are found in Table 10.5.

BASIC PROCEDURE FOR PAN-FRYING FISH AND SHELLFISH

1. Heat enough clarified butter or oil in a heavy sauté pan to immerse one-third to one-half of the item. The fat temperature should be between 165°C and 180°C (325°F and 350°F).

2. Add the floured, breaded or battered item to the pan, being careful not to splash the hot fat. Cook until done, turning once halfway through the cooking process.

3. Remove the food and drain on absorbent paper.

4. Serve it promptly with an appropriate sauce.

1. Blue Crab Cakes: Mixing all ingredients for the crab cakes.

2. Forming the crab cakes.

3. Pan-frying the crab cakes.

APPLYING THE BASICS RECIPE 19.4

 Blue Crab Cakes with Fresh Salsa

Yield: 15 60-g (2-oz.) cakes

Blue crab meat	450 g	1 lb.
Cream, 35%	175 mL	6 fl. oz.
Red bell pepper, small dice	60 g	2 oz.
Green bell pepper, small dice	60 g	2 oz.
Clarified butter	as needed	as needed
Green onions, sliced	1 bunch	1 bunch
Fresh bread crumbs	175 g	6 oz.
Salt and pepper	TT	TT
Dijon mustard, whole seed	15 mL	1 Tbsp.
Parmesan, grated	50 g	5 Tbsp.
Cajun Spice Mix (recipe follows)	30 g	3 Tbsp.
Egg, slightly beaten	1	1
Tomato Salsa (Recipe 10.18)	500 mL	1 pt.

1. Carefully pick through the crab meat, removing any pieces of shell. Keep the lumps of crab meat as large as possible.

2. Place the cream in a saucepan and bring to a boil. Reduce by approximately one-half. Chill the cream well.

3. Sauté the red and green bell peppers in a small amount of clarified butter until tender. Add green onions and sweat 30 seconds.

4. Combine the crab meat, reduced cream, peppers, green onions and approximately 90 g (3 oz.) of the bread crumbs along with the salt, pepper, Dijon mustard, Parmesan, Cajun Spice and egg. Mix to combine all ingredients, trying to keep the lumps of crab meat intact.

continued

5. Using a mould, form the crab mixture into cakes of the desired size.

6. Place the remaining bread crumbs in an appropriately sized hotel pan. Place the crab cakes, a few at a time, in the hotel pan and cover with the bread crumbs. To help them adhere, press the crumbs lightly into the cakes.

7. Heat a sauté pan over moderate heat and add enough clarified butter to cover the bottom, approximately 0.5-cm (1/4-in.) deep.

8. Add the crab cakes to the pan and cook until done, turning once when the first side is nicely browned. Remove and drain on absorbent paper.

9. Serve the crab cakes with fresh Tomato Salsa.

Cajun Spice Mix

Paprika	25 g	3 Tbsp.
Salt	30 g	2 Tbsp.
Onion powder	12 g	2 Tbsp.
Garlic powder	4.5 g	1 Tbsp.
Black pepper	8 g	1 Tbsp.
Cayenne pepper	5.5 g	2 tsp.
Oregano, dry, crushed	2 g	1 Tbsp.
Thyme, dry	3 g	1 Tbsp.
White pepper, ground	2.5 g	1 tsp.

RECIPE 19.4

Approximate values per 60 g serving:

Calories	167
Total fat	8.3 g
Saturated fat	4.5 g
Cholesterol	58 mg
Sodium	891 mg
Total carbohydrates	13.5 g
Protein	9.8 g

Deep-Fat Frying

Deep-fat frying is the process of cooking foods by submerging them in hot fat. Typically, fish or shellfish are breaded or battered before deep-fat frying. Alternatively, they can be formed into croquettes or fritters. Properly deep-fat fried fish and shellfish should be moist and tender, not greasy or tough. Their coating should be crispy and golden brown.

Selecting Fish and Shellfish to Deep-Fat Fry

Whole small fish and fillets of lean fish such as catfish or halibut are excellent for deep-fat frying. The fillets should be of uniform size and relatively thin so that they cook quickly and evenly. Fatty fish, such as salmon, are ideal for croquettes. Peeled shrimp and shucked mollusks, especially clams and oysters, can be breaded, battered or formed into fritters and deep-fat fried. Deep-fat fried breaded or battered sliced squid or octopus served with a dipping sauce makes an excellent hors d'oeuvre.

Seasoning Fish and Shellfish to Be Deep-Fat Fried

Typically, seasonings used for deep-fat fried fish or shellfish are added to the breading or batter, although salt and pepper should be added after frying. Additional flavours come from sauces or accompaniments.

Accompaniments to Deep-Fat Fried Fish and Shellfish

As with pan-fried fish and shellfish, lemon wedges and mayonnaise-based sauces such as tartar sauce and rémoulade sauce are popular accompaniments to deep-fat fried fish and shellfish. Spicy tomato- or soy-based dipping sauces are also excellent choices. Traditional English fish and chips is served with malt vinegar.

BASIC PROCEDURE FOR DEEP-FAT FRYING FISH AND SHELLFISH

1. Shuck, peel, cut, trim or otherwise prepare the fish or shellfish to be deep-fat fried. Season, bread or batter it, as desired.

2. Heat the fat to the desired temperature, usually around 177°C (350°F). Breaded or battered fish or shellfish cook quickly and the fat must be hot enough to cook the food's interior without burning its surface.

3. Carefully place the food in the hot fat using either the basket method or the swimming method.

4. Deep-fat fry the fish or shellfish until done. Doneness is usually determined by colour, timing or sampling.

5. Remove the deep-fat fried food from the fat and hold it over the fryer, allowing the excess fat to drain off. Transfer the food to a hotel pan either lined with absorbent paper or fitted with a rack. Season with salt, if desired.

6. If the deep-fat fried fish or shellfish is to be held for later service, place it under a heat lamp.

Deep-Fried Basa Fillets

RECIPE 19.5

Approximate values per serving:	
Calories	383
Total fat	26 g
Saturated fat	2 g
Cholesterol	98 mg
Sodium	370 mg
Total carbohydrates	2 g
Protein	33 g

APPLYING THE BASICS   **RECIPE 19.5**

Deep-Fried Basa Fillets with Tartar Sauce

Yield: 8 servings

Basa fillets, cut into uniform-sized pieces	1.5 kg	3 lb.
Salt and pepper	TT	TT
Flour	as needed for breading	
Egg wash	as needed for breading	
Bread crumbs	as needed for breading	
Tartar Sauce (Recipe 25.14)	325 mL	12 fl. oz.

1. Dry the fillets and season with salt and pepper.

2. Bread the fillets using the standard breading procedure.

3. Using the basket method, deep-fat fry the fillets until done. Drain well and serve with the Tartar Sauce.

1. Flouring the seasoned fish fillets.

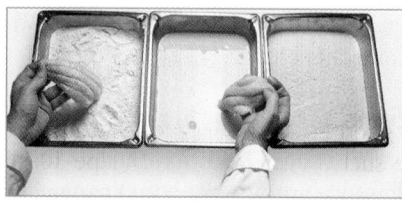

2. Passing the floured fillets through the egg wash.

3. Coating the fillets with bread crumbs.

Moist-Heat Cooking Methods

Fish and shellfish lend themselves well to moist-heat cooking methods, especially steaming, poaching and simmering. Steaming best preserves the food's natural flavours and cooks without adding fat. Poaching is also popular, especially for fish. Poached fish can be served hot or cold, whole or as steaks, fillets or portions. Boiling, which usually means simmering, is most often associated with crustaceans.

Steaming

Steaming is a very natural way to cook fish and shellfish without adding fats. Fish are steamed by suspending them over a small amount of boiling liquid in a covered pan. The steam trapped in the pan gently cooks the food while preserving its natural flavours and most nutrients. The liquid used to steam fish and shellfish can be water or a court bouillon with herbs, spices, aromatics or wine added to infuse the item with the additional flavours. Mussels and clams can be steamed by placing them directly in a pan, adding a small amount of wine or other liquid and covering them. Their shells will hold them above the liquid as they cook. Fish and shellfish can also be steamed by wrapping them in parchment paper together with herbs, vegetables, butters or sauces as accompaniments and baking them in a hot oven. This method of steaming is called **en papillote**.

Steamed fish and shellfish should be moist and tender. They should have clean and delicate flavours. Any accompaniments or sauces should complement the main item without masking its flavour. Fish and shellfish cooked en papillote should be served piping hot so that the aromatic steam trapped by the paper escapes as the paper is cut open tableside.

● **en papillote** a cooking method in which food is wrapped in paper, leaves or foil and then heated so that the food steams in its own moisture

Selecting Fish and Shellfish to Steam

Mollusks (e.g., clams and mussels), fatty fish (e.g., salmon and sea bass) and lean fish (e.g., sole) all produce good results when steamed. The portions should be of uniform thickness and no more than 2.5 cm (1 in.) thick to promote even cooking.

Seasoning Fish and Shellfish to Be Steamed

Steamed fish and shellfish rely heavily on their natural flavours and often require very little seasoning. Nevertheless, salt, pepper, herbs and spices can be applied directly to the raw food before steaming. Flavoured liquids used to steam fish and shellfish will contribute additional flavours. If the liquid is served with the fish or shellfish as a broth or used to make a sauce to accompany the item, it is especially important that the liquid be well seasoned. Lemons, limes and other fruits or vegetables can also be cooked with the fish or shellfish to add flavours. Clams and mussels often do not require additional salt, as the liquor released when they open during cooking is sufficiently salty.

Accompaniments to Steamed Fish and Shellfish

Steamed fish and shellfish are popular partly because they are low in fat. In keeping with this perception, a low-fat or nonfat sauce or a simple squeeze of lemon and steamed fresh vegetables are good accompaniments. If fat is not a concern, then an emulsified butter sauce such as beurre blanc (Recipe 10.14) or hollandaise (Recipe 10.13) may be a good choice. Table 10.5 lists several sauce suggestions.

Classic New England steamed clams are served with a portion of the steaming liquid; steamed mussels are served with a sauce that is created from the wine and other ingredients used to steam them.

1. Steamed Salmon: Placing the fish in the steamer.

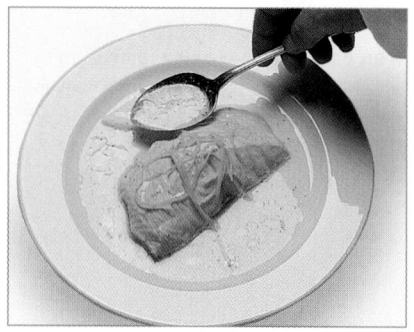

2. Spooning the dressing over the fish.

RECIPE 19.6

Approximate values per serving:	
Calories	638
Total fat	48 g
Saturated fat	7.7 g
Cholesterol	103 mg
Sodium	304 mg
Total carbohydrates	6.9 g
Protein	35 g

RECIPE 19.7

Approximate values per serving:	
Calories	504
Total fat	36 g
Saturated fat	22 g
Cholesterol	156 mg
Sodium	718 mg
Total carbohydrates	7 g
Protein	37.9 g

BASIC PROCEDURE FOR STEAMING FISH AND SHELLFISH

1. Portion the fish to an appropriate size. Clean the shellfish.
2. Prepare the cooking liquid. Add seasoning and flavouring ingredients as desired and bring to a boil.
3. Place the fish or shellfish in the steamer on a rack or in a perforated pan and cover tightly.
4. Steam the fish or shellfish until done.
5. Serve the fish or shellfish immediately with the steaming liquid or an appropriate sauce.

APPLYING THE BASICS	RECIPE 19.6

Steamed Salmon with Lemon and Olive Oil

Yield: 4 servings

Lemon zest, blanched	30 g	3 Tbsp.
Lemon juice	125 mL	4 fl. oz.
Salt and pepper	TT	TT
Virgin olive oil	125 mL	4 fl. oz.
White wine	250 mL	8 fl. oz.
Bay leaf	1	1
Leek, chopped	60 g	2 oz.
Fresh thyme	1 sprig	1 sprig
Peppercorns, cracked	3 g	1 tsp.
Salmon fillet or steak, approximately 175 g (6 oz.)	4	4

1. To make the dressing, combine the lemon zest, lemon juice, salt and pepper. Whisk in the olive oil.
2. Combine the wine, bay leaf, leek, thyme and peppercorns in the bottom of a steamer.
3. Season the salmon with salt and pepper and place it in the steamer basket.
4. Cover the steamer and bring the liquid to a boil. Cook the fish until done, approximately 4–6 minutes.
5. Plate the salmon and spoon the dressing over it.

APPLYING THE BASICS	RECIPE 19.7

Red Snapper en Papillote

Yield: 6 servings

Clarified butter	as needed	as needed
Leek, julienne	100 g	3 oz.
Fennel, julienne	125 g	4 oz.
Carrot, julienne	100 g	3 oz.
Celery, julienne	100 g	3 oz.

continued

Red bell pepper, julienne	100 g	3 oz.
Red snapper fillets, skin on, 175 g (6 oz.) each	6	6
Salt and pepper	TT	TT
Basil Butter (p. 210)	250 g	9 oz.

1. Cut 6 heart-shaped pieces of parchment paper large enough to contain the fish and vegetables when folded in half.

2. Brush each piece of parchment paper with clarified butter.

3. Toss the vegetables together. Place one-sixth of the vegetables on half of each piece of the buttered parchment paper.

4. Place 1 portion of red snapper on each portion of vegetables, skin side up; season with salt and pepper.

5. Top each portion of fish with 40 g (1-1/2 oz.) of Basil Butter.

6. Fold each piece of paper over and crimp the edges to seal it.

7. Place the envelopes (papillotes) on sheet pans and bake in a preheated oven at 230°C (450°F) for 8–10 minutes.

8. When baked, the parchment paper should puff up and brown. Remove from the oven and serve immediately. The envelope should be carefully cut open tableside to allow the aromatic steam to escape.

1. Red Snapper en Papillote: Cutting heart-shaped pieces of parchment paper.

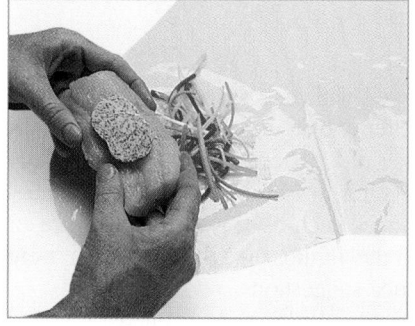

2. Placing the vegetables, red snapper and Basil Butter on the parchment paper.

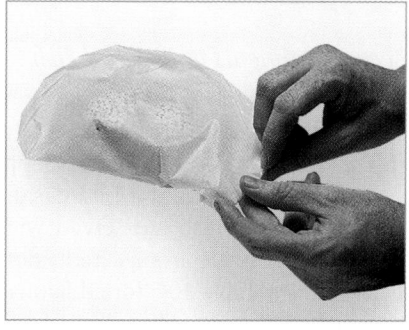

3. Crimping the edge of the parchment paper to seal it.

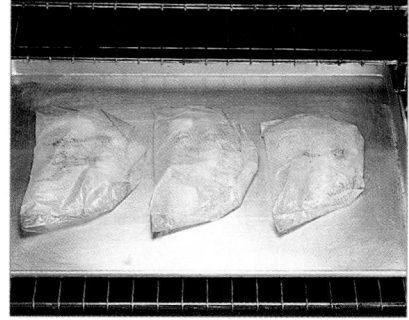

4. The finished papillotes.

Poaching

Poaching is a versatile and popular method for cooking fish. Shellfish are rarely poached, however. The exception is squid, which can be quickly poached and chilled for use in salads and other preparations.

There are two distinct poaching methods. The first is the **submersion method**, in which the fish is completely covered with a liquid, usually a court bouillon, fish stock or fish fumet. It is cooked until just done. The poached fish is then served (either hot or cold) with a sauce sometimes made from a portion of the cooking liquid but more often made separately. Whole fish (wrapped in cheesecloth to preserve its shape during cooking), fillets and steaks can all be cooked by submersion poaching.

The second method, called **shallow poaching**, combines poaching and steaming to achieve the desired results. The main item, usually a fillet or steak, is placed on a bed of aromatic vegetables in enough liquid to immerse half of the item. The liquid, called a **cuisson**, is brought to a simmer on the stove

● **submersion poaching** a poaching method in which the food is completely covered with the poaching liquid

● **shallow poaching** a moist-heat cooking method that combines poaching and steaming; the food (usually fish) is placed on a vegetable bed and partially covered with a liquid (cuisson) and simmered

● **cuisson** the liquid used for shallow poaching

top. The pan is then covered with a piece of buttered parchment paper (cartouche) or a lid, and cooking is completed either on the stove top or in the oven. Shallow-poached fish is usually served with a sauce made with the reduced cooking liquid. Sometimes the main item is sautéed lightly before the cooking liquid is added. If so, the cooking method is more accurately braising, as both dry- and moist-heat cooking methods are used.

Selecting Fish to Poach

Lean white fish such as turbot, bass and sole are excellent for poaching. Some fatty fish such as salmon and trout are also excellent choices.

Seasoning Fish to Be Poached

Fish poached by either submersion or shallow poaching gain all of their seasonings from the liquid in which they are cooked and the sauce with which they are served. Therefore, it is very important to use a properly prepared court bouillon, fish fumet or a good-quality fish stock well seasoned with vegetables such as shallots, onions or fennel as well as ample herbs, spices and other seasonings. Many poached fish recipes call for wine. When using wine, either in the cooking liquid or sauce, be sure to choose a wine of good quality. Most fish are very delicately flavoured, and using poor-quality wine might ruin an otherwise excellent dish. Citrus, especially lemon, is always a popular seasoning; lemon juice or zest may be added to the poaching liquid, the sauce or the finished dish.

Accompaniments to Poached Fish

Poached fish cooked by submersion go well with rich sauces like hollandaise and beurre blanc. If fat is a concern, a better choice may be a vegetable coulis (for example, broccoli or red pepper). Cold poached fish are commonly served with mayonnaise-based sauces such as sauce vert or rémoulade. Shallow-poached fish are served with sauces such as a white wine sauce or beurre blanc made from a reduction of the liquids in which the fish were poached. See Table 10.5 for additional sauce suggestions.

Poached fish are often served with rice or pasta and steamed or boiled vegetables.

BASIC PROCEDURE FOR SUBMERSION POACHING

1. Prepare the cooking liquid. Whole fish should be started in a cold liquid; gradually increasing the liquid's temperature helps preserve the appearance of the fish. Portioned fish should be started in a simmering liquid to preserve their flavour and more accurately estimate cooking time.

2. Use a rack to lower the fish into the cooking liquid. Be sure the fish is completely submerged.

3. Poach the fish at 80°C to 85°C (175°F to 185°F) until done.

4. Remove the fish from the poaching liquid, moisten with a portion of the liquid and hold in a warm place for service. Or remove the fish from the poaching liquid, cover it to prevent drying and allow it to cool, then refrigerate.

5. Serve the poached fish with an appropriate sauce.

APPLYING THE BASICS   RECIPE 19.8

 # Whole Poached Salmon

Yield: 18–20 servings

| Salmon, drawn, 1.8–2.2 kg (4–5 lb.) | 1 | 1 |
| Court bouillon | as needed | as needed |

1. Place the fish on a lightly oiled rack or screen and secure with butcher's twine.

2. Place the rack or screen in a pot and cover with cold court bouillon.

3. Bring the court bouillon to a simmer over moderate heat. Reduce the heat and poach the fish at 80–85°C (175–180°F) until done, approximately 30–45 minutes.

4. If the fish is to be served hot, remove it from the court bouillon, draining well, and serve immediately with an appropriate garnish. If it is to be served cold, remove it from the court bouillon, draining well, cool and refrigerate for several hours before decorating and garnishing as desired.

RECIPE 19.8

Approximate values per serving:	
Calories	144
Total fat	5 g
Saturated fat	1 g
Cholesterol	65 mg
Sodium	293 mg
Total carbohydrates	0 g
Protein	24 g

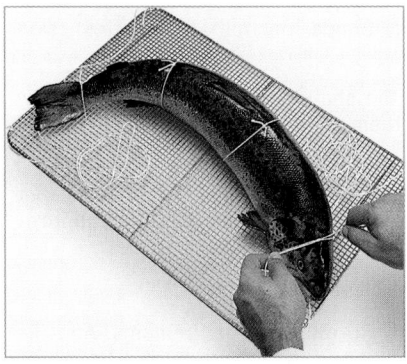

1. Whole Poached Salmon: Arranging the whole fish on a rack.

2. Preparing the court bouillon.

3. Removing and draining the fish. Serve immediately or chill.

BASIC PROCEDURE FOR SHALLOW POACHING

1. Butter a sauteuse and add aromatic vegetables as directed in the recipe.

2. Add the fish to the pan.

3. Add the cooking liquid to the pan.

4. Cover the pan with buttered parchment paper (cartouche) or a lid.

5. Bring the liquid to a simmer and cook the fish on the stove top or in the oven until done.

6. Remove the fish from the pan, moisten with a portion of the liquid and hold in a warm place for service.

7. Reduce the cuisson and finish the sauce as directed in the recipe.

8. Serve the poached fish with the sauce.

Approximate values per serving:	
Calories	485
Total fat	32 g
Saturated fat	19 g
Cholesterol	162 mg
Sodium	614 mg
Total carbohydrates	11 g
Protein	31 g

1. Fillets of Sole Bonne Femme: Arranging the sole on the bed of shallots and mushrooms.

2. Covering the fish with buttered parchment paper after the liquid is added.

3. Adding the velouté to the cuisson.

Fillets of Sole Bonne Femme

Yield: 2 servings

Sole fillets, approximately 75 g (2-1/2 oz.) each	4	4
Salt and pepper	TT	TT
Whole butter	10 g	2 tsp.
Shallots, minced	5 g	1 tsp.
Mushrooms, sliced	125 g	4 oz.
Parsley, chopped	3 g	1 tsp.
White wine	100 mL	3 fl. oz.
Lemon juice	25 mL	1 fl. oz.
Fish stock	100 mL	3 fl. oz.
Fish velouté	125 mL	4 fl. oz.
Butter, softened	50 g	2 oz.

1. Season the sole with salt and pepper. Shape into rolls (paupiettes), skin side in, starting at the head end.

2. Melt the butter in a sauté pan. Add the shallots, mushrooms and parsley and arrange the sole paupiettes over them. Add the wine, lemon juice and fish stock.

3. Bring the liquid to a simmer. Cover the fish with buttered parchment paper and cook on the stove top or in a 175°C (350°F) oven until done, approximately 5–8 minutes.

4. Remove the sole and reserve in a warm place.

5. Reduce the cuisson until approximately 30 mL (1 fl. oz.) remains. Add the velouté and adjust the seasonings. Mount the sauce with butter. Serve the sauce with the fish.

VARIATION: Small whole sole, skinned, or plaice may be used.

Simmering

"Boiled" lobster, crab and shrimp are not actually boiled; rather, they are cooked whole in their shells by simmering. Although they are not as delicate as some fish, these crustaceans can become tough and are easily overcooked if the cooking liquid is allowed to boil.

Selecting Shellfish to Simmer

Lobsters, crabs and shrimp are commonly cooked by simmering. Their hard shells protect their delicate flesh during the cooking process.

Seasoning Shellfish to Be Simmered

The shellfish being simmered are not seasoned. Rather, they gain flavour by being cooked in a seasoned or flavoured liquid, typically salted water or court bouillon. A sachet of pickling spice or Old Bay Seasoning® is sometimes used for additional flavour.

Determining Doneness

Timing is the best method for determining the doneness of simmered shellfish. This varies depending on the size of the shellfish and how quickly the liquid returns to a simmer after the shellfish are added. Shrimp cook in as little as 3 to 5 minutes, crabs cook in 5 to 10 minutes and it can take as little as 6 to 8 minutes for a 450-g (1-lb.) lobster to cook and 15 to 20 minutes for a 1.1-kg (2-1/2-lb.) lobster.

Accompaniments to Simmered Shellfish

The standard accompaniments to simmered shellfish are lemon wedges and melted butter. If the shellfish is being eaten cold, there are a variety of flavourful cold sauces to select from. Nearly any type of vegetable or starch goes well with simmered shellfish, and salad preparations are popular as well as freshly baked breads.

BASIC PROCEDURE FOR SIMMERING SHELLFISH

1. Bring court bouillon or water to a boil.

2. Add the shellfish to the liquid. Bring the liquid back to a boil and reduce to a simmer. Whenever an item is added to boiling water, it lowers the water's temperature. The greater the amount of water, however, the faster it will return to a boil. So, to accelerate the time within which the water returns to a boil after the shellfish are added, use as much water as possible.

3. Cook until done.

4. Remove the shellfish from the liquid and serve immediately. Or cool by plunging them in ice water if they are to be eaten cold.

Boiled Lobster

APPLYING THE BASICS		RECIPE 19.10

Boiled Lobster

Yield: 1 serving

Lobster, 675 g (1 lb. 8 oz.)	1	1
Boiling salted water	8 L	2 gal.
Lemon wedges	4	4
Whole butter, melted	60 mL	2 fl. oz.

1. Drop the lobster into the boiling water. Bring the water back to a boil, reduce to a simmer and cook the lobster until done, approximately 12 minutes.

2. Remove the lobster from the pot, drain and serve immediately with lemon wedges and melted butter on the side.

3. If the lobster is to be eaten cold, plunge it into a sink of ice water to stop the cooking process. When cool enough to handle, remove the meat from the shell following the procedures discussed earlier.

RECIPE 19.10

Approximate values per serving:	
Calories	1095
Total fat	51 g
Saturated fat	30 g
Cholesterol	612 mg
Sodium	3279 mg
Total carbohydrates	20 g
Protein	140 g

Combination Cooking Methods

Combination cooking methods are used with meats, game and poultry in part to tenderize them. Because fish and shellfish are inherently tender, they do not necessarily benefit from such procedures. As noted in the section on shallow poaching, fish can on occasion be lightly sautéed or browned and then poached. Although this procedure is a combination cooking method, it is used to enhance flavours and not to tenderize the product.

You may encounter fish or shellfish recipes with the word "braised" or "stew" in the title. Note, however, that these recipes rarely follow the traditional combination cooking methods discussed in this book.

Conclusion

In part because of consumers' increased health awareness, more and more food service operations are expanding their selections of fish and shellfish. Their task is aided by the tremendous variety of high-quality fish and shellfish now available. A variety of dry-heat and moist-heat cooking methods can be used with these products and a variety of sauces and accompaniments can be served with them. Regardless of how they are served, care and attention are required in order to select, store and avoid overcooking fish and shellfish.

Questions for Discussion

1. Discuss six techniques for determining the freshness of fish and shellfish.
2. What are the physical differences between a flatfish and a round fish? How do fabrication techniques vary for these fish?
3. List four market forms for fish and discuss several factors that may determine the form most appropriate for an operation to purchase.
4. List the three categories of mollusks and give an example of a commonly used food from each category.
5. Discuss four methods for determining the doneness of fish or shellfish. Why is it important not to overcook fish and shellfish?
6. Explain the differences between shallow poaching and submersion poaching. Why is poaching a commonly used method for preparing fish and shellfish?
7. Why are combination cooking methods rarely used with fish and shellfish? Why is boiling rarely used?

Additional Fish and Shellfish Recipes

RECIPE 19.11

Poached Fish Steaks

Yield: 8 servings
Method: Poaching

Court Bouillon (Recipe 10.5)	as needed	as needed
Fish steaks (cod, salmon or turbot), each 200 g (7 oz.)	8	8

1. Bring the court bouillon to a boil.
2. Arrange the steaks on a rack and lower into the court bouillon.
3. Reduce the heat and poach the fish until done, approximately 5–10 minutes.
4. Remove the fish and drain well. Remove the skin or bones, if necessary. Serve with lemon wedges and an appropriate sauce, such as hollandaise, mousseline or beurre noisette.

RECIPE 19.11

Approximate values per serving:

Calories	230
Total fat	2 g
Saturated fat	0 g
Cholesterol	125 mg
Sodium	310 mg
Total carbohydrates	0 g
Protein	52 g

RECIPE 19.12

Teriyaki Salmon with Pineapple Papaya Salsa

Yield: 4 servings
Method: Grilling

Soy sauce	250 mL	8 fl. oz.
Garlic, crushed	5 g	1 tsp.
Ginger, minced	5 g	1 tsp.
Brown sugar	60 g	2 oz.
Sake	125 mL	4 fl. oz.
Salmon fillets, each 120 g (4 oz.)	4	4
Vegetable oil	as needed	as needed
Pineapple Papaya Salsa (Recipe 26.9)	450 g	16 oz.

1. To make the marinade, combine the soy sauce, garlic, ginger, brown sugar and sake.
2. Marinate the salmon fillets in the marinade for 15 minutes.
3. Remove the salmon from the marinade and pat dry. Brush the fillets with vegetable oil and broil or grill until done.
4. Serve the salmon on a bed of warmed Pineapple Papaya Salsa.

Teriyaki Salmon with Pineapple Papaya Salsa

RECIPE 19.12

Approximate values per serving:

Calories	230
Total fat	9 g
Saturated fat	2 g
Cholesterol	65 mg
Sodium	3651 mg
Total carbohydrates	28 g
Protein	35 g

RECIPE 19.13

Red Snapper Veracruz

Yield: 4 servings
Method: Sautéing

Red snapper fillets, skinless, each 175 g (6 oz.)	4	4
Salt and pepper	TT	TT
Flour	as needed	as needed
Olive oil	60 mL	2 fl. oz.
Onions, medium dice	175 g	6 oz.
Garlic cloves, minced	15 g	4
Lemon juice	30 mL	1 fl. oz.
Fish or chicken stock	250 mL	8 fl. oz.
Jalapeño, seeded, small dice	1	1
Tomato concassée	650 g	1 lb. 8 oz.
Pimento-stuffed green olives, quartered	150 g	20
Sugar	5 g	1 tsp.
Cinnamon stick	5 g	1
Dried thyme	0.5 g	1/2 tsp.
Dried marjoram	0.5 g	1/2 tsp.
Capers	25 g	2 Tbsp.
Fresh cilantro for garnish	as needed	as needed

Red Snapper Veracruz

RECIPE 19.13

Approximate values per serving:

Calories	570
Total fat	22 g
Saturated fat	3 g
Cholesterol	80 mg
Sodium	1820 mg
Total carbohydrates	41 g
Protein	51 g

continued

1. Season the fillets with salt and pepper and dredge in flour. Sauté the fillets in olive oil until done. Remove and reserve in a warm place.

2. Add the onions and garlic to the pan and sauté until tender. Deglaze the pan with the lemon juice and add the stock, jalapeño, tomatoes, olives, sugar, cinnamon stick, thyme and marjoram.

3. Simmer 10 minutes. Remove the cinnamon stick and add the capers. Season with salt and pepper to taste.

4. Return the fish to the pan to reheat. Serve on warm plates garnished with fresh cilantro.

VARIATION: Substitute bass or halibut fillets for the red snapper.

1. Paupiettes of Sole: Flattening the fillets slightly with a mallet.

2. Spreading the fillets with the prepared mousseline.

3. Rolling the paupiettes.

RECIPE 19.14

Approximate values per serving:	
Calories	466
Total fat	20 g
Saturated fat	11 g
Cholesterol	267 mg
Sodium	564 mg
Total carbohydrates	6.2 g
Protein	61 g

RECIPE 19.14

Paupiettes of Sole with Mousseline of Shrimp

Yield: 10 servings
Method: Poaching

Shrimp meat	600 g	20 oz.
Egg white	2	2
Cream, 35%	300 mL	10 fl. oz.
Salt and white pepper	TT	TT
Lemon sole fillets, skinless, each 125 g (4 oz.)	20	20
Whole butter	as needed	as needed
Shallots, chopped	85 g	3 oz.
Parsley, chopped	30 g	3 Tbsp.
White vermouth	300 mL	10 fl. oz.
Shrimp stock	575 mL	20 fl. oz.
Beurre manié	approx. 75 g	approx. 2-1/2 oz.

1. Purée the raw shrimp meat in a food processor.

2. Add the egg white and pulse to incorporate.

3. Slowly add 100 mL (3-1/2 fl. oz.) of the cream to the shrimp while pulsing the processor. Season the mousseline with salt and white pepper.

4. Place the sole fillets skin side up on a cutting board and flatten slightly with a mallet.

5. Spread each fillet with a portion of the mousseline. Roll up the fillets, starting with the thickest part and finishing with the tail portion.

6. Butter a sauteuse and sprinkle with the chopped shallots and parsley.

7. Place the sole paupiettes in the sauteuse and add the vermouth and shrimp stock.

8. Bring the liquid to a boil, cover with a piece of buttered parchment paper and place in a 180°C (350°F) oven. Poach until nearly done.

9. Remove the sole from the sauteuse and reserve in a warm place.

10. Return the sauteuse to the heat and reduce the cuisson slightly.

11. Thicken the cuisson to the desired consistency with the beurre manié.

12. Add the remaining cream, bring the sauce to a boil and strain through a fine etâmine. Adjust the seasonings.

13. Serve 2 paupiettes per portion in a pool of sauce.

Oysters Rockefeller

RECIPE 19.15

Oysters Rockefeller

ADAPTED FROM ANTOINE'S RESTAURANT, NEW ORLEANS, LA

Yield: 6 servings

Method: Baking

Oysters, on half shell	36	36
Butter	250 g	8 oz.
Celery, finely chopped	60 g	2 oz.
Garlic, finely chopped	5 g	1 tsp.
Shallots, finely chopped	60 g	2 oz.
Fennel, finely chopped	60 g	2 oz.
Parsley, finely chopped	30 g	1 oz.
Spinach (or watercress)	125 g	4 oz.
Pernod	60 mL	2 oz.
Fresh bread crumbs	60 g	2 oz.
Salt and ground white pepper	TT	TT
Rock salt	as needed	as needed

1. Shuck the oysters; reserve in fridge. Retain as much oyster liquor as possible.
2. Sauté the celery, garlic, shallots, fennel and parsley in butter for 5 minutes.
3. Add the spinach or watercress leaves and sweat 1 minute.
4. Add the Pernod and bread crumbs and season to taste.
5. Transfer mixture to a food processor and purée.
6. Top each oyster with 10 mL (2 tsp.) of purée to coat the oyster.
7. Bake the oysters on a bed of rock salt at 230°C (450°F) until the mixture bubbles; approximately 6–7 minutes.

RECIPE 19.15

Approximate values per serving:	
Calories	438
Total fat	37 g
Saturated fat	22 g
Cholesterol	151 mg
Sodium	834 mg
Total carbohydrates	15 g
Protein	9 g

RECIPE 19.16

Clams Casino

Yield: 36 clams

Method: Baking

Bacon, diced	100 g	4 slices
Onion, minced	30 g	1 oz.
Red bell pepper, minced	30 g	1 oz.
Green bell pepper, minced	30 g	1 oz.
Whole butter	180 g	6 oz.
Lemon juice	15 mL	1 Tbsp.
Worcestershire sauce	10 mL	2 tsp.
Tabasco sauce	TT	TT
Clams, scrubbed	36	36
Fresh bread crumbs	60 g	2 oz.

Clams Casino

1. Fry the bacon until well done. Drain the fat, reserving 30 mL (2 Tbsp.).
2. Sauté the onion and peppers in the bacon fat until tender; remove from the heat and cool.
3. Combine 120 g (4 oz.) of the butter, lemon juice, Worcestershire sauce, Tabasco sauce, bacon pieces and sautéed vegetables and chill.
4. Open the clams, leaving the loosened meat in the bottom shell. Top each clam with 5 mL (1 tsp.) of the vegetable-butter-bacon mixture.
5. Melt the remaining butter in a sauté pan and toss the bread crumbs in the butter. Top each clam with a portion of the bread crumbs.
6. Bake at 200°C (400°F) until light brown and bubbling, approximately 10 minutes. Serve immediately.

RECIPE 19.16

Approximate values per serving:	
Calories	55
Total fat	4.5 g
Saturated fat	3 g
Cholesterol	16 mg
Sodium	107 mg
Total carbohydrates	2 g
Protein	2 g

Pierre Dubrulle, CCC

Born in France, into a family of restaurateurs, Pierre apprenticed in Lille. Soon afterwards, he was drafted into the French army, where he cooked breakfast, lunch and dinner for 2000 men per day for 18 months. Pierre came to Canada in 1966 and worked in a variety of top-notch dining establishments before owning and operating his own delicatessens and restaurants. He founded The Pierre Dubrulle Culinary School in 1983, and in 1992 joined Thomas Haney Secondary School as a Chef Instructor.

RECIPE 19.17

Approximate values per serving:	
Calories	964
Total fat	50 g
Saturated fat	26 g
Cholesterol	218 mg
Sodium	2617 mg
Total carbohydrates	58 g
Protein	63 g

RECIPE 19.17

Mussel Soup

SAMUEL ROBERTSON TECHNICAL SECONDARY SCHOOL, Maple Ridge, BC
Chef Instructor Pierre Dubrulle, CCC

Yield: 4 servings
Method: Simmering

Fresh shell mussels	675 g	1-1/2 lb.
Dry white wine	125 mL	4 fl. oz.
Fish stock	1.5 L	1.5 qt.
Roux, white	100 g	3-1/2 oz.
White pepper, freshly ground	TT	TT
Saffron threads	1 g	1 tsp.
Cream, 35%	250 mL	8 fl. oz.
Carrot, julienne, blanched	125 g	1/2 cup
Leek, julienne, blanched	100 g	1/2 cup
Pernod	5 mL	1 tsp.
Baguette, toasted	1	1
Parmesan cheese, freshly grated	75 g	1/2 cup
Chopped parsley	as needed	as needed

1. Wash, clean and debeard mussels.
2. Cook mussels in the white wine in a sauce pot with a tight lid until all the mussels open. Remove mussels and cool. Strain and reserve liquid.
3. Remove mussels from shell and reserve mussels.
4. Reduce stock and cooking liquid by one-third and thicken reduced liquid with roux to achieve a light coating consistency. Simmer to cook out roux. Season with pepper and saffron.
5. Add cream, boil and strain into clean pot. Keep warm. Add carrot and leek.
6. Warm mussels and place in soup bowls. Pour hot soup over mussels. Sprinkle with Pernod. Place baguette slices, sprinkle with cheese and parsley.

Scott Jaeger

After completing an apprenticeship with Bruno Marti at La Belle Auberge, Scott went to work at the Waldorf Hotel in London, England, the Hotel Eiger in Switzerland, and the Four Seasons in Melbourne, Australia, before opening The Pear Tree Restaurant in Burnaby, BC. Scott was Canada's representative at the 2007 Bocuse d'Or in Lyon.

RECIPE 19.18

Roasted Sablefish with Tomato Jam

THE PEAR TREE RESTAURANT, Burnaby, BC
Vice-Conseiller Culinaire Scott Jaeger

Yield: 10 servings
Method: Searing

Black cod, fresh	1.5 kg	1 lb. 12 oz.
Tiroler spec or prosciutto	250 g	8 oz.
Butter	100 g	3-1/2 oz.
Sea salt and black pepper	TT	TT
Tomato Jam (recipe follows)		

1. Clean, bone and skin cod into long loins.
2. Thinly slice the cured meat and wrap the fish in it. Refrigerate for 2 hours to partially cure the fish.
3. Sear the fish in butter on all sides until just cooked through.
4. Slice and serve over Tomato Jam (recipe follows) with sea salt and fresh black pepper.

continued

Tomato Jam

Roma tomatoes, peeled and seeded	30	30
Brown sugar	80 g	6 Tbsp.
Rice wine vinegar	90 mL	6 Tbsp.
Sachet:		
Cloves	3	3
Star anise pod	1	1
Black peppercorns	6	6
Coriander seeds	10	10
Chile flakes	pinch	pinch

Place all ingredients in a noncorrosive saucepan and reduce to a jam consistency.

RECIPE 19.18

Approximate values per serving, with Tomato Jam:	
Calories	338
Total fat	19 g
Saturated fat	6 g
Cholesterol	94 mg
Sodium	546 mg
Total carbohydrates	26 g
Protein	34 g

Tomato Jam— Approximate values per serving:	
Calories	109
Total fat	1.2 g
Saturated fat	0.1 g
Cholesterol	0 mg
Sodium	36 mg
Total carbohydrates	25 g
Protein	3.1 g

RECIPE 19.19

Shellfish Bouillabaisse with Ginger Aïoli

SHAW CONFERENCE CENTRE, EDMONTON, AB
Executive Chef Simon Smotkowicz, CCC

Yield: 4 servings
Method: Sautéing

Butter, unsalted	50 g	4 Tbsp.
Carrots, medium, peeled and diced	75 g	1
Celery, stalks, peeled and diced	150 g	2
Fennel bulb, cored and diced	150 g	1
Onion, medium, peeled and diced	150 g	1
Ginger root, peeled and minced	40 g	1/4 cup
Clams	12	12
Mussels, cleaned and debearded	12	12
Fish stock	175 mL	6 fl. oz.
Butter, unsalted	60 g	4 Tbsp.
Prawns, shelled	8	8
Lobsters, split lengthwise	2	2
Salt and pepper	TT	TT
Scallops	8	8
White wine	125 mL	4 fl. oz.
Ground ginger	10 g	3 tsp.
Vegetable Broth (recipe follows)	1.25 L	40 fl. oz.
Saffron	pinch	pinch
Butter, unsalted, room temperature	40 g	3 Tbsp.

Ginger Aïoli (recipe follows)

1. In a large saucepan, heat the butter over medium-high heat, add the vegetables and ginger and sauté until softened.
2. Remove from the pan and set aside. Add the clams, mussels and stock, cover the pan and simmer until the shellfish are just opened. Remove the shellfish from the pan and set aside.
3. In the same pan, heat the butter. Season the prawns and lobsters with salt and pepper and place in the pan. Sauté until pink, remove from the pan and set aside. Season the scallops with salt and pepper, add to the pan and sauté until golden brown. Remove from the pan and set aside.

Simon Smotkowicz, CCC
Simon has been a member and a leader of award-winning Canadian culinary teams for many years, managing Team Canada to a world championship in Glasgow in 1997 and 2001. In 1995 he was elected Chef of the Year for the Western Region by his peers in the CFCC, now the CCFCC.

RECIPE 19.19

Approximate values per serving:	
Calories	962
Total fat	74 g
Saturated fat	26 g
Cholesterol	263 mg
Sodium	1824 mg
Total carbohydrates	18 g
Protein	40 g

continued

4. In the same pan, combine the wine, ginger, Vegetable Broth and saffron and reduce by half. Whisk in the butter and season. Remove from the heat and keep warm.

5. To serve, arrange the vegetables and shellfish in individual bowls, pour the reduced and seasoned broth on top, and spoon the Ginger Aïoli over the bouillabaisse as desired.

Vegetable Broth

Yield: 1.25 L (40 fl. oz.)

White wine	250 mL	8 fl. oz.
Carrot, medium, peeled and chopped	75 g	1
Onion, medium, peeled and chopped	150 g	1
Celery stalk, chopped	75 g	1
Tomato, medium, peeled and chopped	150 g	1
Ginger root, peeled and chopped	30 g	3 Tbsp.
Water	1.8 L	64 fl. oz.
Saffron	pinch	pinch
Bouquet garni (celery, bay leaf, thyme and cloves)	1	1

1. Put the wine in a large saucepan, add the vegetables, ginger, water, saffron and bouquet garni and bring to a boil.

2. Reduce the heat and simmer for 20 minutes or until reduced by approximately one-third. Remove from the heat, strain and reserve.

Ginger Aïoli

Yield: 180 mL (6 fl. oz.)

Ginger root, peeled and chopped	10 g	2 tsp.
Garlic clove	5 g	1
White wine	30 mL	1 fl. oz.
Saffron	pinch	pinch
Egg yolk, small	1	1
Olive oil	175 mL	6 fl. oz.
Salt and pepper	TT	TT

1. In a small sauté pan, combine the ginger, garlic, wine and saffron. Bring the mixture to a boil, and reduce until nearly all of the liquid has evaporated.

2. Remove the reduction to the bowl of a food processor fitted with a metal blade and purée the mixture. While processing, incorporate the egg yolk and add the oil in a steady stream until the mixture is emulsified.

3. Season with salt and pepper, remove to another bowl and set aside in the refrigerator.

Vegetable Broth—Approximate values per 300 mL serving:

Calories	38
Total fat	0 g
Saturated fat	0 g
Cholesterol	0 mg
Sodium	17 mg
Total carbohydrates	0.5 g
Protein	0 g

Ginger Aïoli—Approximate values per 30 g serving:

Calories	215
Total fat	24 g
Saturated fat	3 g
Cholesterol	32 mg
Sodium	175 mg
Total carbohydrates	0.5 g
Protein	0.5 g

RECIPE 19.20

Seviche/Escabeche

SASKATOON, SK
Chef/Consultant David Powell, CCC

Yield: 1 kg (2-1/4 lb.)
Method: Marinating

Raw scallops	600 g	1 lb. 4 oz.
Fresh lime juice	175 mL	6 fl. oz.
Scallion, bias cut	1	1
Serrano pepper, minced	1	1
Red onion, fine dice	75 g	2-1/2 oz.
Fresh cilantro, minced	10 g	1 Tbsp.
Olive oil	30 mL	2 Tbsp.
Tomato, peeled, seeded, diced	250 g	9 oz.
Garlic, chopped	8 g	2 tsp.
Salt and pepper	TT	TT

1. Slice the scallops evenly. Place in a nonreactive container and add the lime juice. Cover and marinate in the refrigerator for 4 hours.

2. Toss in the remaining ingredients and season to taste with salt and pepper. Chill thoroughly and serve as a salad, cocktail or canapé.

3. If the seviche is going to be held for more than 2 hours, drain the liquid and refrigerate separately. The reserved liquid can then be tossed with the other ingredients at service time.

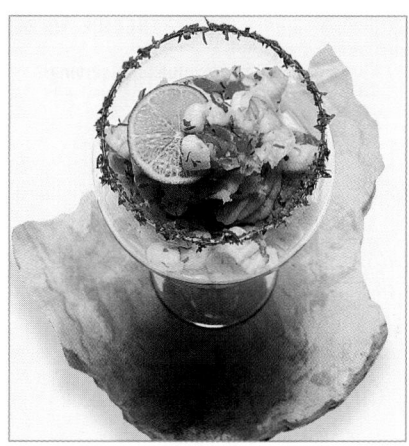

Seviche

RECIPE 19.20

Approximate values per 120 g serving:	
Calories	120
Total fat	4.5 g
Saturated fat	0.5 g
Cholesterol	30 mg
Sodium	250 mg
Total carbohydrates	5 g
Protein	13 g

RECIPE 19.21

Halibut in Banana Leaf with Aromatics

NORTH 44° RESTAURANT, TORONTO, ON
Chef/Co-Owner Mark McEwan

Yield: 2 servings
Method: Baking

Dry rub:

Coriander seeds, toasted and crushed	4.5 g	1 Tbsp.
Cracked black pepper	3 g	1 tsp.
Lemon zest	3 g	1 tsp.
Orange zest	3 g	1 tsp.
Thyme leaves	2 g	1 tsp.
Cumin	pinch	pinch
Curry powder	pinch	pinch
Salt	pinch	pinch
Halibut fillets, each 150 g (5 oz.)	2	2
Banana leaves, each 30-cm (12-in.) square	4	4
Hearts of palm or leek hearts, steamed tender and cooled	4	4
Pearl onions, peeled, blanched, oven-roasted	12	12
Sugar beets, blanched, peeled, cut in half	4	4

Mark McEwan

Mark studied at George Brown College, where he completed two internships and won the Red Seal Award for scholarship. He apprenticed at Switzerland's Grand National Hotel as Commis de Cuisine. Highlights of Mark's career include working at the Sutton Place Hotel, where he cooked for Pope John Paul II in 1984; co-owning and working at Pronto Ristorante, for years Toronto's most prestigious restaurant; and running North 44° restaurant. Mark is also co-owner of One and Bymark, as well as the retail outlet McEwan, all in Toronto.

continued

Approximate values per serving:	
Calories	363
Total fat	18 g
Saturated fat	1.6 g
Cholesterol	48 mg
Sodium	495 mg
Total carbohydrates	16 g
Protein	35 g

Coriander	3 sprigs	3 sprigs
Chiles, halved and seeded	2	2
Ginger, slivered	25 g	2 Tbsp.
Lemon grass, lightly pulverized	2 strands	2 strands
Chervil	4 sprigs	4 sprigs
Salt	pinch	pinch
Coriander oil	30 mL	2 Tbsp.

1. Combine all dry rub ingredients and rub on top of halibut pieces to form crust.
2. Sear fish spice side down until lightly charred, then sear bottom; remove from pan and cool. Fish should be medium-rare.
3. Put banana leaves on table one on top of another, at opposing angles but centred.
4. Place palm hearts (or leeks) on bottom with pearl onions, sugar beets and halibut on top.
5. Place coriander, chiles, ginger, lemon grass and chervil over top of fish. Add pinch of salt and 15 mL (1 Tbsp.) coriander oil on each fish.
6. Fold the top leaf first, then the second leaf to create a neat, airtight package. Tie with string.
7. Place in 180°C (375°F) oven for 15–18 minutes (until they reach an internal temperature of 60°C/140°F).
8. Place on plate, cut and remove strings. Serve with basmati rice.

James Hutton

Vancouver-born James Hutton has been a Culinary Instructor for nearly 24 years, the past 14 at Vancouver Community College. James has been fortunate to have spent his career thus far combining his two greatest passions, cooking and teaching. A virtual who's who of key players in British Columbia's remarkable culinary scene have passed through his classes; although he is unwilling to take credit for the success of these talented chefs, he would like to think that he has offered them both inspiration and a gentle push in the right direction.

Approximate values per serving:	
Calories	1125
Total fat	79 g
Saturated fat	41 g
Cholesterol	485 mg
Sodium	1567 mg
Total carbohydrates	36 g
Protein	61 g

Lobster and Spinach Lasagna with Dijon Mustard Cream and Parmesan Reggiano

VANCOUVER COMMUNITY COLLEGE, Vancouver, BC
Chef Instructor James Hutton

Yield: 2 servings
Method: Sautéing

Pasta dough	60 g	2 oz.
Lobster, live 500 g (1-1/4 lb.)	1	1
Clarified butter	20 mL	4 tsp.
Shallots, minced	10 g	2 tsp.
Garlic, crushed	5 g	1 clove
Spinach, picked, washed, blanched and refreshed, drained well	1 bunch	1 bunch
Salt and fresh-ground black pepper	TT	TT
Salted water	as needed	as needed
Dijon Mustard Cream Sauce (recipe follows)	180 mL	6 fl. oz.
Parmesan Reggiano, shaved	10 g	1 Tbsp.

1. Allow pasta dough to rest at room temperature for 30 minutes. Using a pasta rolling machine, roll out the pasta, gradually reducing the thickness until the thinnest setting is used.
2. Cut the pasta sheet into 6- to 8-cm (2-1/2-in.) squares. Cover and reserve until service.

continued

3. Split the lobster and remove the meat from the tail and claws. Dice into 1.5-cm (1/2-in.) pieces. Chop and reserve the shells for the sauce.

4. Sauté the lobster in 10 mL (2 tsp.) clarified butter over moderate heat. Avoid intense heat as the lobster will become tough and dry.

5. Sweat the shallots and garlic in 10 mL (2 tsp.) of the clarified butter. Add the spinach and cook over moderate heat until the spinach is completely wilted. Season to taste with salt and pepper.

6. Cook the pasta squares in simmering salted water until tender.

7. To serve, place a square of pasta in each of 2 rimmed soup plates. Place one-sixth of the spinach, one-sixth of the lobster and 30 mL (1 fl. oz.) of the sauce on each square.

8. Repeat until 3 layers are completed and top each stack with a sheet of pasta. Nappé the remaining sauce over the top.

9. Top each portion with Parmesan and glaze under a hot salamander until bubbling and lightly golden brown.

Dijon Mustard Cream Sauce

Yield: 400 mL (14 fl. oz.)

Lobster shells, from 500 g (1-1/4 lb.) lobster	1	1
Extra virgin olive oil	20 mL	4 tsp.
Mirepoix, diced roughly	120 g	4 oz.
Garlic, crushed	5 g	1 clove
Bay leaf	1	1
Tomato paste	10 mL	2 tsp.
Cognac	30 mL	1 fl. oz.
White wine	30 mL	1 fl. oz.
Fish stock	300 mL	10 fl. oz.
Cream, 35%	300 mL	10 fl. oz.
Dijon mustard	40 mL	8 tsp.
Salt and fresh-ground black pepper	TT	TT

Dijon Mustard Cream Sauce— Approximate values per 100 mL serving:	
Calories	690
Total fat	66 g
Saturated fat	35 g
Cholesterol	201 mg
Sodium	451 mg
Total carbohydrates	12 g
Protein	5 g

1. Sauté the lobster shells in olive oil in a heavy-bottomed saucepan over medium heat until "toasted" and bright red.

2. Add the mirepoix, garlic and bay leaf and continue sautéing until the mirepoix is lightly caramelized.

3. Add the tomato paste and sweat the mixture until it begins to colour slightly. Do not burn!

4. Flambé the mixture with cognac.

5. Deglaze with white wine, add the fish stock and reduce to half the quantity of liquid.

6. Add the cream and simmer until a light sauce consistency is achieved.

7. Finish with Dijon mustard and salt and pepper.

8. Strain through a very fine sieve or cheesecloth.

9. Reserve, covered, in bain marie until required.

Christopher Mills, CCC

Born in Montreal and raised on Vancouver's North Shore, Chris had his first culinary inspiration in high school. He began his apprenticeship at the Chateau Whistler Resort and in only 10 years rose to the position of Executive Chef at the Metropolitan Hotel. He has secured gold medals from Team BC, the Vancouver Culinary Salon, and the Pierre Dubrulle "Rising Star" competition, and represented Canada at the Bocuse d'Or World Culinary Championship in 2001. Chris is now Product Development Chef for Joey Tomato's Mediterranean Grill restaurants.

RECIPE 19.23

Approximate values per serving not including Cassoulet:	
Calories	305
Total fat	11 g
Saturated fat	1 g
Cholesterol	92 mg
Sodium	386 mg
Total carbohydrates	8 g
Protein	42 g

Cassoulet— Approximate values per serving:	
Calories	439
Total fat	16 g
Saturated fat	8.5 g
Cholesterol	61 mg
Sodium	1437 mg
Total carbohydrates	43 g
Protein	32 g

RECIPE 19.23

Lentil-Crusted Tiger Cod with Cassoulet

JOEY TOMATO'S MEDITERRANEAN GRILL, Coquitlam, BC
Product Development Chef Christopher Mills, CCC

Yield: 3 175-g (6-oz.) servings
Method: Stewing and pan-frying

Fresh tiger or rock cod fillets, scaled	500 g	1 lb.
Salt and white pepper	TT	TT
Red lentils, ground fine in a spice mill, sifted	125 g	4 oz.
Vegetable oil	30 mL	2 Tbsp.
Cassoulet (recipe follows)	125 g	4 oz.

1. Season cod with salt and white pepper, then roll the fillets in the ground red lentils, pressing them into the lentil powder until well coated.

2. In a heavy-based saucepan over medium heat, pan-fry the fish in the vegetable oil until lentils form a crust and lightly brown. Serve on 125 g (4 oz.) of Cassoulet.

Cassoulet

Double-smoked bacon, finely chopped	125 g	1/4 lb.
Unsalted butter	15 g	1 Tbsp.
Small onion, finely chopped	100 g	1
Garlic, finely minced	5 g	1 clove
Small leek, white part only, washed, brunoise	50 g	1
Small carrot, brunoise	50 g	1
Salt and white pepper	TT	TT
French green lentils, organic	175 g	6 oz.
Hearty chicken stock	500 mL	16 fl. oz.
Bouquet garni	1	1
Rich demi-glace (reduced veal stock)	60 mL	2 fl. oz.
Cream, 35%	60 mL	2 fl. oz.
Fresh chopped parsley and thyme to finish		

1. In a heavy-based saucepan over low heat, cook the bacon with 15 mL (1 Tbsp.) of water to slowly render it. Add the butter, onion and garlic to the pan and continue cooking for a few minutes. Add the leek and carrot, cooking a few minutes longer. Adjust seasoning.

2. Once the vegetables are softened, stir in the lentils and add the chicken stock and bouquet garni. Adjust seasoning. Bring the cassoulet to a slow simmer. Cook for 10 minutes and add the demi-glace and cream. Cook for 5–10 minutes. Once the lentils have absorbed most of the liquid and the consistency is similar to stew, the dish is almost finished. Remove the bouquet garni, stir in the fresh chopped herbs and adjust the final seasoning and consistency. The cassoulet can now be served or is even better cooled and heated gently later.

Futaba-Crusted Ahi Tuna in Green Tea Broth

LA CHAUMIÈRE, CALGARY, AB
Chef/Co-Owner Robert Matthews

Yield: 10 servings
Method: Sautéing

Red lentils	200 g	7 oz.
Green lentils	200 g	7 oz.
Fish stock	1 L	1 qt.
Cipollini onions	10	10
Milk	300 mL	10 fl oz.
Garlic	8 g	2 cloves
Salt and pepper	TT	TT
Green tea powder	150 g	5 oz.
Ahi tuna steaks, each 120 g (4 oz.)	10	10
Futaba seasoning	200 g	7 oz.
Tea konnyaku	1 pkg	1 pkg
Asparagus spears	40	40
Bok choy, small	10	10
Okra	20	20
Sesame oil	100 mL	3-1/2 fl. oz.
Shizo (a Japanese herb)	50 g	1-1/2 oz.

1. Soak lentils separately for 1 hour.
2. Boil separately in fish stock until soft. Remove and reserve.
3. Simmer onions in milk until soft, scoop out centres and dice.
4. Sauté diced onion with garlic. Add lentils, season with salt and pepper and fill onion cavities.
5. Bake in a slow oven (145°C/275°F) for 20 minutes.
6. Bring water to 98°C (200°F) and pour over green tea powder.
7. In a hot pan, sauté tuna coated with futaba seasoning until medium-rare. Cut tuna on bias.
8. Prepare julienned noodles of konnyaku and blanch in hot water to warm.
9. Wash and prepare asparagus and bok choy, then blanch in boiling, salted water.
10. Stir-fry lightly in sesame oil. Season lightly with salt and pepper.
11. Blanch okra until tender.
12. Sauté with sesame oil. Season with shizo.
13. Set onion filled with lentils in prewarmed bowl and surround with warm konnyaku.
14. Arrange asparagus, bok choy and okra around onion and top with sliced tuna.
15. Finish with green tea broth.

Robert Matthews

The year Bob began his professional chef training was also the year he represented Canada on the Men's Olympic Cycling Team. Twenty years later, he's an Olympic competitor in the culinary arena! After completing the Professional Cooking Program at the Southern Alberta Institute of Technology, Bob worked in Canada and abroad until finally becoming Personal Chef to the Canadian Ambassador for Japan, a position he held for five years. He returned to Canada in 1999 and became chef/co-owner of the highly regarded La Chaumière.

Approximate values per serving:	
Calories	398
Total fat	12 g
Saturated fat	2 g
Cholesterol	72 mg
Sodium	744 mg
Total carbohydrates	28.5 g
Protein	45 g

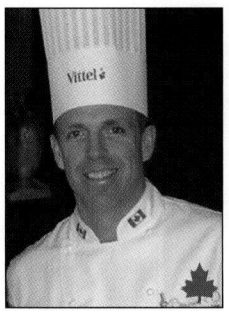

Michael Noble

Michael was fated to become a chef after preparing a perfect Belgian waffle in a high-school cooking class. He began his career in Vancouver, although he gained valuable developmental experience in Europe. In 1996, Michael opened Vancouver's Diva at the Met and, within a year, it had won awards from *Gourmet Magazine, Vancouver Magazine* and *GQ*. Michael went on to open Catch, in a heritage building in downtown Calgary, which was awarded *EnRoute Magazine*'s award for best new Canadian restaurant in 2002. One of Canada's leading chefs, Michael represented Canada three times in international competition and was the only Canadian ever to appear on the Japanese TV show Iron Chef. Read more about his other culinary experiences in the profile on page 425.

RECIPE 19.25

Approximate values per serving, with garnishes:	
Calories	230
Total fat	11 g
Saturated fat	2 g
Cholesterol	46 mg
Sodium	1177 mg
Total carbohydrates	15 g
Protein	17 g

RECIPE 19.25

Potato-Crusted Smoked Black Cod with Tomato Chutney and Scallion Oil

NOTABLE, Calgary, AB
Principal and Chef Michael Noble

Yield: 4 servings
Method: Sautéing

Scallion oil:		
Green onion, green part only, minced	1 bunch	1 bunch
Olive oil, extra virgin	200 mL	7 fl. oz.
Ground white pepper	TT	TT
Rice wine vinegar	15 mL	1 Tbsp.
Smoked black cod fillets, each 60 g (2 oz.)	4	4
Ground black pepper	TT	TT
Baking potato	250 g	1
Egg white	1	1
Chives, chopped	2 g	1 tsp.
Salt	TT	TT
Flour for dredging	as needed	as needed
Olive oil	as needed	as needed
Tomato chutney:		
Shallot, minced	50 g	1
Red pepper, diced fine	10 g	2 tsp.
Olive oil	25 mL	2 Tbsp.
Raspberry vinegar	50 mL	2 fl. oz.
Sugar	50 g	2 oz.
Tomato concassée	250 g	8 oz.
Salt and ground black pepper	TT	TT
Pea shoots	as garnish	as garnish

1. To make the scallion oil, place the minced green onion, olive oil and white pepper in a bowl. Let the mixture stand in a refrigerator for 12–24 hours. Purée it in a blender with the rice wine vinegar.

2. Season the cod portions with the ground black pepper. Sear quickly over a hot grill or in a hot pan and let cool. Grate the potato on a coarse grater. Squeeze out the excess water without rinsing. Place the potato in a bowl. Add egg white, chives and salt. Dredge the cod lightly with flour, pat a little of the potato mixture onto the fish and sauté each piece carefully in olive oil over medium heat until golden brown and cooked through. Drain on paper towel.

3. To make the tomato chutney, sweat the shallot and red pepper in the olive oil. Add the vinegar and sugar and reduce by three-quarters. Add the tomato concassée and continue cooking slowly for approximately 20 minutes, or until the liquid has evaporated and the chutney is deep red in colour. Season with salt and pepper. Set aside.

4. Toss some pea shoots in olive oil. Place on a plate and then top them with the black cod. Put some tomato chutney on the cod, then drizzle some scallion oil on the plate and serve.

RECIPE 19.26

Sautéed Scallops and Shrimps with Orange-Ginger Sauce

HUMBER COLLEGE, Toronto, ON
Chef Jurgen Lindner

Yield: 10 servings
Method: Sautéing

Shallot, brunoise	50 g	2 oz.
Garlic, minced	5 g	1 clove
Butter	60 g	2 oz.
Scallops, 20/30 (4 per serving)	900 g	1 lb. 14 oz.
Shrimps, 21/25 (3 per serving), peeled, deveined	700 g	1 lb. 8 oz.
Salt and pepper	TT	TT
Orange-Ginger Sauce (recipe follows)		

1. Sweat shallot and garlic in butter, then increase heat and sauté scallops and shrimps for 1 minute. Reserve in a warm place.
2. Reserve juice from shellfish sauté for sauce.

Orange-Ginger Sauce

Butter	100 g	3-1/2 oz.
Shallots, brunoise	120 g	4 oz.
Garlic, minced	5 g	1 clove
Fresh ginger purée	50 g	1-1/2 oz.
Bay leaf	1	1
Orange juice concentrate	300 mL	10 fl. oz.
White wine	150 mL	5 fl. oz.
Fish stock	300 mL	10 fl. oz.
Cream, 35%	150 mL	5 fl. oz.
Juice from sautéed shellfish		
Salt and pepper	TT	TT

1. Melt butter in saucepan and sweat shallots, garlic and ginger.
2. Add bay leaf, orange concentrate, white wine and fish stock and simmer for 30 minutes.
3. Add cream and reserved shellfish juice.
4. Adjust seasoning with salt and pepper.
5. Remove bay leaf and blend sauce with hand mixer.
6. Strain through a fine strainer and keep warm.

Note: For service, accompany with grilled eggplant, harlequin rice (with multi-coloured peppers, red onion and parmesan), glazed fennel and beet crisps. Drizzle the sauce around the rice ring and over the shellfish.

Jurgen Lindner
Jurgen was born in Berlin, Germany. He started his apprenticeship at age 16 in hotels and restaurants, and later trained in Zurich, Switzerland; Paris, France; London, England; and the Tunberry Hotel in Scotland. After arriving in Canada, he worked for many years at The Granite Club as a sous-chef and in many hotels as an executive chef. A proud member of the Escoffier Society, Jurgen has worked as a chef for many years at Humber College.

RECIPE 19.26

Approximate values per serving, with sauce:	
Calories	408
Total fat	21 g
Saturated fat	12 g
Cholesterol	198 mg
Sodium	526 mg
Total carbohydrates	21 g
Protein	31 g

Orange-Ginger Sauce—Approximate values per 25 mL serving:	
Calories	207
Total fat	14 g
Saturated fat	8.6 g
Cholesterol	46 mg
Sodium	170 mg
Total carbohydrates	17 g
Protein	1.7 g

John-Carlo Felicella

John-Carlo was born in Vancouver and trained in the Culinary Arts Program at Vancouver Community College. After working as Executive Chef at two well-known golf country clubs in British Columbia, he ventured into private business and opened his own restaurant, La Toque Blanche, in West Vancouver. In 1999, he also decided to become an instructor at Vancouver Community College, because a key priority for him is the education of young chefs. He is currently the Department Head.

RECIPE 19.27

Approximate values per serving, with chutney and salad:	
Calories	640
Total fat	44 g
Saturated fat	11 g
Cholesterol	106 mg
Sodium	818 mg
Total carbohydrates	34 g
Protein	30 g

Sun-Dried Tomato Chutney— Approximate values per serving:	
Calories	196
Total fat	12 g
Saturated fat	1.6 g
Cholesterol	0 mg
Sodium	211 mg
Total carbohydrates	23 g
Protein	2 g

Artichoke and Niçoise Olive Salad— Approximate values per serving:	
Calories	153
Total fat	12 g
Saturated fat	1.6 g
Cholesterol	0 mg
Sodium	260 mg
Total carbohydrates	11 g
Protein	2.1 g

RECIPE 19.27

Seared Sockeye Salmon with Sun-Dried Tomato Chutney and Artichoke and Niçoise Olive Salad

VANCOUVER COMMUNITY COLLEGE, Vancouver, BC
Department Head and Chef John-Carlo Felicella

Yield: 4 servings
Method: Searing

Butter	50 g	2 oz.
Sockeye salmon fillets, scaled, skin on; each 120 g (4 oz.)	4	4
Salt and pepper	TT	TT

1. Preheat a nonstick frying pan on medium heat.
2. Add butter to pan.
3. Season salmon with salt and pepper.
4. Sear salmon skin-side first for approximately 4 minutes; turn salmon over when skin is crisp and continue to sear for another 4 minutes. You may have to reduce the heat to low for the second side.
5. Remove salmon from pan and reserve on a plate.

Sun-Dried Tomato Chutney

Olive oil	50 mL	2 fl. oz.
Onion, small dice	200 g	7 oz.
Sun-dried tomato, presoaked and chopped	20 pieces	20 pieces
Rice vinegar	70 mL	2-1/2 fl. oz.
Sugar	50 g	3 Tbsp.

1. Heat oil in a pan and sauté onions until caramelized.
2. Add tomato, vinegar and sugar and simmer until liquid has evaporated.

Artichoke and Niçoise Olive Salad

Green beans, stemmed, blanched and refreshed	120 g	4 oz.
Artichoke bottoms, tinned, 2-cm dice	70 g	2-1/2 oz.
Shallots, fine dice	50 g	4 Tbsp.
Niçoise olives, pitted, chopped	20 g	3/4 oz.
Pimento, 2-cm (3/4-in.) dice	40 g	1-1/2 oz.
New potatoes, peeled, diced 2 cm (3/4 in.), blanched, cooled	70 g	2-1/2 oz.
Olive oil	50 mL	2 fl. oz.
Lemon juice, fresh	2 lemons	2 lemons
Basil, fresh, chiffonade	10 g	2 Tbsp.
Salt and pepper	TT	TT

1. Bring salted water to a boil and add the vegetables and potatoes. Return to a simmer and strain.
2. Toss the hot vegetables with olive oil, lemon juice, and basil and season to taste.
3. Place a portion of the vegetables on a warm dinner plate and place salmon on top.
4. Spoon chutney on top of salmon.

RECIPE 19.28

Olive Oil Poached Salmon with Oscietra Caviar

BEVERLY HILLS HOTEL AND BUNGALOWS, HOLLYWOOD, CA
Regional Director of Culinary and Food and Beverage Operations
Robert Allen Sulatycky

Yield: 4 servings
Method: Poaching

Olive oil	2 L	2 qt.
Shallots, peeled and sliced	60 g	2 oz.
Fresh basil, bruised	50 g	1-1/2 oz.
Bouquet garni tied with leek to include thyme, parsley, fresh laurel leaf	1	1
Cracked white pepper	10 g	1 Tbsp.
Sea salt	TT	TT
Boneless darnes of Atlantic salmon, each 175 g (6 oz.)	4	4
Freshly ground white pepper	TT	TT
Fresh lemon (for juice)	2 pieces	2 pieces
Oscietra caviar	25 g	1 oz.
Beurre blanc	175 mL	6 fl. oz.
Fleur de sel, French	TT	TT
Sprigs of chervil for garnish		

1. Preheat oven to 63°C (170°F). Place olive oil in an ovenproof dish and add the shallots, basil, bouquet garni, cracked white pepper and 30 g (1 oz.) of sea salt. Place in the low oven and allow the oil to "steep" for up to 2 hours.

2. Season the salmon with sea salt and ground white pepper. Drizzle with lemon juice and place in the oil. Ensure that the oil fully covers the salmon. Poach the salmon in the oil in the oven for approximately 20–25 minutes or until the internal temperature of the salmon reaches 60°C (140°F). When the salmon is done, it will have the appearance of being medium-rare to medium from top to bottom. Remove the container from the oven but leave the salmon in the oil.

3. Stir the caviar into the beurre blanc.

4. Remove the salmon from the oil and drain on paper towel. Remove the skin from each darne.

5. Drizzle more lemon juice on the salmon and sprinkle with fleur de sel. Serve with the caviar sauce and garnish with chervil. Appropriate vegetables would be baby fennel or celery étuvée or asparagus.

Robert Allen Sulatycky

Robert's professional training comes from having worked at top haute cuisine establishments in London and Paris, but he credits the simple cooking methods of his grandmother, who was an accredited cook all her life, as having inspired his culinary passion. Robert's food stylings have been showcased in the namesake Absolut Vodka print ads, his titled "Absolut Sulatycky" (Fall 1998). In 2000, he not only became the first Canadian chef to receive the coveted Robert Mondavi Culinary Award of Excellence, but also was handpicked by the producers of *The Great Canadian Food Show* for an episode that explored the question "What makes a great chef great?" Read more about his other culinary experiences in the profile on page 670.

RECIPE 19.28

Approximate values per serving:	
Calories	1158
Total fat	104 g
Saturated fat	31 g
Cholesterol	253 mg
Sodium	784 mg
Total carbohydrates	12 g
Protein	48 g

Gilbert Noussitou, CCC

A graduate of École Hôtelière des Pyrénées, in Toulouse, France, Gilbert has been practising his trade for 28 years in some of the finest establishments of France, England and Canada. His varied experience includes owning a restaurant, a catering company and a consulting firm, as well as winning many national and international awards. He currently teaches the Cook Apprenticeship Program at Camosun.

RECIPE 19.29

Approximate values per 60 g serving:	
Calories	208
Total fat	17 g
Saturated fat	6 g
Cholesterol	130 mg
Sodium	824 mg
Total carbohydrates	8 g
Protein	8 g

RECIPE 19.29

Corn Flan and Smoked Salmon with Chive Oil

CAMOSUN COLLEGE, VICTORIA, BC
Chef Instructor Gilbert Noussitou, CCC

Yield: 9 60-g (2-oz.) servings
Method: Baking

Corn kernels	300 g	10 oz.
Cream, 35%	200 mL	7 fl. oz.
Eggs	2	2
Egg yolks	2	2
Salt	TT	TT
Lemon juice	10 mL	2 tsp.
Mustard powder	8 g	2 tsp.
Chile oil	TT	TT
Smoked salmon, thinly sliced	225 g	8 oz.
Chives	as needed	as needed
Fried parsley	as needed	as needed
Potato tuiles	as needed	as needed
Chive oil	50 mL	1-1/2 fl. oz.

1. Simmer corn and cream for 3 minutes. Purée and pass through a fine sieve.
2. Whisk eggs and yolks together and whisk in corn purée. Season with salt, lemon juice, mustard and chile oil.
3. Divide the mixture among 9 buttered ramekins. Bake in a bain marie in a 150°C (300°F) oven for approximately 45 minutes or until set.
4. Allow to cool slightly before unmoulding.
5. Place warm flan on plate, arrange smoked salmon attractively and garnish with chives, parsley and tuiles. Drizzle with chive oil.

RECIPE 19.30

Paella

WASHINGTON, DC
Chef Leland Atkinson

Yield: 4 servings
Method: Braising

Chicken thighs	4	4
Salt and pepper	TT	TT
Olive oil	60 mL	2 fl. oz.
Onion, medium dice	60 g	2 oz.
Garlic, chopped	15 g	1 Tbsp.
Red bell pepper, medium dice	75 g	3 oz.
Green bell pepper, medium dice	50 g	2 oz.
Rice, short grain	350 g	12 oz.
Saffron	1 g	1 tsp.
Chicken stock, well seasoned, hot	750 mL	26 fl. oz.
Chorizo, cooked, sliced	125 g	4 oz.
Clams, scrubbed	12	12
Shrimp, 16–20 count	12	12
Lobster (600 g/21 oz.), cut up	1	1
Mussels, bearded and scrubbed	12	12

Paella

continued

1. Season the chicken with salt and pepper. Pan-fry it in the olive oil, browning it well. Cook until done, approximately 20 minutes. Remove the chicken and reserve.

2. Add the onion, garlic and peppers to the pan and sauté until tender.

3. Add the rice and sauté until it turns translucent.

4. Add the saffron to the chicken stock. Stir the chicken stock into the rice and bring to a boil.

5. Add the sliced chorizo and clams to the pan. Cover and place in a 190°C (375°F) oven for 20 minutes.

6. Add the raw shrimp and lobster, and the cooked chicken to the pan. Cover and cook for an additional 15 minutes.

7. Add the mussels to the pan and cook until the shrimp and lobster are done, the chicken is hot and all the shellfish are opened, approximately 5 minutes.

RECIPE 19.30

Approximate values per serving:	
Calories	930
Total fat	41 g
Saturated fat	10 g
Cholesterol	650 mg
Sodium	2050 mg
Total carbohydrates	31 g
Protein	110 g

RECIPE 19.31

Paupiettes of Arctic Char with White Wine Sabayon

Retired Executive Chef Hans U. Herzig

Yield: 10 servings

Method: Baking

Fillets of Arctic char, each 70–80 g (2-1/2 to 2-3/4 oz.)	20	20
Salt and pepper	TT	TT
Bok choy, greens only, blanched	2 large heads	2 large heads
Butter	100 g	3-1/2 oz.
Shallots, finely diced	2	2
White wine	300 mL	10 fl. oz.
Fish stock	500 mL	18 fl. oz.
Roma tomatoes, medium, peeled and cored	10	10
Asparagus spears, peeled and blanched, approximately 7–8 cm (3 in.) long	70	70
Yukon Gold potatoes, 5-mm (1/4-in.) thick slices, blanched	70	70
Egg yolks	5	5

1. Lay out the fish fillets, season lightly with salt and pepper and top with bok choy greens cut into size of fillets.

2. Roll fillets with greens on the inside and fasten with skewers.

3. Butter the baking dish, add paupiettes, sprinkle with shallots, 200 mL (6 fl. oz.) of the wine and 450 mL (16 fl. oz.) of the fish stock and season. Cover with buttered parchment paper and bake at 190°C (375°F) for 10–12 minutes, until firm.

4. Cut tomatoes into large square fillets, season lightly with salt and pepper and sauté. Simmer asparagus and sliced potatoes in water or stock until heated through.

5. To make the sabayon, put the egg yolks into a stainless steel bowl. Add the remaining wine, the remaining fish stock and a pinch of salt and pepper. Whisk vigorously over simmering water until thick.

6. Arrange 2 paupiettes on a plate and place the sliced potatoes around them. Coat the paupiettes with sabayon and garnish with tomato and the asparagus spears.

Hans U. Herzig

Hans was born in Switzerland, trained in Europe and came to Canada to work at the Windsor Arms in Toronto. Among the highlights of his career was captaining the Canadian team that won 10 gold medals at the 1988 World Culinary Olympics. He recently retired after a legendary career at the Westin Prince Hotel in Toronto, Ontario.

RECIPE 19.31

Approximate values per serving, with sabayon:	
Calories	616
Total fat	25 g
Saturated fat	6 g
Cholesterol	129 mg
Sodium	597 mg
Total carbohydrates	53 g
Protein	42 g

James Olberg

James was born and trained near Toronto, and he completed his apprenticeship at the King Edward Hotel. His career continued at places such as the Sutton Place Hotel, the Four Seasons Hotel, the Metropolitan Hotel, and the Delawana Inn. In 2001, he joined the award-winning Crowne Plaza Hotel Georgia. He recently did a stint on Holland America before joining Vintage Hotels.

RECIPE 19.32

Approximate values per serving:	
Calories	903
Total fat	71 g
Saturated fat	22 g
Cholesterol	193 mg
Sodium	1321 mg
Total carbohydrates	17 g
Protein	51 g

RECIPE 19.32

Tea-Smoked Atlantic Salmon Fillets on Lobster Emulsion

VINTAGE HOTELS, QUEEN'S LANDING, NIAGARA-ON-THE-LAKE, ON
Executive Chef James Olberg

Yield: 4 servings
Method: Pan-smoking and Baking

Marinade:		
Sesame oil	250 mL	8 fl. oz.
Soy sauce	20 mL	4 tsp.
Olive oil	250 mL	8 fl. oz.
White wine	125 mL	4 fl. oz.
Garlic, chopped	30 g	1 oz.
Rosemary, chopped	30 g	1 oz.
Black peppercorns, cracked	15 g	1/2 oz.
Atlantic salmon fillets, each 175 g (6 oz.)	4	4
Smoking ingredients:		
Wood chips	500 g	1 lb.
Wood dust	250 g	8 oz.
Earl Grey tea	3 bags	3 bags
Salt and white pepper	TT	TT
Lobster emulsion:		
Lobster fumet	500 mL	16 fl. oz.
Shallots, fine chop	60 g	2 oz.
Butter	125 g	4 oz.
Tarragon, chopped	30 g	1 oz.
Salt and white pepper	TT	TT

1. Combine marinade ingredients and let sit for 1 hour.

2. Immerse salmon fillets in marinade for 5 minutes. Remove and blot dry with paper towels. Place in a perforated pan and cover with plastic wrap.

3. Place smoking ingredients in a deeper pan that fits outside the perforated pan. Set salmon pan on top.

4. Heat pans over open flame until smoke is visible. Remove from heat and let smoke for 10 minutes.

5. Season salmon with salt and pepper and sear in a hot pan to colour. Finish in oven.

6. Reduce lobster fumet and shallots to 175 mL (6 fl. oz.). Whisk in butter and tarragon. Adjust seasoning.

7. Serve salmon on truffled mashed potatoes with baby vegetables. Drizzle with lobster emulsion.

Crayfish Etouffée

Yield: 4 servings
Method: Simmering

Lard	125 g	4 oz.
Flour	125 g	4 oz.
Onion, chopped fine	250 g	1 medium
Celery stalk, chopped fine	75 g	1
Green bell pepper, chopped	100 g	1/2
Garlic cloves, minced	10 g	2
Shrimp broth or clam juice	150 mL	5 fl. oz.
Tomato paste	15 mL	1 Tbsp.
Salt	5 g	1 tsp.
Cayenne	0.5 g	1/4 tsp.
Black pepper	0.5 g	1/4 tsp.
Dried thyme	0.25 g	1/4 tsp.
Crayfish tails, peeled	500 g	1 lb.
Green onions, sliced	4	4
Flat leaf parsley, minced	20 g	2 Tbsp.
White rice, cooked	1 L	1 qt.

1. Heat the lard in a large sauté pan. Whisk in the flour and cook, stirring constantly, to make a medium-dark roux.

2. Add the onion, celery, green bell pepper and garlic and sauté over medium-low heat until the vegetables are wilted, approximately 5 minutes.

3. Slowly add the shrimp broth or clam juice and bring to a boil. Reduce the heat to a simmer and add the tomato paste and the spices. Simmer for 15 minutes to thicken.

4. Add the crayfish tails and simmer for approximately 10 minutes. Add the green onions and parsley and adjust the seasonings. Serve over cooked rice.

Crayfish Etouffée

Approximate values per serving:	
Calories	880
Total fat	32 g
Saturated fat	4 g
Cholesterol	130 mg
Sodium	1154 mg
Total carbohydrates	107 g
Protein	40 g

20 Charcuterie

" There are only two questions to ask about food.
Is it good? And is it authentic? We are open [to]
new ideas, but not if it means destroying our history.
And food is history.

—Giuliano Bugialli, quoted in *The New York Times*, May 9, 1984

Traditionally, charcuterie was limited to the production of pork-based pâtés, terrines and galantines. Over the years, however, it has come to include similar products made with game, poultry, fish, shellfish and even vegetables. Many of these are discussed here.

Charcuterie is an art and science in itself. This chapter is not intended to be a complete guide to the charcutier's art. Instead, we focus on procedures for making common charcuterie items that can be prepared easily in most kitchens. We also discuss the preparation of sausages as well as curing methods, including salt curing, brining and both cold and hot smoking. The chapter ends with information about several cured pork products.

FORCEMEATS AND THEIR USES

A **forcemeat** is a preparation made from uncooked ground meats, poultry, fish or shellfish, seasoned, then emulsified with fat. Forcemeats are the primary ingredient used to make pâtés, terrines, galantines and sausages.

The word *forcemeat* is derived from the French word *farce*, meaning stuffing. Depending on the preparation method, a forcemeat can be very smooth and velvety, well textured and coarse, or anything in between. Regardless of its intended use, it has a glossy appearance when raw and will slice cleanly when cooked. A properly emulsified forcemeat provides a rich taste and a comforting texture on the palate.

Forcemeats are emulsified products. Emulsification is the process of binding two ingredients that ordinarily would not combine. (Emulsified sauces are discussed in Chapter 10, Stocks and Sauces; emulsified salad dressings are discussed in Chapter 25, Salads and Salad Dressings.) The proteins present in the meat, poultry, fish and shellfish combine easily with both fat and liquids. In forcemeats, these proteins act as a stabilizer that allows the fat and liquids, which ordinarily would not combine, to bind. When improperly emulsified forcemeats are cooked, they lose their fat, shrink, and become dry and grainy. To ensure proper emulsification of a forcemeat:

1. the ratio of fat to other ingredients must be precise,
2. temperatures must be maintained below 4°C (40°F), and
3. the ingredients must be mixed properly.

Forcemeat Ingredients

Forcemeats are usually meat, poultry, fish or shellfish combined with binders, seasonings and sometimes garnishes. Selections from each of these basic categories are used to make an array of forcemeats. All ingredients must be of the finest quality and added in just the right proportions.

Meats

The *dominant meat* is the meat that gives the forcemeat its name and essential flavour. The dominant meat does not have to be beef, veal, lamb, pork or game. It can be poultry, fish or shellfish. When preparing meats, poultry or fish for forcemeat, it is important to trim all silverskin, gristle and small bones so that the meat will be more easily ground and will produce a smoother finished product.

● **panada** a starch-based product added to a forcemeat to bind and create a smoother texture

● **curing salt** a mixture of salt and sodium nitrite that inhibits bacterial growth; used as a preservative, often for charcuterie items

Many forcemeats contain some pork. Pork adds moisture and smoothness to the forcemeat. Without it, poultry-based forcemeats tend to be rubbery, while venison and other game-based forcemeats tend to be dry. The traditional ratio is one part pork to two parts dominant meat.

Many forcemeats also contain some liver. Pork liver is commonly used, as is chicken liver. Liver contributes flavour as well as binding to the forcemeat. For a finer texture, grind the livers and then force them through a drum sieve before incorporating them into the forcemeat.

Fats

Here, fat refers to a separate ingredient, not the fat in the dominant meat or pork, both of which should be quite lean in order to ensure the correct ratio of fat to meat. Usually pork backfat or heavy cream is used to add moisture and richness to the forcemeat. Because fat carries flavour, it also promotes the proper infusion of flavours and smoke.

Binders

There are two principal types of binders: panadas and eggs.

A **panada** is something other than fat that is added to a forcemeat to enhance smoothness (especially in fish mousselines, which tend to be slightly grainy in texture), to aid emulsification (especially in vegetable terrines, where the protein levels are insufficient to bind on their own) or both (for example, in liver mousses). It should not make up more than 20% of the forcemeat's total weight. Usually a panada is nothing more than crustless white bread soaked in milk or, more traditionally, a heavy béchamel, velouté or rice.

Eggs or egg whites are used as a binding agent in some styles of forcemeat. If used in forcemeats that have a large ratio of liver or liquids, they also add texture. The proteins in the meat, fish or poultry are the primary binder.

Seasonings

Forcemeats are seasoned with salt, curing salt, marinades and various herbs and spices.

Salt not only adds flavour to a forcemeat but also aids in the emulsification of the meat and fat. As with other foods, a forcemeat that lacks salt will taste flat and may not bind properly. Use approximately 10 grams per kilogram (1 tsp. per pound) of meat.

Curing salt is a mixture of salt and sodium nitrite. Sodium nitrite controls spoilage by inhibiting bacterial growth. Equally important, curing salt preserves the rosy pink colours of some forcemeats that might otherwise oxidize to an unappetizing grey. Although currently regarded as substantially safer than the previously used potassium nitrate (saltpetre), some studies suggest that sodium nitrite is a carcinogen. For a typical consumer, however, the amount of sodium nitrite consumed from cured meats should not pose a substantial health threat.

Traditionally, ingredients for forcemeats were marinated for long periods of time, sometimes days, before grinding. The trend today is for shorter marinating times so that the true flavours of the main ingredients shine through. Both classic and contemporary marinades include herbs, citrus zest, spices and liquors, all of which lend flavour, character and nuance to the forcemeat.

Pâté spice is a mixture of several spices and herbs that can be premixed and used as needed.

Pâté Spice

Yield: 190 g (7-2/3 oz.)

Mace	15 g	3 Tbsp.
Cloves	30 g	5 Tbsp.
Dried ginger	20 g	4 Tbsp.
Nutmeg	15 g	2 Tbsp.
Paprika	15 g	2 Tbsp.
Dried basil	20 g	8 Tbsp.
Black pepper	20 g	2-1/2 Tbsp.
White pepper	20 g	2-1/2 Tbsp.
Bay leaves	2 g	12 leaves
Dried thyme	20 g	7 Tbsp.
Dried marjoram	10 g	6 Tbsp.
Cayenne	3 g	1 tsp.

Grind all ingredients in a spice grinder. Pass through a sieve to remove any large pieces.

NOTE: Either use this mixture as is, or mix 30 g (1 oz.) (or any amount desired) with 450 g (1 lb.) of salt. The salt and spice mixture can then be used to season forcemeats; 10 g (1/3 oz.) per 450 g (1 lb.) of forcemeat usually suffices for most pâtés. Also, 30 g (1 oz.) pulverized dry wild mushrooms may be added.

A forcemeat's seasoning and texture can be tested by cooking a small portion before the entire forcemeat is cooked. (Unlike sauces, stews and other dishes, you cannot taste and adjust a forcemeat's flavouring during the cooking process.) A small portion of a hearty forcemeat can be sautéed; a small portion of a more delicate forcemeat should be poached for three to five minutes. When cooked, the forcemeat should hold its shape and be slightly firm but not rubbery. If it is too firm, add a little cream.

Garnishes

Forcemeat garnishes are meats, fat, vegetables or other foods added in limited quantities to provide contrasting flavours and textures and to improve appearance. The garnishes are usually diced, chopped or more coarsely ground than the dominant meat. Common garnishes include pistachio nuts, diced backfat, truffles or truffle peelings and diced ham or tongue.

Equipment for Preparing Forcemeats

To prepare forcemeats properly, you should have a food chopper or food processor and a heavy-duty drum sieve with a metal band. You will also need a standard meat grinder or meat-grinding attachment with various-sized grinding plates (see Figure 20.1).

FIGURE 20.1 A blade and assorted plates for a standard grinder.

Preparing Forcemeats

The three common forcemeat preparations are country-style, basic (or straight) and mousseline. Each can be produced easily in a typical food service operation. Other types of forcemeat preparations such as the emulsified mixture

Other Forcemeats

The **5/4/3 forcemeat** contains 5 parts meat, 4 parts fat and 3 parts ice. It is finely ground and blended to produce an emulsion. Sausages, often smoked, are the most common use.

Gratin-style forcemeats contain meat or liver that has been sautéed before grinding. Their flavour and texture are very palatable.

Forcemeats based on rice or bread are most often used in hot kitchen applications, but any of the forcemeats may be used as a stuffing mixture. Low-temperature cooking is required to avoid a tough, grainy filling when cooked. Verify the internal temperature for doneness with a probe thermometer.

● **country-style forcemeat** usually a coarse grind or dice of meat, highly aromatic and containing liver. Pork backfat is added to enhance mouth-feel or melt.

● **dominant meat** the main meat in a preparation, giving it an identity (e.g., game, pork, rabbit) and predominant flavour

used to make hot dogs and bratwurst are not commonly encountered in food service operations and are discussed in the sidebar.

When preparing any forcemeat, certain guidelines must be followed:

1. Forcemeat preparations include raw meats, liver, eggs and dairy products. If improperly handled, these potentially hazardous foods create a good environment for the growth of microorganisms. To avoid the risk of food-borne illness, temperatures must be carefully controlled and all cutting boards and food contact surfaces must be as sanitary as possible at all times.

2. To ensure a proper emulsification, the forcemeat must be kept cold—below 4°C (40°F)—at all times. Refrigerate all moist ingredients and keep forcemeats in progress in an ice bath. Chilling or freezing the metal grinder and food processor parts helps keep the ingredients as cold as possible.

3. Cut all foods into convenient sizes that fit easily into grinder openings. Do not overstuff grinders or overfill food processors. When grinding items twice, always begin with a larger plate, followed by a medium or small plate. For exceptional smoothness, press the forcemeat through a sieve after grinding to remove any lumps or pieces of membrane.

Country-Style Forcemeats

A traditional **country-style forcemeat** is heavily seasoned with onions, garlic, pepper, juniper berries and bay leaves. It is the simplest of the forcemeats to prepare and yields the heartiest and most distinctive pâtés and sausages.

The **dominant meat** for a country-style forcemeat is usually ground once through the grinder's large plate, then ground again through the medium plate. This produces the characteristic coarse texture. As with most forcemeats, the dominant meat for a country-style forcemeat is usually marinated and seasoned prior to grinding and then mixed with some liver.

BASIC PROCEDURE FOR PREPARING A COUNTRY-STYLE FORCEMEAT

1. Chill all ingredients and equipment thoroughly. Throughout preparation they should remain at temperatures below 4°C (40°F).
2. Cut all meats into an appropriate size for grinding.
3. Marinate, under refrigeration, the dominant meat and pork with the desired herbs, spices and liquors.
4. If using liver, grind it and force it through a sieve.
5. Cut the backfat into an appropriate size and freeze.
6. Prepare an ice bath for the forcemeat. Then grind the dominant meat, pork and fat as directed in the recipe, usually once through the grinder's largest plate and a second time through the medium plate.
7. If using liver, eggs, panada or garnishes, fold them in by hand with a spoon or spatula, remembering to keep the forcemeat over an ice bath at all times.
8. Cook a small portion of the forcemeat; adjust the seasonings and texture as appropriate.
9. Refrigerate the forcemeat until needed.

APPLYING THE BASICS	RECIPE 20.2

Country-Style Forcemeat

Yield: 1.1 kg (2.5 lb.)

Lean pork, diced	450 g	1 lb.
Pâté spice	3 g	1 tsp.
Salt	7 g	1-1/2 tsp.
Pepper	TT	TT
Brandy	30 mL	1 fl. oz.
Pork liver, cleaned and diced	225 g	8 oz.
Backfat, diced	175 g	6 oz.
Double smoked bacon, diced	60 g	2 oz.
Shallots, small dice	45 g	1-1/2 oz.
Garlic, minced	5 g	1-1/2 tsp.
Fresh parsley, chopped	20 g	1-1/2 Tbsp.
Eggs	3	3

Approximate values per 85 g serving:	
Calories	247
Total fat	21 g
Saturated fat	7.4 g
Cholesterol	134 mg
Sodium	292 mg
Total carbohydrates	1.5 g
Protein	13 g

1. Combine the diced pork with the pâté spice, salt, pepper and brandy; marinate under refrigeration for several hours.

2. Grind the liver and force it through a drum sieve. Reserve.

3. Grind the marinated pork and backfat through the grinder's large plate.

4. Grind half the pork, backfat and bacon a second time through the medium plate along with the sweetened and cooled shallots, garlic and parsley.

5. Working over an ice bath, combine the coarse and medium ground pork with the liver and eggs.

6. Cook and taste a small portion of the forcemeat and adjust the seasonings as necessary.

The forcemeat is now ready to use as desired in the preparation of pâtés, terrines, galantines and sausages.

1. Country-Style Forcemeat: Marinating the meat with herbs, spices and brandy.

2. Pressing the ground liver through a sieve.

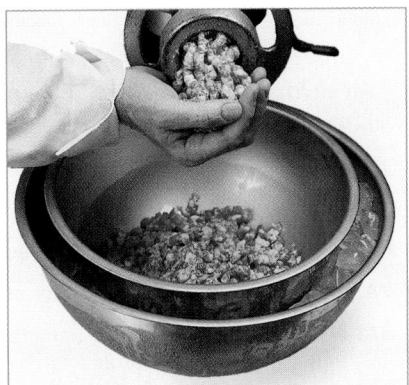

3. Grinding half the meat a second time.

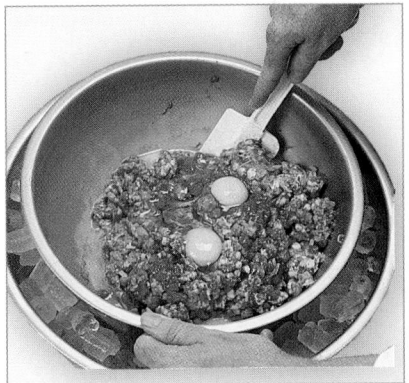

4. Incorporating the liver and eggs into the ground mixture over an ice bath to keep the forcemeat cold.

Straight Forcemeats

Smoother and more refined than a country-style forcemeat, a **straight** or **basic forcemeat** is probably the most versatile of all. It should be well seasoned, but the seasonings should not mask the dominant meat's flavour. Examples of basic forcemeats are most game pâtés and terrines as well as traditional pâtés en croûte.

● **straight forcemeat (basic forcemeat)** comprises a dominant meat plus lean pork to give the finished product a smooth texture

A basic forcemeat is made by grinding the meat and fat separately—the meat twice and the fat once. The fat is then worked into the meat, either by hand or in a food processor or chopper. A quicker method involves grinding the fat and meat together and then blending them in a food processor. Whichever method is used, some recipes call for the incorporation of crushed ice to minimize friction, reduce temperature and add moisture.

BASIC PROCEDURE FOR PREPARING A STRAIGHT FORCEMEAT

1. Chill all ingredients and equipment thoroughly. Throughout preparation they should remain at temperatures below 4°C (40°F).

2. Cut all meats into an appropriate size for grinding.

3. Marinate, under refrigeration, the dominant meat and pork with the desired herbs, spices and liquors.

4. If using liver, grind it and force it through a sieve.

5. Cut the backfat into appropriately sized pieces and freeze.

6. Grind the meats twice, once through the grinder's large plate and then through the medium plate; hold on an ice bath.

7. Grind the chilled or frozen fat once through the medium plate and add it to the meat mixture.

8. Work the fat into the meat over an ice bath or in a well-chilled food processor or chopping machine.

9. Over an ice bath, add any required eggs, panada and/or garnishes and work them into the mixture.

10. Cook a small portion of the forcemeat in stock or water; adjust the seasonings and texture as appropriate.

11. Refrigerate the forcemeat until needed.

An alternative method for preparing a basic forcemeat replaces Steps 6 to 9 with the following procedures:

6A. Grind the meats and fats together twice.

7A. Place them in a food processor or chopper and blend until smooth.

8A. Add any required eggs or panada while the machine is running and blend them in with the meat and fat.

9A. Remove the forcemeat from the machine and, working over an ice bath, fold in any garnishes by hand (use a spatula).

Whichever method is used, a particularly warm kitchen or a lengthy running time in the food processor or chopping machine may necessitate the addition of small quantities of crushed ice to emulsify the forcemeat properly. Add the ice bit by bit while the machine is running.

Straight Forcemeat

SAIT POLYTECHNIC, Calgary, AB
SCHOOL OF HOSPITALITY AND TOURISM
Chef Instructor Gerd Steinmeyer, CCC

Yield: 1.35 kg (3 lb.)

Veal liver	125 g	4 oz.
Shallots	40 g	1-1/2 oz.
Butter	30 g	1 oz.
Veal, diced	250 g	8 oz.
Lean pork, diced	250 g	8 oz.
Double smoked bacon	200 g	7 oz.
Brandy	30 mL	1 fl. oz.
Madeira	30 mL	1 fl. oz.
Pâté spice	3 g	1 tsp.
Salt	7 g	1-1/2 tsp.
Cream, 35%	175 mL	6 fl. oz.
Egg	1	1
Ham, medium dice	80 g	3 oz.
Backfat, diced	80 g	3 oz.
Pistachio nuts, peeled	60 g	2 oz.
Black olives, chopped coarse	60 g	2 oz.

1. Sauté liver and shallots in butter. Cool.

2. Combine the veal, pork, bacon, liver and shallots with the brandy, Madeira, pâté spice, and salt; marinate under refrigeration for several hours.

3. Grind the meats through the grinder's large plate and again through the small plate.

4. Place the meat mixture in the bowl of a food processor and pulse until it is emulsified.

5. Work in the cream and egg until the forcemeat is smooth and well emulsified. Do not overprocess the forcemeat.

6. Fold in the ham, backfat, pistachio nuts and olives.

7. Cook a small portion of the forcemeat by poaching or sautéing it. Taste and adjust the seasonings as necessary.

The forcemeat is now ready to use as desired in the preparation of pâtés, terrines, galantines and sausages.

VARIATIONS: Replace veal with game. Use dried fruits as a garnish. Green and red peppercorns add flavour. Pieces of meat (pork tenderloin) may be added as garnish if wrapped in backfat or seared chicken breast.

Gerd Steinmeyer, CCC
Gerd was born in West Germany and apprenticed at the Hotel School Siegen there. Two highlights of his long and varied career in Alberta include having functioned as Executive Chef to the official German Delegation at the 1988 XV Olympic Winter Games and having successfully coached umpteen young culinarians for local and international culinary competitions. Over the last 10 years, many of his student teams were awarded Best Apprentice Team, Most Outstanding Single Apprentice and/or Top Entry.

RECIPE 20.3

Approximate values per 85 g serving:	
Calories	263
Total fat	23 g
Saturated fat	9.2 g
Cholesterol	93 mg
Sodium	406 mg
Total carbohydrates	3 g
Protein	11 g

1. Straight Forcemeat: Grinding the meat through the chilled grinder.

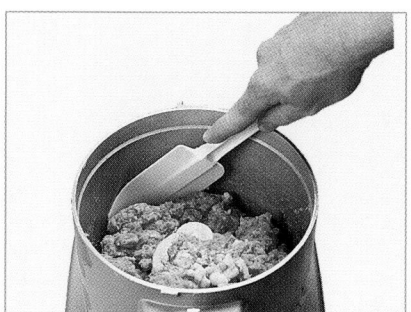

2. Combining the fat with the meat in the food processor.

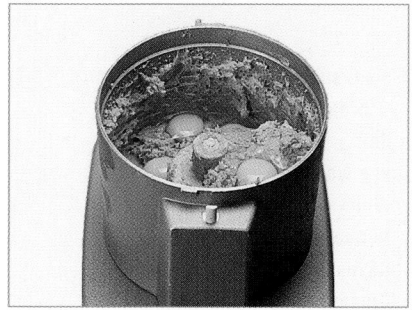

3. Adding the eggs and cream to the meat.

4. Folding the garnishes into the forcemeat.

Mousseline Forcemeats

A properly made **mousseline forcemeat** is light, airy and delicately flavoured. It is most often made with fish or shellfish but sometimes with veal, pork, feathered game or poultry. (A mousseline forcemeat is not the same as a mousse, which usually contains gelatin and is discussed later in this chapter.)

A mousseline forcemeat is prepared by processing ground meats and cream in a food processor; often egg whites are added to lighten and enrich the mixture. The ratio of fish to eggs to cream is very important: too many egg whites and the mousseline will be rubbery; too few and it may not bind together. If too much cream is added, the mousseline will be too soft or will fall apart during cooking.

A mousseline forcemeat can be served hot or cold. It can be used to make fish sausages and a variety of timbales and terrines. Or it can be used to make quenelles, which are discussed later. A shrimp mousseline is used with the Paupiettes of Sole, Recipe 19.14.

BASIC PROCEDURE FOR PREPARING A MOUSSELINE FORCEMEAT

1. Chill all ingredients and equipment thoroughly. Throughout preparation they should remain at temperatures below 4°C (40°F).
2. Cut all meats into an appropriate size for processing.
3. Grind the meat in a cold food processor until smooth. Do not overprocess.
4. Add eggs and pulse until just blended.
5. Add cream and seasonings in a steady stream while the machine is running. Stop the machine and scrape down the sides of the bowl once or twice during the processing. Do not run the machine any longer than necessary to achieve a smooth forcemeat.
6. If desired, pass the forcemeat through a drum sieve to remove any sinew or bits of bone.
7. Over an ice bath, fold in any garnishes by hand.
8. Poach a small amount of the mousseline in stock or water. Taste and adjust the seasonings and texture as necessary.
9. Refrigerate until ready for use.

Cold, Cold, Cold

Working ground meat or fish with salt helps to extract the proteins needed for binding. The amount of heavy cream a forcemeat can hold in emulsion varies with the freshness of the meat or fish used and how cold the cream and forcemeat are. When incorporating them, do not add the cream too quickly. In some cases, only half the cream may be needed. The cream should be at a temperature of 0°C to 1°C (32°F to 34°F) for best results.

APPLYING THE BASICS RECIPE 20.4

Mousseline Forcemeat

Yield: 1.8 kg (4 lb.)

Fish, scallops, skinless chicken breast or lean veal (fresh)	900 g	2 lb.
Salt	15 g	1 Tbsp.
Egg whites	4	4
White pepper	TT	TT
Nutmeg	TT	TT
Cayenne pepper	TT	TT
Cream, 35%, very cold	up to 900 mL	up to 1 qt.

RECIPE 20.4

Approximate values per 85 g serving:	
Calories	186
Total fat	16 g
Saturated fat	10 g
Cholesterol	78 mg
Sodium	327 mg
Total carbohydrates	1.3 g
Protein	9.2 g

continued

1. Grind the chilled dominant fish or meat through a large plate.
2. Process the meat and salt in a food processor until smooth.
3. Add the egg whites one at a time and pulse the processor until they are incorporated.
4. Scrape down the sides of the processor's bowl and add the spices.
5. With the machine running, add the cream in a slow steady stream. Check the consistency; you may not need all the cream. Frozen meats absorb less cream.
6. Scrape down the bowl again and process the mousseline until it is smooth and well mixed. Do not overprocess.
7. Remove the mousseline from the machine and hold in an ice bath. If additional smoothness is desired, force the mousseline through a drum sieve in small batches using a plastic scraper or rubber spatula.
8. Cook a small portion of the forcemeat. Taste and adjust the seasonings and texture as necessary.
9. The forcemeat is now ready to use as desired in the preparation of pâtés, terrines, galantines or sausages. If frozen fish is used, less cream will be needed and you may have to add some fine white fresh bread to make a panada.

1. Mousseline Forcemeat: Processing the ground meat and salt in a cold food processor just until smooth.

2. Adding the egg whites and pulsing until blended.

3. Adding the cream in a steady stream while the machine runs.

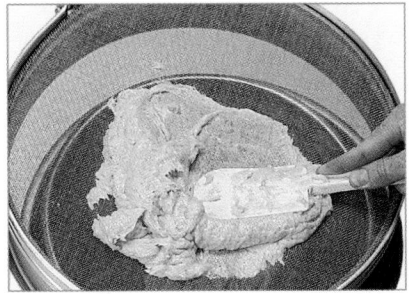

4. Pressing the forcemeat through a drum sieve to ensure a smooth finished product.

Quenelles

Quenelles are small oblong-shaped portions of a mousseline forcemeat poached in an appropriately flavoured stock. Quenelles are a traditional garnish for many soups and a popular appetizer, usually accompanied by a tomato coulis or a fish velouté-based sauce such as sauce nantua (see page 198). The technique used for making and poaching quenelles is also used for testing the seasoning and consistency of a mousseline forcemeat.

● **quenelles** oblong-shaped portions of mousseline forcemeat poached in stock

BASIC PROCEDURE FOR PREPARING QUENELLES

Forming the quenelles using two spoons and poaching gently until done.

1. Prepare a mousseline forcemeat.
2. Bring an appropriately flavoured poaching liquid to a simmer.
3. Use two spoons to form the forcemeat into oblong-shaped dumplings. For small quenelles use small spoons; for larger quenelles use larger spoons.
4. Poach the quenelles until done. Test by breaking one in half to check the centre's doneness.
5. Small soup-garnish-sized quenelles can be chilled in ice water, drained and held for service. Reheat them in a small amount of stock before garnishing the soup.

USING FORCEMEATS

Forcemeats are used as basic components in the preparation of other foods, including terrines, pâtés, galantines and sausages. Many are used in the hot kitchen as stuffings. Aspic jelly is also an important component of these products.

Terrines, Pâtés and Galantines

● **pâté** traditionally, a forcemeat baked in a crust; today, the term may refer generically to most forcemeat preparations

● **terrine** a forcemeat baked in the oven in a terrine mould immersed in a water bath

● **pâté en croûte** a forcemeat baked in a crust

● **galantines** forcemeats wrapped in the skin of the dominant meat, fish or poultry, and poached. Modern galantines are often prepared without the skin; plastic wrap is used and the product poached or steamed.

Traditionally, a **pâté** was a fine savoury meat filling wrapped in pastry, baked and served hot or cold. A **terrine** was considered more basic, consisting of coarsely ground and highly seasoned meats baked in a waterbath in an earthenware mould and generally served cold. (The mould is also called a terrine, derived from the French word *terre*, meaning earth.) Pâtés baked in pastry are called **pâtés en croûte**. Many types of pâté are baked in loaf-type pans, without a crust, which according to tradition would make them terrines. Today, the terms *pâté* and *terrine* are used almost interchangeably. **Galantines** are made from forcemeats of poultry, fish, game or suckling pig wrapped in the skin of the bird or animal and poached in an appropriate stock, or wrapped in plastic wrap and poached or steamed.

Terrines, pâtés and galantines are often made with forcemeats layered with garnishes to produce a decorative or mosaic effect when sliced. A wide variety of foods can be used as garnishes, including strips of ham, backfat or tongue; mushrooms or other vegetables; truffles and pistachio nuts. Garnishes should always be cooked before they are added to the pâté, terrine or galantine or they will shrink during cooking, creating air pockets.

Garnishing Sliced Terrines and Pâtés

Cornichons sliced into decorative fans are an attractive garnish for sliced country terrines and pâtés en croûte.

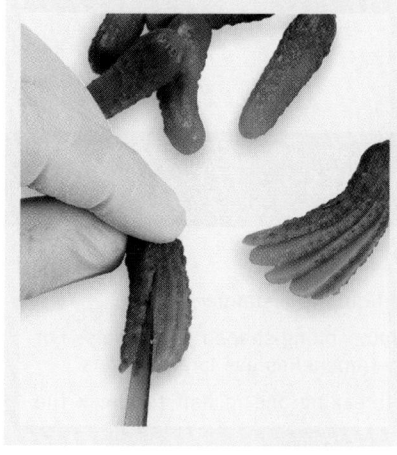

Pâté Pans, Moulds and Terrines

Pâté pans, moulds and terrines come in a variety of shapes and sizes. Pâtés that are not baked in a crust can be prepared in standard metal loaf pans of any shape, although rectangular ones make portioning the cooked pâté much easier. For pâté en croûte, the best pans are collapsible or hinged, thin metal ones. They make it easier to remove the pâté after baking. Collapsible and hinged pans come in various shapes and sizes, from small plain rectangles to large intricately fluted ovals. Traditional earthenware moulds and terrines as well as ones made from enamel, metal, glass or even plastic are available. Most terrines are rectangular or oval in shape. You can see a terrine pan illustrated in Chapter 5, Tools and Equipment.

Terrines

Terrines are forcemeats baked in a mould without a crust. The mould can be the traditional earthenware dish or some other appropriate metal, enamel or glass mould. Any type of forcemeat can be used to make a terrine. The terrine can be as simple as a baking dish filled with a forcemeat and baked until done. A more attractive terrine can be constructed by layering the forcemeat with garnishes to create a mosaic effect when sliced. A terrine can even be layered with different forcemeats; for example, a pink salmon mousseline may be layered with a white pike mousseline.

BASIC PROCEDURE FOR PREPARING A TERRINE

1. Prepare the desired forcemeat and garnishes and keep refrigerated until needed.

2. Line a mould with thin slices of backfat, blanched leafy vegetables or other appropriate liner. (Some chefs claim that the backfat keeps the terrine moist during cooking; most modern chefs do not agree but nevertheless use it for aesthetic purposes.) The lining should overlap slightly, completely covering the inside of the mould and extending over the edge of the mould by approximately 2.5 cm (1 in.). Alternatively, line the mould with plastic wrap.

3. Fill the terrine with the forcemeat and garnishes, being careful not to create air pockets. Tap the mould several times on a solid work surface to remove any air pockets.

4. Fold the liner or plastic wrap over the forcemeat and, if necessary, use additional pieces to completely cover its surface.

5. If desired, garnish the top of the terrine with herbs that were used in the preparation of the forcemeat.

6. Cover the terrine with its lid or aluminum foil and bake in a water bath in a 180°C (350°F) oven. Regulate the oven temperature so the water stays between 77°C and 82°C (170°F and 180°F). The water bath may be replaced by cooking terrines in a combitherm oven with steam.

7. Cook the terrine to an internal temperature of 60°C (140°F) for meat-based forcemeats or 55°C (130°F) for fish- or vegetable-based forcemeats.

8. Remove the terrine from the oven and allow it to cool slightly. If desired, pour off any fat and liquid from around the terrine and cover it with cool liquid aspic jelly.

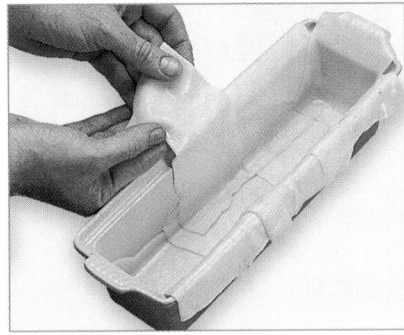

1. Lining a mould with thin slices of backfat.

2. Filling the terrine with the forcemeat and garnish.

3. Decorating the top of the terrine with herbs and placing the terrine in a water bath.

4. Slicing the finished terrine.

Several types of terrines are not made from traditional forcemeats; many others are not made from forcemeats at all. But all are nonetheless called terrines because they are moulded or cooked in the earthenware mould called a terrine. These include liver (and foie gras) terrines, vegetable terrines, brawns or aspic terrines, mousses, rillettes and confits.

Liver terrines are popular and easy to make. Puréed poultry, pork or veal livers are mixed with eggs, seasonings and a panada of cream and bread, then baked in a backfat or bacon-lined terrine. Although most livers purée easily in a food processor, a smoother finished product is achieved if the livers are forced through a drum sieve after or in lieu of puréeing them in the processor.

Aspic Jelly

Aspic jelly is a savoury jelly produced by increasing the gelatin content of a strong stock and then clarifying the stock following the process for preparing consommé discussed in Chapter 11, Soups. Brown stock produces an amber aspic jelly; white stock produces a light aspic jelly.

Although gelatin is a natural ingredient present in all good stocks, its concentration level is not normally high enough to produce a firm aspic jelly. Additional gelatin is usually added to the stock in order to assist gelling (setting). This can be done in two ways. The first is to produce a stock with an extremely high gelatin content by using gelatinous meats and bones such as calves' feet, pigs' ears and pork skin; the second is to add plain gelatin to a finished stock. An easier method of preparing aspic jelly is to add gelatin directly to a flavourful finished consommé.

Aspic jelly has many applications throughout the kitchen. In addition to adding flavour and shine, a coating of aspic jelly prevents displayed foods from drying out and inhibits the oxidation of sliced red meats. Aspic jelly is often lightly flavoured with liquors such as Madeira and cut into decorative garnishes for both plated presentations and buffet displays. It is also used to bind savoury mousses, glaze slices of pâté and coat moulded mousse. Aspic jelly is funnelled into cooked pâtés en croûte to fill the gaps created when the forcemeat shrinks during the cooking process. Aspic jelly is also the basis of aspic moulds or terrines (often simply called *aspics*), in which layers of cooked meats or vegetables are bound together and held in place by the aspic jelly. Many of these uses are discussed in this chapter.

The gelatin content of aspic jelly varies depending upon its intended use. (See Table 20.1.) Verify the bloom strength of the gelatin by testing a small batch. Aspic jelly to be used only on a display can have a very high gelatin content for easier handling. Aspic jelly to be eaten should be fairly firm when cold, gelled at room temperature but tender enough to melt quickly in the mouth when eaten. To test the gelatin content of a liquid, pour 5 mL (1 tsp.) onto a plate and refrigerate the plate for a few minutes. If the liquid does not gel firmly, additional gelatin can be softened in a small amount of cool liquid then added to the hot liquid.

TABLE 20.1	Gelatin Concentrations	
Type of Gel	**Amount of Gelatin per 1 L (1 qt.) of Liquid**	**Typical Use**
Soft	50 g (2 oz.)	Edible glazes for sliced meats, pâtés.
Firm	80–100 g (3–4 oz.)	Complete linings, heavily garnished fillings for terrine (aspic) moulds.
Very firm	100–250 g (4–10 oz.)	Nonedible purposes such as coating nonedible centrepieces or trays for presentations. Humidity and water purity are factors.

● **brawn** also called an aspic terrine; made from simmered meats packed into a terrine and covered with aspic. Head cheese is an old-country European version.

Foie gras terrines are made with fattened geese or duck livers called foie gras. Foie gras is unique, even among other poultry livers, in that it consists almost entirely of fat. (See Chapter 17, Poultry.) It requires special attention during cooking; if it is cooked improperly or too long it turns into a puddle of very expensive fat.

Vegetable terrines can be made with a relatively low fat content and are becoming increasingly popular. Beautiful vegetable terrines are made by lining a terrine with a blanched leafy vegetable such as spinach, then alternating layers of two or three separately prepared vegetable fillings to create contrasting colours and flavours. A different style of vegetable terrine is made by suspending brightly coloured vegetables in a mousseline forcemeat to create a mosaic pattern when sliced.

Brawns or **aspic terrines** are made by simmering gelatinous cuts of meat (most notably, pigs' feet and head, including the tongue) in a rich stock with wine and flavourings. The stock is enriched with gelatin and flavour from the meat, creating an unclarified aspic jelly. The meat is then pulled from the bone, diced and packed into the terrine mould. The stock is reduced to concentrate its gelatin content, strained through cheesecloth and poured over the meat in the terrine. After the terrine has set, it is removed from the mould and sliced for service. The finished product is a rustic and flavourful dish.

A more elegant-appearing brawn is made by lining a terrine mould with aspic jelly, arranging a layer of garnish (for example, sliced meats, vegetables or low-acid fruits) along the mould's bottom, adding aspic jelly to cover the garnish and repeating the procedure until the mould is full.

A **mousse** can be sweet or savoury. Sweet mousses are described in Chapter 32, Custards, Creams, Frozen Desserts and Dessert Sauces. A savoury mousse—which is not a mousseline forcemeat—is made from fully cooked meats, poultry, game, fish, shellfish or vegetables that are puréed and combined with a béchamel or other appropriate sauce, bound with gelatin and lightened with whipped cream. A mousse can be moulded in a decorated, aspic-jelly-coated mould such as that described immediately below, or it can be formed in moulds lined with plastic wrap, which is peeled off after the mousse is unmoulded. A small mousse can be served as an individual portion; a larger moulded mousse can be displayed on a buffet.

BASIC PROCEDURE FOR PREPARING AN ASPIC-JELLY-COATED CHILLED MOUSSE

A mould can be lined with aspic jelly, then decorated and filled with cold mousse. The aspic-jelly-coated mousse is then unmoulded for an attractive presentation.

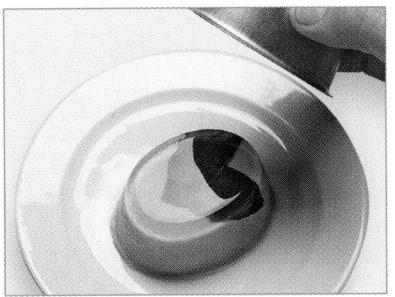

1. Set a metal mould in ice water and add 250 mL (8 fl. oz.) of cool liquid aspic jelly. Swirl the mould so the aspic jelly adheres to all sides. Pour out the excess aspic jelly. Repeat as needed to achieve the desired thickness; 6 mm (1/4 in.) or less is usually sufficient.

2. Garnish the mould by dipping pieces of vegetable or other foods in the liquid aspic jelly and placing them carefully inside the aspic-jelly-coated mould. The mould can now be filled with a cold filling such as a mousse.

3. Refrigerate the mould until it is well chilled. Unmould the aspic by dipping the mould in warm water, then inverting and tapping the mould on a plate.

Rillettes and **confits** are actually preserved meats. Rillettes are prepared by seasoning and slow-cooking pork or fatty poultry such as duck or goose in generous amounts of their own fat until the meat falls off the bone. The warm meat is mashed and combined with a portion of the cooking fat. The mixture is then packed into a crock or terrine and rendered fat is strained over the top to seal it. Rillettes are eaten cold as a spread accompanied by bread or toast.

Confit is prepared in a similar manner except, before cooking, the meat or poultry is often lightly salt-cured to draw out some moisture. The confit is then cooked until very tender but not falling apart. Confits are generally served hot. Like rillettes, confits can be preserved by sealing them with a layer of strained rendered fat. Properly prepared and sealed rillettes and confits will keep for several weeks under refrigeration.

Although it is sometimes incorrectly called chicken liver pâté, chopped chicken liver is prepared in a similar fashion to a rillette. Chopped chicken liver, however, will not have the keeping qualities of traditional rillettes or confits because it is not normally sealed in a crock or terrine with rendered fat. It should be eaten within a day or two of its preparation.

● **rillette** meat cooked in its own fat slowly, then mashed or diced, mixed with fat and potted

● **confit** lightly cured meat, usually duck or goose, stewed in its own fat. Pieces are packed in the fat and chilled for later use. Note that a confit can be made from fruits or vegetables also.

Gerd Steinmeyer, CCC

Gerd was born in West Germany and apprenticed at the Hotel School Siegen there. Two highlights of his long and varied career in Alberta include having functioned as Executive Chef to the official German Delegation at the 1988 XV Olympic Winter Games and having successfully coached umpteen young culinarians for local and international culinary competitions. Over the last 15 years, many of his student teams were awarded Best Apprentice Team, Most Outstanding Single Apprentice and/or Top Entry.

RECIPE 20.5

Approximate values per 30 g serving:	
Calories	100
Total fat	4.4 g
Saturated fat	2.6 g
Cholesterol	23 mg
Sodium	213 mg
Total carbohydrates	13 g
Protein	2.2 g

Pâté en Croûte

Considered by some to be the pinnacle of the charcutier's art, pâtés en croûte are forcemeats baked in a crust. The forcemeat can be country-style, basic or mousseline, but a basic forcemeat is most commonly used. Although pâtés en croûte can be baked without using a mould, a mould helps produce a more attractive finished product.

Pâté Dough (Pâte à Pâté)

The crust surrounding a baking forcemeat must be durable enough to hold in the juices produced as the pâté bakes and to withstand the long baking process. Unfortunately, some of the more durable crusts are tough and unpleasant to eat.

The goal is to achieve a balance so that the crust will hold the juices of the baking pâté and still be relatively pleasant to the palate. Some pâtés, especially more delicate ones such as fish mousselines, can be wrapped in brioche dough (Recipe 29.12).

APPLYING THE BASICS	RECIPE 20.5

Pâté Dough

SAIT POLYTECHNIC, CALGARY, AB
SCHOOL OF HOSPITALITY AND TOURISM
Chef Instructor Gerd Steinmeyer, CCC

Yield: 1.4 kg (3 lb. 3 oz.), enough for 2 pâtés

Flour, all-purpose	800 g	28-1/2 oz.
Salt	20 g	4 tsp.
Butter, soft	225 g	8 oz.
Water, lukewarm	225–250 mL	8–9 fl. oz.
Eggs, medium	3	3

1. Place the flour and salt in the bowl of a food processor with dough hook in place.
2. Combine the butter, 225 mL (8 fl. oz.) of water and eggs; add them to the flour and salt mixture.
3. Mix until smooth and the dough forms a ball (2–3 minutes). Add more water if needed to make a pliable dough. Refrigerate. The dough will be easier to work with if allowed to rest for at least 1 hour.

BASIC PROCEDURE FOR ASSEMBLING AND BAKING PÂTÉ EN CROÛTE

After preparing a forcemeat and pastry dough, all that remains is to assemble and bake the pâté en croûte. The amount of pastry dough and forcemeat needed is determined by the size of the mould or pan chosen.

1. Prepare the pâté dough and the forcemeat, keeping the forcemeat refrigerated until needed.
2. Roll out the dough into a rectangular shape 3-mm (1/8-in.) thick.
3. Using the pâté mould as a pattern, determine how much dough is needed to line the inside; allow enough dough along each side of the mould's length to cover the top when folded over. Mark the dough. Cut the dough slightly

continued

larger than the marked lines. Cut a second rectangular piece of dough that is slightly larger than the top of the mould; it will be used as a lid.

4. Lightly butter the inside of the mould.

5. Lightly dust the large rectangle of dough with flour, fold it over and transfer it to the mould.

6. Use your thumbs and a dough ball made from dough trimmings to form the dough neatly into the corners of the mould. Continue until the dough is of even thickness on all sides and in the corners.

7. Trim the dough, leaving 2 cm (3/4 in.) on the ends and enough dough to cover the top along the sides.

8. Line the mould with thin slices of backfat or ham, allowing 2 cm (3/4 in.) extra around the top of the mould, or as directed in the recipe. This layer helps protect the pastry crust from coming in contact with the moist forcemeat, which would make it soggy.

9. Fill the lined mould with the forcemeat to 1 cm (1/2 in.) below the top of the mould, pressing it well into the corners to avoid air pockets. Layer and garnish as appropriate.

10. Fold the backfat or ham over the top of the forcemeat, using additional pieces if necessary to cover its entire surface. Fold the pastry over the forcemeat.

11. Brush the exposed surface of the pastry with egg wash; carefully cap with the top piece of dough. Press the overlapping dough down inside the sides of the mould with a small spatula.

12. Using round cutters, cut one or two holes in the top to allow steam to escape during cooking. Egg-wash the surface. Place a doughnut-shaped piece of dough around each of the holes. Egg-wash the decorations.

13. Bake the pâté in a preheated 230°C (450°F) oven for 15 minutes. Then mask the surface of the pâté with aluminum foil. Reduce the heat to 180°C (350°F) and continue baking until the internal temperature reaches 60°C (140°F) for meat pâtés or 55°C (130°F) for fish and vegetable pâtés.

14. Allow the pâté to cool for at least one hour or overnight. Using a funnel, pour cool liquid aspic jelly through the holes to fill the space created when the pâté shrank during cooling. Allow the pâté en croûte to chill overnight before slicing.

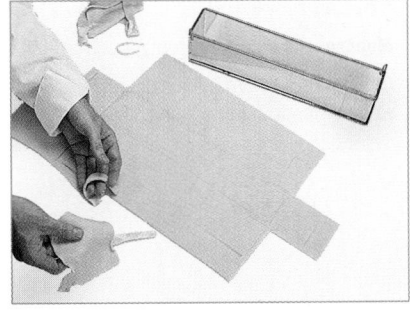

1. Cutting the dough into a large rectangle.

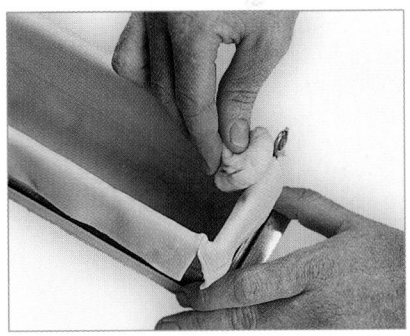

2. Pressing the dough into the mould with a floured dough ball and your thumbs.

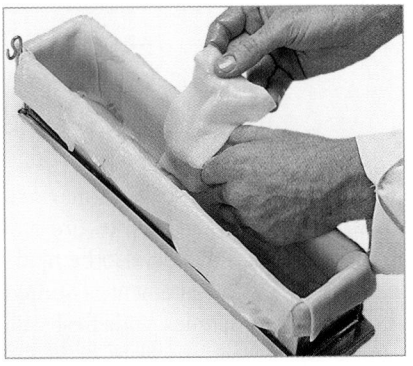

3. Lining the mould with thin slices of backfat.

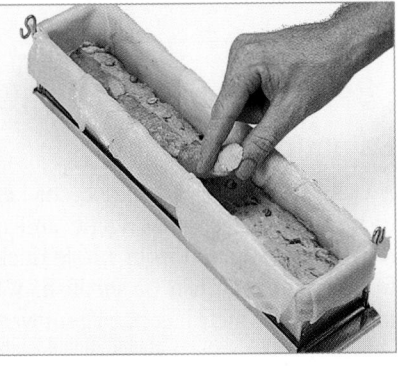

4. Filling the lined mould with the forcemeat and garnish.

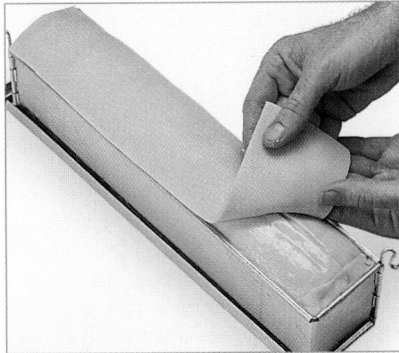

5. Using egg wash on the surface and placing the top on the pâté.

Origins

Galantine—From Old French *galant*, meaning showy.

Ballotine—Possibly from the French *balle*, meaning bale, or *ballot*, meaning bundle.

Terrine—From the Latin *terra*, meaning earth.

Pâté—From the Old French *pasté*, meaning paste.

Mousse—French for "froth."

Quenelle—From Alsatian French *knödel*, meaning dumpling.

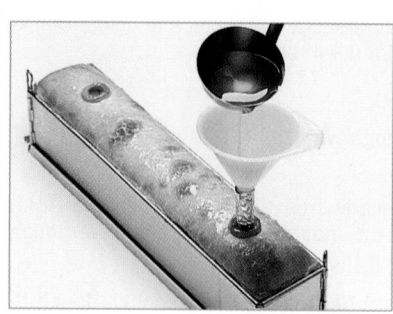

6. Inserting an aluminum chimney in one of the holes of the baked pâté and pouring aspic jelly into the hole.

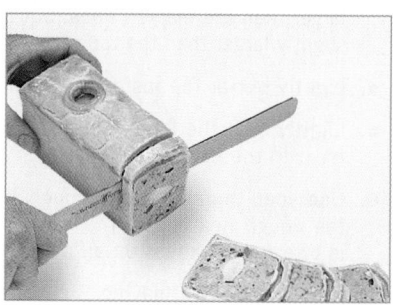

7. Slicing the pâté with a thin-bladed knife.

BASIC PROCEDURE FOR GLAZING PÂTÉ SLICES WITH ASPIC JELLY

Slices of chilled terrines, pâtés en croûte or galantines (discussed below) may be garnished and coated with aspic to preserve their colour, prevent drying and create a more attractive presentation.

1. Stirring slowly to cool the clarified aspic jelly.

2. Brushing or spooning the aspic jelly over slices of chilled pâté arranged on a cooling rack. Repeat the process until the coating reaches the desired thickness.

Technology

Combitherm ovens have revolutionized the way we cook pâtés, galantines and terrines. With dry and moist heat capabilities, precise temperature settings and automatic probe thermometers, the quality of the final product can be better assured.

Galantines

A classic galantine is a boned chicken stuffed with a chicken-based forcemeat to resemble its original shape and then poached. Today, galantines are still most often prepared from whole ducks or chickens, but they can also be made from game, veal, fish or shellfish. When appropriate, the forcemeat is stuffed in the skin, which has been removed in one piece, sometimes with flesh still attached. When the skin is not available or its use is inappropriate or in the case of fish and shellfish where there is no skin, the galantine is made by forming the forcemeat into a cylindrical shape and wrapping it in plastic wrap and foil before poaching. Galantines are served cold and are often displayed on buffets, sliced and glazed with aspic jelly.

A **ballotine** is similar to a galantine but is served hot. It may be poached, braised or roasted. Exercise caution and temperature control if the forcemeat has a high fat content, as the filling can become dry and stringy. The cooking liquid becomes the sauce.

BASIC PROCEDURE FOR PREPARING A POULTRY GALANTINE

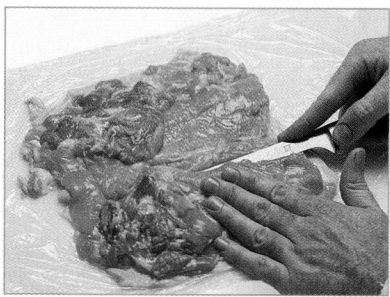

1. Butterflying the breasts and tenderloins and placing a thin layer of meat over the skin.

2. Arranging the forcemeat and garnishes in a cylindrical shape across the centre of the meat.

1. Bone the chicken by cutting through the skin along the length of the backbone and then following the natural curvature of the carcass. Keep all the meat attached to the skin. Remove the legs and wings by cutting through the joints when you reach them; leave the legs and wings attached to the skin. Then cut off the wings. Bone the thighs and legs, leaving the skin and meat attached to the rest of the bird. Trim the skin to form a large rectangle.

2. Prepare a forcemeat using the meat from the skinned bird or any other appropriate meat. Reserve a portion of the meat as garnish if desired. Prepare any other garnishes. Refrigerate the forcemeat and garnishes until ready for use.

3. Spread out the skin and meat on plastic wrap or several layers of cheesecloth with the skin side down and the flesh up.

4. Remove the chicken tenderloins and pull the tendon out of each. Butterfly the breasts and tenderloins and cover the entire skin with a thin layer of meat.

5. Arrange the forcemeat and garnishes in a cylindrical shape across the centre of the skin.

6. Tightly roll the skin around the forcemeat and garnishes to form a tight cylinder. (Use the plastic wrap to assist the process.)

7. Tie the ends of the plastic wrap with butcher's twine and secure the galantine at even intervals using strips of cheesecloth. Wrap the galantine with heavy-duty aluminum foil.

8. Poach the galantine in a water bath of 80°C (175°F) to an internal temperature of 60°C (140°F) for meat-based forcemeats or 55°C (130°F) for fish- or vegetable-based forcemeats.

9. Cool the galantine rapidly in its cooking liquid until it can be handled. Use an ice bath. This helps maintain the round shape. Refrigerate overnight.

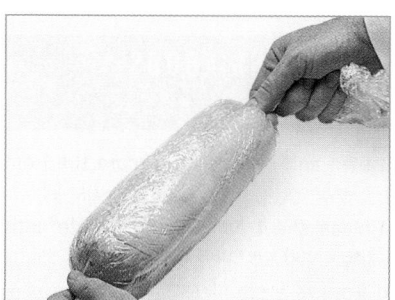

3. Using plastic wrap to roll the galantine into a tight cylinder.

4. Securing the galantine with heavy-duty aluminum foil.

5. Slicing the finished product.

Sauce Chaud-Froid

Sauce chaud-froid (French for "hot-cold") is prepared hot but served cold. Traditionally used to coat meats, poultry or fish that were eaten cold, sauce chaud-froid is now more typically used to coat a whole poached salmon or whole roasted poultry item, which is then further decorated and used as a centrepiece. As with aspic jelly, chaud-froid that is to be eaten should be fairly firm when cold, gelled at room temperature but tender enough to melt quickly in the mouth when eaten. Chaud-froid used for decorative purposes only should have a heavier gelatin content and be quite firm, which makes it easier to work with.

A classic sauce chaud-froid is a mixture of one part cream and two parts stock (veal, chicken and/or fish) strengthened with gelatin. Depending on the stock used, this coating ranges in colour from cream to beige. A more modern sauce chaud-froid (also known as a mayonnaise chaud-froid or mayonnaise collée) is based on mayonnaise; it is easier to make than the classic sauce and provides a whiter product. Chaud-froid may be coloured with tomato purée or spinach purée or infused with saffron. Brown chaud-froid is made with glace de viande and extra gelatin, if needed.

RECIPE 20.6

Approximate values per 100 g serving:	
Calories	182
Total fat	16 g
Saturated fat	9.2 g
Cholesterol	51 mg
Sodium	105 mg
Total carbohydrates	5.8 g
Protein	5.0 g

APPLYING THE BASICS   RECIPE 20.6

Sauce Chaud-Froid

Yield: 1.3 L (48 fl. oz.)

Veal stock, clarified	4 L	4 qt.
Gelatin powder	60 g	2 oz.
Cream, 35%	500 mL	16 fl. oz.
Salt	2 g	1/2 tsp.
White pepper	TT	TT

1. Reduce veal stock to 1 L (1 qt.)
2. Bloom gelatin in cream and stir into the hot veal reduction.
3. Heat carefully to dissolve gelatin and season.
4. Cool to body temperature before pouring over cold galantine or other item.

BASIC PROCEDURE FOR COATING FOODS WITH SAUCE CHAUD-FROID

1. Cook (usually by poaching or roasting), trim and otherwise prepare the item to be decorated.
2. Place the item on a cooling rack over a clean sheet pan and refrigerate until ready to decorate. (Sauce that drips into the clean pan can be reused.)
3. Warm an ample amount of sauce chaud-froid in a stainless steel bowl over a doubleboiler until it is completely melted. Stir the sauce gently with a spoon rather than a whisk in order to prevent air bubbles from forming.
4. When the sauce is warm and smooth, remove the bowl from the doubleboiler and place it in an ice bath.

continued

5. Using the back of a large ladle, stir the sauce by spinning the bowl and holding the ladle stationary. This should be done almost continuously while the sauce cools. Do not scrape the solidified chaud-froid from the sides of the bowl, as lumps will form.

6. When the sauce has cooled to room temperature, remove the item to be decorated from the refrigerator and place it on the work table.

7. Coat the item with the sauce in a single, smooth motion. Use a ladle if the item is small; if it is large, pour the sauce directly from the bowl. The sauce should adhere to the cold food, and the coating should be free of bubbles or runs.

8. Repeat as necessary, reusing the sauce that drips onto the sheet pan, until the desired thickness is achieved.

9. Using a paring knife, carefully cut away any sauce from areas that are to be left uncoated.

10. Decorate the item as desired with vegetable flowers or other garnishes. If desired, finish the item by coating the vegetable garnishes with a layer of clear aspic jelly, using the same procedure.

1. Scoring the skin of the fish.

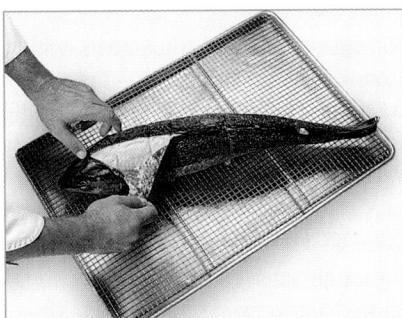

2. Removing the skin.

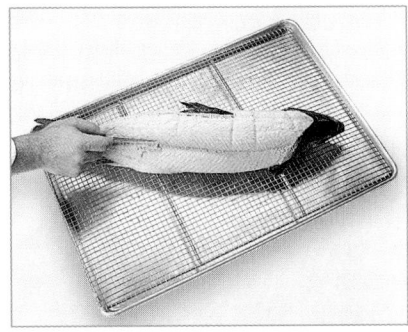

3. Removing the dark flesh and preparing the fish for the first coating of sauce chaud-froid.

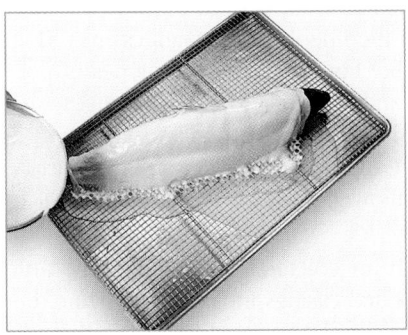

4. Glazing the fish with the sauce chaud-froid.

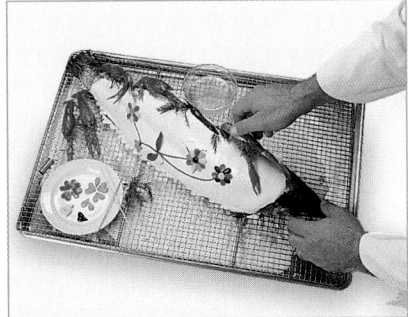

5. Decorating the fish with vegetable flowers.

6. The decorated fish ready for service.

Sausages

Sausages are forcemeats stuffed into casings. For centuries, sausages consisted of ground meat, usually pork, and seasonings. Today sausages are made not only from pork, but also from game, beef, veal, poultry, fish, shellfish and even vegetables.

● **sausage** a seasoned forcemeat usually stuffed into a casing; a sausage can be fresh, smoked or cooked, dried or hard

Types of Sausage

Andouille—A very spicy smoked pork sausage, popular in Cajun cuisine.

Chorizo—A coarse, spicy smoked pork sausage flavoured with ground chiles and removed from its casing before cooking; used in Mexican and Spanish cuisines.

Mortadella—An Italian smoked sausage made with ground beef, pork and pork fat, flavoured with coriander and white wine; it is air-dried and has a delicate flavour; also a large American bologna-type pork sausage studded with pork fat and garlic.

Pepperoni—A hard, thin, air-dried Italian sausage seasoned with red and black pepper.

Soppressata—A hard, aged Italian sausage salami, sometimes coated with cracked peppercorns or herbs.

Slices of Rosette de Lyon, a dry-cured French sausage, also known as saucisson sec.

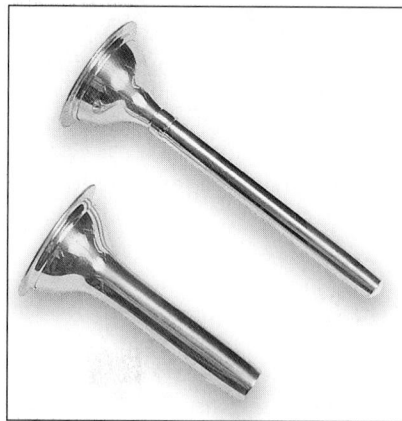

FIGURE 20.2 Sausage nozzles.

There are three main types of sausages:

1. Fresh sausages include breakfast sausage links and Italian sausages. They are made with fresh ingredients that have not been cured or smoked.
2. Smoked and cooked sausages are made with raw meat products treated with chemicals, usually the preservative sodium nitrite. Examples are kielbasa, bologna and hot dogs.
3. Dried or hard sausages are made with cured meats, then air-dried under controlled conditions. Dry sausages may or may not be smoked or cooked. Dried or hard sausages include salami, pepperoni, Lebanon bologna and landjäger.

Smoked and cooked sausages and dry or hard sausages are rarely prepared in typical food service operations. They are produced by specialty shops and will not be discussed here. We do discuss the ingredients and procedures for a variety of fresh sausages that can be prepared in almost any kitchen.

Sausage Components

Sausage Meats

Sausage meats are forcemeats with particular characteristics and flavourings. Coarse Italian and lamb sausages, for example, are simply a country-style forcemeat without liver and with different seasonings, stuffed into casings and formed into links. Hot dogs, bratwurst and other fine-textured sausages are variations of basic forcemeats stuffed into casings and formed into links.

Sausage Casings

Although sausage mixtures can be cooked without casings, most sausages are stuffed into casings before cooking. Two types of sausage casings are commonly used in food service operations:

1. Natural casings are portions of hog, sheep or cattle intestines. Their diameters are measured in millimetres and they come in several sizes depending upon the animal or portion of the intestine used. Hog casings are the most popular; sheep casings are considered the finest-quality small casings. Both hog and sheep casings are used to make hot dogs and many types of pork sausage. Beef casings are quite large and are used to make sausages such as ring bologna and Polish sausage. Most natural casings are purchased in salt packs. In order to rid them of salt and impurities, the casings must be carefully rinsed in warm water and allowed to soak in cool water for at least one hour or overnight before use.
2. Collagen casings are manufactured from collagen extracted from cattle hides. They are generally inferior to natural casings in taste and texture, but they do have advantages: Collagen casings do not require any washing or soaking prior to use and they are uniform in size.

Preparing Sausages

Equipment for Sausage Making

Sausage-stuffing machines are best if you engage in large-scale sausage production. Otherwise, all you need is a grinder with a sausage nozzle attachment such as the ones shown in Figure 20.2. Nozzles are available in several sizes to accommodate the various casing sizes.

BASIC PROCEDURE FOR MAKING SAUSAGES

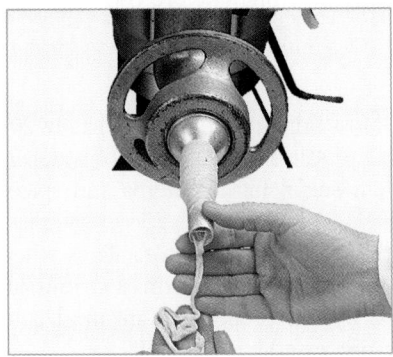

1. Sliding the casing over the nozzle of the sausage stuffer.

1. Prepare a forcemeat.
2. Thoroughly chill all parts of the sausage stuffer that will come in contact with the forcemeat.
3. Rinse and soak the casings if using natural ones. Cut the casings into 1- to 2-m (4- to 6-ft.) lengths.
4. Put the forcemeat in the sausage stuffer.
5. Slide the casing over the nozzle of the sausage stuffer. Tie the end in a knot and pierce with a skewer to prevent an air pocket.
6. Support and guide the casing off the end of the nozzle as the forcemeat is extruded from the nozzle into the casing.
7. After all the forcemeat has been stuffed into the casing, twist or tie the sausage into uniform links of the desired size.

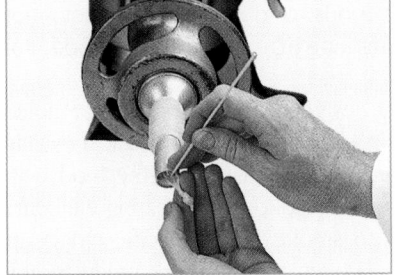

2. Knotting and piercing the casing with a skewer.

3. Supporting and guiding the casing off the end of the nozzle as the forcemeat is extruded from the machine into the casing.

4. Twisting or tying the sausage into uniform links.

SALT-CURING, BRINING AND SMOKING

Curing, brining and smoking are ancient techniques for preserving food. Today, foods such as hams, corned beef and smoked salmon are salt-cured, brined or smoked primarily for flavour. Cured meats have a characteristic pink colour caused by the reaction of sodium nitrite, which is added during processing, with the naturally occurring myoglobin protein in the meat.

Salt-Curing

Salt-curing is the process of surrounding a food with salt or a mixture of salt, sugar, nitrite-based curing salt, herbs and spices. Salt-curing dehydrates the food, inhibits bacterial growth and adds flavour. It is most often used with pork products and fish. Salt-curing is not a quick procedure—and the time involved adds money to production costs. For example, country-style hams are salt-cured. Proper curing requires approximately 1.5 days per 450 g (1 lb.) of ham, which means three weeks for the average ham.

Some salt-cured hams such as Smithfield and prosciutto are not actually cooked. The curing process preserves the meat and makes it safe to consume raw.

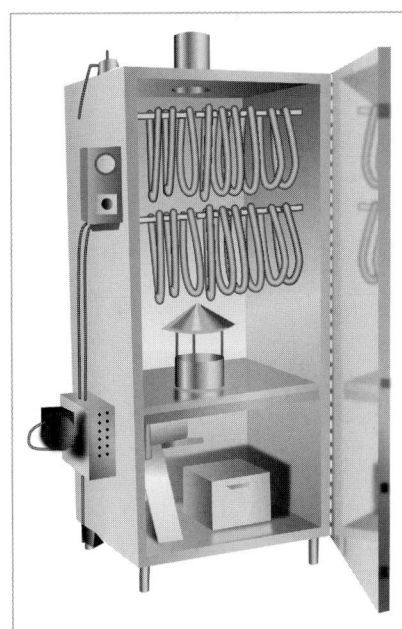

Commercial Smoker

Gravlax is a well-known salmon dish prepared by salt-curing salmon fillets with a mixture of salt, sugar, pepper and dill. A recipe for gravlax (Recipe 20.9) is included later in this chapter.

Duck and goose confit are lightly salt-cured overnight before cooking.

Brining

A brine is actually a very salty marinade. Most brines have approximately 20% salinity, which is equivalent to 450 g (1 lb.) of salt per 4 L (1 gal.) of water. As with dry-salt cures, brines can also contain sugar, nitrites, herbs and spices. Brining is sometimes called pickling.

Today, most cured meats are prepared in large production facilities where the brine is injected into the meat for rapid and uniform distribution. Commercially brined corned beef is cured by this process, as are most common hams. After brining, hams are further processed by smoking.

Smoking

There are two basic methods of smoking foods: cold smoking and hot smoking. The principal difference is that hot smoking actually cooks the food; cold smoking does not.

Both are done in a smoker specifically designed for this purpose. Smokers can be gas or electric; they vary greatly in size and operation. But they have several things in common. All consist of a chamber that holds the food being smoked, a means of burning wood to produce smoke and a heating element.

Different types of wood can be used to smoke food. Specific woods are selected to impart specific flavours. Hickory is often used for pork products; alder is excellent for smoked salmon. Maple, chestnut, juniper, mesquite and many other woods are also used. Resinous woods such as pine give food a bitter flavour and should be avoided. Tea and aromatic herb stems may be used in smoking.

Cold smoking is the process of exposing foods to smoke at temperatures of 10°C to 29°C (50°F to 85°F). Meat, poultry, game, fish, shellfish, cheese, nuts and even vegetables can be cold-smoked successfully. Most cold-smoked meats are generally salt-cured or brined first. Salt-curing or brining adds flavour, allows the nitrites (which give the ham, bacon and other smoked meats their distinctive pink colour) to penetrate the flesh and, most important, extracts moisture from the food, allowing the smoke to penetrate more easily. Cold-smoked foods are actually still raw. Some, like smoked salmon (lox), are eaten without further cooking. Others, such as bacon and hams, must be cooked before eating.

Hot smoking is the process of exposing foods to smoke at temperatures of 93°C to 121°C (200°F to 250°F). As with cold smoking, a great variety of foods can be prepared by hot smoking. Meats, poultry, game, fish and shellfish that are hot-smoked also benefit from salt-curing or brining. Although most hot-smoked foods are fully cooked when removed from the smoker, many are used in other recipes that call for further cooking.

While most smoking requires specialized equipment, two affordable options exist for imparting a smoked flavour to foods. A stove top smoker, which resembles a hotel pan with a tight-fitting lid, can be used to hot-smoke small cuts of meat, fish, poultry or vegetables. Wood chips are scattered inside the bottom of the pan. Foods to be smoked sit on top of a mesh rack placed inside the box. The heat of the stove top ignites the wood chips, permeating the food with a smoky flavour. Foods smoked in this manner must reach proper internal cooking temperatures to be served without additional cooking. Liquid smoke is a flavouring made from smoke, which has been condensed from the burning of wood chips. When used judiciously it can impart a pleasant smoky taste to barbecue sauces and marinades.

Pork Products

Preparing hams and curing and smoking pork products is a traditional part of charcuterie. Although most bacon and ham is now produced in large commercial facilities, the chef still works with these
products and must be able to identify them properly.

Most **bacon** comes from a hog's fatty belly.

Side bacon is produced by brining and cold smoking trimmed pork belly.
It is available in slab or sliced form. Sliced bacon is purchased by count (number of slices) per pound; thick-sliced bacon runs 10 to 14 slices per pound,
while thin-sliced bacon may contain as many as 28 to 32 slices per pound.

Canadian bacon is produced from a boneless pork loin, trimmed so that
only a thin layer of fat remains on its surface. It is then brined and smoked.
When coated in cornmeal, it becomes peameal bacon.

Pancetta is an Italian pork-belly bacon that is not smoked. It is salt-cured, peppered and often rolled into a cylinder shape. It can be sliced into rounds and
fried; it is diced, rendered and combined with sauce to make fettuccine carbonara.

A **fresh ham** is a hog's hind leg; it is a primal cut. Many processed products produced from the primal fresh ham are also called ham.

Ham, in Canada, describes a variety of processed pork products, most of
which come from the primal fresh leg. **Boneless** or **formed hams** are
produced by separating a primal leg into its basic muscles, defatting the meat,
curing it, stuffing the meat into various-sized and -shaped casings and cooking
it. Boneless or formed hams are either smoked or have liquid smoke flavouring
added during the curing process. The quality of boneless or formed hams varies
greatly. The best hams are formed from only one or two large muscles, have
low fat content and no added water other than that used during the curing
process. Hams of lesser quality are formed from many small pieces of muscle
and have a higher fat and water content. B & R (boned and rolled) and Pullman
hams are common. Many boneless or formed hams are listed in *The Meat Buyers
Guide* and are indexed by the IMPS/NAMP system.

Country ham is a specialty of the southeastern United States. Country
hams are dry-cured, smoked and hung to air-dry for a period ranging from
several weeks to more than a year. During drying, a mould develops on the
ham rind that must be scrubbed off before the ham is cooked. It is best
cooked by first soaking, then slow simmering. The most famous country hams
are Virginia hams; those from Smithfield, Virginia, are considered the finest.
Only hams produced in rural areas can be called country hams; others must be
labelled country-style ham.

Prosciutto is Italian for ham. What we call prosciutto in this country is
called **Parma** in Italy. It is available raw (*crudo*) or cooked (*cotto*). Parma
ham, produced near that Italian city, is made from hogs fed on the whey of
cheese processed nearby. The ham is salt-cured and air-dried but not smoked.
The curing process makes it safe and wholesome to consume raw. Several
domestic varieties of prosciutto are produced (the raw variety is more popular), varying widely in quality. Imported prosciuttos are much larger than the
domestic varieties because Italian hogs are larger when butchered.

Jamón (AH-mohn) is the Spanish word for ham. Jamón Serrano or mountain
ham is salt-cured and air-dried but not smoked. Jamón Iberico is a salted, dry-
cured ham from specific breeds of hogs, a Spanish delicacy prized since Roman
times. The most esteemed is that made from the Bellota breed that feed on for-
aged acorns. Like prosciutto, these hams are served raw, thinly sliced.

Westphalian ham is dry-cured, brined and then smoked with beechwood.
Authentic Westphalian hams are produced in the Westphalia region of
Germany and are quite similar to prosciutto. They are sold bone-in or boneless. Their characteristic flavour is derived from the juniper berries used in the
curing process and the beechwood used for smoking.

Canadian Bacon, Sliced Bacon
and Pancetta

IMPS#501, Ham Short Shank,
Cured and Smoked

IMPS#510, Ham, Boneless, Skinless, Cured and
Smoked, Fully Cooked

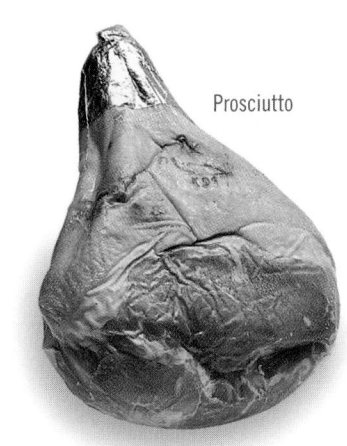

Prosciutto

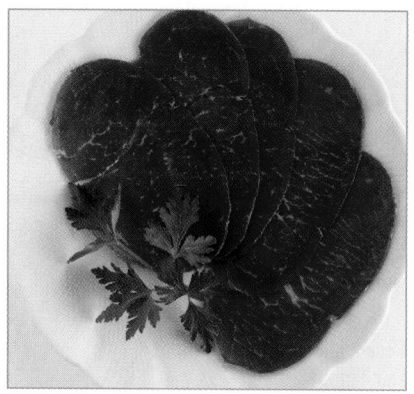

Bresaola, dried beef from the Lombardy region.

Other Cured Meat Products

Although pork is the most common meat in classic charcuterie, other meats and poultry lend themselves to preservation. Beef is used to make pastrami, pickled beef brisket that is spiced and then air-dried. It is steamed, then sliced for sandwiches. **Bresaola**, a specialty of the Lombardy region of Italy, is salted, spiced and dry-aged beef, served raw and thinly sliced. It is made from the eye round of beef and has a subtle flavour of juniper berries. The similar specialty of the Swiss Alps is known as bunderfleisch. Smoked chicken, duck and turkey are delicious alternatives to ham in sandwiches and on salads. But few cured lamb products exist, possibly because of the strong flavour of lamb fat when aged.

Conclusion

The classic art of charcuterie is as popular today as ever. Consumers regularly enjoy high-quality pâtés, sausages, hams and other charcuterie products.

Although production procedures have changed as new technologies and equipment have developed, the basic principles remain the same: terrines, pâtés and sausages should be produced only from high-quality forcemeats, and temperature control is fundamental to the proper production of force-meats and other charcuterie products.

Armed with a basic knowledge of the procedures used for charcuterie, you can use your imagination and creativity to produce a variety of charcuterie products.

Questions for Discussion

1. Explain why the art of charcuterie is relevant to the training of modern cooks.
2. Compare the three styles of forcemeat.
3. In what way is a terrine different from a pâté? How does a pâté differ from a pâté en croûte?
4. Describe the differences and the similarities between a ballotine and a galantine.
5. Describe the typical procedure for making sausages. Why is the selection of casings important?
6. Explain the difference between hot smoking and cold smoking. Describe a food typically prepared by each of these methods.

Additional Charcuterie Recipes

RECIPE 20.7

Carpaccio of Seared Beef with Parmesan Fans and Perfumed Mascarpone

SAIT POLYTECHNIC, CALGARY, AB
SCHOOL OF HOSPITALITY AND TOURISM
Chef Instructor Fred Malley, CCC, B.Ed.

Yield: 10 servings

Beef tenderloin, centre cut, trimmed and cleaned	600 g	20 oz.
Ground black pepper	TT	TT
Oil	as needed	as needed
Watercress sprigs	60	60
Artichoke hearts, halved, grilled and marinated in olive oil vinaigrette	80 pieces	80 pieces
Parmesan fans (shards, sliced from Parmesan block)	60–90	60–90
Mascarpone, flavoured with 4 roasted mashed garlic cloves	250 g	8 oz.
Espresso coffee beans, ground	pinch	pinch
Garlic chips (crisp deep-fat fried slices)	30	30
Cherry tomatoes, sliced or wedged	30	30

1. Sprinkle the meat with pepper and sear in hot oil.
2. Wrap in plastic wrap to make a roll or log shape and chill for 2 hours in the freezer.
3. Slice the beef paper-thin using an electric slicer, then arrange the slices in a ring on a plate.
4. Place watercress and artichokes in the centre of the meat ring with some of the vinaigrette. Top with the Parmesan fans. Pipe 3 rosettes of mascarpone on the plate and sprinkle espresso lightly over each. Top with the garlic chips. Place tomato pieces between the mascarpone rosettes.

Photo by George Webber

Fred Malley, CCC, B.Ed.
Fred's career includes being an educator, chef, food and beverage manager, caterer and food stylist. He currently instructs aspiring culinarians at SAIT, mentors for professional designation and is actively involved in curriculum development. His food styling appears internationally for major corporations, and he has ventured into research and development for food companies.

RECIPE 20.7

Approximate values per serving:	
Calories	459
Total fat	35 g
Saturated fat	15 g
Cholesterol	94 mg
Sodium	503 mg
Total carbohydrates	11 g
Protein	25 g

RECIPE 20.8

Salmon Tartar Mille Feuille

NORTHERN ALBERTA INSTITUTE OF TECHNOLOGY, EDMONTON, AB
THE HOKANSON CENTRE FOR CULINARY ARTS
Chef Instructor Troy Lymburner

Yield: 4 servings

Fresh salmon, finely diced	225 g	8 oz.
Canola oil	5 mL	1 tsp.
Fresh chives	10 g	1 Tbsp.
Tabasco sauce	TT	TT
Salt	TT	TT
Black pepper, freshly ground	TT	TT
Phyllo pastry	3 sheets	3 sheets
Butter, melted	200 g	7 oz.

RECIPE 20.8

Approximate values per serving:	
Calories	844
Total fat	80 g
Saturated fat	32 g
Cholesterol	180 mg
Sodium	1020 mg
Total carbohydrates	14 g
Protein	17 g

continued

Troy Lymburner

Born and raised in Edmonton, Troy graduated from the Culinary Arts program at NAIT and immediately set out to train in Switzerland. Upon returning to Canada, he worked at a number of upscale properties honing his culinary creativity. Most recently, Troy helped to coach Student Culinary Team Alberta to a gold medal at the 2000 International Culinary Olympics.

Grainy mustard sauce:		
Grainy Dijon mustard	50 mL	1-1/2 fl. oz.
Sour cream	50 mL	1-1/2 fl. oz.
Chive oil:		
Fresh chives	125 g	4 oz.
Olive oil	125 mL	4 fl. oz.
Lemon yogurt:		
Plain yogurt	110 mL	3-1/2 fl. oz.
Lemon juice, freshly squeezed	30 mL	1 fl. oz.
Lemon zest, finely chopped	10 g	2 tsp.
Golden whitefish caviar	20 g	3/4 oz.

1. Combine salmon, oil, chives and seasonings in a nonreactive bowl and chill.
2. Brush 1 sheet of phyllo with melted butter and place second sheet on top. Repeat with third sheet. Divide phyllo into 12 equal squares, cut and place on parchment-lined baking sheet. Bake at 180°C (375°F) until golden brown.
3. Combine mustard and sour cream for mustard sauce.
4. Blanch chives briefly and drain well. Add an equal volume of olive oil and purée in blender.
5. Combine ingredients for lemon yogurt.
6. To assemble on plate, divide 60 g (2 oz.) of salmon mixture in three, place first amount in centre of plate and top with phyllo square. Repeat in three equal layers. Top with a dollop of lemon yogurt and a spoonful of caviar.
7. Garnish plate with drizzle of mustard sauce and chive oil.

Shawn Whalen, CCC, CEC

At age 25, Shawn became the youngest chef in Canada to achieve the Certified Chef de Cuisine designation. He has captained seven international culinary teams and has won numerous awards, including the Grand Gold Best of Show Award at the 126th Annual Salon of Culinary Arts of New York City. Shawn was an Executive Chef for 19 years, including 12 years with Marriott. Along with two partners, he is currently Owner and Culinary Director of Liaison College, Toronto West.

RECIPE 20.9

Brandy and Dill Cured Atlantic Salmon, Pickled Vegetable Salad of Golden Beets, Purple Pearl Onions, Cucumber and Green Tomatoes

LIAISON COLLEGE, TORONTO WEST, TORONTO, ON
Executive Chef/Owner Shawn Whalen

Yield: 6 portions

Salmon	400 g	14 oz.
Brandy	30 mL	1 fl. oz.
Lemon juice	30 mL	1 fl. oz.
Brown sugar	15 g	2 Tbsp.
Coarse salt	10 g	1/3 oz.
Dill	20 g	2 Tbsp.
Black pepper, freshly cracked	2 g	1/2 tsp.
Rice vinegar	125 mL	4 fl. oz.
Sugar	125 g	4 oz.
Water	250 mL	8 fl. oz.
Ginger, coarsely chopped	50 g	1/4 cup
Mustard seeds	35 g	1/4 cup
Salt	15 g	1 Tbsp.
Golden beets, cooked, diced	90 g	3 oz.
Purple pearl onions, peeled, halved	90 g	3 oz.
Cucumber, diced	90 g	3 oz.
Green tomatoes, diced	90 g	3 oz.

continued

1. Place salmon in a ceramic dish. Pour brandy and lemon juice over salmon and rotate to coat. Season with sugar, salt, dill and black pepper while rotating to distribute ingredients and flavours. Cover with plastic wrap.

2. Refrigerate for 24–48 hours, turning salmon every 12 hours.

3. To make the salad, combine rice vinegar, sugar, water, ginger, mustard seed and salt in a nonreactive pot and bring to a boil.

4. Reduce the pickling liquid to a simmer and continue cooking for 5 minutes.

5. Place vegetables in another pot and strain the pickling liquid over them. Place a lid on the pot and allow the vegetables to pickle for 10–15 minutes.

6. Remove salmon from the ceramic dish. Remove any excess marinating garnish.

7. Place a spoonful of pickled vegetables on a plate, slice salmon thinly on the bias and serve on top of pickled vegetables.

VARIATIONS: Traditionally, gravlax is marinated in a mixture of 1 part coarse salt, 2 parts sugar, cracked white peppercorns and dillweed. Many variations have been developed such as beet horseradish, tequila/lime, using brown sugar, substituting fennel or young spruce buds for dill or using honey syrup.

RECIPE 20.9

Approximate values per serving:	
Calories	126
Total fat	7 g
Saturated fat	1 g
Cholesterol	39 mg
Sodium	169 mg
Total carbohydrates	1 g
Protein	13 g

Pickled Vegetable Salad Approximate values per serving:	
Calories	29
Total fat	0 g
Saturated fat	0 g
Cholesterol	0 mg
Sodium	111 mg
Total carbohydrates	7 g
Protein	1 g

1. Gravlax: Coating the salmon fillet with the salt cure.

2. Slicing the cured gravlax thinly.

RECIPE 20.10

Duck Confit

Yield: 4 servings

Duck, 1.8 kg (4 lb.), cut into 4 pieces	1	1
Kosher salt	25 g	2 Tbsp.
Black pepper, cracked	3 g	1 tsp.
Bay leaves, crumbled	4	4
Fresh thyme	6 sprigs	6 sprigs
Garlic cloves, crushed	20 g	6
Duck or goose fat, melted	900 g	2 lb.

1. Rub the duck with the salt. Place skin side down in a roasting pan just large enough to hold the pieces in 1 layer; season with the black pepper, crumbled bay leaves, thyme and garlic. Cover and refrigerate overnight.

2. Melt the duck or goose fat. Add the drained and dried duck pieces. Bring to a simmer and maintain a temperature of 105°C (210°F) for 2–2.5 hours. The meat is done when very tender.

3. Remove the duck from the fat and place in a narrow, deep hotel pan. Ladle enough of the cooking fat over the pieces to cover them completely. Be careful not to add any of the cooking juices.

4. Cover the pan and refrigerate for 2 days to allow the flavours to mellow.

5. To serve, remove the duck from the fat and scrape off the excess fat. Bake at 180°C (350°F) until the skin is crisp and the meat is hot, approximately 30 minutes.

Duck Confit: After the duck browns, cover it with melted fat and return it to the oven.

RECIPE 20.10

Approximate values per serving:	
Calories	459
Total fat	35 g
Saturated fat	15 g
Cholesterol	94 mg
Sodium	503 mg
Total carbohydrates	11 g
Protein	25 g

Bruno Marti, CCC

Bruno began his career as a 15-year-old apprentice in Switzerland, moving to Canada in his early 20s and beginning his culinary career at the Queen Elizabeth Hotel in Montreal. After working as the Manager of Catering for Canadian Pacific Airlines for 12 years, he became chef and owner of La Belle Auberge. Over the last 30 years, Bruno has contributed to Canada's regional and national culinary teams as Member, Manager and Coach. In the 2000 Culinary Olympics, he coached Team Canada to a Grand Gold! He now serves as Chairman of the Canadian Culinary Federation. Read more about his other culinary experiences in the profile on page 484.

RECIPE 20.11

Approximate values per serving:	
Calories	46
Total fat	1.3 g
Saturated fat	0.2 g
Cholesterol	0 mg
Sodium	118 mg
Total carbohydrates	7.2 g
Protein	1.3 g

Vegetable Terrine

LA BELLE AUBERGE RESTAURANT, RICHMOND, BC
Chef-Owner Bruno Marti, CCC

Yield: 1 terrine mould, 10 × 10 × 30 cm (4 × 4 × 12 in.),
with lid; 20 servings

Eggplant, cubed	200 g	7 oz.
Garlic clove, chopped	1	1
Olive oil	as needed	as needed
Shallots, chopped fine	75 g	2
Green beans	100 g	3-1/2 oz.
Water	50 mL	2 fl. oz.
Salt and pepper	TT	TT
Butternut squash, peeled, seeded, sliced lengthwise, 1 cm (1/2 in.) thick	200 g	7 oz.
Fresh herbs, chopped: oregano, thyme, basil	TT	TT
Celeriac, peeled, sliced lengthwise, 1 cm (1/2 in.) thick	200 g	7 oz.
Shiitake mushrooms, whole, stems removed	100 g	3-1/2 oz.
Leeks, washed and cleaned, left whole (not split)	2 medium	2 medium
Carrots, peeled, cut into long, thin strips the length of the carrot	4 large	4 large
Gelatin (leaf)	6 sheets	6 sheets
Tomatoes, peeled, halved, seeded	200 g	7 oz.

1. Sauté eggplant in half the garlic and oil. Roast in the oven at 190°C (375°F) for 20 minutes, then purée, adding a little water if needed.

2. Sauté shallots in oil for 1 minute. Add the beans and the water. Season to taste and simmer until cooked, but still crisp. Allow to cool.

3. In a few drops of oil and water, simmer squash in a 200°C (400°F) oven until tender, about 10 minutes. Turn once, and season with herbs.

4. Repeat with celeriac, cover and cook in moderate oven (180–190°C/ 350–375°F) for 30 minutes.

5. Sauté mushrooms in a little oil and water. Season with salt, pepper and the remaining garlic.

6. Blanch leeks for 10 minutes and carrots for 3 minutes in boiling, salted water. Cool them in ice water.

7. Drain vegetables well.

8. Melt package of gelatin according to manufacturer's instructions.

9. Line the mould with plastic wrap. Add carrot slices, placing them across the mould with excess curving up sides and hanging over edges. Brush with gelatin.

10. Layer tomatoes, celeriac, eggplant, beans (arrange them lengthwise), leeks, mushrooms and squash. Alternate ingredients to give an attractive colour combination. Brush each layer with gelatin. After brushing the final layer, fold the carrots over the gelatin to seal. Fold in plastic wrap. Place weight on top and refrigerate for at least 1 day before slicing.

RECIPE 20.12

Chicken Liver Terrine

Chef Marcel Kretz, CM, retired

**Yield: 2 moulds, half-moon shaped, approximately
25 × 10 × 7 cm (10 × 4 × 3 in.); 30 servings**

Chicken livers, cleaned and trimmed	1 kg	2 lb.
Milk	500 mL	16 fl. oz.
Salt	TT	TT
Brandy	100 mL	3 fl. oz.
Fresh pork flank or pork cheeks, ground	250 g	8 oz.
Eggs	2	2
Cream, 35%	100 mL	3 fl. oz.
Neutral gelatin (powder)	20 g	3 Tbsp.
Mace	pinch	pinch
Sugar	pinch	pinch
Curing salt	pinch	pinch
Pepper	pinch	pinch
Dry morels, soaked and chopped	15 g	1/2 oz.
Pork backfat, thinly sliced	175 g	6 oz.

1. Soak the chicken livers overnight in the milk, with a pinch of salt added. Drain and rinse carefully for 15 minutes under running water.

2. Drain the chicken livers thoroughly, place in bowl, then add the brandy and a few grains of salt. Marinate for 10 minutes, then drain again, reserving the brandy marinade.

3. Swiftly blanch 750 g (1-1/2 lb.) of the chicken livers in boiling salted water. Cool rapidly under running water and refrigerate.

4. Purée pork and remaining raw livers in the blender with eggs, cream, gelatin, mace, sugar, marinade, curing salt and pepper. When smooth, add morels, but do not purée them.

5. Line moulds with some of the thinly sliced backfat (reserve the rest for finishing). Line with half the creamy pork and liver farce, then add all the whole chicken livers and cover with remaining farce. Top with more backfat. Wrap in plastic wrap and then cover with foil.

6. Cook in a bain marie in the oven at 250°C (500°F) for 15 minutes, then reduce the heat to 175°C (350°F) and let cook for 30 minutes. The hot water should be three-quarters up the sides of the mould.

7. Remove from oven and put under a press (a foil-covered wooden board the size of the mould). Put some weight on the press and tie it down. Cool for at least 12 hours before unmoulding.

VARIATION: Replace the chicken liver with quail or duck liver.

Marcel Kretz, CM
Born, raised and trained in France, Marcel has had an illustrious, award-winning career in Europe and Canada. He is credited with launching the movement to emphasize Quebec products in top Quebec restaurants. In 1998 Marcel became the first chef ever to receive the Order of Canada.

RECIPE 20.12

Approximate values per serving:	
Calories	126
Total fat	9.2 g
Saturated fat	3.6 g
Cholesterol	174 mg
Sodium	45 mg
Total carbohydrates	1.7 g
Protein	9.1 g

Salmon and Sea Bass Terrine with
Spinach and Basil

Salmon and Sea Bass Terrine with Spinach and Basil

**Yield: 1 terrine, 30 × 10 × 7.5 cm
(12 × 4 × 3 in.); 20 servings**

Salmon fillet, boneless, skinless	700 g	1 lb. 8 oz.
Salt	10 g	2 tsp.
Egg whites	3	3
White pepper	TT	TT
Cayenne pepper	TT	TT
Cream, 35%	up to 700 mL	up to 24 fl. oz.
Basil leaves	12	12
Truffle, brunoise (optional)	20 g	3/4 oz.
Spinach leaves, cleaned	175 g	6 oz.
Sea bass fillets	350 g	12 oz.

1. Grind the salmon through the large plate of a well-chilled meat grinder.
2. Place the salmon in the bowl of a food processor with salt and process until smooth and firm.
3. Add the egg whites, one at a time, pulsing the processor to incorporate. Scrape down the bowl and season with white pepper and cayenne pepper.
4. With the machine running, add the cream in a steady stream. Scrape down the bowl again and process the mousseline until it is smooth and well mixed but still firm. You may not need to use all the cream.
5. Blanch the basil leaves and refresh. Chop them finely.
6. Remove the mousseline from the bowl of the processor. Fold in the basil leaves and truffle and refrigerate.
7. Blanch and refresh the spinach leaves.
8. Spread the spinach leaves on a piece of plastic wrap, completely covering a rectangle approximately the length and width of the terrine mould.
9. Cut the sea bass fillets into strips approximately 2.5-cm (1-in.) wide and place end to end on the spinach leaves. Season with salt and white pepper.
10. Use the plastic wrap to wrap the spinach leaves tightly around the fish fillets.
11. Oil the terrine and line it with plastic wrap.
12. Half-fill the lined terrine with salmon mousseline.
13. Carefully unwrap the spinach and sea bass fillets and place them down the centre of the terrine. Fill the terrine with the remaining mousseline.
14. Tap the terrine mould firmly to remove any air pockets, then fold the plastic wrap over the top.
15. Cover and bake the terrine in a water bath at 150°C (300°F) to an internal temperature of 57°C (135°F), approximately 1.5 hours.
16. Cool the terrine well, unmould, slice or decorate and serve as desired.

RECIPE 20.13

Approximate values per serving:

Calories	198
Total fat	16 g
Saturated fat	8.5 g
Cholesterol	75 mg
Sodium	249 mg
Total carbohydrates	1.4 g
Protein	12 g

RECIPE 20.14

Roasted Red Pepper Mousse

Yield: 700 mL (1-1/2 pt.)

Onion, small dice	100 g	3 oz.
Garlic, chopped	5 g	1 tsp.
Olive oil	30 mL	1 fl. oz.
Red bell pepper, roasted and peeled, small dice	200 g	6 oz.
Salt and pepper	TT	TT
Saffron, ground	1 g	pinch
Tomato paste	30 g	1 oz.
Chicken stock	250 mL	8 fl. oz.
Gelatin	5 leaves	5 leaves
Dry white wine	50 mL	2 fl. oz.
Cream, 35%, whipped	175 mL	6 fl. oz.

1. Sauté the onion and garlic in the olive oil until tender, approximately 2 minutes.

2. Add the bell pepper, salt, pepper, saffron, tomato paste and chicken stock. Bring to a boil, reduce to a simmer and cook until ingredients are tender and liquid is reduced.

3. Soften the gelatin in cold water, squeeze well, then add to the hot pepper mixture with the white wine. Purée the pepper mixture in a blender or food processor and strain through a conical strainer.

4. Place the pepper purée over an ice bath. Stir until cool but do not allow the gelatin to set. Fold in the whipped cream. Pour the mousse into aspic-lined or well-oiled timbales or moulds and refrigerate several hours or overnight.

5. Unmould the mousse and serve as desired.

VARIATIONS: Substitute yellow or green bell peppers for part or all of the red bell peppers. BROCCOLI MOUSSE—Substitute 225 g (8 oz.) of blanched, chopped broccoli for the red bell peppers and omit tomato paste.

Roasted Red Pepper Mousse

RECIPE 20.14

Approximate values per 35 mL serving:	
Calories	56
Total fat	4.8 g
Saturated fat	2.3 g
Cholesterol	12 mg
Sodium	77 mg
Total carbohydrates	2.1 g
Protein	1 g

RECIPE 20.15

Smoked Salmon Mousse

Yield: 900 g (2 lb.)

Smoked salmon, boneless, skinless	300 g	10 oz.
Fish velouté, warm	250 mL	8 fl. oz.
Cream, 35%	250 mL	8 fl. oz.
Granulated gelatin	25 g	3 Tbsp.
Sherry	150 mL	5 fl. oz.
Salt and white pepper	TT	TT
Cayenne pepper	TT	TT

1. Finely chop the salmon and transfer it to the food processor. Add the warm velouté in a steady stream while the machine is running.

2. Whip the cream to soft peaks and reserve.

3. Add the gelatin to the sherry and allow it to soften for 5 minutes. Heat the gelatin mixture to liquefy the gelatin.

4. Transfer the salmon and velouté to a mixing bowl and stir in the gelatin mixture (wine aspic). Season with salt, pepper and cayenne pepper.

5. When the mixture has cooled to near room temperature, fold in the whipped cream with a rubber spatula until just mixed.

6. The mousse is now ready to be formed into timbales, or moulded into various shapes as desired.

RECIPE 20.15

Approximate values per 60 g serving:	
Calories	106
Total fat	8.4 g
Saturated fat	4.8 g
Cholesterol	30 mg
Sodium	465 mg
Total carbohydrates	2.1 g
Protein	5.6 g

Christophe Luzeux, CCC

Christophe comes from Marcq-en-Baroeul in the north of France and is a graduate of Lycée Michel Servet in Lille, France. He honed his skills in several of France's top establishments. His culinary achievements include winning silver in the Individual Competition in the 2000 Culinary Team Canada Competition and functioning as the captain of Team Nova Scotia when it won silver in both 1998 and 1999. Most recently, Christophe was a Gold Medal member of Culinary Team Canada 2004.

RECIPE 20.16

Approximate values per 60 g serving:	
Calories	105
Total fat	3.4 g
Saturated fat	1.4 g
Cholesterol	371 mg
Sodium	2428 mg
Total carbohydrates	6.6 g
Protein	12 g

RECIPE 20.16

Foie Gras

WORLD TRADE AND CONVENTION CENTRE, HALIFAX, NS
Executive Chef Christophe Luzeux, CCC

Yield: 1.5 kg (3-1/2 lb.)
Method: Baking

Goose or duck liver	1.8 kg	4 lb.
Salt	150 g	5 oz.
Pepper	40 g	1-1/2 oz.
Nutmeg	20 g	5 tsp.
Port	125 mL	4 fl. oz.
Cognac	125 mL	4 fl. oz.

1. Soak the liver in water overnight.
2. Mix the salt, pepper and nutmeg together.
3. Cut the liver open and remove all the nerves and built-up blood (keep the liver intact as much as possible).
4. Put the liver in a bowl and add the seasonings, port and cognac. Toss the liver carefully and let set, covered, in the refrigerator for 24 hours.
5. Place the liver in a terrine, press it and cook for 1.5 hours at 75°C (170°F) in a bain marie. Internal temperature should be 55°C (130°F).
6. Remove the terrine from the bain marie. Let it cool. Remove some of the excess grease (set aside for later use) on top and press the liver with a wood plank wrapped in foil. Put in the refrigerator for 4 hours. Remove the plank of wood and pour the reserved melted grease on top to protect your foie gras. Return to the fridge to chill for 24 hours before cutting.

❝ Strange to see how a good dinner and feasting reconciles everybody.

—Samuel Pepys, English diarist (1633–1703)

These interactive online tools will help you master the skills in this chapter:

- Chapter Quizzes

A buffet offers diners all the dishes from a selected menu, usually at one time, in a single, attractive setting. A buffet offers food service professionals the opportunity to exercise their creativity by identifying themes and then creating menus, displays and decorations with these themes in mind.

In this chapter, we use the word "buffet" to describe both the event where all the dishes from a menu are served at once and the table on which these foods are displayed and from which diners serve themselves or are served by wait staff. Buffet foods can be virtually any of those found in this book.

PLANNING THE BUFFET

Buffets must be carefully designed to provide foods from a planned menu in an attractive fashion to a given number of people within a specified time. Doing this well requires a collaborative effort among the chef, the catering sales staff and the dining room manager, banquet manager or other senior front-of-the-house staff. Together, they identify the theme for the event and choose the menu. If the event is designed for a specific client, then the client should be invited to join in the planning.

The theme sets the tone of the event. It defines a motif: an elegant Sunday brunch, a black-and-white formal, a Mexican fiesta, a Hawaiian luau. Regardless of the purpose for the event—a wedding, bar mitzvah, business luncheon, charity ball or the like—the theme defines the menu, decorations, props, linens and dinnerware; it can even define the music, lighting and wait staff uniforms. In Figures 21.1 through 21.3, we present examples of menus, decorations and buffet plans for various themed events.

Once the theme is identified, a menu is designed. Essentially, a lunch or dinner buffet offers an à la carte menu; the only differences are that at a buffet, the foods are presented all at once and the diners generally serve themselves or are served by wait staff stationed at the buffet table. Like an à la carte menu, the buffet menu should contain selections of first courses (soups and/or salads), entrees (hot and/or cold meat, poultry, fish and/or shellfish dishes), accompaniments (vegetables, starches and breads), desserts and beverages. Depending on the event, the menu may need to reflect particular dietary or religious concerns, such as the need for vegetarian entrees or kosher-style selections. Although costs are a consideration, the principal factors limiting a menu are the client's desires and the chef's imagination.

When planning the menu, it is important to offer dishes consistent with the theme. If the theme is a Greek wedding feast, do not offer tortilla chips and salsa. It may be necessary, however, to bend this rule occasionally in order to include one of the client's favourite foods or to offer an item not traditionally associated with the theme, such as beef at a Hawaiian luau.

It is also important to consider visual appeal and avoid repetition. Therefore:

1. *Offer dishes featuring different principal ingredients*—This avoids repetition and offers diners a wider array of choices. Even fussy diners should be able to find something they want to eat. Therefore, if the buffet features two entrees, make one beef and the other poultry; if there is a third, use fish or shellfish. If there are two starch dishes, make one a pasta and the other a potato dish. Also, avoid repeating ingredients in different dishes; for example, if the entree is a stir-fry of beef and broccoli, do not offer steamed broccoli as a vegetable side dish.

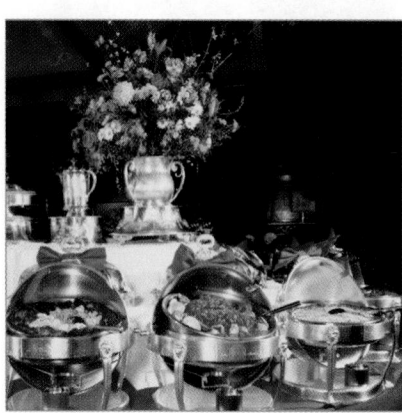

Chafing dishes set up on a curved buffet.

Décor

Linens: buffet and dining tables draped with floor-length coloured linens, buffet table with a contrasting overlay; linen napkins in the same colours as the tablecloths and overlay.

Centrepieces: fresh flowers (tulips, mums, lilies and greenery).

Serviceware: polished stainless steel or brass trays and chafing dishes; ceramic bowls.

Dinnerware: white or ivory china, stainless flatware and plain stemware.

Music: none

Wait staff uniforms: bistro attire (white button-down shirts, long tie, black pants and long aprons).

Menu

Sunset Salad of Mixed Greens, Citrus Wedges and Crispy Beet Frizzles with a Raspberry Vinaigrette

Caesar Salad with Herbed Croutons and Shredded Parmesan

Oven-Roasted Breast of Chicken with Wild Mushroom Sauce

Grilled Salmon Fillet on a Bed of Sautéed Leeks and Greens

Dauphine Potatoes

Medley of Zucchini, Yellow Squash and Carrots

Assorted Rolls with Sweet and Flavoured Butters

Pistachio Citrus Cheesecake with Caramel Sauce

Fresh Fruit Platter

Sacher Torte with Raspberry Sauce

Iced Tea, Lemonade and Sparkling Water French Roast Coffee

A SINGLE-SIDED BUFFET TO FEED 50 PEOPLE

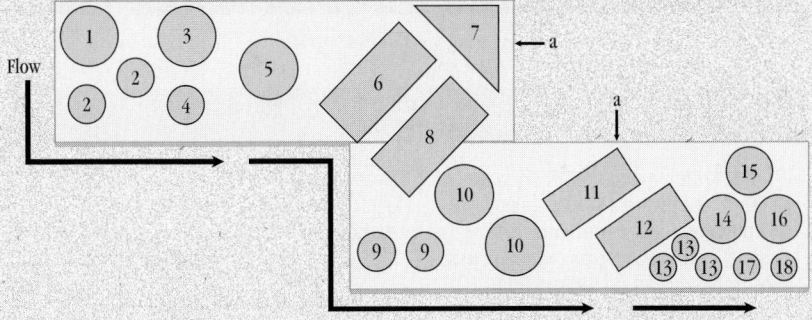

9. Sweet and Flavoured Butters
10. Baskets of Rolls
11. Chafing dish of Chicken with Wild Mushroom Sauce
12. Chafing dish of Salmon Fillets
13. Dessert plates
14. Cheesecake
15. Fruit Platter
16. Sacher Torte
17. Caramel Sauce for the Cheesecake
18. Raspberry Sauce for the Sacher Torte
Note: Beverages will be in pitchers on the table and replenished by the wait staff; coffee will be offered by circulating wait staff.

The key for the buffet table
a. Rectangular table, 8 feet × 30 inches
1. Basket of flatware rolled in linen napkins
2. Dinner plates
3. Sunset Salad
4. Raspberry Vinaigrette
5. Caesar Salad
6. Chafing dish of Vegetable Medley
7. Centrepiece
8. Chafing dish of Dauphine Potatoes

FIGURE 21.1 Business luncheon buffet.

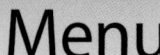

Menu

Crudités of Red and Green Bell Peppers, Carrots, Cauliflower, Broccoli, Jicama and
Snap Peas with Sun-Dried Tomato Dip

Tri-coloured Tortilla Chips with Fresh Tomato Cilantro Salsa,
Zesty Guacamole and Sour Cream

Warm Chorizo Chili Con Queso

Petit Blue Corn and Shrimp Tamales with Cilantro Cream

Soft Tacos of Grilled Pork Loin and Marinated Boneless Chicken Breast,
Served with Ancho-Chile Honey Sauce, Tomato Cilantro Salsa,
Avocado, Grated Queso Blanco and Diced Tomatoes

Goat Cheese and Green Chile Chimichangas with Roasted Habanero Sauce

Fresh Fruit Salad of Watermelon, Honeydew, Cantaloupe, Pineapple, Papaya,
Berries and Grapes with Tequila Lime Splash

Mexican Celebration Cookies

Piñon Nut Tarts

Lemon Curd Tarts

Mocha Mousse Cups with Cinnamon

Fresh Roasted Mexican Coffee

Fresh Mint Lemonade, Peach Iced Tea and Sparkling Water

Assorted Wines and Mexican Beers

Décor

Linens: buffet and dining tables draped in bright colours (yellow, orange, red, fuchsia and/or turquoise) with overlays of brightly coloured Mexican serapes; brightly coloured linen napkins tied with raffia.

Centrepieces: large cacti in pots with raffia ties, surrounded with river rocks and sand.

Buffet, table and room decorations: piñatas, sombreros, fresh chiles, brightly coloured paper flowers, brightly coloured papier mâché vegetables, raffia, small potted cacti in turquoise-painted terracotta pots.

Serviceware: copper or beaten tin trays, copper chafing dishes, wooden or earthenware bowls and platters.

Dinnerware: brightly coloured china (red, yellow and/or turquoise), hammered stainless steel flatware and Mexican green or blue glass stemware.

Music: strolling mariachi band.

Wait staff uniforms: jeans and white shirts with a coloured serape over the shoulders.

FIGURE 21.2 Mexican fiesta buffet.

A DOUBLE-SIDED BUFFET TABLE TO FEED 125 PEOPLE

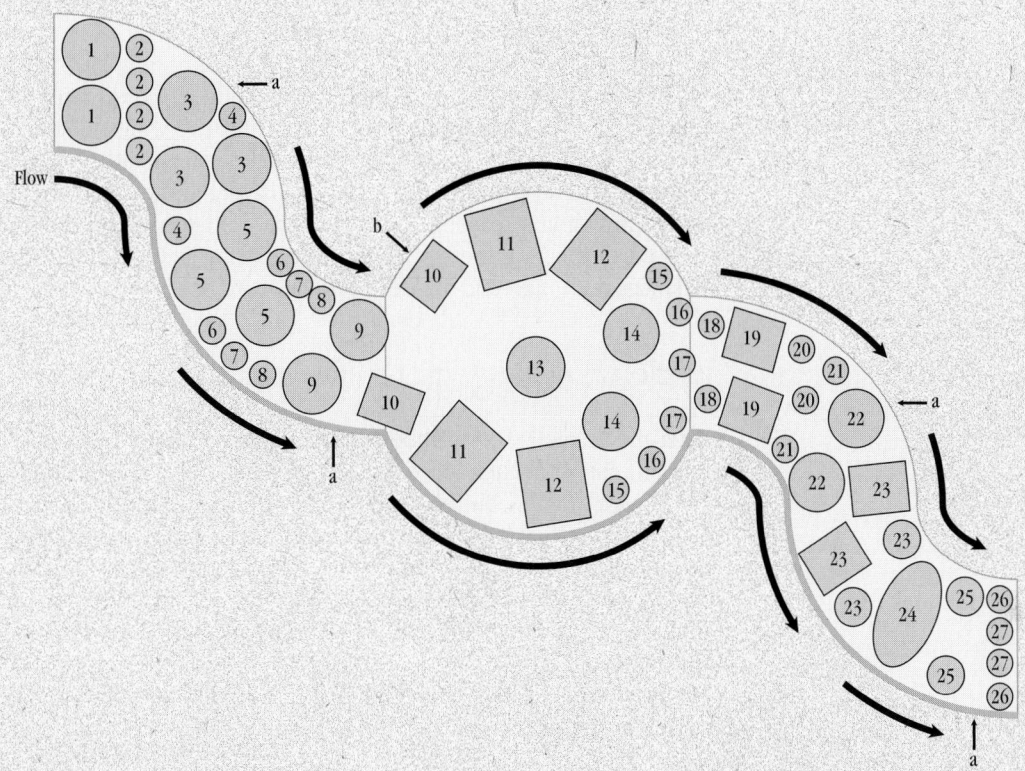

The key for the buffet table

a. Serpentine table, standard size
b. Round table, 72-inch diameter
1. Flatware rolled in linen napkins
2. Plates
3. Crudités
4. Sun-Dried Tomato Dip
5. Tri-Coloured Tortilla Chips
6. Fresh Tomato-Cilantro Salsa
7. Zesty Guacamole
8. Sour Cream
9. Chorizo Chili Con Queso

10. Chafing dish of Blue Corn and Shrimp Tamales
    with Cilantro Cream
11. Chafing dish of Soft Pork Tacos
12. Chafing dish of Soft Chicken Tacos
13. Centrepiece
14. Queso Blanco
15. Ancho-Chile Honey Sauce
16. Tomato Cilantro Salsa
17. Avocado
18. Tomatoes
19. Chafing dish of Goat Cheese and Green Chile
    Chimichangas

20. Habanero Sauce
21. Dessert plates
22. Fruit Salad
23. Platters of Cookies, Tarts and Mousse Cups
24. Coffee cups and spoons
25. Coffee
26. Cream
27. Sweeteners

Note: Beers and wines will be available at a
separate bar; soft drinks will be in pitchers on the
tables and replenished by wait staff.

2. *Offer foods cooked by different methods*—For example, serve beef bourguignon (a hot braised meat dish), roast turkey (a hot or cold roasted poultry dish) and salmon with dill sauce (a cold poached fish dish). Again, this
avoids repetition.

3. *Offer foods with different colours*—Fettuccine Alfredo and poached fish in a
béarnaise sauce may both taste good, but they look boring next to each
other. Offer a tomato and bell pepper salsa instead of the béarnaise sauce,
or a pasta primavera in place of the Alfredo. This will increase the buffet's
visual appeal.

4. *Offer foods with different textures*—If two or more soups are served, make
one a clear soup and the other a cream or purée soup; use a variety of
tossed and bound salads, each with different principal ingredients.

5. *Offer foods appropriate to the time of year*—Buffet menus may be planned months in advance. Consider the availability of the produce needed in the menu being offered. A fresh tomato, basil and mozzarella salad is ideal for a summer buffet but a poor choice in the winter months when hothouse tomatoes may be all that are available.

When defining the theme and creating the menu, costs must be considered. Often a client will place a limit on what he or she wants to spend for the buffet. It is then the responsibility of the chef, sales staff and/or dining room manager to create an attractive and satisfying buffet that meets this budget while providing a reasonable profit to the food service operation. One typical method of meeting these sometimes-conflicting needs is to plan a menu that balances both high-end and less expensive items.

DESIGNING THE BUFFET

After the theme is set, members of the planning group should study the room, garden, patio or other space where the event will be held. They need to allocate space for the buffet table(s), the dining tables and, depending on the function, one or more bars, a dance floor, a stage for musicians, a podium for speakers, audiovisual equipment for presentations and so on. When doing so, common sense should be used. The buffet should be in an area with easy access to both the kitchen and the dining tables—neither the wait staff nor the diners should have to cross a dance floor or walk in front of a podium to get to the food. Similarly, a stage or podium should be within good sightlines of the dining tables.

TABLE 21.1	Standard Buffet Tables	
Shape	**Sizes**	**Sizes for Tablecloths or Skirting**
Rectangle	6 feet × 30 inches	90 × 128 inches (floor length)
	8 feet × 30 inches	60 × 125 inches (lap length) or
		90 × 153 inches (floor length)
Round	24-inch diameter	80-inch diameter (floor length)
	36-inch diameter	96-inch diameter (floor length)
	48-inch diameter	80-inch diameter (lap) or
		108-inch diameter (floor)
	60-inch diameter	96-inch diameter (lap) or
		120-inch diameter (floor)
	72-inch diameter	108-inch diameter (lap) or
		132-inch diameter (floor)
Half-round	30-inch radius at 180° angle (i.e., half of a 60-inch-diameter round)	160 inches of skirting
Quarter-round (wedge)	30-inch radius at 90° angle (i.e., one-quarter of a 60-inch-diameter round)	110 inches of skirting
Serpentine	Outside curve measures 8 feet, inside curve measures 4 feet, ends measure 30 inches (i.e., one-quarter of a circle's circumference)	Specialty cloths needed

Note: Feet and inches are still used to describe table and linen measurements in Canada as well as the U.S. Metric equivalents would be stated in centimetres. The conversion rate is 2.54 cm to 1 in.

A small kitchen becomes the setting for an elegant and unusual brunch buffet.

Once the room's layout is determined, the chef and/or banquet or dining room manager decides on the shape of the buffet table. A buffet table usually comprises one or more standard-sized tables grouped together in a functional and attractive shape. Standard table shapes and sizes are found in Table 21.1; arrangements of the various sizes and shapes are shown in Figures 21.1 through 21.3. The buffet table can then be draped with a floor-length linen tablecloth, or a tablecloth with a detachable skirt can be used. An alternative to standard-sized tables shrouded in linen is to use unique pieces of furniture such as cabinets, sideboards, consoles, armoires, desks or other furniture, draped with linens or not.

The number of diners is a critical consideration when determining the size, arrangement and placement of the buffet table. As a general rule, a single-sided buffet can comfortably serve 50 to 75 people. (See Figure 21.1.) If more than 100 guests are expected, the buffet should be designed with at least two service lines. (See Figure 21.2.) Even so, many guests will still have to wait in line, although their wait should not be excessive.

Several techniques can be used to serve large groups efficiently. One option is to use a double-sided buffet line. On a double-sided buffet, the same foods are served on both sides of the table. (See Figure 21.2.) All diners approach the table from the same direction and at the start of the buffet, the line is split, with half of the diners diverted to either side. Or a single-sided buffet can be divided into two, three or more zones, each of which offers the identical foods. Either option requires that the buffet provide the diners with appropriate visual cues to recognize that the two sides of the table or two ends of the table are offering identical fare.

Another option for serving larger crowds is to divide the menu among various stations that are scattered throughout the room or series of rooms. (See Figure 21.3.) One station can be devoted to cold salads or to an elaborate display of cold fish and shellfish surrounding an ice sculpture. Another can be devoted to pasta prepared to order by a line cook assigned to the station; equipped with a portable gas or electric burner, the chef can finish precooked

Menu

Butlered Hors d'Oeuvre

Red Potatoes with Gorgonzola, Bacon and Walnuts
Mushroom Phyllo Triangles

Popovers with Shrimp and Chive Filling
Asparagus Spears Tied with Red Pepper

Buffet

STATION ONE:

Tropical Fruit Display

Caesar Salad with Herbed Croutons
and Shredded Parmesan

Salad of Bibb Lettuce and Blue Cheese
with Citrus Vinaigrette

Platter of Assorted Pâtés, Galantines and Ballotines

Assorted Rolls with Sweet and Flavoured Butters

Tiered Display of Imported Cheeses including
Stilton, Saint André, Port Salut, Gouda,
Black Diamond Cheddar and Brie Baked in Phyllo
with Apricots and Fresh Basil,
Garnished with Apple Slices and Grape Clusters

Lavosh and Cracker Bread

STATION THREE:

Herb-Rubbed, Grilled Tenderloin of Beef
Carved by the Chef
with Béarnaise Sauce and Sage-Merlot Sauce

Assorted Rolls with Sweet and Flavoured Butters

Chicken Satay with Chile Peanut Sauce

Grilled Shark with Tomatillo Sauce

STATION TWO:

Antipasto of Assorted Salami, Prosciutto, Sliced Cheeses,
Marinated Mushrooms and Artichokes, Olives,
Roasted Peppers and Wedges of Papaya,
Melon and Mango Wrapped with Prosciutto

Penne with Fresh Tomatoes and Basil
Tossed with Extra Virgin Olive Oil

Cheese-Filled Tortellini with Wild Mushroom Alfredo Sauce

Pastas Prepared to Order by the Chef

Wheel of Parmesan

Focaccia, Garlic Twists, Breadsticks and Assorted Rolls

Sweet and Flavoured Butters

STATION FOUR:

Three-Tiered Wedding Cake
bottom layer – Black Forest
middle layer – White Cake with White Chocolate Mousse,
Strawberries and Chocolate Ganache
top layer – Carrot Cake

Petits Fours

Fruit Tartlets

Chocolate-Dipped Strawberries

French Roast Coffee and Tea with Deluxe Condiments

Assorted Beers, Alcoholic Beverages, Still and Sparkling Wines, Sparkling Water and Soft Drinks

Décor

Linens: buffet and dining tables draped with floor-length ivory linens with overlays of tulle and lace, accented with gold ribbons and tassels; linen napkins tied with ribbons and tassels, and decorated with flowers.

Centrepieces and decorations for the buffet stations and dining tables: fresh

flowers (calla lilies, white orchids, roses, tulips, ivy and greenery) and candles (votives, pillars or hurricanes) wrapped in ivy.

Serviceware: fancy silver and mirror trays, silver chafing dishes, china or glass bowls.

Dinnerware: ivory gold-rimmed china on gold chargers, silver flatware and gold-rimmed stemware.

Music: harpist, violinist or quartet.

Wait staff uniforms: tuxedos.

FIGURE 21.3 Formal wedding buffet.

A FOUR-STATION BUFFET (INCLUDING TWO STAFFED BY CHEFS) TO FEED 200 PEOPLE

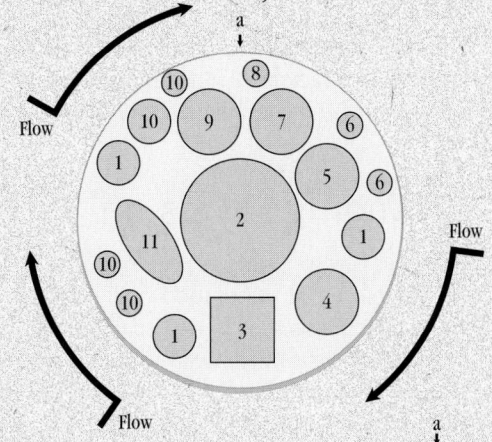

The key for station one:

a. Round table, 72-inch diameter
1. Salad plates
2. Centrepiece
3. Tropical Fruit Display
4. Caesar Salad
5. Basket of Rolls overflowing onto the table

6. Sweet and Flavoured Butters
7. Bibb Lettuce Salad
8. Citrus Vinaigrette
9. Platter of Pâtés, Galantines and Ballotines
10. Baskets of Lavosh and Cracker Breads
11. Tiered Cheese Display

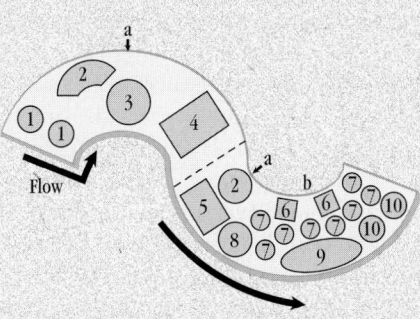

The key for station two:

a. Serpentine table, standard size
b. Chef's station
1. Plates
2. Centrepiece
3. Antipasto
4. Chafing dish of Penne Pasta
5. Chafing dish of Cheese Tortellini
6. Butane burners for chef
7. Garnishes for the pastas made to order, including mushrooms,

grilled chicken, walnuts, peas, roasted bell peppers and shrimp and sauces for the pasta, including Alfredo and tomato basil
8. Large hollowed wheel of Parmesan
9. Basket of Garlic Twists, Focaccia, Breadsticks and Assorted Rolls
10. Sweet and Flavoured Butters

The key for station three:

a. Rectangular table, 6 feet × 30 inches
b. Chef's station
1. Plates
2. Decoration or prop
3. Chafing dish of Shark
4. Tomatillo Sauce
5. Centrepiece

6. Chafing dish of Chicken Satay
7. Chile Peanut Sauce
8. Basket of Assorted Rolls
9. Sweet and Flavoured Butters
10. Carving station with heat lamp for the Tenderloin of Beef
11. Sage-Merlot Sauce
12. Béarnaise Sauce

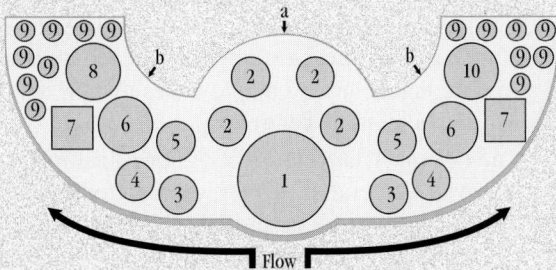

The key for station four:

a. Round table, 48-inch diameter
b. Serpentine table, standard size
1. Three-Tiered Wedding Cake
2. Cake and dessert plates
3. Petits Fours
4. Fruit Tartlets

5. Chocolate-Dipped Strawberries
6. Tray of coffee mugs
7. Carafe of Hot Water with Assorted Tea bags
8. Urn of Regular Coffee
9. Garnishes for Coffee including raw

sugar cubes, artificial sweeteners, cream, whipped cream, candied citrus peel, mint swizzle sticks, cinnamon sticks, rock-sugar sticks and chocolate shavings
10. Urn of Decaffeinated Coffee

Note: Soft drinks as well as assorted wines, beers and other alcoholic beverages will be available at a separate bar; sparkling water, assorted wines and champagne will be served by the wait staff.

pasta in the diner's choice of sauce. Other stations can offer roasted meats and poultry kept warm by an infrared heat lamp and carved to order by the station chef. (See Figure 21.3.)

The excitement and beauty of a well-designed buffet table depends principally on two factors: (1) the arrangement of the foods on their individual serving pieces and (2) the arrangement of the foods and decorations on the buffet table.

Arranging Foods on Serving Pieces

The chef is responsible for determining how the foods will be arranged on their serving pieces. Most hot foods will be presented in chafing dishes, while cold or room-temperature foods are usually served on trays, platters, bowls or mirrors.

Chafing Dish

Chafing dishes are metal dishes, usually rectangular or round, with a heat source (flame or electric) located beneath that is used to keep the foods warm; the foods are usually placed in a hotel pan or other receptacle that sits inside the chafing dish above a pan of hot water. Chafing dishes are usually covered in copper, silver or stainless steel.

Trays, platters and mirrors for presenting foods are available in four basic shapes: square, rectangle, round and oval. They come in a wide variety of materials, including metal (silver, copper, tin and steel), ceramics (china and earthenware), glass, mirrors (glass and acrylic), plastic, wood and stone (especially marble). The choice depends on the theme. Silver and mirror trays create a more formal feel at an event; ceramic and wood lend a more casual look.

Once the tray, platter, bowl or mirror is chosen, the chef must artfully arrange the food on it. When designing the presentation, the chef should consider the following:

● **grosse piece** a centrepiece consisting of a large piece of the principal food offered; for example, a large wheel of cheese with slices of the cheese cascading around it

1. *Height*—The eye is naturally drawn toward the highest point on a tray; typically, this will be the centrepiece. It can be a garnish or a **grosse piece**. Although it is sometimes in the centre of the tray, it is more often located toward the rear, either in the middle or off to one side. Foods placed at a level higher than the centrepiece usually distract from the overall appearance.

2. *Pattern*—Whenever possible, foods should be arranged in an interesting pattern. Three different types of canapés, each chosen for contrasting shapes, colours and textures, can march across a mirrored surface in alternating lines. Crudités can flow from baskets, hollowed squashes or bell peppers. Spirals of different pâtés can swirl around one another. Foods should generally flow toward the diner. Stack foods higher in the centre or rear of the tray so that they cascade toward the front or edges. (Trays that are higher around all the edges than in the centre tend to draw the eye into the hole in the centre.)

3. *Colour*—The colours of the principal foods should complement or contrast with each other. If they cannot (for example, a tray of pâtés or cheeses), they should be garnished with attractively contrasting coloured foods such as fruits, vegetables and herbs.

4. *Texture and shape*—Try to use a variety of shapes and textures. Avoid building trays with circular slices of galantine garnished with circular liver mousse moulds and round tartlets of a vegetable purée; all have the same shape and very similar textures. Instead, try moulding the mousse or tartlets into different shapes or preparing a vegetable salad rather than a purée for the tartlets.

5. *Negative space*—This refers to the areas left unused. It is important because the space enhances the appeal of the object it surrounds and prevents overcrowding. Try leaving a border of space around the tray and some space within clusters of food on the platter.

Arranging Foods and Other Items on the Buffet Table

When designing the shape of the buffet table, the chef and/or banquet or dining room manager must also consider how the various foods, centrepieces and props will be laid out on the table. Besides colour, height, shape and texture, designers should consider the following:

1. *Flow*—Regardless of whether a single buffet table, a main buffet table with one or more stations or only stations are used, the foods should be placed in a logical order that affords the diner the chance to construct a meal in the same order as one that would be served to him or her. The start of the buffet line should be obvious and accessible; usually, it is near the entrance to the room.

A variety of canapés displayed on granite.

Typically, on a single- or double-sided buffet table, the first items offered the diner are plates. (Flatware and napkins can be located at the start or the end of the buffet or on the dining tables.) The first foods to be offered should be soups and salads. These should be followed by appetizers such as cold sliced meats, pâtés, shellfish and the like. Entrees should be next, along with their vegetable and starch accompaniments. Desserts should be the last items on the buffet. (Beverages can be available on the buffet table, at a bar, or on the dining tables or offered by circulating wait staff.)

Stations offer the designer greater flexibility. They also help minimize the line that usually forms at a single buffet table, allowing diners to go in various directions, although this can sometimes cause traffic problems. Like a single buffet table, each station can be designed so that it offers diners sufficient selections to create a complete meal. The stations can also be arranged around a room in a sequence mirroring a meal: soups and salads on the first station diners would approach, appetizers on the next, and so on. A third option is to arrange the stations so that the one with the most spectacular display of centrepiece, foods and decorations or the one featuring a chef making foods to order will be the centre of attention, with the other stations scattered around the room. Regardless of how they are arranged, each should be self-contained, with plates and accompaniments for the main items.

2. *Spacing*—Allow approximately 30 to 35 cm (1 linear foot) for each item on the buffet. Thus, if 16 items are to be placed on the table, including plates, a centrepiece and large props, then the buffet table must be approximately 500 cm (16 ft.) long. If extremely large centrepieces are used or if food is presented on oversized platters, this will, of course, affect the total table space needed.

3. *Reach*—Try to place all foods within easy reach of the diners. Try to avoid stacking one item behind another. But if items must be placed farther back on the table, try setting them on **risers** or on pedestals in order to add height to the platter. This extra height not only adds visual interest, but it also allows the diner to reach over the dish in front without disturbing its arrangement. Also, if possible, place foods that will not drip or splatter behind ones that will; that way, sauce from the back dish will not drip into the front dish on its way to the diner's plate. Trays with foods that will not shift can be propped at a slight angle to make the contents more accessible and attractive.

● **risers** boxes (including the plastic crates used to store glassware) covered with linens, paper or other decorative items and used on a buffet table as a base for platters, trays or displays

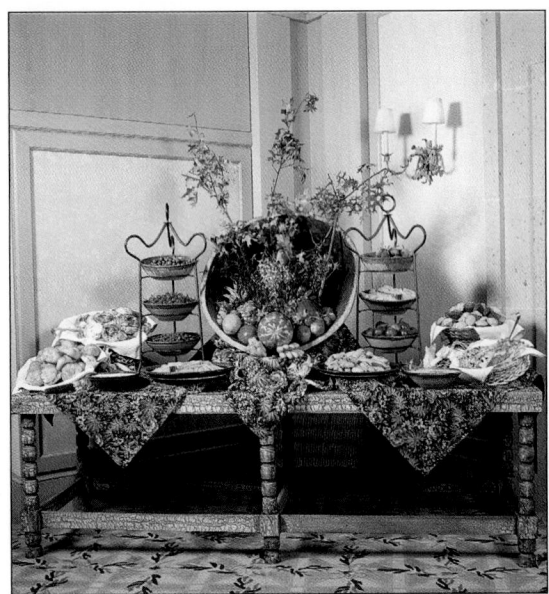

Display of fresh fruit and bread for Sunday brunch buffet.

4. *Accompaniments*—Place the appropriate garnishes, sauces or other accompaniments near their principal foods. Also, place a small plate or napkin near a platter for any serving utensils.

5. *Centrepieces*—A centrepiece brings focus to the buffet, and its height or dominance increases the visual appeal of the overall table design. A centrepiece can be a floral arrangement or a sculpture made of ice, tallow, pastillage, chocolate, blown or pulled sugar or other material. The centrepiece can also be a grosse piece such as a whole roast turkey or whole poached salmon decorated with sauce chaud-froid. (See Chapter 20, Charcuterie.)

6. *Decorations*—In addition to the centrepiece, other nonedible objects or props may grace the buffet table. Sometimes, these are nothing more than smaller or modified versions of the centrepiece, such as flowers or leaves from a floral centrepiece. Of course, anything from a saddle to a silver candelabra can be used, depending on the buffet's theme. Whatever items are chosen, they should be well cleaned and arranged artfully but not in a manner that interferes with a diner's ability to see and reach the food. Props can also be used to mark divisions in the meal; for example, grouping all salads between one set of props divides them from the entrees. Sometimes, unusable or dead space will result because of constrictions of room or food. If it cannot be avoided, try filling the space with props or other decorations.

7. *Labels*—Unlike a restaurant with a printed menu and an attentive wait staff, an unattended buffet may not give the diner an opportunity to inquire about particular dishes. This can be remedied by placing attractively printed cards bearing the name of the dish in front of any items that the chef feels need identification.

PRESENTING AND MAINTAINING THE BUFFET

Portioning Foods

A common problem when planning a buffet is overproduction. Many novice chefs want to make enough of each menu item to serve the entire group. But this is unnecessary. Most people tend to sample a little from many dishes and try not to gorge themselves. Some chefs use a simple, although far from fool-proof, formula of 450 grams (1 pound) of food per person as a starting point and then adjust this number depending upon factors such as the general composition of the group (a luncheon for female executives may require less food than one for male football players), the number of items offered (the more dishes to choose from, the smaller the portions most people will take), the structure of the event (that is, whether it will be convenient for people to return to the buffet for second helpings), and whether diners serve themselves or are served by wait staff or chefs at the buffet.

Generally, portions should be small, especially if more than one item is served in each food category. For example, if a grilled salmon fillet with Lyonnaise potatoes and a medley of sautéed vegetables were served as an entree from an à la carte menu, a typical serving would be 180 grams (6 ounces) of fish, 120 grams (4 ounces) of potato and 120 grams (4 ounces) of vegetables. If the same salmon fillet with its accompaniments were served as one of three

A Block of Ice, a Chain Saw, a Chisel and a Little Caution and Creativity

Ice carvings have long been popular buffet centrepieces; they add elegance and sophistication to the setting and occasion. As with other arts, it may take years to master ice carving. Nevertheless, with some practice and care, you can usually create acceptable ice sculptures after only a few tries.

Blocks of carving ice are specially prepared to remove air bubbles. These large blocks (50 × 25 × 115 centimetres [20 × 10 × 46 inches]) weigh approximately 135 kilograms (300 pounds), and special ice tongs and caution are required when handling them.

At –18°C (0°F), ice is very brittle and difficult to carve without breaking. Therefore, carving ice must be tempered before carving. To temper the ice, remove it from the freezer and allow it to rest at room temperature for approximately one hour. When the surface is clear of frost, carving can begin.

A single carving can take from one to several hours to complete. Although chisels and specially designed saws for ice carving work quite well, chain saws are commonly used to speed up the process. Because most carving is done indoors, electric saws are used; unlike gas saws, they do not leave a greasy residue on the ice's surface. Be very careful when using any chain saw, particularly an electric one, around melting ice and pools of water.

To begin, trace the outline of the figure you want to carve on the surface of all four sides of the block of ice. There are several excellent ice carving books, some of which provide stencils for this purpose.

Then start removing the ice using a large saw or a chainsaw. As the figure begins to take shape, use smaller chisels and specialized tools to create the desired effect. (Some carvers use chain saws for the entire process, however.) After some practice, you will develop your own style and preferences.

When the carving is complete, carefully return the ice to the freezer until needed. When setting it on a buffet, use a pan designed to hold an ice carving and provide drainage. Avoid placing ice sculptures under hot air vents. At room temperature and average humidity, ice melts at the rate of approximately 1.2 centimetres (1/2 inch) per hour from all sides. Keep this in mind when carving thin pieces or small details into the surface.

---

entrees on a dinner buffet for 100 people, the total of available fish should be 60 to 90 grams (2 to 3 ounces) of fish per portion multiplied by 100 portions, 30 to 45 grams (1 to 1.5 ounces) of potatoes per portion multiplied by 100 portions and 30 grams (1 ounce) of vegetables per portion (diners tend to take smaller portions of vegetables than of starches) multiplied by 100 portions. Similarly, if a dessert tart from an à la carte menu had a 10-centimetre (4-inch) diameter, the version offered on a dessert buffet should have a 5-centimetre (2-inch) diameter.

Experience suggests that most diners tend to serve themselves larger portions of foods found at the start of the buffet than at its middle. Thus, if caviar is being served, it may make economic sense to place it somewhere farther down the line than at the start of the buffet.

Ice Carving

Presenting Hot Foods

Keeping hot foods hot on a buffet is a particular challenge, and an important one, for both food safety and presentation concerns. If possible, hot foods should be served in relatively small quantities on warm platters that are exchanged frequently. This is not always possible, however. More often, hot foods are maintained in chafing dishes or under heat lamps.

To maintain the quality of foods kept in a chafing dish, use the following guidelines:

1. Choose foods that hold well. Rare meats and delicate pastas do not hold well in a chafing dish; they become overcooked and unattractive quickly. Instead, try braised meats (which may actually benefit from the extended cooking) or hearty pastas such as tortellini or penne. This guideline also applies to garnishes: bunches of delicate herbs such as basil do not do well in a chafing dish; instead, try sprigs of rosemary or thyme.

2. Cook small amounts of delicate foods at a time and change the insert pan in a chafing dish often. This prevents foods from sitting too long.

3. Ladle a small amount of sauce in the bottom of the pan before placing sliced meats in the pan, or serve sliced meats, poultry or fish on a bed of

vegetables. The sauce or the vegetable bed helps to absorb the heat from the chafing dish, insulating the more delicate items and providing a bit of steam to help keep the foods moist.

4. Keep the chafing dish closed whenever possible. This holds in the steam, which helps keep the food moist. But note too that a closed chafing dish distracts from a buffet's appeal and slows down the flow of diners through the buffet line.

Heat lamps are generally used for keeping large cuts of meats or poultry warm during carving. These foods, however, become dry rapidly and should be replaced periodically. Of course, time and temperature principles of food safety must also be followed.

Presenting Cold Foods

Keeping cold foods cold on a buffet table is a little less of a challenge. As with hot foods, it is best if cold foods are served in relatively small quantities on cold platters that are exchanged frequently. Alternatively, the items can be set on a bed of ice—usually a large bowl filled with ice into which a smaller bowl containing the food is placed.

Replenishing Foods

Dishes from the buffet table should be removed when they are approximately two-thirds empty or have deteriorated in some fashion (for example, when the aspic on pâtés has softened, cut fruits have browned or a hot food has crusted over). Once the old dish has been removed, its fresh replacement should be placed on the buffet immediately, and it should be as carefully arranged and garnished as the original. If items from the old dish are to be combined with a replacement dish, this should be done in the kitchen and not at the buffet table. Batches of temperature-sensitive or potentially hazardous foods should not be combined, however.

Display of fish and shellfish for Sunday brunch buffet.

Serving Foods

Once the banquet or restaurant manager has completed the planning for a buffet, it usually falls to a captain to supervise the actual event. The captain directs the crew setting up the room as well as the stewards who bring the food, flatware, china and glassware from the kitchen to the buffet.

The captain also supervises the wait staff. One of the front waiters' principal responsibilities is to maintain the appearance of the buffet and to replenish items as needed. Depending on the function, front waiters can be stationed behind the buffet table to serve diners, circulate in the crowd with trays of hors d'oeuvre or drinks (passing foods in this fashion is called **butler service**) or serve beverages to diners seated at the dining tables. Back waiters generally police the room and clear tables. They should be particularly vigilant in removing used plates from a dining table after a diner has gone to the buffet for more food and before he or she returns to the dining table with a new plate.

Typically, servers or chefs are placed only at stations where foods are prepared or carved to order. This helps to control portioning. It also provides a greater opportunity for staff to police the buffet and therefore ensure that the table and the individual items remain neat, attractive and fresh. Finally, placing wait staff or kitchen staff at the buffet allows diners to ask questions about the foods presented.

● **butler service** restaurant service in which servers pass foods (typically hors d'oeuvre) or drinks arranged on trays

Conclusion

A buffet is more than a salad bar at a restaurant—that is, merely food laid out for the diner to grab. A buffet is an opportunity for a chef to use his or her creativity to plan and present an entire menu in an attractive fashion. But for a buffet to succeed, it requires careful planning, attention to detail and the help of many professionals in the food services facility.

Questions for Discussion

1. What is a grosse piece? How is it different from a centrepiece?
2. What food safety and sanitation factors must be considered when planning a buffet? Explain your answer.
3. Describe three things that can be done to keep hot foods attractive and fresh when using a chafing dish.
4. Describe two things that can be done to keep cold foods cold on a buffet.
5. List five different stations serving hot foods at a buffet and the equipment necessary for each.
6. Where can you go for current information on new trends and styles of buffet arrangements? What resources are available to assist caterers in business management?

22 Vegetables

" Cuisine is when things taste like themselves.
—Carnonsky (Maurice-Edmond Sailland), French writer (1872–1956)

Long overcooked and underrated, vegetables are enjoying a welcome surge in popularity. Gone are the days when a chef included vegetables as an afterthought to the "meat and potatoes" of the meal. Now, properly prepared fresh vegetables are used to add flavour, colour and variety to almost any meal. Many restaurants are featuring vegetarian entrees, an extensive selection of vegetable side dishes or an entire vegetarian menu. This trend reflects the demands of more knowledgeable and health-conscious consumers as well as the increased availability of high-quality fresh produce.

In this chapter we identify many of the vegetables typically used by food service operations. (Potatoes, although vegetables, are discussed in Chapter 23, Potatoes, Grains and Pasta, and salad greens are discussed in Chapter 25, Salads and Salad Dressings. See also Chapter 24, Vegetarian Cooking.) Here we also discuss how fresh and preserved vegetables are purchased, stored and prepared for service or cooking. Many of the cooking methods analyzed in Chapter 9, Principles of Cooking, are then applied to vegetables.

LEARNING OUTCOMES

After studying this chapter you will be able to:

- identify a variety of vegetables
- purchase vegetables appropriate for your needs
- store vegetables properly
- explain how vegetables are preserved
- prepare vegetables for cooking or service
- apply various cooking methods to vegetables

These interactive online tools will help you master the skills in this chapter:

- Videos
- Chapter Quizzes
- Activities

● **vegetable** any herbaceous plant (one with little or no woody tissue) that can be partially or wholly eaten; vegetables can be classified as cabbages, fruit-vegetables, gourds and squashes, greens, mushrooms and truffles, onions, pods and seeds, roots and tubers and stalks

The term **vegetable** refers to any herbaceous plant that can be partially or wholly eaten. A herbaceous plant has little or no woody tissue. The portions we consume include the leaves, stems, roots, tubers, seeds and flowers. Vegetables contain more starch and less sugar than fruits. Therefore, vegetables tend to be savoury, not sweet. Also, unlike fruits, vegetables are most often eaten cooked, not raw.

IDENTIFYING VEGETABLES

This book presents fruits and vegetables according to the ways most people view them and use them, rather than by rigid botanical classifications. Although produce such as tomatoes, peppers and eggplants are botanically fruits, they are prepared and served like vegetables and are included here under the category we call "fruit-vegetables." Potatoes, although botanically vegetables, are discussed with other starches in Chapter 23, Potatoes, Grains and Pasta.

We divide vegetables into 11 categories, based upon either botanical relationship or edible part. They are flower/bud, fruit type, leafy, fungus, bulb, pod, legume/pulse, root, tuber, stalk and shoot. Some people recognize more or fewer categories. There is no definitive answer to what a vegetable is. A vegetable may have several names, varying across regions or on a purveyor's whim. The names given here follow generally accepted custom and usage.

Flowers/Buds

The *Brassica* or cabbage family includes a wide range of vegetables used for their heads, flowers or leaves. They are generally quick-growing, cool-weather crops. Many are ancient plants with unknown origins. They are inexpensive, readily available and easy to prepare.

Bok Choy

Bok Choy

Bok choy, also known as pok choy, is a white-stemmed variety of southern Chinese cabbage. The relatively tightly packed leaves are dark green, with long white ribs attached at a bulbous stem. The stalks are crisp and mild, with a flavour similar to romaine lettuce. Although bok choy may be eaten raw, it is most often stir-fried or used in soups.

Choose heads with bright white stalks and dark green leaves; avoid those with brown, moist spots. Fresh bok choy is available all year. Jars of pickled and fermented bok choy (known as Korean kim chee) are also available. Baby bok choy is popular with restaurateurs.

Broccoli and Rapini

Broccoli

Broccoli, a type of flower, has a thick central stalk with greyish-green leaves topped with one or more heads of green florets. Broccoli may be eaten raw or steamed, microwaved or sautéed and served warm or cold. Broccoli stalks are extremely firm and benefit from blanching. Stems are often slow-cooked for soups. Generally, broccoli leaves are not eaten.

Choose firm stalks with compact clusters of tightly closed dark green florets. Avoid stalks with yellow flowers. Broccoli is available all year. Rapini or rabé is similar to broccoli with a slightly more bitter and peppery taste. It is popular in Chinese and Mediterranean cuisines. Select stems with bright green leaves and unopened buds.

Broccoli Rabe

BASIC PROCEDURE FOR CUTTING BROCCOLI SPEARS

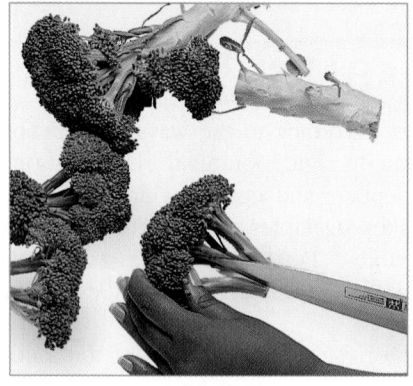

Cut off the thick, woody portion of the stalk, then cut the florets and stems into spears. Peel the stalk and use in stir-frys.

Brussels Sprouts

Brussels Sprouts

Brussels sprouts (Fr. *choux de Bruxelles*) were first cultivated around 1700. The plant produces numerous small heads arranged in neat rows along a thick stalk. The tender young sprouts are similar to baby cabbages and are usually steamed or roasted. Brussels sprouts have a strong, nutty flavour that blends well with game, ham, duck or rich meats.

Choose small, firm sprouts that are compact and heavy. The best size is 2 to 4 cm (3/4 to 1-1/2 in.) in diameter. They should be bright green and free of blemishes. Their peak season is from September through February.

Cauliflower

Cauliflower (Fr. *chou-fleur*) is the king of the cabbage family. Each stalk produces one flower or head surrounded by large green leaves. The head, composed of creamy white florets, can be cooked whole or cut into separate florets for steaming, blanching or stir-frying.

Choose firm, compact heads. Any attached leaves should be bright green and crisp. A yellow colour or spreading florets indicates that the vegetable is overly mature. Cauliflower is available all year, especially from the late fall through the spring. A cross of cauliflower and broccoli called broccoflower is available.

Cauliflower

BASIC PROCEDURE FOR CUTTING CAULIFLOWER FLORETS

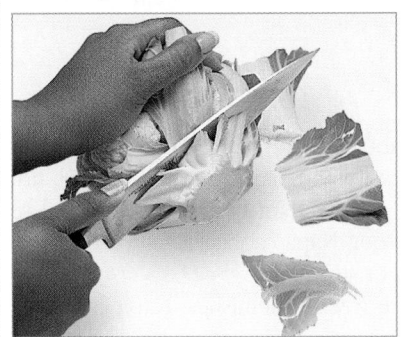

1. Cut off the stem and leaves.

2. Cut the florets off the core.

Green and Red Cabbages

Cabbage (Fr. *chou*) has been a staple of northern European cuisine for centuries. The familiar green cabbages have large, firm, round heads with tightly packed pale green leaves, which are actually flower petals. Flat and conical-shaped heads are also available. Red (or purple) cabbages are a different strain and may be tougher than green cabbages. When cooking red cabbage, an acid (vinegar) is used to preserve the red colour (anthocyanin). Cabbage can be eaten raw (as in coleslaw) or used in soups or stews; it can be braised, steamed or stir-fried. The large, waxy leaves can also be steamed until soft, then wrapped around a filling of seasoned meat and/or rice.

Choose firm heads without dried cores. Cabbages are available all year.

Green and Red Cabbages

Kale

Kale has large ruffled, curly or bumpy leaves. Its rather bitter flavour goes well with rich meats such as game, pork or ham. Kale is typically boiled, stuffed or used in soups.

Choose leaves that are crisp, with a greyish-green colour. Kale is available all year, with peak season during the winter months.

Ornamental or flowering kale is edible but more often used for decorations.

Kale

Ornamental Kale

Kohlrabi

Kohlrabi

Although it looks rather like a round root, kohlrabi is actually a bulbous stem vegetable created by cross-breeding cabbages and turnips. When purchased, both the leaves (which are attached directly to the bulbous stem) and roots are generally removed. Depending on the variety, the skin may be light green, purple or green with a hint of red. The interior flesh is white, with a sweet flavour similar to turnips. (Kohlrabies can be substituted for turnips in many recipes.) Younger plants are milder and more tender than large, mature ones. The outer skin must be removed from mature stems; young stems need only to be well scrubbed before cooking. Kohlrabi can be eaten raw, or it can be cooked (whole, sliced or diced) with moist-heat cooking methods such as boiling and steaming. The stems may also be hollowed out and stuffed with meat or vegetable mixtures.

Choose small, tender stems with fresh, green leaves. Peak season for kohlrabi is from June through September.

Napa Cabbage

Napa Cabbage

Napa cabbage, also known as Chinese cabbage (suey choy), is widely used in Asian cuisines. It has a stout, elongated head with relatively tightly packed, firm, pale green leaves. It is moister and more tender than common green and red cabbages, with a milder, more delicate flavour. Napa cabbage may be eaten raw but is particularly well suited for stir-frying or steaming.

Choose heads with crisp leaves that are free of blemishes. Napa cabbage is available fresh all year.

Savoy

Savoy cabbage has curly or ruffled leaves, often in variegated shades of green and purple. (The term "savoyed" is used to refer to any vegetable with bumpy, wavy or wrinkled leaves.) Savoy cabbage tends to be milder and more tender than regular cabbages and can be substituted for them, cooked or uncooked. Savoy leaves also make an attractive garnish.

Choose heads that are loose or tight, depending on the variety, with tender, unblemished leaves. Peak season is from August through the spring.

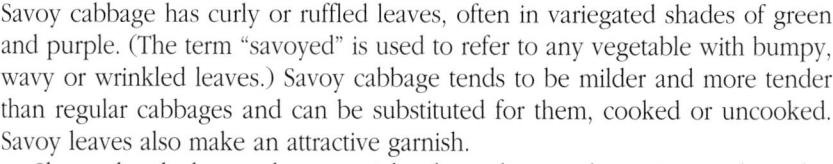
Savoy

Fruit-Vegetables

Botanists classify avocados, eggplants, peppers, tomatoes, gourds and squashes as fruits because they develop from the ovary of flowering plants and contain one or more seeds. Chefs, however, prepare and serve them like vegetables; therefore, they are discussed here.

Avocados

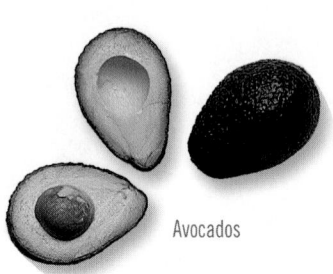
Avocados

Avocados include several varieties of pear-shaped fruits with rich, high-fat flesh. This light golden-green flesh surrounds a large, inedible, oval-shaped seed (pit). Some varieties have smooth, green skin; others have pebbly, almost black skin. Avocados should be used at their peak of ripeness, a condition that lasts only briefly. Firm avocados lack the desired flavour and creamy texture. Ripe avocados should be soft to the touch but not mushy. Ripe Hass avocados have almost black skins; the skins of the other varieties remain green when ripe. Firm avocados can be left at room temperature to ripen, then refrigerated for one or two days. Avocados are most often used raw to garnish salads, mashed or puréed for sauces, sliced for sandwiches or diced for omelettes.

Avocado halves are popular containers for chilled meat, fish, shellfish or poultry salads. Because avocado flesh turns brown very quickly once cut, dip avocado halves or slices in lemon juice and keep unused portions tightly covered with plastic wrap.

Choose avocados that are free of blemishes or moist spots. The flesh should be free of dark spots or streaks. Available all year, the peak season for Hass avocados is April through October; for Fuertes avocados, it is November through April.

BASIC PROCEDURE FOR CUTTING AND PITTING AVOCADOS

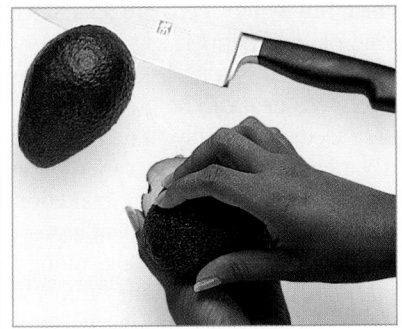

1. Cut the avocado in half lengthwise. Separate the two halves with a twisting motion.

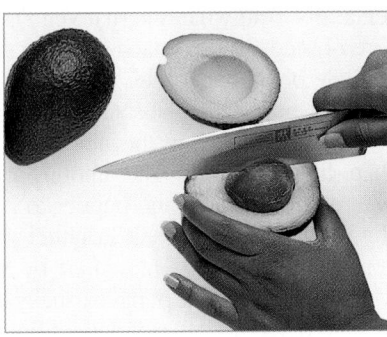

2. Insert a chef's knife into the pit and twist to remove.

3. Scoop the flesh out of the skin with a large spoon.

Eggplants

Two types of eggplants (Fr. *aubergine*) are commonly available: Asian and western. Asian varieties are either round or long and thin, with skin colours ranging from creamy white to deep purple. Western eggplants, which are more common in North America, tend to be shaped like a plump pear with shiny lavender to purple-black skin. Both types have a dense, khaki-coloured flesh with a rather bland flavour that absorbs other flavours well during cooking. Eggplants can be grilled, baked, steamed, fried or sautéed. They are commonly used in Mediterranean and East Indian cuisines (especially in vegetarian dishes), but also appear in European and North American dishes. The skin may be left intact or removed before or after cooking, as desired. Sliced eggplants may be salted and left to drain for 30 minutes to remove moisture and bitterness before cooking and to reduce oil absorption.

Asian Eggplants

Western Eggplant

Japanese Eggplant

Eggplant: To Salt or Not to Salt

Eggplants are filled with cells that contain water and are surrounded by tiny air pockets. The presence of heat will squeeze the air out of the pockets. If the eggplant has not been salted, oil is then free to seep into these pockets and the eggplant becomes soggy when fried.

But when salt is sprinkled on an eggplant, it draws the water out of the cells. The cells then collapse. As a result, no oil can seep into the tiny pockets during the frying process.

—Daniel Zwerdling, senior correspondent with National Public Radio. This sidebar originally appeared in *Gourmet*.

Choose plump, heavy eggplants with a smooth, shiny skin that is not blemished or wrinkled. Asian varieties tend to be softer than western. Eggplants are available all year, with peak season during the late summer.

Peppers

Members of the *Capsicum* family are native to the Americas. When "discovered" by Christopher Columbus, he called them "peppers" because of their sometimes fiery flavour. Interestingly, "New World" peppers were readily accepted in Indian and Asian cuisines, in which they are now considered staples.

Fresh peppers are found in a wide range of colours—green, red, yellow, orange, purple or white—and shapes, from tiny teardrops to cones to spheres. They have dense flesh and a hollow central cavity. The flesh is lined with placental ribs (the white internal veins), to which tiny white seeds are attached. A core of seeds is also attached to the stem end of each pepper.

Chile peppers get their heat from capsaicin, which is found not in the flesh or seeds, but in the placental ribs. Thus, a pepper's heat can be greatly reduced by carefully removing the ribs and attached seeds. Generally, the smaller the chile, the hotter it is. The amount of heat varies from variety to variety, however, and even from one pepper to another depending on growing conditions. Hot, dry conditions result in hotter peppers than do cool, moist conditions. A pepper's heat can be measured by Scoville Heat Units, a subjective rating in which the sweet bell pepper usually rates 0 units, the jalapeño rates from 2500 to 5000 units, the tabasco rates from 30 000 to 50 000 units and the habanero rates a whopping 100 000 to 300 000 units.

When selecting peppers, choose those that are plump and brilliantly coloured with smooth, unblemished skins. Avoid wrinkled, pitted or blistered peppers. A bright green stem indicates freshness.

Sweet Peppers

Common sweet peppers, known as bell peppers, are thick-walled fruits available in green, red, yellow, purple, orange and other colours. They are heart-shaped or boxy, with a short stem and crisp flesh. Their flavour is warm, sweet (red peppers tend to be the sweetest) and relatively mild. Raw bell peppers may be sliced or diced and used in salads or sandwiches. Bell peppers may also be stuffed and baked, grilled, fried, sautéed, roasted or puréed for soups, sauces or condiments. Green bell peppers are available all year; other types are more readily available during the summer and fall. Many coloured peppers are greenhouse-grown.

Green Bell Pepper

Red and Yellow Bell Peppers

BASIC PROCEDURE FOR CUTTING PEPPERS JULIENNE

1. Trim off the ends of the pepper; cut away the seeds and core.

2. Cut away the pale ribs, trimming the flesh to the desired thickness.

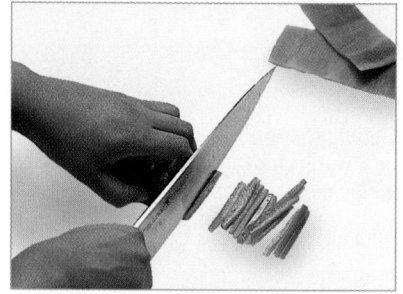

3. Slice the flesh in julienne.

Hot Peppers

Hot peppers, also known as chiles, are also members of the *Capsicum* family. Although a chile's most characteristic attribute is its pungency, each chile has a distinctive flavour, from mild and rich to spicy and sweet to fiery hot.

Chiles are commonly used in Asian, Indian, Mexican and Latin American cuisines. The larger (and milder) of the hot peppers, such as Anaheim and poblano, can be stuffed and baked or sautéed as a side dish. Most chiles, however, are used to add flavour and seasoning to sauces and other dishes. Fresh chiles are available all year and are also available canned in a variety of processed forms such as whole or diced roasted, pickled or marinated, as well as in dried forms.

Dried chiles are widely used in Mexican, Central American and southwestern cuisines. They may be ground to create a powdered spice called chilli or soaked in liquid, then puréed, for sauces or condiments. Drying radically alters the flavour of chiles, making them stronger and more pungent. Dried chiles are often called by names different from those of their fresh versions. For example, the fresh poblano becomes the dried ancho; the fresh jalapeño becomes the dried, smoked chipotle.

Choose dried chiles that are clean and unbroken, with some flexibility. Avoid any with white spots or a stale aroma.

(clockwise from bottom left) Habanero; Red and Green Serrano; Green and Red Jalapeño; Yellow Hot; Poblano; and Anaheim Chiles.

Dried Chiles: (left to right)
California; Ancho; and De Árbol

BASIC PROCEDURE FOR CORING JALAPEÑOS

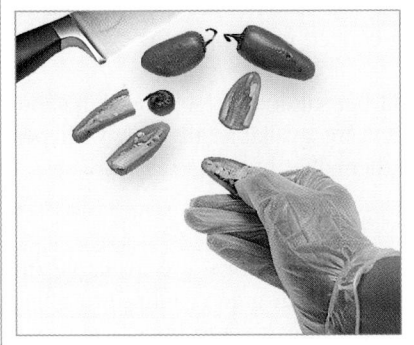

Cut the jalapeño in half lengthwise. Push the core and seeds out with your thumb. You can avoid burning your fingers by wearing rubber gloves when working with hot chiles.

A Pepper by Any Other Name

The popularity of southwestern cuisine, hot condiments and salsas has brought with it a new appreciation and respect for chiles. Diners, and cooks, may find the names given to the various chiles confusing, however. Most chiles can be used either fresh or dried, though drying changes not only the pepper's flavour, but also its name. Regional variations in chile names also add to the confusion. Several of the more frequently encountered chiles are listed here according to the names most commonly used for both their fresh and their dried forms.

Fresh (Fresco)	Dried (Seco)
Anaheim	Mild Red or California
Chilaca	Pasilla or Negro
Jalapeño	Chipotle (smoked)
Mirasol	Guajillo
New Mexico Green	New Mexico Red
New Mexico Red	Chile Colorado
Pimento	Paprika
Poblano	Ancho or Mulato

Chile Pepper Pungency

A pepper's heat can be measured by Scoville Heat Units, a subjective rating created to measure the perception of capsaicin when tasting chile peppers. The higher the rating, the larger the concentration of capsaicin and the hotter the pepper will taste. An example of some of the ranges of heat of common chile peppers as measured in this system is listed here.

Pepper	Pungency (Scoville)
Bell, sweet Italian	0
New Mexico, pimento	500–1000
Anaheim, ancho, pasilla, poblano	1000–1500
Chipotle, jalapeño	2500–10 000
Serrano	5000–23 000
De árbol	15 000–30 000
Aji, cayenne, piquin, tabasco	30 000–50 000
Habanero, Scotch bonnet	80 000–300 000
Pure capsaicin	16 000 000

BASIC PROCEDURE FOR ROASTING PEPPERS

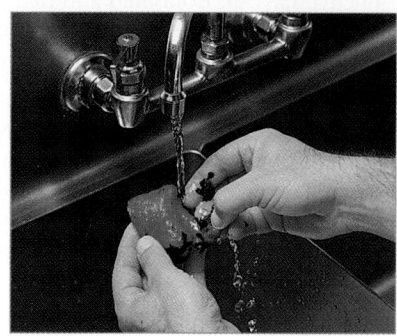

1. Roast the pepper over an open flame until completely charred. Place in a tightly covered bowl to steam.

2. Remove the burnt skin and rinse under running water.

Tomatillos

(clockwise from lower right) Pear, Cherry, Plum and Beefsteak Tomatoes

Sun-Dried Tomatoes

Tomatillos

Tomatillos, also known as Mexican or husk tomatoes, grow on small, weedy bushes. They are bright green, about the size of a small tomato and covered with a thin, papery husk. They have a tart, lemony flavour and crisp, moist flesh. Although an important ingredient in southwestern and northern Mexican cuisines, tomatillos may not be readily available in other areas. Tomatillos can be used raw in salads, puréed for salsa or cooked in soups, stews or vegetable dishes.

Choose tomatillos whose husks are split but still look fresh. The skin should be plump, shiny and slightly sticky. They are available all year, with peak season during the summer and fall. Wash them after husking.

Tomatoes

Tomatoes (Fr. *tomate* or *pomme d'amour*; It. *pomodoro*) are available in a wide variety of colours and shapes. They vary from green (unripe) to golden yellow to ruby red; from tiny spheres (currant tomatoes) to huge, squat ovals (beefsteak). Some, such as the plum tomato, have lots of meaty flesh with only a few seeds; others, such as the slicing tomato, have lots of seeds and juice, but only a few meaty membranes. All tomatoes have a similar flavour, but the levels of sweetness and acidity vary depending on the species, growing conditions and ripeness at harvest.

Because tomatoes are highly perishable, they are usually harvested when mature but still green (unripe), then shipped to wholesalers who ripen them in temperature- and humidity-controlled rooms. The effect on flavour and texture is unfortunate.

Tomatoes are used widely in salads, soups, sauces and baked dishes. They are most often eaten raw but can be grilled, pickled, pan-fried, roasted or sautéed as a side dish.

Choose fresh tomatoes that are plump with a smooth, shiny skin. The colour should be uniform and true for the variety. Tomatoes are available all year, with a summer peak season for most varieties. Many canned tomato products are also available (for example, purée, paste, sauce or stewed whole). Heirloom varieties are now being grown and marketed. Sun-dried tomatoes are available air- or sun-dried. Oil-packed sun-dried tomatoes have better colour and flavour. Dry packs often have to be soaked in hot water to soften.

BASIC PROCEDURE FOR MAKING TOMATO CONCASSÉE

1. With a paring knife, mark an X on the bottom of the tomato just deep enough to penetrate the skin.

2. Blanch the tomato in boiling water for 20 seconds; refresh in ice water.

3. Using a paring knife, cut out the core and peel the tomato.

4. Cut the tomato in half horizontally and squeeze out the seeds and juice. A small melon baller can be used to ensure that all of the seeds are removed.

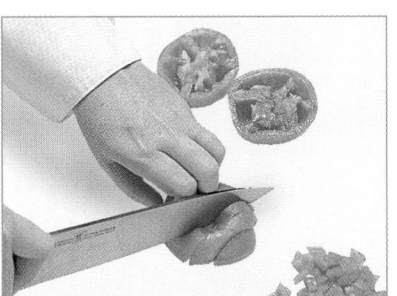

5. Chop or dice the tomato as desired for the recipe. Strain juice for further use.

Tomato Concassée

Traditionally, a concassée is sweated with a small amount of oil and shallots. Current interpretation usually means peeled, seeded and diced tomato flesh. Plum tomatoes have the best yield.

The Olive

Olives are the fruit of a tree native to the Mediterranean area. Green olives are those harvested unripened; black olives are fully ripened. The raw fruit is inedibly bitter and must be washed, soaked and pickled before eating. Green olives should have a smooth, tight skin. Ripe olives will be glossy but softer, with a slightly wrinkled skin. Many varieties and flavours are available, from the tiny black Niçoise to the large purplish Kalamata. Olives are packaged in a range of sizes, from medium (the smallest) to jumbo (the largest). (Colossal and super colossal olives are actually smaller than jumbos.) Pitted olives are also available. The cavity may be filled with strips of pimento, jalapeño pepper, almonds or other foods for flavour and appearance.

Olives are used as a finger food for snacks or hors d'oeuvre, or added to salads or pasta. They may even be cooked in breads, soups, sauces, stews or casseroles. A paste made of minced ripe olives, known as tapenade, is used as a dip or condiment.

Jumbo Spanish Olives

Ripe California Olives

Kalamata Olives

Niçoise Olives

<table>
<tr><td>

BASIC PROCEDURE FOR SEEDING A CUCUMBER

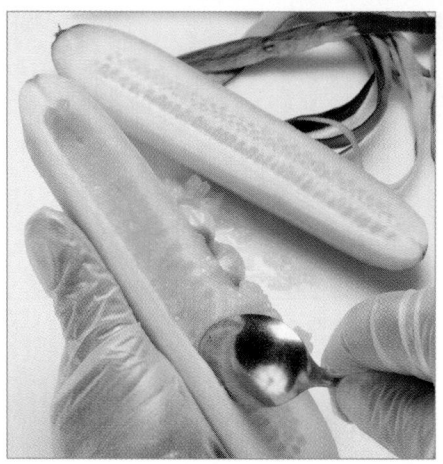

Remove the seeds from a cucumber by slicing it in half lengthwise, then scrape out the seeds with a spoon or melon baller.

</td><td>

BASIC PROCEDURE FOR MAKING DECORATIVE CUCUMBER SLICES

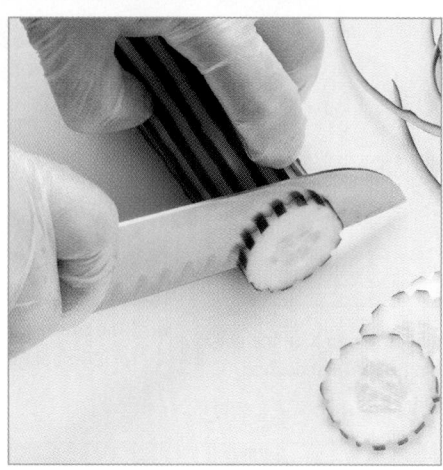

Use a zester or fork to score the rind of a cucumber before slicing.

</td></tr>
</table>

(from top to bottom) Pickling, Green and English (Hothouse) Cucumbers

Cucumbers

Cucumbers can be divided into two categories: pickling and slicing. The two types are not interchangeable. Pickling cucumbers include the cornichon, dill and gherkin. They are recognizable by their sharp black or white spines and are quite bitter when raw. Slicing cucumbers include the burpless, the seedless English (or hothouse), the lemon (which is round and yellow) and the common green field cucumber. Most have relatively thin skins and may be marketed with a wax coating to prevent moisture loss and improve appearance. Waxed skins should be peeled. All cucumbers are valued for their refreshing cool taste and astringency. Slicing cucumbers are usually served raw, in salads or mixed with yogurt and dill or mint as a side dish, especially for spicy dishes. Pickling cucumbers are generally served pickled, without any further processing.

Choose cucumbers that are firm but not hard. Avoid those that are limp, yellowed or have soft spots. The common varieties are available all year, although peak season is from April through October.

Gourds and Squashes

The *Cucurbitaceae* or gourd family includes almost 750 species; its members are found in warm regions worldwide. Gourds are characterized by large, complex root systems with quick-growing, trailing vines and large leaves. Their flowers are often attractive and edible. Although some members of the gourd family originated in Africa, chayotes and most squashes are native to the Americas.

Chayotes

Chayotes

The chayote, also known as merliton or vegetable pear, is a food staple throughout Central America. The vine bears slightly lumpy, pear-shaped fruits with a smooth, light green skin and a paler green flesh. There is a single white, edible seed in the centre. Chayotes are starchy and very bland and are usually

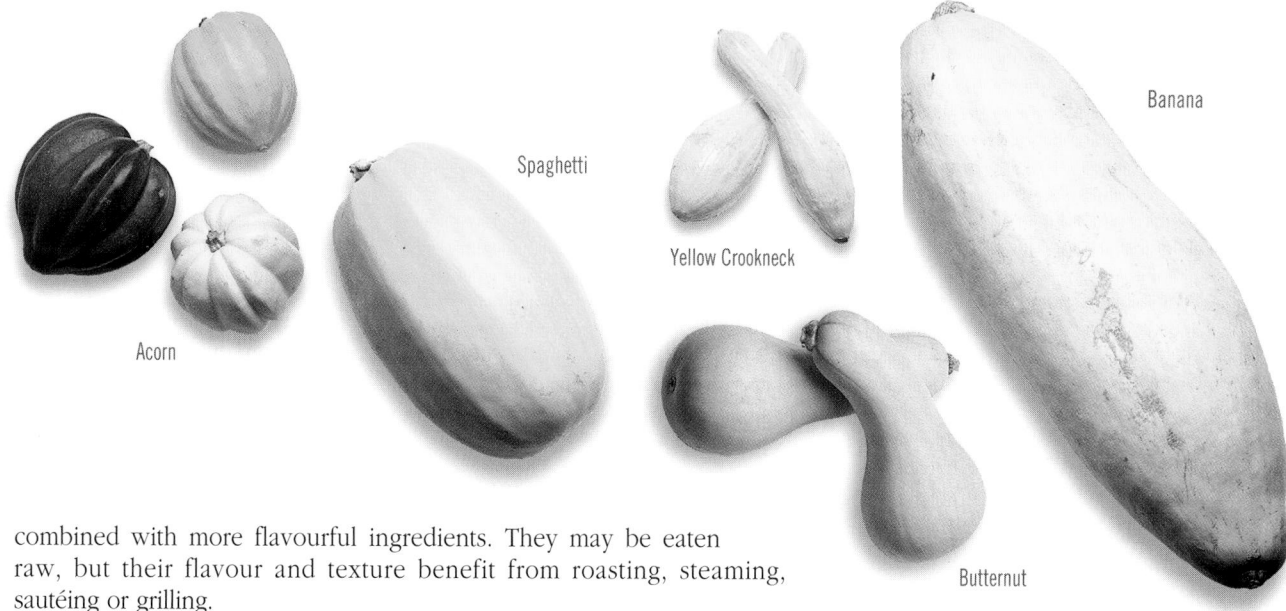

Acorn

Spaghetti

Yellow Crookneck

Banana

Butternut

combined with more flavourful ingredients. They may be eaten raw, but their flavour and texture benefit from roasting, steaming, sautéing or grilling.

Choose chayotes that have well-coloured skin with few ridges. Avoid those with very soft spots or bruises. Their peak season is the late fall and winter.

Squashes

Squashes are the fleshy fruits of a large number of plants in the gourd family. Many varieties are available in a range of colours, shapes and sizes. Squashes can be classified as winter or summer based on their peak season and skin type. All squashes have a centre cavity filled with many seeds, although in winter varieties the cavity is more pronounced. Squash blossoms are also edible. They may be added to salads raw, dipped in batter and deep-fat fried or filled with cheese or meat and baked.

Choose squashes with unbroken skins and good colour for the variety. Avoid any squash with soft, moist spots.

Winter squashes include the acorn, banana, butternut, Hubbard, pumpkin and spaghetti varieties. They have hard skins (shells) and seeds. (Pumpkin seeds are roasted and eaten.) The flesh, which may be removed from the shell before or after cooking, tends to be sweeter and more strongly flavoured than that of summer squash. Winter squashes should not be served raw; they can be baked, steamed or sautéed. Most winter squashes can also be puréed for soups or pie fillings. Their peak season is October through March.

Summer squashes include the pattypan, yellow crookneck and zucchini (courgette) varieties. They have soft edible skins and seeds that are generally not removed before cooking. Most summer squashes may be eaten raw, but are also suitable for grilling, sautéing, steaming or baking. Although summer squashes are now available all year, their peak season is April through September.

Pumpkin

Zucchini

Leafy Greens

The term *leafy* refers to a variety of leafy green vegetables that may be served raw, but are usually cooked. Greens have long been used in the cuisines of India, Asia and the Mediterranean and are an important part of regional cuisine in the southern United States. Most have strong, spicy flavours. Mustard, sorrel, spinach, Swiss chard, dandelion and turnip greens fall into this category. The milder varieties of greens that are eaten almost always raw include the lettuces discussed in Chapter 25, Salads and Salad Dressings.

Mustard

Sorrel

Spinach

Swiss Chard

Turnip Greens

Greens have an extremely high water content, which means that cooking causes drastic shrinkage. As a general rule, allow 250 g (8 oz.) per portion before cooking.

Choose young, tender greens with good colour and no limpness. Avoid greens with dry-looking stems or yellow leaves. Most greens are available fresh all year, especially from November through June. The more popular greens are also available canned or frozen.

Mustard

Mustard, a member of the cabbage family, was brought to North America by early European immigrants. Mustard has large, dark green leaves with frilly edges. It is known for its assertive, bitter flavour. Mustard greens can be served raw in salads or used as garnish. Or they can be cooked, often with white wine, vinegar and herbs.

Choose crisp, bright green leaves without discoloration.

Sorrel

Sorrel is an abundant and rather ordinary wild member of the buckwheat family. Its tartness and sour flavour are used in soups and sauces and to accent other vegetables. It is particularly good with fatty fish or rich meats. Sorrel leaves naturally acquire the texture of a purée after only a few minutes of moist-heat cooking.

Choose leaves that are fully formed, with no yellow blemishes.

Spinach

Spinach (Fr. *épinard*) is a versatile green that grows rapidly in cool climates. It has smooth, bright green leaves attached to thin stems. Spinach may be eaten raw in salads, cooked by almost any moist-heat method, microwaved or sautéed. It can be used in stuffings, baked or creamed dishes, soups or stews. Spinach grows in sandy soil and must be rinsed repeatedly in cold water to remove all traces of grit from the leaves. It bruises easily and should be handled gently during washing. Stems and large mid-ribs should be removed.

Choose bunches with crisp, tender, deep green leaves; avoid yellow, blemished leaves. Picked, washed spinach leaves are readily available.

Swiss Chard

Chard—the reference to "Swiss" is inexplicable—is a type of beet that does not produce a tuberous root. It is used for its wide, flat, dark green leaves. Chard can be steamed, sautéed or used in soups. Its tart, spinachlike flavour blends well with sweet ingredients such as fruit.

Choose leaves that are crisp, with some curliness or savoying. Ribs should be an unblemished white, red, orange or yellow.

Turnip Greens

The leaves of the turnip root have a pleasantly bitter flavour, similar to peppery mustard greens. The dark green leaves are long, slender and deeply indented. Turnip greens are best eaten steamed, sautéed, baked or microwaved.

Fungi

Mushrooms

Mushrooms (Fr. *champignon*; It. *funghi*) are members of a broad category of plants known as fungi. (Fungi have no seeds, stems or flowers; they reproduce through spores.) Mushrooms have a stalk with an umbrellalike top. Although not actually a vegetable, mushrooms are used and served in much the same manner as vegetables.

Several types of cultivated mushroom are available. They include the meadow (or white), shiitake, straw, enokidake (also called enoki) and cloud ear (also known as wood ear or Chinese black). Button mushrooms are the smallest, most immature form of the meadow mushroom. Portobello and crimini are now commonly available, along with chanterelles, lobster, oyster, porcini and morels.

Many wild mushrooms are gathered and sold by specialty purveyors. Because wild mushroom spores are spread around the world by air currents, the same item may be found in several areas, each with a different common name. Wild mushrooms have a stronger earthy or nutty flavour than cultivated mushrooms and should generally be cooked before eating.

Mushrooms, whether cultivated or gathered from the wild, are available fresh, canned or dried. Because mushrooms are composed of up to 80% water, dried products are often the most economical, even though they may cost hundreds of dollars per kilogram. Dried mushrooms can be stored in a cool, dry place for months. When needed, they are rehydrated by soaking in warm water until soft, approximately 10 to 20 minutes.

Choose fresh mushrooms that are clean, without soft or moist spots or blemishes. Fresh cultivated mushrooms are generally available all year; fresh wild mushrooms are available seasonally, usually during the summer and fall. Cultivated mushrooms with exposed gills (the ridges on the underside of the umbrellalike top) are old and should be avoided. Fresh mushrooms can be refrigerated in an open container for up to five days. Normally, it is not necessary to peel mushrooms; if they are dirty, they should be quickly rinsed (not soaked) in cool water just before use.

Truffles

Truffles are actually tubers that grow near the roots of oak or beech trees. They can be cultivated only to the extent that oak groves are planted to encourage truffle growth. The two principal varieties are the Périgord (black) and the Piedmontese (white). Fresh truffles are gathered in the fall and are rarely marketed outside their locale. Truffles, especially white ones, have a strong aroma and flavour, requiring only a small amount to add their special flavour to soups, sauces, pasta and other items. Black truffles are often used as a garnish or to flavour pâtés, terrines or egg dishes. Because fresh imported truffles can cost several hundred dollars per kilogram, most kitchens purchase truffles canned, dried or frozen.

Portobello

Black Trumpet

Pom Pom Blanc

Porcini (cèpe or cep)

White

Morel

Hen of the Woods

Clam Shell

Oyster

Enokidake

Shiitake

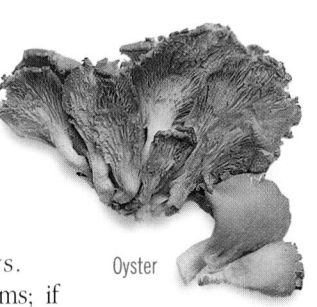

Black Truffles

BASIC PROCEDURE FOR FLUTING MUSHROOMS

Use the sharp edge of a straight paring knife to cut thin curves into the mushroom cap. Fluted mushrooms may be baked or poached, then used as garnish.

Red Onion

Yellow Onion

Pearl Onions

Walla-Walla Sweet Onions

White Onions

Fennel

Garlic

Bulbs

Onions are strongly flavoured, aromatic members of the lily family and are the most widely known bulb. Most have edible grasslike or tubular leaves. Almost every culture incorporates them into its cuisine as a vegetable and for flavouring.

Bulb Onions

Common or bulb onions (Fr. *oignons*) may be white, yellow (Spanish) or red (Bermuda). Medium-sized yellow and white onions are the most strongly flavoured. Larger onions (Vidalia) tend to be sweeter and milder. Widely used as a flavouring ingredient, onions are indispensable in mirepoix. Onions are also prepared as a side dish by deep-fat frying, roasting, grilling, steaming or boiling.

Pearl onions are small, about 1.25 cm (1/2 in.) in diameter, with yellow, red or white skins. They have a mild flavour and can be grilled, boiled, roasted or sautéed whole as a side dish, or used in soups or stews.

Choose onions that are firm, dry and feel heavy. The outer skins should be dry and brittle. Avoid onions that have begun to sprout. They should be stored in a cool, dry, well-ventilated area. Do not refrigerate onions until they are cut. Onions are available all year.

Fennel

Fennel (Fr. *fenouil*) is a Mediterranean favourite used for thousands of years as a vegetable (the bulb), a herb (the leaves) and a spice (the seeds). The bulb (often incorrectly referred to as sweet anise) has short, tight, overlapping celerylike stalks with feathery leaves. The flavour is similar to anise or licorice, becoming milder when cooked. Fennel bulbs may be eaten raw or grilled, steamed, sautéed, baked or microwaved.

Choose fairly large, bright white bulbs on which the cut edges appear fresh, without dryness or browning. The bulb should be compact, not spreading. Fresh fennel's peak season is September through May.

Garlic

Garlic (Fr. *ail*; Sp. *ajo*) is also used in almost all of the world's cuisines. A head of garlic comprises many small cloves. Each clove is wrapped in a thin husk or peel; the entire head is encased in several thin layers of papery husk. Of the 300 or so types of garlic known, only three are commercially significant. The most common is pure white, with a sharp flavour. A Mexican variety is pale pink and more strongly flavoured. Elephant garlic is apple-sized and particularly mild. Although whole bulbs can be baked or roasted, garlic is most often separated into cloves, peeled, sliced, minced or crushed and used to flavour a wide variety of dishes. When using garlic, remember that the more finely the cloves are crushed, the stronger the flavour will be. And cooking reduces garlic's pungency; the longer it is cooked, the milder it becomes.

Choose firm, dry bulbs with tightly closed cloves and smooth skins. Avoid bulbs with green sprouts. Store fresh garlic in a cool, well-ventilated place; do not refrigerate. Fresh garlic is available all year. Jars of processed and pickled garlic products are also available.

Leeks

Leeks (Fr. *poireaux*) look like large, overgrown scallions with a fat white tip and wide green leaves. Their flavour is sweeter and stronger than scallions, but milder than common bulb onions. Leeks must be carefully washed to remove the sandy soil that gets between the leaves. Leeks can be baked, braised or grilled as a side dish, or used to season stocks, soups or sauces.

Choose leeks that are firm, with stiff roots and stems. Avoid those with dry leaves, soft spots or browning. Leeks are available all year.

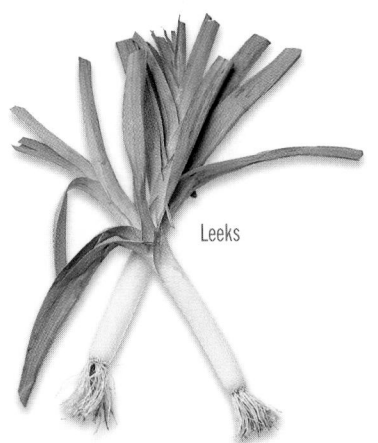
Leeks

BASIC PROCEDURE FOR CLEANING LEEKS

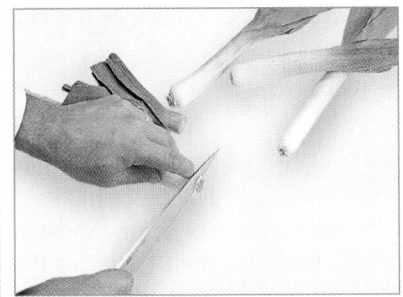
1. Trim the root end from the leek.

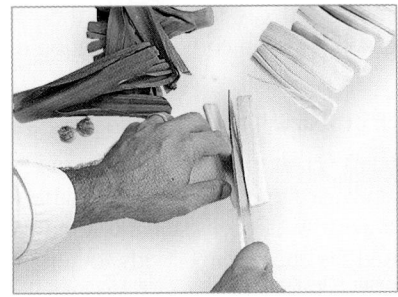
2. Cut away the dark green top and slice the white portion in half lengthwise.

3. Rinse the leek thoroughly under running water to remove soil.

Scallions

Scallions, also known as green onions or bunch onions, are a variety of onion that does not develop a large bulb. The leaves are bright green with either a long and slender or slightly bulbous white base. Green onions are used in stir-fries, salads and as a flavouring in other dishes. The green tops can also be sliced in small rings and used as a garnish.

Choose scallions with bright green tops and clean white bulbs. Avoid those with limp or slimy leaves. Scallions are available all year, with a peak summer season. Store, wrapped in paper, in plastic bags for better shelf life.

Scallions

Shallots

Shallots (Fr. *échalotes*) are shaped like small bulb onions with one flat side. When peeled, a shallot separates into multiple cloves, similar to garlic. They have a mild yet rich and complex flavour. Shallots are the basis of many classic sauces and meat preparations; they can also be sautéed or baked as a side dish.

Shallots

Choose shallots that are plump and well shaped. Avoid those that appear dry or have sprouted. They should be stored in a cool, dry, unrefrigerated place. Shallots are available all year.

Pods and Seeds

Pod and seed vegetables include corn, legumes and okra. They are grouped together here because the parts consumed are all the seeds of their respective plants. In some cases only the seeds are eaten; in others, the pod containing the seeds is eaten as well. Seeds are generally higher in protein and carbohydrates (starch and fibre) than other vegetables.

Corn

Yellow and White Corn

Sweet corn (Fr. *maïs*; Sp. *maíz*) is actually a grain, a type of grass. Corn kernels, like peas, are plant seeds. (Dried corn products are discussed in Chapter 23, Potatoes, Grains and Pasta.) The kernels, which may be white or yellow, are attached to a woody, inedible cob. The cob is encased by strands of hairlike fibres called silks and covered in layers of thin leaves called husks. The silks and husks should be shucked prior to cooking, although the husks may be left on for roasting or grilling. Shucked ears can be grilled, boiled, microwaved or steamed. The kernels can be cut off the cob before or after cooking. Corn on the cob is available fresh or frozen; corn kernels are available canned or frozen.

Choose freshly picked ears with firm, small kernels. Avoid those with mould or decay at the tip of the cob or brownish silks. Summer is the peak season for fresh corn. Refrigeration diminishes quality.

Legumes/Pulses

Green Beans

Beans (Fr. *haricots*; It. *fagioli*) and peas (Fr. *pois*) are members of the legume family, a large group of vegetables with double-seamed pods containing a single row of seeds. Of the hundreds of known varieties of beans, some are used for their edible pods, others for shelling fresh and some only for their dried seeds. Dried beans are actually several varieties of seeds or peas left in the pod until mature, then shelled and dried.

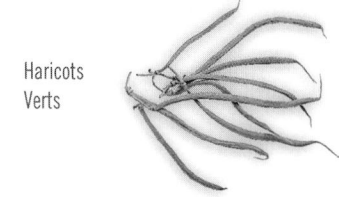

Haricots Verts

Fresh Beans

Beans used for their edible pods, commonly referred to as green beans, string beans, runner beans or snap beans, are picked when immature. Except for the stem, the entire pod can be eaten. This category includes the green bean, the yellow wax bean and the French haricot vert, a long, slender pod with an intense flavour and tender texture. If there are any strings along the pod's seams, they should be pulled off before cooking. Beans may be left whole, cut lengthwise into thin slivers (referred to as french cut) or cut crosswise on the diagonal.

Shelling beans are those grown primarily for the edible seeds inside the pod. Common examples are flageolets, lima beans and fava (broad) beans. Their tough pods are not usually eaten.

Fava Beans

All beans can be prepared by steaming, microwaving or sautéing. They can be added to soups or stews and they blend well with a variety of flavours, from coconut milk to garlic and olive oil. Cooked beans can be chilled and served as a salad or crudité.

Choose beans that have a bright colour without brown or soft spots. Large pods may be tough or bitter. The peak season for fresh beans is from April through December. Most bean varieties are available frozen or canned, including pickled and seasoned products.

Dried Beans

Anthropologists report that for thousands of years cultures worldwide have preserved some members of the legume family by drying. Common dried beans include kidney beans, pinto beans, chickpeas, lentils, black beans, black-eyed peas and split green peas. Shape is the clearest distinction among these products: beans are oval or kidney-shaped; lentils are small, flat disks; peas are round.

Beans and peas destined for drying are left on the vine until they are fully matured and just beginning to dry. They are then harvested, shelled and quickly dried with warm air currents. Some dried legumes are sold split, which means the skin is removed, causing the seed's two halves to separate.

Most dried beans need to be soaked in water before cooking. Soaking softens and rehydrates the beans, thus reducing cooking time. Lentils and split peas generally do not require soaking, however, and will cook faster than beans. After soaking, beans are most often simmered or baked in a liquid until soft and tender. One type may be substituted for another in most recipes, although variations in colour, starch content and flavour should be considered.

Dried beans and peas are available in bulk or in polybags. They should be stored in a cool, dry place, but not refrigerated. Many of these beans are also available fully cooked, then canned or frozen. Some dried beans may be fermented or processed into flour, oil or bean curd.

Red Kidney Beans

Pinto Beans

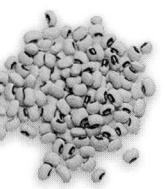

Dried Black-Eyed Peas

Lentils

Great Northern Beans

BASIC PROCEDURE FOR SOAKING DRIED BEANS

1. Pick through the dried beans and remove any grit, pebbles or debris.

2. Place the beans in a bowl and cover with cold water; remove any skins or other items that float to the surface.

3. Drain the beans in a colander, then rinse under cold running water.

4. Return the beans to a bowl and cover with fresh cold water. Allow approximately 750 mL (3 cups) of water for each 250 mL (1 cup) of beans.

5. Soak the beans in the cold water for the time specified in the recipe, usually several hours or overnight. Drain through a colander, discarding the water.

BASIC PROCEDURE FOR QUICK-SOAKING DRIED BEANS

The soaking procedure can be accelerated by the following technique:

1. Rinse and pick through the beans.

2. Place the beans in a saucepan and add enough cool water to cover them by 5 cm (2 in.).

3. Bring to a boil and simmer for two minutes.

4. Remove from the heat, cover and soak for one hour.

5. Drain and discard the soaking liquid. Proceed with the recipe.

Fresh Shelling Peas

Soybeans

Snow Peas

Pea Shoots

Okra

Fresh Shelling Peas

Of the shelling peas that are prepared fresh, the most common are green garden peas (English peas) and the French petit pois. Because they lose flavour rapidly after harvest, most shelling peas are sold frozen or canned. Shelling peas have a delicate, sweet flavour best presented by simply steaming until tender but still al dente. Peas may also be braised with rich meats such as ham or used in soups. Cooked peas are attractive in salads or as garnish.

Choose small fresh pea pods that are plump and moist. Peak season is April and May.

Fresh green soybeans (soya) (Japanese: *edamame*) are becoming a popular shelling pea in the United States. When picked before maturity, soybeans have a light green, fuzzy pod and a tender, sweet pea. Fresh green soybeans are delicious steamed in the pod, then chilled, popped open and eaten out of hand as a snack. Often served in sushi restaurants or with other Asian cuisines, they are extremely high in protein, fibre and phytochemicals. When allowed to mature and then prepared like other dried beans, however, soybeans become extremely tough, hard to digest and bitter. Mature soybeans are best used for processing into oil, tofu, sauce and other foodstuffs.

Edible Podded Peas

Snow peas, also known as Chinese pea pods, are a common variety of edible pea pod. They are very flat and have only a few very small green peas. Snow peas have a string along their seams, which can be removed by holding the leafy stem and pulling from end to end. The pods can be eaten raw, lightly blanched or steamed, or stir-fried.

Another variety of edible pea pod is the sugar snap pea, a cross between the garden pea and snow pea, which was developed during the late 1970s. They are plump, juicy pods filled with small, tender peas. The entire pod is eaten; do not shell the peas before cooking.

Choose pea pods that are firm, bright green and crisp. Avoid those with brown spots or a shrivelled appearance. Pea pods are available all year, with a peak season in March and April. Asian markets also sell pea shoots.

Okra

Okra, a common ingredient in African and Arab cuisines, was brought to the United States by slaves and French settlers. It is now integral to Creole, Cajun, southern and southwestern cuisines. Its mild flavour is similar to asparagus. Okra is not eaten raw; it is best pickled, boiled, steamed, or deep-fat fried. Okra develops a gelatinous texture when cooked for long periods, so it is used to thicken gumbos and stews. To avoid the slimy texture some find objectionable, do not wash okra until ready to cook, then trim the stem end only. Cook okra in stainless steel as other metals cause discoloration.

Choose small to medium pods (3.75 to 5 cm; 1 to 2 in.) that are deep green, without soft spots. Pale spears with stiff tips tend to be tough. Okra's peak season is from June through September. Frozen okra is widely available.

Roots and Tubers

Taproots (more commonly referred to as roots) are single roots that extend deep into the soil to supply the above-ground plant with nutrients. Tubers are fat underground stems. Most roots and tubers can be used interchangeably. All store well at cool temperatures, without refrigeration. Potatoes, the most popular tuber, are discussed in Chapter 23, Potatoes, Grains and Pasta.

Beets

Although records suggest that they were first eaten in ancient Greece, beets are most often associated with the colder northern climates, where they grow for most of the year. Beets can be boiled, then peeled and used in salads, soups or baked dishes.

Choose small to medium-sized beets that are firm, with smooth skins. Avoid those with hairy root tips, as they may be tough. Beets are available all year, with a peak season from March to October.

Carrots

Carrots (Fr. *carotte*), among the most versatile of vegetables, are large taproots. Although several kinds exist, the Imperator is the most common. It is long and pointed, with a medium to dark orange colour. It has a mild, sweet flavour. Carrots can be cut into a variety of shapes and eaten raw, used for a mirepoix or prepared by moist-heat cooking methods, grilling, microwaving or roasting. They are also grated and used in baked goods, particularly cakes and muffins.

Choose firm carrots that are smooth and well shaped, with a bright orange colour. If the tops are still attached, they should be fresh-looking and bright green. Carrots are available all year.

Beets

Carrots

Celery Root

Celery root, also known as celeriac, is a large, round root, long popular in northern European cuisines. It is a different plant from stalk celery, and its stalks and leaves are not eaten. Celery root has a knobby brown exterior; a creamy white, crunchy flesh and a mild, celerylike flavour. Its thick outer skin must be peeled away; the flesh is then cut as desired. Often eaten raw, celery root can be baked, steamed or boiled. It is used in soups, stews or salads and goes well with game and rich meats. Raw celery root may be placed in acidulated water to prevent browning.

Celery Root

Choose small to medium-sized roots that are firm and relatively clean, with a pungent smell. Their peak season is October through April.

Jicama

Jicama is actually a legume that grows underground as a tuber. It is becoming increasingly popular because of its sweet, moist flavour, crisp texture, low calorie content and long shelf life. After its thick brown skin is cut away, the crisp, moist white flesh can be cut as desired. Jicama is often eaten raw in salads, with salsa or as a crudité. It is also used in stir-fried dishes.

Choose firm, well-shaped jicamas that are free of blemishes. Size is not an indication of quality or maturity. They are available all year, with a peak season from January through May.

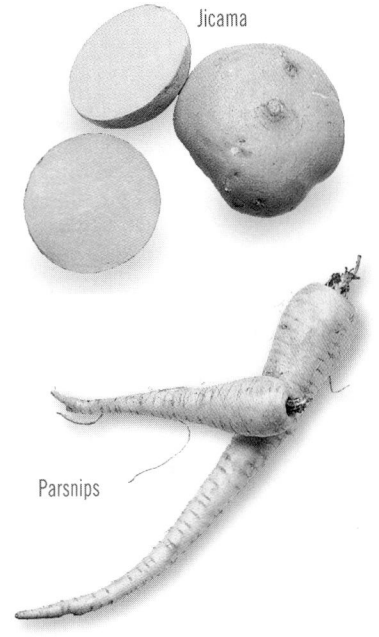

Jicama

Parsnips

Parsnips

Parsnips (Fr. *panais*) are white taproots that look and taste like carrots and have the texture of sweet potatoes. Parsnips should be 12.5 to 25 cm (5 to 10 in.) in length, with smooth skins and tapering tips. Parsnips, peeled like carrots, can be eaten raw or cooked by almost any method. When steamed until very soft, they can be mashed like potatoes.

Sunchokes

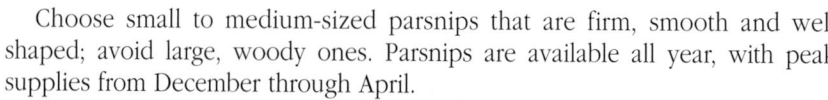

Red Radishes

Daikon

Turnips

Fresh Water Chestnuts

Choose small to medium-sized parsnips that are firm, smooth and well shaped; avoid large, woody ones. Parsnips are available all year, with peak supplies from December through April.

Sunchokes (Jerusalem Artichoke)

Despite their name, Jerusalem artichokes are actually tubers from a variety of sunflower unrelated to artichokes. Consequently, growers are now marketing these vegetables as *sunchokes*. Their lumpy brown skin is usually peeled away (even though it is edible) to reveal a crisp, white interior with a slightly nutty flavour. While they may be eaten raw, it is preferable to cook them before serving to make them easier to digest. Jerusalem artichokes are eaten chopped or grated into salads, or boiled or steamed for a side dish or soup.

Radishes

Radishes (Fr. *radis*) are used for their peppery flavour and crisp texture. Radishes are available in many colours, including white, black and all shades of red; most have a creamy to pure white interior. Asian radishes, known as daikons, produce roots 5 to 10 cm (2 to 4 in.) in diameter and 15 to 50 cm (6 to 20 in.) long. Radishes can be steamed or stir-fried but most often are eaten raw, in salads or used as garnish. Radish leaves can be used in salads or cooked as greens.

Choose radishes that are firm, not limp. Their interior should be neither dry nor hollow. Radishes are available all year.

Rutabagas

Rutabagas are a root vegetable and a member of the cabbage family. Their skin is purple to yellow and they have yellow flesh with a distinctive starchy, cabbagelike flavour. Rutabagas and turnips are similar in flavour and texture when cooked and may be used interchangeably. Rutabaga leaves are not eaten. Rutabagas should be peeled with a chef's knife, then cut into quarters, slices or cubes. They are often baked, boiled and then puréed, or sliced and sautéed. They are especially flavourful when seasoned with caraway seeds, dill or lemon juice.

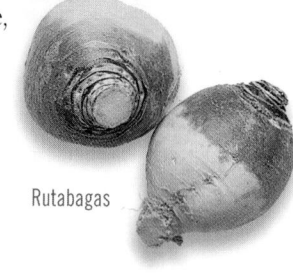

Rutabagas

Choose small to medium-sized rutabagas that are smooth and firm and feel heavy. Their peak season is January through March.

Turnips

Also a root vegetable from the cabbage family, turnips have white skin with a rosy-red or purple blush and white interior. Their flavour, similar to that of a radish, can be rather hot. Turnips should be peeled, then diced, sliced or julienned for cooking. They may be baked or cooked with moist-heat cooking methods and are often puréed like potatoes.

Choose small to medium-sized turnips that have smooth skin and feel heavy. They should be firm, not rubbery or limp. Any attached leaves should be bright green and tender. Spring is their peak season.

Water Chestnuts

Water chestnuts are the tuber of an Asian plant that thrives in water. The brownish-black skin is peeled away to reveal a moist, crisp, white interior, which can be eaten raw or cooked. When cooked, water chestnuts retain their crunchy texture, making them a popular addition to stir-fried dishes. They are also used in salads and casseroles or wrapped in bacon for rumaki hors d'oeuvre.

Stalks and Shoots

Stalk vegetables are plant stems with a high percentage of **cellulose** fibre. These vegetables should be picked while still young and tender. Tough fibres should be trimmed before cooking.

Artichokes

Artichokes (Fr. *artichaut*) are the immature flowers of a thistle plant introduced to America by Italian and Spanish settlers. Young, tender globe artichokes can be cooked whole, but more mature plants need to have the fuzzy centre (known as the choke) removed first. Whole artichokes can be simmered, steamed or microwaved; they are often served with lemon juice, garlic butter or hollandaise sauce. The heart may be cooked separately, then served in salads, puréed as a filling or served as a side dish. Artichoke hearts and bottoms are both available canned.

Choose fresh artichokes with tight, compact heads that feel heavy. Their colour should be solid green to grey-green. Brown spots on the surface caused by frost are harmless. The artichoke's peak season is March through May.

● **cellulose** a complex carbohydrate found in the cell wall of plants; it is edible but indigestible by humans

Artichokes

BASIC PROCEDURE FOR PREPARING FRESH ARTICHOKES

1. Using kitchen shears or scissors, trim the barbs from the large outer leaves of the artichoke.

2. With a chef's knife, cut away the stem and the top of the artichoke. Steam or boil the artichoke as desired.

BASIC PROCEDURE FOR CLEANING ARTICHOKE HEARTS

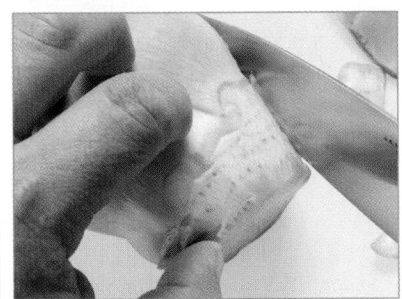

1. Cut off the stem and the outer leaves from the artichoke.

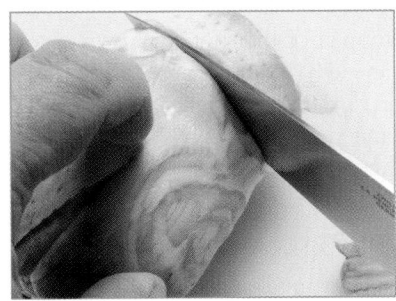

2. Trim the inner stem from the base with a chef's knife.

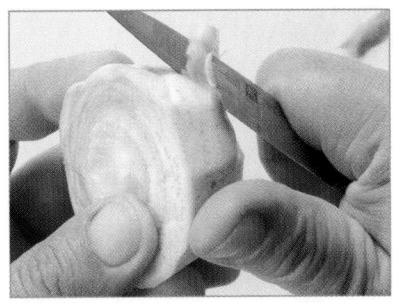

3. Using a paring knife, trim the edges into a neat cup with no tough leaves remaining.

continued

4. Scoop out the fuzzy choke with a melon baller.

5. The cleaned artichoke bottoms are ready to cook.

Asparagus

Fiddleheads

Fresh Bamboo Shoots

Celery

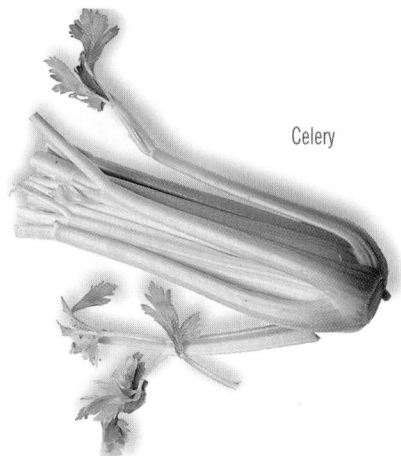

Asparagus

Asparagus (Fr. *asperges*), a member of the lily family, generally has bright green shoots with a ruffle of tiny leaves at the tip. Larger spears or shoots tend to be tough and woody but can be used in soups or for purée. Asparagus are eaten raw or steamed briefly, stir-fried, microwaved or grilled. Fresh spring asparagus is excellent with nothing more than lemon juice or clarified butter; asparagus with hollandaise sauce is a classic preparation.

Choose firm, plump spears with tightly closed tips and a bright green colour running the full length of the spear. Asparagus should be stored refrigerated at 4°C (40°F), upright in 1.25 cm (1/2 in.) of water or with the ends wrapped in moist paper towelling. They should not be washed until just before use. Canned and frozen asparagus are also available. Peak season is March through June.

White asparagus is sometimes available fresh and is readily available canned. It has a milder flavour and soft, tender texture. It is produced by covering the stalks with soil as they grow; this prevents sunlight from reaching the plant and retards the development of chlorophyll.

Fiddleheads

Fiddleheads are a unique Canadian delicacy. The young shoots of a fern, fiddleheads are grown in New Brunswick and Nova Scotia and have a flavour resembling asparagus or broccoli. They are available fresh in the spring and year-round in frozen packages.

Bamboo Shoots

Stripped of their tough brown outer skins, the tender young shoots of certain varieties of bamboo are edible. They make excellent additions to stir-fried dishes or can be served like asparagus. Although fresh shoots are available in Asia, canned peeled shoots packed in brine or water are more common in North America. Canned shoots should be rinsed well before use.

Celery

Once a medicinal herb, stalk celery (Fr. *céleri*) is now a common sight in kitchens worldwide. Stalk celery is pale green with stringy curved stalks (ribs). Often eaten raw in salads or as a snack, it can be braised or steamed as a side dish. Celery is also a mirepoix component.

Choose stalks (ribs) that are crisp, without any sign of dryness. Celery is available all year.

Nopales

The pads of a prickly pear cactus can be prepared as a vegetable known as nopales. Cactus pads have a flavour similar to green bell peppers. Their texture tends to be rather gelatinous or mucilaginous, making them good for stews or sauces. To prepare fresh nopales, hold the pad with tongs and cut off the thorns and "eyes" with a sharp knife or vegetable peeler. Trim off the edge all the way around. Slice the pad into julienne strips or cubes. The pieces can be boiled or steamed and served hot, or chilled and added to salads. Nopales can also be sautéed with onions, peppers and seasonings for a side dish or added to southwestern-style casseroles.

Some cultivated varieties have thin, thornless pads. Choose pads that are stiff and heavy without blemishes. They should not be dry or soggy. Fresh cactus pads are available all year, with peak season in the late spring. Canned and pickled nopales are also available.

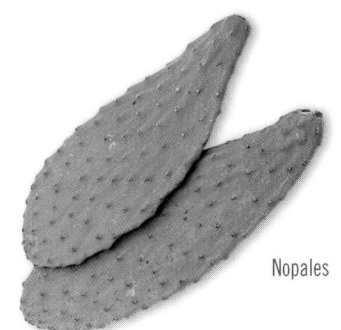

Nopales

Baby Vegetables

Many fine restaurants serve baby vegetables: tiny turnips, finger-length squash, miniature carrots and petite heads of cauliflower. First cultivated in Europe but now widely available elsewhere, baby vegetables include both hybrids bred to be true miniatures as well as regular varieties that are picked before maturity. Baby vegetables are often marketed with blossoms or greens still attached. They tend to be easily bruised and are highly perishable. Many baby vegetables can be eaten raw, but they are usually left whole, then steamed or lightly sautéed and attractively presented as an accompaniment to meat, fish or poultry entrees.

Baby Globe Carrots

NUTRITION

Most vegetables are more than 80% water; the remaining portions consist of carbohydrates (primarily starches) as well as small amounts of protein and fat. The relative lack of protein and fat makes most vegetables especially low in calories.

Much of a vegetable's physical structure is provided by generally indigestible substances such as cellulose and lignin, also known as fibre. This fibre produces the characteristic stringy, crisp or fibrous textures associated with vegetables.

Vegetables are also a good source of vitamins and minerals. Care must be taken during preparation to preserve their nutritional content, however. Once peeled or cut, vegetables lose nutrients to the air, or to any liquid in which they are allowed to soak. Vitamins are concentrated just under the skin, so peel vegetables thinly, if at all.

Chiogghi Beets

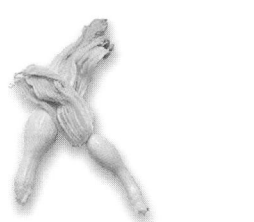

Baby Yellow Squash with Blossoms

PURCHASING AND STORING FRESH VEGETABLES

Fresh vegetables should be selected according to seasonal availability. Using a vegetable at the peak of its season has several advantages: price is at its lowest, selection is at its greatest and the vegetable's colour, flavour and texture are at their best.

Baby Zucchini with Blossoms

Grading

The Canadian Food Inspection Agency has developed a grading system for fresh vegetables traded on wholesale markets. The system is based on appearance, condition and other factors affecting waste or eating quality. Grades for all vegetables include, in descending order of quality, Canada Fancy, Canada No. 1, Canada No. 2 and Canada Domestic Grade.

Consumer or retail grading is required for all domestic and imported vegetables. It uses alphabetical listings, with Canada No. 1 being the finest.

Purchasing

Fresh vegetables are sold by weight or count. They are packed in cartons referred to as cases, lugs, bushels, flats or crates. The weight or count packed in each of these containers varies depending on the size and type of vegetable as well as the packer. For example, celery is packed in 25-kg (55-lb.) cartons containing 18 heads, depending on the size of each head. Celery hearts, however, are packed in pairs in a cello pack of 12 per case.

Some of the more common fresh vegetables (e.g., onions, carrots, celery and lettuces) can be purchased from wholesalers trimmed, cleaned and cut according to your specifications. Although the unit price will be higher for diced onions than for whole onions, for example, the savings in time, labour, yield loss and storage space can be substantial. Processed vegetables may suffer a loss of nutrients, moisture and flavour, however.

Ripening

Although vegetables do not ripen in the same manner as fruits, they do continue to breathe (respire) after harvesting. The faster the respiration rate, the faster the produce ages or decays. This decay results in wilted leaves and dry, tough or woody stems and stalks. Respiration rates vary according to the vegetable variety, its maturity at harvest and its storage conditions after harvest.

Ripening proceeds more rapidly in the presence of ethylene gas. Ethylene gas is emitted naturally by fruits and vegetables and can be used to encourage further ripening in some produce, especially fruit-vegetables such as tomatoes. Items harvested and shipped when mature but green (unripe) are routinely exposed to ethylene gas to induce colour development (ripening) just before sale.

Storing

Some fresh vegetables are best stored at cool temperatures, between 4°C and 16°C (40°F and 60°F), ideally in a separate produce refrigerator. These include winter squash, potatoes, onions, shallots and garlic. If a produce refrigerator is not available, store these vegetables at room temperature in a dry area with good ventilation. Do not store them in a refrigerator set at conventional temperatures. Colder temperatures convert the starches in these vegetables to sugars, changing their texture and flavour.

Most other vegetables benefit from cold storage at temperatures between 2°C and 4°C (34°F and 40°F) with relatively high levels of humidity. Greens and other delicate vegetables should be stored away from apples, tomatoes, bananas and melons, as the latter give off a great deal of ethylene gas.

PURCHASING AND STORING PRESERVED VEGETABLES

Preservation techniques are designed to extend the shelf life of vegetables. These methods include irradiation, canning, freezing and drying. Except for drying, these techniques do not substantially change the vegetable's texture or flavour. Canning and freezing can also be used to preserve cooked vegetables.

Irradiated Vegetables and Other Foods

Exposing foods to controlled amounts of ionizing radiation is called irradiation. Three types are allowed: gamma rays, X-rays and electron beam radiation. The process allows microorganisms to be killed without raising the temperature of the food significantly. The Canadian Food Inspection Agency permits irradiation to (1) prevent food poisoning by reducing the level of harmful bacteria (such as E. coli 0157:H7 in ground beef and salmonella and *Campylobacter* in poultry) and parasites that cause food-borne diseases; (2) prevent spoilage by destroying bacteria, moulds and yeast that cause food to spoil; (3) control insect and parasite infestation; and (4) increase shelf life by slowing the ripening or sprouting in fresh fruits and vegetables. (For more information about irradiation, see the Canadian Food Inspection Agency's website at **www.inspection.gc.ca/english/fssa/concen/tipcon/irrade.shtml**, accessed May 25, 2010.)

Irradiated food is regarded as safe. Currently onions, potatoes, wheat, flour, whole wheat flour and whole or ground spices and dehydrated seasonings are approved for irradiation. Proposed additions are fresh and frozen ground beef; fresh and frozen poultry; prepackaged fresh, frozen, prepared and dried shrimp and prawns; and mangoes.

Irradiated foods must display the international symbol for irradiation (see Figure 22.1). The only exception is prepared food products in which less than 10% of the product is made from irradiated foods.

FIGURE 22.1 Irradiation symbol.

Canned Vegetables

Canned vegetables are an integral part of menu planning for many food service operations. In commercial canning, raw vegetables are cleaned and placed in a sealed container, then subjected to high temperatures for a specific period of time. Heating destroys the microorganisms that cause spoilage, and the sealed environment created by the can eliminates oxidation and retards decomposition. However, the heat required by the canning process also softens the texture of most vegetables and alters their nutritional content; many vitamins and minerals may be lost through the canning process. Green vegetables may also suffer colour loss, becoming a drab olive hue.

Canned vegetables are graded by the Canadian Food Inspection Agency as Canada Fancy, Grade Choice and Grade Substandard. Canada Fancy vegetables must be top quality, tender and free of blemishes. Canada Grade Substandard vegetables may lack uniformity or flavour, but can be used in casseroles or soups if cost is a concern.

Combinations of vegetables as well as vegetables with seasonings and sauces are available canned. For example, corn kernels are available canned in water, in seasonings and sauces, combined with other vegetables or creamed. Canned vegetables are easy to serve because they are essentially fully cooked during the canning process.

Hydroponics: Working Water

Hydroponics is the science of growing plants without soil in water. Plants are grown in an inert medium such as gravel, peat, sand or other sterile material. Nutrients are distributed in water that is circulated over the plant's roots. In a hydroponic farm, the temperatures and light are controlled to maximize production. Because hydroponic farms are indoors, plants can be grown in any climate; both Canada and Holland are major producers of vegetables grown under such conditions.

Canned vegetables are purchased in cases of standard-sized cans (see back endpapers). Canned vegetables can be stored for extended periods at room temperature. Once a can is opened, any unused contents must be transferred to an appropriate storage container and refrigerated. Cans with bulges or dents must be discarded immediately, without opening.

Frozen Vegetables

The Canadian Food Inspection Agency applies the same grading standards for frozen vegetables as for canned or preserved vegetables. Frozen vegetables are almost as convenient to use as canned. However, they often require some cooking, and expensive freezer space is necessary if an inventory is to be maintained. Regardless, freezing is a highly effective method for preserving vegetables. It severely inhibits the growth of microorganisms that cause spoilage without destroying many nutrients. Generally, green vegetables retain their colour, although the appearance and texture of most vegetables may be somewhat altered because of their high water content: ice crystals form from the water in the cells and burst the cells' walls.

Some vegetables are available individually quick frozen (IQF). This method employs blasts of cold air, refrigerated plates, liquid nitrogen, liquid air or other techniques to chill the vegetables quickly. By speeding the freezing process, the formation of ice crystals can be greatly reduced.

Combinations of vegetables as well as vegetables with seasonings and sauces are available frozen. Some frozen vegetables, such as mushrooms, onions and peppers, are raw when frozen; others are blanched before freezing so final cooking time is reduced. Many others are fully cooked before freezing and only need to be thawed or heated for service. Frozen vegetables generally do not need to be thawed before being heated. Once thawed or cooked, they should be stored in the refrigerator and reheated in the same manner as fresh vegetables. Do not refreeze previously frozen vegetables.

Frozen vegetables are graded in the same manner as canned vegetables. They are usually packed in cases containing 1- to 2.5-kg (2- to 5-lb.) boxes or bags. All frozen vegetables should be sealed in moisture-proof wrapping and kept at a constant temperature of –18°C (0°F) or below. Temperature fluctuations can draw moisture from the vegetables, causing poor texture and flavour loss. Adequate packaging also prevents freezer burn, an irreversible change in the colour, texture and flavour of frozen foods.

Dried Vegetables

Except for beans, peas, peppers, tomatoes and mushrooms, few vegetables are commonly preserved by drying. Unlike other preservation methods, drying dramatically alters flavour, texture and appearance. The loss of moisture concentrates flavours and sugars and greatly extends shelf life.

APPLYING VARIOUS COOKING METHODS

Vegetables are cooked in order to break down their cellulose and gelatinize their starches. Cooking gives vegetables a pleasant flavour, creates a softer, more tender texture, and makes them more digestible. Ideally, most vegetables should be cooked as briefly as possible in order to preserve their flavour, nutrients and texture. Unfortunately, sometimes you must choose between

---

SAFETY ALERT

Proper Washing of Vegetables

Surface contaminants from soil, water and handling must be removed from all vegetables before using to avoid the spread of food-borne illnesses. First, remove all labels, tags and ties. Wash whole produce under cold, running water. Soaking is not recommended nor is the use of soap or detergents. Potatoes, turnips and other root vegetables may be scrubbed with a clean brush to remove dirt. Water temperature should be 4.5°C (10°F) warmer than the produce being washed; cold water causes the surface of the vegetable to contract, creating a vacuum that can draw contaminated water into the plant. Refrigerate promptly and prevent cross-contamination during storage.

emphasizing appearance and maintaining nutrition, because cooking methods that preserve colour and texture often remove nutrients.

Acid/Alkali Reactions

The acid or alkaline content of the cooking liquid affects the texture and colour of many vegetables. (See Table 22.1.) This is of greater concern with moist-heat cooking methods, but it is also a consideration with dry-heat cooking methods, as they often call for blanched or parboiled vegetables.

Texture

The acidity or alkalinity of the vegetable's cooking liquid influences the finished product's texture. If an acid such as lemon juice, vinegar or wine is added to the liquid for flavouring, the vegetable will resist softening and will require a longer cooking time. Conversely, an alkaline cooking medium will quickly soften the vegetable's texture and may cause it to become mushy. Alkalinity also causes nutrient loss (especially thiamin) and may impart a bitter flavour. Alkalinity can be caused by tap water, detergent residue on utensils or the addition of baking soda (a base) to the cooking liquid.

Colour

The acidity or alkalinity of the liquid also affects the plant's pigments, causing both desirable and undesirable colour changes. There are three principal pigment categories: chlorophyll, carotenoid and flavonoid (which includes anthocyanins and anthoxanthins). A plant's unique colour is the result of a combination of these pigments. Chlorophyll pigments predominate in green vegetables such as spinach, green beans and broccoli. Carotenoid pigments predominate in orange and yellow vegetables such as carrots, tomatoes, red peppers and winter squashes. Anthocyanin and flavonoid pigments predominate in red, purple and white vegetables such as red cabbage, potatoes and cauliflower. Beets contain a pigment called betalain and are best peeled after cooking.

Initially, as vegetables are cooked, their original colours intensify. Exposure to heat makes pigments, especially chlorophyll, appear brighter. Exposure to acids and bases affects both chlorophyll and flavonoid pigments. Acids will gradually turn green vegetables an olive-drab colour, while a slight alkalinity promotes chlorophyll retention. The opposite occurs with vegetables containing flavonoids: they retain desirable colours in a slightly acidic environment

Metallic Reactions

Some pigments in vegetables react with metal ions. Anthocyanins (red) will react with tin or iron, turning bluish. Anthoxanthins (white) will darken with iron and turn yellowish with aluminum. Choose cooking pots accordingly.

TABLE 22.1	Acid/Alkali Reactions						
		Effect of Acid on		Effect of Alkali on		
Vegetable	Pigment Family	Colour	Texture	Colour	Texture	Cook Covered?
Spinach, Broccoli	chlorophyll	drab olive green	firm	bright green	mushy	no
Carrots, Tomatoes	carotenoid	no change	firm	no change	mushy	no difference
Cauliflower	flavonoid anthoxanthin	white	firm	yellow	mushy	yes
Red cabbage	flavonoid anthocyanins	red	firm	blue	mushy	yes

Note: Alkalinity always causes a loss of thiamin and other nutrients.

1. Spinach cooked with an acid (left) and an alkali.

2. Cauliflower cooked with an acid (left) and an alkali.

3. Red cabbage cooked with an acid (left) and an alkali.

while losing colours in an alkaline one. (Carotenoid is not affected by either acidity or alkalinity.) Colour changes alone do not affect flavour; however, the altered appearance can make the product so visually unappealing as to become inedible.

Colours also change as the naturally occurring acids in vegetables are released during cooking. If the cooking pan is kept covered, the acids can concentrate, creating richer flavonoid pigments but destroying chlorophyll pigments.

Guidelines for Vegetable Cookery

The following general guidelines for vegetable cookery should be considered regardless of the cooking method used:

1. Vegetables should be carefully cut into uniform shapes and sizes to promote even cooking and provide an attractive finished product.

2. Cook vegetables for as short a time as possible to preserve texture, colour and nutrients.

3. Cook vegetables as close to service time as possible. Holding vegetables in a steam table continues to cook them.

4. When necessary, vegetables may be blanched in advance, refreshed in ice water and refrigerated. They can then be reheated as needed.

5. White and red vegetables (those with flavonoid pigments) may be cooked with a small amount of acid such as lemon juice, vinegar or white wine to help retain their colour.

6. When preparing an assortment of vegetables, cook each type separately, then combine them. Otherwise some items will be overcooked in the time required to cook others properly.

Determining Doneness

There are so many types of vegetables, with such varied responses to cooking, that no one standard for doneness is appropriate. Each item should be evaluated on a recipe-by-recipe basis. Generally, however, most cooked vegetables are done when they are just tender when pierced with a fork or the tip of a paring knife. Leafy vegetables should be wilted but still have a bright colour.

You can avoid overcooking vegetables by remembering that some carryover cooking will occur through the residual heat contained in the foods. Always rely on objective tests—sight, feel, taste and aroma—rather than the clock.

Dry-Heat Cooking Methods

Broiling and Grilling

Broiling and grilling use high heat to cook vegetables quickly. This preserves their nutritional content and natural flavours. The radiant heat of the broiler or grill caramelizes the vegetables, creating a pleasant flavour that is not generally achieved when vegetables are cooked by other methods.

Selecting and Preparing Vegetables to Broil or Grill

Broiling is often used to cook soft vegetables such as tomatoes or items that might not rest easily on a grill rack. Broiling is also used to warm and brown items just before service. If necessary, the vegetables can be basted to prevent them from drying out under the broiler's direct heat. Sometimes a cooked vegetable is nappéed with sauce or clarified butter and placed briefly under the broiler as a finishing touch at service time.

A large range of vegetables can be grilled. Carrots, peppers, squashes, eggplants and similar vegetables should be cut into broad, thin slices. They can then be placed on the grill in the same manner as a portion of meat or fish to create attractive crosshatchings. (See Chapter 9, Principles of Cooking.) Smaller vegetables such as mushrooms, cherry tomatoes and pearl onions can be threaded onto skewers for easy handling. Bamboo or wooden skewers should be soaked in cold water for 15 minutes before using to help prevent them from burning on the grill or splintering.

Seasoning Vegetables to Be Broiled or Grilled

Vegetables contain little fat and therefore benefit greatly from added fat when being broiled or grilled. The added fat can be a brushing of clarified butter or a marinade such as one made from olive oil and herbs. Some vegetables may be brushed with butter and crusted with bread crumbs or Parmesan cheese before broiling (gratinée).

BASIC PROCEDURE FOR BROILING OR GRILLING VEGETABLES

1. Heat the grill or broiler.

2. Use a wire brush to remove any charred or burnt particles that may be stuck to the broiler or grill grate. The grate may be wiped with a lightly oiled towel to remove any remaining particles and help season it.

3. Prepare the vegetables to be broiled or grilled by cutting them into appropriate shapes and sizes, then seasoning, marinating or otherwise preparing them as desired or directed in the recipe.

4. Place the vegetables on the broiler grate, broiler platter or grill grate and cook to the desired doneness while developing the proper surface colour.

Grilling skewers of marinated vegetables

Grilled sliced vegetables as an accompaniment to an entree plate.

RECIPE 22.1

Approximate values per skewer:	
Calories	60
Total fat	2.5 g
Saturated fat	0 g
Cholesterol	0 mg
Sodium	534 mg
Total carbohydrates	8 g
Protein	2 g

APPLYING THE BASICS		RECIPE 22.1

Grilled Vegetable Skewers

Yield: 12 skewers

Marinade:		
Rice wine vinegar	125 mL	4 fl. oz.
Vegetable oil	250 mL	8 fl. oz.
Garlic, chopped	30 g	1 oz.
Dried thyme	3 g	2 tsp.
Salt	15 g	1 Tbsp.
Pepper	0.5 g	1/2 tsp.
Zucchini	175 g	6 oz.
Yellow squash	175 g	6 oz.
Broccoli florets, large	12	12
Cauliflower florets, large	12	12
Onions, large dice	24 pieces	24 pieces
Red bell pepper, large dice	12 pieces	12 pieces
Mushroom caps, medium	12	12

1. Combine all ingredients for the marinade and set aside.

2. Cut the zucchini and yellow squash into 1.25-cm-thick (1/2-in.) semicircles.

3. Blanch and refresh the zucchini, yellow squash, broccoli florets, cauliflower florets, onions and red bell pepper as discussed in the section called Moist-Heat Cooking Methods (page 544).

4. Drain the vegetables well and combine them with the marinade. Add the mushroom caps to the marinade. Marinate the vegetables for 30–45 minutes, remove and drain well.

5. Skewer the vegetables by alternating them on 10-cm (6-in.) bamboo skewers (presoaked in water).

6. Place the vegetable skewers on a hot grill and cook until done, turning as needed. The vegetables should brown and char lightly during cooking. Serve hot.

VARIATION: Grilled Sliced Vegetables—slice the vegetables and grill without skewering.

Roasting and Baking

The terms *roasting* and *baking* are used interchangeably when referring to vegetables. Roasting or baking is used to bring out the natural sweetness of many vegetables while preserving their nutritional values. The procedures are basically the same as those for roasting meats.

Selecting and Preparing Vegetables to Roast or Bake

Hearty vegetables such as winter squash and eggplant are especially well suited for roasting or baking. Vegetables such as onions, carrots and turnips are sometimes cooked alongside roasting meats or poultry. The vegetables add flavour to the finished roast and accompanying sauce, and the fats and juices released from the cooking roast add flavour to the vegetables.

Vegetables can be baked whole or cut into uniform-sized pieces. Squash, for example, is usually cut into large pieces. Vegetables may be peeled or left unpeeled, depending on the desired finished product.

Seasoning Vegetables to Be Roasted or Baked

Vegetables may be seasoned with salt and pepper and rubbed with butter or oil before baking, or they may be seasoned afterwards with a wide variety of herbs and spices. Some vegetables, such as winter squashes and sweet potatoes, may be flavoured with brown sugar or honey as well.

BASIC PROCEDURE FOR ROASTING OR BAKING VEGETABLES

1. Wash the vegetables. Peel, cut and prepare them as desired or directed in the recipe.

2. Season the vegetables and rub with oil or butter if desired.

3. Place the vegetables in a baking dish and bake in a preheated oven until done (tender).

APPLYING THE BASICS — RECIPE 22.2

Baked Butternut Squash

Yield: 4 125-g (4-oz.) servings

Butternut squash, medium dice	450 g	1 lb.
Salt and pepper	TT	TT
Cinnamon	0.25 g	1/4 tsp.
Cardamom, ground	0.15 g	1/8 tsp.
Brown sugar	25 g	2 Tbsp.
Lemon juice	30 mL	2 Tbsp.
Whole butter, melted	50 g	2 oz.

1. Place the squash in a buttered pan. Season with salt, pepper, cinnamon, cardamom and brown sugar.

2. Drizzle the lemon juice and butter over the top of the squash.

3. Bake, uncovered, in a 180°C (350°F) oven until tender, approximately 50 minutes.

Baked Butternut Squash

RECIPE 22.2

Approximate values per 125 g serving:	
Calories	160.3
Total fat	10.2 g
Saturated fat	6.3 g
Cholesterol	27.4 mg
Sodium	110.3 mg
Total carbohydrates	18.6 g
Protein	1.2 g

Sautéing or Stir-Frying

Sautéed or stir-fried vegetables should be brightly coloured and slightly crisp when done and show little moisture loss. When sautéing vegetables, all preparation must be complete before cooking begins, because timing is important and cooking progresses rapidly. Have all vegetables, herbs, spices, seasonings and sauces ready before you begin.

Selecting and Preparing Vegetables to Sauté or Stir-Fry

A wide variety of vegetables can be sautéed. Whatever vegetables are used, they should be cut into uniform-sized pieces to ensure even cooking.

Quick-cooking vegetables such as summer squashes, onions, greens, stalks, fruit-vegetables and mushrooms can be sautéed without any preparation except washing and cutting. Other vegetables such as Brussels sprouts, green beans, winter squashes, broccoli, cauliflower and most root vegetables are usually first

Vegetable Sauna

"Sweating vegetables" in a little oil over low heat in a covered pot is, in effect, a vegetable sauna. All of the flavors of the vegetables emerge slowly in a juicy tangle, in a much more intense manner than if you simply added them just-cut to a stock. Like roasting garlic, it is a way to enlarge the natural flavors very dramatically.

—from *China Moon Cookbook* by Barbara Tropp

blanched or otherwise partially cooked by baking, steaming or simmering. They are then sautéed to reheat and finish. Carrots, squash and other vegetables are sometimes finished by sautéing in butter and then adding a small amount of honey or maple syrup to glaze them. Some cooked vegetables are reheated by simply "sautéing" them in a small amount of stock or sauce.

Seasoning Vegetables to Be Sautéed or Stir-Fried

Sautéed vegetables can be seasoned with a great variety of herbs and spices. Seasonings should be added toward the end of the cooking process after all other ingredients have been incorporated in order to evaluate the flavour of the finished dish accurately.

Because sautéing vegetables uses slightly lower temperatures than sautéing meats and poultry, usually whole butter can be used in place of clarified butter. For additional flavours, fats such as bacon fat, olive oil, nut oils or sesame oil can be used in lieu of butter.

BASIC PROCEDURE FOR SAUTÉING VEGETABLES

1. Wash and cut the vegetables into uniform shapes and sizes.

2. Heat a sauté pan and add enough fat to just cover the bottom. The pan should be large enough to hold the vegetables without overcrowding.

3. When preparing an assortment of vegetables, add the ingredients according to their cooking times (first add the vegetables that take the longest to cook). Plan carefully so that all vegetables will be done at the same time. Do not overcrowd the pan; maintain high enough heat so the vegetables do not cook in their own juices.

4. Toss the vegetables using the sloped sides of the sauté pan or wok to flip them back on top of themselves. Do not toss more than necessary. The pan should remain in contact with the heat source as much as possible to maintain proper temperatures.

5. Add any sauces or vegetables with high water content, such as tomatoes, last.

6. Season the vegetables as desired with herbs or spices, or add ingredients for a glaze.

Stir-Fried Asparagus with Shiitake Mushrooms

APPLYING THE BASICS
RECIPE 22.3

Stir-Fried Asparagus with Shiitake Mushrooms

Yield: 450 g (1 lb.)

Asparagus	450 g	1 lb.
Shiitake mushrooms, fresh	175 g	6 oz.
Vegetable oil	15 mL	1 Tbsp.
Sesame oil	15 mL	1 Tbsp.
Garlic, chopped	8 g	2 tsp.
Oyster sauce	125 mL	4 fl. oz.
Crushed red chiles (optional)	TT	TT

continued

1. Wash the asparagus, trim the ends, peel the lower stalks and slice on the bias into 2.5- to 5-cm (1- to 2-in.) pieces.

2. Wash the mushrooms, trim off the stems and slice the caps into 1.25-cm (1/2-in.) slices.

3. Heat the oils in a wok or sauté pan.

4. Add the garlic and stir-fry for a few seconds.

5. Add the mushrooms and asparagus and stir-fry for 1 minute.

6. Add the oyster sauce and crushed red chiles (if using) and continue to stir-fry until the asparagus is nearly tender, approximately 3 minutes.

VARIATIONS: Substitute snow peas or green beans for asparagus.

RECIPE 22.3

Approximate values per 90 g serving:	
Calories	105
Total fat	6 g
Saturated fat	1 g
Cholesterol	8 mg
Sodium	848 mg
Total carbohydrates	10 g
Protein	4 g

Pan-Frying and Deep-Fat Frying

Pan-frying is not as popular as other techniques for cooking vegetables. Green tomatoes, however, are sometimes seasoned, floured and pan-fried; eggplant slices are seasoned, floured, pan-fried and used for eggplant Parmesan. When pan-frying vegetables, follow the procedures outlined in Chapter 9, Principles of Cooking.

Deep-fat frying is a popular method of preparing vegetables such as potatoes, squashes and mushrooms. They can be served as hors d'oeuvre, appetizers or accompaniments to a main dish. Starchy vegetables may be deep-fat fried plain. Most other vegetables are first breaded or battered. Vegetables can also be grated or chopped and incorporated into fritters or croquettes. Any deep-fat fried item should have a crisp, golden exterior with a tender, non-greasy centre. See Chapter 9, Principles of Cooking.

APPLYING THE BASICS **RECIPE 22.4**

Beer-Battered Onion Rings

Yield: 1 L (1 qt.), enough for approximately 1.5 kg (4 lb.) rings

Flour	300 g	10 oz.
Baking powder	7 g	2 tsp.
Salt	10 g	2 tsp.
White pepper	0.5 g	1/4 tsp.
Egg	1	1
Beer	500 mL	16 fl. oz.
Onions, whole	1.5 kg	4 lb.
Flour, for dredging	as needed	as needed

1. Sift the dry ingredients together.

2. Beat the egg in a separate bowl. Add the beer to the beaten egg.

3. Add the egg-and-beer mixture to the dry ingredients; mix until smooth.

4. Peel the onions and cut in 2-cm (1/2-in.) slices.

5. Break the slices into rings and dredge in flour.

6. Dip the rings in the batter a few at a time and fry at 190°C (375°F) until done. Drain on absorbent paper, season with additional salt and white pepper and serve hot.

RECIPE 22.4

Approximate values per 100 g serving:	
Calories	255
Total fat	11 g
Saturated fat	3 g
Cholesterol	6 mg
Sodium	510 mg
Total carbohydrates	34 g
Protein	4.5 g

continued

1. Beer-Battered Onion Rings: Dredging the onion rings in flour.

2. Dipping the floured rings in batter.

3. Frying the onion rings using the swimming method.

Moist-Heat Cooking Methods

Blanching and Parboiling

Blanching and parboiling are variations on boiling; the difference between them is the length of cooking time. Blanched and parboiled vegetables are often finished by other cooking methods such as sautéing.

Blanching is the partial cooking of foods in a large amount of boiling water for a very short period of time, usually only a few seconds. Besides preparing vegetables for further cooking, blanching is used to remove strong or bitter flavours, soften firm foods, set colours or loosen skins for peeling. Kale, chard, snow peas and tomatoes are examples of vegetables that are sometimes blanched for purposes other than preparation for further cooking.

Parboiling is the same as blanching, but the cooking time is longer, usually several minutes. Parboiling is used to soften vegetables and shorten final cooking times. Parboiling is commonly used for preparing root vegetables, cauliflower, broccoli and winter squashes.

Boiling

Vegetables are often boiled. Boiled vegetables can be served as is, or they can be further prepared by quickly sautéing with other ingredients, puréeing or mashing. Boiled vegetables are also chilled, then used in salads.

Starchy root vegetables are generally not boiled but rather simmered slowly so that the heat penetrates to their interiors and cooks them evenly. Green vegetables should be boiled quickly in a large amount of water in order to retain their colour and flavour.

Refreshing

Unless the boiled, blanched or parboiled vegetables will be eaten immediately, they must be quickly chilled in ice water after they are removed from the cooking liquid. This prevents further cooking and preserves (sets) their colours. This process is known as **refreshing** or **shocking** the vegetables.

● **blanching** very briefly and partially cooking a food in boiling water or hot fat; used to assist preparation (for example, to loosen peels from vegetables), as part of a combination cooking method, to remove undesirable flavours or to prepare a food for freezing

● **parboiling** partially cooking a food in a boiling or simmering liquid; similar to blanching but the cooking time is longer

● **refreshing** submerging a food in cold water to quickly cool it and prevent further cooking; also known as shocking; usually used for vegetables

The vegetables are removed from the ice water as soon as they are cold. Never soak or hold the vegetables in the water longer than necessary or valuable nutrients and flavour will be leached away.

Selecting and Preparing Vegetables to Boil

Nearly any type of vegetable can be boiled. Carrots, cabbages, green beans, turnips and red beets are just a few of the most common ones. Vegetables can be large or small, but they should be uniform in size to ensure even cooking. Some vegetables are cooked whole and only require washing before boiling. Others must be washed, peeled and trimmed or cut into smaller or more manageable sizes.

Seasoning Vegetables to Be Boiled

Often vegetables are boiled in nothing more than salted water. Lemon juice, citrus zest, wine and other acidic ingredients are sometimes added to white and red vegetables; if so, they should be added to the liquid before the vegetables. Herbs and spices in a sachet or a bouquet garni are often used to add flavour to boiled vegetables and should be added according to the recipe.

After boiling, vegetables are sometimes finished with herbs, spices, butter, cream or sauces.

BASIC PROCEDURE FOR BLANCHING AND REFRESHING/ BOILING VEGETABLES

1. Wash, peel, trim and cut the vegetables into uniform shapes and sizes.

2. Bring an adequate amount of water, stock, court bouillon or other liquid to a boil. The liquid should cover the vegetables and they should be able to move around freely without overcrowding.

3. Add seasonings if desired or as directed in the recipe.

4. Add the vegetables to the boiling liquid. If more than one vegetable is to be cooked and they have different cooking times, they should be cooked separately to ensure that all are cooked to the proper doneness. The pot may be covered if cooking white, red or yellow vegetables. Do not cover the pot when boiling green vegetables.

5. Cook the vegetables to the desired doneness.

6. Remove the vegetables from the water with a slotted spoon or a spider or drain through a colander.

7. Refresh the vegetables in ice water, drain and refrigerate until needed, or finish the hot boiled vegetables as desired and serve immediately.

1. Blanch, parboil or boil the vegetables to the desired doneness.

2. Remove the vegetables from the cooking liquid and submerge them in ice water just until they are cold.

APPLYING THE BASICS   RECIPE 22.5

Brussels Sprouts in Pecan Butter

Yield: 6 90-g (3-oz.) servings

Brussels sprouts	450 g	1 lb.
Whole butter	50 g	2 oz.
Pecans, chopped	125 g	4 oz.
Salt and pepper	TT	TT

1. Trim the Brussels sprouts and mark an X in the bottom of each with a paring knife to promote even cooking.
2. Boil the sprouts in salted water until tender, approximately 10 minutes.
3. Drain and hold the sprouts in a warm place.
4. Heat the butter in a sauté pan until it turns nut brown (beurre noisette). Add the pecans and toss to brown them.
5. Add the Brussels sprouts and toss to reheat and blend flavours. Adjust the seasonings and serve.

RECIPE 22.5

Approximate values per 90 g serving:	
Calories	227.9
Total fat	21.2 g
Saturated fat	5.4 g
Cholesterol	18.2 mg
Sodium	472 mg
Total carbohydrates	10.3 g
Protein	3.6 g

1. Brussels Sprouts in Pecan Butter: Marking an X in the bottom of each Brussels sprout.

2. Boiling the Brussels sprouts in the appropriate amount of water.

3. Tossing the Brussels sprouts with the butter and pecans.

BASIC PROCEDURE FOR COOKING DRIED BEANS

Dried beans are best rehydrated by soaking as discussed earlier and then cooking in a boiling (actually simmering) liquid. After rehydration and cooking, the beans can be served or further cooked in baked, sautéed or puréed dishes.

1. After soaking, place the drained beans in a heavy saucepan and cover with cold water or stock. Allow approximately three times as much liquid as there are beans. Add flavouring ingredients as directed in the recipe, but do not add acids or salt until the beans have reached the desired tenderness. Acids and salt cause the exterior of beans to toughen and resist any further efforts at tenderizing.
2. Slowly bring the liquid to a boil. Boil uncovered for 10 minutes or as directed in the recipe. Use a ladle to remove any scum that rises to the surface.
3. Cover and reduce the heat. Allow the mixture to simmer until the beans are tender. Whole beans generally require 1 to 2.5 hours, lentils 20 to 35 minutes and split peas 30 to 60 minutes. Add additional hot liquid if necessary. Do not stir the beans during cooking.
4. Drain the cooked beans in a colander.

APPLYING THE BASICS — RECIPE 22.6

Baked Beans

Yield: 2 kg (60 oz.)
Method: Baking

Great Northern beans, soaked	500 g	1 lb.
Onion, small dice	125 g	4 oz.
Bacon lardons	125 g	4 oz.
Anaheim chile, small dice	30 g	1 oz.
Molasses	100 mL	3 fl. oz.
Maple sugar	100 g	3 oz.
Ketchup	250 mL	8 fl. oz.
Dry mustard	2 g	1 tsp.
Cider vinegar	15 mL	1 Tbsp.
Worcestershire sauce	30 mL	2 Tbsp.
Instant coffee powder	2 g	1 Tbsp.
Salt and pepper	TT	TT

1. Simmer the beans in water until almost tender, approximately 45 minutes. Drain well.

2. Combine the remaining ingredients, blending well.

3. Add the sauce to the beans, tossing to coat thoroughly. Adjust the seasonings.

4. Place the beans in a hotel pan or a 2-L (2-qt.) baking dish. Cover and bake in a 180°C (350°F) oven until the beans are completely tender, approximately 30–40 minutes.

Baked Beans

RECIPE 22.6

Approximate values per 100 g serving:	
Calories	120
Total fat	3 g
Saturated fat	1 g
Cholesterol	5 mg
Sodium	1216 mg
Total carbohydrates	19 g
Protein	4.5 g

Steaming

Vegetables can be steamed in a convection steamer or by suspending them over boiling liquid on a rack set over a wok, saucepan or hotel pan. Vegetables can also be pan-steamed by cooking them in a covered pan with a small amount of liquid. Although the food will be touching the cooking liquid, most of the cooking is done by steam because only a small portion of the food is submerged in the liquid. Steamed vegetables can be eaten plain, partially cooked and sautéed lightly to finish, incorporated into casseroles or puréed. If they are not served immediately, they must be refreshed and refrigerated until used.

Properly steamed vegetables should be moist and tender. They generally retain their shape better than boiled vegetables. Vegetables cook very rapidly in steam and overcooking is a common mistake.

Selecting and Preparing Vegetables to Steam

Nearly any vegetable that can be boiled can also be steamed successfully. All vegetables should be washed, peeled and trimmed if appropriate and cut into uniform-sized pieces. Pan-steaming is appropriate for vegetables that are small or cut into fairly small pieces, such as peas and beans or broccoli and cauliflower florets.

Seasoning Vegetables to Be Steamed

Steaming produces vegetables with clean, natural flavours. Foods cooked in convection steamers can be seasoned with herbs and spices; but convection steamers use water to produce steam and the foods being cooked do not gain flavour from the cooking liquid. Vegetables steamed over liquids or pan-steamed in small amounts of liquids can be flavoured by using stocks or court bouillon as the cooking liquid. Herbs, spices and aromatic vegetables can be added to any liquid for additional flavour.

1. Broccoli Amandine: Placing the broccoli spears in a perforated pan for steaming.

2. Drizzling the browned almonds and butter over the broccoli for service.

RECIPE 22.7

Approximate values per 180 g serving:	
Calories	101
Total fat	7 g
Saturated fat	3.5 g
Cholesterol	15 mg
Sodium	453 mg
Total carbohydrates	8 g
Protein	4.5 g

BASIC PROCEDURE FOR STEAMING VEGETABLES

1. Wash, peel, trim and cut the vegetables into uniform shapes and sizes.
2. If a convection steamer is not being used, prepare a steaming liquid and bring it to a boil in a covered pan or doubleboiler.
3. Place the vegetables in a perforated pan in a single layer; do not crowd the pan. Place the pan over the boiling liquid, or add the vegetables to the liquid.
4. Cover the pan and cook to the desired doneness.
5. Remove the vegetables from the steamer and serve, or refresh and refrigerate until needed.

APPLYING THE BASICS	RECIPE 22.7

Broccoli Amandine

Yield: 8 servings

Broccoli, fresh	1 kg	2 lb.
Salt and pepper	TT	TT
Whole butter	50 g	2 oz.
Almonds, sliced	25 g	1 oz.
Garlic clove, minced	5 g	1
Lemon juice	50 mL	2 fl. oz.

1. Cut the broccoli into uniform spears. Rinse and sprinkle lightly with salt and pepper.
2. Place the broccoli in a single layer in a perforated hotel pan and cook in a convection steamer until tender but slightly crisp, approximately 3 minutes.
3. Melt the butter in a sauté pan. Add the almonds and garlic and cook just until the nuts are lightly browned.
4. Arrange the broccoli on plates for service and sprinkle with the lemon juice. Drizzle the almonds and butter over the broccoli and serve immediately.

Combination Cooking Methods

Braising and Stewing

Braised and stewed vegetables are cooked slowly in a small amount of liquid. The liquid, including any given off by the vegetables, is reduced to a light sauce, becoming part of the finished product. Generally, a braised dish is prepared with only one vegetable; a stew is a mixture of several vegetables. The main ingredients are sometimes browned in fat before the liquid is added in order to enhance flavour and colour.

Both braises and stews can be exceptionally flavourful because they are served with all of their cooking liquid. (Boiled vegetables lose some of their flavour to the cooking liquid.) Braised and stewed vegetables generally can be held hot for service longer than can vegetables prepared by other cooking methods.

Selecting and Preparing Vegetables to Braise or Stew

Various lettuces, especially romaine and Boston, are often braised. Cabbages, Belgian endive, leeks and many other vegetables are also commonly braised. Stews may contain a wide variety of vegetables such as summer squashes, eggplant, onions, peppers, tomatoes, carrots, celery and garlic. Leafy green vegetables and winter squashes are less commonly braised or stewed.

The vegetables should be washed and peeled or trimmed if appropriate. Vegetables to be braised may be left whole, cut into uniform pieces or shredded, as desired. Lettuces are usually cut into halves or quarters; cabbage is usually shredded.

Seasoning Vegetables to Be Braised or Stewed

Both braises and stews usually include flavouring ingredients such as garlic, herbs, bacon or mirepoix. The liquid may consist of water, wine, stock or tomato juice. Vegetables can even be braised in butter and sugar or honey to create a glazed dish.

Both braises and stews can be seasoned with a variety of herbs and spices. Add the seasonings before covering the pot to finish the cooking process. Strongly flavoured vegetables such as celery root and turnips are usually parboiled first in order to reduce their strong presence.

BASIC PROCEDURE FOR BRAISING AND STEWING VEGETABLES

1. Wash, peel, trim and cut the vegetables.
2. Sauté or sweat the flavouring ingredients in fat to release their flavours. Or sauté or sweat the main ingredients in fat.
3. For a braise, add the main ingredient in a single layer. For a stew, add the ingredients according to their cooking times or as directed in the recipe.
4. Add the cooking liquid; it should partially cover the vegetables. Bring the liquid to a boil, reduce to a simmer, cover and cook in the oven or on the stove top until done.
5. If desired, remove the main ingredients from the pan and reduce the sauce or thicken it with beurre manié, cornstarch or arrowroot. Then return the main ingredients to the sauce.

APPLYING THE BASICS   RECIPE 22.8

Braised Celery with Basil

Yield: 12 servings

Celery	3 heads	3 heads
Onion, small dice	250 g	8 oz.
Garlic, minced	10 g	2 tsp.
Whole butter	50 g	2 oz.
Olive oil	40 mL	1 fl. oz.
Fresh thyme	2 g	1 tsp.
Fresh basil, chiffonade	20 leaves	20 leaves
Dry white wine	250 mL	8 fl. oz.
Chicken stock	500 mL	1 pt.
Salt and pepper	TT	TT

continued

RECIPE 22.8

Approximate values per 90 g serving:	
Calories	60
Total fat	4.5 g
Saturated fat	1.5 g
Cholesterol	5 mg
Sodium	170 mg
Total carbohydrates	2 g
Protein	1 g

1. Trim the outer ribs from the celery heads, leaving only the tender hearts. Trim the heads to 15-cm (6-in.) lengths. Trim the root slightly, leaving each head together. Cut each head lengthwise into quarters.

2. Sauté the onions and garlic in the butter and olive oil, without colouring, until tender. Add the celery quarters to the pan and sauté, turning occasionally.

3. Add the thyme, basil, wine and chicken stock. Bring to a boil, reduce to a simmer, cover and braise (étuver) in the oven at 180°C (350°F) until tender, approximately 1 hour.

4. Remove the celery and reserve. Reduce the cooking liquid on the stove top until it thickens. Adjust the liquid's seasonings and return the celery to the pan to reheat. Serve the celery with a portion of the sauce.

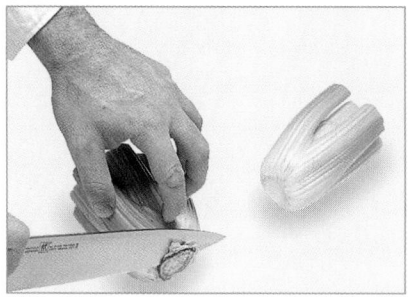
1. Braised Celery: Trimming and cutting the celery.

2. Adding the liquid to the celery.

3. Reducing the sauce.

Microwaving

Fresh vegetables are among the few foods that can be consistently well prepared in a microwave oven. Often microwave cooking can be accomplished without any additional liquid, thus preserving nutrients. With microwaving, colours and flavours stay true and textures remain crisp.

Microwave cooking is actually a form of steaming. As explained in Chapter 9, Principles of Cooking, microwaves agitate water molecules, thus creating steam. The water may be the moisture found naturally in the food or may be added specifically to create the steam.

Cooking time depends on the type of microwave oven as well as on the freshness, moisture content, maturity and quantity of vegetables being prepared.

Selecting and Preparing Vegetables to Microwave

Any vegetable that can be steamed successfully can be microwaved with good results. Because typical microwave ovens are relatively small, they are impractical for producing large quantities of food. They are most useful for reheating small portions of vegetables that have been blanched or partially cooked using another cooking method.

Seasoning Vegetables to Be Microwaved

Microwaving, like steaming, brings out the natural flavours of food and produces a clean, unadulterated flavour. Herbs and spices can be added to the vegetables before they are microwaved. Or, after microwaving, the vegetables can be tossed with butter, herbs and spices or combined with a sauce.

BASIC PROCEDURE FOR MICROWAVING VEGETABLES

1. Wash, peel, trim and cut the vegetables into uniform shapes and sizes.

2. Place the vegetables in a steamer designed for microwave use or arrange the vegetables on a microwaveable dish. Cover the vegetables with the lid or plastic wrap. If plastic wrap is used, it should be punctured to allow some steam to escape during cooking.

3. Cook the vegetables to the desired doneness, allowing for some carryover cooking. Or reheat the previously cooked vegetables until hot. Stir or turn the vegetables as necessary to promote even cooking.

4. Serve the vegetables or refresh and refrigerate until needed.

Puréeing

Puréeing is a technique often used with vegetables. Cooked vegetable purées can be served as is, stuffed into other vegetables or used as an ingredient in other preparations such as pumpkin pie, mashed potatoes or vegetable soufflés. Purées can also be bound with eggs, seasoned and used to make vegetable timbales and terrines.

Puréed vegetables are generally first cooked by baking, boiling, steaming or microwaving. White, red and yellow vegetables should be cooked until quite soft. They are more easily puréed when hot or warm; this also helps ensure a smooth finished purée. For most preparations, green vegetables must be refreshed after cooking and puréed while cold or they will overcook and become discoloured.

Seasoning Vegetables to Be Puréed

Vegetables for purées can be seasoned before they are puréed following the guidelines for the cooking procedure used. They can also be seasoned after they are puréed with a wide variety of ingredients such as herbs or spices, cheese, honey or brown sugar.

Finishing Puréed Vegetables

Purées can be finished with stocks, sauces, butter or cream to add richness and flavour. First purée the main ingredient, then add additional liquids to obtain the desired consistency.

BASIC PROCEDURE FOR PURÉEING VEGETABLES

1. Cook the vegetables. White, red and yellow vegetables should be cooked until very soft. Green vegetables should be cooked until tender but not overcooked to the point of being discoloured.

2. Purée the vegetables in a VCM, food processor or blender or by passing them through a food mill.

3. Season or finish the puréed vegetables as desired or directed in the recipe, or use them in another recipe.

RECIPE 22.9

Approximate values per 100 g serving:	
Calories	158
Total fat	8 g
Saturated fat	5 g
Cholesterol	24 mg
Sodium	291 mg
Total carbohydrates	21.5 g
Protein	2 g

APPLYING THE BASICS   RECIPE 22.9

Parsnip Purée

Yield: 2.5 kg (5 lb.)

Parsnips	2 kg	4 lb.
Russet potatoes	700 g	1 lb. 8 oz.
Cream, 35%, hot	250 mL	8 fl. oz.
Whole butter, melted	125 g	4 oz.
Salt and white pepper	TT	TT
Nutmeg	TT	TT

1. Peel the parsnips and potatoes and cut into large pieces of approximately the same size.

2. Boil the parsnips and potatoes separately in salted water until tender.

3. Drain the parsnips and potatoes well. Purée them together through a food mill.

4. Add the cream and butter and mix to combine. Adjust the consistency by adding cream as desired. Season the mixture with salt, white pepper and nutmeg and serve hot.

VARIATION: Substitute the parsnips with celeriac flavoured with saffron.

1. Parsnip Purée: Passing the parsnips and potatoes through a food mill.

2. The finished parsnip purée.

Conclusion

Vegetables are an essential part of the human diet. They provide the body with vitamins, minerals and fibre. They appeal to the appetite with taste, colour and texture. Increased market availability of fresh, high-quality vegetables as well as new hybrids gives you an ever-increasing variety of vegetables from which to choose. Vegetables are a relatively inexpensive food that can be prepared in limitless ways. They can be served as an entire meal or as an accompaniment to or as part of a wide variety of other dishes. And when cooking vegetables, remember what James Beard (1903–1985), the great American food consultant, culinary educator and writer once said: "No vegetable exists which is not better slightly undercooked."

Questions for Discussion

1. Explain how season affects the price, quality and availability of vegetables.

2. List and describe three processing techniques commonly used to extend the shelf life of vegetables.

3. What special concerns exist regarding the storage of fresh vegetables? Explain why some vegetables should not be refrigerated.

4. Why is it important to cut vegetables into a uniform size before cooking?

5. Discuss several techniques used for determining the doneness of vegetables. Is carryover cooking a concern when preparing vegetables? Explain your answer.

6. Discuss the role of acid in a cooking liquid used for preparing vegetables. Which vegetables, if any, benefit from an acidic cooking environment?

7. Describe the necessary mise en place and procedure for refreshing vegetables.

> ### Tempura
>
> Relatively new to Japanese cuisine, tempura originates from Portugal. The secret to excellent tempura is ice-cold batter and ice-cold ingredients. The tempura must be served immediately upon removal from the fryer.

Additional Vegetable Recipes

RECIPE 22.10

Tempura Shrimp and Vegetables with Dipping Sauce

Yield: 1 L (1 qt.), enough for 1.8 kg (4 lb.) of vegetables or shrimp

Sweet potato	250 g	8 oz.
Dipping sauce:		
Mirin	50 mL	2 fl. oz.
Soy sauce	100 mL	4 fl. oz.
Rice wine vinegar	50 mL	2 fl. oz.
Lemon juice	15 mL	1 Tbsp.
Wasabi powder	0.5 g	1 tsp.
Tempura batter:		
Eggs	2	2
Water, ice cold	450 mL	16 fl. oz.
Baking soda	0.5 g	1/4 tsp.
Flour, bread	220 g	6 oz.
Shrimp, 21/25 count, butterflied		
with tails on	1 kg	2 lb.
Mushrooms, small, whole	450 g	1 lb.
Zucchini, batonnet	250 g	8 oz.

1. Peel the sweet potato and cut in 6-mm (1/4-in.) slices. If the potato is large, cut each slice in half to make semicircles.

2. Combine all ingredients for the dipping sauce. Set aside.

3. To prepare the batter, beat the eggs and cold water until frothy.

4. Add the baking soda and flour to the egg-and-water mixture and mix until it is incorporated. There should still be small lumps in the batter. Overmixing develops gluten, which is undesirable. Keep the batter very cold.

5. Dry the shrimp well and keep them thoroughly chilled. Holding them by the tail, dip them into the batter and drop them into a 190°C (375°F) deep-fat fryer using the swimming method. Cook until done.

6. Drop the vegetables into the batter a few at a time. Remove them from the batter one at a time and drop them into the deep-fat fryer using the swimming method. Cook until batter is a pale, golden colour and crisp.

7. Arrange the tempura shrimp and vegetables on a serving platter and present immediately. Serve the dipping sauce on the side.

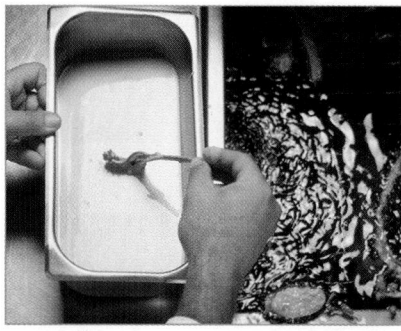

1. Battering the vegetables.

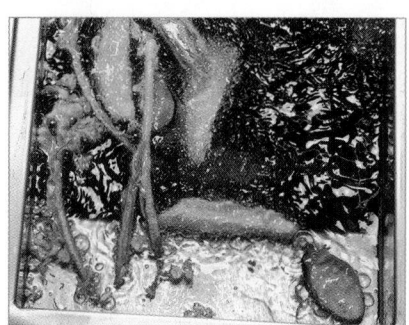

2. Frying the vegetables using the swimming method.

RECIPE 22.10

Approximate values per 125 g serving:	
Calories	500
Total fat	21 g
Saturated fat	4 g
Cholesterol	229 mg
Sodium	1543 mg
Total carbohydrates	42 g
Protein	29 g

Approximate values per 1/2 tomato:	
Calories	98
Total fat	6.5 g
Saturated fat	4 g
Cholesterol	16 mg
Sodium	92 mg
Total carbohydrates	10 g
Protein	1 g

Broiled Tomato

Glazing the onions in butter and sugar.

Approximate values per 60 g serving:	
Calories	78
Total fat	5 g
Saturated fat	3 g
Cholesterol	14 mg
Sodium	337 mg
Total carbohydrates	8 g
Protein	1 g

Approximate values per serving:	
Calories	83
Total fat	0 g
Saturated fat	0 g
Cholesterol	0 mg
Sodium	288 mg
Total carbohydrates	20 g
Protein	2 g

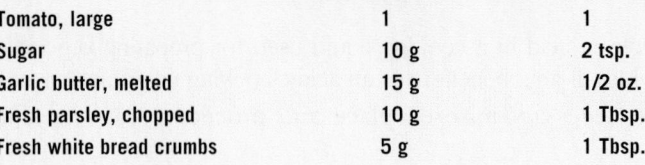

Broiled Tomato

Yield: 2 servings

Method: Broiling

Tomato, large	1	1
Sugar	10 g	2 tsp.
Garlic butter, melted	15 g	1/2 oz.
Fresh parsley, chopped	10 g	1 Tbsp.
Fresh white bread crumbs	5 g	1 Tbsp.

1. Core and halve the tomato.
2. Sprinkle sugar on top of each half. Place on a broiler platter and broil until tender.
3. Drizzle with garlic butter and garnish with parsley and bread crumbs.
4. Quickly brown crumbs under broiler.

Glazed Pearl Onions

Yield: 500 g (1 lb.)

Method: Boiling

Pearl onions, peeled	500 g	1 lb.
Whole butter	50 g	1-1/2 oz.
Sugar	20 g	1 Tbsp.
Salt and pepper	TT	TT

1. Place the onions, butter and sugar in a sauté pan and add enough water to barely cover.
2. Boil the onions, allowing the water to evaporate. As the water evaporates, the butter-and-sugar mixture will begin to coat the onions. When the water is nearly gone, test the doneness of the onions. If they are still firm, add a small amount of water and continue to boil until the onions are tender.
3. Sauté the onions in the butter-and-sugar mixture until they are glazed. Season to taste with salt and pepper.

VARIATIONS: Vegetables such as carrots, turnips, zucchini and other squashes can also be glazed using this procedure. They should be cut into appropriate shapes and be large enough so they glaze properly without overcooking. When preparing a mix of glazed vegetables, cook each type separately because each has a different cooking time.

Harvard Beets

Yield: 10 120-g (4-oz.) servings

Method: Boiling

Sugar	60 g	2 oz.
Cornstarch	15 g	2 Tbsp.
White wine vinegar	125 mL	4 fl. oz.
Salt and pepper	TT	TT
Beets, boiled, peeled, medium dice	1.2 kg	2 lb. 10 oz.

continued

1. Combine the sugar, cornstarch, vinegar, salt and pepper in a heavy saucepan. Whisk until the cornstarch and sugar dissolve.

2. Bring to a boil, then cook, stirring constantly, until the mixture is thick and clear.

3. Add the beets, stirring gently to coat. Serve warm.

VARIATIONS: Add 20 g (2 Tbsp.) orange zest or a pinch of cloves.

Maple-Glazed Carrots

RECIPE 22.14

Maple-Glazed Carrots

Yield: 10 120-g (4-oz.) servings
Method: Sautéing

Carrots	1.4 kg	3 lb.
Whole butter	100 g	3 oz.
Salt and pepper	TT	TT
Maple syrup	100 mL	3 fl. oz.
Fresh parsley, chopped	20 g	2 Tbsp.

1. Peel the carrots and cut into a shape such as oblique, turned or rondelle.

2. Parboil the carrots in salt water and refresh. The carrots should be firm.

3. Sauté the carrots in butter until nearly tender.

4. Season with salt and pepper and add the maple syrup. Garnish with the parsley.

RECIPE 22.14

Approximate values per serving:	
Calories	169
Total fat	8.4 g
Saturated fat	5.1 g
Cholesterol	26 mg
Sodium	328 mg
Total carbohydrates	24 g
Protein	1.6 g

Creamed Corn with Basil

RECIPE 22.15

Creamed Corn with Basil

Yield: 10 120-g (4-oz.) servings
Method: Sautéing

Corn	12 ears	12 ears
Onion, small dice	125 g	4 oz.
Whole butter	60 g	2 oz.
Cream, 10%	250 mL	8 fl. oz.
Basil leaves, chopped	10 g	2 Tbsp.
Salt and white pepper	TT	TT

1. Cut the kernels from the ears of corn.

2. Sauté the onion in the butter without browning.

3. Add the corn and sauté until hot.

4. Add the cream. Bring to a boil, simmer to reduce slightly. When the corn is tender, add the basil and season with salt and white pepper.

RECIPE 22.15

Approximate values per serving:	
Calories	211
Total fat	14 g
Saturated fat	8 g
Cholesterol	44 mg
Sodium	277 mg
Total carbohydrates	19 g
Protein	3 g

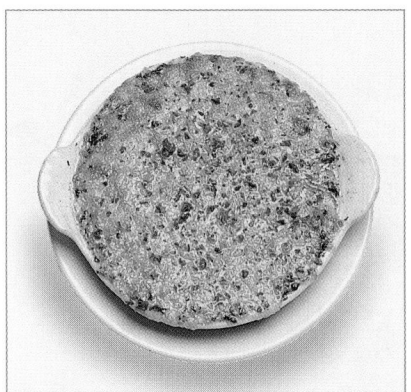

Spinach au Gratin

RECIPE 22.16

Approximate values per 225 g serving:	
Calories	457
Total fat	33 g
Saturated fat	21 g
Cholesterol	101 mg
Sodium	782 mg
Total carbohydrates	16 g
Protein	26 g

RECIPE 22.16

Spinach au Gratin

**Yield: 8 225-g (8-oz.) servings as an entree,
16 servings as a side vegetable**
Method: Gratin

Clarified butter	60 mL	2 fl. oz.
Flour	30 g	1 oz.
Cream, 18%, warm	450 mL	1 pt.
Garlic cloves, minced	10 g	2
Spinach, fresh chopped	1.1 kg	2 lb. 8 oz.
Salt, pepper and nutmeg	TT	TT
Cheddar or Swiss cheese, shredded	650 g	1 lb. 8 oz.

1. Heat half the butter in a saucepan. Add the flour and cook to make a blond roux.
2. Add the cream, whisking to remove any lumps of roux. Bring to a simmer and cook for 15 minutes.
3. Sauté the garlic in the remaining clarified butter. Add spinach and cook for 2 minutes. Remove from the heat and drain well.
4. Combine the hot spinach with the cream sauce and adjust the seasonings.
5. Fill 16 150-mL (3/4-cup) gratin dishes with the creamed spinach. Top each with 40 g (1-1/2 oz.) shredded cheese and place under the broiler until the cheese is melted and browned and the spinach is very hot. Serve immediately.

Ratatouille

RECIPE 22.17

Approximate values per serving:	
Calories	92
Total fat	7.2 g
Saturated fat	1 g
Cholesterol	0 mg
Sodium	587 mg
Total carbohydrates	7 g
Protein	1.6 g

RECIPE 22.17

Ratatouille

Yield: 10 100-g (3-oz.) servings
Method: Sautéing

Eggplant, medium dice	175 g	6 oz.
Onion, medium dice	175 g	6 oz.
Garlic, chopped	5 g	1-1/2 tsp.
Olive oil	75 mL	2 fl. oz.
Green bell pepper, medium dice	100 g	3 oz.
Red bell pepper, medium dice	100 g	3 oz.
Zucchini, medium dice	125 g	4 oz.
Mushrooms, quartered	175 g	6 oz.
Tomato concassée	350 g	12 oz.
Fresh basil, chiffonade	15 g	1/2 oz.
Salt	15 g	1/2 oz.
Pepper	TT	TT
Tomato purée	as needed	as needed

1. Lightly salt the diced eggplant and allow to drain for 45 minutes in a colander.
2. Sauté the onion and garlic in the olive oil.
3. Add the peppers, eggplant, zucchini and mushrooms. Sauté until tender, approximately 10 minutes.
4. Add the tomato, fresh basil and seasonings. Stew for 5 minutes. Adjust the seasonings. If the sauce is too thin, add a small amount of tomato purée to thicken.

VARIATION: Fresh herbs such as oregano, thyme or others may also be used.

RECIPE 22.18

Socca

SHAW CONFERENCE CENTRE, Edmonton, AB
Executive Chef Simon Smotkowicz, CCC

Yield: 4 side dishes/appetizers
Method: Broiling

Chickpea flour	175 g	1-1/2 cups
Extra virgin olive oil	150 mL	2/3 cup
Salt	3 g	1/2 tsp.
Thyme, chopped	0.5 g	1/2 tsp.
Rosemary, chopped	0.5 g	1/2 tsp.
Water	450 mL	16 fl. oz.
Black peppercorns, cracked	TT	TT

1. Combine chickpea flour, 75 mL (2-1/2 fl. oz.) olive oil, salt, herbs and water. Mix and let rest for 1 hour in refrigerator.
2. Preheat a cast-iron frying pan to moderate heat. Preheat broiler/salamander.
3. Ladle batter in pan to coat like a crepe.
4. Place pan under broiler for 2–3 minutes.
5. Remove pan, sprinkle a little olive oil on crepe, return to broiler until flat bread is crisp and golden.
6. Sprinkle with pepper, slide onto plate, keep warm and repeat process.
7. Cut Socca into wedges and serve with ratatouille and cheese.

Simon Smotkowicz, CCC

Simon has been a member and a leader of award-winning Canadian culinary teams for many years, managing Team Canada to a world championship in Glasgow in 1997 and 2001. In 1995 he was elected Chef of the Year for the Western Region by his peers in the CFCC, now the CCFCC.

RECIPE 22.18

Approximate values per 45 g serving:	
Calories	462
Total fat	37 g
Saturated fat	5 g
Cholesterol	0 mg
Sodium	305 mg
Total carbohydrates	27 g
Protein	8.5 g

RECIPE 22.19

Braised Red Cabbage with Apples and Wine

Yield: 10 120-g (4-oz.) servings
Method: Braising

Red cabbage	1 kg	2 lb.
Bacon, medium dice	250 g	8 oz.
Onion, medium dice	150 g	5 oz.
Cider vinegar	50 mL	1-1/2 fl. oz.
Red wine	150 mL	5 fl. oz.
Salt and pepper	TT	TT
White stock	150 mL	5 fl. oz.
Cinnamon sticks	1	1
Medium potato, grated (optional)	100 g	1
Apples, tart, cored and shredded	225 g	8 oz.
Brown sugar	20 g	1/2 oz.
Red currant jelly	80 mL	3 fl. oz.

1. Julienne the cabbage.
2. Render the bacon. Add the onion and sweat in the bacon fat until tender.
3. Add the cabbage and moisten with vinegar and wine. Season with salt and pepper. Add the stock, cinnamon sticks and the potato, if using. Cover and braise until the cabbage is almost tender, approximately 30 minutes. Moisten with additional stock if necessary. (See Variation.)
4. Add the apples, brown sugar and red currant jelly and mix well.
5. Cover and braise until the apples are tender and dissolved, approximately 5 minutes.

Variation: Traditionally, braised red cabbage is thickened with raw grated potato. One medium potato may be added in Step 3.

Braised Red Cabbage with Apples and Wine

RECIPE 22.19

Approximate values per serving:	
Calories	150
Total fat	2.6 g
Saturated fat	0.8 g
Cholesterol	15 mg
Sodium	598 mg
Total carbohydrates	23 g
Protein	8 g

John Cloutier, CCC

John Cloutier is a Chef Instructor for Food and Service Resource Group in Vancouver. He has served on the board of directors of the BC Chefs' Association since 1986, earning Chef of the Year in 1997 and many other awards. His commitment is to the education of young culinarians.

RECIPE 22.20

Approximate values per serving:	
Calories	318
Total fat	19 g
Saturated fat	11 g
Cholesterol	53 mg
Sodium	308 mg
Total carbohydrates	29 g
Protein	11 g

RECIPE 22.20

Artichoke and Mushroom Strudel

FOOD AND SERVICE RESOURCE GROUP, VANCOUVER, BC
John Cloutier, CCC

Yield: 10 servings
Method: Baking

Mushrooms, sliced	1.5 kg	3 lb. 4 oz.
Butter	40 g	1-1/2 oz.
Onion, brunoise	350 g	12 oz.
Garlic, fine chopped	30 g	6 cloves
Olive oil	15 mL	1 Tbsp.
Gewürztraminer (a white wine varietal)	100 mL	3-1/2 fl. oz.
Cornstarch	50 g	6 Tbsp.
Artichoke hearts, tinned, sliced, juice reserved	2 × 450 g	2 × 16 oz.
Chicken or vegetable stock	500 mL	16 fl. oz.
Thyme, minced	3 g	1 tsp.
Marjoram, minced	10 g	1 Tbsp.
Cream, 35%	125 mL	4 fl. oz.
Feta cheese, crumbled	150 g	5 oz.
Salt and pepper	TT	TT
Phyllo sheets	4	4
Butter, clarified	60 g	2 oz.

1. Sweat the mushrooms in butter until soft.
2. In a separate pan, sauté the onion and garlic in olive oil until golden. Deglaze with white wine, then add to the mushrooms.
3. Dissolve the cornstarch in the artichoke juice and add to the mushrooms; bring to a boil and add the stock.
4. Add the artichokes, thyme and marjoram and simmer for 10 minutes. Add the cream and feta and simmer 1 minute. Adjust seasonings. Remove from heat and cool overnight.
5. Butter each sheet of phyllo and stack on top of one another.
6. Place the chilled filling at one end of the phyllo and roll up like a log, tucking in the sides as you roll. Brush with more butter and make a slit in the top of the roll to allow steam to escape.
7. Bake at 175°C (350°F) until golden brown. Let rest for 15 minutes. Slice and serve warm.

RECIPE 22.21

Shrimp Charlotte with Eggplant Wrap

CAMBRIAN COLLEGE, SUDBURY, ON
Chef/Professor Kimberly Coates

Yield: 4 servings

Shrimp, 21/25, shell on	500 g	1 lb.
Eggplant	1	1
Extra virgin olive oil	50 mL	2 fl. oz.
Tomatoes, ripe	2	2
Thyme leaves, fresh	5 g	2 tsp.
Tarragon, fresh, chopped	8 g	2 tsp.
Salt and pepper	TT	TT
Green onions, bias cut	6	6
Red bell pepper, julienne	175 g	1
Yellow bell pepper, julienne	175 g	1
Fish stock	200 mL	7 fl. oz.
Egg white	1	1
Saffron threads	0.25 g	few
Gelatin	6 g	1 sheet
Chives, minced	5 g	2 tsp.
Sauce:		
Shrimp stock	125 mL	4 fl. oz.
Dijon mustard	5 mL	1 tsp.
Balsamic vinegar	50 mL	2 fl. oz.
Peanut oil	200 mL	7 fl. oz.
Salt and pepper	TT	TT
Truffle, slices	4	4

Kimberly Coates
Kim was born and raised in Sudbury, Ontario, and started cooking when she was 17. After completing her apprenticeship, she worked as Chef at the Ontario Provincial Government Building in Sudbury, later moving to Science North, then operating a small catering business. For the past 10 years, Kim has been Chef/Professor and Coordinator of Culinary Programs at Cambrian College in Sudbury. She is a member of both the Canadian Culinary Federation and Women Chefs and Restaurateurs (out of Louisville, Kentucky).

1. Peel and devein the shrimp. Reserve the shells and fortify the fish stock for the sauce.

2. Slice the eggplant lengthways 6 mm (1/4 in.). Lightly salt eggplant and allow it to drain. Brush with some of the olive oil and grill, leaving marks visible. Cool.

3. Peel the tomatoes, cut in half and remove excess seeds. Fry the halves lightly in a small amount of olive oil with the thyme and tarragon. Season lightly with salt and pepper.

4. In the remaining olive oil, sauté the green onions and peppers briefly. Add 50 mL of the fish stock and simmer for 1 minute; drain, reserving the liquid. Chill and reserve the peppers.

5. Poach the shrimp in the cooking liquid from the peppers, adding a bit of water if necessary. Chill the shrimp and reserve the poaching liquid.

6. Cool the poaching liquid, add a lightly beaten egg white and reheat the stock to clarify. Dissolve the saffron threads and the gelatin leaf in the clarified stock.

7. Add the chives to the aspic and cool slightly.

8. For the sauce, boil the shrimp shells in 150 mL of fish stock. Strain and reserve (you should have 125 mL). Cool the stock.

9. Mix the mustard and vinegar with the shrimp stock. Blend while pouring in the peanut oil to emulsify the sauce. Adjust the seasonings.

10. To assemble the charlotte, line 4 ring moulds with slices of eggplant cut in half lengthways to form strips. Place a half tomato in each and drizzle with some of the cooking oil. Top with the pepper onion mixture. Arrange 5 shrimp on each charlotte. Brush lightly with the chive aspic. Place a slice of truffle on top.

11. Place the charlotte on serving plates and remove the ring. Spoon a portion of the sauce around the base.

RECIPE 22.21

Approximate values per serving:

Calories	748
Total fat	61 g
Saturated fat	10 g
Cholesterol	192 mg
Sodium	660 mg
Total carbohydrates	23 g
Protein	32 g

Anne Milne

Having previously held various positions as Executive Chef, including the Butchart Gardens in Victoria and Shangri La Hotels in China, Anne has been a self-employed chef-consultant since 1993. Her company, Kitchen Arts Management, offers services that range from consulting and development to training. She is a home meal replacement specialist and a certified FOODSAFE instructor.

RECIPE 22.22

Approximate values per appetizer:	
Calories	320
Total fat	9 g
Saturated fat	4 g
Cholesterol	22 mg
Sodium	418 mg
Total carbohydrates	39 g
Protein	15 g

RECIPE 22.22

Roasted Vegetable and Bocconcini Stacks on Polenta Rounds

KITCHEN ARTS MANAGEMENT, Vancouver, BC
Chef-Consultant Anne Milne

Yield: 8 appetizers or 4 main course servings
Method: Roasting

Cornmeal	150 g	1 cup
Butter	10 g	2 tsp.
Salt	5 g	1 tsp.
Japanese eggplant, cut into		
1-cm (1/2-in.) rounds	2 large	2 large
Roma tomatoes, cut into		
1-cm (1/2-in.) rounds	4 large	4 large
Zucchini, cut into		
1-cm (1/2-in.) rounds	2 medium	2 medium
Red onions, cut into		
1-cm (1/2-in.) rounds	2 medium	2 medium
Shiitake mushrooms	250 g	8 oz.
Salt and fresh cracked pepper	as needed	as needed
Olive oil	15 mL	1 Tbsp.
Balsamic vinegar	10 mL	2 tsp.
Mozzarella (bocconcini balls), fresh	250 g	8 oz.
Fresh basil leaves	4 large	4 large
Rosemary stems, fresh	4 or 8	4 or 8
Marinara sauce	500 mL	16 fl. oz.

1. To make the polenta, boil 1 L (4 cups) water in a heavy-bottomed pot. Whisk in cornmeal in a slow, steady stream. Stir over reduced heat until cooked, approximately 15 minutes. Stir in butter and salt.

2. Pour the polenta into a greased cookie sheet and spread to 1-cm (1/2-in.) thickness. Cool and cut out circles with a cookie cutter. (Large circles are used for main course and smaller circles for appetizers.)

3. Sprinkle vegetables with salt and pepper and drizzle with olive oil. Heat oven to 225°C (450°F) and brush olive oil on 2 cookie sheets. Spread the vegetables on the sheets and roast in the oven until tender and just starting to brown. (Vegetables may also be grilled.) Remove from oven and sprinkle with balsamic vinegar. Let cool.

4. Arrange the polenta circles on a clean, oiled baking sheet and stack the vegetables and cheese in the following order on top of each polenta round: polenta, bocconcini, one fresh basil leaf, red onion, eggplant, zucchini, tomato and shiitake mushrooms. Secure the stacks by spearing them with a bamboo skewer. Coat tops of stacks with olive oil and bake in a 190°C (375°F) oven for approximately 10 minutes, or just until cheese begins to melt.

5. Remove from the oven and replace the bamboo skewers with a stem of fresh rosemary. Serve stacks on a thin layer of marinara sauce.

> When you become a good cook, you become a good craftsman, first.
> You repeat and repeat and repeat until your hands
> know how to move without thinking about it.

Jacques Pépin, French chef and teacher (1935–)

Fingerlings

Purple Potatoes

Potatoes, grains (corn, rice, wheat and others) and pastas are collectively known as starches. Some of these foods are vegetables; others are grasses. Pastas, of course, are prepared products made from grains. Starches are, for the most part, staple foods: foods that define a cuisine and give it substance. All are high in starchy carbohydrates, low in fat and commonly used as part of a well-balanced meal.

Today's chefs are rediscovering traditional and ethnic dishes that rely on grains seldom used in typical food service operations. Pasta, made from a variety of grains in numerous shapes and flavours and accompanied by countless sauces and garnishes, now regularly appears on many menus alongside the ubiquitous potato prepared in many classic and modern styles.

POTATOES

Potatoes (Fr. *pommes de terre*) are one of the few vegetables native to the New World, probably originating in the South American Andes. Botanically, potatoes are succulent, nonwoody annual plants and members of the nightshade family. The portion we consume is the tuber, the swollen fleshy part of the underground stem. Potatoes are hardy and easy to grow, making them inexpensive and widely available.

Identifying Potatoes

The following are some of the more commonly used types of potatoes. Other varieties are regularly being developed or rediscovered and tested in the marketplace.

Choose potatoes that are heavy and very firm with clean skin and few eyes. Avoid those with many eyes, sprouts, green streaks, soft spots, cracks or cut edges. Most varieties are available all year. New potatoes are small, immature potatoes (of any variety) that are harvested before their starches develop. Although red potatoes can be "new," not all new potatoes are necessarily red-skinned. Conversely, not all red-skinned potatoes are new. True new potatoes are waxy with a high moisture content and a thin, delicate skin.

Fingerlings

Fingerling potatoes are typically heirloom varieties, related to the original potato varieties from the Andes. They are generally small, long and finger-shaped or oblong with good flavour. The Russian Banana looks like a small banana and has a firm texture and rich, buttery flavour. The red-streaked French Fingerling has a nutty flavour, while the red Ruby Crescent has a strong, earthy flavour. All fingerling varieties tend to be low in starch and are good for roasting and in potato salads.

Purple Potatoes

Purple (or blue) potatoes have a deep purple skin. The flesh is bright purple, becoming lighter when cooked. They are mealy, with a flavour and texture similar to russets. The most common varieties are All Blue and Caribe, which were quite popular in the mid-19th century.

Red Potatoes

Red potatoes have a thin red skin and crisp, white, waxy flesh, best suited to boiling or steaming. They do not have the dry, mealy texture successful baking requires.

Red Potatoes

Russet Potatoes

Russet potatoes, also referred to as Idaho potatoes, are the standard baking potato. They are long with rough, reddish-brown skin and mealy flesh. Russets are excellent baked and are the best potatoes for frying. They tend to fall apart when boiled. They are marketed in several size categories and should be purchased in the size most appropriate for their intended use.

Russet Potatoes

White Potatoes

White potatoes are available in round or long varieties. They have a thin, tender skin with a tender, waxy yellow or white flesh. The smaller ones are sometimes marketed as new potatoes (not to be confused with new red potatoes). Round white potatoes are also referred to as all-purpose potatoes. White Rose is a common variety. Bintje (Finnish Yellow) is an increasingly popular variety; it has a golden skin, creamy flesh and buttery flavour. Another variety of white potato known as the Yukon Gold, first bred in Canada, is a medium-sized, slightly flattened, oval potato. It has a delicate pale yellow skin with shallow pink eyes. Its pale yellow flesh has a creamy texture and rich, buttery, nutty flavour. Yukon Gold potatoes are suitable for most cooking methods and will retain their yellow colour when baked, boiled or fried. White potatoes are usually cooked with moist heat or used for sautéing.

White Potatoes

Yukon Gold Potatoes

Sweet Potatoes

Sweet potatoes are from a different botanical family than ordinary potatoes, although they are also tubers that originated in the New World. Two types are commonly available. One has yellow flesh and a dry, mealy texture; it is known as a boniato, white or Cuban sweet potato. The other has a darker orange, moister flesh and is high in sugar; it is known as a red sweet potato. Both types have thick skins ranging in colour from light tan to brownish red. (Sometimes dark-skinned sweet potatoes are erroneously labelled *yams*.) Sweet potatoes should be chosen according to the desired degree of sweetness. They are best suited for boiling, baking and puréeing, although the less sweet varieties can be deep-fat fried. The cooked flesh can also be used in breads, pies and puddings. Sweet potatoes are available canned, often in a spiced or sugary sauce.

Sweet Potatoes

Yams

Yams are a third type of tuber, botanically different from both sweet and common potatoes. Yams are less sweet than sweet potatoes, but they can be used interchangeably. The flesh of yams ranges from creamy white to deep red. Yams are Asian in origin and are now found in Africa, South America and the southern United States.

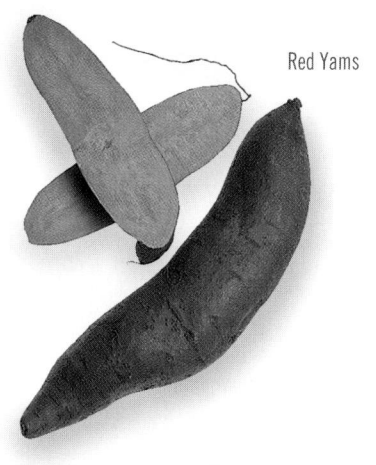
Red Yams

Nutrition

Potatoes contain a high percentage of easily digested complex carbohydrates and little or no fat. They are also a good source of many minerals and some vitamins.

Purchasing and Storing Potatoes
Mealy vs. Waxy

One of the most important considerations in selecting potatoes is choosing between the mealy and waxy varieties. You should understand the differences and purchase the type best suited to your needs. See Table 23.1.

Mealy potatoes (also known as starchy potatoes) have a high starch content and thick skin. They are best for baking and are often ordered from suppliers simply as "bakers." Their low sugar content also allows them to be deep-fat fried long enough to cook the interior fully without burning the exterior. Mealy potatoes tend to fall apart when boiled, making them a good choice for whipped or puréed potatoes.

Waxy potatoes have a low starch content and thin skin. They are best for boiling. They will not develop the desired fluffy texture when baked. Because of their high moisture content, they tend to become limp and soggy when deep-fat fried.

Grading

Potatoes sold in Canada are graded according to size and cleanliness. Canada No. 1 grade potatoes must be "reasonably free from dirt" with "not more than a slight amount of loose dirt or foreign material in the container." Round varieties of potatoes must have a minimum diameter of 57 mm (2-1/4 in.) and a maximum diameter of 89 mm (3-1/2 in.) to be graded as Canada No. 1. Long varieties must have a minimum diameter of 51 mm (2 in.) and a maximum diameter of 70 mm (2-3/4 in.). New potatoes must have a minimum diameter of 48 mm (1-7/8 in.) to be graded Canada No. 1.

Canada No. 2 grade potatoes have an "appreciable amount of dirt adhering to them" and "there is not more than a moderate amount of loose dirt or foreign material in the container" with them. Canada No. 2s must have a minimum diameter of 44 mm (1-3/4 in.) and a maximum diameter of 114 mm (4-1/2 in.).

Purchasing

Potatoes are usually packed in 22-kg (50-lb.) cartons. Counts vary depending on average potato size. For example, in a 100-count carton, each potato would weigh an average of 250 g (8 oz.). Eighty-, 90- and 100-count cartons are the most common. Generally, larger-sized potatoes (i.e., smaller counts) are more expensive. Size does not affect quality, however, and selection should be based on intended use.

Storing

Temperatures between 7°C and 10°C (45°F and 50°F) are best for storing potatoes. Do not store potatoes in the refrigerator. At temperatures below 4°C

- **mealy potatoes** also known as starchy potatoes; those with a high starch content and thick skin; they are best for baking

- **waxy potatoes** those with a low starch content and thin skin; they are best for boiling

TABLE 23.1	Comparison of Mealy and Waxy Potatoes							
		Content of			Best to			
		Starch	Moisture	Sugar	Bake	Boil	Sauté	Deep-fat fry
Mealy: russet, White Rose, purple		high	low	low	✓			✓
Waxy: red, new (red), Bintje, Yukon Gold		low	high	high		✓	✓	

(40°F) potato starch turns to sugar, making the cooked product too sweet and increasing the risk that the potato will turn grey or streaky when cooked. Potatoes with a high sugar content also burn more easily when fried.

Potatoes should be stored in a dark room, as light promotes chlorophyll production, turning them green and bitter. Any green patches indicate the possible presence of solanine, a toxin harmful if eaten in large amounts, and should be peeled away. Solanine is also present in the eyes and sprouts and they, too, should be removed and discarded before cooking.

Under proper conditions, fresh potatoes should last for two months. Do not wash potatoes until ready to use, as washing promotes spoilage.

Once peeled, potatoes should be stored covered in cold water and refrigerated to prevent oxidative enzymatic browning.

Applying Various Cooking Methods

Potatoes have a relatively neutral flavour, making them a perfect accompaniment to many savoury dishes. They can be prepared with almost any dry- or moist-heat cooking method: baking, sautéing, pan-frying, deep-fat frying, boiling or steaming. They can be combined with other ingredients in braises and stews. Potatoes are used in soups (vichyssoise), dumplings (gnocchi), breads, pancakes (latkes), puddings, salads and even vodka.

Many potato dishes, both classic and modern, employ more than one cooking method. For example, lorette potatoes require boiling and deep-fat frying; hash browns require parboiling, then sautéing. Even french fries are best when first blanched in hot oil.

Determining Doneness

Most potatoes are considered done when they are soft and tender or offer little resistance when pierced with a knife tip. Fried potatoes should have a crisp, golden-brown surface; the interior should be moist and tender.

Roasting and Baking

Potatoes may be roasted with meat or poultry, becoming coated with the fat and drippings released from the main item as it cooks. Either mealy or waxy potatoes, peeled or unpeeled, can be roasted successfully.

Mealy potatoes such as russets are ideal for baking. The skin is left intact, although it may be pierced with a fork to allow steam to escape. A true baked potato should not be wrapped in foil or cooked in a microwave; this changes the cooking method to steaming and prevents a crisp skin from forming. A properly baked potato should be white and fluffy, not yellowish or soggy. Once baked, potatoes can be eaten plain (or with butter, sour cream and other garnishes) or used in other recipes.

SAFETY ALERT

Cooked Potatoes

Cooked potato dishes, especially those with cream, butter or custard, are potentially hazardous foods. They must be held for service at 60°C (140°F) or higher. Be sure to reheat potato dishes to 74°C (165°F) or higher.

BASIC PROCEDURE FOR BAKING POTATOES

1. Scrub the potatoes well.
2. Using a fork, pierce the potato skins.
3. Rub the potatoes with oil and salt if desired. Do not wrap them in foil.
4. Bake the potatoes until done. A paring knife should penetrate them easily.

Piercing the potatoes.

RECIPE 23.1

Approximate values per potato:	
Calories	271
Total fat	6 g
Saturated fat	0.5 g
Cholesterol	0 mg
Sodium	1227 mg
Total carbohydrates	51 g
Protein	5 g

APPLYING THE BASICS		RECIPE 23.1

Baked Potatoes

Yield: 8 servings

Russet potatoes	8	8
Vegetable oil	50 mL	3 Tbsp.
Kosher salt	25 g	1 Tbsp.

1. Scrub the potatoes well, but do not peel. Pierce the skin of each potato to allow steam to escape.

2. Rub the potatoes with the oil, then sprinkle with kosher salt.

3. Place the potato on a rack over a sheet pan. Bake in a 200°C (400°F) oven until done, approximately 1 hour. The potatoes should yield to gentle pressure, and a paring knife inserted in the thickest part should meet little resistance.

4. Hold uncovered in a warm spot and serve within 1 hour.

Baking in a Casserole

Many classic potato dishes require baking either raw or parboiled potatoes with sauce, cheese, meat or other seasonings in a baking dish or casserole. Well-known examples include scalloped potatoes, which are baked in béchamel sauce, and au gratin, which are topped with cheese and baked. These dishes usually develop a crisp, brown crust, which is part of their appeal.

The casserole should hold its shape when cut; the potatoes should be tender and the sauce should be smooth, not grainy.

Potato casseroles can be fully baked, then held loosely covered in a steam table for service. Portions can be reheated or browned briefly under a broiler or salamander at service time.

Derivatives of Baked Potatoes

Pommes Macaire—Remove baked potato from skins using a spoon. Mash and mix in butter, season to taste. Using a little flour, mould into 2-cm (1-in.) cakes. Pan-fry.

Stuffed Baked Potato—Cut top off baked potato and scoop out flesh. Mash with sour cream, bacon bits, chives, salt and pepper. Pipe back into shells, sprinkle with grated cheese and bake to heat through. Sometimes referred to as a Jackson potato.

BASIC PROCEDURE FOR BAKING POTATOES EN CASSEROLE

1. Prepare the potatoes by washing, peeling, slicing or partially cooking as desired or as directed in the recipe.

2. Add the potatoes to the baking pan in layers, alternating with the sauce, cream, cheese or other ingredients. Or combine the potatoes with the other ingredients and place in a buttered baking pan.

3. Bake the potatoes until done.

APPLYING THE BASICS		RECIPE 23.2

Gratin Dauphinoise

Yield: 1.8–2.2 kg (4–5 lb.)

Potatoes	1.5 kg	3 lb.
Whole butter	as needed	as needed
Salt and white pepper	TT	TT
Gruyère cheese, grated	250 g	8 oz.

continued

Cream, 18%	700 mL	24 fl. oz.
Nutmeg	0.5 g	1/4 tsp.
Egg yolks	3	3

1. Peel the potatoes and cut into very thin slices.

2. Place a single layer of potatoes in a well-buttered, full-size hotel pan.

3. Season with salt and pepper. Sprinkle on a thin layer of cheese.

4. Add another layer of potatoes and cheese and repeat until all the potatoes and about three-quarters of the cheese are used.

5. Heat the cream and nutmeg to a simmer. Whisk the egg yolks together in a bowl, then gradually add the hot cream.

6. Pour the cream-and-egg mixture over the potatoes. Top with the remaining cheese.

7. Bake uncovered at 180°C (350°F) until the potatoes are tender and golden brown, approximately 50–60 minutes.

Approximate values per 85 g serving:	
Calories	154
Total fat	7 g
Saturated fat	4 g
Cholesterol	48 mg
Sodium	153 mg
Total carbohydrates	17 g
Protein	6 g

1. Gratin Dauphinoise: Layering gratin potatoes.

2. Finished gratin potatoes.

Sautéing and Pan-Frying

Waxy potatoes, such as red- and white-skinned varieties, are best for sautéing or pan-frying. Often they are first parboiled or even fully cooked—a convenient way to use leftover boiled potatoes. They are then cooked in fat following the general procedures for sautéing and pan-frying discussed in Chapter 9, Principles of Cooking.

The fat can be clarified butter, oil, bacon fat or lard, depending on the desired flavour of the finished dish. The fat must be hot before the potatoes are added so that they will develop a crust without absorbing too much fat. Sautéed potatoes should have a crisp, well-browned crust and tender interior. They should be neither soggy nor greasy.

Potatoes can be sautéed or pan-fried by two methods: tossing and still-frying. The tossing method is used to cook relatively small pieces of potatoes in a small amount of fat. The potatoes are tossed using the pan's sloped sides so that they brown evenly on all sides. The still-frying method is used to create a disc-shaped potato product. The shredded or sliced potatoes are added to the pan, usually covering its bottom, and allowed to cook without stirring or flipping until they are well browned on the first side. The entire mass is then turned and cooked on the second side. When the potatoes are done, they can be cut into wedges for service.

BASIC PROCEDURE FOR SAUTÉING AND PAN-FRYING POTATOES

1. Wash, trim, peel, cut and/or cook the potatoes as desired or as directed in the recipe.

2. Heat the pan, add and heat the fat. Add the potatoes to the hot fat. Do not overcrowd the pan. Use enough fat to prevent the potatoes from sticking to the pan. Depending on the recipe, use either the tossing method or still-frying method.

3. Add garnishes, seasonings and other ingredients as desired or as directed in the recipe.

4. Cook the potatoes until done.

Lyonnaise Potatoes

RECIPE 23.3

Approximate values per serving:	
Calories	170
Total fat	12 g
Saturated fat	7 g
Cholesterol	33 mg
Sodium	650 mg
Total carbohydrates	16 g
Protein	1 g

APPLYING THE BASICS   **RECIPE 23.3**

Lyonnaise Potatoes

Yield: 8 120-g (4-oz.) servings

Potatoes, waxy variety	1 kg	2 lb.
Onions, julienne	250 g	8 oz.
Clarified butter	125 mL	4 fl. oz.
Salt and pepper	TT	TT
Parsley, chopped	10 g	1 Tbsp.

1. Partially cook the potatoes by baking, boiling or steaming. Allow to cool.
2. Peel and cut the potatoes into 0.5-cm-thick (1/4-in.) slices.
3. Sauté the onions in half the butter until tender. Remove the onions from the pan with a slotted spoon and set aside.
4. Add the remaining butter to the pan. Add the potatoes and sauté, tossing as needed, until well browned on all sides.
5. Return the onions to the pan and sauté to combine the flavours. Season to taste with salt and pepper and garnish with parsley.

Deep-Fat Frying

Potato chips and french fries (Fr. *pomme frites*) are extremely popular in a variety of shapes, sizes and seasonings. Although a wide range of shapes, sizes and preseasoned frozen products are available, fresh fried potatoes can be a delicious, economical menu item.

Top-quality russet potatoes are recommended for deep-fat frying. The skin may be removed or left attached. If peeled, the potatoes should be soaked in clear, cold water until ready to cut and cook. This keeps them crisp and white by leaching some of the starch that might otherwise make the potatoes gummy or cause smaller cuts to stick together when cooked.

The potatoes are usually blanched in oil ranging in temperature from 120°C to 150°C (250°F to 300°F) until tender and translucent. They are then drained

More Than a French Fry

Thanks to the genius of Carême, Escoffier and others, few vegetables have as extensive a classic repertoire as potatoes. Some of these dishes begin with the duchesse potatoes mixture; in this regard, duchesse potatoes can be considered the mother of many classic potato preparations. For example,

Duchesse + Tomato concassée = Marquis
Duchesse + Chopped truffles + Almond
   coating + Deep-fat frying = Berny
Duchesse + Pâte à choux = Dauphine
Dauphine + Grated Parmesan + Piped
   shape + Deep-fat frying = Lorette

Duchesse + Shaping + Breading +
   Deep-fat frying = Croquettes

Other classic potato preparations not based on duchesse potatoes include:

Anna—Thin slices are arranged in several circular layers in a round pan or mould coated with clarified butter; additional butter is brushed on and the potatoes are baked until crisp, then cut into wedges for service.
Boulangère—Onions and potatoes are sautéed in butter, then transferred to a

baking pan, stock is added and the potatoes are cooked uncovered until done.
Château—Turned potatoes are sautéed in clarified butter until golden and soft.
Parisienne—Small spheres are cut from raw, peeled potatoes with a parisienne scoop; they are seasoned and sautéed in clarified butter, then tossed with a meat glaze and garnished with chopped parsley.
Rösti—Potatoes are shredded, seasoned and pan-fried in the shape of a pie, then cut into wedges for service.

and held for service, at which time they are finished in hotter oil, usually at a temperature between 180°C and 190°C (350°F and 375°F).

Deep-fat frying is also used to finish cooking several classic potato dishes such as croquettes and dauphine, in which fully cooked potatoes are puréed, seasoned, shaped and fried. Deep-fat fried potatoes should be drained on absorbent paper briefly and served immediately. Specific recipes for several types of deep-fat fried potatoes are given at the end of this chapter.

Boiling

Waxy potatoes are best for all moist-heat cooking methods. Boiled potatoes (which are actually simmered) may be served as is or used in multistep preparations such as purées, salads, soups and baked casseroles. Potatoes are usually boiled in water, although stock may be used or milk added for flavour. Always begin cooking potatoes in cold liquid to ensure even cooking. Unlike other vegetables, potatoes should not be refreshed in cold water; it makes them soggy.

BASIC PROCEDURE FOR BOILING POTATOES

1. Wash, peel or trim the potatoes as desired.
2. Cut the potatoes into uniform-sized pieces. The pieces should not be too small or they will absorb a large amount of water as they cook, making the final product soggy.
3. Add the potatoes to enough cool liquid to cover them by several centimetres. Bring to a boil, reduce to a simmer and cook until done. If a slightly firm finished product is desired, remove and drain the potatoes when they are slightly underdone and allow carryover cooking to finish cooking them.
4. Drain the potatoes in a colander and serve or use for further preparation.

APPLYING THE BASICS   RECIPE 23.4

Duchesse Potatoes

Yield: 1 kg (2 lb.)

Potatoes, peeled and quartered	1 kg	2 lb.
Whole butter	50 g	2 oz.
Nutmeg	TT	TT
Salt and pepper	TT	TT
Egg yolks	4	4

1. Boil the potatoes in salted water until tender. Drain and immediately turn out onto a sheet pan to allow the moisture to evaporate.
2. While they are still warm, press the potatoes through a ricer or food mill, or grind through a grinder's medium plate. Blend in the butter and season to taste with nutmeg, salt and pepper.
3. Mix in the egg yolks, blending well.

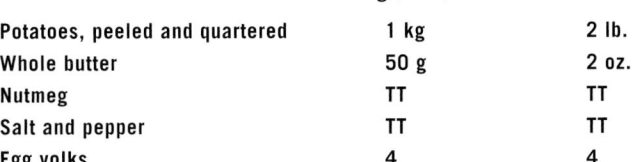

Fried Potato Variations
Cottage fries

Shoestring potatoes

French fries

Steak fries

continued

RECIPE 23.4

Approximate values per 100 g serving:	
Calories	168
Total fat	6 g
Saturated fat	3 g
Cholesterol	97 mg
Sodium	261 mg
Total carbohydrates	25 g
Protein	3.5 g

4. Place the duchesse mixture in a piping bag fitted with a large star tip. Pipe single portion–sized spirals onto a parchment-lined sheet pan. Brush with clarified butter and bake at 190°C (375°F) until the edges are golden brown, approximately 8–10 minutes. Serve immediately.

NOTE: Duchesse Potatoes are often used to decorate platters used for buffets or tableside preparations or to present chateaubriand. To create borders and garnishes, the standard mixture for Duchesse Potatoes is forced through a piping bag while still very hot and relatively soft. Duchesse is the base for other dishes such as croquettes, marquise and lorette.

1. Duchesse Potatoes: Passing boiled potatoes through a food mill.

2. Piping Duchesse Potatoes.

3. The finished potatoes.

GRAINS

● **hull** also known as the husk, the outer covering of a fruit, seed or grain

● **bran** the tough outer layer of a cereal grain and the part highest in fibre

● **endosperm** the largest part of a cereal grain and a source of protein and carbohydrates (starch); the part used primarily in milled products

● **germ** the smallest portion of a cereal grain and the only part that contains fat

Botanically, grains are grasses that bear edible seeds. Corn, rice and wheat are the most significant. Both the fruit (i.e., the seed or kernel) and the plant are called a grain. (See Figure 23.1.)

Most grain kernels are protected by a **hull** or husk. All kernels comprise three distinct parts: the **bran**, **endosperm** and **germ**. The bran is the tough

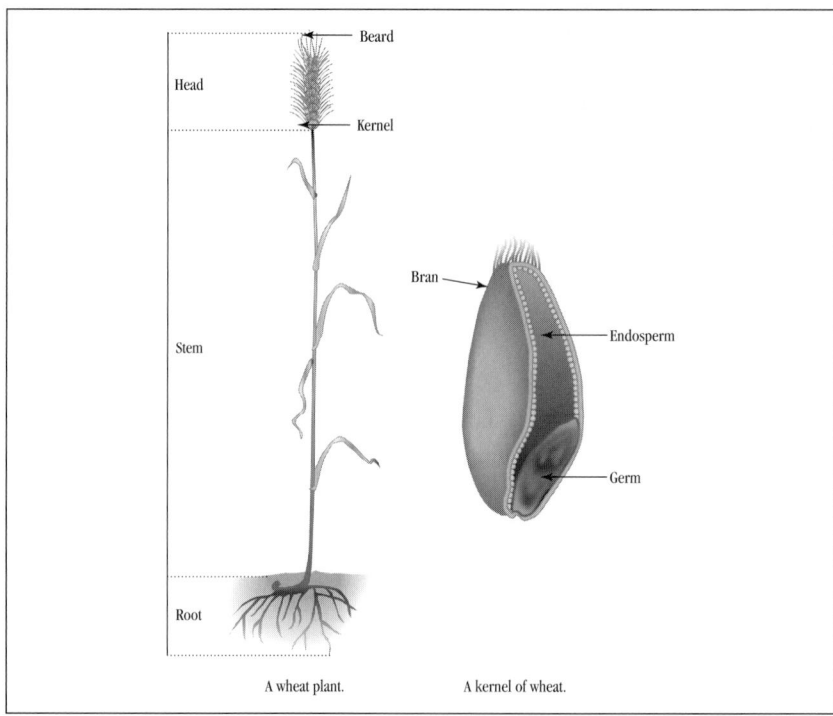

FIGURE 23.1 Parts of a wheat plant.

outer layer covering the endosperm. Bran is a good source of fibre and B vitamins. The endosperm is the largest part of the kernel and is a source of protein and carbohydrates (starch). It is the part used primarily in milled products such as flour. The germ is the smallest portion of the grain and is the only part that contains fat. It is also rich in thiamin. The bran, endosperm and germ are usually separated by milling.

Identifying Grains

This section presents information on corn, rice and wheat as well as several minor grains that are nutritionally significant and gaining popularity.

Some products are available in a stone-ground form. This means that the grains were ground with a stone mill rather than by the steel blades typically used for **cracking**, **grinding**, **hulling** and **pearling**. Stone grinders are gentler and more precise, so they are less likely to overgrind the grain. Stone-ground products will always be labelled as such and are usually more expensive than steel-ground ones.

● **cracking** a milling process in which grains are broken open

● **grinding** a milling process in which grains are reduced to a powder; the powder can be of differing degrees of fineness or coarseness

● **hulling** a milling process in which the hull or husk is removed from grains

● **pearling** a milling process in which all or part of the hull, bran or germ are removed from grains

Corn

Corn (Sp. *maíz*; It. *granturco*) is the only grain that is also eaten fresh as a vegetable. (Fresh corn is discussed in Chapter 22, Vegetables.) Its use as a dried grain dates back several thousand years in Central America and long preceded its use as a vegetable.

Cornmeal

Cornmeal is made by drying and grinding a special type of corn known as *dent*, which may be yellow, white or blue. Cornmeal is most often used in breads, as a coating for fried foods or cooked as polenta or mush. Products made with cornmeal have a gritty texture and a sweet but starchy flavour.

Cornmeal

Hominy

Hominy

Hominy, also known as posole or samp, is dried corn that has been soaked in hydrated lime or lye. This causes the kernels to swell, loosening the hulls. The hulls and germs are removed and the kernels dried. These white or yellow kernels resemble popcorn, but with a soft, chewy texture and smoky-sour flavour. Hominy is available dried or cooked and canned. It may be served as a side dish or used in stews or soups. **Masa harina**, a finely ground flour made from hominy, is used for making breads, tortillas, tamales and other Mexican and southwestern dishes.

Grits

Grits

Grits are traditionally made by grinding dried hominy. These tiny white or yellow (see hominy above) granules may be used in baked dishes but are most often served as a hot breakfast cereal, usually topped with butter or cheese. Quick-cooking and instant grits are available.

Rice

Rice (Fr. *riz*; It. *riso*; Sp. *arroz*) is the starchy seed of a semiaquatic grass. Probably originating on the Indian subcontinent or in Southeast Asia, rice is used as a staple by more than half of the world's population.

Rice can be incorporated into almost any cuisine, from Asian to Spanish to classic French. Its flavour adapts to the foods and seasonings with which the rice is cooked or served. Its texture adds an appealing chewiness to meat and

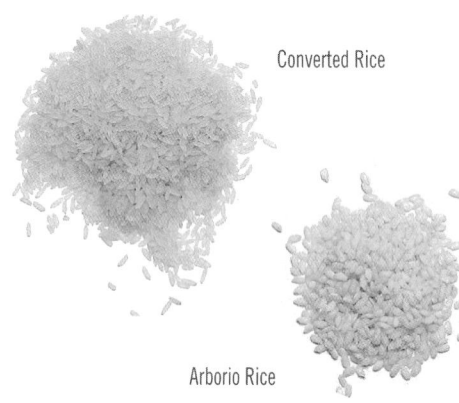

Converted Rice

Arborio Rice

Basmati Rice

Brown Rice

poultry dishes, salads, breads and puddings. Rice is not limited to a side dish but may be used in stews or curries, for stuffing vegetables or game birds, in puddings, salads, beverages (such as *horchata*) and breads.

Rice is divided into three types based on seed size: **long-grain**, **medium-grain** and **short-grain**. Long-grain rice is the most versatile and popular worldwide. The grains remain firm, fluffy and separate when cooked. (Long-grain rice can, however, become sticky if overcooked or stirred frequently during cooking.) Short-grain rice has more starch and becomes quite tender and sticky when cooked. Italian risotto, Japanese sushi and Spanish paella are all traditionally made with short-grain rice. The appearance and starch content of medium-grain rice falls somewhere in between. Medium-grain rice becomes sticky when cool, so it is best eaten freshly made and piping hot.

Long-grain, medium-grain and short-grain rice are available in different processed forms. All rice is originally brown. The grains can be left whole, with the bran attached, for **brown rice**. Or they can be pearled for the more familiar polished **white rice**. Both brown rice and white rice can be processed into converted rice and instant rice.

Converted rice is parboiled to remove the surface starch. This procedure also forces nutrients from the bran into the grain's endosperm. Therefore, converted rice retains more nutrients than regular milled white rice, although the flavour is the same. Converted rice is neither precooked nor instant; in fact, it cooks more slowly than regular milled white rice.

Instant or **quick-cooking rice** is widely available and useful if time is a concern. Instant rice is created by fully cooking then flash-freezing milled rice. Unfortunately, this processing removes some of the nutrients and flavour.

Arborio Rice

Arborio is a round, short-grain rice used primarily in Italian dishes such as risotto. It is very sticky, with a white colour and mild flavour.

Basmati Rice

Basmati is one of the finest long-grain rices in the world. It grows in the Himalayan foothills and is preferred in Indian cuisine. It is highly aromatic, with a sweet, delicate flavour and a creamy yellow colour. Basmati rice is usually aged to improve its aromatic qualities and should be washed well before cooking. Jasmine rice is another aromatic long-grain rice. It is grown in Thailand.

Brown Rice

Brown rice is the whole natural grain of rice. Only the husk has been removed. Brown rice has a nutty flavour; its chewy texture is caused by the high-fibre bran. Brown rice absorbs more water and takes longer to cook than white rice does.

Sticky Rice

Sticky rice is a short-grain rice used in many Asian cuisines. The short grains are fat and round with a high starch content and a pearly white colour. When cooked, the grains tend to clump together, forming a sticky mass. Sticky rice must be soaked for several hours before being cooked. Also known as glutinous rice or sweet rice, it can be ground into flour and used for dumplings and pastries. Japanese sake and mirin and Chinese shaoxing are made from fermented sticky rice, as is rice vinegar.

Wild Rice

Wild rice is prepared in the same manner as traditional rice, although it is actually the seed of an unrelated reedlike aquatic plant. Wild rice has long, slender grains with a dark brown to black colour. It has a nuttier flavour and chewier texture than traditional rice. Three grades are available: *giant* (the best quality, with very long grains); *fancy* (a medium-sized grain, suitable for most purposes); and *select* (a short grain, suitable for soups, pancakes or baked goods). Cultivated in Saskatchewan, Manitoba and Ontario, it is generally served with game, used as a stuffing for poultry or combined with regular rice for a side dish. Wild rice is expensive, but small quantities are usually sufficient.

Wild Rice

Wild Pecan Rice

Wild pecan rice is neither wild nor made with pecans. It is a unique long-grain rice grown only in the bayou country of southern Louisiana. Wild pecan rice has a nutty flavour and exceptionally rich aroma.

Wild Pecan Rice

Guidelines for Cooking Rice

Rice may be rinsed before cooking to remove dirt and debris, but doing so also removes some nutrients. It is not necessary to rinse most North American–grown rice as it is generally clean and free of insects. Rice may also be soaked before cooking. Soaking softens the grains, removes some starch and speeds cooking.

The standard ratio for cooking rice is 2 parts liquid to 1 part rice. The actual ratio varies, however, depending on the type of rice. Guidelines for cooking rice are found in Table 23.2.

Once cooked, rice is highly perishable. Because of its neutral pH and high protein content, cooked rice is a potentially hazardous food. To avoid the risk of food-borne illnesses, be sure to store cooked rice out of the temperature danger zone.

Wheat

Wheat (Fr. *blé*) is most often milled into the wide range of flours discussed in Chapter 27, Principles of the Bakeshop. But wheat and products derived from it are also used as starchy side dishes or ingredients in soups, salads, ground meat dishes and breads. These products include cracked wheat, bulgur and couscous. When cooked they are slightly chewy with a mild flavour. All should be fluffy; none should be soggy or sticky.

TABLE 23.2	Guidelines for Cooking Rice			
Type of Rice	Ratio Rice : Water (by Volume)	Preparation	Cooking Time (simmering)	Yield from 200 g (1 cup) Raw Rice
Arborio	1 : 2.5–3	Do not rinse or soak	15–20 min.	560–675 mL (2.5–3 cups)
Basmati	1 : 1.75	Rinse well; soak	15 min.	675 mL (3 cups)
Brown, long-grain	1 : 2.5	Do not rinse; can soak	45–50 min.	675–900 mL (3–4 cups)
Converted	1 : 2	Do not rinse	20–25 min.	675–900 mL (3–4 cups)
Sticky/glutinous	1 : 0.8	Rinse	20 min.	560–675 mL (2.5–3 cups)
White, long-grain (regular milled)	1 : 2	Do not rinse	15 min.	675 mL (3 cups)
Wild	1 : 3	Rinse	35–60 min., depending on grade	675–900 mL (3–4 cups)

● **berry** the kernel of certain grains such as wheat

● **durum wheat** a species of very hard wheat with a particularly high amount of protein; it is used to make couscous or milled into semolina, which is used for making pasta

Bulgur

Couscous

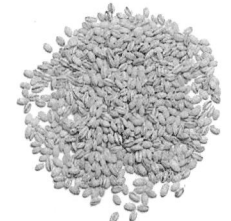

Barley

Buckwheat/
Kasha

Wheat germ and *wheat bran* are widely available and highly touted for their nutritional values. Bran and germ are not generally used alone but may be added to bread or other cooked dishes.

Cracked Wheat

Cracked wheat is the whole wheat kernel (known as a **berry**) broken into varying degrees of coarseness. It is not precooked, and the kernel's white interior should be visible. The bran and germ are still intact, so cracked wheat has a great deal of fibre but a short shelf life. Whole wheat berries must be soaked for several hours before cooking. Cracked wheat can be fully cooked by long, gentle simmering.

Bulgur

Bulgur is a wheat berry that has had the bran removed; it is then steam-cooked, dried and ground into varying degrees of coarseness. Bulgur has a nutlike flavour and texture; it is a uniform golden-brown colour (uncooked cracked wheat is not) and requires less cooking time than cracked wheat. Generally, cracked wheat and bulgur cannot be substituted for each other in recipes.

Bulgur only needs to be soaked in water, then drained, for use in salads, or briefly cooked when used in stews or pilafs. Bulgur is good with grilled meats and as an alternative to rice in stuffings and other dishes. The fine grind is most often used in packaged mixes such as tabouli; the medium grind is most often available in bulk.

Couscous

Couscous is made by removing the bran and germ from **durum wheat** berries. The endosperm is then steamed, pressed to form tiny pellets and dried. Couscous is available in varying degrees of coarseness; medium-fine is the most popular. Couscous is prepared by steaming over water or stock in a pot called a couscousier. Couscous, traditionally served with North African stews, can be used or served like rice.

Other Grains

Barley

Barley is one of the oldest culinary grains, used by humans since prehistoric times. Barley is extremely hardy, growing in climates from the tropics to the near-Arctic. Although much of the barley crop is used to make beer or feed animals, some does find its way into soups, stews and stuffings. The most common type is pearled to produce a small, round white nugget of endosperm. It has a sweet, earthy flavour similar to oats and goes well with onions, garlic and strong herbs. Barley's texture ranges from chewy to soft, depending on the amount of water in which it is cooked. Its starchiness can be used to thicken soups or stews.

Buckwheat/Kasha

Buckwheat is not a type of wheat; it is not even a grain. Rather, it is the fruit of a plant distantly related to rhubarb. Buckwheat is included here, however, because it is prepared and served in the same manner as grains.

The whole buckwheat kernel is known as a groat. The product most often sold as buckwheat is actually kasha, which is a hulled, roasted buckwheat groat. Kasha is reddish brown with a strong, nutty, almost scorched flavour. It is available whole or ground to varying degrees of coarseness. Whole kasha remains in separate grains after cooking; the finer grinds become rather sticky. Kasha can be served as a side dish, usually combined with pasta or vegetables, or it can be chilled and used in salads.

Raw buckwheat groats are ground into flour typically used in pasta, blini and other pancakes. Buckwheat flour contains no gluten-forming proteins and it tends to remain grainy, with a sandy texture. Therefore, it should not be substituted for all of the white or whole wheat flour in breads or baked goods.

Oats

After rice, oats are probably the most widely accepted whole-grain product in the North American diet. Oats are consumed daily as a hot breakfast cereal (oatmeal) and are used in breads, muffins, cookies and other baked goods.

An oat groat is the whole oat kernel with only the husk removed. It contains both the bran and the germ. *Steel-cut oats*, sometimes known as Irish oats, are groats that are toasted then cut into small pieces with steel blades. *Rolled oats*, marketed as "old-fashioned oats," are groats that have been steamed, then rolled into flat flakes. *Quick-cooking oats* are simply rolled oats cut into smaller pieces to reduce cooking time. *Instant oats* are partially cooked and dried before rolling so they need only to be rehydrated in boiling water. Several flavoured versions are also marketed as breakfast cereal. Rolled oats and quick-cooking oats can be used interchangeably, but instant oats should not be substituted in most recipes.

Oat bran is the outer covering of a hulled oat. It is available as a separate product, although rolled and cut oats do contain some oat bran.

The term *oatmeal* is commonly used to refer to both processed groats and the cooked porridge made from them. The processed groats known as oatmeal are a grey-white colour with a starchy texture and sweet flavour. They cook into the soft, thick porridge with a robust flavour called oatmeal.

Quinoa

Quinoa (keen-wa) is native to the South American Andes and was a common food of the Incas, who referred to it as the "mother grain." Although not botanically a true grain, quinoa's tiny seeds are treated as such. The grains (seeds) are small, flattened spheres, approximately 1.5 mm (1/16 in.) in diameter, ringed with the germ. They become translucent when cooked and have a slightly smoky or sesamelike flavour. Several varieties of quinoa are available, ranging in colour from dark brown to almost white. The larger whiter varieties are most common and are considered superior.

Quinoa seeds have a natural, bitter-tasting coating, which protects them from birds and insects. Consequently, they should be placed in a fine-meshed colander and rinsed well with cool water for several minutes before use. Quinoa can then be cooked like rice, and will absorb about twice its volume of water. For a nuttier taste, toast the grain in a hot dry pan for about five minutes before adding the liquid. Quinoa can also be eaten as a hot breakfast cereal, served in lieu of rice or used as a thickener for soups or stews and in salads, casseroles, breads and desserts. Quinoa flour, ground from whole seeds, has a delicate nutty flavour. A gluten-free product, it is suitable for anyone bothered by wheat allergies. Quinoa is marketed as the world's "supergrain" because the seeds form a complete protein (with all of the essential amino acids) and contain important vitamins and minerals as well as carbohydrates and fat. Quinoa should be kept in the refrigerator or freezer for long-term storage. The leaves of the quinoa plant are similar to spinach and can be eaten as a vegetable.

Ancient Grains for Modern Times

As an awareness of the nutritional benefits of eating whole grains grows, long-neglected grains are regaining popularity with chefs and consumers. Farro (*Triticum dicoccum*) is one of the oldest forms of wheat; it was a staple in the diet of ancient Roman armies. Farro is still eaten cooked as a whole grain in Tuscany, where it is prized for its chewy, nutty flavour. Spelt (*Triticum aestivum var. spelta*), a related subspecies of common wheat, is also prized for its taste and consistency. Farro must be soaked like beans before cooking, whereas spelt may be cooked without soaking. Treat these grains like barley. Use them to add texture to soups or cook them to add to salads and vegetable dishes.

Farro

Oats

Quinoa

Nutrition

Grains are an excellent source of vitamins, minerals, proteins and fibre. The amount of milling or refining and the method of preparation affect their nutritional values, however. Unrefined and less-refined grains are excellent sources of dietary fibre. Rice is also quite nutritious: it is low in sodium and calories and contains all the essential amino acids. Some grains, especially white rice and oats, are usually enriched with calcium, iron and B vitamins.

Purchasing and Storing Grains

Purchasing

When buying grains, look for fresh, plump ones with a bright, even colour. Fresh grains should not be shrivelled or crumbly; there should be no sour or musty odours.

Grains are sold by weight. They come in bags or boxes ranging from 450 g to 45 kg (1 to 100 lb.). Units of 4.5, 11 and 22 kg (10, 25 and 50 lb.) are usually available.

Storing

All grains should be stored in airtight containers placed in a dark, cool, dry place. Airtight containers prevent dust and insects from entering. Airtight containers and darkness also reduce nutrient loss caused by oxidation or light. Coolness inhibits insect infestation; dryness prevents mould.

Vacuum-sealed packages will last for extended periods. Whole grains, which contain the oily germ, should be refrigerated to prevent rancidity.

Applying Various Cooking Methods

Three basic cooking methods are used to prepare grains: simmering, risotto and pilaf. Unlike simmered grains, those cooked by either the risotto or the pilaf method are first coated with hot fat. The primary distinction between the pilaf and risotto methods is the manner in which the liquid is then added to the grains. (See Figure 23.2.) When grains are used in puddings, breads, stuffings and baked casseroles, they are almost always first fully cooked by one of these methods.

Determining Doneness

Most grains should be cooked until tender, although some recipes do require a chewier or more al dente product. Doneness can usually be determined by cooking time and the amount of liquid remaining in the pan. Some grains, such as wild rice, are fully cooked when they puff open.

In general, grains will be fully cooked when almost all of the cooking liquid is absorbed. This is indicated by the appearance of tunnel-like holes between the grains. Grains can be cooked until almost all of the liquid is absorbed, then removed from the heat and left to stand, covered, for 5 to 10 minutes. This allows the cooked grains to absorb the remaining moisture without burning.

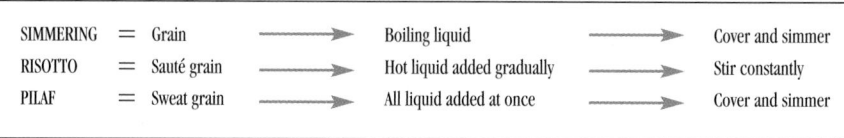

SIMMERING	=	Grain	→	Boiling liquid	→	Cover and simmer
RISOTTO	=	Sauté grain	→	Hot liquid added gradually	→	Stir constantly
PILAF	=	Sweat grain	→	All liquid added at once	→	Cover and simmer

FIGURE 23.2 Grain cooking methods.

Simmering

The most commonly used method for preparing grains is simmering. To do so, simply stir the grains into a measured amount of boiling salted water in a saucepan on the stove top. When the liquid returns to a boil, lower the heat, cover, and simmer until the liquid is absorbed and the grains are tender. The grains are not stirred during cooking.

The grains can be flavoured by using stock as the cooking liquid. Herbs and spices can also be added.

BASIC PROCEDURE FOR SIMMERING GRAINS

1. Bring the cooking liquid to a boil.

2. Stir in the grains. Add herbs or spices as desired or as directed in the recipe.

3. Return the mixture to a boil, cover and reduce to a simmer.

4. Simmer the grains until tender and most of the liquid is absorbed.

5. Remove the grains from the heat.

6. Drain if appropriate or keep covered and allow the excess moisture to evaporate, approximately 5 minutes. Fluff the grains with a fork before service.

Basic Simmered Rice

APPLYING THE BASICS   RECIPE 23.5

 Basic Simmered Rice

Yield: 750 mL (3 cups)

Water	500 mL	16 fl. oz.
Salt	2 g	1/2 tsp.
White rice	200 g	1 cup (7 oz.)

1. Bring the water and salt to a boil in a heavy saucepan. Slowly add the rice.

2. Cover the pan and reduce the heat so that the liquid simmers gently. Cook until the rice is tender and the water is absorbed, approximately 15–20 minutes.

3. Remove from the heat and transfer to a hotel pan. Do not cover. Allow any excess moisture to evaporate for approximately 5 minutes.

4. Fluff the rice and serve, or refrigerate for use in another recipe.

RECIPE 23.5

Approximate values per serving:	
Calories	182
Total fat	0 g
Saturated fat	0 g
Cholesterol	0 mg
Sodium	200 mg
Total carbohydrates	40 g
Protein	4 g

Risotto Method

Risotto is a classic Northern Italian rice dish in which the grains remain firm but merge with the cooking liquid to become a creamy, almost puddinglike dish. True risotto is made with a short-grain starchy rice such as arborio, but the risotto method can also be used to cook other grains such as barley and oats.

The grains are not rinsed before cooking, as this removes the starches needed to achieve the desired consistency. The grains are coated, but not cooked, in a hot fat such as butter or oil. A hot liquid is then gradually added to the grains so that the mixture is kept at a constant simmer. The cooking

Risotto

A properly cooked risotto will have a little crunch left in the centre of the rice kernel. The mixture will have a creamy consistency. Risotto can be par-cooked and cooled for à la carte service and finished off as needed.

liquid should be a rich, flavourful stock. Unlike simmering and the pilaf method, the risotto method requires frequent, sometimes constant, stirring.

When finished, the grains should be creamy and tender, but still al dente in the centre. Grated cheese, 35% cream, cooked meat, poultry, fish, shellfish, herbs and vegetables can be added to create a flavourful side dish or a complete meal.

BASIC PROCEDURE FOR PREPARING GRAINS BY THE RISOTTO METHOD

1. Bring the cooking liquid to a simmer.

2. Heat the fat in a heavy saucepan over moderate heat. Add any onions, garlic or other flavouring ingredients and sauté for one to two minutes without browning.

3. Add the grains to the saucepan. Stir well to make sure the grains are well coated with fat. Do not allow the grains to brown.

4. Add any wine and cook until it is fully absorbed.

5. Begin to add the simmering stock 120 mL (4 fl. oz.) at a time, stirring frequently. Wait until each portion of cooking liquid is almost fully absorbed before adding the next.

6. Test for doneness after the grains have cooked for approximately 18 to 20 minutes. There should be a little crunch remaining. The consistency should be creamy and porridge-like.

7. Remove the saucepan from the heat and stir in any butter, grated cheese, herbs or other flavouring ingredients as directed. Serve immediately.

1. Risotto Milanese: Sautéing the rice and onions in butter.

2. Adding the stock gradually while stirring frequently.

3. Stirring in the remaining butter and grated cheese.

APPLYING THE BASICS		RECIPE 23.6

Risotto Milanese

Yield: 24 120-g (4-oz.) servings

Chicken stock	2.5 L	2-1/2 qt.
Whole butter	125 g	4 oz.
Onion, minced	150 g	5 oz.
Arborio rice	700 g	1 lb. 8 oz.
Dry white wine	250 mL	8 fl. oz.
Saffron threads, crushed	0.5 g	1/2 tsp.
Parmesan cheese, grated	125 g	4 oz.

1. Bring the chicken stock to a simmer.

2. Heat 90 g (3 oz.) of the butter in a large, heavy saucepan. Add the onion and sauté without browning until translucent.

3. Add the rice to the onion and butter. Stir well to coat the grains with butter but do not allow the rice to brown. Add the wine and stir until it is completely absorbed.

4. Add the saffron. Add the simmering stock, 125 mL (4 fl. oz.) at a time, stirring frequently. Wait until the stock is absorbed before adding the next 125-mL (4-fl.-oz.) portion.

continued

5. After approximately 18–20 minutes, all of the stock should be incorporated and the rice should be al dente. Remove from the heat and stir in the remaining butter and the grated cheese. Serve immediately.

VARIATIONS: RISOTTO WITH RADICCHIO (AL RADICCHIO)—Omit the saffron and Parmesan. Just before the risotto is fully cooked, stir in 125 mL (4 fl. oz.) of 35% cream and 100 g (3 oz.) of finely chopped radicchio leaves.

RISOTTO WITH FOUR CHEESES (AL QUATTRO FORMAGGI)—Omit the saffron. When the risotto is fully cooked, remove from the heat and stir in 50 g (2 oz.) each of grated Parmesan, Gorgonzola, fontina and mozzarella cheeses. Garnish with toasted pine nuts and chopped parsley.

RISOTTO WITH SMOKED SALMON (AL SALMONE AFFUMICATO)—Omit the butter, saffron and Parmesan. Sauté the onion in 100 mL (3 fl. oz.) of corn or safflower oil instead of butter. When the risotto is fully cooked, remove from the heat and stir in 250 mL (8 fl. oz.) of 18% cream, 100 mL (3 fl. oz.) of fresh lemon juice and 250 g (8 oz.) of good-quality smoked salmon. Garnish with chopped fresh parsley and dill. Serve with lemon wedges.

RECIPE 23.6

Approximate values per serving:	
Calories	120
Total fat	6 g
Saturated fat	3.5 g
Cholesterol	15 mg
Sodium	483 mg
Total carbohydrates	9 g
Protein	7 g

Pilaf Method

With the pilaf method, the raw grains are lightly sautéed in oil or butter, usually with onions or seasonings for additional flavour. Hot liquid, often a stock, is then added. The pan is covered and the mixture left to simmer until the liquid is absorbed.

BASIC PROCEDURE FOR PREPARING GRAINS BY THE PILAF METHOD

1. Bring the cooking liquid (either water or stock) to a boil.

2. Heat the fat in a heavy saucepan over moderate heat. Add any onions, garlic or other flavourings and sweat for one to two minutes without browning.

3. Add the grains to the saucepan. Stir well to make sure the grains are well coated with fat. Do not allow the grains to brown.

4. All at once, add the hot cooking liquid to the sautéed grains.

5. Return the liquid to a boil, reduce to a simmer and cover.

6. Allow the mixture to simmer, either in the oven or on the stove top, until the liquid is absorbed.

1. Rice Pilaf: Sautéing the rice in butter.

2. Adding the hot stock to the rice.

APPLYING THE BASICS

RECIPE 23.7

Rice Pilaf

Yield: 10 servings
Method: Pilaf

Butter	30 g	1 oz.
Olive oil	30 mL	1 fl. oz.
Onion, fine dice	100 g	3 oz.
Bay leaf	1	1
Long-grain rice	500 g	1 lb.
Chicken stock, boiling	1 L	32 fl. oz.
Salt	TT	TT

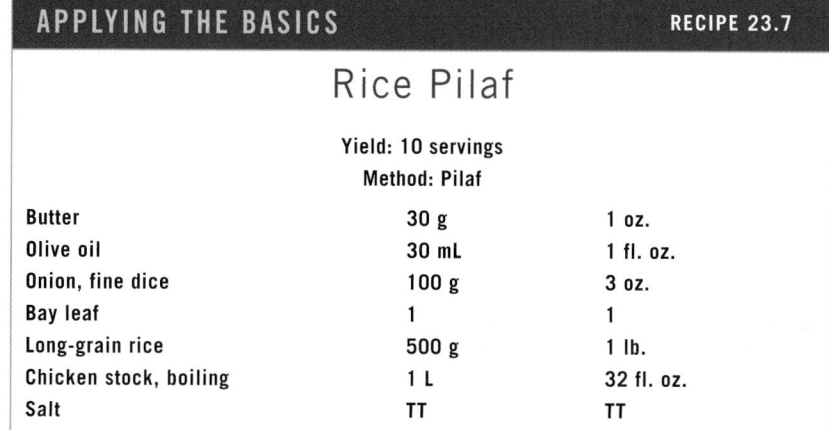

3. Fluffing the finished rice.

continued

Approximate values per 180 g serving:	
Calories	248
Total fat	6 g
Saturated fat	2 g
Cholesterol	7 mg
Sodium	712 mg
Total carbohydrates	41 g
Protein	6 g

1. Heat the butter and olive oil in a heavy sautoir or sauce pot.
2. Add the onion and bay leaf and sweat until tender, but not brown.
3. Add the rice and stir to coat completely with the hot fat. Do not allow the rice to brown.
4. Pour in the boiling chicken stock and season with salt.
5. Cover the pot tightly and place it in a 175°C (350°F) oven. Bake for 18–20 minutes, until the liquid is absorbed and the rice is fluffy and tender.
6. Transfer the cooked rice to a hotel pan and fluff the rice with a fork. Remove the bay leaf and keep the rice hot for service.

● **extrusion** the process of forcing pasta through perforated plates to create various shapes; pasta dough that is not extruded must be rolled and cut

PASTA

Pasta is made from an unleavened dough of liquid mixed with flour. The liquid is usually egg and/or water. The flour can be from almost any grain: wheat, buckwheat, rice or a combination of grains. The dough can be coloured and flavoured with puréed vegetables, herbs or other ingredients and it can be cut or **extruded** into a wide variety of shapes and sizes.

Pasta can be cooked fresh while the dough is still moist and pliable, or the dough can be allowed to dry completely before cooking. Pasta can be filled or sauced in an endless variety of ways. It can stand alone or be used in salads, desserts, soups or casseroles.

Pasta is widely used in the cuisines of Asia, North America and Europe. In Italy, pasta dishes are usually served as a separate course, referred to as the *minestre*; in other European countries, Asia and North America, pasta dishes may be served as an appetizer, entree or side dish.

Identifying Pastas

The better-known pastas are based on the Italian tradition of kneading wheat flour with water and eggs to form a smooth, resilient dough. This dough is rolled very thin and cut into various shapes before being boiled in water or dried (known as "**macaroni**" outside North America) for longer storage.

● **macaroni** any dried pasta made with wheat flour and water; only in North America does the term refer to elbow-shaped tubes

Commercially prepared dried pasta products are usually made with semolina flour. Semolina flour, ground from hard durum wheat and available from specialty purveyors, has a rich cream colour and produces a very smooth, durable dough. Semolina dough requires a great deal of kneading, however, and bread flour is an acceptable substitute when preparing fresh pasta by hand.

Asian pasta, generally known as noodles, is made from wheat, rice, bean or buckwheat flour. It is available fresh or dried from commercial purveyors and at specialty markets.

Semolina

Italian-Style Pasta

Although all Italian-style pasta is made from the same type of dough, the finest commercial pastas are those made with pure semolina flour, which gives the dough a rich, yellow colour. Grey or streaked dough probably contains softer flours. Dried pasta should be very hard and break with a clean snap. The surface should be lightly pitted or dull. (A smooth or glossy surface will not hold or absorb sauces as well.)

Dried pasta, both domestic and imported, is available in a wide range of flavours and shapes. In addition to the traditional white (plain), green

Spinach Fettuccine

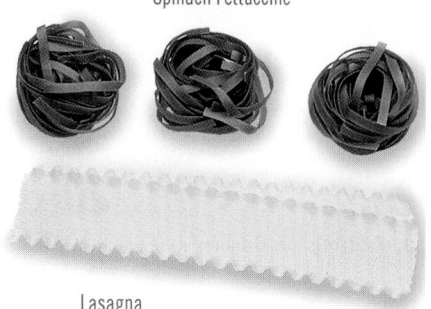

Lasagna

(spinach) and red (tomato) pastas, manufacturers are now offering such unusual flavour combinations as lemon-peppercorn, whole wheat–basil, jalapeño–black bean and carrot–ginger. Small pieces of herbs or other flavourings are often visible in these products.

There are hundreds of recognized shapes of pasta, but only two or three dozen are generally available in Canada. When experimenting with unusual flavours and shapes, be sure to consider the taste and appearance of the final dish after the sauce and any garnishes are added.

Italian-style pasta can be divided into three groups, based on the shape of the final product: ribbons, tubes and shapes. There is no consistent English nomenclature for these pastas, but the Italian names are recognized and applied virtually worldwide. (A specific shape or size may be given different names in different regions of Italy, however. These distinctions are beyond the scope of this text.)

Ribbons

Pasta dough can be rolled very thin and cut into strips or ribbons of various widths. All ribbon shapes work well with tomato, fish and shellfish sauces. Thicker ribbons, such as spaghetti and fettuccine, are preferred with cream or cheese sauces. Sheets of fresh pasta dough can be filled and shaped to create ravioli, cappelletti and tortellini. Filled pasta is usually served with a light cream- or tomato-based sauce that complements the filling's flavours.

Tubes

Cylindrical forms or tubes are made by extrusion. The hollow tubes can be curved or straight, fluted or smooth. Tubes are preferred for meat and vegetable sauces and are often used in baked casseroles.

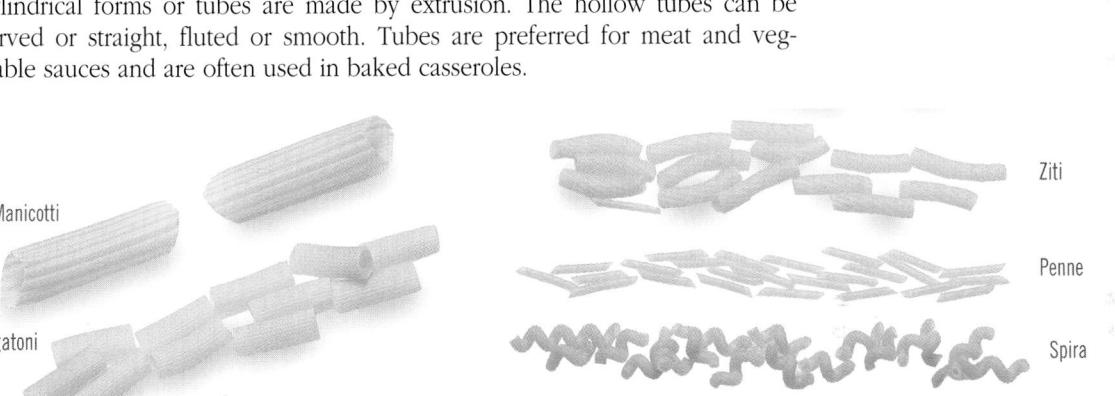

Manicotti

Rigatoni

Ziti

Penne

Spira

Shapes

The extrusion process can also be used to shape pasta dough into forms. The curves and textures produced provide nooks and crevices that hold sauces well. Shaped pastas, such as conchiglie, farfalle and fusilli, are preferred with meat sauces and oil-based sauces such as pesto. Larger-shaped pastas can be cooked, then stuffed with meat or cheese fillings and baked or served as a casserole.

Conchiglie

Farfalle

Fusilli

Rotelle

Orzo

Fettuccine   Spaghetti   Capellini

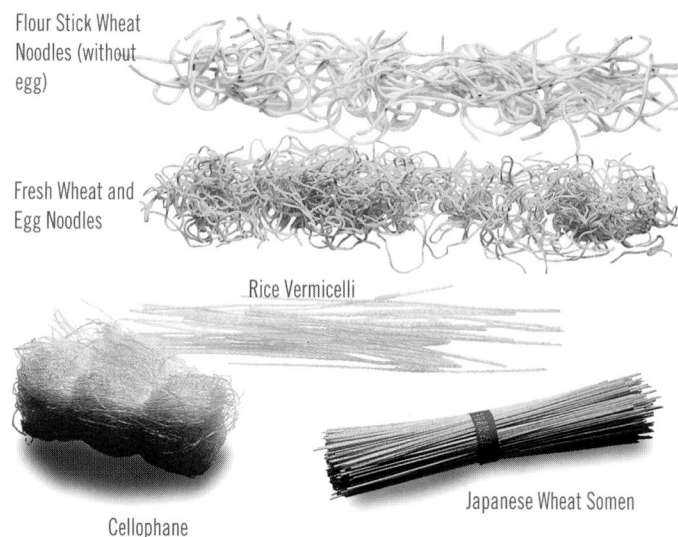

Flour Stick Wheat
Noodles (without
egg)

Fresh Wheat and
Egg Noodles

Rice Vermicelli

Cellophane
Noodles

Japanese Wheat Somen

Dumplings

A **dumpling** is a small mound of dough cooked by steaming or simmering in a flavourful liquid. Dumplings are found in many cuisines: Italian gnocchi, Jewish matzo balls, German spaetzle, Chinese won tons and Polish pierogi. Dumplings can be sweet or savoury, plain or filled.

Plain or **drop dumplings** are made with a breadlike dough, often leavened with yeast or chemical leavening agents. They should be light and tender, but firm enough to hold their shape when cooked. Drop dumplings may be served with stews or broths, or coated with butter or sauce as an appetizer or side dish. Recipes for gnocchi and spaetzle are included at the end of this chapter.

Filled dumplings are made by wrapping noodle dough around seasoned meat, vegetables, cheese or fruit. These parcels are then steamed, fried or baked and served as a snack food, appetizer or side dish. A recipe for Stuffed Won Tons is included in Chapter 34, Appetizers and Sandwiches (Recipe 34.8).

Asian Noodles

Asian noodles are not cut into the same wealth of shapes and sizes as Italian-style pasta, nor are they usually flavoured or coloured with vegetable purées, herbs or other ingredients.

Virtually all Asian noodles are ribbons—some thin, some thick—folded into bundles and packaged. Differences arise because of the flours used for the dough.

Most dried Asian noodles benefit by soaking in hot water for several minutes before further preparation. The water softens the noodle strands; the bundles separate, and the noodles cook more evenly.

Wheat Noodles

Wheat noodles, also known as egg noodles, are the most popular and widely available of the Asian noodles. They are thin, flat noodles with a springy texture; they are available fresh or dried. Dried egg noodles can be deep-fat fried after boiling to create crisp golden noodles (chow mein) used primarily as a garnish.

Japanese wheat noodles, known as somen (if thick) and udon (if thin), may be round, square or flat. They are eaten in broth or with a dipping sauce.

Rice Noodles

Rice noodles are dried, thin noodles made with rice flour. They should be soaked in hot water before cooking and rinsed in cool running water after boiling to remove excess starch and prevent sticking. Rice noodles are often served in soups or sautéed.

Rice vermicelli, which has very fine strands, can be fried in hot oil without presoaking. In only a few seconds the strands will turn white, puff up and become crunchy. Mounds of crunchy rice noodles can be used as a base for sautéed dishes or for presenting hors d'oeuvre.

Bean Starch Noodles

Bean starch noodles are also known as spring rain noodles, bean threads, bean noodles or cellophane noodles. They are thin, transparent noodles made from mung beans. Dried bean noodles can be fried in the same manner as rice vermicelli. Otherwise, they must be soaked in hot water before using in soups, stir-fries or braised dishes.

Buckwheat Noodles

Buckwheat flour is used in the noodles of Northern Japan and the Tokyo region, known as soba noodles. Soba noodles are available fresh or dried and do not need soaking before cooking. They are traditionally served in broth or with a dipping sauce but may be substituted for Italian-style pasta if desired.

Nutrition

Pastas are very low in fat and are an excellent source of vitamins, minerals, proteins and carbohydrates. Also, the processed products are sometimes enriched with additional nutrients.

Purchasing and Storing Pasta Products

Pasta products are purchased by weight, either fresh or dried. Tubes and shapes are not generally available fresh. Dried products, by far the most common, are available in boxes or bags, usually in 500-g, 5- and 20-kg (1-, 10- and 20-lb.) units. They can be stored in a cool, dry place for several months. Fresh pasta can be stored in an airtight wrapping in the refrigerator for a few days or in the freezer for a few weeks.

Preparing Fresh Pasta

Making Fresh Pasta

Fresh pasta is easy to make, requiring almost no special equipment and only a few staples. The basic form is the **sfoglia**, a thin, flat sheet of dough that is cut into ribbons, circles, squares or other shapes.

● **sfoglia** a thin, flat sheet of pasta dough that can be cut into ribbons, circles, squares or other shapes

BASIC PROCEDURE FOR MIXING PASTA DOUGH BY HAND

1. Mound the flour on a workbench. Make a well in the centre. Add the eggs and whip them with a fork.

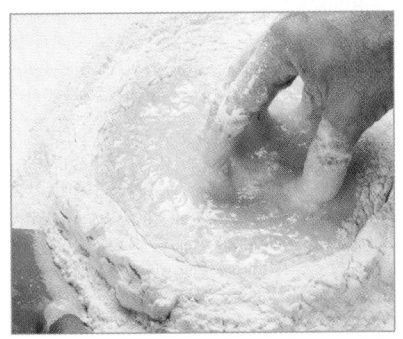

2. Using your fingers, stir the eggs, gradually bringing more flour into the centre.

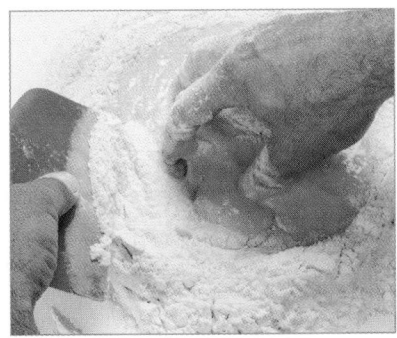

3. Using a dough scraper, add more flour to the egg mixture, stirring constantly until a firm dough is formed.

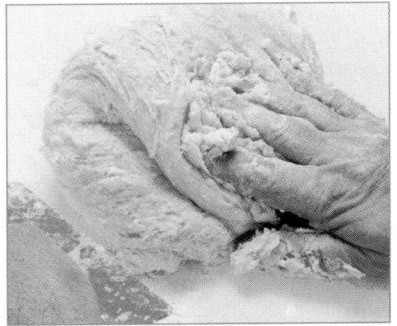

4. Knead the stiff dough until smooth.

Although pasta dough can be kneaded by hand, stretched and rolled with a rolling pin and cut with a chef's knife, pasta machines make these tasks easier. Pasta machines are either electric or manual. Some electric models mix and knead the dough, then extrude it through a cutting disk. An extrusion machine is most practical in a food service operation regularly serving large quantities of pasta. The pasta machine more often encountered is operated manually with a hand crank. It has two rollers that knead, press and push the dough into a thin, uniform sheet. Adjacent cutting rollers slice the thin dough into various widths for fettuccine, spaghetti, capellini or the like.

1. Basic Pasta Dough: Adding flour to the mixing bowl and using the paddle until the mixture forms a soft dough.

2. The finished dough.

RECIPE 23.8

Approximate values per 100 g serving:	
Calories	294
Total fat	6.8 g
Saturated fat	1.7 g
Cholesterol	167 mg
Sodium	443 mg
Total carbohydrates	44 g
Protein	13 g

APPLYING THE BASICS   RECIPE 23.8

Basic Pasta Dough

Yield: 1 kg (2.2 lb.)

Eggs	450 g	8
Olive oil	15 mL	1 Tbsp.
Salt	10 g	2 tsp.
Bread flour or semolina	600 g	1 lb. 6 oz.

1. Place the eggs, oil and salt in a large mixer bowl. Use the paddle attachment to combine.

2. Add one-third of the flour and stir until the mixture begins to form a soft dough. Remove the paddle attachment and attach the dough hook.

3. Gradually add more flour until the dough is dry and cannot absorb any more flour.

4. Remove the dough from the mixer, wrap it well with plastic wrap and set it aside at room temperature for 20–30 minutes.

5. After the dough has rested, roll it into flat sheets by hand or with a pasta machine. Work with only a small portion at a time, keeping the remainder well covered to prevent it from drying out.

6. While the sheets of dough are pliable, cut them into the desired width with a chef's knife or pasta machine. Sheets can also be used for making ravioli, as illustrated on page 586.

VARIATIONS: GARLIC-HERB—Roast 1 head of garlic. Peel and purée the cloves and add to the eggs. Add up to 50 g (2 oz.) of finely chopped assorted fresh herbs just before mixing is complete.

SPINACH—Add 250 g (8 oz.) of cooked, puréed and well-drained spinach to the eggs. Increase the amount of flour slightly if necessary. Use 5 whole eggs and 3 yolks.

TOMATO—Add 100 g (3 oz.) of sweated tomato paste to the eggs; omit the salt. Increase the amount of flour slightly if necessary. Use 5 whole eggs and 3 yolks.

SPICE—Add 12 mL (2-1/2 tsp.) of dry spice of choice.

NOTE: Semolina flour can be substituted in this recipe, although it makes a stronger dough that is more difficult to work with by hand. Try half semolina (durum) and half bread flour.

BASIC PROCEDURE FOR ROLLING AND CUTTING PASTA DOUGH

1. Work with a small portion of the dough. Leave the rest covered with plastic wrap to prevent it from drying out.

2. Flatten the dough with the heel of your hand.

3. Set the pasta machine rollers to their widest setting. Insert the dough and turn the handle with one hand while supporting the dough with the other hand. Pass the entire piece of dough through the rollers.

4. Dust the dough with flour, fold it in thirds and pass it through the pasta machine again.

5. Repeat the folding and rolling procedure until the dough is smooth. This may require four to six passes.

continued

6. Tighten the rollers one or two marks, then pass the dough through the machine. Without folding it in thirds, pass the dough through the machine repeatedly, tightening the rollers one or two marks each time.

7. When the dough is thin enough to see your hand through, but not so thin that it begins to tear, it is ready to use or cut into ribbons. This sheet is the sfoglia.

8. To cut the sfoglia into ribbons, gently feed a manageable length of dough through the desired cutting blades.

9. To dry the pasta, lay it out in a single layer on a sheet pan dusted with flour. Layers of pasta ribbons can be separated with parchment paper.

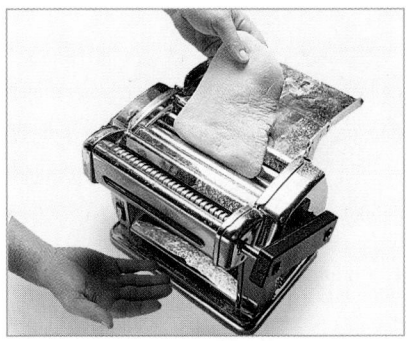

1. Passing the entire piece of dough through the pasta machine.

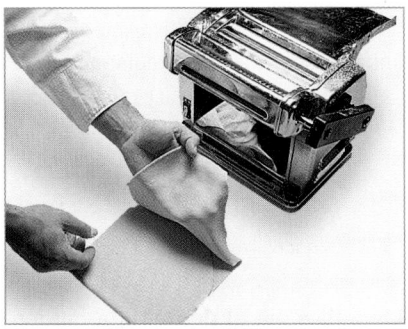

2. Folding the dough in thirds.

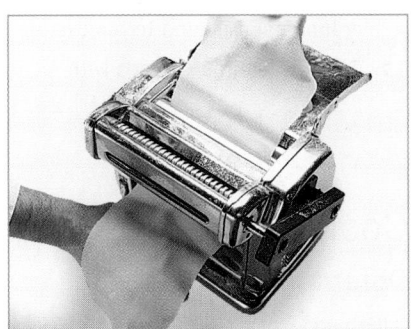

3. Passing the dough through the pasta machine to achieve the desired thickness.

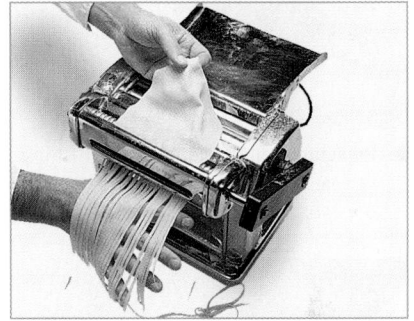

4. Using the pasta machine to cut the pasta into the desired width.

Filling Pasta

Sheets of raw pasta dough can be filled or folded to create ravioli (squares), tortellini (round "hats" with a brim of dough), lunettes (circles of dough folded into half-moons), agnolotti (squares of dough folded into rectangles), cappelletti (squares of dough folded and shaped into rings) and other shapes. The filled pieces of dough are then cooked in boiling water using the procedure for cooking pasta ribbons discussed later. The filling can include almost anything—cheese, herbs, vegetables, fish, shellfish, meat or poultry. It can be uncooked or precooked. However, any meat filling should be fully cooked before the pasta is assembled, as the time it takes for the dough to cook may not be sufficient to cook the filling.

Cannelloni is a different type of filled pasta: a large square of cooked dough is wrapped around a meat or cheese filling and baked. Popular lasagna dishes are similar. Lasagna pasta, which consists of wide, flat sheets, is cooked then layered with cheese, tomato sauce and meat or vegetables as desired. The finished casserole is baked and cut into portions.

Some of the larger, commercially prepared pasta shapes such as large shells (conchigloni or rigate) or large tubes (manicotti) can be partially cooked in boiling water, then filled, sauced and baked as a casserole.

Asian noodle dough is also made into filled items such as dumplings, won tons, egg rolls (made with egg noodle dough) and spring rolls (made with rice paper). These items are usually steamed, pan-fried or deep-fat fried.

When making filled pasta, consider the flavours and textures of the filling, dough and sauce. Each should complement the others. Combinations can range from traditional unflavoured semolina pasta with herb and ricotta filling in a tomato sauce to an elegant escargot in garlic-and-herb pasta served with a beurre blanc to pork, ginger, soy and scallions in Asian egg noodle dough served with a soy-based dipping sauce.

1. Piping the filling onto the dough.

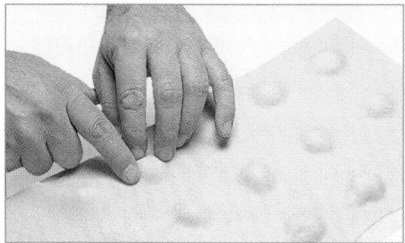

2. Pressing around the mounds of filling to seal the dough and remove any air pockets.

3. Cutting around the mounds with a circular cutter.

BASIC PROCEDURE FOR PREPARING RAVIOLI

1. Prepare a basic pasta dough of the desired flavour.

2. Prepare and chill the desired filling.

3. Roll out two thin sheets of dough between the rollers of a pasta machine. Gently lay the dough flat on the work surface.

4. Using a piping bag or a small portion scoop, place small mounds of filling on one of the dough pieces. Space the fillings evenly, allowing approximately 5 cm (2 in.) between each mound.

5. Brush the exposed areas of dough with water.

6. Gently place the second sheet of dough over the mounds and press firmly around each mound to remove air pockets and seal the dough.

7. Cut between the mounds with a chef's knife, pastry wheel or circular cutter.

Cooking Method

Determining Doneness

Italian-style pastas are properly cooked when they are **al dente**, firm but tender. Cooking times vary depending on the shape and quantity of pasta, the amount of water used, the hardness of the water and even the altitude. Fresh pasta cooks rapidly, sometimes in seconds. Noodles and dried pasta may require several minutes.

Although package or recipe directions offer some guidance, the only way to accurately test doneness is to bite into a piece. When the pasta is slightly firmer than desired, remove it from the stove and drain. It will continue to cook through residual heat.

Unlike Italian pasta, Asian noodles are not served al dente. Rather, they are either boiled until soft or stir-fried until very crisp.

Boiling

All Italian-style pasta and most Asian noodles are cooked by just one method: boiling. The secret to boiling pasta successfully is to use ample water. Allow 4 L (1 gal.) of water for each 500 g (1 lb.) of pasta.

Use a saucepan or stockpot large enough to allow the pasta to move freely in the boiling water, otherwise the starch released by the dough will make the pasta gummy and sticky. The water should be brought to a rapid boil, then all the pasta should be added at once.

Salt should be added to the water. Pasta absorbs water and salt during cooking. Adding salt to the pasta after it is cooked will not provide the same seasoning effect.

Chefs disagree on whether to add oil to the cooking water. Purists argue against adding oil, on the theory that it makes the dough absorb water unevenly. Others think oil should be added to reduce surface foam. Another theory is that oil keeps the pasta from sticking, although this works only when oil is added to cooked, drained pasta.

Asian noodles may be prepared by boiling until fully cooked, or they may be parboiled then stir-fried with other ingredients to finish cooking.

BASIC PROCEDURE FOR COOKING PASTA TO ORDER

1. Bring the appropriate amount of water to a boil over high heat.

2. Add oil to the water if desired.

3. Add the pasta and salt to the rapidly boiling water.

4. Stir the pasta to prevent it from sticking together. Bring the water back to a boil and cook until the pasta is done.

5. When the pasta is properly cooked, immediately drain it through a colander. A small amount of oil may be gently tossed into the pasta if desired to prevent it from sticking together.

6. Serve hot pasta immediately, or refresh in cold water for use in salads or other dishes. (Do not rinse pasta that is to be served hot.)

BASIC PROCEDURE FOR COOKING DRIED PASTA IN ADVANCE

Fresh pasta is so delicate and cooks so rapidly (sometimes in as little as 15 seconds) that it should be cooked to order. Dried pasta, however, can be cooked in advance for quantity service.

1. Follow the above directions for cooking pasta, but stop the cooking process when the pasta is about two-thirds done.

2. Drain the pasta, rinse it lightly and toss it in a small amount of oil.

3. Divide the pasta into appropriate-sized portions. Individual portions can be wrapped in plastic or laid on a sheet pan and covered. Refrigerate until needed.

4. When needed, place a portion in a conical strainer and immerse in boiling water to reheat. Drain, add sauce and serve immediately.

Accompaniments to Pasta

Pasta is widely accepted by consumers and easily incorporated in a variety of cuisines—from Italian and Chinese to Thai and spa. It is used in broths, as a bed for stews, fish, shellfish or meat, or tossed with sauce. Today's creative chefs are constantly developing nontraditional but delicious ways of serving pasta.

Pasta and Broths

Small shapes can be cooked in the broth with which they are served, or cooked separately, then added to the hot liquid at service time. Soups such as cappelletti in brodo and chicken noodle are examples of these techniques.

Pasta Sauces

There are hundreds of Italian pasta sauces as well as sauces for Italian-style pasta, but most can be divided into six categories: ragus, seafood sauces, vegetable sauces, cream sauces, garlic-oil sauces and uncooked sauces. Recipes for a selection of pasta sauces are in Chapter 10, Stocks and Sauces.

Although there are no firm rules governing the combinations of sauces and pasta, Table 23.3 on the next page offers some of the more common combinations.

Sauce	Description	Pasta Shape	Garnish
TABLE 23.3	Combining Sauces, Pasta and Garnishes		
Ragu	Braised dishes used as sauce; flavourings, meat or poultry are browned, then a tomato product and stock, wine, water, milk or cream added	Ribbons, tubes, shapes, filled	Grated cheese
Seafood	White seafood sauces are flavoured with herbs and made with white wine or stock; red seafood sauces are tomato-based	Ribbons (fettuccine and capellini)	Fish or shellfish
Vegetable	Includes both traditional sauces made with tomatoes and stock, flavoured with garlic and red pepper, and modern sauces such as primavera	Ribbons, tubes, filled	Meatballs, sausage, grated cheese
Cream	Uses milk or cream and sometimes roux; usually cheese is added	Thick ribbons (spaghetti and fettuccine), filled	Ham, peas, sausage, mushrooms, smoked salmon, nuts, grated cheese
Garlic-oil	(It. *aglio-olio*) Olive oil flavoured with garlic and herbs; can be hot or cold, cooked or uncooked (pesto is an uncooked, cold sauce)	Ribbons, shapes, filled	Grated cheese (if uncooked or cold), herbs
Uncooked	A variety of dressings and garnishes such as fresh tomatoes, basil and olive oil; or olive oil, lemon juice, parsley, basil and hot red pepper flakes; capers, anchovies, olives, fresh herbs, fresh vegetables, flavoured oils and cubed cheese can also be used	Ribbons, shapes	Cubed or grated cheese, fresh vegetables, herbs

Conclusion

Most meals would seem incomplete without a starch. The most popular starches are potatoes, grains (especially rice) and pasta. All are low in fat and a good source of energy. Most can be prepared with several dry- and moist-heat cooking methods. Starches can be sauced, seasoned or flavoured in limitless ways.

Questions for Discussion

1. Explain the differences between mealy and waxy potatoes. Give two examples of each.
2. Describe the two methods of sautéing or pan-frying potatoes.
3. Explain why duchesse potatoes are regarded as the "mother" of many classic potato dishes. Name and describe two such dishes.
4. All grains comprise three parts. Name and describe each of these parts.
5. Describe and compare the three general cooking methods used to prepare grains.
6. Name the three categories of Italian-style pasta shapes and give an example of each.
7. Why is it necessary to use ample water when cooking pasta? Should pasta be cooked in salted water? Should oil be added to the cooking water? Explain your answers.
8. Discuss the differences between cooking fresh pasta and cooking dried, factory-produced pasta.

Additional Starch Recipes

RECIPE 23.9

Potato Pancakes

Yield: 18 pancakes
Method: Pan-frying

Eggs, whole	2	2
Egg whites	4	4
Milk	350 mL	12 fl. oz.
Onion, grated	150 g	6 oz.
Parsley, chopped	20 g	2 Tbsp.
Garlic clove, minced	5 g	1
Flour	100 g	4 oz.
Sour cream	100 mL	3 fl. oz.
Potatoes, grated	500 g	1 lb.
Bacon, fried, diced	125 g	4 oz.
Canola oil	15 mL	1 Tbsp.
Baking powder	10 g	1 Tbsp.
Salt and pepper	TT	TT
Canola oil	as needed for cooking	

1. Separate the whole eggs and put all the egg whites in a bowl.
2. Whip the egg whites until stiff. In a separate bowl, beat the yolks, then blend into whites.
3. Fold in the milk, onion, parsley, garlic, flour, sour cream, grated potatoes, bacon, oil, baking powder, salt and pepper.
4. Heat the oil in a heavy-bottomed pan. Add the potato mixture to the oil in uniform-sized pancakes. Pan-fry the pancakes until tender, turning once when well browned on the first side. Remove from the pan and drain well.

Potato Pancakes

RECIPE 23.9

Approximate values per 120 g serving:	
Calories	130
Total fat	6 g
Saturated fat	2 g
Cholesterol	35 mg
Sodium	186 mg
Total carbohydrates	12 g
Protein	5 g

RECIPE 23.10

Rösti Potatoes

THE FOUR SEASONS, NEW YORK, NY
Executive Chef Christian Albin

Yield: 6 servings
Method: Pan-frying

Boiling potatoes, large	1 kg	4
Bacon fat	60 g	2 oz.
Lard	60 g	2 oz.
Kosher salt and pepper	TT	TT
Whole butter	30 g	1 oz.

1. Cook the potatoes in salted water until almost done.
2. Drain and cool the potatoes, then peel and coarsely grate them.
3. Heat the bacon fat and lard in a heavy, shallow 25-cm (10-in.) skillet with sloping sides until quite hot. Spread half the potatoes over the bottom of the pan; sprinkle with salt and pepper. Cover with the remaining potatoes and cook over medium-high heat until the bottom turns brown and crusty, approximately 10 minutes.

Rösti Potatoes

RECIPE 23.10

Approximate values per serving:	
Calories	298
Total fat	24 g
Saturated fat	14 g
Cholesterol	30 mg
Sodium	425 mg
Total carbohydrates	20 g
Protein	3 g

continued

4. Turn the potatoes in 1 piece. This is easiest to do by placing a large plate over the pan and turning both together so the potatoes fall onto the plate. Slip the turned-over potatoes off the plate back into the pan, browned side up. Cook until the bottom is browned.

5. Before serving, smooth the edges of the potatoes with a spatula. Sprinkle with salt and brush the edge of the pan with whole butter. It will melt and run into the potatoes.

VARIATION: CHEDDAR CHEESE RÖSTI POTATOES—Make 2 thin potato cakes. Top 1 with a layer of 200 g (7 oz.) sour cream, 60 g (2 oz.) cubed sharp cheddar cheese and 20 g (2 Tbsp.) chopped chives. Top with the other cake. Dot with 15 g (1 Tbsp.) whole butter and bake in a 200°C (400°F) oven for 15 minutes.

RECIPE 23.11

Scalloped Potatoes

Yield: 1 Pan, 9 in. × 12 in. (22 cm × 30 cm)
Method: Baking

Potatoes, mealy russet	5 lb.	2.4 kg
Béchamel (page 198)	36 fl. oz.	1 L
Salt and white pepper	TT	TT
Nutmeg	TT	TT
Whole butter	as needed	as needed

1. Peel the potatoes and hold them in water to prevent browning. Pour the béchamel into a stainless steel bowl. Slice the potatoes thinly (a mandoline works well for this purpose) directly into the béchamel. Stir occasionally so that the sauce coats the potatoes.

2. Season as desired with the salt, white pepper and nutmeg.

3. Layer the potatoes and sauce in a buttered half-size hotel pan. Pour any remaining sauce over the top of the potatoes.

4. Bake covered at 180°C (350°F) for approximately 30 minutes. Uncover and bake until the potatoes are cooked and brown on top, approximately 20 to 30 minutes.

RECIPE 23.11

Approximate values per 20 g serving:	
Calories	122
Total fat	5 g
Saturated fat	3 g
Cholesterol	13 mg
Sodium	270 mg
Total carbohydrates	17 g
Protein	3 g

1. Layering the potatoes in a hotel pan.

2. Pouring the remaining cream sauce over the potatoes.

3. The finished Scalloped Potatoes.

RECIPE 23.12

Candied Sweet Potatoes

Yield: 6 125-g (4-oz.) servings
Method: Baking

Sweet potatoes	1 kg	2 lb.
Brown sugar	150 g	5 oz.
Water	50 mL	2 fl. oz.
Whole butter	50 g	2 oz.
Vanilla extract	5 mL	1 tsp.

1. Wash the sweet potatoes and cut as necessary to promote even cooking.
2. Bake the sweet potatoes on a sheet pan at 180°C (350°F) until cooked but still firm, approximately 30 minutes.
3. Combine the brown sugar, water and butter and bring to a boil. Add the vanilla and remove from the heat.
4. Peel the potatoes and slice or cut as desired. Arrange the potatoes in a baking dish and pour the sugar mixture over them.
5. Sprinkle the potatoes with additional brown sugar if desired and bake for 20 minutes, basting occasionally with the sugar mixture.

Candied Sweet Potatoes

RECIPE 23.12

Approximate values per serving:	
Calories	327
Total fat	7 g
Saturated fat	4 g
Cholesterol	18 mg
Sodium	97 mg
Total carbohydrates	64 g
Protein	3 g

RECIPE 23.13

Château Potatoes

Yield: 10 servings
Method: Boiling/sautéing

Potatoes, waxy	2.2 kg	5 lb.
Salt	TT	TT
Clarified butter	180 mL	6 fl. oz.
White pepper	TT	TT
Whole butter	60 g	2 oz.

1. Peel the potatoes if desired. Cut the potatoes into 5-cm (2-in.) lengths and tournée.
2. Place the potatoes in a pan of salted water. Bring to a simmer and parcook the potatoes for approximately 5 minutes. They should still be raw in the middle.

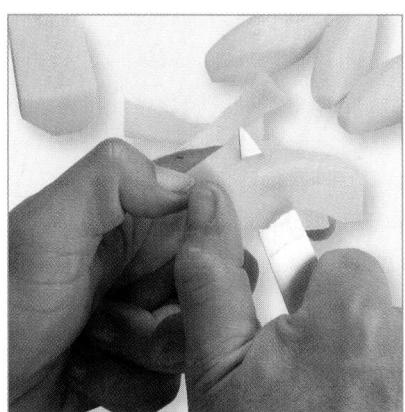

1. Tournéeing the potatoes.

2. Parcooking the potatoes.

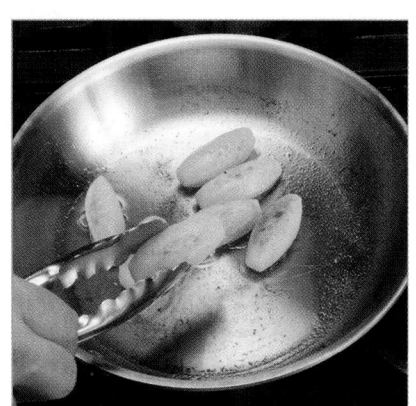

3. Sautéing the potatoes.

continued

3. Remove the potatoes from the water and spread on a pan so that the steam is released and the potatoes dry completely.

4. Heat an appropriately sized sauté pan over medium heat. Add enough clarified butter to cover the bottom of the pan approximately 6 mm (1/4 in.) deep. Sauté the potatoes in batches, adding more butter as necessary and turning them often until all sides are golden brown. If the potatoes are properly browned but not yet fully cooked, place them in a 180°C (350°F) oven for a few minutes until tender.

5. Season the potatoes with salt and white pepper and toss in a small amount of whole butter at service time.

VARIATIONS: PARISIENNE POTATOES AND NOISETTE POTATOES—Parisienne and noisette potatoes are prepared in the same manner as château potatoes but the potatoes are cut into balls with a Parisienne scoop or melon baller. Parisienne potatoes are generally larger than 2.5 cm. (1 in.) and noisette potatoes are generally smaller than 2.5 cm. (1 in.). Parcooking time is greatly reduced; the potatoes can also be cooked from the raw state without parcooking.

RECIPE 23.13

Approximate values per serving:	
Calories	330
Total fat	19 g
Saturated fat	12 g
Cholesterol	60 mg
Sodium	400 mg
Total carbohydrates	36 g
Protein	5 g

RECIPE 23.14

Dauphine Potatoes

Yield: 1.3 kg (3 lb.)

Method: Boiling

Duchesse Potatoes (page 569)	2 lb.	900 g
Basic Choux Paste (page 765)	10 oz.	300 g

1. Combine the Duchesse Potatoes with the Basic Choux Paste while both mixtures are still warm.

2. Pipe the mixture into the desired shapes onto strips of parchment paper. Chill until ready to cook. At service, deep-fat fry by carefully sliding the pieces of paper into the fryer; remove the paper with tongs when the potatoes float loose. Cook until golden brown.

NOTE: Use only half the eggs for the paste. End product has a better texture.

VARIATION: LORETTE—Add 125 g. (4 oz.) grated Parmesan in step 2. Pipe the mixture into small crescents on pieces of parchment paper. Deep-fat fry by carefully sliding the pieces of paper into the fryer; remove the paper with tongs when the potatoes float loose.

RECIPE 23.14

Approximate values per serving:	
Calories	219
Total fat	9 g
Saturated fat	5 g
Cholesterol	89 mg
Sodium	250 mg
Total carbohydrates	27 g
Protein	5 g

1. Deep-fat frying the potatoes using the swimming method.

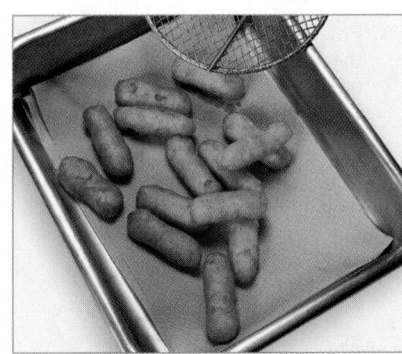

2. The finished potatoes.

RECIPE 23.15

Potato and Fruit Dumplings

Chef Klaus Theyer, CCC
Yield: 12 pieces (4 portions)

Potatoes, mealy	500 g	18 oz.
Egg	1	1
Semolina, quick cooking	70 g	2-1/2 oz.
Nutmeg	1 g	1/4 tsp.
Flour, all-purpose	100 g	3-1/2 oz.
Salt	3 g	1/2 tsp.
Butter, unsalted	250 g	9 oz.
Flour or cornstarch	as needed	as needed
Apricots or plums, pitted	12	12
Sugar cubes	12	12
Salt	TT	TT
Water, boiling	as needed	as needed
Walnuts or hazelnuts, ground	50 g	1-3/4 oz.
Bread crumbs, plain	100 g	3-1/2 oz.
Icing sugar	250 g	9 oz.

Klaus Theyer, CCC

1. Boil potatoes in skins until tender. Drain and peel. Press through a ricer.

2. Mix the riced potatoes while still hot with the egg, semolina, nutmeg, approximately half the flour, salt and 50 g (1-3/4 oz.) of the butter to form a smooth dough. The amount of flour needed will vary according to the dampness of the potatoes.

3. Dust the table with flour or cornstarch. Roll the dough to 1.25 cm (1/2 in.) in a square. Cut into 12 6-cm (2-1/2-in.) squares.

4. Cut a pocket into the fruit and remove the stone. Insert a sugar cube.

5. Place a fruit in the centre of each dough square and bring up the corners to meet at the top; gently squeeze together and carefully roll into a ball-shaped dumpling.

6. Place all 12 dumplings into lightly salted boiling water and simmer for approximately 12 minutes or until they float.

7. Meanwhile, clarify the remaining butter, pour into a sauté pan and heat. Add the nuts and bread crumbs and fry until light golden brown.

8. Remove the dumplings from the water and roll in the crumb-nut mixture until generously coated.

9. Place on serving plate and top with remaining crumbs and dust generously with icing sugar. Serve hot.

RECIPE 23.15

Approximate values per serving:	
Calories	1007
Total fat	61 g
Saturated fat	33 g
Cholesterol	183 mg
Sodium	540 mg
Total carbohydrates	101 g
Protein	17 g

Frank Formella, CCC

Frank Formella has been teaching his
love of cooking to culinary students at
Humber College for more than 22 years.
Before embarking on his teaching career,
Frank enjoyed cooking in a variety of
hotels in places such as Bermuda,
London (England), Germany and
Switzerland.

RECIPE 23.16

Approximate values per serving:	
Calories	310
Total fat	14 g
Saturated fat	7.4 g
Cholesterol	175 mg
Sodium	436 mg
Total carbohydrates	32 g
Protein	16 g

Potato and Squash Timbales

HRT ALLIANCE, HUMBER COLLEGE
OF APPLIED ARTS AND TECHNOLOGY, Toronto, ON
Professor Frank Formella, CCC

Yield: 10 servings

Pumpkin or butternut squash, medium dice	500 g	1 lb.
Butter, unsalted	60 g	2 oz.
Potatoes, cooked and puréed	1 kg	2 lb.
Zucchini, medium dice	1 kg	2 lb.
Red bell pepper, roasted, medium dice	350 g	2
Eggs, beaten	8	8
Grana Padano, grated	160 g	5 oz.
Parsley, fine chopped	30 g	1 oz.
Thyme, fine chopped	20 g	3/4 oz.
Basil, chiffonade	20 g	3/4 oz.
Salt and pepper	TT	TT
Butter, melted	as needed	as needed
Potatoes, thinly sliced (mandoline)	as needed	as needed

1. Lightly sauté the pumpkin in butter.
2. Mix the puréed potatoes with the vegetables, eggs, cheese and herbs.
3. Season with salt and pepper.
4. Brush 10 300-mL ramekins with butter and line bottom and sides with parchment paper. Brush paper with butter.
5. Line bottom and sides of each ramekin with thinly sliced potatoes so that they overlap.
6. Pour the potato mixture into the ramekins and press well to ensure there are no air pockets.
7. Cover with parchment and bake in a 200°C (400°F) oven for 40 minutes or until potato lining is golden brown.

RECIPE 23.17

Saffron Rice

Yield: 10 servings
Method: Simmering

Basmati rice	500 g	16 oz.
Saffron threads	0.5 g	1 tsp.
Boiling water	900 mL	28 fl. oz.
Ghee (or clarified butter)	100 g	3 oz.
Cinnamon stick, 5 cm (2 in.) long	1	1
Cloves, whole	4	4
Onion, fine dice	150 g	5 oz.
Dark brown sugar	15 g	1 Tbsp.
Salt	10 g	2 tsp.
Cardamom, ground	1 g	1/4 tsp.

1. Wash the rice and drain thoroughly.
2. Steep the saffron in 60 mL (2 fl. oz.) of the boiling water.
3. In a saucepan, heat the ghee, add the cinnamon and cloves. Add the onion and stir-fry until it is soft and slightly brown.
4. Add the rice and stir until it is well coated with the ghee and the grains are a light golden colour.
5. Stirring constantly, add the remaining boiling water, brown sugar, salt and cardamom. Bring to a boil and reduce to a simmer.
6. Gently stir in the saffron and its water, cover and simmer until the rice has absorbed all the liquid.
7. Fluff with a fork and serve at once.

Saffron Rice

RECIPE 23.17

Approximate values per 120 g serving:	
Calories	268
Total fat	8.5 g
Saturated fat	5 g
Cholesterol	22 mg
Sodium	477 mg
Total carbohydrates	43 g
Protein	4 g

RECIPE 23.18

Brown Rice Pilaf with Pine Nuts

Yield: 10 90-g (3-oz.) servings
Method: Pilaf

Saffron threads	0.25 g	1/2 tsp.
Chicken stock, hot	500 mL	16 fl. oz.
Sesame oil	15 mL	1 Tbsp.
Vegetable oil	15 mL	1 Tbsp.
Pine nuts	50 g	2 oz.
Onion, medium dice	175 g	6 oz.
Red bell pepper, medium dice	175 g	6 oz.
Garlic, chopped	10 g	2 tsp.
Brown rice	200 g	1 cup
Salt	5 g	1 tsp.
Pepper	TT	TT
Currants, dry	50 g	2 oz.

1. Steep the saffron threads in the hot stock for 5 minutes.
2. Heat the oils and sauté the pine nuts until lightly browned.
3. Add the onion, red pepper and garlic and sauté without browning.
4. Add the rice and stir to coat the rice with the oil.
5. Add the salt and stock to the rice. Season with pepper, bring to a boil, reduce the heat and cover. Cook on the stove top or in the oven until done, approximately 30 minutes.
6. Stir in the currants, cover and allow them to soften for 5 minutes.

RECIPE 23.18

Approximate values per serving:	
Calories	159
Total fat	6 g
Saturated fat	1 g
Cholesterol	0 mg
Sodium	361 mg
Total carbohydrates	23 g
Protein	4.5 g

Paul Rogalski

Paul's passion for cooking was inspired by his grandmother's garden. He began working full-time at the Palliser Hotel in Calgary while still a student at SAIT, then moved to La Chaumière Restaurant, where he became Executive Chef in 1992. After gaining experience at restaurants in North America and abroad, Paul co-founded Rouge Restaurant, noted for fresh ingredients from local purveyors and from the restaurant's own summer garden. Paul is a member of Slow Food Canada and the Chaîne des Rôtisseurs. Read more about his culinary experiences on p. 576.

RECIPE 23.19

Approximate values per serving:	
Calories	471
Total fat	15 g
Saturated fat	6 g
Cholesterol	26 mg
Sodium	884 mg
Total carbohydrates	67 g
Protein	15 g

RECIPE 23.19

Morel and St. Agur Risotto

ROUGE RESTAURANT, CALGARY, AB
Chef/Owner Paul Rogalski

Yield: 6 350-g (12-oz.) portions

Method: Risotto

Morel mushrooms, fresh, cleaned	150 g	5-1/2 oz.
Butter, unsalted	30 g	1 oz.
Extra virgin olive oil	30 mL	1 fl. oz.
Shallots, minced	60 g	2 oz.
Sea salt	5 g	1 tsp.
Black pepper, fresh ground	1 g	1/2 tsp.
Arborio rice	400 g	14 oz.
Chicken stock	1.8 L	64 fl. oz.
St. Agur blue cheese, crumbled	50 g	2 oz.
Dill, fresh, fine chopped	20 g	2 Tbsp.

1. Brush morels under cold running water to remove any sand or dirt. Cut morels into large pieces and reserve.

2. Preheat a brasier and add butter and olive oil. Add shallots and sauté until translucent. Add the morels, season lightly with sea salt and pepper and cook until tender. Remove from brasier and reserve.

3. Add arborio rice to the brasier and stir for 1 minute. Stir in 225 mL (8 fl. oz.) chicken stock and continue stirring until the liquid is almost absorbed. Repeat the process with remaining chicken stock until all stock is absorbed and the rice is tender.

4. Stir in the St. Agur and the reserved morels. Fold in the dill.

5. Adjust seasoning and serve immediately.

RECIPE 23.20

Wild Rice and Cranberry Stuffing

Yield: 2.5 L (5 pt.)

Method: Simmering

Dried morels	30 g	1 oz.
Wild rice	350 g	12 oz.
Onion, minced	250 g	8 oz.
Poultry seasoning	2 g	1 tsp.
Butter or chicken fat	50 g	2 oz.
Chicken stock, hot	approx. 1 L	approx. 1 qt.
Dried cranberries	175 g	6 oz.
Salt and pepper	TT	TT
Fresh parsley, chopped fine	50 g	4 Tbsp.

1. Soak the dried morels overnight in lightly salted water. Drain, reserving the liquid. Rinse well, drain again and chop coarsely.

Wild Rice and Cranberry Stuffing

continued

2. Rinse the wild rice well in cold water.

3. Sauté the onion and poultry seasoning in the butter or chicken fat until tender. Add the morels and wild rice.

4. Strain the reserved liquid from the morels through several layers of cheesecloth to remove all sand and grit. Add enough chicken stock to make 1.5 L (3 pt.). Add the stock mixture and cranberries to the rice. Cover and simmer until the rice is dry and fluffy, approximately 45 minutes.

5. Season to taste with salt and pepper and stir in the parsley. This rice may be served as a side dish or used for stuffing duck or game hens.

RECIPE 23.20

Approximate values per 150 mL serving:	
Calories	130
Total fat	3 g
Saturated fat	2 g
Cholesterol	7 mg
Sodium	235 mg
Total carbohydrates	21 g
Protein	5 g

RECIPE 23.21

Polenta

Yield: 800 g (1 lb. 12 oz.)

Method: Simmering

Shallots, chopped	10 g	2 tsp.
Whole butter	60 g	2 oz.
Milk, white stock or water	1 L	1 qt.
Cornmeal, yellow or white	180 g	6 oz.
Salt and pepper	TT	TT

1. Sauté the shallots in 15 g (1 Tbsp.) of butter for 30 seconds. Add the liquid and bring to a boil.

2. Slowly add the cornmeal while stirring constantly to prevent lumps, then simmer for 30 minutes. Season with salt and pepper. Stir regularly.

3. Scrape the polenta into a buttered nonaluminum dish; spread to an even thickness with a spatula that has been dipped in water. Refrigerate the polenta until well chilled.

4. To serve, unmould the polenta and cut into shapes following the procedure discussed in Chapter 36, Plate Presentation. Sauté or grill the polenta for service, or sprinkle with grated Parmesan cheese and heat under a broiler or salamander.

Cutting the polenta into the desired shape.

RECIPE 23.21

Approximate values per 100 g serving:	
Calories	216
Total fat	11 g
Saturated fat	6.5 g
Cholesterol	34 mg
Sodium	352 mg
Total carbohydrates	23.5 g
Protein	6 g

RECIPE 23.22

Macaroni and Cheese

Yield: 24 250-g (8-oz.) servings

Cheddar sauce (see page 198)	2 L	2 qt.
Worcestershire sauce	TT	TT
Hot pepper sauce	TT	TT
Elbow macaroni, boiled and refreshed	1 kg	2 lb.
Cheddar cheese, grated	1 kg	2 lb.
Whole butter	250 g	8 oz.
Bread crumbs	30 g	1 oz.

1. Season the cheese sauce with Worcestershire and hot pepper sauces.

2. Mix the macaroni with the cheese sauce and the grated cheese.

3. Pour into a buttered full-sized hotel pan. Sprinkle with bread crumbs.

4. Bake uncovered at 180°C (350°F) until hot, approximately 30 minutes.

VARIATION: MACARONI AND CHEESE WITH HAM AND TOMATO—Stir 1 kg (2 lb.) each diced cooked ham and tomato concassée into the macaroni and cheese before pouring it into the hotel pan.

Macaroni and Cheese

RECIPE 23.22

Approximate values per serving:	
Calories	453
Total fat	27 g
Saturated fat	17 g
Cholesterol	80 mg
Sodium	290 mg
Total carbohydrates	35 g
Protein	17 g

Fettucine Alfredo

RECIPE 23.23

Approximate values per serving:	
Calories	546
Total fat	49 g
Saturated fat	30 g
Cholesterol	179 mg
Sodium	437 mg
Total carbohydrates	19 g
Protein	11 g

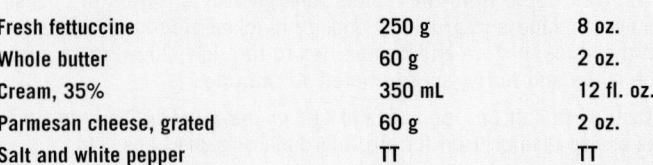

RECIPE 23.23

Fettuccine Alfredo

Yield: 4 180-g (6-oz.) servings

Fresh fettuccine	250 g	8 oz.
Whole butter	60 g	2 oz.
Cream, 35%	350 mL	12 fl. oz.
Parmesan cheese, grated	60 g	2 oz.
Salt and white pepper	TT	TT

1. Boil the pasta, keeping it slightly undercooked. Refresh and drain.
2. To make the sauce, combine the butter, cream and cheese in a sauté pan. Bring to a boil and reduce slightly.
3. Add the pasta to the pan and boil the sauce and pasta until the sauce is thick and the pasta is cooked. Adjust the seasonings and serve.

Goat-Cheese Ravioli in Herbed Cream Sauce

RECIPE 23.24

Approximate values per serving:	
Calories	790
Total fat	64 g
Saturated fat	35 g
Cholesterol	242 mg
Sodium	500 mg
Total carbohydrates	36 g
Protein	18 g

RECIPE 23.24

Goat-Cheese Ravioli in Herbed Cream Sauce

Yield: 72 5-cm (2-in.) ravioli and 750 mL (1-1/2 pt.) sauce

Fresh goat cheese	300 g	11 oz.
Cream cheese	250 g	8 oz.
Fresh basil, chopped fine	30 g	3 Tbsp.
Fresh thyme, chopped fine	8 g	2 tsp.
Fresh parsley, chopped	30 g	3 Tbsp.
Pepper	TT	TT
Pasta, fresh	1 kg	2 lb.
Cream, 35%	1 L	32 fl. oz.
Parmesan cheese, grated	50 g	2 oz.
Salt	TT	TT

1. To make the cheese filling, combine the goat and cream cheese with 20 g (2 Tbsp.) basil, 4 g (1 tsp.) thyme and the parsley; season to taste with pepper.
2. Make ravioli using the cheese mixture and pasta.
3. To make the sauce, combine the cream with the remaining herbs and bring to a boil. Reduce by one-third and add the Parmesan cheese. Season with salt and pepper.
4. Boil the ravioli until done. Drain, toss gently with the sauce and serve.

Pesto Sauce

Yield: 1 kg (30 oz.)

Olive oil	400 mL	12 fl. oz.
Pine nuts	100 g	3 oz.
Fresh basil leaves	200 g	6 oz.
Garlic, chopped	15 g	4 cloves
Parmesan cheese, grated	125 g	4 oz.
Romano cheese, grated	125 g	4 oz.
Salt and pepper	TT	TT

1. Place one-third of the olive oil in a blender or food processor and add all the remaining ingredients.

2. Blend or process until smooth. Add the remaining olive oil and blend a few seconds to incorporate.

VARIATION: Walnut Pesto—Substitute walnuts for pine nuts in the Pesto Sauce recipe.

Approximate values per 50 g serving:	
Calories	243
Total fat	24 g
Saturated fat	5 g
Cholesterol	11 mg
Sodium	192 mg
Total carbohydrates	2 g
Protein	6 g

1. Lasagna Bolognese Style: Layering the pasta, sauce and béchamel in a hotel pan.

Lasagna Bolognese Style

Yield: 15 portions

Pasta sheets, fresh	5	5
Bolognese sauce:		
Olive oil	50 mL	2 fl. oz.
Ground beef	1 kg	2 lb. 4 oz.
Ground pork	1 kg	2 lb. 4 oz.
Onion, small dice	200 g	7 oz.
Carrot, brunoise	400 g	14 oz.
Celery, brunoise	400 g	14 oz.
Tomato paste	200 g	7 oz.
Salt and pepper	TT	TT
Meat stock	1.75 L	1-3/4 qt.
Parsley, minced	50 g	2 oz.
Béchamel sauce, warm	2 L	2-1/4 qt.
Olive oil	as needed	as needed
Parmesan cheese, grated	400 g	14 oz.
Mozzarella, grated	300 g	11 oz.

1. Cut each pasta sheet into 12 rectangles. Parcook in boiling saltwater for approximately 1 minute. Drain on towelling and allow to cool.

2. For the Bolognese sauce, heat 50 mL (2 fl. oz.) olive oil in a brazier, add the meat and fry over fairly high heat to brown. Add the mirepoix and stir in the tomato paste. Fry briefly with the meat, season with salt and pepper and add the stock. Simmer for 30 minutes. Finish with parsley.

3. To assemble, lightly oil an oval ramekin. Place one piece of pasta on the bottom. Layer with 60 g (2 oz.) of meat sauce and place a pasta layer. Spread 60 mL (2 fl. oz.) béchamel sauce and cover with pasta. Repeat. Alternately, prepare in a full-size hotel pan; see below.

4. Distribute the Parmesan and mozzarella over the last layer of béchamel.

5. Bake in a 200°C (400°F) oven for 20 minutes or until cheese layer is browned. Serve immediately. If cooking in a hotel pan, the time will be approximately 40 minutes. Allow lasagna to rest for 10 to 15 minutes before portioning.

2. Pouring a layer of béchamel over the lasagna.

3. The finished lasagna.

Approximate values per serving:	
Calories	949
Total fat	58 g
Saturated fat	26 g
Cholesterol	210 mg
Sodium	1234 mg
Total carbohydrates	52 g
Protein	54 g

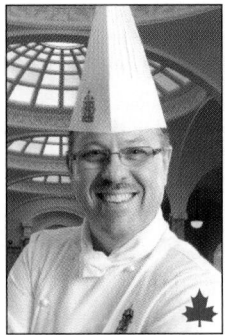

Judson Simpson, CCC

Born, raised and trained in Canada, Judson got his start in a local fish market where he learned the basics of cooking that still serve him well. Later, he decided to enrol at Toronto's George Brown College to study cooking in a formal environment. In 1991, Jud and his family moved to the nation's capital where he continues to practise and teach his artistically personal brand of Canadian cuisine. He was Manager of Gold Medal Culinary Team Canada in 2004. Judson is currently president of the Canadian Culinary Federation.

RECIPE 23.27

Approximate values per serving:	
Calories	590
Total fat	12 g
Saturated fat	2 g
Cholesterol	141 mg
Sodium	626 mg
Total carbohydrates	57 g
Protein	66 g

RECIPE 23.27

Thai Chicken with Canton Noodle Salad

PARLIAMENTARY RESTAURANT, HOUSE OF COMMONS, Ottawa, ON
Executive Chef Judson Simpson, CCC

Yield: 8 servings

Lemon grass, chopped very fine	2 g	1/2 tsp.
Green finger hot chile (Serrano)	1/2	1/2
Lime juice, fresh	50 mL	1-1/2 fl. oz.
Sugar	10 g	2 tsp.
Cilantro, chopped	10 g	1 Tbsp.
Light soy sauce	15 mL	1 Tbsp.
Extra virgin olive oil	30 mL	2 Tbsp.
Shallot, chopped fine	25 g	2 Tbsp.
Water	30 mL	2 Tbsp.
Organic chicken breasts, boneless, skinless	1.5 kg	3 lb.
Rice noodles	150 g	5 oz.
Canton noodles	250 g	8 oz.
Asparagus, blanched, cut on bias	500 g	1 lb.
Shiitake mushrooms, sliced, sautéed	85 g	3 oz.
Baby corn, cut on bias	200 g	6 oz.
Ginger, chopped	2 g	1/2 tsp.
Garlic, minced	5 g	1 clove
Light soy sauce	30 mL	2 Tbsp.
Teriyaki sauce	30 mL	2 Tbsp.
Olive oil	30 mL	2 Tbsp.
Lime juice, fresh	15 mL	1 Tbsp.
White wine vinegar	10 mL	2 tsp.
Radicchio	1/2 head	1/2 head
Endive	1 head	1 head
Sesame seeds	5 g	1 Tbsp.

1. In a nonreactive bowl, combine lemon grass, chile, lime juice, sugar, cilantro, soy sauce, olive oil, shallot and water to make dressing.

2. Lightly brush chicken breasts with one-half of the dressing and bake at 220°C (425°F) until cooked.

3. Cook the rice and canton noodles separately in boiling salted water. Chill.

4. Prepare salad by combining noodles with asparagus, mushrooms, corn, ginger, garlic, soy and teriyaki sauces, olive oil, lime juice and vinegar.

5. To serve, arrange radicchio and endive on plate. Place noodle salad and arrange sliced chicken breast. Drizzle with remaining dressing and sprinkle with sesame seeds.

Gnocchi

Yield: 1.5 kg (3 lb.)

Boiled potatoes	1 kg	2 lb.
Eggs	2	2
Salt, pepper and nutmeg	TT	TT
Flour, all-purpose	400 g	14 oz.

1. Place boiled potatoes on a tray and place in warm oven to dry slightly, then rice them in a food mill.
2. In mixing bowl, incorporate the potatoes, eggs and seasonings.
3. Add 350 g (12 oz.) of the flour to the ingredients in the bowl, all at once.
4. Mix lightly to form a medium-soft dough.
5. If needed, add more flour to adjust the consistency.
6. Roll the dough out to 1-cm (1/2-in.) thickness on lightly floured table, then let it cool. Cut into 1.5 cm × 1.5 cm (3/4 in. × 3/4 in.) squares. Roll the squares over the back of a table fork to make indents, forming a shell shape.
7. Cook in simmering, salted water for 3–4 minutes, or until they double in size.

Gnocchi served with tomato sauce.

Approximate values per 125 g serving:	
Calories	205
Total fat	1 g
Saturated fat	0.5 g
Cholesterol	36 mg
Sodium	115 mg
Total carbohydrates	42 g
Protein	6 g

Spaetzle

Yield: 3.5 kg (7-1/2 lb.)

Eggs	30	30
Water	500 mL	16 fl. oz.
Salt	30 g	1 oz.
Nutmeg	TT	TT
Flour, all-purpose	1.5 kg	3 lb. 4 oz.

1. In the bowl of the food mixer, beat the eggs, water, salt and nutmeg together.
2. With paddle attachment and on low speed, mix in the flour until just incorporated, then mix on high speed for 1 minute. Do not overbeat or the dumplings will be tough.
3. Suspend a large-holed colander over a pot of boiling water. In small batches, press the mixture through the colander so that the batter drops into the water.
4. Cook the dumplings until they float to the surface, approximately 2–3 minutes.
5. Remove them from the water with a skimmer and refresh in ice water. Do not leave them to soak.
6. Drain well and reserve in refrigerator, covered.
7. To serve, sauté the Spaetzle in butter and finish with chopped parsley.

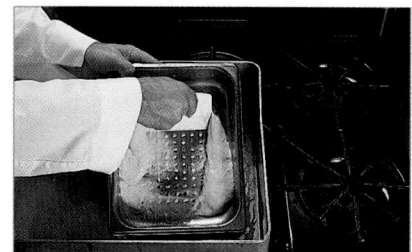

Forcing the Spaetzle through a perforated hotel pan.

Approximate values per 100 g serving:	
Calories	219
Total fat	5 g
Saturated fat	1.5 g
Cholesterol	184 mg
Sodium	453 mg
Total carbohydrates	33 g
Protein	10 g

24 Vegetarian Cooking

> "Cooking should be a carefully balanced reflection of all the good things of the earth.

—Jean and Pierre Troisgros, French chefs

A growing number of people are choosing to forgo some or all animal products in their diets. Given this growing trend, a chef needs to know how to cater to a vegetarian diner. A chef needs to understand that it is not necessarily enough simply to remove the meat from the centre of the plate and replace it with pasta. Nor is it always sufficient to offer a plate composed of several starch and vegetable side dishes as if it were a balanced and inviting meal.

In this chapter we discuss what it is to be a vegetarian and the motivations supporting this diet. We also explore ways in which a chef can offer a variety of flavourful and appealing vegetarian dishes that will satisfy even the most discriminating of vegetarian diners—and maybe a few meat eaters as well.

VARIATIONS ON VEGETARIANISM

Although the term *vegetarian* was not widely used until 1847, when England's Vegetarian Society first adopted it to describe people who excluded all animal products from their diets, millions of people have, for thousands of years, eaten little to no meat. Some have done so for religious or philosophical beliefs, others for environmental or health concerns. Still others have done so simply because they did not have regular access to meat.

One of the earliest known proponents of a vegetarian diet was the Greek mathematician and philosopher Pythagoras (c. 569–475 B.C.E.). He believed that there was a kinship among all living creatures and therefore chose not to eat the flesh of slaughtered animals. Over the next two centuries or so, his beliefs were refined and his followers eventually adopted an ethical code that included vows not to kill living creatures (including animals traditionally sacrificed to the gods) and to never eat meat. His teachings and those of his followers became sufficiently widespread that for centuries—indeed, until the 19th century—the term *Pythagoreans* was used to describe people who chose to eat only plant products.

Other than for small groups of Pythagoreans and some devout, ascetic religious (especially monastic) communities and sects, vegetarianism as a diet of choice never really caught hold in Europe or North America until the 19th and 20th centuries. And even then, until the 1970s, vegetarianism was more often than not chosen as part of a puritanical or spiritual lifestyle devoted to moderation and abstinence from liquor, caffeine and other stimulants.

Today there are many variations on the vegetarian diet. Some vegetarian diets (and lifestyles) exclude the consumption and use of all animal products (and even some plant products), while others allow the adherent to consume some animal or animal-based products. A person who follows a vegetarian diet can be any of the following:

- *Vegan* (VEE-gun)—A person who eats no meat, fish or poultry or any products derived from animals such as milk, cheese, eggs, honey or gelatin; also referred to as a **strict** or **pure vegetarian**.
- *Raw foodist*—Typically, a vegan who eats only raw or slightly warmed plant products (adherents believe that cooking foods to a temperature of 47°C [116°F] or above destroys enzymes and nutrients). A person on a raw foods diet, also referred to as a *living foodist,* may soak certain foods such as nuts and sprouts to soften them and increase nutrient absorption.

● **vegetarian** a person who does not eat any meat, poultry, game, fish, shellfish or animal byproducts such as gelatin or animal fats; may also exclude dairy products or eggs from the diet

- *Fructarian* or *fruitarian*—A person who eats only fruits, nuts, seeds and other plant products that can be gathered without harming the plant (some eat only plant matter that has already fallen off the plant).
- *Ovo-vegetarian*—A vegetarian who eats eggs but not dairy products.
- *Ovo-lacto-vegetarian* or *lacto-ovo-vegetarian*—A person who eats plant products as well as dairy products and eggs (although some may not eat cheeses made with animal-based enzymes such as rennet, or eggs produced by factory farms). This diet is one of the most typical of vegetarian diets and these terms are often used interchangeably with the term *vegetarian.*
- *Lacto-vegetarian*—A vegetarian who eats dairy products but not eggs.
- *Demi-vegetarian*—A vegetarian or ovo-lacto-vegetarian who eats fish.
- *Macrobioticist*—A person who follows a diet devised in the 1920s by a Japanese teacher who adhered to a simple meal plan of brown rice, miso soup and sea vegetables (seaweed). Derived from an ancient style of eating common in Asia, this dietary philosophy is based on Chinese concepts of balancing the opposite forces called *yin* and *yang*. Brown rice, whole grains, and vegetables form the basis of the diet. Fruits, nuts, refined sugars and refined foods are avoided, although fish is occasionally eaten on such diets.

MOTIVATIONS FOR VEGETARIANISM

For millennia, people have followed vegetarian diets for a variety of reasons, including religious and ethical beliefs. More recently, environmental and health concerns have become the major motivations for adopting some sort of vegetarian diet.

Religion

Religion has long played a leading role in defining how and what people eat. Although few religions actually mandate a complete vegetarian diet for their followers, many of the world's major religions promote meatless diets, in part as a spiritual ideal and in part in recognition of man's kinship with animals.

- *Hinduism*. This vast and complex civilization and religion is based, in part, on the Vedas, sacred texts written approximately 4000 years ago. Based on these and later teachings, the priestly caste developed a religious and ethical standard of conduct called *ahimsa*. Ahimsa is the desire not to cause harm or injury; that is, a person should strive to act in a nonviolent fashion. Many observant Hindus (especially members of the priestly caste known as the Brahmins) believe that ahimsa applies to man's relationship with animals. Because they consider the slaughtering of animals for consumption a violent act, they believe that they must follow a vegetarian diet. This diet will, however, often include milk and other dairy products, as animals give these foods willingly and are not injured in the process. Other observant Hindus believe that ahimsa extends only to interactions with other people and therefore will eat meat, although most will abstain from eating beef as the cow is considered sacred. Hinduism is the predominant religion of India, but is practised worldwide by Indian immigrants and their families, as many as 800 million people worldwide.
- *Buddhism*. As with Hindus, not all Buddhists are vegetarians. There are essentially two major schools of Buddhist thought and these schools differ on several important teachings, including vegetarianism. One school of

Buddhism follows certain ancient texts that suggest that the Buddha ate meat, but did so to not offend those who provided him and his fellow monks and nuns with these charitable offerings. These texts also record the Buddha as stating that a person can eat meat provided the person does not hear, see or suspect that the animal was specifically killed for him or her to consume. Thus, this school of Buddhism does not actually prohibit its followers from eating animal products. The second school of Buddhism does not follow these particular texts and practitioners of this school generally adhere to a vegetarian diet. They do so because the Buddha taught that nonviolence, love and compassion are all extremely important virtues that must be extended to all living creatures.

In the modern Buddhist world, attitudes toward vegetarianism also vary by location. In China and Vietnam, monks and other strictly observant Buddhists typically do not eat meat, while in Japan and Korea some will (especially fish), although most do not. In Sri Lanka and Southeast Asia, Buddhists generally do not practise vegetarianism. The Dalai Lama, the spiritual leader of Buddhists worldwide, regularly preaches nonviolence and encourages all Buddhists to maintain vegetarian diets.

- *Jainism.* Based on their blend of Hindu and Buddhist beliefs, observant Jains are vegans. They try to practise as pure a form of ahimsa as possible. Indeed, some Jains continually sweep the path before them and wear gauze masks over their mouths so as not to harm insects by inadvertently treading on them or breathing them in. Similarly, they will not eat root vegetables and bulbs such as garlic and onions as harvesting them may kill worms and other small animals living in the soil. A majority of the world's Jains live in India.

- *Judaism and Christianity.* The book of Genesis suggests that the original diet in the Garden of Eden was vegan. It is only later, after the Deluge, that the descendants of Noah were given permission to eat meat. Based on these scriptures, some Jews and Christians believe that God originally intended humans to be vegetarians, even though the consumption of meat is allowed. Moreover, some observant Jews and Christians are preparing for the coming of the Messiah by practising vegetarianism. They interpret the Bible to suggest that when the Messiah arrives there will be a return to an Eden-like society, including vegetarianism.

Ethics and Animal Rights

Irrespective of religious teachings concerning cruelty to animals, some vegetarians refuse to eat meat because of an emotional aversion to inflicting pain and harm on other living creatures or an objection to the manner in which animals are raised and slaughtered. Early in the 20th century Americans were made aware of cruel and unsanitary practices in slaughterhouses by Upton Sinclair, whose 1906 novel *The Jungle* led to federal regulation of the meat industry. More recently, those beliefs gained much credence with the 1975 publication of *Animal Liberation* by an Australian ethics professor, Peter Singer. Along with lurid descriptions of factory farms, slaughterhouses and scientific laboratories, he presents several ethical arguments on why we should neither eat nor experiment on animals. His book helped spark the animal rights movement in North America, including the founding of PETA (People for the Ethical Treatment of Animals), a strong proponent of vegetarianism. In 2006, a movement started to halt the consumption of foie gras, due to allegations of cruelty to ducks and geese.

Environmental Concerns

Many vegetarians cite environmental concerns as one of the principal reasons they chose to forgo animal products in their diet and to advocate that others do so as well. They often rely on arguments first raised in a scholarly fashion by Frances Moore Lappé in *Diet for a Small Planet*. Published in 1971, *Diet for a Small Planet* explores the problems of world hunger and concludes that world hunger is caused, in great part, by the wasteful use of agricultural resources on supporting animals raised for meat. She notes, for example, that at the time she was writing the book, more than 80% of the grain grown in the United States was fed to livestock. She then argues that if Americans cut their meat consumption by just 10%, there would be enough grain left over to feed many of the world's hungry people. Although she did not necessarily advocate a complete vegetarian diet for all, she did urge people to reduce their consumption of animal products.

Lappé's bestselling book was quickly adopted by the small but growing vegetarian community in North America. They saw it as a manifesto that vegetarianism was good for the body and for the planet. A small number of health food stores and vegetarian restaurants began to open across the United States and Canada. For some, vegetarianism as a lifestyle meshed well with the growing hippie lifestyle of the 1960s and 1970s.

An equally influential text is John Robbins' 1987 book *Diet for a New America*. Robbins explores the prolific use of natural resources and the environmental damage caused by agricultural systems dedicated to raising animals for consumption. He also exposes the perceived horrors of factory farming and related practices such as restricting calves to pens in order to create a whiter, more tender and delicate veal and warehousing thousands of chickens in cramped cages and coops to facilitate egg production. In addition, Robbins documents the unhealthfulness of a meat-based diet and the healthfulness of a vegetarian diet. Robbins' book is sometimes credited with launching the vegan movement in North America.

Today some people strongly believe that the production of meat and animal products at current and likely future levels is environmentally unsustainable. They argue that modern industrial agriculture is changing ecosystems faster than they can adapt. They maintain that while vegetarian agriculture produces some of the same problems as animal production, the environmental impact of animal production is significantly greater. For example, they note that free-range animal production requires land for grazing, which encourages ranchers to encroach on undeveloped lands and clear-cut woodlands. They also point out that overgrazed lands lose their ability to support animal production, which makes further agricultural expansion necessary. While they acknowledge that factory-farm animal production uses less land, they argue that it requires enormous quantities of animal feed that must be grown over large areas of land, requires considerable resources such as water and energy and creates large quantities of polluting wastes. For them, vegetarianism is an environmental imperative. A large and growing body of literature studies the effects of all types of agriculture on the environment.

THE VEGETARIAN DIET

Vegetarianism has become more mainstream over the last century, evolving from a diet followed mainly due to religious or philosophical beliefs to people who now choose a plant-based diet for health reasons. *Canada's Food Guide* (2007), as well as recommendations from the major health groups (Canadian

Cancer Society, Heart and Stroke Foundation, Dietitians of Canada), stresses the importance of fruits, vegetables, legumes and whole grains—the foundation of a plant-based diet. Studies have shown that the incidence of chronic diseases such as obesity, cardiovascular disease, cancer and Type 2 diabetes are lower for vegetarians than for nonvegetarians. It is important to note that other healthy lifestyle factors (not smoking, moderate use or abstinence from alcohol, and exercise) that vegetarians typically follow might also be responsible for the lower disease rates. All of these factors together probably account for the decreased incidence of disease among vegetarians.

Many people who believe that a plant-based diet is associated with a reduced incidence of disease find it difficult to give up all animal foods. They adapt the principles of vegetarianism to their lifestyles by choosing a diet plan loosely based on vegetarianism—the "flextarian" plan. Although it is not recognized as a conventional vegetarian diet, people who follow this eating pattern choose a plant-based diet augmented with lean fish and occasional servings of poultry.

Although plant-based diets offer many healthful qualities, careful planning is vital to ensure that the vegetarian is consuming adequate protein, minerals, vitamins and calories. Eating an assortment of plant foods over the course of a day can provide all the essential amino acids required for good nutrition. Quinoa is an essential grain to eat because it is the only plant source that contains all the essential amino acids. But the quality of plant protein and the ability of the body to absorb it may vary. Vegetarian protein needs can be met by consuming soy foods whose protein has been determined to be as effective a source as animal protein.

A vegetarian diet can meet calcium requirements when plant foods that are good sources of calcium such as greens and cruciferous vegetables are eaten. Vegetarians who elect to consume dairy and eggs do not need to be concerned with meeting adequate calcium intake requirements. Soy products that are fortified with calcium and other vitamins are also readily available. The type of iron found in plant foods may not be as readily absorbed as iron from animal sources; therefore, supplements are recommended.

There are no natural plant sources of vitamin B_{12}, which is crucial for good nutrition, especially for pregnant women and infants. Consumption of dietary supplements, fortified foods or dairy foods is necessary to provide an adequate amount of vitamin B_{12} for vegetarians.

Vegans have to be particularly mindful of their food choices, because they avoid all animal-based foods. Vegans usually supplement their diet with multivitamin mineral supplements and include fortified and enriched foods. Another area in which a vegetarian diet may be lacking is the fatty acids naturally occurring in fish such as salmon and mackerel. To compensate, dietitians advise that vegetarians consume a good quantity of linolenic acid in their diet. A diet rich in nuts, canola oil, flax and other seeds and soy products is recommended.

Vegetarians who consume dairy and/or eggs generally have an easier time meeting their nutrient needs. All vegetarians must choose carefully to be certain to meet their calorie needs, however, if they are also attempting to eat a low-fat diet. High-fibre foods such as vegetables, whole grains, legumes and fruits can reduce calorie intake because these foods tend to make people feel full sooner. Protein intake is not usually a concern for vegetarians who eat a variety of foods. Overall, a carefully planned plant-based diet is a healthy, satisfying way to eat. Those who want to maintain good health while on a vegetarian diet can be helped in making proper food choices by following eating plans such as that shown in Figure 24.1 on the next page.

To Be or Not to Be: Vegetarian

In the not-too-distant past, vegetarianism was linked with aging hippies, musty health food stores and the religiously observant. Not any more. Now most supermarkets stock vegetarian burgers, soy cheeses, tofu and rice milk, while national chains of modern, upscale grocers cater specifically to vegetarian and health-conscious shoppers. Even fast-food restaurants now offer foods such as vegetarian submarine sandwiches and soy-filled tacos.

So just how many vegetarians are there in the United States? The Vegetarian Resource Group has tried to answer this question. In a 2003 poll, it asked adult respondents, "Which of the following foods, if any, [do] you never eat? Meat, Poultry, Fish/Seafood, Dairy Products, Eggs, Honey." Approximately 2.8% of the sample population responded that they did not eat meat, poultry or fish, while 6.5% indicated they did not eat red meat. When the same question was asked in 1994 and again in 1997, only about 1% indicated that they were vegetarian (defined as those who never eat meat, poultry or fish). The Dietitians of Canada reported in June 2003 that approximately 4% of Canadian adults follow a vegetarian diet.

Adults aren't the only vegetarians. According to another Vegetarian Resource Group poll in 2000, 2% of children ages 6 to 17 responded that they never eat meat, fish or poultry, while 6% don't eat red meat.

Significantly, nonvegetarians also enjoy meatless dishes from time to time. According to a 1999 poll, approximately 57% of U.S. adults say they "sometimes, often or always" order a vegetarian entree when dining out.

This growing demand for vegetarian food clearly has an impact on restaurants and institutional food service operations. When more than half of the population sometimes orders vegetarian cuisine, it is no longer sufficient to offer a one-dish-fits-all vegetarian entree. As with nonvegetarian dishes, flavour, freshness, quality and variety will keep customers satisfied and eager to return.

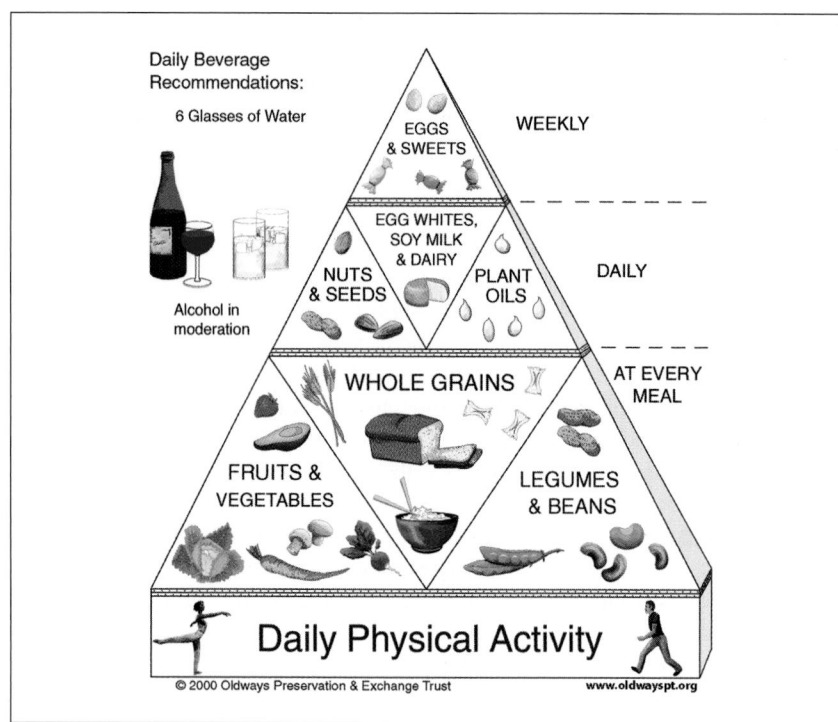

FIGURE 24.1 Traditional Healthy Vegetarian Diet Pyramid

INGREDIENTS FOR VEGETARIAN COOKING

A diet rich in a variety of fruits, vegetables, starches and grains, well prepared and properly seasoned, will satisfy even those adhering to the more strict vegetarian diets. Chefs can prepare flavourful, visually stimulating dishes with a traditional range of ingredients available in most restaurant kitchens. Potatoes, grains, starches, vegetables and fruits form an integral part of vegetarian cooking.

While the professional kitchen offers hundreds of foods appropriate for all vegetarian diets, chefs can use a number of ingredients to enhance the complexity of their vegetarian cooking. Some foods that replace the protein found in animal products are featured here, as well as other ingredients that may mimic more traditional animal-based foods.

Soybean-Based Ingredients

The versatile and protein-rich soybean forms the basis for a wide range of products used in vegetarian and traditional ethnic cuisines worldwide. Soy-based foods have been favourites in Asian cooking for centuries. While there are brown, black and green varieties, most soybeans are yellow. Fresh green soybeans, called edamame, are steamed and eaten as a snack. According to the United Soybean Board, soy protein is the only plant protein that is equivalent to animal protein; it is a rich source of phytochemicals, making soy an ideal ingredient for vegetarian cooking. Soy can be made into a diverse range of foods including flour, "milk," cheese and oil.

Soy milk is made from dried soybeans that are soaked and then finely ground and pressed to extract a milky liquid. (Soy milk can be made in any kitchen by soaking, then cooking dried soybeans in hot water before grinding, straining and simmering the liquid.) Soy milk is believed to have originated in China, where it is traditionally served as a sweet or savoury breakfast beverage or soup base with a distinct beany flavour. Soy milk comes in liquid or powdered form. Liquid soy milk resembles skim milk and has a slight nutty flavour. Most liquid soy milk is sold in aseptic packaging, giving it a one-year shelf life if unopened. Like other dairy products, once opened, liquid soy milk requires refrigeration and lasts from five to seven days or according to recommendations of the manufacturer. Powdered soy milk is shelf-stable and lasts for a year at room temperature. Many dairy substitutes are made from soy milk, such as soy cheese, soy yogurt and flavoured soy beverages.

Soy milk can be used measure-for-measure in all recipes that call for dairy milk. Manufacturing technologies have evolved to produce soy milk products with a richer texture and flavour, more suitable for enriching sauces. When cooking with soy milk, be aware that it can separate at high temperatures. Simmer foods with soy milk gently and add the soy milk near the end of the cooking time to prevent it from separating.

Tofu or bean curd (Fr. *fromage de soja*) is a staple of Japanese and Chinese cuisines and is gaining acceptance in North American kitchens because of its high nutritional value, low cost and flavour adaptability. Tofu is made by processing soybeans into soy milk, which is then coagulated or cultured and formed into a cake. The result is a soft, creamy-white substance similar to cheese. Tofu is easy to digest and is a good source of protein, low in fat and sodium with no cholesterol.

Tofu is an ancient foodstuff, probably created in China during the 2nd century A.D. It was introduced to Japan by Buddhist priests during the 8th century and was "discovered" by Western travellers during the 17th century. Today, Japanese tofu is said to be the finest, perhaps because of the superiority of the soybeans grown in the Yamato region, near the city of Kyoto. Japanese cuisine values the natural flavour and texture of tofu and uses it in a tremendous variety of ways. Chinese cuisine uses it as an additive, not as a principal ingredient.

Tofu may be eaten fresh; added to soup, broth or noodle dishes; tossed in cold salads; grilled, deep-fried or sautéed; or puréed to make a creamy spread. Its flavour is bland, but it readily absorbs flavours from other ingredients.

Two types of tofu are widely available: cotton (or traditional) and silken. **Cotton tofu** is the most common. The soy milk is coagulated (nowadays with calcium sulphate). The curds are then placed in a perforated mould lined with cloth and pressed with a weight to remove the liquid. Cotton tofu is solid, with an irregular surface caused by the weave of the cotton fabric in which it is wrapped for pressing. This traditional tofu comes in three styles: soft, firm and extra firm, each style being progressively drier and firmer. Select the style of tofu suited to the preparation. Firmer tofu is solid enough to be grilled or sautéed. It absorbs the flavours of rubs and marinades. Softer tofu may be scrambled like eggs or processed to form a smooth spread.

Silken tofu (Japanese: *kinugoshi*) has a silky-smooth appearance and texture and a somewhat more delicate flavour than cotton tofu. Silken tofu is made in a process similar to the way yogurt is cultured. No curds are formed, nor is whey produced. This makes a tofu with a custardlike texture suitable for processing into a creamy substance, good to use as a base for dips or in spreads or smoothies. Because the water has not been pressed out of silken tofu, it should not be cooked at high temperatures or for a long time, as it falls apart easily. Silken tofu can also be drained to make a thicker spread with a consistency similar to mascarpone or cream cheese.

Silken Tofu

Fresh tofu is usually packaged in water. It should be refrigerated and kept in water until used. If the water is drained and changed daily, the tofu should

White Miso

Red Miso

Tempeh

Texturized Soy Protein

Seitan

last for one week. Tofu can be frozen for several months, though its texture may be slightly altered after thawing. Weight down the firm tofu while it is thawing to create a denser, firmer product, suitable for grilling. Place a sheet pan on top of the tofu, then place a heavy object such as a #10 can on top of the sheet pan. Drain the liquid from the tofu before using.

Miso (MEE-so) is a thick paste made by salting and fermenting soybeans and rice or barley. After soaking, the soybeans are steamed, then crushed. The mixture is blended with water. Rice or barley is added along with salt before the mixture is inoculated with a living culture, *koji* or aspergillis mould. After fermenting and aging, often in large wooden barrels for as long as a year, the paste is ready to use. In Japan, where the manufacture of miso is a fine art akin to cheese making in France, there are countless styles of miso ranging in colour from pale to rust and in taste from sweet to salty. In Canada, two types of miso are commonly available: sweet **white miso** (*shiro miso*) and dark or **red miso**. Creamy-coloured white miso contains a high percentage of rice and has a mild, somewhat sweet flavour. Dark or red miso, which contains a higher percentage of soybeans, is aged longer and has a stronger, saltier flavour.

Miso can be used in cold and warm preparations but should never be boiled; it contains beneficial enzymes and bacteria that can be killed at high temperatures. A pungent seasoning, miso should be used judiciously so as not to overpower a dish. As little as 5 mL (1 tsp.) per portion can be adequate to flavour a simple broth. With its high salt content, miso will keep indefinitely under refrigeration.

Tempeh (TEHM-pay) is a type of bean cake made from fermented whole soybeans mixed with a grain such as rice or millet. The mixture is inoculated with rhizopus mould, which binds the grains into a firm cake. The traditional food of Indonesia, tempeh has a chewy consistency and a yeasty, nutty flavour.

With its chunky texture, tempeh makes a pleasant meat substitute. It lends itself to being marinated for grilling or sautéing. When crumbled, tempeh can be added to soups or stews to replace ground beef, poultry or pork. A firm cake, tempeh is easily sliced or cut into cubes. Because of the type of live culture used to make it, tempeh should be cooked prior to eating. Proper cooking also tempers its pronounced flavour. Tempeh is sold both fresh and frozen. It lasts for approximately one week in the refrigerator or several months when frozen.

Textured soy protein, also known as textured soy flour or TSP, a proprietary name, is a defatted soy protein that is dried and then compressed into granules or chunks or extruded into shapes. Food manufacturers use it as a meat extender and in commercially produced meat replacements. Granulated texturized soy protein must be rehydrated before cooking which causes it to take on a texture similar to that of meat. Larger forms of texturized soy protein benefit from simmering after rehydration. Adding some vinegar or lemon juice to the simmering liquid helps speed rehydration. A shelf-stable dry product, texturized soy protein can be stored for up to a year when tightly sealed at room temperature. Once it has been rehydrated, texturized soy protein must be refrigerated and should be used within a few days.

Other Popular Ingredients in Vegetarian Cooking

Seitan (SAY-tan), often referred to as "wheat meat," is a form of wheat gluten, the insoluble protein in wheat. A staple in the diets of Buddhist monks for centuries, seitan has a firm, chewy texture and a bland flavour. Seitan is made by preparing a dough from wheat gluten or wheat flour and water. The dough is repeatedly rinsed to remove any remaining starch or bran. The spongy pieces of seitan are then simmered in a broth of soy sauce or tamari with ginger, garlic and kombu (seaweed). Cooking tenderizes seitan and imbues it with the flavours of the cooking liquid. As it absorbs flavours, seitan can be flavoured to mimic many foods. Using seasonings associated with poultry such as thyme and sage brings out a more chickenlike flavour in the seitan, whereas using dark soy sauce and meaty mushrooms can give it a meatlike flavour. Seitan should be added to a dish near the end of cooking, as it is already fully cooked. Fully cooked fresh seitan is sold refrigerated in irregularly sized chunks. Once opened it should be consumed within a few days. Powdered seitan mix is also available.

Grain Beverages

Many grains and nuts can be used to produce beverages that can be used in place of stock or dairy products when making soups, sauces and custards. Almond, hazelnut, oat and rice milks are commercially available. These ingredients tend to be lower in fat but higher in carbohydrates than their dairy counterparts—and they are cholesterol-free.

Analogous Foods

Numerous products made from soy, wheat, grains, or other plant materials are designed to mimic the appearance and texture of popular animal-based products. These commercially prepared products offer a texture and appearance similar to that of their animal-protein-based counterparts. While their flavours are less successful in imitating the actual flavour of their fish, meat or poultry counterparts, many offer consumers the pleasure of eating familiar foods in traditional dishes. Plant-based products are available in the form of "nuggets," "burgers," "sausage," "hot dogs," "ground meat," "bacon," "cold cuts" and even "pastrami." Soy protein extract and judicious use of appropriate seasonings, such as sage in a turkey stuffing analogue, help mimic the flavour of their meat counterparts.

In most cases, these analogous food products may be prepared in the same way as their meat, poultry or fish counterparts. Steaming, sautéing, simmering, grilling and baking work well. Follow the manufacturer's directions, keeping in mind that these products are usually fully cooked, requiring only crisping and heating, and could suffer in overcooking.

VEGETARIAN CUISINE: REBALANCING THE CENTRE OF THE PLATE

The principles of vegetarian cuisine are no different from those of the classic kitchen. When creating an appetizing and satisfying vegetarian dish, chefs use the same professional judgment as when preparing a roast or steak. Flavours must be in balance. Ingredients must be thoughtfully selected and skilfully prepared. Only the ingredients themselves vary. Chefs need to understand the basic principles of cooking and work with the textures and flavours offered by plant-based ingredients.

Fat in meat adds flavour and texture. It may be necessary to add fat to enhance flavour and add moisture to dishes cooked without meats. Replacing animal protein in a main dish with an equal amount of tofu, texturized soy protein, grain, bean purée or plant food may not result in a dish with the same

Haute Vegetables

Today, North America's most respected chefs are elevating plant-based cuisine to the highest culinary art. Internationally acclaimed chefs Thomas Keller of the French Laundry in Yountville, California, and Per Se in New York City and Charlie Trotter of the eponymous restaurant in Chicago both offer a vegetable tasting menu each evening in their respective restaurants. While not strictly vegetarian—dairy products are used in abundance—Chef Keller explores the flavours and versatility of vegetables in his multicourse menu. Chef Trotter regularly offers a strictly raw food menu demonstrating that vegetarian dining can have a place in the finest restaurant.

Some dishes from one of Chef Keller's vegetable tasting menus:

Creamed Ramp Top "Pierogis," French Laundry Garden Shallots, Cipollini Onion "Rissolée," Glazed Ramp Bulbs with "Sauce Soubise" and Chive-Infused Extra Virgin Olive Oil

"Fricassée" of Roasted Marble Potatoes, California Grey Morel Mushrooms, Split English Peas and English Pea "Purée"

Some dishes from one of Chef Trotter's raw vegetable tasting menus:

Root Vegetable Salad with Eggplant and Purple Tomatillo Vinaigrette

Green and White Cauliflower with Shaved Asparagus Salad, Date Purée and Garlic Blossoms

---

appearance and depth of flavour as the original. Vegetables should be chosen for their flavour and texture. The mouth-feel each ingredient contributes to a finished dish should also be considered. Ripe avocados, for example, have a rich, creamy texture that can mimic the mouth-feel of a soft cream cheese.

Baking without eggs poses a number of challenges because of the function eggs perform in many baked goods. Quick-bread formulas using chemical leavening may be better suited to adapting to vegetarian preparation than creaming-style cakes.

With these considerations in mind, here are some suggestions on how to plan and prepare to add vegetarian dishes to a restaurant menu.

- *Use or adapt items from the regular menu.* Many items on existing menus may be vegetarian or can easily be adapted for a vegetarian diner. Soups, salads, stir-fried vegetables and pasta dishes lend themselves to vegetarian ingredients. Prepare tomato sauces without meat stock.

- *Grains and beans add texture and satiation.* Think about these versatile starches as the centre-of-the-plate offerings when planning a vegetarian menu. Chewy grains such as cooked bulgur, barley and millet offer a good textural appeal that can be lacking in plant-based cuisine. Ensuring that a customer feels sufficiently fed is another consideration, something that a plate of steamed vegetables might not offer.

- *Take advantage of meaty vegetables and soy products as main attractions in a vegetarian dish.* Eggplant, mushrooms (especially portobellos), okra, sweet potatoes and parsnips have flavour and body that mimics that of meat. Pan-fried breaded eggplant slices or grilled whole portobello mushroom caps offer hearty vegetable alternatives to a slice of chicken or beef.

- *Compose dishes with an eye to balancing colour.* We eat with our eyes first. When combining grains and beans on a plate, consider using different colours.

- *Balance textures on the same plate.* Look for complementary and contrasting textures in a vegetarian plate. When serving a creamy purée, such as mashed sweet potatoes, for example, balance the texture with something crunchy or crisp such as fried zucchini or a risotto cake.

- *Layer flavours for complexity of taste.* A dish prepared with few ingredients need not be bland or boring. Combine cooking methods in one dish to bring out a complex taste. Sun-dried tomatoes added to a fresh tomato sauce add a rich dimension of taste that might otherwise be lacking.

- *Create a vegetarian pantry stocked with ingredients that help enhance plant-based cooking.* Without base flavour notes created from rich meat stocks, vegetarian dishes can lack depth of flavour. Varieties of fresh and dried mushrooms help enrich flavourful stocks, soups and stews. Dried seaweed such as kombu (sea kelp) adds a briny flavour mimicking seafood stock. Soy sauce and miso can give a vegetable broth a savoury taste and appealing dark colour, as can wine reductions. Richly flavoured nut oils such as sesame oil, hazelnut oil and walnut oil can add complex tastes. Olives and dried fruit have intense flavours and pleasing textures. Toasted sesame and other seeds and nuts add bursts of flavour and a textural contrast to a dish.

- *Seek inspiration from ethnic cuisines in which vegetarian food is traditional.* Asian, Indian, Mexican, Middle Eastern and South American cuisines offer many exciting vegetarian options. Recipes in this book for Indonesian Fried Noodles with Pork and Shrimp (page 341), and Hot and Sour Soup (page 243), for example, are just as frequently prepared without meat or poultry in their native countries, as we have done in our recipe variations on the listed pages.

Vegetarian Recipe Options

On Cooking contains a wealth of recipes suitable for a vegetarian eating plan. Recipes suitable for vegetarians who consume dairy and eggs are marked in this book with a carrot icon (see left). Many other recipes can easily be adapted by substituting vegetable stock for meat stock, for example, or by using oil for sautéing in place of butter. To help adapt recipes for vegetarian cooking, some common alternatives to animal-based foods appear in Table 24.1.

TABLE 24.1	Vegetarian Ingredient Substitutes		
Instead Of	**In This Application**	**Use**	**Comments**
Butter	Sautéing	Vegetable oil or vegetable oil spray	
	Flavouring	Nut oil: hazelnut, pecan or walnut; nut butter: almond, cashew, peanut or sesame butter	Additional oil or liquid may be needed; thin nut butters with oil, fruit juices or nut, rice or soy milks
	Spreading	Ground nut spread: almond, cashew, peanut or sesame butter; vegetable purées: bean, roasted eggplant, red pepper	
	Baking	Dried fruit or cooked vegetable purées	Quick breads, cookies and general baking; may affect colour, taste and texture
Cream	Hot soups, sauces	Soy or rice milk; puréed silken tofu	Add at last moment, heating gently to prevent separation
	Cold creams or spreads	Enriched soy milk	Oil may be needed to improve mouth-feel
Sour cream, yogurt	Beverage or custard	Soy coffee creamer	
	Cold creams or spreads	Puréed silken tofu	
Eggs	Leavening	Chemical leavening	Consider loss of colour from lack of egg yolk; texture will be denser than product containing eggs
	Emulsifier in sauces such as mayonnaise	Form a temporary emulsion; form emulsion using ground nuts or soaked bread	
Beef, fish or poultry stock	Sauces, soups, stews	Vegetable stock; broth made from miso or seaweed	
Demi-glace	Sauces, stews	Rich vegetable stock made with a larger proportion of vegetables, reduced and thickened with starch	
Gelatin	Thickening, gelling	Agar	Gels more firmly than gelatin
Prepared sauces made with fish such as nuoc mam, oyster or Worcestershire	Flavouring	Soy sauce, balsamic or red wine vinegar	

Conclusion

A request for restaurant meals made exclusively with plant foods is no longer exceptional. Consumers choose to forgo eating meat, poultry or fish for a variety of personal and religious reasons. In fact, nutritional science increasingly recommends that all consumers eat a diet high in fibre and the vitamins found in vegetables, grains, fruits and legumes. Today's consumers, accustomed to making their own food choices, are frequently turning to a plant-based diet, and professional chefs need to understand how to create flavourful vegetarian options. While many delicious meals can be prepared using the vegetables, grains and starches studied throughout this book, a number of special ingredients made from soy and other products help vary the flavours and textures of vegetarian dishes.

Questions for Discussion

1. What are the primary motivations for following a vegetarian diet? Have the reasons for such a lifestyle choice changed over time? Discuss what could be the future of this style of eating.

2. What are three important ingredients that can be used to replace meat in a vegetarian dish? Discuss the ingredients used to prepare each product and ways in which it can be used in vegetarian cooking.

3. What are the five most common forms of vegetarianism and what are the types of foods each group permits itself to eat?

4. Identify three popular recipes that use meat, fish or poultry. Discuss how you would adapt such recipes for the vegetarian customer.

Vegetarian Recipes

Pan-Seared Tofu Provençal

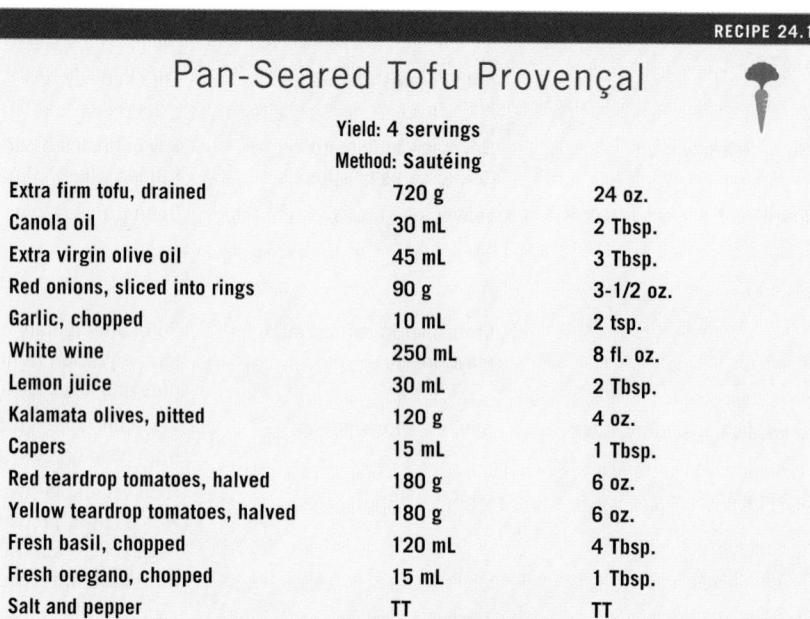

RECIPE 24.1

Pan-Seared Tofu Provençal

Yield: 4 servings
Method: Sautéing

Extra firm tofu, drained	720 g	24 oz.
Canola oil	30 mL	2 Tbsp.
Extra virgin olive oil	45 mL	3 Tbsp.
Red onions, sliced into rings	90 g	3-1/2 oz.
Garlic, chopped	10 mL	2 tsp.
White wine	250 mL	8 fl. oz.
Lemon juice	30 mL	2 Tbsp.
Kalamata olives, pitted	120 g	4 oz.
Capers	15 mL	1 Tbsp.
Red teardrop tomatoes, halved	180 g	6 oz.
Yellow teardrop tomatoes, halved	180 g	6 oz.
Fresh basil, chopped	120 mL	4 Tbsp.
Fresh oregano, chopped	15 mL	1 Tbsp.
Salt and pepper	TT	TT

1. Cut the tofu into eight 90-g (3-oz.) triangles and pat dry on paper towels. Heat the canola oil in a large sauté pan. Sear the tofu on both sides until brown. Remove the tofu to a platter and keep warm.

2. Add the olive oil to the pan. Add the onions and garlic to the pan and sauté for 3 to 4 minutes. Deglaze the pan with the wine and lemon juice.

RECIPE 24.1

Approximate values per serving:	
Calories	567
Total fat	38 g
Saturated fat	5 g
Cholesterol	0 mg
Sodium	823 mg
Total carbohydrates	23 g
Protein	34 g

continued

3. Add the olives and capers to the pan and simmer in the wine sauce until it begins to thicken slightly.

4. Add the tomatoes to the pan and reduce the sauce to the desired consistency. Stir in the basil and oregano. Return the tofu to the sauce to reheat it. Adjust the seasonings. Serve the tofu with some of the sauce spooned over it.

RECIPE 24.2

Fennel and Apple Soufflé with Toasted Walnut Crème Fraîche

CALGARY PETROLEUM CLUB, CALGARY, AB
Executive Chef Liana Robberecht

Yield: 12 servings

Butter	as needed	as needed
Bread crumbs	as needed	as needed
Olive oil	15 mL	1 Tbsp.
Shallots, minced	30 g	1 oz.
Fennel, shaved	500 g	17 oz.
Tarragon, fresh, chopped	20 g	2 Tbsp.
Thyme, fresh, chopped	10 g	1 Tbsp.
Base Mixture (recipe follows)	600 mL	20 fl. oz.
Granny Smith apple, peeled, cored, grated	3	3
Aged white cheddar, grated	150 g	5 oz.
Lemon zest and juice	1	1
Pernod	50 mL	2 fl. oz.
Sea salt and pepper	TT	TT
Egg whites	12	12

1. Butter ramekins and lightly coat the interior with bread crumbs.

2. In a heated sauté pan, add olive oil and quickly sauté shallots and fennel and add herbs. Cool mixture.

3. Mix together Base Mixture, apple, grated cheddar, fennel mixture, lemon zest and juice, Pernod, salt and pepper and combine evenly.

4. Whisk egg whites to soft peaks.

5. Fold one-third of the egg whites into the base mixture. Fold in the remaining eggs whites in two stages.

6. Spoon the batter into the ramekins to within 10 mm (1/2 in.) of the tops. Wipe the rims of the ramekins clean. Tap the ramekins gently to settle the batter.

7. Place the soufflés in a hotel pan, add a small amount of water and place in a 210°C (420°F) oven for approximately 25 minutes. Do not disturb.

8. Remove soufflés from water bath, add Toasted Walnut Crème Fraîche (recipe follows) in small opening on top and serve immediately.

Base Mixture

Milk	725 mL	24 fl. oz.
Bay leaf	1	1
Clove, whole	1	1
Butter	60 g	2 oz.
Flour	60 g	2 oz.

Liana Robberecht

Liana, a BC native, completed her Red Seal training in Alberta and also has a diploma in professional pastry and dessert from the Dubrulle French Culinary School in Vancouver. She is the Executive Chef at the Calgary Petroleum Club, where she focuses on cooking with foods from local Alberta farmers. Read more about her culinary experiences in the profile on page 818.

RECIPE 24.2

Approximate values per serving:	
Calories	288
Total fat	20 g
Saturated fat	10 g
Cholesterol	170 mg
Sodium	332 mg
Total carbohydrates	14 g
Protein	12 g

Base Mixture— Approximate values per portion (24 portions):	
Calories	80
Total fat	6 g
Saturated fat	3 g
Cholesterol	133 mg
Sodium	234 mg
Total carbohydrates	3 g
Protein	3 g

continued

Egg yolks	**15**	**15**
Sea salt and pepper	**TT**	**TT**

1. Heat the milk with bay leaf and clove to infuse.
2. Prepare a white roux from butter and flour.
3. Strain the milk and add the roux to make a béchamel.
4. Simmer approximately 15 minutes, stirring constantly.
5. Temper the egg yolks with some of the béchamel.
6. Incorporate tempered yolks into remaining sauce and bring to just below a simmer. Stir constantly and do not boil.
7. Adjust seasoning and reserve. Chill if being used later.

Toasted Walnut Crème Fraîche

Crème fraîche	**120 mL**	**4 fl. oz.**
Walnuts, whole, toasted, ground	**30 g**	**1 oz.**

1. Fold walnuts into crème fraîche.

Approximate values per serving:

Calories	45
Total fat	5 g
Saturated fat	2 g
Cholesterol	12 mg
Sodium	3 mg
Total carbohydrates	1 g
Protein	1 g

RECIPE 24.3

Soynut Tofu Ice Cream

Adapted from *Soy Desserts* by
Patricia Greenberg, CCP
Regan Books, 2000

Yield: 12 servings

Soynuts	**360 mL**	**1-1/2 c.**
Soft tofu	**1 kg**	**2 lb.**
Granulated sugar	**150 g**	**5 oz.**
Soy milk	**360 mL**	**12 fl. oz.**
Almond extract	**5 mL**	**1 tsp.**

1. In a food processor, grind the soynuts to a coarse consistency. Add the tofu and sugar and purée.
2. With the processor running, add the soy milk and almond extract and continue to process until the mixture is smooth. Pour into an ice cream maker and process according to the manufacturer's directions.

VARIATION: Lemon-Ginger Soy Ice Cream—Omit the soynuts and the almond extract. Add 60 g (2 oz.) crystallized ginger, the zest of three lemons and 3 mL (1/2 tsp.) lemon extract. Process the ginger and lemon zest with the tofu as directed in Step 2.

RECIPE 24.3

Approximate values per serving:

Calories	199
Total fat	8 g
Saturated fat	1 g
Cholesterol	0 mg
Sodium	8 mg
Total carbohydrates	22 g
Protein	12 g

RECIPE 24.4

Braised Tempeh with Morels and Cilantro Ginger Pesto

Yield: 4 servings

Water	**1 L**	**1 qt.**
Dried morel mushrooms	**15 g**	**1/2 oz.**
Dried wild mushrooms	**15 g**	**1/2 oz.**
Tempeh, cut into triangles,		
approx. 2 oz. (60 g) each	**8**	**8**
Peanut oil	**30 ml**	**1 fl. oz.**

RECIPE 24.4

Approximate values per serving:

Calories	370
Total fat	19 g
Saturated fat	3.5 g
Cholesterol	0 mg
Sodium	1190 mg
Total carbohydrates	27 g
Protein	26 g

continued

Lemon grass, chopped	30 g	1 oz.
Garlic, chopped	30 g	1 oz.
Ginger, chopped	30 g	1 oz.
Onion, diced	60 g	2 oz.
Carrot, diced	60 g	2 oz.
Tomato, diced	60 g	2 oz.
Coriander, ground	5 ml	1 tsp.
Black pepper	3 ml	1/2 tsp.
Chile paste	15 ml	1 Tbsp.
White wine vinegar	120 ml	4 fl. oz.
Soy sauce	60 ml	2 fl. oz.
Couscous, cooked	as needed for garnish	
Baby vegetables, steamed	as needed for garnish	
Cilantro Ginger Pesto (recipe follows)	as needed	as needed

1. Combine the water and mushrooms in a small saucepan and bring to a boil. Remove the pan from the heat and allow it to cool to room temperature, approximately 30 minutes. Strain the mushrooms from the liquid through several layers of cheesecloth, reserving both the mushrooms and the liquid. Rinse the mushrooms to remove any sand or grit.

2. Sauté the tempeh in the oil for 3 to 4 minutes or until brown. Turn the pieces and brown on the other side. Remove from the pan and hold in a warm place.

3. Add the lemon grass, garlic, ginger, onion and carrot to the pan and sauté for 3 minutes. Add the tomato, coriander, pepper and chile paste and cook for 1 minute. Deglaze the pan with the vinegar and soy sauce and add the reserved mushroom liquid. Return the tempeh to the pan. Bring to a simmer and cook for approximately 30 minutes or until the sauce is reduced by half and begins to thicken.

4. Remove the tempeh and keep warm. Purée the sauce in a food processor. Strain the sauce through a coarse china cap if desired. Combine the tempeh, sauce and mushrooms in a small sauté pan and bring to a simmer.

5. Plate the tempeh with couscous and steamed baby vegetables and drizzle with Cilantro Ginger Pesto.

Cilantro Ginger Pesto

Yield: 12 fl. oz. (360 mL)

Limes	4	4
Cilantro, picked, washed	60 g	2 oz.
Jalapeño pepper, seeded, chopped	30 g	1 oz.
Ginger, chopped	30 g	1 oz.
Garlic, chopped	30 g	1 oz.
Green onions, chopped	60 g	2 oz.
Vegetable oil	120 mL	4 fl. oz.
Salt and pepper	TT	TT

1. Zest the limes. Cut them in half and juice them.

2. Combine the lime zest and juice with the remaining ingredients in the bowl of a food processor and pulse until well combined. Do not overprocess, as this will cause the sauce to discolour.

Approximate values per 15 mL serving:	
Calories	45
Total fat	4.5 g
Saturated fat	0.5 g
Cholesterol	0 mg
Sodium	0 mg
Total carbohydrates	1 g
Protein	0 g

This chapter discusses all types of salads:

the small plate of crisp iceberg lettuce with tomato wedges, cucumber slices and ranch dressing; the dinner plate of sautéed duck breast fanned across bright red grilled radicchio and toothy green arugula, sprayed with a vinaigrette dressing; the scoop of shredded chicken, mango chutney and seasonings, bound with mayonnaise; and the bowl of artichokes and mushrooms marinated in olive oil and lemon juice.

Each of these dishes fits the definition of a **salad**: a single food or a mix of different foods accompanied or bound by a dressing. A salad can contain meat, grains, fruits, nuts or cheese and absolutely no lettuce. It can be an appetizer, a second course served after the appetizer, an entree (especially at lunch) or served with the main course, a course following the entree or even a dessert.

The colour, texture and flavour of each salad ingredient should complement those of the others, and the dressing should complement all of the ingredients. Harmony is critical to a salad's success—no matter what type of salad is being prepared.

This chapter opens with a section identifying greens commonly used in salads. A discussion of salad dressings follows. Finally, techniques for preparing green salads (both tossed and composed), bound salads, vegetable salads and fruit salads are discussed.

SALAD GREENS
Identifying Salad Greens

Salad greens are not necessarily green: some are red, yellow, white or brown. They are all, however, leafy vegetables. Many are members of the lettuce or chicory families.

Lettuce

Lettuce (Fr. *laitue*; It. *lattuga*) has been consumed for nearly as long as people have kept records of what they and others ate. Archaeologists found that Persian royalty were served lettuce at their banquets more than 2500 years ago. Now grown and served worldwide, lettuces are members of the genus *Lactuca*. The most common types of lettuce are butterleaf, iceberg, leaf and romaine.

Boston and **bibb** are two of the most popular butterleaf lettuces. Their soft, pliable, pale green leaves have a buttery texture and flavour. Boston is larger and paler than is bibb. Both Boston and bibb lettuce leaves form cups when separated from the heads; these cups make convenient bases for holding other foods on cold plates or providing height and texture as part of the garnish.

Iceberg lettuce is the most common of all lettuce varieties in Canada and the United States; it outsells all other varieties combined. Its tightly packed spherical head is made up of crisp, pale green leaves with a very mild flavour. Iceberg lettuce remains crisp for a relatively long period of time after being cut or prepared. Select heads that are firm but not hard and leaves that are free of burnt or rusty tips.

Boston

Iceberg

Red and Green
Leaf Lettuces

Leaf lettuce grows in bunches. It has separate, ruffle-edged leaves branching from a stalk. Because it does not grow into a firm head, it is easily damaged during harvest and transport. Both red and green leaf lettuce have bright colours, mild flavours and tender leaves. Good-quality leaf lettuce should have nicely shaped leaves free of bruises, breaks or brown spots.

Romaine lettuce, also known as cos, is a loosely packed head lettuce with elongated leaves and thick midribs. Its outer leaves are dark green and although they look coarse, they are crisp, tender and tasty without being bitter. The core leaves are paler and more tender but still crisp. Romaine has enough flavour to stand up to strongly flavoured dressings such as the garlic and Parmesan cheese used in a Caesar salad. A good-quality head of romaine has dark green outer leaves that are free of blemishes or yellowing. The hearts are available for separate purchase.

Baby greens have similar but more subtle flavours than their mature versions. They are often less bitter and are always more tender and delicate. Because of their size and variety, they are perfect for composed salads. **Mesclun** is a mixture of several kinds of baby lettuce, herbs and flowers. Field and spring mixes are popular with food service operators. Micro greens are the first true leaves of any edible greens. The tiny, delicate leaves are often used as a garnish for entree and appetizer plates.

Romaine

Chicory

Chicories come in a variety of colours, shapes and sizes; most are slightly bitter. Chicories are quite hardy and can also be cooked, usually grilled or braised.

Belgian endive (witloof) grows in small, tight heads with pointed leaves. It is actually the shoot of a chicory root. The small, sturdy leaves are white at the base with yellow fringes and tips. (A purple-tipped variety is sometimes available.) Whole leaves can be separated, trimmed and filled with soft butters, cheeses or spreads and served as an hors d'oeuvre. Or they can be used for composed salads. The leaves, cut or whole, can also be added to cold salads. Heads of Belgian endive are often braised or grilled and served with meat or poultry. Belgian endive is imported from Belgium or Holland at certain times and is grown in greenhouses locally.

Belgian Endive

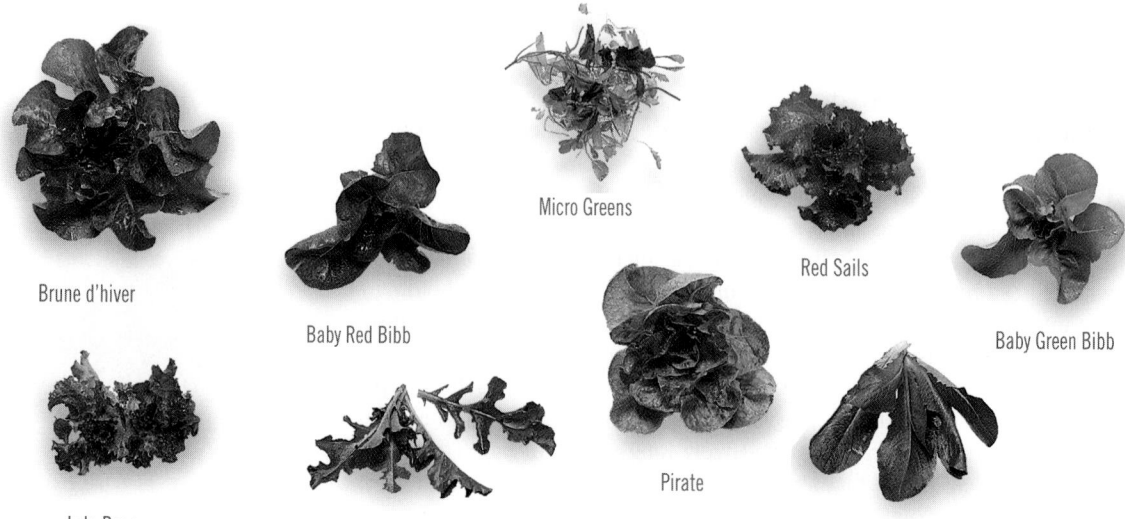

Brune d'hiver

Baby Red Bibb

Micro Greens

Red Sails

Baby Green Bibb

Lola Rosa

Baby Red Oak Leaf

Pirate

Baby Red Romaine

Curly endive is often called by its family name, chicory, or its French name, frisée. The dark green outer leaves are pointed, sturdy and slightly bitter. The yellow inner leaves are more tender and less bitter. Curly endive has a strong flavour that goes well with strong cheeses, game and citrus. It is often mixed with other greens to add texture and flavour.

Escarole, sometimes called broadleaf endive, has thick leaves and a slightly bitter flavour. It has green outer leaves and pale green or yellow centre leaves. Escarole is very sturdy and is often mixed with other greens for added texture. Its strong flavour stands up to full-flavoured dressings. It is a good accompaniment to grilled meats and poultry.

Radicchio resembles a small red cabbage. It retains its bright reddish colour when cooked and is popular braised or grilled and served as a vegetable side dish. Because of its attractive colour, radicchio is popular in cold salads, but it has a very bitter flavour and should be used sparingly and mixed with other greens in a tossed salad. Radicchio is quite expensive and availability is sometimes limited.

Curly Endive

Escarole

Radicchio

Other Salad Greens and Ingredients

Leafy vegetables besides lettuce and chicory, as well as other ingredients, are used to add texture, flavour and colour to salads. A partial listing follows.

Arugula, also known as rocket, is a member of the cabbage family. Its individual leaves are similar to dandelion leaves in size and shape. The best are 5- to 10-cm (2- to 4-in.) long. Arugula has a very strong, spicy, peppery flavour—so strong, in fact, that it is rarely served by itself. It is best when used to add zip to salads by combining it with other greens.

Dandelion grows as a weed throughout most of the world. It has long, thin, toothed leaves with a prominent midrib. When purchasing dandelion for salads, look for small leaves: they are more tender and less bitter. Older, tougher leaves can be cooked and served as a vegetable.

Mâche or lamb's lettuce is very tender and very delicately flavoured. Its small, cuplike, pale to dark green leaves have a slightly nutty flavour. Because its flavour is so delicate, mâche should be combined only with other delicately flavoured greens such as Boston or bibb lettuce and dressed sparingly with a light vinaigrette dressing.

Sorrel, sometimes called sourgrass, has leaves similar to spinach in colour and shape. Sorrel has a very tart, lemony flavour that goes well with fish and shellfish. It should be used sparingly and combined with other greens in a salad. Sorrel can also be made into soups, sauces and purées.

Spinach can be cooked or used as a salad green. As a salad green, it is popular served wilted and tossed with a hot bacon dressing. Spinach is deep green with a rich flavour and tender texture. Good-quality spinach should be fairly crisp. Avoid wilted or yellowed bunches.

Sprouts are not salad greens but are often used as such in salads and sandwiches. Sprouts are very young alfalfa, daikon, sunflower, radish or mustard plants. Alfalfa sprouts are very mild and sweet. Daikon and mustard sprouts are quite peppery.

Arugula

Dandelion

Mâche

Sorrel

Spinach

Sprouts

Watercress has tiny, dime-sized leaves and substantial stems. It has a peppery flavour and adds spice to a salad. Good-quality fresh watercress is dark green with no yellowing. To preserve its freshness, watercress must be kept very cold and moist. It is normally packed topped with ice. Individual leaves are plucked from the stems and rinsed just before service.

Watercress

Many specialty produce growers offer pesticide-free **edible flowers**. They are used for salads and as garnishes wherever a splash of colour would be appreciated. Some flowers such as nasturtiums, calendulas and pansies are grown and picked specifically for eating. Others, such as yellow cucumber flowers and squash blossoms, are byproducts of the vegetable industry.

Squash blossoms and other very large flowers should be cut in julienne strips before being added to salads. Pick petals from large and medium-sized flowers. Smaller whole flowers can be tossed in a salad or used as a garnish when composing a salad. Very small flowers or petals can be sprinkled on top of a salad so they are not hidden by the greens.

Fresh herbs such as basil, thyme, tarragon, oregano, dill, cilantro, marjoram, mint, sage, savory and even rosemary are used to add interesting flavours to otherwise ordinary salads. Because many herbs have strong flavours, use them sparingly so the delicate flavours of the greens are not overpowered. Leafy herbs such as basil and sage can be cut chiffonade. Other herbs can be picked into sprigs or chopped before being tossed with the salad greens. Flowering herbs such as chive blossoms are used like other edible flowers to add colour, flavour and aroma. Refer to Chapter 7, Flavours and Flavourings, for more information on herbs.

Nutrition

Salad greens are an especially healthful food. Greens contain virtually no fat and few calories and are high in vitamins A and C, iron and fibre. But when garnished with meat and cheese and tossed with a dressing (many of which are oil-based), fat and calories are added. In an attempt to maintain the healthful nature of greens, low-fat or fat-free dressings should be available to customers. Due to high nitrate content, greens, as well as broccoli and cauliflower, may be a migraine trigger.

Purchasing and Storing Salad Greens

Purchasing

Lettuces are grown in nearly every part of Canada and the United States, both outdoors and in greenhouses; nearly all types are available year-round. Principal salad greens such as spinach are available all year; many of the specialty greens are seasonal.

Lettuce is generally packed in cases of 24 heads with varying weights. Other salad greens are packed in trays or boxes of various sizes and weights.

Because salad greens are simply washed and eaten, it is extremely important that they be as fresh and blemish-free as possible. Try to purchase salad greens several times per week. All greens should be fresh-looking, with no yellowing. Heads should be heavy, with little or no damage to the outer leaves.

Many types of salad greens are available precut and prewashed. These greens are often modified atmosphere-packed to increase shelf life, although delicate greens are sometimes loosely packaged in 2.5- to 5-kg (5- to 10-lb.) boxes. Precut and prewashed greens are relatively expensive, but can reduce labour costs dramatically.

Storing

Although some types of salad greens are hardy enough to keep for a week or more under proper conditions, all salad greens are highly perishable. Generally, softer-leaved varieties such as Boston and bibb tend to perish more quickly than the crisper-leaved varieties such as iceberg and romaine.

Greens should be stored in their original protective cartons in a specifically designated refrigerator. Ideally, greens should be stored at temperatures between 1°C and 3°C (34°F and 38°F). (Most other vegetables should be stored at warmer temperatures of 4°C to 10°C [40°F to 50°F].) Greens should not be stored with tomatoes, apples or other fruits that emit ethylene gas, which causes greens to wilt and accelerates spoilage.

Do not wash greens until you need them, as excess water causes them to deteriorate quickly.

Preparing Salad Greens

Unless salad greens are purchased precut and prewashed, they will need to undergo some preparation before service, principally tearing, cutting, washing and drying. Do not leave salad greens soaking in water for storage. The nutrients will be leached out.

Tearing and Cutting

Some cooks prefer all salad greens torn by hand. Delicate greens such as butterhead and baby lettuces look nicer and it is less likely they will be bruised if hand-torn. But often it is not practical to hand-tear all greens. It is perfectly acceptable to cut hardy greens with a sharp stainless steel knife.

BASIC PROCEDURE FOR CUTTING ROMAINE LETTUCE

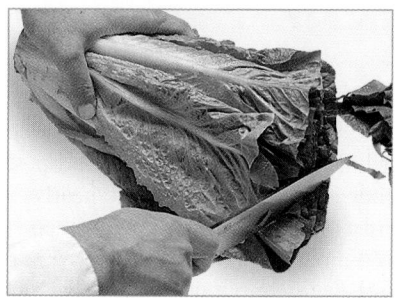

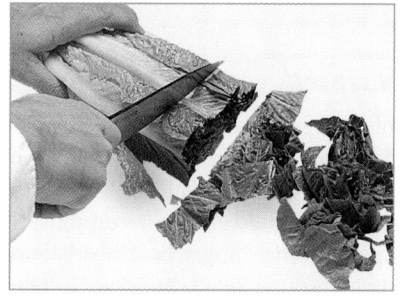

1. To cut romaine lettuce, trim the outer leaves and damaged tips with a chef's knife and split the head lengthwise.

2. Make one or two cuts along the length of the head, leaving the root intact, then cut across the width of the head.

3. Alternative method: Trim the outer leaves and damaged tips with a chef's knife. Pull the leaves from the core and cut the rib out of each leaf. The leaf can then be cut to the desired size. Yield and therefore food cost are affected by this method—there is more wastage.

BASIC PROCEDURE FOR CORING ICEBERG LETTUCE

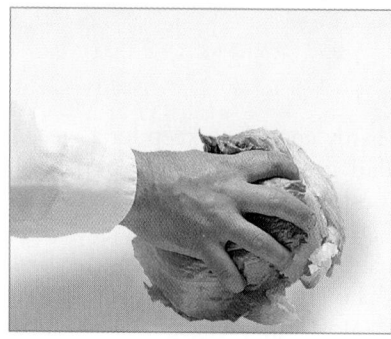

1. Loosen the core by gripping the head and smacking the core firmly on the cutting board.

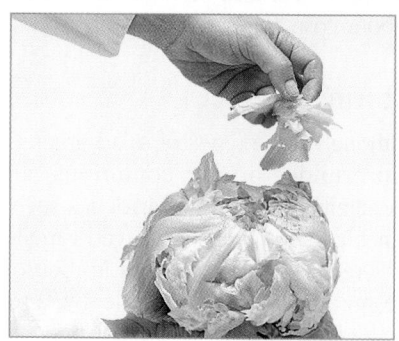

2. Remove the core and cut the lettuce as desired.

BASIC PROCEDURE FOR REMOVING THE MIDRIB FROM SPINACH

Fold the leaf in half and pull off the stem and midrib. Only the tender leaf should remain.

SAFETY ALERT

Handwashing

Because salads are not cooked, it is especially important to be extra careful about proper handwashing when preparing them. Remember that many health departments require single-use gloves to be worn—and changed frequently—whenever working with products that will not be cooked before service.

Washing

All lettuce and other salad greens should be washed before use. Even though they may look clean, greens may harbour hidden insects, sand, soil and pesticides. All greens should be washed after they are torn or cut. Whole heads can be washed by repeatedly dipping them in cold water and allowing them to drain. But washing whole heads is not recommended: it will not remove anything trapped near the head's centre, and water trapped in the leaves can accelerate spoilage.

Drying

Salad greens should be dried after washing. Wet greens do not stay as crisp as thoroughly dried ones. Also, wet greens tend to repel oil-based dressings and

BASIC PROCEDURE FOR WASHING SALAD GREENS

1. Fill a sink with cold water. Place the cut or torn greens in the water.

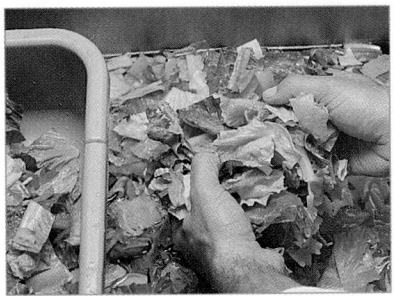

2. Gently stir the water and greens with your hands and remove the greens. Do not allow the greens to soak. Using fresh water each time, repeat the procedure until no grit can be detected on the bottom of the sink after the greens are removed.

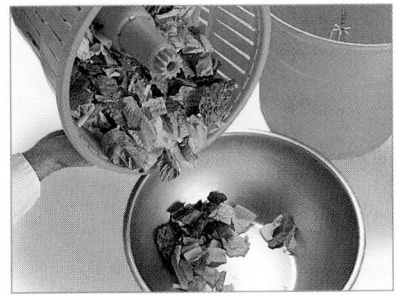

3. Drain greens well and spin if possible to remove excess moisture.

dilute their flavours. Greens may be dried by draining them well in a colander and blotting them with a clean absorbent paper towel, or, preferably, they can be dried in a salad spinner, which uses centrifugal force to remove the water. Spin for 20 to 30 seconds.

SALAD DRESSINGS

A dressing is a sauce for a salad. Just as sauces for hot foods should complement rather than mask the flavour of the principal food, the sauce (dressing) for a salad should complement rather than mask the flavours of the other ingredients. Although a great many ingredients can be used to make salad dressings, most are based on either a mixture of oil and vinegar, called a vinaigrette, or a mayonnaise or other emulsified product.

Vinaigrette-style dressings can be made without oil; creamy dressings similar to mayonnaise-based dressings can be made with sour cream, yogurt or buttermilk instead of mayonnaise. Nevertheless, for all practical purposes these dressings are still prepared like vinaigrettes and mayonnaise-based dressings and they are treated that way here.

Vinaigrette Dressings

The simple vinaigrette, also known as basic **French dressing**, is a temporary emulsion of oil and vinegar seasoned with salt, pepper and mustard. The standard ratio is three parts oil to one part vinegar. The ratio can vary, however. When using strongly flavoured oils, less than three parts oil to one part vinegar generally suffices. In some recipes, all or part of the vinegar is replaced with citrus juice, in which case it may take more than one part vinegar and citrus juice to three parts oil to achieve the proper acidity level. The best way to determine the correct ratio of oil to vinegar is to taste the dressing, preferably on the food it will dress.

Not Just for Salads

With its light taste and texture, vinaigrette dressing makes an appealing sauce where a light touch is desired. It is quick to make and versatile; changing the taste of a vinaigrette is only a matter of switching the type of oil and vinegar and/or citrus juice used. Its balanced acidity makes vinaigrette a good foil for fish dishes, as shown in Seared Sockeye Salmon with Sun-Dried Tomato Chutney and Artichoke and Niçoise Olive Salad (Recipe 19.27 on p. 456).

● **French dressing** classically, a vinaigrette dressing made from oil, vinegar, salt and pepper; in North America, the term also refers to a commercially prepared dressing that is creamy, tartly sweet and red-orange in colour

Oils and vinegars have unique flavours that can be mixed and matched to achieve the correct balance for a particular salad. Olive oil goes well with red wine vinegar; nut oils go well with balsamic or sherry vinegars. Neutral-flavoured oils such as canola, corn or safflower can be mixed with a flavoured vinegar.

Oil and vinegar repel each other and will separate almost immediately when mixed. They should be whisked together immediately before use.

Oils

Many types of oil can be used to make salad dressings. Light, neutral-flavoured oils such as canola, corn, cottonseed, soybean and safflower are relatively low priced and used extensively for this purpose. Other oils can be used to add flavour. Olive oil is very popular; both mild-flavoured pure olive oil and full-flavoured extra virgin olive oil are used. Nut oils such as hazelnut and walnut are expensive but they add unique and interesting flavours. Infused oils are also popular, but great care must be taken in preparing them to avoid botulism.

Vinegars

Many different vinegars can be used to make salad dressings. Red wine vinegar is the most common because it is inexpensive and its flavour blends well with many foods. But other vinegars such as cider, balsamic, white wine and rice are also used. Fruit-flavoured vinegars (particularly raspberry) are extremely popular and widely available, as are herb- and garlic-flavoured ones.

Flavoured vinegars are easy to make. Fruit, herbs or garlic are added to a wine vinegar (either red or white) and left for several days for the flavours to blend. The vinegar is then strained off and used as desired.

Acidic juices such as lemon, orange, lime and verjus are sometimes substituted for all or part of the vinegar in a salad dressing.

Other Flavouring Ingredients

Herbs, spices, shallots, garlic, mustard and sweeteners are only a few of the many flavouring ingredients used to enhance a vinaigrette dressing. Items such as herbs, shallots and garlic should be minced or chopped before being added to the dressing. If dried herbs are used, the dressing should rest for at least one hour to allow the flavours to develop. Other ingredients may be added at any time.

Whisking together the vinaigrette dressing.

BASIC PROCEDURE FOR PREPARING A VINAIGRETTE

1. Choose an oil and vinegar that complement each other as well as the foods they will dress.
2. Combine the vinegar, seasonings and any other flavourings in a bowl.
3. Whisk in the oil.
4. Allow the finished dressing to rest for one hour at room temperature before using so that the flavours can blend.
5. Rewhisk immediately before use. Store in refrigerator. Use in three to four days.

APPLYING THE BASICS   **RECIPE 25.1**

Basic Vinaigrette Dressing

Yield: 500 mL (16 fl. oz.)

Dry mustard	0.75 g	1/2 tsp.
Wine vinegar	125 mL	4 fl. oz.
Salt and pepper	TT	TT
Salad oil	375 mL	12 fl. oz.

1. Dissolve the mustard in a little of the vinegar.

2. Combine all ingredients and mix well. Store in refrigerator.

VARIATIONS: DIJON VINAIGRETTE—Add 60 g (2 oz.) Dijon-style mustard to the vinegar and 50 g (2 oz.) finely chopped shallots. Proceed with the recipe.

HERBED VINAIGRETTE—Add 10 g (1 Tbsp.) fresh herbs or 2.5 g (1-1/2 tsp.) dried herbs such as basil, tarragon, thyme, marjoram or chives to the vinaigrette.

RECIPE 25.1

Approximate values per 15 mL serving:	
Calories	93
Total fat	10.5 g
Saturated fat	1 g
Cholesterol	0 mg
Sodium	38 mg
Total carbohydrates	0 g
Protein	0 g

Mayonnaise

Although most food service operations buy commercially made mayonnaise, every cook should know how it is made to more fully understand how to use it and why it reacts the way it does when used. Knowing how to make mayonnaise also allows you to create a mayonnaise with the exact flavourings you want.

Mayonnaise is an **emulsion**. An emulsion is formed when two liquids that would not ordinarily form a stable mixture are forced together and held in suspension. To make mayonnaise, oil is whisked together with a very small amount of vinegar (it is the water in the vinegar that does not normally mix with oil). As the oil and vinegar are whisked together, the oil breaks into microscopic droplets that are separated from each other by a thin barrier of vinegar. If left alone, the droplets would quickly regroup, forming a large puddle of oil and a small puddle of vinegar. To prevent the oil droplets from regrouping, an emulsifier is added. For mayonnaise, the emulsifier is lecithin, a protein found in egg yolks. Lecithin has the unique ability to combine with both oil and water. It surrounds the oil droplets, binding them together and preventing them from coming in contact with each other and regrouping.

● **emulsion** a uniform mixture of two unmixable liquids

The balance of liquid, oil and lecithin and agitation (whipping) are crucial to achieving a proper emulsion. The higher the proportion of oil to vinegar, the thicker the sauce will be. The higher the proportion of vinegar to oil, the thinner the sauce will be. (For example, the emulsified vinaigrette dressing discussed in Recipe 25.3 is a thin emulsion.)

There is a limit to how much oil each egg yolk can emulsify, however. One large yolk contains enough lecithin to emulsify up to 240 mL (8 fl. oz.) of oil. If more than that amount of oil per egg yolk is added, the sauce will break; that is, the oil and vinegar will separate and the mayonnaise will become very thin and curdled.

Broken mayonnaise is thin and separated or curdled.

Ingredients

A neutral-flavoured vegetable oil is most often used for a standard mayonnaise. Other oils are used to contribute their special flavours. For example, olive oil is used to make a special mayonnaise called aïoli.

Rice or wine vinegar is preferable for a standard mayonnaise. Flavoured vinegars such as tarragon vinegar are often used to create unique flavours.

Seasonings vary according to the intended use but typically include dry mustard, salt, pepper and lemon juice.

Standard white or pickling vinegars are generally too acidic to make a mayonnaise with a balanced flavour.

BASIC PROCEDURE FOR PREPARING MAYONNAISE

1. Gather all ingredients and hold at room temperature. Room-temperature ingredients emulsify more easily than cold ones do.
2. By hand or in an electric mixer, whip the egg yolks on high speed until frothy.
3. Add the seasonings to the yolks and whip to combine. Salt and other seasonings will dissolve or blend more easily when added at this point rather than if added to the finished mayonnaise.
4. Add a small amount of the vinegar from the recipe and whip to combine. This helps to promote the formation of an emulsion by setting the yolks slightly for better binding ability.
5. With the mixer on high or whisking vigorously by hand, begin to add the oil very slowly until an emulsion forms.
6. After the emulsion forms, the oil can be added a little more quickly but still in a slow, steady stream. The mayonnaise can now be whipped at a slightly slower speed.
7. The mayonnaise will become very thick as more oil is added. A small amount of liquid can be added if it becomes too thick. Alternate between oil and liquid two or three times until all the oil is added and the correct consistency is reached.

    Note: A large egg yolk has the ability to emulsify up to 200 mL (7 fl. oz.) of oil; adding more oil may cause the mayonnaise to break.

8. Taste the mayonnaise and adjust the seasonings. Refrigerate immediately.

1. Mayonnaise: Whipping the egg yolks until frothy.

2. Adding the oil very slowly, allowing the emulsion to form.

3. The finished mayonnaise.

RECIPE 25.2

Approximate values per 25 mL serving:	
Calories	170
Total fat	19 g
Saturated fat	1.5 g
Cholesterol	22 mg
Sodium	49 mg
Total carbohydrates	0 g
Protein	0 g

APPLYING THE BASICS   RECIPE 25.2

Mayonnaise

Yield: 1 L (1 qt.)

Egg yolks, large	4	4
Salt	5 g	1 tsp.
White pepper	0.5 g	1/2 tsp.
Dry mustard	1.5 g	1 tsp.
White wine vinegar	50 mL	3 Tbsp.
Salad oil	800 mL	28 fl. oz.
Lemon juice	TT	TT

1. Place the egg yolks in the bowl of a mixer and whip on high speed until frothy. Use pasteurized yolks, if available.
2. Add the dry ingredients and half the vinegar to the yolks; whisk to combine.
3. Begin to add the oil a drop at a time until the mixture begins to thicken and an emulsion begins to form.
4. Add the remaining oil in a slow steady stream, thinning the mayonnaise occasionally by adding a little vinegar. Continue until all oil and vinegar have been incorporated. A little water may be used.
5. Adjust the seasonings and add lemon juice to taste.
6. Store in a covered noncorrosive container. Refrigerate until needed.

Mayonnaise-Based Dressings

Mayonnaise-based salad dressings are sauces that use mayonnaise as a base, with other ingredients added for flavour, colour and texture. These ingredients include dairy products (especially buttermilk and sour cream), vinegar, fruit juice, vegetables (either puréed or minced), tomato paste, garlic, onions, herbs, spices, condiments, capers, anchovies and boiled eggs. Recipes for several mayonnaise-based salad dressings are included at the end of this chapter.

Emulsified Vinaigrette Dressings

An emulsified vinaigrette is a standard vinaigrette dressing emulsified with whole eggs, modified starches or vegetable gums. An emulsified vinaigrette dressing is thinner and lighter than a mayonnaise-based dressing and heavier than a basic vinaigrette. Its taste is similar to a basic vinaigrette, but it will not separate and it clings to greens quite easily. Emulsified vinaigrettes are very popular.

Convenience Products

A great many prepared and dry-mix salad dressings are available. Although they vary greatly in quality, they can be very economical; they reduce labour costs and sometimes food costs. Some of these products use stabilizers, artificial flavourings and colours; nearly all contain preservatives. When considering the advantages of prepared or dry-mix salad dressings, always keep quality in mind.

BASIC PROCEDURE FOR PREPARING AN EMULSIFIED VINAIGRETTE DRESSING

1. Gather all ingredients and hold at room temperature. Room-temperature ingredients emulsify more easily than cold ones do.

2. Whip the eggs until frothy.

3. Add the dry ingredients and any flavourings such as garlic, shallots and herbs.

4. Add a small amount of the liquid from the recipe and whip to incorporate the ingredients.

5. With the mixer on high or whisking vigorously by hand, begin adding the oil very slowly until the emulsion forms.

6. After the emulsion is formed, the oil can be added a little more quickly, but still in a slow, steady stream.

7. Alternate between oil and liquid two or three times until all the oil is added. The dressing should be much thinner than mayonnaise. If it is too thick, it can be thinned with a little water, vinegar or lemon juice. Determine which to use by first tasting the dressing.

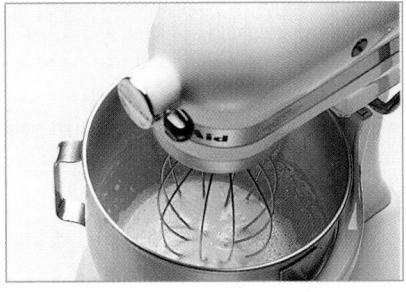

1. Emulsified Vinaigrette Dressing: Whipping the whole eggs.

2. Adding the oil drop by drop to establish the emulsion.

APPLYING THE BASICS   RECIPE 25.3

Emulsified Vinaigrette Dressing

Yield: 500 mL (16 fl. oz.)

Eggs, whole	1	1
Salt	8 g	1-1/2 tsp.
Black pepper, ground	0.5 g	1/4 tsp.
Dry mustard	2.25 g	1-1/2 tsp.
Sugar	8 g	1-1/2 tsp.
Herbes de Provence	2.5 g	1-1/2 tsp.
Cayenne pepper	pinch	pinch
Wine vinegar or cider vinegar	75 mL	2-1/2 fl. oz.
Salad oil	375 mL	12 fl. oz.
Lemon juice	50 mL	2 fl. oz.

3. The finished Emulsified Vinaigrette Dressing.

continued

RECIPE 25.3

Approximate values per 25 mL serving:	
Calories	160
Total fat	18 g
Saturated fat	1 g
Cholesterol	11 mg
Sodium	149 mg
Total carbohydrates	1 g
Protein	0.5 g

1. Place the eggs in the bowl of a mixer and whip at high speed until frothy.

2. Add the dry ingredients and approximately 30 mL (1 fl. oz.) of vinegar to the eggs; whip to combine.

3. While whipping at high speed, begin adding the oil very slowly until an emulsion forms.

4. Add the remaining oil in a slow, steady stream. Occasionally thin the dressing by adding a little vinegar and lemon juice. Continue until all of the oil, vinegar and lemon juice have been incorporated.

5. Adjust the flavour and consistency.

6. Refrigerate until needed.

VARIATION: Omit the herbs and add 3 g (1-1/2 tsp.) paprika and 25 mL (1 fl. oz.) ketchup for an orange-coloured "American French" dressing.

● **tossed salad** a salad prepared by placing the greens, garnishes and salad dressing in a large bowl and tossing to combine

● **composed salad** a salad prepared by arranging each of the ingredients (the base, body, garnish and dressing) on individual plates in an artistic fashion

● **bound salad** a salad composed of cooked meats, poultry, fish, shellfish, pasta or potatoes combined with a dressing

PREPARATION METHODS

There are two types of green salads: tossed and composed. The more informal **tossed salad** is prepared by placing the greens, garnishes and dressing in a large bowl and tossing to combine. A **composed salad** usually has a more elegant look. It is prepared by arranging each of the ingredients on plates in an artistic fashion.

Other types of salads include **bound salads**, which are cooked meats, poultry, fish, shellfish, pasta or potatoes bound with a dressing, vegetable salads and fruit salads.

Traditionally, salads were divided into two categories. Simple salads contain one main featured ingredient. Compound mixed salads contain more than one featured ingredient; unlike composed salads, compound salads are tossed and plated.

Green Salads

Tossed

Tossed salads are made from leafy vegetables such as lettuce, spinach, watercress, arugula or dandelion greens. They may consist only of greens and dressing or they can be garnished with fruits, vegetables, nuts or cheese. They can be dressed with many different types of dressings, from a light oil and vinegar to a hearty hot bacon. It is important that salad dressings be added at the last possible moment before service. Acidic dressings cause most greens to wilt and become soggy.

Matching Dressings and Salad Greens

There is a simple rule to follow when choosing dressings for salads: the more delicate the texture and flavour of the greens or other ingredients, the lighter and more subtle the dressing should be. Vinaigrette-based dressings are much lighter than mayonnaise-based or similar dressings and should be used with butterleaf lettuces, mâche or other delicate greens. Crisp head lettuce such as iceberg and hardy lettuce such as romaine can stand up to heavier, mayonnaise-based or similar dressings. Bitter greens are balanced with tart dressings. (See Table 25.1.)

Salad Garnishes

It is impossible to make a complete list of the garnishes that can be combined with salad greens for a tossed salad. A partial list follows:

• Vegetables—nearly any vegetable (raw, blanched or fully cooked) cut into appropriate sizes and uniform shapes.

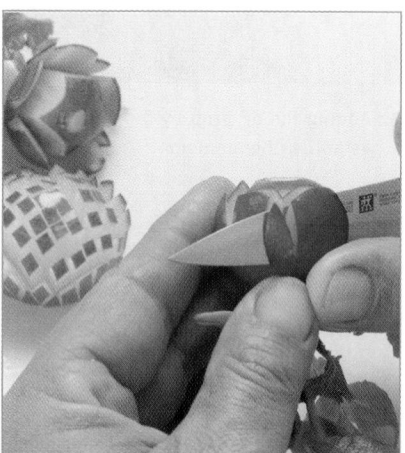

Using a straight paring knife, make parallel horizontal and vertical cuts three-quarters of the way to the root end of a cleaned radish.

TABLE 25.1	Matching Dressings and Salad Greens
Dressing	**Greens**
Vinaigrette dressing made with vegetable oil and red wine vinegar	Any greens: iceberg, romaine, leaf lettuce, butterleaf lettuce, escarole, curly endive, Belgian endive, radicchio, baby lettuces, sorrel, arugula, dandelion
Vinaigrette dressing made with a nut oil and balsamic vinegar	Delicate greens: butterleaf lettuce, bibb lettuce, Belgian endive, radicchio, baby lettuces, arugula, mâche, watercress
Emulsified vinaigrette dressing	Any greens: romaine, leaf lettuce, butterleaf lettuce, escarole, curly endive, Belgian endive, radicchio, baby lettuces, sorrel, arugula, watercress
Mayonnaise-based dressing such as blue cheese or green goddess	Hardy greens: iceberg, romaine, leaf lettuce, escarole, curly endive, sorrel, dandelion

- Fruits—citrus segments, apples or pears; dried fruits such as raisins, currants or apricots.
- Meats, poultry, fish and shellfish—cooked meats and poultry sliced or diced neatly and uniformly; poached, grilled or cured fish, diced or flaked; small, whole cooked shellfish such as shrimp and scallops; lobster or crab, sliced, diced or chopped.
- Cheeses—grated hard cheeses such as Parmesan, Romano or Asiago; semi-hard cheese such as cheddar and Swiss, cut julienne or shredded.
- Nuts—nearly any are appropriate, roasted, candied or smoked.
- Croutons—assorted breads, seasoned in various ways and toasted.

BASIC PROCEDURE FOR PREPARING TOSSED SALADS

1. Select greens with various colours, textures and flavours.
2. Carefully cut or tear, wash and dry the greens.
3. Prepare the garnishes as directed or desired.
4. Prepare the dressing.
5. Combine the greens, garnishes and dressing by tossing them together. Or toss the greens and garnishes and, using a spray bottle, spray the greens with the dressing.

APPLYING THE BASICS
RECIPE 25.4

Mesclun Salad with Raspberry Vinaigrette

Yield: 6 servings

Baby lettuces, assorted	approx. 8 heads	approx. 8 heads
Mâche	125 g	4 oz.
Fresh herbs	20 g	2 Tbsp.

continued

Simple Salads

Green Salad (Salade verte)—any green lettuce served with vinaigrette.

Potato Salad (Salade de pomme de terre)—cooked potatoes diced or sliced. Mixed with mayonnaise or vinaigrette, chopped onion, chives, salt and pepper.

Egg Salad (Salade d'oeufs)—chopped hard-boiled eggs, mustard, chives, salt and pepper.

Artichauts	artichoke !
Aubergine	eggplant !
Betteraves	beetroot !
Céleris	celery ▲
Céleri-rave	celeriac ▲
Chou-rave	kohlrabi ▲
Chou vert	green cabbage ▲
Chou rouge	red cabbage ▲
Concombres	cucumber *
Cresson	watercress *
Endive	chicory ▲
Pissenlit	dandelion ▲
Fenouil	fennel ▲
Laitues	lettuce ▲
Poireau	leek !
Haricots verts	green beans !
Panais	parsnip !
Tomate	tomato *

NOTE: * Raw only
! Cooked only
▲ Raw or cooked

Simple salads should be served tossed or bound with an appropriate dressing.

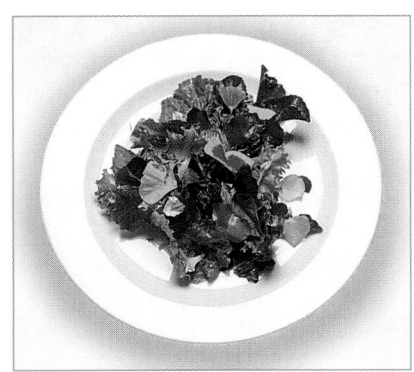
A simple mesclun salad

Edible flowers	approx. 12	approx. 12
Raspberry Vinaigrette		
(Recipe 25.16)	125 mL	4 fl. oz.

1. Trim, wash and dry the baby lettuces and mâche.

2. Pick the fresh herbs from their stems. If using leafy herbs such as basil, cut them chiffonade or leave as whole leaves.

3. Pick the petals from the edible flowers.

4. Place the lettuces and mâche in a bowl and add the herbs. Ladle the dressing over them and toss gently, using 2 spoons.

5. Transfer the salads to cold plates. Some of the larger leaves may be used as liners if desired.

6. Garnish each salad with flower petals.

RECIPE 25.4

Approximate values per serving:	
Calories	155
Total fat	9 g
Saturated fat	1 g
Cholesterol	0 mg
Sodium	189 mg
Total carbohydrates	15 g
Protein	4 g

Garnishing

A garnish is an integral part of a prepared dish. It often uses recipe ingredients cut or arranged specifically to enhance colour, shapes, contrast and overall eye appeal. Sometimes additional items are used to garnish, but the garnish should not change the character of the dish. Traditionally, classical garnishes defined many of the ingredients in a dish and often how it was prepared and served.

● **garnish** food used as an attractive decoration

Transferring composed salads to chilled plates for service

Composed

Composed green salads usually use a green as a base and are built by artistically arranging other ingredients on the plate. There are usually four components: the base, body, garnish and dressing.

The **base** is usually salad greens that partially line or anchor the plate on which the salad will be served. Depending upon the desired effect, the leaves can be cup-shaped or flat.

The **body** is the main ingredient. It can be lettuce or other greens, or another salad made from cooked or blended ingredients, such as chicken salad or fruit.

The **garnish** is added to the salad for colour, texture and flavour. It can be as substantial as a grilled, sliced duck breast or as simple as a sprinkling of chopped herbs; it can be warm or cold. The choice is unlimited but whatever is used should always complement and balance the flavour of the body.

The salad **dressing** should complement rather than mask the other flavours in the salad. If the body already contains a dressing, as in a bound salad, additional dressing may not be necessary.

Composed green salads are usually dressed by ladling the dressing over the salad after it is plated. Alternatively, the individual ingredients can be dressed before they are arranged on the plate. A third method, which may be limited by the intricacy of the salad but which will save precious time during a busy period, is to prepare individual salads on a sheet pan. Just before service, mist them with dressing using a spray bottle designated for this purpose, then transfer them to chilled plates using a spatula as illustrated. Foam beverage cups work well too.

BASIC PROCEDURE FOR PREPARING COMPOSED SALADS

1. Gather all ingredients for the salad and wash, trim, cut, cook, chill or otherwise prepare them as necessary or as called for in the recipe.

2. Arrange all ingredients artistically on the plates, dressing each ingredient as desired or as directed in the recipe.

3. At service time, heat or cook any items that are being served hot and add them to the salad.

1. Salad Niçoise: Lining a cold salad plate with a base of lettuce leaves.

2. The composed Salad Niçoise.

APPLYING THE BASICS		RECIPE 25.5

Salad Niçoise

Yield: 6 servings

Red wine vinegar	125 mL	4 fl. oz.
Salt and pepper	TT	TT
Virgin olive oil	350 mL	12 fl. oz.
Basil leaves, chiffonade	12	12
Belgian endive	1 head	1 head
Tomatoes, peeled	6	6
Waxy potatoes, cooked	700 g	1 lb. 8 oz.
Green beans	350 g	12 oz.
Eggs, hard-boiled	6	6
Artichokes	6	6
Romaine lettuce leaves, washed	12	12
Tuna, fresh, grilled and chilled	750 g	1 lb. 8 oz.
Niçoise olives	125 g	4 oz.
Anchovy fillets	12	12

1. Make a vinaigrette dressing using the red wine vinegar, salt, pepper, olive oil and basil leaves.

2. Wash and dry the endive leaves.

3. Core and cut each tomato into eight wedges.

4. Slice the potatoes and moisten with some of the dressing.

5. Trim and cook the green beans al dente, refresh in ice water.

6. Peel the eggs and cut into wedges.

7. Cook the artichokes. Trim the outer leaves from each artichoke, leaving only the heart. Remove the choke from the heart and cut each heart into quarters.

8. Line each cold plate with romaine lettuce leaves and endive spears, then arrange the ingredients artistically. Use the contrasting shapes, colours and textures to create an attractive presentation.

9. At service, whisk the dressing to combine the ingredients and pour approximately 75 mL (2-1/2 fl. oz.) over each salad.

RECIPE 25.5

Approximate values per serving:	
Calories	957
Total fat	70 g
Saturated fat	11 g
Cholesterol	241 mg
Sodium	777 mg
Total carbohydrates	34 g
Protein	50 g

Bound Salads

The creative cook can prepare a wide variety of salads by combining cooked meats, poultry, fish, shellfish, potatoes, pasta, grains and/or legumes with a dressing and garnishes. Although the combinations vary greatly, these salads are grouped together here because their ingredients are all bound. That is, each salad consists of one or more ingredients held together in a cohesive mass. The binding agent can be either an emulsified vinaigrette or mayonnaise-based or similar dressing. The ingredients should be evenly distributed throughout, and the degree of cohesiveness can range from tightly packed to flaky and easily separated.

The foods that can be used to produce bound salads are so varied that it is impossible to list them all. Preparation generally involves uniformly shaping and cutting the ingredients in smaller pieces. Bound salads hold their shape when moulded or stick together when used as a filling.

Bound salads can be used as the body of a composed salad (for instance, a serving of shrimp salad on a bed of greens). Some are used in sandwiches but not ordinarily as side dishes—for example, egg or ham salad. Some are served as side dishes but not in sandwiches—for example, potato, pasta or cucumber salad. Follow specific recipes and traditional uses for each salad until you are confident enough in your skills to let your imagination take over.

BASIC PROCEDURE FOR PREPARING BOUND SALADS

1. Preparing a salad from cooked foods is a good opportunity to use leftovers, but be sure they are fresh and of good quality. The finished salad can be only as good as each of its ingredients.

2. When making a bound salad, choose ingredients whose flavours blend well and complement each other.

3. Choose ingredients for colour; a few colourful ingredients will turn a plain salad into a spectacular one.

4. To improve appearance, generally cut all ingredients the same size and shape. If the main ingredient is diced, then dice the other ingredients. Be cautious about combining diced, sliced and julienned foods in the same salad.

5. All ingredients should be cut into pieces that are small enough to be eaten easily with a fork.

6. Be sure all meats, poultry, fish and shellfish are fully cooked before using them. Undercooked foods can cause food-borne illness and spoilage.

7. Always chill cooked ingredients well before using them. Warm ingredients promote bacterial growth, especially in mayonnaise-based salads.

8. Always use dressings sparingly. They should enhance the flavours of the other salad ingredients, not mask them.

APPLYING THE BASICS — RECIPE 25.6

Tuna Salad

Yield: 1.5 kg (3 lb.)

Tuna, drained, flaked	1 kg	2 lb.
Celery, small dice	125 g	4 oz.
Green onion, sliced	50 g	2 oz.
Mayonnaise	250 mL	8 fl. oz.
Lemon juice	50 mL	2 fl. oz.
Salt and pepper	TT	TT

Combine the tuna, celery, green onion, mayonnaise and lemon juice in a bowl; mix well. Season to taste with salt and pepper.

VARIATIONS: Diced chicken, turkey, flaked boneless and skinless salmon, chopped hard-boiled eggs or seafood may be substituted for the tuna. Substitute lemon juice with mustard in the egg salad. Use 200 g (7 oz.) diced pineapple for the chicken salad instead of lemon juice.

RECIPE 25.6

Approximate values per 85 g serving:	
Calories	180
Total fat	11 g
Saturated fat	1 g
Cholesterol	19 mg
Sodium	274 mg
Total carbohydrates	1 g
Protein	18 g

Vegetable Salads

Vegetable salads are made from cooked or raw vegetables or a combination of both. They can be served on buffets, as an appetizer or salad course. As with other salads, vegetable salads must successfully combine colour, texture and flavour. Some vegetable salads such as coleslaw and carrot-raisin salad may be made with mayonnaise. Most, however, are made by either marinating the vegetables or combining them in a vinaigrette dressing.

Almost any vegetable can be successfully marinated. The amount of time depends on the vegetables and the marinade, but several hours to overnight is usually sufficient for flavours to blend. Soft vegetables such as mushrooms, zucchini and cucumbers can be added directly to a cold marinade. Hard vegetables such as carrots and cauliflower should be blanched in salted water, refreshed, drained and then added to a cold marinade. Carrots, artichokes, mushrooms, cauliflower, zucchini, pearl onions and the like are sometimes simmered quickly in a marinade flavoured with lemon juice and olive oil, and then served cold. This style is called *à la grecque*.

Many marinated salads will last several days under proper refrigeration. As the salads age in the marinade, they will change in appearance and texture. This may or may not be desirable. For example, mushrooms and artichokes become more flavourful, while green vegetables are discoloured by the acids in the marinade. If marinated salads are prepared in advance, check their appearance as well as their seasonings carefully at service time.

Compound Salads

Cressonnière—Slices of potato, watercress, hard-boiled egg, parsley and vinaigrette.

Japanese/Japonaise—Dice of tomato, pineapple, orange and apple with sour cream.

Waldorf—Dice of celeriac or celery, apples and walnuts bound in mayonnaise.

BASIC PROCEDURE FOR PREPARING VEGETABLE SALADS

1. Gather and wash all vegetables.

2. Trim, cut, shred or otherwise prepare the vegetables as desired or as directed in the recipe.

3. Blanch or cook the vegetables if necessary.

4. Combine the vegetables with the marinade or dressing. Adjust the seasonings.

Caprese Salad

APPLYING THE BASICS   RECIPE 25.7

Caprese Salad

Yield: 10 Servings
Method: Composed

Fresh mozzarella	20 slices	20 slices
Tomatoes	20 slices	20 slices
Fresh basil leaves, chiffonade	20 g	2 Tbsp.
Salt and pepper	TT	TT
Extra virgin olive oil	20 mL	1-1/2 Tbsp.

1. Arrange the mozzarella and tomato slices in overlapping circles on a serving platter, alternating slices of cheese and tomato.

2. Sprinkle the basil, salt and pepper over the salad. Drizzle with the oil. Serve two slices of tomato and two slices of cheese on each individual serving plate.

RECIPE 25.7

Approximate values per serving:	
Calories	186
Total fat	15 g
Saturated fat	8 g
Cholesterol	44 mg
Sodium	408 mg
Total carbohydrates	4 g
Protein	12 g

Fruit Salads

There are so many different fruits with beautiful bright colours and sweet delicious flavours that preparing fruit salads is easy work. Fruit salads are a refreshing addition to buffets and can be served as the first course of a lunch or dinner. A more elaborate fruit salad can be served as a light lunch.

Always prepare fruit salads as close to service time as possible. The flesh of many types of fruit becomes soft and translucent if cut long before service. Other fruits turn brown in a matter of minutes after cutting. Refer to Chapter 26, Fruits, for more information on this browning reaction and for information on specific fruits. Fruit salad recipes are found at the end of that chapter.

If a fruit salad is dressed at all, the dressing is usually sweet and made with honey or yogurt mixed with fruit juices or purées. Melons work well with herbed vinaigrettes when a sweet/sour effect is desired. Alternatively, Grand Marnier, crème de menthe or other liqueurs sprinkled over the salad can serve as a dressing. Fruit salads can be tossed or composed. Either should offer the consumer a pleasing blend of colours, shapes, sizes, flavours and textures.

Conclusion

A salad can be a small part of a meal or the entire meal. There are many styles of salads, and a seemingly endless variety of foods can be used to prepare them. Salads are extremely popular, especially with those interested in lighter dining alternatives. You can tempt these diners by determining the appropriate style of the salads and skilfully combining the main ingredients and dressing to achieve a delicious and appealing balance of colours, textures and flavours.

Questions for Discussion

1. Name several factors that will cause salad greens to wilt or deteriorate.
2. Describe the proper procedure for washing and drying lettuce.
3. Explain the difference between a vinaigrette and an emulsified vinaigrette dressing.
4. Describe the procedure for making mayonnaise. How can the flavour of a mayonnaise be altered?
5. Explain what happens to the ingredients when an emulsion "breaks." How can it sometimes be repaired?
6. Describe a typical bound salad. How does a bound salad differ from a dressed salad?
7. List five ways salads can be presented or offered on a menu.

Additional Salad Recipes

RECIPE 25.8

Caesar Dressing

Yield: 1.5 L (1-1/2 qt.)
Method: Emulsion

Dry mustard	2 g	1/2 tsp.
Lemon juice	150 mL	5 fl. oz.
Salt	5 g	1 tsp.
Eggs, whole	5	5
Anchovy paste	30 g	1 oz.
Worcestershire sauce	5 mL	1 tsp.
Garlic cloves, crushed	2	2
Olive oil	1 L	1 qt.
Black pepper, ground	3 g	1 tsp.
Parmesan cheese (optional)	100 g	3 oz.

1. Dissolve the mustard in the lemon juice with the salt.
2. Whisk mixture with the eggs, anchovy paste, Worcestershire sauce and garlic until frothy.
3. Slowly drizzle the olive oil into mixture while whisking.
4. Once the emulsion forms, add remaining oil in a steady stream.
5. Add the remaining ingredients and adjust seasoning.
6. Store covered in a noncorrosive container under refrigeration. Use within 3–4 days.

RECIPE 25.8

Approximate values per 50 mL serving:	
Calories	301
Total fat	32 g
Saturated fat	5 g
Cholesterol	39 mg
Sodium	176 mg
Total carbohydrates	1 g
Protein	3 g

History of Caesar Salad

Caesar salad originated in Tijuana, Mexico, and was created by Caesar Cardini more than 100 years ago. Today's versions—and there are many—often bear little resemblance to the original. Julia Child documented this salad from memories of Cardini preparing it and input from Rosa, his daughter. The leaves used were the whole centre hearts. The dressing was simply 125 mL (4 fl. oz.) olive oil, juice of 1 lemon, 2 coddled eggs (simmer 1 minute), salt, freshly ground pepper and Worcestershire sauce. The salad was garnished with pan-fried garlic croutons and Reggiano Parmesan, and eaten with the fingers.

Modern restaurateurs have added anchovies, far too much raw garlic, bacon bits and even capers and parsley. This may be due in part to the mistaken notion that the salad is Italian in origin. These varations are more aptly referred to as house-style salads, although the recipes here reflect current style.

RECIPE 25.9

Caesar Salad

Yield: 4 servings

Crisp, chilled romaine, chopped into 3–4-cm (1 to 1-1/2 in.) pieces	1 large	1 large
Garlic clove	1	1
Anchovy fillets, chopped	15 g	1/2 oz.
Coddled eggs (see Step 5)	2	2
English dry mustard	1 g	1/2 tsp.
Juice from 1 lemon	1	1
Salt	2 g	1/2 tsp.
Worcestershire sauce	5 mL	1 tsp.
Olive oil	125 mL	4 fl. oz.
Black pepper, fresh ground	TT	TT
Parmesan cheese, grated	125 g	4 oz.
Garlic Croutons (Recipe 25.17)	250 mL (heaping)	1 cup (heaping)

1. The romaine should be chopped, crisp, dry and chilled.
2. Line up all ingredients ready for use at the tableside. Use only the very best brands of condiments.
3. In a small wooden bowl, crush the garlic with a fork and remove the pieces.
4. Mash the anchovies in the bowl.

Caesar Salad

continued

Approximate values per serving:	
Calories	451
Total fat	41 g
Saturated fat	11 g
Cholesterol	136 mg
Sodium	962 mg
Total carbohydrates	3 g
Protein	18 g

5. To coddle eggs, place shelled eggs in a bowl of hot water to heat through but not set the white.

6. Add the mustard, lemon juice, salt, Worcestershire sauce and coddled eggs. Mix well.

7. Very slowly mix in the oil, creating an emulsion.

8. Mix in pepper and half of the Parmesan cheese.

9. Toss romaine in dressing.

10. Sprinkle on remaining Parmesan and croutons.

11. Serve immediately on chilled plates. Finish with a little Parmesan.

Thousand Island Dressing

Approximate values per 30 mL serving:	
Calories	99
Total fat	9.5 g
Saturated fat	1 g
Cholesterol	24 mg
Sodium	197 mg
Total carbohydrates	3 g
Protein	1 g

RECIPE 25.10

Thousand Island Dressing

Yield: 1 L (1 qt.)

Red wine vinegar	15 mL	1 Tbsp.
Sugar	15 g	1 Tbsp.
Mayonnaise	400 mL	16 fl. oz.
Ketchup	200 g	7 oz.
Red pepper, finely diced	90 g	3 oz.
Green pepper, finely diced	90 g	3 oz.
Hard-cooked eggs, chopped	3	3
Fresh parsley, chopped	30 mL	2 Tbsp.
Green onions, chopped	1	1
Salt and pepper	TT	TT
Worcestershire sauce	TT	TT

1. Combine the vinegar and sugar; stir to dissolve the sugar.

2. Add the remaining ingredients and mix well.

3. Adjust the seasonings with the salt, pepper and Worcestershire sauce.

Approximate values per 30 mL serving:	
Calories	98
Total fat	10 g
Saturated fat	3 g
Cholesterol	17 mg
Sodium	113 mg
Total carbohydrates	1 g
Protein	1 g

RECIPE 25.11

Ranch Dressing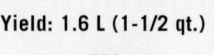

Yield: 1.6 L (1-1/2 qt.)

Sour cream	500 mL	16 fl. oz.
Buttermilk	500 mL	16 fl. oz.
Mayonnaise	500 mL	16 fl. oz.
Cider vinegar	75 mL	2-1/2 fl. oz.
Worcestershire sauce	5 mL	1 tsp.
Parsley, chopped	5 g	2 Tbsp.
Green onion, chopped	50 mL	1/4 cup
Salt	7 g	1-1/2 tsp.
Black pepper, ground	1.5 g	1/2 tsp.

1. Combine all ingredients.

2. Adjust seasoning.

VARIATION: Add 50 g (1-1/2 oz.) crumbled, cooked bacon.

RECIPE 25.12

Cucumber Dressing

Yield: 1.6 L (50 fl. oz.)

Mayonnaise	500 mL	16 fl. oz.
Yogurt, plain	500 mL	16 fl. oz.
English cucumber, grated	500 g	1
Vinegar, white wine or rice	125 mL	4 fl. oz.
Salt	10 g	1-1/2 tsp.
Pepper	0.5 g	1/4 tsp.
Sugar	10 g	2 tsp.

Combine all ingredients.

RECIPE 25.12

Approximate values per 30 mL serving:	
Calories	73
Total fat	7 g
Saturated fat	1 g
Cholesterol	6 mg
Sodium	126 mg
Total carbohydrates	1 g
Protein	1 g

RECIPE 25.13

Creamy Blue Cheese Dressing

Yield: 1.5 L (1-1/2 qt.)

Mayonnaise	700 mL	24 fl. oz.
Sour cream	500 mL	16 fl. oz.
Cream, 35%	200 mL	7 fl. oz.
Blue cheese, grated	200 g	7 oz.
Green onion, finely chopped	10 g	1 Tbsp.
Worcestershire sauce	5 mL	1 tsp.
Salt	15 g	1 Tbsp.
Pepper	1 g	1/4 tsp.
Cider vinegar	50 mL	2 fl. oz.
Lemon juice	20 mL	1 fl. oz.

Combine all ingredients.

Creamy Blue Cheese Dressing

RECIPE 25.13

Approximate values per 30 mL serving:	
Calories	319
Total fat	34 g
Saturated fat	16 g
Cholesterol	91 mg
Sodium	267 mg
Total carbohydrates	2 g
Protein	2 g

RECIPE 25.14

Tartar Sauce

Yield: 500 mL (20 fl. oz.)

Mayonnaise	400 mL	16 fl. oz.
Capers, chopped	50 g	2 oz.
Sour gherkins, chopped	50 g	2 oz.
Shallot, minced	25 g	2 Tbsp.
Fresh parsley, minced	20 g	2 Tbsp.
Lemon juice	15 mL	1 Tbsp.
Salt	TT	TT
Hard-boiled eggs, chopped (optional)	2	2

Stir all of the ingredients together until well blended. Chill thoroughly before serving.

VARIATION: For rémoulade, add 25 g (2 Tbsp.) chopped anchovies and omit eggs.

Tartar Sauce

RECIPE 25.14

Approximate values per 30 mL serving:	
Calories	185
Total fat	20 g
Saturated fat	2 g
Cholesterol	15 mg
Sodium	450 mg
Total carbohydrates	1 g
Protein	0 g

Green Goddess Dressing

RECIPE 25.15

Approximate values per 30 mL serving:	
Calories	189
Total fat	20 g
Saturated fat	2 g
Cholesterol	16 mg
Sodium	167 mg
Total carbohydrates	0.6 g
Protein	0.7 g

RECIPE 25.15

Green Goddess Dressing

Yield: 1 L (1 qt.)

Fresh parsley	30 g	1 oz.
Spinach leaves	60 g	2 oz.
Mayonnaise	900 mL	1-1/2 pt.
Garlic, chopped	15 g	1 Tbsp.
Anchovy fillets, minced	30 g	1 oz.
Fresh chives, chopped	30 g	1 oz.
Fresh tarragon, chopped	10 g	1 Tbsp.
Lemon juice	30 mL	1 fl. oz.
White wine vinegar	30 mL	1 fl. oz.
Salt and white pepper	TT	TT

1. Rinse and chop the parsley and spinach but do not dry it or you will remove some of the chlorophyll.
2. Combine all ingredients up to and including vinegar and mix well. Season to taste with salt and white pepper.

Raspberry Vinaigrette

RECIPE 25.16

Approximate values per 30 mL serving:	
Calories	115
Total fat	11 g
Saturated fat	1 g
Cholesterol	0 mg
Sodium	178 mg
Total carbohydrates	5 g
Protein	0 g

RECIPE 25.16

Raspberry Vinaigrette
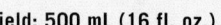

Yield: 500 mL (16 fl. oz.)

Red wine vinegar	65 mL	2 fl. oz.
Rice wine vinegar	60 mL	2 fl. oz.
Lemon juice	15 mL	1 Tbsp.
Dried thyme	0.5 g	3/4 tsp.
Salt	7 g	3/4 tsp.
Pepper, black ground	3 g	3/4 tsp.
Garlic, minced	5 g	3/4 tsp.
Honey	30 g	1 oz.
Raspberry preserves, without seeds	60 g	2 oz.
Olive oil	90 mL	3 fl. oz.
Salad oil	125 mL	4 fl. oz.

1. Whisk together the vinegars, lemon juice, thyme, salt, pepper and garlic.
2. Slowly whisk in the honey and raspberry preserves.
3. Whisk in the oils slowly, emulsifying the dressing.

VARIATION: Prepare Basic Vinaigrette Dressing (Recipe 25.1) using raspberry vinegar.

Roquefort Dressing

Classically, this is a vinaigrette dressing made with olive oil, wine vinegar and crumbled Roquefort whisked in to form an emulsion.

RECIPE 25.17

Garlic Croutons for Salads

Yield: 600 g (1 lb. 4 oz.)

Whole butter	200 g	6 oz.
Garlic, chopped	10 g	1 Tbsp.
French or sourdough bread cubes	750 g	1 lb. 8 oz.
Parmesan cheese, grated	30 g	1 oz.

1. Melt the butter in a small saucepan and add the garlic. Cook the garlic in the butter for 5 minutes.
2. Place the bread cubes in a bowl and add the Parmesan cheese.
3. Pour the garlic butter over the bread cubes and immediately toss to combine.
4. Spread the bread cubes on a sheet pan in a single layer and bake at 180°C (350°F). Stir the croutons occasionally and cook until dry and lightly browned, approximately 15 minutes.

Garlic Croutons for Salads

RECIPE 25.17

Approximate values per 30 mL serving:	
Calories	182
Total fat	10 g
Saturated fat	6 g
Cholesterol	23 mg
Sodium	339 mg
Total carbohydrates	20 g
Protein	4 g

RECIPE 25.18

Chive Essence

FOOD NETWORK CANADA
Chef Michael Smith

Yield: 250 mL (8 fl. oz.)

| Chives, chopped | 70 g | 1 cup |
| Canola oil | 250 mL | 8 fl. oz. |

1. Place chives and oil in a high-speed blender and process until very smooth. Pour into a thick-bottomed pot.
2. Bring mixture to a simmer over medium heat. Do not stir. As soon as it boils, remove from heat.
3. Strain through a fine-meshed sieve. Let mixture drain without squeezing to minimize moisture extraction.
4. Refrigerate until needed. Use within 3 days.

NOTE: This oil's brilliant green colour and delicate chive flavour make it an ideal garnish—you may substitute green onions or leek tops for the chives.

Michael Smith
Chef Michael Smith has dedicated his career to furthering the ideals of Canadian cuisine. He has hosted The Food Network Canada's *Chef at Large*, *Chef at Home*, *Chef Abroad* and *The Inn Chef*, and frequently crisscrosses the country leading cooking classes. He has published a number of cookbooks, including *Open Kitchen: A Chef's Day at The Inn at Bay Fortune*.

RECIPE 25.18

Approximate values per 20 mL serving:	
Calories	171
Total fat	19 g
Saturated fat	1.4 g
Cholesterol	0 mg
Sodium	0 mg
Total carbohydrates	0 g
Protein	0 g

Heirloom Tomato Salad

RECIPE 25.19

Approximate values per serving:	
Calories	186
Total fat	11 g
Saturated fat	1.5 g
Cholesterol	0 mg
Sodium	677 mg
Total carbohydrates	16 g
Protein	5 g

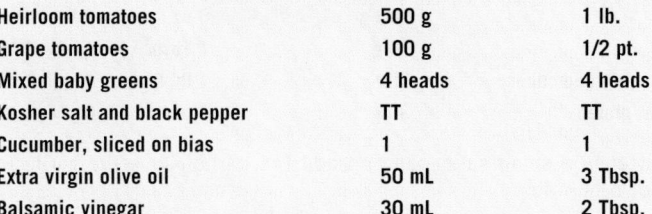

RECIPE 25.19

Heirloom Tomato Salad

Yield: 4 servings

Heirloom tomatoes	500 g	1 lb.
Grape tomatoes	100 g	1/2 pt.
Mixed baby greens	4 heads	4 heads
Kosher salt and black pepper	TT	TT
Cucumber, sliced on bias	1	1
Extra virgin olive oil	50 mL	3 Tbsp.
Balsamic vinegar	30 mL	2 Tbsp.

1. Core the heirloom tomatoes and cut into wedges or thick slices. Pluck the stems from the grape tomatoes; leave whole if small or cut in half if large.
2. Wash the mixed baby greens and dry. Spread the greens on plates or a serving platter and arrange the heirloom tomatoes over them. Season the tomatoes with freshly ground salt and pepper.
3. Garnish the salad with cucumber slices.
4. Drizzle on the olive oil; follow with a light drizzle of vinegar.
5. Arrange the grape tomatoes over the salad.

Couscous Salad

RECIPE 25.20

Approximate values per 100 g serving:	
Calories	166
Total fat	8.5 g
Saturated fat	1.2 g
Cholesterol	0 mg
Sodium	383 mg
Total carbohydrates	21 g
Protein	2.6 g

RECIPE 25.20

Couscous Salad

Yield: 1.3 kg (3 lb.)

Couscous	175 g	6 oz.
Red bell pepper, macedoine	175 g	6 oz.
Green bell pepper, macedoine	175 g	6 oz.
Green onions, bias cut	6	6
Cucumber, peeled, seeded, diced	175 g	6 oz.
Niçoise olives, pitted	125 g	4 oz.
Red onion, julienne	175 g	6 oz.
Dressing:		
Orange juice concentrate	100 mL	3 fl. oz.
Water	60 mL	2 fl. oz.
White wine vinegar	60 mL	2 fl. oz.
Garlic, minced	5 g	1 tsp.
Salt	5 g	1 tsp.
Oregano, fresh, chopped	8 g	2 tsp.
Olive oil	100 mL	3 fl. oz.
Honey	50 g	2-1/2 Tbsp.
Thyme leaves, chopped	5 g	2 tsp.

1. Steam the couscous until tender; set aside to cool.
2. Combine the couscous with the vegetables.
3. Whisk together the dressing ingredients.
4. Combine the salad ingredients with the dressing and chill thoroughly.

RECIPE 25.21

Wilted Spinach Salad with Roasted Peppers

Yield: 2 large or 4 small servings

Red or yellow bell pepper, medium	175 g	1
Olive oil	50 mL	2 fl. oz.
Salt and pepper	TT	TT
Red onion, sliced thin	60 g	2 oz.
Baguette, thin slices for croutons	12	12
Spinach	450 g	1 lb.
Frisée or escarole	1 head	1 head
Balsamic vinegar	45 mL	3 Tbsp.
Niçoise or Gaeta olives, pitted	10	10
Safflower oil	30 mL	1 fl. oz.
Garlic clove, chopped fine	1	1
Parmesan cheese, grated	30 g	1 oz.

1. Roast, peel and cut the pepper into 5-mm (1/4-in.) strips. Toss the pepper strips with 10 mL (1/2 Tbsp.) of olive oil and a few pinches of salt and pepper. Set aside to marinate.
2. Cover the onion slices with cold water to leach the strong onion flavour. Set aside.
3. Place the baguette slices on a baking sheet and brush them lightly with olive oil. Toast in a 190°C (375°F) oven until crisp and lightly browned, approximately 5 minutes.
4. Stem, wash and dry the spinach. Trim the stem end of the frisée or escarole and discard the tough outer leaves. Wash and dry.
5. Drain the onions. In a large bowl, combine the vinegar, 2 mL (1/2 tsp.) salt and a few pinches of pepper. Add the greens, onions, peppers and olives.
6. Heat the safflower oil in a sauté pan with garlic until it is hot. Sauté the spinach quickly. Immediately pour it over the dressing and toss with a pair of metal tongs to coat and wilt the leaves.
7. Plate, sprinkle on the Parmesan cheese and croutons and serve immediately.

Wilted Spinach Salad with Roasted Peppers

RECIPE 25.21

Approximate values per large serving:	
Calories	692
Total fat	52 g
Saturated fat	9 g
Cholesterol	10 mg
Sodium	1163 mg
Total carbohydrates	38 g
Protein	17 g

RECIPE 25.22

Seafood Waldorf Salad

COLLEGE OF THE NORTH ATLANTIC, St. John's, NL
Chef Instructor Gerry Crewe

Yield: 10 servings

Scallops, "catch" removed	300 g	10 oz.
Court bouillon	500 mL	16 fl. oz.
Red apple, diced, skin on	300 g	10 oz.
Green apple, diced, skin on	300 g	10 oz.
Mayonnaise	200 mL	7 fl. oz.
Celery, diced	300 g	10 oz.
Walnut pieces	150 g	5 oz.
Baby shrimp, cooked	300 g	10 oz.
Cream, 35%, whipped (optional)	50 mL	2 fl. oz.
Salt and pepper	TT	TT
Smoked salmon, sliced on bias	300 g	10 slices
Capers	15 g	1 Tbsp.
Garnish: endive spears,		
butterleaf lettuce	as needed	as needed

Gerry Crewe

Gerry has been teaching apprentice cooks for 33 years at the College of the North Atlantic in Newfoundland. He began his training at the Hotel Newfoundland and is a founding member of the CCFCC St. John's Branch. Highlights of his career are the World Cooks Tour in South Africa, winning the Atlantic Chef of the Year and winning the Teaching Excellence Award for Newfoundland.

continued

RECIPE 25.22

Approximate values per serving:	
Calories	362
Total fat	26 g
Saturated fat	2.4 g
Cholesterol	73 mg
Sodium	937 mg
Total carbohydrates	13 g
Protein	21 g

1. Poach scallops in court bouillon, shock in ice water, drain and reserve.

2. Mix the apples with the mayonnaise immediately on dicing. Add the celery, walnuts, shrimp and scallops and whipped cream if desired. Mix gently and adjust seasoning.

3. To plate, place a portion of the salad on chilled plate, arrange a rosette of smoked salmon, dress with capers and garnish with endive spears and butterleaf lettuce.

RECIPE 25.23

Fennel and Mushrooms à la Grecque

Yield: 18 100-g (3-oz.) servings

Method: Simmering

Mushrooms, small	500 g	1 lb.
Pearl onions, peeled	125 g	4 oz.
Olive oil	50 mL	2 fl. oz.
White wine	125 mL	4 fl. oz.
White stock	500 mL	16 fl. oz.
Tomato concassée	400 g	12 oz.
Tomato paste	50 g	1 oz.
Lemon juice	25 mL	1 fl. oz.
Coriander, ground	3 g	1 tsp.
Bouquet garni:		
Carrot stick, 10 cm (4 in.)	1	1
Leek, split, 10-cm (4-in.) piece	1	1
Fresh thyme	1 sprig	1 sprig
Bay leaves	2	2
Salt and pepper	TT	TT
Fennel, batonnet	500 g	1 lb.

1. Wash the mushrooms and trim the stems.

2. Sauté the onions in the olive oil, browning lightly. Add the white wine, stock, tomato concassée, tomato paste, lemon juice, coriander and bouquet garni. Season to taste with salt and pepper and bring to a boil.

3. Add the fennel and mushrooms and simmer for 15 minutes.

4. Remove from the heat and allow to cool to room temperature. Remove the bouquet garni. Adjust the seasonings and refrigerate. Serve chilled.

RECIPE 25.23

Approximate values per 100 g serving:	
Calories	60
Total fat	3.5 g
Saturated fat	0 g
Cholesterol	0 mg
Sodium	245 mg
Total carbohydrates	5 g
Protein	2 g

Potato Salad

RECIPE 25.24

Potato Salad

Yield: 2.5 kg (6 lb. 8 oz.)

Potatoes, waxy, skin on	1.5 kg	4 lb.
Eggs, hard-cooked	5	6
Celery, medium dice	250 g	8 oz.
Green onions, sliced	1 bunch	1 bunch
Mayonnaise	250 mL	10 fl. oz.
Sour cream	150 mL	6 fl. oz.

continued

Red wine or tarragon vinegar	50 mL	2 fl. oz.
Dijon-style mustard	50 mL	2 fl. oz.
Fresh parsley, chopped	30 g	1 oz.
Salt and pepper	TT	TT

1. Boil the potatoes in salted water until nearly cooked. Drain the potatoes, spread them on a sheet pan and refrigerate until cold.

2. Peel and cut the cold potatoes into medium or large dice.

3. Peel and chop the eggs.

4. Combine all ingredients and adjust the seasonings with salt and pepper.

RECIPE 25.24

Approximate values per 85 g serving:	
Calories	134
Total fat	9 g
Saturated fat	1.5 g
Cholesterol	47 mg
Sodium	193 mg
Total carbohydrates	11 g
Protein	3 g

RECIPE 25.25

Creamy Coleslaw

Yield: 1 kg (2 lb.)

Mayonnaise	250 mL	8 fl. oz.
Sour cream or crème fraîche	125 mL	4 fl. oz.
Sugar	50 g	1 oz.
Cider vinegar	50 mL	1 fl. oz.
Green cabbage, shredded	500 g	1 lb.
Celery, julienne	250 g	8 oz.
Carrot, shredded	125 g	4 oz.
Salt and white pepper	TT	TT

1. Combine the mayonnaise, sour cream or crème fraîche, sugar and vinegar in a bowl; whisk together.

2. Add the shredded cabbage, celery and carrot to the dressing and mix well. Season to taste with salt and pepper.

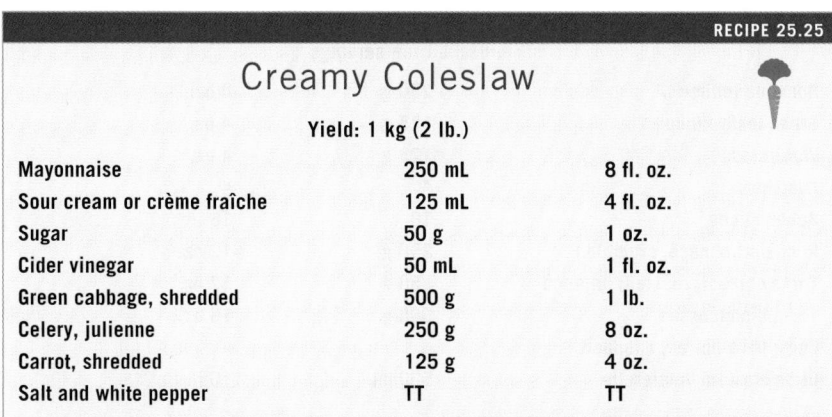

Creamy Coleslaw

RECIPE 25.25

Approximate values per 85 g serving:	
Calories	142
Total fat	13 g
Saturated fat	3 g
Cholesterol	14 mg
Sodium	238 mg
Total carbohydrates	6 g
Protein	1 g

RECIPE 25.26

Greek Salad

Yield: 2.6 kg (5 lb. 8 oz.)

Extra virgin olive oil	125 mL	4 fl. oz.
Lemon juice	25 mL	1 fl. oz.
Red wine vinegar	25 mL	1 fl. oz.
Fresh oregano, chopped	15 g	3 Tbsp.
English cucumbers	2	2
Feta cheese	350 g	12 oz.
Red and green peppers, diced	500 g	1 lb.
Olives, kalamata or other Greek variety	500 g	1 lb.
Tomatoes, cut into 6 wedges	500 g	3
Fresh parsley, chopped	30 g	1 oz.
Red onion	250 g	8 oz.
Black pepper, fresh ground	TT	TT
Romaine lettuce	1 head	1 head

1. To make the dressing, whisk together the olive oil, lemon juice, vinegar and oregano.

2. Dice the cucumbers.

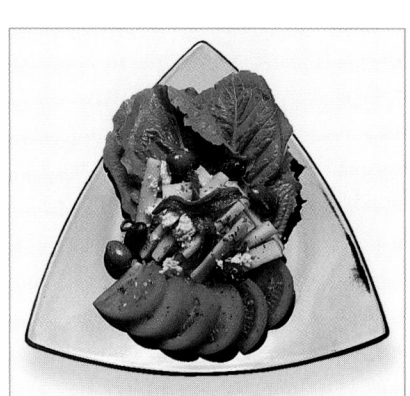

Greek Salad

continued

RECIPE 25.26

Approximate values per 350 g serving:	
Calories	437
Total fat	37 g
Saturated fat	11.5 g
Cholesterol	46 mg
Sodium	1906 mg
Total carbohydrates	19 g
Protein	11 g

3. Dice or crumble the feta cheese into medium pieces.

4. Dice the peppers into 1-cm (1/2-in.) pieces.

5. Combine the olives, cucumbers, tomatoes, chopped parsley and red onion in a bowl and add the dressing. Toss to combine and season to taste with pepper.

6. Line plates or a platter with the romaine lettuce leaves. Add the salad mixture and sprinkle on the feta cheese. Garnish as desired. Toasted fennel seeds may be sprinkled on salad.

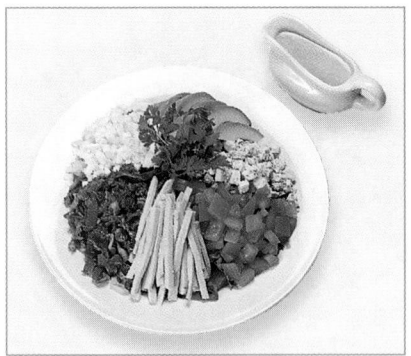

Cobb Salad

RECIPE 25.27

Approximate values per serving:	
Calories	913
Total fat	79 g
Saturated fat	16 g
Cholesterol	210 mg
Sodium	1590 mg
Total carbohydrates	14 g
Protein	41 g

RECIPE 25.27

Cobb Salad

Yield: 8 entree servings

Romaine lettuce	250 g	8 oz.
Green leaf lettuce	125 g	4 oz.
Watercress	125 g	4 oz.
Avocados	4	4
Bacon slices	16	16
Roquefort cheese, crumbled	350 g	12 oz.
Turkey breast, roasted, julienne	350 g	12 oz.
Tomato concassée	500 g	16 oz.
Eggs, hard-boiled, chopped	4	4
Dijon mustard vinaigrette	500 mL	16 fl. oz.

1. Tear, wash and dry the lettuces. Pick over and wash the watercress.

2. Pit, peel and cut the avocados into wedges.

3. Dice the bacon and cook in a sauté pan until crisp. Remove and drain well.

4. Toss the salad greens together and arrange each of the garnishes on top in an artistic fashion.

5. Prepare a simple vinaigrette dressing using Dijon-style mustard; serve on the side.

RECIPE 25.28

Mixed Bean Salad

Yield: 12 90-g (3-oz.) servings
Method: Boiling

Green beans, cut in 1.25-cm (1/2-in.) pieces	125 g	4 oz.
White wine vinegar	50 mL	2 fl. oz.
Vegetable oil	100 mL	3 fl. oz.
Lemon juice	25 mL	1 Tbsp.
Lemon peel, grated	3 g	1 tsp.
Garlic cloves, crushed	8 g	2
White sugar	15 g	1 Tbsp.
Dried red chile, chopped fine	1	1
Red kidney beans, soaked and cooked	250 g	8 oz.
Chickpeas, soaked and cooked	250 g	8 oz.
Lima or cannellini beans, soaked and cooked	250 g	8 oz.

continued

White onion, sliced	125 g	4 oz.
Red and green peppers, julienne	125 g	4 oz.
Salt and pepper	TT	TT

1. Steam the green beans until tender-crisp, approximately 3–4 minutes. Refresh.

2. To make the dressing, combine the white wine vinegar, oil, lemon juice, lemon peel, garlic, sugar and chile.

3. Mix together all the drained beans and peas and pour the dressing over them. Add the onion and peppers. Season with salt and pepper and toss to combine. Marinate for several hours before serving.

RECIPE 25.28

Approximate values per serving:	
Calories	171
Total fat	8 g
Saturated fat	1 g
Cholesterol	0 mg
Sodium	200 mg
Total carbohydrates	20 g
Protein	6 g

RECIPE 25.29

Melon Salad

Yield: 2.5 L (2-1/2 qt.)

Honeydew, medium	1	1
Cantaloupe, medium	1	1
English cucumber	1	1
Tomatoes	4	4
Parsley, chopped	10 g	1 Tbsp.
Oregano, chopped, fresh	5 g	2 tsp.
Black pepper, cracked	3 g	1 tsp.
Lemon juice, fresh	50 mL	2 fl. oz.
Lemon zest	3 g	1 tsp.
Canola oil	150 mL	6 fl. oz.
White wine vinegar	25 mL	1 Tbsp.

1. Split, seed and use a parisienne scoop to form melon balls.

2. Trim ends and split cucumber lengthwise. Slice 1-cm (1/2-in.) thick.

3. Core and cut the tomatoes into wedges.

4. Combine all ingredients and toss to coat.

5. Refrigerate salad for 1 hour before service.

RECIPE 25.29

Approximate values per 250 mL serving:	
Calories	171
Total fat	12 g
Saturated fat	1 g
Cholesterol	0 mg
Sodium	20 mg
Total carbohydrates	17 g
Protein	2 g

RECIPE 25.30

Antipasti Vegetables

Yield: 4 L (4 qt.)

Cauliflower florets	350 g	12 oz.
Zucchini, carrot, green beans, daikon—batonettes, each	200 g	7 oz.
Onion, sliced	100 g	3-1/2 oz.
Baby corn cobs	12	12
Celery, bias-cut	200 g	7 oz.
Red and green pepper triangles, each	100 g	3-1/2 oz.
Pickling salt	300 g	11 oz.
Water	1.5 L	1-1/2 qt.
White vinegar	500 mL	1 pt.

continued

Water	500 mL	1 pt.
Sugar	50 g	2 oz.
Garlic cloves	4	4
Dried chiles	4	4
Mustard seed	10 g	2 tsp.
Whole cloves	16	16

1. Layer cut vegetables in a noncorrosive container and sprinkle with pickling salt. Cover with 1.5 L (1-1/2 qt.) water; weigh down vegetables with a plate to ensure submersion. Refrigerate overnight, covered. Drain, rinse well under running water and drain well.

2. Prepare a brine with the remaining ingredients. Bring to a boil, add vegetables and simmer for 3 minutes. Cool pickled vegetables and store in a noncorrosive container in refrigerator.

RECIPE 25.30

Approximate values per 75 g serving:

Calories	43
Total fat	0.5 g
Saturated fat	0 g
Cholesterol	0 mg
Sodium	4837 mg
Total carbohydrates	10 g
Protein	2 g

Asian Chicken Salad

RECIPE 25.31

Approximate values per 100 g serving:

Calories	101
Total fat	2.9 g
Saturated fat	0.5 g
Cholesterol	29 mg
Sodium	547 mg
Total carbohydrates	6.3 g
Protein	12 g

RECIPE 25.31

Asian Chicken Salad

Yield: 1.4 kg (3 lb.)

Dressing:		
Rice vinegar	185 mL	6 fl. oz.
Soy sauce	125 mL	4 fl. oz.
Brown sugar	30 g	2-1/2 Tbsp.
Ginger, fresh, minced	40 g	3 Tbsp.
White pepper	2 g	1 tsp.
Chicken breast, boneless, skinless	700 g	1 lb. 8 oz.
Sesame oil	30 mL	1 fl. oz.
Snow peas	125 g	4 oz.
Carrot, julienne	125 g	4 oz.
Celery, julienne	125 g	4 oz.
Daikon, julienne	125 g	4 oz.
Red chile, fresh, seeded, julienne (optional)	1	1
Cilantro leaves	10 g	2 Tbsp.

1. To make the dressing, combine the vinegar, soy sauce, sugar, ginger and pepper. Reserve.

2. Cut the chicken into strips approximately 1.25 × 1.25 × 8 cm (1/2 × 1/2 × 3 in.). Stir-fry the chicken in the sesame oil until cooked. Remove from pan, cool and refrigerate.

3. Blanch the vegetables in boiling salt water, except the daikon. Refresh and drain well.

4. Combine the chicken, vegetables and dressing; toss well and finish with cilantro.

RECIPE 25.32

Salad of Ahi Tuna Seared with Lavender and Pepper with Whole-Grain Mustard Sauce

FETZER VINEYARDS, HOPLAND, CA
Culinary Director John Ash

**Yield: 8 servings, each 90 g (3 oz.) tuna
and 30 g (1 oz.) greens**

Lavender-pepper coating:		
Coarse sea salt	7 g	1-1/2 tsp.
Whole black peppercorns	8 g	2 tsp.
Whole fennel seeds	10 g	2 tsp.
White peppercorns	4 g	1 tsp.
Dried lavender flowers	3 g	1-1/2 tsp.
Ahi tuna, a solid 7.5-cm (3-in.)		
square piece, well trimmed	700 g	1 lb. 8 oz.
Olive oil	45 mL	3 Tbsp.
Mustard sauce:		
Whole-grain mustard	60 mL	2 fl. oz.
Olive oil	30 mL	1 fl. oz.
Mustard seeds, toasted	5 g	1 tsp.
Rice wine vinegar	5 mL	1 tsp.
Sugar or honey	5 mL	1 tsp.
Baby greens	250 g	8 oz.

1. Using a mortar and pestle or a rolling pin, crush the ingredients for the lavender-pepper coating.

2. Lightly oil the tuna with 10 mL (2 tsp.) of olive oil; coat lightly and evenly with the lavender-pepper mixture. Heat the remaining oil in a skillet to just smoking and quickly sear the tuna on all sides. This should not take more than 2 minutes. Immediately chill the seared tuna.

3. Mix the ingredients for the mustard sauce. Set aside.

4. To serve, thinly slice the tuna into 3–4 medallions per serving. Arrange on a chilled plate with baby greens and a small dollop of the mustard sauce.

Salad of Ahi Tuna Seared with Lavender and Pepper with Whole-Grain Mustard Sauce

RECIPE 25.32

Approximate values per serving:	
Calories	184
Total fat	10 g
Saturated fat	1.5 g
Cholesterol	35 mg
Sodium	583 mg
Total carbohydrates	3 g
Protein	21 g

Simon Smotkowicz, CCC

Simon has been a member and a leader of award-winning Canadian culinary teams for many years, managing Team Canada to a world championship in Glasgow in 1997 and 2001. In 1995 he was elected Chef of the Year for the Western Region by his peers in the CFCC, now the CCFCC.

RECIPE 25.33

Asparagus and Minted New Potato Salad with Sun-Dried Tomato Mayonnaise

SHAW CONFERENCE CENTRE, EDMONTON, AB
Executive Chef Simon Smotkowicz, CCC

Yield: 4 servings

Asparagus	500 g	1 lb.
Olive oil	75 mL	4 Tbsp.
Raspberry vinegar	25 mL	4 tsp.
Salt and pepper	TT	TT
New potatoes, very small	500 g	1 lb.
Fresh mint, chopped	38 g	4 Tbsp.
Salt	10 g	2 tsp.
Sun-dried tomatoes, finely chopped	15 g	1 Tbsp.
White wine or water	25 mL	2 Tbsp.
Mayonnaise	250 mL	8 fl. oz.
Spinach or pea tops	as needed	as needed

1. To prepare the asparagus, bring a large pot of salted water to a boil. Add the asparagus and cook for 3–5 minutes.
2. Cool at once in a bowl filled with iced water.
3. To prepare the vinaigrette, whisk together the olive oil and raspberry vinegar.
4. In a bowl, toss the asparagus with the vinaigrette. Season with salt and pepper and let sit for 1 hour before serving.
5. To prepare the potato salad, place the potatoes, 30 g (3 Tbsp.) mint and salt in a saucepan. Cover the potatoes with cold water.
6. Bring to a boil and simmer for 15–20 minutes, until done. Drain and let cool.
7. Mix together the sun-dried tomatoes, white wine and mayonnaise.
8. In a bowl, toss the potatoes with the sun-dried tomato mayonnaise.
9. To assemble, lightly cover each plate with springtime greens such as spinach or pea tops.
10. Mound the potato salad on top of the greens, arrange the asparagus on top and sprinkle with 2 g (1 tsp.) mint.

RECIPE 25.33

Approximate values per serving:	
Calories	596
Total fat	56 g
Saturated fat	8 g
Cholesterol	31 mg
Sodium	818 mg
Total carbohydrates	20 g
Protein	6 g

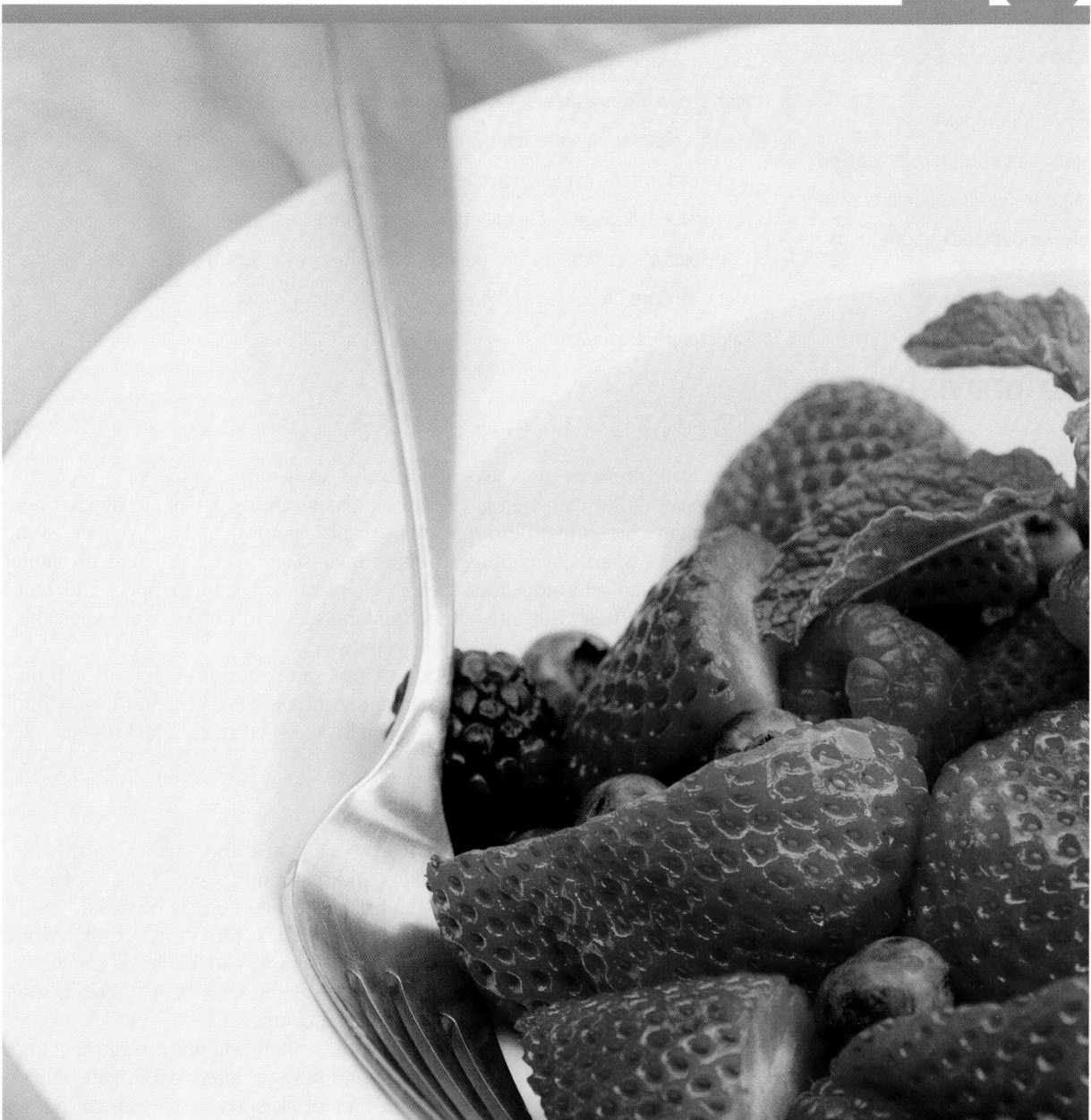

"Talking of pleasure, this moment I was writing with one hand, and with the other holding to my mouth a nectarine—how good how fine. It went down all pulpy, slushy, oozy, all its delicious embonpoint melted down my throat like a large, beatified strawberry.

—John Keats, English poet (1795–1821)

● **ripe** fully grown and developed; the fruit's flavour, texture and appearance are at their peak, and the fruit is ready to use as food

Blackberries

Blueberries

Botanically, a fruit is an organ that develops from the ovary of a flowering plant and contains one or more seeds. Culinarily, a fruit is the perfect snack food; the basis of a dessert, colourful sauce or soup; or an accompaniment to meat, fish, shellfish or poultry. No food group offers a greater variety of colours, flavours and textures than fruit.

This chapter identifies many of the fruits typically used by food service operations. It then addresses general considerations in purchasing fresh and preserved fruits. A discussion follows about some of the cooking methods presented in Chapter 9, Principles of Cooking, as they apply to fruits. Recipes in which a fruit is the primary ingredient are presented at the end of this chapter. Information on juicing appears in Chapter 35, Beverages.

IDENTIFYING FRUITS

This book presents fruits according to the ways most people view them and use them, rather than by rigid botanical classifications. Fruits are divided here into eight categories: berries, citrus, exotics, grapes, melons, pomes, stone fruits and tropicals, according to either their shape, seed structure or natural habitat. Botanically, tomatoes, beans, eggplant, capsicum peppers and other produce are fruits. But in ordinary thinking they are not; they are vegetables and are discussed in Chapter 22, Vegetables.

A fruit may have several names, varying from region to region or on a purveyor's whim. Botanists are also constantly reclassifying items to fit new findings. The names given here follow generally accepted custom and usage.

Berries

Berries are small, juicy fruits that grow on vines and bushes worldwide. Berries are characterized by thin skins and many tiny seeds that are often so small they go unnoticed. Some of the fruits classified here as berries do not fit the botanical definition (for example, raspberries and strawberries), while fruits that are berries botanically (for example, grapes) are classified elsewhere.

Berries may be eaten plain or used in everything from beer to bread, soup to sorbet. They make especially fine jams and compotes.

Berries must be fully **ripened** on the vine, as they will not ripen further after harvesting. Select berries that are plump and fully coloured. Avoid juice-stained containers and berries with whitish-grey or black spots of mould. All berries should be refrigerated and used promptly. Do not wash berries until you are ready to use them, as washing removes some of their aroma and softens them.

Blackberries

Blackberries are similar to raspberries, but are larger and shinier, with a deep purple to black colour. Thorny blackberry vines are readily found in the wild; commercial production is limited. Peak season is mid-June through August. Loganberries, ollalie berries and boysenberries are blackberry hybrids.

Blueberries

Blueberries (Fr. *myrtilles*) are small and firm, with a true blue to almost black skin and a juicy, light grey-blue interior. Cultivated berries (high-bush varieties) tend to be larger than wild (low-bush) ones. Blueberries are native to North

America and are grown commercially in almost all provinces of Canada, with the Lac St. Jean region being the most famous. Peak season is short, from mid-June to mid-August.

Cranberries

Cranberries (Fr. *canneberges*), another native North American food, are tart, firm fruit with a mottled red skin. They grow on low vines in cultivated bogs (swamps) throughout Ontario, British Columbia, Massachusetts, Wisconsin and New Jersey. Rarely eaten raw, they are made into sauce or relish or are used in breads, pies or pastries. Cranberries are readily available frozen, dried (candied) or made into a jelly-type sauce and canned. Although colour does not indicate ripeness, cranberries should be picked over before cooking to remove those that are soft or bruised. Peak harvesting season is from Labour Day through October, leading to the association of cranberries with Thanksgiving dinner.

Cranberries

Currants

Currants are tiny, tart fruits that grow on shrubs in grapelike clusters. The most common are a beautiful, almost translucent red, but black and golden (or white) varieties also exist. All varieties are used for jams, jellies and sauces, and black currants are made into a liqueur, crème de cassis. Fresh North American production is growing. Currants are very popular and widely available in Europe, with a peak season during the late summer. (The dried fruits called currants are not produced from these berries; they are a special variety of dried grapes.)

White Currants

Red Currants

Gooseberries

Several varieties of gooseberry (Fr. *groseille maquereau*) are cultivated for culinary purposes. One well-known variety is the European gooseberry, a member of the currant family that grows on spiny bushes in cool, moist regions of the Northern Hemisphere. Its berries can be relatively large, like a small plum, but are usually less than 2.5 cm (1 in.) in diameter. The skin, which is firm and smooth or only slightly hairy, can be green, white (actually grey-green), yellow or red. The tart berries contain many tiny seeds. They are eaten fresh or used for jellies, preserves, tarts and other desserts or as a traditional accompaniment to rich or fatty dishes, such as goose and mackerel. North American gooseberry varieties are smaller, perfectly round, and pink to deep red at maturity. Although more prolific, these varietals lack flavour and are generally considered inferior to European gooseberries.

Raspberries

Raspberries (Fr. *framboises*) are perhaps the most delicate of all fruits. They have a tart flavour and velvety texture. Red raspberries are the most common, with black, purple and golden berries available in some markets. When ripe, the berry pulls away easily from its white core, leaving the characteristic hollow centre. Because they can be easily crushed and are susceptible to mould, most of the raspberries grown are marketed frozen. They grow on thorny vines in cool climates from British Columbia to the Maritimes and are imported from New Zealand and South America. The peak domestic season is from late May through November.

Raspberries

Strawberries

Strawberries (Fr. *fraises*) are brilliant red, heart-shaped fruits that grow on vines. Actually a perennial herb, the berry's flesh is covered by tiny tan seeds

Strawberries

called achenes, which are the plant's true fruits. Select berries with a good red colour and intact green leafy hull. (The hulls can be easily removed with a paring knife.) Avoid berries with soft or brown spots. Huge berries may be lovely to look at but they often have hollow centres and little flavour or juice. Although available to some extent all year, fresh strawberries are at their peak from April through June.

The tiny wild or Alpine berries, known by their French name *fraises des bois*, have a particularly intense flavour and aroma. They are not widely available commercially in Canada.

Citrus

Citrus fruits include lemons, limes, grapefruits, tangerines, kumquats, oranges and several hybrids. They are characterized by a thick rind, most of which is a bitter white pith (albedo) with a thin exterior layer of coloured skin known as the **zest**. Their flesh is segmented and juicy. Citrus fruits are acidic, with a strong aroma; their flavours vary from bitter to tart to sweet.

Citrus fruits grow on trees and shrubs in tropical and subtropical climates worldwide. All citrus fruits are fully ripened on the tree and will not ripen further after harvesting. They should be refrigerated for longest storage.

Select fruits that feel heavy and have thin, smooth skins. Avoid those with large blemishes or moist spots.

Grapefruits

Grapefruits (Fr. *pamplemousse*) are large and round with a yellow skin, thick rind and tart flesh. They are an 18th-century hybrid of the orange and pummelo (a large, coarse fruit used mostly in Middle and Far Eastern cuisines). Two varieties of grapefruit are widely available all year: white-fleshed and pink- or ruby-fleshed. White grapefruits produce the finest juice, although pink grapefruits are sweeter. Fresh grapefruits are best eaten raw or topped with brown sugar and lightly broiled. Grapefruit segments are available canned in syrup.

Kumquats

Kumquats are very small, oval-shaped, orange-coloured fruits with a soft, sweet skin and slightly bitter flesh. They can be eaten whole, either raw or preserved in syrup, and may be used in jams and preserves.

Lemons

The most commonly used citrus fruits, lemons (Fr. *citrons*), are oval-shaped, bright yellow fruits available all year. Their strongly acidic flavour makes them unpleasant to eat raw but perfect for flavouring desserts and confections. Lemon juice is also widely used in sauces, especially for fish, shellfish and poultry. Lemon zest is candied or used as garnish. Try grilling wedges or slices.

Limes

Limes (Fr. *limons*) are small fruits with thin skins ranging from yellow-green to dark green. Limes are too tart to eat raw and are often substituted for lemons in prepared dishes. They are also juiced or used in cocktails, curries or desserts. Lime zest can be grated and used to give colour and flavour to a variety of dishes. Limes are available all year, with a peak season during the summer.

Ruby Grapefruits

White Grapefruits

Kumquats

Lemons

Limes

Oranges

Oranges are round fruits with a juicy, orange-coloured flesh and a thin, orange skin. They can be either sweet or bitter.

Valencia oranges and navel oranges (a seedless variety) are the most popular sweet oranges. They can be juiced for beverages or sauces and the flesh may be eaten raw, added to salads, cooked in desserts or used as a garnish. The zest may be grated or julienned for sauces or garnish. Sweet oranges are available all year, with peak season from December to April. Blood oranges are also sweet but are small, with a rough, reddish skin. Their flesh is streaked with a blood-red colour. Blood oranges are available primarily during the winter months and are eaten raw, juiced or used in salads or sauces. When selecting sweet oranges, look for fruits that feel plump and heavy, with unblemished skin. The colour of the skin depends on weather conditions; a green rind does not affect the flavour of the flesh.

Bitter oranges include the Seville and bergamot. They are used primarily for the essential oils found in their zest. Oil of bergamot gives Earl Grey tea its distinctive flavour; oil of Seville is essential to curaçao, Grand Marnier and orange flower water. Seville oranges are also used in marmalades and sauces for meats and poultry.

Tangerines

Tangerines, sometimes referred to as mandarins, are small and dark orange. Their rind is loose and easily removed to reveal sweet, juicy, aromatic segments. Tangerines are most often eaten fresh and uncooked, but are available canned as mandarin oranges.

Tangelos are a hybrid of tangerines and grapefruits. The size of a medium orange, they have a bulbous stem end and few to no seeds.

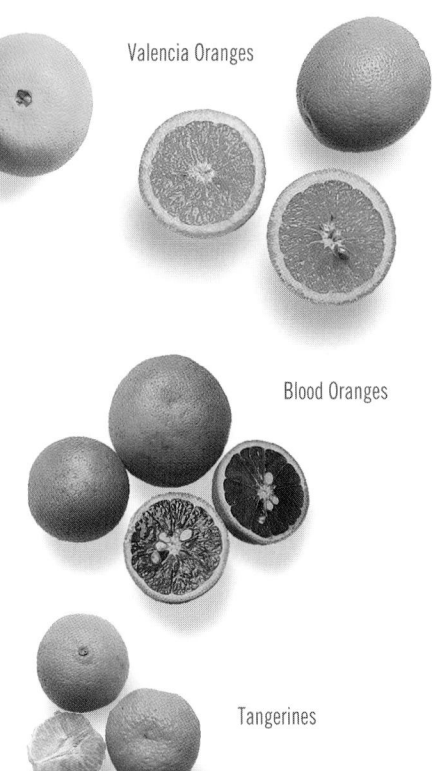

Navel Oranges

Valencia Oranges

Blood Oranges

Tangerines

BASIC PROCEDURE FOR SEGMENTING CITRUS FRUITS

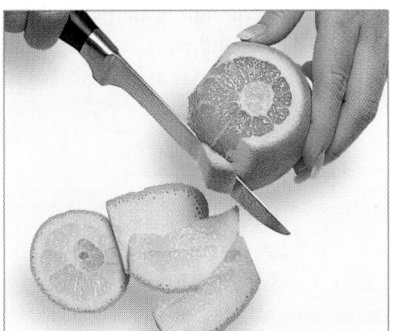

1. Citrus segments, known as fillets or *supremes*, are made by first carefully cutting off the entire peel (including the bitter white pith) in even slices.

2. Individual fillets are then removed by gently cutting alongside each membrane.

Hybrids and Varieties

Several varieties of fruits are extremely responsive to selective breeding and cross-breeding and have been toyed with by botanists and growers since at least the time of ancient Rome. Two distinct products are recognized: hybrids and varieties. **Hybrids** result from cross-breeding fruits from different species that are genetically unalike. The result is a unique product. Citrus is particularly responsive to hybridization. **Varieties** result from breeding fruits of the same species that have different qualities or characteristics. Breeding two varieties of apples, for example, produces a third variety with the best qualities of both parents.

BASIC PROCEDURE FOR ZESTING CITRUS FRUITS

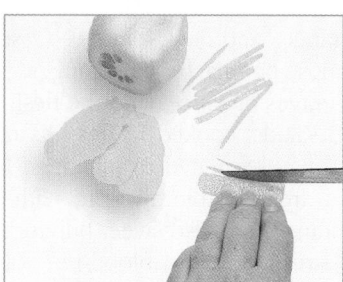

A five-hole zester is used to remove paper-thin strips of the coloured rind.

BASIC PROCEDURE FOR CUTTING CITRUS PEELS

Large strips of citrus zest may be used as a garnish or to flavour soups or sauces.

Cape Gooseberries

Dragon Fruit

Calimyrna Figs

Exotics

Improved transportation has led to the increasing availability (thereby negating the notion of exotic) of specialty fresh fruits such as figs, persimmons, pomegranates, prickly pears, rhubarb and star fruits. Other exotic fruits, such as breadfruit, durian, feijoa and loquat, are available on a regular basis from specialty purveyors but are not discussed here.

Cape Gooseberries

Cape gooseberries, also known as physalis, ground cherries and poha, are unrelated to European and North American gooseberries. Native to Peru, they became popular during the 19th century along the African Cape of Good Hope, for which they are named. Australia and New Zealand are currently the largest producers. Cape gooseberries are covered with a paper-thin husk or calyx. About the size of a cherry, they have a waxy, bright orange skin and many tiny seeds. Their flavour is similar to coconut and oranges, but tarter. Cape gooseberries may be eaten raw, made into jam or used in desserts. Fresh, they make an especially striking garnish.

Dragon Fruit

Dragon fruit are any of several species of the *Cactaceae* family native to South America now widely grown in tropical climates. About the size of an eggplant with a flavour that resembles a kiwi or melon, the fruit is eaten raw and made into a refreshing juice. Dragon fruit are peeled and handled like prickly pears, to which they are related.

Figs

Figs (Fr. *figues*) are the fruit of ficus trees. They are small, soft, pear-shaped fruits with an intensely sweet flavour and rich, moist texture made crunchy by a multitude of tiny seeds. Fresh figs can be sliced and served in salads or with cured meats such as prosciutto. They can also be baked, poached or used in jams, preserves or compotes.

Dark-skinned figs, known as Mission figs, are a variety planted at U.S. Pacific Coast missions during the 18th century. They have a thin skin and small seeds and are available fresh, canned or dried. The white-skinned figs grown commercially include the White Adriatic, used principally for drying and baking, and the all-purpose Kadota. The most important domestic variety, however, is the Calimyrna. These large figs have a rich yellow colour and large nutty seeds. Fresh Calimyrna figs are the finest for eating out of hand; they are also available dried.

For the best flavour, figs should be fully ripened on the tree. Unfortunately, fully ripened figs are very delicate and difficult to transport. Most figs are in season from June through October; fresh Calimyrna figs are available only during June.

Guava

Guava (GWAH-vah) are a small, oval or pear-shaped fruit with a strong fragrance and a mild, slightly grainy flesh. They are excellent in jams and preserves, and guava juice is available plain or blended with other tropical fruit juices. Guava paste, a thick, sliceable gel, is a popular treat throughout Central America and the Caribbean. Guava will ripen if stored at room temperature and should be slightly soft and fully ripened for the best flavour.

Guava

Lychees

The lychee, also spelled *litchi* or *leechee*, is the fruit of a large tree native to southern China and Southeast Asia. The fruits, which grow in clusters, are oval to round, red and about 2.5 cm (1 in.) in diameter. The tough outer skin encloses juicy, white, almost translucent flesh and one large seed. Neither the skin nor the seed are edible. The fruit travels well and is now cultivated in Florida and Hawaii, so supplies are relatively stable. Lychees are eaten fresh out of hand or juiced and are widely available canned or dried. Fresh lychees are mild but sweet with a pleasant perfume.

Lychees

Mangosteens

The mangosteen, another native of Southeast Asia, is cultivated in Java, Sumatra and the Philippines. Mangosteens (no relation to mangos) are the size of a small orange, with flattened ends. They have a thick, hard, deep reddish-purple rind with hard, white, petal-shaped protrusions at the stem end. The interior flesh is snow-white and segmented, looking something like a mandarin orange. The texture is juicy and delicate with a slightly astringent flavour. Because the fruit must ripen on the tree and keeps only a short time, it is rarely found fresh outside of local markets. Mangosteens are usually eaten fresh, although canned fruit and mangosteen juice is available.

Mangosteens

Persimmons

Persimmons, sometimes referred to as kaki or Sharon fruits, are a bright orange, acorn-shaped fruit with a glossy skin and a large papery blossom. The flesh is bright orange and jellylike, with a mild but rich flavour similar to honey and plums. Persimmons should be peeled before use; any seeds should be discarded. Select bright orange fruits and refrigerate only after they are completely ripe. When ripe, persimmons will be very soft and the skin will have an almost translucent appearance.

Ripe persimmons are delicious eaten raw, halved and topped with cream or soft cheese, or peeled, sliced and added to fruit salads. Persimmon bread, muffins, cakes and pies are also popular. Underripe persimmons are almost inedible, however. They are strongly tannic with a chalky or cottony texture.

Persimmons are tree fruits grown in subtropical areas worldwide, although the Asian varieties—now grown in California—are the most common. Fresh persimmons are available from October through January.

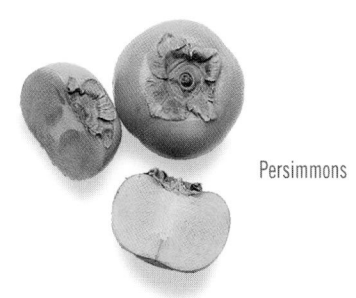

Persimmons

Pomegranates

An ancient fruit native to Persia (now Iran), pomegranates have long been a subject of poetry and a symbol of fertility. Pomegranates are round, about the size of a large orange, with a pronounced calyx. The skin forms a hard shell with a pinkish-red colour. The interior is filled with hundreds of small, red

Pomegranates

seeds (which are, botanically, the actual fruits) surrounded by juicy red pulp. An inedible yellow membrane separates the seeds into compartments. Pomegranates are sweet-sour and the seeds are pleasantly crunchy. The bright red seeds make an attractive garnish. Pomegranate juice is a popular beverage in Mediterranean cuisines and grenadine syrup is made from concentrated pomegranate juice.

Select heavy fruits that are not rock-hard, cracked or heavily bruised. Whole pomegranates can be refrigerated for several weeks. Pomegranates are available from September through December, with peak season in October.

Prickly Pears

Prickly Pears

Prickly pear fruits, also known as cactus pears and barbary figs, are actually the berries of several varieties of cactus. They are barrel- or pear-shaped, about the size of a large egg. Their thick, firm skin is green or purple with small sharp pins and nearly invisible stinging fibres. Their flesh is spongy, sweet and a brilliant pink-red, dotted with small black seeds. Prickly pears have the aroma of watermelon and the flavour of sugar-water.

Once peeled, prickly pears can be diced and eaten raw, or they can be puréed for making jams, sauces, custards or sorbets, to which they give a vivid pink colour. Prickly pears are especially common in Mexican and southwestern cuisines.

Select fruits that are full-coloured, heavy and tender, but not too soft. Avoid those with mushy or bruised spots. Ripe prickly pears can be refrigerated for a week or more. Prickly pears are grown in Mexico and several states of the southwestern U.S. and are available from September through December.

BASIC PROCEDURE FOR PEELING PRICKLY PEARS

1. To avoid being stung by a prickly pear, hold it steady with a fork, then use a knife to cut off both ends.

2. Cut a lengthwise slit through the skin. Slip the tip of the knife into the cut and peel away the skin by holding it down while rolling the fruit away.

Rambutans

Rambutans

Rambutans (ram-BOOT-enz), the fruit of a tree in the soapberry family, are closely related to lychees. Native to Malaysia, they are now cultivated throughout Southeast Asia. The bright red, oval fruit is about the size of a small hen's egg, and is covered with long, soft spines, hence the name "hairy" lychees. The interior has a white, lightly acidic pulp. Rambutans darken with age, so select brightly coloured fruit with soft, fleshy spines. Rambutans are eaten fresh and used in preserves and ice cream; they are also available canned.

Rhubarb

Although botanically a vegetable, rhubarb is most often prepared as a fruit. It is a perennial plant that grows well in temperate and cold climates. Only the pinkish-red stems are edible; the leaves contain high amounts of oxalic acid, which is toxic.

Rhubarb

Rhubarb stems are extremely acidic, requiring large amounts of sugar to create the desired sweet-sour taste. Cinnamon, ginger, orange and strawberry are particularly compatible with rhubarb. It is excellent for pies, cobblers, preserves or stewing. Young, tender stalks of rhubarb do not need to be peeled. When cooked, rhubarb becomes very soft and turns a beautiful light pink colour.

Fresh rhubarb is sold as whole stalks, with the leaves removed. Select crisp, unblemished stalks. Peak season is during the early spring, from February through May. Frozen rhubarb pieces are readily available and are excellent for pies, tarts or jams. Powdered rhubarb juice is now available. It goes well with fish sauces and fruit coulis.

Star Fruits

Star fruits, also known as carambola, are oval, up to 12.5 cm (5 in.) long, with five prominent ribs or wings running their length. A cross-section cut is shaped like a star. The edible skin is a waxy orange-yellow; it covers a dry, paler yellow flesh. Its flavour is similar to plums, sweet but bland. Star fruits do not need to be peeled or seeded. They are most often sliced and added to fruit salad or used as a garnish. Unripe fruits can be cooked in stews or chutneys.

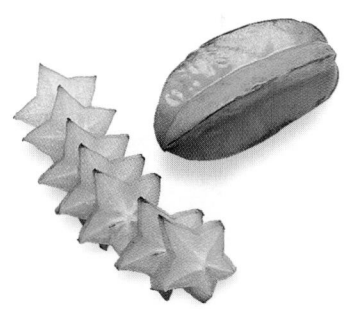

Star Fruit

Colour and aroma are the best indicators of ripeness. The fruits should be a deep golden-yellow and the edge of the ribs should be brown. The aroma should be full and floral. Green fruits can be kept at room temperature to ripen, then refrigerated for up to two weeks. Star fruits are cultivated in Hawaii, Florida, California and Asia, though some are still imported from the Caribbean. Fresh fruits are available from August to February.

Grapes

Grapes are the single largest fruit crop in the world, due, of course, to their use in wine making. This section, however, discusses only table grapes, those grown for eating. Grapes are berries that grow on vines in large clusters. California is the world's largest producer, with more than a dozen varieties grown for table use. Grapes are classified by colour as white (which are actually green) or black (which are actually red). White grapes are generally blander than black ones, with a thinner skin and firmer flesh.

The grape's colour and most of its flavour are found in the skin. Grapes are usually eaten raw, either alone or in fruit salads. They are also used as a garnish or accompaniment to desserts and cheeses. Dried grapes are known as raisins (usually made from Thompson Seedless or muscat grapes), currants (made from Black Corinth grapes and labelled as Zante currants) or sultanas (made from sultana grapes).

Grapes are available all year because the many varieties have different harvesting schedules. Look for firm, unblemished fruits that are firmly attached to the stem. A surface bloom or dusty appearance is caused by yeasts and indicates recent harvesting. Wrinkled grapes or those with brown spots around the stem are past their prime. All grapes should be rinsed and drained prior to use.

Red Flame Grapes

Thompson Seedless Grapes

Concord Grapes

Cantaloupes

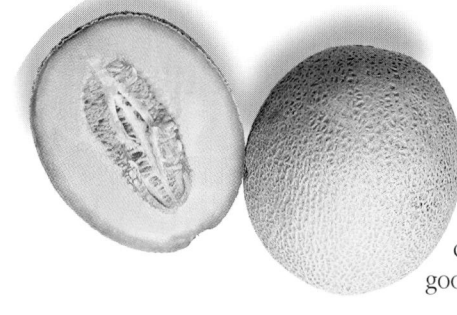

Casaba Melons

Red Flame grapes are a seedless California hybrid, second only in importance to the Thompson Seedless. Red Flame grapes are large and round with a slightly tart flavour and variegated red colour.

Thompson Seedless grapes, which are pale green with a crisp texture and sweet flavour, are the most commercially important table grapes. Peak season is from June to November. Many are dried in the hot desert sun of California's San Joaquin Valley to produce dark raisins. For golden raisins, Thompson Seedless grapes are treated with sulphur dioxide to prevent browning, then dried mechanically.

Concord, **Ribier** and **Emperor** are the most important varieties of the table grapes containing seeds. They range from light red to deep black in colour, and all three are in season during the autumn. Concord grapes, one of the few grape varieties native to the New World, are especially important for making juices and jellies.

Melons

Like pumpkins and cucumbers, melons are members of the gourd family (*Cucurbitaceae*). The dozens of melon varieties can be divided into two general types: sweet (or dessert) melons and watermelons. Sweet melons have a tan, green or yellow netted or farrowed rind and dense, fragrant flesh. Watermelon has a thick, dark green rind surrounding crisp, watery flesh.

Melons are almost 90% water, so cooking destroys their texture, quickly turning the flesh to mush. Most are served simply sliced, perhaps with a bit of lemon or lime juice. Melons also blend well in fruit salads or with rich, cured meats such as prosciutto. Melons may be puréed and made into soups or sorbets.

Melons should be vine-ripened. A ripe melon should yield slightly and spring back when pressed at the blossom end (opposite the stem). It should also give off a strong aroma. Avoid melons that are very soft or feel damp at the stem end. Ripe melons may be stored in the refrigerator, although the flavour will be better at room temperature. Slightly underripe melons can be stored at room temperature to allow flavour and aroma to develop.

Cantaloupes

North American cantaloupes, which are actually musk melons, are sweet melons with a thick, yellow-green netted rind, a sweet, moist, orange flesh and a strong aroma. (European cantaloupes, which are not generally available in this country, are more craggy and furrowed in appearance.) As with all sweet melons, the many small seeds are found in a central cavity. Cantaloupes are excellent for eating alone and are especially good with ham or rich meats.

Avoid cantaloupes with the pronounced yellow colour or mouldy aroma that indicates overripeness. Mexican imports ensure a year-round supply, although their peak season is summer.

Casaba Melons

Casaba melons are a teardrop-shaped sweet melon. They have a coarse, yellow skin and a thick, ridged rind; their flesh is creamy white to yellow. Casaba melons are used like cantaloupes. Casaba melons do not have an aroma, so selection must be based on a deep skin colour and the absence of dark or moist patches. Peak season is during September and October.

Crenshaw Melons

Crenshaw (or cranshaw) melons have a mottled, green-yellow ridged rind and orange-pink flesh. Crenshaws are large and pear-shaped, with a strong aroma. The flesh has a rich, spicy flavour and may be used like cantaloupe. Crenshaws are available from July through October, with peak season during August and September.

Crenshaw Melons

Honeydew Melons

Honeydew melons are large, oval melons with a smooth rind that ranges from white to pale green. Although the flesh is generally pale green, with a mild, sweet flavour, pink- or gold-fleshed honeydews are also available. Like casaba melons, honeydew melons have no aroma. They are available almost all year, with peak season from June through October.

Santa Claus Melons

Santa Claus or Christmas melons are large, elongated melons with a green-and-yellow-striped, smooth rind. The flesh is creamy white or yellow and tastes like casaba. They are a winter variety, with peak availability during December (hence the name).

Green Honeydews

Gold Honeydews

Watermelons

Watermelons are large (up to 13.5 kg or 30 lb.), round or oval-shaped melons with a thick rind. The skin may be solid green, green-striped or mottled with white. The flesh is crisp and extremely juicy with small, hard, black seeds throughout. Seedless hybrids are available, although they are relatively expensive. Most watermelons have pink to red flesh, although golden-fleshed varieties are becoming more common.

Watermelons are of a different genus from the sweet melons described above. They are native to tropical Africa and are now grown commercially in Texas and several of the southern U.S. states.

Santa Claus Melons

Pomes

Pomes are tree fruits with thin skin and firm flesh surrounding a central core containing many small seeds called pips or carpels. Pomes include apples, pears and quince. Almonds are in this family as well.

Apples

Apples (Fr. *pommes*), perhaps the most common and commonly appreciated of all fruits, grow on trees in temperate zones worldwide. They are popular because of their convenience, taste, variety and availability.

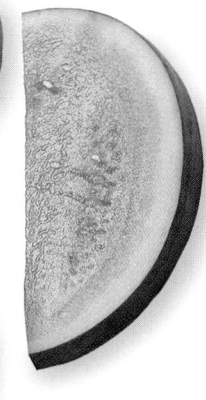
Red Seedless
Watermelon

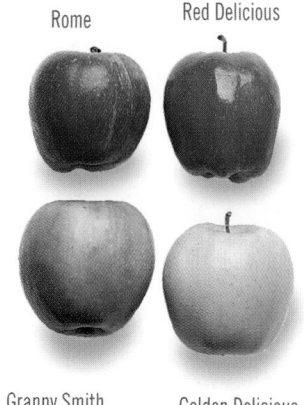

Rome
Red Delicious
Granny Smith
Golden Delicious

McIntosh

Gala

Apples can be eaten raw out of hand, or they can be used in a wide variety of cooked or baked dishes. They are equally useful in breads, desserts or vegetable dishes and go well with game, pork and poultry. Classic dishes prepared with apples are often referred to as *à la Normande*. Apple juice (cider) produces alcoholic and nonalcoholic beverages and cider vinegar.

Of the hundreds of known apple varieties, only 20 or so are commercially significant in Canada. Several varieties and their characteristics are noted in Table 26.1. Most have a moist, creamy white flesh with a thin skin of yellow, green or red. They range in flavour from very sweet to very tart, with an equally broad range of textures, from firm and crisp to soft and mealy.

In Europe, apples are divided into distinct cooking and eating varieties. Cooking varieties are those that disintegrate to a purée when cooked. North American varieties are less rigidly classified. Nevertheless, not all apples are appropriate for all types of cooking. Those that retain their shape better during cooking are the best choices where slices or appearance is important. Varieties with a higher malic acid content break down easily, making them more appropriate for applesauce or juicing. Either type may be eaten out of hand, depending on personal preference.

Although not native to North America, apples are now grown commercially in most provinces of Canada, with Ontario, British Columbia and Nova Scotia leading in production. Apples are harvested when still slightly underripe, then stored in a controlled atmosphere (temperature and oxygen are greatly reduced) for extended periods until ready for sale. Modern storage techniques make fresh apples available all year, although peak season is during the autumn. Also, imports ensure a constant supply.

When selecting apples, look for smooth, unbroken skins and firm fruits, without soft spots or bruises. Badly bruised or rotting apples should be discarded immediately. They emit quantities of ethylene gas that speed spoilage of nearby fruits. (Remember the saying that "one bad apple spoils the barrel.") Store apples chilled for up to six weeks. Apple peels (the skin) may be eaten or removed as desired, but in either case, apples should be washed just prior to use to remove pesticides and any wax that was applied to improve appearance. Apple slices may be frozen (often with sugar or citric acid added to slow spoilage) or dried.

TABLE 26.1	Apple Varieties				
Variety	Skin Colour	Flavour	Texture	Peak Season	Use
Fiji	Yellow-green with red highlights	Sweet-spicy	Crisp	All year	Eating; in salads
Gala	Yellow-orange with red stripes	Sweet	Crisp	Aug.–March	Eating; in salads; sauce
Golden Delicious	Glossy, greenish-gold	Sweet	Semifirm	Sept.–Oct.	In tarts; with cheese; in salads
Granny Smith	Bright green	Tart	Firm and crisp	Oct.–Nov.	Eating; in tarts
Jonathan	Brilliant red	Tart to acidic	Tender	Sept.–Oct.	Eating; all-purpose
McIntosh	Red with green background	Tart to acidic	Soft	Fall	Applesauce; in closed pies
Pippin (Newtown)	Greenish-yellow	Tart	Semifirm	Fall	In pies; eating; baking
Red Delicious	Deep red	Sweet but bland	Soft to mealy	Sept.–Oct.	Eating
Rome	Red	Sweet-tart	Firm	Oct.–Nov.	Baking; pies; sauces
Winesap	Dark red with yellow streaks	Tangy	Crisp	Oct.–Nov.	Cider; all-purpose

BASIC PROCEDURE FOR CORING APPLES

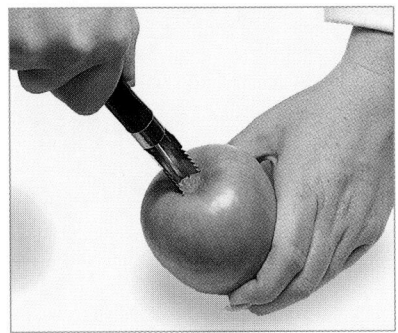 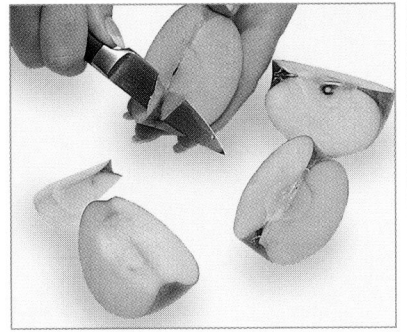

1. Remove the core from a whole apple with an apple corer by inserting the corer from the stem end and pushing out the cylinder containing the core and seeds.

2. Alternatively, first cut an apple into quarters, then use a paring knife to cut away the core and seeds.

● **pectin** a gelatin-like carbohydrate obtained from certain fruits; used to thicken jams and jellies

Anjou

Red d'Anjou

Bosc

Pears

Pears (Fr. *poires*) are an ancient tree fruit grown in temperate areas throughout the world. Most of the pears marketed in this country are grown in British Columbia, California, Washington and Oregon.

Although literally thousands of pear varieties have been identified, only a dozen or so are commercially significant. Several varieties and their characteristics are noted in Table 26.2 on the next page. Pear varieties vary widely in size, colour and flavour. They are most often eaten out of hand, but can be baked or poached. Pears are delicious with cheese, especially blue cheeses, and can be used in fruit salads, compotes or preserves.

Asian pears, also known as Chinese pears or apple-pears, are of a different species than common pears. They have the moist, sweet flavour of a pear and the round shape and crisp texture of an apple. They are becoming increasingly popular in this country, particularly those known as Twentieth Century or Nijisseiki.

When selecting pears, look for fruits with smooth, unbroken skin and an intact stem. Pears will not ripen properly on the tree, so they are picked while still firm and should be allowed to soften before use. Underripe pears may be left at room temperature to ripen. A properly ripened pear should have a good fragrance and yield to gentle pressure at the stem end. Pears can be prepared or stored in the same way as apples.

Bartlett

Asian Pears

Quince

Common quince (Fr. *coing*) resemble large, lumpy yellow pears. Their flesh is hard, with many pips or seeds, and they have a wonderful fragrance. Too astringent to eat raw, quince develop a sweet flavour and pink colour when cooked with sugar. Quince are used in meat stews, jellies, marmalades and pies. They have a high **pectin** content and may be added to other fruit jams or preserves to encourage gelling.

Fresh quince, usually imported from South America or southeast Europe, are available from October through January. Select firm fruits with a good yellow colour. Small blemishes may be cut away before cooking. Quince will keep for up to a month under refrigeration.

Quince

TABLE 26.2	Pear Varieties				
Variety	**Appearance**	**Flavour**	**Texture**	**Peak Season**	**Use**
Anjou (Beurre d'Anjou)	Greenish-yellow skin; egg-shaped with short neck; red variety also available	Sweet and juicy	Firm, keeps well	Oct.–May	Eating; poaching; baking
Bartlett (Williams)	Thin yellow skin; bell-shaped; red variety also available	Very sweet, buttery, juicy	Tender	Aug.–Dec.	Eating; canning; in salads
Bosc	Golden-brown skin; long, tapered neck	Buttery	Dry, holds its shape well	Sept.–May	Poaching; baking
Comice	Yellow-green skin; large and chubby	Sweet, juicy	Smooth	Oct.–Feb.	Eating
Seckel	Tiny; brown to yellow skin	Spicy	Very firm, grainy	Aug.–Dec.	Poaching; pickling

Stone Fruits

Stone fruits, also known as drupes, include apricots, cherries, nectarines, peaches and plums. They are characterized by a thin skin, soft flesh and one woody stone or pit. Although most originated in China, the shrubs and trees producing stone fruits are now grown in temperate climates worldwide.

The domestic varieties of stone fruits are in season from late spring through summer. They tend to be fragile fruits, easily bruised, difficult to transport and with a short shelf life. Do not wash them until ready to use, as moisture can cause deterioration. Avoid ingesting the pits—most contain toxic acids. Stone fruits are excellent dried and are often used to make liqueurs or brandies.

Apricots

Apricots

Apricots (Fr. *abricots*) are small, round stone fruits with a velvety skin that varies in colour from deep yellow to vivid orange. Their juicy orange flesh surrounds a dark, almond-shaped pit. Apricots can be eaten out of hand, poached, stewed, baked or candied. They are often used in fruit compotes or savoury sauces for meat or poultry and are also popular in quick breads, fruit tarts or puréed for dessert sauces, jams, custards or mousses.

Apricots enjoy a short season, peaking during June and July, and do not travel well. Select apricots that are well shaped, plump and fairly firm. Avoid those that are greenish-yellow or mushy. Fresh apricots will last for several days under refrigeration, but the flavour is best at room temperature. If fresh fruits are unavailable, canned apricots are usually an acceptable substitute. Dried apricots and apricot juice (known as nectar) are readily available.

Cherries

Bing Cherries

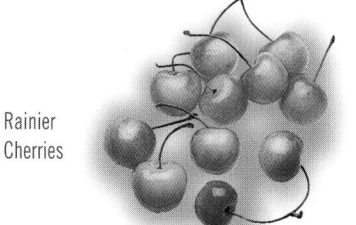
Rainier Cherries

Readily grown in most provinces of Canada are the two most important types of cherry (Fr. *cerises*): the sweet cherry and the sour (or tart) cherry.

Sweet cherries are round to heart-shaped, about 2.5 cm (1 in.) in diameter, with skin that ranges in colour from yellow to deep red to nearly black. The flesh, which is sweet and juicy, may vary from yellow to dark red. The most common and popular sweet cherries are the dark red Bings. Yellow-red Royal Ann and Rainier cherries are also available in some areas.

Sweet cherries are often marketed fresh, made into maraschino cherries or candied for use in baked goods. Fresh sweet cherries have a very short season, peaking during June and July. Cherries will not ripen further after harvesting. Select fruits that are firm and plump with a green stem still attached. There should not be any brown spots around the stem. A dry or brown stem indicates that the cherry is less than fresh. Once the stem is removed, the cherry will deteriorate rapidly. Store fresh cherries in the refrigerator and do not wash them until ready to use.

Sour cherries are light to dark red in colour and are so acidic they are rarely eaten uncooked. The most common sour cherries are the Montmorency and Morello. Most sour cherries are canned or frozen, or cooked with sugar and starch (usually cornstarch or tapioca) and sold as prepared pastry and pie fillings.

Both sweet and sour varieties are available dried.

BASIC PROCEDURE FOR PITTING CHERRIES

Remove the stem and place the cherry in the pitter with the indentation facing up. Squeeze the handles together to force out the pit.

Peaches and Nectarines

Peaches (Fr. *pêches*) are moderate-sized, round fruits with juicy, sweet flesh. Nectarines are a variety of peach, the main difference between the two being their skin. Peaches have a thin skin covered with fuzz, while nectarines have a thin, smooth skin. The flesh of either fruit ranges from white to pale orange. Although their flavours are somewhat different, they may be substituted for each other in most recipes.

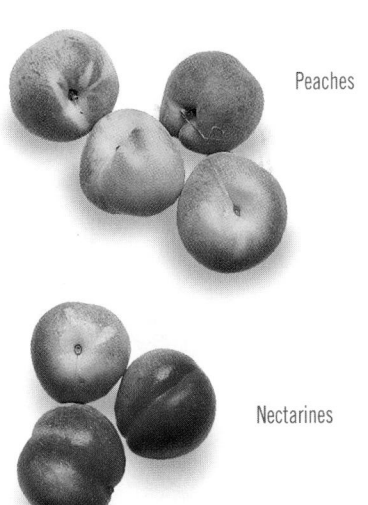

Peaches

Nectarines

Peaches and nectarines are excellent for eating out of hand or in dessert tarts or pastries. They are also used in jams, chutneys, preserves and savoury relishes, having a particular affinity for Asian and Indian dishes. Although the skin is edible, peaches are generally peeled before being used. (Peaches are easily peeled if blanched first.)

Peaches and nectarines are either freestones or clingstones. With freestones, the flesh separates easily from the stone; freestone fruits are commonly eaten out of hand. The flesh of clingstones adheres firmly to the stone; they hold their shape better when cooked and are the type most often canned.

Select fruits with a good aroma, an overall creamy, yellow or yellow-orange colour and an unwrinkled skin free of blemishes. Red patches are not an indication of ripeness. A green skin indicates that the fruit was picked too early and it will not ripen further. Peaches and nectarines will soften but do not become sweeter after harvesting.

The United States, especially California and Georgia, is the world's largest producer of peaches and nectarines. In Canada, Ontario's Niagara Region produces abundant peach crops. Peak season is through the summer months, with July and August producing the best crop. South American peaches are sometimes available from January to May. Canned and frozen peaches are readily available.

Santa Rosa
Plums

Damson Plums

Plums

Plums (Fr. *prunes*) are round to oval-shaped fruits that grow on trees or bushes. Dozens of plum varieties are known, although only a few are commercially significant. Plums vary in size from very small to 7.5 cm (3 in.) in diameter. Their thin skin can be green, red, yellow or various shades of blue-purple.

Plums are excellent for eating out of hand. Plums can also be used in pies, cobblers or tarts, or be baked or poached; they are often used in jams or preserves, and fresh slices can be used in salads or compotes.

Fresh plums are widely available from June through October, with a peak season in August and September. When selecting plums, look for plump, smooth fruits with unblemished skin. Generally, they should yield to gentle pressure, although the green and yellow varieties remain quite firm. Avoid plums with moist, brown spots near the stem. Plums may be left at room temperature to ripen, then stored in the refrigerator. Prunes, discussed later, are produced by drying special plum varieties, usually the French Agen.

Tropicals

Tropical fruits are native to the world's hot, tropical or subtropical regions. Most are now readily available throughout Canada thanks to rapid transportation and distribution methods. All can be eaten fresh, without cooking. Their flavours complement each other and go well with rich or spicy meat, fish and poultry dishes.

Common Yellow Bananas

Bananas

Common yellow bananas (Fr. *bananes*) are actually the berries of a large tropical herb. Grown in bunches called hands, they are about 17.5 to 22.5 cm (7 to 9 in.) long, with a sticky, soft, sweet flesh. Their inedible yellow skin is easily removed. Red bananas are also available seasonally.

Properly ripened bananas are excellent eaten out of hand or used in salads. Lightly bruised or overripe fruits are best used for breads or muffins. Bananas blend well with other tropical fruits and citrus. Their unique flavour is also complemented by curry, cinnamon, ginger, honey and chocolate.

Fresh bananas are available all year. Bananas are always harvested when still green because the texture and flavour will be adversely affected if the fruits are allowed to turn yellow on the tree. Unripe bananas are hard, dry and starchy. Because bananas ripen after harvesting, it is acceptable to purchase green bananas if there is sufficient time for final ripening before use. Bananas should be left at room temperature to ripen. A properly ripened banana has a yellow peel with brown flecks. The tip should not have any remaining green colouring. As bananas continue to age, the peel darkens and the starches turn to sugar, giving the fruits a sweeter flavour. Avoid bananas that have large brown bruises or a grey cast (a sign of cold damage).

Plantains

Plantains, also referred to as cooking bananas, are larger than but not as sweet as common bananas. They are frequently cooked as a starchy vegetable in tropical cuisines.

Medjool Dates

Dates

Dates are the fruit of the date palm tree, which has been cultivated since ancient times. Dates are about 2.5 to 5 cm (1 to 2 in.) long, with a paper-thin skin and a single grooved seed in the centre. Most are golden to dark brown when ripe.

Although dates appear to be dried, they are actually fresh fruits. They have a sticky-sweet, almost candied texture and rich flavour. Dates provide flavour and moisture for breads, muffins, cookies and tarts. They can also be served with fresh or dried fruits, or stuffed with meat or cheese as an appetizer.

Pitted dates are readily available in several packaged forms: whole, chopped or extruded (for use in baking). Whole unpitted dates are available in bulk. Date juice is also available for use as a natural sweetener, especially in baked goods. Although packaged or processed dates are available all year, peak season for fresh domestic dates is from October through December. When selecting dates, look for those that are plump, glossy and moist.

Kiwis

Kiwis, sometimes known as kiwifruits or Chinese gooseberries, are small oval fruits, about the size of a large egg, with a thin, fuzzy brown skin. The flesh is bright green or yellow with a white core surrounded by hundreds of tiny black seeds.

Kiwis

Kiwis are sweet but somewhat bland. They are best used raw, peeled and eaten out of hand or sliced for fruit salads or garnish. Although kiwis are not recommended for cooking because heat causes them to fall apart, they are a perfect addition to glazed fruit tarts and can be puréed for sorbets, mousses or Bavarians. Kiwis contain an enzyme (actinidin), similar to that in fresh pineapple or papaya, that has a tenderizing effect on meat and prevents gelling.

Mangoes

Mangoes are oval or kidney-shaped fruits that normally weigh between 180 and 500 g (6 oz. and 1 lb.). Their skin is smooth and thin but tough, varying in colour from yellow to orange-red, with patches of green, red or purple. As mangoes ripen, the green disappears. The juicy, bright orange flesh clings to a large, flat pit.

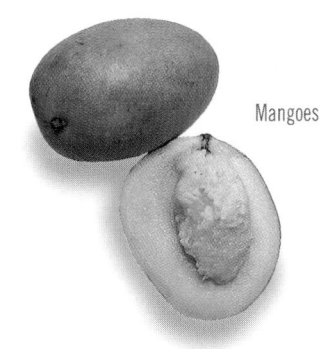

Mangoes

A mango's unique flavour is spicy-sweet, with an acidic tang. Mangoes can be puréed for use in drinks or sauces, or the flesh can be sliced or cubed for use in salads, pickles, chutneys or desserts. Mangoes go well with spicy foods such as curry and with barbecued meats.

Although Florida produces some mangoes, most of those available in North America are from Mexico. Peak season is from May through August. Select fruits with good colour that are firm and free of blemishes. Ripe mangoes should have a good aroma and should not be too soft or shrivelled. Allow mangoes to ripen completely at room temperature, then refrigerate for up to one week.

BASIC PROCEDURE FOR PITTING AND CUTTING MANGOES

1. Cut along each side of the pit to remove two sections.

2. Each section can then be cubed using the "hedgehog" technique: make crosswise cuts through the flesh, just to the skin; then press up on the skin side of the section, exposing the cubes.

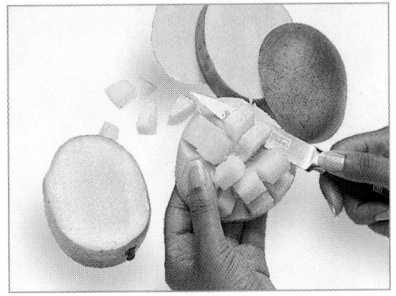

3. The mango may be served like this, or the cubes can be cut off to use in salads or other dishes.

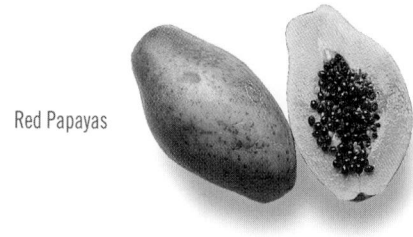

Red Papayas

● **papain** an enzyme found in papayas that breaks down proteins; used as the primary ingredient in many commercial meat tenderizers

Papayas

Papayas, also known as pawpaws, are greenish-yellow fruits shaped rather like large pears and weighing 500 to 1000 g (1 to 2 lb.). When halved, they resemble a melon. The flesh is golden to reddish-pink; the centre cavity is filled with round, silver-black seeds resembling caviar. Ripe papayas can be eaten raw, with only a squirt of lemon or lime juice. They can also be puréed for sweet or spicy sauces, chilled soups or sorbets.

Regular Papayas

Papayas contain **papain**, which breaks down proteins, and therefore papayas are an excellent meat tenderizer. Meats can be marinated with papaya juice or slices before cooking. Papain, however, makes fresh papayas unsuitable for use in gelatins because it inhibits gelling. Unripe (green) papayas are often used in pickles or chutneys, and can be baked or stewed with meat or poultry.

Papaya seeds are edible, with a peppery flavour and slight crunch. They are occasionally used to garnish fruit salads or add flavour to fruit salsas and compotes.

Papayas are grown in tropical and subtropical areas worldwide. Although available year round, peak season is from April through June. Select papayas that are plump, with a smooth, unblemished skin. Colour is a better determinant of ripeness than is softness: the greater the proportion of yellow to green skin colour, the riper the fruit. Papayas may be held at room temperature until completely ripe, then refrigerated for up to one week.

Passion Fruits

Pineapples

Passion Fruits

Passion fruits (Fr. *granadillas*) have a firm, almost shell-like purple skin with orange-yellow pulp surrounding large, black, edible seeds. They are about the size and shape of large hen eggs, with a sweet, rich and unmistakable citrusy flavour. The pulp is used in custards, sauces and ice creams.

Select heavy fruits with dark, shrivelled skin and a strong aroma. Allow them to ripen at room temperature, if necessary, then refrigerate. Passion fruits are in season only during February and March. Bottles or frozen packs of purée are readily available, however, and provide a strong, true flavour.

Pineapples

Pineapples (Fr. *ananas*) are the fruit of a shrub with sharp, spear-shaped leaves. Each fruit is covered with rough, brown eyes, giving it the appearance of a pine cone. The pale yellow flesh, which is sweet and very juicy, surrounds a cylindrical woody core that is edible but too tough for most uses. Most pineapples weigh approximately 1 kg (2 lb.), but dwarf varieties are also available.

Pineapples are excellent eaten raw, alone or in salads. Slices can be baked or grilled to accompany pork or ham. The cuisines of Southeast Asia incorporate pineapple into various curries, soups and stews. Pineapple juice is a popular beverage, often used in punch or cocktails. Canned or cooked pineapple can be added to gelatin mixtures, but avoid using fresh pineapple, as an enzyme (bromelin) found in fresh pineapple breaks down gelatin.

Pineapples do not ripen after harvesting. They must be left on the stem until completely ripe, at which time they are extremely perishable. The vast majority of pineapples come from Hawaii. Fresh pineapples are available all year, with peak supplies in March through June. Select heavy fruits with a strong, sweet aroma and rich colour. Avoid those with dried leaves or soft spots. Pineapples should be used as soon as possible after purchase. Pineapples are also available canned in slices, spears, or cubes or crushed, dried or candied.

BASIC PROCEDURE FOR TRIMMING AND SLICING PINEAPPLES

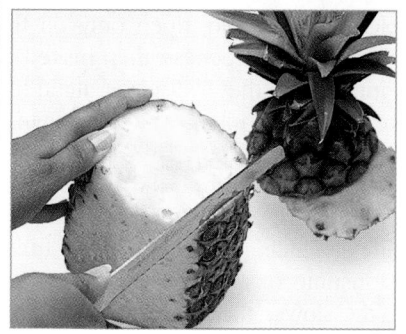

1. Slice off the leaves and stem end. Stand the fruit upright and cut the peel off in vertical strips.

2. Cut the peeled fruit in quarters, then cut away the woody core.

3. The flesh can then be cut as desired.

NUTRITION

Most fruits are quite nutritious. They have a high water content (usually 75% to 95%) and low protein and fat contents, all of which makes them low in calories. They are also an excellent source of fibre, and the sugar content of ripe fruits is a good source of energy. Some fruits, such as citrus, melons and strawberries, contain large amounts of vitamin C (which may be destroyed, however, by cooking or processing). Deep yellow and green fruits, such as apricots, mangoes and kiwis, are high in vitamin A; bananas, raisins and figs are a good source of potassium.

PURCHASING FRESH FRUITS

Fresh fruits have not been subjected to any processing (such as canning, freezing or drying). Fresh fruits may be ripe or unripe, depending on their condition when harvested or the conditions under which they have been stored. In order to use fresh fruits to their best advantage, it is important to make careful purchasing decisions. The size of each piece of fruit, its grade or quality, its ripeness on delivery and its nutritional content may affect your ability to use the fruit in an appropriate and cost-effective manner.

Grading

Fresh fruits traded on the wholesale market may be graded under the standards of the Canadian Food Inspection Agency. The grades, based on size and uniformity of shape, colour and texture as well as the absence of defects, are Canada No. 1, Canada No. 2 and Canada Domestic. Most fruits purchased for food service operations are Canada No. 1. Fruits with lower grades are suitable for processing into sauces, jams, jellies or preserves.

Ripening

Several important changes take place in a fruit as it ripens. The fruit reaches its full size; its pulp or flesh becomes soft and tender; its colour changes. In addition, the fruit's acid content declines, making it less tart, and its starch content converts into fructose and glucose, the sugars that provide the fruit's sweetness, flavour and aroma.

Unfortunately, these changes do not stop when the fruit reaches its peak of ripeness. Rather, they continue, deteriorating the fruit's texture and flavour and eventually causing spoilage.

Depending upon the species, fresh fruits can be purchased either fully ripened or unripened. Figs and pineapples, for example, ripen only on the plant and are harvested at or just before their peak of ripeness, then rushed to market. They should not be purchased unripened as they will never attain full flavour or texture after harvesting. However some fruits, including bananas and pears, continue to ripen after harvesting and can be purchased unripened.

With most harvested fruits, the ripening time as well as the time during which the fruits remain at their peak of ripeness can be manipulated. For instance, ripening can be delayed by chilling. Chilling slows down the fruit's **respiration rate** (fruits, like animals, consume oxygen and expel carbon dioxide). The slower the respiration rate, the slower the conversion of starch to sugar. For quicker ripening, fruit can be stored at room temperature.

Ripening is also affected by ethylene gas, a colourless, odourless hydrocarbon gas. Ethylene gas is naturally emitted by ripening fruits and can be used to encourage further ripening in most fruits. Apples, tomatoes, melons and bananas give off the most ethylene and should be stored away from delicate fruits and vegetables, especially greens. Fruits that are picked and shipped unripened can be exposed to ethylene gas to induce ripening just before sale. Conversely, if you want to extend the life of ripe fruits a day or two, isolate them from other fruits and keep them well chilled.

Fresh fruits will not ripen further once they are cooked or processed. The cooking or processing method applied, however, may soften the fruits or add flavour.

Purchasing

Fresh fruits are sold by weight or by count. They are packed in containers referred to as crates, bushels, cartons, cases, lugs or flats. The weight or count packed in each of these containers varies depending on the type of fruit, the purveyor and the place where the fruits were packed. For example, Texas citrus is packed in cartons equal to 7/10 of a bushel; Florida citrus is packed in cartons equal to 4/5 of a bushel. Sometimes size must be specified when ordering fruit. A 13.5-kg (30-lb.) case of lemons, for example, may contain 96, 112 or 144 individual lemons, depending on their size.

Some fresh fruits, especially melons, pineapples, peaches and berries, are available trimmed, cleaned, peeled or cut, and sugar and preservatives are sometimes added. They are sold in bulk containers, sometimes packed in water. These items offer a consistent product with a significant reduction in labour costs. The purchase price may be greater than that for fresh fruits and flavour and freshness and nutritional qualities may suffer somewhat from the processing.

PURCHASING AND STORING PRESERVED FRUITS

Preserving techniques are designed to extend the shelf life of fruits in essentially fresh form. These methods include irradiation, acidulation, canning, freezing and drying. Except for drying, these techniques do not substantially change the fruits' texture or flavour. Canning and freezing can also be used to preserve cooked fruits.

Preserves such as jellies and jams are cooked products and are discussed later in this chapter.

Irradiated Fruits

Some fruits can be subjected to ionizing radiation to destroy parasites, insects and bacteria. The treatment also slows ripening without a noticeable effect on the fruits' flavour and texture. Irradiated fruits must be labelled "treated with radiation," "treated by irradiation" or with a symbol when sold in the United States. Canada currently is reviewing the practice and is considering applications to add more foods to the list included in the Food and Drug Regulations (2011).

Acidulation

Apples, pears, bananas, peaches and other fruits turn brown when cut. Although this browning is commonly attributed to exposure to oxygen, it is actually caused by the reaction of enzymes.

Enzymatic oxidative browning can be retarded by immersing cut fruits in an acidic solution such as lemon or orange juice. This simple technique is sometimes referred to as **acidulation**. Soaking fruits in water or lemon juice and water (called acidulated water) is not recommended. Unless a sufficient amount of salt or sugar is added to the water, the fruits will just become mushy. But if enough salt or sugar is added, the flavour will be affected.

● **acidulation** the process of adding citric or acetic acid to water, used to preserve colour (to retard enzymatic oxidative browning of some fruits and vegetables), to clean aluminum or to soak kidneys and game

Canned Fruits

Almost any type of fruit can be canned successfully; pineapple and peaches are the largest sellers. In commercial canning, raw fruits are cleaned and placed in a sealed container, then subjected to high temperatures for a specific amount of time. Heating destroys the microorganisms that cause spoilage, and the sealed environment created by the can eliminates oxidation and retards decomposition. But the heat required by the canning process also softens the texture of most fruits. Canning has little or no effect on vitamins A, B, C and D because oxygen is not present during the heating process. Canning also has no practical effect on proteins, fats or carbohydrates.

In *solid pack* cans, little or no water is added. The only liquid is from the fruits' natural moisture. *Water pack* cans have water or fruit juice added, which must be taken into account when determining costs. *Syrup pack* fruits have a sugar syrup—light, medium or heavy—added. The syrup should also be taken into account when determining food costs, and the additional sweetness should be considered when using syrup-packed fruits. Cooked fruit products such as pie fillings are also available canned.

Canned fruits are purchased in cases of standard-size cans. Canned fruits can be stored for extended time periods at room temperature. Once a can is opened, any unused contents must be transferred to an appropriate storage container and refrigerated. Cans with bulges must be discarded immediately, without opening. Canned fruits are graded as follows: Canada Fancy (top quality), Canada Choice and Canada Substandard.

Frozen Fruits

Freezing is a highly effective method for preserving fruits. It severely inhibits the growth of microorganisms that cause fruits to spoil. Freezing does not destroy nutrients, although the appearance or texture of most fruits can be affected because of their high water content. This occurs when ice crystals formed from the water in the cells burst the cells' walls.

Many fruits, especially berries and apple and pear slices, are now individually quick frozen (IQF). This method employs blasts of cold air, refrigerated plates, liquid nitrogen, liquid air or other techniques to chill the produce quickly. By speeding the freezing process, known as shock freezing, the formation of ice crystals can be greatly reduced.

Fruits can be trimmed and sliced before freezing and are also available frozen in sugar syrup, which adds flavour and prevents browning. Berries are frozen whole, while stone fruits are usually peeled, pitted and sliced. Fruit purées are also available frozen.

Frozen fruits are graded as Canada Fancy, Canada Choice or Extra Standard, or Canada Substandard. The "Canada" grade indicates that a government inspector has graded the product, but packers may use grade names without an actual inspection if the contents meet the standards of the grade indicated.

Individually quick frozen fruits can be purchased by the case. All frozen fruits should be sealed in moistureproof wrapping and kept at a constant temperature of –18°C (0°F) or below. Temperature fluctuations can cause freezer burn.

Golden Raisins

Dried Fruits

Currants

Drying is the oldest-known technique for preserving fruits, having been used for more than 5000 years. When ripe fruits are dried, they lose most of their moisture. This concentrates their flavours and sugars and dramatically extends shelf life. Although most fruits can be dried, plums (prunes), grapes (raisins, sultanas and currants), apricots, cranberries and figs are the fruits most commonly dried. The drying method can be as simple as leaving ripe fruits in the sun to dry naturally or the more cost-efficient technique of passing fruits through a compartment of hot, dry air to quickly extract moisture.

Apricots

Apples

Dried fruits actually retain from 16% to 25% residual moisture, which leaves them moist and soft. They are often treated with sulphur dioxide to prevent browning (oxidation) and to extend shelf life.

Dried fruits may be eaten out of hand; added to cereals or salads; baked in muffins, breads, pies or tarts; stewed for chutneys or compotes; or used as a stuffing for roasted meats or poultry. Before use, dried fruits may be softened by soaking them for a short time in a hot liquid such as water, wine, rum, brandy or other liquor. Some dried fruits should be simmered in a small amount of water before use.

Persimmons

Pears

Store dried fruits in airtight containers to prevent further moisture loss; keep in a dry, cool area away from sunlight. Dried fruits may become mouldy if exposed to both air and high humidity.

Kiwis

APPLYING VARIOUS COOKING METHODS

Although most fruits are edible raw and typically served that way, some fruits can also be cooked. Commonly used cooking methods are broiling and grilling, baking, sautéing, deep-fat frying, poaching and simmering.

When cooking fruits, proper care and attention are critical. Even minimal cooking can render fruits overly soft or mushy. To combat this irreversible process, sugar can be added. When fruits are cooked with sugar, the sugar will be absorbed slowly into the cells, firming the fruits. Acids (notably lemon juice) also help fruits retain their structure. (Alkalis, such as baking soda, cause the cells to break down more quickly, reducing the fruits to mush.)

Determining "Doneness"

There are so many different fruits with such varied responses to cooking that no one standard for doneness is appropriate. Each item should be evaluated on a recipe-by-recipe basis. Generally, however, most cooked fruits are done when they are just tender when pierced with a fork or the tip of a paring knife. Simmered fruits, such as compotes, should be softer, cooked just to the point of disintegration.

You can avoid overcooking fruits by remembering that some carryover cooking will occur through the residual heat contained in the foods. Always rely on objective tests—sight, feel, taste and aroma—rather than the clock.

Dry-Heat Cooking Methods
Broiling and Grilling

Fruits are usually broiled or grilled just long enough to caramelize sugars. But cooking must be done quickly in order to avoid breaking down the fruits' structure. Good fruits to broil or grill are pineapples, apples, grapefruits, bananas, persimmons and peaches. The fruits may be cut into slices, chunks or halves as appropriate. A coating of sugar, honey or liqueur adds flavour, as do lemon juice, cinnamon and ginger.

When broiling fruits, use an oiled sheet pan or broiling platter. When grilling fruits, use a clean grill grate or thread the pieces onto skewers. Only thick fruit slices will need to be turned or rotated to heat fully. Broiled or grilled fruits can be served alone, as an accompaniment to meat, fish or poultry or as a topping for ice creams or custards.

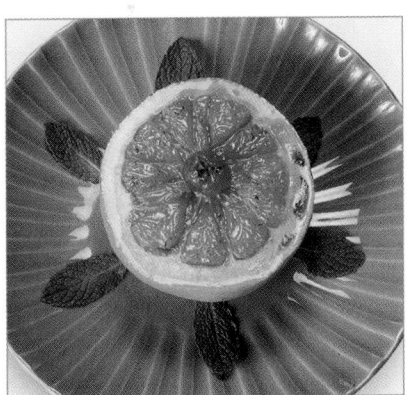
Broiled Grapefruit

BASIC PROCEDURE FOR BROILING OR GRILLING FRUITS

1. Select ripe fruits and peel, core or slice as necessary.
2. Top with sugar or honey to add flavour and aid caramelization.
3. Place the fruits on the broiler platter, sheet pan or grill grate.
4. Broil or grill at a high temperature, turning as necessary to heat the fruits thoroughly but quickly.

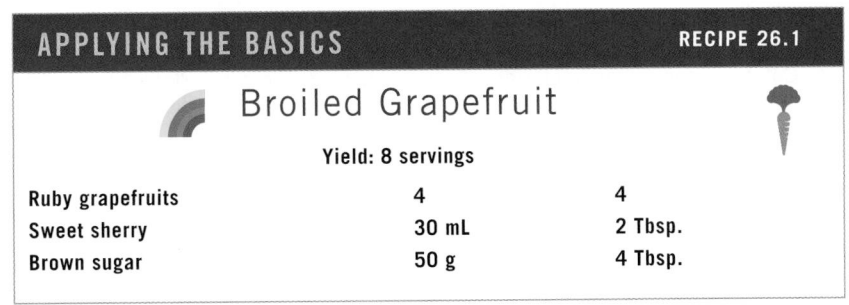

APPLYING THE BASICS   RECIPE 26.1

Broiled Grapefruit

Yield: 8 servings

Ruby grapefruits	4	4
Sweet sherry	30 mL	2 Tbsp.
Brown sugar	50 g	4 Tbsp.

RECIPE 26.1

Approximate values per 1/2 grapefruit:

Calories	70
Total fat	0 g
Saturated fat	0 g
Cholesterol	0 mg
Sodium	0 mg
Total carbohydrates	16 g
Protein	1 g

continued

1. Cut each grapefruit in half (perpendicular to the segments), then section with a sharp knife, carefully removing any visible seeds.
2. Sprinkle the grapefruit halves with the sherry and sugar.
3. Arrange on a baking sheet and place under a preheated broiler. Cook briefly, only until well heated and the sugar caramelizes. Serve immediately.

Baking

After washing, peeling, coring or pitting, most pomes, stone fruits and tropicals can be baked to create hot, flavourful desserts. Fruits with sturdy skins, particularly apples and pears, are excellent for baking alone, as their skin (peel) holds in moisture and flavour. They can also be used as edible containers by filling the cavity left by coring with a variety of sweet or savoury mixtures.

Combinations of fruits can also be baked successfully. Try mixing fruits for a balance of sweetness and tartness (for example, strawberries with rhubarb, apples with plums).

Several baked desserts are simply fruits (fresh, frozen or canned) topped with a crust (and called a *cobbler*), streusel (and called a *crumble* or *crisp*) or batter (and called a *buckle*). (See Recipe 30.32, Blackberry Cobbler.) Fruits, sometimes poached first, can also be baked in a wrapper of puff pastry, flaky dough or phyllo dough to produce an elegant dessert.

BASIC PROCEDURE FOR BAKING FRUITS

1. Select ripe but firm fruits and peel, core, pit or slice as necessary.
2. Add sugar or any flavourings.
3. Wrap the fruits in pastry dough if desired or directed in the recipe.
4. Place the fruits in a baking dish and bake uncovered in a moderate oven until tender or properly browned.

Warm Baked Peaches

RECIPE 26.2

Approximate values per serving:	
Calories	103
Total fat	6 g
Saturated fat	4 g
Cholesterol	16 mg
Sodium	2 mg
Total carbohydrates	12 g
Protein	0 g

APPLYING THE BASICS   **RECIPE 26.2**

 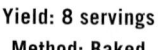

Warm Baked Peaches or Nectarines

Yield: 8 servings

Method: Baked

Freestone peaches or nectarines	4	4
Vanilla bean	1	1
Granulated sugar	60 g	2 oz.
Lemon juice	30 mL	1 fl. oz.
Unsalted butter	60 g	2 oz.
Pastry Cream (Recipe 32.2) or ice cream	as needed	as needed

1. Cut the peaches or nectarines in half. Remove the pits. Place them, cut side up, in a well-buttered half-size hotel pan or ovenproof dish.
2. Split the vanilla bean and scrape the seeds into the sugar. Sprinkle the fruit with the sugar and lemon juice.
3. Place a small piece of butter in the centre of each fruit half and bake at 180°C (350°F) until tender and lightly browned, approximately 20 minutes. Serve warm with Pastry Cream or ice cream.

Sautéing

Fruits develop a rich, syrupy flavour when sautéed briefly in butter, sugar and, if desired, spices or liqueur. Cherries, bananas, apples, pears and pineapples are good choices. They should be peeled, cored and seeded as necessary and cut into uniform-sized pieces before sautéing.

For dessert, fruits are sautéed with sugar to create a caramelized glaze or syrup. The fruits and syrup can be used to fill crepes or to top spongecakes or ice creams. Liquor may be added and the mixture flamed (flambéed) in front of diners, as with Bananas Foster (Recipe 26.15).

For savoury mixtures, onions, shallots or garlic are often added.

In both sweet and savoury fruit sautés, the fat used should be the most appropriate for the finished product. Butter or oil are typical choices.

BASIC PROCEDURE FOR SAUTÉING FRUITS

1. Peel, pit and core the fruits as necessary and cut into uniform-sized pieces.
2. Melt the fat in a hot sauté pan.
3. Add the fruit pieces and any flavouring ingredients. Do not crowd the pan, as this will cause the fruit to stew in its own juices.
4. Cook quickly over high heat.

APPLYING THE BASICS   RECIPE 26.3

Savoury Fruit Chutney

Yield: 750 mL (24 fl. oz.)

Onion, fine dice	175 g	6 oz.
Garlic, minced	25 g	5 cloves
Butter	30 g	1 oz.
Fruit medley, apples (tart) or peaches, pineapple, etc.	500 g	1 lb.
Raisins	100 g	1/2 cup
Ginger, grated	25 g	2 Tbsp.
Malt vinegar	250 mL	8 fl. oz.
Dry chile, seedless	1	1
Granulated sugar	175 g	6 oz.
Allspice	0.5 g	1/3 tsp.
Salt	5 g	1 tsp.

1. Sweat the onion and garlic in the butter without browning.
2. Slice the fruit into thin, even pieces. Add to the onion and cook for 1–2 minutes. Add the remaining ingredients.
3. Cook, uncovered, over medium heat for 10 minutes or until tender.
4. Serve warm or chilled as an accompaniment.

RECIPE 26.3

Approximate values per 75 mL serving:	
Calories	163
Total fat	3 g
Saturated fat	1.5 g
Cholesterol	7 mg
Sodium	222 mg
Total carbohydrates	37 g
Protein	1 g

Deep-Fat Frying

Few fruits are suitable for deep-fat frying. Apples, bananas, pears, pineapples and firm peaches mixed in or coated with batter, however, produce fine results. These fruits should be peeled, cored, seeded and cut into evenly sized slices or chunks. They may also need to be dried with paper towels so that the batter or coating can adhere. The procedures for deep-fat frying are found in Chapter 9, Principles of Cooking.

Moist-Heat Cooking Methods
Poaching

One of the more popular cooking methods for fruits is poaching. Poaching softens and tenderizes fruits and infuses them with additional flavours such as spices or wine. Poached fruits can be served hot or cold and used in tarts, pastries or as an accompaniment to meat or poultry dishes.

The poaching liquid can be water, wine, liquor or sugar syrup. (As noted earlier, sugar helps fruits keep their shape, although it takes longer to tenderize fruits poached in sugar syrup.) The low poaching temperature (85°C/185°F) allows fruits to soften gradually. The agitation created at higher temperatures would damage them.

Cooked fruits should be allowed to cool in the flavoured poaching liquid or syrup. Most poaching liquids can be used repeatedly. If they contain sufficient sugar, they can be reduced to a sauce or glaze to accompany the poached fruits.

BASIC PROCEDURE FOR POACHING FRUITS

1. Peel, core and slice the fruits as necessary.
2. In a sufficiently deep, nonreactive saucepan, combine the poaching liquid (usually water or wine) with sugar, spices, citrus zest and other ingredients as desired or as directed in the recipe.
3. Submerge the fruits in the liquid. Place a circle of parchment paper over the fruits to help them stay submerged.
4. Place the saucepan on the stove top over a medium-high flame; bring to a boil.
5. As soon as the liquid boils, reduce the temperature. Simmer gently.
6. Poach until the fruits are tender enough for the tip of a small knife to be easily inserted. Cooking time depends on the type of fruit used, its ripeness and the cooking liquid.
7. Remove the saucepan from the stove top and allow the liquid and fruits to cool.
8. Remove the fruits from the liquid and then refrigerate. The liquid can be returned to the stove top and reduced until thick enough to use as a sauce or glaze or refrigerated for further use.

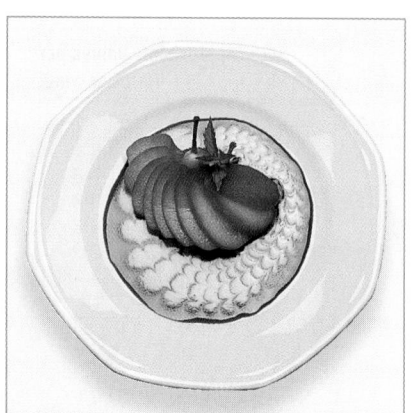
Pears Poached in Red Wine

APPLYING THE BASICS | RECIPE 26.4

 Pears Poached in Red Wine

CULINARY ARTS INSTITUTE, MISSISSIPPI UNIVERSITY FOR WOMEN
Director Sarah Labensky, CCP

Yield: 8 servings

Ripe pears, Anjou or Bartlett	8	8
Zinfandel or Burgundy wine	1.5 L	50 fl. oz.
Whole peppercorns	8–10	8–10
Vanilla bean	1	1
Granulated sugar	350 g	12 oz.
Fresh basil, chopped	30 g	1 oz.
Zest of 1 orange		

continued

1. Peel and core the pears, leaving the stems intact.

2. Combine the remaining ingredients in a large nonreactive saucepan. Arrange the pears in the liquid in a single layer.

3. Place the pears on the stove top over medium-high heat. Bring to just below a boil, then immediately reduce the heat and allow the liquid to simmer gently. Cover with a round of parchment paper if necessary to keep the pears submerged.

4. Continue poaching the pears until tender, approximately 1–1.5 hours. Remove the saucepan from the stove and allow the pears to cool in the liquid.

5. Remove the pears from the poaching liquid and return the liquid to the stove top. Reduce until the liquid is thick enough to coat the back of a spoon, then strain.

6. Serve the pears chilled or at room temperature in a pool of the reduced wine syrup.

RECIPE 26.4

Approximate values per serving:	
Calories	414
Total fat	1.5 g
Saturated fat	0 g
Cholesterol	0 mg
Sodium	35 mg
Total carbohydrates	92 g
Protein	6 g

Simmering

Simmering techniques are used to make stewed fruits and compotes. Fresh, frozen, canned and dried fruits can be simmered or stewed. As with any moist-heat cooking method, simmering softens and tenderizes fruits. The liquid used may be water, wine or the juices naturally found in the fruits. Sugar, honey and spices may be added as desired. Stewed or simmered fruits can be served hot or cold, as a first course, a dessert or an accompaniment to meat or poultry dishes.

BASIC PROCEDURE FOR SIMMERING FRUITS

1. Peel, core, pit and slice the fruits as necessary.

2. Bring the fruits and cooking liquid, if used, to a simmer. Cook until the fruit is tender.

3. Add sugar or other sweeteners as desired or as directed in the recipe.

APPLYING THE BASICS   RECIPE 26.5

Dried Fruit Compote

Yield: 1.5 kg (3 lb.)

Dried apricots	150 g	5 oz.
Prunes, pitted	150 g	5 oz.
Dried pears or apples	150 g	5 oz.
Dried peaches	150 g	5 oz.
Hot water or apple juice	750 mL	24 fl. oz.
Cinnamon stick	1	1
Light corn syrup	350 mL	12 fl. oz.
Cointreau	50 mL	2 fl. oz.

1. Coarsely chop the fruits, if desired. Place the pieces in a nonreactive saucepan and add the liquid and cinnamon stick.

2. Bring the mixture to a simmer, cover and cook until tender, approximately 12–15 minutes.

3. Add the corn syrup and Cointreau. Simmer uncovered until thoroughly heated. Serve warm or refrigerate for longer storage.

Dried Fruit Compote

RECIPE 26.5

Approximate values per 150 g serving:	
Calories	188
Total fat	0 g
Saturated fat	0 g
Cholesterol	0 mg
Sodium	52 mg
Total carbohydrates	47 g
Protein	1 g

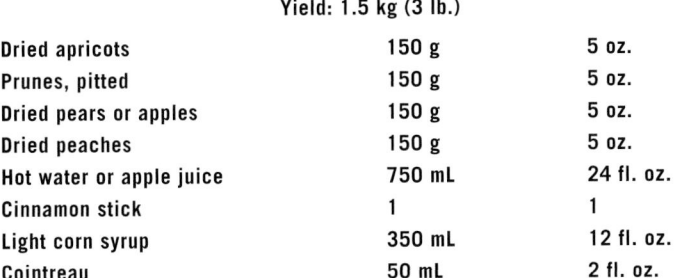

- **concentrate** also known as a fruit paste or compound; a reduced fruit purée, without a gel structure, used as a flavouring

- **jam** a fruit gel made from fruit pulp and sugar

- **jelly** a fruit gel made from fruit juice and sugar

- **marmalade** a citrus jelly that also contains unpeeled slices of citrus fruit

- **preserve** a fruit gel that contains large pieces or whole fruits

Preserving

Fresh fruits can be preserved with sugar if the fruit and sugar mixture is **concentrated** by evaporation to the point that microbial spoilage cannot occur. The added sugar also retards the growth of, but does not destroy, microorganisms.

Pectin, a substance present in varying amounts in all fruits, can cause cooked fruits to form a semisolid mass known as a *gel*. Fruits that are visually unattractive but otherwise of high quality can be made into gels, which are more commonly known as **jams**, **jellies**, **marmalades** and **preserves**.

The essential ingredients of a fruit gel are fruit, pectin, acid (usually lemon juice) and sugar. They must be carefully combined in the correct ratio for the gel to form. For fruits with a low pectin content (such as strawberries) to form gels, pectin must be added, either by adding a fruit with a high pectin content (for example, apples or quinces) or by adding packaged pectin.

BASIC PROCEDURE FOR MAKING FRUIT PRESERVES

1. Clean, peel, core, pit and cut the fruits as necessary.
2. Firm fruits should be simmered in water or juice until tender.
3. Add sugar and other flavourings to the fruits as desired or as directed in the recipe.
4. Simmer until the mixture thickens.

APPLYING THE BASICS   RECIPE 26.6

Strawberry Jam

Yield: 8 225-mL (8-oz.) jars

Strawberries, hulled, crushed	850 mL	3-3/4 cups
Sugar	1575 g	7 cups
Lemon juice, fresh	50 mL	2 fl. oz.
Pectin (Certo®)	1 package	1 package

1. Measure ingredients exactly and combine berries with 50 g (1-1/2 oz.) of the sugar, lemon juice, and pectin in a 6–8 L (6–8 qt.) sauce pot and stir.
2. Bring to a full rolling boil and add remaining sugar. Boil for 1 minute on high heat, stirring constantly.
3. Remove from heat and skim foam.
4. Ladle into sterilized jars to within 30 mm (1/8 in.) of top, and wipe rims and threads. Secure with 2-piece lids and screw bands tightly.
5. Place jars in a nonpressurized steamer (Combi-Therm) set at 100°C (212°F) and 100% moisture and process for 10 minutes. Remove and let cool at room temperature. Check seals. Refrigerate any unsealed jars.

NOTE: Altitude adjustments for water bath—to processing time add 5 minutes for 300–1000 m (900–3000 ft.), 10 minutes for 1001–2000 m (3001–6000 ft.), 15 minutes for 2001–2600 m (6001–7800 ft.), and 20 minutes for 2601–3000 m (7801–9000 ft.).

RECIPE 26.6

Approximate values per 15 mL serving:	
Calories	54
Total fat	0 g
Saturated fat	0 g
Cholesterol	0 mg
Sodium	1 mg
Total carbohydrates	14 g
Protein	0 g

Conclusion

Fruits, whether fresh, frozen, canned or dried, are one of the most versatile and popular of foods. Fruits can be used uncooked or incorporated into a soup, salad, bread, meat dish or dessert. When selecting fresh fruits, it is important to consider seasonal availability, storage conditions and ripeness. It is essential that they be at their peak of ripeness for the best flavour, texture, aroma and appearance.

Questions for Discussion

1. Define ripeness and explain why ripe fruits are the most desirable. How does the ripening process affect the availability of some fruits?

2. Describe the proper storage conditions for most fruits. Which fruits emit ethylene gas and why is this a consideration when storing fruits?

3. Explain why some apple varieties are preferred for cooking, while other varieties are preferred for eating. Which variety is generally preferred for making applesauce?

4. Which types of fruits are best for dry-heat cooking methods? Explain your answer. Why is sugar usually added when cooking any type of fruit?

5. List and describe three ways to prepare fruits for extended storage.

Additional Fruit Recipes

Pressing apples through a food mill.

RECIPE 26.7

Applesauce

Yield: 1 L (1 qt.)

McIntosh apples	1.75 kg	4 lb.
Cinnamon sticks	2	2
Granulated sugar	150 g	5 oz.
Lemon juice	15 mL	1 Tbsp.

1. Peel, core and quarter the apples. Place in a saucepan with just enough cold water to cover the bottom of the pan. Add the cinnamon sticks.

2. Bring to a simmer, cover and cook until the apples are tender, approximately 15 minutes.

3. Add the sugar and lemon juice. Simmer 10 minutes more.

4. Remove the cinnamon sticks and press the apples through a food mill.

RECIPE 26.7

Approximate values per 50 g serving:	
Calories	104
Total fat	0 g
Saturated fat	0 g
Cholesterol	0 mg
Sodium	0 mg
Total carbohydrates	26 g
Protein	0 g

RECIPE 26.8

Cranberry-Orange Sauce

Yield: 1.5 L (1-1/2 qt.)

Granulated sugar	225 g	8 oz.
Orange juice	110 mL	2 fl. oz.
Water	220 mL	4 fl. oz.
Fresh or frozen cranberries	350 g	12 oz.
Cinnamon stick	1	1

Cranberry-Orange Sauce

continued

Orange liqueur	25 mL	1 fl. oz.
Orange zest, finely grated	10 g	1 Tbsp.
Oranges, filleted	1	1

1. Combine the sugar, juice and water in a nonreactive saucepan; bring to a boil.
2. Add the cranberries and cinnamon stick and simmer uncovered until the berries begin to burst, approximately 15 minutes. Skim off any foam that rises to the surface.
3. Add the orange liqueur and zest and simmer for another 5 minutes.
4. Remove from the heat and remove the cinnamon stick. Add the orange fillets. Cool and refrigerate.

RECIPE 26.8

Approximate values per 50 g serving:	
Calories	48
Total fat	0 g
Saturated fat	0 g
Cholesterol	0 mg
Sodium	0 mg
Total carbohydrates	12 g
Protein	0 g

Pineapple Papaya Salsa

RECIPE 26.9

Approximate values per 50 mL serving:	
Calories	12
Total fat	0 g
Saturated fat	0 g
Cholesterol	0 mg
Sodium	115 mg
Total carbohydrates	3 g
Protein	0 g

RECIPE 26.9

Pineapple Papaya Salsa

Yield: 2 L (2 qt.)

Tomatoes	450 g	3
Pineapple, fresh	1	1
Papaya, fresh	1	1
Green onions, sliced	1 bunch	1 bunch
Fresh cilantro, chopped	1 bunch	1 bunch
Jalapeños, seeded, minced	2	2
Lemon juice	50 mL	3 Tbsp.
Garlic, chopped	5 g	1 tsp.
Salt	10 g	2 tsp.

1. Core and dice the tomatoes.
2. Peel and dice the pineapple.
3. Peel, seed and dice the papaya.
4. Combine all ingredients and chill well.

RECIPE 26.10

Approximate values per 50 g serving:	
Calories	142
Total fat	0 g
Saturated fat	0 g
Cholesterol	0 mg
Sodium	2 mg
Total carbohydrates	35 g
Protein	1 g

RECIPE 26.10

Berry Compote

Yield: 450 mL (16 fl. oz.)

Berries, fresh or frozen	350 g	12 oz.
Granulated sugar	125 g	4 oz.
Oranges, juice and zest	2	2
Honey	100 g	3 oz.
Cinnamon stick	1	1
Brandy	50 mL	3 Tbsp.

1. Select an assortment of fresh or frozen berries—strawberries, blueberries, raspberries, blackberries and cherries can be used, depending on availability.
2. Place the fruits and sugar in a nonreactive saucepan. Add the juice of 2 oranges. Bring to a simmer over low heat; cook until the fruits are soft but still intact.

continued

3. Strain the mixture, saving both the fruits and the liquid. Return the liquid to the saucepan. Add the finely grated zest from 1 orange, and the honey, cinnamon and brandy.

4. Bring to a boil and reduce until the mixture thickens enough to coat the back of a spoon. Remove from the heat and cool to room temperature.

5. Gently stir the reserved fruits into the sauce, cover and chill.

Berry Compote

RECIPE 26.11

Cherry Confit

Yield: 125 g (4 oz.)

Red onion, small dice	25 g	2 Tbsp.
Whole butter	10 g	2 tsp.
Dried cherries	100 g	3 oz.
Brandy	25 mL	1 Tbsp.
Port	25 mL	1 Tbsp.
Sherry vinegar	5 mL	1/2 tsp.

1. Sauté the onion in butter without colouring.

2. Add the cherries. Add the brandy and flambé.

3. Add the port and sherry vinegar; cook until almost dry. Serve warm or at room temperature with charcuterie items, or grilled or roasted meats.

4. The confit can be kept, refrigerated, for up to 1 week.

RECIPE 26.11

Approximate values per 50 mL serving:	
Calories	26
Total fat	2 g
Saturated fat	1 g
Cholesterol	6 mg
Sodium	16 mg
Total carbohydrates	2 g
Protein	0 g

RECIPE 26.12

Figs with Berries and Honey Mousse

GREENS RESTAURANT, San Francisco, CA
Executive Chef Annie Somerville

Yield: 4 servings

Raspberries or blackberries	300 g	10 oz.
Fresh figs such as Black Mission, Kadota or Calimyrna	300 g	10 oz.
Honey	175 g	6 oz.
Egg yolks	4	4
Cream, 35%	450 mL	1 pt.

1. Pick through the berries, rinse quickly and drain immediately because water will dilute their flavour.

2. Rinse the figs and cut them in half, leaving the stem attached.

3. To make the mousse, whisk the honey and egg yolks together in a bowl over a pan of barely simmering water. Whisk the mixture continuously for 8 minutes. After 5 minutes, the mousse will begin to thicken and the texture will become creamy. Whisk vigorously until the mousse leaves thick ribbons on its surface when poured over itself. Set aside to cool. The texture of the cooled mousse will be stiff and sticky.

4. Whisk 30 mL (2 Tbsp.) of cream into the mousse, working it until it loosens.

5. Whip the remaining cream until it is firm, fold it into the mousse until it is just incorporated, then whisk the two together. The texture will be light and creamy.

6. Loosely arrange the figs on a platter, sprinkle with the berries and serve with the mousse.

Figs with Berries and Honey Mousse

RECIPE 26.12

Approximate values per serving:	
Calories	689
Total fat	48 g
Saturated fat	28 g
Cholesterol	370 mg
Sodium	214 mg
Total carbohydrates	57 g
Protein	6 g

Tropical Fruit Salad with Yogurt Dressing

RECIPE 26.13

Approximate values per serving:	
Calories	170
Total fat	1 g
Saturated fat	0 g
Cholesterol	0 mg
Sodium	30 mg
Total carbohydrates	38 g
Protein	3 g

Tropical Fruit Salad with Yogurt Dressing

Yield: 4 small salads

Ingredient	Metric	U.S.
Mango, cut into 12-mm (1/2-in.) cubes	175 g	6 oz.
Pineapple, cut into 12-mm (1/2-in.) cubes	175 g	6 oz.
Papaya, cut into 12-mm (1/2-in.) cubes	125 g	4 oz.
Grapefruit segments	16	16
Pineapple or grapefruit juice	50 mL	2 fl. oz.
Yogurt, plain, nonfat	125 mL	4 fl. oz.
Honey	50 g	2 Tbsp.
Lime juice, fresh	15 mL	1 Tbsp.
Butterleaf lettuce, large leaves, separated and cleaned	4	4
Kiwi, peeled and sliced	1	1
Poppy seeds	3 g	1 tsp.

1. Mix the mango, pineapple, papaya and grapefruit together with the pineapple or grapefruit juice.

2. To make the dressing, whisk the yogurt, honey and lime juice together.

3. Line the plates with the butterleaf lettuce. Arrange the kiwi slices and the fruit salad over the lettuce.

4. Drizzle the dressing over the fruits and top with poppy seeds.

Dusting the fritters with powdered sugar.

RECIPE 26.14

Approximate values per serving:	
Calories	60
Total fat	1.5 g
Saturated fat	1 g
Cholesterol	10 mg
Sodium	36 mg
Total carbohydrates	11 g
Protein	1 g

Banana Fritters

Yield: 40 fritters

Ingredient	Metric	U.S.
Egg, beaten	1	1
Milk	250 mL	8 fl. oz.
Unsalted butter, melted	50 g	2 oz.
Vanilla extract	5 mL	1 tsp.
Orange zest, finely grated	20 g	2 Tbsp.
Orange juice	50 mL	2 fl. oz.
Ripe banana	1 large	1 large
Pastry flour, sifted	325 g	12 oz.
Granulated sugar	100 g	4 oz.
Baking powder	10 g	1 Tbsp.
Salt	2 g	1/2 tsp.
Confectioner's sugar	as needed for garnish	

1. Whisk together the egg, milk, butter and vanilla. Add the orange zest and juice.

2. Peel and dice the banana (6-mm or 1/4-in. size) and add to the egg mixture.

3. Sift together the flour, sugar, baking powder and salt. Gently stir in the banana-egg mixture to form a thick batter.

4. Heat deep-fat fryer oil to 180°C (350°F). Fry 15-g (1-Tbsp.) portions of the batter until the fritters are brown and crisp, approximately 5 minutes.

5. Drain on paper towels, dust with confectioner's sugar and serve hot.

RECIPE 26.15

Bananas Foster

BRENNAN'S, NEW ORLEANS, LA
Chef Michael Roussel

Yield: 4 servings
Method: Sautéing

Whole butter	60 g	2 oz.
Brown sugar	225 g	8 oz.
Cinnamon	2 g	1/2 tsp.
Banana liqueur	60 mL	2 fl. oz.
Bananas, cut into quarters	4	4
White rum	60 mL	2 fl. oz.
Vanilla ice cream	4 scoops	4 scoops

1. Combine the butter, sugar and cinnamon in a sauté or flambé pan. Cook over low heat, stirring until the sugar dissolves.

2. Stir in the banana liqueur, then place the bananas in the pan. When the bananas soften and begin to brown, carefully add the rum.

3. Continue to cook until the rum is hot, then tip the pan slightly and ignite the rum. When the flames subside, lift the bananas out of the pan and place 4 pieces over each portion of ice cream. Spoon the warm sauce over the ice cream and serve immediately.

Bananas Foster

Bananas Foster was created in 1951 by Brennan's chef Paul Blangé to promote New Orleans' role as the major port of entry for bananas arriving from Central and South America. The dish was named for Richard Foster, chairman of the New Orleans Crime Commission, a civic group working to clean up the French Quarter. Foster was a good friend to Owen Edward Brennan and a frequent customer at his restaurant. Today Brennan's flambés some 15 875 kg (35 000 lb.) of bananas each year for this world-famous dessert.

RECIPE 26.15

Approximate values per serving:	
Calories	555
Total fat	15 g
Saturated fat	9 g
Cholesterol	40 mg
Sodium	161 mg
Total carbohydrates	93 g
Protein	2 g

RECIPE 26.16

Oven-Roasted Vanilla Pears with Brie-Nut Crumble and Warm Buckwheat-Thyme Honey

ADAPTED FROM OLAF MERTENS, *COOKING FROM THE HIP* (WHITECAP BOOKS, 2002)

Yield: 20 portions
Method: Poaching and Baking

Pears, ripe, peeled	10	10
Vanilla beans, split and scraped	2-1/2	2-1/2
Cinnamon, ground	15 g	2 Tbsp.
Maple syrup	600 mL	16 fl. oz.
White wine	1.5 L	2 bottles
Lemons, zested	2-1/2	2-1/2
Brie-Nut Crumble:		
Brie, rind on	600 g	1-1/4 lb.
Butter, unsalted	150 g	5 oz.
Flour	300 g	10 oz.
Pecans, ground	300 g	10 oz.
Hazelnuts, ground	300 g	10 oz.
Pistachio, ground	300 g	10 oz.
Warm Buckwheat-Thyme Honey:		
Buckwheat honey	200 g	6 fl. oz.
Thyme sprigs	5 g	1

RECIPE 26.16

Approximate values per serving:	
Calories	588
Total fat	42 g
Saturated fat	12 g
Cholesterol	47 mg
Sodium	255 mg
Total carbohydrates	44 g
Protein	15 g

continued

1. Split the pears in half lengthways, remove the core and trim a small slice off the curve to allow each pear to sit flat later on the baking tray.
2. Combine the vanilla, cinnamon, maple syrup, wine and lemon zest in a noncorrosive pot and bring to a boil.
3. Immerse the pear halves and poach for 10 minutes or until pears are tender.
4. Remove pears with a slotted spoon and place on a nonstick baking tray.
5. Place a 30-g (1-oz.) cube of Brie on each pear half.
6. Combine the crumble ingredients and divide among the pears.
7. Bake in a 190°C (375°F) oven for 5 minutes or until golden.
8. Infuse the honey and thyme by heating the honey for 5 minutes.
9. To serve, plate the pear halves and drizzle some of the honey around.

NOTE: This would work well as a buffet dessert in chafing dishes. Half-pears will yield 20 portions and quarter-pears will yield 40 portions.

Clayton Folkers

Born in Canada, Clayton earned his Commercial Cooking Diploma from the Northern Alberta Institute of Technology and was invited by the Four Seasons Hotel to extend his work-study program with them into a permanent position. To enhance his pastry skills, Clayton attended the Provinciaal Hoger Instituut PIVA in Antwerp, Belgium, where he completed a graduate program while gaining experience as a Production Chef in a prominent pastry shop. Back in Edmonton, he honed his pastry skills at the Four Seasons Hotel, at La Favorite Pastry Shop, which he co-owned, and at the Shaw Conference Centre, where he was Pastry Chef. He joined NAIT in 2007.

RECIPE 26.17

Approximate values per leaf:	
Calories	15
Total fat	0 g
Saturated fat	0 g
Cholesterol	0 mg
Sodium	0 mg
Total carbohydrates	4 g
Protein	0 g

RECIPE 26.17

Dried Strawberry Leaves

HOKANSON SCHOOL OF CULINARY ARTS, NAIT, EDMONTON, AB
Pastry Chef Clayton Folkers

Yield: 50 leaves

Red Delicious apples	225 g	2
Lemon juice, fresh	25 mL	1-1/2 Tbsp.
Fresh strawberry purée	600 g	20 oz.
Sugar	100 g	3-1/2 oz.
Orange juice	60 mL	2 fl. oz.

1. Peel and core the apples. Purée with lemon juice until smooth.
2. Continue blending while slowly adding the strawberry purée.
3. Add the sugar and orange juice and blend until smooth.
4. Place template on silicone baking pad and spread the pulp.
5. Dry in a 95°C (200°F) convection oven for 30–35 minutes.
6. Remove leaves from pad while still warm.
7. Store in a warm, dry place.

Joseph Kumar

Joseph trained in his native Singapore, where he gained his first experience at Marco-Polo and Shangri-La. In Canada, he has been Corporate Pastry Chef for the Liberty Group and Promotional Chef for Lindt of Switzerland (Canada). Since 1999, he has been a Baking and Pastry Arts instructor at Humber College, where he has also acted as coach for culinary teams.

RECIPE 26.18

Fruit Sushi

HUMBER COLLEGE, TORONTO, ON
Professor Joseph Kumar

Yield: 4 rolls

Chocolate Plastique

Bitter chocolate	400 g	1 lb.
White corn syrup	160 mL	6-1/2 fl. oz.

1. Warm the corn syrup by placing it over a warm water bath or microwaving it on low power.

continued

2. Melt the chocolate over a bain marie and mix in the warm corn syrup.

3. Wrap and let rest at room temperature for 3 hours. The mixture will be firm. Divide the mixture into 4 pieces and knead each one before rolling out.

Lychee Coconut Rice Pudding

Lychee fruit	200 g	8 oz.
Coconut milk	800 mL	32 fl. oz.
Cream, 35%	800 mL	32 fl. oz.
Jasmine rice	230 g	9 oz.
Sugar	200 g	8 oz.

1. Chop the lychee fruit in a blender and reserve in the refrigerator.

2. Combine the remaining ingredients in a saucepan and simmer, stirring frequently, for approximately 25 minutes or when the rice is cooked and very thick.

3. Transfer to a bowl, cover and cool completely. Add the lychee and mix.

Marinated Fruits

Kiwi, peeled	4	4
Mango, peeled	2	2
Strawberries, washed, hulled	12	12
Grand Marnier	120 mL	5 fl. oz.
Simple syrup	120 mL	5 fl. oz.

1. Slice the fruit into batonettes.

2. Combine Grand Marnier and syrup, pour over fruit and marinate for 2–3 hours.

Garnish

Cocoa powder	as needed	as needed
Kiwi purée	as needed	as needed
Sesame Caramel Sauce		
(see Recipe 32.13)	as needed	as needed

1. To assemble, dust table with cocoa powder and roll out each sheet of kneaded plastique into a rectangle 18 × 28 cm (7 × 12 in.). Trim edges.

2. Spread 225 g of pudding on each sheet, leaving a 6-mm (1/4-in.) strip on the long side.

3. Drain and towel-dry the fruit and arrange in a strip along the long edge with the rice even with it.

4. Roll up firmly to form a log. Trim off both ends and dust off excess cocoa powder. Slice into 2.5-cm (1-in.) pieces.

5. Arrange 3 pieces per plate and garnish with kiwi purée and Sesame Caramel Sauce.

RECIPE 26.18

Approximate values per serving:	
Calories	570
Total fat	41 g
Saturated fat	28 g
Cholesterol	65 mg
Sodium	37 mg
Total carbohydrates	55 g
Protein	6.3 g

Xango

This South American offering can be made with different fruits and flavourings—
a dessert item that works well as part of a breakfast-brunch offering.
We got the idea from Moxie's Restaurants.

Yield: 10 pieces
Method: Deep-fat frying

Bananas, peeled and split in half lengthwise	5	5
Pastry cream	600 mL	20 fl. oz.
Flour tortilla, 22 cm (8 in.)	10	10
Egg white	25 mL	1
Oil for deep-fat frying	as needed	as needed
Cinnamon sugar	as needed	as needed
Caramel sauce	250 mL	8 fl. oz.

1. Place half a banana and 60 mL (2 fl. oz.) of pastry cream along the centre of each tortilla.

2. Fold the sides of the tortilla in and roll the tortilla around the filling. Before you complete the roll, brush the end part with egg white to allow for a positive seal. Finish wrapping the Xango tightly and reserve on a tray, covered. Repeat.

3. Deep-fat fry the Xangos until golden, drain and roll in cinnamon sugar.

4. Arrange on a serving plate with a drizzle of caramel sauce. Chocolate sauce works well too. You may split the Xango in 2 for presentation purposes.

RECIPE 26.19

Approximate values per serving:	
Calories	589
Total fat	28 g
Saturated fat	4.8 g
Cholesterol	58 mg
Sodium	423 mg
Total carbohydrates	81 g
Protein	8.3 g

Principles of the Bakeshop 27

" No one who cooks, cooks alone. Even at her most solitary,
a cook in the kitchen is surrounded by generations of cooks past,
the advice and menus of cooks present, the wisdom of
cookbook writers.

—Laurie Colwin, American writer (1944–1992)

Flour, sugar, eggs, milk, butter, flavourings—

with this simple list of ingredients you can produce a seemingly endless variety of goods, from breads to sauces to pastries. But to produce consistently good brioche, Bavarians, biscuits or the like, you must pay careful attention to the character and quantity of each ingredient, the way the ingredients are combined and how heat is applied to them. Unlike a cut of meat that can be grilled, roasted, sautéed or braised and still be the same cut of meat, bakeshop products depend on careful, precise preparation for their very identity.

Accurate measurements are critical in the bakeshop. It is equally important to follow bakeshop **formulas** carefully and completely. Unlike the rest of the kitchen, mistakes in the bakeshop often cannot be discovered until the product is finished, by which time it is too late to correct them. For example, if you omit the salt when preparing a stew, the mistake can be corrected by adding salt at service time. If you omit the salt from a loaf of bread, however, the mistake cannot be corrected after the bread has baked—and its texture and flavour may be ruined as a result. To follow a written formula, to measure ingredients precisely and to combine them accurately are more important in the bakeshop than anywhere else in the kitchen.

BAKESHOP TOOLS AND EQUIPMENT

As a beginning cook, you may find the tools of the bakeshop a bit complex. Indeed, the tools required for a professional pâtisserie are quite specialized. A well-equipped cook need not be concerned with possessing every gadget

Bakeshop Tools (clockwise from centre back): cake turntable, cake pans, flan ring, tartlet pans, cannoli form, offset spatulas, flat cake spatula, blade for scoring breads, flower nail, rectangular tartlet pans, piping bag and tips, metal spatula, dough cutter, rolling pin, springform pan, copper sugar pot (on cooling rack), nest of round cutters

available, but should recognize and be familiar with most of the items shown in the photograph on page 688. Although many of these hand tools will make a task easier, most can be improvised by a creative cook. Several of the items shown, such as the springform pans, tartlet pans and petit four moulds, are used for shaping or holding batters and doughs. The various spatulas and pallet knives are used for spreading icings or fillings. The piping tools and cake comb are used for decorating and finishing baked goods.

When purchasing tools and equipment, look for quality and durability. As your baking skills grow, so will your equipment selection.

Bakeshop ovens may be conventional, convection or steam injection models. Convection ovens can reduce cooking time, but the air currents may damage delicate products such as spongecake or puff pastry. Steam injection ovens use conventional heat flow but allow the baker to add steam automatically to the cooking chamber as needed to produce crisp-crusted breads. Although expensive, steam injection ovens are a necessity for commercial bakeries and most larger restaurant and hotel bakeshops. Baking instructions in the following chapters are based on the use of a conventional oven. If a convection oven is used instead, remember that the temperature and baking time may need to be reduced.

INGREDIENTS

Although substituting ingredients may have little or no effect on some dishes (you can use carrots instead of turnips in a stew, for instance), this is not the case with baked goods. Different flours, fats, liquids and sweeteners function differently. Bread flour and cake flour are not the same, nor are shortening and butter. If you substitute one ingredient for another, the results will be different.

Understanding ingredients, why they function the way they do and how to adjust for their differences will make your baking experiences more successful and consistent. This chapter discusses **flours**, **sugar** and other sweeteners, **fats**, thickeners and **flavourings** such as chocolate, extracts and liquors. Eggs and dairy products, also common in baked goods, are discussed in Chapter 8, Eggs and Dairy Products.

Flours

Wheat Flour

Wheat flour (Fr. *farine*) is produced by milling wheat kernels (berries). As discussed in Chapter 23, Potatoes, Grains and Pasta, a wheat kernel has an outer covering called bran. It comprises several layers that protect the endosperm, which contains starches and proteins. The innermost part is the germ, which contains fat and serves as the wheat seed (see Figure 23.1). During milling, the kernels first pass through metal rollers to crack them, then the bran and germ are removed through repeated stages of sifting and separation. The remaining endosperm is then ground into flour. Flour derived from the portion of the endosperm closest to the germ (**patent flour**) is finer; flour derived from the portion of the endosperm nearer the bran (**clear flour**) is coarser and darker.

The character of the wheat determines the character of the flour. Wheats are classified as *soft* or *hard* depending on the kernel's hardness. The harder the wheat kernel, the higher its protein content. Soft wheat yields a soft flour with a low protein content. Soft flour, also called weak flour, is best for tender products such as cakes. Hard wheat yields a hard flour with a high protein content. Hard flour, also known as strong or patent flour, is used for yeast breads.

World's Best

The Canadian Prairies produce among the best hard wheat flour in the world. Hard Red Spring #1 is a variety renowned for its protein content and results in superior breads. Pasta manufacturers have many facilities in Western Canada as well. They take advantage of the supply of durum wheat, prized for making the best dried pastas.

● **flour** a powdery substance of varying degrees of fineness made by milling grains such as wheat, corn or rye

● **sugar** a carbohydrate that provides the body with energy and gives a sweet taste to foods

● **fats** (1) a group of compounds comprising oxygen, hydrogen and carbon atoms that supply the body with energy (9 calories per gram); fats are classified as saturated, nonsaturated or polyunsaturated; (2) the general term for butter, lard, shortening, oil and margarine used as cooking media or ingredients

● **flavouring** an item that adds a new taste to a food and alters its natural flavours; flavourings include herbs, spices, vinegars and condiments

● **patent flour** flour made from the portion of the endosperm closest to the germ

● **clear flour** flour made from the portion of the endosperm nearer to the bran; it is coarser and darker than patent flour

Various types of flour are created by mixing or blending flours from different sources. All-purpose flour is a blend of approximately two-thirds hard and one-third soft flours. Widely used in home applications, it can be substituted in some recipes. Professional bakeshops rarely use all-purpose flour; instead, they choose flours specifically milled and blended for industrial uses.

Aging and Bleaching

Any flour develops better baking qualities if allowed to rest for several weeks after milling. Freshly milled flour produces sticky doughs and products with less volume than those made with aged flour. While aging, flour turns white through a natural oxidation process referred to as bleaching.

Natural aging and bleaching are somewhat unpredictable, time-consuming processes, however, so chemicals are now used to do both. Benzoyl peroxide and chlorine dioxide gas rapidly age flour. Chlorine dioxide and other chemicals bleach flour by removing yellow pigments in order to obtain a uniform white colour. Bleaching destroys small amounts of the flour's naturally occurring vitamin E, which is replaced in fortified or enriched products.

Composition of Flour

Flour comprises primarily five nutrients: fat, minerals, moisture, starches and proteins. Fat and minerals each generally account for less than 1% of flour's content. The moisture content of flour is also relatively low—when packaged, it cannot exceed 15% under government standards. However, its actual moisture content varies depending on climatic conditions and storage. In damp areas, flour absorbs moisture from the atmosphere.

Starches compose 63% to 77% of flour and are necessary for the absorption of moisture during baking. This process, known as **gelatinization**, occurs primarily at temperatures above 60°C (140°F). Starches also provide food for yeast during **fermentation**.

Flour proteins are important because of their gluten-forming potential. **Gluten** is the tough, rubbery substance created when wheat flour is mixed with water. Gluten strands are both plastic (i.e., they change shape under pressure) and elastic (they resume their original shape when that pressure is removed). Gluten is responsible for the volume, texture and appearance of baked goods. It provides structure and enables dough to retain the gases given off by leavening agents. Without gluten, there could be no raised breads: the gases created by yeast fermentation or chemical leaveners would simply escape if there were no network of gluten strands to trap them in the dough.

The higher a flour's protein content, the greater that flour's gluten-forming potential. The proteins responsible for gluten formation are *glutenin* and *gliadin*. Flour does not contain gluten; only a dough or batter can contain gluten. Gluten is produced when glutenin and gliadin are moistened and manipulated, as when they are stirred or kneaded. Generally, the longer a substance is mixed, the more gluten will develop. Products requiring a dough that can be kneaded and shaped, such as French rolls, require a flour with a higher protein content than products meant to be tender, such as cakes or muffins.

Table 27.1 on the next page lists the protein content and uses for several common flours. Remember that substitutions will result in a changed and probably less desirable product.

Specialty Flours
Whole Wheat

Whole wheat flour, also referred to as graham flour, is made by milling the entire wheat kernel, except the germ. Whole wheat flour has a nutty, sweet flavour and

● **gelatinization** the process by which starch granules are cooked; they absorb moisture when placed in a liquid and heated; as the moisture is absorbed, the product swells, softens and clarifies slightly

● **fermentation** the process by which yeast converts sugar into alcohol and carbon dioxide; it also refers to the time that yeast dough is left to rise

● **gluten** an elastic network of proteins created when wheat flour is moistened and manipulated

TABLE 27.1	Protein Content of Flours	
Type of Flour	Percent Protein	Uses
Cake	7–9.5	Tender cakes
Pastry	7.5–10	Biscuits, pie crusts
All-purpose	10–13	General baking
Bread (patent or clear)	12–15	Yeast breads
Whole wheat (straight)	13–14	Breads
High gluten (vital)	75–80	Bagels; to increase protein content of weaker flours (such as rye, whole grain and specialty flours) for bread making

brown, flecked colour. Products made with whole wheat flour will be denser and have less volume than those made with white flour. Whole wheat milled with the germ is not a commercial commodity in Canada because the fat content of the germ may cause rancidity. Whole wheat flour with germ is available in health food stores. Toasted wheat germ can replace up to one-third of the wheat flour in a formula if more fibre and flavour and a denser texture are desired. Gluten development is more difficult with whole wheat flour due to the bran content.

Whole Wheat Flour

Self-Rising

Self-rising flour is an all-purpose flour to which salt and a chemical **leavener**, usually baking powder, have been added. It is not recommended for professional use. Chemicals lose their leavening ability over time and may cause inconsistent results. Furthermore, different formulas call for different ratios of salt and leaveners; no commercial blend is appropriate for all purposes.

● **leavener** an ingredient or process that produces or incorporates gases in a baked product in order to increase volume, provide structure and give texture

Nonwheat Flours

Nonwheat flours, also referred to as composite flours, are made from grains, seeds or beans. Corn, soybeans, rice, oats, buckwheat, potatoes and other items provide flours, but none of them contains the gluten-forming proteins of wheat flour. Composite flours are generally blended with a high-protein wheat flour for baking. Substituting a composite flour for wheat flour changes the flavour and texture of the product.

Specialized bakeries produce gluten-free products for people with celiac sprue. Combinations of starches are used in addition to other ingredients to produce products with texture. Care must be taken not to contaminate gluten-free products with flours that form gluten.

Rye flour is commonly used in bread baking. It is milled from the rye berry much as wheat flour is milled from the wheat berry. Rye flour comes in four grades or colours: white, medium, dark and pumpernickel. White rye flour is made from only the centre of the rye berry. Medium and dark rye flours are made from the whole rye berry after the bran is removed. Pumpernickel is made by grinding the entire rye berry, including the bran. All rye flours have a warm, pungent flavour similar to caraway and a grey-brown colour. Although rye flour contains proteins, they will not form gluten, so a bread made with 100% rye flour will be dense and flat. Therefore, rye flour is usually blended with a high-protein wheat flour to produce a more acceptable product.

Vital Wheat Gluten

Vital wheat gluten (gluten flour) is the pure protein extracted from wheat flour. Averaging 75% protein content, it is used to boost the protein content of rye and whole wheat flours.

Rye Flour

Nutrition

Flours are generally high in carbohydrates and low in fat. The grains from which they are milled are often rich in vitamins and minerals. Some of these nutrients, however, are lost during milling. In enriched flours, thiamin, riboflavin, niacin and iron are added at levels set by the government.

Purchasing and Storing

Most flours are purchased in 20- and 40-kg (50- and 100-lb.) bags. They should be stored in a well-ventilated room at temperatures no higher than 27°C (80°F). Flour can be stored in a refrigerator or freezer if necessary to prevent the onset of rancidity if the germ is present. Refrigeration may cause the flour to absorb moisture, however, which will limit the flour's ability to absorb additional moisture during actual use.

An open bag of flour should be transferred to a closed container to prevent contamination. Even unopened bags of flour should not be stored near items with strong odours, as flour readily absorbs odours.

Sugar and Sweeteners

Sugar (Fr. *sucre*) and other sweeteners serve several purposes in the bakeshop. They provide flavour and colour, tenderize products by weakening gluten strands, provide food for yeasts, act as a preservative to increase shelf life (keeping qualities) by retaining moisture and act as a creaming or foaming agent to assist with leavening. Sugars also give colour to crusts.

Sugar

Sugars are carbohydrates. They are classified as either (1) single or simple sugars (monosaccharides) such as glucose and fructose, which occur naturally in honey and fruits, or (2) double or complex sugars (disaccharides), which may occur naturally, such as lactose in milk or in refined sugars.

● **sucrose** the chemical name for common refined sugar; it is a disaccharide, composed of one molecule each of glucose and fructose

The sugar most often used in the kitchen is **sucrose**, a refined sugar obtained from both the large tropical grass called sugar cane and the root of the sugar beet. Sucrose is a disaccharide, comprising one molecule each of glucose and fructose. The chemical composition of beet and cane sugars is identical. The two products taste, look, smell and react the same. Sucrose is available in many forms: white granulated, light or dark brown granulated, molasses or powdered.

Sugar Manufacturing

Common refined or table sugar is produced from sugar cane or sugar beets. The first step in sugar production is to crush the cane or beet to extract the juice. This juice contains tannins, pigments, proteins and other undesirable components that must be removed through refinement. Refinement begins by dissolving the juice in water, then boiling it in large steam evaporators. The solution is then crystallized in heated vacuum pans. The uncrystallized liquid byproduct, known as molasses, is separated out in a centrifuge. The remaining crystallized product, known as raw sugar, contains many impurities and is considered unfit for direct use in food.

Raw sugar is washed with steam to remove some of the impurities. This yields a product known as demerara sugar. Refining continues as the demerara is heated, liquefied, centrifuged and filtered. Chemicals may be used to bleach and purify the liquid sugar. Finally, the clear liquid sugar is recrystallized in vacuum pans as granulated white sugar.

Pure sucrose is sold in granulated and powdered forms and is available in several grades. Because there are no government standards regulating grade labels, various manufacturers' products may differ slightly.

Types of Sugar

Demerara sugar, sometimes called turbinado sugar, is the closest consumable product to raw sugar. It is partially refined, light brown in colour, with coarse crystals and a caramel flavour. It is sometimes used in beverages and certain baked goods. Because of its high and variable moisture content, demerara sugar is not recommended as a substitute for granulated or brown sugar.

Sanding sugar has a large, coarse crystal structure that prevents it from dissolving easily. It is used almost exclusively for decorating cookies and pastries.

Regular granulated sugar is the all-purpose sugar used throughout the kitchen. The crystals are a fine, uniform size suitable for a variety of purposes.

Sugar cubes are formed by pressing moistened granulated sugar into moulds and allowing it to dry. Cube sugar is most often used for beverage service.

Brown sugar is simply regular refined sugar with some of the molasses returned to it. Light brown sugar contains approximately 3.5% molasses; dark brown sugar contains about 6.5%. Molasses adds moisture and a distinctive flavour. Brown sugar can be substituted for refined sugar, measure for measure, in any formula where its flavour is desired. Because of the added moisture, brown sugar tends to lump, trapping air into pockets. It should be measured by weight; if measured by volume, it should be packed firmly into the measuring cup in order to remove any air pockets. Always store brown sugar in an airtight container to prevent it from drying and hardening.

Superfine sugar is granulated sugar with a smaller-sized crystal. Also known as castor sugar, it can be produced by processing regular granulated sugar in a food processor for a few moments. Superfine sugar dissolves quickly in liquids and produces light and tender cakes.

Icing or **confectioner's sugar** (Fr. *sucre en poudre*) is made by grinding granulated sugar crystals through varying degrees of fine screens. Icing sugar cannot be made in a food processor. It is widely available in three degrees of fineness: 10× is the finest and most common; 6× and 4× are progressively coarser. Because of icing sugar's tendency to lump, 3% cornstarch is added to absorb moisture. Icing sugar is most often used in icings and glazes and for decorating baked products.

Clockwise from top left: Demerara Sugar Cubes, Light Brown Sugar, Icing Sugar, Sugar Cubes, Brown Sugar Crystals, Granulated Sugar

Liquid Sweeteners

Liquid sweeteners can be used to achieve the same benefits as sugar, except for leavening, in baked goods. Most of these liquids have a distinctive flavour as well as sweetness. Some liquid sweeteners are made from sugar cane; others are derived from other plants, grains or bees.

Corn syrup (Fr. *sirop de maïs*) is produced by extracting starch from corn kernels and treating it with acid or an enzyme to develop a sweet syrup. This syrup is extremely thick or viscous and less sweet-tasting than honey or refined sugar. Its viscosity gives foods a thick, chewy texture. Corn syrup is available in light and dark forms; the dark syrup has caramel colour and flavour added. Corn syrup is a **hygroscopic** (water-attracting) sweetener, which means it will attract water from the air on humid days and lose water through evaporation more slowly than granulated sugar. Thus, it keeps products moister and fresher longer.

Honey (Fr. *miel*) is a powerful sweetener comprising fructose and glucose. It is created by honey bees from nectar collected from flowers. Its flavour and colour vary depending on the season, the type of flower the nectar came from

● **hygroscopic** describes a food that readily absorbs moisture from the air

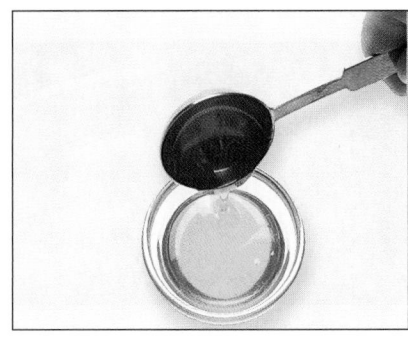

Honey

and its age. Commercial honey is often a blend, prepared to be relatively neutral and consistent. Like corn syrup, honey is highly hygroscopic. Its distinctive flavour is found in several ethnic foods such as baklava and halvah, and beverages such as Drambuie and Benedictine.

Maple syrup (Fr. *sirop d'érable*) is made from the sap of sugar maple trees. Sap is collected during the spring, then boiled to evaporate its water content, yielding a sweet brown syrup. One sugar maple tree produces about 48 L (12 gal.) of sap each season; 120 to 160 L (30 to 40 gal.) of sap will produce about 4 L (1 gal.) of syrup. Pure maple syrup must weigh not less than 1.25 kg per litre; it is graded according to colour, flavour and sugar content. The more desirable products, Canada No. 1, light and medium, have a light amber colour and delicate flavour. Pure maple syrup is expensive, but it does add a distinct flavour to baked goods, frostings and, of course, pancakes and waffles.

Maple-flavoured syrups, often served with pancakes, are usually corn syrups with artificial colourings and flavourings added. Birch tree syrup is a prized product when available.

As mentioned earlier, **molasses** (Fr. *mélasse*) is the liquid byproduct of sugar refining. Edible molasses is derived only from cane sugar as beet molasses has an unpleasant odour and bitter flavour. *Unsulphured molasses* is not a true byproduct of sugar making. It is intentionally produced from pure cane syrup and is preferred because of its lighter colour and milder flavour. *Sulphured molasses* is a byproduct and contains some of the sulphur dioxide used in secondary sugar processing. It is darker and has a strong, bitter flavour.

The final stage of sucrose refinement yields *blackstrap molasses*, which is somewhat popular in the American South. Blackstrap molasses is very dark and thick, with a strong, unique flavour that is unsuitable for most purposes.

Sorghum molasses is produced by cooking down the sweet sap of a brown corn plant, known as sorghum, which is grown for animal feed. The flavour and appearance of sorghum molasses are almost identical to unsulphured sugar cane molasses.

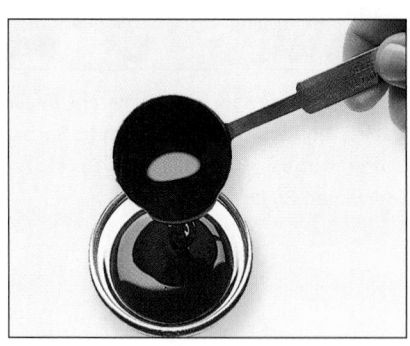
Molasses

Nutrition

Sweeteners are carbohydrates. They are high in calories and contain no fibre, protein, fat, vitamin A or vitamin C. They contain only trace amounts of thiamin, riboflavin and niacin.

Cooking Sugar

Sugar can be incorporated into a prepared item in its dry form or first liquefied into a syrup. **Sugar syrups** (not to be confused with liquid sweeteners such as molasses) take two forms: **simple syrups**, which are mixtures of sugar and water, and **cooked syrups**, which are made of melted sugar cooked until it reaches a specific temperature. Be extremely careful when working with hot sugar syrup. Because sugar reaches very high temperatures, it can cause severe burns.

Simple Sugar Syrups

Simple or stock syrups are solutions of sugar and water. They are used in the bakeshop to moisten cakes and to make sauces, fruit sorbets, buttercreams and candied fruits.

The syrup's density or concentration is dictated by its intended purpose. Cold water will dissolve up to double its weight in sugar; heating the solution forms denser, more concentrated syrups. A **hydrometer**, which measures

● **sugar syrups** either **simple syrups** (thin mixtures of sugar and water) or **cooked syrups** (melted sugar cooked until it reaches a specific temperature)

● **hydrometer** a device used to measure specific gravity; it shows degrees of concentration on the Baumé scale

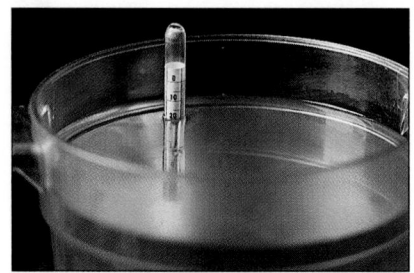
Using a Baumé hydrometer

specific gravity and shows degrees of concentration on the Baumé scale (see photo on page 694), is the most accurate guide to density.

Simple syrups can be prepared without the aid of a hydrometer, however. To make a simple sugar syrup, specific amounts of water and sugar are combined in a saucepan and brought to a boil. Once the solution boils, it is important not to stir it, as this may cause recrystallization or lumping. For successful simple sugar syrups, the following formulas must be followed precisely:

- *Light syrup*—Boil 2 parts water with 1 part sugar by weight for 1 minute. This concentration would measure 17–20° on the Baumé scale. A light syrup can be used for making sorbet or moistening spongecake.

- *Medium syrup*—Boil 1 part sugar with 1.5 parts water by weight for 1 minute. This concentration would measure 21–24° on the Baumé scale. A medium syrup can be used for candying citrus peel.

- *Heavy syrup*—Boil equal weights of water and sugar for 1 minute. This concentration would measure 28–30° on the Baumé scale, and the solution should be at 104°C (220°F). Heavy syrup is a basic, all-purpose syrup kept on hand in many bakeshops and diluted as needed.

Cooked Sugars

Caramel sauce, candy and other confections often need liquid sugar that will have a cooked caramel flavour or be firm when cool. For these purposes, sugar needs to be cooked to temperatures far higher than for simple syrups. A small amount of water is generally added at the beginning to help the sugar dissolve evenly. As the mixture boils, the water evaporates, the solution's temperature rises and its density increases. The syrup's concentration depends on the amount of water remaining in the final solution: the less water, the harder the syrup will become when cool.

The sugar's temperature indicates its concentration. If there is a great deal of water present, the temperature will not rise much above 100°C (212°F). As water evaporates, however, the temperature will rise until it reaches 160°C (320°F), the point at which all water is evaporated. At temperatures above 160°C (320°F), the pure sugar begins to brown or caramelize. As sugar caramelizes, its sweetening power decreases dramatically. At approximately 190°C (375°F), sugar will burn, developing a bitter flavour. If allowed to continue cooking, sugar will ignite.

Sugar solutions are unstable because of their molecular structure. They can recrystallize because of agitation or uneven heat distribution. Several steps should be taken to prevent recrystallization:

1. Always use a heavy, clean saucepan, preferably copper.

2. Stir the solution to make sure all sugar crystals dissolve before it reaches a boil. Do not stir the solution after it begins boiling, however.

3. An interferent may be added when the solution begins to boil. Cream of tartar, vinegar, glucose (a monosaccharide) and lemon juice are known as *interferents* because they interfere with the formation of sugar crystals. Some formulas specify which interferent to use, although most are used in such small quantities that their taste cannot be detected.

4. Brush down the sides of the pan with cold water to wash off crystals that may be deposited there. These sugar crystals may seed the solution, causing more crystals (lumps) to form if not removed. Instead of using a brush to wash away crystals, you can cover the pan for a few moments as soon as the solution comes to a boil. Steam will condense on the cover and run down the sides of the pan, washing away the crystals.

Caramelizing sugar

Washing sugar crystals from the side of the pan

SAFETY ALERT
Hot Sugar Syrups

Sugar syrups can be heated to very high temperatures. They also stick to surfaces, including skin, which causes a deeper, more severe burn. Do not touch liquefied or caramelized sugar with your bare hand until it has cooled completely.

The concentration of sugar syrup should be determined with a candy thermometer that measures very high temperatures. If a thermometer is not available, use the traditional but less accurate ice-water test: Spoon a few drops of the hot sugar into a bowl of very cold water. Check the hardness of the cooled sugar with your fingertips. Each stage of cooked sugar is named according to its firmness when cool—for example, soft ball or hard crack.

Table 27.2 lists the various stages of cooked sugar and the temperature for each. Each stage is also identified by the ice-water test result. Note that even a few degrees makes a difference in the syrup's concentration.

TABLE 27.2	Stages of Cooked Sucrose Sugar	
Stage	**Temperature**	**Ice-Water Test**
Thread	110°C (236°F)	Spins a 5-cm (2-in.) thread when dropped
Soft ball	116°C (240°F)	Forms a soft ball
Firm ball	119°C (246°F)	Forms a firm ball
Hard ball	125°C (260°F)	Forms a hard, compact ball
Soft crack	132°C (270°F)	Separates into a hard, but not brittle, thread
Hard crack	149°C (300°F)	Separates into a hard, brittle sheet
Caramel	170°C (338°F)	Liquid turns dark brown in the pan

Soft ball stage

Hard ball stage

Hard crack stage

Fats

Fat is the general term for butter, lard, oil and margarine. Shortenings are hydrogenated vegetable oils. Fats provide flavour and colour, add moisture and richness, assist with leavening, help extend a product's shelf life and shorten gluten strands.

The flavour and texture of a baked good depends on the type of fat used and the manner in which it is incorporated with other ingredients. In pastry doughs, solid fat shortens or tenderizes the gluten strands; in bread doughs, fat increases loaf volume and lightness; in cake batters, fat incorporates air bubbles and helps leaven the mixture. Fats should be selected based on their flavour, melting point and ability to form emulsions.

Most bakeshop ingredients combine completely with liquids; fats do not. Fats will not dissolve but will break down into smaller and smaller particles through mixing. With proper mixing, these fat particles are distributed, more or less evenly, throughout the other ingredients.

All-Purpose Shortening

Any fat is a shortening in baking because it shortens gluten strands and tenderizes the product. What is generally referred to as shortening, however, is a type of solid, white, generally tasteless fat, specially formulated for baking. Shortenings are made from animal fats and/or vegetable oils that are solidified through hydrogenation. These products are 100% fat, with a relatively high melting point. Solid shortenings are ideal for greasing baking pans because they are tasteless and odourless.

Emulsified Shortening

Emulsifiers may be added to regular shortening to assist with moisture absorption and retention as well as leavening. Emulsified shortenings, also known as high-ratio shortenings, are used in the commercial production of cakes and frostings where the formula contains a large amount of sugar. If a formula calls for an emulsified shortening, use it. If you substitute any other fat, the product's texture suffers.

Lard

Lard (Fr. *saindoux*) is rendered pork fat. It is a solid white product of almost 100% pure fat; it contains only a small amount of water. Lard yields flaky, flavourful pastries, such as pie crusts, but is rarely used commercially because it turns rancid quickly and is not acceptable to some religious beliefs.

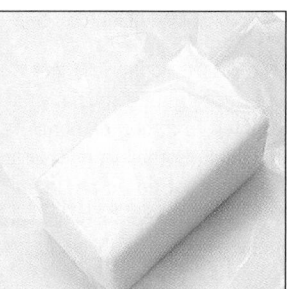

Lard

Butter and Margarine

Butter is prized in the bakeshop for its flavour; however, it melts at a relatively low temperature of 33°C (93°F) and burns easily. Unsalted butter is preferred for baking because it tends to be fresher, and additional salt might interfere with product formulas. Margarine melts at a slightly higher temperature than butter, making it useful for some rolled-in doughs such as puff pastry or danish. For detailed information on butter and margarine see Chapter 8, Eggs and Dairy Products. Whole butter is approximately 80% fat.

Oil

Unlike butter and other fats, oil blends evenly throughout a mixture. It therefore coats more of the proteins, and the gluten strands produced are much shorter, a desirable result in fine-textured products such as muffins or chiffon cakes. For baking, select a neutral-flavoured oil unless the distinctive taste of olive oil is desired, as in some breads. Never substitute oil in a formula requiring a solid shortening. For detailed information on oil, see Chapter 7, Flavours and Flavourings.

Nutrition

Fats are high in calories and contain varying levels of saturated fats. Although they have no carbohydrates, a few fats such as butter have trace amounts of protein and minerals. Butter is also high in vitamin A.

Thickeners

Starches

Starches are often used as thickening agents in bakeshop products. Cornstarch, arrowroot, instant starch, waxy maize and flour can be used as thickeners for pastry creams, sauces, custards and fruit fillings. **Cornstarch** is a grain-based starch. It must be dissolved in cold water, then added to the mixture to be thickened and then heated. Once it reaches just below the boiling point it

Modified Starches

The use of modified corn starches produced from waxy maize is increasing. They are manufactured to provide controlled thickening under various conditions. The best products are precooked and work either hot or cold. Premium products will have acid resistance and a high shear value. Frozen products can be successfully thawed without "breaking," particularly if they were shock-frozen.

must be cooked until it thickens into an opaque gel. Products thickened with cornstarch should not be vigorously stirred once cooled or they can break down and soften. Products thickened with cornstarch tend to separate when thawed after freezing.

Arrowroot is dissolved in cold water and added to a liquid to thicken it. Used primarily to thicken hot sauces, arrowroot can break down if overcooked, making it most appropriate for thickening sauces that will be served immediately.

Although less commonly encountered in professional bakeshops, tapioca can be used to thicken a variety of pastry products. **Tapioca** is a starch produced from the root of the tropical cassava (manioc) plant. It is available as a flour or as balls, referred to as pearls. Tapioca flour can be used in the same manner as cornstarch to thicken sauces and fruit mixtures. Pearl tapioca is used to thicken milk for tapioca pudding or to thicken fruit pie fillings. Most pearl tapioca must be soaked in a cold liquid for several hours before cooking. Instant tapioca, which is smaller, needs to soak for only 20 to 30 minutes before cooking.

Pearl Tapioca

● **gelatin** a flavourless, odourless and brittle mixture of proteins (especially collagen) extracted from boiling bones, connective tissue and other animal parts; when dissolved in a hot liquid and then cooled, it forms a jellylike substance used as a thickener and stabilizer

Gelatin

One of the most commonly used thickeners in the bakeshop is **gelatin**, a natural product derived from the animal protein collagen. It is available in two forms: granulated gelatin and sheet (also called leaf) gelatin. A two-step process is necessary to use either form: the gelatin must first be softened (bloomed) in a cold liquid, then dissolved in a hot liquid.

Granulated gelatin is available in bulk or in 7-g (1/4-oz. or slightly less than 1-Tbsp.) envelopes. One envelope is enough to set 450 mL (1 pt.) of liquid. Granulated gelatin should be softened in four times its weight in cool liquid for at least five minutes, then heated gently to dissolve. The initial softening in a cold liquid is necessary to separate the gelatin molecules so that they will not lump together when the hot liquid is added.

Sheet or leaf gelatin is available in 1-kg boxes, sometimes further packaged in 5- or 6-sheet envelopes. Each sheet weighs approximately 3 g (1/10 oz.). They must be separated and soaked in ice water until very soft, at least 15 minutes. They are then removed from the water, squeezed to remove excess moisture and stirred into a hot liquid to completely dissolve.

Gelatin Bloom

Gelatin sheets or powder is dry and must be rehydrated in a cold liquid before melting. "Blooming" the gelatin is an important step and cannot be skipped, otherwise some of the gelatin will lump and not be available to provide thickening. Use four times by weight of water to bloom granulated gelatin.

BASIC PROCEDURE FOR USING SHEET GELATIN

1. Gelatin sheets are submerged in ice water for 15 minutes to soften. Drain and squeeze water out.

2. Softened gelatin sheets are then incorporated into a hot liquid.

Granulated and sheet gelatin can be substituted weight for weight in any formula. Sheet gelatin, though more expensive, is preferred for its lack of flavour and colour. It also tends to dissolve more readily and evenly and has a longer shelf life than the granulated product.

Once incorporated into a product such as a Bavarian, gelatin can be frozen, or melted and reset once or twice without a loss of thickening ability. Because it scorches easily, gelatin and mixtures containing gelatin should not be allowed to boil; a doubleboiler or steam jacket is recommended.

Gelatin will not set or gel when incorporated with certain fruits. Enzymes in fresh pineapple (bromelain), papaya (papain), melon and kiwi (actinidin) break down the protein in gelatin. Cooking will neutralize the enzymes. Acids such as vinegar, citrus juices and wine weaken gelatin. Alcohol increases the strength of gelatin as does milk. Salt lowers gel strength and sugar increases it.

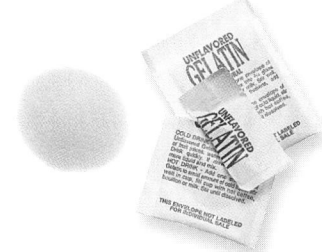

Granulated Gelatin

Flavourings

Many flavouring ingredients are used in the bakeshop. Practically any herb, spice, beverage or extract can be used to give baked goods, creams and confections their characteristic flavours. As with all baking ingredients, select flavouring components for overall quality and freshness, and combine flavourings carefully to achieve a balanced, good-tasting finished product. Recommendations for bakeshop uses for herbs and spices can be found in Chapter 7, Flavours and Flavourings.

Emulsions and Extracts

Emulsions and extracts are liquid flavouring agents derived from various **essential oils**.

Emulsions are flavouring oils mixed into water with the aid of emulsifiers. Lemon and orange are the most common emulsions. Emulsions are much stronger than extracts and should be used carefully and sparingly.

Extracts are mixtures of flavouring oils and ethyl alcohol. Vanilla, almond and lemon are frequently used extracts. An extract may be made with pure flavouring oils or with artificial flavours and colours. Contents are regulated and must be clearly labelled.

Emulsions and extracts are highly volatile. They should be stored in sealed containers in a cool area away from direct light.

Vanilla

Vanilla (Fr. *vanille*) is the most frequently used flavouring in the bakeshop. It comes from the pod fruit, called a bean, of a vine in the orchid family. Vanilla beans are purchased whole, individually or by weight. They should be soft and pliable, with a rich brown colour and good aroma. The finest vanilla comes from Tahiti and Madagascar. Mexico is a major producer.

To use a vanilla bean, cut it open lengthwise with a paring knife. Scrape out the moist seeds with the knife's tip and stir them into the mixture being flavoured. The seeds do not dissolve and will remain visible as small black or brown flecks. After all the seeds have been removed, the bean can be stored in a covered container with sugar to create vanilla sugar.

Vanilla beans should be stored in an airtight container in a cool, dark place. During storage, the beans may develop a white coating. This is not mould but rather crystals of vanilla flavour known as **vanillin**. It should not be removed.

Pure vanilla extract is an easy and less expensive way to give bakeshop products a true vanilla flavour. It is dark brown and aromatic, and comes in several

● **essential oils** pure oils extracted from the skins, peels and other parts of plants used to give their aroma and taste to flavouring agents in foods, cosmetics and other products

● **emulsions** flavouring oils, such as orange and lemon, mixed into water with the aid of emulsifiers

● **extracts** concentrated mixtures of ethyl alcohol and flavouring oils such as vanilla, almond and lemon

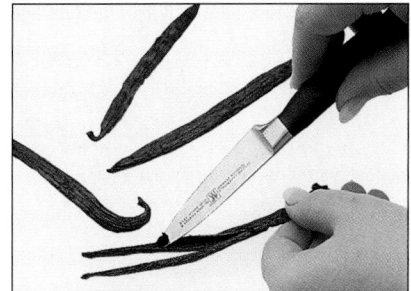

Scraping seeds from the interior of a vanilla bean.

● **vanillin** (1) whitish crystals of vanilla flavour that often develop on vanilla beans during storage; (2) synthetic vanilla flavouring

strengths; the stronger products are used only in manufacturing. Due to varying strengths it is difficult to substitute extracts for beans, but a general guide is 15 mL (1 Tbsp.) extract for each vanilla bean. Taste is the real determining factor. By law, any product labelled vanilla extract must not contain artificial flavourings and must be at least 35% alcohol by volume.

Vanilla extract should be stored at room temperature in a closed, opaque container. It should not be frozen.

Artificial or imitation vanilla flavouring is made with synthetic vanillin. Artificial flavouring is available in a clear form, which is useful for white buttercreams where the dark brown colour of pure vanilla extract would be undesirable. Although inexpensive, artificial vanilla is, at best, weaker and less aromatic than pure extract. It can also impart a chemical or bitter taste to foods.

Chocolate

Chocolate is one of the most—perhaps *the* most—popular flavouring for candies, cookies, cakes and pastries. Chocolate is also served as a beverage and is an ingredient in the traditional spicy Mexican molé sauce. Chocolate is available in a variety of forms and degrees of sweetness.

Chocolate Production

Cocoa Beans

Chocolate (Fr. *chocolat*) begins as yellow fruit pods dangling from the trunk and main branches of the tropical cacao tree. Each pod contains about 40 almond-sized cocoa beans. After the pods ripen, the beans are placed in the sun for several days to dry and ferment. They are then cleaned, dried, cured and roasted to develop flavour and reduce bitterness. Next the beans are crushed to remove their shells, yielding the prized chocolate nib.

● **cocoa butter** the fat found in cocoa beans and used in fine chocolate

Nibs are shipped to manufacturers worldwide where they can be further roasted. They are crushed into a thick (nonalcoholic) paste known as chocolate liquor or chocolate mass. Chocolate mass contains about 53% fat, known as **cocoa butter**. The chocolate mass is further refined depending on the desired product. If cocoa powder is to be produced, virtually all of the cocoa butter is removed. A variety of other products are created by adding more cocoa butter, sugar, milk solids and flavourings to the chocolate mass. Most manufacturers of fine chocolates use the Swiss technique of conching to increase smoothness. **Conching** involves stirring large vats of blended chocolate with a heavy roller or paddle to smooth out sugar crystals and improve the flavour by removing acidity from the chocolate, a process that may last from 12 hours to 3 days.

● **conching** stirring melted chocolate with large stone or metal rollers to create a smooth texture in the finished chocolate

Chocolate Flavours

There are two types of chocolate beans: a very hardy, abundant African variety used as a base bean, and a very flavourful, aromatic variety from Costa Rica used for flavour. Unlike wine or coffee, you cannot taste processed chocolate and tell which beans were used. Most chocolates are blends, created by their manufacturer to be unique yet consistent. However, single-origin chocolate is now available.

Roasting greatly affects the final flavour of chocolate. Generally, German and Spanish manufacturers use a high (or strong) roast; Swiss and American makers use a low (or mild) roast.

Refining is also a matter of national taste. Swiss and German chocolate is the smoothest, followed by English chocolates. North American chocolate tends to be noticeably more grainy.

Cacao—A Brief History

The cacao tree originated in South America. In the 6th century, Mayans introduced it to Mexico, where it was cultivated by the Aztecs and Toltecs. Used as currency, cacao beans were roasted, crushed and steeped in water, then thickened with corn flour to be drunk as cold chocolate. Sometimes honey, vanilla or spices, including chiles, were added to make the bitter, high-caffeine brew more palatable.

Twenty-plus years after Columbus, Cortez took cacao beans from Mexico and planted them on islands on his return to Spain. Some found their way to Africa over time, but Spain controlled the cocoa trade into the 18th century. Cocoa beverages spread though Europe as a result of royal weddings.

Cocoa production was done with mortar and pestle or stone disks until the Industrial Revolution. Cocoa factories proliferated in Europe in the 18th century. Some key dates in the development of chocolate as we know it include:

1825—Van Houten patents "chocolate powder"; he pressed the cocoa butter from the beans

1847—Fry and Sons introduce the first eating chocolate

1876—Swiss chocolatier Daniel Peter invents solid milk chocolate using Nestlé's condensed milk

1894—Hershey sells milk chocolate bars

1939—Nestlé introduces chocolate chips

Chocolate quality is actually the product of several factors besides taste. All these factors should be evaluated when selecting chocolates:

1. *Appearance*—should be even in colour and glossy, without any discoloration.
2. *Smell*—should be chocolatey with no off-odours or staleness.
3. *Break*—should snap cleanly without crumbling.
4. *Texture*—should melt quickly and evenly on the tongue.

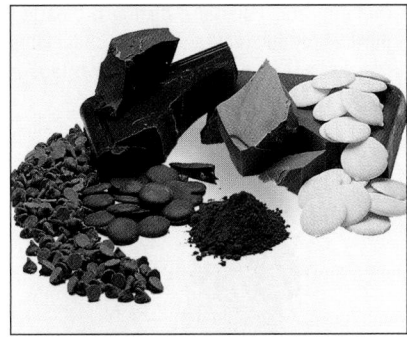

Clockwise from lower left: Semi-Sweet Chips, Disks of Chocolate Liquor, Block of Bittersweet Chocolate, Block of Milk Chocolate, Disks of White Chocolate, Alkalized Cocoa Powder.

Types of Chocolate

Unsweetened chocolate is pure, hardened chocolate liquor without any added sugar or milk solids. It is frequently used in baking and is sometimes referred to as "baking chocolate." Unsweetened chocolate is approximately 53% cocoa butter and 47% cocoa solids. Its flavour is pure and chocolatey, but the absence of sugar makes it virtually inedible as is.

Both **bittersweet** and **semi-sweet chocolates** contain at least 35% chocolate liquor plus additional cocoa butter, sugar, flavourings and sometimes emulsifiers. Generally, semi-sweet chocolate will be sweeter than bittersweet chocolate, but there are no precise definitions, so flavour and sweetness will vary from brand to brand. Both are excellent eating chocolates and can usually be substituted measure for measure in any formula. **Couverture** refers to high-quality chocolate containing at least 32% cocoa butter.

● **couverture** a high-quality chocolate containing at least 32% cocoa butter

Government standards require that **sweet chocolate** contain not less than 15% chocolate liquor and varying amounts of sugar, milk solids, flavourings and emulsifiers. As the name implies, sweet chocolate is sweeter, and thus less chocolatey, than semi-sweet chocolate.

The favourite eating chocolate in North America is **milk chocolate**. It contains sugar, vanilla, perhaps other flavourings and, of course, milk solids. The milk solids that make the chocolate milder and sweeter than other chocolates also make it less suitable for baking purposes. Do not substitute milk chocolate for dark chocolate in any product that must be baked, as the milk solids tend to burn. If melted slowly and carefully, milk chocolate can be used in glazes, mousses or candies.

Chocolate chips are drops of chocolate available in count sizes from 14 to 160 per ounce (the average chips are 1800–2200 per kilogram; 800 to 1000 per pound). They are easy additions to cookies, muffins and cakes. Like the larger **chocolate chunks,** chips are available in many flavours including white chocolate, butterscotch, peanut butter and fruit flavours. **Pistoles** or **calets** are small round pieces of chocolate, often the finest couverture, designed to

Chocolate Pistoles

Melting and Tempering Chocolate

There are two important rules for melting chocolate:

1. Never exceed 49°C (120°F).
2. Never allow even a drop of water or steam to touch melted chocolate.

A water droplet causes the chocolate to become lumpy and seize. If seizing occurs, adding a fat such as cocoa butter, clarified butter or vegetable shortening will restore the chocolate to a workable state. At 49°C (120°F) the different fat fractions are melted. Overheating adversely affects flavour. Larger pieces of chocolate should be chopped or grated to ensure uniform melting, and constant stirring is needed, particularly for milk and white chocolates. Pistoles are now marketed to save labour.

Remove the chocolate from the heat source at 46°C (115°F) and stir constantly to keep the cocoa butter distributed evenly.

Tempering chocolate is a process where couverture is slowly heated and cooled while stirring. The fat crystals in the cocoa butter stabilize. At a cool room temperature the tempered chocolate will dry rapidly to a hard, shiny piece that breaks with a snap. It also shrinks slightly—handy for unmoulding chocolates. Tempered chocolate has a good shelf life at room temperature.

Untempered melted chocolate dries slowly and is soft in texture. It "blooms" —becomes dull and streaky—and sticks to moulds. Refrigeration is usually necessary.

To temper dark chocolate, melt and heat it to a temperature of 46°C to 49°C (115°F to 120°F). Cool it to 26°C to 28°C (80°F to 82°F) and then slowly warm to 30°C to 32°C (87°F to 90°F). Milk and white chocolates use lower temperatures—melt to 43°C to 46°C (110°F to 115°F), cool to 25°C to 26°C (78°F to 80°F) and then warm to 29°C to 30°C (85°F to 87°F). Care must be taken to maintain the final temperature.

Compound coatings do not need to be tempered as they contain palm kernel oil, which allows them to set. The snap associated with fine chocolates will not be evident. If using compound coating, buy a high-quality product.

Dutch-Processed Cocoa Powder (left) and American-Style Nonalkalized Cocoa Powder

eliminate the need for chopping chocolate in the bakeshop—especially useful when tempering.

The brown powder left after the fat (cocoa butter) is removed from cocoa beans is known as **cocoa powder**. It does not contain any sweeteners or flavourings and is primarily used in baked goods. Alkalized or Dutch-processed cocoa powder has been treated with an alkaline solution, such as potassium carbonate, to raise the powder's pH from 5.5 to 7 or 8. Alkalized powder is darker and milder than nonalkalized powder and has a reduced tendency to lump. Either can be used in baked goods, however.

Cocoa Butter

Chocolate liquor is approximately 53% cocoa butter. Cocoa butter has long been prized for its resistance to rancidity and its use as a cosmetic. Cocoa butter has a very precise melting point, just below body temperature.

White Chocolate

This ivory-coloured substance is not the product of an albino cocoa bean. It is actually a confectionery product that does not contain any chocolate solids or liquor. (Thus it cannot be labelled "chocolate" in Canada, though the U.S. FDA has allowed white chocolate to be labelled as chocolate as of January 2004.) The finest white chocolates contain cocoa butter, sugar, milk solids, vanilla or other flavours. Other products replace all or part of the cocoa butter with partially hydrogenated palm kernel oil. These confectionery products will be less expensive than those containing pure cocoa butter, but their flavour and texture will be noticeably inferior. White chocolate melts at a lower temperature than dark chocolate does and burns easily. It is excellent for eating and candy making but is less often used in baked goods.

Compound Coatings

A less expensive product substituted in many prepared foods, compound coating is made with partially hydrogenated palm kernel oil instead of cocoa butter. The resulting product melts at a higher temperature. Products containing compound coating should be labelled "chocolate flavoured." Carob is a common ingredient.

Nutrition

Chocolates are high in calories and fat. They contain minimal amounts of vitamin A and trace amounts of other vitamins, as well as some sodium, phosphorus, potassium and other minerals.

Storing Chocolate

All chocolates should be stored at a cool, consistent temperature, away from strong odours and moisture. Dark chocolate, white chocolate and cocoa powder can be kept for up to one year without loss of flavour. Milk chocolate will not keep as well because it contains milk solids.

Chocolate may develop greyish-white spots during storage. This is called **fatbloom** or **bloom**; it results from the migration of cocoa butter crystals to the surface when temperatures change. Bloom will not affect the flavour or function of chocolate and will disappear when the chocolate is melted.

Nuts

A **nut** (Fr. *noix*) is the edible single-seed kernel of a fruit surrounded by a hard shell. A hazelnut is an example of a true nut. The term is used more generally, however, to refer to any seed or fruit with an edible kernel in a hard shell. Walnuts and peanuts are examples of non-nut "nuts" (peanuts are legumes that grow underground; walnuts have two kernels). Nuts are a good source of protein and B vitamins but are high in fat. Their high fat content makes them especially susceptible to rancidity and odour absorption. Nuts should be stored in nonmetal, airtight containers in a cool, dark place. Most nuts may be kept frozen for up to one year.

Nuts are used in foods to provide texture and flavour. They are often roasted in a low (135°C/275°F) oven before use to heighten their flavour. Allowing roasted nuts to cool to room temperature before grinding prevents them from releasing too much oil.

Almonds (Fr. *amande*) are the seeds of a plumlike fruit. Native to western India, the almond was first cultivated by the ancient Greeks. It is now a major commercial crop in California. Almonds are available whole, sliced, slivered or ground. Blanched almonds have had their brown, textured skins removed; natural almonds retain their skins. Unless the brown colour of natural almond skin is undesirable, the two types can be used interchangeably in recipes. Almonds are frequently used in pastries and candies and are the main ingredient in marzipan.

Brazil nuts (Fr. *noix du Brésil*), sometimes referred to as cream nuts, are the large, oval-shaped seeds of huge trees that grow wild in the rain forests of Central and South America. Their high oil content gives them a rich, buttery flavour and a tender texture. Brazil nuts are available both in-shell and shelled, and are eaten raw, roasted, salted and in ice creams and bakery and confectionery products.

Cashews, native to the Amazon, are now cultivated in India and east Africa. The cashew nut is actually the seed of a plant related to poison ivy. Because of toxins in the shell, cashews are always sold shelled. They are expensive and have a strong flavour. Cashews are used in some Asian cuisines and make a wonderful addition to cookies and candies.

Chestnuts (Fr. *marrons*) are true nuts that must be cooked before using. Available steamed, dried, boiled or roasted, they are often sold as a canned purée, with or without added sugar. Candied or glazed chestnuts are also available. Most chestnuts are grown in Europe, primarily Italy, but new varieties

● **bloom** a white, powdery layer that sometimes appears on chocolate if the cocoa butter separates

● **nut** (1) the edible single-seed kernel of a fruit surrounded by a hard shell; (2) generally, any seed or fruit with an edible kernel in a hard shell

Almonds

Almond Paste

Brazil Nuts

Cashews

Chestnuts

● **coconut water** the thin, slightly opaque liquid contained within a fresh coconut

● **coconut milk** a coconut-flavoured liquid made by pouring boiling water over shredded coconut; may be sweetened or unsweetened. Do not substitute cream of coconut for coconut milk.

● **coconut cream** (1) a coconut-flavoured liquid made like coconut milk but with less water; it is creamier and thicker than coconut milk; (2) the thick fatty portion that separates and rises to the top of canned or frozen coconut milk. Do not substitute cream of coconut for true coconut cream.

● **cream of coconut** a canned commercial product consisting of thick, sweetened coconut-flavoured liquid; used for baking and in beverages

● **praline** hazelnut paste made with sugar

● **gianduja** blend of hazelnut paste and chocolate

Hazelnuts

Macadamias

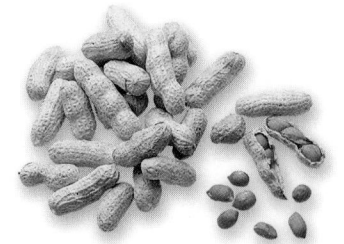

Peanuts

Pine Nuts

Coconuts

are beginning to flourish in North America. Their distinctive flavour is found in many sweet dishes and pastries. Because of their high starch content, chestnuts are also used in soups and sauces and may be served as a side dish.

Coconuts (Fr. *noix de coco*) are the seeds from one of the largest of all fruits. They grow on the tropical coconut palm tree. The nut is a dark brown oval, covered with coarse fibres. The shell is thick and hard; inside is a layer of white, moist flesh. The interior also contains a clear liquid known as **coconut water**. (This is not the same as **coconut milk** or **coconut cream**, both of which are prepared from the flesh.) Coconut has a mild aroma, a sweet, nutty flavour and a crunchy, chewy texture. Fresh coconuts are readily available but require some effort to use. Coconut flesh is available shredded or flaked, with or without added sugar. **Cream of coconut** is available in cans. Coconut is most often used in pastries and candies and is also an important ingredient in Indian and Caribbean cuisines. A good fresh coconut should feel heavy; you should be able to hear the coconut water sloshing around inside. Avoid cracked, moist or mouldy coconuts.

Hazelnuts (Fr. *noisette*) are true nuts that grow wild in the northwest and upper midwest of the United States. The cultivated form, known as a **filbert**, is native to temperate regions throughout the northern hemisphere. A bit larger than the hazelnut, it has a weaker flavour than its wild cousin. Both nuts look like smooth brown marbles. Filberts are generally less expensive. Hazelnuts are often ground for use in cakes or pastries. Their distinctive flavour goes well with chocolate and coffee. **Praline** and **gianduja** are made from hazelnuts.

To remove the hazelnut's bitter skin, roast whole nuts in a 135°C (275°F) oven for 12 to 15 minutes. They should give off a good aroma and just begin to darken. While still hot, rub the nuts in a dry towel or against a mesh sifter to remove the skin.

Macadamias, although commercially significant in Hawaii, are actually native to Australia. This small round nut is creamy white with a sweet, rich taste and high fat content. Its shell is extremely hard and must be removed by machine, so the macadamia is always sold out of the shell. Its flavour blends well with fruits, coconut and white and dark chocolate.

Peanuts (Fr. *arachide*), also known as groundnuts, are actually legumes that grow underground. The peanut is native to South America; it made its way into North America via Africa and the slave trade. Peanuts are a good source of protein and fat and became an important source of food and oil during World War II. They may be eaten raw or roasted and are available shelled or unshelled, with or without their thin red skins. Peanuts are used in Asian cuisines and are ubiquitous ground with a bit of oil into peanut butter.

Pecans (Fr. *noix de pacane*), native to the Mississippi River Valley, are perhaps the most popular nuts in America. Their flavour is rich and mapley and appears most often in breads, sweets and pastries. They are available whole in the shell or in various standard sizes and grades of pieces.

Pecans

Pine nuts (Fr. *pignon*), also known as piñon nuts and pignole, are the seeds of several species of pine tree. The small, creamy white, teardrop-shaped nuts are commonly used in dishes from Spain, Italy and the American Southwest. They are rarely chopped or ground due to their small size and will only need

Gases Are Trapped

The stretchable network of proteins created in a batter or dough either by egg proteins or gluten traps gases in the product. Without an appropriate network of proteins, the gases would just escape without causing the mixture to rise.

Starches Gelatinize

When starch granules reach a temperature of approximately 60°C (140°F), they absorb additional moisture—up to 10 times their own weight—and expand. This contributes to the baked good's structure.

Proteins Coagulate

Gluten and dairy and egg proteins begin to coagulate (solidify) when the dough or batter reaches a temperature of 71°C (160°F). This process provides most of the baked good's structure.

Proper baking temperatures are important for controlling the point at which proteins coagulate. If the temperature is too high, proteins will solidify before the gases in the product have expanded fully, resulting in a product with poor texture and volume. If the temperature is too low, gases will escape before the proteins coagulate, resulting in a product that may collapse.

Fats Melt

As fats melt, steam is released and fat droplets are dispersed throughout the product. These fat droplets coat the starch (flour) granules, thus moistening and tenderizing the product by keeping the gluten strands short. Shortenings melt at different temperatures. It is important to select a fat with the proper melting point for the product being prepared.

Water Evaporates

Throughout the baking process, the water contained in the liquid ingredients will turn to steam and evaporate. This steam is a useful leavener. As steam is released, the dough or batter dries out, starting from the outside, resulting in the formation of a crust.

Sugars Caramelize

As sugars are heated above the boiling point they caramelize, adding flavour and causing the product to darken. Sugars are found in eggs, dairy products and other ingredients, not just in refined sugar and liquid sweeteners.

Carryover Baking

The physical changes in a baked good do not stop when it is removed from the oven. The residual heat contained in a product continues the baking process as the product cools. That is why a cookie or biscuit may seem a bit underbaked when removed from the oven; it will finish baking as it cools.

TABLE 27.3	Gases That Leaven Baked Goods
Leavening Agent	**Present In**
Air	All products, especially those containing whipped eggs or creamed fat
Steam	All products when liquids evaporate or fats melt
Carbon dioxide	Products containing baking soda, baking powder, baking ammonia or yeast

● **staling** also known as **starch retrogradation**; a change in the distribution and location of water molecules wthin baked products; stale products are firmer, drier and more crumbly than fresh-baked goods

Staling

Staling is a change in a baked good's texture and aroma caused by both moisture loss and changes in the structure of the starch granules. Stale products have lost their fresh aroma and are firmer, drier and more crumbly than fresh goods.

Staling is not just a general loss of moisture into the atmosphere; it is also a change in the location and distribution of water molecules within the product. This process, known as **starch retrogradation**, occurs as starch molecules cool, becoming more dense and expelling moisture.

In breads, this moisture migrates from the interior to the drier crust, causing the crust to become tough and leathery. If the product is not well wrapped, moisture will escape completely into the surrounding air. In humid conditions, unwrapped bread crusts absorb moisture from the atmosphere, resulting in the same loss of crispness. The flavour and texture of breads can be revived by reheating them to approximately 60°C (140°F), the temperature at which starch gelatinization occurs. Usually, products can be reheated only once without causing additional quality loss.

The retrogradation process is temperature-dependent. It occurs most rapidly at temperatures of approximately 4°C (40°F). Therefore, baked products should not be refrigerated unless they contain perishable components such as cream fillings. It is better to store products frozen or at room temperature.

Products containing fats and sugars, which retain moisture, tend to stay fresh longer. Commercial bakeries usually add chemical emulsifiers or gums to retard staling, but these additives are not practical for small-scale production.

Conclusion

Of the many stations of the kitchen, the bakeshop often requires the most conscientious attention to detail. The correct use of flour, thickeners, sugar, fat, chocolate and other flavourings is essential. During preparation and baking, doughs and batters go through many physical changes. One of the most important is the development of gluten, the elastic network of wheat proteins created when doughs and batters are prepared, which gives baked goods body and structure. You should understand the changes baked goods undergo and learn to control or adjust them as needed.

Questions for Discussion

1. Name several specialized hand tools or pans often used in the bakeshop.
2. What are the differences between a steam injection oven, a convection oven and a conventional oven? Why might you select one type of oven over another?
3. What is gluten? How is it produced and why is it important in the preparation of baked goods?
4. Discuss four functions of sugar and other sweeteners in baked goods.
5. Describe several steps that can be taken to prevent crystals from forming in sugar solutions.
6. Describe the effect of fat on gluten strands. Why is fat an important ingredient in baked goods?
7. Explain the difference between chocolate liquor and semi-sweet chocolate. Can these two types of chocolate be used interchangeably in most recipes? Explain your answer.
8. List and describe the nine steps in the baking process.

Quick Breads **28**

"When I am in trouble, eating is the only thing that consoles me. . . .
At the present I am eating muffins because I am unhappy.
Besides, I am particularly fond of muffins.

—Oscar Wilde, Irish dramatist and writer (1854–1900)

Buttermilk biscuits, blueberry muffins, banana-nut bread and currant scones are all quick breads. Although the origin of the name may be a mystery, why they are so named is obvious: they are quick to make and quick to bake. With only a few basic ingredients and no yeast, almost any food service operation can provide its customers with fresh muffins, biscuits, scones and loaf breads.

The variety of ingredients is virtually limitless: cornmeal, whole wheat, fruits, nuts, spices and vegetables all yield popular products. And the use of these products is not limited to breakfast service; they are equally appropriate for lunch, snacks and buffets.

CHEMICAL LEAVENING AGENTS

Quick breads are made with chemical leavening agents, principally baking soda and baking powder. This sets them apart from breads that are made with yeast and require additional time for fermentation and proofing. Understanding how chemical leavening agents operate is essential to successful quick-bread production.

Chemical leavening agents release gases through chemical reactions between acids and bases contained in the formula. These gases form bubbles or air pockets throughout the dough or batter. As the product bakes, the dough or batter sets around these air pockets, thus giving the quick bread its rise and texture.

Baking Soda

Sodium bicarbonate ($NaHCO_3$) is more commonly known as household **baking soda**. Baking soda is an alkaline compound (a base) that releases carbon dioxide gas (CO_2) if both an acid and moisture are present. Heat is not necessary for this reaction to occur; however, the chemical reaction will be faster at higher temperatures. Therefore, products made with baking soda must be baked at once, before the carbon dioxide has a chance to escape from the batter.

Acids commonly used with baking soda are buttermilk, sour cream, lemon juice, honey, molasses and fresh fruit. Generally, the amount of baking soda used in a formula is only the amount necessary to neutralize the acids present. If more leavening action is needed, baking powder, not more baking soda, should be used. Too much baking soda causes the product to taste soapy or bitter; it may also cause a yellow colour and brown spots to develop.

Baking Powder

Baking powder is a mixture of sodium bicarbonate and one or more acids, generally cream of tartar ($KHC_4H_4O_6$) and/or sodium aluminum sulphate ($Na_2SO_4 \cdot Al_2[SO_4]_3$). Baking powder also contains a starch to prevent lumping and to balance the chemical reactions. Because baking powder contains both the acid and the base necessary for the desired chemical reaction, the formula does not need to contain any acid. Only moisture is necessary to induce the release of gases.

There are two types of baking powder: single-acting and double-acting. An excess of either type produces undesirable flavours, textures and colours in baked products.

Single-acting baking powder requires only the presence of moisture to start releasing gas. This moisture is supplied by the eggs, milk, water or other liquids in the formula. As with baking soda, products using single-acting baking powder must be baked immediately.

Double-acting baking powder is more popular. With double-acting baking powder, there is a small release of gas upon contact with moisture and a second, stronger release of gas when heat is applied. Products made with double-acting baking powder need not be baked immediately but can sit for a short time without loss of leavening ability. Note: All formulas in this book rely on double-acting baking powder.

Both baking soda and baking powder are sometimes used in one formula. This is because baking soda can release CO_2 only to the extent that there is also an acid present in the formula. If the soda/acid reaction alone is insufficient to leaven the product, baking powder is needed for additional leavening.

Baking Ammonia

Baking ammonia (ammonia bicarbonate or ammonia carbonate) is also used as a leavening agent in some baked goods, primarily cookies and crackers. Baking ammonia releases ammonia and carbon dioxide very rapidly when heated. It is suitable for low-moisture products with large surface areas that are baked at high temperatures, such as crackers. Consequently, it is rarely used in quick breads.

Purchasing and Storing

Purchase chemical leaveners in the smallest unit appropriate for your operation. Although a large can of baking powder may cost less than several small ones, if not used promptly, the contents of a larger container can deteriorate, causing waste or unusable baked goods.

Chemical leavening agents should always be kept tightly covered. Not only is there a risk of contamination if left open, but they can also absorb moisture from the air and lose their effectiveness. They should be stored in a cool place, as heat deteriorates them. A properly stored and unopened container of baking powder or baking soda has a shelf life of approximately one year.

MIXING METHODS

Quick breads are generally mixed by either the **biscuit method**, the **muffin method** or the **creaming method**. (See Table 28.1.) The type and consistency of the fat usually dictates the method used. Quick breads are tender products with a soft **crumb**. Flour is mixed in quickly and gently to minimize gluten development.

Biscuit Method

The biscuit method is used for biscuits and scones and is very similar to the technique used to make flaky pie doughs. The goal is to create a baked good that is light, flaky and tender.

● **biscuit method** a mixing method used to make biscuits, scones and flaky doughs; it involves cutting cold fat into the flour and other dry ingredients before any liquid is added

● **muffin method** a mixing method used to make quick-bread batters; it involves combining liquid fat with other liquid ingredients before adding them to the dry ingredients

● **creaming method** a mixing method in which softened fat and sugar are vigorously combined to incorporate air

● **crumb** the interior of bread or cake; may be elastic, aerated, fine or coarse grained.

TABLE 28.1	Quick Bread Mixing Techniques	
Mixing Technique	**Fat**	**Result**
Biscuit method	Solid (chilled)	Flaky dough
Muffin method	Liquid (oil or melted butter)	Soft, tender, cakelike texture
Creaming method	Softened (room temperature)	Rich, tender, cakelike texture

● **makeup** the cutting, shaping and forming of dough products before baking

Biscuits and Scones: A Genealogy

Biscuit is a French word used to describe any dry, flat cake, whether sweet or savoury. It was perhaps originally coined to describe twice-baked cakes (*bis* = twice + *cuit* = cooked). Crusader chronicles, for example, mention soldiers eating a "bread called 'bequis' because it is cooked twice," and still today the Reims biscuit is returned to the oven for further baking after it is removed from its tin.

Over the centuries the French began to use the term *biscuit* generically and appended modifiers to identify the particular type of dry, flat cake. For example, a *biscuit de guerre* (war) was the very hard, barely risen product of flour and water used from the time of the Crusades to the era of Louis XIV as an army ration; *biscuit de Savoie* is a savoury spongecake; *biscuit de pâtisserie* is a sweet biscuit.

To the British, a biscuit is what North Americans call a cracker or cookie. To the North Americans, the closest relative would be the scone. But because a scone contains eggs and butter, it is much richer than a biscuit.

Elizabeth Alston theorizes that early British colonists in America brought with them traditional scone recipes. Unable to find or afford the necessary fresh butter and eggs, these practical bakers substituted lard and omitted the eggs.

BASIC PROCEDURE FOR PREPARING PRODUCTS WITH THE BISCUIT METHOD

1. Measure all ingredients.
2. Sift the dry ingredients together.
3. Cut in the fat, which should be in a solid form.
4. Combine the liquid ingredients, including any eggs.
5. Add the liquid ingredients to the dry ingredients. Mix just until the ingredients are combined and form a soft dough. Do not overmix, as this causes toughness and inhibits the product's rise.
6. Place the dough on the bench and knead it lightly 10 or 15 times (about 20 to 30 seconds). The dough should be soft and slightly elastic, but not sticky. Too much kneading toughens the biscuits.
7. The dough is now ready for **makeup** and baking.

MAKEUP OF BISCUIT METHOD PRODUCTS

1. Roll out the dough on a floured surface to a thickness of 1.25 to 2 cm (1/2 to 3/4 in.). Be careful to roll it evenly. Biscuits should double in height during baking.
2. Cut into the desired shapes. Cut straight down; do not twist the cutters, as this inhibits rise. Space cuts as closely together as possible to minimize scraps.
3. Position the biscuits on a lightly greased or paper-lined sheet pan. If placed with sides nearly touching, the biscuits will rise higher and have softer sides. Place biscuits farther apart for crusty sides.
4. Scraps may be rerolled one time without overtoughening the product. To do so, press the dough together gently; do not knead.
5. Tops may be brushed with egg wash before baking or with melted butter after baking. Bake immediately in a hot oven.
6. Cool the finished products on a wire rack.

1. Sifting the dry ingredients together.

2. Cutting in the fat.

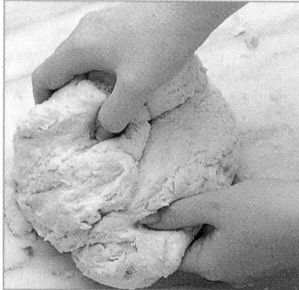

3. Kneading the dough.

4. Cutting the biscuits.

APPLYING THE BASICS	RECIPE 28.1

Fairmont Empress Scones

VANCOUVER ISLAND UNIVERSITY, NANAIMO, BC
Pastry Chef Ken Harper

Afternoon tea at The Empress is a world-renowned tradition.

Yield: 2 dozen (small) or 1 dozen medium

Method: Biscuit

Pastry flour	150 g	5 oz.
Bread flour	150 g	5 oz.
Sugar	60 g	2 oz.
Baking powder	20 g	2 Tbsp.
Butter	75 g	2-1/2 oz.
Cream, 35%	125 mL	4 fl. oz.
Eggs	2	2
Raisins	60 g	2 oz.
Egg wash		

1. Sift the dry ingredients together.
2. Cut in the butter until mealy; do not overmix.
3. Mix cream and eggs together.
4. Add raisins and liquid to dry ingredients; mix until just combined.
5. Knead 2–3 times and roll out 2-cm (3/4-in.) thick. Cut with a floured cutter.
6. Place biscuits on a lined sheet, brush with egg wash (see page 728) and let rest 45 minutes.
7. Bake at 170°C (325°F) for 20–25 minutes until golden brown.

Ken Harper

Born and raised in Victoria, Ken completed his scholarship in Camosun College's culinary program and then joined the Fairmont Empress as an apprentice chef. Highlights of his career include joining the culinary teams at the Fairmont Banff Springs Hotel, the Fairmont Château Whistler Resort and the Pan Pacific Hotel. He became Pastry Chef at the Empress in 1997 and now teaches at Vancouver Island University.

RECIPE 28.1

Approximate values per scone:	
Calories	109
Total fat	5 g
Saturated fat	3 g
Cholesterol	30 mg
Sodium	94 mg
Total carbohydrates	14 g
Protein	2 g

Muffin Method

Muffins are any small, cakelike baked good made in a muffin tin (pan). Batters for muffins and loaf quick breads are generally interchangeable. For example, banana muffin batter may be baked in a loaf pan by altering the baking time.

When preparing baked goods by the muffin method, the goal is to produce a tender product with an even shape and an even distribution of fruits, nuts or other ingredients. The most frequent problem with muffin-method products is overmixing. This causes toughness and may cause large holes to form inside the baked product, a condition known as **tunnelling**.

● **tunnelling** the holes that may form in baked goods as the result of overmixing

BASIC PROCEDURE FOR PREPARING PRODUCTS WITH THE MUFFIN METHOD

1. Measure all ingredients.
2. Sift the dry ingredients together.
3. Combine the liquid ingredients, including melted fat or oil. Melted butter or shortening may resolidify when combined with the other liquids; this is not a cause for concern.
4. Add the liquid ingredients to the dry ingredients and stir just until combined. Do not overmix. The batter may be lumpy.
5. The batter is now ready for makeup and baking.

Improperly mixed corn muffins rise unevenly and have large irregular holes.

MAKEUP OF MUFFIN METHOD PRODUCTS

1. Muffin pans and loaf pans should be greased with butter, shortening or a commercial pan grease. Paper liners may be used and will prevent sticking if the batter contains fruits or vegetables. Paper liners, however, inhibit rise.

2. A portion scoop is convenient for ensuring uniform-sized muffins. Be careful not to drip or spill batter onto the edge of the muffin cups; it will burn and cause sticking.

3. Allow muffins and loaf breads to cool for several minutes before attempting to remove them from the pan.

4. Cool the finished products on a wire rack.

APPLYING THE BASICS   **RECIPE 28.2**

Blueberry Muffins

Yield: 12 muffins
Method: Muffin

All-purpose flour	250 g	8 oz.
Sugar	125 g	4 oz.
Baking powder	10 g	3 tsp.
Salt	1 g	1/4 tsp.
Egg	1	1
Milk	250 mL	8 fl. oz.
Unsalted butter, melted	125 mL	4 fl. oz.
Vanilla	5 mL	1 tsp.
Blueberries, or other frozen berries	175 g	6 oz.
Lemon zest	10 g	1 Tbsp.

1. Sift the dry ingredients together.

2. Stir together the liquid ingredients, including the melted butter.

3. Stir the liquid mixture into the dry ingredients. Do not overmix. The batter should be lumpy.

4. Gently fold in the blueberries and lemon zest.

5. Portion into greased or paper-lined muffin cups and bake at 175°C (350°F) until light brown and set in the centre, approximately 18 minutes.

6. Cool the muffins in the pan for several minutes before removing.

RECIPE 28.2

Approximate values per muffin:	
Calories	218
Total fat	92 g
Saturated fat	5.5 g
Cholesterol	39 mg
Sodium	112 mg
Total carbohydrates	30 g
Protein	4 g

1. Blueberry Muffins: Combining the liquid ingredients.

2. Folding in the blueberries.

3. Portioning the batter.

Creaming Method

The creaming method is comparable to the mixing method used for many butter cakes. The final product will be cakelike, with a fine texture. There is less danger of overmixing with this method because the higher fat content shortens gluten strands and tenderizes the batter.

BASIC PROCEDURE FOR PREPARING PRODUCTS WITH THE CREAMING METHOD

1. Measure all ingredients.

2. Sift the dry ingredients together.

3. Combine softened fat and sugar in a mixer bowl. Cream until the colour lightens and the mixture fluffs.

4. Add eggs gradually, mixing well.

5. Add the dry and liquid ingredients to the creamed fat alternately. In other words, a portion of the flour is added to the fat and incorporated, then a portion of the liquid is added and incorporated. These steps are repeated until all the liquid and dry ingredients are incorporated. By adding the liquid and dry ingredients alternately, you avoid overmixing the batter and prevent the butter and sugar mixture from curdling.

6. The batter is now ready for makeup and baking.

MAKEUP OF CREAMING METHOD PRODUCTS

Panning and baking procedures are the same as those for quick breads prepared with the muffin method.

1. Sour Cream Muffins: Creaming the butter and sugar.

APPLYING THE BASICS   RECIPE 28.3

Sour Cream Muffins

Yield: 15 muffins

Method: Creaming

Unsalted butter, room temperature	250 g	8 oz.
Sugar	250 g	8 oz.
Eggs	2	2
Bread flour	200 g	7 oz.
Cake/pastry flour	100 g	3 oz.
Baking powder	3 g	1 tsp.
Baking soda	3 g	1 tsp.
Salt	5 g	1 tsp.
Sour cream	300 g	10 oz.
Vanilla	5 mL	1 tsp.

1. Cream the butter and sugar until light and fluffy. Add the eggs. Beat well.

2. Sift the dry ingredients together.

3. Stir the dry ingredients and sour cream, alternately, into the butter mixture. Stir in the vanilla.

2. Adding the sour cream.

3. Topping the muffins with streusel.

continued

Approximate values per muffin:

Calories	292
Total fat	17 g
Saturated fat	10 g
Cholesterol	73 mg
Sodium	218 mg
Total carbohydrates	32 g
Protein	4 g

4. Portion and bake at 175°C (350°F) until light brown and set, approximately 20 minutes.

5. Allow the muffins to cool briefly in the pan before removing.

VARIATIONS: Sour cream muffins can be topped with streusel (see Recipe Archive) or flavoured with a wide variety of fruits or nuts by adding approximately 125–175 g (4–6 oz. or 1 cup) fresh or frozen drained fruit to the batter. Blueberries, dried cherries, candied fruits, pecans and diced pears yield popular products. By adding 0.25 g (1/2 tsp.) each of cinnamon and nutmeg, basic spice muffins are produced.

Griddlecakes and Fritters

Griddlecakes, such as **pancakes** and **waffles**, are a type of quick bread. They are usually leavened with baking soda or baking powder and are quickly cooked on a very hot griddle or waffle iron with very little fat. They are described in detail in Chapter 33, Breakfast and Brunch. Fritters are made from leavened batter and deep-fat fried.

APPLYING THE BASICS RECIPE 28.4

Fruit Fritters (Beignets)

Yield: 10 servings (approximately)

Batter:

Pastry flour	250 g	9 oz.
Instant yeast	6 g	2 tsp.
Sugar	15 g	1 Tbsp.
Salt	1 g	pinch
Beer	100 mL	3-1/2 fl. oz.
Milk	150 mL	5 fl. oz.
Egg yolks	2	2
Vegetable oil	50 mL	2 fl. oz.
Egg whites	2	2
Sugar	15 g	1 Tbsp.
Fruit (peeled apples, bananas, pineapple, plums)	1 kg	2 lb. 4 oz.
Icing sugar	as needed	as needed

1. Combine flour, yeast, sugar and salt together.

2. Whisk the beer, half the milk and egg yolks together. Mix into the dry ingredients to make a smooth batter. Add the oil and remaining milk and let rest for 1 hour.

3. Whisk the egg whites to soft peaks and beat in the sugar to form stiff peaks. Fold the meringue into the batter.

4. Coat the fruit pieces with the batter and deep-fat fry at 175°C (350°F). Turn the pieces over to ensure even browning. Remove the fruit fritters from the oil and drain on paper towelling.

5. Dust with icing sugar and serve immediately.

NOTE: Beignets made from a soft dough are popular in New Orleans. They may be sweet or savoury. Beavertails made from sweet dough are popular in Eastern Canada.

Approximate values per fritter:

Calories	393
Total fat	24 g
Saturated fat	2.1 g
Cholesterol	40 mg
Sodium	57 mg
Total carbohydrates	41 g
Protein	4.5 g

TABLE 28.2	Troubleshooting Chart for Quick Breads	
Problem	**Cause**	**Solution**
Soapy or bitter taste	Chemical leaveners not properly mixed into batter	Sift chemicals with dry ingredients
	Too much baking soda	Adjust formula
Elongated holes (tunnelling)	Overmixing	Do not mix until smooth; mix only until moistened
Crust too thick	Too much sugar	Adjust formula
	Oven temperature too low	Adjust oven
Flat top with only a small peak in centre	Oven temperature too low	Adjust oven
Cracked, uneven top	Oven temperature too high	Adjust oven
No rise; dense product	Old batter	Bake promptly
	Damaged leavening agents	Store new chemicals properly
	Overmixing	Do not overmix

Conclusion

First you must master the three mixing methods used in producing quick breads (muffin, biscuit and creaming) and understand the interaction between chemical leaveners and other ingredients. Then, with an imaginative use of flavouring ingredients, you can successfully produce a wide array of fresh-baked breads for almost any food service operation. Table 28.2 provides some troubleshooting guidelines should you encounter difficulties.

Questions for Discussion

1. Name two chemical leavening agents and explain how they cause batters and doughs to rise.
2. List three common methods used for mixing quick breads. What is the significance of the type of fat used for each of these mixing methods?
3. What is the most likely explanation for discoloured and bitter-tasting biscuits? What is the solution?
4. Describe the resulting product when muffin batter has been overmixed.

Howard Selig, RD

Howard Selig is a Chef and Registered Dietitian living in Nova Scotia's bountiful Annapolis Valley. Howard provides a variety of contract services to the food service and continuing care industries. His company, Valley Flaxflour Ltd. (www.flaxflour.com), produces and distributes flax flour, an ingredient gaining in popularity for both its functional and its therapeutic qualities.

RECIPE 28.5

Approximate values per serving:	
Calories	156
Total fat	4 g
Saturated fat	1 g
Cholesterol	2 mg
Sodium	222 mg
Total carbohydrates	26 g
Protein	4 g

Date Bran Muffins

RECIPE 28.6

Approximate values per muffin:	
Calories	260
Total fat	9.1 g
Saturated fat	2.5 g
Cholesterol	27 mg
Sodium	539 mg
Total carbohydrates	44 g
Protein	4.5 g

Additional Quick Bread Formulas

RECIPE 28.5

Buttermilk Apple Cake (gluten free)

VALLEY NUTRITION AND FOOD SERVICES, MIDDLETON, NS
Chef/Registered Dietitian Howard Selig, RD

Yield: 12 servings
Method: Biscuit

Brown sugar	85 g	3 oz.
Buttermilk	500 mL	16 fl. oz.
Brown rice flour	150 g	1 cup
Flax flour	125 g	1 cup
Baking powder	3.5 g	1 tsp.
Baking soda	3.5 g	1 tsp.
Cinnamon	3 g	2 tsp.
Salt	2 g	1/2 tsp.
Apples, medium, cored, chopped fine	2	2

1. Lightly grease and flour a 2-L (2-qt.) Bundt pan or 20-cm (8-in.) square baking pan.
2. Beat sugar and buttermilk together.
3. Combine dry ingredients. Add, with apples, to wet ingredients. Mix to just combine.
4. Spread batter evenly in pan.
5. Bake in a 175°C (350°F) oven for 40–45 minutes. Cool in pan before removing.

RECIPE 28.6

Date Bran Muffins

Yield: 3 dozen (#16 scoop)
Method: Creaming

Brown sugar	550 g	20 oz.
Salt	20 g	3/4 oz.
Shortening	275 g	10 oz.
Date purée	550 g	20 oz.
Eggs	250 g	9 oz.
Bran	300 g	10 oz.
Bread flour	440 g	15 oz.
Baking soda (but see Step 3 for overnight refrigeration)	30 g	1 oz.
Milk	680 g	25 fl. oz.
Whole wheat flour	90 g	3 oz.

1. Cream sugar, salt, shortening and date purée together until well mixed on medium-high speed with a paddle attachment.
2. Add the eggs and beat smooth.
3. Add the remaining ingredients and mix until smooth. The mixture may be refrigerated overnight at this point, but increase baking soda to 35 g (1 oz. + 1 tsp.).
4. Deposit in paper-lined tins using a #16 scoop.
5. Bake at 175°C (350°F) for 18–20 minutes or until done.

RECIPE 28.7

Zucchini Bread

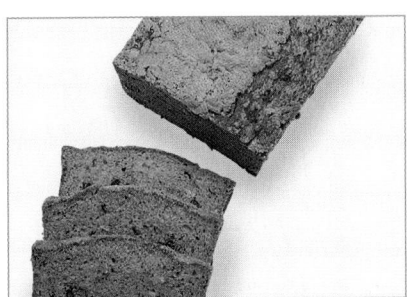

Yield: 2 24-cm × 12-cm (9-in. × 5-in.) loaves
Method: Muffin

Whole eggs	3	3
Canola oil	250 mL	8 fl. oz.
Sugar, white	225 g	8 oz.
Sugar, brown	170 g	6 oz.
Vanilla	10 mL	2 tsp.
Cinnamon	5 g	3 tsp.
Salt	5 g	1 tsp.
Baking soda	3.5 g	1 tsp.
Baking powder	1 g	1/4 tsp.
All-purpose flour	300 g	11 oz.
Zucchini, coarsely grated	350 g	12 oz.
Pecans, chopped	140 g	5 oz.

1. Combine all ingredients using the muffin method.
2. Bake in 2 greased loaf pans at 175°C (350°F), approximately 1 hour.

Zucchini Bread

RECIPE 28.7

Approximate values per slice:	
Calories	246
Total fat	15 g
Saturated fat	1.3 g
Cholesterol	23 mg
Sodium	135 mg
Total carbohydrates	27 g
Protein	2.8 g

RECIPE 28.8

Shortcakes

Yield: 2-1/2 to 3-1/2 dozen, depending on size
Method: Biscuit

Bread flour	500 g	1 lb.
Pastry flour	500 g	1 lb.
Sugar	225 g	8 oz.
Baking powder	60 g	2 oz.
Nutmeg	2 g	1/2 tsp.
Butter	450 g	1 lb.
Eggs, beaten	2	2
Milk	550 mL	20 fl. oz.
Raisins (optional)	180 g	6 oz.

1. Combine all dry ingredients.
2. Cut or rub butter into flour mixture until coarse and crumbly. The butter should be about the size of a pea.
3. Combine eggs and milk and add to flour-butter mixture. Stir until just combined.
4. Turn out onto a lightly floured surface and knead lightly a few times to combine the ingredients. If raisins are being used, add them at this time.
5. Pat the dough out to a thickness of 2.5 cm (1 in.). Use a cutter to shape into rounds. Reshape scrap pieces and cut to shape.
6. Place shortcakes on a parchment-lined baking sheet about 2 cm (3/4 in.) apart and let rest for 15 minutes.
7. Brush lightly with egg wash if desired.
8. Bake in a 200°C (400°F) oven for approximately 15–20 minutes or until done.

VARIATION: For cheese biscuits, cut the sugar to 50 g (2 oz.), the butter to 350 g (12 oz.) and add 250 g (9 oz.) grated cheddar to the crumble mixture. Omit the raisins.

Shortcakes

RECIPE 28.8

Approximate values per biscuit:	
Calories	273
Total fat	13 g
Saturated fat	8.0 g
Cholesterol	52 mg
Sodium	284 mg
Total carbohydrates	34 g
Protein	4.5 g

RECIPE 28.9

Banana Bread

Yield: 2 loaves
Method: Creaming

Bananas, ripe	750 g	1 lb. 12 oz.
Baking soda	25 g	1 oz.
Cake flour	250 g	10 oz.
Bread flour	250 g	10 oz.
Butter	190 g	6-1/2 oz.
Brown sugar	425 g	1 lb.
Whole egg	200 g	7-1/2 oz.
Dates, chopped	60 g	2 oz.

1. Purée bananas and reserve.
2. Combine baking soda and flours (sifted).
3. Using the paddle, beat butter and sugar on #2 speed until light in colour. Scrape down sides of bowl.
4. Add egg, beat and scrape down sides of bowl.
5. Combine half the flour mixture with the dates and stir into creamed mixture.
6. Add banana and mix thoroughly on #1 speed.
7. Add remaining flour and mix thoroughly, scraping down sides of bowl.
8. Oil 2 loaf pans and line bottoms with parchment paper.
9. Divide batter among the pans and level it.
10. Bake at 190°C (375°F) for 65–70 minutes or until done (knife comes out clean).

RECIPE 28.9

Approximate values per slice:	
Calories	244
Total fat	7.7 g
Saturated fat	4.3 g
Cholesterol	51 mg
Sodium	368 mg
Total carbohydrates	42 g
Protein	3.5 g

Morning Glory Muffins

RECIPE 28.10

Approximate values per muffin:	
Calories	527
Total fat	26 g
Saturated fat	4 g
Cholesterol	72 mg
Sodium	278 mg
Total carbohydrates	70 g
Protein	6 g

RECIPE 28.10

Morning Glory Muffins

Yield: 18 muffins
Method: Muffin

All-purpose flour	500 g	1 lb.
Granulated sugar	550 g	18 oz.
Baking soda	15 g	4 tsp.
Cinnamon	10 g	4 tsp.
Carrots, grated	425 g	14 oz.
Raisins	200 g	6 oz.
Pecan pieces	100 g	4 oz.
Coconut, shredded	125 g	4 oz.
Apple, unpeeled, grated	200 g	6 oz.
Eggs	6	6
Canola oil	350 mL	12 fl. oz.
Vanilla extract	20 mL	4 tsp.

1. Sift the dry ingredients together and set aside.
2. Combine the carrots, raisins, pecans, coconut and apple.
3. Combine the eggs, oil and vanilla.
4. Toss the carrot mixture in the dry ingredients. Add the liquid ingredients, stirring just until combined.
5. Bake in well-greased muffin tins at 175°C (350°F) until done, approximately 25 minutes.

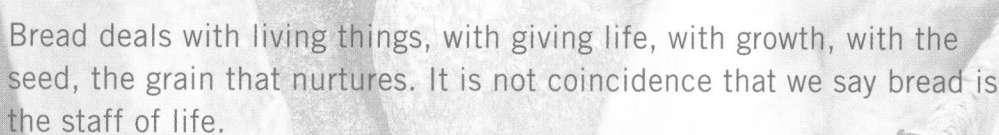

" Bread deals with living things, with giving life, with growth, with the seed, the grain that nurtures. It is not coincidence that we say bread is the staff of life.

—Lionel Poilane, France's most celebrated baker (1946–2002)

After studying this chapter you will be able to:

- select and use yeast
- perform the 10 steps involved in yeast bread production, including kneading by hand
- mix yeast doughs using the straight dough method and sponge method
- prepare rolled-in doughs

These interactive online tools will help you master the skills in this chapter:

- Videos
- Chapter Quizzes
- Activities

● **yeasts** microscopic fungi whose metabolic processes are responsible for fermentation; they are used for leavening bread and in cheese, beer and wine making

● **fermentation** the process by which yeast converts sugar into alcohol and carbon dioxide; it also refers to the time that yeast dough is left to rise

Bread making is an art that dates back to ancient times.
Bakers have learned to manipulate flour, water, salt and leavening to produce a vast variety of breads. A renewed interest in full-flavoured and textured breads has resulted in bakeries and restaurants offering customers exciting varieties of bread products.

Yeast breads can be divided into two categories: lean doughs and rich doughs. Lean doughs, such as those used for French and Italian breads, contain little or no sugar or fat. Rich doughs, such as brioche and some multigrain breads, contain significantly more sugar and fat. Rolled-in doughs, so-called because the fat is rolled into the dough in layers, are a type of rich dough used for baked goods such as croissants and sweetened Danish.

The study of yeast breads could occupy an entire text or course. The focus here is to detail basic production techniques for making lean doughs and other yeast-raised products. Rereading ingredient function in Chapter 28, Quick Breads, is recommended before beginning this chapter.

YEAST

Yeast is a living organism, a one-celled fungus. Various strains of yeast are present virtually everywhere. Yeast feeds on carbohydrates, converting them to carbon dioxide and alcohol in an organic process known as **fermentation**:

Yeast + Carbohydrates = Alcohol + Carbon Dioxide

When yeast produces carbon dioxide gas during bread making, the gas becomes trapped in the dough's gluten network. The trapped gas leavens the bread, providing the desired rise and texture. The small amount of alcohol produced by fermentation evaporates during baking.

As with most living things, yeast is very sensitive to temperature. It prefers temperatures between 21°C and 54°C (70°F and 130°F) depending on the type of yeast. The range used in most bakeries is 32°C to 43°C (90°F to 110°F). At temperatures below 2°C (34°F) it becomes dormant; above 59°C (138°F) it dies. (See Table 29.1.)

TABLE 29.1	Temperatures for Yeast Development	
Temperature		**Yeast Development**
2°C	34°F	Inactive
16–21°C	60–70°F	Slow action
21–32°C	70–90°F	Best temperature for growth of fresh yeast
41–46°C	105–115°F	Best temperature for growth of dry yeast
52–54°C	125–130°F	Best temperature for activating instant yeast
59°C	138°F	Yeast dies

Salt is used in bread making because it conditions gluten, making it stronger and more elastic. Salt also affects yeast fermentation. Because salt inhibits the growth of yeast, it helps control the dough's rise. Too little salt and not only will the bread taste bland, but it will also rise too rapidly. Too much salt, however, and the yeast will be destroyed. By learning to control the amount of food for the yeast and the temperatures of fermentation, you can learn to control the texture of your yeast-leavened products.

The addition of fats or shortenings to a dough will tenderize, moisturize and increase volume, but it will slow down fermentation.

Types of Yeast

Baker's yeast is available in two forms: compressed and active dry. (You may also encounter a product called brewer's yeast; it is a nutritional supplement with no leavening ability.)

Compressed Yeast

Compressed yeast is a mixture of yeast and starch with a moisture content of approximately 70%. Also referred to as fresh yeast, compressed yeast must be kept refrigerated. It should be creamy white and crumbly with a fresh, yeasty smell. Do not use compressed yeast that has developed a sour odour, brown colour or slimy film.

Compressed yeast is available in 17-g (3/5-oz.) cubes and 450-g (1-lb.) blocks. Under proper storage conditions, compressed yeast has a shelf life of two to three weeks. Freeze it if you cannot use it within one week. Liquids added to yeast doughs made with fresh yeast should be between 20°C and 24°C (68°F and 76°F).

Active Dry Yeast

Active dry yeast differs from compressed yeast in that virtually all of the moisture has been removed by hot air. The absence of moisture renders the organism dormant and allows the yeast to be stored without refrigeration for several months. When preparing doughs, dry yeast is generally rehydrated in lukewarm (40°C [105°F to 110°F]) liquid before being added to the other ingredients.

Dry yeast is available in 7-g (1/4-oz.) packages and 450-g or 1-kg (1- or 2-lb.) vacuum-sealed bags. It should be stored in a cool, dry place and refrigerated after opening. Dry yeast can be substituted for fresh yeast by using 40% the amount by weight.

Instant Dry Yeast

Instant dry yeast has gained popularity because of its ease of use; it is added directly to the dry ingredients in a bread formula without rehydrating. The water in the formula activates it. Like all yeasts, instant dry yeast is a living organism and will be destroyed at temperatures above 59°C (138°F). While instant yeast can be added to flour without hydration, some bakers still prefer to hydrate instant yeast before using it in certain types of formulas. When doughs are mixed briefly or are very firm, such as bagel or croissant dough, instant dry yeast may not fully dissolve during mixing. In such cases the yeast is moistened in four to five times its weight of water. Deduct this amount of water from the total water called for in the formula. Beware of the yeast clumping.

Beware!

Yeast is temperature-sensitive and is killed if the liquid temperature is too high.

Too much sugar or salt will also kill yeast. Do not let yeast come in direct contact with concentrations of either.

Yeast stops growing or slows down if too cool.

Instant yeast is not the same as active dry yeast. Mix instant yeast with the flour in a recipe. Direct contact with milk will kill instant yeast.

Note the type of yeast being used and adjust the method and quantity accordingly.

Compressed Yeast

Dry Yeast

TABLE 29.2	Yeast Substitutions				
Use these formulas to convert from one type of yeast to another:					
Compressed (fresh) yeast	×	0.54	=	Active dry yeast	
Compressed (fresh) yeast	×	0.33	=	Instant yeast	
Active dry yeast	×	2	=	Compressed (fresh) yeast	
Active dry yeast	×	0.75	=	Instant yeast	
Instant yeast	×	3	=	Compressed (fresh) yeast	
Instant yeast	×	1.33	=	Active dry yeast	

Substituting Yeasts

The flavours of dry and compressed yeasts are virtually indistinguishable, but dry yeasts are at least twice as strong. Because too much yeast can ruin bread, always remember to reduce the specified weight for compressed yeast when substituting dry yeast or active dry yeast in a formula. Likewise, if a formula specifies dry or active dry yeast, increase the quantity specified when substituting compressed yeast. Do not dissolve instant yeast in milk or water. It will clump and not function properly.

Any type of yeast may be used in the formulas in this book. Use the formulas in Table 29.2 to convert one type of yeast to another.

PRODUCTION STAGES FOR YEAST BREADS

The production of yeast breads can be divided into 10 stages:

1. Scaling the ingredients
2. Mixing and kneading the dough
3. Fermenting the dough
4. Punching down the dough
5. Portioning the dough
6. Rounding the portions
7. Shaping the portions
8. Proofing the products
9. Baking the products
10. Cooling and storing the finished products

Stage 1: Scaling the Ingredients

As with any other bakeshop product, it is important to scale or measure ingredients accurately when making a yeast bread. Be sure that all necessary ingredients are available and at the proper temperature before starting.

The amount of flour required in a yeast bread may vary depending upon the humidity level, storage conditions of the flour and the accuracy with which other ingredients are measured. The amount of flour stated in most formulas is to be used as a guide; experience teaches when more or less flour is actually needed. The moisture content of the flour is an important consideration.

Stage 2: Mixing and Kneading the Dough

The way ingredients are combined affects the outcome of the bread. A dough must be mixed properly in order to combine the ingredients uniformly, distribute the yeast and develop the gluten. If the dough is not mixed properly, the bread's texture and shape suffer.

Yeast breads are usually mixed by either the **straight dough method** or the **sponge method**. A third method used for rich, flaky doughs is discussed later in the section on **rolled-in doughs**.

Once ingredients are combined, the dough must be kneaded to develop gluten, the network of proteins that gives a bread its shape and texture. Kneading can be done by hand or by an electric mixer with its dough hook attachment. Dough should be kneaded until it is smooth and moderately elastic. The presence of a few blisterlike air bubbles on the dough's surface also signals that kneading is complete. Because fat and sugar slow gluten development, rich, sweet doughs are generally kneaded longer than are lean doughs. Overkneading results in dough that is, at best, difficult to shape and, in extreme cases, sticky and inelastic. Overkneading is rarely a problem, however, except when using a high-speed mixer or food processor.

BASIC PROCEDURE FOR KNEADING DOUGH BY HAND

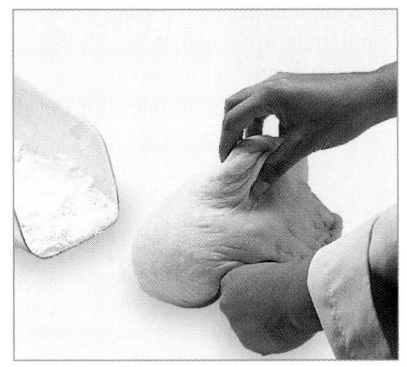

1. First, bring a portion of the dough toward you.

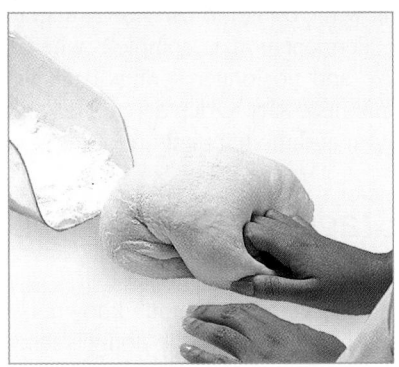

2. Then push the dough away from you with your fist.

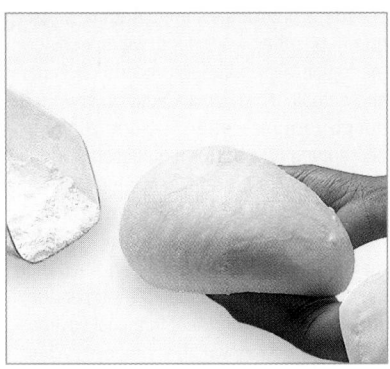

3. Repeat until the dough is properly kneaded.

Straight Dough Method

The simplest and most common method for mixing yeast doughs is known as the straight dough method. With this method, all ingredients are simply combined and mixed. The yeast may or may not be combined first with a warm liquid. Be careful that the temperature of the liquid ingredients does not exceed 59°C (138°F) or the yeast will die.

Once the ingredients are combined, the dough is kneaded until it is smooth and elastic. Kneading time varies according to the kneading method used and the type of dough being produced. The straight dough method is illustrated with Recipe 29.1, Soft Yeast Dinner Rolls.

Sponge Method

The sponge method of mixing yeast doughs has two stages. During the first stage, the yeast, liquid and approximately one-half of the flour are combined to make a thick batter known as a sponge. The sponge is allowed to rise until bubbly and doubled in size. During the second stage, the fat, salt, sugar and remaining flour are added. The dough is kneaded and allowed to rise again. These two fermentations give sponge method breads a somewhat different flavour and a lighter texture than breads made with the straight dough method.

● **straight dough method** a mixing method for yeast breads in which all ingredients are simply combined and mixed

● **sponge method** a mixing method for yeast breads that has two stages; in the first, yeast, liquid and approximately one-half of the flour are combined to create a thick batter (sponge), which is allowed to rise; in the second, fat, salt, sugar and the remaining flour are added, and the dough is kneaded and allowed to rise again

● **rolled-in dough** a dough in which a fat is incorporated in many layers by using a rolling and folding procedure; this method is used for flaky baked goods such as croissants, puff pastry and Danish pastry

Controlling Fermentation

The ingredients in the formula, the dough temperature and the temperature of the environment in which the dough ferments will affect the total fermentation time. Bakers use different strategies to regulate fermentation time to achieve desired results.

Ingredients—Dough with more yeast and more yeast food will ferment more quickly. Increasing the yeast in a formula will increase the rate of fermentation, thus speeding production time. Adding sugar, honey or other yeast food will speed fermentation also, although too much sugar can actually slow yeast's activity; enriched dough formulas often include a higher percentage of yeast for this reason.

Dough Temperature—Using warmer water in the dough and fermenting it in a warm environment will speed up the fermentation process. Conversely, kneading the dough to the proper dough temperature and then letting it ferment in a cool environment will slow down this process. When mixing yeast dough, keep in mind that wintertime baking in colder climates may require very warm water to begin yeast activity. Summertime baking in hot climates may require very cool water to keep bread dough from fermenting too quickly.

Room Temperature—Bakeries often extend the fermentation time of certain doughs in a specially designed refrigerator called a retarder. The cool temperature slows down the yeast activity, giving the dough the maximum opportunity to develop its flavour.

Do not confuse sponge method breads with sourdough starters. The sponge method is most often used to improve the texture of heavy doughs such as rye. Unlike a sourdough starter, the first-stage sponge is prepared only for the specific formula and is not reserved for later use. The sponge method is illustrated with Recipe 29.2, Medium Sour Rye Bread.

Stage 3: Fermenting the Dough

As mentioned earlier, fermentation is the process by which yeast converts sugar into alcohol and carbon dioxide. Fermentation also refers to the time that yeast dough is left to rise—that is, the time it takes for carbon dioxide gas to form and become trapped in the gluten network. Note that fermentation refers to the rise given to the entire mass of yeast dough, while **proofing** refers to the rise given to shaped yeast products just prior to baking.

For fermentation, place the kneaded dough into a lightly oiled container large enough to allow the dough to expand. The surface of the dough may be lightly oiled to prevent drying. Cover the dough and place it in a warm place—that is, at temperatures between 24°C and 29°C (75°F and 85°F). It is better to allow the dough to rise slowly than to rush fermentation.

Fermentation is complete when the dough has approximately doubled in size and no longer springs back when pressed gently with two fingers. The time necessary varies depending on the type of dough, the temperature of the room and the temperature of the dough.

Stage 4: Punching Down the Dough

After fermentation, the dough is gently folded down to expel excessive gas pockets with a technique known as **punching down**. Punching down dough also helps even out the dough's temperature.

Stage 5: Portioning the Dough

The dough is now ready to be divided into portions. For loaves, the dough is scaled to the desired weight. For individual rolls, you can first shape the dough into an even log, then cut off portions with a chef's knife or dough cutter. Weighing the cut dough pieces on a portion scale ensures even-sized portions. When portioning, work quickly and keep the dough covered to prevent it from drying out.

Stage 6: Rounding the Portions

The portions of dough must be shaped into smooth, round balls in a technique known as **rounding**. Rounding stretches the outside layer of gluten into a smooth coating. This helps hold in gases and makes it easier to shape the dough. Unrounded rolls rise unevenly and have a rough, lumpy surface.

Stage 7: Shaping the Portions

Lean doughs and some rich doughs can be shaped into a variety of forms: large loaves, small loaves, free-form or country-style rounds or individual dinner rolls. One shaping or makeup technique is shown in Figure 29.1. Other doughs, particularly brioche, croissant and Danish, are usually shaped in very specific ways. Those techniques are discussed and illustrated with their specific formulas.

Cloverleaf rolls

Bow knot rolls

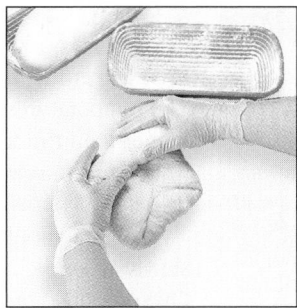
Loaves in a bannaton

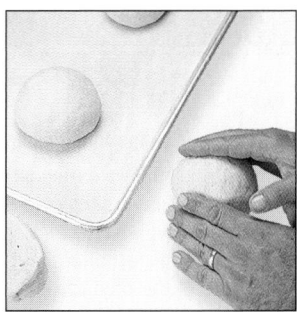
Rounding bread dough.

BASIC PROCEDURE FOR FORMING A TWISTED KNOT ROLL OR LOAF

1. Roll a portion of dough into a long rope. Form a loop by attaching the left end to the middle of the rope. Pinch to seal the dough.

2. Pass the right end of the rope through the loop.

3. Fold down the top of the loop and twist slightly.

4. Thread the loose end of the loaf through the loop.

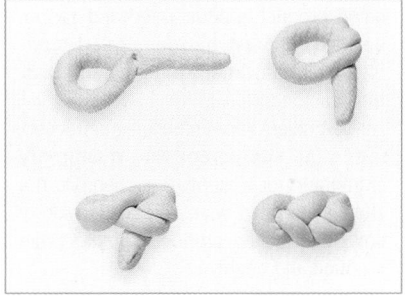
Forming a twisted knot loaf.

BASIC PROCEDURE FOR ROLLING A BAGUETTE

1. Round a portion of dough into a ball by rolling it under cupped hands across the surface of the workbench.

2. Roll the ball of dough out into a short cylinder.

3. With both hands together, roll the dough until it gradually begins to lengthen.

4. Roll to the desired length.

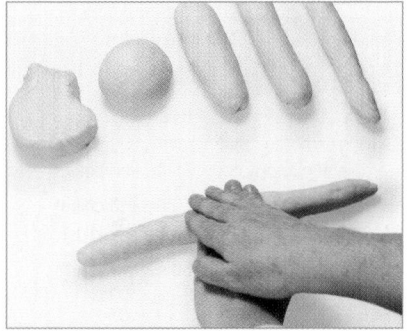
Forming and then rolling a baguette.

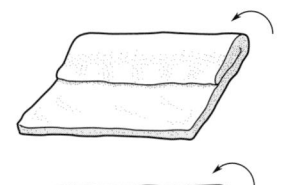
1. Flatten the dough into a rectangle. Fold over one short edge and press the seam together.

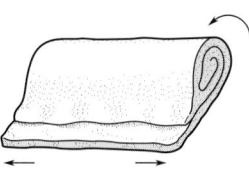
2. Continue to roll the dough, pressing the seam firmly with each turn. Stretch the front corners as necessary to maintain the shape.

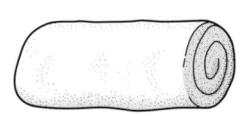
3. Place the finished roll of dough in a greased pan, seam side down. Proof.

FIGURE 29.1 Pan loaves.

Shaped Doughs

The following are some of the most popular shaped doughs:

Bagel—A dense, doughnut-shaped yeast roll; it is cooked in boiling water, then baked, which gives it a shiny glaze and chewy texture.

Bun—Any of a variety of small, round yeast rolls; buns can be sweet or savoury.

Club roll—A small, oval-shaped roll made of crusty French bread.

Kaiser roll—A large, round yeast roll with a crisp crust and a curved pattern stamped on the top; used primarily for sandwiches.

TABLE 29.3	Washes for Yeast Products
Wash	**Use**
Whole egg and water	Shine and colour
Whole egg and milk	Shine and colour with a soft crust
Egg white and water	Shine with a firm crust
Water	Crisp crust
Flour	Texture and contrast
Milk or cream	Colour with a soft crust

● **oven spring** the rapid rise of yeast goods in a hot oven, resulting from the production and expansion of trapped gases

● **wash** a glaze applied to dough before baking; a commonly used wash is made with whole egg and water

● **slashing** cutting the top of bread just before baking with a sharp knife or razor to improve shape and appearance and allow for continued rising and escape of gases from hard-crusted breads

Stage 8: Proofing the Products

Proofing is the final rise of shaped or panned yeast products before baking. The temperatures should be between 35°C and 46°C (95°F and 115°F), slightly higher than the temperatures for fermentation. Some humidity is also desirable to prevent the dough from drying or forming a crust. Temperature and humidity can be controlled with a special cabinet known as a proof box.

Proofing should continue until the product doubles in size and springs back slowly when lightly touched. Underproofing results in poor volume and texture. Overproofing results in a sour taste, poor volume and a paler colour after baking.

Stage 9: Baking the Products

As yeast breads bake, a variety of chemical and physical changes turn the dough into an edible product. These changes are discussed in Chapter 27, Principles of the Bakeshop.

Because of the expansion of gases, yeast products experience a sudden rise when first placed in a hot oven. This rise is known as **oven spring**. As the dough's temperature increases, the yeast dies, the gluten fibres become firm, the starches gelatinize, the moisture evaporates and, finally, the crust forms and turns brown.

Before baking, products can be washed and then, if desired, slashed.

Washes

The appearance of yeast breads can be altered by applying a glaze or **wash** to the dough before baking. The crust is made shiny or matte, hard or soft, darker or lighter by the proper use of washes. (See Table 29.3.) Washes are also used to attach seeds, wheat germ, oats or other toppings to the dough's surface.

The most commonly used wash is an egg wash, composed of whole egg and water. Yeast products can also be topped with plain water, a mixture of egg and milk, plain milk or richer glazes containing sugar and flavourings. Even a light dusting of white flour can be used to top dough. (This is commonly seen with potato rolls.)

Avoid using too much wash, as it can burn or cause the product to stick to the pan. Puddles or streaks of egg wash on the dough will cause uneven browning.

Washes may be applied before or after proofing. If applied after proofing, be extremely careful not to deflate the product.

Occasionally a formula will specify that melted butter or oil be brushed on the product after baking. Do not, however, apply egg washes to already baked products, as the egg will remain raw and the desired effect will not be achieved.

Slashing

The shape and appearance of some breads can be improved by cutting their tops with a sharp knife or razor just before baking. This is referred to as **slashing**. Hard-crusted breads are usually slashed to allow for continued rising and the escape of gases after the crust has formed. Breads that are not properly slashed will burst or break along the sides. Slashing can also be used to make an attractive design on the product's surface. Docking or pricking a dough with small holes will help prevent the formation of irregular air bubbles in flatbreads such as pizza and crackers.

Steam Injection

The crisp crust desired for certain breads and rolls is achieved by introducing moisture into the oven during baking. Professional bakers' ovens have built-in steam injection jets to provide moisture as needed. To create steam in any oven, you can spray or mist the bread with water several times during baking, place ice cubes on the oven floor to melt or keep a pan of hot water on the oven's lowest rack. Rich doughs, which do not form crisp crusts, are baked without steam.

Determining Doneness

Baking time is determined by a variety of factors: the product's size, the oven thermostat's accuracy and the desired crust colour. Larger items require a longer baking time than do smaller ones. Lean dough products bake faster and at higher temperatures than do rich dough products.

Bread loaves can be tested for doneness by tapping them on the bottom and listening for a hollow sound. This indicates that air, not moisture, is present inside the loaf. If the bottom is damp or heavy, the loaf probably needs more baking time. The texture and colour of the crust are also a good indication of doneness, particularly with individual rolls. As you bake a variety of yeast products, you will develop the experience necessary to determine doneness without strict adherence to elapsed time.

Stage 10: Cooling and Storing the Finished Products

The quality of even the finest yeast products suffers if they are cooled or stored improperly. Yeast products should be cooled at room temperature and away from drafts. Yeast breads and rolls should be removed from their pans for cooling. Allow loaves to cool completely before slicing.

Once cool, yeast products should be stored at room temperature or frozen for longer storage. Do not refrigerate baked goods, as refrigeration promotes staling. Do not wrap Italian or French loaves, as this causes crusts to lose the desired crispness.

Frozen Doughs

There are many frozen dough products on the market today. They come shaped and partially or fully proofed. After flash or shock freezing, they are packaged for distribution. The raw product is trayed, allowed to thaw and proof, then baked. Par-baked items are placed directly in a hot oven to finish baking.

APPLYING THE BASICS　　　　　　　　　**RECIPE 29.1**

Soft Yeast Dinner Rolls

Yield: 36 rolls

Method: Straight dough

Instant dry yeast	22.5 g	3/4 oz.
Bread flour	600 g	1 lb. 5 oz.
Salt	15 g	1/2 oz.
Sugar	60 g	2 oz.
Dried milk powder	30 g	1 oz.
Water, lukewarm	300 g	10 oz.
Shortening	30 g	1 oz.
Unsalted butter, softened	30 g	1 oz.
Eggs, whole	60 g	2 oz.
Egg wash	as needed	as needed

RECIPE 29.1

Approximate values per roll:	
Calories	78
Total fat	2 g
Saturated fat	1 g
Cholesterol	9 mg
Sodium	161 mg
Total carbohydrates	13 g
Protein	3 g

continued

1. Soft Yeast Dinner Rolls: Mixing the soft yeast dough. Combining the ingredients in a mixer bowl with the dough hook attached.

1. Combine the dry ingredients in the bowl of an electric mixer with hook attachment.

2. Add the water, shortening, butter and egg (whole); stir to combine.

3. Knead with a dough hook on second speed for 10 minutes.

4. Transfer the dough to a lightly greased bowl, cover and place in a warm spot. Let rise until doubled, approximately 1 hour.

5. Punch down the dough. Let it rest a few minutes to allow the gluten to relax.

6. Divide the dough into 35-g (1-1/4-oz.) portions and round. Shape as desired and arrange on paper-lined sheet pans. Proof until doubled in size.

7. Carefully brush the proofed rolls with egg wash. Bake at 200°C (400°F) until medium brown, approximately 12–15 minutes.

2. Kneading the dough.

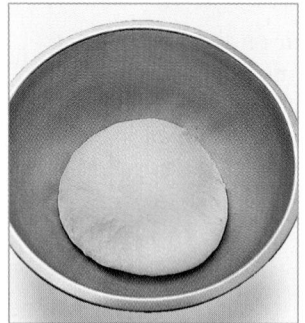

3. The dough before rising.

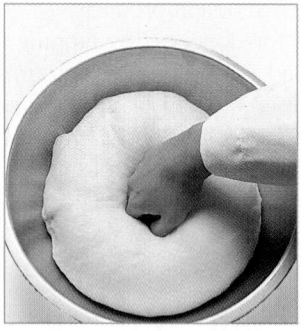

4. Punching down the risen dough:
a) Pressing down on the centre of the dough with your fist.

b) Folding the edges of the dough in toward the centre.

5. Scaling the dough.

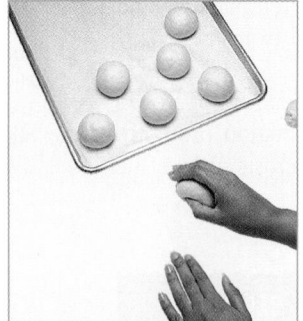

6. Rounding the rolls.

7. Egg-washing the rolls.

RECIPE 29.2

Approximate values per slice:	
Calories	74
Total fat	0.4 g
Saturated fat	0 g
Cholesterol	0 mg
Sodium	163 mg
Total carbohydrates	15 g
Protein	2.6 g

APPLYING THE BASICS   RECIPE 29.2

Medium Sour Rye Bread

Yield: 4.3 kg (9 lb.) (6 loaves)

Dark rye flour	600 g	1 lb. 8 oz.
Light rye flour	600 g	1 lb. 8 oz.
Bread flour	1.25 kg	2 lb. 12 oz.
Salt	50 g	1-3/4 oz.
Dehydrated sourdough starter	40 g	1-1/4 oz.
Yeast, instant	22.5 g	3/4 oz.
Water, 40°C (105°F)	1.7 kg	3 lb. 6 oz.

continued

1. Blend the first 6 ingredients with a hook in mixing bowl for 1 minute on low speed.

2. Verify temperature of water and add to the flour.

3. Mix for 2 minutes on low speed and 5 minutes on second speed.

4. Bench for 30 minutes (benching refers to the time the dough rests in its first proofing stage at room temperature).

5. Divide dough into 700-g (1 lb. 8 oz.) rounds and rest 15 minutes.

6. Bake at 220°C (430°F) for 10–15 minutes, then turn oven down to 180°C (390°F) to finish baking, approximately 30 minutes

1. Medium Sour Rye Bread: Rye bread starter.

2. Mixing the rye dough.

3. Shaping the rye loaves.

ROLLED-IN DOUGHS

Baked goods made with rolled-in doughs include croissants, Danish pastries and the non-yeast-leavened puff pastry. (Puff pastry is discussed in Chapter 30, Pies, Pastries and Cookies.) The dough is so named because the fat is incorporated through a process of rolling and folding. Products made with a rolled-in dough have a distinctive flaky texture created by the repeated layering of fat and dough. As the dough bakes, moisture is released from the fat in the form of steam. The steam is then trapped between the layers of dough, causing them to rise and separate.

Making Rolled-in Doughs

Rolled-in doughs are made following most of the 10 production stages discussed earlier. The principal differences are (1) the butter is incorporated through a folding process after the dough base is fermented and punched down; (2) rolled-in doughs are portioned somewhat differently from other yeast doughs; and (3) the portions are then shaped without rounding.

Butter is often used for rolled-in products because of its flavour. Unfortunately, butter is hard to work with because it cracks and breaks when cold and becomes too soft to roll at room temperature. Margarine, shortening or specially formulated high-moisture fats can be used, sometimes in combination with butter, in order to reduce costs or to make it easier to work with the dough.

The dough base should not be kneaded too much, as gluten will continue to develop during the rolling and folding process. Commercial bakeries, hotels and larger restaurants generally use an electric dough sheeter to roll the dough. This saves time and ensures a more consistent product.

The Cultured Croissant

A croissant brings to mind a Parisian sidewalk café and a steaming cup of café au lait. It is, however, a truly international delicacy. Created by bakers in Budapest (Hungary) to celebrate the city's liberation from Turkey in 1686, its shape was derived from the crescent moon of the Turkish flag. The delicacy was soon adopted as a breakfast pastry by both the French and the Italians. The first machine for mass-producing croissants was designed by a Japanese firm and manufactured in Italy. Although croissants became popular in North America only during the last generation or so, millions of croissants are now consumed each year.

Volker Baumann, CMB
Volker, a Certified Master Baker and instructor at SAIT Polytechnic, comes from a family of bakers, all of whom are passionate about the profession. He began his training in Germany and later moved to Canada, where he ran his own bakery successfully for several years. Volker's accomplishments include acting as the Educational Chair for the Baking Association of Canada and publishing a book, *Baking: The Art and Science*. He has also received several prestigious awards, including an award for excellence in the classroom.

BASIC PROCEDURE FOR PREPARING ROLLED-IN DOUGHS

1. Mix the dough and allow it to rise.
2. Shape the butter or shortening, then chill it.
3. Roll out the dough evenly, then top with the chilled butter.
4. Fold the dough around the butter, enclosing it completely.
5. Roll out the dough into a rectangle, about 0.6 to 1.25 cm (1/4 to 1/2 in.) thick. Always be sure to roll at right angles; do not roll haphazardly or in a circle as you would roll pastry doughs.
6. Fold the dough in thirds. Be sure to brush off any excess flour from between the folds. This completes the first turn. Chill the dough for 20 to 30 minutes.
7. Roll out the dough and fold it in the same manner a second and third time, allowing the dough to rest between each turn. After completing the third turn, wrap the dough carefully and allow it to rest for several hours or overnight before shaping and baking.

APPLYING THE BASICS — RECIPE 29.3

Croissants

SAIT POLYTECHNIC, Calgary, AB
SCHOOL OF HOSPITALITY AND TOURISM
Master Baker Volker Baumann, CMB

Yield: 36 90-g (3-oz.) rolls
Method: Rolled in

Bread flour	1.5 kg	4 lb. 2 oz.
Milk	480 g	16 oz.
Water	480 g	16 oz.
Sugar	150 g	5 oz.
Salt	30 g	1 oz.
Yeast, fresh	30 g	1 oz.
Butter	675 g	1 lb. 8 oz.
Bread flour	125 g	6-1/2 oz.
Egg wash	as needed	as needed

1. Incorporate first 6 ingredients on low speed for 3 minutes using a dough hook. Dough should be a medium-stiff consistency.
2. Increase mixing speed to medium and mix for 4–5 minutes until dough becomes smooth but not fully developed. Dough temperature should be 24°C (75°F).
3. Remove dough from mixer, cover and let proof 30 minutes at room temperature.
4. Shape dough into a rectangle about 1.25 cm (1/2 in.) thick, cover again and refrigerate dough overnight.
5. Mix butter and flour to a paste and shape into a 20 × 27 cm (8 × 11 in.) rectangle between two plastic sheets.
6. Roll the dough into a rectangle just more than twice the size of the butter mixture. Place prepared butter (pliable) on half of the dough rectangle, and then fold over to cover butter. Roll dough to a thickness of about 8 mm (1/2 in.) and fold into 3 equal parts like a business letter (single fold). Maintain the rectangular shape.

continued

7. Refrigerate dough for 30 minutes. Repeat 2 more single folds, chilling between each, for a total of 3. Refrigerate dough at least 1 hour before makeup.

8. Roll dough to a thickness of 3 mm (1/8 in.) (#3 on reversible sheeter) and cut into 90-g (3-oz.) triangles.

9. Shape into croissants starting at the large end, place on a parchment-lined sheet pan and proof until double in size (1–1.5 hours) at 20°C (78°F), covered with plastic sheet.

10. Brush with egg wash and bake 16–18 minutes at 190°C (375°F).

Variations: Fill with grated cheese, chocolate or hazelnut filling. For a deeper shine, brush twice with egg wash before baking.

RECIPE 29.3

Approximate values per serving:	
Calories	325
Total fat	16 g
Saturated fat	10 g
Cholesterol	52 mg
Sodium	441 mg
Total carbohydrates	38 g
Protein	6 g

1. Croissants: Rolling out the butter between two sheets of plastic wrap.

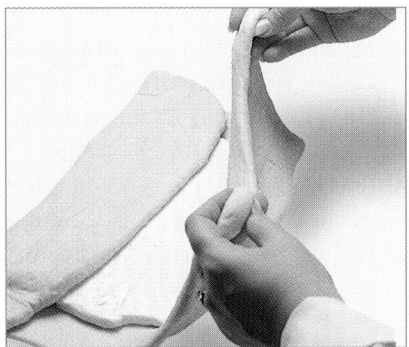

2. Folding the dough around the butter, which has been placed in the centre.

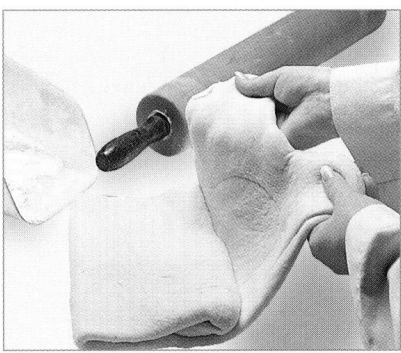

3. Folding the dough in thirds.

4. The finished croissant dough.

5. Cutting the dough into triangles.

6. The baked croissants.

QUALITIES OF BREAD

Bread is judged by its external and internal appearance, flavour, aroma and keeping properties. Well-crafted bread has a pleasing uniform brown surface colour. The crust is neither too thick nor too thin depending on the type of formula. The crust is crisp or tender without being leathery and excessively thick. With the exception of long-fermented sourdough, the crust should be uniform and free from surface blisters. The interior (crumb) of a tender crusted bread or enriched dough product should be even and moist without being sticky. A long-fermented country bread or sourdough may contain an irregular cell structure characteristic of this type of bread. Well-crafted bread has good keeping properties; improperly made bread will stale in a matter of hours.

Conclusion

Fresh yeast breads are a popular and inexpensive addition to any menu and are surprisingly easy to prepare. By understanding and appreciating the importance of each of the 10 production stages described in this chapter, you will be able to create and adapt formulas to suit your specific operation and needs. Table 29.4 provides some troubleshooting guidelines should you encounter difficulties.

Questions for Discussion

1. Describe the characteristics of lean and rich doughs and give an example of each.
2. Explain the differences between active dry yeast and compressed yeast. Describe the correct procedures for working with these yeasts.
3. Explain the differences between a sponge and a sourdough starter. How are each of these items used?
4. Describe the straight dough mixing method and give two examples of products made using this procedure.
5. Briefly describe the procedure for making a rolled-in dough and give two examples of products made from rolled-in doughs.
6. List the 10 production stages for yeast breads. Which of these production stages would also apply to quick-bread production? Explain your answer.

TABLE 29.4	Troubleshooting Chart for Yeast Breads	
Problem	**Cause**	**Solution**
Cannonball of dough	Too much flour forced into the dough	Gradually add water; adjust formula
Crust too pale	Oven temperature too low	Adjust oven
	Dough overproofed	Proof only until almost doubled, then bake immediately
Crust too dark	Oven too hot	Adjust oven
	Too much sugar in dough	Adjust formula or measure sugar carefully
Top crust separates from rest of loaf	Dough improperly shaped	Shape dough carefully
	Crust not slashed properly	Slash dough to a depth of 1.25 cm (1/2 in.)
	Dough dried out during proofing	Cover dough during proofing
Sides of loaf are cracked	Bread expanded after crust had formed	Slash top of loaf before baking
Dense texture	Not enough yeast	Adjust formula or measure yeast carefully
	Not enough fermentation time	Let dough rise until doubled or as directed
	Too much salt	Adjust formula or measure salt carefully
Ropes of undercooked dough running through the product	Insufficient kneading	Knead dough until it is smooth and elastic or as directed
	Insufficient rising time	Allow adequate time for rising
	Oven too hot	Adjust oven
Free-form loaf spreads and flattens	Dough too soft	Add flour
Large holes in bread	Too much yeast	Adjust formula or measure yeast carefully
	Overkneaded	Knead only as directed
	Inadequate punch-down	Punch down properly to knead out excess air before shaping
Blisters on crust	Too much liquid	Measure ingredients carefully
	Improper shaping	Knead out excess air before shaping
	Too much steam in oven	Reduce amount of steam or moisture in oven

Additional Yeast Bread Formulas

RECIPE 29.4

Baguette

Yield: 12.5 kg (25 lb.)

Method: Straight dough	Dough temperature 28°C (82°F)	
Bread flour	7.5 kg	14 lb.
Yeast, instant dry	45 g	1-1/2 oz.
Salt	150 g	4 oz.
Malt	75 g	2-1/2 oz.
Shortening	75 g	2-1/2 oz.
Format (if available)	60 g	2-1/2 oz.
Water, 22°C	4.5 kg	8-1/4 qt.

1. Place flour, yeast, salt, malt, shortening and format (if using) into a mixing bowl.

2. Warm the water and add to mix.

3. Mix with a hook for 1 minute on low speed, then check the dough for consistency and continue mixing for 9–10 minutes at second speed.

4. Bench for 15 minutes at a dough temperature of 28°C (82°F).

5. Divide dough into 600-g (22-oz.) portions and give 10 minutes' intermediate proof.

6. Mould, proof, cut and bake at 215°C (420°F) for 30–35 minutes.

NOTE: Format is a dough conditioner that speeds up fermentation. If unavailable, proceed with the next ingredient but be aware that the proofing will take longer.

RECIPE 29.4

Approximate values per slice:	
Calories	98
Total fat	0.7 g
Saturated fat	0 g
Cholesterol	0 mg
Sodium	203 mg
Total carbohydrates	19 g
Protein	3.2 g

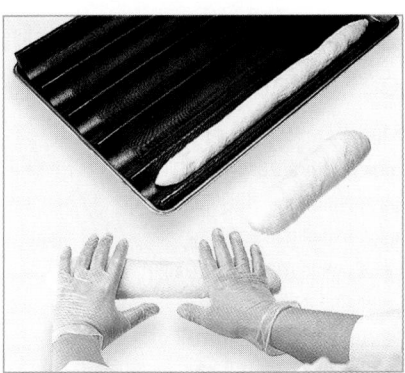

1. Baguette: The dough is portioned and then rolled into baguettes in two stages.

2. The proofed loaves are slashed to allow steam to escape.

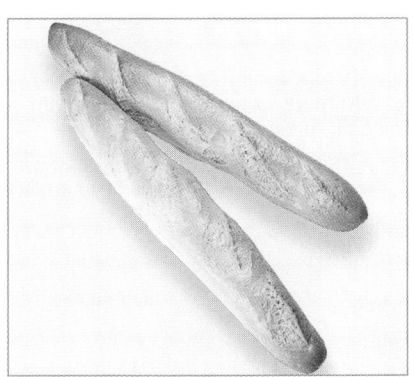

3. The finished baguettes.

RECIPE 29.5

White Pan Bread

Yield: 18 kg (40 lb.)

Method: Straight dough   Dough temperature 28°C (82°F)

Ingredient	Metric	US
Bread flour	10 kg	22 lb.
Yeast, instant	125 g	4-1/3 oz.
Sugar	450 g	15-3/4 oz.
Salt	200 g	7 oz.
Milk powder	300 g	10-1/2 oz.
Shortening	400 g	14 oz.
Water, room temperature	6–7 L	190–220 fl. oz.

1. Place all ingredients except water in a mixing bowl and stir to mix.
2. Add water to the mix.
3. Mix for 2 minutes on low speed.
4. Check dough for consistency and add more flour or water as needed. Continue mixing for 9–10 minutes on second speed.
5. Divide dough into 540-g (18-oz.) units, shape into rounds and give them 10 minutes' intermediate proof.
6. Mould dough pieces and place in bread pans.
7. Proof.
8. Bake at 200°C (400°F) for about 30 minutes.
9. Cool on wire rack before slicing and bagging.

RECIPE 29.5

Approximate values per slice:

Calories	93
Total fat	1.2 g
Saturated fat	0.3 g
Cholesterol	0 mg
Sodium	172 mg
Total carbohydrates	17 g
Protein	2.9 g

RECIPE 29.6

60% Whole Wheat Bread

Yield: 19 kg (42 lb.)

Method: Straight dough   Dough temperature 28°C (82°F)

Ingredient	Metric	US
Bread flour	4.3 kg	9 lb.
Whole wheat flour	6.3 kg	13 lb.
Sugar	450 g	15-3/4 oz.
Shortening	400 g	14 oz.
Milk powder	300 g	10-1/2 oz.
Salt	200 g	7 oz.
Yeast, fresh	350 g	12-1/4 oz.
Water, 22°C	7–8 L	190–260 fl. oz.

1. Place flour and all ingredients except yeast and water in mixing bowl.
2. Dissolve yeast in water and add to mix.
3. Mix 2 minutes on low speed.
4. Check dough for proper consistency and add more water or flour as needed. Continue mixing for 9–10 minutes on second speed.
5. Divide dough into 540-g (18-oz.) units, round and give 10 minutes' intermediate proof.
6. Mould dough pieces and place into bread pans.
7. Proof.
8. Bake at 200°C (400°F) for about 30 minutes.
9. Cool on wire rack before slicing and bagging.

RECIPE 29.6

Approximate values per serving:

Calories	89
Total fat	1.2 g
Saturated fat	0.3 g
Cholesterol	0 mg
Sodium	163 mg
Total carbohydrates	17 g
Protein	3.1 g

RECIPE 29.7

Multigrain Date Bread

Yield: 2 small loaves
Method: Straight dough

Dates, chopped	250 g	8 oz.
Bread flour	725 g	1 lb. 8 oz.
Instant dry yeast	12 g	4 tsp.
Whole wheat flour	175 g	6 oz.
Water, heated to 20°C (70°F)	500 g	16 oz.
Honey	125 g	4 oz.
Unsalted butter, melted	60 g	2 oz.
Nonfat dry milk	35 g	1-1/4 oz.
Salt	15 g	1 Tbsp.
Rye flour	50 g	2 oz.
Wheat germ	50 g	2 oz.
Bran flakes, toasted	50 g	2 oz.
Sesame seeds	10 g	2 Tbsp.
Egg wash	as needed	as needed
Poppy or sesame seeds	10 g	2 Tbsp.

1. In a small bowl, combine the dates with 60 g (2 oz.) of the bread flour; toss to coat and set aside. Mix yeast with whole wheat flour.

2. In a large mixer bowl, add the warm water. Add the honey, butter, milk powder, salt and whole wheat flour–yeast mixture. Beat at medium speed for 2 minutes.

3. Stir in the rye flour, wheat germ, bran flakes, sesame seeds and date mixture.

4. Slowly add enough of the remaining bread flour to make a soft dough. Knead until smooth and elastic, approximately 5 minutes.

5. Place the dough in a lightly greased bowl and cover. Allow to rise until doubled, approximately 1.5 hours.

6. Punch down the dough and knead for a few seconds.

7. Divide the dough in half. Shape each piece and place in a lightly greased loaf pan. Cover and allow to rise until almost doubled, approximately 45 minutes.

8. Slash the top of the loaves as desired and top with egg wash and poppy or sesame seeds. Bake at 190°C (375°F) until golden brown and firm, approximately 40 minutes. Loaves should be dry and sound hollow when tapped on the bottom. Remove the loaves from the pans to cool.

RECIPE 29.7

Approximate values per slice:

Calories	162
Total fat	3 g
Saturated fat	1 g
Cholesterol	4 mg
Sodium	203 mg
Total carbohydrates	32 g
Protein	5.5 g

RECIPE 29.8

Breadsticks

Yield: 36 breadsticks
Method: Straight dough

Water, heated to 20°C (70°F)	450 g	15 oz.
Sugar	45 g	1-1/2 oz.
Instant dry yeast	20 g	2 Tbsp.
Bread flour	750 g	1 lb. 11 oz.
Olive oil	180 mL	6 fl. oz.
Salt	15 g	3 tsp.
Egg wash	as needed	as needed
Sesame seeds	25 g	3/4 oz.

RECIPE 29.8

Approximate values per breadstick:

Calories	128
Total fat	5.3 g
Saturated fat	0.7 g
Cholesterol	0 mg
Sodium	168 mg
Total carbohydrates	17 g
Protein	3.3 g

continued

1. Stir the water and sugar together in a mixer bowl.

2. Mix the yeast with 250 g of the bread flour.

3. Blend in the oil, salt and 250 g (8 oz.) of the flour-yeast mixture.

4. Gradually add the remaining flour. Knead the dough until it is smooth and cleans the sides of the bowl, approximately 5 minutes.

5. Remove the dough from the bowl and allow it to rest for a few minutes. Roll the dough into a rectangle, about 0.5 cm (1/4 in.) thick.

6. Cut the dough into 24 even pieces. Roll each piece into a rope and twist; bring the ends together, allowing the sides to curl together. Place on a paper-lined sheet pan.

7. Brush with egg wash and top with sesame seeds. Let the sticks rise until doubled, approximately 20 minutes.

8. Bake at 190°C (375°F) until golden brown, approximately 12–15 minutes.

VARIATIONS: GARLIC BREADSTICKS—Knead 30 g (1 oz.) grated Parmesan cheese and 25 g (2 Tbsp.) minced garlic into the dough.

HERBED BREADSTICKS—Knead 30 g (3 Tbsp.) chopped fresh herbs such as basil, parsley, dill and oregano into the dough.

1. Breadsticks: Rolling the breadstick dough.

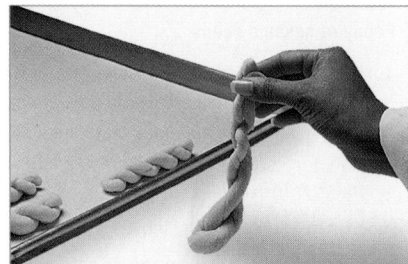

2. Twisting the breadstick dough.

Focaccia: Topping the focaccia (flat-bread) dough with crushed rosemary.

RECIPE 29.9

Approximate values per serving:	
Calories	156
Total fat	2 g
Saturated fat	0 g
Cholesterol	0 mg
Sodium	325 mg
Total carbohydrates	32 g
Protein	6 g

RECIPE 29.9

Focaccia

Yield: 1 sheet pan, 30 × 45 cm (12 × 18 in.)
Method: Straight dough

Sugar	15 g	1 Tbsp.
Water, lukewarm	350 mL	12 fl. oz.
Instant dry yeast	7.5 g	2-1/4 tsp.
Bread flour	500 g	1 lb. 2 oz.
Kosher salt	10 g	2 tsp.
Onion, chopped fine	90 g	3 oz.
Olive oil	10 mL	2 tsp.
Fresh rosemary, crushed	25 g	2 Tbsp.

1. Combine the sugar and water. Stir the yeast into the flour. Stir in the flour mixture 125 g (4 oz.) at a time.

2. Stir in 5 g (1 tsp.) of salt and the onion. Mix well, then knead on a lightly floured board until smooth.

3. Place the dough in an oiled bowl, cover and let rise until doubled.

4. Punch down the dough, then flatten it onto an oiled sheet pan. It should be no more than 2.5 cm (1 in.) thick. Brush the top of the dough with the olive oil. Let the dough proof until doubled, about 15 minutes.

5. Sprinkle the crushed rosemary and remaining salt on top of the dough. Bake at 200°C (400°F) until lightly browned, approximately 20 minutes.

Pizza Dough

Yield: 1 large or 4 individual pizzas
Method: Straight dough

Instant dry yeast	7.5 g	2-1/4 tsp.
Bread flour	450 g	16 oz.
Water, lukewarm	240 g	8 oz.
Salt	5 g	1 tsp.
Olive oil	45 mL	1-1/2 fl. oz.
Sugar	20 g	4 tsp.

1. Stir the yeast into the flour.

2. Stir the water, salt, olive oil and sugar into the flour mixture. Knead with a dough hook or by hand until smooth and elastic, approximately 5 minutes.

3. Place the dough in a lightly greased bowl and cover. Allow the dough to rise in a warm place for 30 minutes. Punch down the dough and divide into portions. The dough may be wrapped and refrigerated for up to 2 days.

4. On a lightly floured surface, roll the dough into very thin rounds and top as desired. Bake at 200°C (400°F) until crisp and golden brown, approximately 8–12 minutes.

NOTE: Substitute all-purpose flour for a more tender crust, but reduce water by 2–3%.

RECIPE 29.10

Approximate values per individual pizza:	
Calories	522
Total fat	12 g
Saturated fat	2 g
Cholesterol	0 mg
Sodium	489 mg
Total carbohydrates	87 g
Protein	14 g

Naan (Indian Flatbread)

Yield: 6 loaves, approximately 300 g (10 oz.) each
Method: Sponge

Compressed yeast	5 g	1 tsp.
Water	500 mL	17 fl. oz.
Bread flour	700 g	24 oz.
Whole-wheat flour	350 g	12 oz.
Yogurt	300 g	10 oz.
Olive oil	30 mL	2 Tbsp.
Baking powder	1.5 g	1/2 tsp.
Baking soda	1.5 g	1/2 tsp.
Salt	20 g	3-1/2 tsp.
Vegetable or olive oil	as needed	as needed
Black sesame seeds	as needed	as needed

1. To prepare the sponge, dissolve 2 mL (1/2 tsp.) yeast in 180 mL (6 fl. oz.) water in the bowl of a mixer fitted with a dough hook. Add 240 g (8 oz.) bread flour and mix until well incorporated. Cover and set aside. Ferment at room temperature until cracks appear on the surface of the starter, approximately 3 hours.

2. Place the sponge and the remaining 460 g (16 oz) bread flour, 320 mL (11 fl. oz.) water, whole-wheat flour, yogurt, olive oil, baking powder and baking soda in the bowl of a mixer fitted with a dough hook. Mix on low speed for 3 minutes. Stop the mixer and scrape down the bowl. Add the remaining compressed yeast and mix on high speed for an additional 3 minutes. Add the salt, then mix until the dough is smooth and elastic, approximately 5 minutes more.

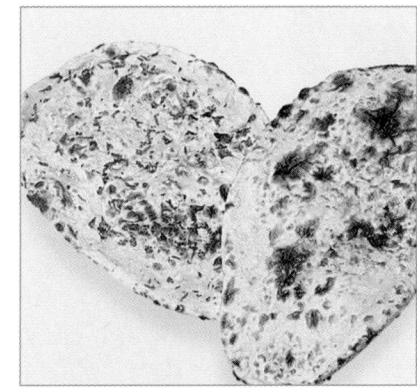

Naan

RECIPE 29.11

Approximate values per 1-1/2-oz. (45-g) serving:	
Calories	104
Total fat	1 g
Saturated fat	0 g
Cholesterol	0 mg
Sodium	214 mg
Total carbohydrates	20 g
Protein	4 g

continued

1. Brioche: Combining the ingredients for brioche.

2. Adding the water to the dough.

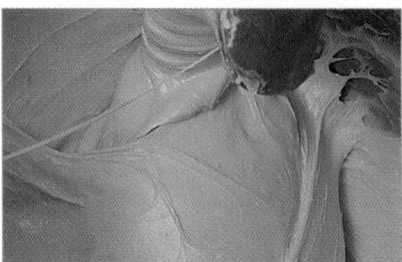

3. Brioche dough after 20 minutes of kneading.

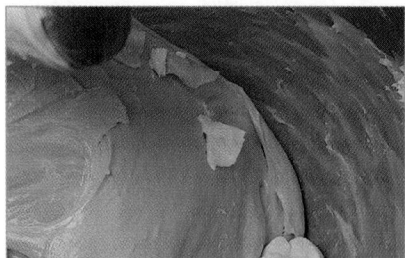

4. Adding the butter to the brioche dough.

3. Let the dough ferment, covered, for 3 hours.

4. Punch down the dough and divide it into 6 uniform pieces. Round the portioned dough. Cover and let rest for 30 minutes.

5. Stretch each piece of dough out until it measures 30 cm (12 in.) long. Place the dough on flour-dusted sheet pans and proof until doubled, approximately 50 minutes.

6. Dimple the surface of the dough with your fingertips. Brush the dough with oil and sprinkle it with black sesame seeds. Place the dough directly on the heated surface of a deck oven at 252°C (485°F) or place the sheet pan of dough on a rack in the oven. Bake until the breads are well browned and crisp, approximately 10–12 minutes. To prevent a soggy crust, open the oven door or vent during the last 2 minutes of baking to remove any excess steam that may build up in the oven. Cool the loaves on cooling racks, then serve immediately.

RECIPE 29.12

Brioche

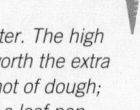

Brioche is a rich, tender bread made with an abundance of eggs and butter. The high ratio of fat makes this dough difficult to work with, but the flavour is well worth the extra effort. Brioche is traditionally made in fluted pans and has a cap or topknot of dough; this shape is known as brioche à tête. The dough may also be baked in a loaf pan, making it perfect for toast or canapés.

Yield: 3 large loaves or 60 7.5-cm (3-in.) rolls

Method: Straight dough

Bread flour	2 kg	4 lb. 7 oz.
Instant dry yeast	30 g	3 Tbsp.
Eggs	1.3 kg	24
Salt	20 g	3/4 oz.
Sugar	100 g	3-1/2 oz.
Water, heated to 20°C (70°F)	225 mL	7 fl. oz.
Unsalted butter, room temperature	1.3 kg	3 lb.

1. Place the flour, yeast, eggs, salt and sugar into the bowl of a large mixer fitted with the dough hook. Stir the ingredients together.

2. Add the water to the other ingredients.

3. Knead for 20 minutes on second speed. The dough will be smooth, shiny and moist. It should not form a ball.

continued

5. The finished brioche dough ready for fermentation.

6. Shaping the brioche à tête.

7. Panning the rolls.

4. Slowly add the butter to the dough. Knead only until all the butter is incorporated. Remove the dough from the mixer and place it into a bowl dusted with flour. Cover and let rise at room temperature until doubled.

5. Punch down the dough, cover well and refrigerate overnight.

6. Shape the chilled dough as desired. Place the shaped dough in well-greased pans and proof at room temperature until doubled. Do not proof brioche in a very warm place; the butter may melt out of the dough before proofing is complete.

7. Bake at 190°C (375°F) until the brioches are a dark golden brown and sound hollow. Baking time will vary depending on the temperature of the dough and the size of the rolls or loaves being baked.

VARIATION: RAISIN BRIOCHE—Gently warm 90 mL (3 fl. oz.) rum with 180 g (6 oz.) raisins. Set aside until the raisins are plumped. Drain off the remaining rum into the mixture and add the raisins to the dough after the butter is incorporated.

BRIOCHE FOR SANDWICHES OR COULIBIAC—Reduce the sugar to 90 g (3 oz.). Ferment the dough, then retard it overnight. Mould in a rectangular loaf pan for slicing. Or use the dough to wrap salmon and fillings for Coulibiac.

SAVOURY CHEESE AND HERB BRIOCHE—Reduce the sugar to 90 g (3 oz.). Add 120 g (4 oz.) grated Parmesan, 120 g (4 oz.) grated Gruyère cheese, 1 mL (1/4 tsp.) black pepper and 1 mL (1/4 tsp.) dried thyme to the dough with the flour. Mould in rectangular or conical pans. Served sliced thin with smoked salmon, pâté or other savoury spreads.

8. A finished loaf of brioche baked in a pullman pan.

RECIPE 29.12

Approximate values per roll:	
Calories	302
Total fat	20 g
Saturated fat	12 g
Cholesterol	141 mg
Sodium	159 mg
Total carbohydrates	25 g
Protein	8 g

RECIPE 29.13

Pecan Sticky Buns

Yield: 12–15 buns

Method: Straight dough

Instant dry yeast	22.5 g	7 tsp.
Bread flour	425 g	14 oz.
Sugar	60 g	2 oz.
Water	15 mL	1 Tbsp.
Buttermilk	175 mL	5-1/2 fl. oz.
Vanilla	5 mL	1 tsp.
Lemon zest, grated	10 g	1 Tbsp.
Lemon juice	5 mL	1 tsp.
Egg yolks	2	2
Salt	2 g	1/2 tsp.
Unsalted butter, very soft	250 g	8 oz.
Topping:		
Honey	175 g	6 oz.
Brown sugar	175 g	6 oz.
Pecans, chopped	100 g	3 oz.
Filling:		
Cinnamon	5 g	2 tsp.
Pecans, chopped	100 g	3 oz.
Brown sugar	125 g	4 oz.
Unsalted butter, melted	100 g	3 oz.

1. Stir yeast and flour together.

2. Stir the sugar, water, buttermilk, vanilla, lemon zest and lemon juice together in mixing bowl.

continued

3. Add the egg yolks, flour–yeast mixture, salt and softened butter to the liquid mixture. Turn out onto a lightly floured board and knead until the butter is evenly distributed and the dough is smooth. Cover and let rise until doubled.

4. Prepare the topping and filling mixtures while the dough is rising. To make the topping, cream the honey and sugar together. Stir in the nuts. This mixture will be very stiff. To make the filling, stir the cinnamon, pecans and sugar together.

5. Lightly grease muffin cups, then distribute the topping mixture evenly, about 20 g (1 Tbsp.) per muffin cup. Set the pans aside at room temperature until the dough is ready.

6. Punch down the dough and let it rest 10 minutes. Roll out the dough into a rectangle about 1.25-cm (1/2-in.) thick. Brush with the melted butter and cover evenly with the filling mixture.

7. Starting with either long edge, roll up the dough. Cut into slices about 1.8 to 2.5 cm (3/4 to 1 in.) thick. Place a slice in each muffin cup over the topping.

8. Let the buns proof until doubled, approximately 20 minutes. Bake at 170°C (350°F) until very brown, approximately 25 minutes. Immediately invert the muffin pans onto paper-lined sheet pans to let the buns and their topping slide out.

RECIPE 29.13

Approximate values per bun:	
Calories	484
Total fat	26 g
Saturated fat	11 g
Cholesterol	79 mg
Sodium	100 mg
Total carbohydrates	55 g
Protein	5 g

1. Pecan Sticky Buns: Brushing melted butter over the sticky bun dough.

2. Rolling up the filling in the sticky bun dough.

3. Cutting and panning the sticky buns.

RECIPE 29.14

Danish Pastries

Danish pastry was actually created by a French baker more than 350 years ago. He forgot to knead butter into his bread dough and attempted to cover the mistake by folding in softened butter. This rich, flaky pastry is now popular worldwide for breakfasts, desserts and snacks. The dough may be shaped in a variety of ways and is usually filled with jam, fruit, cream or marzipan.

Dough for Danish Pastries

Yield: 24 pastries at 60 g (2 oz.) plus filling

Method: Rolled-in

Instant dry yeast	12 g	4 tsp.
Bread flour	400 g	14 oz.
Pastry flour	200 g	6 oz.
Sugar	60 g	2 oz.
Water, cold	125 mL	4 fl. oz.
Milk, cold	125 mL	4 fl. oz.
Eggs, room temperature	3	3
Salt	5 g	1 tsp.
Mace, ground	1.5 g	1/2 tsp.
Unsalted butter, melted	50 g	1-1/2 oz.
Unsalted butter, cold	450 g	1 lb.
Filling (recipes follow)	as needed	as needed
Egg wash	as needed	as needed

1. In a large bowl, stir together the yeast and 350 g (12 oz.) of flour. Add the sugar, water, milk, eggs, salt, mace and melted butter. Stir until well combined.

2. Add the remaining flour gradually, kneading the dough by hand or with a mixer fitted with a dough hook. Knead until the dough is smooth and only slightly tacky to the touch, approximately 2–3 minutes. Do not overmix.

3. Place the dough in a bowl that has been lightly dusted with flour. Cover and refrigerate for 1–1.5 hours.

4. Prepare the remaining butter while the dough is chilling. Soften the butter in a mixer bowl with paddle attachment on low speed.

5. On a lightly floured surface, roll out the dough into a large rectangle about 1.25 cm (1/2 in.) thick. Brush away any excess flour.

6. Spread the butter evenly over two-thirds of the dough. Fold the unbuttered third over the centre, then fold the buttered third over the top. Press the edges together to seal in the butter.

continued

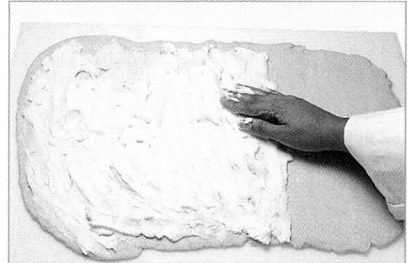

1. Danish Pastries: Spreading the butter over the rolled-out dough.

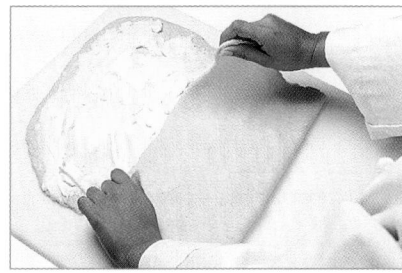

2. Folding the dough in thirds to cover the butter.

3. Rolling out the dough.

4. Folding the dough in thirds to complete a turn.

5. Cutting rectangles of Danish dough.

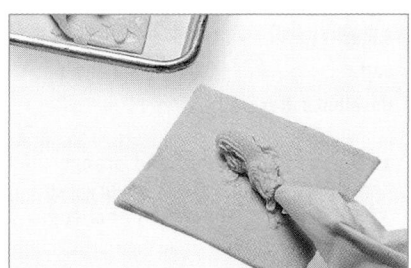

6. Piping the filling onto the Danish dough. Use 15 g (1 Tbsp.) filling for each Danish.

7. Shaping snails from Danish dough.

Approximate values per Danish:	
Calories	263
Total fat	18 g
Saturated fat	11 g
Cholesterol	69 mg
Sodium	94 mg
Total carbohydrates	22 g
Protein	4 g

7. Roll the dough into a rectangle about 30 × 45 cm (12 × 18 in.). Fold the dough in thirds as before. This rolling and folding (called a turn) must be done a total of 3 times. Chill the dough between turns as necessary. After the final turn, wrap the dough well and refrigerate for at least 4 hours or overnight.

8. Shape and fill the Danish dough as desired. Place the shaped pastries on a paper-lined baking sheet and allow to proof for approximately 15–20 minutes.

9. Brush the pastries with egg wash and sprinkle lightly with sugar if desired. Bake at 190°C (375°F) until light brown, approximately 12–15 minutes.

NOTE: In drier climates with low humidity it may be necessary to add 5% more liquid.

Fillings for Danish Pastries:

Cream Cheese

Yield: 450 g (16 oz.)

Cream cheese	225 g	8 oz.
Sugar	125 g	4 oz.
Butter, soft	25 g	1 oz.
Vanilla	3 mL	1/2 tsp.
Flour	10 g	1-1/2 Tbsp.
Egg yolk	1	1
Lemon extract	3 mL	1/2 tsp.
Lemon zest	5 g	1 tsp.

Beat the cream cheese until light and fluffy. Stir in the remaining ingredients.

Cream Cheese—Approximate values per 15 g serving:	
Calories	53
Total fat	3.5 g
Saturated fat	2.1 g
Cholesterol	17 mg
Sodium	31 mg
Total carbohydrates	4.7 g
Protein	0.8 g

Almond Cream

Yield: 480 g (16 oz.)

Almond paste	300 g	10 oz.
Unsalted butter, soft	120 g	4 oz.
Salt	1 g	1/4 tsp.
Vanilla	5 mL	1 tsp.
Egg whites	2	2

Blend the almond paste and butter until smooth. Add the salt and vanilla, then the egg whites. Blend well.

Almond Cream—Approximate values per 15 g serving:	
Calories	76
Total fat	6 g
Saturated fat	2.3 g
Cholesterol	8.8 mg
Sodium	18 mg
Total carbohydrates	4.8 g
Protein	1.2 g

Apricot

Yield: 450 g (16 oz.)

Dried apricots	110 g	4 oz.
Orange juice	225 mL	8 fl. oz.
Sugar	90 g	3 oz.
Salt	0.5 g	1/8 tsp.
Unsalted butter	30 g	1 oz.

1. Place the apricots and orange juice in a small saucepan. Cover and simmer until the apricots are very tender, approximately 25 minutes. Stir in the sugar and salt. When the sugar is dissolved, add the butter and remove from the heat.

2. Purée the mixture in a blender until smooth. Cool completely before using.

Apricot—Approximate values per 15 g serving:	
Calories	31
Total fat	0.8 g
Saturated fat	0.5 g
Cholesterol	2.2 mg
Sodium	7 mg
Total carbohydrates	6 g
Protein	0.2 g

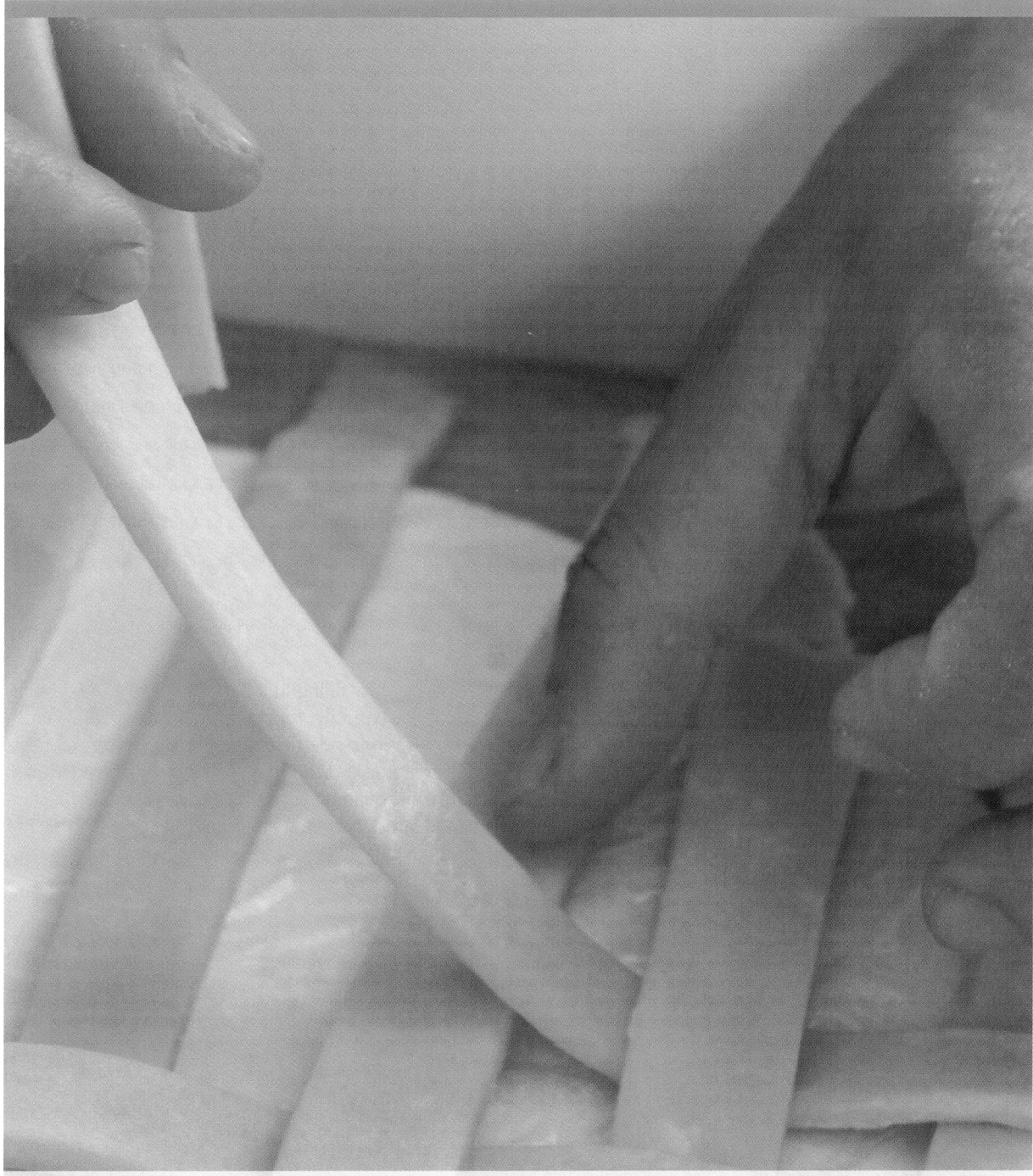

" The pie is an English institution which, planted on American soil, forthwith ran rampant and burst forth into an untold variety of genera and species.

—Harriet Beecher Stowe, American novelist (1811–1896)

LEARNING OUTCOMES

After studying this chapter you will be able to:

- prepare a variety of pie crusts and fillings
- prepare a variety of classic pastries
- prepare a variety of meringues
- prepare a variety of cookies
- prepare a variety of dessert and pastry items, incorporating components from other chapters

These interactive online tools will help you master the skills in this chapter:

- Videos
- Chapter Quizzes
- Activities

● **pie** a sweet or savoury filling in a baked crust, which can be open-faced, lattice or full

● **tart** a sweet or savoury filling in a baked crust made in a shallow, straight-sided pan without a top crust

Mention pastry to diners and most conjure up images of buttery dough baked to crisp flaky perfection and filled or layered with rich cream, ripe fruit or smooth custard. Mention pastry to novice cooks and most conjure up images of sophisticated, complex and intimidating work. Although the diners are correct, the novice cooks are not. Pastry making is the art of creating containers for a variety of fillings. Taken one step at a time, most pastries are nothing more than selected building blocks or components assembled in a variety of ways to create traditional or unique desserts.

Perhaps the most important (and versatile) building block is the dough. Pastries can be made with flaky dough, mealy dough, sweet dough/paste, puff pastry, choux paste or meringue. (See Table 30.1.) Because pies, tarts and cookies are constructed from some of these same doughs (principally pie dough and sweet dough), they, as well as pie fillings, are discussed in the section on pies and tarts; puff pastry, choux paste and baked meringue are discussed in the section on classic pastries. The cream, custard and mousse fillings used in some of the recipes at the end of this chapter are discussed in Chapter 32, Custards, Creams, Frozen Desserts and Dessert Sauces. Cakes and frostings are covered in Chapter 31.

PIES AND TARTS

A **pie** is composed of a sweet or savoury filling in a baked crust. It can be open-faced (without a top crust) or, more typically, topped with a full or lattice crust. A pie is generally made in a round, slope-sided pan and cut into wedges for service. A **tart** is similar to a pie except it is made in a shallow, straight-sided pan, often with fluted edges. A tart can be almost any shape; round, square, rectangular and petal shapes are the most common. It is usually open-faced and derives much of its beauty from an attractive arrangement of glazed fruit.

TABLE 30.1	Classification of Pastry Doughs		
Dough	**French Name**	**Characteristics after Baking**	**Use**
Flaky dough	Pâte brisée	Very flaky; not sweet	Prebaked pie shells; pie top crusts
Mealy dough	Pâte à foncer	Moderately flaky; not sweet	Custard, cream or fruit pie crusts; quiche crusts
Sweet dough	Pâte sucrée (sèche sucrée, sablée)	Very rich; crisp; not flaky	Tart and tartlet shells
Choux paste	Pâte à choux	Hollow, with crisp exterior	Cream puffs; éclairs; savoury products
Puff pastry	Pâte feuilletée	Rich but not sweet; hundreds of light, flaky layers	Tart and pastry cases; cookies; layered pastries; savoury products
Meringue	Meringue	Sweet; light; crisp or soft depending on preparation	Topping or icing; baked as a shell or component for layered desserts; cookies
Phyllo	Phyllo	Very thin, crisp, flaky layers	Middle Eastern pastries and savouries, hors d'oeuvre, baklava

Crusts

Pie crusts and tart shells can be made from several types of doughs or crumbs. Flaky dough, mealy dough and crumbs are best for pie crusts; sweet or short paste is usually used for tart shells. A pie crust or tart shell can be shaped and completely baked before filling (known as baked blind) or filled and baked simultaneously with the filling.

Flaky and Mealy Doughs

Flaky and mealy pie doughs are quick, easy and versatile. Flaky dough, sometimes known as **pâte brisée**, takes its name from its final baked texture. It is best for pie top crusts and lattice coverings and may be used for prebaked shells that will be filled with a cooled filling shortly before service. **Mealy dough** takes its name from its raw texture. It is used whenever a soggy crust would be a problem (for example, as the bottom crust of a custard or fruit pie) because it resists soaking better than flaky dough does. Both flaky and mealy doughs are too delicate for tarts that will be removed from the pan for service. Sweet dough, described later, is better for these types of tarts.

Flaky and mealy doughs contain little or no sugar and can be prepared from the same formula with only a slight variation in mixing method. For both types of dough a cold fat, such as butter or shortening, is cut into the flour. The amount of flakiness in the baked crust depends on the size of the fat particles in the dough. The larger the pieces of fat, the flakier the crust will be. This is because the flakes are actually the sides of fat pockets created during baking by the melting fat and steam. When preparing flaky dough, the fat is left in larger pieces, about the size of peas or peanuts. When preparing mealy dough, the fat is blended in more thoroughly, until the mixture resembles coarse cornmeal. Because the resulting fat pockets are smaller, the crust is less flaky.

The type of fat used affects both the dough's flavour and flakiness. Butter contributes a delicious flavour, but does not produce as flaky a crust as other fats. Butter is also more difficult to work with than are other fats because of its lower melting point and its tendency to become brittle when chilled. All-purpose vegetable shortening produces a flaky crust but contributes nothing to its flavour. The flakiest pastry is made with lard, but because some people cannot eat pork products lard is not often used. Some chefs prefer to use a combination of butter with either shortening or lard. Oil is not an appropriate substitute, as it disperses too thoroughly through the dough; when baked, the crust is stiff and crisp.

After the fat is cut into the flour, water or milk is added to form a soft dough. Less water is needed for mealy dough because more flour is already in contact with the fat, reducing its ability to absorb liquid. Cold water is normally used for both flaky and mealy doughs. The water should be well chilled to prevent softening the fat or shortening. Milk may be used to increase richness and nutritional value. It will produce a darker, less crisp crust, however. If dry milk powder is used, it should be mixed with the flour.

Hand mixing is best for small to moderate quantities of dough. You retain better control over the procedure when you can feel the fat being incorporated. It is very difficult to make flaky dough with an electric mixer or food processor, as they tend to cut the fat in too thoroughly. Overmixing makes the dough elastic and difficult to use. When an electric mixer must be used for large quantities, use the paddle attachment at the lowest speed and be sure the fat is well chilled, even frozen.

● **pâte brisée** a dough that produces a very flaky baked product containing little or no sugar that is used for prebaked pie shells and crusts; **mealy dough** is a less flaky product used for custard, cream or fruit pie crusts

Terminology

Pâte à foncer—Short pastry with a low (10% to 12%) sugar content. Powdered sugar is used for this lining paste.

    Pâte sèche sucrée—Sweet short paste with 40% butter and high egg content.

    Pâte sucrée—Sweet short paste with 80% butter and low egg content.

    Pâte sablée—Sweet short paste with 65% butter and 35% powdered sugar.

    Sweet pastes are the basis of many cookies and can be flavoured accordingly. The butter percentages are approximate and pastry chefs have their own preferred formulas.

BASIC PROCEDURE FOR PREPARING FLAKY AND MEALY DOUGHS

1. Sift flour, salt and sugar (if used) together in a large bowl.

2. Cut the fat into the flour.

3. Gradually add a cold liquid, mixing gently until the dough holds together. Do not overmix.

4. Cover the dough with plastic wrap and chill thoroughly before using.

APPLYING THE BASICS　　　　　　　　　　　　　**RECIPE 30.1**

Basic Pie Dough

Yield: 2.7 kg (5 lb.)

Pastry flour	1.5 kg	3 lb.
Milk powder	85 g	3 oz.
Shortening	800 g	26 oz.
Water, cold	425 mL	14 fl. oz.
Salt	40 g	1-1/2 oz.

1. Blend the flour and milk powder in a mixing bowl.

2. Add the shortening and cut it into the flour with a paddle attachment until the fat is pea-sized.

3. Dissolve the salt in the water.

4. Add the water all at once to the flour and fat mixture. Blend on No. 1 speed only until the mix comes together.

NOTE: For mealy pie crust, the fat should be crumb-sized.

RECIPE 30.1

Approximate values per 30 g serving:	
Calories	144
Total fat	9 g
Saturated fat	2 g
Cholesterol	0 mg
Sodium	178 mg
Total carbohydrates	14 g
Protein	2 g

1. Basic Pie Dough: Cutting the fat into the flour coarsely for flaky dough.

2. Cutting the fat into the flour finely for mealy dough.

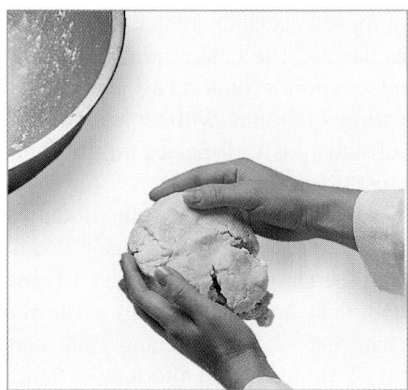

3. The finished dough.

Sweet Paste

● **pâte sucrée** a dough containing sugar that produces a very rich, crisp (not flaky) baked product; also known as sweet dough; it is used for tart shells

Sweet paste or **pâte sucrée** is a rich, nonflaky dough used for sweet tart shells. It is sturdier than flaky or mealy dough because it contains egg yolks and the fat is thoroughly blended in. It is also more cookielike than basic pie dough and has the rich flavour of butter. It creates a crisp but tender crust and is excellent for tartlets as well as for straight-sided tarts that will be removed from their pans before service. Sweet paste crusts may be prebaked then filled, or filled and baked simultaneously with the filling. The raw dough may be kept refrigerated for up to two weeks or frozen for up to three months.

BASIC PROCEDURE FOR PREPARING SWEET PASTE

1. Cream softened butter. Add sugar and beat until the mixture is light and fluffy.
2. Slowly add eggs, blending well.
3. Slowly add flour, mixing only until incorporated. Overmixing toughens the dough.
4. Cover the dough with plastic wrap and chill thoroughly before using.

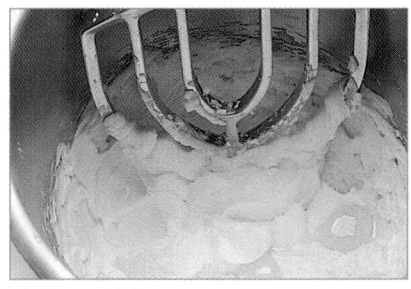

1. Sweet (Short) Paste: Mixing the sweet dough.

APPLYING THE BASICS   RECIPE 30.2

Sweet (Short) Paste

Yield: 2.35 kg (5 lb.)

Unsalted butter, softened	700 g	1 lb. 8 oz.
Sugar	425 g	1 lb.
Whole eggs	225 g	8 oz.
Pastry flour	1 kg	2 lb.

1. Cream the butter and sugar in a large mixer bowl using the paddle attachment.
2. Slowly add the eggs to the creamed butter. Mix until smooth and free of lumps, scraping down the sides of the bowl as needed.
3. With the mixer on low speed, slowly add the flour to the butter-and-egg mixture. Mix only until incorporated; do not overmix. The dough should be firm, smooth and not sticky.
4. Dust a half-sheet pan with flour. Pack the dough into the pan evenly. Wrap well in plastic wrap and chill until firm.
5. Work with a small portion of the chilled dough when shaping tart shells or other products.

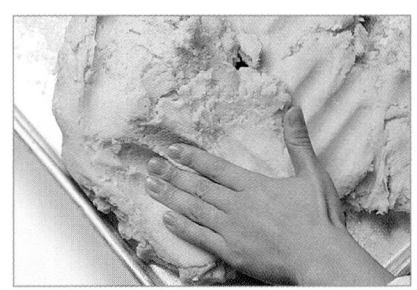

2. The finished sweet dough.

RECIPE 30.2

Approximate values per 30 g serving:	
Calories	136
Total fat	8 g
Saturated fat	5 g
Cholesterol	32 mg
Sodium	5 mg
Total carbohydrates	16 g
Protein	1.5 g

Shaping Crusts

Crusts are shaped by rolling out the dough to fit into a pie pan or tart shell (mould) or to sit on top of fillings. Mealy, flaky and sweet doughs are all easier to roll out and work with if well chilled, as chilling keeps the fat firm and prevents stickiness. When rolling and shaping the dough, work on a clean, flat surface (wood or marble is best). Lightly dust the work surface, rolling pin and dough with bread flour before starting to roll the dough. Also, work only with a manageable amount at a time: usually enough for one pie crust or a standard-sized tart or enough for 10 to 12 tartlet shells.

Roll out the dough from the centre, working toward the edges. Periodically, lift the dough gently and rotate it. This keeps the dough from sticking and helps produce an even thickness. If the dough sticks to the rolling pin or work surface, dust with a bit more flour. Too much flour, however, makes the crust dry and crumbly and causes grey streaks.

BASIC PROCEDURE FOR ROLLING AND SHAPING DOUGH FOR PIE CRUSTS OR TART SHELLS

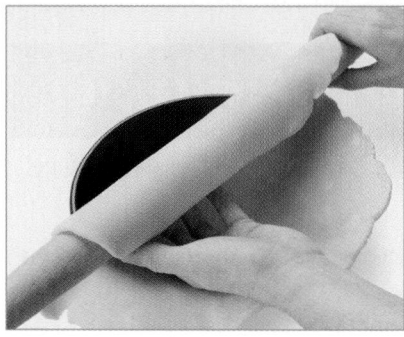

1. A typical pie crust or tart shell should be rolled to a thickness of approximately 3 mm (1/8 in.); it should also be at least 5 cm (2 in.) larger in diameter than the baking pan.

2. Carefully roll up the dough onto a rolling pin. Position the pin over the pie pan or tart shell and unroll the dough, easing it into the pan or shell.

3. Press the dough into the pan and trim the edges as necessary. Bake or fill as desired.

BASIC PROCEDURE FOR ROLLING AND SHAPING DOUGH FOR TARTLET SHELLS

1. A typical crust for tartlets should be approximately 3 mm (1/8 in.) thick.

2. Roll out the dough as described earlier. Then roll the dough up onto the rolling pin.

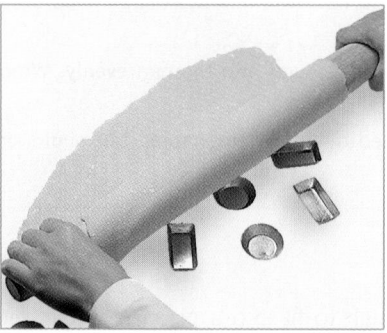

3. Lay out a single layer of tartlet moulds. Unroll the dough over the moulds, pressing the dough gently into each mould.

4. Roll the rolling pin over the top of the tartlet shells. The edge of the moulds will cut the dough. Be sure the dough is pressed against the sides of each mould. Bake or fill as desired.

BASIC PROCEDURE FOR ROLLING AND SHAPING DOUGH FOR A TOP CRUST

1. Roll out the dough as before, making a circle large enough to hang over the pan's edge. The dough may be lifted into place by rolling it onto the rolling pin, as done with the bottom crust. Slits or designs can be cut in the top crust to allow steam to escape.

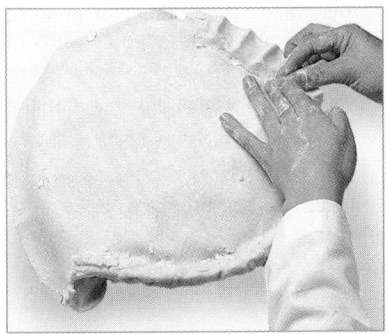

2. Seal the top crust to the bottom crust with egg wash or water. Crimp as desired.

BASIC PROCEDURE FOR ROLLING AND SHAPING DOUGH FOR A LATTICE CRUST

1. Roll out the dough as described earlier. Using a ruler as a guide, cut even strips of the desired width, typically 1.25 cm (1/2 in.). A special cutter is available to stamp out the lattice crust on the table top. The crust is then laid over the pie.

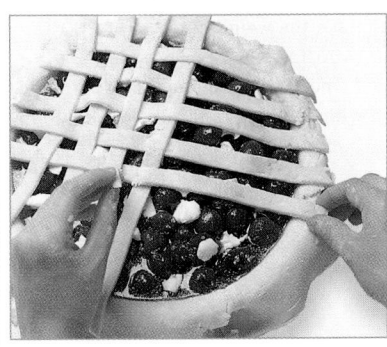

2. Using an over-under-over pattern, weave the strips together on top of the filling. Be sure the strips are evenly spaced for an attractive result. Crimp the lattice strips to the bottom crust to seal.

Streusel topping is also used for some pies, particularly fruit pies. A standard recipe is available in the Recipe Archive.

Baking Crusts

Pie crusts can be filled and then baked, or baked and then filled. Unfilled baked crusts can be stored at room temperature for two to three days or wrapped in plastic wrap and frozen for as long as three months.

● **docking** pricking small holes in an unbaked dough or crust to allow steam to escape and to prevent the dough from rising when baked

BASIC PROCEDURE FOR BAKING UNFILLED (BAKED BLIND) PIE CRUSTS

1. Roll out the dough to the desired thickness and line the pie pan or tart shell. A crimped edge or border can be added.

2. **Dock** the dough with a fork or docking wheel. Cover and allow the dough to rest in the fridge for several hours.

3. Cover the dough with heat-resistant plastic, baking parchment or greased aluminum foil. Press the plastic, paper or foil against the edge or walls of the shell, allowing a portion of it to extend above the pan.

4. Fill the pan with baking weights, dry rice or beans. These will prevent the crust from rising.

5. Bake the weighted crust at 200°C (400°F) for 10 to 15 minutes.

6. Remove the weights and paper and return the crust to the oven. Bake until golden brown and fully cooked, approximately 5 to 8 minutes.

7. Allow to cool, then fill as desired or store.

1. Cover the dough with heat-resistant plastic, baking parchment or greased aluminum foil (greased side down). Press the plastic, paper or foil against the walls of the shell, allowing a portion of it to extend above the pan. Fill the pan with baking weights or dry rice or beans.

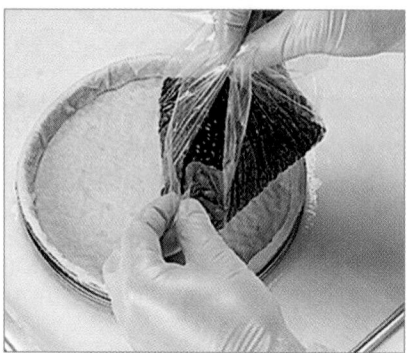

2. Bake the weighted crust at 200°C (400°F) for 10 to 15 minutes. Remove the weights and paper. Brush with egg wash and finish baking for 5 minutes.

Crumb Crusts

A quick and tasty bottom crust can be made from finely ground crumbs moistened with melted butter. Crumb crusts can be used for unbaked pies such as those with cream or chiffon fillings, or they can be baked with their fillings, as with cheesecakes.

Chocolate cookies, graham crackers, gingersnaps, vanilla wafers and macaroons are popular choices for crumb crusts. Some breakfast cereals such as corn flakes or bran flakes are also used. Ground nuts and spices can be added for flavour. Whatever cookies or other ingredients are used, be sure they are ground to a fine, even crumb. If packaged crumbs are unavailable, crumbs can be prepared in a food processor or blender or with a rolling pin.

The typical ratio for a crumb crust is one part melted butter, two parts sugar and four parts crumbs. For example, 250 g (8 oz.) graham crackers mixed with 125 g (4 oz.) sugar and 60 mL (2 fl. oz.) melted butter produce enough crust to line one 22- to 25-cm (9- to 10-in.) pan. The amount of sugar may need to be adjusted depending on the type of crumbs used, however; for example,

Pressing the crumb mixture into the pan.

chocolate sandwich cookies need less sugar than graham crackers. If the mixture is too dry to stick together, gradually add more melted butter. Press the mixture into the bottom of the pan and chill or bake it before filling.

Fillings

Fillings make pies and tarts distinctive and flavourful. Four types of fillings are discussed here: cream, fruit, custard and chiffon. There is no one correct presentation or filling-and-crust combination. The apples in an apple pie, for example, may be sliced, seasoned and topped with streusel; caramelized, puréed and blended with cream; chopped and covered with a flaky dough lattice; or poached, arranged over pastry cream and brushed with a clear glaze. Only an understanding of the fundamental techniques for making fillings—and some imagination—ensures success.

Cream Fillings

A cream filling is really nothing more than a flavoured pastry cream. Pastry cream is a type of starch-thickened egg custard discussed in Chapter 32, Custards, Creams, Frozen Desserts and Dessert Sauces. When used as a pie filling, pastry cream should be thickened with cornstarch so that it gels and is firm enough to hold its shape when sliced. Popular flavours are chocolate, banana, coconut and lemon.

A cream filling is fully cooked on the stove top, so a prebaked or crumb crust is needed. The crust can be filled while the filling is still warm, or the filling can be chilled and later placed in the crust. A cream pie may be topped with meringue, which is then browned quickly in an oven or under a broiler. Chantilly cream is the most popular topping.

APPLYING THE BASICS		RECIPE 30.3

Basic Cream Pie

Yield: 2 22-cm (9-in.) pies

Pastry Cream:		
Granulated sugar	250 g	8 oz.
Milk	1 L	1 qt.
Egg yolks*	10	10
Cornstarch	90 g	3 oz.
Unsalted butter	60 g	2 oz.
Vanilla extract	15 g	1/2 oz.
Pie shells, baked	2	2

*Alternatively, 3 whole eggs and 2 yolks may be used.

1. In a heavy saucepan, dissolve 125 g (4 oz.) of sugar in the milk. Bring just to a boil.

2. Meanwhile, whisk the egg yolks in a large bowl.

3. Sift the cornstarch and remaining sugar (125 g/4 oz.) into the eggs. Whisk until smooth.

4. **Temper** the egg mixture with approximately half of the hot milk. Stir the warmed egg mixture back into the remaining milk and return it to a boil, stirring constantly.

continued

Pastry Cream

The filling for the cream pie is a basic pastry cream. This mixture is used extensively in dessert preparations. Some recipes use a combination of whole eggs and yolks. Pastry cream may be flavoured with fruit compounds. Whipped cream or Italian meringue may be added. Note that no gelatin is used; the resulting gel is solely obtained from the cooked cornstarch.

1. Basic Cream Pie: Filling the pie shell with chocolate pastry cream.

2. Topping with meringue.

● **tempering** heating gently and gradually; refers to the process of slowly adding a hot liquid to eggs or other foods to raise their temperature without causing them to curdle

5. Stirring constantly and vigorously, allow the cream to boil until thick, approximately 30 seconds. Remove from the heat and stir in the butter and vanilla. Stir until the butter is melted and incorporated.

6. Pour the cream into prebaked pie crusts.

7. The pies may be topped with meringue while the filling is still warm. The meringue is then lightly browned in a 210°C (425°F) oven. Chill the pies for service or, when chilled, top with whipped cream.

VARIATIONS: CHOCOLATE—Melt 175 g (6 oz.) bittersweet chocolate. Fold the melted chocolate into the hot milk after adding the butter and vanilla.

BANANA—Layer 250 g (8 oz.) sliced bananas (about 2 medium bananas) into the baked shell. The juice of one-half lemon may be added to the bananas to help prevent browning. Fill shell with pastry cream.

COCONUT I—Substitute 175 mL (6 fl. oz.) cream of coconut for 175 mL (6 fl. oz.) of milk and 60 g (2 oz.) of sugar. Top the pie with whipped cream and shredded toasted coconut.

COCONUT II—Stir 125 g (4 oz.) toasted coconut into the warm milk.

RECIPE 30.3

Approximate values per slice:	
Calories	306
Total fat	16 g
Saturated fat	6 g
Cholesterol	151 mg
Sodium	159 mg
Total carbohydrates	35 g
Protein	5 g

Starches for Pies

Although flour is somewhat unreliable as a thickener, it can be used in traditional baked fruit pies in which the fruit is not excessively juicy, such as Pippin apples or Bosc pears. Cornstarch is preferred for custard and fruit fillings because it sets up into a somewhat firm, clear gel. Be aware that cornstarch loses its potency when combined with sugar or an acid such as lemon juice. When a pie is to be frozen, cornstarch is not recommended as a thickener, however. The gel formed by cornstarch when cooking breaks down during freezing. Use tapioca or tapioca starch instead. Tapioca is a good choice for fruit fillings because it thickens at a lower temperature than cornstarch, withstands freezing and cooks into a clear gel. Instant tapioca can be measured and then ground into a powder before using. Grinding makes it easier to disperse. Modified starch, also known as waxy maize, can also be used for pies that must be frozen.

Fruit Fillings

A fruit filling is a mixture of fruit, fruit juice, spices and sugar thickened with starch. Apple, cherry, blueberry and peach are traditional favourites. The fruit can be fresh, frozen or canned. (See Chapter 26, Fruits, for comments on selecting the best fruits for fillings.) The starch can be cornstarch, tapioca or a packaged commercial instant or pregelatinized starch. The ingredients for a fruit filling are most often combined using one of three methods: cooked fruit, cooked juice or baked fruit.

Cooked Fruit Fillings

The cooked fruit filling method is often used when the fruits need to be softened by cooking (for example, apples, rhubarb or dried fruits). (Poaching fruit, discussed in Chapter 26, Fruits, is a variation of this procedure.) A cooked fruit filling can be used with a prebaked or unbaked crust. If an unbaked raw crust is used, the pie is baked before service. Uncooked raw fruit may be used to make pies—for example, apple pie; however, the filling may be too moist and runny for a clean presentation.

BASIC PROCEDURE FOR PREPARING COOKED FRUIT FILLINGS

1. Combine the fruit, sugar and some juice or liquid in a heavy, nonreactive saucepan and bring to a boil.

2. Dissolve the starch (usually cornstarch) in cold liquid, then add to the boiling fruit.

3. Stirring constantly, cook the fruit-and-starch mixture until the starch is clear and the mixture is thickened.

4. Add any other flavourings and any acidic ingredients such as lemon juice. Stir to blend.

5. Remove from the heat and cool before use.

APPLYING THE BASICS

Apple-Cranberry Pie

Yield: 2 22-cm (9-in.) pies
Method: Cooked fruit filling

Fresh tart apples such as Granny Smiths, peeled, cored and cut in 2.5-cm (1-in.) cubes	1 kg	2 lb.
Brown sugar	250 g	8 oz.
Granulated sugar	250 g	8 oz.
Orange zest	20 g	2 Tbsp.
Ground cinnamon	4 g	2 tsp.
Salt	2 g	1/2 tsp.
Cornstarch	15 g	4 tsp.
Orange juice	175 mL	6 fl. oz.
Fresh cranberries, rinsed	500 g	16 oz.
Partially baked mealy dough pie shell	2	2
Streusel Topping (see Recipe Archive)	250 g	8 oz.

1. Combine the apples, brown sugar, granulated sugar, orange zest, cinnamon and salt in a large, nonreactive saucepan.

2. Dissolve the cornstarch in the orange juice and add it to the apples.

3. Cover and simmer until the apples begin to soften, stirring occasionally. Add the cranberries, cover and continue simmering until the cranberries begin to soften, approximately 2 minutes. Cool the mixture to room temperature.

4. Place the apple-cranberry mixture in the pie shell and cover with the prepared Streusel Topping. Bake at 200°C (400°F) until the filling is bubbling hot and the topping is lightly browned, approximately 20 minutes.

VARIATION: APPLE-RHUBARB PIE—Substitute cleaned rhubarb, cut into 2.5-cm (1-in.) chunks, for the cranberries. Add 0.5 g (1/4 tsp.) nutmeg.

Apple-Cranberry Pie

Approximate values per slice:	
Calories	392
Total fat	13 g
Saturated fat	4.8 g
Cholesterol	12 mg
Sodium	266 mg
Total carbohydrates	69 g
Protein	2.5 g

Cooked Juice Fillings

The cooked juice filling method is recommended for delicate fruits that cannot withstand cooking such as strawberries, pineapple or blueberries and frozen berries. Because only the juice is cooked, the fruit retains its shape, colour and flavour better. A cooked juice filling can be used with a prebaked or unbaked crust.

BASIC PROCEDURE FOR PREPARING COOKED JUICE FILLINGS

1. Drain the juice from the fruit. Measure the juice and add water if necessary to create the desired volume.

2. Combine the liquid with sugar in a nonreactive saucepan and bring to a boil.

3. Dissolve the starch in cold water, then add it to the boiling liquid. Cook until the starch is clear and the juice is thickened.

4. Add any other flavouring ingredients.

5. Pour the thickened juice over the fruit and stir gently.

6. Cool the filling before use.

Blueberry Pie Filling

RECIPE 30.5

Approximate values per 125 g serving:	
Calories	160
Total fat	0.6 g
Saturated fat	0 g
Cholesterol	0 mg
Sodium	1.6 mg
Total carbohydrates	40 g
Protein	0.4 g

APPLYING THE BASICS **RECIPE 30.5**

Blueberry Pie Filling

Yield: 2 kg (4 lb.) filling
Method: Cooked juice filling

Frozen blueberries, unsweetened	1.5 kg	3 lb. 4 oz.
Water	as needed	as needed
Sugar	400 g	13 oz.
Cornstarch	60 g	2 oz.
Water	100 mL	4 fl. oz.
Cinnamon	1 g	1/2 tsp.
Lemon juice	20 mL	2 Tbsp.
Lemon zest, grated fine	7 g	2 tsp.

1. Thaw berries and retain juice.

2. Measure the juice and, if necessary, add enough water to provide 275 mL (10 fl. oz.) of liquid. Bring to a boil, add the sugar and stir until dissolved.

3. Dissolve the cornstarch in water.

4. Add the cornstarch to the boiling juice and return to a boil. Cook until the mixture thickens and clears. Remove from the heat.

5. Add the cinnamon, lemon juice, lemon zest and reserved blueberries. Stir gently to coat the fruit with the glaze.

6. Allow the filling to cool, then use it to fill pie shells or other pastry items.

NOTE: A modified starch (waxy maize) (50 g or 1-1/2 oz.) may be used if the pie will be frozen.

Baked Fruit Fillings

The baked fruit filling method is a traditional technique in which the fruit, sugar, flavourings and starch are combined in an unbaked shell. The dough and filling are then baked simultaneously. Almost any type of fruit and starch can be used. The results are not always consistent, however, because thickening is difficult to control.

BASIC PROCEDURE FOR PREPARING BAKED FRUIT FILLINGS

1. Combine the starch, spices and sugar.

2. Peel, core, cut or drain the fruit as desired or as directed in the recipe.

3. Toss the fruit with the starch mixture, coating well.

4. Add a portion of juice to moisten the fruit. Small lumps of butter are also often added.

5. Fill an unbaked shell with the fruit mixture. Cover with a top crust, lattice or streusel and bake.

APPLYING THE BASICS — RECIPE 30.6

Cherry Pie

Yield: 2 22-cm (9-in.) pies
Method: Baked fruit filling

Tapioca	45 g	1-1/2 oz.
Salt	pinch	pinch
Granulated sugar	450 g	1 lb.
Almond extract	2 mL	1/2 tsp.
Canned pitted cherries, drained		
(reserve the liquid)	1.3 kg	3 lb.
Unbaked pie shells	2	2
Unsalted butter	30 g	1 oz.
Egg wash	as needed	as needed
Sanding sugar	as needed	as needed

1. Stir the tapioca, salt and sugar together. Add the almond extract and cherries.

2. Stir in up to 250 mL (8 fl. oz.) of the liquid drained from the cherries, adding enough liquid to moisten the mixture thoroughly.

3. Allow the filling to stand for 30 minutes. Then stir gently and place the filling in an unbaked pie shell.

4. Cut the butter into small pieces. Dot the filling with the butter.

5. Place a top crust or a lattice crust over the filling; seal and flute the edges. Cut several slits in the top crust to allow steam to escape. Brush with an egg wash and sprinkle with sanding sugar.

6. Place on a preheated sheet pan and bake at 200°C (400°F) for 50–60 minutes.

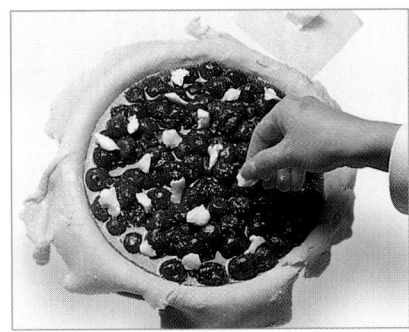

Cherry Pie: Dotting the cherry filling with butter.

RECIPE 30.6

Approximate values per slice:	
Calories	340
Total fat	9 g
Saturated fat	3 g
Cholesterol	5 mg
Sodium	183 mg
Total carbohydrates	63 g
Protein	2 g

Custard Fillings

A **custard** pie has a soft filling that bakes along with the crust. Popular examples include pumpkin, egg custard and pecan pies. As explained in Chapter 32, Custards, Creams, Frozen Desserts and Dessert Sauces, custards are liquids thickened by coagulated egg proteins. To make a custard pie, an uncooked liquid containing eggs is poured into a pie shell. When baked, the egg proteins coagulate, firming and setting the filling.

The procedure for making custard pies is simple: combine the ingredients and bake. But there is often a problem: baking the bottom crust completely without overcooking the filling. For the best results, bake the pie in a 200°C (400°F) oven. After 10 minutes, reduce the heat to 160°C to 180°C (325°F to 350°F) to finish cooking the filling slowly.

To determine the doneness of a custard pie:

1. Shake the pie gently. It is done if it is no longer liquid. The centre should show only a slight movement.

2. Insert a thin knife about 2.5 cm (1 in.) from the centre. The filling is done if the knife comes out clean.

● **custard** any liquid thickened by coagulation of egg proteins; its consistency depends on the ratio of eggs to liquid and the type of liquid used; custards can be baked in the oven or cooked in a bain marie or on the stove top

Convenience Products: Fillings

Prepared or canned pie fillings are available in a variety of fruit and custard flavours. These products offer convenience and the ability to serve fruit pies out of season. The ratio of fruit to pregelled liquid varies greatly from brand to brand, however. Most commercial fillings are stabilized to permit any additional cooking needed to assemble the final product. Shelf life tends to be extremely long, often without the need for refrigeration. Dry custard mixes are also available, needing only the addition of water or milk. Despite the convenience, most prepared pie fillings are a disappointing substitute for a well-made fresh fruit or custard filling.

RECIPE 30.7

Approximate values per 1/8 pie:	
Calories	214
Total fat	10 g
Saturated fat	2.5 g
Cholesterol	30 mg
Sodium	231 mg
Total carbohydrates	26 g
Protein	4 g

Convenience Products: Pastries

Commercially prepared puff pastry is readily available in unbaked frozen sheets or precut into a variety of shapes. Some convenience doughs, especially those made with butter, provide excellent results. Their expense may be offset by the ability to offer a consistent product at a tiny fraction of the labour cost. Keep these frozen doughs well wrapped to prevent drying and freezer burn, and prepare according to package directions.

Fully baked, ready-to-use éclair paste (pâte à choux) items such as éclair and cream puff shells are also available commercially, in both frozen and shelf-stable forms. These are useful when time or labour cost is a concern; just follow package directions for storage and recrisping. High-quality fillings and glazes can then be added to create excellent finished pastries.

APPLYING THE BASICS RECIPE 30.7

Pumpkin Pie

Yield: 2 22-cm (9-in.) pies
Method: Baked custard filling

Eggs, beaten slightly	225 g	4
Pumpkin purée	600 g	1 lb. 6 oz.
Brown sugar	350 g	12 oz.
Pastry flour	30 g	1 oz.
Salt	2 g	1/2 tsp.
Nutmeg, ground	0.5 g	1/4 tsp.
Cloves, ground	0.5 g	1/4 tsp.
Cinnamon, ground	2 g	1 tsp.
Ginger, ground	1 g	1/2 tsp.
Evaporated milk or cereal cream	600 mL	24 fl. oz.
Mealy dough pie shells	2	2

1. Combine the eggs and pumpkin. Blend in the sugar and pastry flour.

2. Add the salt and spices, then the evaporated milk. Whisk until completely blended and smooth.

3. Allow the filling to rest for 15–20 minutes before filling the pie shells. This allows the starch in the pumpkin to begin absorbing liquid, making it less likely to separate after baking.

4. Pour the filling into unbaked pie shells. Place in the oven on a preheated sheet pan at 220°C (400°F). Bake for 15 minutes. Lower the oven temperature to 180°C (350°F) and bake until a knife inserted near the centre comes out clean, approximately 40–50 minutes.

NOTE: The purpose of the flour in this recipe is to prevent weeping of the custard pie filling.

Chiffon Fillings

A chiffon filling is created by adding gelatin to a stirred custard or a fruit purée. Whipped egg whites are then folded into the mixture. The filling is placed in a prebaked crust and chilled until firm. These preparations are the same as those for chiffons, mousses and Bavarians discussed in Chapter 32, Custards, Creams, Frozen Desserts and Dessert Sauces.

Assembling Pies and Tarts

The various types of pie fillings can be used to fill almost any crust or shell, provided the crust is prebaked as necessary. The filling can then be topped with meringue or whipped cream as desired. Garnishes such as toasted coconut, cookie crumbs and chocolate curls are often added for appearance and flavour. (See Table 30.2.) If you encounter quality issues with pies, Table 30.3 provides troubleshooting information.

Storing Pies and Tarts

Pies and tarts filled with cream or custard must be kept refrigerated to retard bacterial growth. Baked fruit pies should be held at refrigerator temperature.

Unbaked fruit pies or unbaked pie shells may be frozen for up to two months. Freezing baked fruit pies is not recommended unless waxy maize or modified starch, not regular cornstarch, is used in preparing the filling. Custard, cream and meringue-topped pies should not be frozen as the eggs will separate, making the product runny.

TABLE 30.2	Suggestions for Assembling Pies		
Filling	**Crust**	**Topping**	**Garnish**
Vanilla or lemon cream	Prebaked flaky dough or crumb	None, meringue or whipped cream	Crumbs from the crust
Chocolate cream	Prebaked flaky dough or crumb	None, meringue or whipped cream	Crumbs from the crust or shaved chocolate
Banana cream	Prebaked flaky dough	Meringue or whipped cream	Dried banana chips
Coconut cream	Prebaked flaky dough	Meringue or whipped cream	Shredded coconut
Fresh fruit	Unbaked mealy dough or sweet dough if shallow tart	Lattice, full crust or streusel	Sanding sugar or cut-out designs if lattice or top crust is used
Canned or frozen fruit	Unbaked mealy dough	Lattice, full crust or streusel	Sanding sugar or cut-out designs if lattice or top crust is used
Chiffon or mousse	Crumb or prebaked, sweetened flaky dough	None or whipped cream	Crumbs, fruit or shaved chocolate
Custard (e.g., pecan or pumpkin)	Unbaked mealy dough	None	Whipped cream
Vanilla pastry cream	Prebaked sweet dough	Fresh fruit	Glaze

TABLE 30.3	Troubleshooting Chart for Pies	
Problem	**Cause**	**Solution**
Crust shrinks	Overmixing	Adjust mixing technique
	Overworking dough	Adjust rolling technique
	Not enough fat	Adjust formula
Soggy crust	Wrong dough used	Use mealier dough
	Oven temperature too low	Adjust oven
	Not baked long enough	Adjust baking time
Crumbly crust	Not enough liquid	Adjust formula
	Too much fat	Adjust formula
Tough crust	Not enough fat	Adjust formula
	Overmixing	Adjust mixing technique
Runny filling	Insufficient starch	Adjust formula
	Starch insufficiently cooked	Allow starch to gelatinize completely
Lumpy cream filling	Starch not incorporated properly	Stir filling while cooking
	Filling overcooked	Adjust cooking time
Custard filling weeps or separates	Too many eggs	Reduce egg content or add starch to the filling
	Eggs overcooked	Reduce oven temperature or baking time

CLASSIC PASTRIES

Puff pastry, choux paste and meringue are classic components of French pastries; they are used to create a wide variety of dessert and pastry items. Many combinations are traditional. Once you master the skills necessary to produce these products, however, you will be free to experiment with other flavours and assembly techniques.

Puff Pastry

● **pâte feuilletée** also known as puff pastry; rolled-in dough used for pastries, cookies and savoury products; it produces a rich and buttery but not sweet baked product with hundreds of light, flaky layers

Puff pastry is one of the bakeshop's most elegant and sophisticated products. Also known as **pâte feuilletée**, it is a rich, buttery dough that bakes into hundreds of light, flaky layers. The term *mille feuille* means 1000 leaves.

Puff pastry is used for both sweet and savoury preparations. It can be baked and then filled or filled first and then baked. Puff pastry may be used to wrap beef (for beef Wellington), pâté (for pâté en croûte) or almond cream (for an apple tart). It can be shaped into shells or cases known as vol-au-vents or bouchées and filled with shellfish in a cream sauce or berries in a pastry cream. Puff pastry is essential for napoleons, pithiviers and palmiers.

Like croissant and Danish dough (discussed in Chapter 29, Yeast Breads), puff pastry is a rolled-in dough. But unlike those doughs, puff pastry does not contain any yeast or chemical leavening agents. Fat is rolled into the dough in horizontal layers; when baked, the fat melts, separating the dough into layers. The fat's moisture turns into steam, which causes the dough to rise and the layers to further separate.

Butter is the preferred fat because of its flavour and melt-in-the-mouth quality. But butter is rather difficult to work with as it becomes brittle when cold and melts at a relatively low temperature. Therefore, specially formulated puff pastry shortenings are used to compensate for butter's shortcomings. They do not, however, provide the true flavour of butter. Some bakers use a combination of butter and specially formulated shortening.

Raw, frozen, commercially prepared puff pastry is readily available in sheets or precut in a variety of shapes. Some convenience products, especially those made with butter, provide excellent, consistent results. Their expense may be offset by the savings in time and labour. Keep these frozen doughs well wrapped to prevent drying and freezer burn, and prepare according to package directions.

Making Puff Pastry

Making Puff Pastry

English method—Fat covers two-thirds of dough and single folds are used to create layers. Either 6 × 3 or 4 × 4 folds (bookfold) can be used.

Blitz method—Fat is incorporated as in flaky pie dough, only fat pieces are larger; dough is given two or three single folds.

The procedure described here for making puff pastry is just one of many. Each chef will have his or her own formula and folding method. All methods, however, depend upon the proper layering of fat and dough through a series of turns or folds to give the pastry its characteristic flakiness and rise.

Some chefs prefer to prepare a dough called **blitz** or *quick puff pastry*. It does not require the extensive rolling and folding procedure used for true puff pastry. Blitz puff pastry is less delicate and flaky but may be perfectly acceptable for some uses such as beef Wellington and pâté en croûte.

● **détrempe** a paste made with flour and water during the first stage of preparing a pastry dough, especially rolled-in (laminated) doughs

BASIC PROCEDURE FOR PREPARING PUFF PASTRY

1. Prepare the dough (**détrempe**) by combining the flour, water, salt and a small amount of fat. Do not overmix. Overmixing results in greater gluten formation; too much gluten can make the pastry undesirably tough.
2. Wrap the détrempe and chill for several hours or overnight. This allows the gluten to relax and the flour to absorb the liquid.
3. Shape the butter into a rectangle of even thickness; wrap and chill until ready to use.
4. Allow the détrempe and butter to sit at room temperature until slightly softened and of the same consistency.
5. Roll out the détrempe into a rectangle of even thickness.

continued

6. Place the butter in the centre of the dough. Fold the dough around the butter, enclosing it completely.

7. Roll out the block of dough and butter into a long, even rectangle. Roll only at right angles so that the layered structure is not destroyed.

8. Fold the dough like a business letter: fold the bottom third up toward the centre so that it covers the centre third, then fold the top third down over the bottom and middle thirds. This completes the first turn.

9. Rotate the block of dough one-quarter turn (90 degrees) on the work surface. Roll out again into a long, even rectangle.

10. Fold the dough in thirds again (single fold). This completes the second turn. Wrap the dough and chill for approximately 20 to 30 minutes. The resting period allows the gluten to relax; the chilling prevents the butter from becoming too soft. Overchilling will harden the butter too much.

11. Repeat the rolling and folding process, chilling between every one or two turns, until the dough has been turned a total of five times.

12. Wrap well and chill overnight. Raw dough may be refrigerated for a few days or frozen for two to three months.

13. Shape and bake as needed. Baked, unfilled puff pastry can be stored at room temperature for two to three days.

Bookfolds

The process of folding the dough and rolling it out and folding it again is referred to as bookfolds or turns. There are single folds (layering the dough in thirds), as described in the Basic Procedure for Preparing Puff Pastry, and bookfolds, bringing both outside edges to the centre and then folding in half again. The more folds, the more layers of fat and the flakier the pastry becomes—to a point. Too many folds results in the dough becoming too thin to support the structure as it develops during baking.

APPLYING THE BASICS	RECIPE 30.8

Puff Pastry

Yield: 1.3 kg (2 lb.)

Method: Rolled-in dough

Shortening	60 g	2 oz.
Bread flour	500 g	1 lb.
Water, cold	300–330 mL	10–11 fl. oz.
Butter or special pastry shortening		
(S.P.S.), softened	460 g	1 lb.

1. To form the détrempe, cut the shortening into small pieces and then rub the pieces into the flour until the mixture resembles coarse cornmeal.

2. Make a well in the centre of the mixture and add all the water at once. Using a rubber spatula or your fingers, gradually draw the flour into the water. Mix until all of the flour is incorporated.

3. Turn the détrempe out onto a lightly floured surface. Knead the dough a few times by hand, rounding it into a ball. Wrap the dough tightly in plastic and chill overnight.

4. To roll in the fat, first prepare the piece of fat by placing it between 2 sheets of plastic wrap. Use a rolling pin to roll the softened fat into a rectangle approximately 12.5 × 20 cm (5 × 8 in.). It is important that the détrempe and butter be of almost equal consistency. If necessary, allow the détrempe to sit at room temperature to soften or chill the butter briefly to harden.

5. On a lightly floured board, roll the détrempe into a rectangle approximately 30 × 37.5 cm (12 × 15 in.). Lift and rotate the dough as necessary to prevent sticking.

6. Use a dry pastry brush to brush away any flour from the dough's surface. Loose flour can cause grey streaks and prevent the puff pastry from rising properly when baked.

7. Peel one piece of plastic wrap from the fat. Position the fat in the centre of the rectangle and remove the remaining plastic. Fold the 4 edges of the détrempe over the fat, enclosing it completely. Stretch the dough if necessary; it is important that none of the butter be exposed.

Roll-in Fat (S.P.S.)

There are several special pastry shortenings (S.P.S.) on the market. Some are coloured and flavoured to resemble butter. The advantages of using them are cost and ease of handling. For superior taste, however, nothing beats a pure butter puff pastry. Concerns about trans fats will see these hydrogenated shortenings being reformulated.

1. Puff Pastry: Détrempe (left) and butter for puff pastry.

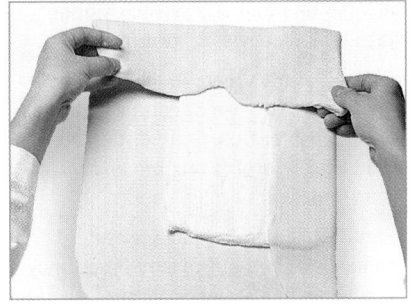

2. Folding the dough around the butter.

continued

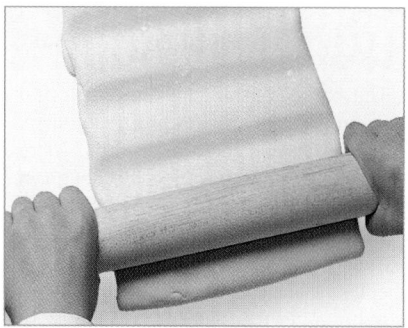

3. Rolling out the dough.

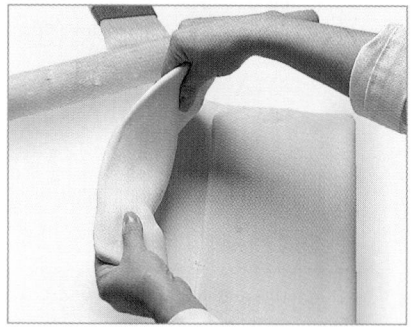

4. Folding the dough in thirds.

RECIPE 30.8

Approximate values per 50 g serving:	
Calories	217
Total fat	17 g
Saturated fat	10 g
Cholesterol	38 mg
Sodium	102 mg
Total carbohydrates	14 g
Protein	3 g

● **bouchées** small puff pastry shells that can be filled and served as bite-sized hors d'oeuvre or petit fours

● **vol-au-vents** deep, individual portion-sized puff pastry shells, often shaped as a heart, fish or fluted circle; they are filled with a savoury mixture and served as an appetizer or main course

● **feuilletés** square, rectangular or diamond-shaped puff pastry boxes; may be filled with a sweet or savoury mixture

8. With the folded side facing up, press the dough several times with a rolling pin. Use a rocking motion to create ridges in the dough. Place the rolling pin in each ridge and slowly roll back and forth to widen the ridge. Repeat until all of the ridges are doubled in size.

9. Using the ridges as a starting point, roll the dough out into a smooth, even rectangle approximately 20 × 60 cm (8 × 24 in.). Be careful to keep the corners of the dough at right angles.

10. Use a dry pastry brush to remove any loose flour from the dough's surface. Fold the dough in thirds, like a business letter. If one end is damaged or in worse condition, fold it in first; otherwise start at the bottom. This completes the first turn.

11. Rotate the block of dough 90 degrees so that the folded edge is on your left and the dough faces you like a book. Roll the dough out again, repeating the ridging technique. Once again, the dough should be in a smooth, even rectangle approximately 20 × 60 cm (8 × 24 in.).

12. Fold the dough in thirds again, completing the second turn. Cover the dough with plastic wrap and chill for 20 to 30 minutes.

13. Repeat the rolling and folding technique until the dough has had a total of 5 turns. Do not perform more than 2 turns without a resting and chilling period. Cover the dough completely and chill overnight before shaping and baking.

VARIATION: For a richer dough, use 50% butter and 50% S.P.S.

NOTES: The détrempe can be made in a food processor. To do so, combine the flour, salt and pieces of butter in a food processor bowl fitted with the metal blade. Process until a coarse meal is formed. With the processor running, slowly add the water. Turn the machine off as soon as the dough comes together to form a ball. Proceed with the remainder of the recipe.

It is not necessary to work with the entire block of dough when making bouchées, cookies or the like. Cut the block into thirds or quarters and work with one of these portions at a time, keeping the rest chilled until needed.

Shaping Puff Pastry

Once puff pastry dough is prepared, it can be shaped into containers of various sizes and shapes. Classic shapes are bouchées, vol-au-vents and feuilletés. **Bouchées** are small puff pastry shells often used for hors d'oeuvre or appetizers. **Vol-au-vents** are larger, deeper shells, often filled with savoury mixtures for a main course. Although they are most often round or square, special vol-au-vent cutters are available in the shape of fish, hearts or petals. **Feuilletés** are square, rectangular or diamond-shaped puff pastry boxes. They can be filled with a sweet or savoury mixture.

When making straight cuts in puff pastry, press the tip of your knife into the dough and cut by pressing down on the handle. Do not drag the knife through the dough or you will crush the layers and deform the pastry.

BASIC PROCEDURE FOR SHAPING VOL-AU-VENTS AND BOUCHÉES

1. Roll out the puff pastry dough to a thickness of approximately 6 mm (1/4 in.).

2. Cut the desired shape and size using a vol-au-vent cutter or rings.

3. Place the vol-au-vent or bouchée on a paper-lined sheet pan. If you used rings, place the base on the paper-lined sheet pan, brush lightly with water, then top it with the dough ring; score the edge with the back of a paring knife. Chill for at least 20 minutes to allow the dough to relax before baking.

continued

4. Brush with egg-wash if desired and dock the centre with a fork.

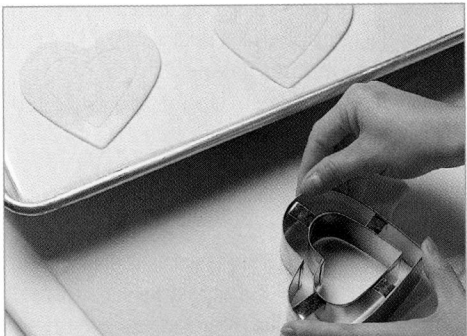

1. A vol-au-vent cutter looks like a double cookie cutter with one cutter about 2.5 cm (1 in.) smaller than the other. To cut the pastry, simply position the cutter and press down.

2. To shape with rings, use two rings, one approximately 2.5 cm (1 in.) smaller in diameter than the other. The larger ring is used to cut two rounds. One will be the base and is set aside. The smaller ring is then used to cut out an interior circle from the second round, leaving a border ring of dough. (The scrap of dough from the dough ring's centre has no further use in making vol-au-vents but may be used to make bouchées or fleurons.)

BASIC PROCEDURE FOR SHAPING FEUILLETÉES

1. Roll out the puff pastry dough into an even rectangle approximately 3 to 6 mm (1/8 to 1/4 in.) thick.

2. Using a sharp paring knife or chef's knife, cut squares that are about 5 cm (2 in.) larger than the desired interior of the finished feuilletée.

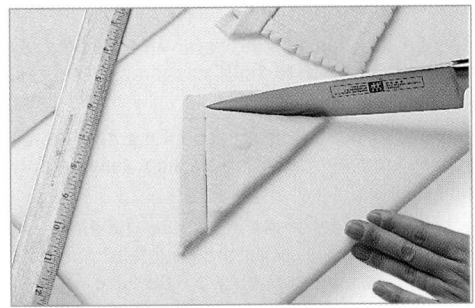

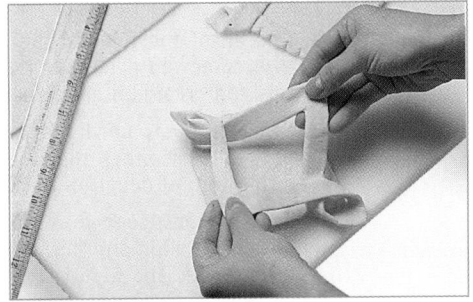

3. Fold each square in half diagonally. Cut through two sides of the dough, about 1.25 cm (1/2 in.) from the edge. Cut a "V," being careful not to cut through the corners at the centre fold.

4. Open the square and lay it flat. Lift opposite sides of the cut border at the cut corners and cross them.

5. Brush water on the edges to seal the dough. Place the feuilletées on a paper-lined sheet pan.

6. Score the edges with the back of a paring knife. Chill for at least 30 minutes to allow the dough to relax before baking.

7. Brush with egg-wash if desired and dock the centre with a fork.

● **pâte à choux** also known as choux paste and éclair paste; a soft dough that produces hollow baked products with crisp exteriors; used for making éclairs, cream puffs and savoury products

● **cream puffs** baked rounds of choux paste cut in half and filled with pastry cream, whipped cream, fruit or other filling

● **profiteroles** small baked rounds of choux paste filled with ice cream and topped with chocolate sauce

● **croquembouche** a pyramid of small puffs, each filled with pastry cream; a French tradition for Christmas and weddings, it is held together with caramelized sugar and decorated with spun sugar or marzipan flowers

● **éclairs** baked fingers of choux paste filled with pastry cream; the top is then coated with chocolate glaze or fondant

● **Paris-Brest** rings of baked choux paste cut in half horizontally and filled with light pastry cream and/or whipped cream; the top is dusted with powdered sugar or drizzled with chocolate glaze

● **beignets** squares or strips of choux paste deep-fat fried and dusted with powdered sugar

● **churros** a Spanish and Mexican pastry in which sticks of choux paste flavoured with cinnamon are deep-fat fried and rolled in sugar while still hot

● **crullers** a Dutch pastry in which a loop or strip of twisted choux paste is deep-fat fried

● **gougère** choux flavoured with cheese, baked and served as an hors d'oeuvre

---

Mastering Choux Paste

Choux paste requires some experience to achieve the proper consistency. If the paste is too firm, it will not rise properly; if it is too soft, it will not hold its shape when piped. For a crisper baked choux, only water is used; however, a small amount of sugar needs to be added for crust colour.

Puff pastry scraps cannot be rerolled and used for products needing a high rise. The additional rolling destroys the layers. Scraps (known as *rognures*), however, can be used for cookies such as palmiers (Recipe 30.22), turnovers, decorative crescents (fleurons), tart shells, napoleons (Recipe 30.23) or any item for which rise is less important than flavour and flakiness.

Most puff pastry products bake best in a hot oven, about 200°C to 220°C (400°F to 425°F).

Choux Paste

Choux paste (**pâte à choux**), sometimes called éclair paste, bakes up into golden brown, crisp pastries. The inside of these light pastries is mostly air pockets with a bit of moist dough. They can be filled with sweet cream, custard, fruit or even savoury mixtures. The dough is most often piped into rounds for **cream puffs**, and **profiteroles**, pyramids for **croquembouches**, fingers for **éclairs** or rings for **Paris-Brest** or gougères. Choux paste may also be piped or spooned into specific shapes and deep-fat fried for doughnut-type products known as **beignets**, **churros**, **crullers** and savoury **gougères**.

Preparing Choux Paste

Choux paste is unique among doughs because the flour is cooked before baking. The cooking occurs when the flour is added to a boiling mixture of water, milk and butter. This process breaks down the starches in the flour, allowing them to absorb the liquid, speeding gelatinization. Eggs are added to the flour mixture for leavening. The paste produced is batterlike with a smooth, firm texture; it does not have the dry, elastic or crumbly texture of other doughs. Without this technique, the paste would not puff up and develop the desired large interior air pockets when baked.

BASIC PROCEDURE FOR PREPARING CHOUX PASTE

1. Combine liquid ingredients and butter and bring to a boil.

2. Add all of the flour to the saucepan as soon as the water-and-butter mixture comes to a boil. If the liquid is allowed to boil, evaporation occurs; this can create an imbalance in the liquid-to-flour ratio.

3. Stir vigorously until the liquid is absorbed. Continue cooking the dough until it forms a ball that comes away from the sides of the pan, leaving only a thin film of dough in the pan.

4. Transfer the dough to a mixing bowl. Add eggs one at a time, beating well after each addition. This may be done in a mixer with the paddle attachment or by hand. The number of eggs used varies depending on the size of each egg and the moisture content of the flour mixture. Stop adding eggs when the paste just begins to fall away from the beaters or it forms a soft peak.

5. The finished paste should be smooth and pliable enough to pipe through a pastry bag; it should not be runny.

6. Pipe the paste as desired and bake immediately. A high oven temperature is necessary at the start of baking; it is then reduced gradually to finish baking and dry the product. Do not open the oven door during the first half of the baking period.

7. Allow the paste to bake until completely dry. If the products are removed from the oven too soon, they will collapse.

8. Baked choux paste can be stored, unfilled, for several days at room temperature or frozen for several weeks. Once filled, the pastry should be served within two or three hours as it quickly becomes soggy.

Basic Choux Paste

Yield: approximately 900 g (2 lb.)

Milk, 2%	200 mL	7 fl. oz.
Water	110 mL	4 fl. oz.
Butter	125 g	4-1/2 oz.
Bread flour	180 g	5-1/2 oz.
Eggs	300 g	5–6

1. Basic Choux Paste: Heating the butter, milk and water.

1. Preheat the oven to 220°C (425°F). Line a sheet pan with parchment. Have a pastry bag with a large plain tip ready.

2. Place the milk, water and butter in a saucepan. Bring to a rolling boil. Make sure the butter is fully melted.

3. Remove from the heat and immediately add all the flour. Vigorously beat the dough by hand. Put the pan back on the heat and continue beating the dough until it comes away from the sides of the pan. The dough should look relatively dry.

2. Adding the flour to the hot liquid.

4. Transfer the dough to a mixing bowl and allow it to cool briefly to a temperature of approximately 54°C (130°F) or lower. Using the mixer's paddle attachment, begin beating in the eggs one at a time on #2 speed and incorporating thoroughly.

5. Continue to add the eggs until the mixture is shiny but firm. It may not be necessary to use all the eggs. The paste should pull away from the sides of the bowl in thick threads; it will not clear the bowl.

6. Put a workable amount of dough into the pastry bag and pipe onto the sheet pan in the desired shapes at once.

3. Stirring the dough to dry it.

7. Bake immediately, beginning at 220°C (425°F) for 10 minutes, then lowering the heat to 190°C (375°F) for another 10 minutes. Continue gradually lowering the oven temperature until the shapes are brown and dry inside. Open the oven door as little as possible to prevent rapid changes in the oven's temperature.

8. Cool completely, then fill as desired. Leftovers can be frozen or stored at room temperature.

Approximate values per 30 g serving:	
Calories	69
Total fat	4.6 g
Saturated fat	2.5 g
Cholesterol	48 mg
Sodium	50 mg
Total carbohydrates	5 g
Protein	2 g

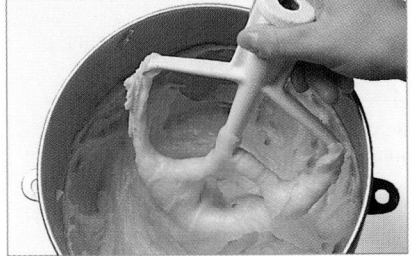

4. The finished batter after the eggs have been incorporated.

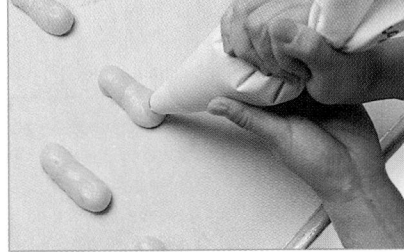

5. Piping éclairs or other shapes.

Meringues

Meringues are egg whites whipped with sugar. The texture—hard or soft—depends on the ratio of sugar to egg whites.

An equal or lesser sugar content in ratio to the egg whites creates a soft meringue. Soft meringues can be folded into a mousse to lighten it or used in a spongecake or soufflé. Meringues with only a small amount of sugar will always be soft; they will not become crisp no matter how they are used.

● **meringue** a foam made of beaten egg whites and sugar

Meringue Guidelines

1. Use clean equipment, completely grease-free.
2. Use clean egg whites—no yolk can be present. Hint: separate egg whites from yolks individually before adding to bowl; if a yolk breaks, only one egg white is ruined.
3. Some chefs add a small amount of acid (cream of tartar or lemon juice) to egg whites before whipping to increase volume and stability.
4. Egg whites should be at room temperature for maximum volume.
5. Do not add the sugar too soon or too fast.
6. Do not overwhip.

SAFETY ALERT

Pasteurized egg products are recommended for any meringue item that will not be fully baked before serving.

Soft meringues can be incorporated into a buttercream or pastry cream or used to top a pie or baked Alaska. These toppings are usually placed briefly under a broiler to caramelize the sugar, creating an attractive brown surface.

Hard meringues are made with twice as much sugar, or more, as egg whites. They can be piped into disks or other shapes and dried in an oven. A low oven temperature evaporates the eggs' moisture, leaving a crisp, sugary, honeycomb-like structure. Disks of baked meringue can be used as layers in a torte or cake. Cups or shells of baked meringue can be filled with cream, mousse, ice cream or fruit. Often baked meringues also contain ground nuts (and are then known as *japonaise*; see Recipe 30.10), cocoa powder or other flavourings.

Making Meringues

There are three methods for making meringues: common, Swiss and Italian. Regardless of which preparation method is used, the final product should be smooth, glossy and moist. A meringue should never be completely dry or spongelike. You should review the procedure for whipping egg whites given in Chapter 8, Eggs and Dairy Products. Table 30.4 provides some troubleshooting guidelines should you encounter quality issues with meringues.

Common Meringues

Common meringues are made by first beating egg whites to a soft foam (soft peaks). Granulated sugar is then added slowly and beaten into the egg whites. The final product may be hard (2:1) or soft (1:1), depending on the ratio of sugar to egg whites.

Swiss Meringues

Swiss meringues are made by combining unwhipped egg whites with sugar and warming the mixture over a bain marie to a temperature of approximately 40°C (105°F). The syrupy solution is then whipped until cool and stiff. The final product may be hard or soft, depending on the ratio of sugar to egg whites. Swiss meringues are extremely stable but rather difficult to prepare. If the mixture gets too hot, it will not whip properly; the result will be syrupy and runny. Swiss meringue is often used as a topping or in buttercream.

TABLE 30.4	Troubleshooting Chart for Meringues	
Problem	**Cause**	**Solution**
Weeps or beads of sugar syrup are released	Old eggs	Use fresher eggs or add starch or stabilizer
	Egg whites overwhipped	Whip only until stiff peaks form
	Not enough sugar	Increase sugar
	Not baked long enough	Increase baking time
	Browning too rapidly	Do not dust with sugar before baking; reduce oven temperature
	Moisture in the air	Do not refrigerate baked meringue
Fails to attain any volume or stiffness	Fat present	Start over with clean bowls and utensils
	Sugar added too soon	Allow egg whites to reach soft peaks before adding sugar
	Too much sugar added too quickly	Add sugar gradually
Lumps	Not enough sugar	Add additional sugar gradually or start over
	Overwhipping	Whip only until stiff peaks form
Not shiny	Not enough sugar	Add additional sugar gradually or start over
	Overwhipping	Whip only until stiff peaks form

Italian Meringues

Italian meringues are made by slowly pouring a hot sugar syrup into whipped egg whites (see Recipe 30.11). The heat from the syrup cooks the egg whites, adding stability. Be sure that the sugar syrup reaches the correct temperature and that it is added to the egg whites in a slow, steady stream. Italian meringues are used in buttercream (see Chapter 31, Cakes and Frostings) or folded into pastry cream to produce crème Chiboust. They may be flavoured and used as a cake filling and frosting called boiled icing.

Piping out the meringue disks.

APPLYING THE BASICS

RECIPE 30.10

Japonaise Meringue

Yield: 2 kg (4 lb.)

Egg whites	500 g	16 oz.
Granulated sugar	500 g	16 oz.
Icing sugar	500 g	16 oz.
Ground hazelnuts	500 g	16 oz.

1. Whip egg whites at medium speed to soft peaks.

2. With the machine still running, add the granulated sugar in small quantities. Whip to soft peaks.

3. Combine icing sugar and nuts, then fold into the meringue.

4. Using a pencil, mark circles on silicone sheets. Turn the sheets over and place on tray.

5. Pipe the japonaise mixture onto the sheets using a plain 12–15 mm (1/2-in.) tube. Using the pencilled circles as a guide, pipe in a spiral.

6. Bake at 120°C (250°F) until crisp, 1.5–2 hours. Use the meringues to make tortes.

RECIPE 30.10

Approximate values per 30 g serving:	
Calories	103
Total fat	4 g
Saturated fat	0 g
Cholesterol	0 mg
Sodium	24 mg
Total carbohydrates	15 g
Protein	2 g

Phyllo Dough

Phyllo, also spelled filo or fillo, is from the Greek *phyllon*, meaning thin sheet or leaf. Although its name is Greek, the origin of phyllo is unknown. Indians, Turks, Syrians, Yugoslavs and Austrians all claim it as their own. Somewhat blandly flavoured phyllo sheets are brushed with melted butter or oil, stacked and then used in many Mediterranean, Middle Eastern and central Asian dishes as a tart crust or a wrapper for various sweet or savoury fillings.

Phyllo dough is made from flour, water, a bit of oil and eggs. The dough must be stretched tissue-paper thin, using techniques that can take years to master. Fortunately, excellent commercially pre-pared phyllo is available in frozen sheets. Sheets of phyllo can stick together if thawed too quickly, so thaw frozen dough slowly for a day or so in the refrigerator. Then temper the package of dough at room temperature for at least one hour before opening. Unused phyllo should not be refrozen; it will keep for several days in the refrigerator if tightly wrapped.

When you are ready to use the phyllo, open the package and unfold the stack of leaves. Place them flat on a sheet pan or work surface and cover with a sheet of plastic wrap topped with a damp towel. Remove one leaf at a time from the stack, keeping the remainder well covered to prevent it from drying out. Brush melted butter or oil over the sheet's entire surface. Chopped nuts, sugar, cocoa powder or bread crumbs can be dusted over the butter or oil for additional flavour. Repeat with additional leaves until the desired number of layers have been prepared and stacked together.

The number of layers will depend on the thickness of the sheets and their use. Generally, a filled tart or casserole requires more leaves than does a folded or wrapped hors d'oeuvre. Cut the stacked phyllo with scissors or a very sharp knife and use as directed in the recipe.

Adding hot syrup to meringue.

RECIPE 30.11

Approximate values per 30 g serving:	
Calories	21
Total fat	0 g
Saturated fat	0 g
Cholesterol	0 mg
Sodium	4 mg
Total carbohydrates	5 g
Protein	0.5 g

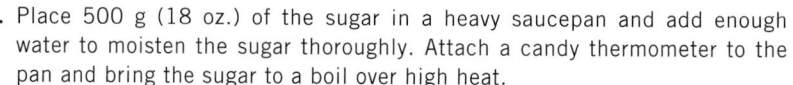

APPLYING THE BASICS	RECIPE 30.11

Italian Meringue

Yield: approximately 8 L (2 gal.)

Granulated sugar	800 g	28 oz.
Egg whites, room temperature	400 g	14 oz.

1. Place 500 g (18 oz.) of the sugar in a heavy saucepan and add enough water to moisten the sugar thoroughly. Attach a candy thermometer to the pan and bring the sugar to a boil over high heat.

2. Place the egg whites in the bowl of an electric mixer fitted with the whip attachment. As the temperature of the boiling sugar approaches 115°C (238°F), begin whipping the egg whites. When the whites form soft peaks, gradually add the remaining 300 g (10 oz.) of sugar. Lower the mixer speed and continue whipping.

3. When the sugar reaches 115°C (238°F), pour it into the whites, with the mixer running. Pour in a steady stream between the side of the bowl and the beater. Continue whipping the whites at medium speed until they are cool.

COOKIES

Cookies are small, flat pastries usually eaten alone (although not singularly) and sometimes used as a component in other desserts. The recent proliferation of cookie shops in malls and office buildings attests to the popularity of freshly baked cookies. They are indeed among the world's best-loved foods.

Part of the pleasure of cookies comes from their versatility. They may be eaten as a midmorning snack or as the elegant end to a formal dinner. Cookies also provide the finishing touch to a serving of ice cream, custard or fruit. Flavours are limited only by the baker's imagination; chocolate, oatmeal, cornmeal, fresh and dried fruit and nuts all find their way into several types of cookies. Several cookie formulas are given at the end of this chapter.

Mixing Methods

Most cookie doughs are mixed by the **creaming** method used for quick breads and cake batters. (See Chapter 28, Quick Breads, and Chapter 31, Cakes and Frostings.) Because cookie dough contains less liquid than these batters, the liquid and flour need not be added alternately, however. Cookies may be leavened with baking soda, baking powder or just air and steam. Most cookies are high in fat, which contributes taste and tenderness and extends shelf life. Overdevelopment of gluten is usually not a problem with cookies because of their high fat and low moisture contents. Careless mixing can cause the dough to become tough and dense instead of tender and flaky. Other mixing methods include **one-stage** and **sponge**.

● **cookies** small, sweet, flat pastries; usually classified by preparations or makeup techniques as drop, icebox, bar, cut-out or rolled, pressed and wafer

● **creaming method** a mixing method in which softened fat and sugar are vigorously combined to incorporate air

● **one-stage method** low-moisture formulas can be mixed all at once; rarely used because you have less control

● **sponge method** like the cake method, foamed egg whites are used; the batter is delicate; makes small quantities (e.g., ladyfingers, madeleines)

BASIC PROCEDURE FOR MIXING COOKIE DOUGHS

1. Cream the fat and sugar together to incorporate air and to blend the ingredients completely.

2. Add the eggs gradually, scraping down the bowl as needed.

continued

3. Stir in the liquid ingredients.

4. Stir in the flour, salt, spices and leaveners.

5. Fold in any nuts, chocolate chips or chunky ingredients by hand or by mixer on low speed.

Makeup Methods

Cookie varieties are usually classified by the way in which the individual cookies are prepared. This section describes six preparation or makeup techniques: drop, icebox, bar, cut-out or rolled, pressed and wafer. Some doughs can be made up by more than one method. For example, chocolate chip cookie dough can be (a) baked in sheets and cut into bars, (b) dropped in mounds or (c) rolled into logs, chilled and sliced like icebox cookies. Regardless of the makeup method used, uniformity of size and shape is important for appearance and baking time. Cookies should also be evenly spaced on sheet pans for proper air circulation and crust formation.

Drop Cookies

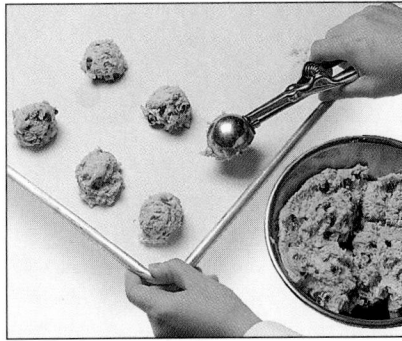

Drop Cookies

Drop cookies are made from a soft dough that is spooned or scooped into mounds for baking. Chunky cookies such as chocolate chip, oatmeal raisin and nut jumbles are common examples. Although a uniform appearance is not as important for drop cookies as for other types, uniform size and placement results in uniform baking time. A portion scoop is recommended for portioning the dough. Drop cookies tend to be thick, with a soft or chewy texture.

Icebox Cookies

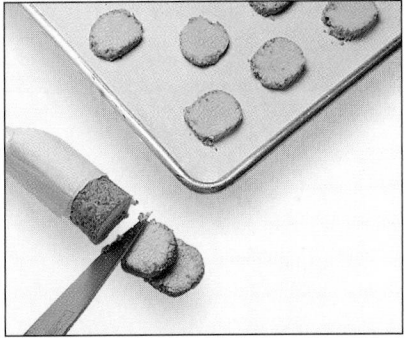

Icebox Cookies

Icebox cookies are made from dough that is shaped into logs or rectangles, chilled thoroughly, then sliced into individual pieces and baked as needed. Icebox cookies can be as simple as a log of chocolate chip dough or as sophisticated as elegant pinwheel and checkerboard cookies assembled with two colours of short dough. This method usually produces uniform, waferlike cookies with a crisp texture.

Bar Cookies

Bar Cookies

Bar cookie dough is pressed or layered in shallow pans and cut into portions after baking, usually squares or rectangles to avoid waste or scraps. This category, also known as sheet cookies, contains a wide variety of layered or fruit-filled products. Brownies, often considered a bar cookie, are discussed in Chapter 31, Cakes and Frostings.

Cut-out or Rolled Cookies

Cut-out or Rolled Cookies

Cut-out or rolled cookies are made from a firm dough that is rolled out into a sheet and then cut into various shapes before baking. A seemingly infinite selection of cookie cutters is available, or you can use a paring knife or pastry wheel to cut the dough into the desired shapes. Always start cutting cookies from the edge of the dough, working inward. Cut the cookies as close to each other as possible to avoid scraps. Cut-out cookies are usually baked on an ungreased pan to keep the dough from spreading.

Cut-out cookies are often garnished or decorated with nuts, glaze, fruit or candies. Raw cookies should be decorated as soon as they are placed on the pan. If the dough is allowed to stand, the surface will dry out and the garnish will not adhere properly.

Pressed Cookies

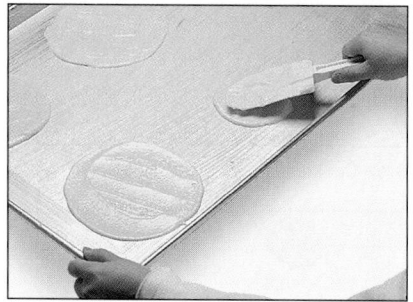

Wafer Cookies

Pressed Cookies

Also referred to as bagged or spritz cookies, these products are made with a soft dough that is forced through a pastry tip or cookie gun. Pressed cookies are usually small, with a distinct, decorative shape. The task of piping out dozens of identical cookies may seem daunting, but the skill can be mastered with practice and an understanding of doughs. Doughs for pressed cookies often include eggs as their only liquid. Egg whites, which are a toughener, contribute body and help the cookies retain their shape. The yolks act as a tenderizer. Using too much fat or too-soft flour (i.e., one low in protein) can cause the cookies to spread and lose their shape.

Wafer Cookies

Wafer cookies are extremely thin and delicate. They are made with a thin batter that is poured or spread onto a baking sheet and baked. Then, while still hot, the wafer is moulded into a variety of shapes. The most popular shapes are the tightly rolled cigarette, the curved tuile and the cup-shaped tulip. Wafer batter is sweet and buttery and is often flavoured with citrus zest or ground nuts.

Cookie Textures

The textures associated with cookies—crispness, softness, chewiness or spread—are affected by various factors, including the ratio of ingredients in the dough, the oven's temperature and the pan's coating. Understanding these factors allows you to adjust formulas or techniques to achieve the desired results. (See Table 30.5.)

Storing Cookies

Most cookies can be stored for up to one week in an airtight container. Do not store crisp cookies and soft cookies in the same container, however. The crisp cookies will absorb moisture from the soft cookies, ruining the texture of both. Do not store strongly flavoured cookies, such as spice cookies, with those that are milder, such as shortbread.

Most cookies freeze well if wrapped airtight to prevent moisture loss or freezer burn. Raw dough can also be frozen, either shaped or unshaped.

TABLE 30.5	Cookie Textures					
		Content of				
Desired Texture	**Fat**	**Sugar**	**Liquid**	**Flour**	**Size or Shape**	**Baking**
Crispness	High	High; use granulated sugar	Low	Bread or pastry	Thin dough	Well done; cool on baking sheet
Softness	Low	Low; use hygroscopic sugars	High	Pastry or cake	Thick dough portion	Use parchment-lined pan; underbake
Chewiness	High	High; use hygroscopic sugars	High	Bread or pastry	Not relevant; chilled dough	Underbake; cool on rack
Spread	High	High; use coarse granulated sugar	High; especially from eggs	Pastry or cake	Not relevant; room-temperature dough	Use greased pan; low temperature

1. Using the blender's paddle attachment at low speed, mix together brown sugar, corn syrup, salt, cinnamon and ginger until blended.

2. With machine running, add eggs one at a time.

3. Pour melted butter into mixture and mix thoroughly.

Rum and Raisin Crème Anglaise

Raisins	75 g	3 oz.
Rum	50 mL	2 fl. oz.
Egg yolks	5	5
Sugar	50 g	2 oz.
Milk	250 g	8-1/2 oz.
Cream, 35%	175 g	6 oz.
Vanilla bean	1	1
Sugar	50 g	2 oz.

1. Boil raisins in water for 1 minute.

2. Strain and add rum. Set aside.

3. Whisk together egg yolks and 50 g (2 oz.) of sugar until pale and thick.

4. Scald milk, cream, vanilla bean and 50 g (2 oz.) sugar. Infuse vanilla for 5 minutes and scald again.

5. Temper the egg mixture with the infused liquid.

6. Transfer to a clean saucepan and cook over low heat, stirring constantly until the mixture coats the back of a wooden spoon (rose stage).

7. Strain and chill quickly and thoroughly over ice.

8. Add rum-flavoured raisins.

Bitter Chocolate Sorbet

Cocoa powder	60 g	2 oz.
Sugar	280 g	10 oz.
Water	800 g	27 oz.
Dark chocolate, chopped	500 g	1 lb. 2 oz.

1. Make a syrup by heating cocoa powder, sugar and water and stirring until the liquid comes to a boil.

2. Add chopped chocolate to the syrup and stir until melted. Chill over an ice bath.

3. Freeze in an ice cream freezer.

Banana Wafers

Bananas, ripe	2	2
Honey	30 g	1 oz.

1. Purée banana.

2. Pass the banana purée through a fine sieve and add the honey.

3. Using a template with 12-cm (5-in.) circles, pour the mixture onto parchment paper. Each wafer should be about 2 mm (1/16 in.) thick.

4. Dry in the oven at 82°C (180°F) until golden brown.

5. Remove one by one and fold in half to form an open-fan shape.

6. If wafers harden, return them to the oven.

7. Store in a sealed container until ready to use.

Rum and Raisin Crème Anglaise— Approximate values per 30 g serving:

Calories	69
Total fat	4 g
Saturated fat	2 g
Cholesterol	61 mg
Sodium	10 mg
Total carbohydrates	7 g
Protein	1 g

Bitter Chocolate Sorbet—Approximate values per 30 g serving:

Calories	66
Total fat	5 g
Saturated fat	3 g
Cholesterol	0 mg
Sodium	2 mg
Total carbohydrates	8 g
Protein	1 g

Banana Wafers—Approximate values per 30 g serving:

Calories	39
Total fat	0.1 g
Saturated fat	0.1 g
Cholesterol	0 mg
Sodium	0.5 mg
Total carbohydrates	10 g
Protein	0 g

Evelyn McManus, Ph.D.
Evelyn holds a Ph.D. in biochemistry, as well as her Red Seal chef papers and her Pâtissière papers. She is a graduate of the Stratford Chef School, where she won the Eckhardt Award for outstanding achievement in pastry. Following several successful years as a chef in fine dining establishments, Evelyn is currently Chef, Hospitality Programs, School of Business & Hospitality, Conestoga College Institute of Technology and Advanced Learning, Waterloo, ON.

RECIPE 30.17

Cream Cheese Pastry—Approximate values per serving:	
Calories	313
Total fat	24 g
Saturated fat	15 g
Cholesterol	67 mg
Sodium	431 mg
Total carbohydrates	20 g
Protein	4 g

Filling— Approximate values per serving:	
Calories	481
Total fat	30 g
Saturated fat	11 g
Cholesterol	203 mg
Sodium	129 mg
Total carbohydrates	50 g
Protein	6.5 g

RECIPE 30.17

Caramel Flan

CONESTOGA COLLEGE INSTITUTE OF TECHNOLOGY AND
ADVANCED LEARNING, WATERLOO, ON
Hospitality Programs, School of Business & Hospitality
Chef Evelyn McManus, Ph.D.

Yield: 1 22-cm (10-in.) flan

Cream Cheese Pastry

Butter	250 g	8 oz.
Cream cheese	250 g	8 oz.
Salt	pinch	pinch
Lemon zest	10 g	1 Tbsp.
Pastry flour	300 g	10-1/2 oz.

1. Cream butter, cheese, salt and lemon zest until light and fluffy.
2. Add flour all at once and mix just until dough forms a ball. Chill at least 1 hour before using.
3. Line flan with pastry.
4. Bake blind at 175°C (350°F) until golden.

Filling

Sugar	280 g	10 oz.
Eggs	450 g	8
Butter, unsalted	225 g	8 oz.
Salt	pinch	pinch
Sugar, caramelized	280 g	10 oz.
Hazelnuts, roasted, skinned, chopped	200 g	7 oz.
Chocolate Ganache (Recipe 31.15)	300 g	10–11 oz.

1. Cream sugar, eggs, butter and salt until light and fluffy.
2. Dry-cook second sugar to dark caramel colour; remove from heat and set the pot in cold water to stop the cooking process.
3. Stir the creamed mixture into the caramel, return to heat and bring to a boil. Cook until all lumps disappear and the mixture is smooth and glossy (about 10 minutes).
4. Add nuts, remove from heat and pour into cooked shell. Cool.
5. Top with Chocolate Ganache. Chill overnight.

RECIPE 30.18

Apple Custard Flan

SAIT POLYTECHNIC, CALGARY, AB
School of Hospitality and Tourism
Pastry Chef Instructor Albert Liu

Yield: 1 20-cm (8-in.) flan

Sweet Paste (Recipe 30.2)	300 g	10-1/2 oz.
Golden apples	5	5
Whole eggs	110 g	2
Granulated sugar	75 g	2-1/2 oz.
Cornstarch	15 g	1/2 oz.
Milk, 2%	125 g	4 oz.
Cream, 35%	125 g	4 oz.
Vanilla	2 mL	1/2 tsp.
Nutmeg, grated	pinch	pinch

1. Line the flan tin with the Sweet Paste. Set aside.
2. Peel and slice the apples.
3. Arrange the apples in the flan, overlapping them in a circle.
4. In a bowl, combine the eggs, sugar and cornstarch.
5. Add the milk, cream, vanilla and nutmeg. Whisk to blend.
6. Pour mixture over apples.
7. Bake at 170°C (350°F) until custard is set, about 45 minutes.

Albert Liu

Albert began his career as a pâtissier at the Four Seasons Hotel in Vancouver, worked as an Executive Pastry Chef in the Bahamas, and then became the Executive Pastry Chef at the Palliser Hotel in Calgary. Currently he is a Pastry Chef Instructor at SAIT in Calgary.

RECIPE 30.18

Approximate values per 1/12 flan:	
Calories	252
Total fat	13 g
Saturated fat	8 g
Cholesterol	86 mg
Sodium	26 mg
Total carbohydrates	33 g
Protein	3.5 g

RECIPE 30.19

Saskatoon-Almond Tart

HARDWARE GRILL, EDMONTON, AB
Chef/Owner Larry Stewart, CCC

Yield: 6 servings

Dough

Unsalted butter, cubed	100 g	3 oz.
Egg	1	1
Icing sugar	50 g	1-1/2 oz.
Pastry flour	175 g	6 oz.
Baking powder	7 g	2 tsp.

1. Beat butter and egg with a paddle attachment until the mixture resembles scrambled eggs. Add icing sugar and beat on high speed until mixture is smooth.
2. On low speed, add flour and baking powder. Mix just until mixture comes away from sides of bowl.
3. Form dough into a ball and chill for at least 1 hour. Divide dough into 6 pieces and roll into 15-cm (6-in.) rounds. Line tart moulds and parbake at 175°C (350°F) for 10 minutes.

Larry Stewart, CCC

In 1996, Larry established Hardware Grill in Edmonton, an A-list dining spot with a reputation that travels beyond city and province. Providing excellent food, an award-winning wine list, outstanding service and serious respect for the history of Canadian cuisine, chef/owner Larry Stewart and his wife Melinda are pioneers in the development of a real Prairie food culture. His restaurant has a two-star rating in *Where to Eat in Canada* and has won *Wine Spectator*'s Best Award of Excellence.

continued

RECIPE 30.19

Dough— Approximate values per serving:	
Calories	270
Total fat	15 g
Saturated fat	9 g
Cholesterol	72 mg
Sodium	98 mg
Total carbohydrates	31.5 g
Protein	3.5 g

Almond Streusel— Approximate values per serving:	
Calories	214
Total fat	13 g
Saturated fat	6 g
Cholesterol	22 mg
Sodium	87 mg
Total carbohydrates	22 g
Protein	4 g

Saskatoon-Almond Filling— Approximate values per serving:	
Calories	329
Total fat	18 g
Saturated fat	7 g
Cholesterol	112 mg
Sodium	128 mg
Total carbohydrates	36 g
Protein	6 g

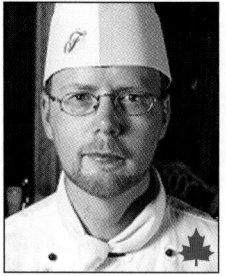

Ken Harper

Born and raised in Victoria, Ken completed his scholarship in Camosun College's culinary program and then joined the Fairmont Empress as an apprentice chef. Highlights of his career include joining the culinary teams at the Fairmont Banff Springs Hotel, the Fairmont Château Whistler Resort and the Pan Pacific Hotel. He became Pastry Chef at the Empress in 1997 and now teaches at Vancouver Island University.

RECIPE 30.19

Almond Streusel

Butter, softened	60 g	2 oz.
Rolled oats	50 g	1-1/2 oz.
Brown sugar	50 g	1-1/2 oz.
Almonds, sliced	50 g	1-1/2 oz.
Flour, pastry	50 g	1-1/2 oz.
Cinnamon	1 g	1/4 tsp.

Combine all ingredients into a crumbly mixture.

Saskatoon-Almond Filling

Almond paste	150 g	5-1/2 oz.
Butter, softened	70 g	2-1/2 oz.
Sugar	120 g	4 oz.
Eggs	120 g	2
Lemon zest	10 g	1 Tbsp.
Grand Marnier	15 mL	1/2 fl. oz.
Flour	20 g	2-1/2 Tbsp.
Baking powder	0.25 g	1/2 tsp.
Saskatoon berries, thawed and drained	175 g	6 oz.

1. Mix the almond paste, butter and sugar with paddle. Add eggs, lemon zest and Grand Marnier and mix well.
2. Add sifted flour and baking powder. Mix to blend. Fold in Saskatoon berries.
3. Divide almond batter among tart shells and top with streusel.
4. Bake at 160°C (325°F) for approximately 20 minutes.

NOTE: Chef Stewart serves this tart warm with cinnamon ice cream and oatmeal praline.

RECIPE 30.20

Lemon Thyme Pear Tart with Jasmine Tea Glaze

VANCOUVER ISLAND UNIVERSITY, NANAIMO, BC
Pastry Chef Ken Harper

Yield: 10 servings

Puff Pastry (Recipe 30.8)	250 g	8 oz.
Lemon Thyme Almond Cream (recipe follows)	450 g	1 lb.
Poached pear halves, fanned	10	10
Jasmine Tea Glaze (recipe follows)	as needed	as needed

1. Roll out Puff Pastry into a circle, approximately 22 cm (9 in.) in diameter and 3 mm (1/8 in.) thick. Lay the dough on a sheet pan lined with parchment paper. Dock with a fork.
2. Using a plain tip, pipe 10 teardrops of Lemon Thyme Almond Cream around the ring of puff pastry.
3. Arrange the pear fans over the almond cream, overlapping slightly.
4. Bake at 180°C (375°F) until the dough is golden, approximately 15 minutes.
5. Serve warm, glazed with Jasmine Tea Glaze and accompanied by vanilla ice cream.

continued

Lemon Thyme Almond Cream (Frangipane)

Yield: 700 g (1.5 lb.)

Unsalted butter, softened	100 g	3-1/2 oz.
Granulated sugar	125 g	4 oz.
Eggs	125 g	2
All-purpose flour	10 g	4 tsp.
Almonds, ground	175 g	6 oz.
Lemon zest	10 g	1
Lemon thyme	2 g	1 tsp.

1. Cream the butter and sugar. Slowly add the eggs, scraping down the sides of the bowl as necessary.

2. Stir the flour, ground almonds, lemon zest and lemon thyme together, then add to the butter mixture. Blend the **frangipane** until no lumps remain.

Jasmine Tea Glaze

Yield: 200 mL (7 fl. oz.)

White wine	180 mL	6-1/2 fl. oz.
Jasmine tea	15 mL	1 Tbsp.
Sugar	60 g	2 oz.
Jelly powder	5 g	1-1/2 tsp.
Apricot jam	15 g	1 Tbsp.

1. Bring wine to a boil, add tea and steep for 2 hours. Strain.

2. Bring back to a boil and whisk in sugar, jelly powder and jam.

RECIPE 30.21

Chocolate Éclairs

Yield: 20 éclairs

Baked éclair shells, 10 cm (4 in.) long, made from Basic Choux Paste (Recipe 30.9)	20	20
Pastry Cream (Recipe 32.2), chocolate flavoured	1 L	1 qt.
Chocolate glaze:		
Unsweetened chocolate	125 g	4 oz.
Semi-sweet chocolate	125 g	4 oz.
Unsalted butter	125 g	4 oz.
White corn syrup	25 mL	4 tsp.
White chocolate, melted (optional)	as needed	as needed

1. Use a paring knife or skewer to cut a small hole into the end of each baked, cooled éclair shell.

2. Pipe the Pastry Cream into each shell using a piping bag fitted with a small plain tip. Be sure that the cream fills the full length of each shell. Refrigerate the filled éclairs.

3. Prepare the glaze by melting all ingredients together over a bain marie. Remove from the heat and allow to cool, occasionally stirring, until slightly thickened.

RECIPE 30.20

Approximate values per serving:

Calories	441
Total fat	27.5 g
Saturated fat	11 g
Cholesterol	146 mg
Sodium	96 mg
Total carbohydrates	43 g
Protein	7 g

Lemon Thyme Almond Cream (Frangipane)—Approximate values per 70 g serving:

Calories	245
Total fat	19 g
Saturated fat	6 g
Cholesterol	76 mg
Sodium	19 mg
Total carbohydrates	17 g
Protein	5 g

Jasmine Tea Glaze— Approximate values per serving:

Calories	41
Total fat	0 g
Saturated fat	0 g
Cholesterol	0 mg
Sodium	3 mg
Total carbohydrates	7 g
Protein	0.5 g

 frangipane a sweet almond and egg filling cooked inside pastry

RECIPE 30.21

Approximate values per serving:

Calories	410
Total fat	31 g
Saturated fat	17 g
Cholesterol	110 mg
Sodium	230 mg
Total carbohydrates	27 g
Protein	5 g

continued

4. In a single, smooth stroke, dip the top of each filled éclair through the glaze. Only the very top of each pastry should be coated with chocolate.

5. Melted white chocolate may be piped onto the wet glaze, then pulled into patterns using a toothpick. (See sauce-pulling techniques in Chapter 36, Plate Presentation.) Keep finished éclairs refrigerated and serve within 8–12 hours.

1. Chocolate Éclairs: Filling the éclairs with Pastry Cream using a piping bag.

2. Dipping the éclairs in chocolate glaze.

RECIPE 30.22

Palmiers

| Puff Pastry (Recipe 30.8) | as needed |
| Granulated sugar | as needed |

1. Roll out the Puff Pastry into a very thin rectangle. The length is not important but the width should be at least 17.5 cm (7 in.).

2. Sprinkle the Puff Pastry sheet lightly with granulated sugar. Using a rolling pin, gently press the granulated sugar into the dough. Flip over and repeat.

3. Along the long edges of the dough, make a 2.5-cm (1-in.) fold toward the centre. Sprinkle on additional sugar.

4. Make another 2.5-cm (1-in.) fold along the long edges toward the centre. The 2 folds should almost meet in the centre. Sprinkle on additional sugar.

5. Fold 1 side on top of the other. Press down gently with a rolling pin or your fingers so that the dough adheres. Chill for 1 hour.

6. Cut the log of dough in thin slices. Place the cookies on a paper-lined sheet pan and bake at 200°C (400°F) until the edges are brown, approximately 8–12 minutes.

RECIPE 30.22

Approximate values per 30 g serving:	
Calories	130
Total fat	5 g
Saturated fat	1 g
Cholesterol	0 mg
Sodium	35 mg
Total carbohydrates	19 g
Protein	1 g

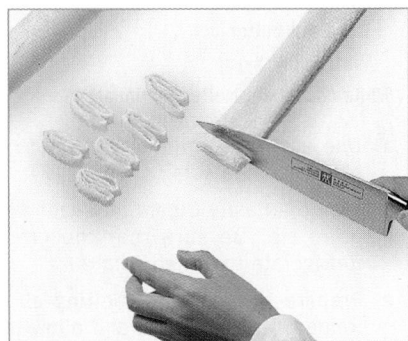

1. Palmiers: Folding the dough toward the centre from both edges.

2. Slicing the log of dough into individual cookies.

RECIPE 30.23

Strawberry Napoleon

Yield: 10 servings

Puff Pastry, cut into		
10 × 37-cm (4 × 15-in.) strips,		
docked and baked (Recipe 30.8)	3	3
Pastry Cream (Recipe 32.2)	500 mL	1 pt.
Fresh strawberries, sliced	1 L	1 qt.
Crème Chantilly (Recipe 32.6)	500 mL	1 pt.
Basic Sugar Glaze (Recipe 31.13)	as needed	as needed
Dark chocolate, melted	30 g	1 oz.

1. Allow the Puff Pastry to cool completely before assembling.

2. Place a strip of Puff Pastry on a cake cardboard for support. Pipe on a layer of Pastry Cream, leaving a clean margin of almost 10 mm (1/2 in.) on all 4 sides.

3. Top the cream with a layer of berries.

4. Spread on a thin layer of Crème Chantilly. Repeat the procedure for the second layer of Puff Pastry.

5. Chill while you prepare the Basic Sugar Glaze. When ready to glaze, place the third strip of Puff Pastry on an icing rack, flat side up. Pour the Basic Sugar Glaze down the length of the pastry and spread evenly with a metal cake spatula. Allow the excess to drip over the sides.

6. Immediately pipe thin lines of chocolate across the glaze. Use a toothpick to pull a spiderweb pattern in the glaze. Chill to set the glaze, then place the top in position on the napoleon.

Strawberry Napoleon

RECIPE 30.23

Approximate values per serving:	
Calories	320
Total fat	20 g
Saturated fat	9 g
Cholesterol	115 mg
Sodium	65 mg
Total carbohydrates	29 g
Protein	4 g

RECIPE 30.24

Chocolate Délice

Yield: 1 20-cm (8-in.) cake

Classic Dacquoise (recipe follows)
Chocolate Ganache (Recipe 31.15)
Crème Chantilly (Recipe 32.6)
Candied Almonds (recipe follows)

1. Spread an even layer of Ganache over 2 of the dacquoise disks.

2. Top 1 disk with about 200 g (7 oz.) of Crème Chantilly. Place the second disk on top, chocolate side up. Top with another 200 g (7 oz.) of Crème Chantilly. Position the third disk on top, flat side up.

3. Spread the remaining Crème Chantilly over the top and sides.

4. Sprinkle Candied Almonds over the top and sides of the cake.

5. Freeze to firm the cream, approximately 1 hour. Remove from freezer and refrigerate for service.

RECIPE 30.24

Approximate values per serving:	
Calories	490
Total fat	32.5 g
Saturated fat	13 g
Cholesterol	50 mg
Sodium	35 mg
Total carbohydrates	39 g
Protein	10 g

continued

Classic Dacquoise

Blanched almonds	60 g	2 oz.
Granulated sugar	180 g	6 oz.
Egg whites	90 g	3 oz.

1. Preheat oven to 110°C (225°F). Line a baking sheet with parchment. Draw 3 20-cm (8-in.) circles on the parchment.

2. Grind the nuts in a food processor. They should be the consistency of cornmeal and as dry as possible. Combine with 60 g (2 oz.) of the sugar and set aside.

3. Whip the egg whites on medium speed until foamy. Increase the speed and gradually add 30 g (1 oz.) of the sugar.

4. Continue whipping until the egg whites form soft peaks. Gradually add the remaining 90 g (3 oz.) of sugar.

5. Continue whipping until smooth and glossy, about 2 minutes.

6. Sprinkle the almond-sugar mixture over the meringue and fold together by hand using a spatula.

7. Take a pastry bag with a plain tip and using the circles on the parchment paper as a guide, pipe the meringue into 3 20-cm (8-in.) disks.

8. Bake until firm and crisp but not brown, approximately 60–75 minutes. Cool completely.

Candied Almonds

Egg whites	2	2
Granulated sugar	60 g	2 oz.
Sliced almonds	250 g	8 oz.

1. Preheat oven to 160°C (325°F).

2. Whisk the egg whites and sugar together. Add the almonds. Toss with a rubber spatula to coat the nuts completely.

3. Spread the nuts in a thin layer on a lightly greased baking sheet. Bake until lightly toasted and dry, approximately 15–20 minutes. Watch closely to prevent burning.

4. Stir the nuts with a metal spatula every 5–7 minutes during baking.

5. Cool completely. Store in an airtight container for up to 10 days.

1. Chocolate Délice: Piping out the meringue disks.

2. Layering the ganache-covered dacquoise.

3. Frosting the délice.

RECIPE 30.25

Sugar Cookies

Yield: 3 dozen
Method: Cut-out cookies

Pastry flour	300–340 g	10–12 oz.
Baking powder	7 g	2 tsp.
Mace, ground	0.75 g	1/4 tsp.
Unsalted butter, softened	125 g	4 oz.
Granulated sugar	250 g	8 oz.
Vanilla extract	5 mL	1 tsp.
Egg	55 g	1

1. Stir together the flour, baking powder and mace. Set aside.

2. Cream the butter and sugar until light and fluffy. Blend in the vanilla. Add the egg and beat again until fluffy. Gradually add the flour mixture, beating just until well combined.

3. Wrap the dough in plastic wrap and refrigerate until firm, about 1–2 hours.

4. Work with about half the dough at a time, keeping the remainder refrigerated. On a lightly floured board, roll out the dough to a thickness of about 3 mm (1/8 in.). Cut as desired with cookie cutters. Carefully transfer the cookies to lightly greased baking sheets.

5. Bake at 160°C (325°F) until golden brown, approximately 10–12 minutes. Let stand for about 1 minute, then transfer to wire racks to cool.

VARIATION: Ken Harper, Vancouver Island University, recommends flavouring with 15 g (5 Tbsp.) dried, crushed lavender.

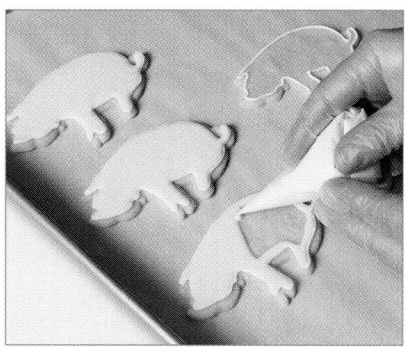

Sugar Cookies

RECIPE 30.25

Approximate values per cookie:	
Calories	92
Total fat	3 g
Saturated fat	2 g
Cholesterol	14 mg
Sodium	17 mg
Total carbohydrates	15 g
Protein	1 g

RECIPE 30.26

Oatmeal Coconut Cookies

Yield: 35 85-g (3-oz.) cookies
Method: Dropped cookies

Shortening	360 g	13 oz.
Brown sugar	540 g	20 oz.
Salt	10 g	2 tsp.
Baking soda	5 g	1-1/2 tsp.
Whole eggs	90 g	3-1/2 oz.
Milk	50 mL	2 fl. oz.
Oatmeal	225 g	8 oz.
Coconut, fine	180 g	6 oz.
Pastry flour	360 g	13 oz.
Baking powder	10 g	1 Tbsp.

1. Cream the shortening, brown sugar, salt and baking soda until light and fluffy.

2. Beat in eggs and milk, scraping down bowl.

3. Add mixture of oatmeal, coconut, pastry flour and baking powder. Blend together until just well combined.

4. Portion with a scoop, flatten slightly and bake in a 190°C (375°F) oven for 15–20 minutes or until lightly browned on the edges.

Oatmeal Coconut Cookies

RECIPE 30.26

Approximate values per cookie:	
Calories	221
Total fat	12 g
Saturated fat	4 g
Cholesterol	11 mg
Sodium	194 mg
Total carbohydrates	26 g
Protein	1.5 g

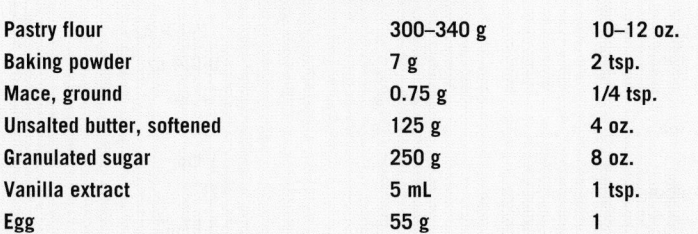

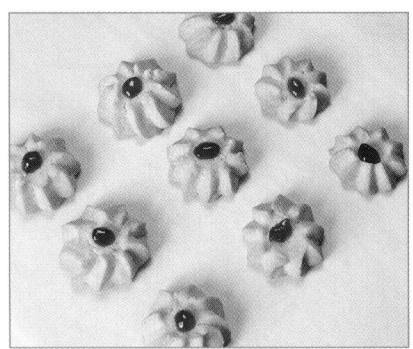

Spritz Piped Cookies

RECIPE 30.27

Approximate values per cookie:	
Calories	81
Total fat	5 g
Saturated fat	2.5 g
Cholesterol	9 mg
Sodium	3 mg
Total carbohydrates	7 g
Protein	1 g

Mark Jorundson

Mark received his Journeyman certification from the Northern Alberta Institute of Technology, earning the title "Canadian Apprentice of the Year." He went on to travel through Europe, eventually catering to the rich and famous at the renowned Anton Mossiman's Belfry in London. Upon returning to Canada, Mark joined Canadian Pacific Hotels and offered Canadian cuisine at the Lodge at Kananaskis and the Hotel Macdonald in Edmonton, Alberta. He operates a catering business in Calgary.

RECIPE 30.28

Approximate values per horn:	
Calories	35
Total fat	2 g
Saturated fat	1 g
Cholesterol	4 mg
Sodium	17 mg
Total carbohydrates	5 g
Protein	0 g

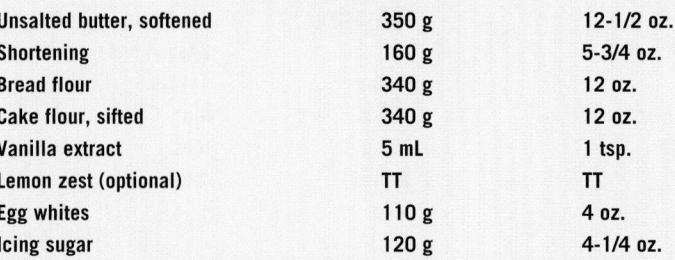

RECIPE 30.27

Spritz Piped Cookies

Yield: 5 dozen
Method: Pressed cookies

Unsalted butter, softened	350 g	12-1/2 oz.
Shortening	160 g	5-3/4 oz.
Bread flour	340 g	12 oz.
Cake flour, sifted	340 g	12 oz.
Vanilla extract	5 mL	1 tsp.
Lemon zest (optional)	TT	TT
Egg whites	110 g	4 oz.
Icing sugar	120 g	4-1/4 oz.

1. Cream the butter and shortening until light and fluffy. Add the flours, vanilla and lemon zest (if desired) and beat well for 6–8 minutes until fluffy.
2. Make a stiff meringue from the egg whites and sugar.
3. Blend the flour and meringue mixtures until smooth.
4. Pipe the dough onto an ungreased sheet pan using a piping bag fitted with a medium or large star tip.
5. Bake at 190°C (375°F) until lightly browned around edges, approximately 10 minutes. Transfer to wire racks to cool.

VARIATION: Cookies may be drizzled with chocolate or the ends may be dipped in chocolate. For Chocolate Spritz, replace 100 g (3-1/2 oz.) of pastry flour with cocoa powder.

RECIPE 30.28

Brandy Snaps

Executive Chef Mark Jorundson

Yield: 100 horns
Method: Wafer

Granulated sugar	200 g	8 oz.
Honey	200 g	8 oz.
Butter	200 g	8 oz.
Bread flour	200 g	8 oz.
Brandy	25 mL	1 fl. oz.
Orange zest, grated fine	25 g	2 Tbsp.

1. Cream the sugar, honey and butter together, then add the flour and brandy. Mix at medium speed for about 5 minutes to form a paste.
2. Add the orange zest.
3. Pipe or spoon an amount of mixture no larger than 1 cm (1/2 in.) onto a silicone-sheeted pan. (Mixture will spread to a circle 10–15 cm/4–6 in. in diameter.)
4. Bake at 200°C (400°F) until mixture spreads and is bubbly. Edges should begin to appear crisp.
5. Remove from oven and shape over a cream horn tube, a dowel or rod, or a cup or glass (to form a basket). If desired, shape hot cookies with a cutter to form perfect circles.

Almond Tulip (Tuile) Mix

Yield: Varies according to template
Method: Wafer

Almond paste	500 g	17-1/2 oz.
Sugar	200 g	7 oz.
Egg whites	275 g	10 oz.
Salt	0.5 g	pinch
Vanilla	1 mL	dash
Cinnamon	0.25 g	pinch
Lemon juice	5 mL	1 tsp.
Cream, 35%	125 mL	4 fl. oz.
Bread flour	300 g	10-1/2 oz.

1. Beat the almond paste, sugar and egg whites until smooth. Add the salt, vanilla, cinnamon, lemon juice and cream and beat until smooth.
2. Add the flour and mix until smooth and free of lumps.
3. Let the batter rest for 1 hour or overnight.
4. Spread the mixture into a template to give it a shape. Bake at 200°C (400°F) until the edges are brown and the dough is dry, approximately 12–18 minutes.

RECIPE 30.29

Approximate values per 30 g serving:	
Calories	96
Total fat	4 g
Saturated fat	1 g
Cholesterol	4 mg
Sodium	26 mg
Total carbohydrates	13 g
Protein	4 g

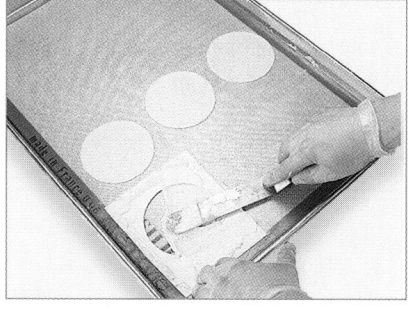

1. Almond Tulip (Tuile) Mix: Spreading the batter into circles on a sheet pan lined with a silicon mat.

2. Shaping the baked wafer cookies into cups while still hot.

Biscotti

Yield: 2-1/2 dozen

Butter	125 g	4 oz.
Sugar	175 g	6 oz.
Salt	5 g	1 tsp.
Eggs	2	2
Orange zest, grated	5 g	2 tsp.
Orange oil	1 g	5 drops
Pastry flour	300 g	10 oz.
Baking powder	5 g	1-1/2 tsp.
Pistachios, skinned	100 g	3-1/2 oz.
Egg wash	as needed	as needed

1. Cream butter, sugar and salt until light.

2. Beat in eggs until smooth with orange zest and oil.

3. Sift together flour and baking powder and stir into creamed mixture on low speed. When combined, mix on high speed for 5–8 seconds.

4. Fold in pistachios.

5. Form into 2 logs about 5 cm (2 in.) in diameter. Place on parchment-lined sheet pans. The dough may be a bit sticky. Brush with egg wash.

6. Bake at 160°C (325°F) for about 35 minutes or until lightly browned.

7. Remove from oven and cool slightly.

8. Cut into 5-mm (1/2-in.) bars on the diagonal and lay them flat on pan.

9. Bake again at 135°C (275°F) until lightly toasted, approximately 30 minutes.

VARIATIONS: Substitute almonds and lemon zest for pistachio and orange. Try 5 g (1-1/2 tsp.) espresso (instant) dissolved in 15 mL (1 Tbsp.) coffee and chocolate chips.

RECIPE 30.30

Approximate values per serving (1 Biscotti):	
Calories	113
Total fat	5.4 g
Saturated fat	2.4 g
Cholesterol	23 mg
Sodium	111 mg
Total carbohydrates	14 g
Protein	2 g

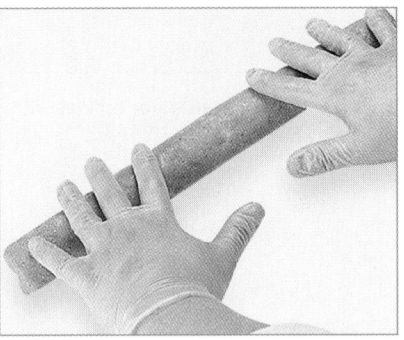

1. Biscotti dough rolled into a log before the first baking.

2. Slicing biscotti before the second baking.

RECIPE 30.31

Apple Strudel

Master Pâtissier Hermann Greineder, MPC
Yield: 4–5 strudels, each 60-cm (24-in.) long

Strudel Dough

Bread flour	1.75 kg	4 lb.
Butter, melted	500 g	17 oz.
Whole eggs	325 g	6
Hot water	750 mL	26 fl. oz.

Combine all ingredients and knead dough until **window test** is accepted. Let rest for 30 minutes.

Filling

Bread crumbs	750 g	1-1/2 lb.
Butter	100 g	3-1/2 oz.
Golden Delicious apples, peeled, cored and sliced	40	40
Cinnamon	50–75 g	2–3 oz.
Sugar	500 g	1 lb. 2 oz.
Butter, whole, melted	600 g	1 lb. 5 oz.
Raisins, marinated in rum (optional)	750 g	1-1/2 lb.
Butter, unsalted, melted	500 g	1 lb.
Icing sugar	250 g	8 oz.
Garnish: Crème Chantilly (Recipe 32.6) or Crème Anglaise (Recipe 32.1)	as needed	as needed

1. Combine bread crumbs and butter and toast until fragrant. Reserve.
2. Cover table with a linen cloth dusted with flour.
3. Place one-fifth of the dough on the cloth and roll it into a long strip (60 cm/24 in.).
4. Stretch the dough out using the back of your hands to form a rectangle. The dough should be paper-thin.
5. Sprinkle one-fifth of the toasted crumbs evenly over the dough.
6. Sprinkle one-fifth of the sliced apples evenly over the crumbs.
7. Combine cinnamon and sugar and sprinkle 110 g (4 oz.) over the apples, followed by 110 g (4 oz.) of melted whole butter.
8. Optional: Scatter one-fifth of the marinated raisins over the apple slices.
9. Trim the thick edges off the dough.
10. Using the cloth, roll up the strudel like a jelly roll into a log.
11. Place the strudel on a well-buttered baking sheet. Repeat the process with the remaining dough and filling.
12. Bake strudels at 200°C (400°F) for approximately 30–45 minutes, depending on the thickness of the strudel. They should have an even, golden brown colour. Remove from oven and brush each strudel with 100 g (3-1/2 oz.) melted unsalted butter. Dust with icing sugar.
13. To serve, slice strudels into portions and plate. Garnish with Crème Chantilly or a rum-flavoured Vanilla Custard Sauce (Crème Anglaise).

Hermann Greineder, MPC
Hermann received his German Master Certification as "Chef Pâtissier" in 1971. He has 48 years of experience in a wide range of establishments and he has won several medals in competition for his beautiful chocolate showpieces. Hermann is now retired.

● **window test** a test in pastry making to determine if dough has been properly kneaded; stretch a small amount of dough between your hands until it is very thin; if it has been kneaded long enough, it will form a thin, translucent sheet that does not tear

RECIPE 30.31

Approximate values per strudel:	
Calories	5956
Total fat	301 g
Saturated fat	177 g
Cholesterol	1024 mg
Sodium	3396 mg
Total carbohydrates	792 g
Protein	86 g

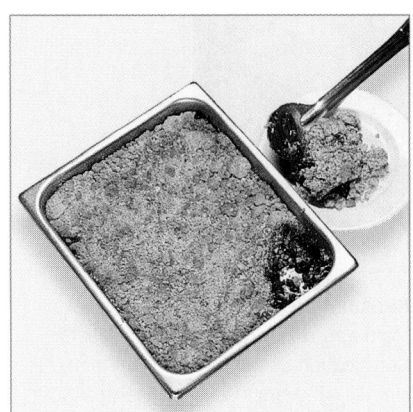

Blackberry Cobbler

RECIPE 30.32

Approximate values per serving:	
Calories	210
Total fat	5 g
Saturated fat	3 g
Cholesterol	20 mg
Sodium	10 mg
Total carbohydrates	39 g
Protein	1 g

RECIPE 30.32

Blackberry Cobbler

A cobbler is a home-style baked fruit dessert, usually made with a top crust of flaky pie dough, biscuit dough or streusel topping. The finished product will be slightly runny and is often served warm in a bowl or rimmed dish, accompanied by whipped cream or ice cream.

Yield: 10 servings

Individually quick-frozen blackberries	**2 L**	**2 qt.**
Sugar	250 g	8 oz.
Tapioca	60 g	2 oz.
Water	300 mL	10 fl. oz.
Unsalted butter	60 g	2 oz.
Lemon zest	10 g	1 Tbsp.
Topping (see Step 3)		

1. Combine all ingredients, tossing the berries gently until well coated with the other ingredients.
2. Transfer to a lightly buttered half-size hotel pan, then set aside for at least 30 minutes before baking.
3. The cobbler can be topped with Basic Pie Dough (about 200 g/7 oz.) (Recipe 30.1), scone dough (300–500 g/10–18 oz.) (Recipe 28.1) or Streusel Topping (300–500 g/10–18 oz.) (see Recipe Archive) before baking.
4. Bake at 180°C (350°F) until the berry mixture bubbles and the crust is appropriately browned, approximately 40–50 minutes.

VARIATION: You may substitute many fresh or frozen fruits.

Cakes and Frostings 31

> Anyone can make you enjoy the first bite of a dish, but only a real chef
> can make you enjoy the last.
>
> —François Minot, Editor, *Guide Michelin*

● **cake** in North American usage, refers to a broad range of pastries, including layer cakes, coffee cakes and gâteaux; can refer to almost anything that is baked, tender, sweet and sometimes frosted

Cakes are popular in most bakeshops because a wide variety of finished products can be created from only a few basic cake, filling and frosting formulas. Many of these components can be made in advance and assembled into finished desserts as needed. Cakes are also popular because of their versatility: they can be served as unadorned sheets in a high-volume cafeteria or as the elaborate centrepiece of a wedding buffet.

Cake making need not be difficult or intimidating, but it does require an understanding of ingredients and mixing methods. This chapter begins by explaining how typical cake ingredients interact. Each of the traditional mixing methods is then explained and illustrated with a recipe. Information on panning batters, baking temperatures, determining doneness and cooling methods follows. The second section of this chapter presents mixing methods and formulas for a variety of frostings and icings. The third section covers cake assembly and presents some simple and commonly used cake decorating techniques. A selection of popular cake formulas concludes the chapter.

CAKES

Most **cakes** are created from liquid batters with high fat and sugar contents. The baker's job is to combine all of the ingredients to create a structure that will support these rich ingredients, yet keep the cake as light and delicate as possible. As with other baked goods, it is impossible to taste a cake until it is fully baked and too late to alter the formula. Therefore, it is extremely important to study any formula before beginning and to follow it with particular care and attention to detail. Accurate scaling of ingredients is essential.

Ingredients

Good cakes begin with high-quality ingredients (see Chapter 27, Principles of the Bakeshop). However, even the finest ingredients must be combined in the proper balance. Too much flour and the cake may be dry; too much egg and the cake will be tough and hard. Changing one ingredient may necessitate a change in one or more of the other ingredients.

Each ingredient performs a specific function and has a specific effect on the final product. Cake ingredients can be classified by function as tougheners, tenderizers, moisteners, driers, leaveners and flavourings. Some ingredients fulfil more than one of these functions. For example, eggs contain water, so they are moisteners, and they contain protein, so they are tougheners. By understanding the function of various ingredients, you should be able to understand why cakes are made in particular ways and why a preparation sometimes fails. With additional experience, you should be able to recognize and correct flawed formulas and develop your own cake formulas.

Tougheners

Flour, milk and eggs contain protein. Protein provides structure and toughens the cake. Too little protein and the cake may collapse; too much protein and the cake may be tough and coarse-textured.

Tenderizers

Sugar, fats and egg yolks shorten gluten strands, making the cake tender and soft. These ingredients also improve the cake's keeping qualities.

Moisteners

Liquids such as water, milk, juice and eggs bring moisture to the mixture. Moisture is necessary for gluten formation and starch gelatinization, as well as improving a cake's keeping qualities.

Driers

Flour, starches and milk solids absorb moisture, giving body and structure to the cake. The lower protein content of cake/pastry flour contributes to producing a tender, short crumb.

Leaveners

Cakes rise because gases in the batter expand when heated. Cakes are leavened by the air trapped when fat and sugar are creamed together, by carbon dioxide released from baking powder and baking soda and by air trapped in beaten eggs. All cakes rely on natural leaveners—steam and air—to create the proper texture and rise. Because baking soda and baking powder are also used in some cake formulas, you should review the material on chemical leaveners in Chapter 28, Quick Breads.

Flavourings

Flavourings such as extracts, cocoa, chocolate, spices, salt, sugar and butter provide cakes with the desired flavours. Acidic flavouring ingredients such as sour cream, chocolate and fruit also provide the acid necessary to activate baking soda.

Cake ingredients should be at room temperature, approximately 21°C (70°F), before mixing begins. If one ingredient is too cold or too warm, it may affect the batter's ability to trap and hold the gases necessary for the cake to rise.

Mixing Methods

Even the finest ingredients will be wasted if the cake batter is not mixed correctly. When mixing any cake batter, your goals are to combine the ingredients uniformly, incorporate air cells and develop the proper texture.

All mixing methods can be divided into two categories: *high fat* (those that create a structure that relies primarily on creamed fat [air] and flour), and *egg foam* (those that create a structure that relies primarily on whipped eggs [air] and flour). Within these broad categories are several mixing methods or types of cakes. Creamed-fat cakes include butter cakes (also known as creaming method cakes) and high-ratio cakes. Egg-foam cakes include genoise, spongecakes, angel food cakes and chiffon cakes. (See Table 31.1 on the next page.) Although certain general procedures are used to prepare each cake type, there are, of course, variations. Follow specific formula instructions precisely.

Creamed Fat

Creamed-fat cakes include most of the popular North American–style cakes: poundcakes, layer cakes, coffee cakes and even brownies. All are based on high-fat formulas containing chemical leaveners. A good high-fat cake has a fine grain, cells of uniform size and a crumb that is moist rather than crumbly. Crusts should be thin and tender.

Equal weights of butter increase in volume when creamed thoroughly (right) and expand very little in volume when creamed insufficiently (left).

TABLE 31.1	Cakes		
Category	Mixing Method/Type of Cake	Key Formula Characteristics	Texture
Creamed fat (high fat)	Butter (creaming method)	High-fat formula; chemical leavener used	Fine grain; air cells of uniform size; moist crumb; thin and tender crust
	High-ratio (two-stage)	Emulsified shortening; two-part mixing method	Very fine grain; moist crumb; relatively high rise
Egg foam whipped	Genoise	Whole eggs are whipped with sugar; no chemical leaveners	Dry and spongy
	Sponge	Egg yolks are mixed with other ingredients, then whipped egg whites are folded in	Moister and more tender than genoise
	Angel food	No fat; large quantity of whipped egg whites; high percentage of sugar	Tall, light and fluffy
	Chiffon	Vegetable oil used; egg yolks mixed with other ingredients, then whipped egg whites folded in; baking powder may be added	Tall, light and fluffy; moister and richer than angel food

Creamed-fat cakes can be divided into two classes: butter cakes and high-ratio cakes.

Butter Cakes

Butter cakes, also known as creaming method cakes, begin with softened butter or shortening **creamed** to incorporate air cells. Because of their high fat content, these cakes usually need the assistance of a chemical leavener to achieve the proper rise.

Modern-day butter cakes—the classic layer cakes, popular for birthdays and special occasions—are made with the creaming method. These cakes are tender yet sturdy enough to handle rich buttercreams or fillings. High-fat cakes are too soft and delicate, however, to use for roll cakes or to slice into extremely thin layers.

When making butter cakes, the fat should be creamed at low to moderate speeds to prevent raising its temperature. An increased temperature could cause a loss of air cells.

● **creaming** vigorously combining fat and sugar while incorporating air

Storage and Food Labelling

Proper food labelling and good record keeping are as important as safe food-handling practices to prevent cross-contamination and food spoilage. Food labels should be used to date all foods that are made for kitchen use as well as leftovers. Systems for labelling foods vary in every operation. Once placed in clean sanitized storage containers, food prepared for later use should be labelled with the product name and the date and time it was made. Some health department regulations require that food be labelled with the day or date by which the food must be consumed on premises, sold or discarded. Once labelled and then refrigerated or frozen, products will be easily identifiable by the entire kitchen staff.

BASIC PROCEDURE FOR PREPARING BUTTER (CREAMING METHOD) CAKES

1. Preheat the oven and prepare the pans.
2. Sift the dry ingredients together and set aside.
3. Add the butter and sugar and cream the mixture until it is light and fluffy. Add the sugar and cream until the mixture is fluffy and smooth.
4. Add the eggs slowly, beating well after each addition.
5. Add the dry and liquid ingredients alternately. Start with flour and finish with flour.
6. Divide the batter into prepared pans and bake immediately.

APPLYING THE BASICS   RECIPE 31.1

Classic Poundcake

Yield: 2 30- × 10-cm (12- × 4-in.) loaves
Method: Creaming

Cake flour	500 g	1 lb.
Baking powder	7 g	2 tsp.
Salt	2 g	1/2 tsp.
Unsalted butter, softened	500 g	1 lb.
Granulated sugar	350 g	12 oz.
Eggs	500 g	16 oz.
Vanilla extract	5 mL	1 tsp.
Lemon extract	5 mL	1 tsp.

1. Sift the cake flour, baking powder and salt together; set aside.

2. Cream the butter and sugar until light and fluffy. Add the eggs one at a time, beating well after each addition. Stir in the extracts.

3. Fold in the dry ingredients by hand. Divide the batter into greased loaf pans.

4. Bake at 160°C (325°F) until golden brown and springy to the touch, approximately 1 hour and 10 minutes.

VARIATION: FRENCH-STYLE FRUITCAKE—Add 175 g (6 oz.) finely diced nuts, raisins and candied fruit to the batter. Substitute vanilla extract for the lemon extract and add 50 mL (3 Tbsp.) rum to the batter. After baking, brush the warm cake with additional rum.

RECIPE 31.1

Approximate values per 1/12 cake:	
Calories	250
Total fat	15 g
Saturated fat	9 g
Cholesterol	108 mg
Sodium	66 mg
Total carbohydrates	25 g
Protein	4 g

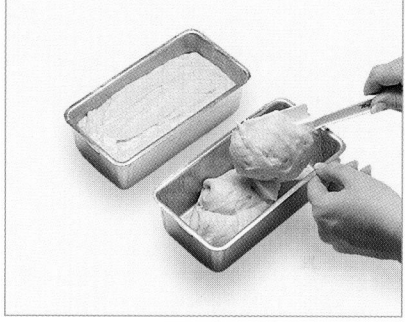

1. Classic Poundcake: Creaming the butter.   **2.** Folding in the flour.   **3.** Panning the batter.

High-Ratio Cakes

Commercial bakers often use a special two-stage mixing method to prepare large quantities of a very liquid cake batter. These formulas require emulsified shortenings and are known as two-stage cakes because the liquids are added in two stages or portions. If emulsified shortenings are not available, do not substitute all-purpose shortening or butter as they cannot absorb the large amounts of sugar and liquid in the formula.

Because they contain a high ratio of sugar and liquid to flour, these cakes are often known as **high-ratio cakes**. They have a very fine, moist crumb and relatively high rise. High-ratio cakes are almost indistinguishable from modern butter cakes and may be used interchangeably.

● **high-ratio cake** a form of creamed-fat cake that uses emulsified shortening and has a two-stage mixing method

BASIC PROCEDURE FOR PREPARING HIGH-RATIO CAKES

1. Preheat the oven and prepare the pans.
2. Place all the dry ingredients and emulsified shortening into a mixer bowl. Blend on low speed for several minutes.
3. Add approximately one-half of the liquid and blend.
4. Scrape down the mixer bowl and add the remaining liquid ingredients. Blend into a smooth batter, scraping down the bowl as necessary.
5. Pour the batter into prepared pans using liquid measurements to ensure uniform division.

APPLYING THE BASICS   **RECIPE 31.2**

High-Ratio Yellow Cake

Yield: 2 sheet pans
Method: High-ratio (2 stage)

Cake flour	1.1 kg	2-1/2 lb.
Granulated sugar	1.65 kg	2 lb. 10 oz.
Emulsified shortening	550 g	1 lb. 4 oz.
Salt	30 g	1 oz.
Baking powder	60 g	2 oz.
Powdered milk	110 g	4 oz.
Light corn syrup	170 g	6 oz.
Water, cold	500 mL	1 pt.
Eggs	550 g	1 lb. 4 oz.
Water, cold	1125 mL	36 fl. oz.
Lemon extract	15 mL	1/2 fl. oz.

1. Combine the flour, sugar, shortening, salt, baking powder, powdered milk, corn syrup and 500 mL (1 pt.) cold water in a large bowl of a mixer fitted with the paddle attachment. Beat for 5 minutes on low speed.
2. Combine the remaining ingredients in a separate bowl. Add these liquid ingredients to the creamed-fat mixture in 3 additions. Scrape down the sides of the bowl after each addition.
3. Beat for 2 minutes on low speed.
4. Divide the batter into greased and floured pans. Pans should be filled only halfway. Four litres (4 qt.) of batter is sufficient for a 45- × 60- × 5-cm (18- × 24- × 2-in.) sheet pan. Bake at 170°C (340°F) until a cake tester comes out clean and the cake springs back when lightly touched, approximately 12–18 minutes.

RECIPE 31.2

Approximate values per serving:	
Calories	313
Total fat	11 g
Saturated fat	2.9 g
Cholesterol	37 mg
Sodium	314 mg
Total carbohydrates	51 g
Protein	3.5 g

Egg Foams

Cakes based on whipped egg foams include European-style genoise as well as spongecakes, angel food cakes and chiffon cakes. Some formulas contain chemical leaveners, but the air whipped into the eggs (whether whole or separated) is the primary leavening agent. Egg-foam cakes contain little or no fat.

Genoise

Genoise is the classic European-style cake. It is based on whole eggs whipped with sugar until very light and fluffy. Chemical leaveners are not used. A small amount of oil or melted butter is sometimes added for flavour and moisture. Genoise is often baked in a thin sheet and layered with buttercream, puréed fruit, jam or chocolate filling to create multilayered specialty desserts. Because genoise is rather dry, it is usually soaked with a flavoured sugar syrup (see Chapter 27, Principles of the Bakeshop) or liquor for additional flavour and moisture.

● **genoise** a form of egg-foam cake that uses whole eggs whipped with sugar

1. Classic Genoise: Whipping the eggs.

BASIC PROCEDURE FOR PREPARING GENOISE

1. Preheat the oven and prepare the pans.
2. Sift the flour with any additional dry ingredients.
3. Combine the whole eggs and sugar in a large bowl and warm over a doubleboiler to a temperature of 40°C (104°F).
4. Whip the egg-and-sugar mixture until very light and tripled in volume.
5. Fold the sifted flour into the whipped eggs carefully but quickly.
6. Fold in oil or melted butter if desired.
7. Divide into pans and bake immediately.

2. Folding in the flour.

3. Adding the melted butter.

APPLYING THE BASICS   RECIPE 31.3

Classic Genoise

Yield: 2 full sheet pans
Method: Egg foam

Cake flour	500 g	16 oz.
Eggs	825 g	1 lb. 13 oz.
Granulated sugar	500 g	16 oz.
Unsalted butter, melted (optional)	85 g	3 oz.

1. Sift the flour and set aside.
2. Whisk the eggs and sugar together in a large mixer bowl. Place the bowl over a bain marie and warm the eggs to about 40°C (104°F). Stir frequently to avoid cooking the eggs.
3. When the eggs are warm, remove the bowl from the bain marie and attach to a mixer fitted with a whip attachment. Whip the egg-and-sugar mixture at medium speed until tripled in volume.
4. Quickly fold the flour into the egg mixture by hand. Be careful not to deflate the batter.
5. Pour the melted, cooled butter around the edges of the batter and fold in quickly.
6. Divide the batter immediately into parchment-lined pans. Bake at 180°C (350°F) until light brown and springy to the touch, approximately 8 minutes.

VARIATION: CHOCOLATE GENOISE—Reduce flour by 100 g (3-1/2 oz.) and sift 100 g (3-1/2 oz.) of cocoa powder with the flour.

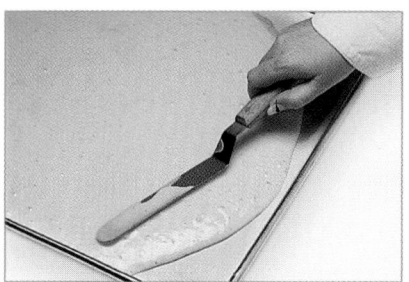

4. Panning the batter.

RECIPE 31.3

Approximate values per serving:	
Calories	99
Total fat	2.8 g
Saturated fat	1.2 g
Cholesterol	58 mg
Sodium	18 mg
Total carbohydrates	16 g
Protein	2.6 g

Spongecakes

Spongecakes (Fr. *biscuits de Savoie*) are made with whole separated eggs. A batter is prepared with the egg yolks and other ingredients, then the egg whites are whipped to firm peaks with a portion of the sugar (common meringue method) and folded into the batter. Spongecakes are primarily leavened with air, but baking powder may be included in the formula. As with genoise, oil or melted butter may be added if desired.

Spongecakes are extremely versatile. They can be soaked with sugar syrup or a liquor and assembled with buttercream as a traditional layer cake. Or they can be sliced thinly and layered, like genoise, with jam, custard, chocolate or cream filling.

BASIC PROCEDURE FOR PREPARING SPONGECAKES

1. Preheat the oven and prepare the pans.

2. Separate the eggs. Whip the egg whites with a portion of the sugar.

3. Sift the dry ingredients together and combine with liquid ingredients, including the egg yolks, as directed.

4. Carefully fold the whipped egg whites into the batter.

5. Pour the batter into the pans and bake immediately.

APPLYING THE BASICS		RECIPE 31.4

 ## Classic Spongecake

Yield: 2 22-cm (9-in.) rounds
Method: Egg foam

Cake flour, sifted	180 g	6 oz.
Granulated sugar	300 g	11 oz.
Eggs	10 large	10 large
Vanilla extract	7 mL	1-1/2 tsp.
Cream of tartar	5.25 g	1-1/2 tsp.

1. Line the bottom of 2 springform pans with parchment. Do not grease the sides of the pans.

2. Sift the flour and 180 g (6 oz.) of the sugar together and set aside.

3. Separate the eggs, placing the yolks and the whites in separate mixing bowls. Whip the yolks on high speed for 3–5 minutes, until thick, pale and at least doubled in volume. Whip in the vanilla extract. The yolks should be whipped "to ribbon," that is, until they fall from the beater in thick ribbons that slowly disappear into the batter's surface.

4. Place the bowl of egg whites on the mixer and, using a clean whip attachment, beat until foamy. Add the cream of tartar and 30 g (2 Tbsp.) of sugar. Whip at medium speed until the whites are glossy and stiff but not dry.

5. Remove the bowl from the mixer. Pour the egg yolks onto the whipped whites. Quickly fold the 2 mixtures together by hand. Sprinkle the remaining sugar (90 g/3 oz.) over the mixture and fold in lightly.

6. Sprinkle one-third of the sifted flour over the batter and fold in. Repeat the procedure until all of the flour is incorporated. Do not overmix; fold just until incorporated.

7. Pour the batter into the prepared pans, smoothing the surface as needed. Bake immediately at 190°C (375°F) until the cake is golden brown and spongy, approximately 30 minutes. A toothpick inserted in the centre will be completely clean.

8. Invert the cake, remove from pan; run a thin metal spatula around the edge of the pan to remove the cakes if they stick. Plate on racks or parchment paper. Sprinkle with granulated sugar, then let cool.

9. When the cake is completely cool, it can be frosted or wrapped in plastic wrap and frozen for 2–3 months.

RECIPE 31.4

Approximate values per 1/16 cake:	
Calories	122
Total fat	2.5 g
Saturated fat	1 g
Cholesterol	105 mg
Sodium	31 mg
Total carbohydrates	22 g
Protein	3 g

1. Classic Spongecake: The eggs whipped to ribbon stage.

2. Folding the flour into the batter.

3. Panning the batter.

APPLYING THE BASICS

RECIPE 31.5

Emulsified Spongecake

Yield: 3 20-cm (8-in.) cakes

Milk powder	35 g	1-1/4 oz.
Sugar	375 g	13-1/2 oz.
Baking powder	5 g	1-1/2 tsp.
Cake flour, sifted	325 g	11 oz.
Cold water	150 mL	6 fl. oz.
Whole eggs, chilled	325 g	11 oz.
K-68 emulsifier, chilled	10 g	1/2 oz.
Melted butter	60 g	2 oz.

1. Place all the dry ingredients into the mixer bowl. Blend together on slow speed, using a whip attachment.

2. Add water, eggs and emulsifier to the dry ingredients. Blend on slow speed, scraping down the bowl, then whip on high speed for 3 minutes exactly.

3. Fold in the melted butter by spatula.

4. Scale 350 g (12 oz.) of batter per cake tin and bake at 190°C (380°F) for 20–30 minutes.

VARIATION: This recipe is adjusted for an altitude of 1000 metres. For chocolate spongecake, add 30 g (1 oz.) cocoa sifted with the flour.

RECIPE 31.5

Approximate values per 1/12 cake:	
Calories	101
Total fat	2.3 g
Saturated fat	1.1 g
Cholesterol	44 mg
Sodium	38 mg
Total carbohydrates	18 g
Protein	2.2 g

Angel Food Cakes

Angel food cakes are tall, light cakes made without fat and leavened with a large quantity of whipped egg whites. Angel food cakes are traditionally baked in ungreased tube pans, but large loaf pans can also be used. The pans are left ungreased so that the batter can cling to the sides as it rises. The cakes should be inverted as soon as they are removed from the oven and left in the pan to cool. This technique allows gravity to keep the cakes from collapsing or sinking as they cool.

Although they contain no fat, angel food cakes are not low in calories as they contain a high percentage of sugar. The classic angel food cake is pure white, but flavourings, ground nuts or cocoa powder may be added for variety. Although angel food cakes are rarely frosted, they may be topped with a fruit-flavoured or chocolate glaze. They are often served with fresh fruit, a fruit compote or whipped cream.

BASIC PROCEDURE FOR PREPARING ANGEL FOOD CAKES

1. Preheat the oven.

2. Sift the dry ingredients together.

3. Whip the egg whites with a portion of the sugar until stiff and glossy.

4. Gently fold the dry ingredients into the egg whites.

5. Spoon the batter into an ungreased pan and bake immediately.

6. Allow the cake to cool inverted in its pan.

APPLYING THE BASICS　　　　　　　　　　　　　　　**RECIPE 31.6**

Chocolate Angel Food Cake

Yield: 1 25-cm (10-in.) tube cake

Method: Egg foam

Cocoa powder, alkalized	30 g	1 oz.
Water, warm	60 g	2 oz.
Vanilla extract	10 mL	2 tsp.
Granulated sugar	340 g	12 oz.
Cake flour, sifted	100 g	3-1/2 oz.
Salt	1 g	1/4 tsp.
Egg whites (large eggs)	480 g	16
Cream of tartar	7 g	2 tsp.

1. Combine the cocoa powder and water in a bowl. Add the vanilla and set aside.

2. In another bowl, combine 150 g (5 oz.) of the sugar with the flour and salt.

3. Whip the egg whites until foamy, add the cream of tartar and beat to soft peaks. Gradually beat in the remaining sugar. Continue beating until the egg whites are stiff but not dry.

4. Whisk approximately 250 g (1 cup) of the whipped egg whites into the cocoa mixture. Fold this into the remaining egg whites.

RECIPE 31.6

Approximate values per 1/16 cake:	
Calories	125
Total fat	0.2 g
Saturated fat	0 g
Cholesterol	0 mg
Sodium	89 mg
Total carbohydrates	28 g
Protein	4 g

continued

5. Sift the dry ingredients over the whites and fold in quickly but gently.

6. Pour the batter into an ungreased tube pan and smooth the top with a spatula. Bake immediately at 180°C (350°F) until the cake springs back when lightly touched and a cake tester comes out clean, approximately 40–50 minutes. The cake's surface will have deep cracks.

7. Remove the cake from the oven and immediately invert the pan onto the neck of a bottle. Allow the cake to rest upside down until completely cool.

8. To remove the cake from the pan, run a thin knife or spatula around the edge of the pan and the edge of the interior tube. If a 2-piece tube pan was used, the cake and tube portion are lifted out of the pan. Use a knife or spatula to loosen the bottom of the cake, then invert it onto a cake board or serving platter.

1. Chocolate Angel Food Cake: Folding the cocoa mixture into the whipped egg whites.

2. Folding in the flour.

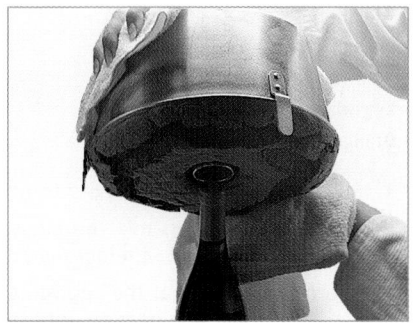

3. Cooling the cake upside down in its pan.

4. Removing the cake from the pan.

Chiffon Cakes

Although chiffon cakes are similar to angel food cakes in appearance and texture, the addition of egg yolks and vegetable oil makes them moister and richer. Chiffon cakes are usually leavened with whipped egg whites but may contain baking powder as well. Like angel food cakes, chiffon cakes are baked in an ungreased pan to allow the batter to cling to the pan as it rises. Chiffon cakes can be frosted with a light buttercream or whipped cream or topped with a glaze. Lemon and orange chiffon cakes are the most popular, but formulas containing chocolate, nuts or other flavourings are also common.

BASIC PROCEDURE FOR PREPARING CHIFFON CAKES

1. Preheat the oven.

2. Whip the egg whites with a portion of the sugar until almost stiff. Set aside.

3. Sift the dry ingredients together. Add the liquid ingredients, including oil.

4. Fold the whipped egg whites into the batter.

5. Spoon the batter into an ungreased pan and bake immediately.

6. Allow the cake to cool inverted in its pan.

Hollywood Classic

Chiffon cake is one of the few desserts whose history can be traced with absolute certainty. According to Gerry Schremp in her book *Kitchen Culture: Fifty Years of Food Fads*, a new type of cake was invented by Henry Baker, a California insurance salesman, in 1927. Dubbed *chiffon*, it was as light as angel food and as rich as poundcake. For years Baker kept the formula a secret, earning fame and fortune by selling his cakes to Hollywood restaurants. The cake's secret ingredient—vegetable oil—became public knowledge in 1947 when Baker sold the formula to General Mills, which promoted it on packages of cake flour. Chiffon cakes, in a variety of flavours, became extremely popular nationwide.

Folding the whipped egg whites into the cake batter.

RECIPE 31.7

Approximate values per 1/16 cake:	
Calories	255
Total fat	10 g
Saturated fat	1 g
Cholesterol	106 mg
Sodium	197 mg
Total carbohydrates	37 g
Protein	4 g

Convenience Products

Packaged cake mixes are a tremendous time saver for commercial food service operations. Almost any operation can serve a variety of cakes made by relatively unskilled employees using prepared mixes. The results are consistent and the texture and flavour are acceptable to most consumers. Indeed, a well-prepared packaged mix cake is preferable to a poorly prepared cake made from scratch. Most packaged cake mixes can be adapted to include flavourings, nuts, spices or fruits, which can improve the product's overall quality. Frostings, fillings and attractive decorations complete these items.

The convenience of mixes is not without cost, however. Packaged cake mixes are often more expensive than the ingredients needed for an equal number of cakes made from scratch. Cakes made from mixes are also softer and more cottony than scratch cakes, and their flavour tends to be more artificial.

APPLYING THE BASICS	RECIPE 31.7

Orange Chiffon Cake

Yield: 1 25-cm (10-in.) tube cake
Method: Egg foam

Cake flour, sifted	250 g	8 oz.
Sugar	375 g	12 oz.
Baking powder	10 g	1 Tbsp.
Salt	5 g	1 tsp.
Vegetable oil	125 mL	4 fl. oz.
Egg yolks (large eggs)	130 g	6
Water, cool	60 mL	2 fl. oz.
Orange juice	125 mL	4 fl. oz.
Orange zest	10 g	1 Tbsp.
Vanilla extract	15 mL	1 Tbsp.
Egg whites	250 g	8 oz.
Orange Glaze (recipe follows)		

1. Sift together the flour, 175 g (6 oz.) of sugar, the baking powder and salt.
2. In a separate bowl, mix the oil, yolks, water, juice, zest and vanilla. Add the liquid mixture to the dry ingredients.
3. In a clean bowl, beat the egg whites until foamy. Slowly beat in the remaining sugar. Continue beating until the egg whites are stiff but not dry.
4. Stir one-third of the egg whites into the batter to lighten it. Fold in the remaining egg whites.
5. Pour the batter into an ungreased 25-cm (10-in.) tube pan. Bake at 160°C (325°F) until a toothpick inserted in the centre comes out clean, approximately 1 hour.
6. Immediately invert the pan over the neck of a bottle. Allow the cake to cool upside down, then remove from the pan.

Orange Glaze

Powdered sugar	90 g	3 oz.
Orange juice	30 mL	2 Tbsp.
Orange zest	8 g	2 tsp.

1. Sift the sugar, then stir in the juice and zest.
2. Drizzle the glaze over the top of the cooled cake.

VARIATION: LEMON CHIFFON CAKE—Substitute 60 mL (2 fl. oz.) fresh lemon juice and 60 mL (2 fl. oz.) water for the orange juice. Substitute lemon zest for the orange zest. Top with Basic Sugar Glaze, Recipe 31.13.

Panning, Baking and Cooling

Preparing Pans

To prevent cakes from sticking, most baking pans are coated with fat or a non-stick baking parchment. (See Table 31.2 on the next page.) Pans should be prepared before the batter is mixed so that they may be filled and the cakes baked as soon as the batter is finished. If the batter stands while the pans are prepared, air cells within the batter will deflate and volume may be lost.

Solid shortening is better than butter for coating pans because it does not contain any water; the water in butter and margarine may cause the cake to

TABLE 31.2 Pan Preparations

Pan Preparation	Used For
Ungreased	Angel food and chiffon cakes
Ungreased sides; paper on bottom	Genoise layers
Greased and papered	High-fat cakes, sponge sheets
Greased and coated with flour	High-fat cakes, chocolate cakes, anything in a bundt or shaped pan
Greased, floured and lined with paper	Cakes containing melted chocolate, fruit chunks or fruit or vegetable purées

stick in places. Solid shortening is also less expensive, tasteless and odourless. Finally, solid shortening does not burn as easily as butter and it holds a dusting of flour better.

Pan-release sprays are useful but must be applied carefully and completely. Although relatively expensive, sprays save time and are particularly effective when used with parchment pan liners.

In kitchens where a great deal of baking is done, it may be more convenient to prepare quantities of pan coating to be kept available for use as needed. Pan coating is a mixture of equal parts oil, shortening and flour, creamed together, that can be applied to cake pans with a pastry brush. It is used whenever pans need to be greased and floured. Pan coating will not leave a white residue on the cake's crust the way a dusting of flour often does.

Applying pan coating.

APPLYING THE BASICS   RECIPE 31.8

Pan Coating

Yield: 1.5 kg (3 lb.)

Vegetable oil	500 g	1 lb.
All-purpose shortening	500 g	1 lb.
Bread flour	500 g	1 lb.

1. Combine all ingredients in a mixer fitted with the paddle attachment. Blend on low speed for 5 minutes or until smooth.
2. Store in an airtight container at room temperature for up to 2 months.
3. Apply to baking pans in a thin, even layer using a pastry brush.

RECIPE 31.8

Approximate values per 3 g serving:	
Calories	21
Total fat	2 g
Saturated fat	0.3 g
Cholesterol	0 mg
Sodium	0 mg
Total carbohydrates	0.7 g
Protein	0.1 g

Pan coating is not appropriate for all cakes, however. Those containing chocolate, raisins or fruit should still be baked in pans lined with parchment paper to prevent sticking.

Angel food and chiffon cakes are baked in ungreased, unlined pans because these fragile cakes need to cling to the sides of the pan as they rise. Spongecakes and genoise are often baked in pans with a paper liner on the bottom and ungreased sides. While the ungreased sides give the batter a surface to cling to, the paper liner makes removing the cake from the pan easier.

Filling Pans

Pans should be filled no more than one-half to two-thirds full. This allows the batter to rise during baking without spilling over the edges.

Brownies

Where do you draw the line between cakes and brownies? The decision must be a matter of texture and personal preference, for the preparation methods are nearly identical. Brownies are generally chewy and fudgy, sweeter and denser than even the richest of butter cakes.

Brownies are a relatively inexpensive and easy way for a food service operation to offer its customers a fresh-baked dessert. Although not as sophisticated as an elaborate gâteau, a well-made brownie can always be served with pride (and a scoop of ice cream).

Brownies are prepared using the same procedures as those for high-fat cakes. Good brownies are achieved with a proper balance of ingredients. A high percentage of butter to flour produces a dense, fudgy brownie; less butter produces a more cakelike brownie. Likewise, the higher the ratio of sugar, the gooier the finished brownie. In some formulas, the fat is creamed to incorporate air, as with butter cakes. In others, the fat is first melted and combined with other liquid ingredients. Brownies are rarely made with whipped egg whites, however, as this makes their texture too light and cakelike.

Each customer and cook has his or her own idea of the quintessential brownie. Some are cloyingly sweet, with a creamy texture and an abundance of chocolate; others are bitter and crisp. Baked brownies can be frozen for two to three months if well wrapped.

Pans should be filled to uniform depths. High-fat and egg-foam cake batters can be ladled into each pan according to weight. High-ratio cake batter is so liquid that it can be measured by volume and poured into each pan. Filling the pans uniformly prevents both uneven layers and over- or underfilled pans. If you are baking three 20-cm (8-in.) layers to be stacked for one presentation and the amount of batter is different in each pan, the baking times will vary and the final product will suffer.

The cake batter should always be spread evenly in the pan. Use an offset spatula. Do not work the batter too much, however, as this destroys air cells and prevents the cake from rising properly.

Baking

Temperatures

Always preheat the oven before preparing your batter. If the finished batter must wait while the oven reaches the correct temperature, valuable leavening will be lost and the cake will not rise properly.

Most cakes are baked at temperatures between 160°C and 190°C (325°F and 375°F). The temperature must be high enough to create steam within the batter and cause that steam and other gases in the batter to expand and rise quickly. If the temperature is *too high*, however, the cake may rise unevenly and the crust may burn before the interior is completely baked. The temperature must also be low enough that the batter can set completely and evenly without drying out. If the temperature is *too low*, however, the cake will not rise sufficiently and may dry out before baking completely.

If no temperature is given in a formula or you are altering the dimensions of the baking pan from those specified, use common sense in setting the oven temperature. Usually, the larger the surface area, the higher the temperature can be. Tall cakes, such as bundt or tube cakes, should be baked at a lower temperature than thin layer or sheet cakes. Tube or loaf cakes take longer to bake than thin sheet cakes; butter cakes, because they contain more liquid, take longer to bake than genoise or spongecakes.

Altitude Adjustments

As you learned in Chapter 9, Principles of Cooking, altitude affects the temperatures at which foods cook. The decreased atmospheric pressure at altitudes above 900 m (3000 ft.) affects the creation of steam and the expansion of hot air in cake batters. These factors must be considered when making cakes. Because gases expand more easily at higher altitudes, the cake may rise so much that its structure cannot support it and the cake can collapse.

Therefore, the amount of leavening should be decreased at higher altitudes. (See Figure 31.1.) Chemical leaveners should usually be reduced by 20% at 1050 m (3500 ft.) and by 40% at altitudes of more than 1500 m (5000 ft.). Eggs should be underwhipped to avoid incorporating too much air, and the volume should be increased by approximately 10%. An additional 10% of liquid may be required. In general, oven temperatures should also be increased by 15°C (25°F) at altitudes of more than 1050 m (3500 ft.) to help the cake's structure to set rapidly.

Because the boiling point decreases at higher altitudes, more moisture will evaporate from your cake during baking. This may cause dryness and an excessive proportion of sugar, which shows up as white spots on the cake's surface. Correct this by reducing every 225 g (8 oz.) of sugar by 15 g (1/2 oz.) at 900 m (3000 ft.) and by 45 g (1-1/2 oz.) at 2100 m (7000 ft.).

Attempting to adjust typical (i.e., sea level) formulas for high altitudes is somewhat risky, especially in a commercial operation. Try to find and use formulas developed especially for your area.

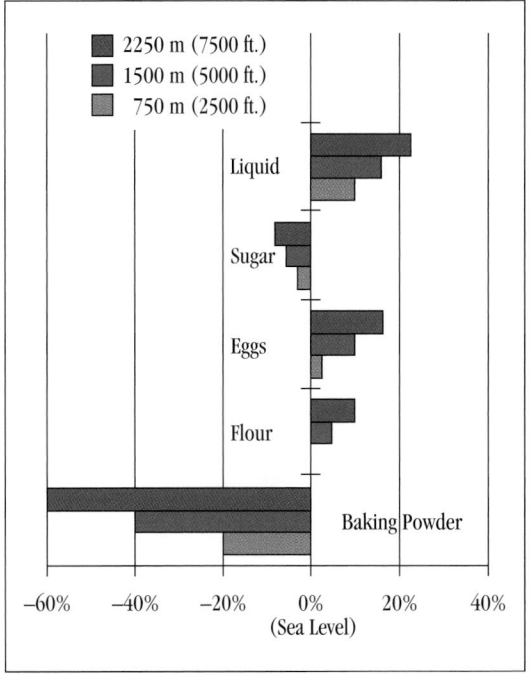

FIGURE 31.1   Altitude adjustments.
Source: Andreas Schwarzer, SAIT.

Determining Doneness

In addition to following the baking time suggested in a formula, several simple tests can be used to determine doneness. Whichever test or tests are used, avoid opening the oven door to check the cake's progress. Cold air or a drop in oven temperature can cause the cake to fall. Use a timer to note the minimum suggested baking time. Then, and only then, should you use the following tests to evaluate the cake's doneness:

- *Appearance*—The cake's surface should be a light to golden brown. Unless noted otherwise in the formula, the edges should just begin to pull away from the pan. The cake should not jiggle or move beneath its surface.
- *Touch*—Touch the cake lightly with your finger. It should spring back quickly without feeling soggy or leaving an indentation.
- *Cake tester*—If appearance and touch indicate that the cake is done, test the interior by inserting a toothpick, bamboo skewer or metal cake tester into the cake's centre. With most cakes, the tester should come out clean. If wet crumbs cling to the tester, the cake probably needs to bake a bit longer.

If a formula provides particular doneness guidelines, they should be followed. For example, some flourless cakes are fully baked even though a cake tester will not come out clean.

Cooling

Generally, a cake is allowed to cool for 10 to 15 minutes in its pan after being removed from the oven. This helps prevent the cake from cracking or breaking after it is removed from its pan.

To remove the partially cooled cake from its pan, run a thin knife or spatula blade between the pan and the cake to loosen it. Place a wire rack, cake board or sheet pan over the cake and invert. Then remove the pan. The cake can be left upside down to cool completely or inverted again to cool top side up. Wire racks are preferred for cooling cakes because they allow air to circulate, speeding the cooling process and preventing steam from making the cake soggy.

Angel food and chiffon cakes should be turned upside down immediately after they are removed from the oven. They are left to cool completely in their pans to prevent the cake from collapsing or shrinking. The top of the pan should not touch the countertop so that air can circulate under the inverted pan.

All cakes should be left to cool away from drafts or air currents that might cause them to collapse. Cakes should not be refrigerated to speed the cooling process, as rapid cooling can cause cracking. Prolonged refrigeration also causes cakes to dry out. (See Table 31.3 for troubleshooting tips should you encounter problems with cakes.)

FROSTINGS

● **frosting** also known as icing, is a sweet decorative coating used as a filling between the layers or as a coating over the top and sides of a cake

Frosting, also known as *icing*, is a sweet decorative coating used as a filling between the layers or as a coating over the top and sides of a cake. It is used to add flavour and to improve the cake's appearance. Frosting can also extend a cake's shelf life by forming a protective coating.

TABLE 31.3	Troubleshooting Chart for Cakes	
Problem	**Cause**	**Solution**
Batter curdles during mixing	Ingredients too warm or too cold	Eggs must be room temperature and added slowly
	Incorrect fat used	Use correct ingredients
	Fat inadequately creamed before liquid was added	Add a portion of the flour, then continue adding the liquid
	Too much liquid was added	Add a portion of the flour, then continue adding the liquid
Cake lacks volume	Flour too strong	Use a weaker flour
	Old chemical leavener	Replace with fresh leavener
	Egg foam underwhipped	Use correct mixing method, do not deflate eggs during folding
	Oven too hot	Adjust oven temperature
Crust burst or cracked	Too much flour or too little liquid	Adjust formula
	Oven too hot	Adjust oven temperature
Cake shrinks after baking	Weak internal structure	Adjust formula
	Too much sugar or fat for the batter to support	Adjust formula
	Cake not fully baked	Test cake for doneness before removing from oven
	Cake cooled too rapidly	Cool away from drafts
Texture is dense or heavy	Too little leavening	Adjust formula
	Too much fat or liquid	Cream fat or whip eggs properly
	Oven too cool	Adjust oven temperature
Texture is coarse with an open grain	Overmixing	Alter mixing method
	Oven too cool	Adjust oven temperature
Poor flavour	Poor ingredients	Check flavour and aroma of all ingredients
	Unclean pans	Do not grease pans with rancid fats
Uneven shape	Butter not incorporated evenly	Incorporate fats completely
	Batter spread unevenly	Spread batter evenly
	Oven rack not level	Adjust oven racks
	Uneven oven temperature	Adjust oven temperature

There are seven general types of frosting: buttercream, foam, fudge, fondant, glaze, royal icing and ganache. (See Table 31.4.) Each type can be produced with a number of formulas and in a range of flavourings.

Because frosting is integral to the flavour and appearance of many cakes, it should be made carefully using high-quality ingredients and natural flavours and colours. A good frosting is smooth; it is never grainy or lumpy. (Table 31.5 below provides some troubleshooting guidelines for frostings.) It should complement the flavour and texture of the cake without overpowering it.

Buttercream

A **buttercream** is a light, smooth, fluffy mixture of sugar and fat (butter, margarine or shortening). It may also contain egg yolks for richness or whipped egg whites for lightness. A good buttercream will be sweet, but not heavy; buttery, but not greasy.

Buttercreams are popular and useful for most types of cakes and may be flavoured or coloured as desired. They may be stored, covered, in the refrigerator for several days but must be softened before use and creamed again.

Although there are many types of buttercream and many formula variations, we discuss the three most popular styles: simple, Italian and French.

● **buttercream** a light, smooth, fluffy frosting of sugar, fat and flavourings; egg yolks or whipped egg whites are sometimes added. There are three principal kinds: simple, Italian and French.

TABLE 31.4	Frostings	
Frosting	**Preparation**	**Texture/Taste**
Buttercream	Mixture of sugar and fat (usually butter); can contain egg yolks or egg whites	Rich but light; smooth, fluffy
Foam	Meringue made with hot sugar syrup	Light, fluffy; very sweet
Fudge	Cooked mixture of sugar, butter and water or milk; applied warm	Heavy, rich and candylike
Fondant	Cooked mixture of sugar and water; applied warm	Thick; opaque; sweet
Glaze	Confectioner's sugar with liquid	Thin
Royal icing	Uncooked mixture of confectioner's sugar and egg whites	Hard and brittle when dry
Ganache	Blend of melted chocolate and cream; may be poured or whipped	Rich, smooth, intense flavour

TABLE 31.5	Troubleshooting Chart for Frostings	
Problem	**Cause**	**Solution**
Frosting breaks or curdles	Fat added too slowly or eggs too hot when fat was added	Add shortening or sifted confectioner's sugar
Frosting is lumpy	Confectioner's sugar not sifted	Sift dry ingredients
	Ingredients not blended	Use softened fat
	Sugar syrup lumps in frosting	Add sugar syrups carefully
Frosting is gritty	Granulated sugar not dissolved	Cook sugar syrups properly; cook fudge frostings as directed
Frosting is too stiff	Not enough liquid	Adjust formula; add small amount of water or milk to thin frosting
	Too cold	Bring frosting to room temperature
Frosting will not adhere to cake	Cake too hot	Cool cake completely
	Frosting too thin	Adjust frosting formula

Flavour Combinations for Cakes

Citrus, coffee, maple, peanut butter and vanilla are popular flavourings for buttercream icings but the possible cake and filling combinations are limitless. Chocolate cakes can be filled with almond, citrus, coffee, hazelnut and red fruit-flavoured icings. Dense chocolate ganache paired with apricot, cherry, raspberry or other jam works well in plain or chocolate butter cakes. Tropical fruit flavours such as kiwi, key lime and pineapple complement butter and sponge cakes as do rich custards and flavoured creams.

Simple Buttercream

Simple buttercream is made by creaming butter and powdered sugar together until the mixture is light and smooth. Cream, eggs (preferably pasteurized—whole, yolks or whites) and flavourings may be added as desired. Simple buttercream is quick and easy to prepare.

If cost is a consideration, high-ratio or emulsified shortening can be substituted for a portion of the butter, but the flavour and mouth-feel will be different. Buttercream made with shortening tends to taste greasier and heavier because shortening does not melt on the tongue like butter. It will be more stable than buttercream made only with butter, however, and is useful for products that will be on display.

BASIC PROCEDURE FOR PREPARING SIMPLE BUTTERCREAM

1. Cream softened butter or shortening until the mixture is light and fluffy.
2. Beat in egg, if desired.
3. Beat in sifted powdered sugar, scraping down the sides of the bowl as needed.
4. Beat in the flavouring ingredients.

Simple Buttercream

RECIPE 31.9

Approximate values per 30 g serving:	
Calories	142
Total fat	8 g
Saturated fat	5 g
Cholesterol	25 mg
Sodium	79 mg
Total carbohydrates	19 g
Protein	0 g

APPLYING THE BASICS	RECIPE 31.9

Simple Buttercream

Yield: 1.5 kg (3 lb.)

Lightly salted butter, softened	450 g	1 lb.
Egg (optional)	1	1
Powdered sugar, sifted	900 g	2 lb.
Vanilla extract	10 mL	2 tsp.

1. Using a mixer fitted with the paddle attachment, cream the butter until light and fluffy.
2. Beat in the egg, if using. Gradually add the sugar, frequently scraping down the sides of the bowl.
3. Add the vanilla and continue beating until the frosting is smooth and light.

VARIATIONS: LIGHT CHOCOLATE—Dissolve 30 g (1 oz.) sifted cocoa powder in 60 mL (2 fl. oz.) cool water. Add to the buttercream along with the vanilla.

LEMON—Decrease the vanilla extract to 5 mL (1 tsp.). Add 5 mL (1 tsp.) lemon extract and the finely grated zest of 1 lemon.

Italian Buttercream

Italian buttercream, also known as meringue buttercream, is based on an Italian meringue, that is, whipped egg whites enriched with hot sugar syrup. (See Chapter 30, Pies, Pastries and Cookies.) Softened butter is then whipped into the cooled meringue and the mixture is flavoured as desired. This type of buttercream is extremely soft and light. It can be used on most types of cakes and is particularly popular for multilayered genoise and spongecakes.

BASIC PROCEDURE FOR PREPARING ITALIAN BUTTERCREAM

1. Whip the egg whites until soft peaks form.

2. Beat granulated sugar into the egg whites and whip until firm and glossy.

3. Meanwhile, combine additional sugar with water and cook to soft ball stage (115°C/238°F).

4. With the mixer on medium speed, pour the sugar syrup into the whipped egg whites. Pour slowly and carefully to avoid splatters.

5. Continue whipping the egg-white-and-sugar mixture until completely cool.

6. Whip softened, but not melted, butter into the cooled egg-white-and-sugar mixture.

7. Add flavouring ingredients as desired.

1. Italian Buttercream: Adding the sugar syrup to the whipped egg whites.

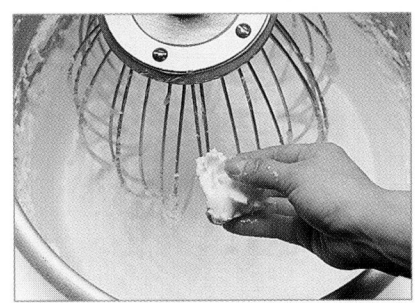

2. Adding the softened butter to the cooled Italian meringue.

APPLYING THE BASICS   RECIPE 31.10

Italian Buttercream

Yield: 2.2 kg (5 lb.)

Egg whites	200 g	7 oz.
Sugar	50 g	2 oz.
Sugar	450 g	1 lb.
Water	125 mL	4 fl. oz.
Lightly salted butter, softened		
but not melted	1.2 kg	2 lb. 10 oz.

1. All ingredients should be at room temperature before beginning.

2. Place the egg whites in a mixer bowl. Have 50 g (2 oz.) of sugar nearby.

3. Place 450 g (1 lb.) of sugar and water in a heavy saucepan. Bring to a boil over high heat.

4. As the sugar syrup's temperature approaches a soft ball stage (115°C/ 238°F), begin whipping the egg whites. Watch the sugar closely so that the temperature does not exceed 115°C (238°F).

5. When soft peaks form in the egg whites, gradually add the 50 g (2 oz.) of sugar to them.

6. When the sugar syrup reaches soft ball stage, immediately pour it into the whites while the mixer is running. Pour the syrup in a steady stream between the side of the bowl and the beater. If the syrup hits the beater it will splatter and cause lumps. Continue beating at medium speed until the meringue is cool and forms stiff peaks.

7. Gradually add the softened butter to the Italian meringue, blending it well. When all of the butter is incorporated, turn mixer to medium speed and beat until fluffy. Add flavouring ingredients as desired.

VARIATION: CHOCOLATE—Add 15 mL (1 Tbsp.) vanilla extract and 300 g (10 oz.) melted and cooled bittersweet chocolate.

3. Finished Italian buttercream.

RECIPE 31.10

Approximate values per 30 g serving:	
Calories	166
Total fat	15 g
Saturated fat	9.5 g
Cholesterol	41 mg
Sodium	160 mg
Total carbohydrates	8 g
Protein	0.5 g

French Buttercream

French buttercream, also known as mousseline buttercream, is similar to Italian buttercream except that the hot sugar syrup is whipped into beaten egg yolks (not egg whites). Softened butter and flavourings are added when the sweetened egg yolks are fluffy and cool. An Italian meringue such as the one created in Recipe 31.10 is *sometimes* folded in for additional body and lightness. French buttercream is perhaps the most difficult type of buttercream to master, but it has the richest flavour and smoothest texture. Like a meringue buttercream, mousseline buttercream may be used on almost any type of cake.

BASIC PROCEDURE FOR PREPARING FRENCH BUTTERCREAM

1. Prepare a sugar syrup and cook to soft ball stage (115°C/238°F).
2. Beat egg yolks to a thin ribbon.
3. Slowly beat the hot sugar syrup into the egg yolks.
4. Continue beating until the yolks are pale, stiff and completely cool.
5. Gradually add softened butter to the cooled yolks.
6. Fold in Italian meringue (optional).
7. Stir in flavouring ingredients.

Adding softened butter.

RECIPE 31.11

Approximate values per 30 g serving:	
Calories	152
Total fat	11 g
Saturated fat	7 g
Cholesterol	77 mg
Sodium	105 mg
Total carbohydrates	13 g
Protein	1 g

APPLYING THE BASICS — **RECIPE 31.11**

French Buttercream

Yield: 1.5 kg (3.3 lb.)

Glucose	100 g	3-1/2 oz.
Granulated sugar	500 g	17-1/2 oz.
Water	200 g	7 oz.
Egg yolks	185 g	8 large
Butter, softened	600 g	21 oz.
Flavouring to taste	50 g	2 oz.

1. Combine the glucose, sugar and water in a small saucepan and bring to a boil. Continue boiling until the syrup reaches 115°C (238°F).
2. Meanwhile, beat the egg yolks in a mixer fitted with a wire whisk on medium speed. When the sugar syrup reaches 115°C (238°F), pour it slowly into the egg yolks, gradually increasing the speed at which they are whipped. Continue beating at medium-high speed until the mixture is very pale, stiff and cool.
3. Gradually add the softened butter to the egg mixture, frequently scraping down the sides of the bowl.
4. Stir in flavouring extracts as desired.

VARIATION: One litre (1 qt.) Italian meringue may be folded in for a lighter buttercream.

Foam Frosting

Foam frosting, sometimes known as boiled icing or 7-minute frosting, is simply a meringue made with hot sugar syrup. Foam frosting is light and fluffy but very sweet. It may be flavoured with extract, liqueur or melted chocolate.

Foam frosting is rather unstable. It should be used immediately and served the day it is prepared. Refrigeration often makes the foam weep beads of sugar. Freezing causes it to separate or melt.

An easy foam frosting can be made by following the formula for Italian Buttercream (Recipe 31.10). As soon as the meringue has cooled to room temperature, it can be flavoured with extracts as desired.

Fudge Frosting

A fudge frosting is a warmed mixture of sugar, butter and water or milk. It is heavy, rich and candylike. It is also stable and holds up well. A fudge frosting should be applied warm and allowed to dry on the cake or pastry. When dry, it will have a thin crust and a moist interior. A fudge frosting can be vanilla- or chocolate-based and is used on cupcakes, layer cakes and sheet cakes.

BASIC PROCEDURE FOR PREPARING FUDGE FROSTINGS

1. Blend sifted powdered sugar with corn syrup, beating until the sugar is dissolved and the mixture is smooth.

2. Blend in warm melted shortening and/or butter.

3. Blend in hot liquids. Add extracts or flavourings.

4. Use fudge frosting while still warm.

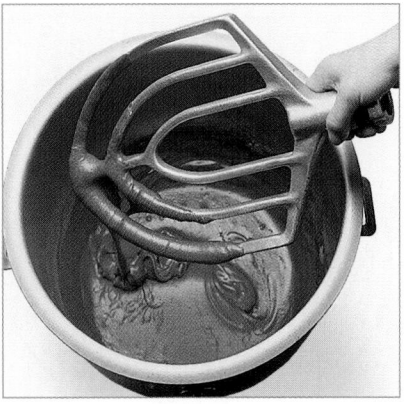

Cocoa Fudge Frosting

APPLYING THE BASICS   **RECIPE 31.12**

Basic Fudge Frosting

Yield: 2 kg (4 lb.)

Icing sugar, sifted	1.5 kg	3 lb.
Salt	1 g	1/4 tsp.
Light corn syrup	60 mL	2 fl. oz.
Shortening, melted	120 g	4 oz.
Water, hot (60°C/140°F)	300 mL	10 fl. oz.
Vanilla extract	30 mL	2 Tbsp.

1. Blend the sugar, salt and corn syrup. Beat until smooth.

2. Add the melted shortening and blend well.

3. Add the hot water and vanilla and blend well. If the fudge is too stiff it may be thinned with a simple sugar syrup. Use before the icing cools.

VARIATION: COCOA FUDGE FROSTING—Sift 125 g (4 oz.) cocoa powder with the powdered sugar. Add 60 mL (2 fl. oz.) melted unsalted butter with the shortening.

RECIPE 31.12

Approximate values per 30 g serving:	
Calories	136
Total fat	2.5 g
Saturated fat	0.5 g
Cholesterol	0 mg
Sodium	17 mg
Total carbohydrates	29 g
Protein	0 g

Fondant

Fondant is a thick, opaque sugar paste commonly used for glazing napoleons, petit fours and other pastries as well as some cakes. It is a cooked mixture of sugar and water, with **glucose** or corn syrup added to encourage the correct type of sugar crystallization. Poured over the surface being coated, fondant quickly dries to a shiny, nonsticky coating. It is naturally pure white and can be tinted with food colouring. Fondant can also be flavoured with melted chocolate.

Fondant is made by boiling a mixture of 100% sugar, 25% water and 20% glucose to 115°C (240°F). Cool to 43°C (110°F) and work on a marble slab

● **fondant** a sweet, thick opaque sugar paste commonly used for glazing pastries such as napoleons or making candies

● **glucose** a thick, sweet syrup made from cornstarch, composed primarily of dextrose; light corn syrup can usually be substituted for it in baked goods or candy making

Rolled Fondant

Rolled fondant is a very stiff doughlike type of fondant that is used for covering cakes and for making flowers and other decorations. As the name implies, it is rolled out to the desired thickness, then draped over a cake or torte to create a very smooth, flat coating. After the fondant dries, the cake may be decorated with royal icing or buttercream. Rolled fondant is available in a ready-to-use form. It can be flavoured or coloured if desired. Be sure to keep the fondant tightly wrapped in plastic and stored in an airtight container to prevent if from drying out and cracking.

until smooth, white and creamy. However, because fondant is rather difficult to make, it is almost always purchased prepared. To use, warm fondant to 37°C (100°F) over medium heat, stirring constantly to prevent overheating. (Overheating will cause fondant to lose its shine and become too hard.) If necessary, thin fondant with water or simple syrup after warming up the fondant. Commercially prepared fondant will keep for several months at room temperature in an airtight container. The surface of the fondant should be coated with simple syrup, however, to prevent a crust from forming.

Glaze

A **glaze** is a thin coating meant to be poured or dripped onto a cake or pastry. A glaze is usually too thin to apply with a knife or spatula. It is used to add moisture and flavour to cakes on which a heavy frosting would be undesirable—for example, a chiffon or angel food cake.

Flat icing or **water icing** is a specific type of glaze used on Danish pastries and coffee cakes. It is pure white and dries to a firm gloss.

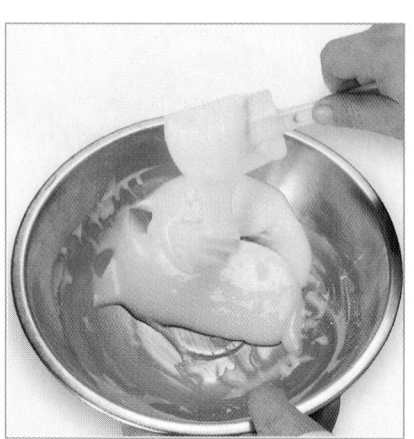

Basic Sugar Glaze

RECIPE 31.13

Approximate values per 10 g serving:	
Calories	32
Total fat	0 g
Saturated fat	0 g
Cholesterol	0 mg
Sodium	0 mg
Total carbohydrates	8 g
Protein	0 g

BASIC PROCEDURE FOR PREPARING GLAZES

1. Blend sifted powdered sugar with a small amount of liquid and flavourings.
2. Use immediately.

APPLYING THE BASICS		RECIPE 31.13

Basic Sugar Glaze

Yield: 300 g (13 oz.)

Icing sugar, sifted	225 g	9-1/2 oz.
Water, warm	50 mL	2 fl. oz.
Glucose or corn syrup	25 g	1 oz.
Vanilla extract	10 mL	2 tsp.

1. Stir the ingredients together in a small bowl until smooth.
2. Adjust the consistency by adding more water to thin the glaze if necessary.
3. Adjust the flavour as necessary.
4. Use immediately, before the glaze begins to dry.

VARIATION: Another extract, such as lemon or almond, may be used in place of vanilla if desired.

● **glaze** a thin, flavoured coating poured or dripped onto a cake or pastry; **flat icing** or **water icing** is a specific glaze used on Danish pastries and coffee cakes

● **royal icing** also known as decorator's icing; an uncooked mixture of confectioner's sugar and egg whites that becomes hard and brittle when dry; used for making intricate cake decorations

Royal Icing

Royal icing, also known as *decorator's icing*, is similar to flat icing except it is much stiffer and becomes hard and brittle when dry. It is an uncooked mixture of icing sugar and egg whites. It may be dyed with food colouring pastes.

Royal icing is used for making decorations, particularly intricate flowers or lace patterns. Prepare royal icing in small quantities and always keep any unused portion covered with a damp towel to prevent hardening.

BASIC PROCEDURE FOR PREPARING ROYAL ICING

1. Combine egg white and lemon juice, if used.
2. Beat in sifted icing sugar until the correct consistency is reached.
3. Beat until very smooth and firm enough to hold a stiff peak.
4. Colour as desired with paste food colourings.
5. Store covered with a damp cloth and plastic wrap.

APPLYING THE BASICS   RECIPE 31.14

Royal Icing

Yield: 200 g (7 oz.)

Icing sugar	180 g	6 oz.
Egg white, room temperature	1	1
Lemon juice	1 mL	1/4 tsp.

1. Sift the sugar and set aside.
2. Place the strained egg white and lemon juice in a stainless steel bowl.
3. Add 125 g (4 oz.) of sugar and beat with an electric mixer or metal spoon until blended. The mixture should fall from a spoon in heavy globs. If it pours, it is too thin and will need the remaining 55 g (2 oz.) of sugar.
4. Once the consistency is correct, continue beating for 3–4 minutes. The icing should be white, smooth and thick enough to hold a stiff peak. Food colouring paste can be added at this time if desired.
5. Cover the icing with a damp towel and plastic wrap to prevent it from hardening.

Convenience Products

A wide selection of prepared icings, glazes and toppings is available. Often, chocolate and vanilla fudge icing bases are purchased, then flavoured or coloured as needed. Foam frostings can be purchased in powder form, to which you add water and then whip. Even prepared "buttercreams" are available, although they contain little or no real butter.

Prepared icings are often exceedingly sweet and overpowered by artificial flavours and chemical preservatives. These products save time but often cost more than their counterparts made from scratch. They should be used only after balancing the disadvantages against the benefits for your particular operation.

RECIPE 31.14

Approximate values per 30 g serving:	
Calories	120
Total fat	0 g
Saturated fat	0 g
Cholesterol	0 mg
Sodium	9 mg
Total carbohydrates	30 g
Protein	1 g

Ganache

Ganache is a blend of chocolate and cream. It may also include butter, liquor or other flavourings. Any bittersweet, semi-sweet or dark chocolate may be used; the choice depends on personal preference and cost considerations.

Depending on its consistency, ganache may be used as a filling, frosting or glaze-type coating on cakes or pastries. The ratio of chocolate to cream determines how thick the cooled ganache will be. Equal parts chocolate and cream generally are best for frostings and fillings. Increasing the percentage of chocolate produces a thicker ganache. Warm ganache can be poured over a cake or pastry and allowed to harden as a thin glaze, or the ganache may be cooled and whipped to create a rich, smooth frosting. If it becomes too firm, ganache can be remelted over a bain marie.

● **ganache** a rich blend of chocolate and heavy cream and, optionally, flavourings, used as a pastry or candy filling or frosting

BASIC PROCEDURE FOR PREPARING GANACHE

1. Melt finely chopped chocolate with cream in a doubleboiler. Or
2. Bring cream just to a boil. Then pour it over finely chopped chocolate and allow the cream's heat to gently melt the chocolate. Do not attempt to melt chocolate and then add cool cream. This will cause the chocolate to resolidify and lump.
3. Whichever method is used, cool the cream and chocolate mixture over an ice bath.

RECIPE 31.15

Approximate values per serving:

Calories	130
Total fat	10 g
Saturated fat	6 g
Cholesterol	15 mg
Sodium	0 mg
Total carbohydrates	10 g
Protein	1 g

APPLYING THE BASICS   RECIPE 31.15

Chocolate Ganache

Yield: 1.1 kg (2 lb. 5 oz.)

Bittersweet chocolate	500 g	1 lb.
Cream, 35%	500 g	1 lb.
Liqueur (e.g., Grand Marnier, Kahlúa, rum)	50 mL	2 fl. oz.
Butter, softened	100 g	3 oz.

1. Chop the chocolate into small pieces and place in a large metal bowl.
2. Bring the cream just to a boil, then immediately pour it over the chocolate, whisking to blend until the mixture is smooth.
3. Stir in the liqueur, followed by the softened butter.
4. Allow to cool, stirring frequently until the desired consistency is achieved. An ice bath may be used to speed the cooling process.

1. Chocolate Ganache: Pouring the hot cream over the chopped chocolate.

2. Cool, firm ganache.

ASSEMBLING AND DECORATING CAKES

Much of a cake's initial appeal lies in its appearance. This is true whether the finished cake is a simple sheet cake topped with swirls of buttercream or an elaborate wedding cake with intricate garlands and bouquets of royal icing roses. Any cake assembled and decorated with care and attention to detail is preferable to a carelessly assembled or garishly overdecorated one.

Thousands of decorating styles or designs are possible, of course. This section describes a few simple options that can be prepared by beginning pastry cooks using a minimum of specialized tools. In planning your cake's design, consider the flavour, texture and colour of the components used as well as the number of guests or portions that must be served. Consider who will be cutting and eating the cake and how long the dessert must stand before service.

Assembling Cakes

Before a cake can be decorated, it must be assembled and coated with frosting. Most cakes can be assembled in a variety of shapes and sizes: sheet cakes, round layer cakes and rectangular layer cakes are the most common. When assembling any cake, the goal is to fill and stack the cake layers evenly and to apply an even coating of frosting that is smooth and free of crumbs.

Most of the photographs in this section show the assembly and decoration of the cake shown to the left.

Celebration cake covered with rolled fondant

Assembled cake

BASIC PROCEDURE FOR ASSEMBLING CAKES

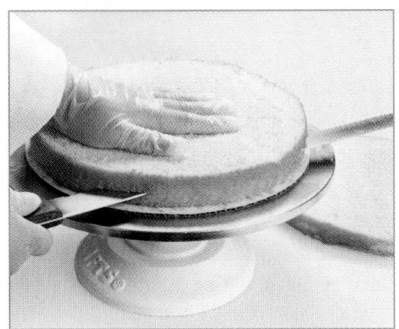

1. Split the cake horizontally into thin layers if desired. Use cake boards to support each layer as it is removed. Brush away any loose crumbs with a dry pastry brush or your hand.

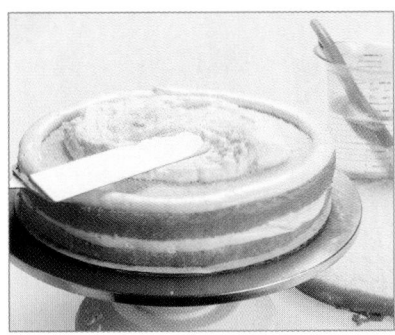

2. Position the bottom layer on a cake board. Place the layer on a revolving cake stand, if available. Pipe a border of buttercream around the cake, then top the layer with a mound of filling. Use a cake spatula to spread it evenly.

3. Position the next cake layer over the filling and continue layering and filling the cake as desired.

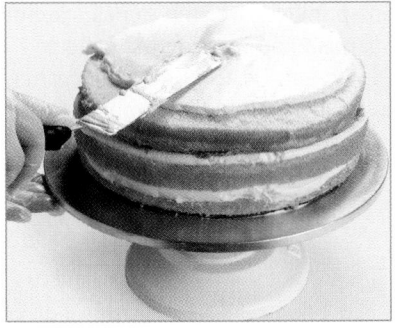

4. Place a mound of frosting in the centre of the cake top. Push it to the edge of the cake with a cake spatula. Do not drag the frosting back and forth or lift the spatula off the frosting, as these actions tend to pick up crumbs.

5. Smooth a thin layer of frosting (the crumb coat) over the top of the cake. Cover the sides with excess frosting from the top. Chill the cake.

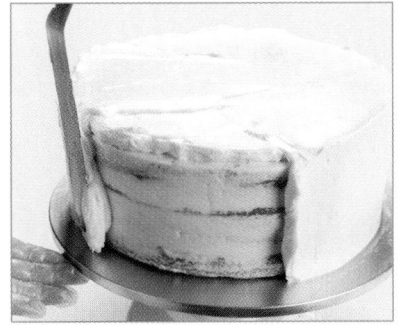

6. Place another mound of frosting in the centre of the cake top. Frost the cake with a second layer of icing. Hold the spatula upright against the side of the cake and, pressing gently, turn the cake stand slowly. This smooths and evens the sides. When the sides and top are smooth, the cake is ready to be decorated as desired.

Simple Decorating Techniques

An extremely simple yet effective way to decorate a frosted cake is with a garnish of chopped nuts, fruit, toasted coconut, shaved chocolate or other foods arranged in patterns or sprinkled over the cake. Be sure to use a garnish that complements the cake and frosting flavours or reflects one of the cake's ingredients. For example, finely chopped pecans would be an appropriate garnish for a carrot cake that contains pecans; shaved chocolate would not.

Side masking is the technique of coating only the sides of a cake with garnish. The top may be left plain or decorated with icing designs or a message. Be sure to apply the garnish while the frosting is still damp enough for it to adhere.

Stencils can be used to apply patterns of finely chopped garnishes, confectioner's sugar or cocoa powder to the top of a cake. A design can be cut

● **side masking** the technique of coating only the sides of a cake with garnish

Side masking—coating the sides of a carrot cake with chopped pecans

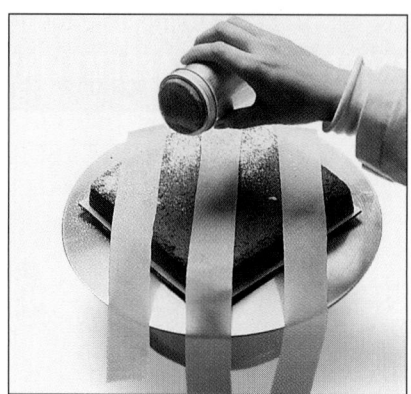

Stencils—creating a design with confectioner's sugar and strips of parchment paper

Cake comb—creating a pattern on a frosted cake

from cardboard, or thin plastic forms can be purchased. Even simple strips of parchment paper can be used to create an attractive pattern. If using a stencil on a frosted cake, allow the frosting to set somewhat before laying the stencil on top of it. After the garnishes have been sprinkled over the stencil, carefully lift the stencil to avoid spilling the excess garnish and messing the pattern.

A cake or baker's comb or a serrated knife can be used to create patterns on a cake iced with buttercream, fudge or ganache. Hold the comb against the frosted cake and rotate the cake slowly and evenly to create horizontal lines in the icing.

Piping Techniques

More elaborate and difficult decorations can be produced with the aid of a piping bag and an assortment of pastry tips. With these tools, frosting or royal icing can be used to create borders, flowers and messages. Before applying

Advanced Pâtisserie

Sugar can be used to create a number of doughs, pastes and syrups used for artistic and decorative work. Mastering even some of these products takes years of experience and practice. Although formulas and preparation methods are beyond the scope of this book, it is important that all pastry cooks be able to recognize and identify certain decorative sugar products.

Blown sugar—A boiled mixture of sucrose, glucose and tartaric acid that is coloured and shaped (in a manner very similar to glass blowing) using an air pump. It is used for making pieces of fruit and containers such as bowls and vases.

Gum paste—A smooth dough made of sugar and gelatin; it dries relatively slowly, becoming very firm and hard. The paste can be coloured and rolled out, cut and shaped, or moulded. It is used for making flowers, leaves and small figures.

Marzipan—A mixture of almond paste and sugar that may be coloured and used like modelling clay for sculpting small fruits, flowers or other objects. Marzipan may also be rolled out and cut into various shapes or used to cover cakes or pastries.

Nougat—A candy made of caramelized sugar and almonds that can be moulded into shapes or containers. Unlike other sugar decorations, nougat remains deliciously edible.

Pastillage—A paste made with sugar, cornstarch and gelatin. It can be rolled into sheets, then cut into shapes. It dries in a very firm and sturdy form, like plaster. Naturally pure white, it can be painted with cocoa or food colourings. Pastillage is used for showpieces and large decorative items.

Pulled sugar—A doughlike mixture of sucrose, glucose and tartaric acid that is coloured, then shaped by hand. Pulled sugar is used for making birds, flowers, leaves, bows and other items.

Spun sugar—Made by flicking dark caramelized sugar rapidly over a dowel to create long, fine, hairlike threads. Mounds or wreaths of these threads are used to decorate ice cream desserts, croquembouche and gâteaux.

any decoration, however, plan a design or pattern that is appropriate for the size and shape of the item being decorated.

When used properly, coloured frostings can bring cake decorations to life. Buttercream, royal icing and fondant are easily tinted using paste food colouring. Liquid food colourings are not recommended as they may thin the frosting too much. Always add colouring gradually with a toothpick. Frosting colours tend to darken as they sit. It is easy to add more later to darken the colour if necessary, but it is difficult to lighten the colour if too much is added.

Piping bags made from plastic, nylon or plastic-coated canvas are available in a range of sizes. A disposable piping cone can also be made from parchment paper.

Most decorations and designs are made by using a piping bag fitted with a pastry tip. Pastry tips are available with dozens of different openings and are referred to by standardized numbers. You can produce a variety of borders and designs by changing the pressure, the angle of the bag and the distance between the tip and the cake surface.

BASIC PROCEDURE FOR FILLING A PIPING BAG

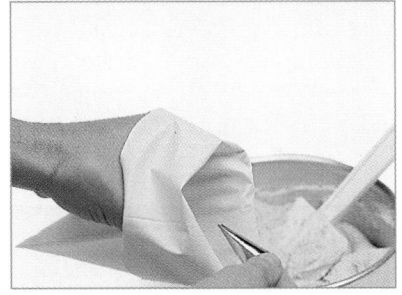

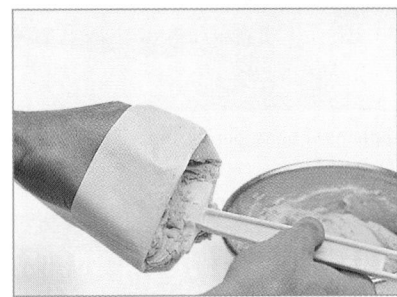

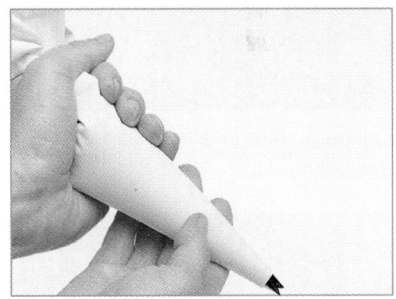

1. Select the proper size piping bag for your task. Insert the desired tip.

2. Fold down the top of the bag, then fill approximately half full with frosting. Do not overfill the bag.

3. Be sure to close the open end tightly before you start piping. Hold the bag firmly in your palm and squeeze from the top. Do not squeeze from the bottom or you may force the contents out the wrong end. Use the fingers of your other hand to guide the bag as you work.

Piped-on Decorating Techniques

Instead of leaving the sides of a frosted cake smooth or coating them with chopped nuts or crumbs, you can pipe on frosting designs and patterns. A simple but elegant design is the basket weave, shown on the next page.

Normally, a border pattern will be piped around the base of the cake and along the top edge. Borders should be piped on after nuts or any other garnishes are applied.

Each slice or serving of cake can be marked with its own decoration. For example, a rosette of frosting or a whole nut or piece of fruit could be used as shown on the next page. This makes it easier to portion the cake evenly.

Delicate flowers such as roses can be piped, allowed to harden, then placed on the cake in attractive arrangements. Royal icing is particularly useful for making decorations in advance because it dries very hard and lasts indefinitely.

Applying a basket weave pattern to the sides of the wedding cake.

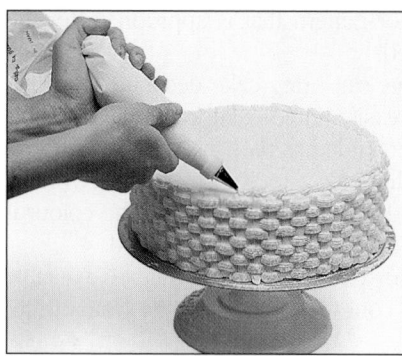

Applying a shell border to the wedding cake.

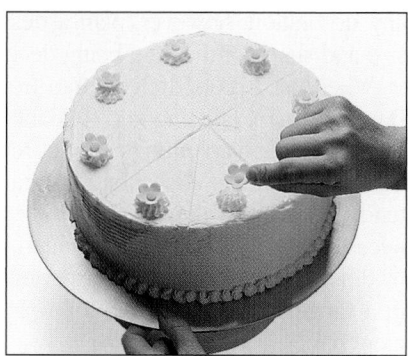

Placing royal icing flowers onto cake portions.

Applying a vine and leaf border onto a celebration cake.

Applying a bead border onto a celebration cake.

BASIC PROCEDURE FOR PIPING A BUTTERCREAM ROSE

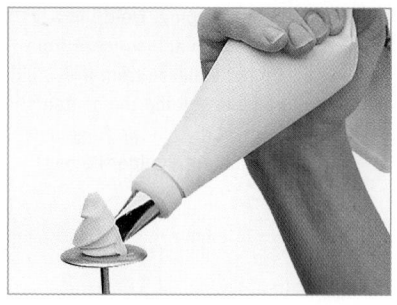

1. Using a #104 tip, pipe a mound of icing onto a rose nail.

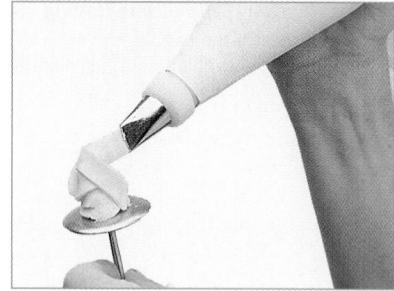

2. Pipe a curve of icing around the mound to create the centre of the rose.

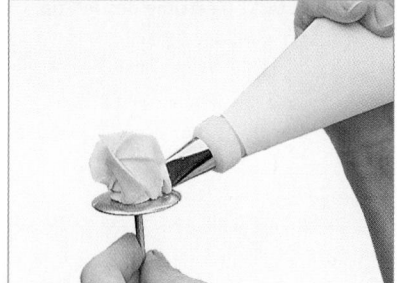

3. Pipe three overlapping petals around the centre.

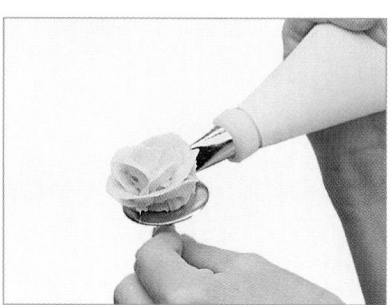

4. Pipe five more overlapping petals around the first three petals.

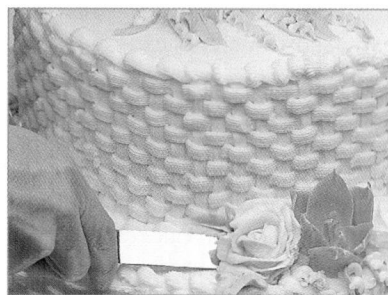

5. The finished rose is placed on the cake.

Making a Parchment-Paper Cone

A disposable piping bag or cone is easily made from parchment paper. Begin with an equilateral triangle of uncreased paper. Shape it into a cone as shown, folding the top edges together to hold the shape. The point of the cone can be cut as desired. Paper cones are especially useful for writing messages or piping melted chocolate.

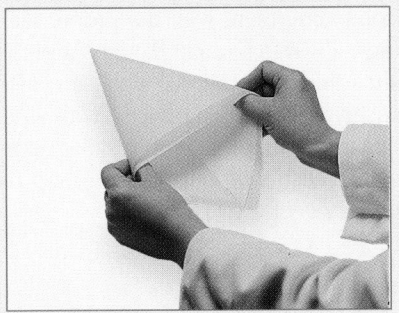

1. With the tip of the triangle pointing toward you, take the left corner and roll it into a cone, with the point at the centre of the long side. The left corner will now be in the tip of the triangle. Roll the right corner over the top of the cone and bring it to the tip.

2. Fold the ends together to seal.

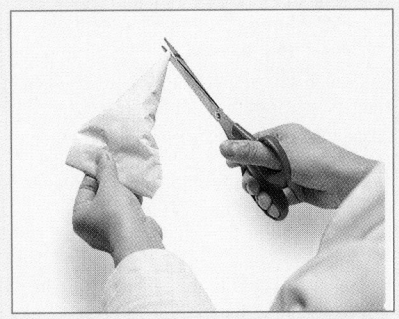

3. Cut the tip of the filled parchment cone.

The key to success with a piping bag is practice, practice, practice. Use plain all-purpose shortening piped onto parchment paper to practise and experiment with piping techniques. Once you are comfortable using a piping bag, you can apply these newfound skills directly to cakes and pastry decorating. Piping skills are also used in other areas of food preparation.

Storing Cakes

Unfrosted cake layers or sheets can be stored at room temperature for two or three days if well covered. Frosted or filled cakes are usually refrigerated to prevent spoilage. Simple buttercreams or sugar glazes, however, can be left at room temperature for one or two days. Any cake containing custard filling or whipped cream, as well as cakes finished with buttercream containing eggs, must be refrigerated. Cakes made with foam-type frosting should be eaten the day they are prepared.

Cakes can usually be frozen with great success; this makes them ideal for baking in advance. Unfrosted layers or sheets should be well covered with plastic wrap and frozen at –18°C (0°F) or lower. High-fat cakes will keep for up to six months; egg foam cakes begin to deteriorate after two or three months.

Frostings and fillings do not freeze particularly well, often losing flavour or changing texture when frozen. Buttercreams made with egg whites or sugar syrups tend to develop crystals and graininess. Foam frostings weep, expelling beads of sugar and becoming sticky. Fondant will absorb moisture and separate from the cake. If you must freeze a filled or frosted cake, it is best to freeze it unwrapped first, until the frosting is firm. The cake can then be covered with plastic wrap without damaging the frosting design. Leave the cake wrapped until completely thawed. It is best to thaw cakes in the refrigerator if time permits. Do not refreeze thawed cakes.

Conclusion

The ability to produce good cakes and frostings depends on using the right balance of high-quality ingredients and combining them with the proper techniques. When preparing cakes and frostings, always combine flavours and textures with care; apply frostings, garnishes and decorations with care also. Avoid overly rich, cloyingly sweet or garishly decorated products. With study and practice, you can learn the mixing techniques and assembly skills necessary for producing good cakes. Additional practice will help you develop the decorating and garnishing skills of a fine pastry chef.

Questions for Discussion

1. Raw cake ingredients can be classified by function into six categories. List them and give an example of each.
2. What is the primary leavening agent in cakes made with the foaming method? How is this similar to or different from cakes made with the creaming method?
3. What is the difference between a spongecake and a classic genoise?
4. Describe the procedures for making three types of frosting or icing as discussed in this chapter.
5. List the steps employed in assembling and frosting a three-layer cake.

Additional Cake and Frosting Formulas

RECIPE 31.16

Chocolate Caramel Maxine Torte

MONTAGE RESORT AND SPA, LAGUNA BEACH, CA
Executive Pastry Chef Richard Ruskell

Yield: 3 domed tortes, 15 cm (6 in.)
or 38 individual tortes, 6.2 cm (2-1/2 in.) each

Chocolate Caramel Mousse (recipe follows)	2400 g	5 lb. 5 oz.
Caramel Filling (recipe follows)	1270 g	2 lb. 14 oz.
Classic Spongecake (Recipe 31.4), chocolate variation, baked into 15-cm (6-in.) rounds	3 rounds	3 rounds
Dark Chocolate Glaze (recipe follows)	1350 g	3 lb.
Chocolate Cutouts (recipe follows)	as needed	as needed

1. Pipe the Chocolate Caramel Mousse into 15-cm (6-in.) moulds with approximately 3-L (3-qt.) capacity. Fill the moulds approximately three-fourths full.

2. Fill another pastry bag with the Caramel Filling and, inserting the nozzle of the pastry bag into the centre of the dome, pipe in approximately 340 g (12 oz.) of Caramel Filling to each mould or just enough to fill the moulds. There may be extra mousse or Caramel Filling.

3. Smooth the tops of the tortes with an offset spatula. Top with the spongecake, cut slightly smaller than the size of the mould. Freeze the tortes until completely firm.

continued

4. Remove the tortes from their moulds and place on a glazing rack. Pour the Dark Chocolate Glaze over the tortes. Place overlapping squares of Chocolate Cutouts along the bottom of each torte as garnish. Serve once thawed.

Chocolate Caramel Mousse

Yield: 3085 g (6 lb. 13 oz.)

Granulated sugar	590 g	1 lb. 5 oz.
Heavy cream	1360 mL	14 fl. oz.
Unsalted butter	200 g	7 oz.
Extra bittersweet chocolate, chopped fine	365 g	13 oz.
Unsweetened chocolate, chopped fine	170 g	6 oz.
Heavy cream, whipped to soft peaks	675 mL	1-1/2 qt.

1. Place the sugar in a large heavy saucepan. Add enough water to make a wet sand, approximately 120 mL (4 fl. oz.). Place the pan over medium-high heat. Cook the sugar to a caramel stage, periodically brushing down the sides of the pot with water to prevent any sugar crystals from building up.

2. Meanwhile, place the cream and butter in a small pot and bring to a boil. Set aside until needed.

3. Combine the chocolates in a large bowl. Set aside.

4. When the caramel reaches a dark brown colour, remove from the heat and slowly add the cream-and-butter mixture. Be very careful of the boiling caramel because serious burns can result. When all of the cream has been added, strain the mixture over the bowl of chopped chocolates. Let the chocolate and cream rest for approximately 1 minute and then whisk together until the chocolate is fully melted.

5. Set aside the chocolate ganache until cooled to room temperature. Once cooled, whisk in half of the whipped cream. Fold in the remaining cream. Use the mousse immediately.

Caramel Filling

Yield: 1270 g (2 lb. 14 oz.)

Unsalted butter	30 g	2 oz.
Granulated sugar	450 g	1 lb.
Heavy cream	450 mL	1 pt.
Glucose or corn syrup	340 g	12 oz.

1. Bring the butter, 120 g (4 oz.) of sugar and the cream to a boil. Set aside.

2. In a separate large saucepan, warm the glucose until it liquefies. Add the remaining sugar.

3. Continue heating the glucose and sugar until the mixture caramelizes to a dark brown. Turn off the heat.

4. Slowly add the cream mixture to the caramel. Be very careful, as this will bubble wildly. Also, to avoid steam burns, do not place your hands above the boiling caramel. When the boiling begins to subside, stir with a wooden spoon. Repeat this process until all of the cream has been added.

5. Return the pan to the heat and cook to a temperature of 113°C (236°F). Strain and allow to cool thoroughly before using.

Dark Chocolate Glaze

Yield: 1800 g (4 lb.)

Evaporated milk	420 mL	14 fl. oz.
Glucose or corn syrup	90 mL	3 fl. oz.
Simple syrup	420 mL	14 fl. oz.

Approximate values per individual torte:	
Calories	560
Total fat	35 g
Saturated fat	21 g
Cholesterol	115 mg
Sodium	51 mg
Total carbohydrates	65 g
Protein	6 g

Chocolate Caramel Mousse— Approximate values per individual torte:	
Calories	260
Total fat	20 g
Saturated fat	12 g
Cholesterol	48 mg
Sodium	12 mg
Total carbohydrates	22 g
Protein	2 g

Caramel Filling— Approximate values per individual torte:	
Calories	116
Total fat	5 g
Saturated fat	3 g
Cholesterol	17 mg
Sodium	11 mg
Total carbohydrates	19 g
Protein	0 g

continued

● **pâte à glacer** a specially formulated chocolate coating compound with vegetable oils designed to retain its shine without tempering; it is used as a coating or frosting chocolate

● **tempering** a process for melting chocolate during which the temperature of the cocoa butter is carefully stabilized; this keeps the chocolate smooth and glossy

Dark chocolate coating or pâte à glacer	480 g	17 oz.
Extra bittersweet couverture, chopped fine	480 g	17 oz.

1. Bring the milk, glucose and syrup to a boil, stirring carefully. Do not whisk vigorously or you will incorporate too much air.
2. In a bowl, combine the dark chocolate coating or pâte à glacer and the bittersweet chocolate.
3. Slowly pour the milk mixture onto the chocolate. Let it sit for approximately 1 minute. Using a whisk, stir the mixture slowly to incorporate the chocolate and milk.
4. Keep the mixture refrigerated. When ready to use, warm it over a water bath to 38°C (100°F). If the temperature gets any hotter the glaze will not be as shiny.

Chocolate Cutouts

Bittersweet chocolate, melted and tempered	as needed	as needed

1. Pour a thin band of melted chocolate onto a sheet of acetate. Spread the chocolate with an offset spatula into a wide band approximately 2 mm (1/16 in.) thick.
2. Allow the chocolate to set, just until the surface of the chocolate loses some of its gloss, then cut into uniform rectangles with a paring knife. Allow the chocolate to harden completely, then peel the pieces from the acetate.

Carrot Cake with Cream Cheese Frosting

RECIPE 31.17

Carrot Cake with Cream Cheese Frosting

Yield: 1 sheet cake or 4 22.5-cm (9-in.) rounds

Method: Muffin

Vegetable oil	650 g	1 lb. 8 oz.
Brown sugar	900 g	2 lb.
Eggs	450 g	8
Vanilla	5 mL	1 tsp.
Carrots, shredded	900 g	2 lb.
Crushed pineapple, with juice	900 g	2 lb.
Baking soda	25 g	1 oz.
Cinnamon	3 g	2 tsp.
Salt	2 g	1/4 tsp.
Bread flour	1 kg	2 lb. 3 oz.
Hazelnut, ground	450 g	1 lb.

1. Blend the oil and sugar in a large mixer bowl fitted with the paddle attachment. Add the eggs and vanilla and incorporate.
2. Blend in the carrots and pineapple.
3. Sift the dry ingredients together, then add them to the batter.
4. Divide the batter into 4 greased and floured pans.
5. Bake at 175°C (350°F) until springy to the touch and a cake tester comes out almost clean.

Cream Cheese Frosting

Unsalted butter, softened	125 g	4 oz.
Cream cheese, softened	350 g	12 oz.
Icing sugar, sifted	125 g	4 oz.
Lemon, zest and juice	1	1

1. Cream the butter and cream cheese until smooth. Add the icing sugar and beat well, scraping down the sides of the bowl.
2. Beat in the lemon juice and finely grated zest.

Cream Cheese Frosting—Approximate values per serving:	
Calories	55
Total fat	5 g
Saturated fat	3 g
Cholesterol	14 mg
Sodium	22 mg
Total carbohydrates	3 g
Protein	1 g

RECIPE 31.18

Sacher Torte

SAIT POLYTECHNIC, CALGARY, AB
School of Hospitality and Tourism
Pastry Chef Instructor Albert Liu

Yield: 2 20-cm (8-in.) cakes
Method: Creaming

Butter	280 g	10 oz.
Sugar	140 g	5 oz.
Almond paste	225 g	8 oz.
Egg yolks	225 g	8 oz.
Dark chocolate, melted	225 g	8 oz.
Egg whites	280 g	10 oz.
Sugar	150 g	5-1/2 oz.
Baking powder	5 g	1-1/2 tsp.
Pastry flour, sifted	280 g	10 oz.
Apricot jam	225 g	8 oz.
Apricot glaze	350 mL	12 fl. oz.
Chocolate glaze	180 mL	6-1/2 fl. oz.

1. Cream butter, sugar and almond paste until light. Gradually add the egg yolks, beating smooth after each addition.
2. Pour in the melted chocolate, beating smooth; reserve.
3. Prepare a common meringue from the egg whites and 150 g (5-1/2 oz.) sugar.
4. Fold the meringue into the creamed mixture.
5. Combine the baking powder and flour and fold into the batter.
6. Divide the batter between 2 greased cake pans or rings.
7. Bake at 180°C (375°F) for 35–45 minutes or until set.
8. Cool cakes for 5 minutes and remove from pans. Cool completely.
9. Slice each cake horizontally into 2 layers. Spread apricot jam between the layers and restack them.
10. Heat the apricot glaze and spread it over the top and sides of each cake. Allow to cool completely.
11. Pour chocolate glaze over each cake to form a complete, smooth, glossy coating.

VARIATIONS: There are many variations of this cake in existence. The original cake from Hotel Sacher in Vienna is made with ground hazelnuts.

Albert Liu
Albert began his career as a pâtissier at the Four Seasons Hotel in Vancouver, worked as an Executive Pastry Chef in the Bahamas, and then became the Executive Pastry Chef at the Palliser Hotel in Calgary. Currently he is a Pastry Chef Instructor at SAIT in Calgary.

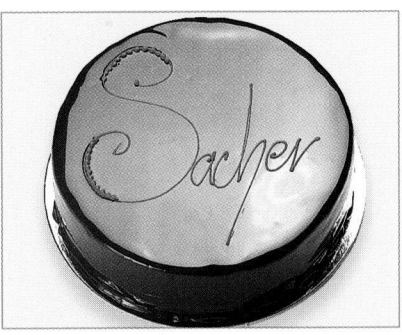

Sacher Torte

RECIPE 31.18

Approximate values per 1/16 of one cake:	
Calories	275
Total fat	16 g
Saturated fat	8 g
Cholesterol	107 mg
Sodium	109 mg
Total carbohydrates	32 g
Protein	4.5 g

Hermann Greineder, MPC

A retired Pastry Instructor at SAIT, Hermann received his German Master Certification as "Chef Pâtissier" in 1971. He has more than 50 years of experience in a wide range of establishments and he has won several medals in competition for his beautiful chocolate showpieces.

RECIPE 31.19

Approximate values per serving:	
Calories	750
Total fat	36 g
Saturated fat	20 g
Cholesterol	274 mg
Sodium	254 mg
Total carbohydrates	104 g
Protein	12 g

RECIPE 31.19

Convoluted Cake

Master Pâtissier Hermann Greineder, MPC, retired

Yield: 1 cake / 16 servings

White spongecake, 20 cm (8 in.)	1	1
Chocolate spongecake, 20 cm (8 in.)	1	1
Simple syrup	300 mL	10 fl. oz.
Brandy	50 mL	2 fl. oz.
French Buttercream (Recipe 31.11)	1000 g	36 oz.
Chocolate Ganache (Recipe 31.15), melted	500 g	17 oz.

1. Trim and slice spongecakes as needed into 3 x 6 mm (1/4 in.) thick layers.
2. Alternate the sponge layers as follows, saving the last white layer for the base of the finished cake: chocolate/white/chocolate/white/chocolate.
3. Starting with the chocolate layer, moisten with a portion of the brandy-flavoured syrup; cover with a 3-mm (1/8-in.) layer of buttercream. Repeat with each alternating layer, starting and finishing with a chocolate layer.
4. Cut an 18-cm (7-1/2-in.) diameter cone from the cake (going all the way to the bottom; see Figure 31.2(a)) and set aside.
5. Moisten the remaining white layer with brandy-flavoured syrup and coat with buttercream. Invert and place on the hollowed cake.
6. Flip the cake over so the white layer is now the bottom.
7. Gently press the cake in the centre to make room for the cone. Moisten the concave hole with syrup and spread with buttercream.
8. Place the cone in the centre of the cake (see Figure 31.2(b)) and coat with buttercream until smooth. Refrigerate the cake to chill it.
9. Glaze with melted ganache and decorate as desired.

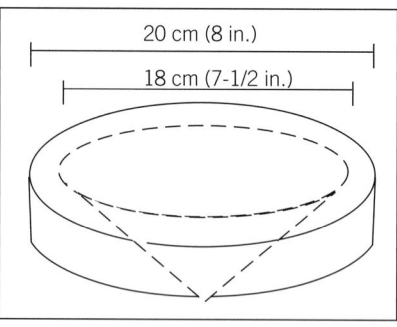

FIGURE 31.2 (a)

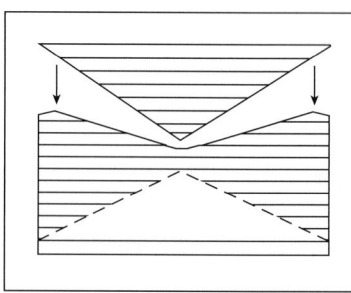

FIGURE 31.2 (b)

Devil's Food Cake

Yield: 1 sheet pan or 6 20-cm (8-in.) rounds
Method: High-ratio (two-stage)

Cake flour	500 g	1 lb.
Granulated sugar	600 g	1 lb. 3 oz.
Emulsified shortening	300 g	9-1/2 oz.
Cocoa powder	100 g	3-1/4 oz.
Salt	25 g	1/2 oz.
Baking powder	20 g	5 Tbsp.
Baking soda	10 g	2-1/2 Tbsp.
Nonfat dry milk powder	55 g	2 oz.
Vanilla extract	15 mL	1 Tbsp.
Corn syrup	100 g	3 oz.
Water, cold	450 mL	14-1/2 fl. oz.
Eggs	400 g	12-1/2 oz.

1. Mix the cake flour, sugar and emulsified shortening in a large mixer bowl on low speed for 5 minutes.
2. Add the cocoa powder, salt, baking powder, baking soda, milk powder, vanilla, corn syrup and 200 mL (7 fl. oz.) of the cold water. Blend well, then scrape down the bowl.
3. Combine the eggs with the remaining cold water and add to the batter in 3 equal parts, blending well and scraping down the bowl after each addition.
4. After all ingredients are incorporated, blend on low speed for 2 minutes.
5. Divide into greased and floured pans, scaling 450 g (1 lb.) for each 20-cm (8-in.) round layer.
6. Bake at 170°C (340°F) until springy and a toothpick inserted in the centre comes out clean.

RECIPE 31.20

Approximate values per serving:	
Calories	169
Total fat	7 g
Saturated fat	2 g
Cholesterol	36 mg
Sodium	308 mg
Total carbohydrates	24 g
Protein	3 g

Bûche de Noël

Yield: 10–12 servings

Classic Genoise (Recipe 31.3), freshly baked	one-half sheet	one-half sheet
Simple syrup	as needed	as needed
Simple Buttercream (Recipe 31.9; coffee, chocolate or vanilla)	1 L	1 qt.

1. Roll up the Classic Genoise in a spiral, starting with the long side. Wrap in parchment paper and cool.
2. Carefully unroll the cake. Brush the interior with simple syrup and coat with buttercream, leaving a 2.5-cm (1-in.) unfrosted rim around each edge.
3. Reroll the cake tightly and position it with the seam down on a cake cardboard.
4. Cut one end from the cake on a diagonal. Place the cut piece on top of the log, securing with skewers until iced in place.

RECIPE 31.21

Approximate values per serving:	
Calories	650
Total fat	21 g
Saturated fat	6 g
Cholesterol	0 mg
Sodium	330 mg
Total carbohydrates	115 g
Protein	2 g

continued

5. Pipe additional buttercream onto the cake log using a large star tip. Remove skewers. Pipe the buttercream onto the ends in a spiral pattern. Decorate as desired with buttercream flowers, baked meringue mushrooms or marzipan figures.

1. Bûche de Noël: Rolling the cake filled with buttercream.

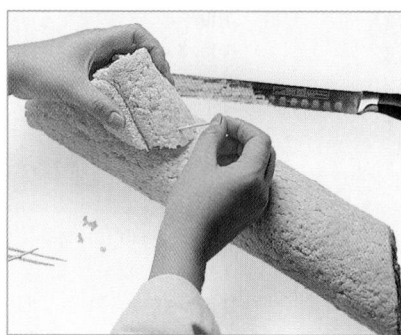

2. Attaching the cut end to the log.

3. Piping on the buttercream.

Pierre Jean St-Pierre

Pierre is a graduate of both George Brown College and SAIT. He began his career in pastries at Jasper Park Lodge and has since gone on to work at the Ritz-Carlton, Buckhead (Atlanta, Georgia), the Ritz-Carlton, Huntington (Pasadena, California) and the Ritz-Carlton, New Orleans. Previously he was the Executive Pastry Chef at the Fairmont, Washington, DC. Highlights of his career include a gold medal finish at the 1996 Grand Salon Culinaire, in Vancouver, and the Grand Prize in the 1999 Southern Pastry Classic in Atlanta, Georgia. He now works as a buyer at Costco.

RECIPE 31.22

Approximate values per piece:	
Calories	103
Total fat	7 g
Saturated fat	4 g
Cholesterol	58 mg
Sodium	40 mg
Total carbohydrates	8 g
Protein	3 g

RECIPE 31.22

Almond Chocolate Sheet Sponge

COSTCO, OTTAWA, ON
Executive Pastry Chef Pierre Jean St-Pierre

Yield: 4 sheet pans

Butter	675 g	1 lb. 8 oz.
Icing sugar	575 g	1 lb. 4 oz.
Eggs	375 g	14 oz.
Egg yolks	625 g	1 lb. 6 oz.
Dark chocolate, melted	940 g	2 lb.
Egg whites	675 g	1 lb. 8 oz.
Icing sugar	225 g	8 oz.
Bread flour	285 g	10 oz.
Almond flour	680 g	1 lb. 8 oz.

1. Cream butter and icing sugar (575 g/1 lb. 4 oz.). Slowly add eggs and yolks, scraping sides of bowl.

2. Add melted chocolate.

3. Make a common meringue of egg whites and icing sugar (225 g/8 oz.).

4. Fold meringue into chocolate mixture.

5. Sift bread and almond flour together and fold into batter.

6. Divide batter evenly among 4 lined sheet pans and spread evenly and thinly.

7. Bake at 190°C (375°F) for approximately 5 minutes.

NOTE: This sponge is an excellent base for individual mousses or opera-style entremets.

RECIPE 31.23

Ladyfingers

Yield: 80 cookies, 10 cm (4 in.) each
Method: Spongecake

Cornstarch	90 g	3 oz.
Bread flour	120 g	4 oz.
Eggs, separated	6	6
Granulated sugar	180 g	6 oz.
Lemon juice	2 mL	1/2 tsp.

1. Sift the cornstarch and flour together.

2. Whip the egg yolks with 60 g (2 oz.) of the sugar until thick and creamy.

3. Whip the egg whites until foamy. Gradually add 60 g (2 oz.) of the sugar and the lemon juice. Continue whipping to soft peaks, then add the remaining sugar gradually and whip to stiff peaks.

4. Fold approximately one-quarter of the egg whites into the whipped yolks to lighten them, then gently fold in the remaining whites. Fold in the flour mixture.

5. Place the batter into a pastry bag fitted with #8 plain tip. Pipe 10-cm (4-in.) long cookies onto paper-lined sheet pans.

6. Bake immediately at 220°C (425°F) until lightly browned, approximately 8 minutes.

Ladyfingers

RECIPE 31.23

Approximate values per cookie:

Calories	24
Total fat	0.4 g
Saturated fat	0.1 g
Cholesterol	14 mg
Sodium	4.7 mg
Total carbohydrates	4.4 g
Protein	0.6 g

RECIPE 31.24

Ribbon Sponge

SAIT POLYTECHNIC, Calgary, AB
Pastry Chef Albert Kurylo

Yield: 1 full sheet pan

Eggs	250 g	8 oz.
Egg yolks	80 g	3 oz.
Sugar	100 g	3-1/2 oz.
Almonds, fine ground	200 g	7 oz.
Bread flour	55 g	2 oz.
Egg whites	120 g	4-1/4 oz.
Sugar	100 g	3-1/2 oz.
Butter, melted	55 g	2 oz.

1. Place eggs, egg yolks and sugar (100 g/3-1/2 oz.) in a bowl. Heat over a bain marie, stirring constantly, to a temperature of 49°C (120°F). Remove from heat and whip at high speed for 1 minute.

2. Thoroughly combine ground almonds and flour.

3. Whip egg whites and sugar (100 g/3-1/2 oz.) until mixture has the appearance of snow (thick and foaming but will not hold a peak).

4. Stir the almond mixture into the whole egg mixture.

5. Stir in the melted butter.

6. Gradually fold in the egg-white mixture.

7. Colour a small portion of the paste and apply in a pattern on a silicone mat.

8. Spread the remaining paste 5-mm (1/4-in.) thick on a silicone mat and bake at 200°C (400°F) until set.

Albert Kurylo

Albert was trained in pastry in Poland and worked in Banff before joining SAIT. He combines classical and contemporary offerings equally well and is quality driven.

Biscuit Joconde

Traditional Joconde sponge is mostly eggs and egg whites with lesser amounts of nut flour, icing sugar and cake flour enriched with butter. The ribbon is created with a stencil paste made of equal weights of butter, icing sugar, egg whites and cake flour. Colour with powder or paste food colours. For chocolate, substitute 20% cocoa for flour.

RECIPE 31.24

Approximate values per piece:

Calories	68
Total fat	4 g
Saturated fat	1 g
Cholesterol	47 mg
Sodium	21 mg
Total carbohydrates	6 g
Protein	2 g

Peter Phillips, CCC

Leaving his home of Nipawin, Saskatchewan, to attend Humber College's Culinary Arts Program, Peter attained top student honours as well as numerous other awards. After his apprenticeship at a golf and country club in Winnipeg, and an exciting position at a ski resort in Japan, Peter returned to Saskatchewan and soon thereafter began managing Boffins Café. Although he has a strong interest in and aptitude for the business and management side of the culinary industry, he continues to develop his artistic talents through national and international competitions.

RECIPE 31.25

Tiramisu Torte

BISON FOOD SERVICES, SASKATOON, SK
Executive Chef-Owner Peter Phillips, CCC

Yield: 1 22.5-cm (9-in.) torte

Gelatin leaves	**4**	**4**
Water, cold	**30 mL**	**1 fl. oz.**
Egg yolks	**125 g**	**6**
Mascarpone	**500 g**	**18 oz.**
Egg whites	**180 g**	**6**
Sugar	**90 g**	**3 oz.**
Espresso	**125 mL**	**4 fl. oz.**
Ladyfingers and Cake (recipe instructions follow)		
Cocoa powder, dutched	**TT**	**TT**

1. Soak gelatin in cold water until soft, approximately 10 minutes. Heat gently to melt the gelatin.
2. At medium speed, whisk the egg yolks until light and fluffy.
3. Add the gelatin to the egg yolks in small quantities and continue mixing until well blended.
4. Add the mascarpone and mix well.
5. In a separate bowl, whip the egg whites until foamy. Continue to whip while gradually adding sugar, until soft peaks form.
6. Fold egg-white mixture into cheese mixture in 3 stages, mixing well.
7. Place the 22.5-cm (9-in.) cake layer in a 22.5-cm (9-in.) cake ring on a 30-cm (12-in.) cake board and brush lightly with espresso.
8. Cut each ladyfinger in half and place upright around the inside of the cake ring.
9. Pour in half the cheese mixture.
10. Place the remaining cake layer on top of the mixture and brush well with espresso.
11. Pour in the remaining cheese mixture.
12. Refrigerate for 2–3 hours.
13. Dust with cocoa powder.

RECIPE 31.25

Approximate values per slice:	
Calories	472
Total fat	24 g
Saturated fat	13 g
Cholesterol	308 mg
Sodium	274 mg
Total carbohydrates	51 g
Protein	16 g

Ladyfingers and Cake

Yield: 20 Ladyfingers, 1 22.5-cm (9-in.) layer and 1 17.5-cm (7-in.) layer

Ladyfingers (Recipe 31.23)

1. To make the ladyfingers, pipe 20 10-cm (4-in.) long cookies onto paper-lined sheet pans. Allow for some spreading during baking.
2. To make the base and centre layers of cake, draw a 22.5-cm (9-in.) circle and a 17.5-cm (7-in.) circle on parchment paper to make a template and turn over onto a sheet pan (allow for some spreading during baking). Pipe batter onto the circles.
3. Sprinkle both trays with sugar and bake at 220°C (425°F) until golden brown, 8–10 minutes.

Ladyfingers and Cake—Approximate values per 30 g serving:	
Calories	77
Total fat	1 g
Saturated fat	0.5 g
Cholesterol	53 mg
Sodium	35 mg
Total carbohydrates	14 g
Protein	2 g

Savarin (Rum Baba)

Yield: 2 20-cm (8-in.) moulds

Dough

Eggs	6	6
Sugar	30 g	1 oz.
Salt	10 g	2 tsp.
Butter	175 g	6 oz.
Water or milk, warm	375 mL	12 fl. oz.
Bread flour	500 g	1 lb. 2 oz.
Yeast	25 g	1 oz.

1. Beat eggs, sugar and salt together until pale and light.
2. Stir in softened butter.
3. Mix in warm water or milk (45°C/110°F).
4. Stir in flour and yeast to make a soft dough.
5. Cover dough and allow to proof in a warm place for 15 minutes.
6. Grease moulds with butter.
7. Fill moulds half full of dough.
8. Proof until dough reaches top of moulds.
9. Bake at 190°C (375°F) until golden. Turn onto rack to cool.

Syrup

Sugar	225 g	8 oz.
Water	375 mL	12 fl. oz.
White wine	175 mL	6 fl. oz.
Rum	150 mL	5 fl. oz.

1. Simmer sugar, water and wine for 6 minutes.
2. Stir in rum and cool slightly.

Assembly:

Soak Savarin in hot syrup to moisten. Brush Savarin with warm apricot glaze. Plate with Crème Chantilly (Recipe 32.6) and fresh or candied fruit.

VARIATION: Add 300 g (10 oz.) of rum-soaked raisins to the dough.

Approximate values per serving:	
Calories	278
Total fat	10 g
Saturated fat	5.5 g
Cholesterol	93 mg
Sodium	304 mg
Total carbohydrates	35 g
Protein	6 g

32 Custards, Creams, Frozen Desserts and Dessert Sauces

"Like a host at a good party, vanilla
encourages all the elements present to
rise to the occasion and make their own contributions to the whole,
without calling undue attention to itself.

—Richard Sax, American food writer, cookbook author and teacher (1954–1995)

The bakeshop is responsible for more than just quick breads, yeast breads, pies, pastries, cookies and cakes. It also produces many delightfully sweet concoctions that are not baked and often not even cooked. These include sweet custards, creams, frozen desserts and dessert sauces. Sweet custards are cooked mixtures of eggs, sugar and milk; starch may be added. Sweet custards can be flavoured in a variety of ways and eaten hot or cold. Some are served alone as a dessert or used as a filling, topping or accompaniment for pies, pastries or cakes. Creams include whipped cream and mixtures lightened with whipped cream such as Bavarians, chiffons and mousses. Frozen desserts include ice cream and sorbet as well as the still-frozen mousses called semifreddi.

Sauces for these desserts, including fruit purées, caramel sauces and chocolate syrup, are also made in the bakeshop and are discussed in this chapter. Indeed, many of the items presented in this chapter are components, meant to be combined with pastries (Chapter 30) or cakes (Chapter 31) to form complete desserts. Guidelines for assembling desserts are given at this chapter's end.

LEARNING OUTCOMES

After studying this chapter you will be able to:

- prepare a variety of custards and creams
- prepare a variety of ice creams, sorbets and frozen dessert items
- prepare a variety of dessert sauces
- use these products in preparing and serving other pastry and dessert items
- plan and prepare assembled desserts

PEARSON
myculinarylab

These interactive online tools will help you master the skills in this chapter:

- Videos
- Chapter Quizzes

CUSTARDS

A **custard** is any liquid thickened by the coagulation of egg proteins. A custard's consistency depends on the ratio of eggs to liquid and the type of liquid used. The more eggs used, the thicker and richer the final product will be. The richer the liquid (cream versus milk, for example), the thicker the final product. Most custards, with the notable exception of pastry creams, are not thickened by starch.

A custard can be stirred or baked. A stirred custard tends to be soft, rich and creamy. A baked custard, typically cooked in a bain marie, is usually firm enough to unmould and slice.

Stirred Custards

A stirred custard is cooked on the stove top, either directly in a saucepan or over a doubleboiler. It must be stirred throughout the cooking process to prevent curdling (overcooking).

A stirred custard can be used as a dessert sauce, incorporated into a complex dessert or eaten alone. The stirred custards most commonly used in food service operations are **vanilla custard sauce** (Recipe 32.1) and **pastry cream** (Recipe 32.2). Other popular stirred custards are lemon curd (Recipe 33.14) and **sabayon** (Recipe 32.3).

Vanilla Custard Sauce (Crème Anglaise)

A custard sauce is made with egg yolks, sugar and milk or cereal cream. Usually flavoured with vanilla bean or pure vanilla extract, a custard sauce can also be flavoured with liquor, chocolate, ground nuts or other extracts.

It is prepared on the stove top over direct heat. Be extremely careful to stir the mixture continually and not allow it to exceed 88°C (190°F), or it will curdle. Remove from the heat at 85°C (185°F). A properly made custard sauce should be smooth and thick enough to coat the back of a spoon. It should not contain any noticeable bits of cooked egg.

● **custard** any liquid thickened by the coagulation of egg proteins; its consistency depends on the ratio of eggs to liquid and the type of liquid used; custards can be baked in the oven or cooked in a bain marie or on the stove top

● **vanilla custard sauce** also known as crème anglaise; a stirred custard made with egg yolks, sugar and milk or half-and-half and flavoured with vanilla; served with or used in dessert preparations

● **pastry cream** also known as crème pâtissière; a stirred custard made with egg yolks, sugar and milk and thickened with starch; used for pastry and pie fillings

● **sabayon** also known as zabaglione; a foamy, stirred custard sauce made by whisking eggs, sugar and wine over low heat

Vanilla custard sauce (Fr. *crème anglaise*) is served with cakes, pastries, fruits and soufflés and is often used for decorating dessert plates. It may be served hot or cold. It is also used as the base for many ice creams.

A very thick version of custard sauce can be made using 35% cream and additional egg yolks. Its consistency is more like a pudding than a sauce. This custard is often served over fruit, or in a small ramekin or other container and then topped with caramelized sugar for a dessert known as **crème brûlée** (burnt cream; see Recipe 32.15).

Pastry Cream

Pastry cream (Fr. *crème pâtissière*) is a stirred custard made with egg yolks, sugar and milk and thickened with cornstarch. Because starch protects the egg yolks from curdling, pastry cream can be boiled. In fact, it must be boiled to fully gelatinize the starch and eliminate the taste of raw starch.

Pastry cream can be flavoured with chocolate, liquors, extracts or fruits. (**Pudding** is nothing more than flavoured pastry cream.) It is used for filling éclairs, cream puffs, napoleons, fruit tarts and other pastries. Pastry cream is also the filling for cream pies (see Chapter 30, Pies, Pastries and Cookies). Pastry cream is thick enough to hold its shape without making pastry doughs soggy.

Pastry cream can be rather heavy. It can be lightened by folding in whipped cream to produce a **mousseline**, or Italian meringue can be folded in to produce a **crème Chiboust**.

● **crème brûlée** French for burnt cream; used to describe a rich dessert custard topped with a crust of caramelized sugar

● **pudding** a thick, spoonable dessert custard, usually made with eggs, milk, sugar and flavourings and thickened with flour or another starch

● **mousseline** a cream or sauce lightened by folding in whipped cream

● **crème Chiboust** a vanilla pastry cream lightened by folding in Italian meringue; traditionally used in a Gâteau St. Honoré

● **tempering** heating gently and gradually; refers to the process of slowly adding a hot liquid to eggs to raise their temperature without causing them to curdle

---

SAFETY ALERT

Eggs and Sanitation

Eggs are high-protein foods that are easily contaminated by bacteria such as salmonella that cause food-borne illnesses. Because custards cannot be heated to temperatures high enough to destroy these bacteria without first curdling the eggs, it is especially important that sanitary guidelines be followed in preparing the egg products discussed in this chapter.

1. Cleanliness is important. Wash your hands thoroughly before beginning; be sure to use clean, sanitized bowls, utensils and storage containers.
2. When breaking or separating eggs, minimize contact between the egg shell and raw egg.
3. Heat the milk to just below a boil before combining it with the eggs. This reduces the final cooking time.
4. Chill the finished product quickly over an ice bath and refrigerate immediately.
5. Do not use your fingers to taste the custard.
6. Do not store any custard mixture, cooked or uncooked, at room temperature.
7. Purchase pasteurized egg products if possible.

BASIC PROCEDURE FOR PREPARING VANILLA CUSTARD SAUCE AND PASTRY CREAM

1. Place milk and/or cream in a heavy, nonreactive saucepan; add scraped vanilla bean if desired.
2. In a mixing bowl, whisk together the egg yolks, sugar and starch (if used). Do not use an electric mixer as it incorporates too much air.
3. Bring the liquid just to a boil. **Temper** the egg mixture with approximately one-third of the hot liquid.
4. Pour the tempered eggs into the remaining hot liquid and return the mixture to the heat. The stove's temperature can be as hot as you dare. The lower the temperature, the longer the custard will take to thicken; the higher the temperature, the greater the risk of curdling or burning. The thickening agent for custard sauce is eggs. The thickener for pastry cream is cornstarch.
5. Cook, stirring constantly, until thickened. Custard sauce should reach a temperature of 85°C (185°F). Pastry cream should be allowed to boil for a few moments.
6. Immediately remove the cooked custard from the hot saucepan to avoid overcooking. Butter or other flavourings can be added at this time.
7. Cool over an ice bath. Store in a clean, shallow container, cover and refrigerate.

BASIC PROCEDURE FOR SALVAGING CURDLED VANILLA CUSTARD SAUCE

1. Strain the sauce into a bowl. Place the bowl over an ice bath and whisk vigorously.
2. If this does not smooth out the overcooked sauce, place the sauce in a blender and process for a few moments.

Vanilla Custard Sauce (Crème Anglaise)

Yield: 600 mL (20 fl. oz.)
Method: Stirred custard

Cereal cream	500 mL	16 fl. oz.
Vanilla bean, split*	1/2	1/2
Egg yolks, large	140 g	6
Granulated sugar	125 g	4 oz.

*If vanilla bean is not available, stir in 30 mL (1 fl. oz.) of vanilla extract when sauce is removed from heat.

1. Using a heavy, nonreactive saucepan, bring the cream and vanilla bean just to a boil.

2. Whisk the egg yolks and sugar together in a mixing bowl. Temper the egg mixture with approximately one-third of the hot cream, then return the entire mixture to the saucepan with the remaining cream.

3. Cook the sauce over medium heat, stirring constantly, until it is thick enough to coat the back of a spoon. Do not allow the sauce to boil.

4. As soon as the sauce thickens, remove it from the heat and pour it through a fine mesh strainer into a clean bowl. Chill the sauce over an ice bath, then cover and keep refrigerated. Use the sauce within 2 days.

VARIATIONS: CHOCOLATE—Stir 90 g (3 oz.) of finely chopped dark chocolate into the strained custard while it is still warm. The heat of the custard will melt the chocolate.

COFFEE—Add 15 mL (1 Tbsp.) of coffee (café) extract or compound to the warm custard.

FRANGELICO—Omit the vanilla bean. Stir in 2 mL (1/2 tsp.) vanilla and 30 mL (2 Tbsp.) of Frangelico, to taste.

PISTACHIO—Omit the vanilla bean. Place 60 g (2 oz.) of finely chopped pistachio nuts in the saucepan with the barely boiling cereal cream. Remove from the heat, cover and steep for up to 1 hour. Uncover the mixture, reheat and continue preparing the sauce as directed. The ground nuts will be strained out in Step 4.

Approximate values per 50 mL serving:

Calories	133
Total fat	8 g
Saturated fat	3.8 g
Cholesterol	153 mg
Sodium	23 mg
Total carbohydrates	12 g
Protein	3.2 g

1. Vanilla Custard Sauce: Mise en place for vanilla sauce.

2. Tempering the eggs.

3. The properly cooked sauce.

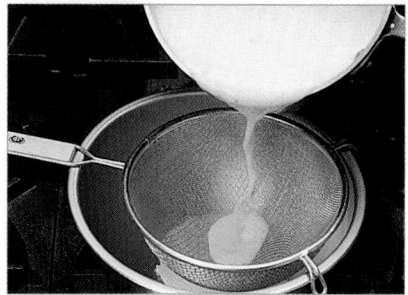

4. Straining the sauce into a bowl.

Pastry Cream (Crème Pâtissière)

Yield: 825 mL (30 oz.)
Method: Stirred custard

Cornstarch	60 g	2 oz.
Sugar	165 g	6 oz.
Milk	650 mL	21 fl. oz.
Egg yolks	1	1

Approximate values per 50 mL serving:

Calories	108
Total fat	4 g
Saturated fat	2 g
Cholesterol	49 mg
Sodium	51 mg
Total carbohydrates	16 g
Protein	2.5 g

continued

1. Pastry Cream: Stirring the Pastry Cream as it comes to a boil.

2. Folding butter and vanilla into the cooked Pastry Cream.

Whole eggs	120 g	2
Butter	40 g	1-1/2 oz.
Vanilla	5 mL	1 tsp.

1. Dilute the cornstarch and half the sugar with 250 mL (8 fl. oz.) of cold milk, egg yolks and whole eggs. Whisk until very smooth.
2. Bring the remaining milk and sugar to a boil.
3. Blend the 2 mixtures together gradually, stirring constantly.
4. Place back on the heat and cook for a few minutes, stirring constantly, until thickened.
5. Remove the pan from the heat and stir in butter and vanilla. Transfer mixture to a clean bowl.
6. Cover surface with plastic film and cool over ice bath. Store in refrigerator.

Sabayon

Sabayon (It. *zabaglione*) is a foamy, stirred custard sauce made by whisking eggs, sugar and wine over low heat. The egg proteins coagulate, thickening the mixture, while the whisking incorporates air to make it light and fluffy. Usually a sweet wine is used; Marsala and champagne are the most popular choices.

The mixture can be served warm, or it can be chilled. Sabayon may be served alone or as a sauce or topping with fruit or pastries such as spongecake or ladyfingers.

BASIC PROCEDURE FOR PREPARING SABAYON

1. Combine egg yolks, sugar and wine in the top of a doubleboiler.
2. Place the doubleboiler over low heat and whisk constantly until the sauce is foamy and thick enough to form a ribbon when the whisk is lifted.
3. Remove from the heat and serve immediately, or whisk over an ice bath until cool. If allowed to sit, the hot mixture may separate.

The thickened sabayon.

RECIPE 32.3

Approximate values per serving:	
Calories	252
Total fat	16 g
Saturated fat	8 g
Cholesterol	256 mg
Sodium	20.5 mg
Total carbohydrates	21 g
Protein	3.5 g

APPLYING THE BASICS	RECIPE 32.3

Champagne Sabayon

Yield: 1 L (1 qt.)

Method: Stirred custard

Egg yolks	8	8
Granulated sugar	150 g	5-1/4 oz.
Champagne	180 mL	6 fl. oz.
Lemon or orange juice	30 mL	1 fl. oz.
Cream, 35% (optional; see Variation)	250 mL	8 fl. oz.

1. Combine the egg yolks and sugar in a stainless steel bowl.
2. Add champagne and juice to the egg mixture.
3. Place the bowl over a pan of barely simmering water. Whisk vigorously until the sauce is thick and pale yellow, approximately 10 minutes. Serve immediately.

VARIATION: To prepare a Sabayon Mousseline, place the bowl of sabayon over an ice bath and continue whisking until completely cold. Whip the cream to soft peaks and fold it into the cold sabayon. For Sabayon Sauce, increase the wine to 200 mL (7 fl. oz.) and flavour with 125 mL (4 fl. oz.) liqueur.

Baked Custards

A baked custard is based on the same principle as a stirred custard: a liquid thickens by the coagulation of egg proteins. However, with a baked custard, the thickening occurs in an oven. The container of custard is usually placed in a water bath (bain marie) to protect the eggs from curdling. Even though the water bath's temperature will not exceed 100°C (212°F), care must be taken not to bake the custards for too long or at too high a temperature. An over-baked custard will be watery or curdled; a properly baked custard should be smooth-textured and firm enough to slice.

Baked custards include simple mixtures of egg yolks, sugar and milk such as crème caramel as well as custard mixtures in which other ingredients are sus-pended—for example, cheesecake, bread pudding and quiche.

Crème Caramel

Crème caramel, crème renversée and flan all refer to an egg custard baked over a layer of caramelized sugar and inverted for service. The caramelized sugar produces a golden-brown surface on the inverted custard and a thin caramel sauce.

● **crème caramel** like crème renversée and flan, a custard baked over a layer of caramelized sugar and inverted for service

APPLYING THE BASICS		RECIPE 32.4

Crème Caramel

Yield: 12 125-mL (4-fl.-oz.) ramekins
Method: Baked custard

Granulated sugar	350 g	12-1/2 oz.
Lemon juice	20 mL	1/2 fl. oz.
Water	60 mL	2 fl. oz.
Milk	1 L	1 qt.
Vanilla bean, split	1	1
Whole eggs	350 g	6
Egg yolks	4	4
Sugar	200 g	7 oz.

1. Combine the granulated sugar, lemon juice and water in a small, heavy saucepan; bring to a boil. Cook until the sugar reaches a deep golden brown. Set the pot into cold water to stop the cooking. Immediately divide the caramel sugar into each of the lightly buttered ramekins. Arrange the ramekins in a 5-cm (2-in.) deep hotel pan and set aside.

2. Combine the milk and vanilla bean in a large saucepan. Bring just to a boil, cover and remove from the heat. Allow this mixture to **steep** for about 30 minutes.

3. Whisk the eggs, egg yolks and sugar together in a large bowl.

4. Uncover the milk mixture and return it to the stove top. Bring just to a boil. Temper the egg-and-sugar mixture with approximately one-third of the hot milk. Whisk in the remaining hot milk.

5. Strain the custard through a fine mesh strainer. Pour into the caramel-lined ramekins, filling to just below the rims.

6. Pour enough warm water into the hotel pan to reach halfway up the sides of the ramekins. Bake at 160°C (325°F) for approximately 30–40 minutes. The custards should be almost set, but still slightly soft in the centre.

7. Completely chill the baked custards before serving. To unmould, run a small knife around the edge of the custard, invert onto the serving plate and give the ramekin a firm sideways shake. Garnish with fresh fruit or caramelized almonds and a rosette of Crème Chantilly (Recipe 32.6).

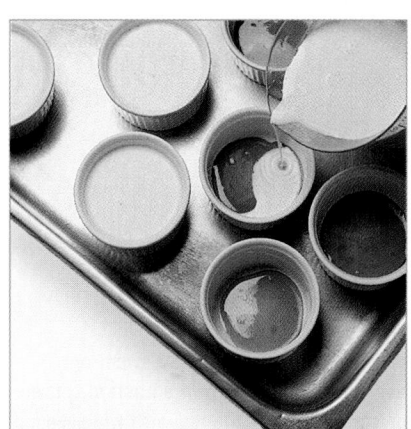

Crème Caramel: Filling the ramekins for flans.

● **steep** to soak food in a hot liquid to either extract its flavour or soften its texture

RECIPE 32.4

Approximate values per ramekin:	
Calories	283
Total fat	6.3 g
Saturated fat	2.5 g
Cholesterol	181 mg
Sodium	81 mg
Total carbohydrates	50 g
Protein	7.4 g

Cheesecake

Cheesecakes, which are almost as old as Western civilization, have undergone many changes and variations since the ancient Greeks devised the first known recipe. Americans revolutionized the dessert with the development of cream cheese in 1872.

Cheesecake is a baked custard that contains a smooth cheese, usually a soft, fresh cheese such as cream, ricotta, cottage or farmer cheese. A cheesecake may be prepared without a crust or it may have a base or sides of short dough, cookie crumbs, ground nuts or spongecake. The filling can be dense and rich (New York style) or light and fluffy (Italian style). Fruit, nuts and flavourings may also be included in the filling. Cheesecakes are often topped with fruit or sour cream glaze. A recipe for cheesecake appears at the end of this chapter (Recipe 32.20).

Some cheesecakes are unbaked and rely on gelatin for thickening; others are frozen. These are not really custards, however, but are more similar to the chiffons or mousses discussed later.

Bread Pudding

Bread pudding is a home-style dessert in which chunks of bread, flavourings and raisins or other fruit are mixed with an egg custard and baked. The result is somewhat of a cross between a cake and a pudding. It is often served with custard sauce, ice cream, whipped cream or a whisky-flavoured butter sauce. Bread pudding is a delicious way to use stale or leftover bread or overripe fruit. Recipes for Bread Pudding with Sauce Anglaise (Recipe 32.17) and Chocolate, Cherry and Croissant Pudding (Recipe 32.18) appear at the end of this chapter.

Soufflés

● **soufflé** an airy textured sweet or savoury dish made from a custard, purée or starch base lightened with whipped egg whites and baked

A **soufflé** is made from a custard, purée or starch-thickened base that is lightened with whipped egg whites and baked. The air in the egg whites expands to create a light, fluffy texture and tall rise. A soufflé is not as stable as a cake and collapses quickly when removed from the oven.

Soufflés can be prepared in a wide variety of sweet or savoury flavours. The flavouring—for example, liqueur, chocolate, cheese or fruit—is incorporated in the base, which can be made ahead.

When making a soufflé, the custard base and egg whites should be at room temperature. First, the egg whites will whip to a better volume, and second, if the base is approximately the same temperature as the egg whites, the two mixtures can be more easily incorporated. The egg whites are whipped to stiff peaks with a portion of the sugar for stability. The whipped egg whites are then gently folded into the base immediately before baking.

A soufflé is baked in a straight-sided mould or individual ramekin. The finished soufflé should be puffy, with a lightly browned top. It should rise well above the rim of the baking dish. A soufflé must be served immediately, before it collapses. A warm custard sauce (crème anglaise) is often served as an accompaniment to a sweet soufflé.

A frozen soufflé is not a true soufflé. Rather, it is a creamy custard mixture lightened with whipped egg whites or whipped cream and placed in a soufflé dish wrapped with a tall paper collar. When the paper is removed, the mixture looks as if it has risen above the mould like a hot soufflé.

BASIC PROCEDURE FOR PREPARING BAKED SOUFFLÉS

1. Butter the mould or ramekins and dust with granulated sugar. Preheat the oven to approximately 220°C (425°F).

2. Prepare the custard base. Add flavourings as desired.

3. Whip the egg whites and sugar to stiff peaks. Fold the whipped egg whites into the base.

4. Pour the mixture into the prepared mould or ramekins and bake immediately.

1. Chocolate Orange Soufflés: Folding the whipped egg whites into the chocolate base.

APPLYING THE BASICS

RECIPE 32.5

Chocolate Orange Soufflés

Yield: 8 servings

Orange juice	450 mL	1 pt.
Sugar	120 g	4 oz.
Butter	50 g	2 oz.
Bread flour	90 g	3 oz.
Bittersweet chocolate, chopped fine	150 g	5-1/2 oz.
Eggs, separated	8	8
Orange liqueur	50 mL	2 fl. oz.
Butter, melted	as needed	as needed
Granulated sugar	as needed	as needed

1. To prepare the base, heat the orange juice and 90 g (3 oz.) sugar and whisk in a paste made from the butter and flour. Bring to a boil and simmer 5–10 minutes while stirring constantly to cook out the flour taste.

2. Add the chocolate and stir until smooth.

3. Cool mixture to below 60°C (140°F).

4. Incorporate the egg yolks and liqueur. This base mixture may be refrigerated but must be brought to room temperature for use.

5. To prepare the soufflés, brush individual-serving-sized ramekins with melted butter and dust with granulated sugar.

6. Preheat the oven to 220°C (425°F). Place a sheet pan in the oven, onto which you will place the soufflés for baking. (This makes it easier to remove the hot soufflé cups from the oven.)

7. Whip the egg whites to soft peaks with the remaining 30 g (1 oz.) of sugar. Fold the meringue into the chocolate base and spoon the mixture into the prepared ramekins. The ramekins should be filled to within 6 mm (1/4 in.) of the rims. Smooth the top of each soufflé with a spatula and bake immediately.

8. Bake for approximately 20–30 minutes. The soufflés are done when well risen and golden brown on top, and the edges appear dry. Do not touch a soufflé to test doneness.

9. Sprinkle the soufflés with powdered sugar if desired and serve immediately with a sabayon sauce.

2. Filling the ramekins.

3. The finished soufflé, ready for service.

RECIPE 32.5

Approximate values per serving:	
Calories	350
Total fat	15 g
Saturated fat	8 g
Cholesterol	210 mg
Sodium	65 mg
Total carbohydrates	48 g
Protein	10 g

TABLE 32.1	Cream (Crème) Components		
For a	**Begin with a Base of**	**Thicken with**	**Then Fold in**
Bavarian	Custard	Gelatin	Whipped cream
Chiffon	Custard or starch-thickened fruit	Gelatin	Whipped egg whites
Mousse	Melted chocolate, puréed fruit or custard	Nothing or gelatin	Whipped cream, whipped egg whites or both

CREAMS

Creams (Fr. *crèmes*) include light, fluffy or creamy-textured dessert items made with whipped egg whites or cream. Some, such as Bavarian creams and chiffons, are thickened with gelatin. Others, such as mousses and Chantilly cream, are softer and lighter. Table 32.1 provides a summary. The success of all, however, depends on the proper whipping and incorporation of egg whites or heavy cream.

You should review the material on whipping cream found in Chapter 8, Eggs and Dairy Products. Note that whipping cream has a butterfat content of 30% to 40%. When preparing any whipped cream, be sure that the cream, the mixing bowl and all utensils are well chilled and clean. A warm bowl can melt the butterfat, destroying the texture of the cream. Properly whipped cream should increase two to two and a half times in volume. Over-whipped cream loses volume, curdles, and separates.

Chantilly Cream/Crème Chantilly

● **crème Chantilly** heavy cream whipped to soft peaks and flavoured with sugar and vanilla; used to garnish pastries or desserts or folded into cooled custard or pastry cream for fillings

Crème Chantilly is simply heavy cream whipped to soft peaks and flavoured with sugar and vanilla. It can be used for garnishing pastry or dessert items, or it can be folded into cooled custard or pastry cream and used as a component in a pastry.

When making crème Chantilly, the vanilla extract and sugar should be added after the cream begins to thicken. Either granulated or icing sugar may be used; there are advantages and disadvantages to both. Granulated sugar assists in forming a better foam than does icing sugar, but it may cause the cream to feel gritty. Icing sugar dissolves more quickly and completely than does granulated sugar, but does nothing to assist with foaming. Whichever sugar is used, it should be added just before the whipping is complete to avoid interfering with the cream's volume and stability.

Properly whipped Crème Chantilly

APPLYING THE BASICS

RECIPE 32.6

Crème Chantilly

Yield: 2 to 2.5 L (2 to 2-1/2 qt.)

Cream, 35%, chilled	1 L	1 qt.
Icing sugar	90 g	3 oz.
Vanilla extract	10 mL	2 tsp.

1. Place the cream in a chilled mixing bowl. Using a balloon whisk, whisk the cream until slightly thickened.

2. Add the sugar and vanilla and continue whisking to the desired consistency. The cream should be smooth and light, not grainy. Do not overwhip.

3. Crème Chantilly may be stored in the refrigerator for several hours. If the cream begins to soften, gently rewhip as necessary.

RECIPE 32.6

Approximate values per 30 g serving:	
Calories	100
Total fat	10 g
Saturated fat	6 g
Cholesterol	35 mg
Sodium	10 mg
Total carbohydrates	3 g
Protein	1 g

Bavarian Cream

A **Bavarian cream** (Fr. *bavarois*) is prepared by first thickening custard sauce with gelatin, then folding in whipped cream. The final product is poured into a mould and chilled until firm enough to unmould and slice. Although a Bavarian cream can be moulded into individual servings, it is most often poured into a round mould lined with jellyroll slices or ladyfingers to create the classic desserts known as charlotte royale and charlotte russe.

Bavarians may be flavoured by adding chocolate, puréed fruit, chopped nuts, extracts or liquors to the custard sauce base. Layers of fruit or liquor-soaked spongecake may also be added for flavour and texture.

When thickening a dessert cream with gelatin, it is important to use the correct amount of gelatin. If not enough gelatin is used or it is not incorporated completely, the cream will not become firm enough to unmould. If too much gelatin is used, the cream will be tough and rubbery. The recipes given here use sheet gelatin, although an equal amount by weight of granulated gelatin can be substituted. Refer to Chapter 27, Principles of the Bakeshop, for information on using gelatin.

● **Bavarian cream** a sweet dessert mixture made by thickening custard sauce with gelatin and then folding in whipped cream; the final product is poured into a mould and chilled until firm

BASIC PROCEDURE FOR PREPARING BAVARIAN CREAMS

1. Prepare a custard sauce of the desired flavour.

2. While the custard sauce is still quite warm, stir in softened gelatin. Make sure the gelatin is completely incorporated.

3. Chill the custard until almost thickened, then fold in the whipped cream.

4. Pour the Bavarian into a mould or charlotte form. Chill until set.

Approximate values per 90 g serving:	
Calories	169
Total fat	12 g
Saturated fat	7 g
Cholesterol	144 mg
Sodium	28.5 mg
Total carbohydrates	12 g
Protein	3 g

Charlotte, Sweet Charlotte

The original charlotte was created during the 18th century and named for the wife of King George III of England. It consisted of an apple compote baked in a round mould lined with toast slices. A few decades later, the great French chef Carême adopted the name but altered the concept in response to a kitchen disaster. When preparing a grand banquet for King Louis XVIII, he found that his gelatin supply was insufficient for the Bavarian creams he was making, so Carême steadied the sides of his sagging desserts with ladyfingers. The result became known as charlotte russe, probably due to the reigning fad for anything Russian. A fancier version, known as charlotte royale, is made with pinwheels or layers of spongecake and jam instead of ladyfingers. The filling for either should be a classic Bavarian cream.

Charlotte Bavarian.

Bavarian Cream (Crème Bavaroise)

Yield: 1.5 L (1-1/2 qt.)

Egg yolks	8	8
Sugar	150 g	5-1/2 oz.
Milk	500 mL	16 fl. oz.
Vanilla or flavouring	TT	TT
Gelatin sheets, softened	9	9
Cream, 35%	400 mL	14 fl. oz.

1. Lightly spray the bottom of moulds with pan release spray.
2. Prepare a Vanilla Custard Sauce using the yolks, sugar, milk and vanilla. Remove from the saucepan when it reaches 80°C–85°C (175°F–180°F).
3. Add softened, squeezed gelatin sheets to the hot custard. Chill until thick, but do not allow the custard to set.
4. Whip the cream until stiff and fold it into the chilled and thickened custard. Fill the moulds with the Bavarian cream. Chill until completely set, approximately 2 hours.
5. Unmould onto a serving dish. Garnish the top with fruit and whipped cream as desired.

NOTE: Gelatin may separate in the freezer, so quick chilling is not recommended. Products made with gelatin keep well for 1–2 days but stiffen with age.

VARIATION: CHARLOTTE—Line a 1- to 1.5-L (1- to 1-1/2-qt.) charlotte mould with Ladyfingers (Recipe 31.23) before filling with layers of fruit and Bavarian. Invert onto a serving platter when firm and garnish with whipped cream.

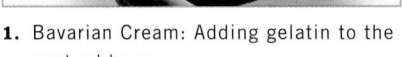

1. Bavarian Cream: Adding gelatin to the custard base.

2. Folding in the whipped cream.

Chiffon

A chiffon is similar to a Bavarian except that whipped egg whites instead of whipped cream are folded into the thickened base. The base may be a custard or a fruit mixture thickened with cornstarch. Although a chiffon may be moulded like a Bavarian, it is most often used as a pie or tart filling.

BASIC PROCEDURE FOR PREPARING CHIFFONS

1. Prepare the base, which is usually a custard or a fruit mixture thickened with cornstarch.
2. Add gelatin to the warm base.
3. Fold in whipped egg whites.
4. Pour into a mould or pie shell and chill.

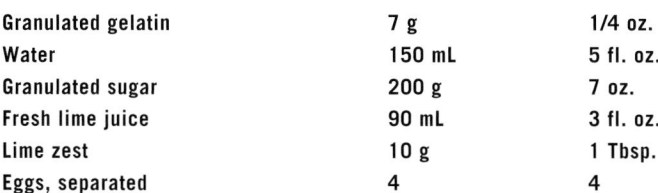

 ## Lime Chiffon

Yield: 1 25-cm (10-in.) pie or 8 servings

Granulated gelatin	7 g	1/4 oz.
Water	150 mL	5 fl. oz.
Granulated sugar	200 g	7 oz.
Fresh lime juice	90 mL	3 fl. oz.
Lime zest	10 g	1 Tbsp.
Eggs, separated	4	4

1. Soften the gelatin in 30 mL (1 fl. oz.) of the water.

2. Combine 120 g (4 oz.) of the sugar, the remaining water, lime juice, zest and egg yolks in a bowl over a pan of simmering water.

3. Whisk the egg-and-lime mixture together vigorously until it begins to thicken. Add the softened gelatin and continue whipping until very thick and foamy.

4. Remove from the heat, cover and refrigerate until cool and as thick as whipping cream.

5. Meanwhile, whip the egg whites to soft peaks. Whip in the remaining sugar and continue whipping until stiff but not dry.

6. Fold the meringue into the egg-and-lime mixture. Pour into a prepared pie crust or serving dishes and chill for several hours, until firm.

VARIATIONS: LEMON CHIFFON—Substitute lemon juice and lemon zest for the lime juice and zest.

ORANGE CHIFFON—Substitute orange juice for the lime juice and for 120 mL (4 fl. oz.) of the water. Substitute orange zest for the lime zest. Reduce the amount of sugar in the egg yolk mixture to 30 g (1 oz.).

Lime Chiffon

RECIPE 32.8

Approximate values per serving:	
Calories	139
Total fat	2.5 g
Saturated fat	1 g
Cholesterol	10 mg
Sodium	35 mg
Total carbohydrates	26 g
Protein	4 g

● **mousse** a soft, creamy or puréed food product, either sweet or savoury, lightened by adding whipped cream, beaten egg whites or both

Mousse

The term **mousse** applies to an assortment of dessert creams not easily classified elsewhere. A mousse is similar to a Bavarian or chiffon in that it is lightened with whipped cream, whipped egg whites or both. A mousse is generally softer than these other products, however, and usually too soft to mould. A small amount of gelatin may be added to stabilize the mousse, but too much will toughen it.

A mousse may be served alone as a dessert or used as a filling in cakes or pastry items. Sweet mousses may be based on a custard sauce, melted chocolate or puréed fruit. Savoury mousses are discussed in Chapter 20, Charcuterie.

BASIC PROCEDURE FOR PREPARING MOUSSES

1. Prepare the base, which is usually a custard sauce, melted chocolate or puréed fruit.

2. If gelatin is used, soften it first, then dissolve it in the warm base.

3. Fold in whipped egg whites, if used. If the base is slightly warm when the egg whites are added their proteins will coagulate, making the mousse firmer and more stable.

4. Allow the mixture to cool completely, then fold in whipped cream, if used.

NOTE: The egg whites are folded in before any whipped cream. Although the egg whites may deflate somewhat during folding, if the cream is added first, it may become overwhipped when the egg whites are added, creating a grainy or coarse product.

Convenience Products

Commercially prepared powders and mixes can be used to make a wide assortment of puddings, custards, mousses, gelatin desserts and creams. Although these mixes are not recommended for fine dining facilities, pastry cooks in institutions such as schools and hospitals base much of their dessert preparation on them. The advantages are speed, cost, quality control and the ability to use semiskilled assistants. Packaged mixes are simply prepared according to the directions provided by the manufacturer, then portioned for service. The pastry cook can often improve on the final product by adding whipped cream, fruit or an appropriate garnish. As with other convenience products, quality varies from merely adequate to very good. Sample and experiment with several brands to select the best for your operation.

Andreas Schwarzer

Andreas worked in pastry shops and bakeries in Germany before coming to Canada. He has won several medals for his pastries and showpieces, and he has worked on banquets for such celebrities as Clint Eastwood, Arnold Schwarzenegger, Margaret Thatcher and Prince Philip.

RECIPE 32.9

Approximate values per 75 g serving:	
Calories	288
Total fat	27 g
Saturated fat	16 g
Cholesterol	136 mg
Sodium	19 mg
Total carbohydrates	15 g
Protein	4.4 g

APPLYING THE BASICS   **RECIPE 32.9**

Classic Chocolate Mousse

SAIT POLYTECHNIC, CALGARY, AB
School of Hospitality and Tourism
Pastry Chef Andreas Schwarzer

Yield: 1.3 kg (3 lb.)

Couverture (see page 701)	425 g	15 oz.
Cream, 35%	600 mL	20 fl. oz.
Egg yolks	140 g	5 oz.
Granulated sugar	125 g	4-1/2 oz.
Water	40 mL	1-1/2 fl. oz.

1. Melt the couverture in a doubleboiler to not more than 40°C (104°F).
2. Whip the cream to soft peaks, being careful not to overwhip.
3. In a bowl, start mixing the yolks on slow speed.
4. At the same time, make the syrup by mixing the sugar and water and bringing to a boil—125°C (256°F).
5. Add the syrup in a steady stream to the egg yolks while mixing at a medium speed.
6. Add the melted couverture to the cool, whipped egg yolk mixture.
7. Fold in the whipped cream, carefully.

NOTE: The temperature of the sugar syrup will determine the thickness of the mousse. If you like a softer chocolate mousse, cook the syrup to only 115°C (240°F). A good couverture (a fine grade of chocolate with a high cocoa butter content) gives the mousse a pure chocolate taste, which chocolate lovers will appreciate. Coating compound will not give as rich and tasteful a chocolate mousse. The mousse will be soft and weaker in flavour.

SAFETY ALERT

Egg Products in Uncooked Mousses

Pasteurized egg products are recommended for most mousse formulas, because mousses require no further cooking. One exception is Italian meringue; the hot sugar syrup cooks the egg whites to a temperature that makes them safe for consumption.

FROZEN DESSERTS

Frozen desserts include ice cream and gelato and desserts assembled with ice cream such as baked Alaska, bombes and parfaits. Frozen fruit purées, known as sorbets and sherbets, are also included in this category. Still-frozen desserts, known as *semifreddi*, are made from custards or mousses that are frozen without churning.

When making any frozen mixture, remember that cold dulls flavours. Although perfect at room temperature, flavours seem weaker when the mixture is cold. Thus, it may be necessary to oversweeten or overflavour creams or custards that will be frozen for service. Although liquors and liqueurs are common flavouring ingredients, alcohol drastically lowers a liquid mixture's freezing point. Too much alcohol as well as too much sugar will prevent the mixture from freezing; thus, any liqueurs or liquors and sugar must be used in moderation.

Ice Cream and Gelato

Ice cream and gelato are custards that are churned during freezing. They can be flavoured with a seemingly endless variety of fruits, nuts, extracts, liqueurs and the like. **Gelato** is an Italian-style ice cream. It is denser than American-style products because less air is incorporated during churning.

● **gelato** an Italian-style ice cream that is denser than North American–style ice cream

The Canadian Food Inspection Agency requires that products labelled "ice cream" contain not less than 10% milk fat and 20% milk solids, and have no more than 50% **overrun**. "Ice milk" refers to products that do not meet the standards for ice cream. Low-fat products made without cream or egg yolks are also available for the health-conscious. Frozen yogurt uses yogurt as its base. Although touted as a nutritious substitute for ice cream, frozen yogurt may have whole milk or cream added for richness and smoothness.

One hallmark of good ice cream and gelato is smoothness. The ice crystals that would normally form during freezing can be avoided by constant stirring or churning. Churning, usually accomplished mechanically, also incorporates air into the product. The air causes the mixture to expand. Gelato has little incorporated air. Good-quality ice creams and sorbets have enough air to make them light; inferior products often contain overrun. The difference becomes obvious when equal volumes are weighed.

Many food service operations use ice cream makers that have internal freezing units to chill the mixture while churning it. Most commercial machines are suitable for churning either ice cream or sorbet. Follow the manufacturer's directions for using and cleaning any ice cream maker.

● **overrun** the amount of air churned into an ice cream

BASIC PROCEDURE FOR PREPARING ICE CREAMS

1. Place the milk and/or cream in a heavy saucepan. If a vanilla bean is being used, it may be added at this time.
2. Whisk the egg yolks and sugar together in a mixing bowl.
3. Bring the liquid just to a boil. Temper the egg mixture with approximately one-third of the hot liquid.
4. Pour the tempered eggs into the remaining hot liquid and return the mixture to the heat.
5. Cook, stirring constantly, until warm (84°C/183°F).
6. Remove the cooked custard sauce from the hot saucepan immediately. If left in the hot saucepan, it will overcook. Flavourings may be added at this time.
7. Cool the cooked custard sauce over an ice bath. Store covered and refrigerated until ready to process.
8. Process according to the machine manufacturer's directions.

SAFETY ALERT
Ice Cream

It is important to exercise extra care when preparing ice cream products because ice cream contains several potentially hazardous foods, such as cream, milk and eggs. Ice cream freezers have many grooves and crevices where bacteria can hide and grow. Always take apart and clean your ice cream maker after each use, and sanitize all pieces according to the manufacturer's directions. Never store frozen ice cream products in a container that held raw or unprocessed custard without first cleaning and sanitizing the container. And, of course, wash your hands thoroughly and wear gloves when working with ice cream products.

APPLYING THE BASICS   RECIPE 32.10

Ice Cream Base

Yield: 2.5 L (2-1/2 qt.)

Whole milk	1.5 L	1-1/2 qt.
Cream, 35%	500 mL	1 pt.
Vanilla bean (optional)	1	1
Egg yolks	325 g	16
Granulated sugar	600 g	20 oz.

continued

Mise en place for Ice Cream Base

1. Combine the milk and cream in a heavy saucepan and bring to a boil. Add the split and scraped vanilla bean, if desired.

2. Whisk the egg yolks and sugar together in a mixing bowl.

3. Temper the eggs with one-third of the hot milk. Return the egg mixture to the saucepan.

4. Cook over medium heat until slightly thickened. Pour through a fine mesh strainer into a clean bowl.

5. Chill the cooked custard sauce completely before processing.

6. Allow the finished ice cream to ripen overnight in the freezer to fully develop the flavours and texture.

VARIATIONS: CHOCOLATE—Add approximately 200 g (7 oz.) of finely chopped bittersweet chocolate per litre (quart) of ice cream base. Add the chocolate to the hot mixture after it is strained. Stir until completely melted.

NUTMEG—Add 5 to 10 g (2-1/2 to 5 tsp.) dry ground nutmeg depending on intensity of flavour desired (e.g., use less nutmeg if a cinnamon-nutmeg version using 10 g/5 tsp. cinnamon is preferred).

CAPPUCCINO—Steep the hot milk and cream with the vanilla bean and 2-3 cinnamon sticks. After the ice cream base is made, stir in 30 mL (2 Tbsp.) coffee extract.

BRANDIED CHERRY—Drain the liquid from 1 500-g (16-oz.) can of tart, pitted cherries. Soak the cherries in 50 mL (2 fl. oz.) brandy. Prepare the ice cream base as directed, omitting the vanilla bean. Add the brandy-soaked cherries to the cooled custard before processing.

RECIPE 32.10

Approximate values per 85 mL serving:	
Calories	209
Total fat	11 g
Saturated fat	6 g
Cholesterol	175 mg
Sodium	37 mg
Total carbohydrates	24 g
Protein	4 g

● **sherbet and sorbet** a frozen mixture of fruit juice or fruit purée that may contain milk and/or egg yolks for creaminess

Sherbets/Sorbets and Granité

Sherbet and **sorbet** (Fr.) are frozen mixtures of fruit juice or fruit purée. Sherbet may contain milk and/or egg yolks for creaminess.

Sherbet or sorbet can be prepared in a wide variety of fruit, herb and some vegetable flavours; it is often flavoured with an alcoholic beverage. It is served as a first course, a palate refresher between courses or a dessert. Sherbets with milk content tend to be richer, so are generally reserved for dessert. The French style of sorbet contains no milk or egg yolks.

For wine sorbets, use 1 L (1 qt.) each wine and base mixture adjusted with water to 15° Baumé and add 50 g (2 oz.) Italian meringue. For liqueur sorbets, use 250 mL (8 fl. oz.) liqueur to 1 L (1 qt.) base and adjust to 16° Baumé. Add 50 g (2 oz.) Italian meringue.

Granité is still or churn frozen and has a grainy texture. The flavoured syrup has a density of 14° Baumé. It usually functions as a palate cleanser.

Lemon Sorbet

APPLYING THE BASICS		RECIPE 32.11

Sorbet

Yield: Approximately 2 kg (4-1/2 lb.)

Water	400 mL	16 fl. oz.
Sugar	400 g	1 lb.
Glucose	80 g	3 oz.
Juice or purée	1 L	32 fl. oz.
Lemon juice	30 mL	1 fl. oz.
Water	as needed	as needed

continued

1. Boil water, sugar and glucose for 2 minutes. Cool. It should be approximately 30° Baumé (base mixture).

2. Add fruit juice or purée and lemon juice and enough water to adjust the density to 17° Baumé. Strain.

3. Pour the syrup into an ice cream machine, filling it half full, and churn freeze for approximately 7–10 minutes or until set.

RECIPE 32.11

Approximate values per 60 g serving:	
Calories	31
Total fat	0 g
Saturated fat	0 g
Cholesterol	0 mg
Sodium	1 mg
Total carbohydrates	18 g
Protein	0 g

Serving Suggestions for Ice Creams and Sorbets

Ice creams and sorbets are usually served by the scoop, often in cookie cones. Or they can be served as **sundaes**. More formal presentations include **baked Alaska**, **bombes**, **coupes** and **parfaits**.

Still-Frozen Desserts

Still-frozen desserts (It. *semifreddi*) are made with frozen mousse, custard or cream. Layers of spongecake and/or fruit may be added for flavour and texture. Because these mixtures are frozen without churning, air must be incorporated by folding in relatively large amounts of whipped cream or meringue. The air helps keep the mixture smooth and prevents it from becoming too hard. Still-frozen desserts develop ice crystals quicker than do churned products, so they tend to have a shorter shelf life than ice creams or sorbets.

Still-frozen products include frozen soufflés, **marquises**, mousses and **neapolitans**. No gelatin is used for a still-frozen dessert.

DESSERT SAUCES

Pastries and desserts are often accompanied by sweet sauces. Dessert sauces provide flavour and texture and enhance plate presentation. Vanilla Custard Sauce (Recipe 32.1) is the principal dessert sauce. It can be flavoured and coloured with chocolate, coffee extract, liquor or fruit compound as desired. Other dessert sauces include fruit purées, caramel sauces and chocolate syrups. Techniques for decorating plates with sauces are discussed in Chapter 36, Plate Presentation.

Fruit Purées

Many types of fruit can be puréed for dessert sauces: strawberries, raspberries, blackberries, apricots, mangoes and papayas are popular choices. They produce thick sauces with strong flavours and colours. Fresh or individually quick frozen (IQF) fruits are recommended.

Puréed fruit sauces, known as **coulis**, are uncooked. Fruit sauce generally denotes a cooked product. Cooking thickens sauces by reduction and allows the starch thickener to gelatinize. Fruit sauces cooked and thickened with waxy maize or modified starches tend to have a better shine than cornstarch achieves. Glucose contributes to a better consistency, particularly for coulis. They can also be sweetened with granulated sugar or a sugar syrup. The amount of sweetener will vary depending upon the fruit's natural sweetness.

● **sundae** a great and gooey concoction of ice cream, sauces (hot fudge, marshmallow and caramel, for example), toppings (nuts, candies and fresh fruit to name a few) and whipped cream

● **baked Alaska** ice cream set on a layer of spongecake and encased in meringue, then baked until the meringue is warm and golden

● **bombe** two or more flavours of ice cream, or ice cream and sherbet, shaped in a spherical mould; each flavour is a separate layer that forms the shell for the next flavour

● **coupe** another name for an ice cream sundae, especially one served with a fruit topping

● **parfait** ice cream served in a long, slender glass with alternating layers of topping or sauce

● **semifreddi** also known as still-frozen desserts; items made with frozen mousse, custard or cream into which large amounts of whipped cream or meringue are folded in order to incorporate air; layers of spongecake and/or fruits may be added for flavour and texture; semifreddi include frozen soufflés, marquises, mousses and neapolitans

● **marquise** a frozen mousse-like dessert, usually chocolate

● **neopolitan** a three-layered loaf or cake of ice cream; each layer is a different colour and flavour, such as chocolate, vanilla and strawberry

● **coulis** a sauce made from a purée of fruits or vegetables

Raspberry Coulis

RECIPE 32.12

Approximate values per 25 mL serving:	
Calories	61
Total fat	0 g
Saturated fat	0 g
Cholesterol	0 mg
Sodium	0 mg
Total carbohydrates	15 g
Protein	0 g

APPLYING THE BASICS	RECIPE 32.12

Raspberry Coulis

Yield: 750 mL (25 fl. oz.)

Raspberries, fresh or IQF	750 g	1 lb. 10 oz.
Granulated sugar	375 g	12 oz.
Lemon juice	20 mL	1-1/2 fl. oz.

1. Purée the berries and strain through a fine etâmine.
2. Stir in the sugar and lemon juice. Adjust the flavour with additional sugar if necessary.

NOTE: A small amount of modified cornstarch may be blended in to make a thicker coulis. If the coulis is too thick, thin with simple syrup.

Caramel Sauce

Caramel sauce is a mixture of caramelized sugar and heavy cream. A liqueur or citrus juice may be used for added flavour. Review the material on caramelizing sugar in Chapter 27, Principles of the Bakeshop, before making caramel sauce.

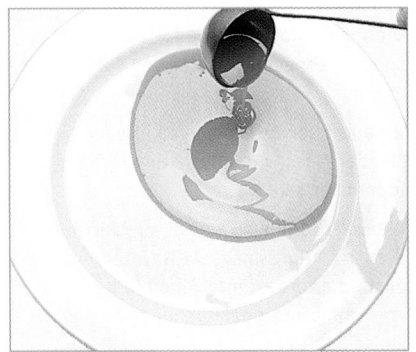

Caramel Sauce

RECIPE 32.13

Approximate values per 25 mL serving:	
Calories	129
Total fat	6.9 g
Saturated fat	4.3 g
Cholesterol	24 mg
Sodium	6 mg
Total carbohydrates	17 g
Protein	0.4 g

APPLYING THE BASICS	RECIPE 32.13

Caramel Sauce

Yield: 750 mL (25 fl. oz.)

Granulated sugar	500 g	1 lb. 2 oz.
Lemon juice	15 mL	1/2 fl. oz.
Water	125 mL	4 fl. oz.
Cream, 35%, room temperature	500 mL	16 fl. oz.
Unsalted butter, cut into pieces	40 g	1 oz.

1. Combine the sugar, lemon juice and water in a large, heavy saucepan. Stir to moisten the sugar completely. Place the saucepan on the stove top over high heat and bring to a boil. Brush down the sides of the pan with water to remove any sugar granules.
2. Do not stir the sugar. Continue boiling until the sugar caramelizes, turning a dark golden brown and producing a rich aroma.
3. Remove the saucepan from the heat. Gradually add the cream. Be extremely careful, as the hot caramel may splatter. Whisk in the cream to blend.
4. Add the pieces of butter. Stir until the butter melts completely. If necessary, return the sauce to the stove to reheat enough to melt the butter.
5. Strain the sauce and cool completely at room temperature. The sauce may be stored for several weeks under refrigeration. Stir before using.

VARIATION: SESAME CARAMEL SAUCE—Add 25 g (5 Tbsp.) sesame seeds at the end of Step 2 and/or add toasted sesame oil to taste with the butter in Step 4.

Chocolate Syrup

Chocolate syrup or sauce can be prepared by adding finely chopped chocolate to warm Vanilla Custard Sauce (Recipe 32.1). A darker syrup can also be made with unsweetened chocolate or cocoa powder. Fudge-type sauces are essentially variations on ganache, discussed in Chapter 31, Cakes and Frostings.

Dark Chocolate Sauce

APPLYING THE BASICS		RECIPE 32.14

Dark Chocolate Sauce

Yield: 750 mL (25 fl. oz.)

Cocoa powder	75 g	3 oz.
Water	450 mL	16 fl. oz.
Chocolate, dark, fine chopped	375 g	12 oz.
Unsalted butter	75 g	3 oz.

1. Mix the cocoa powder with just enough water to make a smooth paste.
2. Bring the remaining water to a boil in a small, heavy saucepan. Immediately add the cocoa paste, whisking until smooth.
3. Pour over the fine-chopped chocolate and bring back to a simmer, stirring constantly, then remove from the heat.
4. Stir the butter into the warm cocoa mixture. Serve warm or at room temperature.

NOTE: The consistency of the sauce can be adjusted with either simple syrup or glucose.

RECIPE 32.14

Approximate values per 25 mL serving:	
Calories	88
Total fat	9 g
Saturated fat	5.4 g
Cholesterol	5.5 mg
Sodium	2 mg
Total carbohydrates	5 g
Protein	1.8 g

ASSEMBLING DESSERTS

As noted previously, many pastries and other desserts are assembled from the baked doughs discussed in Chapter 30, Pies, Pastries and Cookies; the cakes, icings and glazes discussed in Chapter 31, Cakes and Frostings; and the creams, custards and other products discussed in this chapter. Many of these desserts are classic presentations requiring the precise arrangement of specific components. Formulas for some of these desserts are found at the end of the chapters in this part. But once you begin to master the basic skills presented in these chapters, you can use your creativity, taste and judgment to combine these components into a wide selection of new, unique and tempting desserts.

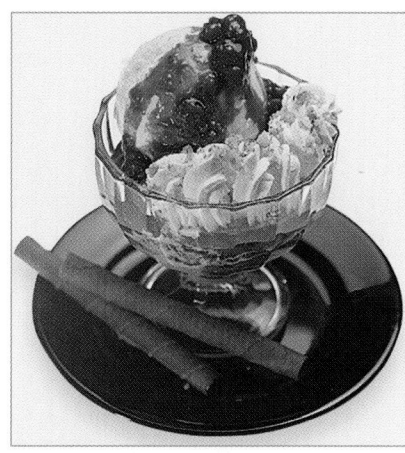

Sundae or coupe with raspberry coulis, Chantilly cream and nuts.

Assembled pastries and other desserts generally consist of three principal components: the base, the filling and the garnish. The base is the dough, crust or cake product that provides structure and forms the foundation for the final product. The filling refers to whatever is used to add flavour, texture and body to the final product. The garnish is any glaze, fruit, sauce or accompaniment used to complete the dish.

BASIC GUIDELINES FOR ASSEMBLING DESSERTS

1. There should be a proper blend of complementary and contrasting flavours. For example, pears, red wine and blue cheese go well together, as do chocolate and raspberries. Do not combine flavours simply for the sake of originality, however.

2. There should be a proper blend of complementary and contrasting textures. For example, crisp puff pastry, soft pastry cream and tender strawberries are combined for a strawberry napoleon.

3. There should be a proper blend of complementary and contrasting colours. For example, a garnish of red raspberries and green mint looks great.

4. Garnishes should not be overly fussy or garish.

5. The base should be strong enough to hold the filling and garnish without collapsing, yet thin or tender enough to cut easily with a fork.

6. The filling or garnish may cause the base to become soft or even soggy. This may or may not be desirable. If you want a crisp base, assemble the product very close to service. If you want this softening to occur, assemble the product in advance of service.

7. Consider the various storage and keeping qualities of the individual components. It may be best to assemble or finish some products at service time.

8. The final construction should not be so elaborate or fragile that it cannot be portioned or served easily or attractively.

9. Consider whether the product would be better prepared as individual portions or as one large item. This may depend on the desired plate presentation and the ease and speed with which a large product can be cut and portioned for service.

Plating Desserts

There are four different ways to plate and present desserts:

1. The dessert by itself.
2. The dessert with fruit, sugar or chocolate garnish.
3. The dessert and sauce painting.
4. The complex presentation: two or more desserts on one plate. One or more sauces, garnishes or both may also be included.

Conclusion

If pastry doughs are the backbone of dessert preparations, then custards, creams, mousses and the like are the heart. The skills and techniques presented in this chapter are essential to successful pastry production. Many of these skills, such as whipping cream or preparing custards, will be useful in other areas of the kitchen as well. Once you have mastered these skills as well as those discussed in Chapter 30, Pies, Pastries and Cookies, and Chapter 31, Cakes and Frostings, you will be able to prepare a wide variety of tempting desserts.

Questions for Discussion

1. Eggs and dairy products are susceptible to bacterial contamination. What precautions should be taken to avoid food-borne illnesses when preparing custards?
2. Explain why pastry cream should be boiled and why custard sauce should not be boiled.
3. Identify three desserts that are based on a baked custard.
4. Compare a classically prepared Bavarian, chiffon, mousse and soufflé. How are they similar? How are they different?
5. Describe the procedure for making a typical still-frozen dessert. What is the purpose of including whipped cream or whipped egg whites?
6. Explain three ways in which sweet sauces can be used in preparing or presenting a dessert.

Additional Custard, Cream, Frozen Dessert and Dessert Sauce Formulas

RECIPE 32.15

Crème Brûlée

SAIT POLYTECHNIC, CALGARY, AB
Pastry Chef Ian Bragoli

Yield: 12 ramekins; 100 mL (3-1/2 fl. oz.)

Cream, 35%	1 L	32 fl. oz.
Sugar	150 g	5 oz.
Vanilla bean, split, scraped	1	1
Egg yolks	240 g	8 oz.
Sugar, for topping	120 g	4 oz.

1. Preheat oven to 165°C (325°F).
2. Place cream, half of the sugar and the vanilla bean in a medium saucepan. Bring to a simmer, whisk, remove from heat, cover and let steep for 15 minutes.
3. Combine egg yolks and remaining sugar in a bowl and whisk until smooth.
4. Uncover cream and reheat to a simmer.
5. Temper the yolk mixture gradually with the cream. Strain the custard through a fine mesh.
6. Place ramekins into a hotel pan and divide the custard between them.
7. Fill the bottom of the hotel pan with hot water to halfway up the sides of the ramekins, cover loosely with foil and bake for 35–50 minutes until the custards are set around the edge and soft in the centre (about the size of a penny).
8. Remove carefully from the water bath and cool custards completely.
9. Sprinkle each custard with 10 g (2 tsp.) of sugar and torch the surface to heat sugar to a deep golden brown. Refrigerate and serve within 1 hour.

Ian Bragoli

Born in Montreal, Ian trained at L'Institut de Tourisme et d'Hôtellerie du Québec. He apprenticed at the Montreal Casino, where he developed a passion for fine-dining desserts. He then held a number of positions, including nine years as part of the pastry team at Victoria's Fairmont Empress Hotel, where he prepared thousands of pastries for the hotel's famous afternoon tea service. After a brief stint with a national pastry ingredients company, Ian enthusiastically took on the challenge of teaching at SAIT.

RECIPE 32.15

Approximate values per serving:	
Calories	434
Total fat	36 g
Saturated fat	20 g
Cholesterol	347 mg
Sodium	39 mg
Total carbohydrates	25 g
Protein	5 g

RECIPE 32.16

Chocolate and Cinnamon Pots de Crème

COSTCO, OTTAWA, ON
Executive Pastry Chef Pierre Jean St-Pierre

Yield: 10 120-mL (4-fl.-oz.) servings

Milk	250 mL	9 fl. oz.
Cream, 35%	750 mL	26 fl. oz.
Granulated sugar	110 g	4 oz.
Cinnamon sticks	6	6
Vanilla bean, scraped	1	1
Egg yolks	170 g	8
Dark chocolate, chopped	140 g	5 oz.
Cocoa powder	30 g	1 oz.

1. Heat the milk, cream, sugar, cinnamon sticks and vanilla bean to a boil.
2. Whisk the egg yolks together, temper with some hot cream and then strain over the chocolate and cocoa powder. Stir until smooth.

Pierre Jean St-Pierre

Pierre is a graduate of both George Brown College and SAIT. He began his career in pastries at Jasper Park Lodge and has since gone on to work at the Ritz-Carlton, Buckhead (Atlanta, Georgia), the Ritz-Carlton, Huntington (Pasadena, California) and the Ritz-Carlton, New Orleans. Previously he was the Executive Pastry Chef at the Fairmont, Washington, DC. Highlights of his career include a gold medal finish at the 1996 Grand Salon Culinaire, in Vancouver, and the Grand Prize in the 1999 Southern Pastry Classic in Atlanta, Georgia. He now works as a buyer for Costco.

continued

RECIPE 32.16

Approximate values per 120 mL serving:	
Calories	549
Total fat	49 g
Saturated fat	28 g
Cholesterol	195 mg
Sodium	401 mg
Total carbohydrates	26.5 g
Protein	9.5 g

3. Pour into ramekins. Pass a torch over top to remove any air bubbles. Place the ramekins in a hotel pan and add enough hot water to reach halfway up the sides of the ramekins.

4. Bake at 150°C (300°F) until custards are almost set in the centre, approximately 30–40 minutes. Remove from the water bath and refrigerate until thoroughly chilled. Serve garnished with whipped cream and chocolate shavings.

Bread Pudding with Sauce Anglaise

RECIPE 32.17

Approximate values per serving:	
Calories	619
Total fat	28 g
Saturated fat	16 g
Cholesterol	216 mg
Sodium	196 mg
Total carbohydrates	81 g
Protein	9.8 g

RECIPE 32.17

Bread Pudding with Sauce Anglaise

Yield: 20 servings

Method: Baked custard

Raisins	250 g	8 oz.
Brandy	125 mL	4 fl. oz.
Unsalted butter, melted	60 g	2 oz.
White bread, day-old	720 g	24 oz.
Cream, 18%	2 L	2 qt.
Eggs	6	6
Sugar	800 g	1 lb. 10 oz.
Vanilla extract	30 mL	1 fl. oz.
Crème Anglaise (Recipe 32.1)	as needed	as needed

1. Combine the raisins and brandy in a saucepan and heat to a simmer. Cover and remove from heat.

2. Coat a 5-cm (2-in.) deep hotel pan with the butter.

3. Tear the bread into chunks and place in a large bowl. Pour the cream over the bread and set aside to soak the bread.

4. Beat the eggs and sugar until thick and smooth. Add the vanilla and raisin-brandy mixture and combine.

5. Gently fold the egg mixture into the bread mixture to blend. Pour into the hotel pan and bake at 180°C (350°F) for approximately 45 minutes or until browned and the custard is almost set.

6. Serve warm with 30–45 mL (2–3 Tbsp.) Crème Anglaise, which may be flavoured with liquor if desired.

Chocolate, Cherry and Croissant Pudding

VANCOUVER COMMUNITY COLLEGE, VANCOUVER, BC
Chef Instructor Glen O'Flaherty

Yield: 20–25 portions

Whipping cream	1 L	32 fl. oz.
Dark couverture, chopped into small pieces	1 kg	2 lb.
Eggs	450 g	8
Granulated sugar	180 g	6 oz.
Vanilla Sauce (recipe follows)	700 mL	25 fl. oz.
Croissants, day old, 1.5-cm (1/2-in.) cubes	20 pieces	20 pieces
Bing cherries, pitted	1.14 kg	40 oz.
Apricot glaze, melted	200 g	7 oz.

1. Scald cream and pour over chocolate chunks. Continue mixing until a smooth ganache is made.

2. Whisk together eggs, sugar and Vanilla Sauce, then mix with chocolate ganache. Add croissant cubes and cherries and continue folding until all ingredients come together.

3. Press into a buttered hotel pan 5 cm (2 in.) deep and bake in an oven at 150°C (300°F) in a bain marie for approximately 75 minutes.

4. Cool. Brush with apricot glaze. Refrigerate to completely set.

5. Cut and serve as required.

Vanilla Sauce

Whipping cream	500 mL	16 fl. oz.
Vanilla bean	1/2	1/2
Egg yolks	125 g	6
Granulated sugar	80 g	3 oz.

1. In a saucepan, combine cream and vanilla bean and bring to a boil.

2. Combine egg yolks and sugar, mixing thoroughly. When the cream has come to a boil, add a small amount to the egg mixture (temper).

3. Combine egg and sugar mixture with hot cream and cook until thickened.

4. Remove from the heat and set aside to cool.

Glen O'Flaherty

Glen was a 15-year-old dishwasher when the chef at the Pillar and Post Restaurant Inn called him in and offered him the position of prep cook! Over the following three-and-a-half years, Glen apprenticed and attended culinary classes at both George Brown College, in Toronto, and Niagara College, in Niagara Falls. He held positions at the Muskoka Sands Inn in Ontario and at two hotels in Nova Scotia before moving to BC and becoming Executive Chef at the Newlands Golf and Country Club. Currently, he is a Chef Instructor at Vancouver Community College.

RECIPE 32.18

Approximate values per serving:	
Calories	771
Total fat	69 g
Saturated fat	41 g
Cholesterol	313 mg
Sodium	125 mg
Total carbohydrates	45 g
Protein	12 g

Vanilla Sauce—Approximate values per 25 mL serving:	
Calories	203
Total fat	19.5 g
Saturated fat	12 g
Cholesterol	146 mg
Sodium	21 mg
Total carbohydrates	6 g
Protein	2 g

Cherry Clafouti

Yield: 1 25-cm (10-in.) flan

Butter	15 g	1 Tbsp.
Dark cherries, pitted, fresh		
or canned	500 g	1 lb.
Eggs	4	4
Milk	350 mL	12 fl. oz.
Sugar	60 g	2 oz.
Vanilla extract	5 mL	1 tsp.
Pastry flour	60 g	2 oz.
Icing sugar	as needed	as needed

Cherry Clafouti

continued

RECIPE 32.19

Approximate values per 1/16 of pan:	
Calories	243
Total fat	7.4 g
Saturated fat	3.2 g
Cholesterol	135 mg
Sodium	92 mg
Total carbohydrates	37 g
Protein	7.9 g

1. Butter the flan. Drain the cherries and pat dry with paper towels. Arrange them evenly on the bottom of the flan. Do not use a springform or removable-bottom pan.
2. Make the custard by whisking together the eggs, milk, sugar, vanilla and flour until there are no lumps.
3. Pour the custard over the cherries and bake at 160°C (325°F) for 60–90 minutes. The custard should be lightly browned and firm to the touch when done.
4. Dust with icing sugar and serve warm.

VARIATION: Other stone fruits, such as plums or peaches, can be used in this recipe.

Albert Liu

Albert began his career as a pâtissier at the Four Seasons Hotel in Vancouver, worked as an Executive Pastry Chef in the Bahamas, and then became the Executive Pastry Chef at the Palliser Hotel in Calgary. Currently he is a Pastry Chef Instructor at SAIT in Calgary.

RECIPE 32.20

Baked Cheesecake

SAIT POLYTECHNIC, CALGARY, AB
School of Hospitality and Tourism
Pastry Chef Instructor Albert Liu

Yield: 2 22-cm (9-in.) cakes

Cream cheese, softened	1350 g	3 lb.
Granulated sugar	425 g	18 oz.
Cornstarch	60 g	2 oz.
Bread flour	60 g	2 oz.
Eggs	400 mL	7
Sour cream	500 mL	18 fl. oz.
Milk (2%)	400 mL	14 fl. oz.
Vanilla extract	10 mL	2 tsp.
Lemon zest and juice	1	1
Short Paste crusts, 22-cm (9-in.), baked (Recipe 30.2)	2	2

1. Cream the cheese and sugar at low speed until smooth. Incorporate the cornstarch and flour.
2. Blend in the eggs slowly, then add the sour cream, milk, vanilla and lemon zest and juice.
3. Divide the batter into 2 cake pans sprayed with pan release.
4. Bake in a hot water bath at 180°C (350°F) for 1 hour. Remove from oven and water bath and let rest 1 minute.
5. Turn cakes out onto oiled, plastic-wrapped cake boards.
6. Place baked Short Paste crusts on cake and flip back onto a clean cake board. Cool.

RECIPE 32.20

Approximate values per 1/12 cake:	
Calories	410
Total fat	28 g
Saturated fat	17 g
Cholesterol	150 mg
Sodium	207 mg
Total carbohydrates	32 g
Protein	8 g

RECIPE 32.21

Crème Chiboust

CONA SUCRE D'ART, Nanaimo, BC
Pâtissier Confiseur George Wagner

Yield: 2 L (2 qt.)

Egg yolks	200 g	7 oz.
Sugar	150 g	5 oz.
Lemon juice	150 mL	5 fl. oz.
Cream, 35%	300 mL	10 fl. oz.
Cornstarch	10 g	1 Tbsp.
Gelatin leaves (soaked in cold water)	6	6
Egg whites	350 g	12-1/4 oz.
Sugar	250 g	8 oz.

1. Whisk egg yolks, 150 g (5 oz.) of sugar and lemon juice in a doubleboiler until warm and foamy.

2. Blend cream and cornstarch in a heavy-bottomed saucepan.

3. Add yolk mixture to cream mixture and bring to a boil for 4 minutes.

4. Squeeze excess moisture from gelatin leaves and add to hot mixture. Stir until dissolved.

5. Whip egg whites and remaining sugar to form soft meringue.

6. Gently fold meringue into hot sauce.

George Wagner

Born and raised in France, George was apprenticed at the age of 14 and later specialized in pâtisserie. He came to Canada in 1966 and was Pastry Instructor at Malaspina University-College (now Vancouver Island University) from 1978 to 1994. George now owns his own school, where he instructs students in the art of sugar and chocolate confections.

RECIPE 32.21

Approximate values per 125 mL serving:	
Calories	220
Total fat	10.5 g
Saturated fat	5 g
Cholesterol	187 mg
Sodium	48 mg
Total carbohydrates	27 g
Protein	5 g

RECIPE 32.22

Raspberry Mousse

Yield: 1 L (1 qt.)

Gelatin	6 sheets	6 sheets
Raspberries, puréed	350 g	12 oz.
Granulated sugar	100 g	3 oz.
Raspberry brandy	30 mL	2 Tbsp.
Cream, 35%	250 mL	8 fl. oz.

1. Soften the gelatin in ice water and set aside.

2. Place the raspberry purée, sugar and brandy in a nonreactive saucepan and warm just to dissolve the sugar. Remove from the heat and strain through a fine etâmine.

3. Add the softened gelatin, stirring until it is dissolved. Chill the mixture until thick but not set.

4. Whip the cream to soft peaks and fold it into the raspberry mixture.

RECIPE 32.22

Approximate values per 100 mL serving:	
Calories	158
Total fat	9 g
Saturated fat	5.5 g
Cholesterol	32 mg
Sodium	20 mg
Total carbohydrates	19 g
Protein	2 g

Michéal McFadden, CCC

Michéal has been helping turn out new chefs at Humber College for the past 18 years. Prior to that, he was the Executive Pastry Chef at the former Harbour Castle Hilton. His love of cooking emerged early in life, as he helped his mother around the house in his native Ireland.

RECIPE 32.23

Approximate values per 30 g serving:	
Calories	72
Total fat	6 g
Saturated fat	3 g
Cholesterol	21 mg
Sodium	11 mg
Total carbohydrates	5 g
Protein	1 g

RECIPE 32.23

Black Currant Mousse

HRT ALLIANCE, HUMBER COLLEGE, TORONTO, ON
Chef Michéal McFadden, CCC

Yield: 1.5 L (1-1/2 qt.)

Granulated sugar	300 g	10-1/2 oz.
Water	100 mL	3-1/2 fl. oz.
Egg whites	110 g	5
Icing sugar	50 g	2 oz.
Gelatin leaves	6	6
Black currants, puréed	500 g	17-1/2 oz.
Cream, 35%	1 L	35 fl. oz.
Whipped cream	TT	TT
Black currants, fresh	TT	TT

1. Bring granulated sugar and water to 118°C (244°F) to make a syrup.
2. Whip egg whites and icing sugar together to make a soft meringue.
3. Pour hot syrup into the meringue and whip until cold.
4. Soak gelatin in ice water until soft and then dissolve over a warm-water bath.
5. Add gelatin to the black currant purée and mix well.
6. Whip cream until it forms soft peaks.
7. Add black currant mixture to the cool meringue.
8. Fold in cream and transfer to a stainless steel bowl.
9. Cover with plastic wrap and refrigerate for approximately 2 hours.
10. Using a piping bag with a #10 star tip, pipe mixture into glasses and decorate with whipped cream and fresh black currants.

Vinod Varshey

After graduating with a Bachelor of Science degree, Vinod's interests in the food and hospitality industry led him to join the Institute of Hotel Management. He completed his apprenticeship in New Delhi and in Germany, where he worked as a Commis Pâtissier. After coming to Canada, he worked at prestigious hotels and lodges before joining the culinary team at NAIT, where he is Culinary Coordinator. Vinod is the Team Manager for Culinary Team Alberta.

RECIPE 32.24

Duo of Nougat and Mango Mousses with Warm Pitted Cherry Compote

NORTHERN ALBERTA INSTITUTE OF TECHNOLOGY, EDMONTON, AB
THE HOKANSON CENTRE FOR CULINARY ARTS
Culinary Coordinator Vinod Varshey

Yield: 8–10 ramekins

Nougat Mousse

Gelatin leaves	3	3
Egg yolks	2	2
Sugar	40 g	1-1/2 oz.
Milk	200 mL	7 fl. oz.
Hazelnut paste	50 g	1-3/4 oz.
Cream, 35%, whipped	200 mL	7 fl. oz.

1. Soak the gelatin leaves in cold water.
2. Whisk the yolks and sugar over doubleboiler until ribbon stage.
3. Boil the milk and add to the sugar mixture.
4. Cook until slightly thickened.

continued

5. Add the softened gelatin to the hot sauce and stir until dissolved.

6. Mix in hazelnut paste.

7. Cool to body temperature and fold in the whipped cream.

8. Pour into ramekin half full. Chill.

Mango Mousse

Gelatin leaves	4	4
Egg yolks	2	2
Sugar	50 g	1-3/4 oz.
Milk	200 mL	7 fl. oz.
Mango purée	50 mL	1-3/4 fl. oz.
Mango, small dice	10 g	1 Tbsp.
Cream, 35%, whipped	200 mL	7 fl. oz.

1. Soak the gelatin leaves in cold water.

2. Whisk the yolks and sugar over doubleboiler until ribbon stage.

3. Boil the milk and add to the sugar mixture.

4. Cook until slightly thickened.

5. Add the softened gelatin and stir until dissolved.

6. Mix in mango purée and pieces.

7. Cool to body temperature and fold in the whipped cream.

8. Pour on top of Nougat Mousse to fill ramekin.

Cherry Compote

Cherry juice	80 mL	3 fl. oz.
Sherry	100 mL	3-1/2 fl. oz.
Lemon juice and zest	1	1
Orange juice and zest	1	1
Sugar	90 g	3 oz.
Freshly ground black peppercorn	10 g	4 tsp.
Cinnamon stick	1	1
Dark, pitted cherries	500 g	1 lb. 2 oz.
Whipped cream, fresh fruits and raspberry–passion fruit coulis to taste and for presentation		

Combine all ingredients except the cherries in a saucepan. Bring to a boil. Add the cherries. Reduce to desired consistency. Remove from heat and serve warm.

Assembly:

Unmould the mousse and place in the centre of a plate. Place the cherry compote on the side of the plate. Drizzle the mousse with coulis and garnish with whipped cream and fresh fruit.

Nougat Mousse—Approximate values per serving:	
Calories	131
Total fat	12 g
Saturated fat	5 g
Cholesterol	68.5 mg
Sodium	12 mg
Total carbohydrates	6 g
Protein	2 g

Mango Mousse—Approximate values per serving:	
Calories	116
Total fat	9 g
Saturated fat	5 g
Cholesterol	72 mg
Sodium	20 mg
Total carbohydrates	8 g
Protein	2 g

Cherry Compote—Approximate values per serving:	
Calories	100
Total fat	1 g
Saturated fat	0 g
Cholesterol	0 mg
Sodium	2 mg
Total carbohydrates	22 g
Protein	1 g

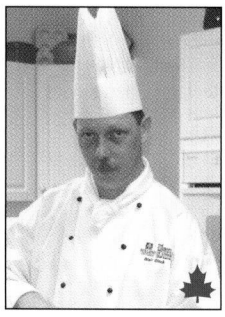

Blair Zinck

Blair has 31 years' experience in cooking, gained from working in various positions that include Executive Chef with Rodd's Hotels and Resorts and Chef Instructor for the Culinary Institute of Canada. Blair has been teaching at Holland College for the past 13 years, and his classes include the basic cooking program at the Summerside Centre, the apprentice-cooking program for the Department of Education, and the Culinary Arts program at the Culinary Institute of Canada.

RECIPE 32.25

Approximate values per serving:	
Calories	596
Total fat	22 g
Saturated fat	12 g
Cholesterol	84 mg
Sodium	457 mg
Total carbohydrates	94 g
Protein	7 g

RECIPE 32.26

Iced Soufflé— Approximate values per serving:	
Calories	189
Total fat	12 g
Saturated fat	7 g
Cholesterol	88 mg
Sodium	16 mg
Total carbohydrates	19 g
Protein	1.5 g

Liquid Filling— Approximate values per serving:	
Calories	36
Total fat	0 g
Saturated fat	0 g
Cholesterol	0 mg
Sodium	1 mg
Total carbohydrates	9 g
Protein	0 g

RECIPE 32.25

Blueberry Buckle

CULINARY INSTITUTE OF CANADA, CHARLOTTETOWN, PEI
Chef Blair Zinck

Yield: 6–8 servings

Sugar	170 g	6 oz.
Butter	60 g	2 oz.
Egg	1	1
Milk	125 mL	4 fl. oz.
Flour, all purpose	200 g	2 cups
Baking powder	6 g	2 tsp.
Salt	3 g	1/2 tsp.
Blueberries	250 g	2 cups
Flour	15 g	2 Tbsp.
Pan grease	as needed	as needed
Topping:		
Sugar	125 g	4 oz.
Flour, all purpose	75 g	1/3 cup
Cinnamon	3 g	2 tsp.
Butter	60 g	2 oz.

1. Cream sugar, butter and egg together until light.

2. Mix in milk and add flour, baking powder and salt.

3. Lightly dust blueberries with 15 g (2 Tbsp.) flour and fold into batter.

4. Spread batter into a 20-cm (8-in.) square baking dish brushed with pan grease.

5. Rub topping ingredients together and spread on top of batter.

6. Bake in a 175°C (350°F) oven until cake is done, approximately 35–45 minutes.

7. Serve warm with Crème Chantilly (Recipe 32.6) or ice cream.

RECIPE 32.26

Strawberry Iced Soufflé

NORTHERN ALBERTA INSTITUTE OF TECHNOLOGY,
THE HOKANSON CENTRE FOR CULINARY ARTS
EDMONTON, AB
Pastry Chef Clayton Folkers

**Yield: 110 servings as part of a composite plate or
25 individual soufflés**

Iced Soufflé

Egg yolks	440 g	20
Granulated sugar	675 g	24 oz.
Cream, 35%, whipped	3 L	3 qt.
White chocolate, melted	450 g	1 lb.
Strawberry purée, fresh	900 g	2 lb.
Strawberry concentrate	75 g	2-1/2 oz.
Liquid Filling (recipe follows)		

continued

1. Warm the egg yolks and sugar to 40°C (105°F), stirring constantly, and whip until cold. Fold in one-third of the whipping cream and mix together with the chocolate.
2. Fold in the remaining cream, strawberry purée and concentrate.
3. Fill cone-shaped moulds three-quarters full. Insert a second cone to form an interior cavity and freeze.
4. When frozen, remove the interior cone and fill the centre with Liquid Filling. Return to freezer.
5. Seal the bottom with the remaining soufflé filling and freeze.

Liquid Filling

Water	500 mL	16 fl. oz.
Granulated sugar	850 g	1 lb. 14 oz.
Corn syrup	70 g	2.5 oz.
Passion fruit concentrate	180 g	6 oz.
Grand Marnier	60 mL	2 fl. oz.

1. Combine the water, sugar and corn syrup. Bring to a boil.
2. Cool the liquid, then add the concentrate and Grand Marnier.

Clayton Folkers
Born in Canada, Clayton earned his Commercial Cooking Diploma from the Northern Alberta Institute of Technology and was invited by the Four Seasons Hotel to extend his work-study program with them into a permanent position. To enhance his pastry skills, Clayton attended the Provinciaal Hoger Instituut PIVA in Antwerp, Belgium, where he completed a graduate program while gaining experience as a Production Chef in a prominent pastry shop. Back in Edmonton, he honed his pastry skills at the Four Seasons Hotel, at La Favorite Pastry Shop, which he co-owned, and at the Shaw Conference Centre, where he was Pastry Chef since 1989. He joined NAIT in 2007.

RECIPE 32.27

Truffles

CHOCOLATERIE BERNARD CALLEBAUT®, CALGARY, AB
Owner Bernard Callebaut

Yield: 1.5 kg (3 lb.)

Semi-sweet or bittersweet chocolate	1 kg	2-1/4 lb.
Whipping cream	500 mL	16 fl. oz.
Flavouring compound (optional)	TT	TT
Cocoa powder and icing sugar	as needed	as needed

1. Melt chocolate over a doubleboiler to 48°C–55°C (118°F–130°F).
2. Warm the whipping cream to 50°C (120°F).
3. Add the melted chocolate to the cream while stirring.
4. Add flavouring if you wish, such as orange or coffee.
5. Pour mixture in baking trays and spread to 2.5 cm (1 in.) thick.
6. Cool in fridge until the mixture is hard.
7. Scoop small pieces with a melon baller or coffee spoon.
8. Roll pieces by hand into round or oval shapes.
9. Roll truffles in cocoa powder, icing sugar or anything light.

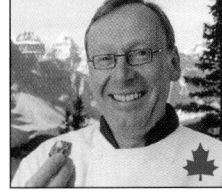

Bernard Callebaut
Bernard arrived in Canada from Belgium in 1982. His family owned the Callebaut Chocolate Factory in Wieze, Belgium, from 1911 until 1980, when it was purchased by the Suchard Toblerone group. Having achieved renown as an innovative creator of unique fillings for chocolates, Bernard manufactures what is considered to be the highest quality line of Canadian-made chocolates and chocolate-related products, including sauces, bars and ice cream.

RECIPE 32.27

Approximate values per 15 g serving:	
Calories	67
Total fat	5 g
Saturated fat	3 g
Cholesterol	8 mg
Sodium	3 mg
Total carbohydrates	7 g
Protein	0.5 g

Shaping chocolate truffles

Chocolate Truffles

Chocolate truffles are suprisingly simple to make. Fine chocolate is melted with cream and perhaps butter. The mixture is flavoured as desired with liqueur, extracts, fruit or coffee and allowed to harden. Once firm, the ganache is scooped into balls and rolled in cocoa powder, confectioner's sugar or melted chocolate. The classic French truffle is a small, irregularly shaped ball of bitter-sweet chocolate dusted with cocoa powder. Canadians, however, seem to prefer larger candies, coated with melted chocolate and decorated with nuts or additional chocolate. Recipe 32.27 can be prepared in either style.

RECIPE 32.28

Chocolate Butter Cream

CHOCOLATERIE BERNARD CALLEBAUT®, CALGARY, AB
Owner Bernard Callebaut

Semi-sweet chocolate	350 g	12 oz.
Unsalted butter, cubed	225 g	8 oz.

1. Melt chocolate over a doubleboiler.
2. Place butter in a metal bowl and let warm to room temperature.
3. Add the chocolate, which is approximately 30°C (86°F), and mix quickly with a whisk or the chocolate will solidify on the cold metal and the filling will become chunky.
4. Fill a pastry bag and pipe shapes on waxed paper.
5. Put in cooler for 30 minutes so the mixture can harden.

RECIPE 32.28

Approximate values per 15 g serving:	
Calories	86
Total fat	7.5 g
Saturated fat	5 g
Cholesterol	15 mg
Sodium	2 mg
Total carbohydrates	6 g
Protein	0.5 g

RECIPE 32.29

Candied Citrus Soufflé

SAIT POLYTECHNIC, CALGARY, AB
Chef Instructor Ian Cowley

Yield: 4 servings

Butter, melted	as needed	as needed
Sugar	as needed	as needed
Crème Pâtissière (recipe follows)	60 g	2 oz.
Egg yolks	6	6
Candied lemon, lime and orange zest	120 g	4 oz.
Egg whites	6	6
Icing sugar	as needed	as needed
Crème Anglaise (recipe follows)	as needed	as needed

1. Preheat oven to 200°C (400°F).
2. Brush the insides of the soufflé moulds with melted butter and coat with sugar.
3. Combine the pastry cream, egg yolks and candied zests.
4. Beat the egg whites to stiff peaks and fold into the pastry cream mixture.
5. Fill the moulds to the brim and bake for 12 minutes.
6. Dust tops of soufflés with icing sugar and serve Crème Anglaise on the side.

Ian Cowley

A graduate of SAIT's Professional Cooking program, Ian spent five years in Europe at Claridges in London and the Michelin-starred Le Petit Nice in Marseille, Troisgros in Roanne and L'Espérance de Marc Meneau in Vézelay. Sous-chef positions followed at the Four Seasons in Vancouver and Boston. His front-of-house management experience includes Hastings House, the Fairmont Chateau Lake Louise and the Fairmont Orchid.

continued

Crème Pâtissière

Cornstarch	25 g	8 tsp.
Milk	170 mL	6 fl. oz.
Egg yolks	4	4
Vanilla extract	5 mL	1 tsp.
Sugar	30 g	1 oz.
Butter	10 g	2 tsp.

1. Stir cornstarch into half of the milk until smooth.
2. Beat the egg yolks and combine with the remaining milk, vanilla and sugar in a saucepan. Bring to a boil.
3. Temper the two mixtures together, stirring constantly. Stir over low heat until the mixture thickens.
4. Remove pan from heat, stir in butter, cover and cool.

Crème Anglaise

Egg yolks	4	4
Sugar	80 g	3 oz.
Milk, 3.25%	375 mL	12 fl. oz.
Vanilla bean, split	1/2	1/2

1. Combine all ingredients and heat to just a boil.
2. Continue heating and stirring until thickened (coats the back of a spoon).
3. Cover and cool.

Candied Citrus Soufflé—
Approximate values per serving:

Calories	566
Total fat	29 g
Saturated fat	13 g
Cholesterol	646 mg
Sodium	211 mg
Total carbohydrates	59 g
Protein	17 g

Crème Pâtissière—
Approximate values per serving:

Calories	163
Total fat	9 g
Saturated fat	3.8 g
Cholesterol	213 mg
Sodium	42 mg
Total carbohydrates	16 g
Protein	4.3 g

Crème Anglaise—
Approximate values per serving:

Calories	195
Total fat	8 g
Saturated fat	3.4 g
Cholesterol	212 mg
Sodium	47 mg
Total carbohydrates	24 g
Protein	5.8 g

33 Breakfast and Brunch

> I had an excellent repast—the best repast possible—which consisted simply of boiled eggs and bread and butter. It was the quality of these simple ingredients that made the occasion memorable. The eggs were so good that I am ashamed to say how many of them I consumed. . . . It might seem that an egg which has succeeded in being fresh has done all that can be reasonably expected of it.
>
> —Henry James, American novelist (1843–1916)

Breakfast (from the expression "to break fast")

gives you the energy to get going after a night's sleep. It should provide at least one-fourth of the calories and nutrients consumed during the day.

Breakfast is often an on-the-go, rushed experience, hence the popularity of breakfast sandwiches, jumbo muffins and take-out coffee. **Brunch**, on the other hand, is a leisurely experience, combining breakfast and lunch into a social occasion. Brunch menus include traditional breakfast foods along with almost anything else, including alcoholic beverages and desserts.

Food service operations offer a variety of breakfast options to appeal to a wide range of consumers. Hotels and resorts may offer a complimentary continental-style breakfast of coffee, juice and rolls, a full-service à la carte dining room, a room service menu and a casual snack bar. From simple to elaborate, buffet-style breakfasts have become common in hotels on a daily basis. The Sunday and holiday brunch buffet is an institution for celebrations and special occasions.

The foods served at breakfast include many of the foods served at other times during the day. A diner's perception of the proper breakfast depends on his or her cultural, ethnic, economic and geographic background as well as sleep patterns and work schedule.

Although few people sit down to a breakfast including multiple components even occasionally, most food service operations find it necessary to offer a range of items in order to meet their customers' expectations.

This chapter discusses cooking methods used for eggs, breakfast meats, pancakes and other griddlecakes and cereals. Other foods typically served at breakfast are noted on the following pages and discussed in more detail elsewhere in this text.

BEVERAGES

Few breakfast menus would be complete without offering coffee, tea or other hot beverages. Whether it's black tea in St. Petersburg or café au lait in Paris, cinnamon-spiced chocolate in Mexico City or a cup of fresh-brewed Colombian in Vancouver, people everywhere enjoy starting their day with hot, aromatic, caffeine-laced beverages. Coffees and teas are identified and discussed in Chapter 35, Beverages.

FRUITS

Fruits are popular breakfast foods because they are light and flavourful, require little or no preparation and provide vitamins and natural sugars for energy. Citrus fruits, melons, berries and bananas are breakfast staples. Fruits, whether raw or cooked, fresh, canned, frozen or dried, can be served alone, with a topping of cream or yogurt or as a garnish for cereals, pancakes or French toast. Fresh seasonal fruits can be served at the beginning of the meal, as garnish with the main course, as a light brunch dessert or as juice. Fruits are identified and discussed in Chapter 26, Fruits.

BREADS

Breads, usually rich, sweet and loaded with fruits and nuts, are a staple of many breakfast menus. Sticky pecan buns, glazed cinnamon rolls, fruit-filled muffins, Danish pastries and buttery croissants, which seem too rich later in the day, somehow seem perfect in the morning. Even a humble slice of toast rounds out a breakfast menu, especially if topped with butter and jam. Breakfast breads can be served as an accompaniment to eggs, fruits or other dishes or they can be the complete meal. Several recipes for breakfast breads and pastries are included in Chapter 28, Quick Breads; Chapter 29, Yeast Breads; and Chapter 30, Pies, Pastries and Cookies.

POTATOES

Potatoes are often served at breakfast and brunch, usually sautéed or pan-fried as hash browns, cottage fries or lyonnaise. Potatoes may be served as a side dish or incorporated into hash or egg casseroles. Unlike breads or fruits, which may be the entire breakfast, potatoes are usually just part of a hearty breakfast, especially one that includes meat and eggs. Potatoes are identified and discussed in Chapter 23, Potatoes, Grains and Pasta.

DAIRY PRODUCTS

Some dairy products are indispensable at breakfast: milk, cream and yogurt, for example. Other dairy products such as crème fraîche and cheese are less commonly served but just as appropriate. Like milk, yogurt and crème fraîche can be used to top cold cereals or fruit. Cheeses are commonly used in omelettes and frittatas, blintzes and Danish pastries; an assortment of mild cheeses offered with crusty bread and fresh fruit is a delicious breakfast or brunch alternative. Dairy products are identified and discussed in Chapter 8, Eggs and Dairy Products.

EGGS

No other breakfast food is as popular or as versatile as the egg. Eggs can be cooked by almost any method and served with a wide array of seasonings, accompaniments and garnishes. Whatever cooking method is selected, be sure to prepare the eggs carefully. Overcooked eggs and those cooked at too high a temperature will be tough and rubbery. Eggs are described in Chapter 8, Eggs and Dairy Products.

The following cooking methods are those most often used for egg-based breakfast dishes. They include dry-heat cooking methods (baking, sautéing and pan-frying) and moist-heat cooking methods (in-shell cooking and poaching).

Dry-Heat Cooking Methods

Baking

Shirred Eggs

Baked eggs, also referred to as shirred eggs, are normally prepared in individual ramekins or baking dishes. The ramekins can be lined or partially filled with ingredients such as bread, ham, creamed spinach or artichokes. The eggs are often

APPLYING THE BASICS   **RECIPE 33.4**

Shrimp and Avocado Omelette

Yield: 1 serving

Shrimp, peeled, deveined and cut into pieces	50 g	2 oz.
Green onion, sliced	10 g	1 Tbsp.
Clarified butter	30 g	1 oz.
Eggs	3	3
Salt and pepper	TT	TT
Avocado, peeled and diced	1/4	1/4
Cilantro, chopped	5 g	2 tsp.

1. Sauté the shrimp and onion in half of the butter for 1 minute. Remove from the heat and set aside.
2. Heat an omelette pan and add the remaining butter.
3. Whisk the eggs together in a small bowl, season with salt and pepper and pour into the omelette pan.
4. Stir the eggs as they cook. Stop when they begin to set. Lift the edges as the omelette cooks to allow the raw eggs to run underneath.
5. When the eggs are nearly set, add the shrimp filling, avocado and cilantro. Fold one-third of the eggs over and roll the omelette onto a plate.

Approximate values per serving:

Calories	576
Total fat	48 g
Saturated fat	21 g
Cholesterol	788 mg
Sodium	753 mg
Total carbohydrates	7 g
Protein	30 g

1. Shrimp and Avocado Omelette: Lifting the edge of the eggs to allow them to cook evenly.

2. Adding the filling to the eggs.

3. Folding the eggs.

4. Rolling the omelette onto the plate. Ensure the seam is on the bottom.

Frittatas

Frittatas are essentially open-faced omelettes of Spanish-Italian origin. They may be cooked in small pans as individual portions or in large pans, then cut into wedges for service. A relatively large amount of hearty ingredients are mixed directly into the eggs. The eggs are first cooked on the stove top, then the pan is transferred to an oven or placed under a salamander or broiler to finish cooking.

BASIC PROCEDURE FOR PREPARING FRITTATAS

1. Fully cook any meats and blanch or otherwise prepare any vegetables that will be incorporated into the frittata.
2. Heat a sauté pan and add clarified butter.
3. Whisk the eggs, flavourings and any other ingredients together; pour into the pan.

Caring for the Omelette Pan

Unless your pan is nonstick, you will need to treat it before you use it.

Wash it well, then dry it and cover the bottom with salt and oil. Heat the oil until it is very hot. Remove it from the heat. Pour away the oil and wipe the pan well with paper towels while the pan is still hot. Do not wash the inside after use, but wipe it with a paper towel. This will season the pan and prevent the omelette from sticking.

continued

4. Stir gently until the eggs start to set. Gently lift the cooked eggs at the edge of the frittata so that the raw eggs can run underneath. Continue cooking until the eggs are almost set.

5. Place the pan in a hot oven or underneath a salamander or broiler to finish cooking and lightly brown the top.

6. Slide the finished frittata out of the pan onto a serving platter.

Tex-Mex Frittata

RECIPE 33.5

Approximate values per serving:	
Calories	1045
Total fat	71 g
Saturated fat	39 g
Cholesterol	764 mg
Sodium	646 mg
Total carbohydrates	12 g
Protein	89 g

APPLYING THE BASICS   **RECIPE 33.5**

Tex-Mex Frittata

Yield: 1 serving

Chicken breast, 120 g (4 oz.), boneless, skinless	1	1
Garlic, chopped	5 g	1 tsp.
Cumin	1 g	1/4 tsp.
Salt and pepper	TT	TT
Mushrooms, sliced	50 g	2 oz.
Unsalted butter	50 g	3 Tbsp.
Jalapeño, seeded, minced	3 g	1 tsp.
Red bell pepper, roasted, seeded, peeled, julienne	60 g	2 oz.
Green onions, sliced	30 g	1 oz.
Cilantro	5 g	2 tsp.
Eggs, beaten	2	2
Monterey Jack or cheddar cheese	50 g	2 oz.

1. Rub the chicken breast with the garlic, cumin, salt and pepper. Grill or broil the chicken until done. Allow it to rest briefly, then cut into strips.

2. In a well-seasoned 23-cm (9-in.) sauté pan, sauté the mushrooms in the butter until tender. Add the jalapeño and sauté for 30 seconds. Add the chicken, roasted pepper, green onions and cilantro and sauté until hot.

3. Add the eggs and season with salt and pepper. Cook the mixture, stirring and lifting the eggs to help them cook evenly, until they begin to set.

4. Sprinkle the cheese over the eggs and place under a salamander or broiler to melt the cheese and finish cooking the eggs. Slide the frittata onto a plate or cut into wedges for smaller portions.

Pan-Frying

Pan-fried eggs are commonly referred to as sunny-side-up or over-easy, over-medium or over-hard. These are visibly different products produced with proper timing and technique. Very fresh eggs are best for pan-frying as the yolk holds its shape better and the white spreads less.

Sunny-side-up eggs are not turned during cooking; their yellow yolks remain visible. They should be cooked over medium-low heat long enough to firm the whites and partially firm the yolks—approximately 4 minutes if cooked on a 120°C (250°F) cooking surface.

For "over" eggs, the egg is partially cooked on one side, then gently flipped and cooked on the other side until done. The egg white should be firm and its edges should not be brown. The yolk should never be broken regardless of the degree of doneness. Not only is a broken yolk unattractive, the spilled yolk will coagulate on contact with the hot pan, making it difficult to serve.

For over-easy eggs, the yolk should remain very runny; on a 120°C (250°F) cooking surface, the egg should cook for about 3 minutes on the first side and 2 minutes on the other. Eggs fried over-medium should be cooked slightly longer, until the yolk is partially set. For over-hard eggs, the yolk should be completely cooked.

Most establishments prepare this style of egg on a griddle.

1. Over-Easy Eggs: Pouring the eggs into the sauté pan.

BASIC PROCEDURE FOR PREPARING PAN-FRIED EGGS

1. Select a sauté pan just large enough to accommodate the number of eggs being cooked. (A 20-cm [8-in.] diameter pan is appropriate for up to three eggs.)

2. Add a small amount of clarified butter and heat until the fat just begins to sizzle.

3. Carefully break the eggs into the pan.

4. Continue cooking over medium-low heat until the eggs reach the appropriate degree of firmness. Sunny-side-up eggs are not flipped during cooking; "over" eggs are flipped once during cooking.

5. When done, gently flip the "over" eggs once again so that the first side is up, then gently slide the cooked eggs out of the pan onto the serving plate. Use a lifter to move the eggs. Blot the lifter on a clean towel before placing the eggs on a plate. Serve immediately.

NOTE: Some restaurants prepare fried eggs on a griddle.

2. Flipping the eggs.

3. Sliding the eggs onto a plate for service.

Basted eggs are a variation of sunny-side-up eggs. Basted eggs are cooked over low heat with the hot butter from the pan spooned over them as they cook. Another version of basted eggs is made by adding 5 to 10 mL (1 to 2 tsp.) of water to the sauté pan and then covering the pan. The steam cooks the top of the eggs.

Moist-Heat Cooking Methods

In-Shell Cooking (Simmering)

The difference between soft-boiled eggs (also called soft-cooked) and hard-boiled eggs (also called hard-cooked) is time. Both styles refer to eggs cooked in their shell in hot water. Despite the word "boiled" in their names, eggs cooked in the shell should never be boiled. Boiling toughens eggs and causes discoloration (see Figure 33.1 on the next page). Instead, eggs should be simmered. Soft-boiled eggs are usually simmered for 3 to 5 minutes; hard-boiled eggs may be simmered for as long as 12 to 15 minutes, depending on customer preference and the altitude where you are.

Sometimes it is difficult to remove the shell from very fresh eggs. Eggs that are a few days old are better for cooking in the shell and peeling.

Tips and Techniques

- Cool boiled eggs quickly once the cooking time is up. This rapid cooling helps prevent a green ring from forming around the yolk.
- Handle eggs with care to minimize cracking egg shells before cooking.

Coddling an Egg

To coddle an egg (e.g., to make Caesar salad dressing; see Recipe 25.9), place the shelled egg in a bowl of hot water to heat through but not set the white.

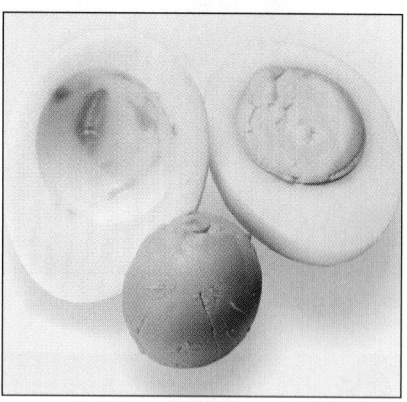

FIGURE 33.1 Properly hard-boiled eggs (top) are uniformly cooked through and gold coloured. A green discoloration covers the yolk when in-shell eggs are overcooked (bottom).

BASIC PROCEDURE FOR PREPARING SOFT-BOILED EGGS

1. Fill a saucepan or stockpot with sufficient water to cover the eggs. Bring the water to a simmer. Add salt.
2. Carefully lower each egg into the simmering water. Simmer uncovered for three to five minutes, depending on the firmness desired and the altitude.
3. Lift each egg out of the water with a slotted spoon or spider. Crack the large end of the shell carefully and serve immediately.

BASIC PROCEDURE FOR PREPARING HARD-BOILED EGGS

1. Follow Steps 1 and 2 for soft-boiled eggs, simmering the eggs for 12 to 15 minutes depending on the altitude and the size of the eggs.
2. Lift each egg out of the water with a slotted spoon or spider and place in an ice bath.
3. When the eggs are cool enough to handle, peel them and use as desired or cover and refrigerate for up to five days.

Poaching

Eggs that are to be poached should always be very fresh. They should also be kept very cold until used. Cold egg whites stay together better when dropped into hot water. Poached eggs should be soft and moist; the whites should be firm enough to encase the yolk completely, but the yolk should still be runny.

Some chefs add salt to the poaching water for flavour; others feel the salt causes the egg whites to separate. To help the egg whites cling together, add 30 mL (2 Tbsp.) of white vinegar per 1 L (1 qt.) of water.

BASIC PROCEDURE FOR PREPARING POACHED EGGS

1. Fill a saucepan or stockpot with at least 7.5 cm (3 in.) of water. Add salt and vinegar if desired. Bring the water to a simmer and hold at a temperature of approximately 90°C (200°F).
2. One at a time, crack the eggs into a small ramekin or cup. If a piece of shell falls into the egg, it can be removed; if the yolk breaks, the egg can be set aside for some other use.
3. Gently slide each egg into the simmering water and cook for three to five minutes.
4. Lift the poached egg out of the water with a slotted spoon. Trim any ragged edges with a paring knife. Serve immediately.

For quantity service, eggs can be poached in advance and held for up to one day. To do so, cook the eggs as described in the Basic Procedure. As each egg is removed from the hot water, set it in a hotel pan filled with ice water. This stops the cooking process. The eggs can be stored in the ice water until needed. For banquet-style service, all of the eggs can be reheated at once by placing the entire pan on the stove top. Or, the eggs can be reheated one or two at a time by placing them in a pan of barely simmering water until they are hot.

APPLYING THE BASICS   RECIPE 33.6

Poached Eggs

Yield: 1 serving

Water	1 L	1 qt.
Salt (optional)	5 g	1 tsp.
Vinegar (optional)	30 mL	2 Tbsp.
Eggs	2	2

1. Bring the water to a simmer; add the salt and vinegar if desired.

2. Crack 1 egg into a cup and carefully add it to the water. Repeat with the other egg.

3. Cook the eggs to the desired doneness, approximately 3–5 minutes. Remove them from the water with a slotted spoon and serve as desired or carefully lower them into ice water and refrigerate for later use.

RECIPE 33.6

Approximate values per serving:	
Calories	140
Total fat	10 g
Saturated fat	3 g
Cholesterol	425 mg
Sodium	280 mg
Total carbohydrates	1 g
Protein	12 g

1. Poached Eggs: Adding eggs to a pot of simmering water.

2. Lowering the eggs into ice water to cool them for future use.

BREAKFAST MEATS

At other meals, meat is typically the principal food, but at breakfast it is usually an accompaniment. Breakfast meats tend to be spicy or highly flavoured. A hearty breakfast menu may include a small beef steak (usually sirloin and often pan-fried) or pork chop. Corned beef, roast beef or roast turkey can be diced or shredded, then sautéed with potatoes and other ingredients for a breakfast hash. Fish, particularly smoked products, are also served at breakfast.

But the most popular breakfast meats are bacon, ham and sausages. They are all discussed in Chapter 20, Charcuterie. Bacon can be cooked on a flat griddle or in a heavy skillet or baked on a sheet pan. Regardless of the method used, the cooked bacon should be drained on absorbent paper towels to remove excess fat. Canadian back bacon is very lean and requires little cooking, although slices are usually sautéed briefly before serving. The round slices may be served like ham and are essential for eggs Benedict. A ham steak is simply a thick slice ideal for breakfast. Fully cooked ham needs only to be heated briefly on a griddle or in a sauté pan before service. The most popular breakfast sausages are made from uncured, uncooked meats. They can be mild to spicy, slightly sweet or strongly seasoned with sage. Recipes for country-style and other sausages are included in Chapter 20. Breakfast sausage is available in bulk, links or preformed patties. Link sausage is often steamed, then browned by sautéing at service time. It should be drained on absorbent paper towels to remove excess fat before service.

GRIDDLECAKES AND FRENCH TOAST
Griddlecakes

Pancakes and waffles are types of griddlecakes or griddle breads. They are usually leavened with baking soda or baking powder and are quickly cooked on a very hot griddle or waffle iron with very little fat. Griddlecakes should be more than just an excuse for eating butter and maple syrup, however. They should have a rich flavour and a light, tender, moist interior.

Pancake and waffle batters may be flavoured with tangy buckwheat flour, flaxseed, fruits, whole grains or nuts. Both pancakes and waffles are usually served with plain or flavoured butter and fruit compote or syrup.

Waffles must be cooked in a special waffle iron that gives the cakes a distinctive gridlike pattern and crisp texture. Electric waffle irons are available with square, round and even heart-shaped moulds. The grids should be seasoned well, then never washed. (Follow the manufacturer's directions for seasoning.) Crispy Belgian waffles are made in a waffle iron with extra deep grids. They are served for breakfast or as a dessert, topped with fresh fruit, whipped cream or ice cream. Waffle batter is richer than pancake batter.

BASIC PROCEDURE FOR PREPARING PANCAKES

1. Prepare the batter.

2. Heat a flat griddle or thick big-bottomed flat pan over moderately high heat. Lightly coat with vegetable oil.

3. Portion the pancake batter onto the hot griddle using a portion scoop, ladle or adjustable batter dispenser. Pour the portioned batter in one spot; it should spread into an even circle. Pour the batter so that no two pancakes will touch after the batter spreads.

4. Cook until bubbles appear on the surface and the bottom of the cake is set and golden brown. Flip the pancake using an offset spatula.

5. Cook the pancake until the second side is golden brown. Avoid flipping the pancake more than once as this causes it to deflate.

Buttermilk Pancakes

APPLYING THE BASICS   RECIPE 33.7

Buttermilk Pancakes

Yield: 24 pancakes

Bread flour	300 g	10 oz.
Pastry flour	150 g	6 oz.
Granulated sugar	60 g	4 Tbsp.
Baking powder	15 g	4 tsp.
Baking soda	8 g	2 tsp.
Salt	5 g	1-1/2 tsp.
Buttermilk	1 L	32 fl. oz.
Unsalted butter, melted	125 g	4 oz.
Eggs, beaten	4	4

continued

1. Sift the flour, sugar, baking powder, baking soda and salt together.

2. Combine the liquid ingredients and add them to the dry ingredients. Mix just until the ingredients are combined. Do not overmix.

3. If the griddle is not well seasoned, coat it lightly with vegetable oil. Once its temperature reaches 190°C (375°F), drop the batter onto it in 60-g (2-oz.) portions using a ladle, portion scoop or batter portioner. If the batter is too thick and does not spread enough, thin with a little water.

4. When bubbles appear on the pancake's surface and the bottom is browned, flip the pancake to finish cooking.

RECIPE 33.7

Approximate values per pancake:	
Calories	145
Total fat	5.7 g
Saturated fat	3.2 g
Cholesterol	44 mg
Sodium	274 mg
Total carbohydrates	19 g
Protein	4.5 g

Crepes and Blintzes

Crepes are thin, delicate, unleavened pancakes. They are made with a very liquid batter cooked in a small, very hot sauté pan. Crepe batter can be flavoured with buckwheat flour, cornmeal or other grains. Crepes are not eaten as is, but are usually filled and garnished with sautéed fruits, scrambled eggs, cheese or vegetables. Crepes can be prepared in advance, then filled and reheated in the oven.

Blintzes are crepes that are cooked on only one side, then filled with cheese, browned in butter and served with sour cream, fruit compote or preserves. A recipe for cheese blintzes is provided at the end of this chapter (Recipe 33.13).

BASIC PROCEDURE FOR PREPARING CREPES

1. Prepare the batter.

2. Heat a well-seasoned crepe pan over moderately high heat. Add a small amount of clarified butter.

3. Ladle a small amount of batter into the pan. Tilt the pan so that the batter spreads to coat the bottom evenly.

4. Cook until the crepe is set and the bottom begins to brown, approximately one minute. Flip the crepe over with a quick flick of the wrist or by lifting it carefully with a spatula.

5. Cook for an additional 30 seconds. Slide the finished crepe from the pan. Crepes can be stacked between layers of parchment paper for storage.

1. Sweet Crepes: Coating the bottom of the pan evenly with the batter.

2. Flipping the crepe. Notice the proper light brown colour.

APPLYING THE BASICS	RECIPE 33.8

Sweet Crepes 🥕

Yield: 30 15-cm (6-in.) crepes

Whole eggs	6	6
Egg yolks	6	6
Water	350 mL	12 fl. oz.
Milk	500 mL	18 fl. oz.
Granulated sugar	175 g	6 oz.
Salt	5 g	1 tsp.
Flour	400 g	14 oz.

Sweet Crepes (serving suggestion)

continued

| Unsalted butter, melted | 150 g | 5 oz. |
| Clarified butter | as needed | as needed |

1. Whisk together all liquid ingredients except the melted butter. Add the sugar, salt and flour; whisk together. Stir in the melted butter. Cover and set aside to rest for at least 1 hour before cooking.

2. Heat a small sauté or crepe pan; brush lightly with clarified butter. Pour in 30 to 45 mL (1 to 1-1/2 fl. oz.) of batter; swirl to coat the bottom of the pan evenly.

3. Cook the crepe until set and light brown, approximately 30 seconds. Flip it over and cook a few seconds longer. Remove from the pan.

4. Cooked crepes may be used immediately or covered and held briefly in a warm oven. Crepes can also be wrapped well in plastic wrap and refrigerated for 2–3 days or frozen for several weeks.

VARIATION: For savoury crepes, reduce sugar to 50 g (1-1/2 oz.), add 5 g (1 tsp.) salt and 10 g (2 tsp.) finely chopped parsley or other herbs.

RECIPE 33.8

Approximate values per crepe:	
Calories	144
Total fat	7 g
Saturated fat	3.5 g
Cholesterol	99.5 mg
Sodium	88 mg
Total carbohydrates	17 g
Protein	4 g

French Toast

Like a pancake, French toast is sautéed on a griddle and served with butter and syrup. Unlike a pancake, French toast begins with slices of day-old bread. (It is known in France as *pain perdu*, meaning "lost bread," probably because it provided a way to use bread that would otherwise have been discarded.) French bread, raisin bread, challah, whole wheat, even stale croissants can be used. The bread is dipped into a batter of eggs, sugar, milk or cream and flavourings, then sautéed in butter. French toast should be served very hot. It may be topped with powdered sugar, fresh fruit, fruit compote or maple syrup as desired.

BASIC PROCEDURE FOR PREPARING FRENCH TOAST

1. Prepare the batter. Store the batter in a hotel pan that is large enough to accommodate the bread slices. Keep the batter refrigerated until ready to use.

2. Slice the bread as desired. Dip each slice of bread into the batter. Allow the bread to absorb the batter through to the centre. Turn the bread so that both sides are coated.

3. Heat a griddle or sauté pan and add clarified butter.

4. Place the batter-dipped bread onto the hot griddle. Cook until the bottom is set and golden brown. The cooking time will be determined by the thickness of the bread.

5. Flip the bread with an offset spatula and cook the toast on the other side. The toast is done when it is not runny in the middle; however, it should not be dry. Remove and serve immediately.

APPLYING THE BASICS

RECIPE 33.9

Cinnamon French Toast

Yield: 6 servings

Eggs, beaten	10	10
Cream, 35%	125 mL	4 fl. oz.
Sugar	75 g	3 oz.
Cinnamon, ground	2 g	1/2 tsp.
Thick-sliced bread such as		
cinnamon, French or brioche	12 slices	12 slices
Unsalted butter	as needed	as needed
Powdered sugar	as needed	as needed

1. Whisk together the eggs, cream, sugar and cinnamon.

2. Place the egg mixture in a shallow pan. Place the slices of bread in the egg mixture and let soak for 2–3 minutes, turning them over after the first minute or so.

3. Cook the slices of French toast in a lightly buttered, preheated sauté pan or griddle set at 180°C (350°F) until well browned. Turn the slices and cook on the second side until done.

4. Cut each slice of bread into 2 triangles if square slices are used.

5. Arrange 4 triangles on each plate and dust with powdered sugar.

VARIATION: Replace the eggs, cream and sugar with a sauce anglaise. The finished product is called "pain perdu" and is soft and rich in texture. Serve with a fruit sauce or compote.

Cinnamon French Toast

RECIPE 33.9

Approximate values per serving:

Calories	438
Total fat	20 g
Saturated fat	10 g
Cholesterol	310 mg
Sodium	487 mg
Total carbohydrates	48 g
Protein	15 g

CEREALS AND GRAINS

Oats, rice, corn and wheat are perhaps the most widely eaten breakfast foods. Processed breakfast cereals are ready-to-eat products made from these grains. Most consumers now think of breakfast cereal as a cold food, but not so long ago only hot grains were breakfast staples. Oatmeal served as a hot porridge is still popular, especially with toppings such as cream, brown sugar, fresh or dried fruit or fruit preserves. Oats and oatmeal, grits and other grains are discussed in Chapter 23, Potatoes, Grains and Pasta.

Ready-to-eat (cold) cereal is usually topped with milk or light cream and sugar. Fresh or dried fruits may be added. Many products are enriched or fortified with vitamins and minerals to compensate for the nutrients lost during processing. Creative cooks can avoid overly sweet, artificially flavoured commercial products by making their own ready-to-eat breakfast cereals such as granola, a toasted blend of whole grains, nuts and dried fruits. The results are less expensive, more nutritious and far more interesting.

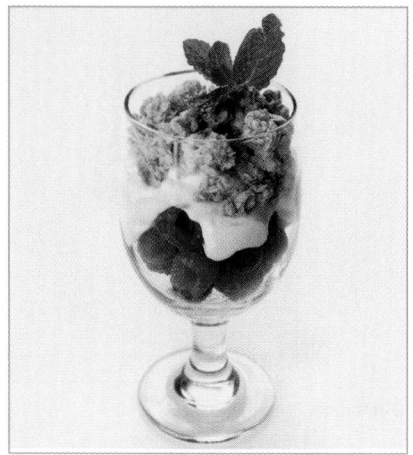

Granola topping berries and yogurt

APPLYING THE BASICS

RECIPE 33.10

Crunchy Granola

Yield: 3 L (12 cups)

Brown sugar	250 g	8 oz.
Water, hot	125 mL	4 fl. oz.
Canola oil	175 mL	6 fl. oz.
Old-fashioned oats	500 g	18 oz.
Wheat germ	125 g	4 oz.
Coconut, shredded	75 g	2-1/2 oz.
Salt (optional)	15 g	1 Tbsp.
Whole wheat flour	60 g	2 oz.
Amaranth flour		
(ancient grain of the Aztecs)	60 g	2 oz.
Unbleached all-purpose flour	60 g	2 oz.
Yellow cornmeal	60 g	2 oz.
Pecans, chopped	125 g	4 oz.

1. Dissolve the brown sugar in the hot water. Add the oil.
2. Combine the dry ingredients in a large bowl. Mix thoroughly by hand.
3. Add the brown-sugar-and-oil mixture to the dry ingredients; toss to combine.
4. Spread out the granola in a thin layer on a sheet pan. Bake at 90°C (200°F) until crisp, approximately 1.5–2 hours. Toss lightly with a metal spatula every 30 minutes.
5. Let the baked granola cool completely at room temperature, then store in an airtight container. Chopped dried fruits, additional nuts or fresh fruits can be added at service time.

RECIPE 33.10

Approximate values per 30 g serving:	
Calories	118
Total fat	7 g
Saturated fat	1 g
Cholesterol	15 mg
Sodium	120 mg
Total carbohydrates	15 g
Protein	3 g

NUTRITION

Most nutritionists agree that you and your customers should start the day with a nutritious breakfast. Depending upon what is eaten, a breakfast can supply a good percentage of the day's proteins, carbohydrates, fats, vitamins and minerals.

From Health Food to Sugar Snack

The century-old, multibillion-dollar-a-year North American breakfast cereal industry, unlike any other in the world, is rooted in health foods. During the 1890s, Dr. John Harvey Kellogg directed a sanitarium in Battle Creek, Michigan. Among the healthful foods prescribed for his patients was his special mixture of whole grains called "granula." John, along with his brother Will, next created and began marketing wheat flakes as a nutritious breakfast food. They were not an immediate success, however; people found a cold breakfast unappealing. Undeterred, Will continued toying with cold cereals, eventually creating flakes made from toasted corn and malt. Thanks to a massive advertising campaign, the American public finally embraced corn flakes and a financial empire was born.

Charles W. Post was a patient of Dr. Kellogg's Battle Creek Sanitarium in 1891. He adopted the principles of healthful eating espoused by the Kellogg brothers and soon opened his own spa, complete with a factory producing his "Post Toasties" and grape nuts. He promoted them as a cure for appendicitis, consumption and malaria.

Soon Battle Creek became a boomtown, home to more than 40 breakfast cereal companies. Unfortunately for the consumer, not all manufacturers—then and now—were as concerned about health as John, Will and C. W. The addition of sugar, sometimes totalling more than half the cereal's weight, makes some of today's breakfast products more sugary than candy bars. Even some of the granola cereals touted as a healthier alternative to other breakfast cereals and snacks contain 20% or more sugar. But at least they no longer claim to cure malaria.

Conclusion

Breakfast is an important meal for consumers and food service operations alike. Breakfast menus may offer a variety of items, including fruits, cereals, eggs, pancakes and cured meats, or they can be devoted to one or two specialty items such as coffee and cinnamon rolls. Whatever is served should be prepared and served with care.

Questions for Discussion

1. Explain the differences between a typical breakfast and a typical brunch. Create a sample menu for each of these meals.
2. Explain the difference between an omelette and a frittata.
3. Describe four different types of fried eggs and explain how each is prepared.
4. What is the difference between a soft-boiled egg and a hard-boiled egg? Why are these eggs simmered instead of boiled?
5. List three types of griddlecakes and explain how they are prepared.
6. What problems might be encountered when preparing French toast with very thick slices of bread? How can you avoid these problems?
7. Should meats be fully cooked before being incorporated into egg dishes such as omelettes and quiches? Explain your answer.

Additional Breakfast and Brunch Recipes

RECIPE 33.11

Waffles

Yield: 20 17-cm (7-in.) waffles

Eggs, large	9	9
Buttermilk	1 L	1 qt.
Bread flour	325 g	12 oz.
Pastry flour	180 g	6 oz.
Baking powder	20 g	5-1/2 tsp.
Baking soda	10 g	3 tsp.
Salt	7 g	1-1/2 tsp.
Butter, softened	325 g	12 oz.

1. Beat eggs and buttermilk together in a mixing bowl with whisk attachment.
2. Combine the dry ingredients, mix and add to the wet mixture.
3. Add the butter to the bowl and mix together until smooth.
4. Reserve mixture in refrigerator if not using immediately. This mixture will hold up for a service period but not overnight.
5. Cook the waffles in a preheated waffle iron according to the manufacturer's instructions. A cooking spray helps to ensure the waffle will release from the iron.
6. Serve hot with a whipped flavoured butter, whipped cream, fresh marinated or stewed fruits or your favourite syrup.

VARIATIONS: NUT WAFFLES—Sprinkle 15 g (2 Tbsp.) chopped nuts on the batter as soon as it is ladled onto the iron.

BLUEBERRY WAFFLES—Scatter 25 g (2 Tbsp.) berries on the batter as soon as it is ladled onto the iron.

Waffles

RECIPE 33.11

Approximate values per waffle:	
Calories	262
Total fat	16 g
Saturated fat	9.2 g
Cholesterol	127 mg
Sodium	562 mg
Total carbohydrates	22 g
Protein	7.3 g

Yogurt Pancakes

Yield: 10–12 pancakes

Eggs, large	4	4
Plain yogurt	250 mL	8 fl. oz.
Water	50 mL	2 fl. oz.
Rice flour	175 g	3/4 cup
Potato starch flour	15 g	1-1/2 Tbsp.
Baking soda	3 g	3/4 tsp.
Salt	2 g	1/2 tsp.

1. Beat eggs until light and lemon coloured.
2. Blend in yogurt and water.
3. Sift dry ingredients together and add to liquid ingredients. Beat until smooth.
4. Cook 50- to 60-mL (1-3/4- to 2-fl.-oz.) portions of batter on a lightly greased griddle. Turn when puffy, bubbly and browned on 1 side. Brown other side.

NOTE: This recipe meets the needs of both celiac sprue and diabetic diets. The pancakes are wonderful with fruit compote and do not taste like a modified diet product. Use for breakfast or as a dessert.

RECIPE 33.12

Approximate values per pancake:	
Calories	101
Total fat	2 g
Saturated fat	0.5 g
Cholesterol	45 mg
Sodium	191 mg
Total carbohydrates	17 g
Protein	4 g

Cheese Blintzes

Cheese Blintzes

Yield: 16 blintzes

Eggs	3	3
Milk	250 mL	8 fl. oz.
Vegetable oil	30 mL	1 fl. oz.
Salt	2 g	1/2 tsp.
Flour	125 g	4 oz.
Clarified butter	as needed	as needed
Ricotta cheese	350 g	12 oz.
Egg yolk	1	1
Salt	1 g	1/4 tsp.
Lemon juice	5 mL	1 tsp.
Vanilla extract	5 mL	1 tsp.
Butter	60 g	2 oz.

1. To make the batter, whisk together the eggs, milk and oil. Add the salt. Stir in the flour and mix until smooth. Allow the batter to rest for 30 minutes.
2. Heat a crepe pan and add a small amount of clarified butter.
3. Add 30 g (1 oz.) of the batter to the pan. Tip the pan so the batter coats the entire surface in a thin layer.
4. Cook the pancake until lightly browned on the bottom. Remove it from the pan and reserve. Do not stack the pancakes.
5. To make the filling, drain the cheese in a conical strainer. Combine the remaining ingredients (except the butter) with the cheese and mix well.
6. To assemble, place a pancake on the work surface with the uncooked side down. Place 30 g (1 oz.) of the filling in the centre of the pancake. Fold the opposite ends in and then roll up to form a small package.
7. Sauté each blintz in butter until hot. Serve with sour cream or fruit compote as desired.

RECIPE 33.13

Approximate values per serving:	
Calories	110
Total fat	7 g
Saturated fat	3.5 g
Cholesterol	65 mg
Sodium	170 mg
Total carbohydrates	7 g
Protein	5 g

RECIPE 33.14

Banana French Toast with Lemon Curd

THE SHERATON HOTEL NEWFOUNDLAND, St. John's, NL
Executive Chef Roary MacPherson, CCC
Yield: 1 serving

Banana Bread, sliced (Recipe 28.9)	2 slices	2 slices
Whole egg, beaten	as needed	as needed
Clarified butter	15 g	1/2 oz.
Lemon Curd (recipe follows)	30 mL	1 fl. oz.
Macedoine of strawberries	30 g	1 oz.
Crème Chantilly (Recipe 32.6)	as needed	as needed
Maple syrup, warm	as needed	as needed

1. Dip slices of Banana Bread quickly in egg. Sauté in butter until golden.
2. Arrange Banana Bread, Lemon Curd and strawberry macedoine attractively on plate. Pipe a rosette of Crème Chantilly.
3. Serve warm maple syrup on the side.

Lemon Curd

Lemons	8	8
Sugar	350 g	12 oz.
Eggs	8	8
Butter	350 g	12 oz.

1. Juice the lemons and strain.
2. Mix sugar and eggs together, then add lemon juice.
3. Cook on a doubleboiler, stirring frequently until very thick.
4. Whisk in butter and cool quickly in an ice bath, strain through a fine sieve.

VARIATION: Zest of 2 lemons can be included.

Roary MacPherson, CCC
The youngest of 14 children, Roary took turns with his brothers and sisters helping out in the kitchen and knew he was hooked while regularly cooking for a table of 16. He received his Journeyman's Red Seal from the Cabot Institute of Technology and his Chef-de-Cuisine designation from the Southern Alberta Institute of Technology. Roary began his career with Fairmont Hotels & Resorts when he secured a position with The Fairmont Newfoundland. He is currently Executive Chef at the Sheraton Hotel Newfoundland.

RECIPE 33.14

Approximate values per serving, including lemon curd and Crème Chantilly:	
Calories	970
Total fat	47 g
Saturated fat	26 g
Cholesterol	419 mg
Sodium	1030 mg
Total carbohydrates	130 g
Protein	17 g

Lemon Curd— Approximate values per 50 mL serving:	
Calories	232
Total fat	16 g
Saturated fat	9.5 g
Cholesterol	124.5 mg
Sodium	171 mg
Total carbohydrates	22 g
Protein	3 g

RECIPE 33.15

Shirred Italian Eggs

HUMBER COLLEGE, Toronto, ON
Professor Francisco Rivera, CCC

Yield: 1 serving

Olive oil	5 mL	1 tsp.
Prosciutto, sliced	15 g	1 slice
Roma tomato, sliced	2	2
Basil, chiffonade	5 g	2 leaves
Salt and pepper	TT	TT
Eggs	2	2
Buffalo mozzarella, sliced	30 g	1 oz.
Half-and-half cream	15 mL	1 Tbsp.
Extra virgin olive oil	5 mL	1 tsp.

Francisco Rivera, CCC
Francisco trained in Toronto, working his way through the ranks and eventually leading culinary brigades in the city as a Chef de Cuisine. Italian cuisine is his passion and he also shares his talents with the students at Humber College. He is a member of the Canadian Federation of Chefs and Cooks (CCFCC) and an active member of the Escoffier Society in Toronto.

continued

RECIPE 33.15

Approximate values per serving:	
Calories	353
Total fat	27 g
Saturated fat	8.7 g
Cholesterol	402 mg
Sodium	628 mg
Total carbohydrates	4.9 g
Protein	23 g

1. Preheat an oval ramekin in a 200°C (400°F) oven.
2. Brush the ramekin with olive oil and lay in the prosciutto, tomato slices and basil chiffonade. Season lightly with salt and pepper.
3. Crack the eggs on top, cover with the mozzarella and add the cream.
4. Bake in hot oven for approximately 15 minutes, remove, drizzle with extra virgin olive oil and serve immediately.

Eggs Benedict

RECIPE 33.16

Approximate values per serving:	
Calories	466
Total fat	27 g
Saturated fat	10.5 g
Cholesterol	462 mg
Sodium	1596 mg
Total carbohydrates	33 g
Protein	23 g

RECIPE 33.16

Eggs Benedict

Yield: 1 serving

English muffin, split	1	1
Canadian back bacon slices, 5 mm (1/4 in.) thick	2	2
Eggs, poached	2	2
Hollandaise Sauce (Recipe 10.13)	100 mL	3 fl. oz.
Truffle slices or black olive halves	2	2

1. Toast the English muffin.
2. Sauté or griddle the bacon slices until hot.
3. Remove eggs from poaching liquid. Drain well and dress.
4. Place the muffins on a plate and top with the bacon slices. Place an egg on each slice of bacon and cover with the Hollandaise Sauce. Gratinée until golden.
5. Garnish each egg with a truffle slice or black olive half and serve.

VARIATIONS: POACHED EGGS SARDOU—poached eggs and creamed spinach on an artichoke bottom with Hollandaise Sauce.

POACHED EGGS PRINCESS STYLE—poached eggs on an English muffin with asparagus tips and Hollandaise Sauce.

Try "Bennys" with smoked salmon slices or crabcakes.

Corned Beef Hash

RECIPE 33.17

Corned Beef Hash

Yield: 5–6 servings
Method: Sautéing

Onion, diced fine	125 g	4 oz.
Vegetable oil	30 mL	2 Tbsp.
Corned beef, cooked and diced fine	500 g	1 lb.
Potatoes, cooked, diced	250 g	8 oz.
Tomato paste	25 g	1 oz.
Tomato concassée	500 g	1 lb.
Parsley, chopped fine	15 g	1/2 oz.
Salt and pepper	TT	TT

1. Sauté onion in oil until clear.
2. Add the corned beef and sauté until meat is heated through.
3. Add potatoes and sauté mixture until it is lightly browned. Stir periodically.
4. Add tomato paste and concassée. Simmer until liquid is reduced by two-thirds.

continued

5. Add chopped parsley and adjust seasoning with salt and pepper.

6. Cool the mixture and refrigerate until needed.

7. To serve, preheat the skillet and lubricate it with a small amount of oil. Place a portion of the hash in the skillet and sauté until lightly browned, stirring constantly.

8. Shape and transfer to plate.

9. Serve with fried or poached eggs.

ALTERNATIVE METHOD: Reheat and brown mixture in a sauté pan and shape like a cigar.

RECIPE 33.17

Approximate values per serving:	
Calories	247
Total fat	14 g
Saturated fat	3 g
Cholesterol	82 mg
Sodium	1218 mg
Total carbohydrates	14 g
Protein	17 g

RECIPE 33.18

Cheese Soufflé

Yield: 12 individual servings

Butter	as needed	as needed
Bread crumbs	as needed	as needed
Base Mixture (recipe follows)	600 mL	20 fl. oz.
Sharp cheddar, grated	150 g	5 oz.
Ermite cheese, grated	25 g	1 oz.
Dry mustard	0.5 g	1 tsp.
Salt and pepper	TT	TT
Egg whites	12	12

1. Butter ramekins and lightly coat the interior with bread crumbs.

2. Mix together the Base Mixture, grated cheeses, mustard, salt and pepper. Blend evenly.

3. Whisk egg whites to soft peaks.

4. Fold one-third of the egg whites into the cheese mixture. Fold in the remaining egg whites in 2 stages.

5. Spoon the batter into the ramekins to within 10 mm (1/2 in.) of the top. Wipe the rims clean. Tap the ramekins gently to settle the batter.

6. Place the soufflés on a baking sheet and bake in a 210°C (420°F) oven for 15–18 minutes. Do not disturb. Serve immediately.

Base Mixture

Yield: 600 mL (20 fl. oz.)

Milk	725 mL	24 fl. oz.
Bay leaf	1	1
Clove, whole	1	1
Butter	60 g	2 oz.
Flour	70 g	2-1/2 oz.
Egg yolks	15	15
Salt and pepper	TT	TT

1. Heat milk with bay leaf and clove to infuse.

2. Prepare a white roux from the butter and flour.

3. Strain the milk and add to the roux to make a béchamel.

4. Simmer approximately 15 minutes, stirring constantly.

5. Temper the egg yolks with some of the béchamel.

6. Incorporate tempered egg yolks into remaining sauce and bring to a simmer for 3–4 minutes. Do not boil. Stir constantly.

7. Adjust seasoning with salt and pepper and reserve. Chill if being used later.

RECIPE 33.18

Approximate values per serving:	
Calories	247
Total fat	18 g
Saturated fat	9 g
Cholesterol	304 mg
Sodium	722 mg
Total carbohydrates	9 g
Protein	14 g

Base Mixture—Approximate values per serving:	
Calories	170
Total fat	13 g
Saturated fat	6 g
Cholesterol	289 mg
Sodium	316 mg
Total carbohydrates	8 g
Protein	6 g

Doug Overes

An Alberta native, Doug has cooked at a variety of establishments in that province, including the Paradise Canyon Golf and Country Club, as well as at a Michelin-starred restaurant in Holland. He has been a member of Culinary Team Alberta since 2000, winning awards in competitions such as Expogast Culinary World Cup (2002) and the IKA Culinary Olympics (2004). Doug has been an instructor at Lethbridge College since 1998.

RECIPE 33.19

Approximate values per 4 beignets:	
Calories	196
Total fat	9 g
Saturated fat	0.7 g
Cholesterol	0 mg
Sodium	743 mg
Total carbohydrates	25 g
Protein	3.3 g

RECIPE 33.19

Roasted Garlic Beignets

LETHBRIDGE COLLEGE, LETHBRIDGE, AB
Chef Instructor Doug Overes

Yield: 2 dozen

All-purpose flour	150 g	1-1/2 cups
Baking powder	14 g	5 tsp.
Sugar	15 g	1 Tbsp.
Kosher salt	2.5 g	1-1/2 tsp.
Cayenne	2.75 g	1 tsp.
Black pepper, ground	1.3 g	1/2 tsp.
Garlic, split and roasted, coarsely chopped	2 heads	2 heads
Chives, fresh, minced	20 g	2 Tbsp.
Ice water	225 mL	8 fl. oz.
Oil	for frying	for frying
Salt	TT	TT

1. Combine flour, baking powder, sugar, salt, cayenne, black pepper, garlic, and chives in a medium bowl.

2. Whisk in ice water until the mixture is smooth. Cover and refrigerate batter while heating the oil.

3. Heat frying oil to 180°C (360°F) and line a hotel pan with paper towels.

4. Carefully drop tablespoonfuls of batter into the hot oil, deep-frying no more than 6 at a time. Turn beignets often, until they are golden brown on all sides.

5. Transfer beignets to hotel pan to drain and season lightly with salt while still hot.

Appetizers and Sandwiches 34

" The gentle art of gastronomy is a friendly one. It hurdles the language barrier, makes friends among civilized people, and warms the heart.

—Samuel Chamberlain, American author (1895–1975)

LEARNING OUTCOMES

After studying this chapter you will be able to:

- prepare and serve a variety of cold and hot hors d'oeuvre

- prepare a variety of appetizers

- choose hors d'oeuvre and appetizers that are appropriate for the meal or event

- select high-quality sandwich ingredients

- identify different types and styles of sandwiches

- prepare sandwiches to order

These interactive online tools will help you master the skills in this chapter:

- Chapter Quizzes
- Activities

● **hors d'oeuvre** very small portions of hot or cold foods served before the meal to stimulate the appetite

● **appetizers** also known as first courses; usually small portions of hot or cold foods intended to whet the appetite in anticipation of the more substantial courses to follow

Un Artiste de l'Hors d'oeuvre

Well may it be said that a good hors d'oeuvre artist is a man to be prized in any kitchen, for, although his duties do not by any means rank first in importance, they nevertheless demand of the chef the possession of such qualities as are rarely found united in one person, reliable and experienced taste, originality, keen artistic sense, and professional knowledge.

Auguste Escoffier,
Le Guide culinaire

Hors d'oeuvre and canapés, whether hot or cold, are very small portions of foods served before or at the beginning of the meal to stimulate the appetite or at a reception as the accompaniment to liquid refreshments. **Hors d'oeuvre** can be passed elegantly by waiters or displayed on buffets. **Appetizers**, whether hot or cold, are generally the first course or introduction to a meal; they are more typically served with dinner than with lunch. Sometimes there is very little difference between an hors d'oeuvre and an appetizer.

Sandwiches, which are usually quick and easy to assemble, also lend themselves to a cook's creativity. Fancy sandwiches can become sensational menu additions in even the most formal restaurants, and amazing sandwiches can keep lunch customers visiting regularly.

The preparation of hors d'oeuvre and sandwiches uses skills from almost every work station. Because they can consist of meat, poultry, fish, shellfish, vegetables, potatoes, grains, pasta, fruits, baked goods and sauces, they require a detailed knowledge of these foods and how they are prepared.

Although hors d'oeuvre and sandwiches can be divided into hot and cold varieties, it is difficult (and unnecessary) to categorize them further because of the vast variety possible and the absence of any one dominant food type or style.

HORS D'OEUVRE

The French term *hors d'oeuvre* translates as "outside the work," although we generally use it to mean appetizer. Its usage was correct under the classic kitchen brigade system, for it was the service staff's responsibility to prepare small tidbits for guests to enjoy while the kitchen prepared the meal. Today, however, the kitchen staff prepares the hors d'oeuvre as well as the meals. Cold hors d'oeuvre are usually prepared by the *garde-manger*; hot ones are prepared in the main kitchen.

There are really only two limitations on the type of food and manner of preparation that can be used for hors d'oeuvre: the cook's imagination and the foods at his or her disposal. There are, however, a few guidelines.

BASIC GUIDELINES FOR PREPARING HORS D'OEUVRE

1. Hors d'oeuvre should be small, one to two bites.
2. They should be flavourful and well seasoned without being overpowering.
3. They should be visually attractive.
4. They should complement the foods to follow without duplicating their flavours.

Cold Hors d'oeuvre

Cold hors d'oeuvre are divided here into five broad categories based upon preparation method, principal ingredient or presentation style. They are canapés, caviars, crudités, dips and sushi. These categories may vary somewhat from classical teachings, but they are completely appropriate for modern menus and food service operations.

Canapés

Canapés are, essentially, tiny, open-faced sandwiches. They are constructed from a base, a spread and one or more garnishes.

The most common canapé base is a thin slice of bread cut into an interesting shape and toasted. Although most any variety of bread can be used, spiced, herbed or otherwise flavoured breads may be inappropriate for some spreads or garnishes. Melba toasts, crackers, or slices of firm vegetables such as cucumbers or zucchini or meat slices are also popular canapé bases. The base must be strong enough to support the weight of the spread and garnish without falling apart when handled.

The canapé spread provides some of the canapé's flavour and moistness. Spreads are usually flavoured butters, cream cheese or a combination of the two. (Examples of spreads are listed in Table 34.1.) Each of the spreads is made by adding the desired amount of the main ingredient (chopped or puréed as appropriate) and seasonings to softened butter or cream cheese and mixing until combined. Quantities and proportions vary according to individual tastes. Other canapé spreads include bound salads (for example, tuna or egg), finely chopped shrimp or liver mousse. Any of a number of ingredients can be combined for spreads, provided the basic guidelines are followed.

● **canapé** a tiny open-faced sandwich served as an hors d'oeuvre, usually composed of a small piece of bread or toast topped with a savoury spread and garnish

Salmon Rosette Canapés

Salami Cornet Canapés

Shrimp and Caviar Canapés

BASIC GUIDELINES FOR PREPARING CANAPÉ SPREADS

1. The spread's texture should be smooth enough to produce attractive designs if piped through a pastry bag fitted with a decorative tip.

2. The spread's consistency should be firm enough to hold its shape when piped onto the base, yet soft enough to stick to the base and hold the garnishes in place.

3. The spread's flavour should complement the garnishes and be flavourful enough to stimulate the appetite without being overpowering.

TABLE 34.1	A Selection of Canapé Spreads and Suggested Garnishes
Spread	**Suggested Garnishes**
Anchovy butter	Hard-cooked eggs, capers, green or black olive slices
Blue cheese	Grape half, walnuts, roast beef roulade, pear slice, currants, watercress
Caviar butter	Caviar, lemon, egg slice, chives
Devilled ham	Cornichons, mustard butter, sliced radish
Horseradish butter	Smoked salmon, roast beef, smoked trout, marinated herring, capers, parsley
Lemon butter	Shrimp, crab, caviar, salmon, chives, parsley, black olive slices
Liver pâté	Truffle slice, cornichons
Mustard butter	Smoked meats, pâté, dry salami coronet, cornichons
Pimiento cream cheese	Smoked oyster, sardine, pimiento, parsley
Shrimp butter	Poached bay scallops, shrimp, caviar, parsley
Tuna salad	Capers, cornichons, sliced radish

A spread may be a substantial portion of the canapé as well as its distinguishing characteristic. Or it can be applied sparingly and used more as a means of gluing the garnish to the base than as a principal ingredient.

Canapés with bread bases tend to become soggy quickly from both the moisture in the spread and the moisture in the refrigerator where they are stored. Using a spread made with butter will help keep the bread bases crispier, as will buttering the base with a thin coat of softened plain butter before piping on the spread. The best way to ensure a crisp base is to make the canapés as close to service time as possible.

The variety of canapé garnishes is vast. The garnish can dominate or complement the spread, or it can be a simple herb sprig intended to provide visual appeal but little flavour. Although several ingredients can be used to garnish the same canapé, remember the limitations imposed by the canapé's size and purpose.

1. Slicing bread into the desired shapes.

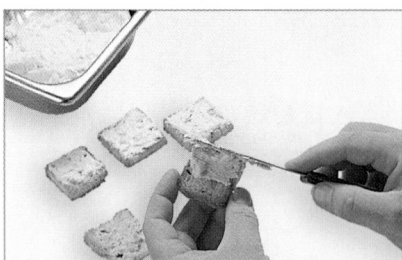

2. Applying the spread to the base with a palette knife.

3. Piping the spread onto the base.

BASIC PROCEDURE FOR PREPARING CANAPÉS

This procedure can be adapted and used with a variety of ingredients to produce a variety of canapés. If the canapé base is a bread crouton, begin with Step 1. If some other product is used as the base, prepare that base and begin with Step 4.

1. Trim the crust from an unsliced loaf of bread. Slice the bread lengthwise approximately 8 mm (1/3 in.) thick.
2. Cut the bread slices into the desired shapes using a serrated bread knife or canapé cutter.
3. Brush the bread shapes with melted butter or olive oil and bake in a 180°C (350°F) oven until they are toasted and dry. Remove and cool.
4. If desired, spread each base with a thin layer of softened plain butter.
5. Apply the spread to the base. If a thin layer is desired, use a palette knife. If a thicker or more decorative layer is desired, pipe the spread onto the base using a pastry bag and decorative tip.
6. Garnish the canapé as desired.
7. If desired, glaze each canapé with a thin coating of aspic jelly. The aspic jelly can be applied with a small spoon or a spray bottle designated for that purpose.

4. Coating the entire slice of toasted bread with a spread before cutting it into canapés.

5. Garnishing the canapés.

6. Spraying the finished canapés with aspic.

Barquettes, Tartlets and Profiteroles

Barquettes, tartlets and profiteroles are all adaptations of the basic canapé. A *barquette* is a tiny boat-shaped shell made from a savoury dough such as pâte brisée. A *tartlet* is simply a round version of a barquette. A *profiterole* is a small puff made from pâte à choux. These three items can be prepared like canapés by filling them with flavoured spreads and garnishing as desired.

BASIC PROCEDURES FOR PREPARING BARQUETTES

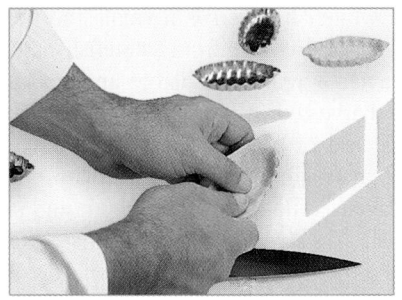

1. Pressing the dough into the barquette shells.

2. Pricking the dough with a fork to allow steam to escape during baking.

3. Placing a second barquette shell on top of the dough to prevent it from rising as it bakes.

Other Types of Canapés

Vegetables such as cherry tomatoes, blanched snow peas, mushroom caps and Belgian endive leaves are sometimes used as canapé bases. Thickly sliced rounds of cucumber or hollowed-out small potatoes can also be used as containers for canapés, as well as hard-cooked eggs or mussel shells. They are filled and garnished in the same manner as barquettes, tartlets and profiteroles. Bruschetta or crostini are slices of country bread that are grilled, brushed with garlic and olive oil and then garnished with diced tomatoes or other toppings. These Italian-style canapés are versatile and easy to prepare. Buffet platters can be garnished with canapés.

Steamed Mussel, Cream-Cheese-Filled Endive and Tartlet Canapés

Caviars

Caviar, considered by many to be the ultimate hors d'oeuvre, is the salted roe (eggs) of the sturgeon fish. In Canada, only sturgeon roe can be labelled as simply "caviar." Roe from other fish must be qualified as such on the label (e.g., salmon caviar or lumpfish caviar).

Beluga Caviar

Most of the world's caviar comes from sturgeon harvested in the Caspian Sea and imported from Russia and Iran. Imported sturgeon caviar, classified

Sevruga Caviar

according to the sturgeon species and the roe's size and colour, includes beluga, osetra and sevruga as well as pressed caviar. Beluga is the most expensive caviar. It comes from the largest species (the sturgeon can weigh up to 800 kg/ 1750 lb.); the dark grey and well-separated eggs are the largest and most fragile kind. Osetra is considered by some connoisseurs to be the best caviar; the eggs are medium-sized, golden yellow to brown in colour and quite oily. Sevruga is harvested from small sturgeon; the eggs are quite small and light to dark grey in colour. Pressed caviar is a processed caviar from osetra and sevruga roes. The eggs are cleaned, packed in linen bags and hung to drain; as salt and moisture drain away, the natural shape of the eggs is destroyed and the eggs are pressed together. Approximately 1.3 kg (3 lb.) of roe produce only 450 g (1 lb.) of pressed caviar. Pressed caviar has a spreadable, jamlike consistency.

Most of the roe consumed in Canada comes from other fish species and is labelled appropriately as golden whitefish, lumpfish or salmon caviar. Sturgeon caviar and sturgeon products are produced in aqua farms in New Brunswick; they have a medium grain and a colour range of amber to golden to dark brown, similar to osetra. American sturgeon roe is harvested in the Tennessee River and the coastal northwest. Golden whitefish caviar is a small and very crisp roe; the roe is a natural golden colour and comes from whitefish native to the northern Great Lakes. Lumpfish caviar is readily available and reasonably priced; it is produced from lumpfish harvested in the North Atlantic. The small and very crisp eggs are dyed black, red or gold; the food colouring is not stable, however, and when used to garnish foods, coloured lumpfish caviar has a tendency to bleed. Salmon caviar is the eggs of the chum and silver salmon and is a very popular garnish. The eggs are large with a good flavour and natural orange colour. Tobiko or flying fish roe is widely used.

Osetra Caviar

Salmon Roe

Purchasing and Storing Caviars

Although all caviar is processed with salt, the best caviar is labelled *malassol*, which means "little salt." Caviar should smell fresh, with no off-odours. The eggs should be whole, not broken, and they should be crisp and pop when pressed with the tongue. Excessive oiliness may be caused by a large number of broken eggs. The best way to test a caviar's quality is to taste it. Remember, price alone does not necessarily indicate quality.

Most caviar can be purchased fresh or pasteurized in tins or jars ranging from 28 g (1 oz.) to more than 2 kg (4 lb.). Some caviars are also available frozen. (Frozen caviar should be used only as a garnish and should not be served by itself.) In order to ensure the freshest possible product, always purchase caviar in small quantities as often as necessary based on your needs.

Fresh caviar should be stored at 0°C (32°F). Because most refrigerators are considerably warmer than that, store the caviar on ice in the coldest part of the refrigerator and change the ice often. If properly handled, fresh caviar will last one to two weeks before opening and several days after opening. Pasteurized caviar does not require refrigeration until it is opened and will last several days in the refrigerator after opening.

Serving Caviars

Fine caviar should be served in its original container or a nonmetal bowl on a bed of crushed ice, accompanied only by lightly buttered toasts or blinis and sour cream. Connoisseurs prefer china, bone or other nonmetal utensils for serving caviar because metal reacts with the caviar, producing off-flavours.

Lesser quality caviars are often served on ice, accompanied by minced onion, chopped hard-cooked egg whites and yolks (separately), lemon, sour cream and buttered toasts.

Lumpfish and other nonsturgeon caviars are usually not served by themselves. Rather, they are used as ingredients in or garnishes for other dishes.

Crudités

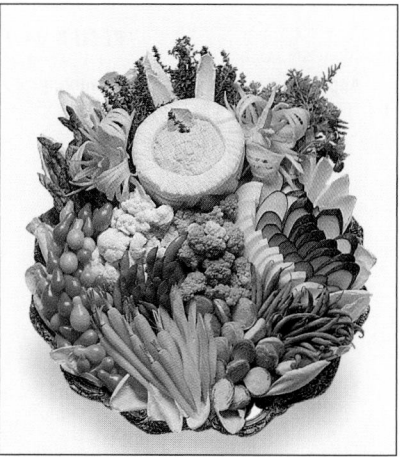

An artful array of crudités and dip

Crudité, a French word meaning "raw thing," generally refers to raw or slightly blanched vegetables served as an hors d'oeuvre. Although almost any vegetable will do, the most commonly used are broccoli, cauliflower, carrots, celery, asparagus and green beans, all of which are often blanched, and cucumbers, zucchini, yellow squash, radishes, green onions, cherry tomatoes, Belgian endive leaves, mushrooms, peppers and jicama, which are served raw.

When preparing crudités, use only the freshest and best-looking produce available. Because crudités are displayed and eaten raw, blemishes and imperfections cannot be disguised. Vegetables, both blanched and raw, should be cut into attractive shapes. Crudités are usually served with one or more dips.

Dips

Dips can be served hot or cold and as an accompaniment to crudités, crackers, chips, toasts, breads or other foods.

Cold dips often use mayonnaise, sour cream or cream cheese as a base. The methods for preparing mayonnaise- and sour cream–based dips are identical to those for making mayonnaise-based salad dressings discussed in Chapter 25, Salads and Salad Dressings. The principal difference is that dips are normally thicker than dressings.

To use cream cheese as a base, first soften it by mixing it in an electric mixer with a paddle attachment. Then add the flavouring ingredients such as chopped cooked vegetables, chopped cooked fish or shellfish, herbs, spices, garlic or onions. Adjust the consistency of the dip by adding milk, buttermilk, cream, sour cream or other appropriate liquid.

Some cold dips such as guacamole and hummus use purées of fruits, vegetables or beans as the base.

Hot dips often use a béchamel, cream sauce or cheese sauce as a base and usually contain a dominant flavouring ingredient such as chopped spinach or shellfish. The traditional Italian bagna cauda is an example of a hot, oil-based dip. It is made with olive oil, garlic and anchovies and is kept hot over a small burner while guests dip raw vegetables in it.

Dips can be served in small bowls or hollowed-out cabbages, squash, pumpkins or other vegetables. Hot dips are often served in **chafing dishes**.

The combinations of ingredients and seasonings that can be used to make dips as well as the foods that are dipped in them are limited only by the chef's imagination.

● **chafing dish** a metal dish with a heating unit (flame or electric); used to keep foods warm at tableside or during buffet service

APPLYING THE BASICS		RECIPE 34.1
Baba Ghanoush		
Yield: Approximately 1.2 L (40 fl. oz.)		
Eggplants	3	3
Virgin olive oil	120 mL	4 fl. oz.
Salt and pepper	TT	TT
Fresh lemon juice	120 mL	4 fl. oz.
Garlic cloves	30 g	6
Tahini	200 g	7 oz.

Baba Ghanoush

continued

RECIPE 34.1

Approximate values per 30 mL serving:	
Calories	64
Total fat	5 g
Saturated fat	1 g
Cholesterol	0 mg
Sodium	55 mg
Total carbohydrates	4 g
Protein	0 g

1. Cut the eggplants in half and score the cut surface of each half from edge to edge in a crosshatch pattern approximately 1.2 cm (1/2 in.) deep.
2. Brush the cut surfaces with 60 mL (2 fl. oz.) of the oil, season with salt and pepper and place cut side down on a sheet pan. Roast in a 350°F (180°C) oven until very soft, approximately 45 minutes.
3. Cool the eggplants and scoop out the flesh. Purée the flesh in a food processor with the lemon juice, garlic, tahini, salt and pepper. Add the remaining oil and blend in. Adjust the seasonings. Serve in a bowl, drizzled with additional oil, if desired, and accompanied by pita bread or crudités.

- **sushi** cooked or raw fish or shellfish rolled in or served on seasoned rice
- **sashimi** raw fish eaten without rice; usually served as the first course of a Japanese meal

Sushi Seasonings

Shoyu—Japanese soy sauce, which is lighter and more delicate than the Chinese variety.

Wasabi—A strong aromatic root, purchased as a green powder. It is sometimes called green horseradish, although it is not actually related to the common horseradish.

Pickled ginger—Fresh ginger pickled in vinegar, which gives it a pink colour.

Nori—A dried seaweed purchased in sheets; it adds flavour and is sometimes used to contain the rolled rice and other ingredients.

Sushi

Generally, **sushi** refers to cooked or raw fish and shellfish rolled in or served on seasoned rice. **Sashimi** is raw fish eaten without rice. In Japan, the word sushi (or *zushi*) refers only to the flavoured rice. Each combination of rice and another ingredient or ingredients has a specific name. These include: *nigiri zushi* (rice with raw fish), *norimaki zushi* (rice rolled in seaweed), *fukusa zushi* (rice wrapped in omelette), *inari zushi* (rice in fried bean curd) and *chirashi zushi* (rice with fish, shellfish and vegetables). Although a Japanese sushi master spends years perfecting style and technique, many types of sushi can be produced in any professional kitchen with very little specialized equipment.

Ingredients

Fish—The key to good sushi and sashimi is the freshness of the fish. All fish must be of the highest quality and absolutely fresh, preferably no more than one day out of the water. Ahi and yellowfin tuna, salmon, flounder and sea bass are typically used for sushi. Cooked shrimp and eel are also popular.

Rice—Sushi rice is prepared by adding seasonings such as vinegar, sugar, salt and rice wine (sake or mirin) to steamed short-grain rice. The consistency of the rice is very important. It must be sticky enough to stay together when formed into finger-shaped oblongs, but not too soft.

APPLYING THE BASICS · RECIPE 34.2

Zushi (Sushi Rice)

Yield: 1 kg (2 lb.)

Short-grain sushi rice	425 g	1 lb.
Water	550 mL	20 fl. oz.
Sugar	45 g	3 Tbsp.
Salt	12 g	2-1/2 tsp.
Rice vinegar	60 mL	2 fl. oz.

1. Wash the rice until the water runs clear. Leave to soak in water for 30 minutes and then allow it to drain for 30 minutes.

continued

2. Combine the rice and water in a saucepan with a tight-fitting lid. Bring to a boil and simmer for 15 minutes (remove from heat and let set for 20 minutes). Most of the water will be absorbed. Do not open the lid.

3. To make the *sushi-zu*, dissolve the sugar and salt in some warmed rice vinegar. Add the remaining rice vinegar and cool.

4. Spread the rice in a shallow bowl or tray.

5. Plough the rice with a paddle (*shamoji*). Go up and down, then across, again and again to separate the grains. As you toss and plough the rice, sprinkle it with the sushi-zu. Fan the rice at the same time. It will take 10–15 minutes to cool down. The finished rice should be glossy and just stick together.

6. Keep cooled mixture covered with a damp cloth. Use immediately.

RECIPE 34.2

Approximate values per 35 g serving:	
Calories	61
Total fat	0 g
Saturated fat	0 g
Cholesterol	0 mg
Sodium	167 mg
Total carbohydrates	14 g
Protein	1 g

APPLYING THE BASICS   **RECIPE 34.3**

Nigiri Zushi

Yield: 24 pieces

Sushi-quality fish fillets such as		
ahi tuna, salmon, flounder or sea bass	450 g	1 lb.
Wasabi powder	30 g	1 oz.
Water	30 mL	1 fl. oz.
Zushi (Recipe 34.2)	900 g	2 lb.
Pickled ginger, sliced	60 g	2 oz.
Shoyu	90 mL	3 fl. oz.

1. Trim the fish fillets of any skin, bone, imperfections or blemishes. Cut the fillets into 24 thin slices approximately 5 cm long × 2.5 cm wide (2 in. × 1 in.).

2. Mix the wasabi powder and water to form a paste.

3. With your hands, form a 50-g (1-1/2-oz.) portion of rice into a finger-shaped mound.

4. Rub a small amount of wasabi on one side of a slice of fish.

5. Holding the rice mound in one hand, press the fish, wasabi side down, onto the rice with the fingers of the other hand.

6. Serve with additional wasabi, pickled ginger and shoyu.

RECIPE 34.3

Approximate values per serving:	
Calories	80
Total fat	2 g
Saturated fat	0 g
Cholesterol	10 mg
Sodium	310 mg
Total carbohydrates	11 g
Protein	5 g

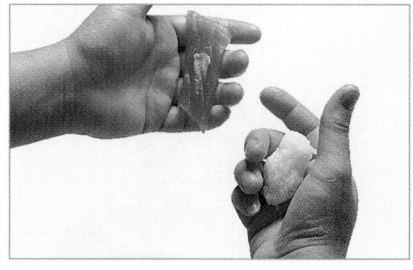

1. Nigiri Zushi: Forming a finger-shaped rice mound.

2. Pressing the fish onto the rice.

RECIPE 34.4

Approximate values per serving:	
Calories	40
Total fat	0 g
Saturated fat	0 g
Cholesterol	5 mg
Sodium	220 mg
Total carbohydrates	6 g
Protein	2 g

APPLYING THE BASICS		RECIPE 34.4

Norimaki Zushi

Yield: 36 pieces

Dried shiitake mushrooms	4	4
Shoyu	125 mL	4 fl. oz.
Brown sugar	15 g	1 Tbsp.
Cucumber	1/2	1/2
Sushi-quality fish fillets such as ahi tuna, salmon, flounder or sea bass	150 g	5 oz.
Nori	3 sheets	3 sheets
Zushi (Recipe 34.2)	500 g	18 oz.
Wasabi paste	60 mL	2 fl. oz.
Pickled ginger	60 g	2 oz.

1. Soak the mushrooms in hot water for 20 minutes. Remove the mushrooms and reserve 125 mL (4 fl. oz.) of the liquid. Trim off the mushroom stems.

2. Julienne the mushroom caps. Combine the reserved soaking liquid with 30 mL (2 Tbsp.) of the shoyu and the brown sugar. Simmer the caps in this liquid and reduce au sec. Remove from the heat and refrigerate.

3. Peel and seed the cucumber; cut it into strips the size of pencils, approximately 15 cm (6 in.) long.

4. Trim the fish fillets of any skin, bone, imperfections or blemishes. Cut the fillets into strips the same size as the cucumbers.

5. Cut the sheets of nori in half and place one half sheet on a napkin or bamboo rolling mat. Divide the rice into 6 equal portions; spread 1 portion over each half sheet of nori, leaving a 12-mm (1/2-in.) border of nori exposed.

6. Spread 5 mL (1 tsp.) of wasabi evenly on the rice.

7. Lay one-sixth of the mushrooms, cucumber and fish strips in a row down the middle of the rice.

8. Use the napkin or bamboo mat to roll the nori tightly around the rice and garnishes.

9. Slice each roll into 6 pieces and serve with the remaining shoyu, pickled ginger and remaining wasabi.

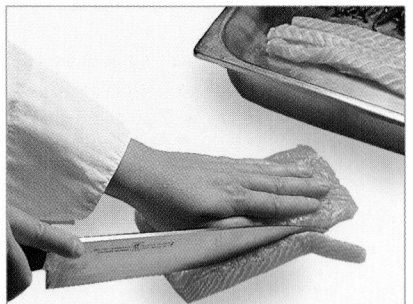

1. Norimaki Zushi: Preparing the garnishes for the sushi roll.

2. Spreading the rice over the nori.

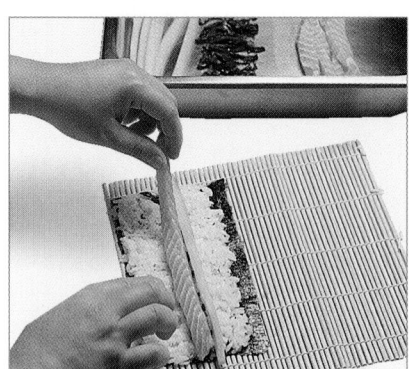

3. Adding the garnishes in a row down the middle of the rice.

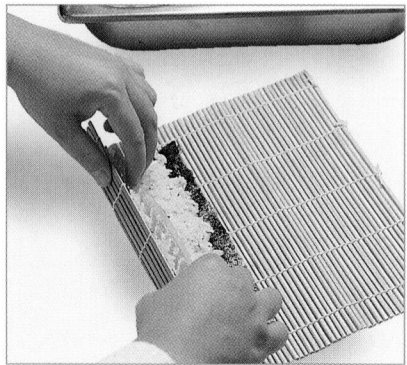

4. Rolling the nori around the rice and garnishes using the mat.

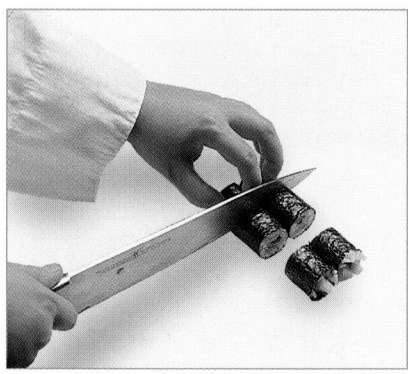

5. Slicing the roll into six pieces.

Hot Hors d'oeuvre

To provide a comprehensive list of hot hors d'oeuvre would be virtually impossible; therefore, we discuss just a few of the more commonly encountered ones that can be easily made in almost any kitchen.

Filled Pastry Shells

Because savoury (unsweetened) barquettes and tartlets, choux puffs (profiteroles) and bouchées can hold a small amount of liquid, they are often baked, then filled with warm meat, poultry or fish purées, ragouts or salpicons, garnished and served hot. They become soggy quickly, however, and must be prepared at the last possible minute before service.

Brochettes or Kebabs

Hors d'oeuvre **brochettes** are small skewers holding a combination of meat, poultry, game, fish, shellfish or vegetables. They are normally baked, grilled or broiled and are often served with a dipping sauce. Brochettes or kebabs can be small pieces of boneless chicken breast marinated in white wine and grilled; beef cubes glazed with teriyaki sauce; lamb or chicken satay (saté) with peanut sauce or rabbit and shiitake mushrooms skewered on a sprig of fresh rosemary (see Recipe 34.5).

In order to increase visual appeal, the main ingredients should be carefully cut and consistently sized and shaped. The ingredients are normally diced, but strips of meat and poultry can also be threaded onto the skewers. Often, ingredients are first marinated.

As hors d'oeuvre, the skewers should be very small, slightly larger than a toothpick. Bamboo skewers work well, but remember to soak them in water for 20 minutes to prevent splintering of the wood. When assembling brochettes, leave enough exposed skewer so diners can pick them up easily. Wooden skewers have a tendency to burn during cooking. Soaking them in water before using them helps reduce the risk of burning.

● **brochettes** skewers, either small hors d'oeuvre or large entree size, threaded with meat, poultry, fish, shellfish and/or vegetables and grilled, broiled or baked; sometimes served with a dipping sauce

---

APPLYING THE BASICS		RECIPE 34.5

Rabbit and Shiitake Skewers

Yield: 12 skewers

Rabbit	1	1
Shiitake mushrooms, stemmed	6–8	6–8
Rosemary sprigs	12	12
Salt and pepper	TT	TT
Olive oil	60 mL	2 fl. oz.
Mushroom ragout (optional)	600 g	22 oz.

1. Bone the rabbit and cut the pieces into 1.25-cm (1/2-in.) cubes. One rabbit should produce 36 cubes.
2. Wash the mushrooms. Trim and discard the stems.
3. Cut enough of the mushrooms into 1.25-cm (1/2-in.) dice to produce 24 pieces.
4. Skewer 3 pieces of rabbit and 2 pieces of mushroom alternately onto each rosemary sprig.
5. Season the skewers with salt and pepper and brush with olive oil. Grill the skewers over medium heat, being careful not to burn the rosemary sprigs.
6. Heat the mushroom ragout. Arrange a portion of ragout and 2 rabbit skewers on each plate.

Rabbit and Shiitake Skewers

RECIPE 34.5

Approximate values per serving:	
Calories	160
Total fat	8 g
Saturated fat	1.5 g
Cholesterol	31 mg
Sodium	20 mg
Total carbohydrates	11 g
Protein	12 g

Meatballs

Meatballs made from ground beef, veal, pork or poultry and served in a sauce buffet-style are a popular hot hors d'oeuvre. One of the best known is the Swedish meatball. It is made from ground beef, veal and pork bound with eggs and bread crumbs and served in a velouté or cream sauce seasoned with dill. Other sauces that can be used in the same manner are mushroom sauce, red wine sauce or any style of tomato sauce.

Swedish Meatballs

APPLYING THE BASICS		RECIPE 34.6

Swedish Meatballs

Yield: 1 kg (2 lb. 4 oz.)

Onions, small dice	125 g	4 oz.
Whole butter	25 g	1 oz.
Ground beef	500 g	1 lb.
Ground pork	500 g	1 lb.
Bread crumbs, fresh	75 g	2-1/2 oz.
Eggs	2	2
Salt	8 g	1-1/2 tsp.
Pepper, ground black	3 g	1 tsp.
Nutmeg	2 g	1/2 tsp.
Allspice	2 g	1/2 tsp
Lemon zest, grated	2 g	1/2 tsp.
Demi-glace, hot	500 mL	16 fl. oz.
Cream, 35%, hot	125 mL	4 fl. oz.
Dill, fresh, chopped	10 g	1 Tbsp.

1. Sauté the onions in butter without colouring. Remove and cool.

2. Combine the onions with all the ingredients except the demi-glace, cream and dill. Mix well.

3. Portion the meat with a #20 scoop; form into balls with your hands and place on a sheet pan.

4. Bake the meatballs at 200°C (400°F) until firm, approximately 15 minutes. Remove the meatballs from the pan with a slotted spoon, draining well, and place in a hotel pan.

5. Combine the demi-glace, cream and dill; pour over the meatballs.

6. Cover the meatballs and bake at 180°C (350°F) until done, approximately 20 minutes. Skim off the grease from the surface and serve.

RECIPE 34.6

Approximate values per 50 g serving:	
Calories	188
Total fat	12.5 g
Saturated fat	5.5 g
Cholesterol	72 mg
Sodium	224 mg
Total carbohydrates	3 g
Protein	15 g

Rumaki

Traditionally, rumaki were made by wrapping chicken livers in bacon and broiling or baking them. Today, however, many other foods prepared in the same fashion are called rumaki. For example, blanched bacon can be wrapped around olives, pickled watermelon rind, water chestnuts, pineapple, dates or scallops. These morsels are then broiled, baked or fried and served piping hot.

APPLYING THE BASICS   RECIPE 34.7

Rumaki

Yield: 60 pieces

Chicken livers	500 g	1 lb.
Marinade:		
Brown sugar	10 g	1 Tbsp.
Water, hot	15 mL	1 Tbsp.
Soy sauce	15 mL	1 Tbsp.
Garlic, minced	15 g	1 Tbsp.
Bacon, sliced thin	30 slices	30 slices
Water chestnuts, sliced	60 slices	60 slices
Toothpicks (for assembly)	60	60

1. Rinse the livers, drain and pat dry. Trim and cut 60 equal-sized pieces. Place the livers in a stainless steel bowl.

2. Combine the marinade ingredients. Pour the marinade over the livers and toss gently. Refrigerate, covered, for 1 hour.

3. Cut the bacon slices in half, spread them on a baking sheet and parcook at 180°C (375°F) for approximately 5 minutes. Drain off and discard the excess fat and liquid.

4. Drain the marinated livers. Roll 1 piece of liver and 1 water chestnut slice in half a bacon slice and secure with a toothpick. Place on a parchment-lined baking sheet seam side down.

5. Bake the rumaki in a 200°C (400°F) convection oven until the bacon is crisp and the liver is cooked, approximately 10 minutes. Do not overcook. Serve hot.

RECIPE 34.7

Approximate values per piece:	
Calories	42
Total fat	1.4 g
Saturated fat	0.4 g
Cholesterol	43 mg
Sodium	200 mg
Total carbohydrates	2.8 g
Protein	4.5 g

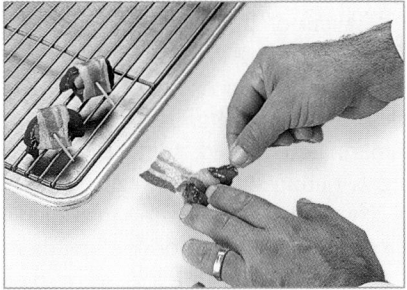

1. Rolling rumaki.

2. The finished rumaki.

Stuffed Won Ton Skins

Won ton skins are an Asian noodle dough used to produce a wide variety of hors d'oeuvre such as a miniature version of the traditional egg roll or a puff filled with a mixture of seasoned cream cheese and crab. Or they can be stuffed with a wide variety of pork, chicken, shellfish and vegetables before cooking. As hors d'oeuvre, stuffed won ton skins can be steamed, but they are more often pan-fried or deep-fat fried.

Folding the wontons and sealing the edges.

RECIPE 34.8

Approximate values per won ton:	
Calories	57
Total fat	2 g
Saturated fat	0.5 g
Cholesterol	13 mg
Sodium	180 mg
Total carbohydrates	7 g
Protein	3 g

APPLYING THE BASICS		RECIPE 34.8

Stuffed Won Tons

Yield: 40 pieces

Shiitake mushrooms, stemmed, finely chopped	75 g	6
Green onions, finely chopped	4	4
Ground pork	250 g	8 oz.
Shrimp, deveined, chopped	125 g	4 oz.
Salt	8 g	1-1/2 tsp.
Soy sauce	15 mL	1 Tbsp.
Sesame oil	5 mL	1 tsp.
Wraps, thawed	450 g	1 lb.

1. Combine all ingredients, except wraps, and mix well to bind.
2. Lay a few wraps at a time on a table and keep remainder covered with plastic to prevent drying.
3. Place a 12 g (1 Tbsp.) portion of filling in the centre of each wrap. Wet 2 adjacent sides of wrap lightly with water. Fold the wrap in half to form a triangle. Seal the edges well.
4. If the won tons are to be deep-fat fried as hors d'oeuvre, leave in triangle shapes. For won ton soup, moisten 1 bottom corner of the won ton and press the other point on top of it. The shape should resemble a tortellini.

Other Hot Hors d'oeuvre

Other types of hot hors d'oeuvre include layers of phyllo dough wrapped around various fillings; vegetables such as mushrooms that are stuffed and baked; tiny red potatoes filled with sour cream and caviar or Roquefort cheese and walnuts; tiny artichoke or clam fritters; or any of the hundreds of varieties of chicken wings that are seasoned or marinated, baked, fried, broiled or grilled and served with a cool and soothing or outrageously spicy sauce.

The secret is to let your imagination be your guide, to keep the ingredients harmonious and, if the hors d'oeuvre are to precede dinner, not to allow them to duplicate the foods to be served or overpower them with excessively spicy flavours.

Serving Hors d'oeuvre

Hors d'oeuvre are not only served as a precursor to dinner. At many events, the only food served may be butlered hors d'oeuvre, an hors d'oeuvre buffet or a combination of the two. Whether the hors d'oeuvre are being served before dinner or as dinner, butler style or buffet style, they must always be attractively prepared and displayed.

All events have themes and varying degrees of formality. Long buffets with overflowing baskets of crudités and sweet potato chips with dips presented in hollowed squashes and cabbages may be appropriate for one event, while elegant silver trays of carefully prepared canapés passed among guests by white-gloved, tuxedoed service staff may be appropriate for another. When preparing and serving hors d'oeuvre, always keep the event's theme in mind and plan accordingly.

When choosing hors d'oeuvre, select an assortment that contrasts flavours, textures and styles. There are no limits to the variety of hors d'oeuvre that can be served, but three to four cold and three to four hot selections are sufficient for most occasions. Generally, calculating three hors d'oeuvre per person per hour is sufficient when determining how many to prepare. If no other food will be available, four or five pieces may be appropriate. One must also consider whether the hors d'oeuvre are a meal replacement, in which case larger quantities may be needed.

Butler Service

Butler service hors d'oeuvre or "passed" hors d'oeuvre are presented to guests on trays by the service staff. The hors d'oeuvre can be hot or cold and should be very small to make it easier for the guests to eat them without the aid of a knife or fork. Hot and cold hors d'oeuvre should be passed separately so that they can be kept at the correct temperatures. For a one-hour cocktail reception before a dinner, three to five hors d'oeuvre per person is usually sufficient. Four to five pieces per person per hour may be needed if hors d'oeuvre are the only food being served.

Buffet Service

An hors d'oeuvre buffet should be beautiful and appetizing. It may consist of a single table to serve a small group of people or several huge multilevel displays designed to feed thousands. Colours, flavours and textures must all be taken into account when planning the menu.

Both hot and cold hors d'oeuvre may be served on buffets. Hot hors d'oeuvre are often kept hot by holding them in chafing dishes. Alternatively, hot hors d'oeuvre can be displayed on trays or platters; the trays and platters, however, must be replaced frequently to ensure that the food stays hot. Cold hors d'oeuvre can be displayed on trays, mirrors, platters, baskets, leaves, papers or other serving pieces to create the desired look.

Arranging Buffet Platters

When displaying hors d'oeuvre and other foods on mirrors, trays or platters, the foods should be displayed in a pattern that is pleasing to the eye and flows toward the guest or from one side to the other. An easy and attractive method for accomplishing this is to arrange the items on a mirror or tray with an attractive centrepiece. The food can be placed in parallel diagonal lines, alternating the various styles and shapes. Be careful not to make the tray or mirror too fussy or cluttered, however; often the best approach is to keep it simple. The photos in Figure 34.1 on the next page may be used as guides for arranging canapés and other foods on trays.

Seared Scallops in Hors d'Oeuvre Spoons

Small Portions of Soup

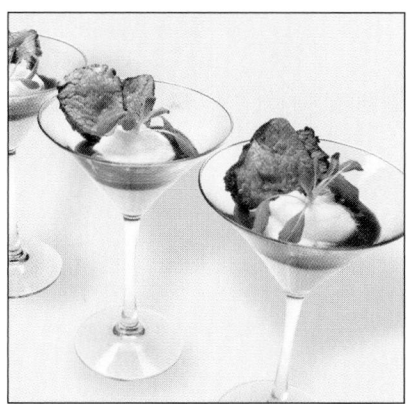

Individual Servings of Beef Tenderloin and Puréed Potatoes for an Hors d'Oeuvre Buffet

APPETIZERS OR FIRST COURSES

Because eating habits have changed over the years, the types of foods chefs prepare have also changed. Today, only the most elaborate banquets include hors d'oeuvre, soup, salad, entree and dessert and perhaps separate fish and cheese courses. A more likely progression may be soup (which serves as the appetizer), salad, entree and dessert, or a salad with a small portion of grilled meat or fish that doubles as both appetizer and salad, followed by an entree and dessert. Because of these changes, the term *first course* may be more fitting than appetizer.

FIGURE 34.1 Simple patterns can be used to effectively display canapés and other foods on trays or mirrors.

Generally, appetizers and first courses are small portions of foods intended to whet the appetite in anticipation of more substantial courses to follow. Some appetizers may contain a combination of protein, vegetable and starch. More often, appetizers consist only of the main item accompanied by a sauce and/or garnish. Appetizers do not need to contain any meat, poultry, fish or shellfish, however. Soups, salads, charcuterie items, vegetables, pizzas, pastas and other starch dishes may be served as appetizers. Because they are very rich, some foods such as foie gras and escargots are traditionally served as appetizers. These foods are generally consumed in small amounts and are rarely served as entrees.

BASIC GUIDELINES FOR PREPARING APPETIZERS

1. The first course should be small. Remember, there are other, more substantial courses to follow. As the name implies, an appetizer should stimulate the appetite rather than satisfy it. Remember that rich cream-based sauces tend to satisfy appetites quickly, even when the portions are small. Sixty to 90 g (2 to 3 oz.) of pasta and 60 g (2 oz.) of sauce is an ample appetizer portion. Many recipes can be prepared as an appetizer by simply serving smaller portions.

2. Avoid very spicy foods that may deaden the palate and detract from any more delicate flavours that follow.

3. The first course should harmonize with the rest of the meal with respect to the types of foods as well as the style. For example, an appetizer of a

continued

roasted Anaheim chile stuffed with grilled corn and goat cheese followed by an entree of paupiettes of sole vin blanc would be a poor combination. The strong spices and flavours of the chile would overpower the delicate flavours of the sole; the chile has strong southwestern ties, while sole is a classic French dish.

4. Avoid duplication of foods within the meal. If fish or shellfish is served as the first course, try not to serve fish or shellfish as the main course.

5. For more variety, use several methods of preparation within the meal. If the entree will be grilled or roasted, serve a first course that is poached or sautéed.

6. A first course should always be attractively presented. Remember that often it is the first food the customer sees. It should set the standard for the rest of the meal.

SANDWICHES

A sandwich is often the first meal a person learns to prepare. Even those who claim to be unable to cook often make delicious hot and cold sandwiches without considering it cooking. Mastering a grilled cheese sandwich or assembling the quintessential BLT may not require a degree in culinary arts, but it does require the ability to select and use ingredients wisely.

Sandwiches offer food service operations economical opportunities for using leftovers and offer customers, especially those with smaller budgets or appetites, meals to eat out of hand. Thus, the ability to correctly prepare hot and cold sandwiches to order is a fundamental skill in many food service operations.

Ingredients for Sandwiches

Sandwiches are constructed from bread, a spread and one or more fillings. These components should be selected and combined carefully so that the finished sandwich is flavourful and visually appealing.

Bread

Bread provides more than a convenient means for handling a sandwich. It holds or contains the spread and fillings and gives the sandwich its shape. Bread also adds flavour, texture, nutrition and colour, and often determines the overall look of the finished product.

Health consciousness and consumer willingness to try new and unusual foods give today's cooks the freedom to create sandwiches without relying on two slices of white bread. Virtually any bread can be used in sandwich making: rolls, biscuits, bagels, croissants, fruit and nut breads, whole grain breads and savoury breads, as well as flatbreads such as naan, lavosh and tortillas, pocket breads such as pitas and flavourful breads such as focaccia and Swedish limpa.

Whatever bread is used and whether its flavour is mild or intense, the bread should complement the fillings and not overpower them. The bread should be fresh (although day-old bread is easier to slice and is excellent toasted) and its texture should be able to withstand moisture from the spread and fillings without becoming soggy or pasty. An overly hard or crusty bread, however, may make the sandwich difficult to eat.

History of Sandwiches

One of the earliest recorded references to foods eaten between two pieces of bread tells of Rabbi Hillel, a great Jewish teacher who lived sometime between 70 B.C.E. and 70 C.E. He created the Passover custom of eating haroseth (chopped nuts and apples) and mohror (bitter herbs) between two slices of matzo (unleavened bread). This "sandwich" was intended to represent the mortar used by the Jews to build the Egyptians' pyramids and the bitter sadness of their internment away from the land of Israel.

The term *sandwich* came into use approximately 200 years ago. The Fourth Earl of Sandwich, Sir John Montague (1718–1792), is credited with popularizing the concept of eating meats and cheeses between two slices of bread. Apparently the earl, not wanting to leave the gaming tables that he loved so much, would demand that his servants bring him meat and bread. He combined the two and ate them with one hand, allowing him a free hand to continue playing at the tables. Some historians argue that a more likely scenario is that, as the head of defence, the earl was kept busy planning British strategy for the Revolutionary War underway in the American colonies. Whichever the case, the name stuck.

Sandwiches became more popular in North America when soft white bread became common in the early 20th century. Today, sandwiches are found on breakfast, lunch and dinner menus and are served by every type of food service operation, from the most casual diner to the fanciest four-star dining room.

Spread

A spread is used to add flavour, moisture and richness to the sandwich; sometimes it helps hold or bind it together. Some spreads, especially plain or flavoured butters, also act as a barrier to prevent the moisture in the filling from soaking into the bread.

There are three principal spreads:

Butter—One of the most common spreads, plain butter adds flavour and richness; it is also an excellent moisture barrier. Flavoured or compound butters, discussed in Chapter 10, Stocks and Sauces, make excellent sandwich spreads, adding flavour dimensions to the finished product. For example, try caper butter on a Cajun-style blackened beef sandwich or a red chile honey butter on a smoked turkey sandwich. Any butter spread should be softened or whipped so that it will spread easily without tearing the bread.

Mayonnaise—Perhaps the most popular sandwich spread, mayonnaise adds moisture, richness and flavour and complements most meat, poultry, fish, shellfish, vegetable, egg and cheese fillings. Like butter, mayonnaise can be made more exciting by adding flavouring ingredients. Condiments (for example, coarse-grained mustard or grated horseradish), herbs, spices and spice blends (for example, curry or chilli powder) and other ingredients such as sun-dried tomatoes and pesto sauce can be stirred into fresh or commercially prepared mayonnaise. Fresh mayonnaise can also be prepared with flavoured oils, such as olive oil, walnut oil or chile oil. See Chapter 25, Salads and Salad Dressings, for recipes and additional information on mayonnaise.

Vegetable purées—Puréed vegetables are often used as sandwich spreads; after all, many lunch boxes would be incomplete without a purée of roasted peanuts (more commonly known as peanut butter) and fruit jam. More sophisticated examples include finely chopped black olives flavoured with fresh thyme, oregano and a few drops of olive oil (tapenade) for a sandwich of Italian meats and cheeses, or a well-seasoned chickpea purée with lemon and tahini paste for a vegetarian sandwich. Unlike butter, vegetable purées usually will not provide a moisture barrier between the bread and the fillings.

Filling

The filling is the body of the sandwich, providing most of its flavour. A sandwich often contains more than one filling. For example, the filling in a Reuben sandwich is corned beef, Swiss cheese and sauerkraut; in a BLT it is bacon, lettuce and tomato. Most fillings for cold sandwiches must be precooked and properly chilled, although some hot sandwich fillings may be cooked to order.

When choosing fillings, be sure that the flavours complement each other. Their textures may be similar or contrasting. If an ingredient such as lettuce is supposed to be crisp, it should be very crisp, not limp. If an ingredient is supposed to be tender and moist, make sure it is so. Improperly prepared, poor quality or mishandled filling ingredients can ruin an otherwise wonderful sandwich.

Popular Fillings

Beef—Although the classic hot beef sandwich is the hamburger, other hot or cold beef products are commonly used. For example, hot or cold small steaks, slices of larger cuts such as the tenderloin, thin slices of roast beef, and so on, make excellent fillings. Also popular are hot or cold slices of cured beef products, including corned beef, pastrami and tongue, as well as beef sausages such as salami, bologna and hot dogs.

Pork—Various ham and bacon products, served either hot or cold, are extremely popular. In addition, pork loin and tenderloin are light, white meats that adapt well to various flavour combinations and cooking methods. Barbecued pork, pork sausages and pork hot dogs are also popular.

Poultry—Sliced turkey breast, either roasted or smoked, and processed turkey are often used in hot or cold sandwiches. Moreover, food substitutes such as turkey bologna, pastrami, hot dogs and ham are becoming increasingly popular because they generally have a lower fat content than the beef or pork original. Boneless chicken breast, either sliced or whole, is also quite popular, as it can be prepared by a variety of methods, it complements a broad range of flavours and it has a relatively low fat content.

Fish and shellfish—Although fried fish fillets are an old standard, grilled fish sandwiches are gaining in popularity. Canned fish products, particularly tuna and salmon, are also widely used. Often fish and shellfish, especially tuna, shrimp and crab, are used for mayonnaise-based bound salads. Sardines and anchovies are less popular than other fish, but they are sometimes mixed into bound salads or arranged on open-faced sandwiches.

Vegetables—Vegetables add texture, moisture, flavour and nutrition to almost any sandwich. Fresh vegetables such as lettuce, onions and tomatoes are commonly used in combination with meat, cheese and other fillings. Vegetables, however, can stand on their own as sandwich fillings. Marinated, grilled vegetables can be used in hot or cold sandwiches and a combination of sliced, fresh vegetables and a flavourful dressing wrapped in soft lavosh or a tortilla becomes a portable salad.

Eggs—Hard-boiled eggs are most often used as an ingredient in a mayonnaise-based salad, where they are chopped and combined with pickle relish and seasonings. Hard-boiled eggs can also be sliced thin and used as an attractive garnish on open-faced sandwiches. Fried or scrambled eggs can be layered between pieces of bread or rolled in a tortilla for a breakfast sandwich.

Cheese—Cheese is available in such a variety of textures, flavours, colours and styles that it is a welcome addition to nearly any sandwich. Sliced cheese can be used as a filling in hot or cold sandwiches; melted cheese or a cheese sauce makes an excellent topping for hot open-faced sandwiches. Flavoured cream cheese is also used as a spread or filling, particularly with bagels and fruit or nut breads.

Bound salads—Protein salads bound with mayonnaise or salad dressing are popular sandwich fillings. Examples include chicken, tuna, egg and ham salads. Bound salads are discussed in Chapter 25, Salads and Salad Dressings.

Types of Sandwiches

Sandwiches can be hot or cold, closed or open-faced, depending on the way in which the ingredients are assembled and presented.

Hot Sandwiches

Hot closed sandwiches include those in which the filling ingredients are served hot, such as a hamburger or hot dog, and those where the entire sandwich is heated for service, such as a grilled cheese or Monte Cristo. Hot closed sandwiches can be categorized as basic, grilled or deep-fat fried.

Basic hot closed sandwiches are generally those in which the principal filling is served hot between two pieces of bread. These sandwiches may also include fillings that are not hot, such as tomato slices and lettuce leaves. Variations of the basic hot closed sandwich include tacos, quesadillas, burros (or burritos) and wraps, in which the hot and/or cold fillings are folded or wrapped in a tortilla or other supple flatbread.

BASIC PROCEDURE FOR PREPARING WRAP SANDWICHES

1. The tortilla is topped with a spread or dressing.

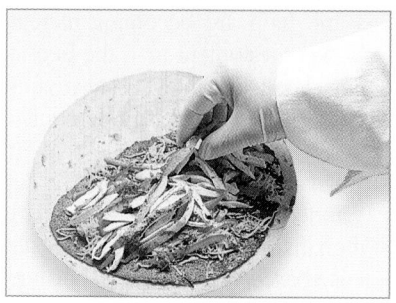

2. Vegetables and meat, fish or poultry items are mounded across the tortilla.

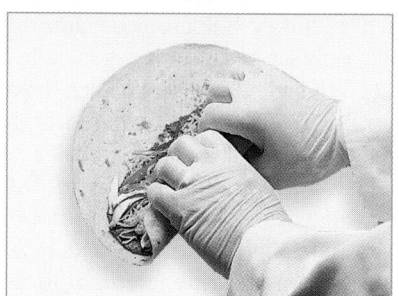

3. The tortilla is rolled tightly around the filling.

Grilled Cheese Sandwiches

Grilled sandwiches are those in which the filling is placed between two pieces of bread, which are buttered on the outside and then browned on a griddle or in a sauté pan. The filling will be warmed during this procedure but will not cook. Therefore, fillings such as bacon or sliced meat should be fully cooked before the sandwich is assembled and grilled.

BASIC PROCEDURE FOR PREPARING SANDWICHES ON A PANINI GRILL

1. Place filled sandwich on a preheated panini grill, then close the lid.

2. Remove sandwiches when heated through and visibly browned.

Deep-fat fried sandwiches are made by dipping a closed sandwich in egg batter or bread crumbs and then deep-fat frying it. The most common example is the Monte Cristo: white bread filled with sliced ham, turkey, Swiss cheese and Dijon mustard.

The hot open-faced turkey or steak sandwich proved long ago that sandwiches do not need to be eaten out of hand. In the typical **hot open-faced sandwich**, bread (grilled, toasted or fresh) is placed on a serving plate, covered with hot meat or other filling and topped with an appropriate gravy, sauce or cheese. (Figure 34.2 illustrates a suggested service style.) The completed dish is often browned under a broiler before service. Condiments and garnishes are usually served on the side.

Perhaps the ultimate hot open-faced sandwich is the pizza. Bread dough is topped with sauce, cheese, meat and vegetables, then baked. Small personal-sized pizzas are a popular menu item even in upscale restaurants.

Cold Sandwiches

Cold sandwiches are simply sandwiches that are eaten cold. They are made with raw ingredients that are not intended to be cooked, such as vegetables and cheese, or with meat, poultry, fish or shellfish that is precooked, then chilled before use as a filling. As with hot sandwiches, cold sandwiches may be closed or open-faced.

Cold closed sandwiches are those that contain two or more pieces of bread with one or more fillings and one or more spreads. Cold closed sandwiches are usually eaten with the hands and come in three styles: basic, multi-decker and tea.

Basic cold sandwiches are made with two pieces of bread or one split roll, one spread and one or more fillings. A tuna salad sandwich or an Italian-style submarine are both examples of basic cold closed sandwiches. A variation of the basic cold sandwich is a wrap with cold fillings, for example, a herb-flavoured tortilla spread with peanut sauce and wrapped around spinach leaves, diced grilled chicken and cold cooked rice.

Multi-decker cold sandwiches are made with three or more pieces of bread, one or more spreads and two or more fillings. The clubhouse sandwich, in which sliced turkey, bacon, lettuce and tomato are layered with three slices of toasted bread, is a classic example of a multi-decker sandwich, although it is actually served warm.

Tea sandwiches are small, fancy constructions made with light, soft, trimmed breads and delicate fillings and spreads. They are usually cut or rolled into shapes such as diamonds, circles or pinwheels and served as a finger food at parties and receptions.

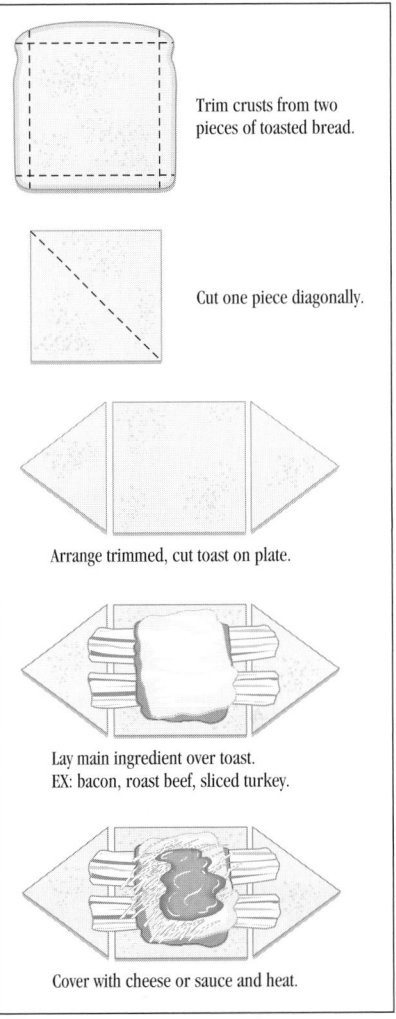

Trim crusts from two pieces of toasted bread.

Cut one piece diagonally.

Arrange trimmed, cut toast on plate.

Lay main ingredient over toast. EX: bacon, roast beef, sliced turkey.

Cover with cheese or sauce and heat.

FIGURE 34.2 Arranging hot open-faced sandwiches.

BASIC PROCEDURE FOR PREPARING COLD MULTI-DECKER SANDWICHES

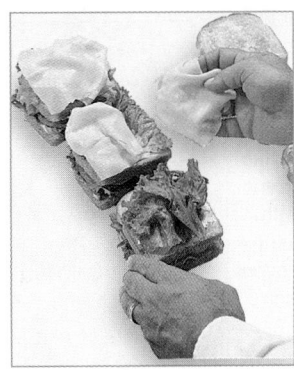

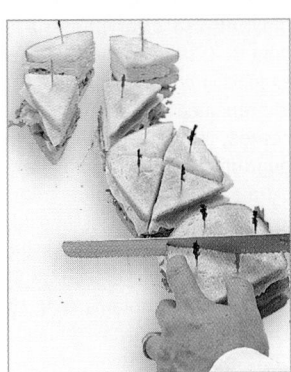

1. Spread butter or mayonnaise on the first slice of toasted bread and top with meat and vegetables.

2. Add the second slice of bread and spread with mayonnaise.

3. Add a second layer of vegetables and meat.

4. Cut the finished sandwich into quarters for service.

● **smørbrød** Norwegian cold open-faced sandwiches; similarly, the Swedish term *smörgåsbord* refers to a buffet or bread-and-butter table of salads, open-faced sandwiches, pickled or marinated fish, sliced meats and cheeses

Cold open-faced sandwiches are simply larger versions of canapés, discussed earlier in this chapter. The most popular style is the open-faced Norwegian sandwich known as **smørbrød**. As with canapés, much emphasis is placed on visual appeal. A single slice of bread is coated with a spread; a small lettuce leaf may be used, then covered with thin slices of meat, poultry or fish, or a portion of a bound salad. Carefully cut and arranged garnishes such as hard-boiled eggs, fresh herbs, pickles, onions and radishes are used to complete the presentation. (See Figure 34.3 for serving suggestions.) A simpler version of an open-faced cold sandwich is a delicatessen classic—a bagel with lox and cream cheese.

Preparing Sandwiches

Sandwiches are generally prepared to order and their preparation usually requires a great deal of handwork. Therefore, the goal is to assemble all ingredients and equipment so that your motions will be as quick and efficient as possible at the time of final assembly. Because each menu and food service operation has its own requirements, there is no one correct station setup, but there are a few basic guidelines.

1. *Prepare ingredients.* All sandwich ingredients should be cooked, mixed, sliced and prepared ahead of service to facilitate quick, efficient assembly at service time. So before service, slice the meats, cheeses and vegetables, blend the flavoured spreads, mix the bound salads, and so on.

2. *Arrange and store ingredients.* Arrange all sandwich ingredients within easy reach of the work area. Cold items must be properly refrigerated at all times. A sandwich bar, similar to a steam table but with refrigerated compartments, is frequently used for this purpose (see Figure 34.4 on the next page). Under-counter refrigeration can be used for backup supplies and less frequently used ingredients. Sliced meats, cheeses and vegetables must be well covered to prevent dehydration or contamination. Many ingredients can be preportioned, either by weight or count, then wrapped in individual portions for storage.

3. *Select and arrange equipment.* The heavy equipment needed for making sandwiches can include preparation equipment such as meat slicers, griddles, grills, fryers and broilers, as well as storage equipment such as

FIGURE 34.3 Cold open-faced sandwiches.

FIGURE 34.3 A typical sandwich bar.

refrigerated sandwich bars for cold ingredients and steam tables for hot ingredients. Even the simplest sandwich menu requires the use of basic hand tools such as spatulas, spreaders, portion scoops, knives and cutting boards. Be sure that the supply of such items is adequate to permit quick handwork and to avoid delays at service time.

Presenting and Garnishing Sandwiches

Sandwiches, especially cold closed sandwiches, are usually cut into halves, thirds or quarters for service. See Figure 34.5 for examples. Cutting makes a sandwich easier for the customer to handle and allows for a more attractive presentation: the sandwich wedges can be arranged to add height to the plate and to expose the fillings' colours and textures. Hot closed sandwiches such as hamburgers are often presented open-faced. Condiments, such as mustard and mayonnaise, and garnishes, such as sliced tomatoes, onions, relish and lettuce leaves, are served on the side or on one of the open bun halves. This tends to be a more attractive presentation and it allows the customer to assemble and add ingredients to the sandwich as desired.

Although a sandwich can be a meal unto itself, it may be served with a salad or starch accompaniment. Potato chips or french-fried potatoes are, of course, standard fare, perhaps because they also are finger foods and they provide a crunchy texture. Bound salads, such as potato and macaroni, are also common starch accompaniments. Plated sandwiches have long been served with coleslaw, fruit salad or a small mixed green salad as side dishes. Even the standard soup-and-sandwich combo—half of a sandwich with a cup of soup—remains a popular lunch selection.

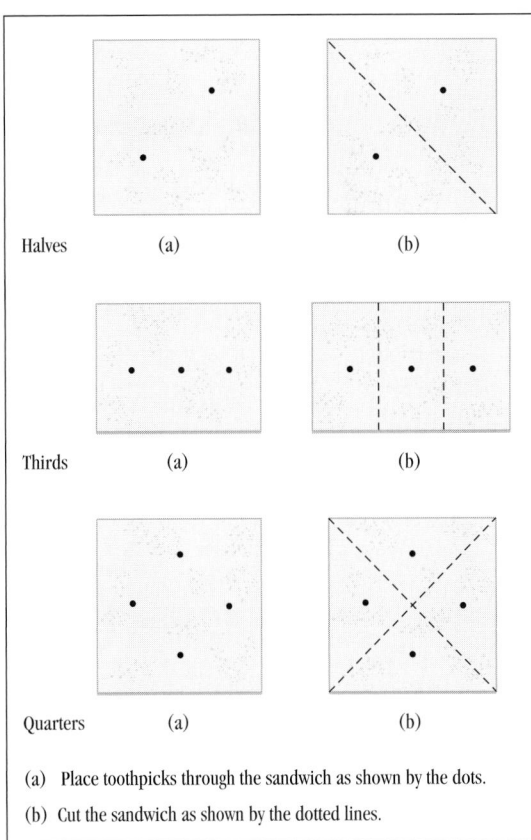

Halves (a) (b)

Thirds (a) (b)

Quarters (a) (b)

(a) Place toothpicks through the sandwich as shown by the dots.

(b) Cut the sandwich as shown by the dotted lines.

FIGURE 34.5 Cutting sandwiches.

Conclusion

The preparation of hors d'oeuvre and sandwiches provides an opportunity for the cook to demonstrate his or her creativity, knowledge of food and skills in presentation and garnishing. Because hors d'oeuvre and canapés often serve as the guests' introduction to the foods you serve, it is especially important that these foods be properly prepared and of the highest quality.

Quality is equally important for sandwiches, which should be made from fresh, carefully prepared ingredients presented in an appetizing and appealing manner. Flavours, colours and textures of the bread, spread and filling should be appropriate and complementary. Breads should be fresh, never stale, and appropriate for the finished sandwich. Spreads should be carefully chosen to add extra flavours and moisture to the sandwich but should not be used to cover or mask dry or poor-quality fillings or breads. Fillings provide the dominant flavour and are usually the source of the sandwich's name; they should be flavourful and properly prepared. The appearance of even the most basic sandwich can be improved by careful assembly and precise trimming and cutting.

Questions for Discussion

1. Discuss four guidelines that should be followed when preparing hors d'oeuvre.
2. Identify and describe the three parts of a canapé.
3. Describe the differences among beluga, osetra and sevruga caviars, and explain how these foods differ from domestic caviars.
4. Create an hors d'oeuvre menu for a small cocktail party. Include three hot and three cold items and explain the reasons for your selections.
5. List and explain five guidelines that should be followed when preparing appetizers or first courses.
6. List examples for each of the three primary sandwich components.
7. Explain the differences between a hot open-faced and a hot closed sandwich.
8. List several hand tools used in sandwich production and explain the need for an ample supply of these tools.
9. Why is cross-contamination a concern when preparing sandwiches? What simple steps can be taken to avoid the spread of pathogenic microorganisms?

Additional Appetizer and Sandwich Recipes

RECIPE 34.9

Spanakopita

Yield: 90 triangles

Onion, small dice	125 g	4 oz.
Unsalted butter, melted	175 g	6 oz.
Fresh spinach, cooked and cooled, or frozen spinach, thawed	700 g	24 oz.
Fresh mint, chopped	10 g	1 Tbsp.
Feta cheese, crumbled	450 g	1 lb.
Eggs, beaten	3	3
Salt and pepper	TT	TT
Phyllo dough	450 g	1 lb.

1. Sauté the onion in 15 g (1 Tbsp.) of melted butter until tender. Remove and cool.

2. Squeeze the water from the spinach. Combine the cooled onion, spinach, mint, feta cheese and beaten eggs. Season with salt and pepper and mix well.

3. Spread 1 sheet of phyllo dough on the work surface; brush with melted butter. Place another sheet of phyllo on top of the first; brush it with butter. Place a third sheet of phyllo on top of the second and brush it with butter as well.

4. Cut the dough into 5-cm (2-in.) wide strips.

5. Place 15 g (1 Tbsp.) of the filling on the end of each strip of phyllo.

6. Starting at the end with the filling, fold 1 corner of the dough over the spinach to the opposite side of the strip to form a triangle. Continue folding the dough, keeping it in a triangular shape, like point-folding a flag (see photograph).

7. Place the phyllo triangles on a sheet pan and brush with melted butter. Bake at 190°C (375°F) until brown and crispy, approximately 20 minutes.

RECIPE 34.9

Approximate values per serving:	
Calories	45
Total fat	3 g
Saturated fat	2 g
Cholesterol	15 mg
Sodium	105 mg
Total carbohydrates	3 g
Protein	2 g

1. Spanakopita: Brushing and stacking the layers of phyllo pastry with butter.

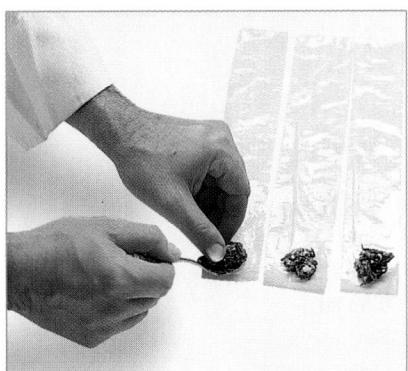

2. Placing the filling on the pastry.

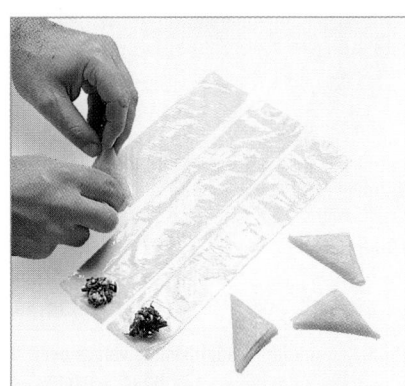

3. Folding the pastry and filling into triangles.

RECIPE 34.10

Approximate values per serving:	
Calories	491
Total fat	47 g
Saturated fat	29 g
Cholesterol	153 mg
Sodium	58 mg
Total carbohydrates	7 g
Protein	12 g

Escargot in Garlic Butter

Yield: 6 8-piece servings

Snails, canned	48	48
Butter, softened	500 g	1 lb.
Shallots, minced	20 g	2 Tbsp.
Garlic, chopped	10 g	2 tsp.
Fine bread crumbs	20 g	2 Tbsp.
Brandy	15 mL	1 Tbsp.
Parsley, chopped	20 g	3 Tbsp.
Salt and pepper	TT	TT
Nutmeg	pinch	pinch
Mushroom caps, medium	48	48

1. Drain and rinse the snails.

2. Combine the butter, shallots, garlic, bread crumbs, brandy, parsley, salt, pepper and nutmeg in a mixer or food processor and mix or process until well blended.

3. Sauté the mushroom caps in a small amount of the butter mixture until cooked but still firm. Remove from the heat and place 6 caps in each of 8 shallow ramekins.

4. Place a snail in each cap and top with a generous amount of the garlic butter.

5. Bake the mushrooms and snails at 230°C (450°F) for 5–7 minutes and serve hot.

VARIATIONS:

1. If snail shells are available, place a small amount of the butter in each shell. Push a snail into the buttered shell and add more butter to completely cover the snail. Place the shells in a specially designed escargot dish or a shallow ramekin with 10 mm (1/2 in.) of rock salt to hold them in place and cook as above.

2. Prepare 48 small bouchées from puff pastry or brioche. Sauté the snails in a generous amount of the garlic butter and place 1 snail in each bouchée. Drizzle the snail with the garlic butter and serve as a hot hors d'oeuvre.

Hummus

RECIPE 34.11

Approximate values per 85 mL serving:	
Calories	267
Total fat	19 g
Saturated fat	3 g
Cholesterol	0 mg
Sodium	20 mg
Total carbohydrates	19 g
Protein	8 g

Hummus

Yield: 1 L (1 qt.)

Chickpeas, cooked	500 g	1 lb.
Tahini paste	250 g	8 oz.
Garlic, chopped	10 g	2 tsp.
Cumin	1 g	1/2 tsp.
Lemon juice	150 mL	5 fl. oz.
Olive oil	100 mL	3 fl. oz.
Salt	5 g	1 tsp.
Cayenne pepper	TT	TT
Fresh parsley, chopped	10 g	2 tsp.

1. Combine the chickpeas, tahini, garlic, cumin, lemon juice and olive oil in a food processor; process until smooth. Season with salt and cayenne.

2. Spoon the hummus onto a serving platter and smooth the surface. Drizzle a little olive oil over the hummus and garnish with the chopped parsley. Serve with warm pita bread that has been cut into quarters.

Guacamole

RECIPE 34.12

Guacamole

Yield: 1 L (1 qt.)

Avocados	6	6
Lemon juice	75 mL	2-1/2 fl. oz.
Green onion, sliced	30 g	4 Tbsp.
Cilantro, chopped	30 g	3 Tbsp.
Tomatoes, seeded, diced	50 g	3 Tbsp.
Garlic, chopped	5 g	1 tsp.
Jalapeños, seeded, chopped	1	1
Salt	TT	TT

1. Cut each avocado in half. Remove the seed and scoop out the pulp.
2. Add the lemon juice to the avocado pulp and mix well, mashing the avocado pulp.
3. Add the remaining ingredients. Season with salt and mix well.

RECIPE 34.12

Approximate values per 50 mL serving:	
Calories	100
Total fat	9 g
Saturated fat	1.5 g
Cholesterol	0 mg
Sodium	243 mg
Total carbohydrates	5 g
Protein	1 g

RECIPE 34.13

Sun-Dried Tomato and Basil Aïoli

Yield: 1 L (1 qt.)

Garlic cloves, mashed to a paste	4	4
Egg yolks	4	4
Lemon juice	30 mL	2 Tbsp.
Olive oil	700 mL	1-1/2 pt.
Sun-dried tomatoes, packed in olive oil	125 g	4 oz.
Fresh basil, chopped	30 g	4 Tbsp.
Salt	5 g	1 tsp.
Pepper	2 g	1/2 tsp.

1. Combine the garlic, egg yolks and a few drops of the lemon juice in a bowl and whip until frothy.
2. While whipping the egg yolk mixture, slowly add the olive oil until an emulsion begins to form. Continue adding the oil while whipping until all of the oil is incorporated. A few drops of lemon juice may be added from time to time to thin the sauce.
3. Finely chop the sun-dried tomatoes. Add them, a portion of the olive oil in which they were packed, and the basil to the aïoli.
4. Season with salt, pepper and lemon juice.

RECIPE 34.13

Approximate values per 15 mL serving:	
Calories	95
Total fat	10 g
Saturated fat	1.4 g
Cholesterol	13 mg
Sodium	70 mg
Total carbohydrates	1 g
Protein	0.5 g

Mezze: Little Bites

Mezze are small plates of assorted salads such as hummus and baba ghanoush that are served with drinks to allow guests to linger and relax before the main meal. Mezze (also spelled meze and mezedes) form part of the dining tradition in countries from North Africa, Greece and Turkey to the Middle East. Spaniards observe a similar custom. Tapas, small portions of savoury foods such as shrimp in garlic sauce or deep-fried olives, are served in bars at lunch or dinner. These little bites serve two purposes; they whet the appetite and keep patrons drinking.

RECIPE 34.14

Approximate values per 15 mL serving:

Calories	38
Total fat	4 g
Saturated fat	0.5 g
Cholesterol	1 mg
Sodium	141 mg
Total carbohydrates	1 g
Protein	0 g

RECIPE 34.14

Tapenade

Yield: 360 mL (12 fl. oz.)

Garlic cloves	4	4
Kalamata olives, pitted	300 g	1 pt.
Anchovies	30 g	1 oz.
Capers	25 g	2 Tbsp.
Fresh thyme	5 g	1 tsp.
Fresh rosemary	5 g	1 tsp.
Fresh oregano	5 g	1 tsp.
Fresh lemon juice	45 mL	3 Tbsp.
Extra virgin olive oil	60 mL	2 fl. oz.

1. Place all of the ingredients in the bowl of a food processor and pulse or process until the mixture forms a coarse paste. Refrigerate.

Pamela Good

Pamela was born and grew up in Montreal. She graduated from the Culinary Institute of Canada in 1991. After gaining experience in Switzerland, Asia and various parts of Canada, she settled in Prince Edward Island. Currently, Pamela is a Chef Instructor at the Culinary Institute of Canada.

RECIPE 34.15

Approximate values per serving:

Calories	334
Total fat	32 g
Saturated fat	17 g
Cholesterol	200 mg
Sodium	194 mg
Total carbohydrates	5.8 g
Protein	6.6 g

RECIPE 34.15

Crimini Mushroom Flans

CULINARY INSTITUTE OF CANADA, CHARLOTTETOWN, PEI
Chef Instructor Pamela Good

Yield: 12 60-mL (2-oz.) ramekins

Crimini (or other) mushrooms, brunoise	600 g	1 lb. 5 oz.
Shallots, brunoise	45 g	3 Tbsp.
Garlic, minced	25 g	5 cloves
Olive oil	50 mL	2 fl. oz.
White wine	50 mL	2 fl. oz.
Rosemary, fresh, minced	10 g	1 Tbsp.
Italian parsley, minced	10 g	1 Tbsp.
Cream, 35%	800 mL	28 fl. oz.
Eggs, beaten	7	7
Salt and pepper	TT	TT
Clarified butter	as needed	as needed

1. Prepare a duxelles with the mushrooms, shallots, garlic, olive oil, wine, rosemary and parsley (see Recipe 10.23).
2. Reduce the cream to 550 mL (16 fl. oz.); temper into the beaten eggs. Fold in the duxelles and season to taste.
3. Brush the ramekins with clarified butter and ladle the mixture into them.
4. Set the ramekins in a hotel pan lined with cloth and pour boiling water in the pan until it is halfway up the sides of the ramekins. Cook in a 155°C (300°F) oven until just set. Let cool and chill. Unmould and reheat gently.
5. To serve, place on a bed of zucchini julienne sautéed in butter, seasoned and garnished with red bell pepper brunoise. Drizzle with herb oil.

RECIPE 34.16

Buckwheat Blinis

Yield: 24 blinis

Granulated sugar	10 g	2 tsp.
Dry yeast	7 g	1/4 oz.
Milk, lukewarm	400 mL	14 fl. oz.
Buckwheat flour	125 g	4 oz.
All-purpose flour	100 g	3 oz.
Salt	2 g	1/2 tsp.
Unsalted butter, melted	50 g	3 Tbsp.
Vegetable oil	30 mL	2 Tbsp.
Egg yolks	3	3
Egg whites	2	2

1. Stir the sugar and yeast into the warmed milk and let stand until foamy, approximately 5 minutes.

2. Whisk in the flours, salt, butter, oil and egg yolks. Beat until smooth.

3. Cover the batter and allow it to rise in a warm place until doubled, approximately 1 hour.

4. Beat the egg whites to stiff peaks, then fold them into the risen batter.

5. Lightly oil and preheat a large sauté pan. Drop 30 mL (2 Tbsp.) of batter into the sauté pan, spacing the blinis at least 2.5 cm (1 in.) apart. Cook until the bottom of each blini is golden, approximately 1 minute. Turn the blini and cook an additional 30 seconds. Remove from the pan and keep warm for service.

Blini may be used as a canapé base and are frequently topped with crème fraîche and garnished with caviar.

RECIPE 34.16

Approximate values per serving:	
Calories	43
Total fat	1 g
Saturated fat	0.5 g
Cholesterol	2 mg
Sodium	90 mg
Total carbohydrates	8 g
Protein	2 g

RECIPE 34.17

Malpeque Oysters Dressed in Fennel Citrus with Carrot Gazpacho

DELTA DAILYFOOD CANADA, INC., MONTREAL, QC
Chef Stephan Czapalay, CCC
Yield: 10 servings

Carrot Gazpacho

Carrot juice	500 mL	17 fl. oz.
Cucumber, peeled, seeded	1	1
Golden tomatoes	2	2
Ginger, chopped	8 g	2 tsp.
Celery heart	450 g	1 lb.
Carrots, sliced	500 g	8
Onion, sliced	350 g	1
Water	2 L	2 qt.
Orange juice	125 mL	4 fl. oz.
Fennel seeds	4	4

1. Purée carrot juice, cucumber, tomatoes, ginger and celery heart; pass through a fine sieve and reserve, chilled.

2. Cook remaining ingredients until tender. Purée and pass through a fine sieve.

3. Combine raw and cooked purées and pass through a sieve again.

4. Chill well.

Stephan Czapalay, CCC
Stephan began his cooking career in 1984 in Wolfville, Nova Scotia, and worked in a variety of prestigious restaurants in PEI, Nova Scotia, Quebec, France, Italy and Switzerland in the years that followed. Between 1997 and 2001, he functioned as the proud chef-owner of Seasons in Thyme Restaurant in Summerside, PEI, which was awarded a three-star rating from *Where to Eat in Canada* and a four-diamond rating by AAA. He regularly upgrades his skills, has instructed at the Canadian Culinary Institute in Charlottetown and has competed in many competitions. Stephan is also Corporate Chef for Clearwater Fine Foods and McCain Foods Canada. He is currently Director, Culinary Innovation and Development, at Delta Dailyfood (Canada) Inc. in Montreal.

continued

Fennel Citrus Salad

Fennel, shredded	350 g	12 oz.
Orange juice	30 mL	2 Tbsp.
Lemon juice	15 mL	1 Tbsp.
Olive oil	50 mL	3 Tbsp.

Mix all ingredients together and chill.

Assembly:

Malpeque oysters, shucked	40	40
Fresh dill	40 sprigs	40 sprigs

1. Ladle 150 mL (5 fl. oz.) of Carrot Gazpacho into a chilled soup cup or ice bowl.
2. Place 10 g (1 Tbsp.) Fennel Citrus Salad on each oyster shell and set oyster on top. Garnish with a dill sprig.
3. On a doily-lined plate, place soup and arrange oysters.

RECIPE 34.17

Approximate values per serving:

Calories	134
Total fat	3 g
Saturated fat	1 g
Cholesterol	30 mg
Sodium	202 mg
Total carbohydrates	21 g
Protein	6 g

RECIPE 34.18

Spring Rolls

Yield: 24 rolls

Shiitake mushrooms, diced	8	8
Peanut oil	50 mL	2 fl. oz.
Sesame oil	15 mL	1 Tbsp.
Garlic, chopped	5 g	1 tsp.
Fresh ginger, grated	2 g	1/2 tsp.
Pork, ground	250 g	8 oz.
Raw shrimp, deveined, chopped	250 g	8 oz.
Daikon, shredded	175 g	6 oz.
Napa cabbage, julienne	175 g	6 oz.
Bean sprouts	125 g	4 oz.
Water chestnuts, chopped	175 g	12
Bamboo shoots, chopped	175 g	6 oz.
Green onion, finely chopped	6	6
Light soy sauce	15 mL	1 Tbsp.
Oyster sauce	15 mL	1 Tbsp.
Salt and pepper	TT	TT
Cornstarch	10 g	1 Tbsp.
Spring roll wrappers	24	24

1. Remove stems from mushrooms. If dry mushrooms are used, rehydrate.
2. Heat the oils and sauté the garlic and ginger for 5 seconds.
3. Add the pork; sauté for 30 seconds and then add shrimp and stir-fry until cooked. Reserve in refrigerator.
4. Add the prepared vegetables, sauces, salt and pepper. Cook for 30 seconds more. Tilt pan and add cornstarch, dissolved in a little water. Boil and mix thoroughly.
5. Remove from the heat, cool and refrigerate.
6. Combine both mixtures. Place 50 g (2 oz.) of filling at 1 end of wrap, start to roll, fold the sides over toward the middle and roll up into a cigar shape. Brush the edge with water and press to seal.
7. Deep-fat fry the spring rolls at 180°C (350°F) until hot and crispy, approximately 45 seconds.

RECIPE 34.18

Approximate values per serving:

Calories	144
Total fat	9 g
Saturated fat	1.5 g
Cholesterol	26 mg
Sodium	332 mg
Total carbohydrates	8 g
Protein	6.5 g

RECIPE 34.19

Cha Gio

(DEEP-FRIED VIETNAMESE SPRING ROLLS)
Yield: 32 pieces (approximately)

Cellophane noodles	60 g	2 oz.
Vegetable oil	15 mL	1 Tbsp.
Garlic, minced	10 g	2 cloves
Shrimp, peeled, deveined and chopped	125 g	4 oz.
Pork, minced	125 g	4 oz.
Carrots, julienne	75 g	2-1/2 oz.
Green onions, sliced	3	3
Mung bean sprouts	30 g	1 oz.
Fish sauce	10 mL	2 tsp.
Vietnamese chile sauce	15 mL	1 Tbsp.
Cornstarch	6 g	2 tsp.
Water, cold	10 mL	2 tsp.
Rice wraps	32	32
Hot water	as needed	as needed

1. Soak the cellophane noodles in boiling water for 5 minutes. Drain and cut into 2.5- to 5-cm (1- to 2-in.) pieces.

2. Heat a wok and add the oil. Stir-fry the garlic for a few seconds. Add the shrimp and pork and stir-fry, breaking up any clumps. Add the carrots, green onions, bean sprouts, fish sauce, chile sauce and drained noodles. Cook until the carrots are slightly softened. Remove from heat and cool completely.

3. Mix the cornstarch and water together in a small bowl.

4. Moisten the rice wraps a few at a time in hot water. Lay out on damp towelling.

5. Place approximately 25 g (2 Tbsp.) of filling in the centre of each wrapper. Fold the sides toward the middle and roll in a cigar shape. Brush the edge with the cornstarch mixture to seal.

6. Using the swimming method, deep-fat fry the spring rolls at 165°C (325°F) until hot and crispy, approximately 45 seconds. Drain on absorbent paper and serve immediately with Nuoc Cham Sauce (recipe follows).

continued

RECIPE 34.19

Approximate values per roll, without sauce:	
Calories	58
Total fat	3.8 g
Saturated fat	0.5 g
Cholesterol	8.8 mg
Sodium	45 mg
Total carbohydrates	4.2 g
Protein	1.7 g

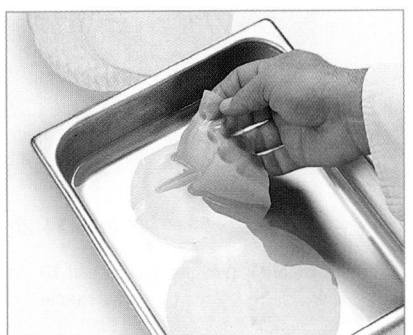

1. Cha Gio: Soaking the spring roll wrappers.

2. Filling the spring roll wrappers.

3. Folding the wrapper around the filling.

4. Sealing the spring roll with cornstarch water.

Nuoc Cham Sauce

Yield: 300 mL (10 tsp.)

Sugar	75 g	5 Tbsp.
Water	50 mL	3 Tbsp.
Fish sauce (nuoc mam)	75 mL	5 Tbsp.
Lemon juice, fresh	125 mL	4 fl. oz.
Garlic, minced	5 g	1 clove
Red chile, seeded, minced	1	1
Shallot, minced	25 g	2 Tbsp.

Whisk all ingredients together and let stand at room temperature for 30 minutes before serving.

Nuoc Cham Sauce—Approximate values per 300 mL serving:	
Calories	12
Total fat	0 g
Saturated fat	0 g
Cholesterol	0 mg
Sodium	217 mg
Total carbohydrates	3.1 g
Protein	0.2 g

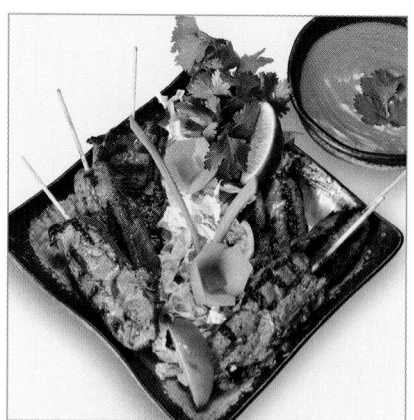

Satay with Peanut Sauce

RECIPE 34.20

Approximate values per skewer and 10 mL sauce:	
Calories	100
Total fat	5 g
Saturated fat	1 g
Cholesterol	27 mg
Sodium	248 mg
Total carbohydrates	4 g
Protein	10 g

RECIPE 34.20

Satay with Peanut Sauce, Singapore Style

Yield: 16 skewers

Chicken breast, beef inside round, pork fillet or lamb leg	500 g	1 lb.
Lemon zest	10 g	2 tsp.
Onion, chopped	200 g	7 oz.
Vegetable oil	25 mL	2 Tbsp.
Light soy sauce	15 mL	1 Tbsp.
Coriander, ground	3 g	2 tsp.
Cumin, ground	3 g	1 tsp.
Turmeric, ground	3 g	1 tsp.
Cinnamon, ground	0.25 g	1/4 tsp.
Salt	5 g	1 tsp.
Sugar	5 g	1 tsp.
Peanut Sauce (recipe follows)		

1. Cut the meat into 1-cm (1/2-in.) cubes.
2. Blend remaining ingredients until smooth, coat meat and marinate for at least 1 hour.
3. Soak bamboo skewers in water for 1 hour before threading 5–6 pieces of meat on top half of skewer.
4. Grill or broil just until meat is cooked.
5. Serve with Peanut Sauce.

Peanut Sauce

Vegetable oil	50 mL	4 Tbsp.
Lemon grass, sliced	1 stalk	1 stalk
Onion, finely chopped	100 g	3 oz.
Garlic, finely chopped	10 g	3 cloves
Dried shrimp paste (blacan)	5 g	2 tsp.
Roasted peanuts, skinless	185 g	6 oz.
Dried tamarind	25 mL	1-1/2 Tbsp.
Hot water	250 mL	8 fl. oz.
Sambal olek (crushed fresh chiles)	5 g	1 tsp.
Ginger powder	3 g	1-1/2 tsp.
Sugar	30 g	1 oz.

continued

| Salt | 5 g | 1 tsp. |
| Soy sauce | 50 mL | 3 Tbsp. |

1. In a blender place half of the oil, lemon grass, onion, garlic and shrimp paste. Blend to a paste.
2. Scrape out blender and add peanuts. Crush finely.
3. Soak tamarind in hot water, squeeze to dissolve pulp and strain. Reserve liquid.
4. Place remaining oil in a hot wok and cook purée mixture over medium heat for a few minutes to cook it out.
5. Add remaining ingredients and simmer until gravy thickens, about 7–8 minutes.

VARIATIONS: 100 g (3 oz.) peanut butter may be substituted for the peanuts. Lemon juice can be used for tamarind. A little coconut milk may be added for additional flavour.

Peanut Sauce—Approximate values per 10 mL serving:

Calories	34
Total fat	3 g
Saturated fat	0.5 g
Cholesterol	0 mg
Sodium	95 mg
Total carbohydrates	2 g
Protein	1 g

RECIPE 34.21

Grilled Shrimp with Prosciutto and Basil

Yield: 12 pieces

Shrimp, 16–20 count, peeled and deveined, tails removed	12	12
Dry white wine	50 mL	2 fl. oz.
Rice wine vinegar	30 mL	1 fl. oz.
Thyme, fresh	5 g	2 tsp.
Onion, minced	25 g	1 oz.
Cumin, ground	5 g	1 Tbsp.
Salt and pepper	TT	TT
Vegetable oil	100 mL	3 fl. oz.
Dried basil	2 g	2 tsp.
Garlic cloves, chopped	2	2
Prosciutto slices	3	3
Fresh basil leaves	6	6

1. Combine all of the ingredients except the prosciutto and fresh basil in a stainless-steel bowl. Marinate for 30 minutes.
2. Remove the shrimps from the marinade and drain them well.
3. Cut each slice of prosciutto into quarters.
4. Wrap each shrimp first with one-half leaf of basil, then a piece of prosciutto; secure with a toothpick.
5. Grill for 1–1.5 minutes per side. Be careful not to overcook. Remove the toothpick and serve hot or cold.

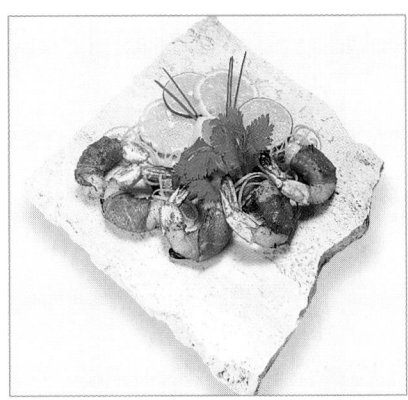

Grilled Shrimp with Prosciutto and Basil

RECIPE 34.21

Approximate values per serving:

Calories	220
Total fat	15 g
Saturated fat	2 g
Cholesterol	170 mg
Sodium	250 mg
Total carbohydrates	2 g
Protein	18 g

Melissa Craig

Melissa completed her Apprenticeship Program at Sooke Harbour House Restaurant and Camosun Community College, in Victoria, BC. Hard work and dedication have won her top honours: she was the CCFCC, 2001 Junior Cook Champion and Canada 2008 Gold Medal Plates Culinary Champion.

RECIPE 34.22

Approximate values per serving:	
Calories	204
Total fat	6 g
Saturated fat	0.5 g
Cholesterol	15 mg
Sodium	811 mg
Total carbohydrates	30 g
Protein	10.5 g

RECIPE 34.22

Seared Weathervane Scallops with Pickled Daikon, Pumpkin Seed, Sea Lettuce and Lamanaria Salad

BEARFOOT BISTRO, WHISTLER, BC
Executive Chef Melissa Craig

Yield: 4 servings

Pickle Marinade:		
Pear cider vinegar	50 mL	2 fl. oz.
Sugar	50 g	2 oz.
Sea salt	5 g	1 tsp.
Ginger, minced	4 g	1 tsp.
Water	125 mL	4 fl. oz.
Daikon radish, julienne	50 g	1/4 cup
Sea lettuce	50 g	1/4 cup
Pumpkinseed oil	30 mL	1 fl. oz.
Shallots, minced	20 g	1 Tbsp.
Garlic, minced	2 g	1/2 tsp.
Salt and pepper	TT	TT
Lamanaria (a type of seaweed)	50 g	1/4 cup
Weathervane scallops	12	12
Leek strips, blanched	4	4
Vegetable oil	as needed	as needed
Pumpkin seeds, toasted	25 g	2 Tbsp.
Arugula flowers	TT	TT
Mustard flowers	TT	TT
Sea salt	TT	TT

1. Combine pickle marinade ingredients, bring to a boil and cool.
2. Add daikon to pickle marinade.
3. Rinse sea lettuce thoroughly and slice into thin strips.
4. In a bowl, combine pumpkinseed oil, shallots, garlic, salt and pepper. Drain daikon and add to dressing along with sea lettuce and lamanaria.
5. Tie scallops together in bunches of 3 with the leek strips.
6. Sear scallops in vegetable oil in a hot pan for approximately 2 minutes per side.
7. Meanwhile, toss pumpkin seeds and flowers with salad. Assemble on plates and place scallop bundles on top. Season with sea salt and garnish with wasabi mayonnaise.

VARIATION: Wrap scallops individually and set on Asian soup spoons.

RECIPE 34.23

Salt-Cured Foie Gras with
Mango Pineapple Salsa on Brioche

CALGARY, AB

Chef/Food Writer dee Hobsbawn-Smith

Yield: 350–400 g (12–14 oz.)

Foie gras	1 lobe	1 lobe
Kosher salt	as needed	as needed
Mango Pineapple Salsa		
(recipe follows)		

1. Remove any connective tissue and veins from foie gras. Wrap in cheese-cloth and tie securely.
2. Place in a bowl lined with kosher salt and completely cover with more salt. Chill for at least 24 hours.
3. Remove any fat and the cheesecloth.
4. Slice thinly. Serve on warm brioche with Mango Pineapple Salsa.

Mango Pineapple Salsa

Mango, diced	1	1
Pineapple, diced	1/2	1/2
Oranges, diced, filleted	4	4

Combine all ingredients gently and chill.

dee Hobsbawn-Smith

dee—a Calgary-based professional chef, caterer, culinary educator and author—has been delighting Calgary diners and readers since 1983. She studied cooking at Vancouver Vocational Institute, completed her Red Seal in Calgary and studied with eminent chef and educator Madeleine Kamman in Annecy, France. Since selling her restaurant, Foodsmith, in 1994, dee has turned to food writing and now has four cookbooks and many magazine articles and columns under her belt.

RECIPE 34.23

Approximate values per 30 g serving:	
Calories	74
Total fat	1.4 g
Saturated fat	0.5 g
Cholesterol	150 mg
Sodium	1220 mg
Total carbohydrates	9.5 g
Protein	6 g

Mango Pineapple Salsa— Approximate values per 1/12 recipe:	
Calories	34
Total fat	0 g
Saturated fat	0 g
Cholesterol	0 mg
Sodium	0 mg
Total carbohydrates	8.5 g
Protein	0.5 g

Hamburger

RECIPE 34.24

Approximate values per serving:	
Calories	580
Total fat	32 g
Saturated fat	9 g
Cholesterol	99 mg
Sodium	355 mg
Total carbohydrates	40 g
Protein	29 g

RECIPE 34.24

Hamburger

Yield: 1 sandwich

Ground round or chuck	125–175 g	4–6 oz.
Salt and pepper	TT	TT
Hamburger bun or an appropriate bread	1	1
Garnishes	as desired	as desired

1. Form the ground round or chuck into a patty, handling the beef as little as possible.

2. Season the patty with salt and pepper and broil or grill to the desired doneness, turning once. While the patty is cooking, toast the bun or bread if desired.

3. Remove the patty from the broiler or grill, place on one-half of the bun or on 1 slice of bread and garnish the other half with a lettuce leaf, a slice of onion, a slice of tomato and/or pickles. Serve with condiments such as ketchup and mustard.

NOTE: It is recommended that ground beef products be cooked to an internal temperature of 74°C (165°F).

VARIATIONS: CHEESEBURGER—Place 25 g (1 oz.) cheddar, Swiss or other cheese on the cooking patty approximately 1 minute before it is done.

BACON CHEESEBURGER—Prepare a cheeseburger and place 2 slices of crisp bacon on top of the cheese when the patty is done.

MUSHROOM BURGER—Sauté 50 g (2 oz.) of sliced mushrooms in 5 mL (1 tsp.) of butter. Top the cooked hamburger or cheeseburger with the cooked mushrooms.

CALIFORNIA BURGER—Grill a boneless, skinless chicken breast and serve on a whole wheat bun, accompanied by 50 g (2 oz.) of guacamole, 25 g (1 oz.) of alfalfa sprouts, 2 slices of ripe tomato and 1 thin slice of red onion.

Reuben Sandwich

RECIPE 34.25

Approximate values per sandwich:	
Calories	556
Total fat	27 g
Saturated fat	10 g
Cholesterol	85 mg
Sodium	2150 mg
Total carbohydrates	39 g
Protein	39 g

RECIPE 34.25

Reuben Sandwich

Yield: 1 sandwich

Dark rye bread	2 slices	2 slices
Thousand Island Dressing (Recipe 25.10)	30 mL	1 fl. oz.
Cooked corned beef, hot, sliced very thinly	125 g	4 oz.
Sauerkraut, hot, drained well	50 g	2 oz.
Swiss cheese	30 g	2 slices
Whole butter, softened	as needed	as needed

1. Spread each slice of bread with half of the Thousand Island Dressing.

2. Place the hot corned beef, hot sauerkraut and Swiss cheese on 1 slice of bread. Top with the second slice of bread, keeping the dressing side down.

3. Butter the top slice of bread and place the sandwich on a hot griddle, top down. Carefully butter the second slice of bread.

4. Fry the sandwich, turning once when the first side is well browned. The sandwich is done when both sides are well browned, the fillings are very hot and the cheese is melted.

5. Cut the sandwich in half diagonally and arrange as desired for service.

RECIPE 34.26

Monte Cristo Sandwich

Yield: 1 sandwich

Cooked turkey breast, sliced thinly	30 g	1 oz.
Swiss cheese	20 g	2 slices
White bread	3 slices	3 slices
Ham, sliced thinly	30 g	1 oz.
Egg	1	1
Milk	30 mL	1 fl. oz.
Oil	as needed	as needed

1. Arrange the turkey breast and 1 slice of cheese on top of the first slice of bread.
2. Place the second slice of bread on top of the turkey, then place the ham and second slice of cheese. Place the third slice of bread.
3. Beat the egg and milk together. Dip the sandwich in the egg batter and allow the batter to soak into the bread.
4. Pan-fry the sandwich in oil until it is evenly browned. Remove from the oil and drain well. Cut the sandwich into 4 pieces and arrange as desired.

VARIATION: Wedge the sandwich before dipping and soaking. Originally this sandwich was deep-fat fried.

Monte Cristo Sandwich

RECIPE 34.26

Approximate values per sandwich:	
Calories	627
Total fat	19 g
Saturated fat	7 g
Cholesterol	279 mg
Sodium	932 mg
Total carbohydrates	74 g
Protein	37 g

RECIPE 34.27

Arugula, Capicola Ham and Provolone Panino

Yield: 1 serving

Ciabatta or hard roll, 10 cm × 6 cm (4 in. × 2-1/2 in.)	1	1
Mayonnaise	30 mL	2 Tbsp.
Pesto Sauce (recipe 23.25)	10 mL	2 tsp.
Arugula	15 g	1/2 oz.
Capicola, prosciutto or ham, sliced thin	60 g	2 oz.
Provolone, sliced thin	30 g	1 oz.
Oven-dried tomato wedges	30 g	1 oz.
Black pepper	TT	TT
Olives	as needed for garnish	
Tomatoes, quartered	as needed for garnish	

1. Cut the roll in half horizontally. Spread the interior of the roll generously with the mayonnaise and pesto.
2. Arrange the arugula, **capicola**, provolone and tomatoes in layers on the bottom portion of the roll. Season the layers with pepper as desired.
3. Place the sandwich on a preheated panini grill or on a griddle. Cook until heated through and browned, approximately 3–5 minutes. (If using a griddle, place a weight on the sandwich as it cooks, then flip it halfway through to brown on both sides.)
4. Cut on the diagonal and serve immediately garnished with olives and fresh tomato wedges on the side.

Arugula, Capicola Ham and Provolone Panino

● **capicola** Italian dry-cured salami made from pork shoulder that is seasoned with garlic, hot pepper, spices and wine, then smoked and cured

RECIPE 34.27

Approximate values per serving:	
Calories	616
Total fat	31 g
Saturated fat	10 g
Cholesterol	65 mg
Sodium	2238 mg
Total carbohydrates	58 g
Protein	29 g

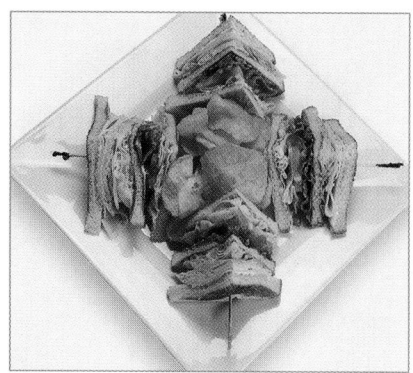

Clubhouse Sandwich

Approximate values per sandwich:	
Calories	530
Total fat	24 g
Saturated fat	6 g
Cholesterol	95 mg
Sodium	821 mg
Total carbohydrates	38 g
Protein	39 g

Clubhouse Sandwich

Yield: 1 sandwich

Bread, toasted	3 slices	3 slices
Mayonnaise	as needed	as needed
Lettuce leaves	2	2
Tomato	3 slices	3 slices
Bacon, cooked crisp	3 slices	3 slices
Salt and pepper	TT	TT
Cooked turkey breast, sliced thinly	90 g	3 oz.

1. Spread 1 side of each slice of toasted bread with mayonnaise.
2. Arrange the lettuce, tomato and bacon on 1 slice of toast. Season with salt and pepper.
3. Place another slice of toast on top of the bacon.
4. Arrange the turkey breast on top of the second slice of toast.
5. Place the third slice of toast on top of the turkey breast, mayonnaise side down.
6. Place 4 frilled toothpicks in the sandwich, 1 on each side, approximately 2.5 cm (1 in.) in from the edge. Cut the sandwich diagonally into quarters and arrange as desired for service.

Veggie Wrap

Yield: 1 sandwich

Spinach-flavoured tortilla	1	1
Garlic Yogurt Dressing (recipe follows)	30 mL	2 Tbsp.
Jasmine rice, cooked	90 g	3 oz.
Roma tomato, diced	30 g	2 Tbsp.
Cucumber, julienne	30 g	1 oz.
Alfalfa sprouts	as needed	as needed
Broccoli florets	30 g	1 oz.
Red onion, sliced thinly	30 g	1 oz.
Capers	10 g	1 Tbsp.

1. Spread the tortilla with half of the Garlic Yogurt Dressing.
2. Arrange the rice in a mound across the centre of the tortilla. Top the rice with the vegetables and capers.
3. Drizzle the remaining Garlic Yogurt Dressing over the vegetables.
4. Using a piece of parchment paper as a wrapper, roll the tortilla tightly around the filling, then chill and serve.

Garlic Yogurt Dressing

Yield: 500 mL (1 pt.)

Nonfat yogurt, plain	500 mL	1 pt.
Parsley, minced	10 g	1 Tbsp.
Garlic, minced	25 g	2 Tbsp.
Dijon-style mustard	30 g	2 Tbsp.
Black pepper	1 g	1/4 tsp.
Tabasco sauce	TT	TT

Combine all of the ingredients and chill until ready to use.

Approximate values per serving:	
Calories	460
Total fat	3 g
Saturated fat	0.5 g
Cholesterol	0 mg
Sodium	296 mg
Total carbohydrates	94 g
Protein	12 g

Garlic Yogurt Dressing—Approximate values per 30 mL serving:	
Calories	19
Total fat	0 g
Saturated fat	0 g
Cholesterol	1 mg
Sodium	46 mg
Total carbohydrates	3 g
Protein	2 g

RECIPE 34.30

Southwestern Grilled Chicken Wrap

Yield: 12 sandwiches

Chicken breast, boneless, skinless	1.4 kg	3 lb.
Salt and pepper	TT	TT
Avocados	3	3
Red bell peppers	300 g	2
Red onion	350 g	1
Tomatoes	350 g	2
Tortillas, 24 cm (10 in.)	12	12
Black Bean Spread (recipe follows)	1.3 kg	3 lb.
Black olives, sliced	175 g	6 oz.
Cilantro, chopped	2 bunches	2 bunches
Cheddar cheese, grated	750 g	1 lb. 8 oz.
Jalapeños, minced	2	2

1. Season the chicken breast with salt and pepper and grill or broil until done. Chill and cut into strips.
2. Peel the avocados and cut each into 12 slices. Clean the bell peppers and cut into strips. Slice the onion thinly. Dice the tomatoes.
3. To make each sandwich, place 1 tortilla on a cutting board and spread with approximately 120 g (4 oz.) of Black Bean Spread.
4. Sprinkle one-twelfth of the pepper, onions, tomatoes, olives, cilantro, cheese and jalapeños over the bean spread.
5. Top with one-twelfth of the chicken.
6. Roll the tortilla around the ingredients tightly enough so the sandwich will hold its shape. Cut the sandwich as desired for service.

Black Bean Spread

Yield: 1.3 kg (3 lb.)

Black beans, soaked and drained	750 g	1 lb. 8 oz.
Water	4 L	4 qt.
Onion, diced	125 g	4 oz.
Tomatoes, diced	175 g	6 oz.
Cilantro, chopped	20 g	2 Tbsp.
Salt and pepper	TT	TT
Cumin	3 g	1 tsp.
Chilli powder	3 g	1 tsp.

1. Combine the beans and the water, bring to a boil, reduce to a simmer and cook until tender, approximately 1 to 1.5 hours.
2. Add the remaining ingredients and simmer for 10 minutes.
3. Drain the beans, reserving the cooking liquid. Chill the beans and the liquid.
4. Purée the beans in a food processor, adding enough of the cooking liquid to make a soft, spreadable purée.

Southwestern Grilled Chicken Wrap

RECIPE 34.30

Approximate values per sandwich:	
Calories	642
Total fat	37 g
Saturated fat	16 g
Cholesterol	118 mg
Sodium	695 mg
Total carbohydrates	37 g
Protein	41 g

Black Bean Spread—Approximate values per 60 g serving:	
Calories	100
Total fat	0.5 g
Saturated fat	0 g
Cholesterol	0 mg
Sodium	51 mg
Total carbohydrates	37 g
Protein	12 g

New Orleans–Style Muffaletta Sandwich

New Orleans–Style Muffaletta Sandwich

Yield: 1 sandwich, 4–6 servings

Red bell pepper, roasted, chopped	1	1
Niçoise or Gaeta olives, pitted, chopped	125 g	4 oz.
Olives, green, pitted, chopped	125 g	4 oz.
Virgin olive oil	125 mL	4 fl. oz.
Italian parsley, chopped	20 g	2 Tbsp.
Anchovy fillets, mashed	2	2
Dried oregano	1 g	1 tsp.
Lemon juice	15 mL	1 Tbsp.
Round Italian bread/focaccia, 18-cm (8-in.) diameter	1	1
Arugula or curly endive, chiffonade	45 g	1-1/2 oz.
Tomato concassée	175 g	6 oz.
Mortadella, sliced thinly	175 g	6 oz.
Soppressata, sliced thinly (see page 482)	125 g	4 oz.
Provolone or fontina, sliced thinly	125 g	4 oz.
Pepper	TT	TT

1. To make the olive salad, combine the red pepper, olives, olive oil, parsley, anchovies, oregano and lemon juice and marinate for several hours.

2. Cut the loaf of bread in half horizontally. Remove some of the soft interior of the bread to create a slight hollow area.

3. Drain the olive salad, reserving the oil. Brush the interior of the bread with the reserved oil, using it all.

4. Arrange the olive salad, greens, tomato, mortadella, soppressata and cheese in layers on the bottom portion of the loaf of bread, finishing with a thick layer of olive salad. Season the layers with pepper as desired.

5. Place the top on the sandwich and wrap tightly with plastic wrap. Refrigerate the sandwich for several hours so that the layers will remain in place when the sandwich is cut.

6. Cut the sandwich into 4–6 wedges and arrange as desired for service.

RECIPE 34.31

Approximate values per serving:

Calories	670
Total fat	57 g
Saturated fat	14 g
Cholesterol	60 mg
Sodium	2201 mg
Total carbohydrates	16 g
Protein	24 g

Blackened Steak Sandwich

Blackened Steak Sandwich

Yield: 2 sandwiches

Strip loin steak, 280 g (10 oz.)	1	1
Blackened Steak Seasoning (recipe follows)	as needed	as needed
Clarified butter	30 mL	1 fl. oz.
Capers	10 g	1 Tbsp.
Whole butter, softened	30 g	1 oz.
French bread, cut on the bias	2 slices	2 slices
Baby lettuce, cleaned	125 g	4 oz.
Roma tomatoes, sliced	2	2
Red onions, sliced	30 g	1 oz.

1. Heat a cast-iron skillet over high heat for 10 minutes. Pat the steak dry with paper towelling. Coat the steak in the Blackened Steak Seasoning.

2. Carefully place the steak into the hot skillet and ladle 15 mL (1/2 fl. oz.) of clarified butter over the steak. Be very careful, as the butter may flare up. There will be intense smoke and the steak will form a dark crust. Cook the steak for approximately 2 minutes. Do not burn the spice crust.

3. Turn the steak; ladle the remaining clarified butter over it and allow it to cook to the desired degree of doneness. Finish in oven for medium-well and well done. Remove the steak from the pan and hold in a warm place.

4. Chop the capers and combine them with the softened butter. Spread each slice of bread with half of the caper butter.

5. Slice the steak on the bias.

6. To assemble each sandwich, place one-half of the warm steak on a slice of buttered bread, arrange half of the lettuce, tomatoes and onions attractively on the plate and serve.

VARIATION: To serve this sandwich cold, allow the steak to cool after cooking, then refrigerate it until completely cold. Proceed with the recipe.

Blackened Steak Seasoning

Yield: 50 g (6 Tbsp.)

Paprika	12 g	2 Tbsp.
Salt	20 g	4 tsp.
Onion powder	4 g	2 tsp.
Garlic powder	3.5 g	2 tsp.
Cayenne pepper	4 g	2 tsp.
White pepper	3 g	1 tsp.
Black pepper	2 g	1 tsp.
Dried thyme	1 g	1 tsp.

Combine all ingredients and mix well.

Blackened Does Not Mean Burnt!

There is a popular misconception that foods cooked by this method must be charred. Not so! Burning imparts a bitter taste and is not palatable. Whether "blackening" beef, fish or chicken, the spice coating should be a deep mahogany colour with the red evident. If thicker pieces of meat are cooked to a more well-done state, it may be necessary to finish the items in the oven.

RECIPE 34.32

Approximate values per sandwich:	
Calories	610
Total fat	38 g
Saturated fat	20 g
Cholesterol	180 mg
Sodium	650 mg
Total carbohydrates	21 g
Protein	44 g

RECIPE 34.33

Grouper Sandwich with Lemon Rémoulade

PHOENIX BREWING CO., ATLANTA, GA
Executive Chef Kevin Fonzo

Yield: 6 sandwiches

Olive oil	30 mL	2 Tbsp.
Grouper fillets, each 150 g (5 oz.)	6	6
Salt and pepper	TT	TT
Lemon Rémoulade (recipe follows)	90 mL	6 Tbsp.
Kaiser rolls, sliced, toasted	6	6
Mixed greens	350 g	12 oz.
Tomato slices	6	6

1. Heat the olive oil in a large sauté pan. Season the grouper fillets with salt and pepper and then sauté the fish until golden brown and cooked through.

2. To assemble each sandwich, spread 15 mL (1 Tbsp.) of the Lemon Rémoulade on the bottom half of each roll, then top with 60 g (2 oz.) of mixed greens, a tomato slice and the cooked fish. Cover with remaining half of the roll and serve.

Grouper Sandwich with Lemon Rémoulade

RECIPE 34.33

Approximate values per serving:	
Calories	330
Total fat	8 g
Saturated fat	1 g
Cholesterol	40 mg
Sodium	380 mg
Total carbohydrates	36 g
Protein	28 g

Lemon Rémoulade

Yield: 600 mL (20 fl. oz.)

Mayonnaise	500 mL	16 fl. oz.
Sweet pickle relish	100 g	3 oz.
Onion, chopped fine	20 g	2 Tbsp.
Parsley, chopped	20 g	2 Tbsp.
Fresh lemon juice	30 mL	2 Tbsp.
Salt and black pepper	TT	TT
Worcestershire sauce	TT	TT
Tabasco	TT	TT

Mix all of the ingredients together until thoroughly blended.

Lemon Rémoulade— Approximate values per serving:	
Calories	170
Total fat	18 g
Saturated fat	2.5 g
Cholesterol	15 mg
Sodium	160 mg
Total carbohydrates	2 g
Protein	0 g

RECIPE 34.34

Falafel

Yield: 12 sandwiches

Chickpeas, dry	500 g	1 lb.
Garlic cloves, minced	6	6
Parsley, chopped	15 g	1/2 oz.
Chives, minced	15 g	1/2 oz.
Cumin, ground	10 g	1 Tbsp.
Coriander, ground	8 g	2 tsp.
Cayenne pepper	TT	TT
Eggs	3	3
Salt	TT	TT
Flour	150 g	5 oz.
Plain yogurt	175 mL	6 fl. oz.
Lemon juice	50 mL	2 fl. oz.
Pita bread	12	12
Iceberg lettuce, shredded	175 g	6 oz.
Tomatoes, diced	175 g	6 oz.

1. To make the falafel, soak the chickpeas following the procedures for dried beans outlined in Chapter 22, Vegetables. Drain the chickpeas, place them in a pot and cover with cool water. Simmer until tender, approximately 2–3 hours, remove from the heat and drain well.

2. Process the chickpeas in a food processor or a food chopper until coarsely chopped. Add the garlic, parsley, chives, cumin, coriander and cayenne pepper and process for a few seconds.

3. Add the eggs, salt and flour and process briefly. Remove the falafel from the machine and chill in the refrigerator for 1 hour.

4. Combine the yogurt and lemon juice and mix well. Set aside.

5. Portion the falafel using a #50 scoop (there should be approximately 60 balls) and deep-fat fry the balls at 190°C (375°F) until crisp and hot. Drain well and hold in a warm place.

6. To assemble each sandwich, cut a pita in half or open it to form a pocket, stuff with several balls of falafel and 30 g (1 oz.) of the shredded lettuce and diced tomatoes, and dress with the yogurt sauce. Arrange the sandwiches as desired and serve hot.

RECIPE 34.34

Approximate values per sandwich:	
Calories	294
Total fat	3 g
Saturated fat	0.5 g
Cholesterol	55 mg
Sodium	471 mg
Total carbohydrates	56 g
Protein	12 g

RECIPE 34.35

Artichoke, Chicken and Sun-Dried Tomato Pizza

Yield: 1 37-cm (15-in.) or 2 22-cm (9-in.) pizzas

Pizza Dough (Recipe 29.10)	500 g	1 lb.
Extra virgin olive oil	30 mL	1 fl. oz.
Basic Tomato Sauce (Recipe 10.12)	125 mL	4 fl. oz.
Grilled chicken breast, sliced	175 g	6 oz.
Sun-dried tomatoes, oil packed, diced	5	5
Smoked Gruyère, grated	125 g	4 oz.
Mozzarella cheese, grated	50 g	2 oz.
Marinated artichoke hearts, sliced	50 g	2 oz.
Fresh basil	12 leaves	12 leaves

1. Preheat the oven to 260°C (500°F). Roll out the dough and place it on a lightly oiled pizza pan or well-floured wooden peel; brush it lightly with the olive oil. Spread the tomato sauce.

2. Lay the chicken and sun-dried tomatoes on top. Toss the Gruyère and mozzarella cheeses together and sprinkle onto the pizza.

3. Sprinkle the artichoke pieces and basil leaves on pizza.

4. Bake the pizza until the crust is golden and crisp, approximately 8–12 minutes.

Artichoke, Chicken and Sun-Dried Tomato Pizza

RECIPE 34.35

Approximate values per slice:	
Calories	761
Total fat	48.5 g
Saturated fat	18 g
Cholesterol	158.5 mg
Sodium	601 mg
Total carbohydrates	29 g
Protein	57 g

35 Beverages

> "
> Drink! for you know not whence you came, nor why:
> Drink! for you know not why you go,
> nor where
>
> —*The Rubaiyat of Omar Khayyam* (1859)

Water, coffee and tea are the staples of most beverage menus.

Despite their relatively low but rising price, bottled water or a good cup of coffee or tea can be extremely important to a customer's impression of a food service operation. A cup of coffee is often either the very first or the very last item consumed by a customer. Tea, whether iced or hot, is often consumed throughout the meal. Consequently, it is important to learn to prepare and serve these beverages properly. Many varieties of water are now available and some customers prefer these specialty waters to that from the tap.

Wines, beers and liquors make up a significant beverage offering in many establishments. They are used as an aperitif to stimulate the appetite, as an accompaniment to the meal, to round out a dessert offering or as a key ingredient in many dishes. Guest cheque averages are positively affected as is the contribution margin.

Not only do these beverages complement a meal, they are important profit centres for restaurant owners. Appreciation of the proper preparation and service of these beverages is an important part of a culinary student's training.

These interactive online tools will help you master the skills in this chapter:

- Chapter Quizzes
- Activities

WATER

At one time in Canada a glass of iced water was more than likely the first thing placed in front of the customer as the menu was presented. The origin of this practice is lost to time; perhaps it was thought that sipping water would ease the waiting time until the food was served. There were also those who believed that water aided digestion. Whatever the reasons, water service has evolved as the preference for bottled water has grown. In other countries, because of suspect local water supplies, if water is ordered by a customer it is usually bottled.

Bottled water is the fastest-growing segment of the beverage industry, in part because of increased health consciousness, in part because of a perception that bottled water is safer. Waters are available from all over the globe, from Australia, France, Fiji, Germany, Italy, Wales and many points between. The list is endless and always growing. All waters imported into Canada are subject to federal regulation.

Types of Water

Current regulations allow for bottled water to be sold as "spring" or "mineral" water only if it is sourced from underground and is not part of a community water supply. It must be potable at its point of origin and may not have its original chemical composition altered. The only permitted treatments are carbonation, addition of ozone as a disinfectant or addition of fluoridation to prevent dental cavities. When not labelled "spring" or "mineral," the bottled water may be from any source and treated to make it fit for human consumption, and it may have its original composition altered.

In Canada, the following names must appear on the label:

- **distilled water**, when the treatment includes distillation (that is, vaporization and condensation)

● **distilled water** water that has had all the minerals and impurities removed through distillation; it is generally used for pharmaceutical purposes

- **demineralized water** water that has had all the minerals and impurities removed by passing it over a bed of ion-exchange resins

- **carbonated water** water that has absorbed carbon dioxide resulting in an effervescent mouth-feel

- **juice** the liquid extracted from any fruit or vegetable

- **nectar** the diluted, sweetened juice of peaches, apricots, guavas, black currants or other fruits, the juice of which would be too thick or too tart to drink straight

- **cider** mildly fermented apple juice; nonalcoholic apple juice may also be labelled cider

- **demineralized water**, when the treatment, by means other than distillation, results in the mineral content being reduced to less than 10 parts per million
- **carbonated water**, when the water contains added carbon dioxide, making it effervescent

When bottled water cannot be categorized as any of the above, it may be named with another appropriate name/category, which must not be misleading.

JUICE

Fruit **juice** is used as a beverage, alone or mixed with other ingredients, and as the liquid ingredient in other preparations. Juice may also be the basis of **nectar** and **cider**. Juice can be extracted from fruits (and some vegetables) in two ways: pressure and blending.

Pressure is used to extract juice from fruits such as citrus that have a high water content. Pressure is applied by hand-squeezing or with a manual or electric reamer. All reamers work on the same principle: a ribbed cone is pressed against the fruit to break down its flesh and release the juice. Always strain juices to remove seeds, pulp or fibrous pieces.

A blender or an electric juice extractor can be used to liquefy less juicy fruits and vegetables such as apples, carrots, tomatoes, beets and cabbage. The extractor pulverizes the fruit or vegetable, then separates and strains the liquid from the pulp with centrifugal action.

Interesting and delicious beverages can be made by combining the juice of one or more fruits or vegetables: pineapple with orange, apple with cranberry, strawberry with tangerine and papaya with orange. Colour should be considered when creating mixed-juice beverages, however. Some combinations can cause rather odd colour changes. Although yellow and orange juices are not a problem, those containing red and blue flavonoid pigments (such as Concord grapes, cherries, strawberries, raspberries and blueberries) can create some unappetizing colours. Adding an acid such as lemon juice helps retain the correct red/blue hues.

RECIPE 35.1

Approximate values per 175 mL serving:	
Calories	110
Total fat	0 g
Saturated fat	0 g
Cholesterol	0 mg
Sodium	3.5 mg
Total carbohydrates	29 g
Protein	1 g

APPLYING THE BASICS — **RECIPE 35.1**

Spiced Cider

Yield: 2 L (64 fl. oz.)

Apple cider	1 L	32 fl. oz.
Orange or cranberry juice	1 L	32 fl. oz.
Brown sugar	50 g	2 oz.
Cinnamon sticks	2	2
Cloves, whole	5	5
Allspice, whole	5	5

1. Combine all ingredients in a nonreactive saucepan over medium-low heat.
2. Bring the mixture to a simmer, cover and remove from the heat. Let steep for 10–15 minutes. Strain and serve garnished with sliced lemon or a cinnamon stick.

COFFEE

Coffee (Fr. *café*) begins as the fruit of a small tree grown in tropical and sub-tropical regions throughout the world. The fruit, referred to as a cherry, is bright red with translucent flesh surrounding two flat-sided seeds. These seeds are the coffee beans. When ripe, the cherries are harvested by hand, then cleaned, fermented and hulled, leaving the green coffee beans. The beans are then roasted, blended, ground and brewed. Note that any coffee bean can be roasted to any degree of darkness, ground to any degree of fineness and brewed by any number of methods.

Only two species of coffee bean are routinely used: *arabica* and *robusta*. Arabica beans are the most important commercially and the ones from which the finest coffees are produced. Robusta beans do not produce as flavour-ful a drink as arabica. Nevertheless, robusta beans are becoming increasingly significant commercially, in part because robusta trees are hardier and more fer-tile than arabica trees. The conditions in which the beans are grown have almost as much effect on the final product as subsequent roasting, grinding and brew-ing. Because coffee takes much of its flavour and character from the soil, sun-light and air, the beans' origin is critical to the product's final quality. Each valley and mountain produces coffee distinct from all others, so geographic names are used to identify the beans whether they are from arabica or robusta trees. Thus, purveyors may offer beans known as Colombian, Chanchamayo (from Peru), Kilimanjaro (from Tanzania), Blue Mountain (from Jamaica), Java and Sumatra (from Indonesia) or Kona (from Hawaii), to name a few.

Although many so-called gourmet coffees are made from a single type of bean, nearly all coffee sold in Canada is a blend of various qualities and types of bean.

Roasting Coffee

Roasting releases and enhances the flavours in coffee. It also darkens the beans and brings natural oils to the surface. Traditionally, almost everyone roasted their own coffee beans because all coffee beans were sold green. Today, however, roasting is left to experts who possess the necessary equipment. It is important to recognize and understand some of the standard descriptions used for various types of roasting. No single international organization controls the naming of roasted coffee, however, so a coffee roaster may refer to products by any name. In general, roasts fall into four categories based on their colour—light, medium, medium-dark or dark. The following descriptions are based on the most com-mon terminology:

Green Coffee Beans

- **City roast:** Also called American or brown roast, city roast is the most widely used coffee style in this country. City roast, which is medium brown in colour, produces a beverage that may lack brilliance or be a bit flat, yet it is the roast most Canadians assume they prefer because it is the roast most often used in grocery store blends.

City Roast Beans

- **Brazilian:** Somewhat darker than a city roast, Brazilian roast should begin to show a hint of dark-roast flavour. The beans should show a trace of oil. In this context, the word *Brazilian* has no relationship to coffee grown in Brazil.

- **Viennese:** Also called medium-dark roast, Viennese roast generally falls somewhere between a standard city roast and French roast.

- **French roast:** French roast, also called New Orleans or dark roast, approaches espresso in flavour without sacrificing smoothness. The beans should be the colour of semi-sweet chocolate, with apparent oiliness on the surface.

French Roast Beans

- **Espresso roast:** Espresso roast, also called Italian roast, is the darkest of all. The beans are roasted until they are virtually burnt. The beans should be black with a shiny, oily surface.

Grinding Coffee

Unlike roasting, which is best left to the experts, the grinding of coffee beans is best left to the consumer or food service operation. Whole coffee beans stay fresh longer than ground coffee. Ground coffee kept in an airtight container away from heat and light will stay fresh for three or four days. Whole beans will stay fresh for a few weeks and may be kept frozen for several months, as long as they are dry and protected from other flavours. Frozen coffee beans do not need to be thawed before grinding and brewing. Do not refrigerate coffee.

The fineness of the grind depends entirely on the type of coffee maker being used. The grind determines the length of time it takes to achieve the optimum (19%) extraction from the beans. The proper grind is simply whatever grind allows this to happen in the time it takes a specific coffee maker to complete its brewing cycle. As a general rule, the finer the grind, the more quickly the coffee should be prepared. Follow the directions for your coffee maker or ask your specialty coffee purveyor for guidance.

Brewing Coffee

● **decoction** (1) boiling a food until its flavour is removed; (2) a procedure for making coffee

● **infusion** (1) the extraction of flavours from a food at a temperature below boiling; (2) a group of coffee-brewing techniques, including steeping, filtering and dripping; (3) the liquid resulting from this process

Coffee is brewed by one of two methods: decoction or infusion. **Decoction** means boiling a substance until its flavour is removed. Boiling is the oldest method of making coffee, but is no longer used except in preparing extremely strong Turkish coffee. **Infusion** refers to the extraction of flavours at temperatures below boiling. Infusion techniques include steeping (mixing hot water with ground coffee), filtering (slowly pouring hot water over ground coffee held in a disposable cloth or paper filter) and dripping (pouring hot water over ground coffee and allowing the liquid to run through a strainer). Percolating is undesirable, as the continuous boiling ruins the coffee's flavour.

The secrets to brewing a good cup of coffee are knowing the exact proportion of coffee to water as well as the length of time to maintain contact between the two. This varies depending on the type of coffee brewing equipment being used.

Drip Brewing

Drip Coffee Maker

Drip coffee is most commonly made from a machine that operates on the principle of gravity and a filter. Water is placed in a reservoir, heated by an element and released slowly over the coffee grounds.

For drip coffee, the best results are usually achieved by using 55 g (2 oz.) of ground coffee per litre (quart) of filtered water. This yields approximately 5.5 "cups" of coffee; a coffee cup is 175 mL (6 fl. oz.). The brew temperature of the water should be 90°C to 93°C (195°F to 205°F). The best coffee is brewed in a French-press coffee maker or a Vacuum coffee pot.

Premeasured packages of ground coffee are generally used with commercial brewing equipment. These packages are available in a range of sizes for making single pots or large urns of coffee. If stronger coffee is desired, use more coffee per cup of water, not a longer brewing time. For weaker coffee, prepare regular-strength coffee and dilute it with hot water. Never reuse coffee grounds.

Espresso Brewing

Espresso (from the Latin *exprimo*, "to press out") is made with a pump-driven machine that forces hot water through compressed, finely ground coffee. An espresso machine also has a steaming rod to froth the milk for espresso-based beverages, as illustrated in Figure 35.1.

Finely ground coffee that is lightly roasted makes the best espresso. It can be purchased in bulk but the best espresso results from freshly grinding the beans with a conical burr grinder. A single serving of espresso uses 7 to 8 g (1/4 oz.) coffee for 25 to 30 mL (1 fl. oz.) of purified water at 88°C to 95°C (190°F to 203°F). It is forced through the grounds at 9 to 10 atmospheres of pressure for 22 to 28 seconds. The pressure creates the *crema* or foam on top of the espresso. It is important that the espresso be made quickly: If the machine pumps water through the coffee for too long, too much water will be added to the cup and the intense espresso flavour will be ruined. Because the single or double "shot" of espresso forms the foundation of so many beverages, this is an important consideration.

Conditions That Affect the Quality of Brewed Coffee

Most coffees are affected by the quality of the water used to brew them. Many commercial establishments have their machines tied into their water supply, so water quality may be beyond the maker's control. Unless equipment is properly cleaned, oils from coffee form an invisible film on the inside of the maker and pots, imparting a rancid or stale flavour to each subsequent batch. Coffeepots and carafes should be cleaned well with hot water between each use; coffee makers should be disassembled and cleaned according to the manufacturer's directions. Calcification on heating elements can also reduce their effectiveness.

Finally, all coffee should be served as soon as it is brewed. Oxidation takes a toll on the aroma and flavour, which soon becomes flat and eventually bitter. Drip coffee may be held for a short time on the coffee maker's hot plate at temperatures of 85°C to 88°C (185°F to 190°F). A better holding method, however, is to immediately pour freshly brewed coffee into a thermal carafe. Never attempt to reheat cold coffee, as drastic temperature shifts destroy flavour.

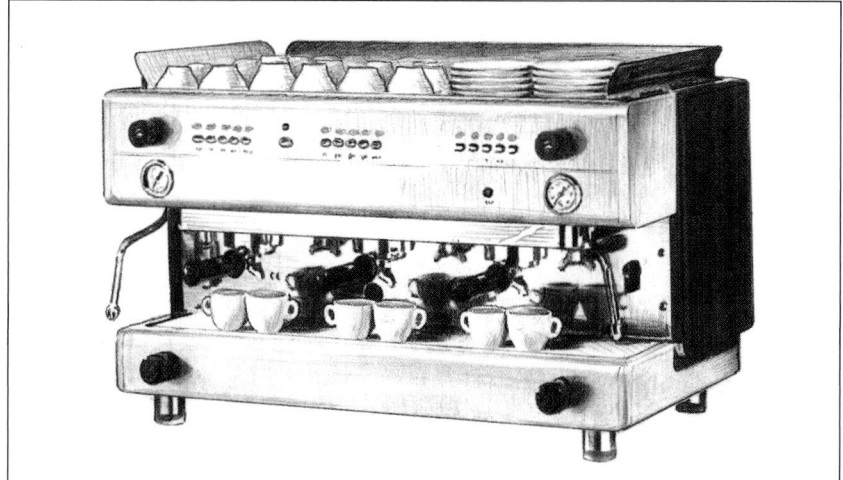

FIGURE 35.1   Espresso coffee machine with steaming rods.

A Cup of Coffee History

Some anthropologists suggest that coffee was initially consumed by central African warriors in the form of a paste made from mashed coffee beans and animal fat rolled into balls. Eaten before battle, the animal fat and bean protein provided nourishment; the caffeine provided a stimulant.

A hot coffee drink may first have been consumed sometime during the 9th century c.e. in Persia. By the year 1000, the elite of the Arab world were regularly drinking a decoction of dried coffee beans. The beans were harvested in Abyssinia (Ethiopia) and brought to market by Egyptian merchants. Within a century or so, kahwa became immensely popular with members of all strata of Arab society. Coffeehouses opened throughout the Levant, catering to customers who sipped the thick, brown brew while discussing affairs of heart and state.

Although European travellers to the Ottoman Empire had tasted coffee, it did not become popular in Europe until the 17th century. Its popularity is due in great part to Suleiman Aga, the Grand Panjandrum of the Ottoman Empire. In 1669, he arrived at the court of King Louis XIV of France as ambassador, bringing with him many exotic treasures, including coffee, which soon became the drink of choice for the French aristocracy.

Coffee became popular in Vienna as a fortune of war. By 1683, the Turks were at the gates of Vienna. A decisive battle was fought, and the Turks fled, leaving behind stores of gold, equipment, supplies and a barely known provision—green coffee beans. One of the victorious leaders, Franz George Kolschitzky, recognized the treasure and opened the first coffeehouse in Vienna, The Blue Bottle.

Despite its growing popularity, coffee was exorbitantly expensive, in part the result of the sultan's monopoly on coffee beans. By the end of the 17th century, the Dutch had stolen coffee plants from Arabia and began cultivating them in Java. By the early 18th century, the French had transported seedlings to the West Indies; from there coffee plantations spread throughout the New World.

Tasting Coffee

Coffee can be judged on four characteristics: aroma, acidity, body and flavour. As a general rule, coffee will taste the way it smells. Some coffees, particularly Colombian, are more fragrant than others, however.

Acidity, also called wininess, refers to the tartness of the coffee. Acidity is a desirable characteristic that indicates snap, life or thinness. Kenyan and Guatemalan are examples of particularly acidic coffees.

Body refers to the feeling of heaviness or thickness that coffee provides on the palate. Sumatran is generally the heaviest, with Mexican and Venezuelan being the lightest.

Flavour, of course, is the most ambiguous as well as the most important characteristic. Terms such as *mellow, harsh, grassy* and *earthy* are used to describe the rather subjective characteristics of flavour.

Serving Coffee

Coffee beverages can be made with specific additions and provide value-added menu alternatives. The most common ways of serving coffee are described here.

Drip Coffee or Filtered Coffee

Drip or filter coffee is the most common style of coffee served in Canada. It is served unadorned, unsweetened and black (without milk or cream). The customer then adds the desired amount of sweetener and/or milk.

- *Black:* A plain cup of unsweetened coffee with no milk or cream added.
- *Café au lait:* The French version of the Italian *caffè latte, café au lait* (or *café crème*) is made with strong coffee instead of espresso and hot, not steamed, milk. It is traditionally served in a handleless bowl.
- *Demitasse:* A small cup of strong black coffee or espresso; also refers to the small cup in which it is served.
- *Iced coffee:* Strong coffee served over ice. If desired, it is best to add sweetener before the coffee is poured over ice or shaken. Iced coffee can also be served with milk or cream. In Australia, a dollop of vanilla ice cream is often added. In Vietnam it is made with a small Vietnamese filter pot using condensed milk as a sweetener. Under no circumstances should leftover coffee be used to make iced coffee.
- *After-dinner coffee:* Strong coffee with the addition of liquor, liqueurs, or spices, and often sweetened and garnished with whipped cream; examples include Irish coffee, made with Irish whiskey, or café brûlot, made with orange, cloves and brandy.

Espresso

Espresso refers to a unique brewing method in which hot water is forced through finely ground and packed coffee under high pressure. Properly made espresso is strong, rich and smooth, not bitter or acidic. As the coffee drains into the cup it will be golden brown, forming a *crema* or foam that lies on top of the black coffee underneath. It is important that the small espresso cups be prewarmed. In Europe an espresso is often served with a twist of lemon on the saucer and a small glass of water on the side.

- *Espresso:* A single (shot) or double serving, black, served in a demitasse.
- *Espresso machiatto:* Espresso "marked" with a tiny portion of **steamed milk**.

Espresso

● **steamed milk** milk that is heated with steam generated by an espresso machine; it should be approximately 66°C to 77°C (150°F to 170°F)

- *Cappuccino:* One-third espresso, one-third steamed milk and one-third **foamed milk**; the total serving is still rather small, about 120 to 180 mL (4 to 6 oz.).
- *Caffè latte:* One-third espresso and two-thirds steamed milk without foam; usually served in a tall glass.
- *Caffè mocha:* One-third espresso and two-thirds steamed milk, flavoured with chocolate syrup; usually topped with whipped cream and chocolate shavings or cocoa.
- *Caffè freddo:* A double serving of sweetened espresso served chilled with ice or shaken with crushed ice. Can be served with milk or whipped cream, usually in a tall glass.
- *Espresso con panna:* Espresso with a dollop of whipped cream.
- *Espresso corretto:* A shot of espresso "corrected" with the addition of liquor such as brandy or liqueur.
- *Espresso ristretto:* Espresso made with half the water normally used for a regular espresso.

Any type of milk can be used to make cappuccino, latte and other espresso beverages. Milk with higher fat content will produce a creamier tasting beverage. To froth the milk for these beverages, pour the milk into a jug, then position it under the steam spout of the espresso machine. Activate the steam control only when the head of the spout is under the surface of the milk. Moving the jug around while keeping the spout under the surface of the milk helps the steam aerate the milk, giving it a consistency resembling frothed cream. Heat to 66°C to 77°C (150°F to 170°F).

Flavoured Coffees

Dried, ground chicory root has long been added to coffee, particularly by the French, who enjoy its bitter flavour. Toasted barley, dried figs and spices have also been used by various cultures for years. Coffees flavoured with vanilla, chocolate, liquors, spices and nuts have recently become popular in Canada. These flavours are added to roasted coffee beans by tumbling the beans with special flavouring oils. The results are strongly aromatic flavours such as vanilla hazelnut, chocolate raspberry or maple walnut.

Decaffeinated Coffee

Caffeine is an alkaloid found in coffee beans (as well as in tea leaves and cocoa beans). It is a stimulant that can improve alertness or reduce fatigue. In excess, however, caffeine can cause some people to suffer palpitations or insomnia. Regular filtered coffee contains 85 to 100 milligrams of caffeine per cup. Robusta beans contain more caffeine than the better-quality arabica beans. Decaffeinated coffee (with 97% or more of the caffeine removed) is designed to meet consumer desires for a caffeine-free product.

Other Uses for Coffee

In addition to its use as a beverage, coffee is also used in stews, sauces and pan gravy. It may be added to breads (such as rye and pumpernickel), cakes, custards, ice creams, dessert sauces and frostings. The flavour of coffee has a strong affinity for chocolate, nuts and rum.

● **foamed milk** milk that is heated and frothed with air and steam generated by an espresso machine; it will be slightly cooler than steamed milk

● **barista** Italian for "bartender"; now used to describe someone who has been professionally trained in the art of preparing espresso and espresso-based beverages

Cappuccino

Caffè Latte

Kopi Luwak

Kopi Luwak is the most unusual and expensive coffee in the world. The palm civet (*Paradoxurus hermaphroditus*) or luwak, as it is called in Indonesia, eats only the ripest of the coffee cherries. Unable to digest the coffee beans, they pass through the civet's digestive tract and are excreted whole. The journey through the civet's digestive tract creates an unusual fermentation environment, where the beans are affected by stomach acids and enzymes, which creates this very expensive coffee delight. It retails at $180 and higher for 454 g (1 lb.).

TEA, TISANES AND RELATED BEVERAGES

Tea and tisanes are made from dried leaves, herbs, spices, flowers or fruits that are prepared by infusion, that is, steeping in fresh boiling water. Tea is the beverage of choice for more than half the world's population and may be served hot or cold. **Tisanes**, or herbal infusions, have long been popular for their perceived health benefits and healing properties in Europe and Asia. As customers in Canada have become familiar with herbal teas, demand for them is growing.

● **tisanes** herbal infusions that do not contain any "real" tea, examples include chamomile, ginseng and lemon balm

Tea

Tea (Fr. *thé*) is the name given to the leaves of *Camellia sinensis,* a tree or shrub that grows at high altitudes in damp tropical regions. Although tea comes from only one species of plant, there are three general types of tea—black, green and oolong. The differences among the three are the result of the manner in which the leaves are treated after picking.

Tea Varieties

Fruit Tea

Gunpowder

Darjeeling

Black tea is amber-brown and strongly flavoured. Its colour and flavour result from fermenting the leaves. Black tea leaves are named or graded by leaf size. Because larger leaves brew more slowly than smaller ones, teas are sorted by leaf size for efficient brewing. *Souchong* denotes large leaves, *pekoe* denotes medium-sized leaves and *orange pekoe* denotes the smallest whole leaves. (Note that orange pekoe does not refer to any type of orange flavour.) Broken tea, graded as either broken orange pekoe or broken pekoe, is smaller, resulting in a darker, stronger brew. Broken tea is most often used in tea bags. These grades apply to both Chinese and Indian black teas.

Green tea is yellowish-green in colour with a bitter flavour. Leaves used for green tea are not fermented. Chinese green tea leaves are also graded according to leaf size and age. The finest green tea is Gunpowder, followed by Imperial and Hyson.

Oolong tea is partially fermented to combine the characteristics of black and green teas. Oolong is popular in China and Japan, often flavoured with jasmine flowers. Oolong tea leaves are also graded by size and age.

As with coffee, tea takes much of its flavour from the geographic conditions in which it is grown. Teas are named for their place of origin—for example, Darjeeling, Ceylon (now Sri Lanka) or Assam.

Many commercial teas are actually blends of leaves from various sources. Blended and unblended teas may also be flavoured with oils, dried fruit, spices, flowers or herbs; they are then referred to as **flavoured teas**. Spices such as allspice, cinnamon, nutmeg and black pepper are often used to create teas flavoured for cold-weather drinking. Bright herbs such as mint and citrus rind or oil, especially bergamot, which gives Earl Grey tea its flavour, add complexity to brewed teas. Chai tea is flavoured black tea and milk.

● **flavoured tea** tea to which flavourings such as oils, dried fruit, spices, flowers and herbs have been added

Tea Flavours

Tea can be described according to three key characteristics: astringency or briskness, body and aroma. *Astringency* is not bitterness, which is undesirable, but a sharp, dry feeling on the tongue that contributes to the refreshing taste of a tea. *Body* refers to the feeling of thickness on the tongue. Teas range from light to full bodied. *Aroma* is the smell and flavours of the tea when brewed.

The following descriptions apply to some of the teas frequently available through wholesalers or gourmet suppliers. Taste several different ones to determine the best choice. Remember that the same tea from different blenders or distributors may taste different, and that different flavours will be more or less appropriate for different times of the day. A selection of flavours may be offered.

Black Teas

- *Assam*—A rich black tea from northeastern India with a reddish colour. It is valued by connoisseurs, especially for breakfast.
- *Ceylon*—A full-flavoured black tea with a golden colour and delicate fragrance. Ideal for serving iced, it does not become cloudy when cold.
- *Darjeeling*—The champagne of teas, grown in the foothills of the Himalayas in northeastern India. It is a full-bodied, black tea with a muscat flavour.
- *Earl Grey*—A blend of black teas, usually including Darjeeling, flavoured with oil of bergamot. A popular choice for afternoon tea.
- *English Breakfast*—An English blend of Indian and Sri Lankan black teas; it is full-bodied and robust, with a rich colour.
- *Keemum*—A mellow black Chinese tea with a strong aroma. It is less astringent than other teas and is delicious iced.
- *Lapsang Souchong*—A large-leafed (souchong) tea from the Lapsang district of China. It has a distinctive tarry, smoky flavour and aroma, appropriate for afternoon tea or dinner.

Variety of cups of brewed tea (from left): Chinese tea, Japanese tea, Moroccan mint tea and black tea with milk

Green Teas

- *Gunpowder*—A green Chinese tea with a tightly curled leaf and grey-green colour. It has a pungent flavour and a light straw colour. It is often served after the evening meal.
- *Matcha (Liquid Jade)*—A very high-quality Japanese powdered green tea used in the tea ceremony. The powder will dye foods green and impart flavour to dishes such as soba noodles or mousse.
- *Sencha (Common)*—A delicate Japanese green tea that has a light colour with a pronounced aroma and a bright, grassy taste.
- *White tea*—A delicate green tea made from new buds picked before they open. Allowed to wither so that natural moisture evaporates, these leaves are lightly dried to a pale silvery colour. White tea has a subtle flavour.

Oolong Teas

- *Formosa Oolong*—A unique and expensive large-leafed oolong tea with the flavour of ripe peaches. It is appropriate for breakfast or afternoon tea.

Tisanes (Herb Teas)

Tisanes are herbal infusions that do not contain any "real" tea. They are commonly made from fresh or dried flowers, herbs, seeds or roots; chamomile, ginseng, linden flowers (Fr. *tilleul*) and lemon balm are among the more popular tisanes. In most countries there is a tradition of indigenous herbal medicine often administered in an infused form, as a tea. In Europe, a tisane may be served after a meal to aid digestion or taken before bed as an aid to sleep. (Herbal teas usually contain no caffeine, so they do not act as stimulants.) In Canada, herbal teas are gaining in popularity. In a professional food service establishment herbal teas are prepackaged blends and require no mixing.

Tea Bags

The invention of the tea bag was apparently inadvertent. According to the Tea Association of America, in 1904, Thomas Sullivan, a New York tea merchant, sent potential customers samples of tea in small muslin or silk bags. Finding that they could make tea by simply pouring boiling water over the bags, Sullivan's new customers clamoured for more.

Throughout the 20th century tea companies experimented and claimed supremacy for their bags, but the quality of the tea within is more important than the shape of the bag.

Some believe that the Chinese emperor Shen Nung discovered tea drinking in 2737 B.C.E. Legend holds that the emperor was boiling his drinking water beneath a tree when some leaves fell into the pot. Whether this is myth or truth, it is known that a hot drink made from powdered dried tea leaves whipped into hot water was regularly consumed in China sometime after the 4th century. Later, decoctions of tea leaves (as well as rice, spices and nuts) became popular. But it was not until the Ming dynasty (1368–1644) that infusions of tea leaves became commonplace.

By the 9th century, tea drinking had spread to Japan. In both Chinese and Japanese cultures, tea drinking developed into a ritual. For the Chinese, a cup of tea became the mirror of the soul. For the Japanese, it was the drink of immortality.

Tea was first transported from China to Europe by Dutch merchants during the early 1600s. By midcentury, it was introduced into England. To ensure a steady supply, the English surreptitiously procured plants from China and started plantations throughout the Indian subcontinent, as did the Dutch. Tea drinking became fashionable in England in court circles.

The social custom of afternoon tea began in the late 1700s. The late-afternoon ritual of snacking on sandwiches and pastries accompanied by tea was intended to quell hunger pangs between breakfast and dinner (which was typically served at 9:30 or 10:00 p.m.).

Eventually, two distinct types of teatime evolved. Low tea was aristocratic in origin and consisted of a snack of pastries and sandwiches, with tea, served in the late afternoon as a prelude to the evening meal. High tea was bourgeois in origin, consisting of leftovers from the typically large middle-class lunch, such as cold meats, bread and cheeses. High tea became a substitute for the evening meal.

Brewing Tea

Tea may be brewed by the cup or the pot. In either case, it is important to use the following procedure.

BASIC PROCEDURE FOR BREWING TEA

1. Always begin with clean equipment and freshly drawn cold water. Water that has been sitting in a kettle or hot water tank contains less air and will taste flat or stale. Tea should never be brewed using a drip coffee system because the water is not hot enough. The resulting product will be refused by any discerning tea drinker.

2. Warm the teapot by rinsing its interior with hot water. This will help relax the tea leaves and ensure that the water will stay hot when it comes in contact with the tea.

3. Place 5 mL (1 tsp.) loose tea or one tea bag per 3/4 cup (180 mL/6 fl. oz.) of water capacity in the warmed teapot.

4. As soon as the water comes to a boil, pour the appropriate amount over the tea. Do not allow the water to continue boiling as this removes the oxygen, leaving a flat taste. The water should be at a full boil when it comes in contact with the tea so that the tea leaves will uncurl and release their flavour.

5. Replace the lid of the teapot and allow the tea to infuse for 3 to 5 minutes. Time the brew. Colour is not a reliable indication of brewing time; tea leaves release colour before flavour, and different types of tea will be different colours when properly brewed.

6. Remove the tea bags or loose tea from the water when brewing is complete. This can be accomplished easily if the teapot is fitted with a removable leaf basket or if a tea bag or a perforated tea ball is used. Otherwise, decant the tea through a strainer into a second warmed teapot.

7. Serve immediately, accompanied with sugar, lemon, milk (not cream) and honey as desired. Dilute the tea with hot water if necessary.

8. Do not reuse tea leaves. Four hundred and fifty grams (1 lb.) of tea yields 200 cups, making it the most inexpensive beverage after tap water.

For iced tea, prepare regular brewed tea using 50% more tea. Then pour the tea into a pitcher or glass filled with ice. The stronger brew will hold its flavour better as the ice melts. If iced tea is not to be used immediately, it should be brewed at room or refrigerator temperature for some hours to prevent clouding.

Serving Tea

Black and oolong tea may be served hot or cold, but green tea is best served hot. Black tea is served with milk or lemon and sugar; green and oolong tea are most often served plain. Adding milk to hot tea is a British preference (not normally followed in Europe or Asia) that reduces the astringency of the tea. Iced tea, an American invention, may be served plain or sweetened, and is often garnished with lemon, orange or fresh mint.

Tea Beverages

The popular tea beverage—iced tea—claims its invention in the United States. Brewed-tea-and-milk beverages called *chai*, from the Chinese word for "tea," are also gaining in popularity, as are iced herbal teas. Moroccan tea is highly sweetened green tea brewed with fresh mint and served hot.

HOT CHOCOLATE AND HOT COCOA

Theobroma cacao (food of the gods) has an ancient history; cacao is believed to have originated in the Amazon basin. The first highly developed civilization in Mesoamerica, the Olmec, enjoyed chocolate as a beverage, as did their successors the Maya and the Aztec. The original chocolate drink, which the Maya called "xocolatl," which means bitter water, lacked sweetness. It was the Spanish who first mixed chocolate with sugar to offset the bitterness.

Today chocolate is enjoyed in its many forms and hot chocolate drinks are a favourite the world over. Typically, hot chocolate can be made from milk, dark chocolate, white chocolate and sugar and spices such as cinnamon and vanilla, while hot cocoa is made by substituting cocoa powder for the chocolate.

Cocoa powder is the unsweetened powder formed from the solid left over after extracting the cocoa butter content from chocolate liquor. There are two types: American or natural, and Dutch or European process. The American process or natural cocoa is recommended for baking purposes while the "Dutched" cocoa is recommended for beverages and frozen desserts. Natural cocoa is more acidic and reacts more favourably with leavening agents used in baking, while the "Dutched" cocoa has been treated with an alkali, which makes the cocoa darker in colour, less bitter and richer in flavour. Some assert that many flavour subtleties are lost during the Dutch process.

APPLYING THE BASICS		RECIPE 35.2
Mayan Hot Chocolate		
Yield: 2 servings		
Milk	450 mL	16 fl. oz.
Vanilla bean, split lengthwise	1/2	1/2
Hot red chile pepper, split with seeds removed	1	1
Cinnamon stick	7.5–10 cm	3–4 in.
Bittersweet chocolate, grated	55 g	2 oz.

1. Into the milk add the vanilla bean, chile pepper and cinnamon stick.
2. Bring almost to a boil, lower heat to just below a simmer and allow to infuse for 10 minutes. Strain.
3. Return milk to heat and whisk in grated chocolate until dissolved. Serve immediately.

NOTE: The Maya would probably have used water instead of milk.

RECIPE 35.2

Approximate values per serving:	
Calories	256
Total fat	15 g
Saturated fat	9 g
Cholesterol	17 mg
Sodium	118 mg
Total carbohydrates	26 g
Protein	10 g

WINES, BEERS, BRANDIES, LIQUORS AND LIQUEURS

Wines, **beers**, **brandies**, **liquors** and **liqueurs** are frequently used in the kitchen, most often as flavourings, but also as primary ingredients in marinades and sauces or even as a cooking medium (pears poached in red wine, for instance). Wines are used to flavour and frequently to tenderize foods in marinades, to add flavour during or at the end of cooking, and to deglaze a pan to add flavour to a sauce. Brandy, especially the classic orange-flavoured Grand Marnier, is a common bakeshop flavouring. Brandy complements fruits and rounds off the flavours of custards and creams. Liqueurs are selected for their

● **wine** an alcoholic beverage made from the fermented juice of grapes; may be sparkling (effervescent) or still (non-effervescent) or fortified with additional alcohol

● **beer** an alcoholic beverage made from water, hops and malted barley, fermented by yeast

● **brandy** an alcoholic beverage made by distilling wine or the fermented mash of grapes or other fruits.

● **liquor** an alcoholic beverage made by distilling grains, fruits, vegetables or other foods; includes rum, whisky and vodka

● **liqueur** a strong, sweet, syrupy alcoholic beverage made by mixing or redistilling neutral spirits with fruits, flowers, herbs, spices or other flavourings; also known as a cordial

specific flavours: amaretto for almond, Kahlúa for coffee, crème de cassis for black currant. They are used either to add flavours or to enhance other flavours in a dish. Liquors such as rum, bourbon and whisky can be used for their own distinctive flavours or to blend with other flavours such as chocolate and coffee.

Because alcoholic beverages are used as flavourings, basic information about them is included here. This information is not intended to be a mini-course on wine tasting or Scotch tasting. Rather, it is to familiarize the student chef with the basics of wine, beer and spirits. Brief guidelines for choosing appropriate wines or other alcoholic beverages as flavourings as well as guidelines on how to use them as flavourings are also included. As with other flavouring ingredients, patience, research, experimentation and practice will help develop a chef's feel for what alcoholic beverage—and how much—is the best flavouring for a specific dish.

Wine

The Wine-Making Process

The process of transforming grapes into a still wine is called *vinification*. Freshly harvested grapes are gently crushed in order to release their juices. While in the crusher, stems and other undesirable matter are separated from the juice and grape skins.

● **vintner** a winemaker

If the **vintner** is making a **red wine**, both the crushed grapes (typically black-skinned grapes) and the juice (collectively called a *must*) are then transferred to a fermentation tank and allowed to ferment. Stainless steel fermentation tanks are used to create crisper red wines; oak casks are used for a more mellow product. As the red wine ferments, the grape skins release tannins, which give many red wines their distinctive astringent characteristic and slightly bitter taste. In order to increase a wine's tannin content, some vintners allow grape stems to remain in the must.

If the vintner is making a **white wine**, the grape skins (typically from white-skinned grapes, although occasionally black-skinned grapes are used) and juice pass through a wine press, where the juice is separated from the skins. For white wines, only the juice is allowed to ferment. If the vintner is making a **rosé wine** (ro-zay) or a blush wine, the grape skins (typically black) are left in contact with the fermenting juice just long enough to add the desired amount of colour.

● **fermentation** the process by which yeast converts sugar into alcohol and carbon dioxide

After the must or juice is transferred to a fermentation tank, the vintner adds yeast and sugar to start the **fermentation** process. The type of yeast and amount of sugar depends on the type of grape used and the style of wine the vintner wants to create. During fermentation, the yeast converts the sugars (both those naturally occuring in the grapes and those added by the vintner) to alcohol and carbon dioxide. Fermentation generally lasts for two to four weeks and creates many of the resulting wine's flavours and aromas.

Once fermentation is complete, red wines are pressed to remove the skins from the wine and then filtered to remove the yeast. White wines are allowed to settle and the yeast filtered out. The wines are then stored in either stainless steel tanks or oak barrels for aging. Aging wines in oak barrels or casks adds a mellow, oaky flavour. (Vintners often subject many red wines and, occasionally, some white wines to a second, brief, fermentation during aging; called a *malolactic fermentation,* it generally reduces the wine's acidic qualities.) White wines are normally aged for less time than red wines, usually no more than a year. When the vintner has determined that the wine has aged sufficiently, the wine is removed from the tank or barrel and bottled, corked and labelled.

A Goblet of Wine History

People have been consuming wine for thousands of years. Wine making probably began 5000 or 6000 years ago in Mesopotamia (today's Iraq) and probably as a happy accident—airborne yeasts came into contact with stored grapes or grape juice and over time the mixture fermented, producing a sweet alcoholic beverage.

Grape cultivation and wine making spread throughout the Middle East. Stone tablets recording grape harvests, paintings of grapes and even vessels with traces of the wine that once filled them have been found in the tombs of Egyptian Pharaohs. The many images and hieroglyphic records pertaining to wine suggest that the upper classes of ancient Egypt valued their wine—a sweet white wine, sometimes flavoured with herbs or sea water—as both a social drink and a component of funerary and other religious rituals.

Wine was also prized in ancient Greece, where it was believed that wine was a gift from the god Dionysus. The Greeks stored their wines in clay vessels lined with pine pitch, giving the wines a resinous flavour probably similar to modern Retsina.

As the Romans came to dominate the Mediterranean basin following the end of the Golden Era of Greece, upper-class Romans absorbed or emulated many Greek traits, including the appreciation of wine. The Roman god of wine—Bacchus—is the Romanized version of Dionysus. The proliferation of vineyards brought the price of wines down remarkably, allowing the lower classes of Rome to enjoy what had once been available to only the upper classes of Egypt and

Greece. It was during the Roman era that bars offering patrons a place to drink wine and sometimes consume food first appeared. The wines were generally red, fruity and sweet (although drier white wines were being produced), sometimes flavoured with ingredients such as fermented fish sauce, garlic or onions.

Following the fall of Rome (mid-5th century C.E.), much of Europe's grape-growing and wine-making activities shifted to the large Christian monasteries scattered throughout what is now northern Italy, France and Germany. Charlemagne (ca. 742–814) established vineyards throughout the kingdom, some of which are still in use today, especially in Burgundy. During the Middle Ages, the white wine/red wine divide became more standardized and the ancient practice of adding flavourings fell out of taste. By the 14th century, the wine-producing regions of France, especially Bordeaux, were already becoming known for the excellence of their products.

As England became a naval power under Queen Elizabeth I (1533–1603), many English merchants became wine importers, especially of sherries from Spain, ports from Portugal and Madeira from the island of the same name.

By the 1700s, France was recognized as the greatest of the European wine-making nations, especially for the fine wines of Bordeaux. Champagne also appeared during this period. The French widow Nicole-Barbe Clicquot-Ponsardin is credited with improving production techniques and creating the cachet that champagne still enjoys today.

In the United States, Thomas Jefferson, convinced that the lack of fine American wines was driving his fellow citizens to drink too much hard liquor, encouraged Americans to plant European wine grapes (from the botanical family of *Vitis vinifera*). These early attempts to plant European grapes, first in the Ohio River Valley and later in California, were generally unsuccessful and ultimately—for Europe—catastrophic. As *Vitis vinifera* grape vine cuttings were brought back and forth between Europe and America, a very destructive vine louse from America called phylloxera took hold in Europe.

By the 1860s, many of the *Vitis vinifera* vineyards in France and elsewhere were destroyed. European vintners eventually resolved this crisis by grafting the *Vitis vinifera* vines onto a hardy New World grape stock naturally resistant to phylloxera. During this turmoil, many French vintners relocated throughout Europe, Australia, North America and elsewhere, bringing their talents with them and the foundations for those regions' wine industries.

The European wine industry has long since recovered, but it is no longer the dominant market leader that it once was. Wines from the United States, Australia, South Africa, Canada, New Zealand, Chile and Argentina, among other countries, now command respect throughout the world. Their development involves harnessing modern technologies that give the vintner near total control over virtually every aspect of the grape-growing and wine-making process.

Sparkling Wines

Sparkling wines are still wines that undergo a complete second fermentation. The carbon dioxide generated during this second fermentation gives a sparkling wine its effervescence. The process for making sparkling wines is similar to that used for making still white or rosé wines from the planting of the grapes through the still wine's fermentation stage. From there, the processes diverge. After the initial fermentation, a sparkling wine is allowed to age for approximately five months. The vintner then adds extra yeast and sugar to the wine and allows it to undergo a second fermentation that lasts for a year or so. (This second fermentation should not be confused with the malolactic fermentation noted previously.)

For champagne (shahm-PAHN-ya) and sparkling wines made like champagne (only a sparkling wine from the Champagne region of France can be called champagne), the second fermentation takes place in the bottle. Called

Wooden Cork Pull

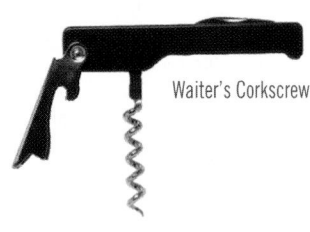

Waiter's Corkscrew

Lever-Type
Corkscrew

● **Vintners Quality Alliance (VQA)** sets standards for the production of VQA wine and appellations; most active in Niagara region and British Columbia

méthode champenoise, the process requires that the wine be aged for one to two years after its second fermentation. After aging, the yeast is removed from the bottles through a two-step process. First, the bottle is placed neck down in a rack at a 45-degree angle and rotated one-eighth of a turn every day (this is called *riddling*); during riddling, the dead yeast cells settle into the neck of the bottle. They are then removed through a process called disgorging: the neck of the bottle is frozen in an ice-and-saltwater bath and the bottle cap is removed. The internal pressure forces the frozen plug of dead yeast cells out of the bottle. Alternatively, the vintner can use the charmat process. With this process, the second fermentation takes place in a tank, eliminating riddling and disgorging.

Regardless of whether the second fermentation takes place in the bottle or tank, once it is completed, the vintner adds a mixture of white wine brandy and sugar called a *dosage*. The sparkling wine is then bottled, corked and secured with a wire, ready for distribution. Champagne and other sparkling wines are classified by their degree of sweetness. From driest to sweetest, they are Natural or Au Sauvage, Brut, Extra Dry, Dry or Sec, Demi-Sec and Doux.

Grape Varietals

With the notable exception of some European, particularly French, wines, most wines sold in Canada are varietal wines. That is, they are labelled and sold according to the grape variety from which they are made. (Canadian **VQA** regulations require that 85% of the wine come from a particular grape before that varietal can be named on the label.)

Most of the world's wine is made from one or more of the many red, black or green grape varieties of the *Vitis vinifera* family of grapes. Several of these varietals are called *noble,* as they are considered to give rise to the world's most regal wines. The red wine grapes generally recognized as noble are Cabernet Sauvignon, Merlot, Nebbiolo, Pinot Noir, Syrah and Sangiovese. Noble white wine sources are Chardonnay, Riesling and Sauvignon Blanc.

Wines not sold as varietal wines may be classified by their place of origin. Thus, for example, Chablis, a popular white wine from the district of Chablis in France's northern Burgundy region, is made from Chardonnay grapes and would be called Chardonnay if made in Canada. A number of countries, led by France and Italy, have implemented systems to ensure that wines bottled and sold under such district names are exclusively from grapes produced in that geographic area. French labels will state "*appelation controlée*" and Italian labels "DOC" (for "*denominazione di origine controllata*") to designate such wines.

In recent years, particularly in the United States, some wines have been given proprietary names in lieu of varietal or geographic designations. Current examples include "Conundrum" by Caymus and "Opus One" by Mondavi-Rothschild, but the practice began in the 1950s with products imported to North America, such as Lancers and Blue Nun. These made-up trademarked names can be used for blended wines when use of a specific varietal would not be possible because no one grape makes up 75% or more of the blend. They are also popular with winemakers, who wish to create something unique in the marketplace.

Fortified Wines

Wines usually have an alcohol content of 10 to 15%. Fortified wines are wines whose alcohol content has been increased to 18 to 22% by the addition of neutral grape spirits or grape brandy made from the same grapes used to make the wine. If the brandy is added before fermentation is complete, the fortified wine will be quite sweet, as the extra alcohol stops the fermentation process. If the brandy is added after fermentation is complete, the fortified wine will be drier. The best-known fortified wines—and the ones most often used as flavourings—are listed next.

Grapes into Wine

Virtually all the fine wine made in the world comes from varieties of a single grape species, *Vitis vinifera*. Although a European species, it is also grown in Canada, the United States, South Africa, South America, the Middle East, Australia and wherever fine wine is made. The variety of grapes used in any given wine determines the wine's character, and most wine-producing countries carefully regulate the growing areas and production of grapes.

North American wines are known by their varietal names, whereas European wines are generally known by the vineyard's location. The major varietals of wine grapes and the wines in which they are used are listed at right.

Grape Varietal	Wine
Pinot Noir	Red Burgundy and champagne
Chardonnay	White Burgundy, Chablis and champagne
Syrah	Côte Rotie and Hermitage
Cabernet Sauvignon	Bordeaux and red Graves
Sauvignon Blanc	Sauterne, white Graves, Fumé Blanc and Sancerre
Merlot	Saint-Emilion and for blending with Cabernet Sauvignon
Zinfandel	Red and white Zinfandel (California claims a virtual monopoly)
Chenin Blanc	Vouvray

Port is the only significant fortified wine made from red wine. Traditionally, port wine is produced in the Duoro valley of Portugal from a blend of five red wine grape varieties. Ports are generally divided into three categories. Tawny ports have a pale brown hue and a mellower, subtle, less fruity flavour than other ports. They are aged in wooden casks, sometimes for 20 or 30 years, and then typically blended with other ports, bottled and consumed. Vintage ports have a darker, more brick or burgundy hue and a richer, sweeter flavour than tawny ports. Vintage ports are aged in their bottles, sometimes as long as several decades, before being consumed. They are among the finest of ports, as the vintage designation is given only to ports considered of exceptional quality. Ruby ports are blends of younger ports of lesser quality than those designated as vintage ports. They tend to have a bright, almost crimson colour and a smooth, sweet, fruity flavour.

Sherry is a fortified white wine from the Jerez region of southern Spain. It is made by an extremely complicated process called *solera* that relies on strict temperature controls and the blending and reblending of wines from different years as they age in wooden casks. During this process, the developing sherry is often exposed to oxygen and, to one degree or another, to a yeast called *flor*. Flor both protects the sherry from too much oxidation and contributes a distinct, somewhat nutty flavour to it. Depending on alcohol content, degree of exposure to flor and other factors, a sherry will be classified as one of six types: manzanilla, the driest sherry, which has a very pale golden-yellow colour; fino, a very dry sherry with a pale golden-brown colour; amontillado, which has a rich, slightly dry, nutty flavour and a light brown, amber colour; oloroso, which has a somewhat dry, rich flavour, a full-body and a medium-brown colour; amoroso, which has a sweet flavour and a medium-brown colour that is sometimes artificially darkened; or cream sherry, the sweetest sherry, with a dark brown colour.

Madeira, a fortified wine from the island of Madeira, is made from white wine grapes. Its characteristic light brown colour and toffee-caramel flavour are produced when the developing wine is heated, a process called *estufagem*. This can occur naturally when the Madeira is left in barrels in warm attics for up to 20 years, or artificially when the wine is placed in containers and heated to a temperature of 40°C (105°F) for three to six months. The four principal types of Madeiras differ depending on the grape used. They are, from the driest to sweetest, Sercial, Verdelho, Bual and Malmsey.

Marsala, a fortified wine from western Sicily that is named for the town associated with its production, is made from grapes that are dried prior to fermentation. This increases the resulting wine's sugar content. After fermentation and fortification, Marsala is often darkened and sweetened with grape juice syrup and then allowed to age in wooden barrels, which mellows its flavours. Marsalas are brown-coloured and available in two styles, dry and sweet; the latter has a richer flavour.

Vermouth is a flavoured wine, sometimes fortified with brandy. Depending on the producer, vermouths are usually made by steeping various flavouring ingredients such as rose petals, citrus peels, hyssop, elderberries, chamomile, juniper berries, cloves, quinine, nutmeg and coriander in white wine. After a month or so, the flavourings are removed and brandy is added, then the vermouth is aged for two to four years in oak casks. There are two styles of vermouth. One, which is a brick- or ruby-red colour, is variously called red (*rosso*), sweet or Italian vermouth. The other, which is clear, is variously called white (*bianco*), dry or French vermouth.

Evaluating Wines

Each grape varietal used to make a wine displays certain hallmark aroma and flavour characteristics in the finished product. This does not mean, however, that all wines made from the same grape varietal will have exactly the same aromas and flavours. Take, for example, a Merlot from Australia and one from California. They may share a certain smooth, juicy, mellow flavour with strong plum, black currant, black cherry and herbal or minty notes. But they will not be identical beverages. Rather, differences in the conditions under which the grapes were grown or the techniques the vintners used to make the wines will create noticeable differences between them. That said, the hallmark flavour and aroma characteristics of several of the world's most popular wine grapes are set forth in Tables 35.1 and 35.2 (see pages 941 and 942). Often vintners blend two or more grape varietals in order to create a wine with the best attributes of a number of grapes. The infinite combinations account for the wide number of wines available and the vast differences between them.

As with any other flavouring, a chef should evaluate wines before using them. Although this text is not intended as a mini wine-tasting course, a chef should consider some basics when evaluating a wine: aroma, flavour and body.

- **Aromas**—Most wines present a collection of different aromas. Called a bouquet or nose, individual aromas can often be distinguished (especially with practice) from a complex bouquet; these aromas are usually described by analogy. That is, the aroma reminds the person of some other aroma, usually that of a fruit, flower, herb, spice or other easily distinguished item. For example, when evaluating the bouquet of a Cabernet Sauvignon, many people recognize the aromas of black currants, green bell peppers, chocolate, mint and/or leather as well as fruit jams if the wine is young (new) and cedar and tobacco when it is aged. Likewise, the hallmark aromas of a Sauvignon Blanc are cut grass, fresh green herbs, asparagus and other vegetables. The quickly dissipating first aromas discerned while evaluating a wine's bouquet are often called top notes; the longer-lasting aromas are its medium or base notes.
- **Flavours**—The alcohol in wine contributes very little to its flavour. Rather, vintners try to create flavours by adjusting the balances between the sugars and acids in the wine. These sugars and acids interact, exciting the taste buds to recognize the wine as sweet, dry or somewhere between the two. The resulting flavour attributes are usually described with words based on a sweet/sour continuum (syrupy, sweet, crisp, tart or dry, for example), a general theme (for instance, fruity, herbaceous or spicy) or a reference to

TABLE 35.1	**Principal Red Wine Grapes**				
Grape Varietals	**Hallmark Flavour and Aroma Characteristics**	**Acidity**	**Tannins**	**Body**	**Common Food Pairings**
Cabernet Sauvignon (KA-bair-nay so-veen-yawn)	Assertive, rich, full flavour with fruity, black currant, chocolate, green bell pepper, mint or spice notes; jams when young, cedar and tobacco when older	Moderate	Moderate to prominent	Medium to full	Lamb and beef, especially if grilled; game, especially venison; strong cheeses
Grenache (gruh-NAHSH)	As a red wine, has a hearty flavour with black pepper notes; as a rosé, has a sturdy flavour with raspberry and cherry notes	Moderate	Moderate to low	Medium to full	Highly seasoned, cold-weather dishes such as meaty soups and stews
Merlot (mare-low)	Soft, smooth, juicy, mellow flavour with strong plum, black currant, black cherry and herbal or minty notes	Low	Low to moderate	Medium	Highly spiced dishes; savoury foods with a hint of sweetness; grilled meats; fish and shellfish; strong cheeses; chocolate
Nebbiolo (nay-BYOH-low)	Very robust flavour with raspberry, plum, violet and earthy notes	High	Prominent, especially in younger wines	Medium	Game, especially venison; beef; dishes with rich sauces; mushrooms
Pinot Noir (pee-noe nwahr)	Rich, complex, flavour with cherry, raspberry and smoky or earthy notes and a velvety, silky texture	Moderate to high	Low to moderate	Light to medium	Game birds; rich, fatty fish or shellfish; roast beef; strong cheeses
Red Zinfandel (zin-fahn-DELL)	Robust, ripe, fruity, spicy flavours with blackberry or raspberry jam and black pepper notes	Low to moderate	Moderate to substantial	Medium to full	Roasted lamb; dishes flavoured with garlic, black pepper and other strong flavourings; chili con carne and other hearty, spicy dishes; vegetable dishes; strong cheeses
Sangiovese (sahn-joe-VAY-zeh)	Earthy, hearty flavour with black cherry, raisin or floral (especially violet) notes	Moderate to high	Moderate	Light to medium	Veal; beef; lamb; hearty chicken dishes; tomato-based dishes
Syrah (see-rah) or Shiraz (shih-rhaz)	Rich flavour with sweet fruity, spice, floral or black pepper notes	Low to moderate	Moderate to prominent	Medium	Peppery, tangy, spicy foods; grilled meats; game

an attribute more akin to mouth-feel than flavour: smooth, velvety, silky and so on. Initial taste is the first impression of a wine's flavours; when constructing a wine's flavour profile, these would be the top notes. Finish is how long the flavour lasts after the wine is swallowed.

Tannins are complex organic compounds concentrated in the grape's skin, pits and stems. Tannins give red wines their characteristic astringent sensation and slightly bitter taste. Because grape parts are separated from the juice early in the white wine–making process, for the most part, tannins present in a white wine are usually the result of the wine being aged in oak casks.

TABLE 35.2	Principal White Wine Grapes			
Grape Varietals	**Hallmark Flavour and Aroma Characteristics**	**Acidity**	**Body**	**Common Food Pairings**
Chardonnay (shar-doe-nay)	Full, rich flavour with a buttery texture and apple, green apple or tropical fruit notes; if aged in oak, may have vanilla or spicy notes	Moderate to high	Light to medium	Fish; shellfish, especially lobster; veal; chicken; foods flavoured with herbs; foods served with rich or creamy sauces
Chenin Blanc (sheh-nan blahn)	Somewhat muted, tart acidic flavour with pine, melon or citrus notes; also used for a slightly sweet wine with similar notes	Very high	Light to medium	Light, summer foods; sweet or delicately flavoured shellfish or fish; chicken; most cheeses; Asian foods
Pinot Blanc (pee-noe blahn)	Dry, full flavour with apple, melon or almond notes	Moderate to high	Medium to full	Duck or goose
Pinot Grigio (pee-noe gree-joe) or Pinot Gris (pee-noe gree)	Crisp, dry, somewhat muted flavour with pine, orange rind and earthy or metallic notes	Moderate	Medium	Vegetables; fish; shellfish; pasta dishes; chicken
Riesling (REESE-ling)	Usually sweet but balanced by a strong steely acidity; apricot, citrus, peach or floral notes	Moderate to high	Light; medium to heavy as a dessert wine	Spicy foods; Asian foods; highly seasoned chicken dishes; shellfish; most cheeses
Sauvignon Blanc (so-veen-yawn blahn)	Bright, crisp, green, tangy flavour with grassy, herb or citrus notes	High	Medium	Spicy foods; tomato-based dishes; rich or fatty fish, especially salmon; most cheeses

Because the skins are present during fermentation in red wines, red wines tend to have more dominant and complex fruity flavours than white wines. These fruity flavours tend to mask the acidity more commonly associated with white wines. White wines are generally served chilled because acidic flavours (the tart or sour taste) are less pronounced at colder temperatures.

Body is the weight of the wine in the mouth and is generally related to the amount of alcohol and/or glycerin it contains. A wine's body is usually described as light, medium or full.

Wine and Food Pairings

For more information on wine and food pairings, see the CD-ROM that accompanies this text. It contains additional tables that list meats, seafoods, and cheeses and suggest appropriate wines.

Matching Wine and Food

The only rule about matching wine and food is that there are no rules. With this in mind, consider the following guidelines.

Match Colours

Traditionally, red wines were served with only beef, veal, pork and lamb; white wines with only fish, shellfish and poultry. Although this rule may still be true for many pairings, do not be afraid to ignore it once in a while. Try, for example, a strong, oaky Chardonnay with grilled beef or a highly acidic, low-tannin red such as Sangiovese (Chianti), Pinot Noir or Beaujolais with fish or shellfish.

Match Tastes

- *Sweet.* Dishes with an element of sweetness often pair well with sweet or slightly sweet wines—the sweetness of one complements the sweetness of the other. If the same dish were served with a dry wine, the sweetness in the dish could make the wine taste a bit sour. Because **dessert wines** are so sweet, they are often difficult to pair with any food. A sweet dessert wine such as Sauternes does, however, complement the fatty richness in foie gras or lobster with a rich cream sauce.

- *Sour.* If a dish has a citrus, especially lemony, top note, usually an acidic wine goes well with it. Wines with a high acid content frequently taste less acidic when paired with salty or sweet foods.
- *Salty.* Salty foods will mute the sweetness and enhance the fruitiness of a wine.
- *Bitter.* Be careful of pairing a wine high in tannins such as a Syrah or Cabernet Sauvignon with a food equally rich in tannins, such as walnuts. The combination will render the wine almost unbearably bitter, dry and astringent.
- *Umami.* The richer the food, often the more robust the wine needed to complement it.

Match Strengths

A delicate dish often goes best with a light, gentle wine, usually a white wine. A richly sauced or meaty dish might be best served with a strong, assertive wine, generally a red wine.

Match Opposites

Sometimes the perfect wine for pungent, spicy foods is a sweet or slightly sweet wine. Similarly, an acidic wine sometimes goes well with rich creamy or buttery sauces. Along the same vein, pair complex wines with simple dishes and simple wines with complex dishes.

Match Origins

Wines often developed alongside regional cuisines and thus they often have an affinity for each other. For example, cheeses or other foods from the Loire Valley of France pair exceptionally well with wines from that region, such as Sancerre (Sauvignon Blanc) or Chenin Blanc.

Vegetarian Cuisine

Vegetarianism, of one form or another, has in more recent years become an increasingly popular cuisine/lifestyle option for many. Wine is as much of a beverage complement to vegetarian foods as it is to other types of more traditional protein-centred cuisine. The same wine and food pairing rules apply when considering vegetarian foods.

Two additional and fundamental concepts are involved in pairing wine with vegetarian foods: the herbaceous, fruity, or occasionally *grassy* flavours exhibited by some fruits and vegetables, and the firm acidity imparted to many vegetable dishes in the form of vinegar-based dressings—particularly in the case of salads.

The principles involved are simple. Intense, full-bodied, barrel-aged reds with high levels of naturally occurring tannins typically fare poorly with vegetarian cuisine because grape and oak tannin has a tendency to clash with the organic compounds present in most fruits and vegetables. The result is that both food and wine will taste rather harsh and grassy—sometimes even slightly metallic. Instead, the best options when choosing red wines to be paired with vegetarian dishes are light reds low in tannin, preferably unoaked with an upfront, dry and fruity profile.

● **dessert wines** sweet wines made from grapes left on the vine until they are overly ripe, such as Sauternes or wines labelled "Late Harvest"; during fermentation, some of the sugar is not converted to alcohol, but remains in the wine, giving it its characteristic intense sweet taste

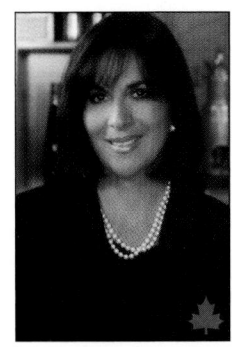

Rossana Di Zio Magnotta

Magnotta Winery Corporation—President
Festa Juice—President

Rossana Di Zio Magnotta sits on many boards and has long been recognized for her outstanding community service. She has a vested interest in the marriage of food and wine, has published books on wine making, and continues to be a resource for many in her field in the art of food and wine pairing. She continues her success in this art form as President of Magnotta Winery, which is recognized as one of Canada's 50 best-managed companies, and is Ontario's third largest and Canada's most award-winning winery.

Whites are *low* in tannin. Opt for a dry, light and again preferably unoaked white with a lively fruit-driven and aromatic character. For salads, the best choices are whites with lively levels of natural acidity. Spicy vegetarian cuisine is at its best accompanied by whites with some measure of residual sweetness.

The two aforementioned principles are not as important, however, when considering grilled vegetables. As grilling has the effect of diminishing the water content of food, the food's flavours in turn are intensified. As a result, the best wine choices are full-bodied, barrel-aged wines, either red or white, with bold flavours to match those of the foods being served.

Desserts

The principles of dessert and wine pairing are easily understood. Three things need to be considered when pairing sweet wines with desserts:

- The sweetness of the wine relative to the sweetness of the dessert
- The "weight" or mouth-feel of the wine relative to the mouth-feel of the dessert
- The flavours of the wine relative to the flavours of the dessert

The dessert should never be sweeter than the wine being paired with it. If it is, the wine will taste harsh and overly tart.

Desserts with creamy, rich, mouthfilling textures should be served with wines of an equally rich and mouthfilling nature. If the dessert wine is too light in mouth-feel (regardless of how sweet it is), it will taste watery relative to the mouth-feel of a rich dessert. The reverse holds true as well. A light, delicately textured dessert offering will be overwhelmed by an overly rich-tasting wine. Light, refreshing desserts, such as those involving fresh fruit, are best served with lighter wines matching both the sweetness and the acidity levels of the dessert itself. Examples of popular dessert wines are icewine, port, sherry, Madeira, Sauternes, Tokaji, and Pineau Des Charentes.

Regardless of how rich or delicate the dessert or wine, ultimately the flavours and aromatics of both must complement and not clash with each other.

Selecting Wines to Use as Flavourings

The concepts just described for matching wines with foods have some bearing on what wines a chef should choose as flavouring ingredients. If a chef is wedded to a particular food-and-wine pairing and the dish calls for wine as an ingredient, it is often best to use the same or a similar wine (that is, a less expensive wine made from the same grape varietal) as the flavouring.

Otherwise, the only rules for choosing wines as flavourings are:

- Avoid using anything called cooking wine. These are usually inferior products with added salt and other flavourings.
- Do not cook with a wine that you would not drink.

A chef should choose good-quality wines at cost-effective prices. Finding such wines may take time, but they are available. Often recipes will specify only a general type of wine. Here are some suggestions on what to use if a recipe calls for specific wines:

- *White wine or dry white wine*—Consider a simple, fruity Chardonnay or a dry, herby Sauvignon Blanc; even a dry Vermouth might be used. Avoid wines with a sharp, acidic flavour, and those with an excessive oaky or woody flavour. When a dessert calls for white wine, such as for poached pears, a sweet wine might be appropriate.
- *Sweet or slightly sweet white wine*—Consider a Riesling or Chenin Blanc or even a white Zinfandel.

- *Red wine or dry red wine*—Consider a simple, fruity red wine with a low to moderately low tannin content. A Pinot Noir or a medium-bodied Merlot or red Zinfandel is usually a good choice.
- *Sweet red wine*—Consider the rich flavour of a ruby port or possibly a red Zinfandel.
- *Sparkling wine*—Consider using a sweet, fruity one (sparkling wines lose their effervescence once exposed to air and heat).
- *Dessert wine*—Consider using the classic dessert wine Sauternes, or one labelled "Late Harvest."
- *Port*—Consider using a ruby port with its rich, sweet, deeply winey flavour; because they are blends, ruby ports offer a greater degree of flavour consistency.
- *Sherry*—Consider using an Amontillado with its roasted, nutty flavour. Generic cream sherry will be sweeter and fruity.
- *Madeira*—Consider a medium-bodied Bual with its toffee-caramel flavour or a more full-bodied, sweet Malmsey.
- *Marsala*—Consider using sweet Marsala with its richer, light caramel-like fruity flavour.
- *Vermouth*—Consider using a dry white Vermouth, a good complement to many savoury foods.

Beer

The Beer-Making Process

Beer is made from water, hops and malted barley, fermented by yeast. In Germany, by law only these four ingredients may be used, but in Canada and elsewhere another unmalted, less expensive grain such as rice or corn is often added to lighten the product.

Barley is converted into malt by steeping the dry grain in cool water for five to nine days, allowing it to germinate and produce the sugar-producing enzymes required for the fermentation process. Once the barley has reached the desired sugar and enzyme levels, the grain is dried with warm air (kilned) to establish colour and flavour. The longer the malting period, the darker the resulting malt. A slow, gentle dry produces pale malts and a corresponding light-coloured and -bodied brew, while more intense heat develops dark malts that may be characterized as "caramelized" or "toasted." To brew beer, the ground barley malt is "mashed" or soaked in hot water, producing a brown liquid called the wort. Hops, the cone-shaped female flowers of the vine *Humulus lupulus,* provide bitterness from their resins and aroma from their oil. They are added to the wort, which is then boiled for one to two hours, allowing the hops to flavour the brew.

Fermentation yeasts, selected according to the type of beer produced, are then added to the cooled wort. The fermentation process, which produces alcohol, can last from a few days in the case of ales to several weeks for lagers. Once fermentation is complete, the beer is transferred to storage vats for conditioning, a process that removes unwanted flavours and develops natural carbonation. This stage can also vary widely, from a few days to a few months. During this stage some brewers subject the beer to such procedures as lagering, *kräusening,* dry hopping, or the addition of other additives to adjust the flavour.

Unlike wine, beer does not improve with age, and is best consumed as soon as possible after production. Light and heat both adversely alter beer's flavour. Brown bottles are generally used to filter damaging rays. Beer is best stored between 10°C and 13°C (50°F and 55°F). Although Canadians have a tendency

Hops Flowers

to serve beer ice-cold, this practice limits the appreciation of its full flavour. Lagers are ideally served at approximately 10°C (50°F), while ales should be served at about 15°C (60°F).

Evaluating Beers

Many characteristics influence the final outcome of the brewing process: the quality of the water, the type of malt, the hops used, the species of yeast selected for fermentation, the length of the fermentation and conditioning stages, as well as any additives. The combined effects of these elements determine the colour, body, astringency, taste, alcohol content, and aroma of the finished product. Beers may be divided into two broad groups: ales and lagers. Ales are made with yeast that rises to the top during the fermentation process, producing an aromatic, cloudy brew; porter and stout are the darkest and most potent ales. Lagers are made with yeast that falls to the bottom during fermentation and are characteristically light, clear and crisp. Pilsner is a popular style of pale, light lager associated with the ancient brewing centre in Plzen in the Western Czech Republic. Most of the beer produced and consumed today is lager, with Britain and Belgium the only two markets preferring ale.

The alcohol content of beer ranges from 3% to 12% by volume. North America has historically preferred lighter beers than Europe or Australia, and in recent decades, in response to calorie consciousness and a desire for lower alcohol content, so-called "light" beers have been developed. These, however, frequently sacrifice taste for the other desired characteristics. There have been many darker beers produced and consumed in Canada in recent years. Nonalcoholic beers, made by removing the alcohol or adjusting the fermentation process to lower the alcohol content, are produced for consumers who enjoy beer's taste but do not consume alcohol for medical, religious or other reasons.

Although all ales and lagers share certain general characteristics, within each group there are immense variations, as demonstrated in Table 35.3.

Matching Beer and Food

Beer can be served with far more than pizza or barbecue; simply consider the following guidelines. (See also the CD-ROM.)

TABLE 35.3	Characteristics of Beer				
Type of Beer	Colour	Alcohol Content	Body	Flavour	Common Food Pairings
American pilsner	Light	Very low	Light	Little aroma or bitterness	Spicy foods
Belgian lambic	Light	Moderate	Light	Sour	Sharp cheese; fruit desserts; dark chocolate
Brown ale	Red to brown	Low	Full-bodied	Sweet, nutty	Sausages; smoked fish; game; salad
European lager	Light	Moderate	Moderate	Bitter, floral finish	Most meat and fish dishes; German sausage; pretzels
Pale ale	Light	Low	Moderate	Bitter, fruity, floral	Spicy foods; smoked or fried seafood; beef; lamb; game
Porter	Dark	Moderate	Full-bodied	Bitter	Barbecue; hearty meat dishes; oysters; shellfish; smoked salmon; strong cheeses
Stout; bock	Very dark	High	Full-bodied	Sweet; malty	Chocolate, nut or fruit desserts; heavy meat dishes; goulash; spicy desserts

Match Tastes

Fruit beers, such as Belgian *kriek,* are often paired with meat or dessert dishes based on fruits.

Match Strengths

Strong beers, such as porter and stout ales or bock lager, are frequently paired with strong tastes, such as sharp cheeses, game and spicy desserts.

Match Opposites

Beer, particularly lighter brew, is often preferable as a pairing with particularly spicy foods of East and Southeast Asia, Africa, the southwestern United States or Latin America, which might overpower wine. In Italy, beer is often drunk with pizza, which frequently contains such acidic ingredients as anchovies or artichokes, or multiple ingredients, which would challenge a single wine.

Match Origins

Beers of a given country are often paired with foods of that country—for example, German bratwurst or pretzels with German lager, or fiery Thai food with Thai pilsners.

Selecting Beers to Use as Flavourings

Beer is frequently used as a flavouring in the cuisines of northern France and Belgium, where it appears in such dishes as *carbonnade,* a stew flavoured with beer. Because of beer's slight bitterness, sugar or brown sugar is often added to balance the flavour. Beer can also be used in marinades and to deglaze and prepare sauces in the same manner as wine. In Canada, beer is frequently used in batters for foods being deep-fat fried, such as fish and vegetables, for example Beer-Battered Onion Rings (Recipe 22.4).

Brandy

Brandy is an alcoholic beverage made by distilling fermented fruit juice or fruit pulp and skin. Brandies typically fall into one of three categories:

- **Grape brandy** is a brandy distilled from white wine or fermented grape pulp and skins. It is aged in wooden casks (usually oak), which contributes to its rich, amber-brown colours and imparts additional mellowing flavours and aromas. **Cognac,** one of the best-known brandies, is made in France's Cognac region (and only brandy made there can be called Cognac). Cognac is twice distilled from blends of various wines that tend to be thin, tart and low in alcohol—bad for drinking but great for brandy making. After distillation, the brandy is aged in oak casks. Virtually all Cognacs sold are blends of brandies from different vintners and different years. Traditionally Cognacs are labelled according to their age. Some common grades are V.S. (Very Special, at least 2.5 years old), V.S.O.P. (Very Superior Old Pale, at least 4.5 years old) and XO, Napoleon or Extra, at least 6 years old. **Armagnac** is another well-known French brandy from the Armagnac region of southwestern France; it is slightly drier and heavier than Cognac or Cognac-style brandies. **Metaxa** is a Greek brandy with a strong resin flavour. **Brandy de Jerez** is a Spanish brandy aged in a solera system similar to that used for sherry; it is generally heavier and sweeter than Cognac and Cognac-style brandies.

- **Pomace brandy** is a brandy made from pomace, the pressed grape pulp, skins and stems that remain after the grapes are crushed and pressed to extract the juices used to make wine. They are minimally aged, and usually not in wooden casks. They tend to have a harsh flavour. Examples include Italian Grappa and French Marc.
- **Fruit brandy** is any brandy made from fermenting fruits other than grapes. This term should not be confused with fruit-flavoured brandy, which is a grape brandy that has been flavoured with the extract of another fruit. Well-known fruit brandies include **Calvados**, an apple brandy from Normandy, France; **Kirschwasser**, a cherry brandy from Bavaria, Germany; **Framboise**, a raspberry brandy from Alsace, France; **Poire**, a pear brandy from Alsace, France; and **Slivovitz**, a plum brandy from eastern Europe and the Balkans.

As with wines, when choosing a brandy as a flavouring, it does not necessarily pay to skimp on costs. The brandy does not have to be the most expensive brand, but it should have a rich, full, mellow flavour. Try, for example, an inexpensive but genuine Cognac (one that is graded V.S.). If the recipe calls for a fruit brandy, make sure to use one. Do not use a fruit brandy with added artificial flavours, a fruit-flavoured brandy or a fruit-flavoured liqueur. These products have different flavours, bodies, degrees of sweetness and alcohol contents than fruit brandies.

Liquors

Liquors are distilled alcoholic beverages such as gin, rum, tequila, vodka and whisky. To create these beverages, a liquid made from grains, vegetables or the like is fermented, then the water component is cooked off and the alcohol is concentrated through **distillation**. The resulting clear liquid can be coloured or flavoured during aging, or bottled for immediate sale. From time to time, a chef may decide to add a distinctive liquor flavour to foods, especially sauces and desserts.

Gin is a clear spirit distilled from grains and flavoured with juniper berries as well as herbs, peels and spices. There are various styles of gin; London dry gin, which is a generally recognized style, not a brand, is considered heavier and drier than American gin; Dutch gin is the sweetest.

Rum is distilled from sugar cane and most of it comes from the cane-producing Caribbean countries. Its character varies according to its colour: White rums, which are clear and colourless, are relatively dry and light; amber or gold rums are similar to white rums but with a slightly stronger flavour and a pale golden colour; dark rums have a strong molasses flavour, a dark brown colour and a heavy body.

Tequila is a clear to amber-coloured spirit made in Mexico from the fermented sap of the agave. Mezcal, which is made from sap extracted from fire-roasted blue agave, is similar to tequila but with a harsher flavour.

Vodka is, traditionally, a flavourless and colourless liquor distilled from potatoes, fruits, grains and/or other plant products. Most of the world's vodka is actually made from wheat. Many newer types of vodka are flavoured, either by including the flavourings in the mash during distillation or by adding flavours afterward.

Whisky is a spirit distilled from various grains that have been pounded and cooked into a mash and allowed to ferment before distillation. After distillation, it is aged in oak barrels until the flavours are mellow and smooth. There are many types of whiskies. Blended whisky is a mixture of straight whiskies and neutral spirits; it is usually aged after blending. Bourbon or bourbon whisky is produced in Kentucky and is distilled from a mash containing at

distillation the separation of alcohol from a liquid (or, during the production of alcoholic beverages, from a fermented mash); it is accomplished by heating the liquid or mash to a gas that contains alcohol vapours; this steam is then condensed into the desired alcoholic liquid (beverage)

Whiskey or Whisky?

The Irish lay claim to having been the first to produce whiskey, which they spell with an e, while the Scottish omit the e—whisky. The word "whiskey" is derived from the Irish *Uisce Beatha* (issge-baha), which means "the water of life." It was the inability of the English to pronounce the Irish that corrupted the original, and the pronunciation morphed into the modern "whisky" that we are familiar with today.

The general differences between Irish and Scotch whisk(e)y are

1. Scotch uses peat during the malting process, which imparts a smoky flavour; the Irish method does not expose the grains to the smoke.
2. Scotch is generally distilled twice, whereas Irish whiskey is triple-distilled, which yields a smoother finish.

least 51% corn, then aged in charred new oak barrels. Canadian whisky is usually a blended product with a light body. Irish whiskey resembles Scotch, but without the smoky flavour. Scotch whisky has a very distinctive, smoky flavour. A single-malt Scotch whisky tends to have a stronger, more complex flavour than a blended Scotch whisky, which is a mixture of malt whiskies and grain whiskies.

Liqueurs

Liqueurs are traditionally made from herbs, fruits, nuts, spices, flowers or other flavourings infused into an alcohol base. The base can be **neutral spirits**, brandy, rum or whisky. All liqueurs have varying degrees of added sugar. Many newer liqueurs, especially generic off-brand products, are made with flavouring extracts, essential oils and even artificial flavours. Cream liqueurs are liqueurs blended with cream. They are thick, with mild, comforting flavours. They do not keep long once opened, so they need to be stored in the refrigerator. Crème liqueurs, such as crème de cacao, crème de menthe and crème de cassis, contain no cream. Rather, additional sugar gives them a thick, syrupy, creamy texture and a very sweet flavour.

When using a liqueur as a flavouring, look for products with rich, true, natural flavours. In addition, bear in mind that a liqueur and a crème liqueur flavoured with the same ingredients are not the same products and should not be used interchangeably. So if a recipe calls for the coffee-flavoured liqueur Kahlúa, use it and not a crème de café product; the latter will have a more syrupy texture and a sweeter flavour. Similarly, if a recipe calls for a proprietary blend such as Drambuie or Chambord, do not skimp with some lesser-quality generic product; customers may know the difference. Many of the liqueurs commonly used as flavourings are listed in Table 35.4 on the next page.

● **neutral spirits or grain spirits** pure alcohol (ethanol or ethyl alcohol); they are odourless, tasteless and a very potent 190 proof (95% alcohol)

GUIDELINES FOR COOKING WITH WINES, BEERS, BRANDIES, LIQUORS AND LIQUEURS

- *Use quality products.* Heating a mediocre wine, brandy, liqueur or liquor tends to bring out the worst characteristics of the product, especially its acidic properties.
- *Pay attention to cooking time once wine or other alcoholic beverages have been added.* The longer a dish cooks, the more alcohol evaporates, thus concentrating its flavours, especially acidic flavours. Because alcohol evaporates at a lower temperature than water (86°C/172°F), the flavourings suspended in the alcohol are reduced and concentrated faster than flavourings suspended in water.
- *Brown foods before adding wine or other alcoholic beverages to a dish such as a sauce or stew.* This allows the surface of the foods to caramelize before liquid is added. As the wine is reduced, all of the flavours will blend together.
- *Understand that alcohol and acids in wine may interact with aluminum or cast-iron cookware.* Some chefs therefore prefer to use nonreactive cookware when cooking with wine or other alcoholic beverages.

For many, the consumption of alcohol is a concern. The amount of alcohol left after a wine or other alcoholic beverage has been added as a flavouring depends on how and for how long the dish is cooked. A dish flambéd tableside with Cognac

Flambéing: Cooking with Alcohol

Often a dish will require flaming or flambéing, which means igniting brandy, rum or other liquor so that the alcohol burns off and the flavour of the liquor is retained. When alcohol comes into contact with a flame, it can ignite. So, in order to avoid singed eyebrows and kitchen fires, be careful when adding wine, brandy, liqueurs or liquor to a dish on or near the stove.

When a dish calls for flambéing, stand away from the pan being flamed. Never pour alcohol directly from a bottle into a hot pan because the flames can travel up into the bottle, causing it to explode. Heat the liquor until warm. This can be done in the pan in which the food is cooking, such as for Pepper Steaks (Recipe 13.4), or in a separate pan. Tilt the pan away from you before igniting the liquor to avoid having the flames leap from the pan. The flame from a gas burner or match will ignite the alcohol. Allow the flame to subside before finishing the preparation.

TABLE 35.4	Liqueurs Commonly Used as Flavourings	
Liqueur	**Alcohol Base**	**Flavourings**
Amaretto	Grape brandy	Almonds and apricots
B&B	Grape brandy	Bénédictine and brandy
Bénédictine	Grape brandy	Herbs, spices and citrus peels
Campari	Neutral spirits	130 different herbs, plants, peels and aromatics
Cassis	Neutral spirits	Black currants, herbs, roots, plants and peels
Chambord	Grape brandy	Black raspberries
Chartreuse	Grape brandy	More than 125 herbs and other flavourings
Cointreau	Neutral spirits	Bitter orange peel
Crème de cacao	Neutral spirits	Chocolate
Crème de café	Neutral spirits	Coffee
Crème de cassis	Grape brandy	Black currants
Crème de menthe	Neutral spirits	Peppermint
Curaçao	Neutral spirits	Bitter orange
Drambuie	Scotch whisky	Honey
Frangelico	Neutral spirits	Hazelnuts
Galliano	Neutral spirits	Anise, licorice and vanilla
Grand Marnier	Grape brandy	Bitter oranges
Irish Cream	Irish whiskey	Cream and sugar
Kahlúa	Neutral spirits	Coffee
Kirsch	Neutral spirits	Cherries
Limoncello	Neutral spirits, vodka	Lemons
Malibu	White rum	Coconut
Midori	Neutral spirits	Melons
Ouzo	Neutral spirits	Anise seed and herbs
Pernod	Neutral spirits	Anise seed and licorice
Pimm's No. 1 Cup	Gin	Herbs, botanicals and fruit extracts
Sambuca	Neutral spirits	Anise seed and elderberries
Sloe Gin	Gin	Sloe berries
Southern Comfort	American whisky	Peaches and oranges
Tia Maria	Cask-aged rum	Coffee beans and spices
Triple Sec	Neutral spirits	Bitter orange peel

that is allowed to burn out before being served, for example, may retain very little of its original alcohol content. But a chicken breast that has been marinated in white wine and then quickly sautéed could retain as much as 75% of the alcohol from the marinade. If, however, the same chicken breast is cooked over medium heat for 15 minutes, as much as 60% of the alcohol will evaporate out. Simmering the same chicken breast over low heat for approximately two hours or more will reduce the alcohol content to 10% or even less.

Conclusion

The role of the chef has evolved beyond the food menu. Understanding how to prepare and serve coffee and tea is an essential skill. Contemporary chefs also pride themselves on their ability to pair food with wine, beer or other suitable beverages, and this skill is often called upon when dealing directly with the public or making recommendations on menus. Like quality food production, quality beverage production requires high-quality ingredients, dedication and skill.

Questions for Discussion

1. Discuss the role of beverages on a menu.
2. Describe the similarities and differences among the four coffee-roasting categories.
3. List and briefly explain five guidelines for food and wine pairing.
4. Choose three different styles of beer and taste several different cheeses with each. Note the effects on taste at the beginning, and at the finish.

36 Plate Presentation

" I want order and taste. A well displayed meal is enhanced one hundred percent in my eyes.

—Marie-Antoine Carême, French chef (1783–1833)

Although food preparation is very much a science, food presentation is an art. Good plate presentation results from careful attention to the colours, shapes, textures and arrangements of the foods. Great plate presentation requires experience and style.

In this chapter, we describe several methods of presenting foods. We realize that for every guideline we suggest, there are exceptions. Our examples are not meant to take the place of more traditional techniques. They are intended only to spark your imagination. As you gain experience, you will undoubtedly develop your own style.

LEARNING OUTCOMES

After studying this chapter you will be able to:

- understand the basic principles of plate presentation
- use a variety of techniques to add visual appeal to plated foods

These interactive online tools will help you master the skills in this chapter:

- Chapter Quizzes

The final step in food preparation is to justify the hours of hard work spent cooking the food by presenting and serving it properly.

Service is the process of delivering the selected foods to diners in the proper fashion. Hot foods should be served very hot and on heated plates; cold foods should be served very cold and on chilled plates. Foods should be cooked to the proper degree of doneness. A roast rack of lamb ordered medium rare should be medium rare—not medium, not rare. Pasta should be served al dente—slightly chewy, not mushy. Bread should be fresh, not stale. Portion sizes should be appropriate. First courses and appetizers should be small enough so that the diner can still appreciate the courses that follow. Rich foods should be served in smaller portions than for other foods.

Presentation is the process of offering the selected foods to diners in a fashion that is visually pleasing. When presenting foods, always bear in mind that diners eat first with their eyes and then with their mouths. The foods must be pleasantly and appropriately coloured and shaped. And the colours, textures, shapes and flavours of all foods must work together to form a pleasing composition on the plate. Any decorative touches such as sauce placement or the addition of garnishes should be done thoughtfully. Most important, plates should be neat and clean. Inspect all plates before they leave the kitchen; wipe drops of sauce, specks of food and fingerprints from plate rims with a clean towel.

Presentation techniques are divided here into two broad categories: those applied to specific foods and those applied to the plate as a whole. The techniques described here can be applied to some foods or recipes that appear elsewhere in the text.

THE FOOD

The appearance of food is contingent on the skilful application of techniques: fabrication, cooking, carving, shaping, placement and garnishing. Coupled with the procurement of the best-quality ingredients, the integrity of the food will be preserved and the diner's enjoyment enhanced.

A sirloin steak grilled medium rare should be pink inside; its surface should glisten and be branded with well-defined and neatly executed crosshatch marks. When serving asparagus with hollandaise, the stalks should be bright green and tender-crisp; the hollandaise sauce should be smooth and shiny, not grainy or separated. A lemon meringue pie should be attractively browned on top; the filling should be a true lemony yellow and the crust golden brown and without cracks.

Whether a recipe calls for browning foods under a salamander before service, poaching a galantine of chicken wrapped in cheesecloth to maintain its shape or adding vinegar when braising red cabbage, proper cooking

Garnishes (an admittedly cranky admonition)

I am a strong believer in the simple, edible garnish that has a close flavor kinship to the dish. In my world, dyed daikon flamingos, writhing carrot dragons, and blinking Christmas lights in the empty eye sockets of a stir-fried lobster—all garnishes of the Hong Kong sort—are out. So, too, are radish flowers, tomato rosettes, and vegetable pellets sculpted to look like suppositories. I find all of this loathsome.

In my own rather minimalist style, the fanciest I get is an occasional scallion brush. Otherwise, a leggy piece of coriander or a flourish of scallion rings are all that our already colorful dishes require. Or, if the dish is green, a confetti of finely diced red bell pepper will do the job.

The issue is a visible one, but it needs to make sense on your tongue. A garnish is primarily designed to tickle the eye, but it also should meld seamlessly with the other flavors on the plate or contrast with them in a meaningful way.

Garnishing the rims of plates—a current feature of trendy restaurants in the 90s—is something I find very peculiar. I spill and splatter my own food quite nicely, thank you, and don't want the kitchen to do it for me.

Ditto the rage for a whole chive aloft each appetizer or a cage of spun sugar looming above a dessert. It is admittedly wonderful to give a little height to a dish: One can arrange cold shrimp, for example, in a lively tumble with just a touch or two. But the unrelated vertical garnish is often absurd, a bit of Dr. Seuss on the plate.

I sound cranky, and perhaps I am! Restaurant cooks frequently spend too much time decorating their food, and too little time paying attention to its taste. This, I think, is sad.

—from *China Moon Cookbook*
by Barbara Tropp

procedures can enhance the texture, shape and colour of many cooked foods. Throughout this text we have discussed the proper cooking procedures for many, many foods. Use them.

Cutting Foods

The careful cutting of foods often increases their visual appeal and reflects the chef's attention to detail. Here we distinguish between cutting foods to decorate the plate and cutting the foods to be consumed. Decorative garnishes such as tomato and radish roses, frizzed scallions, watermelon boats and the like fall within the former category. Cutting foods into beautiful garnishes is an art unto itself, requiring skill and practice. Although beyond the scope of this text, books on creating food garnishes are listed in References and Recommended Reading.

The latter category includes the meats, poultry, fish, vegetables and starches that are the meal. Each should be carefully shaped. Vegetables can be cut into uniform shapes and sizes such as julienne, batonnet or turned. If serving sliced meats or poultry, the slices should be of even thickness; fish can be cut into fillets. Individual stew ingredients and soup or salad garnishes should be of uniform sizes. All of these techniques are simple, fundamental and effective.

Some foods take the shape of the pan in which they are cooked. Polenta and gratin or scalloped potatoes, for example, can be presented attractively when baked in and removed from individual casseroles, or they can be baked in a hotel pan and then cut into various shapes.

Fried Julienned Red Beets

Fried Sliced Lotus Root

Cutting polenta into various shapes.

BASIC PROCEDURE FOR CUTTING POLENTA

1. Cook the polenta according to the recipe. When it is done, pour it onto a well-oiled or buttered half sheet pan. Then chill it in the refrigerator until firm.

2. Once the polenta is firm, flip the pan over onto a work table. Lift off the pan; the polenta will come out easily. Using a chef's knife or circular cutters, cut the polenta into the desired shape. The polenta can be sautéed or grilled for service.

BASIC PROCEDURE FOR CUTTING GRATIN OR SCALLOPED POTATOES

1. Select a recipe that produces a firm finished product so that the finished dish will hold its shape after cutting.
2. Bake the potatoes in a well-greased hotel pan and refrigerate until cold and firm. Then cut the potatoes into various shapes with a chef's knife or circular cutters and remove them to a clean pan using a spatula.
3. For service, reheat the potatoes in a 160°C (325°F) oven until hot.

Cutting potatoes with a circular cutter.

Moulding Foods

Some foods, particularly grains or vegetables bound by sauces, can be moulded into attractive, hard-edged shapes by using metal rings, cutters or timbales. These moulded forms create height and keep the plate neat and clean.

BASIC PROCEDURE FOR MOULDING GRAINS

1. Fill a timbale, soup cup or other mould of the appropriate size and shape with the hot grains, firmly pressing them together.
2. For à la carte service, immediately unmould the grains onto the serving plate by placing the mould upside down on the plate and tapping its rim.
3. For banquet service, place the filled moulds in a hotel pan and refrigerate until needed. Shortly before service, fill the hotel pan with hot water to a point about two-thirds up the side of the moulds. Be careful not to splash any water onto the grains. Cover the pan with foil and place in the oven. Heat until the grains are hot, then plate as desired.

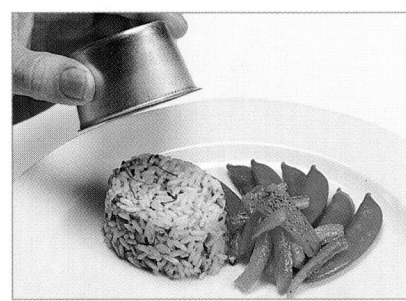

Unmoulding a timbale of rice.

BASIC PROCEDURE FOR MOULDING VEGETABLES

1. Position a ring mould on the plate and fill it with the vegetables. Press the foods into the ring to help them hold the shape. Level the top.

2. Carefully lift off the ring.

Forming grapefruit sorbet into a quenelle shape using two spoons.

THE PLATE

Properly cooked, carefully cut and appropriately moulded foods should not be haphazardly slapped onto a plate. Rather, you should choose and position the foods carefully to achieve a plate presentation with a balanced, harmonious composition.

The composition can be further enhanced by decorating the plate with garnishes or sauces. Some of these techniques (for example, decorating the plate with powdered sugar) do not substantially affect the flavours of the foods, they only make the completed presentation more attractive. Other techniques (for example, garnishing a dessert with finely chopped nuts or painting a plate with two sauces) add flavour and texture to the finished dish.

Choosing Plates

Restaurant china designed to withstand the rigours of repeated use is available in many different shapes, sizes, colours and styles. It is often the chef's responsibility to choose the china appropriate for the food being served. Frequently, specific plates will be used for specific dishes, such as a tulip sundae glass for an ice cream dish.

Sizes and Shapes

Chewy Date Bars with Caramel Ice Cream

Most plates are round, but oval plates (also referred to as platters) and rectangular, square and triangular plates are becoming more common. Plates are available in a variety of sizes from a small 10-cm (4-in.) bread plate to a huge 35-cm (14-in.) charger or base plate. Plates are typically concave; their depths vary within a limited range of about 2.5 cm (1 in.). Most plates have rims; rim widths also vary. Soup bowls can be rimmed or rimless. Soup plates are usually larger and shallower than soup bowls and have wide rims. Soup cups are also available. There are also dozens of plate designs intended for a specific purpose, such as plates with small indentations for holding escargots, or long, rectangular plates with grooves for holding asparagus.

Choose plates large enough to hold the food comfortably without overcrowding or spilling. Oversized, rimmed soup plates are popular for serving any food with a sauce. Be careful when using oversized plates, however, as the food may look sparse, creating poor value perception.

Whether a round, oval or less conventionally shaped plate is used, be sure to choose one with a size and shape that best highlights the food and supports the composition. For example, in the photograph to the left, the rectangular dish with round corners and raised rim accentuates the geometrically simple yet effective composition of the square date bar and spherical scoop of ice cream.

Colours and Patterns

Grilled Prawn Brochette with Butternut Squash Risotto

White and cream are by far the most common colours for restaurant china. Almost any food looks good on these neutral colours.

Coloured and patterned plates can be used quite effectively to accent food, however. The obvious choice is to contrast dark plates with bright- or light-coloured foods and light plates with dark-coloured foods. The food should always be the focal point of any plate. The colours and shapes in the pattern should blend well and harmonize with the foods served. The crisp pattern of blue dots along the plate rim shown to the left, for example, harmonizes well with the beige sauce and symmetrically placed shrimp skewers.

Arranging Foods on Plates

You should strive for a well-balanced plate composition. This can be achieved by carefully considering colours, textures, shapes and arrangements.

Colours

Foods come in a rainbow of colours and, to the extent appropriate, foods of different colours should be presented together. Generally, the colours should provide balance and contrast. But no matter how well prepared or planned, some dishes simply have dull, boring or similar colours. If so, try adding another ingredient or garnish for a splash of colour. The vivid red lobster claws and the shiny black mussel shells shown to the right add striking colour notes to a paella dish that would otherwise be dominated by yellow rice, tan chicken, brown sausages and grey clam shells.

Paella

Textures

Visual texture refers to how smooth or rough, coarse or fine a food looks. Mashed potatoes and carrot purée both look smooth and soft. Salmon mousseline and spinach soufflé both have slightly grainy surfaces. Rösti potatoes and meatloaf both appear coarse. The flavours of each food in these pairs differ; their visual textures do not.

Typically, foods with similar textures look boring together; foods with different textures look more exciting. Serve carrots cut julienne with the mashed potatoes to achieve a balance of hard and soft textures, steamed leaf spinach with the salmon mousseline for a combination of smooth and grainy textures, and a baked potato with the meatloaf for pairing fluffy and coarse textures. These pairs generally maintain the same range of flavours as the first set of pairs while providing different visual textures.

Achieving a balance of texture on a plate can be as simple as adding a crisp garnish such as the fried julienned vegetables shown to the right served with a rack of lamb.

The cassoulet shown to the right harmoniously combines several textures in one dish: the pebbly beans, the slices of smooth slab bacon and coarse sausage and the bumpy skin of the duck leg. Indeed, the variation in textures is so dramatic and appealing that many diners may not even notice that all the principal ingredients are essentially the same colour.

Rack of Lamb Garnished with Fried Julienned Vegetables

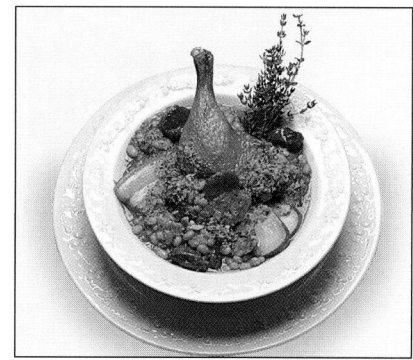

Cassoulet

Shapes

For a more dramatic presentation, combine foods with different shapes on one plate. The plate shown to the right is an excellent example of simple shapes artfully combined: ovals of evenly sliced lamb loin with cleanly cut triangles of crisp potatoes and long, thin spears of asparagus. The three very different shapes lend contrast and character to the dish.

Arrangements

Having decided on the colours, textures and shapes of the foods that will go on the plate, you must next decide where to place each individual item to achieve a balanced and unified composition. Mostly this takes judgment and style, but there are a few general guidelines.

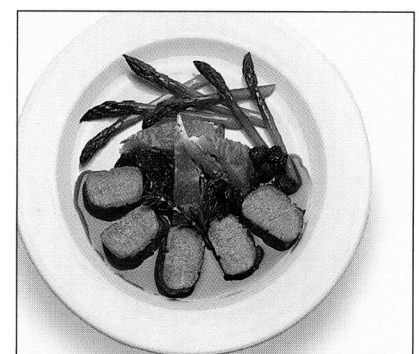

Lamb Loin with Rösti Potatoes

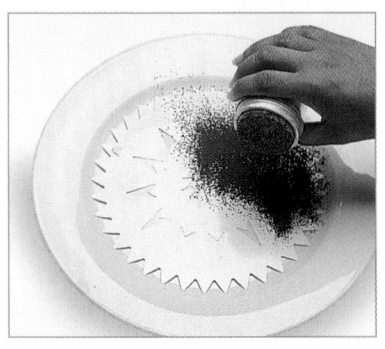

Grilled Duck with Roasted Vegetables

The grilled duck with roasted vegetables shown to the left elegantly illustrates these principles. Height is established by a structure composed of the duck leg and thigh, sliced turnips and baby carrots. The structure sits toward the back of the plate. Its height, placement and striking appearance make it the focal point. The neatly sliced duck breast is then fanned across the plate in front of this focal point, drawing the viewer's attention into the plate.

Decorating Plates

The colours, textures, shapes and arrangements of foods on a plate can be improved or highlighted by decorating a plate with herbs, spices and other garnishes, baked hippen masse dough and sauces. If any of these are to be applied after the principal food is placed on the plate, be prepared to do so quickly so that the food is served at its proper temperature.

Plate Dusting

An attractive method for decorating dessert plates is to cover part of the plate with a dusting of powdered sugar, cocoa powder or both before placing the dessert on the plate. Use sugar on dark-coloured plates and cocoa on light-coloured plates. These items can be dusted onto the plate with a shaker can or sifter in a free-form fashion or into any desired pattern by using a template. The template can be a doily or a stencil placed over the plate before it is dusted. Leave sufficient rim clear to facilitate service without smudges.

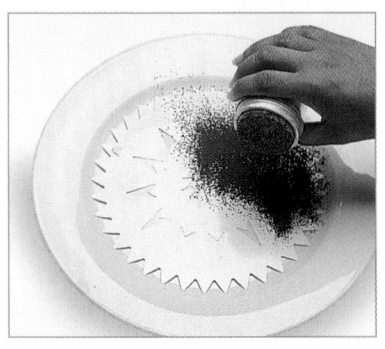

1. Place a template over the plate. Dust the sugar or cocoa over the template.

2. Carefully remove the template.

Using herbs to garnish a plate.

Provided they complement the food, very finely chopped nuts can also be used to decorate plates for sweet or savoury foods. See, for example, the plate of French toast garnished with chopped macadamia nuts shown to the right. Plates for savoury foods can be decorated in a similar fashion by sprinkling them with finely chopped herbs such as thyme or diced vegetables such as a combination of brightly coloured peppers.

Garnishing Plates with Herbs

Using fresh herbs and greens is one of the easiest ways to add colour, texture and flow to a plate. Whether the herbs or greens are an ingredient in the dish or merely a decoration, they should always complement the foods and be consistent with their seasonings. A sprig of fresh rosemary garnishing a beautifully roasted rack of lamb, or tiny leaves of chervil garnishing delicately poached fillets of sole are natural combinations. Sprigs of fresh green mint (often with a fresh berry or two or a strawberry cut in a fan) are often the perfect decoration for a dessert plate. Microgreens add a delicate-tasting, light and lacy garnish to many dishes.

Garnishing Plates with Hippen Masse and Tuiles

An increasingly popular presentation technique is to pipe batters into intricate designs and then bake them to form crisp, rigid, cookielike garnishes. These garnishes are then used to create height and add texture.

Banana Brioche French Toast

Slicing strawberry fans to use as plate garnish.

APPLYING THE BASICS	RECIPE 36.1

Savoury Hippen Masse

ARIZONA BILTMORE, PHOENIX, AZ
Yield: 450 g (1 lb.)

Egg whites, room temperature	250 g	8 oz.
Bread flour	125 g	4 oz.
Cream, 35%	90 mL	3 fl. oz.
Granulated sugar	30 g	1 oz.
Salt and white pepper	TT	TT
Dried thyme, crushed	0.5 g	1 tsp.

1. Stir the egg whites together to blend. Stir in all of the flour at once.

2. Blend in the cream, then add the remaining ingredients.

3. Strain the batter through a conical strainer and allow to rest for 30 minutes.

4. Lightly oil the back of a very flat sheet pan. Pipe the hippen masse onto the pan using a plastic squeeze bottle. Pipe the batter into decorative patterns appropriate for the desired plate presentation.

5. Bake at 190°C (375°F) until set and lightly browned. Remove from the oven, then remove the decorations from the sheet pan while still slightly warm.

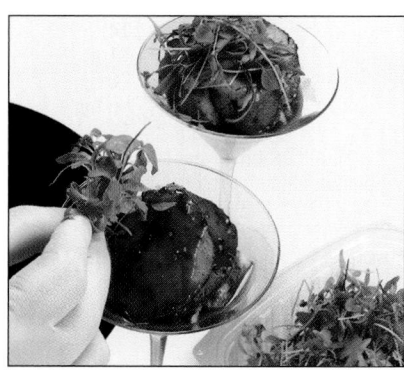

Garnishing an appetizer with microgreens.

RECIPE 36.1

Approximate values per 25 g serving:	
Calories	52
Total fat	2 g
Saturated fat	1 g
Cholesterol	6.5 mg
Sodium	260 mg
Total carbohydrates	7 g
Protein	2.5 g

Gilbert Noussitou, CCC

A graduate of École Hôtelière des Pyrénées, in Toulouse, France, Gilbert has been practising his trade for 32 years in some of the finest establishments of France, England and Canada. His varied experience includes owning a restaurant, a catering company and a consulting firm, as well as winning many national and international awards. He currently teaches the Cook Apprenticeship Program at Camosun.

RECIPE 36.2

Approximate values per tuile:	
Calories	14
Total fat	1 g
Saturated fat	0.5 g
Cholesterol	3 mg
Sodium	13 mg
Total carbohydrates	1 g
Protein	0 g

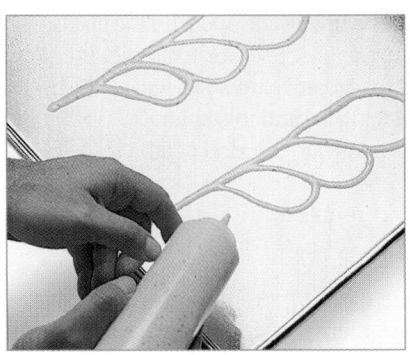

1. Savoury Hippen Masse: Piping the batter onto an oiled sheet pan.

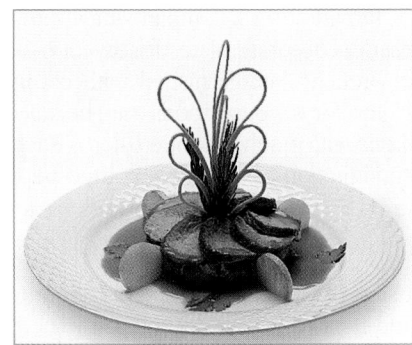

2. The baked batter as a component of the finished design.

APPLYING THE BASICS   RECIPE 36.2

Potato Tuiles

CAMOSUN COLLEGE, VICTORIA, BC
Chef Instructor Gilbert Noussitou, CCC

Yield: 36 7.5-cm (3-in.) tuiles/pieces

Duchesse Potatoes (Recipe 23.4)	50 g	1-3/4 oz.
Egg white, slightly beaten	35 g	1
All-purpose flour	20 g	8 tsp.
Butter, melted	50 g	1-3/4 oz.

1. Combine cool Duchesse Potatoes with egg white.
2. Add flour and mix to a smooth paste.
3. Stir in the butter.
4. On a parchment-lined baking sheet, brush batter into template.
5. Bake in 200°C (400°F) oven until golden brown and crisp.

Decorating Plates with Sauces

The sauce is an integral part of most any dish. It adds flavour and moisture; it also adds colour, texture and flow to the plate. A rich, glossy Bordelaise or Madeira sauce pooled beneath sautéed tournedos of beef is a classic example. A chunky salsa of tomatoes, papaya and pineapple beside a juicy piece of grilled salmon is a more contemporary approach.

Grilled Quail with Balsamic Raspberries

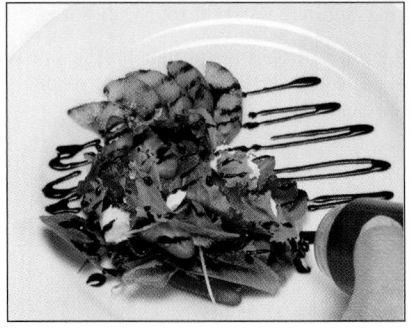

Squirting a salad plate with a balsamic vinegar reduction.

Adding a foamed sauce to a risotto appetizer plate.

Sauces are also used in other, less traditional ways to add visual appeal. For example, if using a vinaigrette dressing for grilled foods, let the oil and vinegar separate and pool on the plate, creating the interesting effect illustrated here.

One or more coloured sauces can also be used to paint plates. One technique is simply to drizzle or splatter the sauce onto the plate.

Alternatively, one or more coloured sauces can be applied to a plate using squirt bottles to create abstract patterns or representational designs. Painting plates with different-coloured sauces also facilitates flow and adds colour. Although this technique can be used with hot sauces, it is more often used with cold sauces (such as vanilla, caramel, chocolate and fruit-flavoured ones) for dessert presentations. The sauces must be thick enough to hold the pattern once it is created and they should all be of the same viscosity.

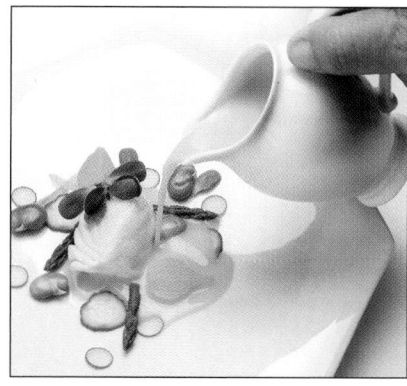

Pouring sauce over a fish and vegetable plate tableside.

BASIC PROCEDURE FOR PAINTING A DESIGN WITH SAUCES

1. Pool one sauce evenly across the entire base of the plate, then apply a contrasting sauce onto the base sauce in a spiral.

2. Draw a thin-bladed knife or a toothpick through the sauces from the centre point toward the edge. Then, leaving a 1.2-cm (1/2-in.) space along the edge, draw a knife blade or toothpick from the edge to the centre.

Other patterns can be produced by squirting the sauces onto the plate in different patterns or by pulling the knife or toothpick through the sauces in different directions. As shown to the left, a circle of chocolate-sauce dots in a pool of vanilla sauce is pulled to create a leaf wreath.

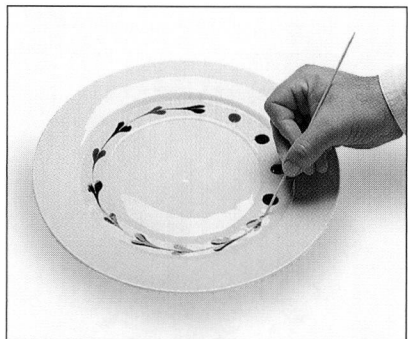

Pulling a skewer through chocolate and raspberry-sauce dots to create a border of hearts.

Painting balsamic reduction on a plate with a pastry brush.

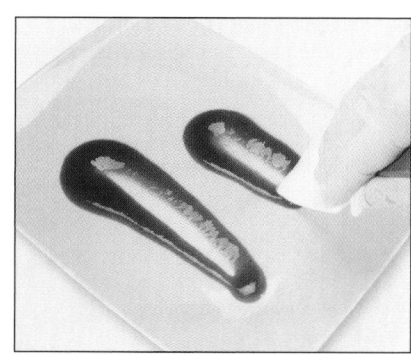

Running a spatula through a line of fruit coulis to create a shadow effect.

SMALL PLATES

Diminutive dishes once reserved for the start of a meal have taken hold as an eating style all its own, referred to as small-plate dining. For consumers seeking variety, eating three or more small plates can replace ordering a traditional appetizer and entree. Each dish on a small-plate menu is usually reduced in size and price, often reducing the cost of dining out. Exposure to chef tasting menus where numerous dishes are served in dainty portions may be one reason why many are comfortable with this style of dining. Or perhaps ethnic dining styles such as Spanish tapas, Chinese dim sum and Middle Eastern mezze are giving consumers a taste for eclectic eating. Studies suggest that consumers view eating a variety of small plates as a less formal, more relaxed way of dining. Small plates allow customers to experiment and try new dishes while offering an alternative to larger portions of protein-dominated entrees at a lower cost.

Whatever the reason for the popularity of such menu offerings, the principles for composing a small plate are the same as for preparing and presenting any dish. Shapes, colours and textures of food should be chosen to enhance each item on the plate. Foods should be arranged with eye appeal, an essential component in ensuring guests' satisfaction. Although composition on each plate is important, balance in the selections of dishes offered on a small-plate menu is of prime consideration because guests often order three or more dishes to create a meal.

BASIC GUIDELINES FOR CREATING SMALL PLATES

1. **Reduce the portion size of a conventional entree.** From stews to sautés, any entree can be adapted by reducing the portion size. In the photograph shown to the left, a 60- to 90-g (2- to 3-oz.) portion of seared salmon accompanied by braised cabbage and sauce makes an appealing yet satisfying miniature dish.

2. **Reduce the number of units served.** A single crab cake, grilled sausage or soft-shell crab, as shown below, would make an appealing small plate. Or serve an unconventionally large diver scallop accompanied by mushrooms and a few crisp potatoes (see below). This dish satisfies the palate without satiating the diner.

3. **Use an unexpected garnish with a traditional protein.** Pairing a dish with a salad or vegetable instead of a heavier starch garnish lightens a conventional entree. In the photograph below, baby greens dressed with hazelnut vinaigrette accompany a grilled duck breast more commonly served with scalloped potatoes or wild rice.

1. Small portion of grilled salmon on a bed of braised cabbage and sauce.

 continued

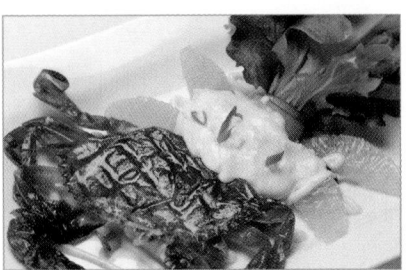

2a. Grilled soft-shell crab with citrus aïoli.

2b. Seared diver scallop with chanterelles, potato gaufrettes and blood orange cream.

3. Warm duck breast salad with Asian spices and hazelnut vinaigrette.

4. **Present entree items in a new format.** Grilled brochettes or skewers of fish, game, meat or poultry served without garnishes are candidates for small-plate menus, as shown to the right. A solitary jumbo shrimp wrapped in potato perched on a mould of spinach and two sauces (see right) is an elegant dish that provides visual appeal as well as a palate-pleasing textural contrast between the crisp potato crust and creamy spinach.

5. **Offer an assortment of starch dishes.** Small potato or grain dishes complement a variety of dishes. Perfectly crisp french-fried potatoes or a more unexpected plate of grilled sweet potato make excellent accompaniments to any number of foods. Do not overlook pasta, risotto or a bread salad served in small portions. Guests are free to compose their own menu by combining a few small plates with a suitable starch.

6. **Highlight vegetables as centre of the plate items.** Vegetable dishes, especially in season, shine on small-plate menus. Early vegetables such as the grilled baby squash shown below make compelling small plates. Salads presented in a novel manner such as a mould of beet and corn salad or in a trio that can be shared among guests at the table satisfy the need for variety on small-plate menus (see photos below).

7. **Look to the breakfast, lunch and appetizer menu for inspiration.** Crepes, quiche and egg dishes make compelling small plates. Scotch eggs, hard-boiled eggs with assorted fillings, individual cheese soufflés, crepes stuffed with mushrooms or mini quiches are often overlooked as components on small-plate menus. Also bear in mind the diminutive size of many appetizers, which naturally work well in the lineup of smaller dishes.

8. **Simplify the plating to compensate for the increased number of dishes needed.** When portions are small, customers will order more dishes, which means more plates to send out from the kitchen. Consider the time and labour needed to compose each plate when designing small-plate menus. Streamline the presentation accordingly.

4a. Veal kebabs.

4b. Freshwater shrimp wrapped in potato.

5. Panzanella (Italian bread salad).

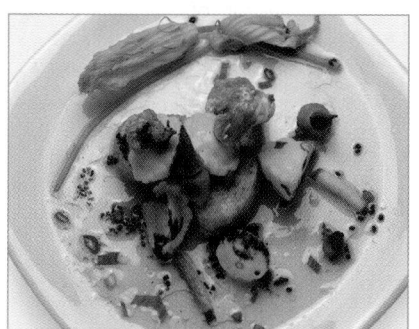

6a. Grilled baby squash with honey cardamom butter.

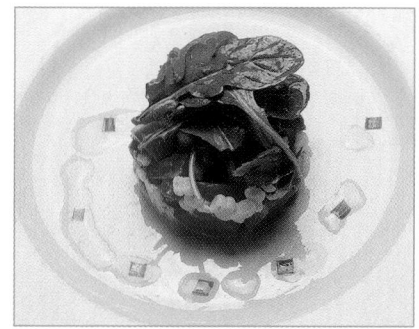

6b. Beet and corn salad.

6c. Trio of salads.

7. Spinach and mushroom crepe.

Conclusion

Although the techniques described in this chapter—as well as many other ones—can be used to create a variety of effects, often the most elegant plates are those with the simplest designs. Thoughtful presentation improves the appeal and appearance of any food as well as the completed plate, but it cannot mask poor-quality, poorly prepared or bland-tasting foods.

Questions for Discussion

1. Explain why proper service and presentation are important in food service operations.
2. Distinguish between cutting and moulding foods for visual appeal and creating garnishes out of foods.
3. How can the selection of serviceware such as bowls and platters affect the visual appeal of the foods served?
4. List and describe four techniques for garnishing plates.
5. Describe how colour, texture, shape and arrangement can be used to create a well-balanced plate composition.
6. Use the Internet to find at least three restaurants that offer small plates on their menus. Analyze the offerings to determine how a complete, balanced meal can be created from these menu selections.

Glossary

À la—(ah lah) French for "in the manner or style of"; used in relation to a food, it designates a style of preparation or presentation

À la carte—(ah lah kart) a menu on which each food and beverage is listed and priced separately

À la grecque—(ah la grehk) a preparation style in which vegetables are marinated in olive oil, lemon juice and herbs, then served cold

À point—(ah PWEN) (1) French term for cooking to the ideal degree of doneness; (2) when applied to meat, refers to cooking it medium rare

Acid—a substance that neutralizes a base (alkaline) in a liquid solution; foods such as citrus juice, vinegar and wine that have a sour or sharp flavour (most foods are slightly acidic); acids have a pH of less than 7

Acidulation—the process of adding citric or acetic acid to water, used to preserve colour (to retard enzymatic oxidative browning of some fruits and vegetables), to clean aluminum or to soak kidneys and game

Additives—substances added to many foods to prevent spoilage or to improve appearance, texture, flavour or nutritional value; they may be synthetic materials copied from nature (for example, sugar substitutes) or naturally occurring substances (e.g., lecithin). Some food additives may cause allergic reactions in sensitive people.

Aerate—to incorporate air into a mixture through sifting and mixing

Aerobic bacteria—those that thrive on oxygen

Aging—(1) the period during which freshly killed meat is allowed to rest so that the effects of rigor mortis dissipate; (2) the period during which freshly milled flour is allowed to rest so that it will whiten and produce less sticky dough; the aging of flour can be chemically accelerated

Airline breast—a boneless chicken breast with the first wing bone attached

Al dente—(ahl DEN-tay) Italian for "to the tooth"; used to describe a food, usually pasta, that is cooked only until it gives a slight resistance when bitten into

Albumen—the principal protein found in egg whites

Alkali—also known as a base, any substance with a pH higher than 7; baking soda is one of the few alkaline foods

Alkaloid—a number of bitter organic substances with alkaline properties; found most often in plants and sometimes in drugs

Allemande—(ah-leh-MAHND) a sauce made by adding lemon juice and a liaison to a velouté made from veal stock

Allumette—(al-yoo-MEHT) a matchstick cut 3 mm × 3 mm × 5 to 6 cm (1/8 in. × 1/8 in. × 2 to 2-1/2 in.) long, usually used for potatoes

American service—restaurant service in which the waiter takes the orders and brings the food to the table; the food is placed on dishes (plated) in the kitchen, making it a relatively fast method for seated service

Amino acid—the basic molecular component of proteins; each of the approximately two dozen amino acids contain oxygen, hydrogen, carbon and nitrogen atoms

Anadromous—a fish that migrates from a saltwater habitat to spawn in fresh water (e.g., salmon)

Anaerobic bacteria—those that are able to live and grow without the presence of oxygen

Angus beef, Certified—a brand created in 1978 to distinguish the highest-quality beef produced from descendants of the black, hornless Angus cattle of Scotland

Animal husbandry—the business, science and practice of raising domesticated animals

Anterior—at or toward the front of an object or place; opposite of posterior

Appetizers—also known as first courses, usually small portions of hot or cold foods intended to whet the appetite in anticipation of the more substantial courses to follow

Aquafarming—also known as aquaculture, the business, science and practice of raising large quantities of fish and shellfish in tanks, ponds or ocean pens. Health and food safety issues are critical.

Aroma—the sensations as interpreted by the brain, of what we detect when a substance comes in contact with sense receptors in the nose

Aromatic—a food added to enhance the natural aromas of another food; aromatics include most flavourings, such as herbs and spices, as well as some vegetables

As purchased (A.P.)—the condition or cost of an item as it is purchased or received from the supplier

Aspic; aspic jelly—a clear jelly usually made from a clarified stock thickened with gelatin; used to coat foods, especially charcuterie items, and for garnish

Au gratin—(oh GRAH-tan) foods with a browned or crusted top; often made by browning a food with a bread-crumb, cheese and/or sauce topping under a broiler or salamander

Au jus—(oh zhew) roasted meats, poultry or game served with their natural, unthickened juices

Au sec—(oh sek) cooked until nearly dry

Backfat—fresh pork fat from the back of the pig, used primarily for barding

Bacteria—single-celled microorganisms, some of which can cause diseases, including food-borne diseases

Bain marie—(bane mah-ree) (1) a hot-water bath used to gently cook food or keep cooked food hot; (2) a container for holding food in a hot-water bath

Baked Alaska—ice cream set on a layer of spongecake and encased in meringue, then baked until the meringue is warm and golden

Baking—a dry-heat cooking method in which foods are surrounded by hot, dry air in a closed environment; similar to roasting, the term "baking" is usually applied to breads, pastries, vegetables and fish

Baking powder—a mixture of sodium bicarbonate and one or more acids, generally cream of tartar and/or sodium aluminum sulphate, used to leaven baked goods; it releases carbon dioxide gases if moisture is present. Single-acting baking powder releases carbon dioxide gas in the presence of moisture only; double-acting baking powder releases some carbon gas upon contact with moisture, and more gas is released when heat is applied.

Baking soda—sodium bicarbonate, an alkaline compound that releases carbon dioxide gas when combined with an acid and moisture; used to leaven baked goods

Ballotine—(bahl-lo-teen) boneless poultry leg stuffed with a forcemeat and gently roasted or braised; traditionally shaped in a ball

Barbecue—(1) to cook foods over dry heat created by the burning of hardwood or hardwood charcoals; (2) a tangy tomato- or vinegar-based sauce used for grilled foods; (3) foods cooked by this method and/or with this sauce

Barding—tying thin slices of fat, such as bacon or pork backfat, over meats or poultry that have little to no natural fat covering in order to protect and moisten them during roasting

Barista—Italian for "bartender"; now used to describe someone who has been professionally trained in the art of preparing espresso and espresso-based beverages

Base—A substance that neutralizes an acid in a liquid solution; ingredients such as sodium bicarbonate (baking soda) that have an alkaline or bitter flavour; bases have a pH of more than 7

Basic sauces—also known as leading or mother sauces, the foundations for the entire classic repertoire of hot sauces; the five leading sauces (béchamel, velouté, espagnole [also known as brown], tomato and hollandaise) are distinguished by the liquids and thickeners used to make them; they can be seasoned and garnished to create a wide variety of derivative or compound sauces

Baste—to moisten foods during cooking (usually grilling, broiling or roasting) with melted fat, pan drippings or a sauce of other liquids to prevent drying and to add flavour

Baton—a stick-shaped cut 12 mm × 12 mm × 6 cm (1/2 in. × 1/2 in. × 2-1/2 in.)

Batonnet—(bah-toh-nah) foods cut into matchstick shapes of 6 mm × 6 mm × 5 to 6 cm (1/4 in. × 1/4 in. × 2 to 2-1/2 in.)

Batter—a semiliquid mixture containing flour or other starch used to make cakes and breads; the gluten development is minimized and the liquid forms the continuous medium in which other ingredients are disbursed; generally contains more fat, sugar and liquids than a dough

Baumé scale—(boh-may) see **Hydrometer**

Bavarian cream—a sweet dessert mixture made by thickening custard sauce with gelatin and then folding in whipped cream; the final product is poured into a mould and chilled until firm

Beard—a clump of dark threads found on a mussel

Béarnaise—(bare-NAYZ) a sauce made of butter and egg yolks and flavoured with a reduction of vinegar, shallots, tarragon and peppercorns

Beating—vigorously agitating foods to incorporate air or develop gluten; use a spoon or electric mixer with its paddle attachment

Béchamel—(beh-shah-MELL) a basic sauce made by thickening milk (infused with a studded onion) with a white roux and adding seasonings

Beer—an alcoholic beverage made from water, hops and malted barley, fermented by yeast

Beignets—squares or strips of choux paste deep-fat fried and dusted with powdered sugar

Berry—the kernel of certain grains such as wheat

Beurre blanc—(burr BLANHK) French for "white butter"; an emulsified butter sauce made from shallots, white wine and butter

Beurre composé—(burr kom-poh-ZAY) see **Compound butter**

Beurre manié—(burr man-YAY) a combination of equal amounts by volume of flour and soft, whole butter; it is whisked into a simmering sauce at the end of the cooking process for quick thickening and added sheen and flavour

Beurre noir—(burr NWAR) French for "black butter"; whole butter cooked until dark brown (not black) sometimes flavoured with vinegar or lemon juice

Beurre noisette—(burr nwah-ZEHT) French for "brown butter"; whole butter heated until it turns light brown, giving off a nutty aroma

Beurre rouge—(burr ROOGE) French for "red butter"; an emulsified butter sauce made from shallots, red wine and butter

Biological hazard—a danger to the safety of food caused by disease-causing micro-organisms such as bacteria, moulds, yeasts, viruses or fungi

Biscuit method—a mixing method used to make biscuits, scones and flaky doughs; it involves cutting cold fat into the flour and other dry ingredients before any liquid is added

Bisque—(bisk) a purée soup made from crustacean shells; classic versions are thickened with rice

Bivalves—mollusks such as clams, oysters and mussels that have two bilateral shells attached at a central hinge

Blanching—very briefly and partially cooking a food in boiling water or hot fat; used to assist preparation (e.g., to loosen peels from vegetables), as part of a combination cooking method, to remove undesirable flavours or to prepare a food for freezing

Blanquette—(blahn-KEHT) a white stew in which the meat is first blanched, then added to a stock or sauce to complete the cooking and tenderizing process. Blanquettes are finished with a liaison of egg yolks and heavy cream.

Blending—mixing two or more ingredients until evenly distributed; use a spoon, rubber spatula, whisk or electric mixer with its paddle attachment

Bloom—(1) a white, powdery layer that sometimes appears on chocolate if the cocoa butter separates; (2) rehydrating dried gelatin in a cold liquid

Blown sugar—a boiled mixture of sucrose, glucose and tartaric acid that is coloured and shaped; used for making pieces of fruit and containers such as bowls and vases

Blue cheese—(1) a generic term for any cheese containing visible blue-green moulds that contribute a characteristic tart, sharp flavour and aroma; also known as a blue-veined cheese or bleu; (2) a group of Roquefort-style cheeses made in Canada and the United States from cow's or goat's milk rather than ewe's milk and injected with moulds that form blue-green veins; also known as blue mould cheese or blue-veined cheese

Boiling—a moist-heat cooking method that uses convection to transfer heat from a hot (approximately 100°C/212°F) liquid to the food submerged in it; the turbulent waters and higher temperatures cook foods more quickly than do poaching or simmering

Bombe—two or more flavours of ice cream, or ice cream and sherbet, shaped in a spherical mould; each flavour is a separate layer that forms the shell for the next flavour

Bordelaise—(bor-dil-AYZ) a brown sauce flavoured with a reduction of red wine, shallots, pepper and herbs and garnished with poached marrow

Bouchées—(boo-SHAY) small puff pastry shells that can be filled and served as bite-sized hors d'oeuvre or petits fours

Bound salad—a salad comprising cooked meats, poultry, fish, shellfish, pasta or potatoes combined with a dressing

Bouquet garni—(boo-KAY gar-NEE) fresh herbs and vegetables tied into a bundle with twine and used to flavour stocks, sauces, soups and stews

Bouquetière—(boo-duh-TYEHR) a garnish (bouquet) of carefully cut and arranged fresh vegetables

Boxed beef—industry terminology for primal and subprimal cuts of beef that are vacuum-sealed and packed into cardboard boxes for shipping from the packing plant to retailers and food service operators

Braising—a combination cooking method in which foods are first browned in hot fat, then covered and slowly cooked in a small amount of liquid over low heat; braising uses a combination of simmering and steaming to transfer heat from the liquid (conduction) and the air (convection) to the foods

Bran—the tough outer layer of a cereal grain and the part highest in fibre

Brandy—an alcoholic beverage made by distilling the fermented mash of grapes or other fruits

Brawn—also called an aspic terrine; made from simmered meats packed into a terrine and covered with aspic

Brazier; brasier—a pan designed for braising; usually round with two handles and a tight-fitting lid

Breading—(1) a coating of bread or cracker crumbs, cornmeal or other dry meal applied to foods that will typically be deep-fat fried or pan-fried; (2) the process of applying this coating

Brigade—a system of staffing a kitchen so that each worker is assigned a set of specific tasks; these tasks are often related by cooking method, equipment or the types of foods being produced

Brine—a mixture of salt, water and seasonings used to preserve or flavour foods

Brioche—(bree-OHSH) a rich yeast bread containing large amounts of eggs and butter

Brochettes—(bro-SHETTS) skewers, either small hors d'oeuvre or large entree size, threaded with meat, poultry, fish, shellfish and/or vegetables and grilled, broiled or baked; sometimes served with a dipping sauce

Broiling—a dry-heat cooking method in which foods are cooked by heat radiating from an overhead source

Broth—a flavourful liquid obtained from the long simmering of meats and/or vegetables

Brown stew—a stew in which the meat is first browned in hot fat

Brown stock—a richly coloured stock made of chicken, veal, beef or game bones and vegetables, all of which are caramelized before they are simmered in water, flavourings and tomato purée

Brunch—a late-morning to early-afternoon meal that takes the place of both breakfast and lunch; a brunch menu often offers breakfast foods as well as almost anything else

Brunoise—(BROO-nwaz) (1) foods cut into cubes of 1 to 2 mm × 1 to 2 mm × 1 to 2 mm (1/16 in. × 1/16 in. × 1/16 in.); (2) foods garnished with vegetables cut in this manner

Buffet service—restaurant service in which diners generally serve themselves foods arranged on a counter or table or are served by workers assigned to specific areas of the buffet. Usually buffet-service-style restaurants charge by the meal; restaurants offering buffet service that charge by the dish are known as cafeterias.

Butcher—(1) to slaughter and/or dress or fabricate animals for consumption; (2) the person who slaughters and fabricates animals

Butler service—restaurant service in which servers pass foods (typically hors d'oeuvre) or drinks arranged on trays

Buttercream—a light, smooth, fluffy frosting of sugar, fat and flavourings; egg yolks or whipped egg whites are sometimes added. There are three principal kinds: simple, Italian and French.

Butterfly—to slice boneless meat, poultry, fish or shrimp nearly in half lengthwise so that it spreads open like a book; used to increase surface area and speed cooking

Cafeteria—see **Buffet service**

Caffeine—an alkaloid found in coffee beans, tea leaves and cocoa beans that acts as a stimulant

Cake—in North American usage, refers to a broad range of pastries including layer cakes, coffee cakes and gâteaux; can refer to almost anything that is baked, tender, sweet and sometimes frosted

Calf—a young cow or bull

Calorie—the unit of energy measured by the amount of heat required to raise 1 kg of water 1°C. Calories may be expressed as joules; one calorie (kilocalorie) equals 4185.5 joules

Canada's Food Guide to Healthy Eating—a dietary guide published by Health Canada that prioritizes and proportions food choices among food groups and promotes nutritious eating

Canapé—(KAN-ah-pay) a tiny open-faced sandwich served as an hors d'oeuvre; usually composed of a small piece of bread or toast topped with a savoury spread and garnish

Capicola—Italian dry-cured salami made from pork shoulder that is seasoned with garlic, hot pepper, spices and wine, then smoked and cured

Capon—(kay-pahn) the class of surgically castrated male chickens; they have well-flavoured meat and soft, smooth skin

Capsaicin—(kap-SAY-ee-zin) alkaloid found in a chile pepper's placental ribs that provides the pepper's heat

Caramelization—the process of cooking sugars; the browning of sugar enhances the flavour and appearance of foods

Carbohydrates—a group of compounds comprising oxygen, hydrogen and carbon that supply the body with energy (4 calories per gram); carbohydrates are classified as *simple* (including certain sugars) and *complex* (including starches and fibre)

Carbonated water—water that has absorbed carbon dioxide resulting in an effervescent mouth-feel

Carotenoid—a naturally occurring pigment that predominates in red and yellow vegetables such as carrots and red peppers

Carryover cooking—the cooking that occurs after a food is removed from a heat source

Cartilage—also known as gristle, a tough, elastic, whitish connective tissue that helps give structure to an animal's body

Carve—to cut cooked meat or poultry into portions

Casings—membranes used to hold forcemeat for sausages; they can be natural animal intestines or manufactured from collagen extracted from cattle hides

Casserole—(1) a heavy dish, usually ceramic, for baking foods; (2) foods baked in a casserole dish

Caul fat—fatty membrane from pig or sheep intestines; it resembles fine nettings and is used to bard roasts and pâtés and to encase forcemeat for sausages

Cellulose—a complex carbohydrate found in the cell wall of plants; it is edible but indigestible by humans

Cephalopods—mollusks with a single, thin internal shell called a pen or cuttlebone, well-developed eyes, a number of arms that attach to the head and a sac-like fin-bearing mantle, including squid and octopus

Chafing dish—a metal dish with a heating unit (flame or electric) used to keep foods warm at tableside or during buffet service

Chalazae cords—thick, twisted strands of egg white that anchor the yolk in place

Charcuterie—(shahr-COO-tuhr-ree) the production of pâtés, terrines, galantines, sausages and similar foods

Cheesecloth—light, fine mesh gauze used to strain liquids and make sachets

Chef de cuisine—(chef duh qui-zine) also known simply as chef; the person responsible for all kitchen operations, developing menu items and setting the kitchen's tone and tempo

Chef de partie—(chef duh par-tee) also known as station chef; produces the menu items under the direct supervision of the chef or sous-chef

Chef's knife—an all-purpose knife used for chopping, slicing and mincing; its tapering blade is 20–35 cm (8–14 in.) long

Chemical hazard—a danger to the safety of food caused by chemical substances, especially cleaning agents, pesticides and toxic metals

Chèvre—(SHEHV-ruh) French for "goat"; generally refers to a cheese made from goat's milk

Chiffonade—(chef-fon-nahd) a preparation of finely sliced or shredded leafy vegetables or herbs

Chile—a member of the capsicum plant family; may be used fresh or dried or dried and ground into powder

Chili—a stewlike dish containing chiles

Chilli—a commercial spice powder containing a blend of seasonings

China cap—a cone-shaped strainer made of perforated metal

Chinois—(sheen-WAH) a conical strainer made of fine mesh, used for straining and puréeing foods

Chlorophyll—a naturally occurring pigment that predominates in green vegetables such as spinach

Cholesterol—a fatty substance found in foods derived from animal products and in the human body; it has been linked to heart disease

Chop—(1) to cut into pieces where uniformity of size and shape is not important; (2) a cut of meat including part of the rib

Choux pastry—(shoo paste-re) soft, pipable dough used for eclairs, profiteroles, churros, gougères, etc.

Chowder—a hearty soup made from fish, shellfish and/or vegetables, usually containing milk and potatoes and often thickened with roux

Churros—a Spanish and Mexican pastry in which sticks of choux paste flavoured with cinnamon are deep-fat fried and rolled in sugar while still hot

Chutney—a sweet-and-sour condiment made of fruits and/or vegetables cooked in vinegar with sugar and spices; some chutneys are reduced to a purée; others retain recognizable pieces of their ingredients

Cider—mildly fermented apple juice; non-alcoholic apple juice may also be labelled as cider

Citrus—fruits characterized by a thick rind, most of which is bitter white pith (albedo) with a thin exterior layer of coloured skin (zest); their flesh is segmented and juicy and varies from bitter to tart to sweet

Clarification—(1) the process of transforming a broth into a clear consommé by trapping impurities with a clearmeat consisting of the egg white protein albumen, ground meat, an acidic product, mirepoix and other ingredients; (2) the clearmeat used to clarify a broth

Clarified butter—purified butterfat; the butter is melted and the water and milk solids are removed

Classic cuisine—a late 19th- and early 20th-century refinement and simplification of French *grande cuisine*. Classic (or classical) cuisine relies on the thorough exploration of culinary principles and techniques, and emphasizes the refined preparation and presentation of superb ingredients.

Clean—to remove visible dirt and soil

Clear flour—flour made from the portion of the endosperm nearer to the bran; it is coarser and darker than patent flour

Clear soups—unthickened soups, including broths, consommés and broth-based soups

Clearmeat—see **Clarification**

Coagulation—the irreversible transformation of proteins from a liquid or semiliquid state to a drier, solid state; usually accomplished through the application of heat

Cocoa butter—the fat found in cocoa beans and used in fine chocolate

Coconut cream—(1) a coconut-flavoured liquid made like coconut milk but with less water; it is creamier and thicker than coconut milk; (2) the thick fatty portion that separates and rises to the top of canned or frozen coconut milk. Do not substitute cream of coconut for true coconut cream.

Coconut milk—a coconut-flavoured liquid made by pouring boiling water over shredded coconut; may be sweetened or unsweetened. Do not substitute cream of coconut for coconut milk.

Coconut water—the thin, slightly opaque liquid contained within a fresh coconut

Coenzyme—any of various small substances, many of which contain a B vitamin, that promote or assist an enzyme's activities

Cojita—(ko-HEE-ta) an aged, hard, salty Mexican cow's-milk cheese; similar to feta, although not soaked in or flavour

Colander—a perforated bowl, with or without a base or legs, used to strain foods

Collagen—a protein found in nearly all connective tissue; it dissolves when cooked with moisture

Combination cooking methods—cooking methods, principally braising and stewing, that employ both dry-heat and moist-heat procedures

Composed salad—a salad prepared by arranging each of the ingredients (the base, body, garnish and dressing) on individual plates in an artistic fashion

Compound butter—also known as *beurre composé*; a mixture of softened whole butter and flavourings used as a sauce or to flavour and colour other sauces

Compound sauces—see **Derivative sauces**

Concassée—(kon-kaas-SAY) peeled, seeded and diced or chopped tomato

Concasser—(kon-kaas-SAY) to pound or chop coarsely; usually used for tomatoes or parsley

Concentrate—also known as a fruit paste or compound; a reduced fruit purée, without a gel structure, used as a flavouring

Conching—stirring melted chocolate with large stone or metal rollers to create a smooth texture in the finished chocolate

Condiment—traditionally, any item added to a dish for flavour, including herbs, spices and vinegars; now also refers to cooked or prepared flavourings such as prepared mustards, relishes, bottled sauces and pickles

Conduction—the transfer of heat from one item to another through direct contact

Confit—(kohn-FEE) lightly cured meat, usually duck or goose, stewed in its own fat. Pieces are packed in the fat and chilled for later use.

Connective tissue—tissue found throughout an animal's body that binds together and supports other tissues such as muscles

Consommé—(kwang-soh-MAY) a rich stock or broth that has been clarified with clearmeat to remove impurities

Contaminants—biological, chemical or physical substances that can be harmful when consumed in sufficient quantities

Contamination—the presence, generally unintentional, of harmful organisms or substances

Contribution margin—the money, including profit, that pays for all costs except food

Convection—the transfer of heat caused by the natural movement of molecules in a fluid (whether air, water or fat) from a warmer area to a cooler one

Conversion factor (C.F.)—the number used to increase or decrease ingredient quantities and recipe yields

Cookery—the art, practice or work of cooking

Cookies—small, sweet, flat pastries; usually classified by preparation or makeup techniques as drop, icebox, bar, cut-out or rolled, pressed and wafer

Cooking—(1) the transfer of energy from a heat source of a food; this energy alters the food's molecular structure, changing its texture, flavour, aroma and appearance; (2) the preparation of food for consumption

Cooking medium—the air, fat, water or steam in which a food is cooked

Coring—the process of removing the seeds or pit from a fruit or fruit-vegetable

Cost of goods sold—the total cost of food items sold during a given period; calculated as beginning inventory plus purchases minus ending inventory; also known as raw food cost

Cost per portion—the amount of the total recipe cost divided by the number of portions produced from that recipe; the cost of one serving

Coulis—(koo-lee) a sauce made from a purée of vegetables and/or fruit; may be served hot or cold

Count—the number of individual items in a given measure of weight or volume

Country-style forcemeat—usually a coarse grind or dice of meat, highly aromatic and containing liver. Pork backfat is added to enhance mouth-feel or melt.

Coupe—(1) another name for an ice cream sundae, especially one served with a fruit topping; (2) type of glass

Court bouillon—(kort boo-yon) water simmered with vegetables, seasonings and an acidic product such as vinegar or wine; used for simmering or poaching fish, shellfish or vegetables

Couverture—a high-quality chocolate containing at least 32% cocoa butter

Cows—female cattle after their first calving, principally raised for milk and calf production

Cracking—a milling process in which grains are broken open

Cream filling—a pie filling made of flavoured pastry cream thickened with cornstarch

Cream of coconut—a canned commercial product consisting of thick, sweetened coconut-flavoured liquid; used for baking and in beverages

Cream puffs—baked rounds of choux paste cut in half and filled with pastry cream, whipped cream, fruit or other filling

Cream sauce—a sauce made by adding cream to a béchamel sauce

Cream soup—a soup made from vegetables cooked in a stock that is thickened with a roux; cream is then incorporated to add richness and flavour

Creaming—vigorously combining fat and sugar while incorporating air; use an electric mixer with its paddle attachment on medium speed

Creaming method—a mixing method in which softened fat and sugar are vigorously combined to incorporate air

Creams—also known as crèmes; include light, fluffy or creamy-textured dessert foods made with whipped cream or whipped egg whites, such as Bavarian creams, chiffons, mousses and crème Chantilly

Crème anglaise—(khrem ahn-GLEHZ) also known as crème à l'anglaise; see **Vanilla custard sauce**

Crème brûlée—(krehm bru-LEH) French for burnt cream; used to describe rich dessert custard topped with a crust of caramelized sugar

Crème caramel—(krehm kair-ah-MEHL) like crème renversée and flan, a custard baked over a layer of caramelized sugar and inverted for service

Crème Chantilly—(krehm shan-TEE) heavy cream whipped to soft peaks and flavoured with sugar and vanilla; used to garnish pastries or desserts or folded into cooled custard or pastry cream for fillings

Crème Chiboust—(krehm chee-BOOS) a vanilla pastry cream lightened by folding in Italian meringue; traditionally used in gâteau St. Honoré

Crème pâtissière—(khrem pah-tees-SYEHR) see **Pastry cream**

Crepe—(krayp) a thin, delicate unleavened griddlecake made with a very thin egg batter cooked in a hot sauté pan; used in sweet and savoury preparations

Critical control point—any step in the food-handling process at which a prescribed action will reduce the likelihood of a food-borne illness or hazard

Croissant—(krwah-SAHN) a crescent-shaped roll made from a rich, rolled-in yeast dough

Croquembouche—(krok-ahm-BOOSH) a pyramid of small choux, each filled with pastry cream; a French tradition for Christmas and weddings, it is held together with caramelized sugar and decorated with spun sugar or marzipan flowers

Croquette—(crow-keht) a food that has been puréed or bound with a thick sauce (usually béchamel or velouté) made into small shapes and then breaded and deep-fat fried

Cross-contamination—the transfer of bacteria or other contaminants from one food, work surface or piece of equipment to another

Croûte, en—(awn KROOT) describes a food encased in a bread or pastry crust

Crouton—(KROO-tawn) a bread or pastry garnish, usually toasted or sautéed until crisp

Crudités—(kroo-dee-TAYS) generally refers to raw or blanched vegetables served as an hors d'oeuvre and often accompanied by a dip

Cruller—(kruh-ler) a Dutch pastry in which a loop or strip of twisted choux paste is deep-fat fried

Crumb—the interior of bread or cake; may be elastic, aerated, fine or coarse grained

Crustaceans—shellfish characterized by a hard outer skeleton or shell and jointed appendages, including lobsters, crabs and shrimp

Cuisine—the ingredients, seasonings, cooking procedures and styles attributable to a particular group of people; the group can be defined by geography, history, ethnicity, politics, culture or religion

Cuisson—(kwee-sohn) the aromatic cooking liquid resulting from shallow poaching fish

Curdling—the separation of milk or egg mixtures into solid and liquid components; caused by overcooking, high heat or the presence of acids

Curing salt—a mixture of salt and sodium nitrite that inhibits bacterial growth; used as a preservative, often for charcuterie items

Custard—any liquid thickened by the coagulation of egg proteins; its consistency depends on the ratio of eggs to liquid and the type of liquid used; custards can be baked in the oven or cooked in a bain marie or on the stove top

Cutlet—a relatively thick, boneless slice of meat

Cutting—incorporating solid fat into dry ingredients only until lumps of the desired size remain; use pastry cutters, fingers or an electric mixer with its paddle attachment

Cutting loss—the unavoidable and unrecoverable loss of food during fabrication; the loss is usually the result of food particles sticking to the cutting board or the evaporation of liquids

Cuttlebone—also known as the pen, the single, thin internal shell of cephalopods

Cycle menu—a menu that changes every day for a certain period and then repeats the same daily items in the same order (e.g., on a seven-day cycle, the same menu is used every Monday)

Dairy products—include cow's milk and foods produced from cow's milk such as butter, yogurt, sour cream and cheese; sometimes other milks and products made from them are included (e.g., goat's milk cheese)

Decline phase—a period during which bacteria die at an accelerated rate, also known as the negative growth phase

Decoction—(1) boiling a food until its flavour is removed; (2) a procedure used for making coffee

Decorator's icing—see **Royal icing**

Deep-fat frying—a dry-heat cooking method that uses convection to transfer heat to a food submerged in hot fat; foods to be deep-fat fried are usually first coated in batter or breading

Deglaze—to swirl or stir in a liquid (usually wine or stock) in a sauté pan or other pan to dissolve cooked food particles remaining on the bottom; the resulting mixture often becomes the base for a sauce

Degrease—to remove the fat from the surface of a liquid such as a stock or sauce by skimming, scraping or lifting congealed fat

Demi-glace—(deh-me glass) French for "half glaze"; a mixture of half brown stock and half espagnole sauce reduced by half

Demineralized water—water that has had all the minerals and impurities removed by passing it over a bed of ion-exchange resins

Derivative sauces—also known as small or compound sauces; made by adding one or more ingredients to a basic sauce; they are grouped together into families based on their basic sauce; some small sauces have a variety of uses, while others are traditional accompaniments for specific foods

Dessert wines—sweet wines made from grapes left on the vine until they are overly ripe, such as Sauternes or wines labelled

"Late Harvest"; during fermentation, some of the sugar is not converted to alcohol, but remains in the wine, giving an intense, sweet taste

Détrempe—(day-trawnp) a paste made with flour and water during the first stage of preparing pastry dough

Deveining—the process of removing a shrimp's digestive tract

Devilled—describes meat, poultry or other food seasoned with mustard, vinegar and other spicy seasonings

Diagonals—oval-shaped slices

Dice—(1) to cut foods into cubes: 3 mm (1/8 in.) for small dice, 6 mm (1/4 in.) for medium dice, and 12 mm (1/2 in.) for large dice; (2) the cubes of cut food

Dietary fibre—indigestible carbohydrates found in grains, fruits and vegetables; fibre aids digestion

Dip—a thick, creamy sauce, served hot or cold, to accompany crudités, crackers, chips or other foods, especially as an hors d'oeuvre; dips are often based on sour cream, mayonnaise or cream cheese

Direct contamination—the contamination of raw foods in their natural settings or habitats

Distillation—the separation of alcohol from a liquid (or, during the production of alcoholic beverages, from a fermented mash); it is accomplished by heating the liquid or mash to a gas that contains alcohol vapours; this steam is then condensed into the desired alcoholic liquid (beverage)

Distilled water—water that has had all the minerals and impurities removed through distillation; it is generally used for pharmaceutical purposes

Diver scallops—scallops that are harvested from the ocean by divers who hand-pick each one; diver scallops tend to be less gritty than those harvested by dragging, and hand-harvesting is more ecologically friendly

Docking—pricking small holes in an unbaked dough or crust to allow steam to escape and to prevent the dough from rising when baked

Dominant meat—the main meat in a preparation, giving it an identity (e.g., game, pork, rabbit) and predominant flavour

Dough—a mixture of flour and other ingredients used in baking; has a low moisture content, and gluten forms the continuous medium into which other ingredients are embedded; it is often stiff enough to cut into shapes

Drawn—a market form for fish in which the viscera are removed

Dredging—coating a food with flour or finely ground crumbs; usually done prior to sautéing or frying or as the first step of the standardized breading procedure

Dress—to trim or otherwise prepare an animal carcass for consumption

Dressed—a market form for fish in which the viscera, gills, fins and scales are removed

Dressing—(1) another name for a bread stuffing used with poultry; (2) sauce for salad or applying it

Drupes—see **Stone fruits**

Dry-heat cooking methods—cooking methods, principally broiling, grilling, roasting and baking, sautéing, pan-frying and deep-fat frying, that use air or fat to transfer heat through convection; dry-heat cooking methods allow surface sugars to caramelize

Drying—a preservation method in which the food's moisture content is dramatically reduced; drying changes the food's texture, flavour and appearance

Duchesse potatoes—(duh-shees) a purée of cooked potatoes, butter and egg yolks, seasoned with salt, pepper and nutmeg; can be eaten as is or used to prepare several classic potato dishes

Duckling—a duck slaughtered before it is eight weeks old

Dumpling—any of a variety of small starchy products made from doughs or batters that are simmered or steamed; can be plain or filled

Durum wheat—a species of very hard wheat with a particularly high amount of protein; it is used to make couscous or milled into semolina, which is used for making pasta

Duxelles—(dook-SEHL) a coarse paste made of finely chopped mushrooms sautéed with shallots in butter

Eau de vie—(oh duh-vee) fruit spirits made by distilling fruit; includes kirsch (cherry), slivovitz (plum), framboise (raspberry) and poire (pear)

Éclairs—(ay-clahr) baked fingers of choux paste filled with pastry cream; the top is then coated with chocolate glaze or fondant

Edible portion (E.P.)—the amount of a food item available for consumption or use after trimming or fabrication; a smaller, more convenient portion of a larger or bulk unit

Egg wash—a mixture of beaten eggs (whole eggs, yolks or whites) and a liquid, usually milk or water, used to coat dough before baking to add sheen or to coat items for breading or frying

Elastin—a protein found in connective tissues, particularly ligaments and tendons. It also appears as a white or silver covering on meat known as silverskin.

Émincé—(eh-manss-say) a small, thin boneless slice of meat

Emulsification—the process by which generally unmixable liquids, such as oil and water, are forced into a uniform distribution

Emulsions—(1) a uniform mixture of two unmixable liquids; (2) flavouring oils such as orange and lemon, mixed into water with the aid of emulsifiers

En papillote—(awn pa-pee-yote) a cooking method in which food is wrapped in paper, leaves or foil and then heated so that the food steams in its own moisture

Endosperm—the largest part of a cereal grain and a source of protein and carbohydrates (starch); the part used primarily in milled products

Entree—(ahn-tray) the main dish of a North American meal, usually meat, poultry, fish or shellfish accompanied by a vegetable and starch; in France, the first course, served before the fish and meat courses

Enzymes—proteins that aid specific chemical reactions in plants and animals

Escallope—(eh-SKAL-ohp) a thin, boneless slice of meat (paillarde, scallopini)

Escargot—(ays-skahr-go) French for "snail"; those used for culinary purposes are land snails (genus *Helix*)

Espagnole—(ess-spah-nyol) also known as brown sauce, a basic sauce made of brown stock, mirepoix and tomatoes thickened with brown roux; often used to produce demi-glace

Essence—(1) a sauce made from a concentrated vegetable juice; (2) concentrated stock

Essential nutrients—nutrients that must be provided by food because the body cannot or does not produce them in sufficient quantities

Essential oils—pure oils extracted from the skins, peels and other parts of plants used to give their aroma and taste to flavouring agents in foods, cosmetics and other products

Ethnic cuisine—the cuisine of a group of people having a common cultural heritage, as opposed to the cuisine of a group of people bound together by geography or political factors

Ethylene gas—a colourless, odourless hydrocarbon gas naturally emitted from fruits and fruit-vegetables that encourages ripening

Evaporation—the process by which heated water molecules move faster and faster until the water turns to a gas (steam) and vaporizes; evaporation is responsible for the drying of foods during cooking

Extracts—concentrated mixtures of ethyl alcohol and flavouring oils such as vanilla, almond and lemon

Extrusion—the process of forcing pasta dough through perforated plates to create various shapes; pasta dough that is not extruded must be rolled and cut

Fabricate—to cut a large item into smaller portions; often refers to the butchering of fish or shellfish and meats

Fabricated cuts—individual portions of meat cut from a subprimal

Facultative bacteria—those that can adapt and will survive with or without oxygen

Fancy—(1) the fish that has been previously frozen; (2) a quality grade for fruits, especially canned or frozen

Farm-to-table movement—an awareness of the source of ingredients with an emphasis on serving locally grown and minimally processed foods in season

Fats—(1) a group of compounds comprising oxygen, hydrogen and carbon atoms that supply the body with energy (9 calories per gram); fats are classified as saturated, monounsaturated or polyunsaturated; (2) the general term for butter, lard, shortening, oil and margarine used as cooking media or ingredients

Fermentation—the process by which yeast converts sugar into alcohol and carbon dioxide; it also refers to the time that yeast dough is left to rise

Feuilletés—(fuh-YET-eh) square, rectangular or diamond-shaped puff pastry boxes; may be filled with a sweet or savoury mixture

Fibre—also known as *dietary fibre*, indigestible carbohydrates found in grains, fruits and vegetables; fibre aids digestion

FIFO—first in, first out; a system of rotating inventory, particularly perishable and semiperishable goods, in which items are used in the order in which they are received

Filé—(fee-lay) a seasoning and thickening agent made from dried, ground sassafras leaves

Fillet—(fee-lay) the side of a fish removed intact, boneless or semi-boneless, with or without skin

Fish velouté—a velouté sauce made from fish stock

Flambé—(flahm-BAY) food served flaming; produced by igniting brandy, rum or other liquor

Flash-frozen—describes food that has been frozen very rapidly using metal plates, extremely low temperatures or chemical solutions

Flatfish—fish with asymmetrical compressed bodies that swim in a horizontal position and have both eyes on the top of their heads, including sole, flounder and halibut

Flavonoids—plant pigments that dissolve readily in water, found in red, purple and white vegetables such as blueberries, red cabbage and beets

Flavour—an identifiable or distinctive quality of a food, drink or other substance perceived with the combined senses of taste, touch and smell

Flavoured tea—tea to which flavourings such as oils, dried fruit, spices, flowers and herbs have been added

Flavouring—an item that adds a new taste to a food and alters its natural flavours; flavourings include herbs, spices, vinegars and condiments. The terms "seasoning" and "flavouring" are often used interchangeably.

Fleuron—(fluh-rawng) a crescent-shaped piece of puff pastry used as a garnish

Flour—a powdery substance of varying degrees of fineness made by milling grains such as wheat, corn or rye

Foamed milk—milk that is heated and frothed with air and steam generated by an espresso machine; it will be slightly cooler than steamed milk

Foie gras—(fwah grah) liver of specially fattened geese or ducks

Fold—a measurement of the strength of vanilla extract

Folding—very gently incorporating ingredients, such as whipped cream or whipped eggs, with dry ingredients or a batter; use a rubber spatula

Fond—(fahn) (1) French for "stock" or "base"; (2) the concentrated juices, drippings and bits of food left in a pan after foods are roasted or sautéed; it is used to flavour sauces made directly in the pan

Fond lié—(fahn lee-ay) see **Jus lié**

Fondant—(FAHN-dant) a sweet, thick opaque sugar paste commonly used for glazing pastries such as napoleons or making candies

Fondue—a Swiss specialty made with melted cheese, wine and flavourings; eaten by dipping pieces of bread into the mixture with long forks

Food allergy—adverse reaction to foods that involves an immune response; also called food hypersensitivity reaction

Food cost—the cost of the materials that go directly into the production of menu items

Food cost percentage—the ratio of the cost of foods served to the food sales dollars during a given period

Food intolerance—adverse reaction to a food that does not involve the immune system

Forcemeat (stuffing)—ground, uncooked meat, fish or poultry emulsified with fat

Fork tender—describes braised meat that is so tender it offers little resistance when pierced with a fork

Formula—standard term used throughout the industry for a bakeshop recipe; ingredients are usually weighed

Frangipane—(fran-juh-pahn) a sweet almond and egg filling cooked inside pastry

Free-range chickens—chickens allowed to move freely and forage for food as opposed to chickens raised in coops

Free-range veal—the meat of calves that are allowed to roam freely and eat grasses and other natural foods; this meat is pinker and more strongly flavoured than that of milk-fed calves

Freezer burn—the surface dehydration and discoloration of food due to moisture loss at below-freezing temperatures. Poor or improper wrapping for storage is the main cause.

French dressing—classically, vinaigrette dressing made from oil, vinegar, salt and pepper; in North America, the term also refers to a commercially prepared dressing that is creamy, tartly sweet and red-orange in colour

French service—restaurant service in which one waiter (a captain) takes the order, does the tableside cooking and brings the drinks and food; the secondary or back waiter serves bread and water, clears each course, crumbs the table and serves the coffee

Frenching—a method of trimming racks or individual chops of meat, especially lamb, in which the excess fat is cut away leaving the eye muscle; all meat and connective tissue are removed from the rib bone

Fresh-frozen—describes a food that has been frozen while still fresh

Fricassee—(FRIHK-uh-see) a white ragout usually made from white meat or small game, seared without browning and garnished with small onions and mushrooms

Frittata—(free-tah-ta) an open-faced omelette of Spanish-Italian heritage

Frosting—also known as icing, is a sweet decorative coating used as a filling between the layers or as a coating over the top and sides of a cake

Fruit—the edible organ that develops from the ovary of a flowering plant and contains one or more seeds (pips or pits)

Frying—a dry-heat cooking method in which foods are cooked in hot fat; includes sautéing and stir-frying and deep-fat frying

Fumet—(foo-may) a stock made from fish bones and vegetables simmered in a liquid with flavourings

Fungi—a large group of plants ranging from single-celled organisms to giant mushrooms; the most common are moulds and yeasts

Fusion cuisine—the blending or use of ingredients and/or preparation methods from various ethnic, regional or national cuisines in the same dish; also known as transnational cuisine

Galantines—(GAL-uhn-teen) forcemeats wrapped in the skin of the dominant meat, fish or poultry, and poached. Modern galantines are often prepared without the skin; plastic wrap is used and the product poached or steamed.

Game—birds and animals hunted for sport or food; many game birds and animals are now ranch-raised and commercially available

Game hen—the class of young or immature progeny of Cornish chickens or of a Cornish chicken and White Rock chicken; they are small and very flavourful

Ganache—(ga-nosh) a rich blend of chocolate and heavy cream and, optionally, flavourings, used as a pastry or candy filling or frosting

Garde-manger—(gar mawn-zhay) (1) also known as the pantry chef, the cook in charge of cold food production, including salads and salad dressings, charcuterie items, cold appetizers and buffet items; (2) the work area where these foods are prepared

Garnish—(1) food used as an attractive decoration; (2) a subsidiary food used to add flavour or character to the main ingredients in a dish

Gastrique—(gas-streek) caramelized sugar deglazed with vinegar, used to flavour tomato or savoury fruit-based sauces

Gastronomy—the art and science of eating well

Gâteau—(gah-toe) (1) in North American usage, refers to any cake-type dessert; (2) in French usage, refers to various pastry items made with puff pastry, éclair paste, short dough or sweet dough

Gaufrette—(goh-FREHT) ridged slices of potato, usually cut in a waffle pattern

Gelatin—a flavourless and odourless mixture of proteins (especially collagen) extracted from boiling bones, connective tissue and other animal parts; when

dissolved in a hot liquid and then cooled, it forms a jellylike substance used as a thickener and stabilizer (aspic)

Gelatinization—the process by which starch granules are cooked; they absorb moisture when placed in a liquid and heated; as the moisture is absorbed, the product swells, softens and clarifies slightly

Gelato—(jah-laht-to) an Italian-style ice cream that is denser than North American–style ice cream

Genoise—(zhen-waahz) a form of egg-foam cake that uses whole eggs whipped with sugar

Germ—the smallest portion of a cereal grain and the only part that contains fat

Ghee—a form of clarified butter in which the milk solids remain with the fat and are allowed to brown; originating in India and now used worldwide as an ingredient and cooking medium, it has a long shelf life, a high smoke point and a nutty, caramel-like flavour

Gianduja—blend of hazelnut paste and chocolate

Giblets—the collective term for edible poultry viscera, including gizzards, hearts, livers and necks

Gizzard—a bird's second stomach

Glaçage—(glah-sahge) browning or glazing a food, usually under a salamander or broiler

Glace de poisson—(glahss duh pwah-sawng) a syrupy glaze made by reducing a fish stock

Glace de viande—(glahss du veeawnd) a dark, syrupy meat glaze made by reducing a brown stock

Glace de volaille—(glahss du volahy) a light brown, syrupy glaze made by reducing a chicken stock

Glaze—(1) the dramatic reduction and concentration of a stock; (2) a thin, flavoured coating poured or dripped onto a cake or pastry; flat icing or water icing is a specific glaze used on Danish pastries and coffee cakes; (3) coat cold food with aspic

Gliaden—see **Gluten**

Global cuisine—foods (often commercially produced items) or preparation methods that have become ubiquitous throughout the world; for example, curries and french-fried potatoes

Glucose—a thick, sweet syrup made from cornstarch, composed primarily of dextrose; light corn syrup can usually be substituted for it in baked goods or candy making

Gluten—an elastic network of proteins created when wheat flour is moistened and manipulated

Glutenin—see **Gluten**

Gougère—choux flavoured with cheese, baked and served as an hors d'oeuvre

Gourmand—a connoisseur of fine food and drink, often to excess

Gourmet—a connoisseur of fine food and drink

Gourmet foods—foods of the highest quality, perfectly prepared and beautifully presented

Grading—designation of a food's overall quality

Grains—(1) grasses that bear edible seeds, including corn, rice and wheat; (2) the fruit (i.e., the seed or kernel) of such grasses

Gram—the basic unit of weight in the metric system; equal to approximately 1/30 of an ounce

Grande cuisine—the rich, intricate and elaborate cuisine of the 18th- and 19th-century French aristocracy and upper classes. It is based on the rational identification, development and adoption of strict culinary principles. By emphasizing the how and why of cooking, *grande cuisine* was the first to distinguish itself from regional cuisines, which tend to emphasize the tradition of cooking.

Grate—to cut a food into small, thin shreds by rubbing it against a serrated metal plate known as a grater or microplane

Gravy—a sauce made from meat or poultry juices combined with a liquid and thickening agent; usually made in the pan in which the meat or poultry was cooked

Green meats—freshly slaughtered meats that have not had sufficient time to age and develop tenderness and flavour

Gremolada—(greh-moa-LAH-dah) an aromatic garnish of chopped parsley, garlic and lemon zest used for osso buco

Grilling—a dry-heat cooking method in which foods are cooked by heat radiating from a source located below the cooking surface; the heat can be generated by electricity or by burning gas, hardwood and hardwood charcoals

Grind—to pulverize or reduce food to small particles using a mechanical grinder and food processor

Grinding—a milling process in which grains are reduced to a powder; the powder can be of differing degrees of fineness or coarseness

Gristle—see **Cartilage**

Grosse piece—a centrepiece consisting of a large piece of the principal food offered; for example, a large wheel of cheese with slices of the cheese cascading around it

Gum paste—a smooth dough of sugar and gelatin that can be coloured and used to make decorations, especially for pastries

HACCP—see **Hazard Analysis Critical Control Points**

Halal—describes food prepared in accordance with Muslim dietary laws

Hanging—the practice of allowing eviscerated (drawn or gutted) game to age in a dry, well-ventilated place; hanging helps tenderize the flesh and strengthen its flavour

Hazard Analysis Critical Control Points—a rigorous system of self-inspection used to manage and maintain sanitary conditions in all types of food service operations; it focuses on the flow of food through the food service facility to identify any point or step in preparation (known as a critical control point) where some action must be taken to prevent or minimize a risk or hazard

Herb—any of a large group of aromatic plants whose leaves, stems or flowers are used as a flavouring; used either dried or fresh

High-ratio cake—a form of creamed-fat cake that uses emulsified shortening and has a two-stage mixing method

Hollandaise—(ohll-uhn-daze) an emulsified sauce made of butter, egg yolks and flavourings (especially lemon juice)

Homogenization—the process by which milk fat is prevented from separating out of milk products

Hors d'oeuvre—(ohr durv) very small portions of hot or cold foods served before the meal to stimulate the appetite

Hotel pan—a rectangular, stainless steel pan with a lip allowing it to rest in a storage shelf or steam tables; available in several standard sizes

Hull—also known as the husk, the outer covering of a fruit, seed or grain

Hulling—a milling process in which the hull or husk is removed from grains

Hybrid—the result of crossbreeding different species that are genetically unalike; often a unique product

Hybrid menu—a menu combining features of a static menu with a cycle menu or a market menu of specials

Hydrogenation—the process used to harden oils; hydrogen atoms are added to unsaturated fat molecules, making them partially or completely saturated and thus solid at room temperature

Hydrometer—a device used to measure specific gravity; it shows degrees of concentration on the Baumé scale

Hygroscopic—describes a food that readily absorbs moisture from the air

Icing—see **Frosting**

Incidental food additives—those inadvertently or unintentionally added to foods during processing, such as pesticide residues on fruits

Induction cooking—a cooking method that uses a special coil placed below the stove top's surface in combination with specially designed cookware to generate heat rapidly with an alternating magnetic field

Infection—in the food safety context, an illness caused by the ingestion of live pathogenic bacteria that continue their life processes in the consumer's intestinal tract

Infrared cooking—a heating method that uses an electric or ceramic element heated to such a high temperature that it gives off waves of radiant heat that cook the food

Infusion—(1) the extraction of flavours from a food at a temperature below boiling; (2) a group of coffee-brewing techniques, including steeping, filtering and dripping; (3) the liquid resulting from this process

Instant-read thermometer—a thermometer used to measure the internal temperature of foods, the stem is inserted in the food, producing an instant temperature readout

Intentional food additives—those added to foods on purpose, such as the chemicals used to ensure longer shelf life or food colourings

Intoxication—in the food safety context, an illness caused by the toxins that bacteria produce during their life processes

Inventory—the listing and accounting of all foods in the kitchen, storerooms and refrigerators

IQF (individually quick-frozen)—describes the techniques of rapidly freezing each individual item of food such as slices of fruit, berries or pieces of fish before packaging; IQF foods are not packaged with syrup or sauce

Irradiation—a preservation method used for certain fruits, vegetables, grains, spices, meat and poultry in which ionizing radiation sterilizes the food, slows ripening and prevents sprouting

Jacquarding—a process of piercing muscle tissue with needles to tenderize

Jam—a fruit gel made from fruit pulp and sugar

Jelly—a fruit gel made from fruit juice and sugar

Juice—the liquid extracted from any fruit or vegetable

Julienne—(ju-lee-en) (1) to cut foods into stick-shaped pieces, approximately 1 to 2 mm × 1 to 2 mm × 2.5 to 5 cm (1/16 in. × 1/16 in. × 1 to 2 in.); (2) the stick-shaped pieces of cut food

Jus lié—(zhoo lee-ay) also known as fond lié; a sauce made by thickening brown stock with cornstarch or similar starch

Kneading—working a dough to develop gluten; use hands or an electric mixer with its dough hook; if done by hand, the dough must be vigorously and repeatedly folded and turned in a rhythmic pattern

Kobe beef—an exclusive type of beef traditionally produced in Kobe, Japan, from Wagyu cattle fed a special diet

Kosher—describes food prepared in accordance with Jewish dietary laws

Lactose—a disaccharide that occurs naturally in mammalian milk; milk sugar

Lag phase—a period, usually following transfer from one place to another, during which bacteria do not experience much growth

Lamb—the meat of sheep slaughtered under the age of one year

Lard—the rendered fat of hogs

Larding—inserting thin slices of fat, such as pork backfat, into low-fat meats in order to add moisture

Lardon—diced, blanched, fried bacon

Leading sauces—see **Basic sauces**

Leavener—an ingredient or process that produces or incorporates gases in a baked product in order to increase volume, provide structure and give texture

Lecithin—a natural emulsifier found in egg yolks and cocoa

Legumes—(lay-gyooms) (1) French for "vegetables"; (2) a large group of vegetables with double-seamed seed pods; depending upon the variety, the seeds, pod and seeds together, or the dried seeds are eaten

Liaison—(lee-yeh-zon) a mixture of egg yolks and heavy cream used to enrich sauces

Liqueur—a strong, sweet, syrupy alcoholic beverage made by mixing or redistilling neutral spirits with fruits, flowers, herbs, spices or other flavourings; also known as a cordial

Liquor—an alcoholic beverage made by distilling grains, vegetables or other foods, includes rum, whisky and vodka

Litre—the basic unit of volume in the metric system, equal to slightly more than a quart

Log phase—a period of accelerated growth for bacteria

Lozenges—diamond-shaped pieces, usually of firm vegetables

Macaroni—any dried pasta made with wheat flour and water; only in North America does the term refer to elbow-shaped pasta tubes

Macerate—to soak foods in a liquid, usually alcoholic, to soften them

Macronutrients—the nutrients needed in large quantities: carbohydrates, proteins, fats and water

Madeira—(muh-DEH-rah) a Portuguese fortified wine heated during aging to give it a distinctive flavour and brown colour

Maillard reactions—the process of browning of non-sugar foods

Maître d'hotel (maître d')—(maytr doh-tel) (1) the leader of the dining room brigade, also known as the dining room manager; oversees the dining room or "front of the house" staff; (2) a compound butter flavoured with chopped parsley and lemon juice

Makeup—the cutting, shaping and forming of dough products before baking

Mandoline—a stainless steel, hand-operated slicing device with adjustable blades

Marbling—whitish streaks of inter- and intramuscular fat

Marinade—the liquid used to marinate foods; it generally contains herbs, spices and other flavouring ingredients as well as acidic product such as wine, vinegar or lemon juice

Marinate—to soak a food in a seasoned liquid in order to tenderize the food or add flavour to it

Market menu—a menu based on product availability during a specific period; it is written to use foods when they are in peak season or readily available

Marmalade—a citrus jelly that also contains unpeeled slices of citrus fruit

Marquise—a frozen mousse-like dessert, usually chocolate

Marsala—(mar-SAH-lah) a flavourful fortified sweet-to-semidry Sicilian wine

Marzipan—(MAHR-sih-pan) a paste of ground almonds, sugar and egg whites used to fill and decorate pastries

Matignon—a standard mirepoix plus diced smoked bacon or smoked ham and, depending on the dish, mushrooms and herbs; sometimes called an edible mirepoix, it is usually cut more uniformly than a standard mirepoix and left in the finished dish as a garnish

Matzo—thin, crisp unleavened bread made only with flour and water; can be ground

into meal that is used for matzo balls and pancakes

Mayonnaise—a thick, creamy sauce consisting of oil and vinegar emulsified with egg yolks, usually used as a salad dressing

Meal—(1) the coarsely ground seeds of any edible grain such as corn or oats; (2) any dried, ground substance (such as bonemeal)

Mealy potatoes—also known as starchy potatoes; those with a high starch content and thick skin; they are best for baking

Mechanical convection—the circulation of heat caused by fans or stirring

Medallion—a small, round relatively thick slice of tender meat

Melting—the process by which certain foods, especially those high in fat, gradually soften and then liquefy when heated

Menu—a list of foods and beverages available for purchase

Meringue—(muh-reng) a foam made of beaten egg whites and sugar

Metabolism—all the chemical reactions and physical processes that occur continuously in living cells and organisms

Metre—the basic unit of length in the metric system, equal to slightly more than one yard

Mezzaluna—a two-handled knife with one or more thick, crescent-shaped blades used to chop and mince herbs and vegetables

Micronutrients—the nutrients needed only in small amounts; vitamins and minerals

Microorganisms—single-celled organisms as well as tiny plants and animals that can be seen only through a microscope

Microwave cooking—a heating method that uses radiation generated by a special oven to penetrate the food: it agitates water molecules, creating friction and heat; this energy then spreads throughout the food by conduction (and by convection in liquids)

Mignonette—(mee-nyohn-EHT) (1) a small cut or medallion of tenderloin; (2) cracked black pepper

Milk-fed veal—also known as formula-fed veal; the meat of calves fed only a nutrient-rich liquid and kept tethered in pens; this meat is whiter and more mildly flavoured than that of free-range calves

Milling—the process by which grain is ground into flour or meal

Mince—to cut into very small pieces where uniformity of shape is not important

Minerals—inorganic micronutrients necessary for regulating body functions and proper bone and tooth structures

Mirepoix—(meer-pwa) a mixture of coarsely chopped onions, carrots and celery used to flavour stocks, stews and other foods; generally, a mixture of 50 percent onions, 25 percent carrots and 25 percent celery, by weight, is used

Mise en place—(meez on plahs) French for "putting in place"; refers to the preparation and assembly of all necessary ingredients and equipment

Miso—(me-so) a thick paste made by salting and fermenting soybeans and rice or barley; generally used as a flavouring

Mix—to combine ingredients in such a way that they are evenly dispersed throughout the mixture

Moist-heat cooking methods—cooking methods, principally simmering, poaching, boiling and steaming, that use water or steam to transfer heat through convection; moist-heat cooking methods are used to emphasize the natural flavours of foods

Molecular gastronomy—a contemporary scientific movement that investigates the chemistry and physics behind the preparation of foods and dishes

Mollusks—shellfish characterized by a soft, unsegmented body, no internal skeleton and a hard external shell

Monounsaturated fats—see **Unsaturated fats**

Monter au beurre—(mohn-tay ah burr) to finish a sauce by swirling or whisking in butter (raw or compound) until it is melted; used to give sauces shine, flavour and richness

Mortar and pestle—a hard bowl (the mortar) in which foods such as spices are ground or pounded into a powder with a club-shaped tool (the pestle)

Mother sauces—(French *sauce mère*), see **Basic sauces**

Moulding—the process of shaping foods, particularly grains and vegetables bound by sauces, into attractive, hard-edged shapes by using metal rings, circular cutters or other forms

Moulds—(1) algaelike fungi that form long filaments or strands; for the most part, moulds affect only food appearance and flavour; (2) containers used for shaping foods

Mousse—(moose) (1) a purée of fully cooked product, combined with a sauce, whipped cream and gelatin; (2) a soft, creamy or puréed food product, either sweet or savoury, lightened by adding whipped cream, beaten egg whites or both

Mousseline—(moose-uh-leen) (1) meat, fish or poultry is finely ground, then puréed; whipping cream and egg whites are incorporated. Used to make quenelles. (2) A

cream or sauce lightened by folding in whipped cream.

Mouth-feel—the sensation created in the mouth by a combination of a food's taste, smell, texture and temperature

Muesli—(MYOOS-lee) a breakfast cereal made from raw or toasted cereal grains, dried fruits, nuts and dried milk solids and usually eaten with milk or yogurt; sometimes known as granola

Muffin method—a mixing method used to make quick-bread batters; it involves combining liquid fat with other liquid ingredients before adding them to the dry ingredients

Muscles—animal tissue consisting of bundles of cells or fibres that can contract and expand; they are the portions of a carcass usually consumed

Mushrooms—members of a broad category of plants known as fungi; they are often used and served like vegetables

Mutton—the meat of sheep slaughtered after they reach the age of one year

NAMP/IMPS/CMC—the United States Department of Agriculture publishes Institutional Meat Purchasing Specifications (IMPS); the IMPS are illustrated and described in *The Meat Buyers Guide* published by the National Association of Meat Purveyors (NAMP); the Canadian Meat Council (CMC) also publishes full-colour manuals that name and number cuts of meat

Nappe—(nap) (1) the consistency of a liquid, usually a sauce, that will coat the back of a spoon; (2) to coat a food with sauce

National cuisine—the characteristic cuisine of a nation

Natural convection—circulation caused by hot molecules rising and cool molecules falling

Navarin—(nah-veh-rahng) a brown ragout generally made with turnips, other root vegetables, onions, peas and lamb

Neapolitan—a three-layered loaf or cake of ice cream; each layer is a different colour and flavour, such as chocolate, vanilla and strawberry

Nectar—the diluted, sweetened juice of peaches, apricots, guavas, black currants or other fruits, the juice of which would be too thick or too tart to drink straight

Needling—a process in which a solution is injected into the muscle to provide moisture and flavour. Products are referred to as marinated or enhanced. The moisture retention must be declared.

Neutral spirits—pure alcohol (ethanol or ethyl alcohol); they are odourless, tasteless and a very potent 190 proof (95% alcohol)

Noisette—(nwah-zet) (1) a small, usually round portion of meat cut from the rib or loin; (2) lightly browned butter

Noodles—the strips of pasta-type dough made with eggs; may be fresh and dried

Nougat—a candy made of caramelized sugar and almonds that can be moulded into shapes or containers

Nouvelle cuisine—French for "new cooking"; a mid-20th-century movement away from many classic cuisine principles and toward a lighter cuisine based on natural flavours, shortened cooking times and innovative combinations

Nut—(1) the edible single-seed kernel of a fruit surrounded by a hard shell; (2) generally, any seed of fruit with an edible kernel in a hard shell

Nutrients—the chemical substances found in food that nourish the body by promoting growth, facilitating body functions and providing energy; there are six categories of nutrients: proteins, carbohydrates, fats, water, minerals and vitamins

Nutrition—the science that studies nutrients

Oblique cuts—small pieces with two angle-cut sides

Offal—(OFF-uhl) also called variety meats; the edible entrails and extremities of an animal

Oignon brûlé—(ohn-nawng brew-LAY) French for "burnt onion"; made by charring onion halves; used to flavour and colour stocks and sauces as a remedial action

Oignon piqué—(ohn-nawng pee-KAY) French for "pricked onion"; a bay leaf tacked with a clove to a peeled onion; used to flavour sauces and soups; also known as oignon clouté

Oil—a type of fat that remains liquid at room temperature

One-stage method—low moisture formulas can be mixed all at once; rarely used because you have less control

Organic farming—a method of farming that does not rely on synthetic pesticides, fungicides, herbicides or fertilizers

Oven spring—the rapid rise of yeast goods in a hot oven, resulting from the production and expansion of trapped gases

Overrun—the amount of air churned into an ice cream

Paillarde—(pahy-lahrd) a scallop of meat pounded until thin; usually grilled

Palate—(1) the complex of smell, taste and touch receptors that contribute to a person's ability to recognize and appreciate flavours; (2) the range of an individual's recognition and appreciation of flavours

Pan gravy—a sauce made by deglazing pan drippings from roast meat or poultry and combining them with a roux or other starch and stock

Panada—(pah-nahd) a starch-based product added to a forcemeat to bind and create a smoother texture

Pan-broiling—a dry-heat cooking method that uses conduction to transfer heat to a food resting directly on a cooking surface; no fat is used and food remains uncovered

Pan-dressed—a market form for fish in which the viscera, gills and scales are removed and the fins and tail are trimmed

Pan-frying—a dry-heat cooking method in which food is placed in a moderate amount of hot fat

Papain—(puh-pay-in) an enzyme found in papayas that breaks down proteins; used as the primary ingredient in many commercial meat tenderizers

Parboiling—partially cooking a food in a boiling or simmering liquid; similar to blanching but the cooking time is longer

Parchment (paper)—heat-resistant paper used throughout the kitchen for tasks such as lining baking pans, wrapping foods to be cooked en papillote and covering foods during shallow poaching

Parcooking—partially cooking a food by any cooking method

Parfait—(par-fay) ice cream served in a long, slender glass with alternating layers of topping or sauce

Paring knife—a short knife used for detail work, especially cutting fruits and vegetables; it has a rigid blade approximately 5 to 10 cm (2 to 4 in.)

Paris-Brest—rings of baked choux cut in half horizontally and filled with light pastry cream and/or whipped cream; the top is dusted with powdered sugar or drizzled with chocolate glaze

Parisienne—a sphere of fruit or vegetable cut with a small melon ball cutter

Parstock (par)—the amount of stock necessary to cover operating needs between deliveries

Pasta—(1) an unleavened paste or dough made from wheat flour (often semolina), water and eggs; the dough can be coloured and flavoured with a wide variety of herbs, spices or other ingredients and cut or extruded into a wide variety of shapes and sizes; it can be fresh or dried and is boiled for service; (2) general term for any macaroni product or egg noodle

Pasteurization—the process of heating a product to a prescribed temperature for a specific time to destroy pathogenic bacteria

Pastillage—(pahst-tee-azh) a paste made of sugar, cornstarch and gelatin; it may be cut or moulded into decorative shapes

Pastry cream—also known as crème pâtissière, a stirred custard made with egg yolks, sugar and milk and thickened with starch; used for pastry and pie fillings

Pâte—(paht) French for "dough"

Pâté—(pah-TAY) traditionally, a forcemeat baked in a crust; today, the term may refer generically to most forcemeat preparations

Pâte à choux—(paht ah shoo) also known as choux paste and éclair paste; a soft dough that produces hollow baked products with crisp exteriors; used for making éclairs, cream puffs and savoury products

Pâte à glacer—a specially formulated chocolate coating compound with vegetable oils designed to retain its shine without tempering; it is used as a coating or frosting chocolate

Pâte au pâté—(paht ah pah-TAY) specially formulated pastry dough used for wrapping pâté when making pâté en croûte

Pâte brisée—(paht bree-zay) a dough that produces a very flaky baked product containing little or no sugar that is used for prebaked pie shells or crusts; mealy dough is a less flaky product used for custard cream or fruit pie crusts

Pâté en croûte—(pah-tay awn croot) a forcemeat baked in a crust

Pâte feuilletée—(paht fuh-yuh-tay) also known as puff pastry; a rolled-in dough used for pastries, cookies and savoury products; it produces a rich and buttery but not sweet baked product with hundreds of light, flaky layers

Pâte sucrée—(paht soo-kray) a dough containing sugar that produces a very rich, crisp (not flaky) baked product; also known as sweet dough; it is used for tart shells

Patent flour—flour made from the portion of the endosperm closest to the germ

Pathogen—any organisms that cause illness; usually refers to bacteria; undetectable by smell, sight or taste, pathogens are responsible for as much as 95 percent of all food-borne illnesses

Pâtissier—(pah-tees-sir-yair) a pastry chef; the person responsible for all baked items, including breads, pastries and desserts

Paupiette—(po-pee-et) a thin slice of meat, poultry or fish spread with a savoury stuffing and rolled, then braised or poached

Paysanne—(pahy-sahn) foods cut into flat squares of 12 mm × 12 mm × 3 mm (1/2 in. × 1/2 in. × 1/8 in.)

Pearling—a milling process in which all or part of the hull, bran and germ are removed from grains

Pectin—a gelatin-like carbohydrate found in the skin and seeds of some fruits (apples, apricots, cranberries, red currants); when boiled with sugar and an acid, it gels when cooked; used to thicken jams and jellies

Persillade—(payr-se-yad) (1) a food served with or containing parsley; (2) a mixture of bread crumbs, parsley and garlic used to coat meats, usually lamb

pH—a measurement of the acid or alkali content of a solution, expressed on a scale of 0 to 14.0. A pH of 7.0 is considered neutral or balanced. The lower the pH value, the more acidic the substance. The higher the pH value, the more alkaline the substance.

Physical hazard—a danger to the safety of food caused by particles such as glass chips, metal shavings, bits of wood or other foreign matter

Pickle—(1) to preserve food in a brine or vinegar solution; (2) food that has been preserved in a seasoned brine or vinegar, especially cucumbers. Pickled cucumbers are available whole, sliced, in wedges or chopped as a relish, and may be sweet, sour, dill-flavoured or hot and spicy.

Pie—a sweet or savoury filling in a baked crust, which can be open-faced, lattice, or full

Pigment—any substance that gives colour to an item

Pilaf—a cooking method for grains in which the grains are lightly sautéed in hot fat and then a hot liquid is added; the mixture is simmered without stirring until the liquid is absorbed

Poaching—a moist-heat cooking method that uses convection to transfer heat from a hot (approximately 71°C–82°C [160°F–180°F]) liquid to the food submerged in it

Poêlé—a combination cooking method that involves browning the meat in butter and braising with a mirepoix

Polyunsaturated fats— see **Unsaturated fats**

Pomes—members of the *Rosaceae* family; tree fruits with a thin skin and firm flesh surrounding a central core containing many small seeds (called pips and carpels); includes apples, pears and quince

Pork—the meat of hogs, usually slaughtered under the age of one year

Posterior—at or toward the rear of an object or place; opposite of anterior

Potentially hazardous foods—foods on which bacteria can thrive

Poultry—the collective term for domesticated birds bred for eating; they include chickens, ducks, geese, guineas, pigeons and turkeys

Praline—hazelnut paste made with sugar

Preserve—a fruit gel that contains large pieces or whole fruits

Primal cuts—primary divisions of muscle, bone and connective tissue produced by the initial butchering of the carcass

Prix fixe—(pree feks) French for "fixed price"; a menu offering a complete meal for a set price; also known as *table d'hôte*

Professional cooking—a system of cooking based on a knowledge of and appreciation for ingredients and procedures

Profiteroles—(pro-feet-uh-rolls) small baked rounds of choux pastry filled with ice cream and topped with chocolate sauce

Proofing—the rise given to shaped yeast products just prior to baking

Proteins—a group of compounds composed of oxygen, hydrogen, carbon and nitrogen atoms necessary for manufacturing, maintaining and repairing body tissues and as an alternative source of energy (4 calories per gram); protein chains are constructed of various combinations of amino acids

Pudding—a thick, spoonable dessert custard, usually made with eggs, milk, sugar and flavourings and thickened with flour or another starch

Puff pastry—see **Pâte feuilletée**

Pulled sugar—a doughlike mixture of sucrose, glucose and tartaric acid that can be coloured and shaped by hand

Pulses—dried seeds from a variety of legumes

Pumpernickel—(1) coarsely ground rye flour; (2) bread made with this flour

Punching down—folding down dough after fermentation in order to expel excessive gas pockets and even out the dough's temperature

Purée—(pur-ray) (1) to process food to achieve a smooth pulp; (2) food that is processed by mashing, straining or fine chopping to achieve a smooth pulp

Purée soup—a soup usually made from starchy vegetables or legumes; after the main ingredient is simmered in a liquid, the mixture, or a portion of it, is puréed

Putrefactives—bacteria that spoil food without rendering it unfit for human consumption

Quality grades—a guide to the eating qualities of meat—its tenderness, juiciness and flavour—based on an animal's age and the meat's colour, texture and degree of marbling

Quenelles—(kuh-nehls) oblong-shaped portions of mousseline forcemeat poached in stock

Quiche—a savoury tart or pie consisting of a custard baked in a pastry shell with a variety of flavourings and garnishes

Quick bread—a bread, including loaves and muffins, leavened by chemical leaveners or steam rather than yeast

Radiation cooking—a heating process that does not require physical contact between the heat source and the food being cooked; instead, energy is transferred by waves of heat or light striking the food. Two kinds of radiant heat used in the kitchen are infrared and microwave.

Raft—a crust formed during the process of clarifying consommé; it comprises the clearmeat and impurities from the stock, which rise to the top of the simmering stock and release additional flavours

Ragout—(rah-goo) (1) traditionally, a well-seasoned, rich stew containing meat, vegetables and wine; (2) any stewed mixture

Ramekin—a small ovenproof dish, usually ceramic

Rancidity—a chemical change in fats caused by exposure to air, light or heat that results in objectionable flavours and odours

Ratites—a family of flightless birds with small wings and flat breastbones; they include the ostrich, emu and rhea

Recipe—a set of written instructions for producing a specific food or beverage; also known as a formula

Recovery time—the length of time it takes a cooking medium such as fat or water to return to the desired cooking temperature after food is submerged in it

Red fish—a name applied to various species of fish around the world. In North America it generally refers to a member of the drum family found in the Southern Atlantic and the Gulf of Mexico. It has a reddish-bronze skin, firm, ivory flesh with a mild flavour and a typical market weight of 0.9–3.6 kg (2–8 lb.), and is also known as channel bass, red drum and red bass.

Red rice—a unmilled, short- or long-grain rice from the Himalayas; it has a russet-coloured bran and an earthy, nutty flavour

Reduction—cooking a liquid such as a sauce until its quantity decreases through evaporation. To reduce by one-half means that one-half of the original amount remains. To reduce by three-quarters means that only one-quarter of the original amount remains. To reduce au sec means that the liquid is cooked until nearly dry.

Refreshing—submerging a food in cold water to quickly cool it and prevent further cooking; also known as shocking; usually used for vegetables

Regional cuisine—a set of recipes based upon local ingredients, traditions and practices; within a larger geographical, political, cultural or social unit, regional cuisines are often variations of one another that blend together to create a national cuisine

Relish—a cooked or pickled sauce usually made with vegetables or fruits and often used as a condiment; can be smooth or chunky, sweet or savoury and hot or mild

Remouillage—(rhur-moo-yahj) French for "rewetting"; a stock produced by reusing the bones left from making another stock

Render—(1) to melt and clarify fat; (2) to cook meats in order to remove the fat

Respiration rate—the speed with which the cells of a fruit use up oxygen and produce carbon dioxide during ripening

Ricer—a sievelike utensil with small holes through which soft food is forced; it produces particles about the size of a grain of rice

Rillette—(ree-yeh) meat cooked in its own fat, slowly, then mashed or diced, mixed with fat and potted

Ripe—fully grown and developed; the fruit's flavour, texture and appearance are at their peak, and the fruit is ready to eat

Risers—boxes (including the plastic crates used to store glassware) covered with linens, paper or decorative items and used on a buffet table as a base for platters, trays or displays

Risotto—(re-zot-toe) (1) a cooking method for grains in which the grains are lightly sautéed in butter and then a liquid is gradually added; the mixture is simmered with near-constant stirring until the still-firm grains merge with the cooking liquid; (2) a Northern Italian rice dish prepared this way

Roasting—a dry-heat cooking method that heats food by surrounding it with hot, dry air in a closed environment or on a spit over an open fire; similar to baking, the term "roasting" is usually applied to meats, poultry, game and vegetables

Roe—(roh) fish eggs

Roll cuts—see **Oblique cuts**

Rolled-in dough—a dough in which a fat is incorporated in many layers by using a rolling and folding procedure; it is used for flaky baked goods such as croissants, puff pastry and Danish pastry

Rondeau—(ron-doe) a shallow, wide, straight-sided pot with two loop handles

Rondelles—(ron-dellz) disk-shaped slices

Rotate stock—to use products in the order in which they were received; all perishable and semi-perishable goods, whether fresh, frozen, canned or dry, should be used according to the first in, first out (FIFO) principle

Rotisserie—cooking equipment that slowly rotates meat or other foods in front of a heating element

Roulade—(roo-lahd) (1) a slice of meat, poultry or fish rolled around a stuffing; (2) a filled and rolled spongecake

Round fish—fish with round, oval or compressed bodies that swim in a vertical position and have eyes on both sides of their heads, including salmon, swordfish and cod

Rounding—the process of shaping dough into smooth, round balls; used to stretch the outside layer of gluten into a smooth coating

Roux—(roo) a cooked mixture of equal parts flour and fat, by weight; used as a thickener for sauces and other dishes

Royal icing—also known as decorator's icing, an uncooked mixture of confectioner's sugar and egg whites that becomes hard and brittle when dry; used for making intricate cake decorations

Rub—a mixture of fresh or dried herbs and spices ground together; it can be used dried or it can be mixed with a little oil, lemon juice, prepared mustard or ground fresh garlic or ginger to make a wet rub

Russian service—restaurant service in which the entree, vegetables and starches are served from a platter onto the diner's plate by a waiter

Sabayon—(sa-by-on) also known as zabaglione; a foamy, stirred custard sauce made by whisking eggs, sugar and wine over low heat

Sachet d'épices—(sah-shay day-peace) French for "bag of spices"; aromatic ingredients tied in a cheesecloth bag and used to flavour stocks and other foods; a standard sachet contains parsley stems, peppercorns, dried thyme, bay leaves, cloves and (optionally) garlic

Salad—a single food or mix of different foods accompanied or bound by a dressing

Salad dressing—a sauce for a salad; most are based on a vinaigrette, mayonnaise or other emulsified product

Salad greens—a variety of leafy vegetables that are usually eaten raw

Salamander—a small broiler used primarily for browning or glazing the tops of foods

Salsa—(sahl-sah) Spanish for "sauce"; generally, a cold chunky mixture of fresh herbs, spices, fruits and/or vegetables used as a sauce for meat, poultry, fish or shellfish

Salt-curing—the process of surrounding a food with salt or a mixture of salt, sugar, nitrite-based curing salt, herbs and spices; salt-curing dehydrates the food, inhibits bacterial growth and adds flavour

Sanding sugar—granulated sugar with a large, coarse crystal structure that prevents it from dissolving easily; used for decorating cookies and pastries

Sanitation—the creation and maintenance of conditions that will prevent food contamination or food-borne illness

Sanitize—to reduce pathogenic organisms to safe levels

Sashimi—(sah-shee-mee) raw fish eaten without rice; usually served as the first course of a Japanese meal

Saturated fats—fats found mainly in animal products and tropical oils; usually solid at room temperature; the body has more difficulty breaking down saturated fats than either monounsaturated or polyunsaturated fats

Sauce—generally, a thickened liquid used to flavour and enhance other foods

Sausage—a seasoned forcemeat usually stuffed into a casing; a sausage can be fresh, smoked and cooked, dried or hard

Sautéing—(saw-tay-ing) a dry-heat cooking method that uses conduction to transfer heat from a hot pan to food with the aid of small amount of hot fat; cooking is usually done quickly over high temperatures

Sauteuse—(saw-toose) the basic sauté pan with sloping sides and a single long handle

Sautoir—(saw-twahr) a sauté pan with straight sides and a single long handle

Savoury—(1) describes spiced or seasoned, as opposed to sweet, foods (2) a highly seasoned last course of a traditional English dinner

Scald—to heat a liquid, usually milk, to just below the boiling point

Score—to cut shallow gashes across the surface of a food before cooking

Scoville Heat Units—a subjective rating for measuring a chile's heat; the sweet bell pepper usually rates 0 units, the tabasco pepper rates 30 000 to 50 000 units and the habanero pepper rates from 100 000 to 300 000 units

Seafood—an inconsistently used term encompassing some or all of the following: saltwater fish, freshwater fish, saltwater shellfish, freshwater shellfish and other edible marine life

Sear—to brown food quickly over high heat; usually done as a preparatory step for combination cooking methods

Season—(1) traditionally, to enhance flavour by adding salt; (2) more commonly, to enhance flavour by adding salt and/or pepper as well as herbs and spices; (3) to mature and bring a food (usually beef or game) to a proper condition by aging or special preparation; (4) to prepare a pot, pan or other cooking surface to prevent sticking

Seasoning—an item added to enhance the natural flavours of a food without dramatically changing its taste; salt is the most common seasoning

Seitan—(SAY-tan) a form of wheat gluten; it has a firm, chewy texture and a bland flavour; traditionally simmered in a broth of soy sauce or tamari with ginger, garlic and kombu (seaweed)

Semi à la carte—a menu on which some foods (usually appetizers and desserts) and beverages are priced and ordered separately, while the entree is accompanied by and priced to include other dishes such as a salad, starch or vegetable

Semifreddi—(seh-mee-frayd-dee) also known as still-frozen desserts; items made with frozen mousse, custard or cream into which large amounts of whipped cream or meringue are folded in order to incorporate air; layers of spongecake and/or fruits may be added for flavour and texture; semifreddi include frozen soufflés, marquises, mousses and neapolitans

Semolina—see **Durum wheat**

Sfoglia—(fo-lee-ah) a thin, flat sheet of pasta dough that can be cut into ribbons, circles, squares or other shapes

Shallow poaching—a moist-heat cooking method that combines poaching and steaming; the food (usually fish) is placed on a vegetable bed and partially covered with a liquid (cuisson) and simmered

Shellfish—aquatic invertebrates with shells or carapaces

Sherbet and sorbet—a frozen mixture of fruit juice or fruit purée that may contain milk and/or egg yolks for creaminess

Shortening—(1) a white, flavourless, solid fat formulated for baking or deep-fat frying; (2) any fat used in baking to tenderize the product by shortening gluten strands

Shred—to cut into thin but irregular strips

Shuck—(1) a shell, pod or husk; (2) to remove the edible portion of a food (e.g., clam meat, peas or an ear of corn) from its shell, pod or husk

Side masking—the technique of coating only the sides of a cake with garnish

Sifting—passing one or more ingredients through a wire mesh to remove lumps and combine and aerate ingredients; use a rotary or drum sifter or mesh strainer

Silverskin—the tough connective tissue that surrounds certain muscles; see **Elastins**

Simmering—(1) a moist-heat cooking method that uses convection to transfer heat from a hot (approximately 85°C–96°C [185°F–205°F]) liquid to the food submerged in it; (2) maintaining the temperature of a liquid just below the boiling point

Skim—to remove fat and impurities from the surface of a liquid during cooking

Slashing—cutting the top of bread just before baking with a sharp knife or razor to improve shape and appearance and allow for continued rising and escape of gases from hard-crusted breads

Slice—to cut an item into relatively broad, thin pieces

Slurry—a mixture of raw starch and cold liquid used for thickening

Small sauces—see **Derivative sauces**

Smoke point—the temperature at which a fat begins to break down and smoke

Smoking—any of several methods for preserving and flavouring foods by exposing them to smoke; includes cold smoking (in which the foods are not fully cooked) and hot smoking (in which the foods are cooked)

Smørbrød—(SMURR-brur) Norwegian cold open-faced sandwiches; similarly, the Swedish term *smörgåsbord* (SMORE-guhs-bohrd) refers to a buffet or bread-and-butter table of salads, open-faced sandwiches, pickled or marinated fish, sliced meats and cheeses

Solid pack—canned fruits or vegetables with little or no water added

Sorbet—(sore-bay) a frozen mixture of fruit juice or fruit purée that may include egg and milk products; sherbet

Soufflé—(soo-flay) an airy textured sweet or savoury dish made from a custard, purée or starch base lightened with whipped egg whites and baked

Sous-chef—(soo-shef) a cook who supervises food production and who reports to the executive chef; he or she is second in command of a kitchen

Specifications; specs—standard requirements to be followed in procuring items from suppliers

Spice—any of a large group of aromatic plants whose bark, roots, seeds, buds or berries are used as a flavouring; usually used in dried form, either whole or ground

Sponge method—(1) a mixing method for yeast breads that has two stages; in the first, yeast, liquid and approximately one-half of the flour are combined to create a thick batter (sponge), which is allowed to rise; in the second, fat, salt, sugar and the remaining flour are added, and the dough is kneaded and allowed to rise again; (2) like the cake method, foamed egg whites are used; the batter is delicate; makes small quantities (e.g., ladyfingers, madeleines)

Spring lamb—the meat of sheep slaughtered before they have fed on grass or grains

Springform pan—a circular baking pan with a separate bottom and a side wall held together with a clamp that is released to free the baked product

Spun sugar—a decoration made by flicking dark caramelized sugar rapidly over a dowel to create long, fine, hairlike threads

Squab—the class of young pigeon used in food service operations

Staling—also known as starch retrogradation; a change in the distribution and location of water molecules within baked products; stale products are firmer, drier and more crumbly than fresh-baked goods

Standard breading procedure—the procedure for coating foods with crumbs or meal by passing the food through flour, then an egg wash and then the crumbs; it gives foods a relatively thick, crisp coating when deep-fat fried or pan-fried

Standardized recipe—a recipe producing a known quality and quantity of food for a specific operation

Staples—certain foods regularly used throughout the kitchen

Starch—(1) complex carbohydrates from plants that are edible and either digestible or indigestible (fibre); (2) a rice, grain, pasta or potato accompaniment to a meal

Starch retrogradation—see **Staling**

Starchy potatoes—see **Mealy potatoes**

Static menu—a menu offering patrons the same foods every day

Station chef—the cook in charge of a particular department in a kitchen

Steak—a cross-section slice of a round fish with a small section of the backbone attached

Steamed milk—milk that is heated with steam generated by an espresso machine; it should be 65°C to 76°C (150°F to 170°F)

Steamer—(1) a set of stacked pots with perforations in the bottom of each pot; they fit over a larger pot filled with boiling or simmering water and are used to steam foods; (2) a perforated insert made of metal or bamboo placed in a pot and used to steam foods; (3) a type of soft-shell clam from the East Coast; (4) a piece of gas or electric equipment in which foods are steamed in a sealed chamber

Steaming—a moist-heat cooking method in which heat is transferred from steam to the food being cooked by direct contact; the food to be steamed is placed in a basket or rack above a boiling liquid in a covered pan

Steel—a tool, usually made of steel, used to hone, true or straighten knife blades

Steep—to soak food in a hot liquid in order to either extract its flavour or impurities or soften its texture

Steers—male cattle castrated prior to maturity and principally raised for beef

Sterilize—to destroy all living microorganisms

Stewing—a combination cooking method similar to braising but generally involving smaller pieces of meat that are first blanched or browned, then cooked in a small amount of liquid that is served as a sauce

Stir-frying—a dry-heat cooking method similar to sautéing in which foods are cooked over very high heat using little fat while stirring constantly and briskly; often done in a wok

Stirring—gently mixing ingredients by hand until blended; use a spoon, whisk or rubber spatula

Stock—(French *fond*) a clear, unthickened liquid flavoured by soluble substances extracted from meat, poultry or fish and their bones as well as from a mirepoix, other vegetables and seasonings

Stone fruits—members of the genus *Prunus*, also known as drupes; tree or shrub fruits with a thin skin, soft flesh and one woody stone or pit; include apricots, cherries, nectarines, peaches and plums

Straight dough method—a mixing method for yeast breads in which all ingredients are simply combined and mixed

Straight forcemeat (basic forcemeat)—comprises a dominant meat plus lean pork and backfat to give the finished product a smooth texture

Strain—to pour foods through a sieve, mesh strainer or cheesecloth to separate or remove the liquid component

Streusel—a crumbly mixture of fat, flour, sugar and sometimes nuts and spices; used to top baked goods

Subcutaneous fat—exterior fat; the fat layer between the hide and muscle

Submersion poaching—a poaching method in which the food is completely covered with the poaching liquid

Subprimal cuts—basic cuts produced from each primal

Suckling pig—(Fr. *cochon de lait*) very young, small whole pig used for roasting or barbecuing whole

Sucrose—the chemical name for common refined sugar; it is a disaccharide, composed of one molecule each of glucose and fructose

Sugar—a carbohydrate that provides the body with energy and gives a sweet taste to foods

Sugar syrups—either simple syrups (thin mixtures of sugar and water) or cooked syrups (melted sugar cooked until it reaches a specific temperature)

Sundae—a concoction of ice cream, sauces (hot fudge, marshmallow and caramel, for example), toppings (nuts, candies and fresh fruit to name a few) and whipped cream

Suprême—(su-prem) (1) a sauce made by adding cream to a velouté made from chicken stock; (2) boneless breast of chicken with wing bone attached

Sushi—(szu-she) seasoned rice often accompanied by cooked or raw fish, shellfish, wasabi and nori

Sweat—to cook a food in a pan (usually covered) without browning, over low heat until the food softens and releases moisture; sweating allows the food to release its flavour more quickly when cooked with other foods

Sweetbreads—the thymus glands of a calf or lamb

Syrup—sugar that is dissolved in liquid, usually water, and often flavoured with spices or citrus zest

Syrup pack—canned fruits with a light, medium or heavy syrup added

Table d'hôte—(tab-bluh dote) see **Prix fixe**

Tagarishi—a Japanese spice that is available at Asian markets

Tahini—(tah-HEE-nee) a thick, oily paste made from crushed sesame seeds

Tang—the portion of a knife's blade that extends inside the handle

Tart—a sweet or savoury filling in a baked crust made in a shallow, straight-sided pan without a top crust

Tartlet—a small, single-serving tart

Taste—the sensations, as interpreted by the brain, of what we detect when food, drink or other substances come in contact with our taste buds

Tempeh—(TEHM-pay) fermented whole soybeans mixed with a grain such as rice or millet; it has a chewy consistency and a yeasty, nutty flavour

Temperature danger zone—the broad range of temperatures between 4°C and 60°C (40°F and 140°F) at which bacteria multiply rapidly

Tempering—(1) heating gently and gradually; refers to the process of slowly adding a hot liquid to eggs or other foods to raise their temperature without causing them to curdle; (2) a process for melting chocolate during which the temperature of the cocoa butter is carefully stabilized; this keeps the chocolate smooth and glossy

Terrine—(teh-reen) a forcemeat baked in the oven in a terrine mould immersed in a water bath

Thickening agents—ingredients used to thicken sauces; include starches (flour, cornstarch and arrowroot), gelatin and liaisons

Timbale—(tim-bull) (1) a small pail-shaped mould used to shape foods; (2) a preparation made in such a mould

Tisanes—(teh-zahns) herbal infusions that do not contain any "real" tea; examples include chamomile, ginseng and lemon balm

Tofu—also known as bean curd; it is created from soymilk using a method similar to the way animal milk is separated into curds and whey in the production of cheese

Tomato concassée—peeled, seeded and diced or chopped tomato

Tomato sauce—a basic sauce made from tomatoes, vegetables, seasonings and white stock; it may or may not be thickened with a roux

Toque—(toke) the tall white hat worn by chefs

Torte—in Central and Eastern European usage, refers to a rich cake in which all or part of the flour is replaced with finely chopped nuts or bread crumbs

Tossed salad—a salad prepared by placing the greens, garnishes and salad dressing in a large bowl and tossing to combine

Total recipe cost—the total cost of ingredients for a particular recipe; it does not reflect overhead, labour, fixed expenses or profit

Tourner—(toor-nay) to shape vegetables while peeling them. Modern practice is to peel the vegetables first, then shape them. The trimmings may then be utilized.

Toxin-mediated infection—illness from toxins produced in the intestine after ingesting living bacteria

Toxins—byproducts of living bacteria that can cause illness if consumed in sufficient quantities

Tranche—(tranch) an angled slice cut from fish fillets

Trans fat—a type of fat created when vegetable oils are solidified through hydrogenation

Tripe—the edible lining of a cow's stomach

Truffles—(1) flavourful tubers that grow near the roots of oak or beech trees; (2) rich chocolate candies made with ganache

Truss—to tie poultry with butcher's twine into a compact shape for cooking

Tube pan—a deep round baking pan with a hollow tube in the centre

Tuber—the fleshy root, stem or rhizome of a plant from which a new plant will grow; some, such as potatoes, are eaten as vegetables

Tumbling—a process in which solid muscle meat is tumbled with crushed ice and/or a seasoned liquid until the meat absorbs a prescribed percentage of its weight in liquid

Tunnelling—the holes that may form in baked goods as the result of overmixing

Unit cost—the price paid to acquire one of the specified units

Univalves—single-shelled mollusks with a single muscular foot, such as abalone

Unsaturated fats—fats that are normally liquid (oils) at room temperature; they may be monounsaturated (from plants such as olives and avocados) or polyunsaturated (from grains and seeds such as corn, soybeans and safflower as well as from fish)

Vacuum packaging—a food preservation method in which fresh or cooked food is placed in an airtight container (usually plastic); virtually all air is removed from the container through a vacuum process, and the container is then sealed

Vanilla custard sauce—also known as crème anglaise; a stirred custard made with egg yolks, sugar and milk or half-and-half and flavoured with vanilla; served with or used in dessert preparations

Vanillin—(1) whitish crystals of vanilla flavour that often develop on vanilla beans during storage; (2) synthetic vanilla flavouring

Variety—the result of breeding plants of the same species that have different qualities or characteristics; the new plant often combines features from both parents

Variety meats—see **Offal**

Veal—the meat of calves dressing out at less than 160 kg (350 lb.)

Vegan—(VEE-gun) a vegetarian who does not eat dairy products, eggs, honey or any other animal product; vegans usually also avoid wearing and using animal products such as fur, leather or wool

Vegetable—any herbaceous plant (one with little or no woody tissue) that can be partially or wholly eaten; vegetables can be classified as cabbages, fruit-vegetables, gourds and squashes, greens, mushrooms and truffles, onions, pods and seeds, roots and tubers and stalks

Vegetarian—a person who does not eat any meat, poultry, game, fish, shellfish or animal byproducts such as gelatin or animal fats; may not eat dairy products and eggs

Velouté—(veh-loo-tay) a basic sauce made by thickening a white stock (fish, veal or chicken) with roux

Venison—flesh from any member of the deer family, including antelope, elk, moose, reindeer, red-tailed deer, white-tailed deer, mule deer and axis deer

Vent—(1) to allow the circulation or escape of a liquid or gas; (2) to cool a pot of hot liquid by setting the pot on blocks in a cold water bath and allowing cold water to circulate around it

Vin blanc—a wine-enriched sauce made by reducing the cooking liquid from shallow poaching fish and adding a velouté

Vinaigrette—(vin-nay-greht) a temporary emulsion of oil and vinegar (usually three parts oil to one part vinegar) seasoned with herbs, salt and pepper; used as a salad dressing or sauce

Vinegar—a thin, sour liquid used as a preservative, cooking ingredient and cleaning solution

Vintner—a winemaker

Vintners Quality Alliance (VQA)—sets standards for the production of VQA wine and appellations; most active in Niagara region and British Columbia

Viruses—the smallest known form of life; they invade the living cells of a host and take over those cells' genetic material, causing the cells to produce more viruses; some viruses can enter a host through the ingestion of food contaminated with those viruses

Viscera—internal organs

Vitamins—compounds present in foods in very small quantities; they do not provide energy but are essential for regulating body functions

Vol-au-vents—(vul-oh-vanz) deep, individual portion-sized puff pastry shells; often shaped as a heart, fish or fluted circle; they are filled with a savoury mixture and served as an appetizer or a main course

Volume—the space occupied by a substance; volume measurements are commonly expressed as millilitres, litres, cups, quarts, gallons, teaspoons, fluid ounces and bushels

Wash—a glaze applied to dough before baking; a commonly used wash is made with whole egg and water

Water bath—see **Bain marie**

Water pack—canned fruits with water and fruit juice added

Waxy potatoes—those with a low starch content and thin skin; they are best for boiling

Weight—the mass or heaviness of a substance; weight measurements are commonly expressed as grams, kilograms, ounces and pounds

Whetstone—a dense, grained stone used to sharpen or hone a knife blade

Whipping—beating vigorously to incorporate air; use a whisk or an electric mixer with its whip attachment

White stew—see **Blanquette** and **Fricassee**

White stock—a light-coloured stock made from chicken, veal or beef bones simmered in water with vegetables and seasonings

White wash—a thin mixture or slurry of flour and cold water used like cornstarch for thickening

Whole butter—butter that is not clarified, whipped or reduced fat

Window test—a test in pastry making to determine if dough has been properly kneaded; stretch a small amount of dough between your hands until it is very thin; if it has been kneaded long enough, it will form a thin, translucent sheet that does not tear

Wine—an alcoholic beverage made from the fermented juice of grapes; may be sparkling (effervescent) or fortified with additional alcohol

Work section—see **Work station**

Work station—a work area in the kitchen dedicated to a particular task, such as broiling or salad making; work stations using the same or similar equipment for related tasks are grouped together into *work sections*

Yeasts—microscopic fungi whose metabolic processes are responsible for fermentation; they are used for leavening bread and in cheese, beer and wine making

Yield—the total amount of a product made from a specific recipe; also, the amount of food item created or remaining after cleaning or processing

Yield grades—a grading program for meat that measures the amount of usable meat on a carcass

Zabaglione—see **Sabayon**

Zest—the coloured outer portion of the rind of a citrus peel; contains the oil that provides flavour and aroma

Zushi—(zhoo-she) the seasoned rice used for sushi

References and Recommended Reading

General Interest

Bartlett, Jonathon. *The Cook's Dictionary and Culinary Reference*. Lincolnwood, Ill: Contemporary Books, 1995.

Bennion, Marion, and Barbara Scheule. *Introductory Foods*. 12th ed. Upper Saddle River, NJ: Pearson Education, 2004.

Bickel, Walter, ed. and trans. *Hering's Dictionary of Classical and Modern Cookery*. 13th ed. Culinary & Hospitality Industry Publication Services, 1994.

Casselman, Bill. *Canadian Food Words: The Juicy Lore & Tasty Origins of Foods That Founded a Nation*. Toronto: McArthur & Co., 1998.

Coco: 10 World-Leading Masters Choose 100 Contemporary Chefs. New York: Phaidon, 2009.

Cox, Jeff. *The Organic Cook's Bible*. New York: Wiley, 2006.

The Culinary Institute of America. *The Professional Chef's Techniques of Healthy Cooking*. 2nd ed. New York: Wiley, 2000.

Davidson, Alan. *The Oxford Companion to Food*. Oxford: Oxford University Press, 1999.

Escoffier, Auguste. *Le Guide culinaire*. (Translation entitled *The Escoffier Cookbook and Guide to the Fine Art of Cookery for Connoisseurs, Chefs, Epicures*). New York: Crown, 1969.

Fuller, John and Edward Renold. *The Chef's Compendium of Professional Recipes*. 3rd ed. Oxford: Butterworth-Heinemann, 1992.

Herbst, Sharon Tyler, and Ron Herbst. *The Deluxe Food Lover's Companion*. New York: Barron, 2009.

Kamman, Madeleine. *The New Making of a Cook*. New York: Morrow, 1997.

Keller, Thomas. *Bouchon*. New York: Artisan, 2004.

———. *The French Laundry Cookbook*. New York: Artisan, 1999.

Knight, Chris. *Cook Like a Chef: Techniques, Tips and Secrets from the Professional Kitchen to Yours*. Vancouver: Whitecap, 2004.

Kunz, Gray and Peter Kaminsky. *The Elements of Taste*. Boston: Little Brown, 2001.

Larousse Gastronomique. English ed. New York: Crown, 2009.

Marranca, Bonnie, ed. *A Slice of Life: Contemporary Food Writers on Food*. New York: Overlook, 2003.

Molt, Mary. *Food for Fifty*. 12th ed. Upper Saddle River, N.J.: Prentice Hall, 2005.

Pepin, Jacques. *The Art of Cooking*. New York: Knopf, 1987.

———. *La Technique*. New York: Pocket Books, 1987.

Peterson, James. *Essentials of Cooking*. New York: Artisan, 2000.

Point, Fernand. *Fernand Point: Ma Gastronomie*. English ed. Wilton, Conn.: Lyceum, 1974.

Richard, Michel. *Happy in the Kitchen: The Craft of Cooking, the Art of Eating*. New York: Artisan, 2006.

Rolland, Jacques & Sherman, Carol. *The Food Encyclopedia: Over 8,000 Ingredients, Tools, Techniques and People*. Toronto: Robert Rose, 2006.

Saulnier, Louis. *Le Répertoire de la Cuisine*. Revised ed. New York: Barron's Educational Series, 1976.

Stern, Lise. *How to Keep Kosher: A Comprehensive Guide to Understanding Jewish Dietary Laws*. New York: HarperCollins, 2004.

Trotter, Charlie. *Workin' More Kitchen Sessions with Charlie Trotter*. Berkeley, Calif.: Ten Speed Press, 2004.

Walt, James. *Araxi: Seasonal Recipes from the Celebrated Whistler Restaurant*. Vancouver: Douglas & McIntyre, 2009.

Waltuck, David. *Chanterelle: The Story and Recipes of a Restaurant Classic*. Newtown, Conn.: Taunton Press, 2008.

Waters, Alice. *The Art of Simple Food: Notes, Lessons, and Recipes from a Delicious Revolution*. New York: Clarkson Potter, 2007.

Waverman, Lucy, and James Chatto. *A Matter of Taste: Inspired Seasonal Menus with Wines and Spirits to Match*. Toronto: HarperCollins, 2004.

Willan, Anne. *La Varenne Pratique*. New York: Crown, 1989.

Food History

Anderson, Jean. *The American Century Cookbook: The Most Popular Recipes of the 20th Century*. New York: Potter, 1997.

Coe, Sophie D., and Michael D. Coe. *The True History of Chocolate*. New York: Thames & Hudson, 1996.

Cooper, Ann. *A Woman's Place Is in the Kitchen: The Evolution of Women Chefs*. Stamford, Conn.: Thomson, 1997.

Fussell, Betty. *The Story of Corn*. New York: Borzoi Books, Knopf, 1992.

Kurlansky, Mark. *Cod: A Biography of the Fish That Changed the World*. New York: Walker, 1997.

Lovegren, Sylvia. *Fashionable Food: Seven Decades of Food Fads*. New York: Macmillan General Reference, 1995.

Mintz, Sidney W. *Sweetness and Power: The Place of Sugar in Modern History*. New York: Viking Press, 1995.

Norman, Barbara. *Tales of the Table: A History of Western Cuisine*. Englewood Cliffs, N.J.: Prentice-Hall, 1972.

Revel, Jean-François. *Culture and Cuisine*. (Trans. of *Un Festin en paroles*.) New York: Da Capo, 1982.

Rupp, Rececca. *Blue Corn and Square Tomatoes*. Pownal, Vt.: Garden Way, 1987.

Schlossberg, Eli W. *The World of Orthodox Judaism*. Northvale, N.J.: Aronson, 1996.

Shapiro, Laura. *Perfection Salad: Women and Cooking at the Turn of the Century*. New York: Farrar, Straus and Giroux, 1986.

Tannahill, Reay. *Food in History*. Revised ed. New York: Crown, 1995.

Toussaint-Samat, Maguelonne. *A History of Food*. Translated by Anthea Bell. Cambridge, Mass.: Blackwell, 1992.

Wheaton, Barbara Ketcham. *Savoring the Past: The French Kitchen and Table from 1300 to 1789*. Reprint ed. New York: Touchstone, 1996.

Willan, Anne. *Great Cooks and Their Recipes: From Taillevent to Escoffier*. Boston: Little, Brown, 1992.

Sanitation and Safety

Canadian Restaurant and Food Services Association publications.

Loken, Joan. *The HACCP Food Safety Manual*. New York: Wiley, 1995.

McSwane, David, Nancy Rue, Richard Linton, and Dan Reeves. *Essentials of Food Safety and Sanitation*, Cdn. ed. Toronto: Pearson Education Canada, 2006.

National Assessment Institute. *Handbook for Safe Food Service Management*. 2nd ed. Upper Saddle River, N.J.: Prentice Hall, 1998.

National Restaurant Association Educational Foundation. *ServSafe Essentials*. New York: Wiley, 2004.

———. *ServSafe: Serving Safe Food*. Workbooks and videos. New York: Wiley.

Nutrition

Baskette, Michael, and Eleanor Mainella. *The Art of Nutritional Cooking*. 2nd ed. Upper Saddle River, N.J.: Prentice Hall, 1999.

Drummond, Nina, and Lisa M. Brefore. *Nutrition for Foodservice and Culinary Professionals*. New York: Wiley, 2003.

Food Costing and Menu Pricing

Cullen, Noel. *Life Beyond the Line: A Front-of-the-House Companion for Culinarians*. Upper Saddle River, N.J.: Prentice Hall, 2001.

Drysdale, John, and Paula Kerr. *Profitable Menu Planning*. Cdn. ed. Toronto: Pearson Education Canada, 1999.

Labensky, Sarah R. *Applied Math for Food Service*. Upper Saddle River, N.J.: Prentice Hall, 1998.

Miller, Jack E. *Menu Pricing and Strategy*. 4th ed. Toronto: Wiley, 1996.

Schmidt, Arno. *Chef's Book of Formulas, Yields, and Sizes*. 3rd ed. Toronto: Wiley, 2003.

Tools

Bridge, Fred, and Jean F. Tibbetts. *The Well-Tooled Kitchen*. New York: Morrow, 1991.

Williams, Chuck, ed. *Williams-Sonoma Kitchen Companion*. New York: Time-Life Books, 2000.

Wolf, Burton, ed. *The New Cooks' Catalogue*. New York: Knopf, 2000.

General Ingredients

Bateman, Michael. *The World of Spice*. Vancouver: Whitecap, 2003.

Chiarello, Michael. *Michael Chiarello's Flavored Oils and Vinegars*. San Francisco: Chronicle, 2006.

Gayler, Paul. *Flavours: Magical Flavors and Tastes to Transform Your Cooking*. London: Kyle Cathie, 2005.

Hemphill, Ian. *The Spice and Herb Bible: A Cook's Guide*. Toronto: Robert Rose, 2002.

Morris, Sallie, and Lesley Mackley. *The Spice Ingredients Cookbook*. New York: Lorenz Books, 1997.

Ortiz, Elisabeth Lambert. *The Encyclopedia of Herbs, Spices and Flavorings*. 1st American ed. New York: Dorling Kindersley, 1992.

Stobart, Tom. *Herbs, Spices and Flavorings*. Woodstock, N.Y.: Overland, 2000.

Eggs, Dairy and Cheese

Callec, Christian. *The Complete Encyclopedia of Cheese*. Lisse, The Netherlands: Rebo Productions, 2002.

Dairy Farmers of Canada. *Fundamentals of Canadian Cheeses and Their Use in Fine Cuisine*. Montreal: Les Éditions de la Chenelière, 1992.

Fletcher, Janet. *The Cheese Course*. San Francisco: Chronicle, 2002.

Jenkins, Steven. *Steven Jenkins' Cheese Primer*. New York: Workman, 1996.

Lambert, Paula. *The Cheese Lover's Cookbook & Guide*. New York: Simon & Schuster, 2000.

Masui, Kazuko, and Tomoko Yamada. *French Cheese*. New York: Dorling Kindersley, 1996.

Flavours and Food Science

Corriher, Shirley O. *Cookwise*. New York: Morrow, 1997.

Delwiche, Jeannine. "Are there 'basic' tastes?" *Trends in Food Science & Technology,* 7, Special Issue on Flavor Perception (December 1996): 411–415.

Freeland-Graves, H., and Gladys C. Peckham. *Foundations of Food Preparation*. 5th ed. New York: Macmillan, 1987.

Heath, Henry B. *Source Book of Flavors*. Norwalk, Conn.: AVI, 1981.

Joachim, David, and Andrew Schloss. *The Science of Good Food*. Toronto: Robert Rose, 2008.

McGee, Harold. *The Curious Cook: More Kitchen Science and Lore*. New York: Macmillan General Reference, 1990.

———. *On Food and Cooking: The Science and Lore of the Kitchen*. Revised and updated ed. New York: Scribner, 2004.

McWilliams, Margaret. *Foods: Experimental Perspectives*. 4th ed. Upper Saddle River, N.J., Prentice Hall, 2001.

——— *Food Fundamentals*. 7th ed. Redondo Beach, Calif.: Plycon Press, 1998.

Page, Karen, and Andrew Dornenburg. *The Flavor Bible*. New York: Little, Brown, 2008.

Parsons, Russ. *How to Read a French Fry*. Boston: Houghton Mifflin, 2001.

New Techniques: Molecular Cooking and Sous Vide

Achatz, Grant. *Alinea*. Berkeley, Calif.: Ten Speed Press, 2008.

Adrià, Ferran. *A Day at elBulli*. New York: Phaidon, 2008.

Blumenthal, Heston. *The Fat Duck Cookbook*. New York: Bloomsbury, 2009.

Keller, Thomas. *Under Pressure: Cooking Sous Vide*. New York: Artisan, 2008.

Stocks, Sauces and Soups

Clayton, Bernard. *The Complete Book of Soups and Stews*. New York: Simon & Schuster, 1987.

Davis, Deidre. *A Fresh Look at Saucing Foods*. Reading, Mass.: Addison-Wesley, 1993.

Editors of *Cook's Illustrated* Magazine. *The Best Recipe: Soup and Stew*. Boston: Boston Common Press, 2001.

Kafka, Barbara. *Soup: A Way of Life*. New York: Artisan, 1998.

Larousse, David Paul. *The Sauce Bible: Guide to the Saucier's Craft*. New York: Artisan, 1998.

Peterson, James. *Sauces: Classical and Contemporary Sauce Making*. 2nd ed. New York: Wiley, 1998.

Schwartz, Oded. *Sauces and Salsas*. Toronto: Random House Canada, 2000.

Sokolov, Raymond A. *The Saucier's Apprentice*. New York: Knopf, 1976.

Meat, Poultry and Game

Aidells, Bruce, and Denis Kelly. *The Complete Meat Cookbook*. New York: Houghton Mifflin, 1998.

Cameron, Angus, and Judith Jones. *The L.L. Bean Game and Fish Cookbook*. New York: Random House, 1983.

Hibler, Jane. *Wild about Game: 150 Recipes for Cooking Farm-Raised and Wild Game from Alligator and Antelope to Venison and Wild Turkey*. New York: Broadway Books, 1998.

Knox, Luc, and Keith Richmond. *The World Encyclopedia of Meat, Game and Poultry*. New York: Lorenz Books, 2000.

Little, Carolyn. *The Game Cookbook*. Wiltshire, England: Crowood Press, 1988.

Marrone, Teresa. *Dressing and Cooking Wild Game*. New York: Prentice Hall Press, 1987.

North American Meat Processors Association. *The Meat Buyers Guide*. New York: Wiley, 2004.

Romans, John R., et al. *The Meat We Eat*. 14th ed. Upper Saddle River, NJ: Prentice Hall, 2000.

Webster, Harold W., Jr. *The Complete Venison Cookbook*. Brandon, Miss.: Quail Ridge Press, 1996.

Fish and Shellfish

Howarth, A. Jan. *The Complete Fish Cookbook*. New York: St. Martin's, 1983.

Kambolis, Harry, and Robert Clark. *C Food*. Vancouver: Whitecap, 2009.

King, Shirley. *Fish: The Basics*. New York: Chapters, 1996.

Loomis, Susan Herrmann. *The Great American Seafood Cookbook*. New York: Workman, 1988.

McClane, A. J. *The Encyclopedia of Fish Cookery*. New York: Holt, Rinehart & Winston, 1989.

Peterson, James. *Fish and Shellfish*. New York: Morrow, 1998.

The Seafood Handbook: Seafood Standards. Rockland, Maine: Seafood Business Magazine, 1991.

Charcuterie

The Editors of Time-Life Books. *The Good Cook: Terrines, Pâtés and Galantines*. London: Time Life International (Nederland) B.V., 1981.

Ehlert, Friedrich W., et al. *Pâtés and Terrines*. Reprint. London: Hearst Books, 1990.

Grigson, Jane. *The Art of Charcuterie*. Reprint. New York: Echo Press, 1991.

Kinsella, John, and David T. Harvey. *Professional Charcuterie*. New York: Wiley, 1996.

Vegetables and Fruits

Andrews, Jean. *Peppers: The Domesticated Capsicums*. Updated ed. Austin, Tex.: University of Texas Press, 1995.

Brown, Marlene. *International Produce Cookbook and Guide*. Los Angeles: HP Books, 1989.

Davidson, Alan. *Fruit: A Connoisseur's Guide and Cookbook*. New York: Simon & Schuster, 1991.

DeWitt, Dave, and Nancy Gerlach. *The Whole Chile Pepper Book*. Boston: Little, Brown, 1990.

Ingram, Christine. *The New Guide to Vegetables*. New York: Hermes House, 1997.

Miller, Mark, with John Harrisson. *The Great Chile Book*. Berkeley, Calif.: Ten Speed Press, 1991.

National Geographic Society. *Edible: An Illustrated Guide to the World's Food Plants*. Lane Cove, Australia: Global Book Publishing, 2008.

Payne, Rolce Redard, and Dorrit Speyer Senior. *Cooking With Fruit*. New York: Crown, 1992.

Peterson, James, and Justin Schwartz. *Vegetables*. New York: Morrow, 1998.

Prince, Thane. *Jellies, Jams and Chutneys*. London: DK Publishing, 2008.

Routhier, Nicole. *Nicole Routhier's Fruit Cookbook*. New York: Workman, 1996.

Schmidt, Jimmy. *Cooking for All Seasons*. New York: Macmillan, 1991.

Schneider, Elizabeth. *Vegetables from Amaranth to Zucchini: The Essential Reference*. New York: Morrow, 2001.

Ziedrich, Linda. *The Joy of Pickling*. Revised ed. Boston: Harvard Common Press, 2009.

Grains and Pasta

Bugialli, Giuliano. *On Pasta*. New York: Simon & Schuster, 1988.

Della Croce, Julia. *Pasta Classica*. San Francisco: Chronicle, 1987.

Greene, Bert. *The Grains Cookbook*. New York: Workman, 1988.

Leblang, Bonnie Tandy, and Joanne Lamb Hayes. *Rice*. New York: Harmony Books, 1991.

Teubner, Christian, Silvio Rizzi, and Tang Lee Leng. *The Pasta Bible*. New York: Penguin, 1996.

Vegetarian

Bauer, Cathy, and Juel Andersen. *The Tofu Cookbook*. Emmaus, Pa.: Rodale Press, 1979.

Bergeron, Ken. *Professional Vegetarian Cooking*. New York: Wiley, 1999.

Cotter, Denis. *Café Paradiso Seasons: Vegetarian Cooking Season by Season*. Irvington, NY: Hylas, 2003

Gifford, K. Dun, and Sara Baer-Sinnott. *The Oldways Table: Essays & Recipes from the Culinary Think Tank*. Berkeley, CA: Ten Speed Press, 2006.

Greenburg, Patricia. *The Whole Soy Cookbook*. New York: Random House, 1998.

Harris, William. *The Scientific Basis of Vegetarianism*. Honolulu: Health Publishers, 1995.

Holthaus, Fusako. *Tofu Cookery*. Tokyo: Kodansha International, 1992.

Madison, Deborah. *Vegetarian Cooking for Everyone*. New York: Broadway Books, 1997.

Melino, Vesanto, and Brenda Davis. *The New Becoming Vegetarian: The Essential Guide to a Healthy Vegetarian Diet*. Summertown, Tenn.: Healthy Living Publications, 2003.

Messina, Mark, and Virginia Messina. *The Vegetarian Way*. New York: Three Rivers Press, 1996.

Solomon, Charmaine. *Complete Vegetarian Cookbook*. Australia: Collins/Angus & Robertson, 1990

Salads and Salad Dressings

Ingram, Christine. *Sensational Salads*. London: Lorenz Books, 1999.

Kolpas, Norman. *Whole Meal Salads*. Chicago: Contemporary Books, 1992.

Nathan, Amy. *Salad*. San Francisco: Chronicle, 1985.

Breads

Alford, Jeffrey and Naomi Duigood. *Home Baking: The Artful Mix of Flour and Tradition Around the World*. Toronto: Random House, 2003.

Alston, Elizabeth. *Biscuits and Scones*. New York: Clarkson N. Potter, Inc., 1988.

Clayton, Bernard. *Bernard Clayton's New Complete Book of Breads*. Rev. ed. New York: Simon & Schuster, 1995.

David, Elizabeth. *English Bread and Yeast Cookery*. New ed. New York: Penguin, 2001.

Glezer, Maggie. *Artisan Baking Across America*. New York: Artisan, 2000.

Hensperger, Beth. *The Bread Bible: Beth Hensperger's 300 Favorite Recipes*. San Francisco: Chronicle Books, 1999.

Ortiz, Joe. *The Village Baker: Classic Regional Breads from Europe and America*. Berkeley, Calif.: Ten Speed Press, 1993.

Reinhart, Peter. *The Bread Baker's Apprentice*. Berkeley, Calif.: Ten Speed Press, 2001.

Pastries and Desserts

American Culinary Federation. *Baking Fundamentals*. Upper Saddle River, N.J.: Pearson Education, 2007.

Boyle, Tish and Timothy Moriarity. *Grand Finales: The Art of The Plated Dessert*. New York: Van Nostrand Reinhold, 1997

Braker, Flo. *The Simple Art of Perfect Baking*. Shelburne, Vt.: Chapters Publishing, 1992.

Daley, Regan. *In the Sweet Kitchen: The Definitive Baker's Companion*. New York: Artisan, 2001.

Desaulniers, Marcel. *Death by Chocolate*. Toronto: Random House, 1993.

Friberg, Bo. *The Professional Pastry Chef*. 4th ed. New York: Wiley, 2002

———. *The Advanced Professional Pastry Chef*. Hoboken, NJ: Wiley, 2003.

Healy, Bruce, and Paul Bugat. *Mastering the Art of French Pastry*. Woodbury, NY: Barron's, 1984.

Heatter, Maida. *Maida Heatter's Book of Great Desserts*. Kansas City, Mo.: Andrews McMeel, 1999.

Hyman, Philip, and Mary Hyman, trans. *The Best of Gaston Lenotre's Desserts*. Woodbury, NY: Barron's, 1983.

Labensky, Sarah, and Eddy Van Damme. *On Baking: A Textbook of Baking and Pastry Fundamentals*. Upper Saddle River, N.J.: Prentice Hall, 2005.

London, Sheryl, and Mel London. *Fresh Fruit Desserts: Classic and Contemporary*. New York: Prentice Hall Press, 1990.

Luchetti, Emily. *A Passion for Desserts*. San Francisco: Chronicle, 2003.

Purdy, Susan G. *A Piece of Cake*. Reprint ed. New York: Macmillan, 1993.

Silverton, Nancy. *Desserts by Nancy Silverton*. New York: Harper & Row, 1986.

Teubner, Christian, ed. *The Chocolate Bible*. New York: Penguin Studio, 1997.

Thuries, Yves. *The Classic and Contemporary Recipes of Yves Thuries: Restaurant Pastries and Desserts*. New York: Van Nostrand Reinhold, 1996.

Meal Service

Aloni, Nicole. *Secrets from a Caterer's Kitchen*. Tuscon, Ariz.: HP Books, 2001.

Bristow, Linda Kay. *Bread and Breakfast*. San Ramon, Calif.: 101 Productions, 1985.

Culinary Institute of America. *Garde Manger: The Art and Craft of the Cold Kitchen*. New York: Wiley, 2000.

Duffy, Gillian. *Hors d'Oeuvres*. New York: Morrow, 1998.

Fox, Margaret S., and John Bear. *Morning Food from Café Beaujolais*. Berkeley, Calif.: Ten Speed Press, 1994.

Ingram, Christine, ed. *Appetizers, Starters & Hors d'oeuvres: The Ultimate Collection of Recipes to Start a Meal in Style*. London: Lorenz Books, 2000.

Janericco, Terence. *The Book of Great Hors d'Oeuvre*. New York: Van Nostrand Reinhold, 1990.

Larousse, David Paul. *The Professional Garde Manger: A Guide to the Art of the Buffet*. New York: Wiley, 1996.

Megel, Christophe, and Anton Kilayko. *Asian Tapas*. North Clarendon, VT: Tuttle, 2004.

Sanders, Ed, et al. *Catering Solutions*. Upper Saddle River, N.J.: Prentice Hall, 2000.

Schmidt, Arno, and Inja Nam. *The Book of Hors d'Oeuvres and Canapes*. New York: Van Nostrand Reinhold, 1996.

Simmons, Bob, and Coleen Simmons. *Tapas Fantasticas: Appetizers with a Spanish Flair*. San Leandro, Calif.: Bristol, 1999.

Tramonto, Rick. *Amuse-Bouche: Little Bites of Delight Before the Meal Begins*. New York: Random House, 2002.

Beverages

Coates, Clive. *An Encyclopedia of the Wines and Domaines of France*. Davis, Calif.: University of California Press, 2001.

Davids, Kenneth. *Coffee: A Guide to Buying, Brewing, and Enjoying*. 5th ed. New York: St. Martin's Griffin, 2001.

Duby, Dominique, and Cindy Duby. *Wild Sweets: Exotic Desserts and Wine Pairings*. Vancouver: Douglas and McIntyre, 2003.

MacNeil, Karen. *The Wine Bible*. New York: Workman, 2001.

Maresca, Tom. *The Right Wine: Matching Wine with Food for Every Occasion*. New York: Grove Press, 1990.

Pettigrew, Jane. *The Tea Companion*. Jackson, Tenn.: Running Press, 2004.

Robinson, Jancis. *The Oxford Companion to Wine*. 3rd ed. Oxford: Oxford University Press, 2006.

Schapira, Joel, Karl Schapira, and David Schapira. *The Book of Coffee and Tea*. 2nd ed. New York: St. Martin's Griffin, 1996.

Schmid, Albert. *Hospitality Managers Guide to Wines, Beers and Spirits*. Upper Saddle River, N.J.: Prentice Hall, 2004.

Sharp, Andrew. *Winetaster's Secrets*. Toronto: Warwick Publishing, 1998.

Presentation and Garnishing

Budgen, June. *The Book of Garnishes*. Los Angeles: HP Books, 1986.

Haydock, Robert, and Yukiko Haydock. *Japanese Garnishes*. New York: Holt, Rinehart & Winston, 1980.

Huang, Su-Huei. *Great Garnishes*. Monterey Park, Calif.: Wei-Chuan, 1990.

Lynch, Francis Talyn. *Garnishing: A Feast for Your Eyes*. Los Angeles: HP Books, 1987.

Rosen, Harvey. *How to Garnish*. Lakewood, N.J.: International Culinary Consultants, 1998.

Texido, Amy. *Glorious Garnishes: Crafting Easy & Spectacular Food Decorations*. Asheville, N.C.: Lark Books, 1996.

International Cuisines

Alford, Jeffrey, and Naomi Duigood. *Hot Sour Salty Sweet: A Culinary Journey Through Southeast Asia*. Toronto: Random House Canada, 2000.

Alford, Jeffrey, and Naomi Duigood. *Mangoes and Curry Leaves: Culinary Travels Through the Great Subcontinent*. Toronto: Random House Canada, 2005.

Anderson, Burton. *Treasures of the Italian Table: Italy's Celebrated Foods and the Artisans Who Make Them*. New York: Morrow, 1994.

Bayless, Rick, with Deann Groen Bayless. *Authentic Mexican: Regional Cooking from the Heart of Mexico*. New York: Morrow, 1987.

Besh, John. *My New Orleans: The Cookbook*. Kansas City, Mo.: Andrews McMeel, 2009.

Bouley, David. *East of Paris: The New Cuisines of Austria and the Danube*. New York: HarperCollins, 2003.

Bugialli, Giuliano. *The Fine Art of Italian Cooking*. New York: Random House, 1990.

Casas, Penelope. *The Foods and Wines of Spain*. New York: Knopf, 1991.

Cormier-Boudreau, Marielle, and Melvin Gallant. *A Taste of Acadie*. Fredericton, NB: Goose Lane, 1991.

Contaldo, Gennaro. *Gennaro's Italian Year*. Toronto: McArthur & Co., 2006.

Cost, Bruce. *Asian Ingredients: A Guide to Foodstuffs of China, Japan, Korea, Thailand and Vietnam*. New York: Quill Harper Collins, 2000.

Curnonsky [Maurice Edmond Sailland]. *Traditional French Cooking*. Translation of *Cuisine et vins de France*, English ed. Jeni Wright. New York: Doubleday, 1989.

Desjardins, Anne. *Anne Desjardins Cooks at L'Eau à La Bouche: The Seasonal Cuisine of Quebec*. Vancouver: Douglas and McIntyre, 2003.

Devi, Yamuna. *The Art of Indian Vegetarian Cooking*. New York: E.P. Dutton, 1987.

Doeser, Linda. *Food of the World: Italy*. Bath, UK: Paragon, 2003.

Downer, Lesley. *At the Japanese Table*. San Francisco: Chronicle, 1993.

Field, Carol. *Celebrating Italy*. New York: Morrow, 1990.

Gin, Maggie. *Regional Cooking of China*. San Francisco: 101 Productions, 1984.

Harris, Jessica. *The Africa Cookbook: Tastes of a Continent*. New York: Simon & Schuster, 1998.

Hazan, Marcella. *Essentials of Classic Italian Cooking*. New York: Knopf, 1993.

Hsiung, Deh-Ta. *The Food of China*. Australia: Murdoch Books, 2001.

Jaffrey, Madhur. *An Invitation to Indian Cooking*. New York: Vintage Books, 1973.

———. *A Taste of India*. New York: Atheneum, 1986.

Joelson, Daniel. *Tasting Chile*. New York: Hippocrene Books, 2004.

Kasper, Lynn Rossetto. *The Splendid Table: Recipes from Emilia-Romagna the Heartland of Northern Italian Food*. New York: Morrow, 1992.

Kennedy, Diana. *The Cuisines of Mexico*. Rev. ed. New York: Harper & Row, 1986.

Kijac, Maria Baez. *The South American Table*. Boston: The Harvard Common Press, 2003.

LeBlanc, Beverly. *Food of the World: Spain*. Bath, UK: Paragon, 2003.

Lo, Kenneth. *The Encyclopedia of Chinese Cooking*. New York: Bristol Books, 1979.

Mallos, Tess. *The Complete Middle East Cookbook*. North Clarendon, Vt.: Tuttle, 2006.

Matsuhisa, Nobu. *Nobu Now*. New York: Clarkson Potter, 2005.

Matsuhisa, Nobu, and Mark Edwards. *Nobu West*. Kansas City, Mo.: Andrews McMeel, 2007.

McCausaland-Gallo. *The Secrets of Colombian Cooking*. New York: Hippocrene, 2004.

McDermott, Nancie. *Real Thai: The Best of Thailand's Regional Cooking*. San Francisco: Chronicle, 1992.

McWilliams, Margaret, and Holly Heller. *Food Around the World: A Cultural Perspective*. Upper Saddle River, NJ: Prentice Hall, 2003.

Olaore, Ola. *Traditional African Cooking*. London: Foulsham, 1990.

Ortega, Simone, and Ines Ortega. *The Book of Tapas*. New York: Phaidon, 2010.

Pham, Mai. *Pleasures of the Vietnamese Table*. New York: HarperCollins, 2001.

Richie, Donald. *A Taste of Japan*. New York: Kodansha, 1985.

Riley, Gillian. *The Oxford Companion to Italian Food*. New York: Oxford University Press, 2007.

Roden, Claudia. *The New Book of Middle Eastern Food*. New York: Knopf, 2000.

Rodriguez, Douglas. *Neuvo Latino: Recipes that Celebrate the New Latin-American Cuisine*. Berkeley, Calif.: Ten Speed Press, 2002.

Rojas-Lombardi, Felipe. *The Art of South American Cooking*. New York: HarperCollins, 1991.

Rose, Evelyn. *The New Complete International Jewish Cookbook*. New York: Carroll & Graf, 1992.

Routhier, Nicole. *Foods of Vietnam*. New York: Stewart, Tabori & Chang, 1989.

Rozin, Elisabeth. *Ethnic Cuisine: The Flavor-Principle Cookbook*. Lexington, Mass.: S. Green Press, 1983. Reprint. New York: Viking Penguin, 1992.

Sandler, Bea. *The African Cookbook*. New York: World Publishing, 1970.

Solomon, Charmaine. *The Complete Asian Cookbook*. New York: McGraw-Hill, 1976.

———. *Charmaine Solomon's Thai Cookbook*. Rutland, Vt.: Tuttle, 1991.

———. *Encyclopedia of Asian Food*. Boston: Periplus Editions, 1998.

Stewart, Anita. *The Flavours of Canada: A Celebration of the Finest Regional Foods*. Vancouver: Raincoast Books, 2000.

Takakashi, Kuwako. *The Joy of Japanese Cooking*. Singapore: Tuttle Publishing, 2002.

Tsai, Ming and Boehm, Arthur. *Blue Ginger: East Meets West Cooking*. New York: Clarkson Potter Publishers, 1999.

Volokh, Anne, with Mavis Manus. *The Art of Russian Cuisine*. New York: Collier Books, 1983.

Von Bremzen, Anya, and John Welchman. *Please to the Table: The Russian Cookbook*. New York: Workman, 1990.

Williams, Patrick. *The Caribbean Cook*. London: Penguin, 2003.

Wolfert, Paula. *Couscous and Other Good Food from Morocco*. New York: Harper & Row, 1973.

Yamamoto, Katsuji and Hicks, Roger. *Step by Step Sushi*. London: New Burlington Books, 1990.

Books by Contributing Chefs

Ash, John, and Sid Goldstein. *American Game Cooking*. Reading, Mass.: Addison-Wesley (Aris Books), 1991.

Beranbaum, Rose Levy. *The Cake Bible*. New York: Morrow, 1988.

Bishop, John, and Dennis Green. *Simply Bishop's Easy Seasonal Recipes*. Vancouver: Douglas & McIntyre, 2002.

Carpenter, Hugh, and Teri Sandison. *Chopstix: Quick Cooking with Pacific Flavors*. New York: Stewart, Tabori & Chang, 1990.

Chavich, Cindy, Pam Fortier, Rosemary Hartbrecht, dee Hobsbawn-Smith, et al., *Dishing: Calgary Women Cook*. Vancouver: Whitecap, 2001.

Golden, Harris. *Golden's Kitchen: The Artistry of Cooking and Dining on the Light Side*. Rev. 2nd ed. Phoenix, Ariz.: Quail Run Books, 1989.

Hobsbawn-Smith, dee. *Food in a Flash: Fabulous Meals in Minutes*. Vancouver: Whitecap, 1998.

———. *Skinny Feasts: Deceptively Rich Cooking the Low-Fat Way*. Vancouver: Whitecap, 1996.

Kennedy, Jamie. *Jamie Kennedy's Seasons*. Vancouver: Whitecap Books, 2000.

Kennedy, Jamie, and Christopher Freeland. *Great Soup Empty Bowls: Recipes from the Empty Bowls Fundraiser*. Vancouver: Whitecap, 2002.

Kerr, Graham. *Graham Kerr's Minimax Cookbook*. New York: Doubleday, 1992.

Medrich, Alice. *Cocolat*. New York: Warner Books, 1990.

Mertens, Olaf. *Cooking from the Hip: Amazing Recipes from a Master Chef*. Vancouver: Whitecap, 2002.

Roberts, Michael. *Secret Ingredients*. New York: Bantam Books, 1988.

Smith, Michael. *Chef at Home*. Vancouver: Whitecap, 2005.

———. *The Inn Chef: Creative Ingredients, Sensational Flavour*. Montreal: Callawind, 2000.

———. *Open Kitchen: A Chef's Day at The Inn at Bay Fortune*. Montreal: Callawind Publications, 1998.

Somerville, Annie. *Fields of Greens: New Vegetarian Recipes from the Celebrated Greens Restaurant*. New York: Bantam Books, 1993.

Tropp, Barbara. *China Moon Cookbook*. New York: Workman, 1992.

Index

Credits

p. 561: Teubner Foodfoto/Stock Food/Maxx Images

p. 602: Leigh Beisch/Jupiter Images – FoodPix – Creatas

p. 618: © Richard Embery/Pearson Education/PH College

p. 651: © Reggie Casgrande/Stockbyte RF/Getty Images, Inc.

p. 656 (dragon fruit): SGM/Stock Connection

p. 687: © Food Collection/Stock Food America

p. 709: © Stockphoto

p. 721: © Tracey Kusiewicz/Food Collection RF/Stockfood America

p. 745: © Eric Futari/Stockfood America

p. 789: © Carrie Bottomley/Stockphoto

p. 828: © Paolo Scarlata/iStockphoto

p. 858: Ann Stratton/Jupiter Images – FoodPix – Creatas

p. 881: © Stockfood America

p. 924: Tom Grill/Iconica/Getty Images

p. 933: David Murray © Dorling Kindersley

p. 952: © Darryl Jacobson/Blend Images/SuperStock

Text credits:

p. 22: Trichonosis in Canada. *Meat Hygiene Manual of Procedures*, chapter 5, http://www.inspection.gc.ca/english/fssa/meavia/man/ch5/5-5e.shtml, Canadian Food Inspection Agency, 2010.

p. 27: Canadian Food Inspection Agency. *Food Safety Enhancement Program Manual*, www.inspection.gc.ca/english/fssa/polstrat/haccp/manue/tablee.shtml, Canadian Food Inspection Agency, 2010.

pp. 42–43: Figure 3.1. Source: Canadian Food Guide, http://www.hc-sc.gc.ca/fn-an/food-guide-aliment/index-eng.php, Minister of Public Works and Government Services Canada, [2010].

p. 48: Figure 3.3. Used with permission of Canadian Food Inspection Agency.

p. 49: Table 3.6. *Summary Table of Acceptable Function Claims as Applied to Food or Food Constituents, Table 8-2, (May 2009)*, www.inspection.gc.ca/english/fssa/labeti/guide/ch8e.shtml#tab8-2, Canadian Food Inspection Agency, 2010.

p. 50: Foods Causing Allergies. *Foods Causing Allergies and Sensitivities,* http://www.inspection.gc.ca/english/fssa/labeti/allerg/allergense.shtml, Canadian Food Inspection Agency, 2010.

p. 74: CSA International certification mark. Used with permission of CSA International.

pp. 213, 214: Jamie Kennedy's Tomato Consommé, Piquante Lemon Grass Bouillon. We would like to thank Whitecap Books Ltd. and Jamie Kennedy for the use of his recipes.

p. 214: Flavour Units and Basic Procedure for Making a Flavoured Oil. Used with permission of Canola Info, www.canolainfo.org.

p. 249: Figure 12.3. Source: Canadian Food Inspection Agency. Reproduced with the permission of the Minister of Public Works and Government Services Canada, [2010].

p. 250: Figures 12.4 and 12.5. Source: Canadian Food Inspection Agency. Reproduced with the permission of the Minister of Public Works and Government Services Canada, [2010].

p. 349: Figures 17.1 and 17.2. Source: Canadian Food Inspection Agency. Reproduced with the permission of the Minister of Public Works and Government Services Canada, [2010].

pp. 380–81: Recipe 17.16. Used with permission of Chef Shawn G. Whalen, CCC, CEC.

p. 413: Figure 19.4. Source: Canadian Food Inspection Agency. Reproduced with the permission of the Minister of Public Works and Government Services Canada, [2010].

p. 413: Figure 19.5. Used with permission of Ketchum Manufacturing Inc. Brockville, Ontario.

pp. 488–89: Recipe 20.9. Used with permission of Chef Shawn G. Whalen, CCC, CEC.

p. 534: Canada Organic logo. Used with permission of the Organic Office, Canadian Food Inspection Agency, 2010.

p. 535: Figure 22.1. *Food Irradiation*, www.inspection.gc.ca/english/fssa/concen/tipcon/irrade.shtml, Canadian Food Inspection Agency, 2010.

p. 608: Figure 24.1. © 2000 Oldways Preservation & Exchange Trust, www.oldwayspt.org.

pp. 683–84: Recipe 26.16. We would like to thank Whitecap Books Ltd. and Olaf Mertens for the use of his recipes.

pp. 732–33: Recipe 29.3. Used with permission of Volker Bauman, CMB, CBS.

p. 847: Recipe 32.15. Used with permission of JF Ian Bragoli.

Measurement and Conversion Charts

Measurement Conversion Chart

Formulas for Exact Measures

	When you know:	Multiply by:	To find:
Mass (Weight)	ounces	28.35	grams
	pounds	0.45	kilograms
	grams	0.035	ounces
	kilograms	2.2	pounds
Volume (Capacity)	teaspoons	5.0	millilitres
	tablespoons	15.0	millilitres
	fluid ounces	29.57	millilitres
	cups	0.24	litres
	pints	0.47	litres
	quarts	0.95	litres
	gallons	3.785	litres
	millilitres	0.034	fluid ounces
Temperature	Fahrenheit	5/9 (after subtracting 32)	Celsius
	Celsius	9/5 (then add 32)	Fahrenheit

Rounded Measures for Quick Reference

1 oz.		= 30 g
4 oz.		= 120 g
8 oz.		= 225 g
16 oz.	= 1 lb.	= 450 g
32 oz.	= 2 lb.	= 900 g
36 oz.	= 2-1/4 lb.	= 1000 g (1 kg)
1/4 tsp.	= 1/24 oz.	= 1 mL
1/2 tsp.	= 1/12 oz.	= 2 mL
1 tsp.	= 1/6 oz.	= 5 mL
1 Tbsp.	= 1/2 oz.	= 15 mL
1 c.	= 8 oz.	= 250 mL
2 c. (1 pt.)	= 16 oz.	= 500 mL
4 c. (1 qt.)	= 32 oz.	= 1 L
4 qt. (1 gal.)	= 128 oz.	= 3-3/4 L
32°F	= 0°C	
122°F	= 50°C	
212°F	= 100°C	

Conversion Guidelines

1 gallon	=	4 quarts
		8 pints
		16 cups (8 ounces)
		128 ounces
1 fifth bottle	=	approximately 1-1/2 pints or exactly 26.5 ounces
1 measuring cup	=	8 ounces (a coffee cup is generally 6 ounces)
1 large egg white	=	1 ounce (average)
1 lemon	=	1 to 1-1/4 ounces of juice
1 orange	=	3 to 3-1/2 ounces of juice

Christopher Mills
- Lentil-Crusted Tiger Cod with Cassoulet (p. 452)

Anne Milne
- Roasted Vegetable and Bocconcini Stacks on Polenta Rounds (p. 560)

Mona Moghadasian
- Chocolate Truffle Cake

Marcel Mundel
- Ginger Maple Marinated Trout

Tony Murakami
- Roasted Pheasant with Prairie Baby Lettuce Leaves, Walnut Oil and Balsamic Vinaigrette (p. 393)

Michael Noble
- Parsnip and Rhubarb Soup with Dried Pear Chips
- Roast Rack of Lamb with Crisp Potato and Vegetable Napoleon and Kalamata Olive Butter
- Cinnamon Smoked Breast of Duck with Huckleberry Verjus Brown Butter
- Potato-Crusted Smoked Black Cod with Tomato Chutney and Scallion Oil (p. 454)
- Grilled Pacific Shrimp with Baked Garlic and Butternut Squash Risotto and Pistachio Brown Butter
- Marinated Field Berries with Lemon Cookies and Ice Wine Sabayon

Gilbert Noussitou
- Corn Flan and Smoked Salmon with Chive Oil (p. 458)
- Potato Tuiles (p. 960)

Glen O'Flaherty
- Chocolate, Cherry and Croissant Pudding (p. 849)

Hayato Okamitsu
- Pork Shoulder, Spiced and Roasted, Black Pepper and Thyme Gnocchi
- Lemon and Lime Seared Ahi Tuna

James Olberg
- Tea-Smoked Atlantic Salmon Fillets on Lobster Emulsion (p. 460)

Doug Overes
- Roasted Garlic Beignets (p. 880)
- Berbere Spice
- Moroccan Charmula

Carol Paradis
- Braised Lamb Shanks with Rosemary Jus (p. 322)
- Marinated Sir Laurier d'Arthabaska Cheese

Peter Phillips
- Duck Prosciutto with Melon and Fig Salad
- Tiramisu Torte (p. 826)

Alain Pignard
- Evantail of Semi-Smoked Brome Lake Duckling with Blueberry Cranberry Chutney

David Powell
- Seviche/Escabeche (p. 449)

Francisco Rivera
- Italian Shirred Eggs (p. 877)
- Poached Pear Appetizer

Liana Robberecht
- Gingered Cantaloupe Soup, Spiced West Coast Dungeness Crab and Spot Prawns
- Fennel and Apple Soufflé with Toasted Walnut Crème Fraîche (p. 615)

Nigel Robinson
- Dandelion and Spring Asparagus Salad with Caramelized Quince Dressing

Paul Rogalski
- Morel and St. Agur Risotto (p. 596)

Dave Ryan
- Chicken Malibu

Pierre Jean St-Pierre
- Almond Chocolate Sheet Sponge (p. 824)
- Chocolate and Cinnamon Pots de Crème (p. 847)

Felix Sano
- Grilled Beef Tenderloin with Spicy Red Onion Marmalade (p. 292)
- Jerk Sea Bass with Black Bean Mango Salsa

Karen Schoenrank
- Orange Ginger Pecan Biscotti

Peter Schuster
- Braised Beef Roulade with Bread Dumplings (p. 272)

Andreas Schwarzer
- Classic Chocolate Mousse (p. 840)

Howard Selig
- Buttermilk Apple Cake (gluten free) (p. 718)

Settimio Sicoli
- Osso Buco (p. 309)

Judson Simpson
- Thai Chicken with Canton Noodle Salad (p. 600)

Michael Smith
- Oxtail Jus (p. 219)
- Tomato Anchovy Sauce
- Chive Essence (p. 641)
- Tomato Anchovy Vinaigrette

Teddi Smith
- Pain à l'Ancienne
- Walnut Bread
- Banana Caramel Cake

Simon Smotkowicz
- Pine Nut and Pistachio Relish
- Shellfish Bouillabaisse with Ginger Aïoli (p. 447)
- Pan-Seared Scallops and Ragout of Summer Vegetables in a Phyllo Frying Pan with Minted Orange Sauce
- Socca (p. 557)
- Asparagus and Minted New Potato Salad with Sun-Dried Tomato Mayonnaise (p. 650)

Joerg Soltermann
- Baked Chicken in a Sea-Salt Crust (p. 381)

Gerd Steinmeyer
- Straight Forcemeat (p. 469)
- Pâté Dough (p. 476)

Larry Stewart
- Prairie Black Bean Soup with Cilantro Sour Cream (p. 242)
- Saskatoon-Almond Tart (p. 777)

Robert Sulatycky
- Olive Oil Poached Salmon with Oscietra Caviar (p. 457)
- Roasted Scallops with Green Pea and Butter Lettuce Purée and Mint Vinaigrette
- Salad of Lobster with Tomato Tartare, Haricot Vert and Basil "Crackling"

Suzanne Taylor
- Blueberry Yogurt Flan
- Chocolate Hazelnut Parfait

Klaus Theyer
- Potato and Fruit Dumplings (p. 593)

Vinod Varshey
- Duo of Nougat and Mango Mousses with Warm Pitted Cherry Compote (p. 852)

Mikael Volke
- Roulade of Bison, Fire-Roasted Peppers on a Soft Oka and Wild Forest Mushroom Polenta

George Wagner
- Crème Chiboust (p. 851)
- Pear Tart Chiboust
- Banana Galette with Nutmeg Ice Cream

John Walker
- Sticky Toffee Pudding

Anthony Walsh (with Todd Clarmo)
- Parsnip, Potato and Goat Cheese Pie

Nigel Webber
- Charred Tomato Vinaigrette (p. 220)

Konrad Weinbuch
- Pan-Seared Lamb Loin with Rosemary Mousseline in Crispy Phyllo Crust (p. 323)

Philippe Wettel
- Old-Fashioned Gingerbread

Shawn Whalen
- Muscovy Duck Breast and Confit Leg à l'Orange (p. 380)
- Brandy and Dill Cured Atlantic Salmon, Pickled Vegetable Salad of Golden Beets, Purple Pearl Onions, Cucumber and Green Tomatoes (p. 488)

Morgan Wilson
- Lobster Bisque Scented with Vanilla and Basil (p. 233)

Georg Windisch
- Blanquette of Veal—Sous Vide (p. 277)
- (with Simon Dunn) Bison Medallions on Roasted Parsnip and Onion Bread and Butter Pudding, Espresso Jus (p. 395)

Fred Zimmermann
- Venison Loin in Wild Rice Mantle (p. 396)

Blair Zinck
- Blueberry Buckle (p. 854)